International Directory of
COMPANY
HISTORIES

International Directory of
COMPANY HISTORIES

VOLUME 59

Editor
Jay P. Pederson

ST. JAMES PRESS®

THOMSON

GALE

Detroit • New York • San Diego • San Francisco • Cleveland • New Haven, Conn. • Waterville, Maine • London • Munich

THOMSON
™
GALE

International Directory of Company Histories, Volume 59

Jay P. Pederson, Editor

Project Editor
Miranda H. Ferrara

Editorial
Erin Bealmear, Joann Cerrito, Jim Craddock,
Stephen Cusack, Peter M. Gareffa,
Kristin Hart, Melissa Hill, Margaret
Mazurkiewicz, Carol A. Schwartz, Christine
Tomassini, Michael J. Tyrkus

Imaging and Multimedia
Randy Bassett, Lezlie Light

Manufacturing
Rhonda Williams

LIBRARY OF CONGRESS CATALOG NUMBER 89-190943

ISBN: 1-55862-504-6

BRITISH LIBRARY CATALOGUING IN PUBLICATION DATA

International directory of company histories. Vol. 59
I. Jay P. Pederson
33.87409

Printed in the United States of America
10 9 8 7 6 5 4 3 2 1

CONTENTS _____

Company Histories

PREFACE

The St. James Press series *The International Directory of Company Histories (IDCH)* is intended for reference use by students, business people, librarians, historians, economists, investors, job candidates, and others who seek to learn more about the historical development of the world's most important companies. To date, *IDCH* has covered over 6,250 companies in 59 volumes.

Inclusion Criteria

Most companies chosen for inclusion in *IDCH* have achieved a minimum of US$25 million in annual sales and are leading influences in their industries or geographical locations. Companies may be publicly held, private, or nonprofit. State-owned companies that are important in their industries and that may operate much like public or private companies also are included. Wholly owned subsidiaries and divisions are profiled if they meet the requirements for inclusion. Entries on companies that have had major changes since they were last profiled may be selected for updating.

The *IDCH* series highlights 10% private and nonprofit companies, and features updated entries on approximately 45 companies per volume.

Entry Format

Each entry begins with the company's legal name, the address of its headquarters, its telephone, toll-free, and fax numbers, and its web site. A statement of public, private, state, or parent ownership follows. A company with a legal name in both English and the language of its headquarters country is listed by the English name, with the native-language name in parentheses.

The company's founding or earliest incorporation date, the number of employees, and the most recent available sales figures follow. Sales figures are given in local currencies with equivalents in U.S. dollars. For some private companies, sales figures are estimates and indicated by the abbreviation *est.* The entry lists the exchanges on which a company's stock is traded and its ticker symbol, as well as the company's NAIC codes.

Entries generally contain a *Company Perspectives* box which provides a short summary of the company's mission, goals, and ideals, a *Key Dates* box highlighting milestones in the company's history, lists of *Principal Subsidiaries, Principal Divisions, Principal Operating Units, Principal Competitors,* and articles for *Further Reading.*

American spelling is used throughout *IDCH*, and the word ''billion'' is used in its U.S. sense of one thousand million.

Sources

Entries have been compiled from publicly accessible sources both in print and on the Internet such as general and academic periodicals, books, annual reports, and material supplied by the companies themselves.

Cumulative Indexes

IDCH contains three indexes: the **Index to Companies**, which provides an alphabetical index to companies discussed in the text as well as to companies profiled, the **Index to Industries**, which allows researchers to locate companies by their principal industry, and the **Geographic Index**, which lists companies alphabetically by the country of their headquarters. The indexes are cumulative and specific instructions for using them are found immediately preceding each index.

Suggestions Welcome

Comments and suggestions from users of *IDCH* on any aspect of the product as well as suggestions for companies to be included or updated are cordially invited. Please write:

The Editor
International Directory of Company Histories
St. James Press
27500 Drake Rd.
Farmington Hills, Michigan 48331-3535

AB	Aktiebolag (Finland, Sweden)
AB Oy	Aktiebolag Osakeyhtiot (Finland)
A.E.	Anonimos Eteria (Greece)
AG	Aktiengesellschaft (Austria, Germany, Switzerland, Liechtenstein)
A.O.	Anonim Ortaklari/Ortakligi (Turkey)
ApS	Amparteselskab (Denmark)
A.Š.	Anonim Širketi (Turkey)
A/S	Aksjeselskap (Norway); Aktieselskab (Denmark, Sweden)
Ay	Avoinyhtio (Finland)
B.A.	Buttengewone Aansprakeiijkheid (The Netherlands)
Bhd.	Berhad (Malaysia, Brunei)
B.V.	Besloten Vennootschap (Belgium, The Netherlands)
C.A.	Compania Anonima (Ecuador, Venezuela)
C. de R.L.	Compania de Responsabilidad Limitada (Spain)
Co.	Company
Corp.	Corporation
CRL	Companhia a Responsabilidao Limitida (Portugal, Spain)
C.V.	Commanditaire Vennootschap (The Netherlands, Belgium)
G.I.E.	Groupement d'Interet Economique (France)
GmbH	Gesellschaft mit beschraenkter Haftung (Austria, Germany, Switzerland)
Inc.	Incorporated (United States, Canada)
I/S	Interessentselskab (Denmark); Interesentselskap (Norway)
KG/KGaA	Kommanditgesellschaft/Kommanditgesellschaft auf Aktien (Austria, Germany, Switzerland)
KK	Kabushiki Kaisha (Japan)
K/S	Kommanditselskab (Denmark); Kommandittselskap (Norway)
Lda.	Limitada (Spain)
L.L.C.	Limited Liability Company (United States)
Ltd.	Limited (Various)
Ltda.	Limitada (Brazil, Portugal)
Ltee.	Limitee (Canada, France)
mbH	mit beschraenkter Haftung (Austria, Germany)
N.V.	Naamloze Vennootschap (Belgium, The Netherlands)
OAO	Otkrytoe Aktsionernoe Obshchestve (Russia)
OOO	Obschestvo s Ogranichennoi Otvetstvennostiu (Russia)
Oy	Osakeyhtiö (Finland)
PLC	Public Limited Co. (United Kingdom, Ireland)
Pty.	Proprietary (Australia, South Africa, United Kingdom)
S.A.	Société Anonyme (Belgium, France, Greece, Luxembourg, Switzerland, Arab speaking countries); Sociedad Anónima (Latin America [except Brazil], Spain, Mexico); Sociedades Anônimas (Brazil, Portugal)
SAA	Societe Anonyme Arabienne
S.A.R.L.	Sociedade Anonima de Responsabilidade Limitada (Brazil, Portugal); Société à Responsabilité Limitée (France, Belgium, Luxembourg)
S.A.S.	Societá in Accomandita Semplice (Italy); Societe Anonyme Syrienne (Arab speaking countries)
Sdn. Bhd.	Sendirian Berhad (Malaysia)
S.p.A.	Società per Azioni (Italy)
Sp. z.o.o.	Spólka z ograniczona odpowiedzialnoscia (Poland)
S.R.L.	Società a Responsabilità Limitata (Italy); Sociedad de Responsabilidad Limitada (Spain, Mexico, Latin America [except Brazil])
S.R.O.	Spolecnost s Rucenim Omezenym (Czechoslovakia
Ste.	Societe (France, Belgium, Luxembourg, Switzerland)
VAG	Verein der Arbeitgeber (Austria, Germany)
YK	Yugen Kaisha (Japan)
ZAO	Zakrytoe Aktsionernoe Obshchestve (Russia)

ABBREVIATIONS FOR CURRENCY

$	United States dollar	KD	Kuwaiti dinar
£	United Kingdom pound	L	Italian lira
¥	Japanese yen	LuxFr	Luxembourgian franc
A$	Australian dollar	M$	Malaysian ringgit
AED	United Arab Emirates dirham	N	Nigerian naira
B	Thai baht	Nfl	Netherlands florin
B	Venezuelan bolivar	NIS	Israeli new shekel
BD	Bahraini dinar	NKr	Norwegian krone
BFr	Belgian franc	NT$	Taiwanese dollar
C$	Canadian dollar	NZ$	New Zealand dollar
CHF	Switzerland franc	P	Philippine peso
COL	Colombian peso	PLN	Polish zloty
Cr	Brazilian cruzado	PkR	Pakistan Rupee
CZK	Czech Republic koruny	Pta	Spanish peseta
DA	Algerian dinar	R	Brazilian real
Dfl	Netherlands florin	R	South African rand
DKr	Danish krone	RMB	Chinese renminbi
DM	German mark	RO	Omani rial
E£	Egyptian pound	Rp	Indonesian rupiah
Esc	Portuguese escudo	Rs	Indian rupee
EUR	Euro dollars	Ru	Russian ruble
FFr	French franc	S$	Singapore dollar
Fmk	Finnish markka	Sch	Austrian schilling
GRD	Greek drachma	SFr	Swiss franc
HK$	Hong Kong dollar	SKr	Swedish krona
HUF	Hungarian forint	SRls	Saudi Arabian riyal
IR£	Irish pound	TD	Tunisian dinar
ISK	Icelandic króna	VND	Vietnamese Dong
J$	Jamaican dollar	W	Korean won
K	Zambian kwacha		

International Directory of
COMPANY
HISTORIES

A. Moksel AG

Rudolf-Diesel-Strasse 10
86807 Buchloe
Germany
Telephone: +49/82 41/5 03-0
Fax: +49/82 41/5 03-210
Web site: http://www.moksel.com

Public Company
Incorporated: 1948
Employees: 2,313
Sales: EUR 1.8 billion (2002)
Stock Exchanges: Munich Frankfurt Berlin Hamburg
Ticker Symbol: MOK
NAIC: 424470 Meat and Meat Product Merchant
    Wholesalers; 311611 Animal (Except Poultry)
    Slaughtering; 311612 Meat Processed From Carcasses

A. Moksel AG runs a meat production and trading concern in the heart of southern Bavaria, one of Germany's major cattle-producing areas. The company operates a large slaughterhouse and trading concern in its home town in Buchloe and oversees a network of slaughterhouses, processors, and trading companies throughout Germany that together form the Moksel Group. Founded just after World War II, the company began importing, exporting, and slaughtering meat in the earliest decades of its existence. Its business activities later grew to encompass cutting and storage of meat. In the mid-1990s, Moksel increased its activity in the area of meat processing and developed a line of convenience foods marketed under the Food Family brand name. The company is majority owned by Bestmeat Company of The Netherlands.

Founding and Steady Growth After World War II

In 1948 Alexander Moksel built a slaughterhouse in Buchloe, a town of several thousand located about 40 miles west of Munich. The slaughterhouse was favorably situated close to producers in an area known for the quality of its livestock. The ''Alexander Moksel Grossschlächterei, Fleisch-Wurst- und Konservenfabrik'' slaughtered and produced meat and sausage, as well as trading locally in meat and livestock. Because livestock did not have to travel far to the slaughterhouse, Moksel expected that he would be able to produce a higher-quality product than the meat that came from slaughterhouses in urban centers.

A decade after its founding Moksel had annual revenues of DM 9 million. Around 1957 the company expanded its trading business and began importing meat from Austria into Bavaria. As imports grew, Moksel achieved revenues of DM 30 million in 1964. That year, Moksel started exporting meat more extensively, particularly to Italy. In the early 1970s the company developed export markets in Eastern Europe as well. In 1970 annual revenues reached DM 130 million.

Five years later Moksel had nearly doubled in size again. It branched out into new areas of the meat industry, buying a stake in a refrigerating and cutting plant. More acquisitions followed in the later 1970s: Moksel took over an importing and exporting concern in Hamburg known as Peter Paulsen as well as a trading company in Berlin. The company was becoming more vertically integrated and could now offer storage and logistics services in addition to slaughtering and trading. With the new subsidiaries, net revenue rose from DM 235 million in 1974 to DM 1 billion in 1980. That year Moksel formally divided its business activities into separate production and trading branches. While beef remained Moksel's most profitable product, the company acquired subsidiaries that dealt in breeding cattle, fine meat cuts, and wild game.

Moksel's expanded activities had outgrown its original headquarters by the mid-1980s. In 1984 the company began construction of a new slaughterhouse in Buchloe and opened the facility a year later. In addition to state-of-the-art slaughtering capabilities, the facility was designed to accommodate extensive refrigerated and frozen storage capacity. Cattle from all over southern Bavaria met their demise at the Buchloe slaughterhouse. In 1986 Moksel also acquired a slaughterhouse in Furth im Wald, a city northeast of Munich in an area known for its quality cattle. The longstanding Furth slaughterhouse was in need of an investor to modernize it to meet new requirements. Moksel spent DM 3 million to bring the facility up to speed.

Continued Expansion As a Public Company: 1987–92

After 40 years of growth and acquisitions, Moksel was ripe for a public offering. By 1987, the firm's subsidiaries included seven trading concerns in Buchloe, Munich, Hamburg, Dortmund, and Madrid, Spain; slaughterhouses in Buchloe, Furth im Wald, Regensburg, Berlin, and Bordertown, Australia; refrigeration operations in Nuremberg, Buchloe, and Fallingbostel; and processing plants in Berlin and Germaringen, all in addition to the original Moksel concern with trading, storage, and slaughtering operations in Buchloe. The entire group employed about 880 people, 220 of them at the central facilities in Buchloe. Net revenues for the group in 1986 were about DM 1.4 billion, with slightly more than 60 percent of revenues coming from livestock trading operations and the remainder from meat slaughtering, storage, and processing.

In preparation for the initial public offering (IPO), Moksel combined its two parent companies—the slaughtering branch and the trading branch—into one entity, Alexander Moksel Schlachtbetriebe, Import-Export GmbH u. Co. KG. In June 1987 that entity was restructured into A. Moksel AG. In October the company offered DM 24.9 million, just under half of its base capital, for sale on the Frankfurt and Munich stock exchanges.

Moksel nearly tripled its size in the few years after the IPO. After a period of stagnant exports due to international overproduction, trade picked up again in 1988 and exports accounted for the majority of the firm's proceeds. In 1987 the company renovated slaughterhouses in Regensburg and Berlin and founded a breeding cattle company in Munich to take advantage of demand from countries that were beginning to develop their milk and meat industries. A trading company was founded in Regensburg in 1989 and construction began on a new slaughterhouse in Gelsenkirchen. In 1990 the company acquired a majority share in Fleischzentrale Südwest GmbH, a slaughterhouse in Crailsheim near Stuttgart, and founded the EGN Erzeugergemeinschaft für Qualitätsfleisch slaughterhouse in Vilshofen east of Munich.

In the late 1980s, Moksel began to increase its activity in the area of meat processing. By 1987 revenues from the processing sector had reached DM 579 million. The following year Moksel introduced a line of exclusive certified meat under the name "Almox premium." The brand name indicated that the livestock came only from certain longtime partners who met strict criteria. The livestock was then slaughtered and stored in a way that would preserve its high quality and freshness. Group sales in 1991 were about DM 4 billion. In the fall of 1992 company founder Alexander Moksel sold his 34 percent stake in the company to the März family, owners of a fellow German meat company.

A String of Crises: 1992–98

Moksel's advance came to a sudden halt in 1992. That year the company acquired G.u.P. Salomon AG, a meat trader and processor near Frankfurt, for DM 40 million. The company was strong in the production of prepared food and had a contract with Burger King. But the deal turned sour after Moksel looked through the firm's accounts and found hidden debt and irregularities costing more than DM 100 million. Moksel reported a DM 125 million net loss in 1992 and was forced to cancel its regular dividend payment.

Meanwhile, Moksel was in the midst of investment and expansion. Aside from a new cutting facility in Buchloe, three new slaughterhouses in the former East Germany were almost ready in the towns of Neustrelitz, Kasel-Golzig near Luckau, and Rodleben near Dessau. Moksel also gained a majority share in Eyckeler & Malt AG, a company near Düsseldorf involved in livestock trade, slaughtering, and processing. In the early 1990s, however, Moksel was investigated for possible illegal dealings with East German companies. The company was suspected of having undeservedly profited from special credits designed to rejuvenate the East German economy. Loans to East Germany had been negotiated by a Bavarian leader with ties to Moksel, and commissions meant for the East may have found their way back to Moksel. When Finance Department leaders of the Christian Social Union made rule changes that absolved Moksel of responsibility, opposition parties on the left accused the government of favoring Moksel because the company was a major contributor to the right-wing party. The investigation was reopened, and the final report in 1994 found that Moksel appeared to have acted illegally in its dealings with East Germany, receiving a share in commissions that were meant for East Berlin. Parties on the left suggested that Moksel's imports from the East resulted in lower livestock prices for Bavarian farmers.

In the mid-1990s a drop in demand for meat was putting even more pressure on Moksel. In particular, the highly modern new slaughterhouses in the East were losing money due to overcapacity. The beleaguered Moksel hit a crisis point in 1994, which Chief Executive Herbert Wüst referred to as "the most difficult year in the company's history." The company reported a group loss of DM 179.1 million. Wüst came to Moksel to lead the company through a drastic restructuring. In his opinion, the *Süddeutsche Zeitung* reported, the company's dire situation was in part due to "a strategy of size without use of market synergies." Under Wüst's leadership, Moksel laid off several hundred employees in 1994, cutting its payroll to about 2,200. Over the next year Wüst carried out cost-cutting measures, cut back slaughtering activities, and called for a greater focus on processing, international trade, and product branding.

After the restructuring, Moksel's capital reserves were used up almost completely. If not for the support of its banks, the

Key Dates:

1948: Alexander Moksel builds a slaughterhouse in Buchloe.
1957: Moksel begins importing meat from Austria.
1964: Moksel increases exports, particularly to Italy.
1974: Through acquisitions, Moksel expands activities into refrigeration and storage.
1987: Moksel is floated on the stock exchange.
1992: Hidden debt discovered at a recently acquired subsidiary starts off a series of difficult years.
1998: Moksel introduces the ''Food Family'' line of convenience products.
2000: Mad cow disease desolates the meat industry.
2002: Bestmeat of The Netherlands acquires majority control of Moksel.

company would have gone bankrupt. Over the course of the mid-1990s, Moksel's creditors refrained from collecting DM 293 million in debt. About DM 50 million was forgiven and the rest converted into rights to Moksel's future profits.

By 1997 the restructuring was showing some tentative results. Moksel reported a small profit of about DM 6 million, its first since 1991, but dividends were still out of the question. Chief Financial Officer Uwe Tillman took leadership of the company after Wüst's early resignation in February. The tough times were not over yet. Creutzfeldt-Jakob or ''mad cow'' disease had just appeared in Britain, causing a drawn-out drop in demand for beef products. The company's financial situation remained poor. The März food company, which held a third of the company's shares, had gone bankrupt. Moksel was in dire need of an investor that could pump some capital into the company, but the search for a partner took years.

Emphasis on Processing: 1998–2003

Tillman carried on with Moksel's focus on the processing sector of the meat business. Because of demographic changes in Germany, more and more people were buying convenience foods. Moksel introduced the ''Food Family'' brand name in 1998 and planned to move forward aggressively in marketing prepared food. ''Meat must not be anonymous anymore,'' Tillman announced that year. Moksel also won organic certification for its slaughterhouse in Landshut, opening up another potential special market. The company reported another small profit in 1998: EUR 3.2 million (DM 6.3 million) on sales of EUR 1.7 billion (DM 3.3 billion). Moksel had added to its workforce a bit, bringing its employees up to 2,570. But a debt totaling nearly DM 500 million was coming due in the near future.

Moksel further diversified its activities in 1999 in an effort to expand the more profitable areas of its business. In response to growing economic globalization, the company's activities grew in the European Union, Eastern Europe, and the Near and Middle East, although the economic crisis in Russia hurt Moksel's export business there. Now that consumers were wary of beef, lamb and poultry accounted for nearly a quarter of Moksel's sales and the company planned for further expansion

in those areas. Moksel also continued to develop an even greater range of prepared and packaged convenience products.

Meanwhile, the search for an investor with capital reserves dragged on. Werner Folger, a board member at Moksel and the liquidator for the bankrupt März AG, had searched unsuccessfully since the late 1990s for a buyer for März's 34 percent stake in Moksel. In 2000 he acquired shares from smaller shareholders and bundled them with his existing holdings to create a nearly 49 percent stake, hoping that the prospect of majority control would make the package more attractive to an investor. The sale also was complicated because the meat industry in Germany was quite fractured, so that no acquisition could give the buyer a large market share. While a single company in Denmark or The Netherlands, for example, had about an 80 percent market share, there were about 240 different slaughterhouses in Germany.

In 2000 a renewed crisis hit the meat industry. Mad cow disease was discovered in some cattle in northern Germany. At the same time consumers discovered that some sausage packages had been incorrectly labeled as being free of beef. Meat sales plummeted 20 to 30 percent; grocery stores quit buying and farmers quit selling cattle in the face of low prices. France was an important customer for the high-quality Bavarian beef, but exports there fell drastically after three French citizens died of mad cow disease. Sales of organically produced meat, on the other hand, went way up. Moksel's banks refrained from collecting another DM 50 million in debt to save the company from total collapse.

In 2001 the industry began to recover from the mad cow disease crisis and there was hope that Moksel's decade-long string of troubles might be over. The company reported net income of EUR 10.3 million that year—its best showing in ten years—on sales of EUR 1.89 billion. Exports were growing, the company's operations were more efficient after all the restructuring, and Moksel's modern facilities, a burden during times of overcapacity, now gave it a competitive advantage. The company increased its organic meat offerings and anticipated substantial growth in sales of convenience foods. In 2001 Moksel increased its share in Eyckeler & Malt, an important producer of prepackaged meats, to nearly 75 percent.

In 2002 Moksel finally found an investor. The Dutch firm Sobel acquired Werner Folger's 50 percent stake for EUR 100 million, took on Moksel's debt and announced plans to invest EUR 40 million over the next two years. Moksel's shares rose 70 percent on the news. Sobel formed the Bestmeat Company as a holding company for Moksel. Bestmeat eventually increased its stake in Moksel to 85 percent and acquired Dumeco, the Dutch meat industry's market leader, as a sister company to Moksel. Moksel's sales and net income in 2002 fell slightly to EUR 1.8 billion and EUR 7.2 million, respectively, but sales in the convenience products division rose 23 percent. Overall, sales of frozen and convenience products had grown five times since 1997. The slaughtering business, however, continued to stagnate. Moksel leadership said the company was still in no position to pay dividends. In 2003 Bestmeat announced that it was planning to take Moksel off the market. Tillman reportedly was being considered for a leadership position at Bestmeat, leading to speculation that Moksel and Dumeco might merge.

Principal Subsidiaries

Alexander Moksel Import-Export GmbH; ALMOX Süddeutsche Häutehandelsgesellschaft mbH; Eyckeler & Malt AG; Eyckeler & Malt Geflügel-GmbH; G.u.P. Salomon GmbH; IFT International Food Trading GmbH; Paulsen-Gruppe; PROMOX Handelsgesellschaft mbH; Thomsen Im- und Export GmbH; EGN Erzeugergemeinschaft für Qualitätsfleisch Ndb. Schlachtbetrieb GmbH; Fleischkontor Moksel GmbH; Fleischzentrale Südwest GmbH; Fleischzentrum Anhalt GmbH; Fleischzentrum Lausitz GmbH; Fleischzentrum Neustrelitz GmbH; Klaus-Dieter Fuchs GmbH; SBL Schlachtbetrieb für Qualitätsfleisch GmbH Landshut; Voss & Co. GmbH; Landhof "Drömling" Köckte GmbH; Otto Nocker GmbH; Salomon Hitburger GmbH; Salomon Meat GmbH; Tatiara Meat Company Pty. Ltd. (Australia).

Principal Competitors

Südfleisch; Cremonini S.p.A.; Nutreco Holding N.V.; Campofrio Alimentación; ConAgra, Inc.; Smithfield Foods, Inc.; Frimancha.

Further Reading

Bauchmüller, Michael, "Niederländer kaufen Moksel," *Süddeutsche Zeitung,* December 12, 2002, p. 21.

Brost, Marc, et al., "Mahlzeit! Es ist angerichtet," *Die Zeit,* January 4, 2001.

"Company Said the Extremely Negative Development of the 1994 Market," *AFX News,* February 2, 1995.

"Fleischkonzern Moksel schwer angeschlagen," *Süddeutsche Zeitung,* February 3, 1995, p. 21.

Köhn, Rüdiger, "Banken retten Fleischhersteller Moksel," *Financial Times Deutschland,* April 19, 2001.

——, "Moksel Seeks Investor," *Financial Times Deutschland,* December 29, 2000, p. 16.

Krill, Hannes, "Freispruch für den verstorbenen Franz Josef Strauß," *Süddeutsche Zeitung,* July 13, 1994, p. 46.

Maier-Mannhart, Helmut, "Moksel hofft auf eine bessere Zukunft," *Süddeutsche Zeitung,* May 30, 2001, p. 30.

"Moksel Chairman Wuest Steps Down Effective Feb 18," *AFX News,* February 13, 1997.

"Moksel drängt in die Veredelung," *Süddeutsche Zeitung,* June 3, 1992.

"Moksel forciert Börsen-Abschied," *Süddeutsche Zeitung,* July 18, 2003, p. 23.

"Moksel ist auf Partnersuche," *Süddeutsche Zeitung,* June 3, 1998, p. 33.

"Moksel übersteht BSE mit blauem Auge," *Süddeutsche Zeitung,* June 19, 1996, p. 19.

"Moksel weiter auf schwachen Beinen," *Süddeutsche Zeitung,* June 7, 2000, p. 31.

Roth, Terence, "Bonn Backs Waigel, Calls Reports Untrue," *Wall Street Journal,* March 23, 1993, p. 2.

"Salomon läßt Moksel blutrote Zahlen schreiben," *Süddeutsche Zeitung,* July 13, 1993, p. 17.

"Schlachten allein genügt nicht mehr," *Bayerische Staatszeitung,* June 13, 2003, p. 21.

Tagliabue, John, "Mad Cow Disease (and Anxiety)," *New York Times,* February 1, 2001, p. C1.

—Sarah Ruth Lorenz

Africare

Africare House
440 R Street, N.W.
Washington, D.C. 20001-1935
U.S.A.
Telephone: (202) 462-3614
Fax: (202) 387-1034
Web site: http://www.africare.org

Nonprofit Company
Founded: 1970
Employees: 60
Operating Revenues: $39.7 million (2002)
NAIC: 624110 Child and Youth Services; 624229 Other
   Community Housing Services; 624210 Community
   Food Services; 624221 Temporary Shelters; 624230
   Emergency and Other Relief Services; 813212
   Voluntary Health Organizations; 813311 Human
   Rights Organizations; 81331 Social Advocacy
   Organizations

While many Americans may not have heard of Africare, it is the oldest and largest African American service organization in the United States. Africare ministers specifically to Africa and its peoples, and has done so quietly and effectively for over three decades. Since its formation in 1970, Africare has delivered almost $400 million in aid to nations both within and around Africa, spearheading HIV/AIDS awareness and treatment, building communities, and providing emergency aid in times of need. Many well-known names in American business and government have been involved with Africare, while its board of directors past and present is a veritable *Who's Who* list of prominent African Americans.

Exploring Africa: 1961–71

The story of Africare is linked to another well known service organization, the Peace Corps. Though Africare was never a part of the Peace Corps nor a federal program, several former Corps volunteers were Africare's founding members. Key among them were Dr. William Kirker, who originally founded Africare, and C. Payne Lucas, who took the unknown service association and turned it into the leading relief organization it is today. The story of Africare begins with Kirker and Lucas.

When John F. Kennedy entered the White House, Democratic Party supporter C. Payne Lucas sought a government position with the new administration. He was sent to talk to the president's brother-in-law (Robert) Sargent Shriver, who was director of a new volunteer organization called the Peace Corps. The Peace Corps, officially established in March 1961, had first emerged during Kennedy's presidential campaign in 1960.

Lucas had little idea of what the Peace Corps was when he went to talk to Shriver. He found out firsthand when he was sent to Africa in 1962. Lucas was headed for Togo, a nation formerly known as French Togoland until its independence from France in 1960. Lucas landed in Lome, Togo's capital, and ended up staying for six years. In 1967 he was awarded the President's Award for Distinguished Federal Civilian Service from President Lyndon B. Johnson for his years in Togo. He then headed northeast to the Republic of Niger, which like Togo had gained its independence in 1960 from France. Lucas met and began working with the nation's president, Hamani Diori. Also in Niger was William O. Kirker, M.D., and his wife Barbara Jean, who had come to Niger the year before to work with the Maina-Soroa Hospital in the city of Diffa. Kirker saw an urgent need for what he called a "new breed of assistance organization" in Niger and Africa as a whole. Kirker and President Diori wanted the world to know the plight of Africans, who were too often hungry and ravaged by disease.

Kirker formed his new organization and called it "Africare," which he incorporated in Hawaii in 1970. Kirker then sought donations and aid, but found little interest until Niger and other regions of Africa were devastated by drought and famine. The need was so great that President Diori reached out to Lucas, who had accepted a Peace Corps post back in the United States assisting returning volunteers. Diori urged Lucas to spread the word to African Americans that the country of their ancestors desperately needed their help. Lucas publicized Africa's plight in Washington, D.C., with surprising results— donations began to flow in but not from wealthy D.C. philan-

Company Perspectives:

Africare helps Africa. Over the course of its 32 years, Africare has become a leader among private, charitable U.S. organizations assisting Africa. It is the oldest and largest African-American organization in the field. And Africa is Africare's specialty.

thropists or aid organizations, but from area churches attended by many of the city's poorest African Americans.

Over $75,000 in aid was raised for Africare in 1970 and by the following year, in 1971, it was decided to reincorporate the organization in Washington, D.C., with Lucas as its president, Kirker on the new group's board of directors, and President Diori as chairman. Due to the close ties between Kirker, Lucas, and President Diori, Africare was allowed to work out of Niger's embassy in Washington, D.C., at virtually no cost and began with an operating budget of just over $39,000.

Gaining Notice and Funding: 1972–89

While Africare's earliest years were spent combating the horrors of drought in West Africa, the organization expanded into other areas of the continent with agricultural projects, healthcare programs, and environmental initiatives. At the helm of Africare, Lucas was an eyewitness to Africa's evolution and realized the service organization must grow to accommodate the country's changing needs. By 1978 Africare had ventured into South Africa for the first time, and continued to expand throughout Africa. Working around civil wars and apartheid as much as possible, Africare developed irrigation and purification systems for water, planting and harvesting assistance for crops, brought in healthcare professionals to fight diseases, and continually offered emergency assistance to nations in need.

The 1980s brought the plight of Somalian refugees to the world and Africare was there to help. Another devastating drought, like the one a decade earlier which had spurred the formation of Africare, took millions of Ethiopians to the brink of starvation and Africare was there, providing emergency aid, receiving donations from disparate sources such as a Saudi prince, other service organizations, religious groups, multinational companies, federal programs, foreign governments, and the United Nations. For his extraordinary efforts on behalf of Africa, Lucas was given the 1984 U.S. Presidential End Hunger Award for Outstanding Individual Achievement, bestowed by then President Ronald Reagan.

In 1987 Africare began a critical healthcare initiative to combat the epidemic of HIV and AIDS in Africa. Medical professionals from around the world came to the country and both local and national programs were instituted to educate Africans about the spread of HIV/AIDS and the various treatments available at the time. In 1989, Africare began the Career Development Internship (CDI) program in South Africa, placing black South Africans in professional internships in the United States. The internees worked in a host of businesses, gaining immeasurable experience they were unable to receive in South Africa because of apartheid. This same year, Bishop John

T. Walker, Washington, D.C.'s first African American Episcopal bishop, who had served as an Africare chairman, died. In his honor, Africare established the Bishop John T. Walker Dinner and Humanitarian Award in 1990.

Leading by Example: 1990s

The new decade found Africare responding to different needs in Africa as many parts of the continent erupted in brutal civil wars. Angola, Burundi, Liberia, Rwanda, Sierra Leone, and Somalia were torn by violent clashes in the 1990s and Africare volunteers, often in danger themselves, rushed in with emergency services for the wounded and displaced. One of the highlights of the decade, however, began with a small effort in Zambia to turn sunflower seeds into cooking oil. Part of southern Africa, Zambia was home to rural farmers who grew particularly hardy sunflowers. Given a small manual press, the villagers were taught how to crush sunflower seeds and make edible cooking oil. Many of the area's farmers, who had lived well below the poverty line for years, were soon successful entrepreneurs. Africare began to supply more presses and a credit program to get more villagers involved. Simple business courses were then made available, and the Zambian program spread to nearby Mozambique and Zimbabwe.

In addition to the cooking oil projects, Africare stepped up literacy programs and health initiatives as HIV and AIDS continued to spread. In South Africa, Nelson Mandela was freed after more than two decades of imprisonment, and the binds of apartheid were loosened. Back in the United States, the Bishop John T. Walker Distinguished Humanitarian Service Award was given to Archbishop Desmond Tutu in 1992, followed by Peace Corps legend Sargent Shriver in 1993. The dinner and award ceremony would soon become Africare's major annual fundraiser, growing each year in donations and Washington, D.C. stature.

The year 1994 brought about the extraordinary, as former prisoner Nelson Mandela was elected the first president of South Africa. Africare celebrated Mandela's achievement by awarding him the Bishop Walker award the same year. In 1995, for the first time in its history, Africare was touched by controversy through a sizable donation from Democratic businessman Johnny Chung. Chung said he made a $25,000 donation to Africare at the suggestion of the U.S. Department of Energy's Hazel O'Leary. While O'Leary disputed the donation was anything other than a charitable contribution, Chung said it secured him a meeting with visiting Chinese dignitaries and industrialists with whom Chung wanted to do business. The Department of Justice investigated the alleged money scheme and though the flap eventually blew over, it was the first negative publicity attached to Africare or its operations.

The later 1990s brought in increased funding for Africare and many new initiatives for Africa. Key among them was South Africa's first "digital village," which was established in Soweto in 1997. Bringing technology to the community was a major step towards the future and such a success that other digital villages were slated for other regions. In 1998 Nelson Mandela was named Africare's Honorary chairman of the board, the same year Africare began a new crop initiative in Uganda, growing pest-resistant plants, helping villagers plant small gardens, and build-

Key Dates:

1961: C. Payne Lucas starts work for the Peace Corps in Africa.

1965: Lucas is sent to Republic of Niger on behalf of the Peace Corps and begins working with President Hamani Diori.

1966: William O. Kirker, M.D., begins healthcare work in Niger.

1970: Kirker founds Africare and incorporates the non-profit organization in Hawaii.

1971: Africare is reincorporated in Washington, D.C., with Lucas as president and Kirker on the board.

1978: Africare begins working in the southern areas of Africa.

1989: The Career Development Internship program is launched in South Africa.

1990: The Bishop John T. Walker Memorial Dinner and Humanitarian Award program is established.

1992: Archbishop Desmond Tutu is awarded the Bishop John T. Walker Distinguished Humanitarian Service Award.

1993: Apartheid ends in South Africa; Sargent Shriver is named the recipient of the Bishop Walker Humanitarian Award.

1994: Nelson Mandela, the newly elected president of South Africa, is awarded Africare's Bishop Walker Award.

1997: Africare's first "digital village" is established in Soweto.

2001: Africare joins the Magic Johnson Foundation and others to combat HIV and AIDS in Africa.

2002: C. Payne Lucas retires; Julian E. Coles is appointed Africare's new president.

2003: Bill and Melinda Gates are awarded the Bishop John T. Walker Distinguished Humanitarian Service Award.

ing roads to get harvested foods to nearby markets. In 1999 the Bill and Melinda Gates Foundation, founded by Microsoft mogul Bill Gates and his wife, awarded Africare nearly $2 million to combat HIV and AIDS in the southern regions of Africa. The donation was the first in a series of collaborations between the Gates Foundation and Africare.

A New Era: 2000s

The new century found Africare doing just what it had in the previous century: dispensing aid to those in need in Africa, through over two dozen field offices offering a total of some 150 different programs. Agriculture programs had vastly improved the lot of many rural farmers; irrigation systems allowed others to water their crops even in near-drought conditions; well construction pooled clean, safe water for villages; and HIV/AIDS prevention and treatment centers were funded in part by a grant from the Magic Johnson Foundation in 2001.

Also in 2001 U.S. Secretary of State Colin Powell visited Africa and saw firsthand the efforts put forth by Africare's

volunteers. Later in the year he was the keynote speaker at the Bishop Walker dinner and fundraiser, which honored Dr. Louis Sullivan as the recipient of the Bishop Walker Distinguished Humanitarian Award. Sullivan, a cabinet member of former president George Bush, had been a founding member of Morehouse College's School of Medicine, and had served as its president. The dinner, like its predecessors, was well attended and raised more than $1 million for Africare's causes.

In 2002 Africare underwent a changing of the guard when Lucas retired as president after more than three decades of service. His successor was Julius E. Coles, an Africare board member and veteran of the U.S. Agency for Independent Development. Coles had also served as director of the Andrew Young Center for International Affairs at Morehouse College and Howard University's Ralph J. Bunche International Affairs Center. While Coles officially began his tenure in June, Lucas stayed through July to ensure a smooth transition and remained a member of Africare's board.

In late 2002 Africare's annual fundraiser was awash in controversy when its honoree, Harry Belafonte, made inflammatory remarks about Secretary of State Colin Powell and National Security Advisor Condoleeza Rice several weeks before the October event. Powell, the keynote speaker the previous year, and Rice, who was scheduled to deliver the keynote speech in 2002, did not respond to Belafonte's comments. Atlanta Mayor Andrew Young replaced Rice as the keynote speaker at the last minute, and the dinner was held without further incident. Africare organizers remained mum about Belafonte and his opinions.

In 2003 Africare responded to crises in Ethiopia, suffering from critical shortages in food and water, and launched a $10 million mission in Liberia, torn apart by warring factions and widespread hunger and disease. The organization also continued its battle with HIV and AIDS, which killed about 6,500 people each day in Africa, according to Africare's figures. To this end, the 2003 Bishop Walker Distinguished Humanitarian Service Award was given to Bill and Melinda Gates for their efforts to combat HIV/AIDS in Africa and beyond.

Africare's sole aim continued to be the creation of better living conditions for the peoples of Africa. For several decades the organization's leaders and volunteers had made a remarkable difference in the lives of millions, from HIV/AIDS treatment and prevention and safer food and water programs to education and business partnerships. Leaders near and far had lauded Africare's efforts and many had contributed to its causes, donating their time and money to Africare's more than 2,000 projects throughout the African continent.

Further Reading

"African-Americans Respond to the Horrors of Rwanda," *Ebony*, October 1994, p. 128.

"Africare Launches $10 Million Health Program in Liberia," *Africa News Service*, January 29, 2003.

"Africare, Magic Johnson, Others Kick Off New Partnership Combating HIV/AIDS," *Africa News Service*, February 22, 2001.

"Africare Receives Grant from Eastman Kodak for HIV/AIDS Programs," *Africa News Service*, December 10, 2001.

Beinart, Peter, "Tough Love," *New Republic*, August 3, 1993, p. 15.

"Black Churches Give Donation to Africare for People of Somalia," *Jet,* March 15, 1993, p. 17.

"C. Payne Lucas Ends 31 Years with Africare, Major U.S. Aid Agency on African Continent," *Jet,* June 17, 2002, p. 5.

Cloud, John, "The Trouble with Hazel," *Time,* September 29, 1997, p. 28.

Cobb, Charles, Jr., "Africare at 'Crossroads' Says New Africare Head," *Africa News Service,* October 24, 2002.

——, "Africare President, Cofounder C. Payne Lucas to Retire," *Africa News Service,* May 22, 2002.

——, " 'Extraordinary Leadership' Needed in Africa, Says Africare Chief," *Africa News Service,* November 6, 2001.

Gamarekian, Barbara, "His Pitch Is Hunger, His Market, the World," *New York Times,* November 29, 1984, p. 12.

"Saudi Arabia Prince Gives $200,000 to Africare," *Jet,* November 19, 1984, p. 32.

—Nelson Rhodes

Ag Services of America, Inc.

1309 Technology Parkway
Cedar Falls, Iowa 50613
U.S.A.
Telephone: (319) 277-0261
Toll Free: (800) 395-8505
Fax: (319) 277-0144
Web site: http://www.agservices.com

Public Company
Incorporated: 1985
Employees: 158
Sales: $197.9 million (2002)
Stock Exchanges: New York
Ticker Symbol: ASV
NAIC: 422910 Farm Supplies Wholesalers

With its headquarters located in Cedar Falls, Iowa, Ag Services of America, Inc. (ASA) provides financing, products, and agricultural-related services to farmers located in 38 states. Primary customers are corn and soybean producers in Illinois, Indiana, Iowa, Minnesota, Nebraska, North Dakota, Ohio, South Dakota, and Texas. The ASA business model is based on the company's financial services, providing funding to farmers who have difficulty securing bank loans or need additional finances to expand operations. All production supplies ("farm inputs") must then be purchased through ASA. The loans are secured by a first lien on the borrower's crop. ASA products, while not the least expensive on the market, are competitively priced. As a result, some farmers turn to ASA simply for the sake of convenience, opting for a single source of farm inputs, financing, as well as the production expertise ASA makes available to its customers. The company makes a negligible income on financing, generating most of its revenues from farm inputs, which are mostly comprised of seed, chemicals, and fertilizer. ASA offers seed from 30 national and regional seed companies and works with customers to determine the proper hybrid or variety of seed needed. Agricultural chemicals are available through major distributors or suppliers. ASA offers fertilizer from more than 500 suppliers. Company profits from all of these inputs are the result of standard dealer discounts, negotiated pricing, manufacturers' rebates, and opportunistic purchasing. In addition, ASA generates fees by acting as an agent for multi-peril crop insurance. Because it is in the company's interest that farmers succeed and become repeat customers, ASA works closely with its borrowers, paying visits to farms to offer suggestions on harvest plans and marketing strategies. Aside from making seasonal loans to farmers, ASA, through its AgriFlex Credit program, also offers long-term financing. ASA also operates Powerfarm.com, a robust web site that serves farmers in a variety of ways. They can not only apply for financing, but also buy supplies and lease equipment on line. In addition, they can stay informed on agricultural news, weather forecasts, and market quotes, and take advantage of sophisticated web-based crop production tools.

Founding the Company in 1985

ASA was formed in October 1985 by cousins Gaylen D. Miller and Henry C. Jungling, who were both raised on Iowa farms, along with Jungling's nephew, Kevin D. Schipper. Miller had experience in agribusiness, serving in administrative and accounting positions with cooperative Land-O-Lakes, Inc. and international seed company DEKALB Genetics Corporation. Jungling came to ASA after running his own farm for 18 years. The youngest of the three, Schipper, worked in product sales for Scoular Grain Company. They recognized an opportunity caused by declining commodity prices and the tightening of credit that left a number of farmers with no means of financing their next crop. The simple idea behind the company was to take a security interest in farmers' crops in order to lend them the money they needed to buy supplies, which ASA would sell to them at a profit. At first, the company did not make any direct loans, nor did it make any money on the financing, relying on the markup on inputs for their profits. Charging an interest rate of 12.5 percent, ASA simply financed the purchase of seed, chemicals, and fertilizers—areas in which the three non-bankers had some expertise. Providing the capital was Community Bank in Chillicothe, Missouri. Although ASA might approve a customer, Community Bank made the final decision on whether to make the loan. In fiscal 1987, its first full year in business, ASA served 88 farmers and recorded $2.8 million in sales and a profit of

Company Perspectives:

Our Mission: Provide farmers the most convenient form of crop inputs and financing with the highest quality of products and services at competitive prices while increasing profitability and maximizing shareholders' wealth.

$47,006. From that positive start, the company grew steadily over the balance of the decade, posting revenues of $4.4 million in fiscal 1988 and $8.5 million in fiscal 1989. Net income during this period totaled $56,598 and $284,212.

ASA enjoyed a major growth spurt in fiscal 1990, more than doubling revenues over the previous year to $21 million while recording a profit of $411,000. In April 1990 a New York financial services company, Harris & Harris Group (H&H), acquired a 50 percent interest in ASA for $3.25 million in cash. At the same time, ASA received a trade credit of $2.75 million and a new line of bank credit totaling $16 million. H&H was controlled by Charles E. Harris, who now became the chairman of ASA. Harris brought with him nearly 20 years of experience in the investment industry, and prior to his days with H&H served as chairman of Wood Struthers and Winthrop Management Corp., the investment advisory subsidiary of Donaldson, Lufkin & Jenrette. His tenure at ASA would be short-lived, however. In December 1990 H&H announced that it was selling its 50 percent stake in ASA.

Going Public in 1991

As a way to both allow H&H to cash in and to help ASA maintain its momentum, ASA chose to make a public offering of stock. As Miller explained to *National Hog Farmer* in a 1998 article, "We simply could not have borrowed the funds needed from traditional sources to enable the business to cash flow at the growth rate we were experiencing. We needed equity capital to secure the line of credit we needed to support our rapid growth." Harris's Wall Street experience was helpful in ASA finding contacts to make the offering a reality. After a potential underwriter was engaged, according to Miller, "A team came in and scrutinized the business and financial statements to ensure everything was in order. They also looked closely at our management team. Once we passed those scrutiny tests, it was a matter of selling our program, our concept and our ideas." Company officials then made a presentation to investor groups, a road show that mostly visited major East Coast cities. On August 1, 1991, the initial public offering was completed, netting $4.7 million for ASA and allowing H&H to sell approximately three-quarters of its interest in the company. ASA stock was subsequently listed on the NASDAQ. (In addition, a public offering of convertible subordinated debentures was completed in April 1993, netting an additional $12.9 million.)

In the 1990s ASA continued its string of strong results, topping $35.5 million in revenues for fiscal 1992 and approaching $55 million a year later, and recording net income of $1.2 million in 1992 and more than $1.8 million in 1993. Because of swings in interest rates, ASA moved from fixed-rate financing to variable-rate in 1994. Business also was impacted by unusu-

ally heavy rains in the Midwest that hurt crop yields and by extension crimped ASA's balance sheet. The company generated revenues in excess of $65.5 million in 1994 and net income just short of $2 million, a healthy increase over the year before but short of ASA's track record of growing 25 to 35 percent each year. ASA achieved a measure of diversity in 1995 by starting to do business in the Texas Panhandle and southeastern Alabama. Strong growth resumed in the mid-1990s, as sales totaled $87.3 million in 1995, $114.7 million in 1996, and $147.6 million in 1997. Net income during this period kept pace, improving from $2.4 million in 1995 to more than $3.1 million in 1996 and $4.3 million in 1997. A dozen years earlier, ASA had serviced less than 100 farmers; now in 1997 its customers totaled more than 1,250. ASA's upward trend was so strong that in 1996 the company moved to the New York Stock Exchange in a bid to widen its investor base.

ASA launched a number of initiatives in the late 1990s to maintain its growth rate. An alliance with MCS Consulting Service was forged in 1998 to provide crop consulting services to customers. ASA also established its AgriFlex Credit Program, which offered qualified farmers intermediate financing, loans amortized over three to seven years that could be used to purchase land, facilities, machinery, and other equipment. (Because ASA was not a bank, it was not bound by per farm lending limits imposed upon banks.) Another effort launched in 1999 was Powerfarm.com, ASA's e-commerce Internet site, which offered financing online as well as brand-name seed and chemicals for sale. ASA even tried to become involved in real world retailing, opening three retail service centers in northwestern Illinois. The venture failed to deliver strong results, however, and in fiscal 2000 the operations were discontinued.

Entering a New Century with Optimism

As the 20th century came to a close, ASA expressed optimism about its position. Agribusiness was undergoing a consolidation trend, as family and small farms were rolled up by big players. ASA's management team believed that even larger operations could benefit from the efficiencies and financing flexibility ASA had to offer. A slowing farm economy also made ASA an attractive option to farmers of all sizes. The company's revenues totaled $186.1 million in 1998, and topped $225 million a year later. Net income during this period increased from $5.2 million to $6.5 million. Despite a successful history and promising future, the price of Ag Services stock languished, selling at just 11 times earnings.

In 2000 ASA took steps to grow its Powerfarm Internet subsidiary. It formed an alliance with Everdream Corporation, based in Fremont, California. In conjunction with Powerfarm, Everdream would offer outsourced IT services on a subscription basis. As a result, customers received such services as a 24-hour solutions center, automated backup, virus protection, and bug fixes, as well as DSL connectivity, Internet access, and a web-based e-mail account. In addition, in 2000 ASA teamed with Agritech Inversora S.A. to form Powerfarm S.A. in order to offer the company's Internet services to South American farmers. In 2001 ASA beefed up the Powerfarm web site through a number of additions. In partnership with Zions Agricultural Finance, ASA was now able to offer long-term, real estate financing online to supplement the work of its field sales

Key Dates:

1985: The company is formed.
1991: The company goes public.
1996: Company stock is listed on the New York Stock Exchange.
1999: Powerfarm.com is launched.

managers. New crop production tools also were added to the web site, such as calculators capable of determining economic thresholds for specific pests such as European Corn Borer and Bean Leaf Beetles, and a weed identification system developed by the University of Illinois and the Illinois Council of Food and Agricultural Research.

Business continued to be strong in the early 2000s, with revenues surging to $294.6 million in 2000 and $345.7 million in 2001, while net income for these years totaled $7.6 million and $7.5 million, respectively. During the 2001 planting season, cool, wet spring weather and falling interest rates (11 cuts in total) combined to make fiscal 2002 a challenging year. While revenues continued to grow, to $387.4 million, net income dropped to $5.5 million. In a conference call held in April 2002 to discuss the year's financial results, Chairman Miller confessed, "It's been a tough, challenging year for reasons we couldn't control." He went on to say, "I'm glad it's behind us, but I'm optimistic about the future." One reason that the company was optimistic about fiscal 2003 was that applications to AgriFlex Credit were up by 20 percent over the previous year. But an unexpected complication would soon place all these hopes in jeopardy.

The financial institution that had provided credit to the company for the past six years elected to cease its relationship with ASA for the 2003 crop season, in the process erasing 80 percent of ASA's $460 million credit line. Management imposed a November deadline to secure new financing, a time frame that appeared sufficient. But the task proved difficult. With no arrangement in place by November the company would be unable to finance the 2003 crop season. ASA retained Rabobak International, a Netherlands-based investment bank specializing in food and agribusiness, to explore alternatives, which included selling the company. Because credit was tight, how-

ever, the same difficulties ASA faced in funding the next season would also hinder an attempt to land a buyer. In mid-November the company announced that it had signed a letter of agreement with New York-based American Securities Capital Partners (ASCP) in a deal that would give ASCP a 51.7 percent controlling interest in ASA in exchange for an investment as high as $70 million. The deal called for ASCP to make an initial payment of $35 million at the end of February, at which point ASCP would gain voting control of the company. Two further payments of $17.5 million were to be made in subsequent years, contingent upon the meeting of economic thresholds.

The deal with ASCP, however, proved to be difficult to close. Since ASA was working with a reduced credit line, it was unable to offer financing to all of its potential customers. Although revenues fell dramatically over the previous year, tumbling to less than $198 million in 2003, the company improved on its earnings over 2002, posting $5.9 million instead of $5.5 million. Because of its problems in securing adequate credit lines, ASA was forced to cut about a quarter of its workforce in May 2003. In July ASA shareholders approved the ASCP arrangement, but by September the deal fell through. With ASA's temporary credit line set to expire in a matter of weeks, ASA faced liquidation as a very real possibility.

Principal Subsidiaries

Ag Acceptance Corporation; Powerfarm, Inc.

Principal Competitors

AGriBank, FCB; Farmland Industries, Inc.; GROWMARK, Inc.

Further Reading

Buelt, Jamie Guttula, "Investors Find Farm Openings," *Business Record,* May 26, 1986, p. 1.
"Cedar Falls, Iowa-Based Ag Supplier Cuts Work Force," *Waterloo Courier,* May 9, 2003.
Dunaway, Bob, "Going Public Raises Money," *National Hog Farmer,* May 1, 1998.
Palmer, Joel, "Cedar Falls, Iowa-Based Ag Services of America Considers Selling Firm," *Waterloo Courier,* November 6, 2002, p. 1.

—Ed Dinger

Agfa Gevaert Group N.V.

Septestraat 27
B-2640 Mortsel
Belgium
Telephone: (+32) 3 444-2111
Fax: (+32) 3 446-0094
Web site: http://www.agfa.com

Public Company
Incorporated: 1964 as Agfa-Gevaert NV
Employees: 19,341
Sales: EUR 4.68 billion ($4.5 billion) (2002)
Stock Exchanges: Euronext Brussels
Ticker Symbol: AGFB
NAIC: 333315 Photographic and Photocopying
    Equipment Manufacturing; 334510 Electromedical and
    Electrotherapeutic Apparatus Manufacturing

One of the world's most renowned names in photographic films and equipment, Belgium-based Agfa Gevaert Group N.V. has been transforming itself into a high-end imaging solutions provider, with an emphasis on developing innovative and cutting-edge hardware, software, and other digital imaging products. These products make up a rising share of the group's sales, accounting for 37 percent of Agfa's total revenues of EUR 4.68 billion in 2002. Medical imaging is also an important part of Agfa's business, and the group is one of the world's largest producers of films, chemicals, software, and printing equipment for radiography and other medical imaging needs. Meanwhile, Agfa continues to produce its highly popular branded line of photographic film, paper, developing chemicals, and equipment for the photography, cinema, graphic arts, and design industries. Agfa has been restructuring its operations since 2001, creating three core business segments: Graphic Systems; Technical Imaging (comprising the Healthcare, Non-Destructive Testing, and Industrial Imaging business groups); and Consumer Imaging. Agfa's main manufacturing and research and development facilities are located at its headquarters in Mortsel, Belgium, and in Leverkusen, Germany, and Wilmington, Delaware, in the United States. The company operates subsidiaries and sales offices in more than 120 countries worldwide. Long held by Germany's Bayer, Agfa has been an independent company since 1999, listed on the Brussels stock exchange.

Photographic Pioneers in the 19th Century

Agfa-Gevaert Group's origins lay in the pioneering days of photography in Europe in the late 19th century. In Germany, a group of investors, including Carl Alexander von Martius and Paul Mendelssohn-Bartholdy (brother of composer Felix Mendelssohn) set up a factory for the production of color dyes. That company began operations in 1867 and went public in 1873, taking the name Aktien Gesellschaft fur Anilin-Fabrikation, or Agfa.

Agfa became one of Europe's pioneers in the newly emerging photography sector as well, and by 1888 the company had already begun producing its first photographic chemicals and equipment. An Agfa researcher developed a new photographic chemical, Rodinal, in 1891, which became an industry standard for black-and-white development, unrivaled throughout the next century. By 1897, Agfa had trademarked its name, which quickly became a reference in Europe for high-quality imaging products. This was especially so when Agfa began producing plates and film for the newly developing X-ray.

In Belgium, meanwhile, the photographer Lieven Gevaert had begun to produce his own photographic papers, setting up shop in Antwerp in 1890. In 1894, Gevaert incorporated his company as L. Gevaert & Cie, and began producing a wider range of photographic chemicals, papers, and equipment. In 1904, Gevaert moved to the town of Mortsel, and, with a full range of photographic equipment, supplies, and chemicals, as well as its own branded film rolls, the company changed its name to Gevaert Photo Producten in 1920.

Agfa expanded its own production in 1908 with the construction of a new film factory, at the time the largest in Europe. In 1905, the company had also joined a "community of interests" with two other rising German dye and chemicals companies, Bayer and BASF. By the end of World War I, as German chemicals companies scrambled to regain their international positions, the informal group moved toward a more formal

14

Company Perspectives:

Agfa strives to be the partner of choice in imaging, by offering leading edge technology, new ways of working and an understanding of the businesses and individual needs of our customers that goes beyond that of our nearest competitor, this with the fundamental goal to deliver profitable growth.

structure. Under the leadership of Bayer Chairman Friedrich Carl Duisberg, Bayer, Agfa, BASF, together with chemical and dye companies Hoechst, Cassella, and Kalle, began merger negotiations that resulted in the creation of the infamous IG (Interessengemeinschaft) Farben in 1925. Under Farben, Agfa took over Bayer and other group members' photographic equipment and supplies activities.

Both Agfa and Gevaert remained at the forefront of the photographic and imaging industries. Agfa brought out its first film roll camera, the Billy, in 1928, while Gevaert launched its own x-ray films the following year. Innovation continued through the 1930s, especially with Agfa's 1936 launch of the first color films using the substractive color process.

IG Farben's involvement in the Nazi regime, especially in its development of the Zyklon B gas used in the Nazi death camps and its use of slave labor during the war, led to the group's dismantling following the war. The division of Germany between the Allied and Soviet governments severed Agfa from its main production site in Wolfen; instead, production of photographic materials resumed at the Bayer headquarters in Leverkusen in 1945. Agfa itself officially returned to business only in 1952, and became a wholly owned subsidiary of Bayer AG the following year. Over the next decade, Agfa continued its legacy of innovation, introducing the first fully automatic camera in 1956, and the first European color paper processing machine the same year. In 1959, Agfa also introduced the world's first fully automatic 35 mm camera.

European Photographic Giant in the 1960s

At the beginning of the 1960s, Agfa took over all of Bayer's photographic and imaging operations. Agfa then agreed to merge with Gevaert, forming Europe's largest photographic equipment and supplies company in 1964. Under terms of the merger, Bayer retained a 50 percent share of the new company, Agfa-Gevaert. During the 1970s, Agfa-Gevaert entered new categories, launching, for example, the first European-designed copy machine in 1972. At the same time, the company continued to develop its medical imaging interests. Yet heightened competition, notably from Japan's rising photographic industry stars, hit Agfa hard. By the beginning of the 1980s, the company was struggling, and Bayer took 100 percent control of Agfa-Gevaert.

Agfa-Gevaert remained one of the world's leading manufacturers of analog film technologies; during the 1980s, however, the company began making a name for itself as an innovative digital technologies group as well, releasing such products as the world's first digital LED printer in 1983 and a CCD flatbed scanner in 1985. The company also played a part in revolu-

tionizing the film development industry with the launch of the first mini-lab in 1989.

By then, Agfa had raised its profile in the graphics industry with the acquisition of the United States' Compugraphic, a manufacturer of electronic pre-press equipment in 1988. Compugraphic's Wilmington, Delaware headquarters then became the home base for much of Agfa's American operations, renamed Agfa Corporation. That year, also, Agfa expanded its medical imaging division with the acquisition of another U.S. company, Matrix.

Bayer began a restructuring of its U.S. holdings in 1992, placing Agfa Corporation under its Pittsburgh-based Miles Inc. subsidiary, which itself took on the name of Bayer Corporation in 1995. Agfa then was refocused as Bayer's imaging division and underwent a restructuring that brought the struggling division back into profitability by the end of the decade.

International Digital Imaging Solutions Provider for the New Century

Agfa began acquiring new operations in the mid-1990s, purchasing Hoechst's printing plate and proofing equipment business Ozasol, with a manufacturing plant in Wiesbaden and sales of DM 420 million (approximately $200 million). The acquisition represented Agfa's largest to date. Agfa struck again in 1998, this time buying the offset printing and graphic arts film operation from DuPont, adding some $600 million in sales. After that acquisition, Agfa sold off its copy machine business to Lanier Worldwide. The following year, Agfa acquired another U.S. company, Sterling Diagnostic Imaging, expanding the company's medical imaging division.

With Agfa once again showing profits, Bayer decided the time was right to refocus its own operations, and in 1999 the company spun off 75 percent of Agfa in a public offering on both the Frankfurt and Euronext Brussels stock exchanges. The Agfa-Gevaert Group's headquarters then relocated to the company's Mortsel site, although its Leverkusen operation remained one of its primary manufacturing facilities. Bayer exited its holding in Agfa completely in 2002, selling its stake to Goldman Sachs.

The newly public and independent company returned to acquisitions in 2000, buying up Krautkramer, the world's leading manufacturer of NDT (non-destructive testing) systems. That year, the company also bought Quadrat, the number one developer of hardware and software for radiology systems.

These acquisitions forecasted a central component of the group's reorganization, launched in 2001. Designed to slash costs by more than EUR 400 million per year, the reorganization called for Agfa's transition toward becoming a digital imaging solutions specialist. As part of that effort, Agfa regrouped its operations under three primary business units: Graphic Systems; Technical Imaging (comprising the Healthcare, Non-Destructive Testing, and Industrial Imaging business groups); and Consumer Imaging. The company also began cutting away at its payroll, with job cuts slated ultimately to reach more than 4,000 of the group's 22,000 employees.

With the launch of its reorganization, the company embarked on a buying spree, picking up Autologic, Talk Technol-

Key Dates:

1873: Paul Mendelssohn-Bartholdy and Carl Alexander von Mathius found color dye factory in Germany, which becomes Aktien Geschellschaft fur Anilinfabrikation (Agfa) in 1873.

1888: Agfa begins production of photographic materials.

1890: Photographer Lieven Gevaert begins producing photographic papers, then incorporates business as L. Gevaert & Cie in Antwerp in 1894.

1897: Agfa is registered as a trademark.

1904: Gevaert moves production and headquarters to Mortsel.

1905: Agfa joins grouping of interests with Bayer and BASF.

1925: Bayer, BASF, Agfa, Hoechst, and others merge to form IG Farben.

1953: Agfa becomes wholly owned subsidiary of Bayer.

1964: Agfa and Gevaert merge, forming Agfa-Gevaert NV, which is 50 percent controlled by Bayer.

1972: Agfa introduces first European-designed copy machine.

1981: Bayer assumes full control of Agfa.

1988: Agfa acquires U.S.-based Compugraphic, and U.S. operation adopts the name Agfa Corporation.

1992: Agfa Corporation is placed under Bayer subsidiary Miles Inc., based in Pittsburgh.

1996: Agfa acquires Hoechst's printing plate and proofing equipment business Ozasol.

1998: Agfa acquires DuPont's offset printing and graphic arts film operation.

1999: Bayer spins off Agfa-Gevaert as a public company, retaining a 25 percent stake.

2000: Agfa acquires Krautkramer, the world's leading manufacturer of NDT (non-destructive testing) systems and Quadrat, the number one developer of hardware and software for radiology systems.

2001: Agfa launches restructuring to emphasize digital imaging products and cut costs; acquires Autologic, Talk Technology, and Pantak in the United States and Seifert inGermany.

2002: Company acquires Mitra, a supplier of imaging and information systems for the healthcare market; Bayer sells its stake in Agfa to Goldman Sachs.

2003: Company buys U.K.-based Printing Techniques Ltd.; sells NDT unit to General Electric; completes new production facility in China in a move to increase its share of Asian market.

---

ogy, X-ray and NDT specialist Pantak, and Seifert, all in 2001. The following year, Agfa added Mitra, a supplier of imaging and information systems for the healthcare market. Then in 2003, the company bought Printing Techniques Ltd., based in the United Kingdom, a maker of printing and proofing plates. The company also targeted expansion in the Asian market, with a new plant in China scheduled to begin operations in late 2003. In that year, also, Agfa announced its agreement to sell its NDT unit to General Electric in a deal worth EUR 400 million.

By then, Agfa was well on its way to achieving the aims of its restructuring. Digital imaging sales represented a fast-rising proportion of the group's total sales, topping 37 percent of its nearly EUR 4.7 billion in revenues. With its restructuring scheduled for completion at the end of 2003, the company expected to start reaping the benefits as early as 2004. By refocusing its commitment onto the digital market, Agfa-Gevaert remained true to its long heritage as one of the world's leading and most innovative imaging specialists.

Principal Subsidiaries

Agfa (Wuxi) Printing Plate Co. Ltd. (China) 100; Agfa Belgie N.V. (Belgium); Agfa Corporation Inc. (U.S.A.); Agfa Deutschland Vertriebsgesellschaft mbH & Cie; Agfa Europe N.V. (Belgium); Agfa Hong Kong Ltd.; Agfa Hungaria Kft. (Hungary); Agfa Inc. (Canada); Agfa Korea Ltd. (South Korea); Agfa Monotype Corp. (U.S.A.), Inc.; Agfa Monotype, Ltd. (U.K.); Agfa s.r.o. (Czechlosovakia); Agfa Singapore Pte. Ltd.; Agfa-Gevaert A/S (Denmark); Agfa-Gevaert AB (Sweden); Agfa-Gevaert AG (Germany); Agfa-Gevaert Argentina S.A.; Agfa-Gevaert AS (Norway); Agfa-Gevaert Colombia Ltd.; Agfa-Gevaert de Venezuela S.A.; Agfa-Gevaert do Brasil Ltda.

(Brazil); Agfa-Gevaert International N.V. (Belgium); Agfa-Gevaert Japan, Ltd.; Agfa-Gevaert Limited (U.K.); Agfa-Gevaert Ltda. (Chile); Agfa-Gevaert New Zealand Ltd.; Agfa-Gevaert S.A. (France); Agfa-Gevaert S.A. (Spain); Autologic Information International, Ltd. (U.S.A.); CEA Deutschland GmbH (Germany); International Typeface Corp. (U.S.A.); Mitra Corporation (U.S.A.); Nutronik GmbH (Germany); Quadrat N.V. (Belgium); Shanghai Agfa Imaging Products Co., Ltd.; Xitron Europe Ltd. (U.K.).

Principal Competitors

Tomoegawa Paper Company Ltd.; Canon Inc.; Fuji Photo Film Company Ltd.; Sony USA Inc.; Xerox Corp.; Ricoh Company Ltd.; Eastman Kodak Co.; Carl-Zeiss-Stiftung; Konica Minolta Holdings Inc.

Further Reading

"Agfa Shrinks to Grow," *Graphic Arts Monthly*, October 21, 2001, p. 29.

"Agfa Streamlines, Acquires Autologic," *American Printer*, November 2001, p. S10.

Dombey, Daniel, "Deal Founders on Agfa Name," *Financial Times*, June 12, 2001, p. 19.

Eodice, Lynne, "Agfa: A Century of Innovative Products," *Peterson's Photographic*, August 1997, p. 33.

Harnischfeger, Uta, "Agfa Buys Sterling of US," *Financial Times*, January 12, 1999, p. 26.

Meller, Paul, "Agfa Sells a Unit to GE," *New York Times*, January 21, 2003, p. C4.

"Plate Supplier PTL Bought up by Agfa," *Print Week*, February 28, 2003, p. 11.

—M. L. Cohen

AIR CANADA

Air Canada

Air Canada Centre
7373 Côte Vertu Boulevard West
Saint-Laurent, Quebec H4Y 1H4
Canada
Telephone: (514) 422-5000
Fax: (514) 422-5909
Web site: http://www.aircanada.ca

Public Company
Incorporated: 1937 as Trans-Canada Air Lines
Employees: 36,000
Sales: C$9.83 billion (US$6.23 billion) (2002)
Stock Exchanges: Toronto
Ticker Symbol: AC
NAIC: 481111 Scheduled Passenger Air Transportation;
    481112 Scheduled Freight Air Transportation; 481211
    Nonscheduled Chartered Passenger Air
    Transportation; 481212 Nonscheduled Chartered
    Freight Air Transportation; 561520 Tour Operators

Air Canada is the only national, full-service airline based in Canada. The corporation ranked as the seventh largest airline in North America and the 13th largest in the world in 2002. That year, Air Canada carried about 29 million passengers. In addition to its flagship full-service carrier, Air Canada also runs Tango, a low-fare air service operating on many Canadian and some U.S. routes; Zip, a low-fare carrier based in Calgary; and Air Canada Jazz, a regional carrier. Overall, the company serves nearly 170 destinations on five continents—but mainly North America—using a fleet of 330 aircraft, 100 of which are part of Air Canada Jazz's regional fleet. Through its membership in the Star Alliance, which also includes United Airlines, Lufthansa, Scandinavian Airlines System, and Thai Airways International, among several others, Air Canada offers service to more than 700 destinations in more than 100 countries. Air Canada provides both scheduled and chartered air transportation for passengers as well as cargo and also owns Air Canada Vacations, a major Canadian tour operator. Aeroplan, Air Canada's frequent flyer program, has more than six million members. Having survived privatization, the threat of scandal, and the industry's usual crises throughout its 65-years-plus history, Air Canada faced a whole host of challenges in the early 2000s that severely affected its financial health and led ultimately to the firm filing for bankruptcy protection in April 2003.

Interwar Origins

Under the administration of Prime Minister Mackenzie King, the Canadian government created Trans-Canada Air Lines (TCA) as a Crown corporation in 1937 to provide transcontinental airline service within Canada's borders. It was originally a wholly owned subsidiary of the government-owned Canadian National Railway Corporation. From its founding through 1959, the government-owned company had a complete monopoly on all of Canada's domestic air routes; it also had a monopoly on all trans-border routes (routes that crossed the Canadian border with the United States) until 1967. The federal Cabinet of Canada approved all of the airline's routes and fares, and government regulators issued licenses approved by the Cabinet for the airline.

But government sponsorship did not rule out competition. Canadian Pacific Limited, one of the country's railway giants, acquired and combined nine small private carriers to form Canadian Pacific Airlines (also known as CP Air), based in Vancouver, British Columbia, in the 1940s. In 1959 the Canadian government allowed CP Air to provide one flight each day in each direction between Vancouver and Montreal, Quebec. From that small bit of business, CP Air grew through 1965 to acquire an average of 12.7 percent—the total it was allowed by federal regulations—of the domestic intercontinental traffic formerly held by Air Canada. In 1967 the Canadian government further relaxed its regulations and allowed CP Air two flights per day and, by 1970, CP Air was permitted to gain 25 percent of the intercontinental traffic in Canada. Also in 1967 the Canadian government allowed CP Air, which was given the right to establish international air routes across the Pacific Ocean in 1948, to establish a route from Vancouver to San Francisco, California—the first trans-border route not flown by TCA. Despite the encroaching competition from CP Air and that airline's dominance in international routes across the Pacific Ocean, TCA

Company Perspectives:

Air Canada together with its regional airline subsidiary, Air Canada Jazz, provides scheduled and charter air transportation for passengers and cargo to more than 150 destinations, vacation packages to over 90 destinations, as well as maintenance, ground handling and training services to other airlines.

Canada's flag carrier is recognized as a leader in the global air transportation market by pursuing a strategy based on value-added customer service, technical excellence and passenger safety.

held, by government fiat, a monopoly on all other international routes and intercontinental domestic air travel.

Changes in the 1960s and 1970s

TCA adopted the name Air Canada in 1965. Government regulations set forth the next year prevented regional air carriers from competing with both Air Canada and CP Air, which were directed to work with the regional carriers to establish joint fare and commission arrangements and to cooperate on technical and servicing matters, including service to specific areas that required special equipment. Later, in 1969, the Canadian government established specific regions in which each of the five regional Canadian airlines could operate; those regulations lasted through the early 1980s.

Throughout the 1970s several pressures (many of which arose or were centered in the United States) challenged the Canadian government and the Air Canada monopoly. Larger jets for airline service provided air carriers with roomier vehicles, but high air fares, which were regulated in both the United States and Canada by federal agencies, prevented the efficient use of those vehicles. The power of consumers increased during the decade, and customers used that power to demand lower air fares from more competitive airlines. Information on how deregulated industries would perform was persuading many regulators, airline executives, and consumers that a regulated airline industry was not in the best interest of anyone. In the late 1970s these forces combined to gain the support of leading politicians in the United States. The deregulation process of the U.S. airline industry began, with Canadian politicians watching closely, especially as Canadian passengers increasingly chose U.S. airlines for their international and transcontinental flights to take advantage of lower fares and improved services.

When Parliament passed the Air Canada Act of 1978, the Crown corporation was finally subjected to the same regulations and regulatory agencies that other Canadian airlines faced, bringing it more fully into competition with CP Air and the other regional airlines that were then operating. That act ended the government's unique regulatory control over Air Canada's routes, fare structures, and services—control the government wielded over the company throughout its first 41 years of business. (The act also reorganized its ownership structure; Air Canada would no longer be a subsidiary of Canadian National Railway, becoming a direct wholly owned subsidiary of the

Canadian government.) On March 23, 1979, the minister of transport removed all capacity restraints on CP Air's share of transcontinental traffic, and it was given a license to provide domestic transcontinental flights. CP Air established transcontinental service in May 1980 to compete directly with Air Canada. While these changes were occurring in its domestic competition, Air Canada was also facing increasing competition in international routes from American Airlines, British Airways, SwissAir, and Lufthansa.

The Competitive 1980s

By 1984 Air Canada hinted in its annual report that, to continue to compete with other international airlines, it would require a tremendous amount of new capital to replace its aging fleet of airliners with state-of-the-art jets. To upgrade its fleet, Air Canada was considering buying, between the years 1984 and 1993, more than 40 new airliners at a cost of more than C$135 million each; the company also stated that it did not believe it could finance such purchases from retained earnings. At that time, six airline companies were operating in Canada, and Air Canada, which had more than a 50 percent share of the market, owned and operated the country's only computer reservations system. This provided them with access to all of the major travel agents in Canada and enabled them to collect a fee from other airlines when their tickets were sold on the computerized system. CP Air, which was acquired by Pacific Western Airlines (an Alberta-based regional carrier) and renamed Canadian Airlines International Ltd. in the mid-1980s, established its own computerized reservation system, but in 1987 the two airlines' systems were merged into a single network called the Gemini Group Limited Partnership.

In 1985 then Transport Minister Donald Mazankowski said that the Canadian government was planning to allow Air Canada and the Canadian National Railways the freedom to operate as private companies. The Canadian public appeared to support that move. In its annual report for the year 1985, Air Canada said it was determined to resolve the challenges it faced from its competition by managing its own destiny and achieving "a standard of financial credibility that will ultimately enable the shareholder to pursue a course of private and employee equity participation." This statement pointed toward the direction the company intended to move and coincided with further relaxation of regulations that encouraged its domestic and international competitors.

The complete deregulation of Canada's airline industry was first proposed in a policy paper from Mazankowski to Parliament in July 1985. That policy was not enacted until Parliament passed the National Transportation Act of 1987, which became effective January 1, 1988. On April 12, 1988, Mazankowski, who was then the minister responsible for privatization, announced that Air Canada would be sold to the public as "market conditions permit" with an initial treasury issue of up to 45 percent of its shares. When it was announced, the sale was seen as the most ambitious act of privatization that the Canadian government had attempted thus far; Air Canada had assets of C$3.18 billion and revenues of C$3.13 billion in 1987. The sale was subjected to several conditions that were placed into the enabling legislation, which Parliament approved in August 1988.

Key Dates:

1937: The Canadian government creates Trans-Canada Air Lines (TCA) as a Crown corporation to provide transcontinental airline service within Canada's borders; it is originally a wholly owned subsidiary of the government-owned Canadian National Railway Corporation.

1964: TCA changes its name to Air Canada.

1978: Air Canada Act transforms Air Canada into a wholly owned subsidiary of the Canadian government, but limits the regulatory control the government has over the airline.

1988: National Transportation Act of 1987 goes into effect, stipulating the complete deregulation of the Canadian airline industry and the privatization of Air Canada; 43 percent of Air Canada's shares are sold to the public.

1989: The sale of the remaining 57 percent of Air Canada's shares completes the corporation's move to privatization.

1997: Air Canada becomes a founding member of the Star Alliance, along with Lufthansa, Scandinavian Airlines System, Thai Airways International, and United Airlines.

1999: Robert Milton is named CEO, fends off a takeover bid from Onex Corporation, and reaches an agreement to acquire arch-rival Canadian Airlines.

2000: Acquisition of Canadian is finalized; the two airlines' various regional carriers are merged into Air Canada Regional Inc.

2001: Low-cost airline Tango is launched.

2002: Air Canada Regional is relaunched as Air Canada Jazz; corporation launches Zip, a Calgary-based low-cost carrier serving western Canada.

2003: Escalating travails force Air Canada to file for bankruptcy protection.

The legislation stipulated several things: the company's headquarters would remain in Montreal, Quebec; the airline, for the indefinite future, would maintain major operational and overhaul centers at Winnipeg, Manitoba, and in Montreal and Toronto; no more than 45 percent of the company's shares would be sold and the proceeds would go to the airline, not to the government; employees would be given the first chance to buy shares in the company, small shareholders the second opportunity, followed by institutional investors and, finally, foreign investors; no individual shareholder would be allowed to hold more than 10 percent of the company's shares and foreign ownership was limited to 25 percent of the initial offering; and the government's 55 percent holding in the company would be voted in accordance with the private sector shareholders to give the company an arm's length relationship to the government.

On September 26, 1988, Air Canada filed the prospectus on its stock, stating that its net income after taxes was C$101 million for the year ended March 31, 1988. The price of the stock was set at C$8 per share. The company completed its IPO in October 1988, issuing 30.8 million shares—42.8 percent of the company's total. The company netted C$225.8 million on the C$246.2 million sale, with underwriting fees taking C$12.3 million and with the airline absorbing C$8 million in discounts to its employees. By the end of March 1989 the company's shares were trading at C$11.75 per share, and the stock hit a high of C$14.83 in August that same year.

Air Canada's efficacious move to becoming a private company was seen as a result of a successful public relations program directed by the company's chairman, Claude I. Taylor, and its president and chief executive officer, Pierre J. Jeanniot. The executives focused the public relations program on the company's employees, the media, communities, customers, and potential shareholders; this was done in two carefully structured parts—pre-announcement and post-announcement—that were designed to ensure the success of the move to privatization by emphasizing the company's strengths and competitive position as it worked to improve its service and operations.

In July 1989 the company completed its move to privatization with the filing of a prospectus for its second issue of stock. The company sold 41.1 million shares—for a total of 57 percent of its equity in the filing—at C$12 per share. Proceeds from that sale went to the government. As an indication of the issue's success, by the end of the first week after the shares were issued the company's stock was trading at C$12.75 per share. The company subsequently updated its fleet by ordering almost three dozen Airbus A320s jets. (The Canadian government later accused Brian Mulroney, prime minister at the time, of taking "kickbacks" in the deal, a charge that was eventually retracted.)

Finding Its Wings in the 1990s

The company's operating results, however, did not reflect the enthusiastic welcome that its stock had met in the market. Air Canada reported losses of C$74 million in 1990 and C$218 million in 1991, and it reported that it had nearly two million fewer passengers in 1991 than in the previous year. The company blamed its losses and decreased passenger load on the combined effects of the economic recession and the falloff in travel that resulted from the war in the Persian Gulf. It also, however, was seen as being hurt extensively by the pressures of competition with other international carriers.

In July 1990 Jeanniot surprised his colleagues at Air Canada by announcing his retirement. Jeanniot, who spent 35 years with the company, told *Traffic World* magazine that he believed the time was right for him to retire: "I have done my time. A chief executive should not hang around forever." Jeanniot was replaced in early 1992 by Hollis L. Harris, a former top executive at Delta Airlines and Continental Airlines; he was named vice-chairman, president, and CEO.

The year that Harris joined Air Canada was a difficult one for his company and for the airline industry in general. Air Canada restructured its operations, eliminating five senior management positions, including four senior vice-presidents and the position of executive vice-president and chief operating officer; it also cut 250 other management positions and 100 administrative and technical support positions, all in an effort to save C$20 million a year. The restructuring was part of the move to cut operating expenses by 10 percent—C$300 million a year—by 1993 and was expected to be accompanied by a reduction of nonmanagement union employees later in 1992. The restructuring enhanced Harris's position in day-to-day operations and gave him direct responsibility for the six divisions that were formed in the restructuring. The Harris regimen would make Air Canada more competitive and, beginning in 1994, profitable once again.

The restructuring also resulted in the sale of Air Canada's "En Route" credit card operations to Diners Club of America, the selling of its Montreal headquarters building, and the relocating of its headquarters staff from downtown Montreal to Dorval Airport; in addition, the company enacted a plan to sell and lease back three of the Boeing 747-400s in its fleet. The restructuring was seen as a move to make Air Canada more efficient.

To gain further efficiencies, Air Canada proposed a merger in early 1992 with Canadian Airlines International, its primary Canadian competitor; the merger would have made Air Canada once again Canada's only international carrier. Canadian Airlines rebuffed Air Canada's merger proposal, however, and the idea was viewed as politically unpopular in Canada where it would have likely eliminated more than 10,000 jobs.

In 1994 Air Canada won long-coveted entree into the Japanese market (it had been prohibited by law from competing in Asia and South America since 1987) when the Canadian government appointed it to serve Osaka's new Kansai International Airport. The corporation took to warmer climes with relish after the signing of an "open skies" agreement between Canada and the United States in early 1995. Beginning with Atlanta, the carrier opened almost 30 new U.S. routes, mostly nonstop, within the year. They proved enduringly popular and profitable. The airline renovated its fleet of smaller aircraft with Canadair regional transports to provide flexibility on its shorter routes. Montreal and Vancouver airports were opened to U.S. carriers in 1997; Toronto followed in 1998.

Air Canada initiated code sharing agreements with U.S. carriers after gaining access to that market. Its networking took on a much larger scale with the creation of the Star Alliance in 1997, through which Air Canada, Lufthansa, Scandinavian Airlines System, Thai Airways International, and United Airlines (later joined by VARIG of Brazil) linked their routes. Each carrier also agreed to honor each other's frequent flyer miles. International fares accounted for more than half of passenger revenue, and the company continued to expand its services in this area while leveling off domestic growth.

Short-Lived Prosperity, Late 1990s

Air Canada had record profits as well as a 60th anniversary to celebrate in 1997. As the company wooed patrons with refinements and innovations such as the Xerox Business Centres located in Maple Leaf Lounges and the Skyriders frequent flyer program for children, it reaped a net income of C$427 million on total revenues of more than C$5 billion. The airline's young fleet of 157 planes boasted one of the continent's best on-time records, carrying 40,000 passengers a day. The positive performance was tempered somewhat by a labor disruption among pilots for its regional subsidiaries. Air Canada divested itself of

Northwest Territorial Airways Ltd. in June 1997 and the next month sold most of its interest in Galileo Canada Distribution Systems Inc.

Harris was succeeded by Lamar Durrett as president and CEO in May 1996. Durrett was a protégé of Harris's, having come to Air Canada with Harris in 1992 as executive vice-president and chief administrative officer; Durrett, like Harris, was an American. John Fraser succeeded Harris as chairman in August 1996.

Durrett's stint at the helm turned out to be short-lived and troubled. Despite the cost-cutting efforts of the early to mid-1990s, Air Canada remained one of the least efficient carriers in North America, and Durrett failed to move quickly enough with further efficiency initiatives. Durrett and his managers were also caught by surprise when the company's pilots went on strike in September 1998 to back up their demands for higher salaries. The strike lasted 13 days, costing Air Canada C$250 million and resulting in a loss of C$16 million for the year. Flight attendants, emboldened by their knowledge that management was desperate to avoid another strike, took the company to the brink of a walkout in July 1999, securing healthy wage increases in the process. Durrett suffered two further black eyes in 1999. In January a blizzard shut down Toronto's Pearson International Airport, and Air Canada did not respond well during the crisis, leaving thousands of angry passengers waiting for hours only to find out that their flights had been canceled. Air Canada also refused to pay fee increases that had been imposed at Pearson, and Durrett tried to get other airlines to do the same—an effort that was an embarrassing failure. By July 1999 Air Canada stock was trading at C$6.30, less than half its value 12 months earlier and more than 20 percent below its 1988 IPO price of C$8.

Durrett resigned under pressure in August 1999 and was replaced by Robert Milton, who at age 39 had been named president just three months earlier. Milton, another American, had been involved with Air Canada since 1992 when he was hired as a consultant to assist in reorganizing the airline's cargo division. Almost immediately after being appointed CEO, Milton found himself in the middle of a very public takeover battle.

Early 2000s Turbulence: Takeover of Canadian Airlines, Dire Economic Environment, Bankruptcy

By mid-1999 Canadian Airlines was in grave financial straits and verging on bankruptcy. Soon after taking the helm as CEO, Milton began pursuing a possible buyout of Canadian Airlines' lucrative international routes, but was quickly turned down. Canadian had already entered into secret negotiations with Onex Corporation, a Toronto-based leveraged buyout firm, and AMR Corporation, the parent of American Airlines and owner of a 25 percent stake in Canadian, about a possible takeover. Gerry Schwartz, head of Onex, soon started pursuing the takeover and merger of both Canadian and Air Canada. Milton responded with his own takeover bid, of Canadian Airlines, backed by Star Alliance partners United Airlines and Lufthansa. He also took Onex to court where he won a verdict that upheld a law stipulating that no single shareholder could own more than 10 percent of Air Canada. This scuttled the Onex bid, and Milton in December 1999 secured an agreement to take over Canadian Airlines at a bargain-basement price of C$61 million—but with a burdensome assumption of C$3.5 billion in Canadian Airlines debt and lease obligations. The acquisition was officially completed in July 2000, although integration moves began even earlier that year.

After discovering that Canadian Airlines was losing C$2 million per day, Milton and his managers put the integration of Canadian into Air Canada on a very fast track. The speed with which the two carrier networks were brought together triggered a period of mass chaos, particularly during the summer of 2000, when many customers were driven irate by canceled flights, departure delays, lost luggage, unhelpful agents, and other difficulties. The situation got so bad that Milton took to the airwaves in early August, promising in a series of ads that within 180 days, or by January 2001, the integration of the two carriers would be complete and the problems plaguing Air Canada would end. He did in fact meet this goal, and service gradually began to improve. Meanwhile, during 2000, the regional carriers of Air Canada and Canadian Airlines—AirBC, Air Nova, Air Ontario, and Canadian Regional Airlines—were merged into a single entity called Air Canada Regional Inc. (which was relaunched as Air Canada Jazz in April 2002).

Although Air Canada was now the sole Canadian full-service air carrier—controlling 80 percent of the nation's air-travel market and about 43 percent of the traffic between Canada and the United States—it was not without competition, and stiff competition at that. WestJet Airlines Ltd. had been operating out of Calgary since 1996, bringing to Canada the low-cost, no-frills airline concept pioneered by the very successful U.S. firm Southwest Airlines Co. Like Southwest, WestJet was a nonunion outfit, giving it a tremendous cost advantage over Air Canada and its heavily unionized workforce. It was in fact competition from WestJet that had brought Canadian Airlines to the brink of insolvency. WestJet, which also quickly established itself as one of the most profitable airlines in North America, expanded throughout western Canada during the late 1990s and then seized upon the opening offered by the Air Canada—Canadian Airlines merger to move into the eastern part of the country in the early 2000s. Milton responded in turn by launching two separate low-cost airlines. Tango began operations in November 2001 and was operated alongside the flagship Air Canada line, sharing its fleet. Zip, a low-fare carrier based in Calgary, began serving western Canada in September 2002; it was operated independently with its own management and fleet.

Competition was far from the only challenge facing Air Canada in the early 2000s. The company along with the entire North American airline industry was battered by an extremely negative operating environment. Business travel slowed down quite suddenly in late 2000 in concert with the faltering global economy and the implosion of the technology sector. The events of September 11, 2001, took a serious toll on the airline industry, and during 2002 air travel continued to be curtailed because of the ongoing economic slowdown and the threat of a U.S. war against Iraq. Air Canada consequently posted net losses of C$1.32 billion in 2001 and C$828 million in 2002. The launching of the Iraq war by the United States in early 2003, coupled with an outbreak of a different sort—that of sudden acute respiratory syndrome (SARS), which seriously affected Air Can-

ada's Asian routes and operations at its Toronto hub—placed the company itself on the brink of bankruptcy, C$13 billion in debt. On April 1, 2003, Air Canada was forced to file for bankruptcy protection, despite several cost-cutting and capacity-reduction initiatives undertaken throughout this period of crisis. Air Canada's filing followed that of several major U.S. carriers, which had entered bankruptcy proceedings in 2002.

Air Canada initiated a host of restructuring efforts while moving toward an emergence from bankruptcy. Perhaps most crucially, the company attempted to reduce its annual operating expenses by 25 percent, or C$2.4 billion. New labor agreements were reached with the unions that involved wage cuts, layoffs, and more flexible work rules. One-quarter of the workforce, or about 10,000 workers, were likely to lose their jobs. Another important move was Air Canada's seeking of an infusion of at least C$700 million (US$517 million) in new equity from an outside investor. In September 2003 the corporation announced two finalists in the bidding for a major Air Canada stake: Victor Li, a powerful Hong Kong businessman with Canadian citizenship, and New York private-equity firm Cerberus Capital Management, L.P. Putting aside the pending emergence from bankruptcy, Air Canada faced the longer term challenge of finding a new business model under which it could successfully compete with WestJet and other discount upstarts.

Principal Subsidiaries

Jazz Air Inc.; ZIP Air Inc.; Aeroplan Limited Partnership; Touram Inc.; Wingco Leasing Inc.; Air Canada Capital Ltd.; Destina.ca Inc.

Principal Divisions

Passenger Operations; Cargo Operations; Air Canada Technical Services.

Principal Competitors

WestJet Airlines Ltd.; AMR Corporation; Delta Air Lines, Inc.; Continental Airlines, Inc.; UAL Corporation.

Further Reading

"Calling the Tune," *Flight International,* September 2, 2003, p. 37.
Came, Barry, " 'Straight Out of Kafka': Mulroney Lashes Out at the Federal Government's Allegations," *Maclean's,* April 29, 1996.
Collins, David H., *Wings Across Time: The Story of Air Canada,* Toronto: Griffin House, 1978.
Dawson, Phil, "Air Canada: Sixty Years of Innovation and Progress," *Airways,* January/February 1998, pp. 19–27.
DeCloet, Derek, and Sean Silcoff, "Be Nice for a Change," *Canadian Business,* October 8, 1999, pp. 37–38, 40.
Enchin, Harvey, Geoffrey Rowan, and Stephen McHale, "An Airline Merger Fails to Fly," *Globe and Mail,* August 24, 1992, p. A1.
Flint, Perry, "The Business Is Actually Fun Again!," *Air Transport World,* June 1995.
——, "The World Has Changed Forever," *Air Transport World,* March 2003, pp. 22–24, 26.
Foster, Cecil, "Air Canada Searching for a New CEO After Jeanniot's Surprise Retirement," *Traffic World,* August 13, 1990.
——, "Tough Guys Don't Cuss," *Canadian Business,* February 1995.
Gibbon, Ann, "Harris, Managers Take Pay Cut," *Globe and Mail,* February 23, 1993, p. B1.

Goldenberg, Susan, *Troubled Skies: Crisis, Competition and Control in Canada's Airline Industry,* Whitby, Ont.: McGraw-Hill Ryerson, 1994.

Libin, Kevin, "Hard Reign," *Canadian Business,* May 26, 2003, pp. 107–10.

Macklem, Katherine, "Air Rage: After Months of Chaos, Air Canada's Tough-Guy Boss Insists the Worst Is Over," *Maclean's,* November 6, 2000, p. 68.

McKenna, Edward, "Air Canada Restructures," *Aviation Week and Space Technology,* May 4, 1992.

McMurdy, Deirdre, "The Style of Dixie," *Maclean's,* July 6, 1992, p. 96.

Millan, Luis, "Can No. 2 Fly Higher?," *Canadian Business,* May 29, 1998, pp. 50–53, 55.

Nicol, John, "Unfriendly Skies," *Maclean's,* May 22, 2000, p. 34.

Ouellet, Francine Vallee, "The Privatization of Air Canada," *Canadian Business Review,* Winter 1989, pp. 19+.

Oum, Tae Hoon, W.T. Stanbury, and Michael W. Tretheway, "Airline Deregulation in Canada and Its Economic Effects," *Transportation Journal,* Summer 1991.

Pigott, Peter, *National Treasure: The History of Trans Canada Airlines,* Madeira Park, B.C.: Harbour Publishing, 2001.

Shiffrin, Carole A., "Aggressive Start for Canadian Carriers in Open Skies Pact," *Aviation Week and Space Technology,* March 25, 1996.

Smith, Philip, *It Seems Like Only Yesterday: Air Canada, the First 50 Years,* Toronto: McClelland and Stewart, 1986.

Tower, Courtney, "Air Canada Charting Its Own Unique Flight Path(s)," *Journal of Commerce and Commercial,* August 13, 1997, p. 14A.

Turner, Craig, "Air Canada's Aboot-Face," *Los Angeles Times,* August 8, 1996.

Van Velzen, Andrew, and Craig Turner, "Canada Settles Suit, Apologizes to Ex-Premier; Courts," *Los Angeles Times,* January 1, 1997.

Verburg, Peter, "Dogfight," *Canadian Business,* September 17, 2001, p. 23.

—Bruce Vernyi
—updates: Frederick C. Ingram, David E. Salamie

Albemarle Corporation

330 South 4th Street
Richmond, Virginia 23210
U.S.A.
Telephone: (804) 788-6000
Toll Free: (800) 535-3030
Fax: (804) 788-6020
Web site: http://www.albemarle.com

Public Company
Incorporated: 1994
Employees: 3,000
Sales: $980.20 million (2002)
Stock Exchanges: New York
Ticker Symbol: ALB
NAIC: 325211 Plastics Material and Resin Manufacturing;
    325188 All Other Inorganic Chemical Manufacturing

Albemarle Corporation is a leading producer of polymer and fine chemicals. The company's products are used as additives to or intermediates for a wide range of products manufactured by pharmaceutical companies, cleaning product manufacturers, water treatment companies, agricultural companies, and paper and photographic companies. These companies are Albemarle's customers. The company operates on a global scale, serving customers in North America, Europe, the Middle East, Africa, and Asia. Albemarle operates several production plants in the United States, maintaining a presence in Houston, Texas; Orangeburg, South Carolina; Magnolia, Arkansas; Tyrone, Pennsylvania; and Dayton, Ohio. In Europe, Albemarle production plants are located in Thann, France; Teesport, England; Port-de-Bouc, France; Bergheim, Germany; and St. Jakobs/Breitenau, Austria. In Asia, the company operates a plant in Osaka, Japan, as well as offices and warehouses in China and Singapore.

19th-Century Origins

The history of Albemarle involved the development of two companies and the legacy of one family. The earliest predecessor organization of Albemarle that existed in the 21st century began operating in 1887 as Albemarle Paper Manufacturing Company. The company was small, employing less than ten workers who produced Kraft and blotting paper. The first signal moment in the paper manufacturer's development occurred in 1918, when Floyd D. Gottwald joined the firm. Gottwald was hired to work in the company's export department, beginning as a clerk. From his modest station as a clerk, the young Gottwald began his climb toward distinction, eventually becoming Albemarle's leader. Gottwald's influence over the fortunes of Albemarle extended to another much larger company, Ethyl Corporation, whose early history was instrumental to the development of the modern-day Albemarle.

Against the backdrop of Gottwald's rise from clerk to company president—a 30-year climb—Ethyl, then known as Ethyl Gasoline Corporation, was enjoying its own steady rise in the petroleum industry. Ethyl's principal product for nearly a half-century was discovered in 1921, three years after Gottwald joined Albemarle. In 1921, a General Motors research chemist named Charles Kettering discovered a way to reduce the engine "knock" produced by gasoline. Kettering's discovery led to the revelation of the antiknock properties of tetraethyl lead (TEL) as a gasoline additive. In 1923, a joint venture between General Motors and Standard Oil was formed to develop and to produce TEL. One year later, the name of the joint venture became Ethyl Gasoline Corporation.

Although TEL served as the foundation for Ethyl for decades, the company diversified into a range of related businesses. In the early 1940s, the name of the company was changed to reflect its broader interests. Ethyl Gasoline Corporation became Ethyl Corporation at roughly the same time Gottwald completed his ascent from clerk to president at Albemarle. It was through Gottwald that the corporate lives of Albemarle and Ethyl became intertwined, a union that was predicated upon Ethyl's diversification beyond TEL. During the 1950s, Ethyl hit its stride, using the market success of TEL to expand physically and operationally. The company opened a plant in Pasadena, Texas, in 1952, a facility that complemented its TEL production site in Baton Rouge, Louisiana, which was opened in 1937. One year after the Pasadena plant opened, Ethyl acquired a specialty chemical plant from Wannamaker Chemical Company.

The acquisition of the plant, located in Orangeburg, South Carolina, marked a pivotal juncture in the development of the

Gottwald family's business interests. Specialty chemicals eventually became the chief business of the Gottwalds and of the later version of Albemarle. The foray into specialty chemicals also built the bridge that connected Albemarle and Ethyl. Ethyl's diversification answered a need of Albemarle's, serving as the nexus of a company founded as a paper manufacturer and a company founded to produce gasoline additives. Gottwald was the protagonist, his actions stemming from the pressures of his position as the leader of a paper manufacturer that was well known as a maker of premium blotting paper.

Acquisition of Ethyl in 1962

During the late 1950s, the development of new materials such as polyethylene film posed a threat to paper makers such as Gottwald's Albemarle. Gottwald had orchestrated the expansion of Albemarle during his tenure, guiding the company toward an emphasis on converting its paper production into finished products, but the emergence of new materials asked new questions of paper makers. The threat demanded one of two responses: either embrace new technological advancements or dismiss the advancements as justification for investment. Gottwald chose to bank the future health of Albemarle on the development of novel materials and began looking for a partner to help him stay on the vanguard of technology. During his search for assistance in producing polyethylene, Gottwald discovered Ethyl. Gottwald's discovery and his desire to obtain Ethyl made business history. Gottwald became the figure behind the largest leveraged buyout ever completed at the time. It was a deal that newspaper headlines described as ''Jonah Swallows the Whale,'' according to Ethyl's web site-published history.

The marriage of Albemarle and Ethyl occurred in 1962. Gottwald borrowed $200 million and acquired a company 13 times larger than Albemarle, creating a new, Virginia-registered concern named Ethyl Corporation that embodied the assets of the Delaware-registered Ethyl Corporation and Albemarle Paper Manufacturing Company. Gottwald was appointed chairman of the new company he had created. Under his leadership, the company expanded. In 1964, Ethyl S.A. was formed as a European subsidiary to ease the company's entry into foreign markets. In 1968, Gottwald's son, Floyd D. Gottwald, Jr., replaced his father as chairman and continued to spearhead Ethyl's diversification and expansion.

Under Floyd Gottwald, Jr., Ethyl developed into a multifaceted concern, directing its growth in four directions. The company followed the general corporate trend that emerged during the late 1960s. Industrial concerns of all types diversified their operations in a new era of holding companies and sprawling conglomerates, assembling a number of different, sometimes eclectic, business interests. Ethyl chose to concentrate on four business areas: chemicals, plastics, aluminum, and energy. Conspicuous by its absence was the company's original business, paper manufacturing. In 1969, a portion of the company's paper making properties was sold to a group of employees who used the assets as the foundation for a new company, James River Corporation. In 1976, after nearly 90 years in the business, the company exited paper manufacture entirely when it divested Oxford Paper.

In paper's place, Ethyl built a presence in its four business groups. In 1968, when Floyd Gottwald, Jr., took the helm as chairman, the company strengthened its interests in plastics by acquiring IMCO Container Company. In 1975, the company purchased a global supplier of lubricant additives named Edwin Cooper, adding to its chemicals portfolio. During the 1980s, Ethyl continued to build on four foundations, making two important acquisitions. In 1986, the company announced that it had reached an agreement to acquire the bromine chemicals business belonging to Dow Chemical, an agreement of significant importance to the future of Albemarle. (Bromine is a nonmetallic liquid element used in producing gasoline anti-knock mixtures, fumigants, dyes, and photographic chemicals.) The acquisition, completed in 1987, included Dow Chemical's plant in Magnolia, Arkansas, where bromine production had begun in 1969. The addition of bromine production capabilities, which became a central component of Albemarle's flame retardant business, was followed in 1989 by the acquisition of Russ Pharmaceuticals, Inc., based in Birmingham, Alabama.

1994 Spinoff

By the time the Russ Pharmaceuticals acquisition was completed, Ethyl had begun to adopt a profoundly different operating strategy. The change mirrored the actions of many companies as the 1990s neared. After years of diversifying their operations, corporations embraced a new mindset toward streamlining their operations. A sharpened focus on core businesses became the ideal, prompting companies to divest businesses that distracted their attention. Ethyl's actions typified the general corporate trend, as the company spun off several divisions into separate companies. The first such instance of the company's move toward consolidation occurred in 1989, when the company spun off its aluminum, plastics, and energy units, forming a new company named Tredegar Industries, later renamed Tredegar Corporation. In 1994, the company spun off its specialty chemicals business, the divestiture that created Albemarle Corporation. The spinoff left Ethyl focused on fuel additives and Albemarle focused on Ethyl's polymer and fine chemicals business, which included olefin and derivative chemicals, specialty chemicals, and brominated chemicals. Starting out on its own, Albemarle operated a publicly traded concern with more than $900 million in annual revenue.

In the wake of the spinoff from Ethyl, Albemarle tailored its operations to suit its future as a company that would be focused on polymer and fine chemicals. The adjustments resulted in divestitures and acquisitions, as the company took charge of shaping its own identity. In 1995, Albemarle sold its electronic materials business. The following year a major divestiture was completed when the company sold its alpha olefins, polyalphaolefins, and synthetic alcohols assets to Amoco. The transaction netted $500 million for Albemarle. Although the divestitures stripped the company of some of its financial might—Albemarle's revenues in 1998 were roughly $100 million less than the total registered five years earlier—the moves were made to realign its structure for the future. In 1997, the new structure of the company was created. Albemarle reorganized into two business units: Polymer Chemicals and Fine Chemicals. Once stripped to assets that corresponded to the scope of these two business units, Albemarle began to build again, seeking to bolster its stance in each of its markets.

During the late 1990s, there were several significant acquisitions completed and one daring bid at expansion that collapsed. In 1998, Albemarle completed two important deals, one in the Middle East and one in Europe. Through a subsidiary named Albemarle Holdings Company Limited, the company forged a joint venture agreement with Jordan Dead Sea Industries Company and Arab Potash Company. According to the terms of the agreement, the company gained the capability to manufacture bromine and bromine derivatives at a production facility to be constructed in Safi, Jordan. In Europe, the company acquired an oilfields chemicals plant in Teesport, England, for $14 million. Formerly the Hodgson Specialty Chemical division belonging to BTP PLC, the addition of the plant improved Albemarle's access to customers in the North Sea.

Albemarle made a bold attempt to increase its stature in 1999. The company launched a $900 million bid to acquire British phosphates producer Albright & Wilson PLC, a deal that would more than double the company's annual sales to $2 billion. "This will significantly strengthen our global capabilities and reach, particularly in Europe, Latin America, and the Asia-Pacific region," an Albemarle spokesperson declared in the March 15, 1999 issue of *Chemical Market Reporter*. Aside from the tremendous boost to sales, the proposed acquisition of Albright & Wilson promised to solidify Albemarle's leading position in the flame retardants market. The company ranked as one of the three largest competitors in the brominated flame retardants market. The addition of Albright & Wilson, which operated as a second-tier phosphorus flame retardants supplier, would result in the second largest producer of flame retardants in the world. The union of the two companies was perceived as ideal in many respects, but the deal's attractiveness became its

own undoing. An industry analyst, in a March 15, 1999 interview with *Chemical Market Reporter*, explained: "Given the level of earnings accretion Albemarle is likely to generate with this transaction and the availability of that accretion to other buyers, we believe there is a possibility that another bidder will emerge." One week after Albemarle submitted its $900 offer, France-based Rhodia S.A. countered with a bid 11.5 percent higher than Albemarle's offer. The deal fell through, forcing Albemarle's management to look elsewhere for acquisitions.

In the years following the collapse of the Albright & Wilson acquisition, Albemarle increased the size and scope of its business through smaller acquisitions. In 2000, the company acquired a plant in Port-de-Bouc, France, as part of a deal that gave the company the flame retardant business of Ferro Corporation. In 2001, the company purchased the custom and fine chemicals business of ChemFirst. The $74 million acquisition gave Albemarle two new production plants, one in Tyrone, Pennsylvania, and another in Dayton, Ohio. During the year, the company also acquired a German company, Martinswerk GmbH, with manufacturing facilities that produced nonhalogen, mineral-based flame retardants for the plastic and rubber markets. In 2003, Albemarle purchased the fuel and lubricant antioxidants business of its former parent, Ethyl. In the years ahead, further acquisitions were expected, as Albemarle completed its first decade as an independent company and geared itself for the future.

Principal Subsidiaries

Albemarle Holdings Company Limited.

Principal Operating Units

Polymer Chemicals; Fine Chemicals.

Principal Competitors

A. Schulman, Inc.; Champion Technologies, Inc.; Ciba Specialty Chemicals Holding Inc.; The Dow Chemical Company; E.I. du Pont de Nemours & Company; Great Lakes Chemical Corporation; NCH Corporation; Hercules Inc.

Further Reading

"Albemarle Outlines Ambitious Plans for Major Global Growth," *Chemical Market Reporter*, March 29, 1999, p. 4.
Chang, Joseph, "Albemarle Launches $900 MM Bid for A&W," *Chemical Market Reporter*, March 15, 1999, p. 1.
Mirasol, Feliza, "Albemarle Targets Growth in Pharma, Fine Chemicals," *Chemical Market Reporter*, December 20, 1999, p. 5.
Scheraga, Dan, "Albemarle to Buy A&W Garners Praise from Analysts," *Chemical Market Reporter*, March 15, 1999, p. 1.
Walsh, Kerri, "Albemarle: Slow and Steady Wins the Race," *Chemical Week*, January 22, 2003, p. 14.
——, "Albemarle to Acquire ChemFirst's Fine Chemicals Business," *Chemical Week*, June 20, 2001, p. 14.

—Jeffrey L. Covell

Allen Systems Group, Inc.

1333 3rd Avenue South
Naples, Florida 34102
U.S.A.
Telephone: (239) 435-2200
Fax: (239) 263-3692
Web site: http://www.asg.com

Private Company
Incorporated: 1986
Employees: 900
Sales: $175 million (2002 est.)
NAIC: 511210 Software Publishers

Allen Systems Group, Inc. (ASG) is a Naples, Florida-based company offering products to enhance the performance of clients' information technology systems. ASG's myriad of product suites deliver more than 150 solutions, divided into six major categories: Identity Management, Applications Management, Operations Management, Performance Management, Information Management, and Infrastructure Management. Identity Management controls who in an enterprise is allowed access to information and how much. ASG solutions are capable of maintaining the full lifecycle of information access, from the issuance of an account to its termination. Applications Management Solutions helps clients keep abreast of new and emerging technologies. ASG is capable of analyzing existing systems, enhancing those systems, and integrating new applications. Operations Management Solutions assists in the efficient and cost-effective management of workloads on clients' IT systems, whether the environment is mainframe or multi-platform. ASG's Information Management Solutions helps to organize and deliver vital business information, either structured (in the form of a database) or unstructured (i.e. paper/electronic documents and enterprise reports). Performance Management Solutions helps clients to efficiently monitor the performance of, and spot potential problems in, specific operating systems. Last, ASG's Infrastructure Management Solutions offers an integrated set of tools that can be used to detect, manage, and resolve problems throughout a client's IT environment. ASG serves more than 7,000 customers worldwide from some 40 offices spread around the globe, 17 of which are located in North and South America and another 19 in Europe, the Middle East, and Africa. ASG also maintains five software development offices in Australia, China, Indonesia, and Japan. Approximately 90 percent of Global 5000 companies rely on ASG in some form. Major clients include American Express, Coca-Cola, DaimlerChrysler, General Electric, HSBC, IBM, Lockheed Martin, Toyota, and Wells Fargo.

Founding of ASG: 1986

The man behind the founding of ASG was Arthur L. Allen, who had a significant background in the software industry before ASG. In 1976 he formed Allen Services Corporation, which he sold in 1981 for $18 million and then retired to Naples, Florida. Still retaining old connections and an interest in the software industry, Allen came out of retirement in 1986 when a friend asked if he could help him market a performance-monitoring product for IDMS databases. As a result, Allen, using just $2,000 in savings and a $100,000 line of credit, formed a new company, Allen Systems Group. In his previous company, Allen had a partner but decided to go it alone this time. According to a Fort Myers, Florida newspaper, *News-Press,* "A decision with a partner to sell an earlier software venture resulted in one of Allen's current chief competitors owning—and profiting greatly—from his work. 'In my first business, I had one partner and I have determined that is one too many,' Allen said." Although the outlay in cash he committed to his new enterprise was modest, Allen's ambitions were not. He told the *News-Press,* "The true vision from the beginning was to be a global company and to exceed $100 million (in revenue) by 2001."

ASG's first marketing effort, the IDMS monitoring tool called ShopMon, was joined a few months later by a product called Fast Access, which helped to increase the throughput for IDMS databases. Believing that the product held great potential, Allen bought Fast Access from the Christian Broadcasting Network, the first of what would become more than 30 acquisitions. Most of these acquisitions during the first dozen years were small, ranging in cost from $1 million to $5 million. In addition to acquisitions, Allen also looked to organic growth.

Company Perspectives:

To partner with clients. To improve productivity. To significantly enhance performance through the intelligent use of technology.

By either means, ASG diversified its customer base and distribution channels, and as a consequence it also built a highly diverse staff. By the end of the 1980s the company had accumulated a varied line of automation and performance software products supporting IBM mainframe software, and boasted sales and technical offices throughout the United States, Canada, Denmark, Norway, the United Kingdom, and Sweden. ASG encountered some cash flow problems because of lengthy delays involved in collecting from international customers, who paid weeks and in some cases months later than domestic customers. Most of the delay was the result of banking bottlenecks, prompting ASG to open bank deposit accounts in key foreign banks and to institute a daily, global cash management system. By mid-afternoon each day, Allen received a consolidated cash report telling him the status of all ASG's bank accounts and the company's line of credit. He then had all excess international funds transferred to a U.S. account, where they were invested on a short-term basis. Allen estimated that he only had to devote an hour of staff time and ten minutes of his own time each day to make the system work. But as a result of this modicum of effort, ASG improved its margins and greatly mitigated any cash flow problems that might hinder the growth of the small company.

European Push in 1996

After establishing a solid base in the mainframe marketplace, ASG expanded into a number of PC and mid-range platform markets. The company also launched in 1996 a concerted effort to expand its European business. By 1997 ASG was generating $23 million in annual revenues and employed some 175 people. The company's slate of products totaled more than 30, providing solutions for enterprise service management, CA-IDMS, data center automation, job control management, file transfer, and data entry. Starting in 1998 ASG completed a series of significant acquisitions that resulted in explosive growth for the company over the next five years. In March 1998 ASG acquired Impact Software Technologies, thereby adding a rapid maintenance and enhancement tool to analyze mainframe systems. A graphical user interface provided an instant, in-depth presentation of the attributes and relationships of an IT system in an easy-to-grasp format. A month later ASG announced that it had bought IMPACT Software Technologies, a French software development firm that developed a computer program which was a strategic fit for ASG's suite of data center automation products. Another important pickup occurred in July 1998, when ASG purchased Firesign Computer Company and bolstered its slate of data center automation products with the addition of Outbound, Firesign's signature product, which provided a high-speed and reliable way to implement on-demand and automated data transfer across multiple platforms. Next, in September 1998, ASG completed two acquisitions. In its largest acquisition to date, ASG bought the oldest and largest

vendor of repository solutions, Amsterdam-based Manager Software Products, with solutions that included the management of information assets, IT infrastructure, data, and process models. ASG also purchased Emprise Technologies, adding the CATS and CSD/Auditor products for CICS change management. Moreover, in 1998 ASG initiated a plan to move aggressively into the Mexican, Latin American, and Caribbean Basin markets, similar to its successful European plan of two years earlier. The strategy called for expansion in both direct and indirect sales, targeting the key markets of Brazil, Argentina, Chile, Mexico, Central America, and Venezuela. Latin America, boasting the world's fastest growing technology market, offered especially promising opportunities for ASG. In 1998 the company also forged strategic alliances with FirstSense and Harris Corporation to integrate complementary products.

ASG completed one major deal in 1999, acquiring several mainframe scheduling and intelligent management tools from Computer Associates, which had months earlier picked them up as part of a purchase of Platinum Technologies. In order to comply with U.S. antitrust regulations, CA was required to divest the products in question. As a result, ASG added such orphaned products as AutoSys/Zeke, AutoRerun, AutoMedia, and CCC/Life Cycle Manager, thus establishing a strong foundation in the Operations Management category. Furthermore, the procurement of the Platinum Technology products put ASG in line to become a $70 million company in 2000, thus making it the third largest private software company in the country, according to *Software Magazine*.

More important acquisitions followed in 2000. In January ASG acquired SISRO, adding a distributed platform scheduler, a production repository, and JCL Generation tool to its list of products. Also in January, ASG bought BETA Systems Software's line of workload products, rounding out its Operations Management tools. Later in 2000 ASG acquired Network Software Associates, adding Report.Web, a multihost publishing and distribution tool for corporate intranet/extranet environments that allowed immediate access to reports from any host source using a standard web browser. ASG also bought the Safari suite of data access, management, and reporting tools from Condor Technology Solutions, Inc. ASG followed with an even more noteworthy deal, the $152 million purchase of Viasoft, a former Wall Street darling. Viasoft first came into prominence after going public in 1995 when it became involved in the Y2K business, helping corporations prepare their systems for the change to 2000. Viasoft, initially priced at $8 a share, saw its stock soar beyond $55 before beginning a long decline. ASG agreed to pay approximately $8.40 a share (essentially double the IPO price when a 2-for-1 stock split was taken into account). As a result of the deal, ASG added Viasoft's Existing Systems Workbench, a tool that nicely complemented its Applications Management product line, and Viasoft's Rochade repository that greatly enhanced ASG's position as major world player in repository and metadata management. In other developments in 2000, ASG entered into an important development partnership with Sybase, Inc., one of the largest, global, independent software companies. ASG was now able to offer a Sybase product bundle to round off its ASG-replication Suite, allowing users to more easily update databases with the assurance of data integrity. ASG announced in September 2000 the establishment of an Enterprise Application Integration division, able to assist clients

---

Key Dates:

1986: Arthur Allen forms his second software company, Allen Systems Group.
1996: Company begins expanding its European business.
1998: Company begins expanding its Latin American business.
2000: Allen Systems Group purchases Viasoft for $152 million.
2002: Landmark Systems acquisition is completed.

---

in making their enterprise applications available for use in e-business. With so many products and initiatives becoming a part of ASG, management in 2000 also opened ASG University to train new sales recruits as well as its existing sales force. In addition, during 2000 ASG opened its first office in Africa, established in Johannesburg, South Africa. A second South African office would open in 2001.

Completion of Landmark Systems Acquisition: 2002

ASG completed one major deal in 2001, acquiring SNMP Frameworks, which led to the development of a Web-based network management and remote network monitoring system. The company also established a strategic alliance with Viaserv Inc. to co-market and promote their e-business solutions. During the course of 2000 ASG opened its 30th international office, adding Sao Paulo, Brazil. Later in the year, ASG formed a distribution partnership with SCI-Tecnologia da Informacao Ltda., which would serve as the exclusive distributor of ASG's Viasoft and Cortex product lines in Brazil. Another major acquisition was agreed to in 2001 but not completed until early in 2002: the $62 million purchase of Reston, Virginia-based Landmark Systems Corporation, maker of management software for mainframe computers.

Founded in 1983, Landmark had been successful for a number of years, but fell on tough times in the late 1990s. Art Allen first attempted to acquire Landmark in 1991 but was turned down by the company's founders, Patrick McGettican and Kathy Clark. Clark was Landmark's CEO in 1998, when according to the *Washington Post,* ''she found herself in what she called the public company equivalent of 'no man's land,' the leader of a technology company that wasn't failing but wasn't in a sexy business that many Wall Street analysts chose to cover. ... Something needed to change. Clark figured she'd start acquiring smaller companies to build Landmark into a super-player. But those she targeted laughed her off—they were raising venture capital and eyeing their own public offerings. 'It was frustrating,' says Clark. 'We were doing okay. We weren't a star performer, but we were doing okay.' '' An attempt to move into a new product failed and soon Landmark became the object of suitors, including ASG's Allen, who pulled out his ten-year-old file on the company.

An offer from ASG made in late 2000 came to nothing, followed by another bid in July 2001. In the meantime, Landmark's condition continued to deteriorate. In the words of the *Washington Post,* ''Clark was terrified of the 'death spiral' of layoffs, lost customers, more layoffs, and more lost customers. 'I could not bear to watch us shrivel up and die a slow death.' '' Because Allen remained persistent about buying Landmark, he maintained contact with Clark until she was finally receptive to a bid. She presented it to her board, which agreed to the sale in December 2001. For ASG the acquisition of Landmark was important because it brought with it a new core competency. To that point, ASG had been involved in three major areas: applications management, operations management, and information management. According to Allen, Landmark's performance management capabilities represented ''the fourth leg on the stool,'' adding tremendous value to ASG's customer base.

Also in 2002, ASG acquired Entact Information Security Corporation, adding new Identity Management solutions to its product line. As a result of a five-year-long acquisition spree, ASG had enjoyed a compounded annual growth rate of 44 percent, with worldwide revenues reaching $175 million during this period, a total that eclipsed Allen's long cherished goal to be a $100 million company by 2001. In 2003 the company was poised to see revenues top $200 million. Set in the autumn of 2003 to launch its first products to enable business service management, ASG was positioned to continue its impressive rate of growth. Allen, who professed he had no interest in taking ASG public, established a new and even more ambitious target, to generate $500 million in annual revenues within the next three years.

Principal Subsidiaries

Allen Systems Group Inc.; Landmark Systems Corporation; Safari Solution.

Principal Competitors

BMC Software, Inc.; Computer Associates International, Inc.; Compuware Corporation.

Further Reading

Dagenais, Bernard, ''Florida Exec Takes Reins at Landmark,'' *Washington Business Journal,* February 24, 2002.

Engstrom, Tim, ''Naples' ASG Flourished on Worldwide Stage,'' *News-Press,* April 28, 2003, p. 15.

Fraser, Jill Andresky, ''By-the-Minute Monitoring,'' *Inc.,* June 1993, p. 45.

Henry, Shannon, ''Not with a Bang, More Than a Whimper,'' *Washington Post,* January 24, 2002, p. E1.

Lais, Sami, ''Allen Systems Gets CA Buyout Spoils,'' *Computerworld,* January 3, 2000, p. 102.

—Ed Dinger

AMCOL International Corporation

1500 West Shure Drive, Suite 500
Arlington Heights, Illinois 60004-7803
U.S.A.
Telephone: (847) 394-8730
Fax: (847) 506-6199
Web site: http://www.amcol.com

Public Company
Founded: 1924 as Bentonite Mining & Manufacturing
   Company
Employees: 1,134
Sales: $298.9 million (2002)
Stock Exchanges: New York
Ticker Symbol: ACO
NAIC: 212325 Clay and Ceramic Refractory Minerals
   Mining; 212399 All Other Nonmetallic Mineral
   Mining; 484120 General Freight Trucking, Long-
   Distance; 488510 Freight Transportation Arrangement

AMCOL International Corporation is one of the world's leading suppliers of bentonite and bentonite-related products and is also a major supplier of other specialty minerals. These materials have a variety of applications, such as a bonding agent for foundry sand molds, a lubricating agent for well drilling, a binder for pharmaceutical tablets, an additive in body lotions, and a clumping material in cat litter; these mineral operations generated 55 percent of 2002 revenues. Additionally, the company is the world leader in geosynthetic clay liners for landfills, sewage lagoons, and mining sites and also produces water treatment products and building materials such as moisture barriers; these environmental-related operations comprised 34 percent of 2002 sales. The remaining 11 percent of revenues came from AMCOL's transportation business, which provides long-haul trucking and freight brokerage services for both the company's other operations as well as outside customers. Through its Nanocor, Inc. subsidiary, AMCOL has been involved in the nanotechnology field since 1995, focusing on the use of nanometer-size (one-billionth of a meter) bentonite-based particles as an additive for plastics. The company operates 33 production/research facilities in the United States, Canada,

the United Kingdom, Poland, Australia, China, South Korea, and Thailand. About 30 percent of revenues are generated outside the United States.

Origins of the Bentonite Industry

AMCOL International Corporation was built on a single product: bentonite clay. Although various types and grades of bentonite clay were in existence, the material that the company began selling in the early 1900s was located in deposits as deep as 100 feet in the northern plains of the United States. That clay was formed from volcanic ash that, over millions of years, was transformed into a highly absorbent, pastelike substance. Native Americans used the clay in several applications, including as a soap for buffalo hide, an ingredient in soils for decorative plants, and possibly even as a dietary supplement during pregnancy. Later, settlers began using the clay to seal log homes, pack inflamed horses' hooves, and grease wheel axles.

In the late 1800s a Wyoming rancher named William Taylor sent some of the clay that he found on his ranch to the University of Wyoming to be studied. He first dubbed the clay "taylorite," but soon thereafter changed the name to "bentonite" because he had found it near Fort Benton. In the early 1900s that deposit became one of the first commercial bentonite mines in the world. The substance was originally mined from the earth's surface by horse and wagon, shipped to Chicago, milled into a fine powder, and processed into a skin-wrinkle cream called "Denver Mud"—the clay was still a chief ingredient in beauty mask products in the 1990s. Bentonite was later used in the manufacture of laundry detergent, asphalt, and insulation. Because few other commercial uses were known for the absorbent material, the bentonite industry languished for several years.

It was eventually discovered that bentonite could be used in foundries to improve the quality of molding sands used to manufacture metal castings. That important discovery was followed by the realization that bentonite was a useful additive to the slurry applied as a lubricant to oil and gas well drills. Among the few bentonite mining companies that emerged early was the Bentonite Mining & Manufacturing Company, which was located in the gold-mining town of Deadwood, South

Dakota. The company was formed one night in 1924—by a group of frustrated gold miners in a local tavern—and was extracting bentonite from nearby deposits shortly afterward.

Enter Paul Bechtner, an entrepreneur, inventor, and workaholic with a background in the foundry industry. Bechtner was born in Wisconsin in 1882, served in a stateside cavalry unit during World War I after typhoid nearly took his life, and then started a chicken farm in his home state. When he tired of that venture, he took a job with a sand company, quickly rising to the position of vice-president and then promptly quitting in 1922. Next, he was employed by a metal casting company, where he worked on developing better foundry molds to make engine blocks for the burgeoning automobile industry. After experimenting with numerous additive and bonding materials, Bechtner became convinced that bentonite was superior to all other materials. Armed with that knowledge, Bechtner left his job and headed west.

Founding of American Colloid, 1927

Bechtner struck a partnership with the founders of Bentonite Mining in 1927. The two parties each agreed to contribute $15,000 to form two new companies: American Colloid Company, which would be headed by the original founders and based in Lead, South Dakota, and Chicago-based American Colloid Company Sales Division, which would buy bentonite from its sister company and sell it in the East for a profit. The name "Colloid" was derived from the Greek *kolloid,* meaning glue-like, and the English "colloid," which defined a degree of fitness. American Colloid built its first bentonite processing plant in Upton, Wyoming, in 1928 adjacent to the original mining facility. Bechtner named the bentonite material that he sold "Volcay," referring to its volcanic origin, and he even advertised that "Bentonite is our sole product."

Bechtner had finally discovered his niche. Indeed, during the 1930s and through the 1950s he became a sort of apostle of bentonite (Volcay). He worked relentlessly, often from early morning until late at night, to build the business. During the start-up, Bechtner effectively lived out of his Ford, traveling nonstop to promote his product before setting up shop in a Chicago apartment. Then, when he was not on the road he was writing literature and responding to customer inquiries in an effort to build American Colloid's client base. At a rate of about two tons per hour, the South Dakota mine generated about 740 tons of bentonite during its first full year of production. As a result of Bechtner's sales push, that figure bolted to more than 3,000 tons in 1929. In addition, demand was growing.

The Great Depression slowed American Colloid's growth. To make matters worse, a fire destroyed the Upton plant. But the enterprise managed to survive the downturn and even to record meager profits during most of the 1930s. In fact, Bechtner managed to turn the misfortune into a positive experience. When he and his crew were surveying the fire damage, one of the men angrily picked up a handful of bentonite clay and hurled it against a burned wall. The clay stuck to the wall extremely well, sending Bechtner's mental gears into motion. Within several weeks he had filed a patent covering the use of vermiculite bonded with bentonite as insulation. He then sold the patent to help pay for reconstruction costs. Although output rose during the early 1930s to more than 4,500 tons, American Colloid struggled. At one point, when the company was on the edge of bankruptcy, an investor named John Owen paid just $5,000 for 17 percent of the organization's stock to keep it afloat.

By 1935 American Colloid's shipments had grown to the point where a second processing plant had to be built. The second plant, located in Belle Fourche, South Dakota, was capable of producing granular and powder bentonite products, for which demand was growing. By 1936, American Colloid was shipping 9,000 tons from the new plant and about 8,000 from the old facility. Two years later, the sales and production divisions of American Colloid merged to form a single company: American Colloid Company. In the late 1930s, the company began mining and processing "southern" bentonite clay in Mississippi. Southern bentonite clay, found primarily in Mississippi and Alabama, was similar to material in the plains states, but the former had significant amounts of calcium rather than sodium and swelled much less when exposed to moisture. Southern bentonite was preferred over plains clay for many foundry applications, though combining the two materials often produced the best effect.

By 1940 American Colloid was selling more than 35,000 tons of clay annually. Because of the U.S. war effort, that figure leapt to 60,000 in 1941. Unfortunately, the company's profit growth failed to keep pace with output, largely because of increased competition from new bentonite manufacturers. As competition increased, the company's profit per ton plunged to 20 cents. Worse yet, in 1941 fire again destroyed the Upton plant. American Colloid quickly rebuilt as its order backlog swelled. Three years later, however, a third blaze wreaked havoc and leveled the Upton plant. Just as before, American Colloid rebuilt. Soon after the plant reopened, however, demand plunged with the end of the war. Bechtner and his discouraged associates struggled for a few years to reposition the company for growth in the postwar era.

New Markets, New Products in the Postwar Era

Fortunately, a major new market opened up for American Colloid in the late 1940s. Because a competitor's patent expired, American Colloid was able to start selling bentonite as an ingredient in oil-drilling lubricants. That new product line quickly took off and the company was forced to expand its manufacturing operations and headquarters to keep up with demand. Despite a fourth fire—this time at the Mississippi plant—and a 1954 tornado that wrecked the rebuilt facility, the company steamed into the mid-1950s with record revenues and profits. Boosting sales were new minerals being mined and

Key Dates:

1924: Group of frustrated gold miners enter the bentonite mining industry through the formation of Bentonite Mining & Manufacturing Company, based in Deadwood, South Dakota.

1927: Entrepreneur Paul Bechtner joins with the founders of Bentonite Mining in transforming that company into American Colloid Company, with a sales division established in Chicago.

1928: Company builds its first bentonite processing plant in Upton, Wyoming.

1963: A Scottsbluff, Nebraska, trucking company is purchased.

1965: First overseas production plants—in Duisburg, Germany, and Birkenhead, England—are inaugurated.

1986: Chemdal Corporation is established as a subsidiary to produce and market superabsorbent polymer.

1987: Company goes public.

1988: Absorbent Clay Products, Inc., an Illinois cat litter company, is acquired.

1991: Colloid Environmental Technologies Company (CETCO) is formed as a subsidiary.

1995: Company changes its name to AMCOL International Corporation; Nanocor, Inc. is created as a subsidiary focused on nanotechnology.

2000: Chemdal is sold to BASF Aktiengesellschaft for $656.5 million; a significant portion of the proceeds are distributed to shareholders via partial liquidation involving payment of $14 per share.

processed by Bechtner's team including lignite/leonardite, a type of low-grade coal used in the petroleum industry and later as a fertilizer. To keep pace with gains, the company opened another plant in Mississippi in 1957.

Paul Bechtner died from a stroke in 1961 at the age of 79. Until his death, he had been intimately involved in the leadership of the company, overseeing its growth from a single plant to the world's largest bentonite producer with sales throughout the world. Bechtner was succeeded by Everett Weaver. Weaver had joined the company straight out of high school in 1940. After a two-year stint in Europe during the war, he had returned to American Colloid to develop the company's marketing program for the oil well drilling industry and to manage some manufacturing plants. He was also joined at the company by his younger brother, Bill. Everett was handpicked by Bechtner to lead the company and assumed the chief executive slot in 1960.

Under Weaver's direction, American Colloid continued to flourish. The company opened a new Alabama calcium bentonite processing center in 1964. In 1965, moreover, the company inaugurated its first overseas production plants, which were located in Duisburg, Germany, and Birkenhead, England. In addition, Weaver purchased a Scottsbluff, Nebraska-based trucking company in 1963 as part of an effort to vertically integrate the company and reduce distribution costs. Everett Weaver handed off some of the day-to-day control of American

Colloid to his brother, Bill, in 1968. Before doing so, he added a new production facility in Lovell, Wyoming, initiated a distribution agreement with a Japanese company that eventually became American Colloid's biggest overseas customer, and broke ground for a new production facility in Granite City, Illinois. That new facility reflected American Colloid's increasing emphasis on the growing well-drilling market.

The Weaver brothers continued to expand the company's reach overseas in the 1970s. In the early 1970s they oversaw the creation of divisions in Spain and Australia, for example. They also purchased a foundry blend processing center in Albion, Michigan, that allowed the company to create new products in demand by the foundry industry. Throughout the 1970s the brothers helped to boost the company's international exposure and to raise sales and profits. Importantly, American Colloid benefited from growing demand, among oil and gas drillers, for its lubricating mud products. That increase was largely a result of the OPEC oil embargo that began in 1973 and buoyed the U.S. oil industry through the early 1980s.

Indeed, American Colloid's revenues went from $20 million in the early 1970s to more than $100 million by the decade's end. During the same period, the company's workforce increased from 450 to more than 1,000. By the early 1980s, at the height of the oil industry boom, American Colloid was shipping more than 80,000 tons of its clay-based gel each month. To keep up with growing demand, the organization invested millions of dollars in new facilities. At the same time, American Colloid began a concerted effort to diversify its product lines to include specialty, high-margin items. The Weaver brothers relinquished hands-on control of the company when it was at its height in terms of sales and profits. That left Roy Harris, who became chief executive in 1981, holding the bag when the bottom dropped out of the U.S. oil industry.

Because American Colloid had become so dependent on the oil industry, but also because of a downturn in its industrial and export divisions, the early 1980s dealt an ugly blow to the company. Almost instantly, orders from the company's oil accounts stopped. American Colloid's management was stunned by the almost unimaginable drop in business. Sales plunged from $134.3 million in 1981 to $77.3 million in 1986. As management scrambled to cut costs and pay its bills, the company's workforce shrunk from 1,250 to just 475 during the same period. American Colloid was eventually forced to shutter its gleaming, eight-year-old, state-of-the art bentonite plant in Malta, Montana.

Diversifying into High-Margin Specialty Products, Late 1980s and 1990s

Roy Harris, one of the last top executives to have worked with Bechtner in the early days, stepped aside in 1985. He was replaced by John Hughes, who would face the task of revitalizing American Colloid and leading it onto a new path toward growth and prosperity. The hard-charging, outspoken Hughes had joined American Colloid straight out of college in 1965 as a research chemist. Almost from the start, he had pressed top management to reduce its dependence on the oil well market. In fact, it was he who had pushed for American Colloid to diversify into other specialty products derived from bentonite, rather than commodity goods, during the late 1970s. As he rose through the ranks, Hughes became known as a tough taskmaster, and some executives had even left the company upon discovering that they would be required to report to him.

After the oil market crashed, Hughes was tapped to help engineer the company's consolidation and workforce reduction. His efforts during that period only added to his intimidating presence within the company. Still, Hughes's aggressive, hard-driving style was exactly what American Colloid needed during the mid-1980s to turn it around. Just as important as his management style and personality, though, was his strategy. "When he first started ... John had a dream: to develop a line of specialized products and decentralized management," explained Everett Weaver in the May 1989 *Business Marketing*. "He doesn't waste time when he knows what he wants to do," Weaver said.

Indeed, Hughes did not waste time. In 1986 he moved the company's corporate offices to Arlington Heights, Illinois, demolished the Malta plant, sold the plant in Germany, and opened a new polymer processing operation in Wyoming. The company raised cash in 1987 by going public for the first time, and Hughes launched aggressive new cost-control and quality initiatives. As American Colloid slashed costs and reorganized during the mid-1980s, Hughes pursued his goal of developing a diverse mix of high-margin specialty applications for bentonite. To that end, the company set up several relatively autonomous industry-specific divisions designed to attack key market niches. The units usually had about 12 people, depending on the market, and were headed by a profit manager. For example, American Colloid's desiccant division was set up to develop and market clays used to absorb moisture in packaging. Similarly, in 1988 American Colloid purchased Absorbent Clay Products, Inc., a cat litter company in southern Illinois. Other bentonite niches included winemaking and new uses in the fertilizer industry.

An important new arena for American Colloid beginning in the late 1980s was an absorbent powder that it sold primarily to manufacturers of diapers and feminine products. The powder was first developed in Japan for the drilling industry, but American Colloid managed to get rights to the product in all countries but Japan and was marketing the powder for new specialty applications. The amazing powder was capable of expanding to hold more than 40 times its volume in water, making it potentially useful in a range of applications that Hughes believed American Colloid could develop and market. An added benefit of the polymer was that it could be shipped much more inexpensively than bentonite. In 1986 Hughes formed a subsidiary—Chemdal Corporation—to produce and market the superabsorbent polymer. Chemdal Limited, a separate European division of that subsidiary, was established in Birkenhead, England, in 1989. That same year, American Colloid purchased a feed processing operation in York, Pennsylvania, which was converted into a foundry blend processing center. The firm's cat litter business received a large boost through the 1991 patenting of a breakthrough clumping cat litter product (also known as "scoopable" cat litter); scoopable cat litter quickly captured more than 40 percent of the U.S. market by the mid-1990s. American Colloid also created a new subsidiary in 1991 called Colloid Environmental Technologies Company (CETCO). CETCO specialized in groundwater chemicals,

building materials, wastewater treatment products, and other environmental products.

Meanwhile, the company continued to cut operating costs and to update manufacturing facilities. The results of Hughes's strategy were quickly visible. After falling to a 1980s low of $77 million in 1986, revenues shot up to $85 million in 1987 and then to $111 million in 1988; the oil well industry accounted for less than 10 percent of those sales. Profits rose similarly, jumping 21 percent in 1987 and then 20 percent in 1988 to a healthier $4.6 million. The profit gains reflected Hughes's financial goal of raising sales at double the rate at which operating costs increased. As demand for American Colloid's new products surged, revenues continued to climb to $125 million in 1989 and then to nearly $150 million in 1991.

Early 1990s gains were largely the result of the success of American Colloid's superabsorbent polymer division, Chemdal. That division was churning out 20,000 tons of product annually by 1993 after more than doubling sales to $31 million between 1990 and 1992; by 1994 Chemdal was generating one-quarter of the company's revenues. The kitty litter division was also posting gains. At the same time, American Colloid's bentonite operations were enjoying steady sales and profit jumps, and they continued to account for the bulk of the company's income. As American Colloid expanded production capacity and bolstered product lines, sales reached $265.4 million in 1994, far surpassing the company's revenues during the oil-industry peak of the early 1980s. Meanwhile, net income rose 17 percent to more than $15 million.

During 1995 American Colloid changed its name to AMCOL International Corporation. CETCO expanded that year through the acquisition of Claymax Corporation, a producer of geosynthetic clay liners for landfills, sewage lagoons, and other applications. AMCOL also formed a new subsidiary called Nanocor, Inc. that year. Nanocor was created to pursue opportunities in the nascent field of nanotechnology, specifically the development of nanometer-size (one-billionth of a meter) bentonite-based composites as additives for plastics. Nanocor began building its first production facility in Aberdeen, Mississippi, in 1997.

Late in 1997 CETCO acquired two France-based distributors of its geosynthetic clay liners, and AMCOL also acquired the cat litter business of LaPorte PLC, which included Cassius, a well-known European brand. Then in January 1998 Chemdal acquired the superabsorbent polymers business of the U.K. firm Allied Colloids Group PLC, securing a strengthened position in the European market. Later in 1998, Chemdal began building a new superabsorbent polymers plant in Thailand. AMCOL also gained a foothold in the bentonite market in the Middle East through the purchase of a minority interest in two Egyptian companies. In April 1998, meantime, the company sold its traditional (i.e., nonscoopable) cat litter business to Oil-Dri Corporation of America. In August of that year, Hughes was promoted to chairman and CEO, while Larry E. Washow was named president and chief operating officer. Washow had most recently served as senior vice-president and COO, after a decade-long stint as the head of Chemdal. Finally, in September, AMCOL's stock was shifted from the NASDAQ to the New York Stock Exchange.

AMCOL gained a presence in the bentonite industry of south Asia in May 1999 via the purchase of a 20 percent stake in Ashapura Minechem Limited of India. That same month, CETCO announced that it would construct a manufacturing facility for geosynthetic clay liners in Szczytno, Poland, to pursue opportunities in Eastern Europe.

A Chemdal-less AMCOL, Early 2000s and Beyond

By the late 1990s, Chemdal had grown to become AMCOL's largest business, accounting for about 42 percent of revenues in 1998, compared to nearly 32 percent for the company's traditional minerals operation and 20 percent for the CETCO environmental operation. Chemdal was at a disadvantage compared with its main competitors, however, because neither it nor AMCOL was a producer of the main raw material of superabsorbent polymers, acrylic acid. AMCOL began investigating the potential of gaining this vertical integration through entering the production of acrylic acid. But while it was doing so, Germany's BASF Aktiengesellschaft approached AMCOL about a possible sale of Chemdal. AMCOL's management concluded that it was in the best interests of the company's shareholders to sell the unit, and in November 1999 the corporation reached an agreement with BASF. The transaction was concluded in June 2000, with BASF paying AMCOL $656.5 million. AMCOL recorded a net gain of $316.3 million on the sale. A significant portion of these proceeds was distributed to the company's shareholders through a plan of partial liquidation involving a payment of $14 per share. In May 2000, meantime, Washow was promoted to president and CEO, with Hughes remaining chairman.

Post-Chemdal, AMCOL was a much smaller company— 2001 revenues of $275.3 million amounting to less than half of the firm's record total of $552.1 million two years earlier. The company now had two main business operations: minerals and the CETCO environmental business. There were further strategic adjustments to the remaining operations. Late in 2000 AMCOL's U.K. cat litter business was closed down, and early the next year the firm sold its U.K. metalcasting business—a jettisoning of two underperforming units. AMCOL also seriously discussed selling its Nanocor subsidiary but instead began entering into strategic alliances with other companies in order to develop commercial applications for the unit's nanocomposites. In 2001 a subsidiary called AMCOL Health & Beauty Solutions, Inc. was established to develop mineral additives for use in personal care products, cosmetics, and pharmaceutics. In May of the following year the corporation completed the acquisition of Colin Stewart Minchem Limited (CSM), a U.K. mineral and chemical company specializing in intermediate products, industrial minerals, inorganic chemicals, and additives for laundry detergents, packaging, oil exploration, construction, and water treatment. Annual sales for CSM were about $25

million. The more focused AMCOL of the early 2000s seemed likely to continue to seek out similar avenues of organic and acquisitive growth.

Principal Subsidiaries

ACP Export, Inc. (U.S. Virgin Islands); AMCOL Europe Limited (U.K.); AMCOL Health & Beauty Solutions, Inc.; AMCOL Holdings B.V. (Netherlands); AMCOL (Holdings) Ltd. (U.K.); AMCOL Holdings Canada Ltd.; AMCOL Specialties Holdings, Inc.; American Colloid Company; Ameri-Co Carriers, Inc.; Ameri-Co Logistics, Inc.; Ashapura Volclay Private Limited (India; 50%); Baker Sillavan Limited (U.K.; 50%); CETCO (Europe) Limited (U.K.); CETCO Australia Pty. Ltd.; CETCO Holdings B.V. (Netherlands); CETCO Korea Ltd.; CETCO-POLAND Sp. z o. o; Colin Stewart Minchem Limited (U.K.); Colloid Environmental Technologies Company; Montana Minerals Development Company; Nanocor, Inc.; Nanocor, Ltd. (U.K.); Silgel Packaging Limited (U.K.); Volclay Dongming Industrial Minerals Co., Ltd. (China; 75%); Volclay Holdings B.V. (Netherlands); Volclay International Corporation; Volclay Korea Ltd.; Volclay Pty. Ltd. (Australia); Volclay Siam Ltd. (Thailand).

Principal Competitors

Halliburton Company; Smith International, Inc.; Süd-Chemie Aktiengesellschaft; Oil-Dri Corporation of America.

Further Reading

"American Colloid Company," *Foundry Management & Technology,* February 1994, p. 51.

Chang, Joseph, "Amcol to Distribute Chemdal Cash Proceeds to Shareholders," *Chemical Market Reporter,* November 29, 1999, pp. 1, 8.

Cleaver, Joanne, "Polymer Broadens Colloid's Markets," *Crain's Chicago Business,* June 27, 1988, p. 23.

Cochran, Thomas N., "American Colloid Co.," *Investment News & Views,* May 23, 1988, pp. 65–66.

Kapp, Sue, "Niche Nitter," *Business Marketing,* May 1989, pp. 10–11.

Lerner, Ivan, "Amcol Closes $657 Million Sale of Polymers Unit to BASF," *Chemical Market Reporter,* June 5, 2000, p. 22.

Murphy, H. Lee, "Colloid Polymer Group Bolsters Bottom Line," *Crain's Chicago Business,* May 31, 1993, p. 68.

Rountree, David, "Company Celebrates Anniversary," *Montgomery Advertiser,* October 30, 1994, p. F6.

Scheraga, Dan, "Amcol's Chemdal Unit in Deal to Acquire Allied Colloids SAP," *Chemical Market Reporter,* December 1, 1997, p. 34.

Young, Linda, "Aberdeen Polymer Plant to Double Production," *Mississippi Business Journal,* December 7, 1992, p. 11.

—Dave Mote
—update: David E. Salamie

American Greetings Corporation

One American Road
Cleveland, Ohio 44144-2398
U.S.A.
Telephone: (216) 252-7300
Fax: (216) 252-6777
Web site: http://www.americangreetings.com

Public Company
Incorporated: 1944 as American Greeting Publishers, Inc.
Employees: 32,600
Sales: $1.99 billion (2003)
Stock Exchanges: New York
Ticker Symbol: AM
NAIC: 511191 Greeting Card Publishers; 322215
    Nonfolding Sanitary Food Container Manufacturing;
    322222 Coated and Laminated Paper Manufacturing;
    322233 Stationery, Tablet, and Related Product
    Manufacturing; 322291 Sanitary Paper Product
    Manufacturing; 339115 Ophthalmic Goods
    Manufacturing; 339950 Sign Manufacturing; 339999
    All Other Miscellaneous Manufacturing; 453220 Gift,
    Novelty, and Souvenir Stores; 516110 Internet
    Publishing and Broadcasting; 533110 Lessors of
    Nonfinancial Intangible Assets (Except Copyrighted
    Works)

Founded in 1906 as a small Cleveland jobber's shop, American Greetings Corporation, which advertises itself as "the world's largest publicly owned creator, manufacturer, and distributor of social expression products," is second only to Hallmark Cards, Inc. (a privately held corporation) in the increasingly competitive and tight-margin greeting card industry. The company's main U.S. greeting card brands are Carlton Cards, American Greetings, and Gibson, the latter having been acquired in 2000; the sale of everyday and seasonal greeting cards generates more than 55 percent of total revenues. Other product lines include DesignWare party goods, GuildHouse candles, and Designers' Collection stationery. Among the firm's domestic sub-

sidiaries are Plus Mark, Inc. (gift wrap), Magnivision, Inc. (reading glasses), Learning Horizons, Inc. (supplemental educational products), and A.G. Industries, Inc. (display fixtures). Another subsidiary, Carlton Cards Retail, Inc., owns and operates about 600 card and gifts shops in the United States and Canada. The majority-owned AmericanGreetings.com, Inc. subsidiary markets online greeting cards and related products through several web sites and Internet services. American Greetings also creates, markets, and licenses characters, including the Care Bears, Holly Hobbie, and Strawberry Shortcake. Non-U.S. subsidiaries operate in Canada, Mexico, the United Kingdom, South Africa, Australia, New Zealand, and Malaysia, and American Greetings distributes its products through a network of more than 125,000 retail outlets in more than 70 countries. About 18 percent of sales originate outside the United States.

Early History

The birth of American Greetings roughly coincides with the birth of the U.S. greeting card industry, which was marked by the advent of occasional cards to complement the seasonal Christmas card trade. A Polish émigré named Jacob Sapirstein entered the fledgling industry in 1906 as an independent salesman. Sapirstein (known as "J.S.") had had some experience working with relatives in a hotel card shop. When the shop closed he established his own business, which consisted of buying picture postcards and reselling them to local outlets such as novelty shops, candy stores, and drugstores. Conducting his wholesaling enterprise from a horse-drawn wagon, J.S. enjoyed modest success and by 1918 welcomed his eldest son, nine-year-old Irving, as the first partner. In 1926 the Sapirstein Greeting Card Company solidified itself as a family business with the additional employment of Irving's brother Morris. Two years later, through the sales efforts of Morris and Irving, the company received its largest order since inception, a postcard contract worth $24,000. During 1929, a year after the Hall Brothers Company (Hallmark) had begun to advertise nationally, the Sapirsteins greatly furthered their eventual position as a mainstay of the market by becoming the first distributor to use self-serve display cabinets for its greeting cards. Three years later, the company began phasing out its dependency on suppliers, whose products were often inferior, by manufacturing its own line of greeting cards.

Company Perspectives:

American Greetings helps people everywhere express their innermost thoughts and feelings, enhance meaningful relationships and celebrate life's milestones and special occasions.

Although Hallmark would retain until the 1980s a formidable industry lead because of its well-established name and high-quality image, the Sapirstein business was at least preparing itself to compete with the market leader.

The Great Depression had minimal negative impact on the company, as evinced by a continuing string of "firsts" during the 1930s. These included the hiring of the first sales representative in 1934; youngest son Harry's first year with the company in 1935; the opening of the first branch office and the first major manufacturing facility in 1936; and the introduction of the first line of Forget-Me-Not cards in 1939. With the advent of the next decade the company, which had renamed itself American Greetings Publishers in 1938, catapulted to national prominence with annual sales exceeding $1 million. In 1944 the family-owned and family-run business incorporated as American Greeting Publishers, Inc. Five years later the firm signed its first licensing agreement, with John Sands Pty. Ltd. of Sydney, Australia. Then in 1952, because of rapid population growth and subsequent plans for both acquisitions and expansion, the company went public as American Greetings Corporation, issuing 200,000 shares at $12 per share. American Greetings introduced Hi Brows, an innovative line of humorous studio cards, in 1956, and also established a Canadian subsidiary, Carlton Cards, Ltd.

Creation of Characters Beginning in 1967

A new era dawned in 1960 when J.S. became chairman of the board and Irving (who, like his brothers, had changed his last name to Stone in the 1940s) became president. This same year the company launched a cabinet manufacturing plant in Forest City, North Carolina, the first of many large capital expenditures necessary to keep pace with growth and fortify the company's large position in the industry. In 1967 the company introduced the Holly Hobbie character to wide public approval; this important creative move, which had huge potential for licensing spinoffs, eventually led to the formation of Those Characters From Cleveland, Inc., a subsidiary operation active since 1980 that became a valuable contributor to the company's financial health. The year following Holly Hobbie's debut, overall sales surpassed $100 million. In 1969 American Greetings ventured south of the border via the establishment of a subsidiary in Mexico City.

The 1970s were marked by a number of major events. The decade opened with the introduction of Soft Touch cards, so labeled for their combination of soft-focus photography and touching sentiment. This new line became the most successful of any introduced in American Greetings' history. In 1971 the company created a retail subsidiary called Summit Corporation (later renamed Carlton Cards Retail, Inc.) to operate its own card shops. In 1972 the world was introduced to Ziggy, "the world's most lovable loser." Even more so than Holly Hobbie (who by 1977 was the most popular female licensed character in the world), Ziggy became a perennial money-maker for the company, due especially to the royalty profits and publicity generated by his syndicated newspaper cartoon series, the creative rights for which were sold to Universal Press. In 1978 Irving Stone became chairman and CEO and Morry Weiss, Irving's son-in-law, was named president. During this changeover year, two new subsidiaries were established: Plus Mark, Inc., a manufacturer of Christmas gift wrap, boxed cards, and accessories, and A.G. Industries, Inc., the largest display fixture company in the country. By this time American Greetings possessed a view of itself as a leading mass-marketer to pharmacies, variety stores, discount stores, and supermarkets of lower-cost cards. Hallmark, which had ignored such venues until 1959, was now beginning to represent a serious threat to American's market share through its Ambassador card line. The most comforting news for American was that it, indisputably, dominated in terms of licensing revenue; the company reinforced this fact in 1980 with the unveiling of Strawberry Shortcake, whose array of products generated $500 million in retail sales in 1981 alone. The Care Bears soon followed, debuting in 1983; the Care Bears were even more of a phenomenon, accounting for $2 billion in sales within two years of introduction.

Increasing Industry Competition in the 1980s and 1990s

American celebrated its 75th anniversary in 1981 by recreating its 21-year-old emblem of the rose. This symbolic affirmation of quality and beauty dovetailed nicely with other key components of the new corporate identity program, including American's first foray into national television advertising as the Fresh Idea Company. Investors sensed a new surge in growth as they nearly doubled the stock price of American shares from October 1981 to May 1982. It was around this time that Weiss fueled investor fever by proclaiming, "We want to be the dominant force in the industry." *Forbes* writer Jeff Blyskal noted that the company was "actively upgrading its products and prices" and opined: "American Greetings is making a bold move. Weiss is pouring his licensing profits into an aggressive and well-timed campaign to challenge Hallmark." From 1981 to 1985 American grew from a half-billion to a billion-dollar company and thus attained one of the key corporate objectives it had set for itself. More important than this increase in total revenue, however, was American's astonishing net income increase of 613 percent in a ten-year period. What the company had failed to do, unfortunately, was enhance its market share with respect to Hallmark.

Gibson Greetings, the number three card-seller, shook the industry in 1986 with a vicious price war, which it commenced in an effort to increase its own 10 percent share. The price war ended the following year, but all three companies suffered profit losses from it, with virtually no change in their respective market positions (Hallmark still led with 45 percent and American followed with 35 percent; the bottom tier was still composed of Gibson and several hundred much smaller manufacturers). American's recovery from this siege, as well as from downswings in noncard sales, was difficult. A 1988 *Forbes* article labeled the company "Flounder," finding support for its

Key Dates:

1906: Jacob Sapirstein begins a card wholesaling business in Cleveland, calling it Sapirstein Greeting Card Company.

1929: The company becomes the first in the industry to use self-serve display cabinets for its greeting cards.

1932: The firm begins manufacturing its own line of greeting cards.

1938: The name of the company is changed to American Greetings Publishers.

1939: The first line of Forget-Me-Not cards is launched.

1944: The company is incorporated as American Greeting Publishers, Inc.

1949: The first overseas licensing deal is reached, with John Sands Pty. Ltd. of Australia.

1952: The company goes public as American Greetings Corporation.

1958: A Canadian subsidiary, Carlton Cards, Ltd., is established.

1967: Holly Hobbie first appears on a greeting card; the popularity of the character leads American Greetings into character licensing.

1970: The Soft Touch line of cards debuts.

1971: American Greetings establishes a retail subsidiary.

1978: Two new subsidiaries are formed: Plus Mark, Inc., maker of gift wrap, boxed cards, and accessories; and A.G. Industries, Inc., the nation's largest maker of display fixtures.

1980: Strawberry Shortcake character debuts.

1981: The company launches its first national television advertising campaign.

1983: The Care Bears characters are introduced.

1993: Magnivision, maker of reading glasses, is acquired.

1995: An 80 percent stake in S.A. Greetings Corporation of South Africa is acquired.

1996: John Sands, leading greeting card company in both Australia and New Zealand, is acquired; a party goods line is relaunched under the name DesignWare; the company enters the e-commerce realm with launch of a company web site.

1997: A line of candles is relaunched as GuildHouse; Learning Horizons, Inc. is created as a subsidiary specializing in supplemental educational products.

2000: Gibson Greetings, Inc. is acquired for $163 million; the company launches a major restructuring.

dismal forecast in new earnings estimates ($1.05 per share versus $2.35 in 1985) and a 60 percent drop in stock price from its mid-1986 high of 42. Nevertheless, after hitting bottom in 1988 with a devastating drop in profits from $63 million to $33 million, American rebounded in 1989 to $44 million.

By 1991, American more than doubled its net income and once again became a feisty contender for the number one position. Although Hallmark's revenues were roughly double those of American, American showed 10 percent growth in sales for cards and related goods in 1991 while Hallmark reported only 1 percent. At least some of this renewed vigor was due to the appointment of longtime employee Ed Fruchtenbaum as the fourth and first non-family president and the elevation of Weiss to CEO. Under Weiss, American cut costs, streamlined its operations, and improved its idea-to-market development time (Desert Storm cards were shipped to retailers within a mere three-week period from initiation). With Fruchtenbaum, American further honed its day-to-day operations by placing special emphasis on its information systems (IS) technology. Through its IS department, the company created software to aid management, the sales force, and their retail customers in tracking inventories and reacting to buying trends. With the ability to supply sales managers and retailers with block-by-block demographic data, IS was an indispensable component of Fruchtenbaum's future plans, for pinpoint marketing represented the cutting edge of the industry.

In 1992 American purchased Custom Expressions, Inc., maker of the CreataCard units, which initially featured approximately 1,000 card options and were capable of producing cards for consumers, priced at $3.50 each, in less than four minutes. In October 1992 American installed a few thousand of the kiosks in mass-merchandise outlets nationwide and had more than 7,000

of them installed by early 1994, by which time they were generating healthy revenue but only modest profits. Hallmark, owner of Touch Screen Greetings and the Personalize It! method, had filed suit against American in 1992 for patent infringement, but the suit was settled in 1995 with each company getting a worldwide, nonexclusive license to use the technology.

Also in 1992, Weiss became both chairman and CEO of American Greetings. Fruchtenbaum was promoted to president and chief operating officer, while Irving Stone assumed the title founder-chairman. Starting the following year, the company began to reconfigure its mix of non-greeting card operations. In 1993 American acquired Magnivision, the leading manufacturer and distributor of nonprescription reading glasses in the United States and 15 other countries. Three years later, American entered into talks with BEC Group Inc. to buy BEC's Foster Grant Group, a maker of sunglasses, but in the midst of the negotiations American decided that it did not wish to pursue the purchase. Also in 1996, American began to reorganize portions of its consumer products group by converting product categories into strategic business units, a move designed to elevate these products from mere sidelines to semi-autonomous units. Subsequently, the company's party goods line was relaunched in 1996 as DesignWare, while its candle line reemerged the following year as GuildHouse. Further such moves were planned for other lines. In March 1997, American announced that it had formed a new subsidiary, Learning Horizons, Inc., to manufacture and distribute supplemental educational products for preschool and elementary school students, including workbooks, science kits, flash cards, math kits, posters, audiocassettes, educational stickers, rubber stamps, and puzzles. The company in August 1997 sold two subsidiaries to Newell Co.: Acme Frame Products, Inc., maker of picture frames, and Wilhold Inc., producer of hair accessory products.

During this same period, American Greetings became more aggressive in pursuing markets outside the United States, whose maturing greeting card industry was seeing flat sales through most of the 1990s. In 1993 American launched the Forget-Me-Not brand in Canada, where it became that country's largest and broadest line of social expression cards. South Africa was the next target for company expansion, which came in the form of the 1995 purchase of an 80 percent stake in S.A. Greetings Corporation, one of the leading players in the $30 million South African greeting card market. The following year, American acquired John Sands, the number one greeting card company in both Australia and New Zealand, for $85.1 million. During the first several months of 1998 the company increased its share of the U.K. greeting card market from 11 to 20 percent by acquiring two London-based firms, Camden Graphics Group and Hanson White Ltd. Finally, in 1999 American Greetings gained a base in Asia through the purchase of a majority stake in a Malaysian greeting card company, Memory Lane SDN BHD.

By late 1995 the kiosk technology that showed such early promise was rapidly being rendered technologically obsolete by the increasing use of PCs and the Internet to make and deliver greeting cards. Lagging CreataCard sales led the company to take a charge of $52.1 million in November 1995 to reflect the decreased value of its kiosks. At the same time, however, American was moving quickly into the home PC and online arenas itself. By early 1996, the company had marketing tie-ins with three online services—Prodigy, CompuServe, and Microsoft Network. During fiscal 1997, American launched a web site, which allowed visitors to design cards and have them printed and mailed from the company fulfillment center in Cleveland. That year also saw the debut of two CD-ROM products, Personal CardShop for Home and Office and Creata-Card Plus. The former enabled users to select from among 150 cards, personalize them, order them by modem, and have the card printed by the Cleveland fulfillment center. CreataCard Plus featured more than 3,000 predesigned greeting cards, invitations, stationery, and announcements, which could be printed at home on a color printer, sent by e-mail, or once again printed and delivered by the fulfillment center.

In the midst of all of this activity, of course, the greeting card war between American Greetings and Hallmark raged on. American gained ground in the 1990s, despite its market share remaining at the same level—35 percent—in 1996 as in 1990. During this same period, however, Hallmark's share fell from 50 percent to 42 percent. American nearly caught up with Hallmark in March 1996 when it tried to acquire the still-number-three Gibson, which claimed 10 percent of the market. But that month, Gibson turned down American's $292 million takeover bid. In July 1997 American Greetings launched a massive revamping of its everyday card lines, aiming to replace, over the next 18 months, 80 percent of its everyday greeting cards as part of a new marketing strategy called ''The All New American Way.'' The company hoped to gain market share by offering cards that met new marketplace needs arising from nine trends in American culture—for example, the increase in cultural diversity, changes in family dynamics, and longer and healthier lives. In 1998 American Greetings' stock was switched from the NASDAQ to the New York Stock Exchange because of the greater exposure offered by the latter. In August 1999 the DesignWare unit was bolstered through the acquisition of Contempo Colours, a Michigan party goods firm whose licenses included Monopoly and Sesame Street.

New Century Struggles

During the 1990s net sales grew from $1.29 billion to $2.21 billion. While the fiscal 1999 results marked the company's 93rd consecutive year of increasing revenue, this streak came to an end the next year when sales fell 1.5 percent. About $100 million in revenues was lost that year because the company slowed shipments to retailers in order to implement a new inventory system that shortened the amount of time necessary to design, produce, and ship cards, thereby allowing the ongoing inventory to be reduced. Furthermore, greeting card sales had been flat for some time, and the Internet was providing consumers with plenty of alternative communication methods. Of course, American Greetings itself was involved online, but the AmericanGreetings.com venture had yet to show a profit. In June 1999 the company announced plans to take its online unit public, but the early 2000 tech stock meltdown forced the initial public offering to be withdrawn. Meantime, revenues came under further pressure from another price war, this one initiated in March 1999 by Hallmark, which introduced a new line of 99-cent cards. Forced to respond, American began selling more inexpensive cards at deep-discount outlets.

In March 2000 American Greetings won a long-sought-after prize, acquiring Gibson Greetings for $163 million in cash. The purchase price was much lower than the offer that had been spurned in 1996 because in the meantime Gibson's stock had plummeted as a series of setbacks reduced the company's U.S. market share to about 6 percent. Among other problems, Gibson had been forced to abandon manufacturing, and some of the firms that had been contracted as outsourcers had been unable to handle Gibson's massive orders. In addition to the Gibson card line, American also gained Gibson's fairly strong subsidiary in the United Kingdom, making American that nation's greeting card leader, as well as the company's 27 percent stake in Egreetings Network Inc., an online greeting card company.

In June 2000 Fruchtenbaum was fired from his position as president and COO after other company officials learned that he had violated the company's insider trading policy in December 1998 when he exercised options on some 30,000 shares of American Greetings stock and then sold them, just before the company made its announcement about the new inventory system (the projected drop in earnings sent the company's stock down by 32 percent on the day the news was released). Fruchtenbaum, who was alleged to have avoided nearly $500,000 in stock losses as a result of his actions, was later sued by the Securities and Exchange Commission for insider trading; he reached a deal with the commission in July 2003, agreeing to pay back nearly $80,000 of his gains plus more than $267,000 in fines and court costs.

Following Fruchtenbaum's departure, James C. Spira, a management consultant who was a longtime American Greetings adviser and a member of the board of directors since 1998, was named vice-chairman. His role soon became a pivotal one when he was charged with overseeing a massive restructuring that was announced in November 2000. American was forced to take drastic measures because of a host of factors: the stagnant retailing climate, fewer and more powerful retailers thanks to retail sector consolidation, increasing competition from lower-priced cards, and the negative effects of the Internet on greeting card sales. The company said that it would cut 1,500 jobs from the workforce, shutter six manufacturing and distribution centers, eliminate one of its four main U.S. card brands—Forget-Me-Not, and slash the number of different greeting cards it offered from 15,000 to 10,000. American also would begin to shift to scan-based trading systems with selected retailers. In the company's traditional system, it would record a sale when a retailer stocked a card on its shelf; in the new system, a card on a retailer's shelf would be kept on American's books as inventory, and it would only be when a card was scanned at the register that American would record a sale. Through the new system, American hoped to gain greater control over inventory, although the shift would be an expensive one. Overall, the restructuring would cost the company more than $300 million, and it sent the company deep into the red for both fiscal 2001 and 2002.

As the restructuring was being implemented in 2001, American Greetings made two Internet-related acquisitions. The company acquired the shares of Egreetings Network it did not already own for about $28 million, and it also purchased another online greeting card company, BlueMountain.com, from At Home Corporation for $35 million. American now operated four online greeting card sites (the fourth being BeatGreets.com, which offered musical greetings); combined, the sites were drawing 100 million visitors per year. However, American's Internet ventures were still operating at a loss, although the loss for fiscal 2002 was much smaller than that of the previous year.

During fiscal 2003 American Greetings suspended its dividend payments in order to free up more cash and pay down its $950 million in debt. Having generated $90 million in savings through the restructuring, American returned to the black that year with a profit of $121.1 million. In June 2003, a few months after this encouraging news was released, a major shift in the executive suite was effected. Morry Weiss named his sons, both of whom had joined the company about a decade earlier, to the firm's top posts—Zev Weiss became CEO and Jeffrey Weiss, president and COO. Spira retired but retained a seat on the board, still headed by Morry Weiss. Continuing the momentum that appeared to have been established during fiscal 2003 was the challenge facing the new leaders.

Principal Subsidiaries

AGC Inc.; A.G. Industries, Inc.; AmericanGreetings.com, Inc. (92%); Carlton Cards Retail, Inc.; Gibson Greetings, Inc.; John Sands (Australia) Ltd. (U.S.A.); Learning Horizons, Inc.; Magnivision, Inc.; Plus Mark, Inc.; Those Characters From Cleveland, Inc.; The Ink Group PTY Ltd. (Australia); Carlton Cards (Canada) Limited; Carlton Cards Ltd. (Ireland); Memory Lane SDN BHD (Malaysia; 85%); Carlton Mexico, S.A. de C.V.; The Ink Group NZ Ltd. (New Zealand); John Sands (N.Z.) Ltd. (New Zealand); S.A. Greetings Corporation (PTY) Ltd. (South Africa); Camden Graphics Group (U.K.); Carlton Cards (United Kingdom) Limited; Gibson Greetings International Limited (U.K.); Hanson White Ltd. (U.K.); The Ink Group Publishers Ltd. (U.K.).

Principal Competitors

Hallmark Cards, Inc.; Taylor Corporation; CSS Industries, Inc.; Amscan Holdings, Inc.; Factory Card & Party Outlet Corp.; Party City Corporation.

Further Reading

''American Greetings Launches Custom Card System,'' *Greetings Magazine,* September 1992, p. 14.

Blyskal, Jeff, ''Greetings from the Competition,'' *Forbes,* March 29, 1982, pp. 36–37.

Bounds, Wendy, and Matt Murray, ''Card Makers Try New Ways to Greet a Paperless World,'' *Wall Street Journal,* March 19, 1996, pp. B1, B8.

Caminiti, Susan, ''The Fortune 500: America's Fastest-Growing Companies,'' *Fortune,* April 22, 1991, pp. 67–76.

Canedy, Dana, ''Wish You Weren't Here: It's Been Live and Let Live Until Today, But Now the Greeting Card Wars Are Under Way,'' *New York Times,* November 20, 1997, p. D1.

Chiu, Tony, and Joyce Wansley, ''Who's Red and Sweet and Filthy Rich? Strawberry Shortcake, Toyland's Newest Tyke-Coon,'' *People Weekly,* May 10, 1982, pp. 91–93.

Cimperman, Jennifer Scott, ''Next Generation Inherits the Passion: Morry Weiss of American Greetings Names Sons Jeffrey, Zev to Top Posts,'' *Cleveland Plain Dealer,* February 19, 2003, p. C1.

Dorfman, John R., and Wendy Bounds, ''American Greetings Stock Gets Warm 'Hello' from Investment Pros Who Cite Mass Market,'' *Wall Street Journal,* June 11, 1994, p. C2.

Fitzgerald, Kate, '' 'Happy Birthday, (Name Here),' '' *Advertising Age,* February 21, 1994, p. 17.

Frazier, Mya, ''American Greetings' Big Slide: Company Didn't Realize Extent of Its Problems, CEO Admits,'' *Cleveland Plain Dealer,* September 16, 2001, p. G1.

——, ''AmericanGreetings.com Buys Rival: Gets BlueMountain for $35 Million,'' *Cleveland Plain Dealer,* September 14, 2001, p. C1.

——, ''American Greetings Stuns Wall St.: Stock Plummets As Card Maker Slashes Profit Outlook, Announces Restructuring,'' *Cleveland Plain Dealer,* November 17, 2000, p. 1C.

——, ''American Greetings Will Cut 1,500 Jobs, Shut Down Six Facilities,'' *Cleveland Plain Dealer,* March 28, 2001, p. 1A.

Geddes, Annmarie L., ''American Greetings' Vision Helps It Hold the Cards,'' *Small Business News-Cleveland,* February 1, 1995, p. 24.

''Hallmark, American at Odds Over Custom Card Patents,'' *Greetings Magazine,* November 1992, p. 13.

Jaffe, Thomas, ''Flounder,'' *Forbes,* April 25, 1988, p. 352.

Laurel, Touby, ''Congratulations on Your Big Earnings Increase!,'' *Business Week,* August 17, 1992, p. 58.

Maturi, Richard J., ''High Tech Makes for High Touch: Managerial Know-How Keeps American Greetings Close to Customers,'' *Industry Week,* August 17, 1992, pp. 50–51.

McCune, Jenny C., ''Street Smart Selling,'' *Success,* May 1991, p. 22.

McMurray, Scott, ''Dealing a Whole New Deck of Cards: American Greetings Gets the High-Tech Message,'' *U.S. News and World Report,* December 4, 1995, pp. 68–69.

Melvin, Chuck, ''The Card Shop Goes Electronic,'' *Cleveland Plain Dealer,* December 31, 1996, p. 1C.

Mendelson, Seth, ''Above the Crowd,'' *Supermarket Business,* June 1996, p. 41.

Miller, James P., ''Stock of American Greetings Plunges on Inventory Plan,'' *Wall Street Journal,* February 25, 1999.

Murakami, Tomoeh, ''American Greetings Returns to Profitability,'' *Cleveland Plain Dealer,* April 4, 2003, p. C1.

Nelson, Emily, ''American Greetings Says It May Sell Certain Noncore Consumer Businesses,'' *Wall Street Journal,* January 14, 1997, p. B9.

——, ''Dearest Mom, Greetings from My CD-ROM,'' *Wall Street Journal,* September 4, 1996, pp. B1, B4.

Oliver, Suzanne, "Christmas Card Blues," *Forbes,* December 24, 1990, p. 100.

Osborne, Eleanore, "Licensing 'Bears' Watching at American Greetings," *Ohio Business,* October 1985, p. 39.

Pledger, Marcia, "Greeting the New America: American Greetings Is Revising Its Line of Cards, Notes, and Calendars to Reflect Today's Lifestyles," *Cleveland Plain Dealer,* June 29, 1997, p. 1H.

——, "The Near-Fall of Gibson," *Cleveland Plain Dealer,* March 9, 2000, p. 1C.

——, "Trans-Ohio Greeting-Card Rivals to Unite: American Greetings Plans to Buy Cincinnati-Based Gibson Greetings," *Cleveland Plain Dealer,* November 3, 1999, p. 1C.

Rifkin, Glenn, "A Sentimental Journey to Success," *Computerworld,* August 28, 1989, pp. 55, 59.

Sanger, Elizabeth, "Salutes for American Greetings," *Barron's,* October 27, 1986, p. 83.

Schwartz, Ela, "The Next Cycle in Greeting Cards," *Discount Merchandiser,* July 1990, pp. 68–69.

Sparks, Debra, "The Card Game," *Financial World,* July 5, 1994, pp. 28–29.

Stodghill, Ron, II, "Roses Are Red, Card Sellers Blue," *Time,* April 19, 1999, pp. 34+.

Weiss, Morry, *American Greetings Corporation,* New York: Newcomen Society in North America, 1982.

—Jay P. Pederson
—update: David E. Salamie

American Pop Corn Company

P.O. Box 178
Sioux City, Iowa 51102
U.S.A.
Telephone: (712) 239-1232
Fax: (712) 239-1268
Web site: http://www.jollytime.com

Private Company
Incorporated: 1926
Employees: 185
NAIC: 311999 All Other Miscellaneous Food Manufacturers

American Pop Corn Company is the oldest processor of popcorn in the United States, as well as one of the largest. The company's products are sold to consumers under the Jolly Time brand. White and yellow popcorn are available dry or packaged for cooking in a microwave oven. Microwave flavors include butter, light, and fat-free varieties, as well as cheddar cheese and sweetened kettle corn. The company offers a premium popcorn under the brand American's Best, available dry in plastic jars. Vendors can purchase bulk quantities of Little Wonder white popcorn and Gold Mine yellow popcorn.

American Pop Corn purchases popcorn from 130 farmers who tend more than 20,000 acres in Iowa and Nebraska. Processing involves slow-drying popcorn on-the-cob to obtain a balance of moisture and dryness for a high volume of fluff. The company's facilities are located in Sioux City, Leeds, and Schaller, Iowa.

Beginnings in 1914

American Pop Corn Company founder Cloid H. Smith spent his childhood in the center of the country, Sac County, Iowa, where climate conditions for growing pop corn are ideal. Smith enjoyed popped "pop corn" frequently as a child, before "popcorn" became a regular part of American life. Enterprising as a young man, Smith opened a drugstore in Odebolt, Iowa, at the age of 20. In 1899 he founded Odebolt Telephone Company, the first local exchange. When that company merged with other telephone exchanges, forming New State Telephone Company, Smith became general manager and moved to Sioux City with his family in 1905. Smith stayed with the company after Bell Telephone Company acquired New State in 1912. With the funds he received from the sale of New State stock C.H. bought farmland north of Odebolt.

Smith stumbled into the popcorn business after the farmer working his land sold the corn for a price Smith considered too low. When Smith discussed the matter with the buyer, the buyer challenged him to start his own business. Smith entered the popcorn trade in 1914 with the idea of packaging a high-quality product that would be easy for grocers to sell and ready for customers to cook. At this time popcorn was sold on the cob in bulk. The bulk bags took space in the stores and were inconvenient for grocers who had to weigh the orders. Customers had to shuck and wash the corn themselves. Also, quality popcorn had not been developed yet, and people accepted that many kernels would not pop.

American Pop Corn was the first company to process and sell popcorn. Smith picked the corn in Odebolt and took it home where he and his son, Howard, shucked corn from the cob, then washed and packaged the kernels. The company sold popcorn in bulk to vendors in 100-pound and 150-pound burlap sacks and in one-pound cardboard cartons to grocers. The Jolly Time name "just happened to pop up." On consumer packaging the name "Jolly Time" was printed in bright green above a picture of three children sitting on the floor, toys strewn around them, eating popcorn from a large bowl. Its first season in business, from April to November 1914, American Pop Corn sold more than 75,000 pounds of popcorn.

Smith's boyhood experience with pop corn influenced the development of the company. Smith knew that freshly harvested corn did not pop as readily as corn dried on the cob for several months. After some experimentation with natural air-drying, Smith and Howard designed a storage crib that would provide the proper level of ventilation. In the fall of 1914 American Pop Corn completed construction of a storage crib in Leeds, Iowa, with the capacity to hold 500,000 pounds of corn. As the family basement and backyard shed no longer provided enough space to handle operations, the following year American Pop Corn built a shelling and washing facility adjacent to the storage crib.

As American Pop Corn's rapid success required more involvement, Smith resigned from Bell Telephone in 1915. After Howard graduated from high school in 1916, he joined the company on a full-time basis as well. American Pop Corn began to establish relationships with brokers who sold Jolly Time Pop Corn to grocers and Smith hired Stanley Thatcher in 1920 to cultivate relationships with vendors who sold popcorn at carnivals and circuses, at busy intersections of larger towns and cities, and near movie theaters. American Pop Corn simplified business for vendors by offering all of the supplies needed: corn oil, salt, and cartons and glassine bags for serving hot, freshly popped popcorn. Thatcher maintained contact through personal letters and the *Jolly Time Booster,* published from 1924 to 1941, which provided information about the company and stories about successful vendors.

Marketing Programs Furthering Growth During 1920s and 1930s

A problem developed in the retail trade as popcorn continued to dry while sitting on grocery store shelves, becoming too dry to pop to its full volume. In 1920 the company experimented with packaging popcorn in glass jars, but it proved to be costly, especially due to breakage. An engineer at American Can Company in Chicago designed an airtight metal can to meet American Pop Corn's needs. Not only was the can a revolutionary way to package popcorn, it was a precursor to the beer can. American Pop Corn introduced Jolly Time in a red, white, and blue can in 1925, which carried the message, "It's guaranteed to pop!" The company hired Jim Coates to promote the product to brokers and the company's first national advertising campaign coincided with the new packaging. American Pop Corn advertised in *Good Housekeeping* magazine and received the magazine's Seal of Approval for quality.

Advertisements in national magazines and major newspapers promoted the appeal of popcorn to people of all ages. In 1929 Jolly Time appeared in many popular magazines, including the *Saturday Evening Post, Holland's Magazine, Liberty,* and the *Farmer's Wife.* Advertising in 162 metropolitan newspapers in every state and in Canada, American Pop Corn reached nearly nine million readers. Full-page advertisements in *Progressive Grocer* exemplified the success of grocers who offered Jolly Time popcorn. In 1929 the company sold more than ten million pounds of popcorn.

American Pop Corn launched a weekly radio show in 1930, hosted by General Jolly Time and his Pop Corn Colonels. The orchestra played popular music and took requests from listeners across the country. The show's theme song, "A Bowl of Pop Corn, a Radio, and You," was a popular hit. A trade advertisement listed 30 cities where the radio show played, along with broadcast stations and times. The promotion stated "Push Jolly Time—For the Largest Profits and Quickest Turnover."

During the 1930s popcorn grew in popularity because it was an inexpensive snack during economically difficult times, at the movies and at home. A ten-ounce can of Jolly Time cost ten cents, and popcorn could be enjoyed at home while listening to the radio. To promote popcorn as a snack, American Pop Corn offered an electric popcorn popper and a can of Jolly Time pop corn for one dollar, shipped anywhere in the country. Thousands of customers responded.

The Smith family encountered its own difficulties in 1931 when the storage crib in Sioux City burned to the ground. The entire stock of corn was destroyed. Construction of a new facility, completed a year later, accommodated the company's patented "Volumized" process for slow-drying.

Post-World War II Era: Marketing to the Consumer

During the late 1930s American Pop Corn began marketing a variety of popcorn brands, including Thunderbolt, Magic-Pop, and Giant Yellow South American Popcorn, designed for different markets, usually at lower prices. The minor brands sold well but not remarkably, so Howard decided to simplify the company's brand marketing to emphasize the Jolly Time brand. The idea proved to be appropriate to a new era that emerged for the company after C.H. Smith died in 1939, when Howard became president of American Pop Corn Company, and after World War II, when a new consumer era developed.

During the early stages of the company's history, American Pop Corn focused most of its marketing efforts toward bulk buyers, the vendors and grocers. After World War II the company marketed directly to consumers on a national basis. Howard maintained the Little Wonder and Gold Mine brands for vendors and positioned Jolly Time for consumers. He hired renowned package designer Jim Nash to give Jolly Time a new look; Nash designed Jolly Time's signature banner. Fresh advertising copy by Bob Savage complemented the new style.

The popularity of movies and the advent of television played a vital role in the company's growth, for both bulk and consumer brands. However, consumer packages showed the most dramatic growth. In 1939 the company sold 75,000 cases of ten-ounce cans of popcorn. By 1947 sales increased to 250,000, then doubled to 500,000 cases in 1949.

New competition slowed sales during the early 1950s as new national brands emerged to take advantage of a growing market. The company hired different advertising agencies to maintain a fresh approach to promotion. Celebrity endorsements from Danny Kaye, Bob Hope, and Ozzie and Harriet Nelson added excitement to magazine advertising. Advertisements appeared in more than 20 national magazines, such as *Ladies' Home Journal, Good Housekeeping, Better Homes and Gardens,* and *Sunset,* as well as in more than 800 newspapers weekly. For 26 weeks during the fall and winter of 1956–57 the company advertised on Arthur Godfrey's national radio show. Godfrey himself endorsed Jolly Time Pop Corn as "the world's best." In 1958 the company offered a hand-carved Black Forest Clock for $1.50 plus a lid or label from a package of Jolly Time popcorn. The ornate wood clocks were shipped directly from Germany.

Key Dates:

1914: American Pop Corn Company sells more than 75,000 pounds of white pop corn its first season in business.

1925: Company introduces revolutionary packaging of popcorn in airtight cans; incorporates the following year.

1930: Radio show is launched to promote Jolly Time popcorn nationwide.

1942: New Jolly Time logo is launched with signature banner and new lettering.

1949: Sales double in two years as company sells 500,000 cases of popcorn in ten-ounce cans.

1968: Jolly Time Pop Corn appears on the popular game show *Let's Make a Deal*.

1973: Jolly Time logo is updated with a sleek style.

1984: Jolly Time Microwave Pop Corn is introduced.

1997: Blast O Butter becomes the company's most popular flavor.

2002: KettleMania Outrageously Fun Kettle Corn is introduced.

2003: American Pop Corn produces its billionth bag of microwave popcorn.

New technology provided American Pop Corn with new packaging options during the 1950s. With some reluctance Howard Smith began to offer Jolly Time Pop Corn in transparent plastic bags. His concern for the quality of the corn—that a torn bag would lead to corn too dry to pop properly—was outweighed by consumer preference for plastic bags. In 1957 the company began to sell popcorn in a polyethylene bag that provided moisture-proof containment and durability to minimize tears. The introduction of a new fiber can in 1958 provided a convenient method of dry storage as a string easily opened the resealable lid. Consumers liked the container, so the company introduced an Economy Size 20-ounce can in 1959.

A third generation took the lead at American Pop Corn Company after Howard died in 1966. His sons, Chesley and Wrede Smith, applied successful methods they learned since working at the company, beginning in the 1940s. Their programs for continued growth and development involved hybrid research, new products, and new marketing and public relations programs.

Marketing and public relations emphasized brand recognition on a national level, particularly on television. In 1968 the company began to promote the Jolly Time brand through popular game shows. Monty Hall offered Jolly Time popcorn on *Let's Make a Deal*, displaying an eight-foot replica of a can of Jolly Time Pop Corn. Over the next decade Jolly Time appeared frequently on more than a dozen game shows.

To support its national advertising effort American Pop Corn sought to cultivate stronger relationships with its brokers. The company hired Shelby Johnstone as a full-time national sales representative in 1971 and began to publish *Jolly Time News* to provide brokers with information about new programs and new products. In 1972 Johnstone launched an annual display contest, to encourage grocers to attract attention to Jolly Time products. Designating October as Pop Corn Month, American Pop Corn offered prizes to grocers and brokers for the best display. Grocers responded with spectacular results, using hundreds of cases of Jolly Time products and increasing sales substantially.

Wrede and Chesley Smith decided to modernize the look of Jolly Time packaging. In 1973 Jolly Time donned a new label, featuring a streamlined version of the banner and sleek lettering for the name. Newspaper advertising featured a new character, Mr. Jolly, who wore a can of Jolly Time Pop Corn as a top hat. To attract attention in small advertisements Mr. Jolly was shown in lively situations, such as holding a sign that said, ''Fun,'' and as a jack-in-the-box.

American Pop Corn introduced several new products in the early 1970s. The company began testing Jolly Time Pop Corn in Oil in certain markets in 1964 and introduced the product nationwide in 1972. Jolly Time Instant Buttery Seasoning, launched in 1974, provided an easy way to add butter and salt to popcorn, as well as meats and vegetables. Jolly Time Popping Oil was introduced in 1975.

Public relations involved providing articles about popcorn to food editors at newspapers and magazines. In 1973 American Pop Corn hired a home economist, Christine Pines, to write stories and present them for publication. The company expanded the program two years later to include recipes, photographs, and news; distribution included radio and television stations in large and small cities nationwide. In 1977 Patricia Fox Sheinwold wrote and published *Jolly Time Party Book: Games, Puzzles, Recipes, and Creative Party Ideas for All Occasions.*

Microwave Ovens, Health Concerns Directing Development: 1980s–90s

New appliances and new health guidelines provided a boost to all popcorn producers during the late 1970s and early 1980s. The hot air popper increased interest in popcorn as a healthy, fat-free snack and nutritionists acknowledged popcorn as a good source of fiber. In 1980 Weight Watchers gave popcorn a ''legal'' status for members of its weight management program. Between 1981 and 1986 the sales nearly doubled industrywide. More than half of all popcorn was eaten at home as network and cable television stations began to show feature films and as video cassette recorders (VCRs) became widely available for viewing movies at home.

Together with home videos, the widespread use of microwave ovens had an immense impact on increasing consumption of popcorn. American Pop Corn responded with the introduction of Jolly Time Microwave Pop Corn in 1984. By 1988 the boom in sales of microwave popcorn required construction of another production facility. Microwave packaging was instrumental in the company's introduction of popcorn to international markets as well, and the company began to export popcorn to Europe.

American Pop Corn sought to improve its product in all areas of consumer interest. In 1987 the company's hybrid research program, initiated in 1976, resulted in a premium popcorn product, American's Best yellow pop corn, which provided superior popping qualities in volume and popcorn size, as well as a sweet taste. As good health continued to be of concern, in late 1989 American Pop Corn reduced the fat-to-calorie ratio of its microwave popcorn to 42 percent, then introduced two light versions, Natural Butter Flavor Light Microwave Pop Corn and Natural Flavor Light Microwave Pop Corn made with 50 percent less fat, as well as less sodium and fewer calories.

The company continued to apply proven marketing techniques. Jolly Time appeared on popular game shows, such as *Wheel of Fortune, The Price Is Right,* and *Jeopardy,* and Paul Harvey and Dick Clark endorsed Jolly Time on their popular radio programs. An innovation in newspaper advertising involved free-standing inserts, packages of product coupons inserted into Sunday newspapers nationwide. American Pop Corn issued more than 200 million coupons annually, seeking to retain loyal customers and attract new ones. National magazine advertising involved newer publications, such as *Family Circle, People, Seventeen,* and the *Disney Channel Magazine.*

In a 1994 promotional campaign, American Pop Corn gave away a free package of Jolly Time microwave popcorn with titles from the Walt Disney Studio Film Collection. The promotion included a rebate program that paid three dollars to buyers who returned four proof-of-purchase UPCs with cash register receipts from Jolly Time Products.

1997: Putting Fun into Marketing

In 1997 American Pop Corn launched a new packaging and marketing concept to emphasize fun, especially family fun. The change occurred in conjunction with the introduction of Jolly Time Blast O Butter Ultimate Movie Theater Butter Microwave Popcorn, packaged in a bright red box with pictures of big popcorn puffs. The marketing involved new cartoon characters, the Funn family, featured in television advertising and on the company's web site. In a promotion of popcorn as fun, the company began to sell kits for making popcorn balls, providing molds for shaping popcorn into balls with a sugar syrup coating.

In November 2000 American Pop Corn launched a unique promotional program, the Search for America's Most Fun Family. The grand prize was an adventure vacation to Maui, Hawaii, including air transportation, accommodations, adventure activities, and $1,000 spending money. To enter families provided pictures and a 100-word essay on why their family was the nation's "most fun" family. After examining over 1,000 entries, in June 2001 American Pop Corn chose the Kostrubanic family of Erie, Pennsylvania. Their entry emphasized that money was not necessary to have fun and included original drawings and a mystery story, "A Case of Who & Where Is America's Most Fun Family."

American Pop Corn's celebration of family fun accompanied the Smith family's own commemorative moment. In late 2001 Wrede Smith retired, with C.H. Smith's great-grandsons heading the company. Wrede's son Garry became president and Carlton, son of Chesley, who died in 1978, became chairman. Only 3 percent of family owned-businesses have passed from the third to the fourth generation. At the time of Wrede's retirement members of the fifth generation remained undecided about managing the family business.

Microwave products introduced in 2002 and 2003 continued American Pop Corn's fun marketing theme with fun flavors and fun product names. These included KettleMania Outrageously Fun Kettle Corn, in a light coating of sugar and salt; Big Cheez Ultimate Cheddar Cheese; Butter Licious; and Healthy Pop Kettle Corn 94% Fat Free. In June 2003 American Pop Corn commemorated the one-billionth bag of microwave popcorn to come off the assembly line.

Principal Competitors

ConAgra Foods, Inc.; General Mills, Inc.

Further Reading

American Pop Corn Company: An American Tradition Since 1914, Sioux City, Ia.: American Pop Corn Company, 1994.

"An American Pop Corn Co. Timeline," *Associated Press State & Local Wire,* July 2003.

Doherty, Katherine, "Jolly Time Extends Its Popcorn Line," *U.S. Distribution Journal,* March 15, 1990, p. 44.

"Double Play," *Grocery Marketing,* October 1995, p. 36.

"Eighty Nine Years—One Billion Bags; Smith Family Innovation Readies Jolly time for Next Billion," *PR Newswire,* June 27, 2003.

Farley, Mary Ann, "Disney's Studio Film Set Sports On-Pack Popcorn," *Video Business,* April 1, 1994, p. 42.

"For a Jolly Good Time," *Food Processing,* May 2002, p. 20.

"Guests Will Gobble Bird Dressed with Pop Corn," *PR Newswire,* November 14, 1994.

"Jolly Time on Mission to Find America's Most Fun Family," *PR Newswire,* November 1, 2000.

"Jolly Time Pop Corn Introduces America's Most Fun Family," *Pr Newswire,* June 21, 2001.

Lorentzen, Amy, "Jolly Time Makers Aim Toward Bigger Sales," *Associated Press State & Local Wire,* July 2003.

Sheinwold, Patricia Fox, *Jolly Time Party Book: Games, Puzzles, Recipes, and Creative Party Ideas for All Occasions,* Cambridge, Mass.: Dorison House Publishers, 1977.

Smith, Andrew F., *Popped Culture: A Social History of Popcorn in America,* Washington, D.C.: Smithsonian Institute Press, 2001.

—Mary Tradii

STIHL®

Andreas Stihl AG & Co. KG

Badstrasse 115
71336 Waiblingen
Baden-Württemberg
Germany
Telephone: (07151) 26 0
Fax: (07151) 26 1119
Web site: http://www.stihl.de

Private Company
Incorporated: 1926
Employees: 7,317
Sales: EUR 1.54 billion ($1.61 billion) (2002)
NAIC: 333991 Power-Drive Hand Tool Manufacturing;
333112 Lawn and Garden Tractor and Home Lawn
and Garden Equipment Manufacturing; 333319 Other
Commercial and Service Industry Machinery
Manufacturing; 335212 Household Vacuum Cleaner
Manufacturing

Based in Waiblingen, Germany, Andreas Stihl AG & Co. KG is one of the world's leading manufacturers of chain saws. The Stihl product line also features a variety of other outdoor power tools, including brushcutters, edgers, trimmers, leaf blowers, earth augers, power washers and sprayers, and wet-and-dry vacuum cleaners. The firm's Viking line of garden equipment encompasses shredders, lawn mowers and tractors, grass and hedge trimmers, blowers, and rototillers. In addition, Stihl offers lines of accessories that include protective work-wear, such as hard hats, safety glasses, and safety boots, and the Stihl Timbersports Collection, which includes apparel for such outdoor activities as hiking and other items such as backpacks, knives, and binoculars. Stihl (pronounced precisely like the metal ''steel'') operates seven manufacturing plants in Germany and five abroad in Switzerland, Brazil, the United States (in Virginia Beach, Virginia), China, and Austria (where the Viking line is produced). The company maintains marketing subsidiaries in 29 countries worldwide, and its products are sold in more than 160 countries through a network of 35,000 dealer-servicers. Foreign sales accounted for more than 87 percent of

Stihl's 2002 revenues. The company's largest single market is the United States, where the Stihl Incorporated subsidiary generates about 30 percent of sales. Stihl's history of innovation, which includes numerous advances in the development of the chain saw, is shown by the company having received or applied for more than 1,000 patents worldwide by the early 2000s.

The Invention of the Chain Saw

An engineer, Andreas Stihl nonetheless began his career as a salesman for a German mill and industrial supply house during the 1920s. Stihl's work brought him in contact with loggers in the Black Forest, where the felling and bucking of trees was done with stationary saws or by hand, and the larger pieces of timber needed to be transported to saw mills for cutting. Stihl sought to introduce more modern methods to the logging trade.

In 1925, Stihl opened a small workshop in his home in Stuttgart and began designing a portable ''tree-felling machine.'' The Stihl workshop manufactured a number of other products, including forehearths for steam boilers, in order to support these efforts. But by 1926, Stihl was ready with his first prototype, a 140-pound electric ''cross-cutting chain saw.'' The saw's bulk required it to be operated by two people, and its reliance on an electric motor limited its portability to areas where a power source was available. Stihl set to work creating a lighter, gasoline-driven saw. Nonetheless, the electric saw found its market, with 50 units sold in 1927. In that year, Stihl opened his first factory in Stuttgart. The following year, as sales of the electric saw reached 100, the company opened a sales office for northern Germany.

Stihl's gasoline saw—the first ever—was ready by 1929. This saw achieved a rating of 6 horsepower (hp); its weight of 101 pounds still required two people to operate it. Yet the saw was fully portable and would change the logging trade forever. In 1930, the saw was featured at the Leipzig trade fair, and sales of the saw soon spread beyond Germany into Holland, Belgium, Switzerland, and France. From the start, Stihl emphasized service along with the sale of his saws. Customers were trained in the operation, maintenance, and repair of Stihl's products. As international sales increased, Stihl trained specialists in each

Company Perspectives:

Progress based on tradition. The basic values of STIHL's company culture have grown historically and evolved over a long period. STIHL has reached its leading position on world markets with a company philosophy formulated for the long term. The continuity in company management and the personal commitment of the owner family are guarantees for the future, too. STIHL is well equipped for future challenges with its strict customer focus, competitive quality products, innovative strength and international positioning.

country, who provided customer instruction and service, along with sales. As one of Stihl's earliest salesmen wrote: "It won't do to sell saws to people without teaching, assisting and offering good service to users later."

Not everyone welcomed the chain saw. Many loggers resisted the new device, fearing the loss of their jobs, and often attacked Stihl's salesmen. But the rise of the chain saw became inevitable, and sales increased. By 1930, Stihl saws were being shipped to the United States. After a trip to the Soviet Union, Stihl received orders for several hundred saws. The Stihl factory moved to Bad Cannstatt, which later became part of Stuttgart, and during the 1930s the number of the company's employees swelled to 200.

Stihl continued to work on improving the saw's design. In 1931, Stihl introduced his second gas-powered saw, which weighed nearly 105 pounds—with a full gas tank—but achieved 8 hp. Other improvements were made, such as an automatic chain lubrication system introduced in 1934. Two years later, the company opened its first foreign sales and distribution office in Vienna. By 1937, Stihl managed to bring the weight of the chain saw down to 88 pounds. Stihl traveled to North America, broadening the saw's reach through the United States and into the Canadian market. Stihl also introduced courses in power saw technology in an effort to increase the chain saw's acceptance throughout the logging and forestry trades.

The Nazi rise to power encouraged Stihl's domestic growth but hampered its international development. In an effort to standardize production within industries, the Nazis held competitions and Stihl's design became the authorized German chain saw. All other German chain saw manufacturers were required to license the Stihl design. However, the outbreak of World War II ended Stihl's international growth. During the war, the Bad Cannstatt plant was destroyed by bombs, and production was moved to Waiblingen. The German capitulation ending the European war also forced Stihl to a halt.

Postwar Growth

By 1947, Stihl's factory reopened and was soon producing 90 chain saws each month. International sales also resumed; in the United States, Stihl bought out its former U.S. importer, and began assembling saws in the United States for the North American market. In 1948, the first Stihl Service Center was opened, offering a higher degree of customer service. Meanwhile, the company continued to improve the chain saw's

design, with weight reduction a primary concern. This led to the development of the one-person chain saw, which would revolutionize the chain saw industry by the end of the decade.

Stihl's first one-person saw was introduced in 1950. This saw was still too heavy for comfortable operation, but it led the way to the introduction of the Stihl BLK saw in 1954. At 31 pounds and 4.5 hp, the BLK was the first truly portable chain saw. Two years later, the BLK was chosen by the German army as its official chain saw; the BLK became the standard saw for many other military services and government organizations as well.

Yet the true revolution in chain saw technology—and the development that led to the worldwide acceptance of the chain saw—was the Stihl Contra, introduced in 1959. The Contra, which featured a direct drive and diaphragm carburetor, weighed only 26.65 pounds, yet achieved 6 hp. Stihl's sales boomed, and production rose from 104 to 500 saws per day by 1964. By then, the company was outgrowing its plant, and a second facility was built in Neustadt. The company's workforce grew to over 1,000. U.S. and Canadian demand surged with the introduction of the Stihl Lightning saw, prompting the company to open its first North American warehouses.

In 1965, Stihl introduced an innovation in chain saw design with its antivibration system, which absorbed the impact of the saw's vibration, allowing steadier and less fatiguing control. This design change was quickly copied by Stihl's competitors. Three years later, Stihl added an electronic ignition system to its saws, improving their reliability. Other design changes included a more efficient chain lubrication system, an inertial chain braking system, which stopped the chain in the event of kickback, and a master control lever, which allowed the user to control the saw's starting and stopping functions without releasing the saw's handle.

By 1971, Stihl's 2,000-strong workforce was producing 340,000 saws annually. In that year, Andreas Stihl's son, Hans Peter, took over as head of the company. Andreas Stihl died two years later. By then the company had added a new plant in Prüm, and a plant in Wiechs am Randen, near the Swiss border. The company's first overseas plant, Andreas Stihl Moto-Serras Ltda. in Sao Leopoldo, Brazil, began chain saw production in 1973. That year, Stihl, with 2,500 employees, saw its revenues top DM 222 million.

The international oil crisis prompted by the Arab Oil Embargo of 1973 sent most industries into a recession. But in response to rising oil prices, the demand for wood as an alternative fuel skyrocketed, and with that demand came an increase in Stihl sales. The company increased its foreign manufacturing base, transferring chain production to a plant in Wil, Switzerland, and opening a U.S. plant in Virginia Beach, Virginia, in 1974. The company also established an assembly plant in Scoresby, Australia. By 1978, Stihl's revenues had more than doubled, to approximately DM 500 million ($245 million). By the mid-1980s, about 50 percent of the company's production took place outside of Germany.

Diversifying Products in the 1980s and 1990s

In 1980, worldwide chain saw sales reached a peak of 5.8 million units, with Stihl holding a commanding share of the market. But as oil prices leveled, and as the world entered the recession of the 1980s, sales slumped in the following years, dropping to 3.4 million units by 1984. Stihl's revenues continued to rise, from $355 million in 1981 to $489 million in 1986, increasing its share to 25 percent of the chain saw market; however, much of this revenue growth could be attributed to the falling value of the dollar against the German mark.

In response to the pressures on chain saw sales, the company began to diversify its product line in the 1980s. In 1986, the company began producing protective apparel and accessories, such as safety glasses, helmets, gloves, boots, and hearing protectors. Two years later, the company introduced specialized clearing saws for professional use, and in 1989 began production of trimmers and blowers.

Further diversification was derived through the Viking line of products. Viking GmbH was founded in Kufstein, Austria, in

1981 as a manufacturer of garden shredders. Three years later, lawn mowers were added to the Viking line, which later expanded to include riding mowers, grass and hedge trimmers, blowers, and rototillers. Eventually the Austria-made Viking line was being marketed throughout Europe. In 1992 Viking became 100 percent owned by Stihl.

Until the 1990s, most Stihl saws were designed exclusively for professional uses. Further improvements in design had decreased the weight of even the company's most powerful model to 20 pounds. Toward the middle of the decade, however, Stihl moved to tap into the small saw market—which represented about half of all chain saw sales—hitting below the $200 price point. Because the United States was the biggest market for small and nonprofessional chain saw purchases, the company moved production of all small saws to its Virginia Beach plant in 1994. By the following year, Stihl's U.S. facilities were producing more machines than its German plants for the first time in the company's history. Also in 1995, Stihl established a manufacturing, marketing, and distribution subsidiary in China, Taicang Andreas Stihl Powertools Co., Ltd. The diversification of the Stihl's product line, meanwhile, helped drive the company's growth. Sales in 1995 topped $1 billion, with foreign sales accounting for roughly 80 percent.

During the late 1990s Andreas Stihl continued to expand its network of marketing subsidiaries around the world. A Mexican subsidiary commenced operation at the beginning of 1996, a South African subsidiary was formed in October 1996 to serve the southern African region, and in May 1997 a further expansion in Eastern Europe resulted in the formation of a subsidiary in Romania. Stihl had already established subsidiaries in the Czech Republic, Hungary, and Poland, and by 1997 operated three representative offices in the former Soviet Union, in St. Petersburg, Russia; Ternopol, Ukraine; and Minsk, Belarus. During 1998 three more marketing subsidiaries were formed in Greece, Portugal, and Argentina.

Shifting to Nonfamily Management: Early 2000s

By 2002 sales outside of Germany were accounting for 87 percent of overall revenues. Despite the rough economic waters of the new decade, revenues maintained their steady rise, reaching EUR 1.54 billion ($1.61 billion), nearly three times the level of 1990. This was the 11th straight year of record revenues. Stihl continued to pump out new products, with an increased emphasis on their environmental impacts. Tougher antipollution laws in the United States, the company's largest market, forced Stihl to develop new technologies to meet the new standards. For example, in 2002 the company unveiled its 4-Mix engine, which reduced emissions of pollutants by combining characteristics of both two-stroke and four-stroke engines. The new engine was initially featured on brushcutters and edgers. Another important development in the early 2000s was the company's increased emphasis on power tools; on a worldwide basis, in terms of units, more power tools than chain saws were being sold. The year 2002 also saw the launch of the Stihl Timbersports Collection, which grew out of the company's long established line of protective clothing for loggers. The new line was more fashion-oriented and was aimed at hikers, campers, and other outdoors enthusiasts; it featured not only clothing but also such accessories as backpacks, knives, and compasses.

Meanwhile, Stihl established a new Eastern European marketing subsidiary based in Kiev, Ukraine.

Although Stihl remained a family-owned business in the early 2000s, there were important developments in the management structure and makeup that gave more power to people outside the Stihl family. The company had created a sister company called Stihl AG in 1998 that was placed in charge of managing the entire Stihl group. Hans Peter Stihl was chairman of the board of management of Stihl AG—essentially serving as chief executive—until June 2002, when he stepped down from that post as part of a thorough overhaul of the board's composition. All other Stihl family members on this board stepped down as well, with Stihl and some of the others taking positions on the supervisory board. Harald J. Joos, who had been the head of the German operations of Schindler Holding AG, a Swiss maker of elevators and escalators, was named chairman of the board of management, but he resigned from this position in February 2003. One month later, Bertram Kandziora was named spokesperson of the board of management. Kandziora had been brought onboard in February 2002 as senior vice-president of manufacturing and materials, having previously served as an executive at BSH Bosch und Siemens Hausgeräte GmbH, a major European appliance manufacturer. Despite these changes, which created a completely nonfamily management board for the first time, the Stihl family continued to wield considerable power through its dominance of the company's advisory board, of which Hans Peter Stihl remained chairman, and which was the company's highest decision-making body. Nevertheless, it seemed likely that these fundamental changes marked the beginning of a new era at Andreas Stihl.

Principal Subsidiaries

Stihl International GmbH; Stihl Vertriebszentrale AG & Co. KG; Andreas Stihl Verwaltungs-GmbH; Stihl Verwaltungsgesellschaft mbH; Stihl Vertriebszentrale Verwaltungs-GmbH; Stihl & Co. (Switzerland); Stihl Incorporated (U.S.A.); Andreas Stihl Moto-Serras Ltda. (Brazil); Viking GmbH (Austria); Stihl Ges.m.b.H. (Austria); Stihl Vertriebs AG (Switzerland); Andreas Stihl Ltd. (U.K.); Andreas Stihl N.V. (Belgium); Andreas Stihl S.A.R.L. (France); Andreas Stihl S.A. (Spain); Andreas Stihl S.A. (Portugal); Andreas Stihl S.p.A. (Italy); Andreas Stihl S.A. (Greece); Andreas Stihl A/S (Norway); Andreas Stihl Norden AB (Sweden); Andreas Stihl Sp. z.o.o. (Poland); Andreas Stihl spol. s.r.o. (Czech Republic); Andreas Stihl Kereskedelmi Kft. (Hungary); Stihl Limited (Canada); Andreas Stihl S.A. de C.V. (Mexico); Andreas Stihl (Pty.) Ltd. (South Africa); Kabushiki Kaisha Stihl (Japan); Stihl Pty. Ltd. (Australia); Stihl Limited (New Zealand); Stihl Motoimplementos S.A. (Argentina).

Principal Competitors

AB Electrolux; The Black & Decker Corporation; Makita Corporation; The Toro Company.

Further Reading

Bruce, Peter, ''Andreas Stihl Cuts Larger Overseas Niche,'' *Financial Times,* January 7, 1986, p. 21.
''A Company Making a Buzz in the Mittelstand,'' *Financial Times,* December 12, 2001, p. 14.
Tagliabue, John, ''Stihl: A Worldwide Family Business,'' *New York Times,* March 17, 1982, p. D4.
Wagner, Lon, ''Expansion Is Routine at Equipment Maker Stihl's U.S. Plant in Virginia,'' *Virginian Pilot,* November 13, 1995.

—M. L. Cohen
—update: David E. Salamie

Annie's Homegrown, Inc.

395 Main Street
Wakefield, Massachusetts
U.S.A.
Telephone: (781) 224-9639
Toll Free: (800) 664-7336
Fax: (781) 224 -9728
Web site: http://www.annies.com

Private Company
Incorporated: 1989
Employees: 20
Sales: $17 million (2003 est.)
NAIC: 311422 Specialty Canning

Annie's Homegrown, Inc. is one of the fastest expanding producers of organic and natural foods pasta products. Finding a niche in the convenient foods category of macaroni and cheese dinners and canned pasta meals, Annie's offers a healthy, natural or organic alternative in its product line. It ranks number two nationally in macaroni and cheese sales behind the blue box of food giant Kraft.

Discovering a Market Niche: 1980s

A piece of the Annie's Homegrown story began in 1982 when Annie Withey and Andrew Martin created an entrepreneurial enterprise in their Boston kitchen. Martin had invented a plastic bag with a tear-off top and had enticed Withey to create a healthy snack food that would help bring about the success of Martin's invention. The bag did not gain the public's attention but persistence paid off when the healthier snack food Withey developed became an instant success. Withey had spent hours perfecting an all-natural cheese sauce and popcorn snack that helped launch what they named Smartfoods. Smartfoods cheesy popcorn snack and its signature green and black box skyrocketed as a natural foods alternative to the neon-orange, chemical-enhanced snack foods that were being marketed at the time. Smartfoods gained a solid foothold in the snack foods industry and Martin and Withey managed the company for several years before selling it in 1986 to Pepsico/Frito Lay for $15 million.

Ready to try their luck again, in January 1989 the same cheese sauce that had proven so successful on popcorn was introduced by Withey and Martin as a key ingredient in Annie's Homegrown Shells and Cheddar, a convenience stovetop macaroni and cheese dinner. The macaroni and cheese hit a market niche by being free of the standard chemical additives that were a part of other packaged macaroni and cheese products. Annie's Shells and Cheddar relied on the natural ingredient annatto to color its cheese sauce. Once again the formula for success had paid off. Annie's had banked on the fact that health-conscious consumers were seeking unadulterated versions of familiar favorites and were willing to pay the almost 20 percent markup in cost.

From the beginning, Annie's Homegrown set itself apart as a company with a corporate commitment to giving back to the community. Annie's linked itself with progressive causes and remained aligned to environmental efforts including its role as stated in its mission statement: "To serve as an ethically, socially and environmentally conscious business model," and further "to expand its role as a responsible corporate citizen." The company was focused on remaining all-natural or organic in its products, and on using sound environmental practices in its production and packaging.

Tasteful Marketing and Development: 1990s

The company's marketing approach was consistent with its natural, no fuss corporate image. Annie's used homespun letters from Withey to capture the hearts and minds of customers. Boxes made from post-consumer recycled paper featured Bernie the Rabbit and told of life on the Withey's organic farm in the Connecticut countryside.

In addition to its first product offering in 1989, the company went on to develop and produce a variety of natural "mac & cheese" products averaging roughly one new product each calendar year. The company continued to buy up shelf space at regional supermarkets and natural food specialty stores nationwide. Withey and Martin's experience with Smartfoods had prepared the way for their new enterprise. Regional supermarkets and natural foods stores had found them capable and dependable and were readily willing to stock their new merchandise.

Annie's Homegrown began to develop its product line, and in August 1989 it introduced its alfredo pasta and sauce and its whole wheat shells and cheddar.

Annie's Homegrown had quickly grown beyond the small home operation and into a national brand. Martin set up a regional office in California and he and Withey separated. The two later divorced and Martin kept the California company presence while Withey remarried and remained on the organic farm running the Massachusetts production facility. The company moved much of its operations from a former railroad station near Withey's home to a warehouse in Massachusetts in 1995.

By July 1996 Annie's was thriving but was quickly outgrowing its resources. Company leadership decided that the best way to continue to develop itself was to reach out to its many devoted customers in a direct public offering (DPO). The stock offering was equal to $3.6 million or 600,000 shares of its common stock. The public offering was advertised in several ways, including a flyer in boxes of its mac & cheese products. The stock deal was limited to customers in 11 states, namely California, Oregon, Washington, Maine, New Hampshire, Vermont, Massachusetts, Rhode Island, Connecticut, New York, and New Jersey. The company also promoted the DPO in the politically and socially progressive magazine *Mother Jones*.

The DPO was conducted by Drew Field Direct Public Offerings in San Francisco, and cost comparatively less than a standard initial public offering, yet still provided the company with the financial reserves it was seeking. Records indicated that the DPO expenses totaled $250,000, with reported investment dollars recorded at $3.35 million.

The company continued to expand its supermarket presence and its product inventory, introducing mild cheddar, a family-size boxed macaroni and cheese, and a bunny-shaped pasta in 1997.

In 1998 the company bought a line of Indian Entrees under the Tamarind Tree label. The food products were sold by Taste of India and included several different varieties of Indian cuisine. Tamarind Tree Entrees were also categorized as convenience natural foods. The entrees were fully prepared and cooked. The Indian food was packaged in heat-and-serve plastic pouches.

In 1998 Annie's Homegrown developed a line of canned pasta products. Canned p'sghetti and p'sghetti with mooless meatballs, a whimsical vegetarian take on a classic kids favorite, proved to meet the demands of discerning health food connoisseurs. As with most organic and natural foods alternatives, the canned pasta meals averaged a 20 percent markup compared with their mainline alternatives.

With every new addition to the company's expanding repertoire of natural foods knock-offs Annie's banked on the fact that consumers were willing to pay more for convenience foods made from natural ingredients. The public wanted convenience but still cared about the content of their food product, and were willing to pay more for healthy alternatives.

Financing Further Expansion: 1999–2000s

In October 1999 company cofounders Withey and Martin signed an agreement with Homegrown Holdings Corporation to sell off a portion of their shares of Annie's common stock. The transaction was completed over a mutually determined length of five years.

Homegrown Holdings Corporation was a private investment group founded by John Foraker and Mike Moone. Both Foraker and Moone had previous high-level experience with food specialties. Foraker served as CEO of Napa Valley Kitchens and as chairman of Calio Groves, and Moone was CEO of food giant Stouffer Foods and the Beringer Wine Estates label.

Homegrown Holdings Corporation purchased one million shares of the company at $2 a share. The deal allowed Annie's to further develop its product assortments and expand its consumer base through increased marketing efforts. Anne Withey commented on the transaction in a company released financial statement saying, "Of all the strategic and financial partners we interviewed, Homegrown Holdings best understood Annie's culture and brand personality. It is comforting to know that our national expansion will be carried out in a manner consistent with our mission statement."

The financial backing from Homegrown Holdings did in fact allow Annie's to expand its product development and become a national brand with solid recognition. Keeping up with food trends in the convenience foods industry, Annie's introduced a microwavable variety of natural macaroni and cheese in 2000. The microwavable mac & cheese could easily be prepared by older children without having to use the stovetop. Kraft had launched a similar product called Easy Mac that had quickly developed a niche in the market.

In December 2001 Annie's introduced a line of organic boxed semolina flour pastas. The company contracted with North Dakota, Montana, and California organic wheat growers to supply the company with good quality organic wheat. Annie's featured organic pasta in several forms, including spaghetti, whole wheat spaghetti, rotini, gemelli, and penne. The products received certification as organic and kosher.

When other food manufacturers began to produce shaped macaroni and cheese characters, Annie's was quick to offer its own versions of popular kid-friendly shapes. Annie's first introduced its bunny-shaped pasta in 1997. The pasta was consistent with the Annie story of Bernie the Rabbit, a company icon. The company followed with its peace sign pasta in 1998. The peace sign pasta appealed to the slightly older child or nostalgic adult consumer. In 2002 Annie's signed a licensing agreement with Marc Brown, the creator of literary and television personality Arthur the Aardvark, to produce Arthur-shaped mac & cheese.

Key Dates:

1982: Annie Withey develops cheese mix; Withey and husband Andrew Martin start Smartfoods.
1986: Withey and Martin sell Smartfoods to Pepsico/Frito Lay for $15 million.
1989: Annie's Homegrown, Inc. is founded.
1995: A direct public offering is completed.
1998: Annie's Homegrown buys Taste of India's Tamarind Tree food line; Annie's introduces pasta meals and peace pasta.
1999: Homegrown Holdings Corporation acquires stake in the company.
2002: Annie's Homegrown launches national advertising campaign; Solera Capital buys majority share of the company.

Annie's Homegrown sponsored many programs in keeping with its various commitments to social causes. Through its Cases for Causes program, for example, Annie's donated thousands of cases of its products to organizations benefiting women, children, and environmental protection. Annie's also created a scholarship program for students majoring in environmental studies and provided 25 $1,000 scholarships to deserving university students. Another program introduced in 2001, Growing Naturally, was designed to foster interest in all things organic among school-aged children. The children were given resources and direction for keeping their own organic gardens.

In August 2001, Solera Capital, a women's private investment firm based in New York City, acquired 80 percent of Annie's Homegrown. The capital investment of $20 million was used to promote the company's lines in natural and mainstream supermarkets and to advertise via national media outlets. It was announced that John Foraker, CEO of Homegrown Holdings, would remain as a board director, Paul Nardone would continue as chief executive officer, and a new addition—Tim Fallon, CEO of Vermont Pure Holdings—would be made to the board.

In 2002 Annie's continued to expand its products by introducing an organic cheese ravioli in tomato sauce. The canned pasta meal was vegetarian and made from 95 percent organic ingredients. This addition to the previously released canned pasta brought the company a total of four canned meal types.

According to industry analysts, the organic foods sector of the food industry was expected to grow at a rate of 20–25 percent annually over the next few years. That compared to the regular food products category with a predicted 1–2 percent growth. Natural foods were predicted to expand at 8–10 percent. With Annie's Homegrown's eye on national food trends and its remarkable ability to create organic or natural alternatives to mainstream products, it appeared well poised to capture its piece of the organic pie.

Principal Subsidiaries

Tamarind Tree.

Principal Competitors

Kraft Foods Inc.; Amy's Kitchen; The Hain Celestial Group, Inc.

Further Reading

"Annie's Homegrown Arthur Macaroni & Cheese," *Product Alert,* December 23, 2002.

"Annie's Homegrown Organic Cheesy Ravioli," *Product Alert,* December 23, 2002.

"Annie's Homegrown to Complete Direct Offering," *Natural Business,* July 1996.

"Deal Should Help Natural Mac & Cheese Maker Boost Presence in Supermarkets," *Food Institute Report,* August 19, 2002.

Fisher, Marshall Jon, "At Home with Annie," *Country Journal,* July/August 2000.

Laliberte, Carol, "Peace Pasta," *Vegetarian Baby and Child,* March/April 2001.

Moran, Michelle, "A License to Sell," *Gourmet Retailer,* December 2002.

Reidy, Chris, "N.Y. Firm Acquires Majority Stake in Annie's Homegrown," *Boston Globe,* August 13, 2002, p. C3.

Tenorio, Vyvyan, "Solera Dishes up Organic Food Deal," *Daily Deal,* August 13, 2002.

—Susan B. Culligan

Apple Bank for Savings

122 East 42nd Street
New York, New York 10017
U.S.A.
Telephone: (212) 224-6400
Toll Free: (800) 722-6888
Fax: (212) 224-6580
Web site: http://www.theapplebank.com

Wholly Owned Subsidiary of Apple Bancorp Inc.
Incorporated: 1863 as Harlem Savings Bank
Employees: 760
Total Assets: $5.93 billion (2002)
NAIC: 522110 Commercial Banking; 522291 Consumer
 Lending; 522310 Mortgage and Other Loan Brokers;
 551111 Offices of Bank Holding Companies

Apple Bank for Savings is a state-chartered savings bank that is the fifth largest of its kind in the state of New York. It offers the usual retail products and services to its customers in the metropolitan New York City area and continues its traditional emphasis on mortgage lending for home residences and to finance multifamily buildings as well.

Harlem Savings Bank: 1863–1983

Originally a Dutch farming settlement, Harlem was still only a village in northern Manhattan in 1863, when a group of local merchants opened a community-based mutual savings bank: that is, a bank owned by its own depositors. The Harlem Savings Bank began its existence at a small storefront location at 1948 Third Avenue, between East 125th and 126th streets. In 1869 it moved to a building of its own construction at Third Avenue and East 124th Street. By mid-1876 the bank had 5,074 depositors. Harlem Savings Bank was a midsized Manhattan savings bank at the beginning of 1900, with 32,108 accounts and deposits of $9.2 million. In 1908 it completed, at a cost of $350,000, a larger building on 125th Street—Harlem's main street—just west of Lexington Avenue. Although seemingly sound, the bank experienced panic withdrawals in 1900 and 1907. No depositor was shortchanged, yet lines ran for blocks as customers feared that the bank might fail in the wake of the demise of less stable thrift institutions.

Harlem became part of New York City in 1873. The imminent arrival of three elevated railway lines soon set off a boom in which speculators bought and resold land to builders—financed by commercial banks, thrift institutions, and insurance companies—who put up brownstones, tenements, and apartment houses. Immigrant Jews prosperous enough to escape the Lower East Side began moving into central Harlem in the 1890s, while immigrant Italians settled in adjacent East Harlem. But excessive construction led to a collapse of real estate values in 1904–05. Financial institutions ceased to make loans to Harlem speculators and building loan companies. Many foreclosed on their mortgages. Realtors found a new market in the rapidly expanding African American population, and whites began moving out of the area. Harlem was by far the largest African American neighborhood in the United States by the end of the 1920s, when Harlem Savings Bank ranked 22nd in size among U.S. mutual savings banks. It weathered the Great Depression without incident and, on the last day of 1932, during the depths of the economic crisis, absorbed the Commonwealth Savings Bank, which had two offices in the Washington Heights neighborhood north of West Harlem. This acquisition brought its totals to 101,052 accounts and $84.82 million in deposits at the end of 1933.

Harlem Savings Bank was active in foreclosure auction sales during the 1930s. The properties were typically four- or five-story walk-up tenements in northern Manhattan and the Bronx. One exception was its 1937 foreclosure of the 15-story Hotel Emerson on the Upper West Side, which it quickly resold. Harlem Savings Bank also held a $600,000 mortgage on Sydenham Hospital in 1950, when the financially strapped Harlem institution was taken over by the city.

Harlem Savings Bank opened branches in the Washington Heights and Inwood neighborhoods of northern Manhattan in 1939 and 1940, respectively. By 1958 it also had a branch on East 42nd Street in midtown Manhattan. The post-World War II exodus of the middle class to the suburbs impelled the bank to reach out to other parts of the metropolitan area. It opened a branch in Manhasset, Long Island, in 1966 and moved its headquarters from Harlem to the 42nd Street branch by 1968. During the 1970s it added a branch on the flourishing Upper East Side, at 81st Street and First Avenue. By contrast, although the Harlem branch still had some 10,000 accounts in 1978, more money was being withdrawn than deposited. During the energy crisis of the early 1970s many residential property owners in northern Manhattan and the Bronx found their unregulated maintenance costs outstripping their regulated rental collections and simply abandoned their tenements rather than pay their bills, leaving Harlem Savings Bank holding nonperforming assets. Over the next few years, the bank amortized the bad mortgage loans, built up its capital, and accumulated cash.

On the one hand, Harlem, Washington Heights, and Inwood activists and politicians charged financial institutions that had served their communities with redlining: labeling low-income and minority neighborhoods as bad risks for loans and declining to issue mortgages in these areas. As late as 1993 Ralph Nader's public interest group accused the bank and four other mortgage lenders in the city with racial redlining—in effect drawing a no-loan red line around areas with a minority population of 75 percent or more. On the other hand, the Harlem Savings Bank's very name had the power to provoke racial hostility. When the bank was building a branch in Massapequa, Long Island, in 1978, the plate-glass windows had to be replaced seven times after they were shattered by bricks. The message, concluded Jerome McDougal, chairman and chief executive of the bank, in an article for *Across the Board,* "was that the name Harlem Savings Bank was unwelcome in the suburbs, where it was unfairly associated with drugs, crime, and general deterioration." Although Harlem had an investment in its existing name, it was the smallest savings bank still headquartered in Manhattan and, according to McDougal, "demographic studies of our own depositors [indicated] that we would be a dead institution by the year 2000, when most of our customers would have passed away."

The name change to Apple Bank for Savings—evoking New York City's reputation as "The Big Apple"—was suggested by a small consulting firm, Selame Design, and championed by McDougal, who pushed it through in 1983 despite some feeling that the name was not dignified compared to the names of other banking companies and would be a liability in seeking large corporate accounts. However, the institution saw its future as a retail bank with younger customers and new, deregulated financial services. Selame Design developed the new logo, a bright red apple with a brown stem and green leaf, and a slogan: "We're good for you." Within the first month of the name change, Apple Bank gained 4,943 new accounts—three times the normal rate—and $116 million in deposits, compared to a loss of $26 million during the corresponding period in 1982.

Expanding in the 1980s

The high inflation of the 1970s and early 1980s caused great strain among thrift institutions, which typically had put their money in mortgages and long-term bonds yielding lower interest rates than those they now had to pay out in order to retain their depositors. But Harlem Savings Bank—soon to be Apple—was in better financial shape than many of the other 36 savings banks in New York City. It ranked 25th, with nine branches—including two on Long Island—146,000 depositors, and $843 million in assets, when, in December 1981, the Federal Deposit Insurance Corp. (FDIC) provided about $160 million so that it could acquire larger but deficit-ridden Central Savings Bank. Harlem thereby gained seven more branches, including three on Long Island (and a landmarked bank building on Manhattan's Upper West Side that resembled a Florentine palazzo).

Two years after changing its name, Apple Bank converted from a mutual savings bank to a stock-issuing public institution, selling 4.6 million shares for a total of $53.5 million. The following year, it acquired Eastern Savings Bank of Scarsdale, New York, which was operating three or four branches in the Bronx, two on Long Island, and two in Westchester County, north of the city. It added a branch in the Westchester County seat of White Plains in 1987. Apple Bank now ranked 17th among the New York metropolitan area's thrift institutions, with assets of $2.7 billion.

Apple Bank began deviating in the 1980s from the traditional role of savings bank: conservative investments in residential mortgages, corporate bonds, and Treasury investments. Commercial loans, virtually zero in 1985, rose to $313.5 million in 1988—10.5 percent of its loan portfolio. Many of these loans were made to small and midsized businesses on Long Island, where Apple had nine of its 28 branches. In 1989 the bank added five more retail offices on Long Island when it acquired Sag Harbor Savings Bank for $29.5 million. Cooperative-apartment loans also grew rapidly, reaching $385.2 million, and credit card loans reached $67.9 million.

Apple Bank also established a foreign-trade desk to provide letters of credit, document clearing, and currency transactions for customers doing business abroad, and an acceptance corporation to offer loans, through a network of dealers and service companies, for the purchase of automobiles and recreational vehicles; the leasing of cars, boats, and equipment, and shelter-product loans. This unit, Apple Acceptance Corp., also offered various commercial products to the dealers, such as floor-plan financing, dealership mortgages, and working capital loans. For the retail client, a customer-service initiative included the training of both frontline and support personnel. Members of a family program were assigned to a personal family banker and were offered free checking, reduced rates on loans, rebates on credit card interest charges, and refunds on mortgage application fees, plus assistance from a team of experts with regard to savings, investment, credit, and life insurance.

Retrenchment in the 1990s

Stanley Stahl, a prominent New York City real estate investor and for years Apple Bank's largest depositor and leading customer, began buying the bank's stock in 1986 and had bought enough shares by the spring of 1989 to hold a 15 percent stake in the company. Over the next six months he doubled his stake. Apple's alarmed management, fearing a takeover,

Key Dates:

1863: Founding of Harlem Savings Bank in the northern Manhattan community of Harlem.

1932: Harlem Savings acquires Community Savings Bank, adding two branches.

1966: The bank expands to the suburbs, opening a Long Island branch.

1981: Harlem Savings acquires the troubled Central Savings Bank.

1983: Harlem Savings Bank changes its name to the Apple Bank for Savings.

1985: Apple Bank converts to a public stockholding savings bank.

1990: Stanley Stahl acquires Apple and converts it to a privately held bank.

1992: Apple Bank withdraws from commercial lending after serious losses.

adopted a "poison-pill" defense in November 1989 that was intended to make it ruinous for Stahl to buy more stock. Stahl had once been good friends with McDougal, but in March 1990 he attempted a hostile takeover of the bank, offering $38 a share for another 46 percent of the stock. Since the book value of the bank was more than $56 a share, management thought it could block Stahl, but share prices dropped in the summer of 1990 as a national economic recession took hold. Stahl won the bank in October 1990, converted it into a private company, fired Mc-Dougal, and moved headquarters to the high-rise office building he owned at 277 Park Avenue.

Under the new chief executive, William J. Laraia, Apple Bank reduced its commercial and industrial lending portfolio from $422.7 million at the end of 1990 to $232.4 million in mid-1992. "Commercial lending is a business that thrifts have not been in, and we didn't have the critical mass," Laraia explained to Robert McNatt of *Crain's New York Business.* "In keeping with Mr. Stahl's business philosophy, we focused attention and capital resources on the activities the bank knew well and in which it could prudently grow." The bank also sold Apple Acceptance Corp. and decided to stop issuing credit card loans. Apple was now primarily in the business of financing real estate, with a special emphasis on commercial real estate and multifamily housing. Its residential mortgage portfolio remained sound despite the recession, with 14 of its 33 branches forming the heart of Apple's home-lending activities. The commercial portfolio had been weakened by the bad economy, however; some $200 million of the $1 billion on its books in commercial real estate was in bad loans and repossessed real estate.

Apple Bank lost $49.4 million in 1991 but was profitable in 1992 after cutting operating expenses by one-fifth, reducing staff by one-third, and installing more rigorous credit controls. By late 1993 it had reduced its nonperforming loans to about 3.5 percent of total assets and was seeking to increase its number of mortgage loans. "We're considering introducing satellite mortgage offices, possibly six in the coming year," Alan Shamoon, the bank president, told Miriam Leuchter of *Crain's New York Business.* "We also haven't fully exploited bringing in residen-

tial products through correspondents, such as brokers and lawyers." The bank's total assets reached $4.47 billion and its net income, $56.2 million. Shamoon succeeded Laraia as chief executive in 1994.

By 1997 banks in New York City were loosening their purse strings in a hot real estate market, offering innovative mortgage-loan packages, some of which, like combining a mortgage with a home equity loan, allowed lower down payments than the usual 20 percent. Brokers mentioned Dime Savings Bank and the Apple Bank of Savings as especially active in the mortgage market. In the worst case—if the buyer could not repay the loan—lenders like Apple were confident that they could recover their investment because residences were selling so well.

At the end of 2002 Apple Bank for Savings had $5.93 billion in assets, $5.2 billion in deposits, and net income of $58 million for the year. Of the bank's 47 branches, 31 were in New York City: 12 in Manhattan, 13 in Brooklyn, four in the Bronx, and two in Queens. There were another 14 on Long Island, and two in Westchester County, including the former Eastern Savings headquarters in Scarsdale, now also the site of the bank's data center.

Principal Subsidiaries

ABS Associates of New York, Inc.

Principal Competitors

Emigrant Savings Bank; Flushing Savings Bank; GreenPoint Bank; Independence Community Bank; Ridgewood Savings Bank.

Further Reading

Alson, Amy, "Apple Merger Adds to Suburb Expansion," *Crain's New York Business,* June 30, 1986, p. 2.

"Apple Bank for Savings," *Wall Street Transcript,* December 1, 1986.

Basch, Mark, "Making Room for Growth," *American Banker,* August 20, 1985, pp. 12, 14.

Bennett, Robert A., "Central Bank Is Merged," *New York Times,* December 5, 1981, pp. 31, 35.

——, "Lesson Plan for the Savings Industry," *New York Times,* August 7, 1988, Sec. 3, pp. F1, F6.

"Harlem Savings Bank Panic Continues," *New York Times,* December 14, 1900, p. 3.

Manning, James Hilton, *A Century of American Savings Banks,* New York: B.F. Buck & Co., vol. 2, 1917.

McDougal, Jerome, "Banking a Name Change," *Across the Board,* January 1987, pp. 55–56.

——, "Name Change Polishes Image for N.Y. Thrift," *Bank Marketing,* February 1987, pp. 18–19.

"Nader Group Cites 'Redlining' in Study of Lenders," *New York Times,* August 13, 1993, p. D2.

Osofsky, Gilbert, *Harlem: The Making of a Ghetto,* New York: Harper & Row, 2nd ed., 1971.

Rozibon, Tracie, "Banks, Flush, Getting Eager to Lend," *New York Times,* February 28, 1997, p. B6.

Selame, Elinor, "Image Counts," *Management Review,* February 1985, p. 43.

"Two Uptown Savings Banks Combine," *New York Times,* January 1, 1933, Sec. 2, p. 7.

—Robert Halasz

Profit from Intelligent Information™

Ascential Software Corporation

50 Washington Street
Westboro, Massachusetts 01581
U.S.A.
Telephone: (508) 366-3888
Toll Free: (800)966-9875
Fax: (508) 366-3669
Web site: http://www.ascential.com

Public Company
Incorporated: 2001
Employees: 900
Sales: $113.0 million (2002)
Stock Exchanges: NASDAQ
Ticker Symbol: ASCL
NAIC: 511210 Software Publishers

Although Ascential Software Corporation is a relatively new company that was established in 2001, it has its roots in Informix Corporation, a database software developer founded in 1980. Following Informix's acquisition of Ardent Software Inc. in early 2000, the company reorganized into two independent, wholly owned subsidiaries. One became Ascential Software Corporation, while the other specialized in database software. After the latter was sold to IBM Corporation in 2001 for $1 billion, Informix Corp. changed its name to Ascential Software Corporation and used the proceeds from the sale of its database business to acquire companies and technology that extended its data integration platform for enterprise usage. Following the acquisition of Mercator Software in 2003, Ascential was positioned as a leading provider of enterprise data integration solutions to Global 2000 enterprises.

Informix Specializing in Database Software in the 1980s

Ascential Software Corporation has its origins in a software company called Informix Corporation, which was established in 1980 by Roger Sippl. Informix began as a developer of relational database-management software for minicomputers, Unix workstations, and personal computers. By 1986 the company had about 350 employees and revenue of $18.9 million.

In 1987 Informix merged with Innovative Software Inc. of Lenexa, Kansas. Innovative Software's principal line of business was developing integrated business software mainly for personal computers. Its flagship product was Smart, a family of integrated business programs that included spreadsheet, word processing, and data storage modules. Innovative Software was founded in 1979 by Michael J. Brown and Mark Callegari. It went public in 1983, raising $4.5 million. The company formally launched Smart in August 1984. In 1985 Innovative had revenue of approximately $6 million and was offering substantial discounts on high-volume purchases.

Informix's acquisition of Innovative gave it an entry into the MS-DOS office automation market. Informix had enjoyed rapid sales growth by selling relational database software primarily for the mid-range Unix market. Revenue increased from $10.6 million in 1985 to $18.9 million in fiscal 1987 ending June 30. While the acquisition was initially valued at about $76 million, a sudden crash in stock market prices in October 1987 reduced the value of the deal to around $37 million. The acquisition was completed in January 1988, with Michael Brown becoming president of the new entity, named Informix Software. The new company had about 600 employees.

A Difficult Decade for Informix: 1990s

At the beginning of 1989 Phillip White, formerly of Wyse Technology Inc., was hired as Informix Software's chief executive officer (CEO). According to the *San Francisco Business Times,* White found a company that had mismanaged its acquisition of Innovative Software, with extensive duplication and an "out-of-control payroll." White immediately laid off about 200 employees and replaced virtually the entire management team. The firm was restructured into two product divisions: the Workstation Products Division, headed by the company's former president, Michael Brown, and headquartered in Lenexa, Kansas; and the Advanced Products Division, which was headed by Phillip White at Informix's headquarters in Menlo Park, California. Informix's database, network, and application-development products fell within the Advanced Products Division, while the Workstation Products Division was responsible for the development and marketing of the company's office productivity software.

Under White's leadership, Informix experienced a turnaround over the next few years. After losing $46.3 million in 1990, Informix turned a profit of $12.6 million in 1991 and $47.8 million in 1992 on revenue of nearly $284 million. As a result, White was named one of 1993's CEOs of the Year by *Financial World* magazine, along with Bill Gates of Microsoft Corporation, John Sculley of Apple Computer, Andrew Grove of Intel Corporation, and Ray Noorda of Novell Inc.

The second half of the 1990s again found Informix in financial straits. The company announced that it may have overstated revenue for 1995 and 1996 by as much as $250 million. In 1997 Informix had to restate its losses for 1996 to $200 million and $50 million for 1995. Several years later in 2000, the Securities and Exchange Commission (SEC) charged the company with inflating revenue by $295 million and earnings by $244 million between 1994 and the first quarter of 1997. In 2002 White was indicted by a federal grand jury on eight counts of financial accounting fraud.

Robert Finocchio replaced White in 1997 and became Informix's president, CEO, and chairman, following $140 million and $120 million quarterly losses and the layoff of 10 percent of the company's employees. Finocchio was an industry veteran who had spent nine years at 3Com Corp. Although Oracle Chairman Larry Ellison predicted Informix's demise in 1997, the company appeared headed for a turnaround in 1998. Among the steps taken by Finocchio to right the company were selling land for $60 million, cutting costs by $200 million and firing 600 employees, raising $150 million through the sale of stock, and arranging for a $75 million bank line of credit. Finocchio also reformed the firm's accounting methods. He organized the company into three groups: one to sell high-end transaction software for Informix's relational database software; another that specialized in data warehousing; and a third group devoted to electronic commerce. Informix's largest competitors in database software were market leader Oracle and IBM.

In July 1999 Jean-Yves Dexmier was named CEO of Informix, with Finocchio remaining as chairman. In December the company announced that it would acquire Ardent Software Inc. of Westboro, Massachusetts, in a transaction valued at $1.1

billion when it was completed in March 2000. Ardent produced data integration infrastructure software for data warehousing, business intelligence, and e-business applications under the brand names UniVerse, UniData, and DataStage. In May 2000 Informix announced the release of Ardent DataStage 4.0, which enabled firms to analyze their electronic commerce data for decision making. DataStage 4.0 supported clickstream analysis and provided tools for capturing and managing Internet-based data.

In July 2000 Jean-Yves Dexmier was replaced by board member Peter Gyenes as president and CEO of Informix. Gyenes was formerly chairman, president, and CEO of Ardent Software. Over the next six months Informix focused on reorganizing for profitability. After consolidating five business units into two operations, Database Business Operations and Solutions Business Operations, in August, the company established two independent operating companies in September. The first, Informix Software, focused on providing database management systems for data warehousing, transaction processing, and electronic commerce applications. The second, which was to be named at a later date, was launched to focus on providing database and platform-independent software solutions and infrastructure for the e-business marketplace. This new company was to be headed by Pete Fiore, a senior vice-president at Informix, and headquartered in Westboro, Massachusetts. Both companies were wholly owned subsidiaries of Informix, which also announced that it was moving its corporate headquarters to Westboro. Around this time Gyenes added the title of chairman, following the resignation of Robert Finocchio as chairman in September 2000.

Ascential Software Providing Asset Management Solutions: 2001–03

Informix's new e-business solutions company became Ascential Software in January 2001. By then its focus had changed to include not just e-business solutions, but also a broader range of information management software. Its product line was designed to enable customers to easily collect, validate, organize, administer, and deliver information. Its strategy was to assist enterprises in treating information as an asset.

Ascential began operations under its new name with more than 1,500 customers globally and about 1,500 employees. It was a dominant provider of data integration infrastructure and content management software that powered such areas as data warehousing and business intelligence, customer relationship management (CRM) analytics, and media asset management. Its key markets included insurance and financial services, media and entertainment, healthcare, telecommunications, retail, and transportation and hospitality companies. Its products included DataStage XE, which managed the collection, validation, organization, and administration of information assets; Media360, a media asset management solution; Axielle Portal, a corporate portal that organized and delivered data to a firm's employees; and i.Decide, a series of analytic solutions that addressed specific customer-related business concerns.

For 2000 Informix reported revenue of $929.3 million, with Ascential Software contributing $121.7 million and Informix Software $807.6 million. Pete Fiore predicted that Ascential's license revenue would increase by 80 to 100 percent in 2001. In March 2001 Ascential announced a partnership with Torrent

Key Dates:

1980: Informix Corporation is founded in Menlo Park, California.

1987: Informix merges with Innovative Software Inc., a Kansas-based publisher of the Smart data program for personal computers and workstations, and becomes Informix Software Inc.

1989: Informix reorganizes into two divisions, with its Advanced Products Division headquartered in Menlo Park, California, and its Workstation Productions Division headquartered in Lenexa, Kansas.

1998: Informix forms two new divisions, one for data warehousing products and one for web and e-commerce products.

2000: Informix acquires Ardent Software Inc. in a deal valued at $1.1 billion and splits into two independent operating companies, one for database software and the other for business solutions software.

2001: Informix's business solutions software company is renamed Ascential Software Corporation; IBM acquires Informix's database software business for $1 billion; Ascential Software Corporation acquires Torrent Systems.

2002: Ascential Software Corporation acquires Vality Technology Inc. and the data profiling technology of Metagenix.

2003: Ascential Software Corporation acquires Mercator Software.

Systems, Inc., a Cambridge, Massachusetts-based developer of customer applications that enabled e-commerce firms to analyze large volumes of clickstream and transaction data. The partnership resulted in the first enterprise-level, fully scalable data warehousing solution, which was a combination of Ascential's DataStage XE and Torrent's Orchestrate. Later in the year Ascential acquired Torrent Systems for $46 million in cash.

In April 2001 Informix Corp. announced that it had signed a definitive agreement with IBM Corp. to sell its database business for $1 billion in cash. The company expected to receive about $800 million after taxes, which it would use in part to fuel the growth of Ascential Software through acquisitions. Following completion of the sale, Informix Corp. changed its name to Ascential Software Corporation; its ticker symbol was changed to ASCL effective July 3, 2001. Ascential subsequently entered into a strategic partnership with IBM.

During 2001 Ascential released new versions of Media360 and DataStage. Version 2.0 of Media360 extended the solution's existing support for video, audio, image, and text asset management. It also included two new modules, one for desktop publishing and one for web publishing. Version 2.1, an upgrade that offered improved functionality, was released later in the year in September. In November the company released a new generation of DataStage XE products, including DataStage XE 5.0, DataStage XE Portal Edition 1.0, DataStage PACK 1.0, and DataStage XE/390 5.0. The new generation of DataStage solutions enabled corporations for the first time to comprehen-

sively integrate data from all corporate information sources within a single, companywide business integration framework.

Although revenue did not increase as much as expected for 2001, due in part to a depressed corporate spending environment, Ascential ended the year in a strong financial position with $758.6 million in cash on hand. For 2001 it reported overall revenue of $124 million. Revenue from DataStage, the firm's core data integration product, increased 33 percent to $104.4 million from $78.3 million in fiscal 2000. Revenue from Media360 and related content management products continued to decline, and the company announced that it had hired an investment bank to help it divest its content management business.

During the next two years Ascential acquired other software companies and integrated new technology into its product releases. In April 2002 Ascential acquired Vality Technology Inc. for $92 million in cash. Boston-based Vality was a recognized industry leader in enterprise data quality management. It had annual revenue of $21.2 million in 2001 and about 500 customers. The acquisition added about 100 employees to Ascential's workforce. Vality's data quality and cleansing product line, Integrity, complemented Ascential's newly released MetaRecon data profiling solution, which it acquired in April from Metagenix Inc. for $4.5 million. These products offered enterprises an integrated and comprehensive, infinitely scalable, data integration solution.

In the second half of 2002 Ascential released version 6.0 of DataStage, its data integration software. The new release incorporated profiling, quality management, and parallel-processing technology that the company had recently acquired. Pricing for DataStage began at $400,000. Ascential also received recognition as a company to watch in 2003 by *Intelligent Enterprise* magazine. It also rose from 43rd to 16th on *DM Review* magazine's 2002 list of the top business intelligence vendors as selected by its readers. For 2002 Ascential reported revenue of $113 million, including $59.6 million in license revenue, and a net loss of $63.6 million.

In June 2003 Ascential released version 7.0 of its Enterprise Integration Suite, the company's flagship enterprise integration solution. The suite combined three data integration products: ProfileStage for data profiling, QualityStage for data quality, and DataStage for data transformation. For the second quarter of 2003 Ascential reported record revenue and profitability since becoming Ascential Software in July 2001. It was the company's first quarterly profit since becoming an independent company and fifth consecutive quarter of revenue growth.

In August 2003 Ascential announced that it would acquire Mercator Software for about $106 million. Based in Wilton, Connecticut, Mercator was a leading provider of data transformation and routing solutions for complex, high-volume transaction processing environments. The acquisition was expected to create the largest independent software vendor focused exclusively on enterprise data integration. Annual revenue was projected to be $250 million, with a base of 3,000 customers. The acquisition was completed in September 2003. Having successfully integrated acquisitions made over the previous two years with cash it received from the sale of Informix's database business to IBM, Ascential was positioned to play a dominant role in the market for enterprise integration solutions.

Principal Competitors

Business Objects S.A. (France); Crystal Decisions, Inc.; Data Junction Corporation; DataMirror Corporation; Evolutionary Technologies International, Inc.; Firstlogic Inc.; Group 1 Software, Inc.; Hummingbird Ltd. (Canada); International Business Machines Corporation; Informatica Corporation; SAS Institute; Tibco Software Inc.; Vitria Technology Inc.; WebMethods Inc.

Further Reading

April, Carolyn A., "Settlement: Informix Settles Securities Charges," *InfoWorld,* January 17, 2000, p. 22.

"Ascential Expands Integration Capabilities with Mercator Acquisition," *InformationWeek,* August 7, 2003.

"Ascential Reports First Independent Profit," *InformationWeek,* July 22, 2003.

"Ascential Software Corp. to Buy Boston-Based Data Management Firm," *Knight Ridder/Tribune Business News,* March 13, 2002.

Burriesci, Jeanette, "Higher Ground," *Intelligent Enterprise,* February 1, 2002, p. 12.

Burriesci, Jeanette, et al., "Integration," *Intelligent Enterprise,* January 1, 2003, p. 31.

"Business Intelligence Bucks IT Spending Slowdown," *InformationWeek,* January 30, 2003.

Cain, Matthew, "Informix Sets $76M Deal for Innovative," *Electronic News,* October 19, 1987, p. 26.

Darrow, Barbara, "An Ascential Acquisition," *Computer Reseller News,* August 11, 2003, p. 26.

"Data Launched on Path to Integration," *eWeek,* September 9, 2002.

Doler, Kathleen, "Informix to Undergo Restructuring, Delays Its Database Engine," *PC Week,* January 30, 1989, p. 54.

Faloon, Kelly, "Informix to Continue Support for Databases," *Supply House Times,* April 2000, p. 33.

"Financial Tools Ease Data Handling," *eWeek,* March 17, 2003.

"Former Informix Exec Indicted," *InformationWeek,* November 23, 2002.

Glenn, David J., "Massachusetts Company Acquires Mercator," *Fairfield County Business Journal,* August 18, 2003, p. 3.

Houston, Patrick, "Backseat Strategist," *PC Week,* July 26, 1993, p. A5.

Hutheesing, Nikhil, "Is Informix Back?," *Forbes,* September 21, 1998, p. 202.

"Informix Adds Divisions," *Information Week,* August 10, 1998, p. 30.

"Informix Buys Ardent," *Washington Business Journal,* December 10, 1999, p. 37.

"Informix Spins Out Ascential Software," *Client Server News,* January 22, 2001.

"Informix Taps Board Member As New CEO," *TechWeb,* July 14, 2000.

"Informix to Sell Database Business to IBM for $1B," *Boston Business Journal,* April 27, 2001, p. 61.

"It's Heads-Up at Informix," *Business Week,* October 16, 2000, p. 217.

Kaberline, Brian, "Merged Informix Yet to Find Wings in Software Market," *Kansas City Business Journal,* January 23, 1989, p. 1.

Kiesnoski, Kenneth, "Robert Finocchio," *Computer Reseller News,* November 10, 1997, p. 131.

LaMonica, Martin, and Paul Krill, "Universal Server Slow to Catch On," *InfoWorld,* July 14, 1997, p. 14.

Leeke, Jim, " 'Smart Packages' Renown Balloons Beyond Kansas," *PC Week,* January 15, 1985, p. 107.

Lyons, Daniel J., "Informix and Innovative Unite, Surprise Industry Observers," *PC Week,* October 20, 1987, p. 179.

——, "Innovative, Informix Merger Still On," *PC Week,* November 3, 1987, p. 245.

Mael, Susan, "Ascential Wants to Be Essential to Info Asset Management," *Online Reporter,* February 26, 2001.

Mulqueen, John T., "Informix Alive and Kicking," *InternetWeek,* May 11, 1998, p. 75.

Rauber, Chris, "Prime Times: Database Company Bounces Back," *San Francisco Business Times,* May 21, 1993, p. 8A.

Rutledge, Tanya, "Financially Strained Informix Looking to Dump Some Land," *Business Journal,* October 6, 1997, p. 4.

Sullivan, Tom, "Informix Splits Operations," *InfoWorld,* September 25, 2000, p. 20.

——, "Two Faces of Informix Look Forward, Refining Consolidation," *InfoWorld,* November 6, 2000, p. 24.

Sweeney, Phil, "Sale of Informix Means Independence for Ascential," *Boston Business Journal,* July 13, 2001, p. 12.

Taschek, John, "Informix Still Has a Long Way to Go," *PC Week,* December 1, 1997, p. 74.

"A Union of Data," *eWeek,* August 18, 2003.

Whiting, Rick, "Ascential Buys Data-Profiling Software," *InformationWeek,* April 4, 2002.

——, "Ascential Does Data," *InformationWeek,* October 5, 2002.

——, "Ascential Integrates the Fruits of Its Buyouts," *InformationWeek,* October 1, 2002.

Whiting, Rick, and Larry Greenemeier, "Making the Most of Data," *InformationWeek,* December 3, 2001, p. 16.

Wiener, Daniel P., "Innovative Software Inc.," *Fortune,* July 8, 1985, p. 72.

—David P. Bianco

Asia Pacific Breweries Limited

#21-00 Alexandra Point
438 Alexandra Road
119958
Singapore
Telephone: (+65) 6272-9488
Fax: (+65) 6271-0811
Web site: http://www.apb.com.sg

Public Company
Incorporated: 1931 as Malayan Breweries
Employees: 2,624
Sales: S$1.09 billion (US$616 million) (2002)
Stock Exchanges: Singapore
Ticker Symbol: APBB
NAIC: 312120 Breweries

Asia Pacific Breweries Limited is one of the largest brewers in the Asian region. The company produces a variety of beers, including its prize-winning premium flagship Tiger Beer, as well as a number of other international, regional, and local beers, such as Anchor, Raffles, Heineken, and its latest brew, Touché, released in 2003. In all, Asia Pacific brews more than 40 beers. Originally focused on the Malaysia and Singapore markets, the company has expanded steadily throughout the region since the early 1990s, and now includes operations in Singapore, Malaysia, New Zealand, Indochina, Cambodia, China, Thailand, and Papua New Guinea. Singapore remains the company's largest market, while New Zealand and Indochina are both strong revenue generators for Asia Pacific. The product of a 1930s joint venture between Singapore's Fraser & Neave and The Netherlands' Heineken, the public company remains controlled by both groups, with its shares listed on the Singapore stock exchange. Asia Pacific Breweries is led by Chairman and CEO Koh Poh Tiong.

Founding a Beer Legend in the 1930s

Fraser & Neave had been present in Singapore since the 1880s and had grown into the region's leading soft drinks manufacturer by the late 1920s, when it decided to enter the beer industry as well. By then, too, Heineken, seeking to take advantage of The Netherlands' colonial influence in the region, had begun making plans to launch its beer on the international market, in part to compensate for the effects of the Depression on its European sales.

The two companies came together in 1931 to found Malayan Breweries. Heineken contributed its brewing expertise, while Fraser & Neave added its regional distribution strengths, with branches and production facilities located throughout Malaysia and Singapore and extending into Thailand and Vietnam as well. By 1932, construction on the new brewery was completed, and in that year Malayan Breweries debuted the Tiger Beer brand. The new beer was said to resemble Heineken's own beer in flavor, a natural outcome of Heineken's contribution to the company's industrial development.

The Tiger Beer brand enabled Malayan Breweries to grow quickly into the dominant beer brand in Malaysia and Singapore. The company began exporting to Hong Kong and Thailand during the decade as well. Soon it was forced to increase production capacity, expanding the brewery in 1937, and then again two years later.

In 1941, Malayan Breweries acquired the Archipelago Brewing Company. That purchase gave the company a second brewery and a new brand, Anchor Beer, a pilsener beer that was to remain the company's second main brand into the next century.

World War II had an unexpected consequence for Malayan Breweries, as soldiers returning home after the war created new international demand for Tiger Beer. Foreign sales were to remain a minor portion of the company's business, however, as Malayan Breweries focused its efforts on its core markets in Malaysia and Singapore. Nonetheless, the company made a new international expansion effort in 1958, when it purchased South Pacific Brewery of Papua New Guinea, giving it that company's premium beer brand, SP Lager. At the same time, the company had been expanding its own beer list, launching its stout and ale varieties in the 1950s.

International Expansion in the 1990s

Malayan Breweries took on new business in the early 1970s when it began production of Heineken-branded beer as well.

Company Perspectives:

Corporate Vision: To be the Leading Brewer in the Asia Pacific Region.

Key Dates:

1931: Heineken and Fraser & Neave set up a joint venture, called Malayan Breweries, to brew beer for the Malaysia and Singapore markets.
1932: Malayan Breweries begins production, launching the Tiger Beer brand.
1941: The company acquires Archipelago Brewing Company and its Anchor Beer brand.
1958: The company acquires South Pacific Brewery in Papua New Guinea and that company's SP Lager.
1973: Production of Heineken beer begins for the export market.
1984: Production of Heineken beer begins for the domestic market.
1988: The company takes a stake in the Shanghai Mila Brewery in China.
1989: A new state-of-the-art brewery is inaugurated in Tuas.
1990: The company changes its name to Asia Pacific Breweries as part of its regional expansion strategy; the company enters Cambodia.
1991: A stake in New Zealand's DB Group is acquired.
1995: The company builds breweries in Cambodia and Myanmar.
1997: The company acquires full control of Hainan, China brewery.
2000: The company acquires full control of DB Group.
2002: The company begins construction of its second Vietnam brewery.
2003: The Touché beer brand is launched.

This move was part of the Dutch parent company's move toward a decentralized brewing effort, and Malayan Breweries' production of the Heineken brand remained focused on the export market through the 1970s. In 1984, however, the company began marketing Heineken beer in Singapore as well. By the following year, Heineken had succeeded in capturing the number five position among top-selling beers in that market.

Malayan Breweries' growing portfolio of brands, as well as its market dominance in the Malaysian and Singapore markets, led it to adopt a new branding strategy. The company began a successful repositioning of its flagship Tiger Beer brand into the premium beer category. In this effort, the company was aided by strong advertising spending—including a long-running series of television and cinema advertisements—and also in its growing international recognition. Indeed, by the end of the 1980s, Tiger Beer had come to be viewed by many as among the world's best beers.

The repositioning of its other major shareholder, Fraser & Neave, provided more opportunities for the company. Fraser & Neave had engaged in a diversification drive in the 1980s, in part in response to Malaysia's new nationalization laws, which left the company in need of cash. In 1985, Fraser & Neave decided to convert its prime Singapore city locations—including the Anchor and Tiger Beer breweries—into commercial development, and construction began on a new state-of-the-art brewery, in Tuas. The highly automated facility opened in 1989 and boasted a production capacity of one million hectoliters per year.

The move heralded a new era for the company. At the end of the 1980s, the company's dominance in the Singapore and Malaysian markets had also left it heavily dependent on those countries for its sales and its profits. At the beginning of the 1990s, more than 75 percent of Malayan Breweries' profits came from its domestic sales. Under the leadership of General Manager, and later Chairman and CEO, Koh Poh Tiong, Malayan Breweries began developing a new international growth strategy.

Koh compared its new international strategy to a boxing match. "Tiger was an amateur fighter. So we thought: forget about countries like Japan and the USA with their heavyweight brands. Let's forget about Europe, but focus on Asia Pacific, a very large area. Let's grow in our own front yard and backyard. Markets like Vietnam, China and Thailand—those fit in our strategy perfectly."

The first step in the company's new plans was a change of name, to Asia Pacific Breweries, as a clear signal of the company's international growth plans. Asia Pacific then began targeting its new markets. The expertise gained from the construction of its Tuas facility, backed by Heineken's own expertise on the export market, enabled it to build new and highly efficient breweries in the region at the start of the 1990s.

Thailand, Cambodia, and Vietnam were among Asia Pacific's first targets, but the company's major interest developed in China—soon to become the world's second largest beer market after the United States. Asia Pacific began positioning itself in that country in 1988 with the purchase of a controlling stake in Shanghai Mila Brewery. Backed by Heineken's brewing expertise, that company, later renamed Shanghai Asia Pacific Co., launched its own beer brand for the Chinese market, Reeb Beer. The success of that brand led the company to add two more breweries in the early 1990s.

Asia Pacific also targeted New Zealand, when, in 1991, it paid S$245 million to acquire a 27 percent stake in that country's DB Group. Formerly known as Magnum, that company operated as a brewer and winemaker, but had extensive hotel and pub holdings as well. Under the influence of Asia Pacific—and Fraser & Neave—DB Group began shedding its nonbeverage holdings, selling off its hotels and pubs in 1993. The following year, Asia Pacific stepped up its shareholding in DB to more than 54 percent.

In support of its expansion, the company began adding production sites, building its new breweries on the model established by its Tuas site. The company opened new facilities in Thailand and Vietnam and elsewhere, while it continued to supply other markets with its Tuas brewery. Among these markets was Cambodia, which the company entered in 1990. By the middle of the decade, however, Asia Pacific had succeeded in grabbing 60 percent of the Cambodian market. Based on its success there, the company opened a new S$36 million brewery near Phnom Penh.

That same year, Asia Pacific turned to Myanmar, setting up a joint venture with that country's Union of Myanmar Economic Holdings, in order to construct a S$42.7 million (US$309 million) brewery near Yangon City. The joint venture, Myanmar Brewery Ltd., held at 60 percent by Asia Pacific, began brewing Tiger Beer in 1996. By then, the company operated more than 15 breweries in Singapore and abroad.

Asia Pacific acquired full control of its Hainan brewery in 1997. Yet despite the company's early success in China, by the late 1990s these operations had begun posting losses. Part of the company's difficulties there came from the slumping sales of Reeb Beer, which had been hard hit by the entry of a number of other, larger competitors, such as Suntory and Tsingtao, into the Chinese market. Asia Pacific struck back in 2001 by deciding to launch a new brand into the Chinese market, and gradually phase out the Reeb brand.

By then, Asia Pacific had gained full control of DB Group, paying NZ$117 million for the remaining shares in the company. The company then shed DB's winemaking operations to concentrate exclusively on brewing. Asia Pacific had also continued to expand into new markets, entering India in 1999.

Asia Pacific's strategy of striving to become a big fish in the small ponds of the Asia Pacific region appeared to be paying off, as its portfolio of brands gave it strong shares in most of its chosen markets at the start of the 21st century. Asia Pacific continued to expand its production capacity, such as launching the construction of a second brewery in Vietnam in 2002. That project was expected to be completed in the fall of 2003. In the meantime, Asia Pacific was celebrating the launch of its first new-style beer, Touché. Launched in March 2003, the new beer featured a yeast cultured from champagne grapes, and marked the company's first effort to adopt micro-brewing techniques. With more than 70 years of brewing success behind it, Asia Pacific—and its flagship Tiger brand—remained a key player in the region's beer industry.

Principal Subsidiaries

Asia Pacific Breweries (Singapore) Pte Ltd; Cambodia Brewery Ltd. (80%); DB Breweries Limited (New Zealand; 76.9%); GAPL Pte Ltd. (50%); Hainan Asia Pacific Brewery Company Ltd. (China); Hatay Brewery Limited (Vietnam; 96.6%); Sino Brew Investments Pte Ltd. (Thailand; 50%); South Pacific Brewery Limited (Papua New Guinea; 75%); Thai Asia Pacific Brewery Co. Ltd.; Tiger Export Pte Ltd.; Tiger Marketing Pte Ltd.; Vietnam Brewery Limited (60%).

Principal Competitors

Madhvani Group; Kirin Brewery Company Ltd.; Asahi Breweries Ltd.; Sapporo Holdings Ltd.; Press Corporation Ltd.

Further Reading

"APB to Build Second Beer Brewery in Vietnam," *Vietnam News Briefs,* March 29, 2002.
"Fraser & Neave Has No Plans to Take Asia Pacific Breweries Private," *AFX Europe,* May 17, 2002.
Hall, Terry, "Singapore Group in NZ Offer," *Financial Times,* January 31, 2000, p. 22.
Khuen, Foo Tiang, "Tiger Burning Bright," *Asia Image,* July 2002, p. 24.
"Singapore's Asia Pacific Breweries Hikes Stake in Vietnam Brewery," *Asia Pulse,* May 5, 2003.

—M. L. Cohen

ASPLUNDH

Asplundh Tree Expert Co.

708 Blair Mill Road
Willow Grove, Pennsylvania 19090-1701
U.S.A.
Telephone: (215) 784-4200
Toll Free: (800) 248-TREE
Fax: (215) 784-4493
Web site: http://www.asplundh.com

Private Company
Founded: 1928
Employees: 28,000
Sales: $1.65 billion (2002 est.)
NAIC: 561730 Landscaping Services; 235310 Electrical
Contractors; 422910 Farm Supplies Wholesalers;
441110 New Car Dealers; 532412 Construction,
Mining, and Forestry Machinery and Equipment
Rental and Leasing; 541990 All Other Professional,
Scientific, and Technical Services; 561990 All Other
Support Services

Asplundh Tree Expert Co. is the world's leading line clearance and tree-trimming company. While most of the company's business is in the United States and Canada, Asplundh (pronounced "AH-splund") also has operations in Australia and New Zealand. Asplundh's primary business, and the one on which it was founded more than 75 years ago, is trimming trees for telephone and electric utility companies and municipalities. The company has diversified its operations over the years, however, and by the early 2000s was also involved in keeping railroad rights-of-way clear, removing storm debris and providing other emergency services for government agencies, inspecting and maintaining telephone poles, installing overhead and underground lines and cables, reading meters, locating and marking underground utility lines, constructing and maintaining traffic signals and highway lighting, leasing utility equipment, and operating a truck dealership. Still owned by the Asplundh family, the company is managed by the third generation of Asplundhs and all board members are family members.

The Early Years: 1928–45

Griffith (Griff) Asplundh was seven years old when his Swedish immigrant father died in 1903. His brother Lester was two, his brother Carl an infant. "Asplundh" in Swedish refers to a grove of aspen trees, so perhaps it is not surprising that, 25 years later, the boys decided to make trees the family business. They got their training working for their big brother Oswald E. (O.E.), who started a nursery and tree-trimming company to help support his widowed mother and his seven siblings. Griff, Lester, and Carl trimmed trees to pay for college, with Griff majoring in forestry at Penn State, Lester in electrical engineering at Swarthmore, and Carl in finance at the University of Pennsylvania.

In 1928 they decided to combine their talents and go into business for themselves, using $2,500 in borrowed capital to set up shop in Glenside, Pennsylvania. Not wanting to compete with O.E.'s residential business, the Asplundh Tree Expert Co. focused on commercial customers—the fast-growing telephone and electric companies whose overhead lines needed to be kept clear of tree branches. The first customers were Philadelphia Electric Co., Public Service Electric & Gas, Co., Jersey Central Power & Light Co., Pennsylvania Power & Light Co., and American Telephone and Telegraph.

Their decision proved a wise one, as the telephone and electric companies continued to expand, despite the Great Depression. The company in fact opened its first branch office in Columbus, Ohio, in 1931. Three years later, the company moved to larger quarters in nearby Jenkintown, Pennsylvania, and in 1936 O.E. left his nursery business and joined his brothers, helping them move into new territory in the Midwest. While Griff oversaw the trimming and Carl kept the books, Lester concentrated on research and development to bring the latest technology to the company and its customers. Able to offer the first power saws (operated by two men) and hand-cranked aerial platforms, Asplundh attracted more customers. Mother Nature also aided the company's growth via several major storms that hit the East Coast in the late 1930s, creating storm emergency work for Asplundh. By the end of the decade, the company had employees working throughout the Mid-Atlantic region, in the Carolinas and Georgia, in the Midwest, and as far west as Texas

---

Company Perspectives:

At Asplundh, our mission is to be the recognized world leader in providing professional, safe and cost-effective vegetation management and other utility-related services. With this goal in mind, each person on our team is challenged to consistently exceed the expectations of the customers for whom we work, and the people they serve.

---

and New Mexico. To keep in touch with their far-flung workforce, the company introduced *The Asplundh TREE*, a quarterly magazine, in 1940. Business slowed significantly during World War II as workers left to join the military and rationing made it difficult to buy fuel, tools, and supplies.

New Services, New Technology in the Postwar Era

The Asplundh brothers thought the "chemical brush killers" developed during the war might prove useful for clearing rights-of-way and, in conjunction with American Chemical and Paint Co., tested these new herbicides. Liking what they found, Asplundh developed special formulae and, in 1946, began offering brush control services for utility rights-of-way, the company's first step in diversification. To make it easier and faster to clear and dispose of brush, Lester invented the first wood chipper, which was field-tested in 1949; the company began assembling these for commercial sale in 1952 through a subsidiary called Asplundh Chipper Co. The demand for electricity mushroomed to supply the housing developments and apartment complexes being built for veterans and their families. To meet that need, utility companies had to expand their rights-of-way networks in order to erect new transmission towers. This meant clearing and cutting lots of brush, bushes, and trees. In 1956 the brothers created another subsidiary, the Asplundh Brush Control Co., to handle the right-of-way clearing work.

Lester was elected president in January 1949, following Griff's death, but stepped down from that position in 1952 because of a health problem. Carl became president and Lester continued to use his engineering skills to expand Asplundh's capabilities. His next project dealt with the company's core business, tree trimming.

By the early 1950s, the technology of tree-trimming had progressed from ladders and ropes to a vehicle called a turret or ladder truck. A tree worker still climbed a ladder, but that was attached to the back of the truck, making it easier to reach branch ends. Then came the introduction of the hydraulic aerial lift, called a "Skyworker." Asplundh started leasing the lifts in 1953, but found their insulation poor. Lester used a new material called fiberglass in designing a stronger and better insulated lift which the company began producing in 1958 at a plant in Chalfont, Pennsylvania; three years later, this plant was merged with the operations of Asplundh Chipper Co. to form the Asplundh Manufacturing Division. Meantime, also in 1958, the company established its Pole Maintenance Division for treating and reinforcing utility poles.

In 1954 Asplundh sent crews to help restore service in Mid-Atlantic states following Hurricanes Carol and Hazel. As a result of those experiences, the company produced a formalized storm emergency procedure for its crews and customers. Seven members of the second generation, sons of the founders, completed college and began training in the field and home office. The company began participating in a research project to study the safe use of herbicides along utility rights-of-way and initiated its supervisory training program for general foremen. Company operations spread throughout New England.

The early 1960s saw Asplundh continue to extend its operations—into Florida and the Pacific Northwest—and to expand its services as it offered underground utility construction. In 1967 the company pioneered commercial thermographic/infrared inspections to detect "hot spots"—short circuits, overheating, and equipment failures—in a power distribution system and prevent power outages. In 1968 Barr Asplundh, Griff's son, was elected president; by this time, all second generation family members working for the company had become board members. That same year, the company established the Asplundh Utility Services Ltd. subsidiary for the start-up of its Canadian operations and formed Asplundh GMC, its own commercial truck dealership.

New Markets: 1970s and 1980s

The company continued to grow and diversify during the next two decades. Street lights seemed a logical place to use its lifts, and Asplundh began cleaning, inspecting, and repairing street lighting and traffic signals for utilities and municipalities in 1972 through the Asplundh Street Lighting Division. In need of larger quarters to manage its expanding operations, Asplundh relocated to Willow Grove, Pennsylvania, in 1974. The company opened its first One-Call Center in New Jersey the following year. Initially called the Underground Location Communications Division, the center served as a link between excavators and utilities with underground lines. Before beginning to dig, a contractor could call the center and describe where the work was to be done. Personnel at the center would notify member utilities with facilities in the work area so they could mark where their underground cables and pipes were. Within 20 years the company had eight such centers around the country using computers and specialized software.

Also in 1975, the company established its Railroad Division, turning its vegetation sprays on the weeds, brush, and trees along railroad tracks. Asplundh began working on large railroads east of the Mississippi, using three spray trucks equipped with Hy-rail wheels that could run on both highway and railroad tracks. To meet the special needs of its new clients, Asplundh designed new equipment, including a high-production spray train car that could operate while attached to a train. In the early 1980s, the division began offering rights-of-way clearing as well as vegetation management, putting Hy-rail wheels on aerial lifts and chippers to trim and remove trees. Soon the equipment shop facility was designing and building specialized equipment including brush cutters that ran on a railroad track and had arms spanning the line, clearing an area 56 feet wide along the track. Both services proved popular and the division was soon working on railroads of all sizes, from coast to coast, from Canada to Mexico. In 1982, meantime, Barr Asplundh was named chairman, and Edward Asplundh, son of Carl, was elected president.

Key Dates:

1928: Three brothers, Griffith, Lester, and Carl Asplundh, form Asplundh Tree Expert Co., based in Glenside, Pennsylvania, to offer tree-trimming services to utility companies.

1931: First branch office opens in Columbus, Ohio.

1934: Headquarters are relocated to Jenkintown, Pennsylvania.

1939: Company is operating throughout the Mid-Atlantic Region and in the Carolinas, Georgia, the Midwest, Texas, and New Mexico.

1946: Using newly developed herbicides, Asplundh begins offering brush control services for utility rights-of-way.

1949: Field-testing begins on the first wood chipper, invented by Lester Asplundh.

1956: Asplundh Brush Control Co. is created as a subsidiary to handle the right-of-way clearing work.

1968: Second generation of Asplundhs begin to lead the company with the election of Barr Asplundh, son of Griff, to the presidency; subsidiary is created to begin expansion into Canada.

1974: Asplundh moves to larger quarters in Willow Grove, Pennsylvania.

1989: American Lighting & Signalization, Inc., which constructs and maintains traffic signal and highway lighting systems, is acquired.

1990: Utility line construction firm B & J Maintenance Co., Inc. is acquired and later renamed Asplundh Construction Corp.; operations in New Zealand commence through a joint venture.

1992: Canadian operations are consolidated under Asplundh Canada, Inc.; company sells its manufacturing division to Altec Industries, Inc.; expansion into meter reading services begins; subsidiary is established in Australia.

1996: Utility Meter Services, Inc. is established as the firm's meter reading services subsidiary.

1997: Central Locating Service Limited is acquired and becomes the center of the firm's utility line marking services; revenues surpass $1 billion for the first time.

2001: Third Asplundh generation is at the management controls with the election of Scott M. Asplundh to the presidency.

2002: Asplundh Environmental Services, Inc. is formed as a disaster recovery subsidiary to help cities, states, and other government entities clean up after storms.

During the 1980s, Asplundh expanded into western Canada through several acquisitions; bought a Buick franchise which it combined with its GMC truck operations; began its first "overseas" line clearance operations in the U.S. Virgin Islands; expanded line clearance operations to serve Hawaii (thus working in all 50 states); created the Municipal Tree Division for trimming trees for cities and towns; and established Asplundh Canada, Inc. to serve Quebec and eastern Canada. In 1989 Asplundh acquired American Lighting & Signalization, Inc., a Florida-based heavy equipment contractor that specialized in constructing and maintaining traffic signal and highway lighting systems. The decade also saw the introduction of a self-propelled, portable backyard chipper developed in the company's Alabama region.

One of the company's greatest strengths was evident following the disruption in telephone and electrical services caused along the East Coast by Hurricane Gloria in 1985 and in the Caribbean and North and South Carolina by Hurricane Hugo in 1989. Asplundh could shift large numbers of employees (1,500 for Gloria and 1,600 for Hugo) to the damaged areas to repair lines and restore service, augmenting the crews of the local utility companies. These emergency storm services, providing quick mobilization of trained crews and specialized equipment, proved to be an important marketing tool for the company and led to the establishment of a weather center at Asplundh's headquarters that monitored every storm in the country. As President Chris Asplundh explained in a 1995 *Forbes* article, "Santa Ana winds in California, that's our problem. Nor'easter in Boston, that's our problem; ice storm in Minnesota, that's our problem."

In 1987 the first of 13 third-generation Asplundh family members completed the Family Management Development Program. An Asplundh must graduate from college, spend three years working outside the company, and then be recommended by three family members, including at least one board member, before being accepted for the eight-year training program. Once in the program, the young Asplundh works in the field as a crew foreman, general foreman, supervisor, and then manager, moving around the country with each promotion, before coming to work at headquarters. In 1989 members of the second generation began to retire.

Aggressively Expanding Its Portfolio of Services in the 1990s

Asplundh started the 1990s with a buying spree. In 1990 it acquired New York-based B & J Maintenance Co., Inc. to increase its utility line construction activities in the Northeast; L. Fulcher Electric, a traffic signal contractor, which became a subsidiary of American Lighting & Signalization; and five small line clearance firms in France. The French companies retained their names and management and operated as partners of Asplundh's French subsidiary, Robert S.A., named for Chairman of the Board Robert Asplundh, who helped negotiate the business arrangements. Located in different regions of the country, the firms' primary client was the government-owned power company, Electricité de France.

Later that year, Asplundh formed a joint venture with a large electrical and engineering contractor in New Zealand called Electrix Limited. The new company, Electrix Asplundh, offered line clearance tree maintenance, right-of-way clearing, mowing, and spraying to municipal councils and electric supply authorities. Asplundh bought out its partner in 1995 and thereupon changed the venture into a subsidiary called Asplundh Tree Expert (N.Z.) Limited.

Training had long been a tradition at Asplundh, beginning with informal training schools for crews. The Supervisory

Training Program for general foremen was initiated in 1953, and the Supervisory Skills Seminars started in 1986. As a regional manager stated in *The Asplundh TREE,* ''Our people have become more professional. This is especially true of crew personnel. They used to be considered 'just tree trimmers.' Now they have Commercial Driver's Licenses, Pesticide Applicator's Licenses, better first aid training, arborist training. . . .'' In 1990, the company established Professional Line Clearance Training Crews who came in and provided two-weeks, hands-on training to crews working on utility properties. That training experience was in addition to the normal on-the-job training crews received.

Equipment development was another company tradition, and 1991 witnessed the unveiling of the manufacturing division's LRIII-55, an aerial lift with a reach of 55 feet, well beyond anything then available.

The year 1992 was busy as all Canadian operations came under the company's Asplundh Canada, Inc. subsidiary; the Asplundh Manufacturing Division was sold to Altec Industries, Inc.; B & J Maintenance was renamed Asplundh Construction Corp. and began to move beyond its Northeast base; Christopher Asplundh, the youngest member of the second generation, took over as president from his brother Edward; and some 3,000 workers from seven states helped clean up and restore service in Florida and Louisiana after Hurricane Andrew. During the year the company began a new service, reading meters on the property of Chattanooga Electric Power Board, and, in cooperation with the Philadelphia Electric Co., Asplundh promoted its Philly Foam, a low-volume foliage spraying system that made it easier for a sprayer to see what had been treated, thus reducing skips and misses. On the international scene, the company formed a wholly owned subsidiary in Australia and acquired Read & Co. Utility Services, Ltd., a long-established firm in England. Asplundh financed the firm's restructuring to help it expand in England and Wales and offer services to the newly privatized electric utilities in England. Late in the year Asplundh bought Ginnifer Tree Care Service in the Republic of Ireland. A commercial/residential tree service company, Ginnifer broadened its services by clearing lines for Ireland's Electric Supply Board around Dublin.

According to Randall Lane in his *Forbes* article, much of the company's growth and service expansion in the 1980s and early 1990s occurred to provide more opportunities for family members in the company. There were 65 members in the fourth generation, and the eldest ones were in college by the mid-1990s, creating a need for a larger company to hold those who complete the family training program.

Asplundh's 65th year of business began with the mobilizing of more than 1,300 crews to restore power all along the East Coast following the Blizzard of '93 in March. The company continued to expand, buying the assets of five subsidiaries of Southeastern Public Service Company, one of its line clearance competitors; among the acquired businesses were Blume Tree Services, Inc. and Farrens Tree Surgeons, Inc. By 1995, the company's revenues had grown from $100 million in 1984 to $850 million. Four of its original five customers were still doing business with the company and some 20 utilities had been using Asplundh crews for 40 or more years.

During 1996, Asplundh turned several of its divisions into wholly owned subsidiaries. The relatively new meter reading operations became Utility Meter Services, Inc.; the renting and leasing of equipment and vehicles was placed under Compass Equipment Leasing, Inc.; and the division handling pole maintenance became Utility Pole Technologies, Inc. Expanding beyond the middleman role of the One-Call operations, Asplundh moved into the actual marking of underground utility lines in 1996 through the acquisition of Underground Utility Locating, Inc. One year later, Central Locating Service Limited, a long established firm in Syracuse, New York, was acquired. Central Locating expanded into Arkansas, Illinois, and Texas through the 1998 purchase of certain assets of NORAM Damage Protection. Further diversification came in 1997 through the purchase of Southern Outdoor Maintenance, which was renamed Outdoor Maintenance Co., Inc. This subsidiary served the outdoor advertising (i.e., billboard) industry, offering vegetation maintenance and construction services. Also in 1997, revenues surpassed the $1 billion mark for the first time.

Although the overseas operations in Australia and New Zealand were proving successful, Asplundh pulled back elsewhere. In 1996 the operations in France were closed down, and in 1999 the company sold Read & Co., its U.K. subsidiary, to Fountain Forestry for an interest in that company. Closer to home, Asplundh ended the decade with three of its largest disaster mobilizations ever. Following the massive ice storm that hit upstate New York, New England, and southern Quebec in January 1998, Asplundh sent more than 580 tree crews and 100 construction crews to help restore power. In September of the following year, 1,650 crews consisting of almost 5,000 employees mobilized on the East Coast in response to Hurricane Floyd. Just one month later, 600 Asplundh crews helped Florida Power & Light restore electrical service that had been interrupted by Hurricane Irene.

Third Generation Leading the Way in the New Millennium

By the early 2000s, all of the second-generation Asplundhs had retired from daily operations, except for Chris, who in January 2001 moved from president to chairman and CEO. Seven members of the third generation shared management responsibility, including the newly appointed president, Scott M. Asplundh. The new leaders had to contend with the challenging economic environment of the new decade, particularly the collapse of the telecommunications industry, which brought an end to the massive line building of the previous several years.

Asplundh nevertheless continued its program of expansion. Having responded to yet another major natural disaster—the back-to-back ice storms that hit the south-central United States in December 2000—Asplundh established a disaster recovery subsidiary to help cities, states, and other government entities clean up after storms. Called Asplundh Environmental Services, Inc. (AES), the new unit was formed in April 2002. Just six months later, AES had its first major test when Hurricane Lili knocked out power to 450,000 homes in southern Louisiana. Mobilizing more than 1,400 crews from 27 Asplundh management regions, AES helped restore power within 48 hours and then spent another three weeks clearing away storm debris. Asplundh also established a new line construction subsidiary called Utility Line Construction Service, Inc. during 2000.

On the acquisitions front, Asplundh acquired a utility line locating service called NOCUTS, a subsidiary of Sprint Corporation, in 2000. Asplundh's line marking operations, which were doubled through this latest purchase, were consolidated into Central Locating Service by the end of 2001. The company also acquired two more utility line clearing businesses: the line clearance operations of F.A. Bartlett Tree Expert Company of Stamford, Connecticut, bought in 2001; and the line clearing business of Trees Inc., a unit of the ServiceMaster Company, purchased in late 2003.

Asplundh Tree Expert's fastest growing businesses in the early 2000s were its utility construction and line locating operations. The company's decades-long diversification drive had greatly expanded its menu of services, but vegetation management continued to generate about 70 percent of the revenues. Perhaps Asplundh's most remarkable achievement was maintaining such a high degree of family control, both in terms of ownership and management, after more than 75 years in business. Asplundh was well-positioned to continue to capture a growing share of the outsourced business of public utilities and cost-conscious municipalities.

Principal Subsidiaries

ALS of North Carolina, Inc.; American Lighting & Signalization, Inc.; Arborchem Products Co.; Asplundh Brush Control Co.; Asplundh Buick/Pontiac-GMC Inc.; Asplundh Construction Company; Asplundh Environmental Services, Inc.; Blume Tree Services, Inc.; Central Locating Service Limited; Compass Equipment Leasing Inc.; Farrens Tree Surgeons, Inc.; Utility Line Construction Service, Inc.; Utility Meter Services, Inc.; Utility Pole Technologies, Inc.; Utility Tree Service, Inc.; Asplundh Tree Expert (Australia) Pty. Ltd.; Asplundh Canada Inc.; Asplundh Tree Expert (N.Z.) Limited (New Zealand).

Principal Competitors

The Davey Tree Expert Company; Wright Tree Service Inc.

Further Reading

The Asplundh TREE, 75th Anniversary Edition, Willow Grove, Pa.: Asplundh Tree Expert Co., 2003.

Chung, Sharon, "Pa.-Based Firm Has Climbed to Industry Top," *York (Pa.) Daily Record* (from Associated Press), June 27, 1994.

Lane, Randall, "Let Asplundh Do It," *Forbes,* October 16, 1995, p. 56.

"Whacking Weeds with Water," *Railway Age,* July 1994, p. 57.

—Ellen D. Wernick
—update: David E. Salamie

August Schell Brewing Company Inc.

1860 Schell Road
New Ulm, Minnesota 56073
U.S.A.
Telephone: (507) 354-5528
Toll Free: (800) 770-5020
Fax: (507) 359-9119
Web site: http://www.schellsbrewery.com

Private Company
Incorporated: 1902
Employees: 42
Sales: $15.9 million (2001)
NAIC: 312120 Breweries; 311930 Beer and Root Beer

August Schell Brewing Company Inc. is the nation's second oldest family-owned brewery. Located in New Ulm, Minnesota, the brewery is operated by the fifth generation of family members since August Schell founded the company in 1860. The company is well known throughout the Midwest as a regional ''craft brewery'' with a combination of beers, lagers, and ales, including specialty and seasonal beers. Schell's beverages are available through distributors in Minnesota, Illinois, Iowa, North Dakota, Pennsylvania, South Dakota, and Wisconsin. The company brews 38 different beers; about 16 of those are varieties of contracted brews distributed under different names. Schell brews approximately 110,000 barrels of beer each year. In 2002 Schell became the state's largest and oldest brewer following the demise of the 150-year-old Minnesota Brewing Company.

Schell Brewing has thrived over the decades by adapting to the changing market, anticipating future trends, and building on its regional popularity. Like most breweries, Schell offers visitors' tours, but Schell's facilities have the added allure of being surrounded by beautiful gardens and grounds along the Cottonwood River. The family incorporates its rich German heritage into the brewery business as well as into the aesthetics of the surrounding property, earning the brewery and its grounds a spot on the National Register of Historic Sites. The brewery hosts thousands of visitors each year who come for tours, beer tasting, and special events such as the annual Bock Fest in

March. The company's events and marketing efforts have helped create a strong local and regional brand loyalty to Schell's products.

Putting Down Roots to Brew a ''Good German Beer'' in the Mid-19th Century

It all began when August Schell, born in Durbach, Germany, left his homeland at age 20 to search for new opportunities in the United States. After living in New Orleans and Cincinnati, August settled in Minnesota in 1856 with his wife, Theresa, and their two daughters. August and Theresa helped found the town of New Ulm with a small group of German friends and acquaintances from Cincinnati.

After a few years working as a machinist in a flour mill, August Schell's desire for a good German beer led him to open a small brewing company just outside of town. His partner was Jacob Bernhardt, who had experience working as a brewmaster in a St. Paul, Minnesota, brewery. Their small brewery along the banks of the Cottonwood River produced 200 barrels of beer that first year. (One barrel is equal to 31.5 gallons or 13.75 cases of 24 12-ounce cans or bottles of beer.) The partners chose to build the brewery near an artesian spring, which provided clean, pure water for the brewing process. The nearby river also enabled the small brewery to easily transport beer and supplies, as well as provide access—at least in wintertime—to ice for refrigeration.

In the early days, the brewery location was in the heart of Dakota Indian territory. When the Sioux Uprising (also referred to as the Dakota Conflict) threatened the region in 1862, the brewery, like everything else, was a vulnerable target for the Native Americans' wrath. Fortunately, Theresa Schell had established herself as a friend to the local Dakota people, and they repaid her kindness by keeping damage well away from the brewery.

In 1866 Bernhardt became ill and decided to sell out his portion of the business. Schell became sole owner of the company for a price of $12,000. Throughout the next several years, the business blossomed under Schell's management. He built several additions to the original brewery facility.

Company Perspectives:

At Schell's, we believe that not all beer is created equal. And passionately so. Any beer with true substance must start with the very finest malts and hops. No exceptions. Both ingredients greatly affect the taste, aroma and color of the beer, and are carefully selected to match the style that's being brewed. From our legendary Pilsner to our award-winning Schell's FireBrick lager to our seasonal favorites, you can rest assured that what only takes you minutes to finish, took weeks to create and over 140 years to perfect.

Second Generation Taking Over in the Late 1800s

In 1878 August Schell turned over daily operations to his sons Adolph and Otto, but remained as chief executive of the company. Adolph managed the business, and Otto, who had spent time studying brewing in Germany, became brewmaster. Later, after Adolph moved out of state, Otto and his brother-in-law George Marti partnered to operate the brewery. Back in those days the beer was delivered to bars by horse-drawn wagon in oak barrels. When trucks were used in later years, Schell even delivered to people's homes.

In 1885, August and Theresa Schell built the Schell mansion and had the brewery property beautifully landscaped with gardens and a deer park. The picturesque landscaping still encompasses the brewery complex today, more than 100 years later. Their attention to detail earned the mansion and grounds a spot on the National Register of Historic Sites.

Sometime before he died, August Schell commissioned a Copper brew kettle for the brewery, which held 3,520 gallons of beer. It cost $25,000. At the time copper was the best metal to use in the brewing process. It helped brewers avoid problems due to the acidic content of wort and beer.

August Schell died in 1891, leaving the brewery to his wife. His youngest son Otto was the manager. The family incorporated August Schell Brewing Company in 1902, with Otto serving as president, Theresa as vice-president, and George Marti as secretary-treasurer. In 1911, Otto died suddenly. Theresa died just four months later, leaving George Marti to run the brewery.

From Prohibition to Expansion of the Product: 1920s–80s

The brewery continued to flourish under George Marti's leadership until Prohibition was signed into law in 1919. Prohibition laws banned the manufacture, sale, and transportation of alcoholic beverages in the United States. Wisely, Marti responded by shifting the brewery's production to ''near beer,'' soft drinks, and candy. When Prohibition laws were finally repealed in 1933, Schell's brewery easily made the transition back to brewing malt beverages. The brewery was fortunate; during that time period, approximately 1,300 breweries in the country went out of business.

The next generation, represented by Alfred Marti, took over brewery management in 1934 after George Marti passed away.

The younger Marti added entertainment to the brewery's local allure by establishing the Schell's Hobo Band, which still performs in the community today. In 1969, Alfred Marti retired, passing on leadership to his son Warren.

Warren Marti expanded the product line, adding new types of beer such as Schell's Export and Schell's Light. He also collaborated with Arneson Distributing in nearby Sleepy Eye, Minnesota, to make 1919 Root Beer, which the brewery still produces.

Beer cans also were introduced during Warren Marti's tenure as head of the business. The company made its products more attractive to consumers and collectors by putting scenic designs on Schell's beer cans. When Marti retired in 1985 the company was flourishing despite the growth of large breweries throughout the country, which were dominating the industry and squeezing market share from small regional breweries.

August Schell's great-great-grandson Ted Marti took hold of the brewery reins in 1985. In addition to the education Marti received growing up around the brewery, he studied at Siebel's Institute of Brewing in Chicago and at several breweries in Germany. Marti's entrepreneurial spirit led the brewery to begin brewing specialty beers—including malts, pilsners, pale ales, and weizens, some of which won national awards in the beer industry. At the 1988 Great American Beer Festival, Schell's Pilsner earned a gold medal in the domestic premium category and Hefeweizen earned a gold medal in the wheat beer category. Pilsner also won first place in 1991 at the Great International Beer Tasting Festival. Schell's Octoberfest and Hefeweizen were awarded silver medals at the 1991 and 1993 Great American Beer Festivals. Schell's Bock earned regional exposure as the Best Dark Super Premium Lager in a *Twin Cities Reader* magazine poll in 1991.

By 1989 Schell was producing eight varieties of beer, from hometown favorite Deer Brand to Weiss Beer. Schell's premium beers including Pilsner and Weiss were well known and well regarded nationally. Schell also began brewing contract beers for a St. Louis-based microbrewery. Among other varieties, Schell brewed their Shlafly's Pale Ale and Oatmeal Stout.

Joining the Specialty Craft Beer Market in the 1990s

Under Ted Marti's leadership, the brewery expanded its offerings and began to focus more on specialty beers, positioning beers such as Firebrick Lager against Killian's Red and Leinie's Red. Innovative executive Marti led the pack of American brewers by bringing bocks and pilsners to the United States before most of the competition. Despite Marti's strong leadership, in 1998 Schell brewed barely more than 40,000 barrels of beer, just two-thirds of its potential capacity. About half of that was contract beers for outside companies, a shrinking piece of the brewery market.

Schell gained regional exposure and added to its historical image in 1998, when the Twin Cities airport opened a theme bar that looked like a brew pub, highlighting Schell's brewery history and several of Schell's beers. Schell marketers encouraged its customers to become beer connoisseurs by distributing recipes that included Schell beverages as ingredients in addition to providing suggestions about which Schell beers were best to accompany a particular dinner menu. Recipe order forms were distributed in six-packs of Schell's beer. Clever packaging also added to Schell's appeal with consumers and helped distinguish its products. For example, Schell marketed Spanish Peaks Black Dog Sweetwater with a label that featured a black paw print and the phrase ''no whiners.''

Demise of Regional Breweries in the Late 20th Century

The last half of the 1990s proved to be a difficult time for small and regional breweries. Beer consumption nationwide had leveled off, prompting the big brewers to lower prices. The mega-breweries dominated the market, with price wars between Miller and Anheuser-Busch luring market share from the smaller players. Together the two brewing giants secured 75 percent of annual beer sales in 1998.

Minnesota saw the closure of Stroh Brewing's East St. Paul plant in 1997, and nearby G. Heileman Brewing Company in La Crosse, Wisconsin, in 1999. At the same time, the state's largest brewery, Minnesota Brewing, was struggling and dealing with a labor strike. While large national brewers across the country closed inefficient plants, small player August Schell Brewing hung on. Schell had experienced modest gains in sales of its proprietary brands, an increase of 5 percent over 1997, which surpassed the 4.1 percent growth in the rest of the industry during the same period.

Ted Marti knew Schell could not compete with the huge advertising budgets of the nation's top breweries. Marti instead expanded the brewery's emphasis to specialty brews. The popularity of Schell craft beers grew in part due to local consumers'

pride. Schell began to gain an image as a specialty craft beer maker. That image, founded in a quality product, combined with clever packaging and an image campaign, helped boost sales 20 percent. Schell competed where it mattered and where the brewery excelled—in taste, rather than pricing.

In 1999 Schell took what some in the industry viewed as a risk by building a new state-of-the art brewery and retiring the old copper brew kettle system. The company made a $600,000 investment in a new, more reliable and efficient brewhouse at a time when the sales outlook was uncertain. The result was four new stainless steel brewing kettles—the mash tun, lauter tun, brew kettle, and the whirlpool—one for each step in the brewing process, and subsequent improved brewing quality. The new brewhouse was built alongside the old one, and it boasted a capacity of 560 barrels a day. At the time Schell brewed 14 of its own beers (four premium and ten specialty) and 50 beers under other brands.

2000 and Beyond

In 2002 Schell purchased the Grain Belt product line, a 109-year-old Minnesota beer tradition. Schell rescued the piece of Minnesota history from disappearing off the shelves for good. Minnesota Brewing closed in June of that year after filing for Chapter 7 bankruptcy. It had been the state's largest volume brewer prior to its closing. Adding the Grain Belt line made Schell the state's top producing brewery, with annual gallonage expected to reach 110,000, up from Schell's 70,000 the previous year.

The acquisition of a beer with such a strong history fit well with Schell's own emphasis on history and heritage. In addition, Grain Belt connoisseurs were thrilled that a Minnesota brewer would take over their product. Fortunately, there was not a lot of market overlap between the two brands. Initially, Schell brewed Grain Belt Premium, the top-selling Minnesota-brewed beer in the state. Schell planned to begin eventually brewing Grain Belt Light and Golden.

The brewery gained national recognition again in 2002 when its new Firebrick Lager, ''an all-malt Vienna style lager made from roasted malt and imported hops,'' earned a bronze medal at the 21st Annual Great American Beer Festival in Denver. Firebrick was awarded the third place medal in the American Amber Lager category. More than 1,400 breweries in the country competed in the annual contest.

By the end of 2002, Grain Belt Premium had become Schell's best-selling beer. Schell also produced and distributed the packaged beers for James Page brewery, and by January 2003 Schell produced the entire James Page brand for the small, struggling Minnesota brewery.

Schell was expected to brew about 110,000 barrels in 2003, its largest volume ever. With the addition of the Grain Belt line, Schell's market share could approach its closest competitors in the state—Leinenkugel, with a 2 percent share of the Minnesota market, and Coors, with about a 4 percent share.

Under Ted Marti's leadership, August Schell Brewing Company had in a sense reinvented itself by branching out into upscale specialty brews. It also had earned a national reputation for some of its premium beers, with Pilsners and Weiss beers distributed nationwide. But its primary market continued to be regional—85 percent of Schell's beer is sold to Minnesota consumers. Throughout southern Minnesota and parts of Iowa, Schell competed well with the big players in the industry.

But in the Twin Cities of Minneapolis and St. Paul the company excelled in the specialty beer market. At the beginning of the 21st century its products included Schell original, light, dark, Pilsner, Bock, Firebrick Lager, German Pale Ale, Schmalt's Alt, Doppel Bock, Miafest, Zommerfest, Hefeweizen, Octoberfest, and Snowstorm Beer. Snowstorm is a special brew of Ted Marti's available only during November and December and reinvented each year. As the company web site explains, "legendary Snowstorms of the past have included a cherry-vanilla porter, a mead/ale, a raspberry-chocolate brew and a Scottish ale,"—no doubt, evidence of Marti's creativity.

Although growth had been phenomenal in its 142-year history, the brewery business remained in the family of August Schell's descendants. Family members comprised the board of directors and stockholders. The company had built and fostered a strong regional loyalty by maintaining a small-town, quality image. Keeping that heritage alive helped to ensure the "old world" quality often lacking in the efficiency-driven 21st century.

Principal Competitors

Jacob Leinenkugel Brewing Company; Adolph Coors Company; Pabst Brewing Company; Miller Brewing Company; Anheuser-Busch Companies, Inc.

Further Reading

"August Tradition Expands," *Beverage World*, July 15, 1999, p. 34.

Egerstrom, Lee, "James Page Brewery Closes," *St. Paul Pioneer Press,* January 3, 2003, p. 1C.
——, "Regional Brewers Buck the Trend," *St. Paul Pioneer Press,* February 22, 1998, p. 1D.
——, "Schell Brews Up Cooking, Dining Guide for Beers," *St. Paul Pioneer Press,* August 9, 1994, p. 2E.
Feyder, Susan, "Can the Man Behind 'The Claw' Help August Schell Brewing Company Sell Grain Belt Premium Beer?," *Minneapolis Star Tribune,* March 25, 2003, p. 1D.
——, "Schell's Game; New Ulm's August Schell Brewing Co. Has Added Minnesota's Venerable Grain Belt to Its Stable of Beers," *Minneapolis Star Tribune,* January 15, 2003, p. 1D.
Flannery, William, "Local Microbrews Headed for Stores," *St. Louis Post Dispatch,* June 28, 1996, p. 1C.
Franklin, Jennifer, "Schell Drafts Compass to Build Branding," *City Business,* November 5, 1999.
Kennedy, Tony, "Brewing: Stroh Shows Industry Gone Flat," *Minneapolis Star Tribune,* November 18, 1997.
——, "Good Things Brewing at August Schell," *Minneapolis Star Tribune,* April 30, 1999, p. 1D.
——, "Revenge Is a Beer That's Best Served Cold," *Minneapolis Star Tribune,* February 20, 1998, p. 1D.
——, "Schell Wins Auction for Grain Belt Brand Name, New Ulm Brewery Upholds Tradition," *Minneapolis Star Tribune,* July 23, 2002, p. 1D.
Lileks, James, "Let's Go to the Hops; As Breweries Continue to Sell Out and Consolidate, We Lose Some of Our Regional Flavor," *St. Paul Pioneer Press,* September 29, 1989, p. 1C.
"Long Time Brewing: Ted Marti Is the Fifth Generation to Run the Family-Owned-and-Operated Brewery Founded by His Great-Great Grandfather August Schell in 1860," *St. Paul Pioneer Press,* September 26, 1999, p. 2B.
"Spanish Peaks Ale—Black Dog Sweetwater Wheat," *Product Alert,* April 3, 1995.
Welbes, John, "Buying a Brand," *St. Paul Pioneer Press,* July 23, 2002, p. 1C.

—Mary Heer-Forsberg

The Bank of Nova Scotia

Scotia Plaza
44 King Street West
Toronto, Ontario M5H 1H1
Canada
Telephone: (416) 866-6161
Fax: (416) 866-3750
Web site: http://www.scotiabank.com

Public Company
Incorporated: 1832
Employees: 43,869
Total Assets: C$282.16 billion (US$200.48 billion)
   (2003)
Stock Exchanges: Toronto New York London
Ticker Symbol: BNS
NAIC: 551111 Offices of Bank Holding Companies;
   522110 Commercial Banking; 522210 Credit Card
   Issuing; 523110 Investment Banking and Securities
   Dealing; 523120 Securities Brokerage; 523920
   Portfolio Management; 523930 Investment Advice;
   523991 Trust, Fiduciary, and Custody Activities;
   525910 Open-End Investment Funds

The Bank of Nova Scotia, the second oldest bank in Canada, was the second largest Canadian bank in 2003 in term of assets (trailing only Royal Bank of Canada). Scotiabank, as it is usually called, conducts its activities through four major divisions: domestic banking, wealth management, Scotia Capital, and international. The domestic banking unit provides a full range of banking services to individuals, small businesses, and commercial accounts; its more than six million customers are served through a network of nearly 1,000 domestic offices and close to 2,200 automatic bank machines (ABMs), in addition to telephone banking, wireless services, and the Scotia OnLine Internet banking service. The wealth management unit, which encompasses Scotiabank's retail brokerage, mutual funds, and private clients services, has nearly three-quarters of a million clients and in excess of $82 billion in assets under management. Active in Canada, the United States, and Europe, Scotia Capital

provides the bank's corporate, institutional, and government clients with corporate and investment banking services. The Bank of Nova Scotia is considered to be the most international of the "Big Five" Canadian banks. Its international banking operations range across more than 40 countries and include more than 720 branches and offices and more than 1,500 ABMs. Scotiabank ranks as the Caribbean's leading provider of financial services, has the largest presence in Asia of any Canadian bank, and maintains major holdings in Latin America, including majority ownership of Grupo Financiero Scotiabank Inverlat, S.A. de C.V. in Mexico and subsidiary operations in Chile, Costa Rica, and El Salvador.

Early Decades of Tentative Growth

The first public financial institution in the colonial port city of Halifax, the Bank of Nova Scotia was formed on March 30, 1832, to handle the economic activity associated with the area's lumber, fishing, farming, and foreign trade. None of the members of the first board of directors had any practical banking experience, but this did not deter them from setting up the necessary operations and appointing James Forman, a prominent citizen of Halifax, to serve as the first cashier (as the general manager was then called).

The bank officially opened in August 1832, a time of unfavorable economic conditions because of massive crop failures and a cholera outbreak. Early development, therefore, focused on establishing a foreign exchange business with agents in New York, London, and Boston, while local agencies and the main office in Halifax concentrated on making domestic loans.

Over the next 30 years, the bank grew slowly in the face of increased competition from existing institutions, such as the Halifax Banking Company and the Bank of British North America, as well as from new banks opening throughout Nova Scotia. It was not until the early 1870s that the staff also determined that growth had been stunted by Mr. Forman's embezzlement of C$315,000 since 1844.

The bank gradually recovered from these losses through the efforts of Forman's successor, William C. Menzies, who guided an expansion program that increased total assets to C$3.5 million by 1875. Though local industry was declining, growth continued throughout the decade as the bank found opportunities in financing coal mining, iron, and steel businesses serving the railway and steamship lines. These improvements in transportation stimulated manufacturing throughout Canada, which also served to fuel the bank's development.

The Bank of Nova Scotia expanded outside the Maritime Provinces in 1882, when it opened a branch in Winnipeg to take advantage of opportunities created by a real estate boom in the area. The boom collapsed within six months, however, saddling the bank with enormous losses and forcing the branch to close three years later.

In 1883, the Bank of Nova Scotia acquired the Union Bank of Prince Edward Island. This bank had sought a larger, stronger institution to help it weather hard times that had already forced the liquidation of one local bank and were seriously affecting others in the area. By the end of that year, the Bank of Nova Scotia was operating 23 branches in Prince Edward Island, New Brunswick, and Nova Scotia.

Although a depression in Canada in the early 1880s caused heavy losses stemming from the failure of several businesses, the bank had rebounded enough by 1885 to consider further expansion, this time in the United States. Minneapolis was chosen, because of its strong grain and manufacturing industries, to be the initial site for a direct lending and foreign exchange business. This office closed seven years later when the local environment became less favorable and other cities, such as Chicago, showed more potential.

In 1888 the bank opened an office in Montreal in a second attempt to establish a domestic presence outside of the Maritime Provinces. This office was followed a year later by an office in Kingston, Jamaica, the first time a Canadian bank had expanded outside North America or the United Kingdom. The next new branch opened in St. John's, Newfoundland, in 1894 to handle the business of two local institutions that had dissolved suddenly; this was the first move by a Canadian bank into Newfoundland, which would not become a province for another 55 years. Credit for this vigorous expansion goes to Thomas Fyshe, who became cashier in 1876 and resigned in 1897 after 21 years with the bank.

Accelerating Expansion, Early 20th Century

In March 1900 the bank moved its headquarters to Toronto, to be better able to take advantage of opportunities offered by the Klondike Gold Rush and the completion of the Canadian Pacific Railway, as well as to be closer to its other branches in Canada and the United States. Its move into Western Canada

was only somewhat successful, however; several unprofitable branches closed soon after they opened, while others in Edmonton, Calgary, and Vancouver were slow to make a profit. Nonetheless, the bank considered expansion a necessary part of its overall strategic plan to achieve national growth and avoid takeover by another institution. Development in the East was more successful; 19 new branches opened in Nova Scotia and New Brunswick, 16 opened in Ontario, and four opened in Quebec between 1897 and 1909.

Beginning in 1901, Henry C. McLeod, who served as general manager from 1897 to 1910, waged a campaign to require all Canadian banks to undergo external inspection by the Canadian Department of Finance. This effort, prompted by the large number of bank failures that had occurred since 1895, was intended to win the public's confidence in its financial institutions. None of the other Canadian banks supported him, so, impatient with the government's inactivity on the issue, McLeod subjected the Bank of Nova Scotia to examination by two Scottish accountants, making his the first Canadian chartered bank to be verified by an independent, external audit. McLeod did not win his battle until 1913, when the Bank Act was revised and such inspection became compulsory.

Between 1910 and 1920 the bank embarked upon a series of major acquisitions that significantly altered its size and the scope of its operations. After two years of informal discussions, the bank officially merged with the oldest Canadian chartered bank, the Bank of New Brunswick, on December 11, 1912. Established in 1820, the Bank of New Brunswick was a relatively small institution, confined to 31 branches in a single region and lacking the resources to expand because of its traditional practice of returning capital to shareholders. In 1914, with the acquisition of the 12-year-old Toronto-based Metropolitan Bank, the Bank of Nova Scotia became the fourth largest financial institution in Canada. Five years later, the Bank of Nova Scotia acquired the Bank of Ottawa, allowing it to expand westward again without having to establish new branches.

Joining other Canadian financial institutions in the war effort during World War I, Scotiabank experienced only minor disruptions in operations and staffing and returned to normal upon the war's end.

Consolidation and a Growing Asset Base, 1920s to Early 1990s

During the early 1920s, the bank slowed the pace of external growth to focus its attention on consolidating the operations of its three prewar acquisitions and reorganizing its departments for greater efficiency. An Investment Department was formed to handle securities transactions, which represented a significant amount of the bank's business in Toronto, Montreal, and New York.

The strong postwar recovery brought healthy earnings throughout most of the decade, until the 1929 stock market crash and subsequent depression. Between 1933 and 1935, the bank closed 19 domestic branches as profits dropped by half a million dollars, to C$1.8 million. Business conditions in Newfoundland deteriorated, the Social Credit Party rose to power in Alberta and enacted troublesome legislation there, and political difficulties in Cuba and Puerto Rico pressured international activities.

Key Dates:

1832: The Bank of Nova Scotia (or Scotiabank) is born; it is the first public financial institution in Halifax.

1883: The Union Bank of Prince Edward Island is acquired.

1889: Scotiabank makes its first move into the Caribbean, opening a branch in Kingston, Jamaica.

1900: Headquarters are moved to Toronto.

1912: Bank of Nova Scotia merges with the Bank of New Brunswick, the oldest Canadian chartered bank.

1914: Toronto-based Metropolitan Bank is acquired, making Scotiabank the fourth largest financial institution in Canada.

1919: The Bank of Ottawa is acquired.

1954: Passage of the National Housing Act leads Scotiabank to create a mortgage department.

1958: Changes to Bank Act of 1954 enable Scotiabank to introduce a consumer credit program.

1981: Bank of Nova Scotia expands into Asia with the opening of a branch in Japan.

1987: Scotia Securities is formed to provide discount brokerage and security underwriting services.

1988: Brokerage firm McLeod Young Weir Ltd. is acquired.

1994: Scotiabank acquires Montreal Trustco Inc.

1997: National Trustco Inc. is acquired for C$1.25 billion.

2000: Scotiabank increases to 55 percent its stake in Mexican bank Grupo Financiero Inverlat, which is subsequently renamed Grupo Financiero Scotiabank Inverlat.

2002: Economic turmoil in Argentina leads to the bank's sale of its subsidiary there and a C$540 million writedown on its investment.

2003: Stake in Scotiabank Inverlat is increased to 91 percent.

Economic recovery went up and down between 1936 and 1939 as the positive effects of the growing Canadian mining industry were offset by a drought in the West. The bank's asset base continued to grow, but not without some managerial concern—it consisted largely of loans to the government for relief funds, rather than higher-yielding commercial transactions.

World War II increased the demand for banking services, particularly by the government for financing the war. By the end of the war the bank's assets had surpassed C$600 million, but federal government securities represented 50 percent of the total.

Offering New Services and Financial Products in the Prosperous Postwar Period

In 1945 the new general manager, Horace L. Enman, renewed prewar efforts to explore new business opportunities and improve shareholders' returns. Buoyed by heavy immigration to Canada and the nation's need for capital, the bank's commercial loan activity increased after the war to restore a more favorable balance between lending to business concerns and to the government. In 1949 Enman became president and C. Sydney Frost became general manager. By this time the bank's

rapid growth and extensive reach demanded greater decentralization. Regional offices gradually assumed responsibility for staffing and maintaining branch activities and credit supervision. By 1950 the bank had opened 90 new branches, half in British Columbia and Alberta.

The 1950s were a period of economic prosperity throughout Canada. Resource development and improvements in transportation increased immigration levels in major Canadian cities and provided a stimulus to growth. The change from a fixed to a floating official exchange rate allowed the bank to take advantage of the open market for the Canadian dollar and enhance its exchange-trading skills. When the National Housing Act was passed in 1954, the bank established a mortgage department, and it later developed a secondary mortgage market among pension funds to offset decreased lending activity. The bank also introduced an insured savings plan that brought in a substantial amount of new business, and more importantly, gave the bank a competitive advantage in selling banking services.

A change in the Bank Act in 1954 permitted banks to make automobile and household loans, prompting the bank to introduce a consumer credit program in 1958. In order for the bank to observe the 6 percent interest rate ceiling mandated by the Bank Act yet successfully operate in the consumer lending area on a large-scale basis, these loans required customers to deposit payments every month into a bank account that would pay off the loan by the due date and return a higher rate of interest to the bank over the life of the loan. By its second year, this plan had generated C$100 million in loans and become a major contributor to the bank's overall earnings. When, in 1959, a money squeeze threatened its lending activity volume, the bank introduced a one-to-six-year term note that allowed it to compete successfully with finance and trust companies.

The bank continued its international expansion during this period, particularly in Jamaica, Trinidad, and Barbados, although the nationalization of Cuban banks in 1961 forced it, regretfully, to close the eight branches it had established there at the beginning of the century.

In 1958 the bank joined with British financial interests to form the Bank of Nova Scotia Trust Company to engage in offshore and trust operations which were off-limits to foreign banks. A year later, the Bank of Nova Scotia Trust Company of New York was established.

Beginning in 1960, the bank aggressively pursued a strategy to increase its volume of deposits by resuming the establishment of new branches in Canada as well as abroad. This inflow of funds was required to support the bank's consumer credit operations while also meeting the demand for mortgages and short-term commercial loans. More than 60 percent of these new branches were in convenient suburban locations to attract new customers in and around Toronto, Montreal, Edmonton, and Calgary. Coupled with new products such as term notes, certificates of deposit, and six-year certificates, this campaign increased the volume of personal savings deposits by 50 percent between 1960 and 1965.

This increased activity also enabled the bank to maintain its presence in the financial services industry despite the ceiling on lending rates, which had virtually eliminated the bank from competing effectively against trust and finance companies in all areas except for personal loans. During this time, the bank also increased its mortgage involvement by joining with two other partners to form three new ventures: Markborough Properties, a real estate company; the Mortgage Insurance Company of Canada; and Central Covenants, a mortgage financing company.

In 1963 the bank underwent a major internal reorganization, and a new profit planning system was introduced that required each branch and region to submit annual loan and deposit forecasts to be incorporated into the bank's overall plan. This system allowed the bank to further decentralize operations, to encourage competition among branches, and to better identify the services its customers wanted.

Meanwhile, business in the Caribbean continued to grow, despite losses in Cuba. Much of this growth was hotel and resort financing in areas such as Jamaica and Puerto Rico, where tourism was becoming big business. The bank also opened branches in London, Glasgow, Amsterdam, Munich, Beirut, and Tokyo. Its international division became a major player in the Eurodollar market at this time.

During the early 1960s, the bank also worked to establish a stronger presence in the United States, particularly in Los Angeles and Houston, by offering financing and deposit opportunities for U.S. corporations in addition to international tax services. These efforts fueled the bank's accelerated growth in the second half of the decade.

Focusing on Existing Operations in the 1970s

At home, the early 1970s saw strong personal and small business lending activity, leading the bank to launch a number of new services, including automobile financing and a farm program to meet credit needs in the agricultural sector. Lending activity shifted significantly toward commercial concerns, particularly retail accounts, later that decade as inflation increased daily operational costs for Canadian businesses.

Actively involved in the precious metals market since 1958, the bank expanded this business throughout the 1970s by buying two-thirds of the country's annual production and then selling actual bullion and bullion certificates. It was also during this period that the rising expenses of branch development caused the bank to refocus its emphasis from opening new offices within Canada to improving existing operations and relocating branches to more lucrative areas.

In 1972, the bank was sued by VK Mason Construction Ltd. for negligent misrepresentation related to the building of an office and shopping complex. The contractor had required assurance from the bank that the developer, Courtot Investments, had sufficient financing to finish the construction before it would agree to take on the job, and Scotiabank had informed Mason that interim financing was available to Courtot if needed. When the project was completed, Mason was paid C$1 million less than had been agreed and found that, rather than helping the developer pay its creditors, the bank called in its own loan and sold the complex when Courtot defaulted.

The Supreme Court of Canada found against the bank, though it affirmed the bank's right of first claim on the devel-oper's assets as the mortgagee. Mason was permitted to collect damages by placing a lien on the bank's assets without having to compete with other Courtot creditors.

Organizational changes at the general office were made in the second half of the 1970s which created separate departments for each of the bank's three main customer categories: individual, commercial, and large corporate. In 1980 an operations department was formed to consolidate many of the branch, regional, and head office functions into one area, a move which signaled a shift away from decentralization toward more direct headquarters control.

Negative Publicity from Series of Cases: Early 1980s

The bank's total assets reached C$50 billion by the end of 1981, with international business growing twice as fast as domestic operations and at a higher rate than that of any other Canadian bank. This growth was attributed to many factors, including the bank's established European and American presence, its expansion into the Asia-Pacific region with the 1981 opening of branch in Japan, and the development of a worldwide foreign exchange and banking system that operated around the clock. The year also saw the historic opening of the first Canadian banking representative office in China.

Although a downturn in the economy during 1983 forced the bank to curtail expansion temporarily, its focus on smaller companies saved it from the large-scale losses other Canadian banks suffered from loans made to failing firms such as Dome Petroleum and Massey-Ferguson, and to Mexico, Brazil, and Poland.

This focus on smaller companies and individuals did create image problems in the corporate and commercial areas. To counter the perception that the bank was not fully committed to businesses, Scotiabank embarked upon an extensive, innovative advertising campaign in 1986 using customers' case histories and games of visual illusion to show the various ways that the bank had helped companies.

During the first half of the 1980s, the bank was accused of wrongdoing in a series of cases stemming from its activities both at home and abroad. In March 1983, the bank was asked by a Miami court to release records from its Cayman Islands branch concerning certain customers under investigation for narcotics and tax violations. Although the bank was protected under Cayman Island law from such releases, a Florida judge ruled that the bank stood in contempt of court and fined it US$25,000 a day, retroactive to November 1983, for each day it did not produce the records. In order to end a stalemate that could have forced the bank into bankruptcy, the Cayman Islands Governor-in-Council intervened to authorize the bank to supply the required information, but not before the fine had reached US$1.8 million. The bank lost its appeal to the U.S. Supreme Court in January 1985.

In 1984 the bank, along with four other Canadian banks, was the subject of a one-year investigation by the Royal Commission of the Bahamas into drug dealing and money laundering by Bahamian Prime Minister Pindling and his wife. Scotiabank had lent more than C$1 million to Pindling between 1977 and 1983 and had also accepted deposits from the couple totaling C$114,000 from an unidentified source. Although the investigation was inconclusive, it cast a cloud on a 1985 case alleging that the bank had committed fraud against the Investment Dealers Association of Canada in its involvement in the failure of Atlantic Securities Ltd. in 1981. Although this case generated much controversy, the Nova Scotia County Court acquitted the bank.

Continued Global Expansion in the Late 1980s and Early 1990s

In 1987 Scotiabank further penetrated the financial services market with the formation of Scotia Securities. That subsidiary, which provided discount brokerage and security underwriting services, allowed the bank to compete more effectively with investment banking firms. In addition to acquiring other banks during the late 1980s and early 1990s, the Bank of Nova Scotia pursued a strategy of global expansion to assure profitability regardless of any fluctuations in individual markets. It also worked to improve the quality of the loans in its portfolio and to increase the efficiency of its operations. Among the acquisitions during this period was the 1988 purchase for C$419 million of the brokerage firm McLeod Young Weir Ltd., which was later merged with Scotia Securities to form ScotiaMcLeod. Scotiabank also acquired a 40 percent stake in Solidbank Corp. in the Philippines in 1998 and a 24 percent stake in Banco Sud Americano, S.A., the sixth largest bank in Chile, in 1991. Also, in 1992, in the wake of the enactment of the North American Free Trade Agreement, Scotiabank became the first Canadian bank to move into Mexico, spending US$75 million for a 5 percent interest in Grupo Financiero Inverlat, S.A. de C.V. The Bank of Nova Scotia also opened its first bank branch in China, which it located in Guangzhou (formerly Canton).

The early 1990s also saw a gradual transition in the top leadership at the Bank of Nova Scotia. Cedric Ritchie, president and CEO since 1972 and chairman since 1974, handed over the presidency to Peter Godsoe, native of Halifax and career banker at Scotiabank, in 1992. Godsoe gained the CEO position the following year and became chairman at the beginning of 1995.

Scotiabank's efforts during the late 1980s and early 1990s were clearly paying off by the mid-1990s. Indeed, the bank's asset base ballooned from about C$94 billion in 1992 to nearly C$138 billion by early 1995—making it the third largest Canadian bank. About C$12 billion in assets were gained in one fell swoop in 1994 when Scotiabank acquired Montreal Trustco Inc. for about C$290 million. The purchase bolstered two areas of weakness for Scotiabank: its retail banking presence in Central Canada and its wealth management operations; also gained were Montreal Trustco's corporate trust services activities. The bank's sales also spiraled upward to about C$9.4 billion in 1994. Net income slipped in 1994 as a result of charges related to restructuring, but profitability had been improving steadily since the late 1980s.

By 1995, Scotiabank had more operations in Latin America and Asia than any other Canadian bank, and Scotiabank executives were working to set up new partnerships with banks in India, Malaysia, Brazil, Peru, and Venezuela. That year the bank purchased 25 percent of Argentina's Banco Quilmes S.A. and 80 percent of Corporacion Mercaban, among whose holdings was Banco Mercantil de Costa Rica, a commercial and consumer bank with a large business in auto loans. The Bank of

Nova Scotia was also branching out into new markets, such as insurance, opened up by Canadian deregulation of the banking industry. As a base for the move into insurance Scotiabank acquired two inactive insurance firms in the mid-1990s, Glacier National Life Assurance and property and casualty insurer Canada Security Assurance Co.

Late 1990s and Beyond

Following Mexico's peso crisis in 1994, that nation's banking industry collapsed under 100 percent interest rates and the inability of borrowers to repay their loans. Scotiabank's Mexican affiliate fell into bankruptcy and was put under the administration of the government, and Scotiabank took a C$145 million writedown on its investment in Grupo Financiero Inverlat in late 1995. The following year, however, the bank repurchased a 10 percent interest in Inverlat and also gained the right to increase its stake to 55 percent in 2000. Meantime, profits at the Bank of Nova Scotia surpassed the C$1 billion mark for the time in 1996.

Scotiabank stepped up its acquisition activity in 1997. It spent US$55 million for 35 percent of a small Indonesian bank, PT Bank Arya Panduarta, as well as C$260 million to acquire the 75 percent of Banco Quilmes, its Argentinean affiliate, it did not already own. The biggest deal that year, however, was Scotiabank's C$1.25 billion purchase of National Trustco Inc., the second largest independent trust company in Canada with 175 branches and C$14.6 billion in assets. The operations of the two companies meshed well, given that 80 percent of National Trustco's branches were in Ontario, a historically weak market for the Bank of Nova Scotia. In the integration process over the next three years, about 50 overlapping branches were closed and about 1,000 jobs were eliminated. This acquisition helped propel Scotiabank's asset base beyond the C$200 billion mark by 1998.

The Canadian banking industry appeared to be headed for the biggest shakeup in its history in 1998 when Royal Bank of Canada and Bank of Montreal agreed to a merger, as did the Toronto-Dominion Bank and Canadian Imperial Bank of Commerce—two mergers involving the four other members of Canada's "Big Five" banks, with Scotiabank the odd bank out. Godsoe lobbied intensely in opposition to the mergers, arguing that they would lead to job cuts numbering 20,000, massive branch closures, and other negative outcomes not in the public interest. In December 1998 Finance Minister Paul Martin scotched both of the deals, having concluded that the mergers would create two banks wielding too much power in the Canadian market, with competition in the industry being severely reduced.

Scotiabank also felt some of the aftershocks of the Asian economic crisis that erupted in 1997. The bank was forced in 1998 to write off its equity stake in its Indonesia affiliate, PT Bank Arya, and to set aside provisions of US$67 million for nonperforming loans in various emerging markets. On the positive side, however, the bank's stake in Banco Sud Americano was increased to 61 percent, and that Chilean bank was subsequently renamed Scotiabank Sud Americano, S.A. In 2000 the Bank of Nova Scotia sold its holding in Solidbank for C$140 million, a move that cleared the way for that bank to merge with a larger Philippine bank. It also exercised an option to increase its stake in Grupo Financiero Inverlat to 55 percent, with the purchase price being US$184 million; the Mexican bank was subsequently renamed Grupo Financiero Scotiabank Inverlat. At the same time, Scotiabank also cut back on its Canadian operations, selling 43 branches in Quebec to Laurentian Bank.

During 2002 the Bank of Nova Scotia acquired Charles Schwab Canada Co. from the Charles Schwab Corporation, the huge U.S. discount broker. The newly acquired Canadian operations were merged with Scotiabank's existing discount brokerage, which was rebranded ScotiaMcLeod Direct Investing. Now both the full-service and the discount brokerages of Scotiabank operated under the ScotiaMcLeod name. Also in 2002, Scotiabank bought a modest equity stake in Xi'an City Commercial Bank, which was based in the capital city of the Shaanxi province of northern China.

Another severe economic crisis, this time in Argentina, had a major impact on Scotiabank in 2002. In the political and economic chaos that followed Argentina's defaulting on its foreign debt in December 2001, the operations of Banco Scotiabank Quilmes were suspended by the local government because of liquidity problems, after Scotiabank refused to inject more capital into the troubled bank. In September 2002 Scotiabank sold the assets of its Argentinean bank to two small local banks, and it also took a C$540 million aftertax writedown on its investment there. One result was that net income fell to C$1.8 billion for the year, down 17 percent from the $2.17 billion figure recorded the year previous.

By 2002 Godsoe had changed his tune on mergers between the big Canadian banks. He now not only favored them but also attempted to quietly engineer one with the Bank of Montreal that summer. But this deal was squashed as well, with the veto this time reportedly coming directly from the office of Prime Minister Jean Chrétien. The federal government said that it would not consider approving any bank mergers before September 2004.

The following year was another year of executive transition at the bank. In January 2003 Richard E. Waugh was named president of Scotiabank, having joined the bank in 1970 and most recently served as vice-chairman, wealth management and international banking. In August 2003 the bank announced that Waugh would succeed Godsoe as CEO in December of that year, and that Godsoe would remain chairman until March 2004, when a nonexecutive chairman would replace him. Meanwhile, Scotiabank paid C$465 million to the Mexican government's bank bailout agency for an additional 36 percent of Scotiabank Inverlat, increasing its stake to 91 percent. It was expected to acquire the remaining 9 percent stake in relatively short order. In July 2003 Scotiabank announced that it would double its operations in the Dominican Republic by buying 40 branches and selected financial assets of the defunct Banco Intercontinental S.A.

The Bank of Nova Scotia was well-positioned in the early 2000s with a nice balance of operations: about half of earnings came from its domestic banking and wealth management units, one-quarter from international banking activities, and the other quarter from Scotia Capital, its investment and corporate banking unit. Scotiabank was likely to continue to seek opportunities for expansion outside of Canada, but it appeared that gaining a major presence in the U.S. retail banking sector had reached the top of the bank's agenda, ahead of further ventures into emerging markets. According to Godsoe, the bank could afford to spend as much as C$2 billion in cash on a U.S. acquisition. Whether the Bank of Nova Scotia would actually go ahead with a major U.S. purchase prior to September 2004, when the federal government's prohibition on bank mergers was slated to end, remained an open question.

Principal Subsidiaries

BNS Capital Trust; BNS Investments Inc.; The Bank of Nova Scotia Properties Inc.; e-Scotia Commerce Holdings Limited; Montreal Trust Company of Canada; MontroServices Corporation; Scotia Merchant Capital Corporation; The Mortgage Insurance Company of Canada; National Trustco Inc.; The Bank of Nova Scotia Trust Company; National Trust Company; RoyNat Inc.; Scotia Capital Inc.; Scotia Cassels Investment Counsel Limited; Scotia Life Insurance Company; Scotia Mortgage Corporation; Scotia Mortgage Investment Corporation; Scotia Securities Inc.; Scotiabank Capital Trust; The Bank of Nova Scotia Berhad (Malaysia); The Bank of Nova Scotia International Limited (Bahamas); BNS International (Barbados) Limited; BNS Pacific Limited (Mauritius); The Bank of Nova Scotia Asia Limited (Singapore); The Bank of Nova Scotia Channel Islands Limited; The Bank of Nova Scotia Trust Company (Bahamas) Limited; The Bank of Nova Scotia Trust Company (Cayman) Limited (Cayman Islands); Scotia Insurance (Barbados) Limited; Scotia Subsidiaries Limited (Bahamas); Scotiabank (Bahamas) Limited; Scotiabank (British Virgin Islands) Limited; Scotiabank (Cayman Islands) Ltd.; Scotiabank (Hong Kong) Limited; Scotiabank (Ireland) Limited; The Bank of Nova Scotia Jamaica Limited (70%); Grupo Financiero Scotiabank Inverlat, S.A. de C.V. (Mexico; 91%); Nova Scotia Inversiones Limitada (Chile); Scotiabank Sud Americano, S.A. (Chile; 98%); Scotia Capital (USA) Inc.; Scotia Holdings (US) Inc.; The Bank of Nova Scotia Trust Company of New York (U.S.A.); Scotia International Inc. (U.S.A.); Scotiabanc Inc. (U.S.A.); Scotia International Limited (Bahamas); Corporacion Mercaban de Costa Rica, S.A.; Scotia Mercantile Bank (Cayman Islands); Scotiabank Anguilla Limited; Scotiabank de Puerto Rico; Scotiabank El Salvador, S.A.; Scotiabank Europe plc (U.K.); Scotiabank Trinidad & Tobago Limited (47%); ScotiaMocatta Limited (U.K.).

Principal Operating Units

Domestic Banking; Wealth Management Group; International Banking; Scotia Capital.

Principal Competitors

Royal Bank of Canada; The Toronto-Dominion Bank; Canadian Imperial Bank of Commerce; Bank of Montreal.

Further Reading

Anderson, Mark, "The Lost Picture Show," *Canadian Business,* May 1, 1997, p. 93.

Blackwell, Richard, "Bank of Nova Scotia Looks to Branching Out," *Financial Post,* October 5, 1994, sec. 1, p. 8.

——, "Scotiabank Expects Big Fall in Loan Losses," *Financial Post,* January 18, 1995, sec. 1, p. 8.

Darroch, James L., *Canadian Banks and Global Competitiveness,* Montreal: McGill-Queen's University Press, 1994.

Haliechuk, Rick, "Scotiabank Profit Hits Record in 4th Quarter," *Toronto Star,* December 1, 1994, p. E2.

Kalawsky, Keith, "Bank Mergers No Longer a Hot Political Issue," *Financial Post,* March 25, 2003, p. FP1.

——, "Scotiabank Looks South for Future," *Financial Post,* March 26, 2003, p. FP1.

Kraus, James R., "Scotiabank Weathers Growing Pains Overseas," *American Banker,* July 28, 1999, p. 4.

Laver, Ross, "Banking in Bad Times," *Maclean's,* November 26, 1990, pp. 44+.

Partridge, John, "Scotiabank Bids for National Trustco," *Globe and Mail,* June 25, 1997, p. A1.

——, "Scotiabank Gets New Spin: CEO Provides 'Stark Contrast' to Former Management Style," *Globe and Mail,* June 21, 1993, p. B1.

——, "Scotiabank Takes Hit over Mexican Bank," *Globe and Mail,* November 30, 1995, p. B1.

——, "Scotiabank Vaults to No. 3: Montreal Trust Gives It Stronger Presence in Central Canada, Personal Finance," *Globe and Mail,* December 4, 1993, p. B17.

Partridge, John, Karen Howlett, and Sinclair Stewart, "Scotiabank Names President," *Globe and Mail,* January 16, 2003, p. B1.

Posner, Michael, "Titans at the Altar: Two Financial Giants Link Up with New Partners," *Maclean's,* July 7, 1997, pp. 50–51.

Schull, Joseph, and J. Douglas Gibson, *The Scotiabank Story: A History of the Bank of Nova Scotia, 1832–1982,* Toronto: Macmillan of Canada, 1982.

Stewart, Sinclair, "Scotiabank Chief to Step Down in 2003," *Globe and Mail,* December 4, 2002, p. B1.

Wood, Chris, "The Trials of a Banking Giant," *Maclean's,* November 18, 1985, pp. 34+.

—updates: Dave Mote, David E. Salamie

Blue Martini Software, Inc.

2600 Campus Drive
San Mateo, California 94403
U.S.A.
Telephone: (650) 356-4000
Toll Free: (800) 258-3627
Fax: (650) 356-4001
Web site: http://www.bluemartini.com

Public Company
Incorporated: 1998
Employees: 255
Sales: $33.6 million (2002)
Stock Exchanges: NASDAQ
Ticker Symbol: BLUE
NAIC: 511210 Software Publishers

Blue Martini Software, Inc.'s principal business is to provide software solutions that streamline and enhance the selling process for retailers and manufacturers. The company began in 1998 by offering solutions for electronic commerce, then expanding into customer relationship management (CRM). While the company's first retail customers utilized Blue Martini to run their online stores, they later came to adopt Blue Martini's in-store CRM solutions for their brick-and-mortar operations. Blue Martini first offered support for business-to-business transactions in 2000. Following the acquisition of Cybrant Corporation in the first half of 2002, Blue Martini began to offer more CRM software solutions for manufacturers as well as retailers.

Providing Software for Electronic Commerce: 1998–99

Blue Martini Software was launched in December 1998 by Monte Zweben. Zweben had founded Red Pepper Software Co. in 1992 and served as its president, CEO, and chairman until it was acquired by PeopleSoft, Inc. in December 1996. Following the acquisition Zweben was vice-president and general manager at PeopleSoft. Prior to founding Red Pepper Software, Zweben co-managed NASA's principal artificial intelligence laboratory.

Blue Martini began with a distinguished board of directors that included James C. Gaither, a senior partner in Cooley Godward LLP; Thomas M. Siebel, chairman and CEO of Siebel Systems, which he founded in 1993; Michael Spence, dean of the graduate school of business at Stanford University; and William F. Zuendt, retired president and chief operating officer of Wells Fargo & Company and its principal subsidiary, Wells Fargo Bank. In March 1999, Blue Martini raised $5 million in its first round of venture capital financing led by Matrix Partners.

When it was founded, Blue Martini's mission was to develop a complete software solution for companies selling directly to consumers over the Internet. The company released its E-Merchandising Suite 1.0 in March 1999, followed by version 2.0 later in the year. Levi Strauss & Co. became the company's flagship customer, choosing Blue Martini's E-Merchandising System for its global electronic commerce efforts. The software system integrated a scalable, high-availability commerce server with features for dynamic merchandising, targeted selling, and tailored customer service. It consisted of five modules: merchandise management, customer management, micro marketing, webstore operations, and tools. Pricing for the suite began at $500,000.

Version 2.0 was a major upgrade that offered enhanced capabilities in the same areas and added a sixth module for content management. With the content management module, clients could develop, manage, and deliver personalized images, text, HTML templates, and video content to shoppers. Version 2.0 also added new features such as click-stream analysis, a more detailed enterprise reporting system, expanded rules-based cross-selling and promotional capabilities, enhanced gift registries, and one-click buying.

Blue Martini continued to raise capital, receiving $12.5 million in September 1999 in its second round of venture capital financing led by U.S. Venture Partners. Proceeds were expected to be invested in sales and marketing. The company also announced a strategic alliance with Andersen Consulting to provide advanced business-to-consumer Internet selling and electronic merchandising solutions for manufacturers, retailers, media companies, and telecommunications firms. A partnership with JDA Software Group, Inc. leveraged the two companies'

Company Perspectives:

Blue Martini Software is the leading provider of intelligent selling systems. Innovative companies use our software to slash sales costs and improve customer and channel loyalty.

Blue Martini intelligent selling systems deliver the expertise of a company's best sales and marketing people through advisory applications for customers, sales people and partners. Our software uses unique "decide and act" capabilities to monitor key customer events and transactions, suggest optimal multi-channel responses, guide transactions, and measure the effectiveness of each action.

strengths to create an integrated solution that added JDA's merchandising, warehouse, and financial applications to Blue Martini's E-Merchandising System. In November Harley-Davidson, Inc. selected Blue Martini to support a new online, dealer-driver sales effort. The first phase of Harley-Davidson's program was an online catalog, with actual online sales occurring through a group of independent Harley-Davidson dealers.

At the end of 1999 Blue Martini introduced version 3.0 of its software suite, now called the Customer Interaction System. The new solution went beyond merchandising to deliver solutions for marketing and service related to Internet-based sales. Two new modules were added, a TeleConnect module for customer interaction through call centers, and the Customer Collaboration module, which allowed shoppers in different locations to visit online storefronts together and engage in an online dialog while shopping. Pricing for Version 3.0 began at $1 million.

Gained New Customers and Alliances As a Public Company: 2000–01

Blue Martini reported revenue of $11.2 million and a net loss of $10.9 million in 1999. In 2000 the company went public and enjoyed substantially higher revenue. Its first quarter revenue of $10.7 million nearly equaled the previous year's total. However, the company cautioned that it did not expect to be profitable for several years, due to high operating expenses. Blue Martini had about 35 customers when it filed its initial public offering (IPO) registration statement in May 2000. The IPO was held in July and raised $150 million, with 7.5 million shares sold at $20 each. On the first day of trading the stock opened at $40 a share and ended the day around $54.

During 2000 Blue Martini introduced new versions of its e-commerce software, expanded into Europe and Asia, and signed several high-profile customers, including Saks Fifth Avenue and the United States Olympic Committee, both of which utilized Blue Martini software to launch online storefronts. Early in the year the company introduced its E-Business Intelligence Service (E-BIS) to help clients build their brands, increase revenue, and retain customers using Blue Martini's tools and partner resources. The company also opened a training center in Redwood City, California, to train partners and customers in deploying and operating Blue Martini's Customer Interaction System. Version 3.1 of the CIS was introduced in May; it was an internationalized version that supported multi-

lingual, multi-currency web sites. The new version also included a module to support mobile wireless delivery of product and service information directly to customers and in-store sales staff. Other new features included new data visualization tools and an integration suite that linked web site operations with back office fulfillment using SAP, PeopleSoft, and other industry standards-based systems. Version 3.1 was priced at $1 million, plus consulting fees.

While previous versions of Blue Martini's Customer Interaction System focused on business-to-consumer (B2C) e-commerce, Version 4.0, introduced in October 2000, added support for business-to-business (B2B) transactions and processes. The new version incorporated software from Ariba, Inc., called "adapters," which enabled companies to distinguish themselves when participating in online marketplaces. When prospective buyers entered an online marketplace, they could click back to a seller's site, where product data aggregated by Blue Martini software would be available. The software also enabled sellers and buyers to fill purchase orders and agree on a price at the seller's site. From there, buyers returned to the marketplace to complete their purchase. Blue Martini expected the new application would help it enter new vertical markets and sell to more functional groups within targeted accounts, as well as offer more options to its existing customer base.

In the second half of 2000 Blue Martini formed strategic alliances with Hewlett-Packard Co. and Arthur Andersen to deliver customer interaction solutions to enterprise-level clients. Before the end of the year, Blue Martini shipped a version of its Customer Interaction System to run on Hewlett-Packard's HP-UX 11.0 platform for Unix. As part of the strategic agreement, HP's global sales force would offer this package as an integrated e-business solution to enterprise customers worldwide. The agreement with Arthur Andersen focused on business-to-business customers, with Arthur Andersen training its consultants on Blue Martini software and implementing it in their solution centers in the United States, Europe, and the Asia-Pacific region. Under another agreement signed toward the end of 2000, Blue Martini and Intel Corp. agreed to work together to optimize and market the Customer Interaction System for Intel-based platforms.

In an effort to build its brand among business-to-business and business-to-consumer executives, Blue Martini launched a print ad campaign in October 2000, which was estimated to cost between $5 million and $10 million and ran in a variety of business publications. The ads featured photographs of a blue martini and copy promoting the company's ability to deliver a highly personalized, branded experience. In November, *Computerworld* magazine included Blue Martini in its list of the top 100 Emerging Companies to Watch in 2001.

For 2000 Blue Martini reported revenue of $74.3 million and a pro forma net loss of $29 million. During the year the company's customer base grew to 87, including new customers in strategic vertical markets outside retail, such as those participating in online marketplaces, manufacturing, financial services, consumer packaged goods, technology, and service companies.

The year 2001 was more challenging for Blue Martini in the face of tough economic conditions. Revenue for the year de-

Key Dates:

1998: Blue Martini Software is founded by software industry veteran Monte Zweben.
1999: Levi Strauss & Co. is the first customer for Blue Martini's E-Merchandising System.
2000: Blue Martini has a successful initial public offering (IPO).
2001: Blue Martini introduces Blue Martini 4.0 and expands in Europe.
2002: Blue Martini introduces customer relationship management (CRM) software designed specifically for manufacturers and retailers.

creased to $57.5 million, while the company's pro forma net loss increased to $45.9 million. After widening losses in the first quarter and a decline in revenue in the second quarter, Blue Martini announced mid-year that it would move aggressively to cut costs, including a 25 percent workforce reduction and a corresponding consolidation in operations. Later in the year Michael J. Borman was hired as president and chief operating officer, reporting to Chairman and CEO Monte Zweben. Borman was formerly with IBM Corp., where he most recently served as vice-president for Unix sales worldwide. Also during the year Zweben was recognized by *Brandweek* magazine as one of the top ten "Marketers of the Next Generation."

Blue Martini's principal new product release in 2001 was Blue Martini 4. The tightly integrated software suite consisted of four new applications: Blue Martini Marketing, Blue Martini Commerce, Blue Martini Channels, and Blue Martini Service. The marketing application allowed companies to create a unified picture of their customers, analyze customer behavior, and implement those findings through outbound marketing and personalization. The commerce module was an e-commerce application for selling directly to businesses and consumers through multiple touch-points, including web sites and mobile devices. Channels was a complete channel management application that helped companies establish and manage their relationships with partners. It included the ability to drive sales through partner extranets, portals, and online marketplaces. The service module was a customer service application that supported customer service representative activities online and over the phone. Each of the four applications was available separately or as a suite, with pricing for each module starting at $250,000.

Internationally, Blue Martini entered into a strategic alliance with Netyear Group Corp. for the purpose of establishing a Japanese subsidiary. In Europe, Blue Martini announced it had offices in Paris, France; Munich, Germany; Maidenhead, England; Stockholm, Sweden; Milan, Italy; and Amsterdam, Netherlands. The company also offered training in London and Paris. In mid-2001 Blue Martini released localized versions of Blue Martini 4 in German, French, Spanish, and Japanese.

Toward the end of 2001 Blue Martini released the next generation of Blue Martini Integrated Analytics. The suite consisted of an analysis portal, discovery tools, online analytic processing, and an automatically generated data warehouse.

Shipped as part of Blue Martini's external customer relationship management (eCRM) application suite, the new software helped companies study and analyze customer behavior, marketing campaigns, promotions, and operations.

Another new release announced at the end of 2001 and shipped in 2002 was Blue Martini Manufacturing, an industry specific solution for manufacturers. The new solution combined Blue Martini's eCRM application suite with business processes specific to manufacturing, including catalog and content management, marketing, commerce, channel management, and service.

Expanding Customer Relationship Management (CRM) Software: 2002–03

Blue Martini's revenue continued to decline in 2002 in the face of a challenging environment for software sales. The company reported revenue of $33.6 million and a pro forma net loss of $30.2 million. During the year the company shipped Blue Martini Manufacturing and introduced Blue Martini 5, in addition to offering new applications for retailers. Early in the year at the National Retail Federation Show, the company demonstrated the use of its marketing and sales applications in physical stores through IBM point of sale (POS) devices. By integrating its software with POS devices, Blue Martini moved offline from its web-based applications to provide in-store customer information to sales associates, allowing them to personalize their service in real time. At the same show Blue Martini conducted a retail survey that showed a majority of retailers could not identify their most valuable customers.

In March 2002 Blue Martini released Blue Martini Retail, the first comprehensive customer relationship management (CRM) solution for retailers. Blue Martini Retail consisted of nine applications that worked in conjunction with its Customer Engine. The Customer Engine was the heart of the solution, collecting data from all channels, segmenting and scoring customers with integrated analytics, and presenting real-time, content-rich offers and information personalized for each shopper.

Also in March, Blue Martini released Blue Martini 5, an upgrade of its flagship suite of applications for personalized marketing, sales, and self-service across multiple channels. The suite consisted of four modules—marketing, commerce, channels, and service—underpinned by content management and integrated analytics. Each of the four modules was priced at $85,000. Later in the year, separate editions of Blue Martini 5 were released for IBM and for manufacturers.

In April 2002 Blue Martini acquired Cybrant Corporation, a company that provided interactive selling applications. Cybrant's applications were used to provide cost savings and streamline operations for companies that sold, priced, and quoted complex products, or who needed to help customers match their needs to the best available products and services. Blue Martini felt the acquisition of Cybrant's interactive selling applications helped them better serve selected vertical markets, including high-tech, electronic, medical instrument, automobile, and industrial manufacturing markets.

Another new release in 2002 was Blue Martini Relationship Marketing, an application that enabled marketers to centrally manage customer communications across all channels and points of contact. The stand-alone application was designed to work independently with any e-commerce, CRM, and enterprise resource planning (ERP) system via industry-standard protocols. Among the marketing initiatives the application could optimize were loyalty programs, gift registries, promotional campaigns, and the returns process.

In 2003 Blue Martini released Blue Martini Clienteling, an upgrade of its in-store point-of-sale customer information system for retailers launched the previous year. Blue Martini Clienteling enabled store associates to access relevant customer information, service-related messages, targeted promotions, event details, and other information through store-based kiosks, POS devices, personal computers, and wireless handheld devices.

Blue Martini's founder, CEO, and Chairman Monte Zweben was honored in 2003 by retail publication *Chain Store Age* and the manufacturing publication *MSI* magazine. *Chain Store Age* cited Zweben and Blue Martini for turning intelligent systems into proven, real-world business applications and helping retailers improve the consumer experience. *MSI* magazine noted that Blue Martini's interactive selling applications helped manufacturers sell more effectively.

With the overall economy and software spending improving during the year, Blue Martini was able to report that its revenue during the first three quarters of the year increased 110 percent over the same period in 2002. The company also reduced its net loss and cash burn rate. Looking ahead, the company remained focused on improving its execution and expanding its customer base as more companies adopted its intelligent selling systems.

Principal Competitors

Art Technology Group, Inc.; BroadVision, Inc.; E.piphany, Inc.; i2 Technologies, Inc.; International Business Machines Corporation; Microsoft Corporation; Oracle Corp.; PeopleSoft, Inc.; SAP AG; Siebel Systems, Inc.; Trilogy; Unica Corp.; Vignette Corp.

Further Reading

Arroyo, Arnaldo, "Networking Dot-Coms Gain Ground," *Equities,* October 2000, p. 44.

Bacheldor, Beth, "B-to-B Software Mixes Blue Martini and Ariba," *TechWeb,* September 14, 2000.

"Blue Martini Issues Q2 Warning," *San Francisco Business Times,* July 13, 2001, p. 62.

"Blue Martini Launches into B2B," *Online Reporter,* October 16, 2000.

"Blue Martini Losses Widen," *Online Reporter,* April 30, 2001.

"Blue Martini Moves CRM Offline," *eWeek,* March 4, 2002.

"Blue Martini Readies New CRM, Commerce Apps," *TechWeb,* February 10, 2001.

"Blue Martini Software," *IPO Reporter,* July 24, 2000.

"Blue Martini Toasts IPO," *San Francisco Business Times,* August 4, 2000, p. 10.

Callaghan, Dennis, and John S. McCright, "New Software to Support Marketers," *eWeek,* February 12, 2001, p. 38.

Colkin, Eileen, "Blue Martini's Revenue Drops, but Losses Are Lower," *InformationWeek,* October 29, 2001, p. 80.

Dignan, Larry, "The Week Ahead," *Inter@ctive Week,* July 24, 2000, p. 58.

Dyck, Timothy, "Blue Martini Is Site Lightning," *eWeek,* June 12, 2000, p. 79.

"E-Commerce, Portal Vendors Struggle," *eWeek,* October 25, 2002.

Elgin, Ben, "Will Blue Martini Stir the Market?," *Sm@rt Reseller,* May 8, 2000, p. 34.

"Full-Featured CRM," *InformationWeek,* April 24, 2000, p. 193.

Hibbard, Justin, "Retail's Human Touch," *InformationWeek,* March 22, 1999, p. 79.

Hickey, Kathleen, "True Blue," *Traffic World,* October 11, 1999, p. 34.

Hill, Sidney, Jr., "Maybe This Is Rocket Science," *MSI,* December 2002, p. 51.

Hill, Sidney, Jr., "A Toast to Manufacturers," *Manufacturing Systems,* February 2002, p. 14.

Kerstetter, Jim, "Commerce Suites Offer Missing Link," *PC Week,* March 22, 1999, p. N12.

LaMonica, Martin, "Blue Martini Helps Pull Together E-Commerce Components," *InfoWorld,* July 26, 1999.

Maselli, Jennifer, "CRM Help for Manufacturers," *InformationWeek,* December 10, 2001, p. 79.

"Monte Zweben," *San Francisco Business Times,* August 20, 1999, p. 30.

"Monte Zweben – Founder, President and CEO, Blue Martini," *VARbusiness,* November 13, 2000, p. 90.

O'Connor, Colleen, "Feature: Blue Martini Looking to Shake up Market," *IPO Reporter,* July 24, 2000.

Sapp, Geneva, "Blue Martini's Retail Platform Helps In-Store Cross-Selling," *InfoWorld,* May 8, 2000, p. 26.

Schaff, William, "Not a Perfect Tonic for the Market Upset," *InformationWeek,* October 30, 2000, p. 194.

Spirrison, J. Bradley, "Investors Fill up Blue Martini Software," *Private Equity Week,* October 4, 1999, p. 3.

Trott, Bob, "Blue Martini Readies Channel Solution for B-to-B Partners," *InfoWorld,* March 5, 2001, p. 20.

Wasserman, Todd, "Blue Martini Stirs $5M+ to Tell Us What They Do," *Brandweek,* October 16, 2000, p. 8.

——, "Monte Zweben," *Brandweek,* March 26, 2001, p. 35.

Whiting, Rick, "Monte Zweben Keeps Blue Martini Focused on Customers' Needs," *InformationWeek,* January 1, 2001, p. 73.

—David P. Bianco

BMC Industries, Inc.

One Meridian Crossings, Suite 850
Minneapolis, Minnesota 55423-3938
U.S.A.
Telephone: (952) 851-6000
Fax: (952) 851-6050
Web site: http://www.bmcind.com

Public Company
Incorporated: 1907 as Buckbee-Mears Company
Employees: 2,405
Sales: $248.1 million (2002)
Stock Exchanges: OTC Bulletin Board
Ticker Symbol: BMMI
NAIC: 334419 Other Electronic Component Manufacturing;
     339115 Ophthalmic Goods Manufacturing

BMC Industries, Inc. is a leading manufacturer of aperture masks and optical lenses. Its Buckbee-Mears group, responsible for about 56 percent of 2002 revenues, is the only North American producer of aperture masks, a key component in color television picture tubes that precisely direct electron beams onto the proper phosphor color stripes, resulting in a sharp image. BMC pioneered the development of the photochemical machining process used to make these masks. Two of BMC's largest customers are purchasers of the aperture masks of Buckbee-Mears: Thomson, S.A. of France accounted for 19 percent of BMC's 2002 revenues, while sales to Samsung Display Co., Ltd. of South Korea amounted to 13 percent of the total. The main production facility of the Buckbee-Mears group is located in Cortland, New York. The Optical Products group, which operates under the trade name Vision-Ease Lens, is one of the world's leading manufacturers of polycarbonate and glass lenses and is also a supplier of plastic lenses sourced through third-party manufacturers. Vision-Ease sells both semifinished and finished lenses—including single-vision, multifocal, progressive, and prescription sunglass lenses, some of which feature antireflective and scratch-resistant coatings—to wholesale optical laboratories and retail eyewear chains throughout the United States and Europe. Optical production facilities are cen-

tered in Ramsey, Minnesota; and Jakarta, Indonesia. Because of lagging demand for aperture masks and fierce competition from Asian manufacturers of the masks, as well as management problems, BMC Industries fell into the red in 2001 and by late 2003 was teetering on the brink of a bankruptcy filing.

Roots in the Graphic Arts

Founded in 1907 by cousins Charles E. Buckbee and Norman T. Mears, Buckbee-Mears Company operated one of the Twin Cities' first photoengraving plants. The St. Paul, Minnesota, company quickly added photography to its engraving and creative art departments, and thus became a full-line graphic arts supplier. By 1927, offset printing—a photomechanical process—had been developed and Buckbee-Mears later rendered that service as well.

"It was World War II that brought Norman B. Mears to the forefront in the then-conservative family operation," wrote Dick Caldwell in a 1967 *Minneapolis Star* article. The younger Mears, son of the cofounder, had left his farming operation in South Dakota in 1928 and joined Buckbee-Mears. He then pushed for expansion of the business into photomechanical production. Mears got a big opportunity to experiment with the process when the U.S. Navy needed grids etched on the eyepieces of military equipment. Mears not only led the successful development of a vacuum-etching production line for metal and glass reticles used in fire control (gun sights), radar, and guided missiles, but he created a new industrial division for the company.

A New Focus in the Postwar Years

The industrial skills BMC acquired during the war were transferred to the television industry in peacetime. The Radio Corporation of America (RCA) enlisted Buckbee-Mears to develop a crucial part for color television tubes. In 1963 the company perfected an automated process for the production of the "shadow mask," an extremely thin metal sheet punctured by hundreds of thousands of perfectly positioned holes that directed electron beams toward phosphorous strips that generate the color. The automated chemical etching process had evolved over a 13-year period and several generations of equipment.

Company Perspectives:

We have what we believe to be a clear plan to return BMC to growth. At its core, we must efficiently operate our two restructured businesses. In 2003, we are focused on returning to profitability by: Improving the performance of our global polycarbonate lens franchise; Managing our core mask operations for maximum cash flow; Stabilizing the earnings stream for consistent and predictable results; and Using free cash flow to further reduce debt and increase financial flexibility. We also seek to leverage the applications for our technology and develop new, higher-margin products that we can introduce in growing market segments. These are the yardsticks by which we will measure our success.

Norman B. Mears became company president in 1957 and at one point owned up to 92 percent of the stock. He and Buckbee-Mears were direct beneficiaries of the wave of color television sales they helped set in motion. By 1966 about five million color televisions were sold in the United States; 99 percent of those TV sets contained a Buckbee-Mears mask. The industrial division had doubled its sales from 1965 to 1966, largely because of the shadow masks. The company went public in September 1966.

According to a 1982 *Business Week* article, Buckbee-Mears enjoyed a short-lived high-tech image because of its pioneering work in the television manufacturing field. Growth of the company's other division was steady but less dramatic. When Buckbee-Mears reached its 60th year of business, the graphic arts division primarily served a 13-state area and held a big share of the important Twin Cities' market.

Internal and External Changes in the 1970s

The makeup of the company began to change in the late 1960s and into the mid-1970s. Buckbee-Mears exited the graphics arts business and entered the ophthalmic lens business, acquiring Vision-Ease Lens, Inc. in 1968; this St. Cloud, Minnesota, firm had been founded in 1930. Norman B. Mears stepped down from his position as company president. The business environment that had been favorable for Buckbee-Mears also began to change. Color television imports rose from 18 percent of U.S. sales in 1975 to 37 percent in 1976; major domestic television manufacturers, Westinghouse Electric Corp., Motorola Inc., Admiral, and Philco, stopped producing color picture tubes. The loss of business resulted in cutbacks at Buckbee-Mears. Nearly one-third of the workers (75) were laid off at its St. Paul aperture mask plant, and 45 salaried employees also lost their jobs. The company also had aperture mask plants in New York and West Germany.

In December 1976, Everett F. Carter replaced James Bourquin as president. Carter had come to Buckbee-Mears from GTE Sylvania Inc. in 1969, the year Bourquin succeeded Mears as president. The company lost over $300,000 in 1976, but became profitable again under Carter; earnings reached $4.3 million in 1979.

Acquisitions Boom of the Early 1980s

Buckbee-Mears Company began the 1980s earning steady profits from its ophthalmic products and the precision metal parts operations of its industrial division. But aperture mask sales stagnated. The company planned to gradually diversify by moving from parts to subassembly to end-product manufacturing. That strategy changed dramatically when the board brought on Ryal Poppa, a high profile manager. Poppa had a number of successful turnarounds associated with his name including Pertec Corp., a southern California computer equipment maker. His eight-year acquisition drive at Pertec had increased Pertec's annual sales from $28 million to $200 million. Poppa, along with a $1 million investment in Buckbee-Mears, stepped into the CEO and chair positions in January 1982. Everett F. Carter retained his position as president, but Norman C. Mears retired from the board. (Carter resigned his position as president as well at the end of 1982.)

As he had with other businesses, Poppa acted quickly and aggressively. A new management team, a new company name, and an ambitious acquisition plan were put in place. Ryal Poppa intended to make the company, renamed BMC Industries, Inc. in 1983, a major player in the electronic interconnections field. But his first acquisitions were in the optics area. Bolstered by the purchase of Camelot Industries, the optics division contributed about two-thirds of 1982 revenues.

The next year, 1983, was marked by an announcement for a joint venture with Control Data Corporation in the production of semiconductor chip equipment. Four important high-tech businesses were acquired. Total sales reached $155 million with earnings of $4.5 million. With Honeywell's Tampa operations and Advanced Controls of Irvine California included in the electronics division, Poppa was predicting sales to double in 1984. Investors were taking notice of what was happening in St. Paul. *St. Paul Pioneer Press Dispatch* reporter Dave Beal wrote, "Wall Street loved Ryal Poppa's big adventure; the stock doubled to $27 in just two years."

The Boom Goes Bust

The adventure, however, came to an end. The environment in which Poppa was trying to diversify BMC was inhospitable: the U.S. electronics industry was struggling under foreign competition and a soft consumer demand. In addition, the new Interconics division, which served the semiconductor and electronic equipment industries, had been funded largely by debt. In December 1984, $30 million in debentures were sold to four companies to pay off some of the heavy debt load.

Return on stockholders equity fell to 2.5 percent in 1984, from over 10 percent in the previous three years. Ryal Poppa left BMC early in 1985. The debenture holders sued BMC in order to rescind the notes and call in the debt. Robert J. Carlson, formerly a top executive with United Technologies Corp. and Deere & Co., joined BMC as chief executive in mid-1985. Carlson tried cost-cutting measures in an attempt to keep the electronics division Poppa had built intact. But the recession in the industry and BMC's debt were both too deep. In November 1985 BMC announced that the electronics division would be sold off. Losses in 1985 were nearly $70 million, largely because of business divestment reserves.

BMC's outlook had changed drastically from the aggressive optimism of the Poppa days; 13 high-technology operations—

Key Dates:

1907: Cousins Charles E. Buckbee and Norman T. Mears establish Buckbee-Mears Company, which operates a photoengraving plant in St. Paul, Minnesota.

1963: Company perfects production of the shadow mask, a key component in color televisions.

1966: Buckbee-Mears is taken public.

1968: Company enters the ophthalmic lens business through the purchase of Vision-Ease Lens, Inc. of St. Cloud, Minnesota.

1982: Turnaround specialist Ryal Poppa is named CEO, and he engineers an acquisitions-led drive into electronics.

1983: Company changes its name to BMC Industries, Inc.

1985: Poppa leaves the company, having saddled it with a high debt load; BMC announces it will divest its nascent electronics business.

1998: BMC acquires polycarbonate lens maker Orcolite, which is merged into Vision-Ease; plunging demand for aperture masks leads to a net loss for the year.

2002: Restructuring efforts include the closure of two plants and the elimination of hundreds of jobs.

2003: Worsening conditions in the aperture mask market lead to the closure of mask operations in Europe and a refocusing of the company on its Vision-Ease unit; company stock is delisted from the New York Stock Exchange; BMC verges on bankruptcy as it falls out of compliance with its bank loan.

one-third of BMC's assets—were on the sales block, and its $100 million debt was in default. Sales of color television aperture masks and optical lenses both rose in 1986, but profits were drained by the interest on debt and from operating losses in the discontinued businesses. BMC lost another $6.5 million in 1986. Stock prices dropped as low as $3.25 a share, and the company had to ward off a takeover bid.

In 1987, BMC settled the lawsuit by agreeing to pay off the notes, and it began restructuring negotiations on the remaining debt. BMC received $65 million in new loans from institutional investors and used cash from the divestitures to pay off the $100 million debt, as well as $5 million in interest. The company was back to its pre-Poppa product lines, optical products and precision-etched products, but still held $65 million in long-term debt accumulated from its failed diversification attempt. In terms of production, BMC made a deal with IBM for precision-etched computer parts to be made out of its West German plant. It also entered into a joint venture with an Italian plastic eye-glass lens maker, and made an aperture mask engineering and manufacturing service contract with the Soviet Union. The company also marked 1987 by moving its corporate headquarters from its longtime St. Paul location to a smaller facility in Bloomington, Minnesota.

Growth in the Early 1990s Still Hampered by Debt

Debt hampered capacity expansion in the years following BMC's restructuring, and stock prices generally bounced back and forth between the $5 and $10 per share mark. The company struggled with: production problems in the New York aperture mask plant; slow sales in the St. Paul plant where electronic components and etched glass and large printed circuit boards were made; and a general economic recession. Net earnings for 1990 dropped to $1.8 million, down 66 percent from 1989.

An $18.6 million aperture mask equipment and technology deal with a Chinese company sent BMC earnings upward again in the beginning of 1991. Paul Burke rose to the position of president; Carlson retained his positions as chairman and CEO. Burke had joined BMC in 1983 as an associate general counsel and at age 29 was appointed general counsel by Carlson. Burke played an instrumental role in the successful divestiture and debt restructuring, and then requested a move to the operations side of the company in 1987. He managed a turnaround at the Florida Vision-Ease Lens plant and became president of the $75 million division two years later. Carlson left BMC in July 1991 and was succeeded by Burke, then 35 years old. Sales for the year reached $203.2 million with record earnings of $8.2 million.

BMC continued to make steady progress toward increasing sales and profits and reducing debt. In 1993 BMC made another deal with a Chinese firm for aperture mask equipment and technology: this time for $26 million. The company was moving away from the manufacturing of the lower-end aperture masks it was licensing, to higher-margin, high-resolution computer monitors and televisions. The precision-etched products division, which made the aperture masks and specialty photo-etched glass and metal parts, provided just under two-thirds of BMC's sales. Eyewear lens sales through the optical products division provided the other third.

BMC debt was down to $32 million toward year-end 1993 and the stock price had doubled from the previous year to about $16 per share. A breakthrough deal with a Japanese television manufacturer in 1994 and rising worldwide demand for high-end aperture masks had pushed BMC plants to near capacity. BMC also saw progress in its optical products division in 1994, polycarbonate lens sales jumping 44 percent compared with industry growth of 25 percent. In September 1994 BMC paid off its debt, giving the company room for capital investment.

Expansion Moves in the Mid- to Late 1990s

In 1995 BMC accelerated expansion of its aperture masks production lines, announcing plans for two additional television and one additional computer mask lines. Japanese firms were its only competitors in the high-end market, and they were being hurt by the strong yen which drove up their prices relative to BMC's. The company's other business segment was also doing well with its higher-margin product; in the fast-growing polycarbonate lens market BMC ranked second in sales behind Gentex Optics of Massachusetts. Riccardo A. Davis wrote in July 1995, "BMC has produced 16 consecutive quarters of increased earnings as it has focused on higher margin masks and lenses." In October 1995 BMC stock was split two-for-one.

Buckbee-Mears St. Paul (BMSP), a business unit that had been struggling for survival in the early 1990s, increased earnings by 200 percent in 1995 because of increased sales, sales mix changes, and improved production efficiencies. As a world leader in the field of photochemical machining BMSP provided thinner, more detailed pieces, and a greater range of sizes than stamped metal parts. Its products were used in automotive, electronics, medical, office, consumer, industrial, military and aerospace applications.

The year 1995 also marked a milestone for the company that began as Buckbee-Mears. Norman B. Mears had retired from the board in 1994, leaving the company without Mears's family leadership for the first time. Company-wide profits for 1995 were $24.5 million on total sales of $255.4 million. The precision imaged products group, which included aperture masks and BMSP, brought in 70 percent of BMC's consolidated revenues. The aperture masks alone provided 58 percent total revenue. Optical products brought in 30 percent.

BMC had expanded its polycarbonate lens production capacity in 1993, 1994, and 1995. In 1996 the company announced plans to build a $10 million state-of-the-art facility in Ramsey, Minnesota, near Minneapolis, for polycarbonate manufacturing, as well as centralized distribution and research and development. (Polycarbonate lenses—thinner, lighter, and more impact resistant than plastic or glass lenses—were manufactured through a highly automated injection process.) While polycarbonate lenses were the fastest growing segment of the U.S. market, it was actually the smallest segment among BMC's three lens types. BMC held more than 50 percent of the domestic fused multifocal glass lens market and was a major supplier internationally. BMC, like other U.S. manufacturers, began contracting overseas for more labor-intensive hard-resin lenses, which held about half of the U.S. market.

In addition to the new plant, which opened in 1998, there were several other notable developments for the Vision-Ease Lens subsidiary in the mid- to late 1990s. In 1993 Vision-Ease introduced the first progressive polycarbonate lenses; a progressive lens was a type of multifocal lens designed with a continuous gradient of different corrective power without the line separating different powers that was typically present in other multifocal lenses. Vision-Ease two years later introduced its SunRx line of polarized lenses. The company's position in Europe was bolstered via the January 1996 purchase of the London-based Optical Manufacturing Supplies Limited, a distributor of lenses throughout the United Kingdom and Continental Europe. Then in 1997 Vision-Ease began manufacturing lenses at a new plant in Jakarta, Indonesia, where it could take advantage of the lower costs associated with production there. The company that year also introduced its Tegra brand of premium polycarbonate lenses, which, when compared to most other lenses then marketed, were lighter, clearer, more scratch resistant, and had less distortion. Tegra Outlook premium progressive lenses made their debut two years later. Meanwhile, in May 1998, BMC paid approximately $100 million to acquire Orcolite from Monsanto Company. Orcolite manufactured premium polycarbonate eyeglass lenses at its plant in Azusa, California. Orcolite, which had 1997 revenues of about $34 million, was merged into Vision-Ease, making that company the largest manufacturer of polycarbonate lenses in the United States.

Struggling from Weakness in Aperture Mask Market, Late 1990s and Early 2000s

Although BMC's optical products operations were now its biggest growth area, and a solidly profitable one at that, the company's core product remained aperture masks, and the market for that component collapsed in the late 1990s. BMC had sunk $85 million into the expansion of its Cortland, New York, plant so that it could begin producing masks for computer monitors. The new lines, however, were not ready until 1998. By that time, it had lost two of its key customers in North America—Zenith because it went into bankruptcy, Samsung because it cut back on its monitor production. BMC was forced to try to sell its masks into an Asian market flooded by production overcapacity; adding to the difficulties was the Asian economic crisis, which had battered the local currencies, thereby making BMC's products hopelessly expensive. The company had to take a $42 million writedown on its investment in the Cortland plant, leading to a net loss of $30.6 million for 1998. In addition, more than 500 workers were laid off from that plant. BMC's stock suffered tremendously during this difficult year: It had traded above $22 per share early in the year, but finished 1998 at $6.25.

BMC returned to modest levels of profitability over the next two years as sales of aperture masks recovered in tandem with the rebounding economies of southeast Asia. Overall revenues, however, were stagnating at about $354 million. Vision-Ease continued to grow, acquiring an optical lens laboratory located outside Paris, France, that specialized in polycarbonate eyewear lenses in March 2000. This added to Vision-Ease's lens processing capabilities in Europe, where it had an existing lab in Germany. That same month, BMC announced a reorganization in which the firm's mask operations and the Buckbee-Mears St. Paul unit were combined into a new operating group called simply Buckbee-Mears.

Sales plunged more than 15 percent in 2001 to $302.3 million as the sluggish economy weakened demand for both televisions and computers. Computer monitor prices dropped sharply, prompting BMC to exit from that segment of the aperture mask only a few years after entering it. During the fourth quarter of 2001, BMC recorded a $12.2 million restructuring charge related to this exit as well as two plant closures that were completed in 2002—the Vision-Ease plant in Azusa, California, and the Buckbee-Mears facility in St. Paul. The production that had been done in Azusa was shifted to Vision-Ease's remaining plants in Ramsey and Jakarta. The St. Paul plant produced various precision metal products that comprised less than 5 percent of BMC revenues; some of these operations were sold off, and the rest were assigned to the Buckbee-Mears facilities in Cortland, New York, and Müllheim, Germany. BMC reported a net loss of $22.6 million in 2001.

The company's restructuring efforts during 2001 and 2002 included the elimination of more than 1,100 jobs, or nearly one-third of the workforce. In early 2002 Vision-Ease's Optifacts unit, a wholesaler of optical lens laboratory software, was divested. As BMC continued to pile up losses in 2002, Burke retired from the company in June. Douglas C. Hepper, a 28-year veteran manager with PPG Industries, Inc., was brought onboard as chairman, president, and CEO. By this time, BMC's stock had plummeted further to $1.52 per share. In the final months of 2002, Hepper managed to restore some credibility to the company by restructuring its credit, with most of the short-term debt converted into long-term debt, and by suspending dividend payments. The company late in the year also settled a lawsuit that had been brought by a shareholder who had accused BMC of improperly forgiving a $2.6 million loan to Burke. The Burke era received an additional degree of notoriety when it was revealed that the CEO had run the Minnesota-based company out of Paris for a yearlong period in 2000 and 2001. Revenues dropped another 18 percent in 2002, hitting $248.1 million, while the net loss of $61.9 million reflected $2.8 million in restructuring costs and a $52.7 million charge connected with a change in accounting principles.

Worsening conditions in the aperture masks market necessitated more drastic measures in 2003. In June BMC announced that it would shut down its Buckbee-Mears operations in Europe, including its main plant in Germany as well as a facility in Hungary where product inspection and other services were conducted. BMC's mask operations were consolidated at Buckbee-Mears's one remaining plant in Cortland. In addition, all nonmask operations of Buckbee-Mears were discontinued. For the second quarter of 2003, a net loss of $95.3 million was reported, which included $46.9 million in asset impairment charges mainly connected with the Buckbee-Mears restructuring and a $24.1 million loss from discontinued operations. The latest round of bad news once again hammered the stock, which fell below $1 per share for an extended period. Consequently the New York Stock Exchange in August 2003 delisted the stock, which then began trading on the OTC Bulletin Board. At the same time, BMC fell out of compliance with the terms of its bank loan, lacking enough cash on hand to make certain principal payments. It received a series of waivers from its bankers, but a bankruptcy filing appeared imminent. The company had hired an investment bank to explore strategic options, leading to speculation about a sale of the company or perhaps a divestment of the troubled aperture mask business. It seemed certain in any event that if BMC had a future as an independent company, it would be as a supplier of eyeglass lenses given that Vision-Ease Lens appeared to be BMC's only viable business long-term.

Principal Subsidiaries

Buckbee-Mears Medical Technologies, LLC; Vision-Ease Lens, Inc.; Vision-Ease Lens Azusa, LLC; Vision Ease Lens Limited (U.K.); Vision-Ease Canada, Ltd.; P.T. Vision-Ease Asia (Indonesia); Vision-Ease France SAS; Buckbee-Mears Netherlands B.V.

Principal Operating Units

Buckbee-Mears Group; Optical Products Group.

Principal Competitors

Essilor International SA; Sola International Inc.; LG Group.

Further Reading

"All Ryaled Up at BMC," *Corporate Report-Minnesota,* May 1984, pp. 22–23.

Beal, Dave, "BMC May Close Plant in St. Paul to Cut Costs," *St. Paul Pioneer Press,* October 2, 1993, pp. 1B, 7B.

——, "Tumult Passed, BMC Now Braves the 90s," *St. Paul Pioneer Press,* October 25, 1993, pp. 1E, 6E.

Beran, George, "BMC Chief Advises Patience for Earnings Growth," *St. Paul Pioneer Press Dispatch,* April 29, 1988.

——, "BMC Completes Debt Restructuring," *St. Paul Pioneer Press Dispatch,* July 17, 1987.

Bjorhus, Jennifer, "BMC Faces Losses, Layoffs," *St. Paul Pioneer Press,* August 20, 2003, p. C1.

"BMC Industries Inc.," *Minneapolis/St. Paul CityBusiness,* April 8, 1994.

Breimhurst, Henry, "Asia's Woes, Other Forces Bite BMC," *Minneapolis/St. Paul Business Journal,* September 14, 1998.

Caldwell, Dick, "Buckbee-Mears Expanding," *Minneapolis Star,* January 12, 1967, p. 15B.

Carlin, Bing, and Mark Hoonsbeen, "Clear Vision," *Twin Cities Business Monthly,* July 1995.

Carlson, Scott, "BMC Reversal Makes Stock More Attractive," *St. Paul Pioneer Press Dispatch,* February 15, 1988.

Davis, Riccardo, "BMC Poised to Be Big Part of High-Definition TV Picture," *St. Paul Pioneer Press,* January 9, 1997, p. 1B.

——, "BMC's Bright Picture," *St. Paul Pioneer Press,* July 19, 1995.

——, "BMC's Vision," *St. Paul Pioneer Press,* May 30, 1996.

——, "4Q Warning Topples BMC Stock," *St. Paul Pioneer Press,* November 20, 1997, p. 1B.

DePass, Dee, "BMC Restructures in Europe," *Minneapolis Star Tribune,* June 28, 2003, p. 1D.

DeSilver, Drew, "BMC Again Has Its Eye on Acquisitions," *Minneapolis/St. Paul CityBusiness,* June 14–20, 1996.

Feyder, Susan, "BMC Industries Swallows a Strong Dose," *Minneapolis Star Tribune,* March 31, 1986, p. 1M.

——, "Group Buys into BMC Industries," *Minneapolis Star Tribune,* January 21, 1987, pp. 1M-2M.

Fifty Years, Minneapolis: Buckbee-Mears Company, 1957.

Fredrickson, Tom, "BMC Breaks into the Japanese TV Market," *Minneapolis/St. Paul CityBusiness,* February 25, 1994.

Greenwald, John, "TV Imports Hurt Buckbee-Mears," *Minneapolis Star,* March 25, 1977.

Gross, Steve, "Drastic Changes Apparently Working at Buckbee-Mears," *Minneapolis Star Tribune,* February 13, 1983, pp. 1D, 3D.

Hannagan, Charley, "Profit Masks Trouble," *Syracuse (N.Y.) Post-Standard,* May 19, 2003, p. 11.

Hequet, Marc, "Let's Make a Deal," *Corporate Report-Minnesota,* December 1983, pp. 76–78.

Hughlett, Mike, "BMC Severs Its Last Link to St. Paul," *St. Paul Pioneer Press,* December 22, 2002, p. A1.

McDonnell, Lynda, "A Bet on BMC Is a Bet on Bob Carlson," *St. Paul Pioneer Press Dispatch,* July 27, 1987, pp. 1, 10.

Men, Minds, Microns, Minneapolis: Buckbee-Mears Company, 1967.

"Periscope: BMC Industries, Inc.," *Corporate Report-Minnesota,* February 1985, pp. 134–35.

Peterson, Susan E., "BMC CEO Plans to Step Down; PPG Veteran Will Replace Him," *Minneapolis Star Tribune,* May 16, 2002, p. 1D.

——, "BMC Chooses Paul Burke As New Second-In-Command," *Minneapolis Star Tribune,* May 10, 1991.

——, "BMC Industries Plans to Buy Orcolite in $100 Million Deal," *Minneapolis Star Tribune,* March 26, 1998, p. 1D.

——, "BMC Reports Sharp Rise in Earnings; Carlson Retires," *Minneapolis Star Tribune,* July 16, 1991, pp. 1D-2D.

——, "A Sharper Focus," *Minneapolis Star Tribune,* August 16, 2002, p. 1D.

——, ''Young Executive Credited with BMC's Turnaround,'' *Minneapolis Star Tribune,* September 9, 1991, pp. 1D, 7D.

Phelps, David, ''BMC Faces Lawsuit over CEO's Stock Deal,'' *Minneapolis Star Tribune,* June 17, 2002, p. 1D.

''Poppa Tests His Golden Touch,'' *Business Week,* January 18, 1982, p. 102.

Sarkes Neaville, Lisa, ''BMC Industries Building Plant for Lens Molding,'' *Plastic News,* August 19, 1996.

Strand, Phil, ''Checking in Again,'' *Corporate Report-Minnesota,* August 1984, pp. 97–98.

Taylor, Jeff A., ''BMC Industries' Paul Burke,'' *Investor's Business Daily,* March 28, 1996.

Weinberger, Betsy, ''After BMC Exec Leaves, Turmoil Follows,'' *Minneapolis/St. Paul CityBusiness,* May 22, 1992, pp. 1, 30.

——, ''Galileo Discovers BMC,'' *Minneapolis/St. Paul CityBusiness,* February 5, 1993.

Young, Robin, ''Profile: Ryal Poppa:'' *Corporate Report-Minnesota,* October 1982, pp. 76–77, 135–36, 138.

—Kathleen Peippo
—update: David E. Salamie

Bridgestone Corporation

10-1, Kyobashi 1-chome
Chuo-ku
Tokyo 104-8340
Japan
Telephone: (03) 3567-0111
Fax: (03) 3535-2553
Web site: http://www.bridgestone.co.jp

Public Company
Incorporated: 1931 as Bridgestone Ltd.
Employees: 106,846
Sales: ¥2.25 trillion ($18.75 billion) (2002)
Stock Exchanges: Tokyo Nagoya Osaka Fukuoka
Ticker Symbol: 5108
NAIC: 326211 Tire Manufacturing (Except Retreading);
  314992 Tire Cord and Tire Fabric Mills; 325182
  Carbon Black Manufacturing; 325212 Synthetic
  Rubber Manufacturing; 326212 Tire Retreading;
  326291 Rubber Product Manufacturing for
  Mechanical Use; 332611 Spring (Heavy Gauge)
  Manufacturing; 336399 All Other Motor Vehicle Parts
  Manufacturing; 336991 Motorcycle, Bicycle, and
  Parts Manufacturing; 339920 Sporting and Athletic
  Goods Manufacturing; 441320 Tire Dealers

Bridgestone Corporation is the world's leading manufacturer of tires, and the company is number three in the North American tire market, trailing the other two of the world's "Big Three" tiremakers, Michelin and The Goodyear Tire & Rubber Company. In addition to its flagship Bridgestone and Firestone brands, the company makes and markets tires under the names Dayton, Seiberling, Road King, Gillette, and Peerless, as well as private and house brand tires. Bridgestone also makes the raw materials that go into tires and maintains an extensive network of company-owned tire retail outlets, including nearly 2,300 in North America and about 700 in Japan. The company's tires also are sold through tens of thousands of independent retailers operating in more than 150 countries around the world. Nontire products, which account for about 20 percent of sales, include automotive components, particularly vibration- and noise-isolating parts, such as engine mounts and air springs; industrial products, such as polyurethane foam, conveyor belts, and rubber tracks for crawler tractors; construction and civil engineering materials; and sporting goods—golf balls and clubs, tennis balls and rackets, and bicycles. Products are manufactured within more than 40 tire plants and more than 60 nontire plants on six continents. Geographically, sales break down as follows: 44 percent from North and South America, 37 percent from Japan, 11 percent from Europe, and the remaining 8 percent from elsewhere (Africa and the Asia-Pacific region outside of Japan).

Origins of Pioneering Japanese Tiremaker

Bridgestone was founded by Shojiro Ishibashi, whose name means "stone bridge." Prior to founding the company, Ishibashi, along with his brother, had led the family clothing business, which produced *tabi*—Japanese workers' footwear; Ishibashi made a fortune by adding rubber soles. Deciding that his future lay in the rubber business, he began intensive research and development in 1929, founding Bridgestone Ltd. two years later in Kurume, Japan, as the first local tire supplier for the nascent Japanese automotive industry. Headquarters were moved to Tokyo in 1937. In 1942 the company changed its name to the Nippon Tire Co., Ltd., but was renamed Bridgestone Tire Co., Ltd. in 1951 and became Bridgestone Corporation in 1984. Ishibashi was an aggressive businessman with strong marketing skills whose main business principle was to expand during recessionary periods. He also thrived on business connections made through his children's marriages. It was said in Japan that his family connections to government officials allowed Bridgestone to secure orders during the Korean War of the 1950s, helping the company to gain its strong position in the domestic market. Meantime, production of nontire products began early on, with golf balls added to the portfolio in the 1930s and bicycles in 1946.

Before World War II, Bridgestone's business—like that of other major Japanese industrial concerns—was focused on supplying military requirements; at the same time, Bridgestone tires also supplied the growing Japanese automobile industry.

Company Perspectives:

"Serving society with superior quality." Those words of our founder, Shojiro Ishibashi, state our mission simply and precisely. That mission is what the trust we earn and the pride we feel are all about.

Production was based at two plants, one in Kurume, the other in Yokohama. Growth after the war was rapid, with the establishment of four new production facilities in the 1960s and six during the 1970s. Bridgestone's first overseas factory was established in Singapore in 1963, with further factories built in Thailand in 1967 and Indonesia in 1973. Bridgestone Singapore ceased operations in 1980 following the Singapore government's lifting of tariff protection for locally made tires. In 1976 Bridgestone set up a sales company in Hamburg, Germany, in partnership with Mitsui. This new company, named Bridgestone Reifen G.m.b.H., was intended to increase tire sales in the important West German market. In 1990 Bridgestone set up a new subsidiary in London, Bridgestone Industrial, to handle industrial rubber products throughout Europe.

Expansion Through 1980s Acquisitions

Since the 1980s Bridgestone's most significant expansion has been by acquisition, acquiring majority interests in Uniroyal Holdings Ltd. (UHL), the South Australian tire manufacturer, in 1980 and a Taiwanese company in 1986. In 1983 Bridgestone gained its first U.S. production base by purchasing a plant in LaVergne, Tennessee, belonging to the Firestone Tire & Rubber Company. This proved to be the first step toward Bridgestone's acquisition of that U.S. company in 1988, for a total of $2.65 billion.

Before acquiring Firestone, Bridgestone had first approached Goodyear in 1987, with proposals for a merger that would have created the world's largest tire manufacturer. Talks in Hawaii, however, failed to reach agreement as Bridgestone would not accept the high value that Goodyear had placed on its loss-making Trans-American oil pipeline. Bridgestone then turned to Firestone as a U.S. production base for the manufacture of heavy-duty radial truck tires. They were encouraged in this by the acquisition of an ailing Firestone plant in LaVergne, Tennessee, in 1983, which Bridgestone had turned into a success. Bridgestone originally agreed to buy Firestone's tire operations for $1.25 billion, but Pirelli, the Italian manufacturer, intervened with a rival bid, forcing the Japanese company to increase the offer. Bridgestone finally paid $2.65 billion for the whole company, with 54,000 employees and two headquarters, in 1988. The following year Bridgestone's North American operations were integrated with those of Firestone under the Bridgestone/Firestone, Inc. subsidiary. One year later, Bridgestone/Firestone Europe S.A. was created to manage European operations.

The Firestone deal gave Bridgestone its sought-after foothold in the United States and strengthened its position in Europe, as Firestone also owned plants in Portugal, Spain, France, and Italy. In addition, it gave Bridgestone instant access to high-quality manufacturing facilities, with an extensive na-

tional marketing system for replacement tires, as well as large research and development laboratories. The Firestone name and sales network gave the Japanese company access to Detroit carmakers for original equipment sales and for the sale of Firestone brand tires for the two million cars a year produced by Japanese automobile firms. In North America, Bridgestone's sales in the replacement market were through independent dealers and through their MasterCare network of more than 1,500 tire and service centers. These independent dealers also strengthened sales in the United States and Canada, and the company's marketing strategy widened further in the early 1990s through mass merchandisers such as Sears and Kmart. Another highlight of its international sales network was the chain of Cockpit retail outlets, which offered car audio equipment and accessories such as wheels, as well as tires. The 200th Cockpit shop opened in the spring of 1990.

Within six months of the Firestone purchase, Bridgestone announced a $1.5 billion modernization program. Firestone's auxiliary head office in Chicago and Bridgestone's own U.S. base in Nashville were closed to concentrate operations in Akron, and Firestone's management was reduced through a voluntary early retirement scheme. The investment in Firestone coincided with a slowdown in North American and European car production, however, heralding a period of much tougher competition in tire markets. The renovation of Firestone turned out to be more expensive and time-consuming than expected. Other problems included weak markets in Latin America and the Middle East and intense competition in European markets. Fortunately for Bridgestone, not all of the massive investment came from borrowings but in part from Bridgestone's hidden assets, including land, buildings, and securities, purchases made decades ago. Company founder Shojiro Ishibashi also had invested heavily in art, mostly Western, opening the Bridgestone Museum of Art in 1952.

Bridgestone continued to retain its position in Asia, where Bridgestone and Firestone brands maintained the largest share of the market. This region promised to display rapid growth in the world's tire markets over the next decade, and Bridgestone was positioned to remain in a strong position to capitalize on this with local production operations and large market shares, particularly in Thailand, Indonesia, and Taiwan.

Bridgestone's production, however, was not limited to tires. Its technical research and development laboratories worked on the development of rubber and nonrubber items. Rubber technology featured prominently with such items as conveyor belts, inflatable rubber dams, and marine fenders. Multi-rubber bearings were produced for use in the construction of buildings in areas prone to earthquakes as the rubber element in the construction enabled the buildings to vibrate with the earth's movement. Bridgestone's other innovative ideas included rubber "muscles" for robots and grease-free conveyor belts. Bridgestone became a Japanese leader in vibration-isolating components for automobiles and through Bridgestone/Firestone gained a large share of the North American market for rubberized roofing materials. It was also a major supplier in the United States of air springs for trucks, automobiles, trailers, and other vehicles.

In 1988 Bridgestone Cycle Co., Ltd. gave cyclists the first opportunity to design their own machines. Cyclists were able to choose, from a list of standard parts, the shape, color, and materials for the frame, brakes, handlebars, and seat, to make their own unique "mix and match" bicycle. Bridgestone's advance in metallurgy made it possible to produce bicycles that were lighter than ever in weight. The Radac line of racing, touring, and recreational bicycles was introduced in 1990, with a model that featured the world's lightest frame, thanks to an aluminum-ceramic composite, the first ceramic material ever to be used on a bicycle. Nonrubber products included items from special batteries for electronic equipment to weighing systems for aircraft. Bridgestone was also a leading supplier of golf balls and clubs, tennis rackets, and other sporting goods. The Bridgestone Sports Co., Ltd. was established in 1972 and subsequently won many awards, including one from the Japanese Ministry for International Trade and Industry for a line of windsurfing boards. In 1987 the company introduced the Science Eye system, which gave a high-speed photographic analysis of a golfer's swing, for use in department stores and professional shops. Bridgestone also operated swimming schools and health clubs.

Although Bridgestone Corporation entered the 1990s with the ability to compete on equal terms with the industry's two other giants, Goodyear of the United States and Michelin of France, its international expansion came late. Bridgestone had concentrated on the domestic market while other Japanese companies were developing production plants and overseas markets. Japanese customers bought whatever Bridgestone sold, which did little to encourage Bridgestone to develop new products; in addition, Bridgestone's production of radial tires came late by Western standards. Japanese manufacturers were reluctant to import European or American tires in the 1960s and 1970s, even though foreign tires were considered superior to Bridgestone's. These factors conspired to give the company a commanding share of the Japanese market, 46 percent in 1990, while exports were 50 percent.

Difficulties with U.S. Operations in the Forefront in the 1990s

By 1991, Bridgestone's acquisition of Firestone generally was being called a huge blunder. Bridgestone, not wishing to step on American toes, was slow to push for changes that were needed at a Firestone bloated with bureaucracy. Bridgestone even waited until late 1991 to integrate the U.S. headquarters of Bridgestone and Firestone into one location (which turned out to be Nashville, not Akron, where Firestone had resided). Bridgestone also had difficulty with the size of its new foreign subsidiary, finding it hard to manage from Japan. Finally, in March 1991 Yoichiro Kaizaki, who spoke little English and had a background in the company's nontire operations, was sent to the United States to head up Bridgestone/Firestone, the first Japanese person to do so. Meanwhile, Bridgestone/Firestone had lost $1 billion in the United States from 1990 to 1992. Bridgestone's profits consequently suffered, totaling only ¥4.5 billion in 1990 and ¥7.47 billion in 1991 before rebounding slightly to ¥28.4 billion in 1992.

Kaizaki immediately began to turn around the company's U.S. operations. In addition to consolidating headquarters in Nashville, he also tightened the management structure by setting up 21 operating divisions at Bridgestone/Firestone, each with its own president whose pay was tied to his or her division's performance. Money was pumped in from Japan to raise productivity at the plants and to improve the quality of the tires produced there. After two years of improving the American operation, Kaizaki returned to Japan as president of Bridgestone Corporation. Kaizaki appointed Masatoshi Ono, a trusted lieutenant, to head up Bridgestone/Firestone.

Bridgestone executives believed that its U.S. plants would not be profitable until the wages of its workers were cut and the workers agreed to operate the plants 24 hours a day. With labor and management on a collision course, United Rubber Workers (URW) contracts with major tiremakers expired in April 1994. Goodyear was chosen that year as the target company, and it reached an agreement in June with the URW. Bridgestone, however, refused to accept the "pattern" agreement. The union rejected the company's contract proposal, and on July 12, more than 4,000 URW workers at five Bridgestone/Firestone plants went out on strike. In January 1995 Bridgestone hired more than 2,000 permanent "replacement workers" (scabs), bringing criticism from both Labor Secretary Robert Reich and President Bill Clinton and much negative publicity for Bridgestone/Firestone. In May the URW called off the ten-month-old strike, with the workers agreeing to return to work without a contract. Nevertheless, not all of the workers were rehired immediately. In July 1995 the URW was absorbed into the United Steelworkers of America.

In September 1996 Bridgestone/Firestone recalled almost all of the workers it had replaced, and a little more than a month later, in early November, a three-year agreement was reached, which both the Steelworkers and Bridgestone claimed as victory. Among the provisions favoring the workers were the 4.4 percent wage hike and the rehiring of all workers dismissed during the long conflict. Bridgestone won the key concession on operating the factories around the clock.

In the midst of this labor strife, Bridgestone/Firestone managed to turn a 1996 profit of $180 million in part because it had unilaterally imposed an around-the-clock schedule. Back in Japan, meanwhile, Kaizaki was trimming domestic operations to contain costs, cutting the workforce 14 percent from 1993 to 1996. The company was also in the midst of building new tire plants in central Europe and China and a plant in India scheduled to open in 1998 through a joint venture with Tata Industries. In addition, despite its difficulties in the United States, Bridgestone spent $430 million in 1997 and 1998 to upgrade existing American plants and announced in mid-1997 that it would build its eighth U.S. tire factory, a $435 million plant scheduled to open in Aiken, South Carolina, in early 1999. The new factory would manufacture about 25,000 car and light-truck tires at its peak, and reach full employment of 800 workers by 2000. The company needed the new plants to satisfy the increasing demand for its tires; the U.S. plant also was designed specifically to reduce the need to import tires from Japan. Indeed, tire sales had increased nearly 19 percent in 1996, a year in which Bridgestone earned a record ¥70.34 billion ($645.28 million) on a record ¥1.96 trillion ($17.96 billion) in sales.

Despite slumping sales of automobiles in Japan and other Asian nations because of the Asian economic crisis of 1997–98, Bridgestone closed out the decade strongly. In fact, the results for 1998 set new records: ¥104.63 billion ($921 million) in profits on ¥2.24 trillion ($19.69 billion) in revenues. The company was aided by its more efficient and productive U.S. operations, which showed steadily increasing profits in the late 1990s, reaching $300 million by 1999. The balance sheet of the U.S. subsidiary also was bolstered through a 1999 infusion of cash from the parent company aimed at reining in Bridgestone/Firestone, Inc.'s $3 billion debt.

On the negative side, Kaizaki had received much criticism in Japan for his aggressive, U.S.-style restructuring initiatives, including the launch of an early retirement program in the early 1990s; such moves were, in large part, still considered anathema in Japan. The criticism of Kaizaki came to a head in March 1999. That month a Bridgestone manager who had agreed to take early retirement went into Kaizaki's office to demand that the company's personnel policies be changed. When Kaizaki refused to change course, the manager took out a knife and committed hara-kiri. The resulting firestorm of negative publicity was only heightened by Kaizaki's failure to speak publicly about the incident for four months; when he did break his silence during a meeting with reporters, the company president came off as defiant and unfeeling.

Surviving a Potentially Devastating Tire Recall in the Early 2000s

In mid-2000 Kaizaki found himself embroiled in another crisis when reports began surfacing of possible defects in several Firestone tire models. Some of the tires, many of which had been used as the original tires on Ford Explorer sport utility vehicles, were shredding on the highway, leading to rollover accidents and more than 200 deaths and some 800 injuries, according to investigators with the U.S. National Highway Traffic Safety Administration. In August 2000 Bridgestone announced that its U.S. subsidiary would recall 6.5 million Firestone-brand ATX, ATX II, and Wilderness AT tires and replace them at the cost of hundreds of millions of dollars. Bridgestone's stock nosedived, and the company was once again hurt by missteps on the public relations front: Kaizaki, as he had in the prior crisis, maintained a long public silence over the issue, and Ono, the head of the U.S. subsidiary, made a belated public apology that was further marred by the suggestion that the drivers were to blame for the accidents because they had failed to keep their tires properly inflated.

Bridgestone gained control over the crisis soon after new executives were installed. In October 2000 Ono was replaced by John Lampe, who had been marketing chief for Bridgestone/Firestone. In early 2001, Shigeo Watanabe, a senior vice-president, took over the helm at Bridgestone, replacing Kaizaki. One of Watanabe's key early moves was to give Lampe more authority to make autonomous decisions concerning the crisis without constantly needing to gain approval from the Tokyo headquarters. As an American, Lampe was better able to communicate the Bridgestone/Firestone line: While acknowledging that the company had made some bad tires, and after expressing regret for the tragic accidents, Lampe was aggressive in contending that the design of the Ford Explorer had played a key role in the rollover accidents. When Ford Motor Company announced in May 2001 that it would spend $3 billion to replace an additional 13 million Firestone tires on Ford vehicles, Lampe made the stunning announcement that the Bridgestone/Firestone unit would end its 95-year relationship with Ford—at least in North and South America. (The two companies had more than just a business relationship: William Clay Ford, Jr., chairman of Ford, was the great-grandson of the founder of Firestone, Harvey Firestone.) While dramatic, cutting ties with Ford represented the loss of only 4 percent of Bridgestone's total revenues.

To escape the bankruptcy of the U.S. unit that many observers were predicting at the height of the crisis, Lampe engineered other moves. He took to the airwaves, starring in television commercials that had the theme ''Making It Right'' to begin repairing the damaged Firestone image. To the surprise of a number of analysts, the Firestone brand was not jettisoned but was instead retained as a mass market brand in the United States—though repositioned slightly downmarket—while the Bridgestone brand received greater emphasis as a premium brand. Lampe worked hard to keep Bridgestone/Firestone dealers onboard in particular by picking up the costs of the recall. He also launched a cost-cutting initiative to stem the unit's sea of red ink. Most notably, the company's plant in Decatur, Illinois, where many of the recalled tires had been made, was shut down at the end of 2001, costing about 1,500 workers their jobs.

Recall-related costs led to a $511 million loss at Bridgestone/Firestone in 2000, and the following year the unit lost a whopping $1.7 billion thanks not only to recall and restructuring costs but also to $285 million paid out to settle lawsuits filed in connection with the rollover accidents. The crisis meantime had a major impact on the company's U.S. market share, cutting its portion of the replacement tire market from 10.5 percent in

1999 to 7.5 percent in 2001, while its share of the new car market fell in the same period from 25 percent to 22 percent. To shore up the finances at Bridgestone/Firestone, the parent company injected it with $1.3 billion in January 2002. Despite the retention of the Firestone brand, Bridgestone began dropping that moniker from the names of its subsidiaries, with the U.S. unit renamed Bridgestone Americas Holding, Inc. at the beginning of 2003 and the company's European holding company renamed Bridgestone Europe N.V./S.A. This rebranding was part of an effort to build a global corporate identity under the Bridgestone name.

The remarkable turnaround at Bridgestone was evident in its results for 2002, which included a 5 percent increase in revenues, a 161 percent jump in profits, and the return of the U.S.-based subsidiary to profitability. Growing ever more confident that the crisis was over, Bridgestone announced late in 2002 that it was earmarking ¥56 billion ($467 million) for an expansion of its global passenger tire production capacity at plants in Japan, Poland, Thailand, Indonesia, China, Costa Rica, and Mexico. An additional ¥27 billion ($225 million) was set aside to increase production capacity at plants in Thailand, China, and Spain, where truck and bus tires were made. In March 2003 Bridgestone bolstered its European operations by purchasing an 18.9 percent interest in Finnish tire manufacturer Nokian Tyres PLC for ¥78.3 million. Nokian was the largest tire producer in the Nordic region with sales of ¥479 million in 2002. Still the world's leading tire maker, Bridgestone had managed not only to survive the potentially crippling tire recall but also to return quickly to a policy of aggressive growth.

Principal Subsidiaries

Bridgestone Cycle Co., Ltd.; Bridgestone Finance Corporation; Bridgestone Flowtech Corporation; Bridgestone Elastech Co., Ltd.; Bridgestone Sports Co., Ltd.; Asahi Carbon Co., Ltd. (99.4%); Bridgestone Tire Tokyo Hanbai K.K.; Bridgestone Tire Chubu Hanbai K.K. (99.7%); Bridgestone Tire Osaka Hanbai K.K.; Bridgestone Tire Hokkaido Hanbai K.K.; Bridgestone Tire Kyushu Hanbai K.K.; Bridgestone/Firestone Argentina S.A.I.C.; Bridgestone Australia Ltd. (60.3%); Bridgestone Earthmover Tyres Pty. Ltd. (Australia); Bridgestone Europe N.V./S.A. (Belgium); Bridgestone Aircraft Tire (Europe) S.A. (Belgium); Bridgestone/Firestone do Brasil Industria e Comercio Ltda. (Brazil); Bridgestone/Firestone Canada Inc.; Bridgestone/Firestone Chile, S.A. (89.7%); Bridgestone Off-the-Road Tire Latin America S.A. (Chile; 90%); Bridgestone (Tianjin) Tire Co., Ltd. (China; 94.5%); Bridgestone (Shenyang) Tire Co., Ltd. (China; 73.5%); Bridgestone Aircraft Tire Company (Asia) Limited (China); Bridgestone/Firestone de Costa Rica, S.A. (98.6%); Bridgestone France S.A.; Bridgestone Deutschland G.m.b.H. (Germany); Bridgestone ACC India Ltd. (64%); P.T. Bridgestone Tire Indonesia (51%); Bridgestone Italia S.p.A. (Italy); Bridgestone/Firestone de Mexico, S.A. de C.V.; Bridgestone Benelux B.V. (Netherlands); Bridgestone Finance Europe B.V. (Netherlands); Bridgestone/Firestone New Zealand Ltd.; Bridgestone Poland Limited Liability Company; Bridgestone Portuguesa, Lda. (Portugal); Bridgestone C.I.S. L.L.C. (Russia); Bridgestone Singapore Pte., Ltd.; Bridgestone/Firestone South Africa Holdings (Pty) Ltd. (93.7%); Bridgestone Hispania S.A. (Spain; 99.7%); Bridgestone Sweden AB; Bridgestone (Schweiz) AG (Switzerland); Bridgestone Taiwan Co., Ltd. (80%); Thai Bridgestone Co., Ltd. (Thailand; 67.2%); Brisa Bridgestone Sabanci Lastik Sanayi ve Ticaret A.S. (Turkey; 42.9%); Bridgestone U.K. Ltd.; Bridgestone Industrial Ltd. (U.K.); Bridgestone Americas Holding, Inc. (U.S.A.); Bridgestone/Firestone North American Tire, LLC (U.S.A.); BFS Retail & Commercial Operations, LLC (U.S.A.); BFS Diversified Products, LLC (U.S.A.); Morgan Tire & Auto, Inc. (U.S.A.; 58.5%); Bridgestone APM Company (U.S.A.); Bridgestone Aircraft Tire (USA), Inc.; Bridgestone/Firestone Venezolana C.A. (Venezuela).

Principal Competitors

Compagnie Générale des Établissements Michelin; The Goodyear Tire & Rubber Company; Continental AG; Sumitomo Rubber Industries, Ltd.; The Yokohama Rubber Co., Ltd.; Cooper Tire & Rubber Company; Toyo Tire & Rubber Co., Ltd.; Kumho Industrial Co., Ltd.

Further Reading

Aeppel, Timothy, Norihiko Shirouzo, and Michael Williams, ''Pit Crew: Firestone Team Faces Challenge of Steering Company Past Crisis,'' *Wall Street Journal,* October 11, 2000, pp. A1 + .

Belson, Ken, and Micheline Maynard, ''Big Recall Behind It, Tire Maker Regains Its Footing,'' *New York Times,* August 10, 2002, p. C1.

Bernstein, Aaron, Zachary Schiller, and Edith Hill Updike, ''Rubber Workers with Nerves of Steel,'' *Business Week,* December 18, 1995, p. 44.

''Bridgestone: America Holds the Key for Its Expanding Horizons,'' *Modern Tire Dealer,* December 1983, p. 22.

Chappell, Lindsay, ''Bridgestone Waxes As Firestone Wanes,'' *Tire Business,* November 19, 2001, p. 20.

Dickson, Martin, ''Bridgestone Wakes from an American Nightmare,'' *Financial Times,* August 24, 1993, p. 15.

Fahey, Jonathan, ''Flats Fixed,'' *Forbes,* May 27, 2002, pp. 40–41.

''Goodyear Drops Suit Against Bridgestone Over Ad Campaign,'' *Wall Street Journal,* July 1, 1997, p. B8.

''Goodyear Files Suit Over Firestone Ad Touting Tire Traction,'' *Wall Street Journal,* June 4, 1997, p. A8.

Griffiths, John, ''World Tyre Industry May Face Shake-Out,'' *Financial Times,* March 14, 1997, p. 4.

Holden, Ted, and Zachary Schiller, ''Now Akira Yeiri Really Has to Burn Rubber,'' *Business Week,* May 27, 1991, pp. 72–73.

How Bridgestone Works, Tokyo: Bridgestone Corporation, 1995.

Kindel, Stephen, ''Firestone: Sayonara to Tires,'' *Financial World,* March 22, 1988, p. 12.

Krisher, Bernard, ''A Different Kind of Tiremaker Rolls into Nashville,'' *Fortune,* March 22, 1982, p. 136.

Morris, Kathleen, ''A Bridge Far Enough,'' *Financial World,* June 9, 1992, pp. 52–54.

Narisetti, Raju, ''Bridgestone Takes on Goodyear in Aggressive Campaign,'' *Wall Street Journal,* April 16, 1997, p. B2.

Nelson, Emily, ''Anatomy of a Long, Bitter Labor Fight,'' *Wall Street Journal,* November 6, 1996, pp. B1, B4.

——, ''Bridgestone-Steelworker Accord Gives Firm Key Victory on Operating Plants,'' *Wall Street Journal,* November 7, 1996, p. A8.

Nevin, John J., ''The Bridgestone-Firestone Merger: An Insider's Account,'' *Journal of Business Strategy,* July/August 1989.

Schiller, Zachary, ''Bridgestone Is Nearing Some Hairpin Curves,'' *Business Week,* April 22, 1991, pp. 32–33.

——, ''Skid Marks at Bridgestone,'' *Business Week,* August 22, 1994, p. 31.

Schiller, Zachary, and Douglas Harbrect, ''Blowup at Bridgestone,'' *Business Week,* January 30, 1995, pp. 30–32.

Schiller, Zachary, and Roger Schreffler, ''So Far, America Is a Blowout for Bridgestone,'' *Business Week,* August 6, 1990, pp. 82–83.

Shibouta, Seishi, ''Bridgestone's Restructuring: Necessary But Painful,'' *Tokyo Business Today,* April 1995, p. 20.

Shuchman, Lisa, ''Bridgestone Stock May Keep Climbing,'' *Wall Street Journal,* April 17, 1998, p. B7D.

Stoyer, Lloyd, ''Bridgestone/Firestone's Kaizaki: U.S. Competition's Toughest in the World,'' *Modern Tire Dealer,* August 1992, p. 22.

——, ''Old Values, New Methods,'' *Modern Tire Dealer,* July 1998, pp. 32+.

Weinberg, Neil, ''The Buck Stops Here,'' *Forbes,* March 10, 1997, pp. 44–45.

Welch, David, ''Firestone: Is This Brand Beyond Repair?,'' *Business Week,* June 11, 2001, p. 48.

——, ''Meet the New Face of Firestone,'' *Business Week,* April 30, 2001, pp. 64, 66.

''When the Bridge Caught Fire,'' *Economist,* September 7, 1991, pp. 72–73.

Zaun, Todd, ''A Blowout Blindsides Bridgestone,'' *Wall Street Journal,* August 7, 2000, p. A8.

Zaun, Todd, et al., ''Pushing Back: Bridgestone Boss Has Toughness, But Is That What Crisis Demands?,'' *Wall Street Journal,* September 12, 2000, p. A1+.

Zaun, Todd, and Phred Dvorak, ''The Recall Rolls On: Firestone's Japan Parent Appears Anxiety-Free Despite U.S. Recall,'' *Wall Street Journal,* September 5, 2000, p. A16.

—Lois Glass
—update: David E. Salamie

BUDGENS
A **Musgrave** Company

Budgens Ltd.

Stonefield Way
Ruislip
Middlesex HA4 0JR
United Kingdom
Telephone: + 44 208-966-6000
Toll Free: 0800-526002
Fax: + 44 208-423-2263
Web site: http://www.budgens.co.uk

Wholly Owned Subsidiary of Musgrave Group Plc
Incorporated: 1896 as Budgen & Company Limited
Employees: 6,000
Sales: £500 million ($794 million) (2002 est.)
NAIC: 445110 Supermarkets and Other Grocery (Except
    Convenience) Stores

Although the smallest of the United Kingdom's top supermarket groups, Budgens Ltd. has successfully carved out a niche for itself among its behemoth rivals by focusing on local and city-center markets. Budgens operates more than 235 supermarkets and convenience stores, primarily in England's southern and Midlands regions—in 2003, however, the company opened its first stores in the northern region. The company's stores range from 700-square-foot forecourt shops, to 1,500-square-foot convenience stores, to the larger 10,000-square-foot Budgens supermarket concept. Altogether, the company operates more than 800,000 square feet of selling space throughout England. In addition to its emphasis on local markets, and the so-called "top up" trade, Budgens has differentiated itself through the high proportion of fresh foods at its stores—representing as much as 40 percent of total store items. The company's convenience format operates under the Budgens Express signage, and features a 24-hour, seven-day-per-week opening schedule, while Budgens Forecourts operates smaller shops within service stations. Budgens has also been developing its own franchising concept, Budgens Local. By 2003, more than 30 independent grocers have converted to the new signage. Ireland's retail leader Musgrave Group Plc acquired 100 percent control of Budgens since 2002; however, Musgrave has

pledged to maintain Budgens' independent operations, while seeking synergies between the two retail groups.

From Button to Booker to Barker in the 20th Century

Budgens started as a small, local grocer in England's southeast, founded in 1872 in Notting Hill. The Budgens name later appeared on a number of stores throughout the south, establishing a reputation for servicing the local communities around England's High Streets and suburban towns. In 1896, the company formally incorporated as Budgen & Company Limited.

Into the mid-20th century, however, the chain remained a small one, and had become part of the wholesale and retail group Alfred Button & Sons, itself founded in 1798. As part of Button, Budgen represented one of half a dozen retail store brands, which, by the middle of the century, had reached a total of some 82 stores.

In 1957, Button was acquired by the trading group Booker, McConnell & Co. That company's history dated back to the early 19th century, when the Booker brothers began trading operations between Liverpool and Guyana, then known as the British colony Demerra. The Booker brothers later expanded into sugar plantations as well as shipping and steamship services. Booker, McConnell then added food retailing and wholesaling operations in Guyana. After going public in 1927, the company began expanding beyond Guyana, adding operations in Trinidad and central Africa.

The political crises that swept through British Guyana in the early 1950s threatened Booker, McConnell's core business. In 1953, the company's board took the decision to diversify its operations. For this, Booker, McConnell proposed to add new operations in England, with an early emphasis on engineering on the one hand, and grocery distribution on the other. As part of that latter effort, Booker, McConnell acquired majority control of Alfred Button & Sons in 1957.

Under Booker, McConnell, Button's operations were restructured into its two core branches. Alfred Button represented Booker, McConnell's wholesale interests, while the company's

Company Perspectives:

Budgens' aim is to operate in every small town, large village & city centre, offering customers the finest fresh foods, the friendliest service and great Value for money. The aim is to be the viable alternative to the superstore and the first choice local supermarket where customers know they can trust the products they buy and where it is convenient for them to shop.

English retail stores were placed under Budgen & Co. (the latter eventually became known as Budgens). By the early 1970s, with its Guyana operations under continued pressure (these were sold to the Guyana government in 1976), Booker, McConnell stepped up its grocery distribution operations, with an emphasis on expanding its wholesale distribution business. At the same time, the Budgens chain of supermarkets grew to more than 100 stores by the end of the 1970s. Nonetheless, Budgens retained its regional focus, with nearly all of its stores concentrated in the country's southeast.

Continued expansion of the chain brought its store numbers to nearly 150 by the mid-1980s. By then, however, Booker had decided to concentrate its future development on its wholesale operations. Booker had also come under attack in a takeover bid from Dee Corporation in early 1984.

After its failure to acquire Booker, Dee, which had been formed from the Linfood Holdings wholesale business, began to convert its focus to the retail market under the Gateway supermarket banner. In that process, Dee sold its Linfood wholesale operation to Booker in 1987. In the meantime, Booker itself had completed the reorientation of its grocery distribution wing, selling off the Budgens retail operation in 1986 to confectioner Barker & Dobson for £80 million. That purchase, described as ''audacious,'' was greeted by a great deal of skepticism from the market.

Barker & Dobson itself had a long history as a prominent maker of confectionery—especially licorice—products, but had fallen on hard times in the 1970s. In 1985, Barker & Dobson's institutional shareholders insisted on new management for the company, bringing in John Fletcher to lead a turnaround. The young Fletcher, who held an M.B.A. from Harvard Business School, had already earned a reputation as something of a corporate hotshot, following his successful refocus of regional supermarket group Asda into one of the country's largest national chains.

Fletcher initially attempted to resurrect Barker & Dobson's confectionery brands. Yet the company's immediate efforts were met with continued losses. Instead, Fletcher decided to concentrate the company's growth efforts on its supermarket operation. Barker & Dobson announced its decision to sell off its confectionery arm, striking a deal at the end of 1988 to sell that business, including the Barker & Dobson name, to Scotland's Alma Caledonia. Following that transaction, the company renamed itself Budgens Plc.

In the meantime, Fletcher had led the company into an even more audacious direction. In 1987, Fletcher launched a £2 billion takeover attempt against Dee Corporation. If successful, the deal would have transformed Budgens into a major, nationally operating supermarket group. In anticipation of the group's impending expansion, Budgens commissioned a new, oversized warehouse and distribution facility in Wellingborough. Yet, the largely paper-based transaction failed, in part because the Budgens operation simply did not provide enough cash flow, or profits, to convince shareholders to support the bid. Dee Corporation was later transformed into the publicly listed Somerfield group.

Licking his wounds, Fletcher next attempted to merge Budgens with William Low in 1989. Yet that deal, too, ended unsuccessfully. By the beginning of the 1990s, Budgens' institutional shareholders—who had installed Fletcher in 1985—were becoming impatient. Added to these worries was the collapse of the British economy at the end of the 1980s, which resulted in the shedding of a number of Budgens stores. Finally, in 1991, Fletcher was dismissed, replaced by a three-man management team, led by John von Spreckelson, who had recently completed the turnaround of Germany's REWE supermarket group. By then, Budgens represented just 95 stores.

Convenience in the 1990s

Yet Budgens' new management appeared equally at a loss to find a position for the company in the rapidly changing British retail climate. The bruising economic climate had encouraged a wide-scale consolidation of the British supermarket industry, resulting in the emergence of a smaller number of powerful super-groups, led by Tesco and Sainsbury. At the same time, supermarkets were shifting their focus to the growing ''out-of-town'' shopping centers, which were springing up on the outskirts of the country's towns and cities, draining shoppers from the traditional High Street city centers. Meanwhile, a new breed of discount supermarket formats, led by Germany's Lidl and Aldi hard-discount chains, grabbed a stake in the United Kingdom's shrinking retail market. In response, supermarkets were forced to choose between an emphasis on differentiation—notably, the addition of new services and product categories—or a focus on price/cost, such as the discount model.

Budgens, however, attempted to achieve on both fronts, positioning itself as committed to local, High Street neighborhoods, while still continuing to differentiate with an emphasis on fresh foods in order to capture a stronger share of the ''top-up'' consumer market (that is, daily and weekly purchases as supplements to the main shopping excursion). As part of that effort, the company acquired Gilsons Bakers, a supplier of fresh baked goods to retailers, in 1992.

On the other hand, Budgens' new management led it, briefly, into the discount market as well. In 1992, Budgens agreed to sell more than 26 percent of its stock (with an option to increase that stake to more than 46 percent) to Germany's REWE. In return, REWE agreed to provide technical and financial support to Budgens in importing its highly successful Penny Market Discount store formula.

With more than 2,000 Penny Markets in Germany, the new formula appeared a good bet to attract the increasingly price-conscious British consumer, despite REWE's inexperience on

Key Dates:

1872: First Budgens supermarket opens.
1896: Budgens incorporates as Budgen & Company.
1957: Part of Albert Button & Sons, Budgen is acquired by Booker, McConnell.
1986: Booker, McConnell sells the business, now known as Budgens, to Barker & Dobson, led by John Fletcher.
1987: Barker & Dobson attempts but fails in takeover of Dee supermarket group.
1988: Barker & Dobson sells confectionery business and changes name to Budgens.
1992: Budgens sells 26 percent of stock to Germany's REWE and begins rollout of REWE's Penny Market discount retail format in United Kingdom.
1994: Budgens abandons Penny Market format and focuses instead on building convenience store network.
1997: Company acquires 55-store 7-11 chain in United Kingdom and converts it to Budgens Express format.
1998: Company acquires Teleshop Services and launches Budgens Direct home shopping and delivery service (abandoned in 2000).
2000: Musgrave Group of Ireland acquires 28 percent stake in Budgens.
2002: Musgrave Group acquires full control of Budgens.
2003: Budgens begins 20-store-per-year opening schedule as part of a strategy to double sales.

the international market. Budgens began converting stores to the new format in 1992, and by the following year had converted nearly 10 percent of its total portfolio. Budgens also proposed to build five new stores featuring the Penny Market signage starting in 1994.

In 1995, however, Budgens pulled the plug on the Penny Market experiment. The company had been unable to impose the new brand on the British market, succeeding only in draining sales away from its own stores. Penny Market's losses in the meantime had dragged down Budgens' total profits. Rather than fight for market share, Budgens quickly abandoned the discount formula, selling five of its Penny Markets to Lidl.

Instead, Spreckelson led Budgens into a new arena that proved closer to the company's traditional base, that of the convenience sector. After converting the remaining Penny Markets to a new format (Freshsave, evoking the larger company's growing emphasis on its fresh foods selection), Budgens began exploring other areas of growth in the convenience sector. In 1996, the company added a second Gilsons Bakers to support its commitment to its fresh foods strategy.

By then, the company was back on the expansion track, adding ten new supermarkets, and moving into the service station forecourt market with an agreement to open ten stores in Q8 and Mobil outlets. The company's association with Kuwait Petroleum strengthened the following year with an agreement to open 40 more Budgens shops in the Q8 network.

In 1997, Budgens' convenience arm took a major step forward when the company purchased the 55-store U.K. network of 7-11 convenience stores from Jardine Matheson. That deal cost Budgens nearly £6 million, yet included a cash treasury of some £2 million, offsetting the purchase price. Budgens immediately began converting the 7-11 stores under the company's newly developed convenience store format, Budgens Express. The addition of the new stores helped boost Budgens' total to more than 170 stores, and enabled it to extend into the Midlands region from its traditional southeast base.

Fresh Focus and Fresh Owners for the New Century

With REWE seeking to exit its shareholding, Budgens began looking for new partners in the late 1990s. The company nearly found a partner in former owner Booker—which had been struggling in the 1990s—which proposed a reverse takeover, creating a larger wholesale and retail distribution group under the Booker name, but with Budgens management in control. Yet Budgens' shareholders ultimately balked at the deal after the two sides could not agree upon a price.

Instead, in 2000, REWE sold its stake to Ireland's Musgrave Group, that country's largest privately held retailer, which had been seeking to enter the U.K. market since the late 1990s. Under that sale, Musgrave Group agreed not to launch a full takeover offer of Budgens for at least one year. Yet similarities between the two groups, including their emphasis on local markets, appeared to offer strong potential for an ultimate merger.

In the meantime, Budgens continued to expand its three retail formats, building up a chain of more than 230 stores by the new millennium. Budgens also tried to extend into a fourth formula, that of Internet shopping and home delivery, acquiring Teleshop Services in 1998. Yet the company ran up against heavy competition from Tesco and others, and the service, dubbed Budgens Direct, was shut down in 2000. Spreckelson stepped down that year, replaced by Martin Hyson.

Hyson returned the company's focus to its core local retail formats, introducing a new franchise concept, Budgens Local, in 2001. The company began signing on independent retailers, who agreed to adopt the Budgens signage, while Budgens provided product purchasing, distribution, marketing, and other services. Initially, the company hoped to expand its Budgens Local branch to 200 or more stores; yet by 2003, the company had succeeded in signing on just 30 stores.

In the meantime, the company had added four new supermarkets, through its acquisition of Sewards in 2001, which strengthened its position in the Berkshire region. The company also announced plans to step up its expansion of its convenience store network, with new store openings to reach as much as 20 per year.

Fueling that effort was the company's new majority shareholder, Musgrave, which moved to take full control of the company in 2002. At the time of the takeover, however, Musgrave announced its commitment to maintaining Budgens as an independent operation, while pledging to use its own strong financial position to help Budgens double its revenues within five years, to top the £1 billion mark. With its strong emphasis on fresh food and local service, as well as a new parent company, Budgens appeared to have found the formula for its future success.

Principal Subsidiaries

Budgens Express; Budgens Forecourts; Budgens Local; Convenience; Metro; Village.

Principal Competitors

Co-operative Group CWS Ltd.; Marks and Spencer PLC; John Lewis Partnership PLC; Somerfield PLC; Associated British Foods PLC; Wm. Morrison Supermarkets PLC; Waitrose Ltd.; Aldi Stores Ltd.; Food Brokers Ltd.

Further Reading

Addy, Rod, "Expansion Takes Budgens to York," *Grocer*, March 22, 2004, p. 8.

"Budgens Launches Customer Loyalty Scheme," *Marketing*, September 4, 2003, p. 5.

Daynes, Paul, "Training up Our Foodies," *Grocer*, May 31, 2003, p. 56.

Don, Andrew, "Budgens Awaits the Midas Touch," *Super Marketing*, October 25, 1991, p. 30.

Hawkesworth, Richard I., "Budgens plc: Coping with Competition in UK Grocery Retailing," *International Journal of Retail & Distribution Management*, January 1998, p. 38.

Murray-West, Rosie, "Budgens Backs Musgrave's £232m Bid," *Daily Telegraph*, June 22, 2002, p. 28.

Watson, Elaine, "Budgens Goes for 1bn," *Grocer*, October 12, 2002, p. 4.

——, "Mr. McGettigan's Local Ambitions," *Grocer*, October 19, 2002, p. 36.

Urny, Maggie, "Refocused Budgens to Accelerate Expansion," *Financial Times*, July 6, 2001, p. 20.

—M. L. Cohen

Budweiser Budvar, National Corporation

Karoliny Světlé 4
370 21 České Budějovice
Czech Republic
Telephone: 420 387 705 111
Fax: 420 387 311 135
Web site: http://www.budweiser.cz

Government-Owned Company
Incorporated: 1895 as Český akciový pivovar
Employees: 651
NAIC: 312120 Breweries; 424810 Beer and Ale
    Merchant Wholesalers

Small but feisty Czech brewer Budweiser Budvar, National Corporation has been battling mighty Anheuser-Busch (A-B) for nearly a century over the right to use the famed Budweiser brand. Budweiser Budvar National Corp., which remains wholly owned by the Czech government's National Property Fund, hails from the town of České Budějovice, also known as Budweis, leading to the company's claim as the brewer of the "Original" Budweiser—and not the A-B version, which, despite being the world's largest-selling beer brand, remains what many consider a pale imitation of a full-bodied beer. On the other hand, the Budweiser Budvar version is recognized by many beer experts and consumers as among the world's finest lagers. Since the beginning of the 1990s, Budvar has succeeded in winning its case in a number of markets, and especially in Eastern and Western Europe, and now holds the exclusive trademark to the Budweiser name in more than 50 countries. In North America, however, the company is forced to market its beers under the Czechvar name in accordance with an agreement made with A-B in 1939. Since emerging from Communist domination, during which period Budweiser Budvar existed primarily as one of the country's three authorized export beers, the company has successfully gained a strong share of its domestic market as well, and by the beginning of the 2000s ranked as the country's number four brewer, producing more than 1.3 million hectoliters per year. Budweiser Budvar operates sales and marketing subsidiaries in a number of countries, notably in the United Kingdom—the only country where both Budvar and A-B have the rights to the Budweiser brand name—as well as in Germany and Croatia. In these markets, and others such as Austria, Budvar ranks among the top-selling imported beers. In the Czech Republic, Budvar operates its own chain of retail stores, which sell wine and other alcoholic beverages, in addition to its Budweiser Budvar, Budweiser Free (nonalcoholic), and Bud Super-Strong brews. Budvar is slated for possible privatization, but remains under control of the Czech government; the company is led by Jiří Boček.

Czech Beer History 101

For many beer enthusiasts, the history of "real" beer began in the region known as Bohemia, later known as the Czech Republic, and the development of the "lager" style of beer. This brewing style, which owed as much to its recipe and to the use of the region's Zatec (Saaz) hops, centered on a number of small towns, such as Pilsen, which gave its name to a whole class of beers, and the small village of Budějovice—formerly known by its German name of Budweis. That village was established by royal decree in 1265 and was given a license to brew beer by King Přemysl Otakar II.

At first, beer brewing rights were granted to a broad spectrum of citizens, but by the early 18th century, the town's beer-making activity had come almost entirely under the province of a small number of professional brewers, with the exception of a "public" brewery owned by the town council and operated in the town center. Political struggles between the town's rival Czech and German populations, however, resulted in the public brewery being transferred to a group of "burghers," or citizens, who, under the control of the Austro-Hapsburg empire were to enjoy a great deal of political and economic control in the region. The citizens group finally won out, taking over the brewery in 1795 and founding Měšťanský pivovar ("Burghers' Brewery"). In German, the new company's name became Die Budweiser Bräuberechtigten Bürgerliches Bräuhaus gegründet 1795.

The new Budweiser brewery soon became the town's dominant brewer, as the fame of the Budějovice brews spread throughout the region. Under the Austro-Hapsburg empire, brewers were restricted to selling beers only within their own regions. Nonetheless, the Budweiser brewery production grew strongly. In 1847 a new, larger facility was built outside of

Company Perspectives:

Budweiser Budvar pays as much attention as possible to the way its beer is made, it uses the very best home ingredients and the beer is made by the best brewing experts. For more than one hundred years, many generations of ordinary customers as well as renowned experts have valued the wonderful taste, aroma and body of the original Budweiser.

town. By the 1870s, Měšt'anský had begun exporting its beers, including to the United States starting in 1872.

Political tensions between the German and Czech populations in Budějovice began building during the late 19th century, exacerbated in part by the empire's system of attributing voting rights according to wealth—thereby giving the wealthier, but smaller German population in town control of its political structure. The abolition of the brewing laws restricting breweries to sales in their region in 1860 opened the prospect for new growth in the Bohemian brewing industry. Yet the German control of the town's main Budweiser brewer, as well as the two other major breweries in the region, effectively cut out Czech brewers and investors from entering the field.

In response, a group of Czech brewers began preparations to build their own brewery in the early 1890s. In 1894, the group organized its first meeting for prospective shareholders in order to gather the funds necessary to launch a new business. Over the next year, the group succeeded in raising the funds—and overcoming the political obstacles—needed to create and build their brewery, and Český akciový pivovar, or the Czech Joint Stock Brewery, was founded in 1895.

The new brewery, built using then modern, industrial techniques, was an instant success, producing more than 51,000 hectoliters of beer in its first year, with sales fueled in part by nationalist sentiments—as the region's Czech population became the company's first customers. Yet the new brew proved to be more than an exercise in national pride—by the end of 1896, the company had already won its first awards, the Gold Medal at the Prague trade fair and the Silver Medal at the Industrial and Pharmaceutical Exhibition, also in Prague. By the following year, the Budějovice brew's fame had already begun to cross borders, with a new Gold Medal at the Stuttgart food and drink exhibition. At the same time, the company's sales expanded throughout the Austro-Hapsburg empire, becoming a popular brew in Trieste and Vienna and other European capitals.

By World War I, the Budějovice brewery's production had already doubled that of the Měšt'anský brewery. The beer had by then achieved worldwide fame, far beyond the empire, as beer drinkers around the world embraced the so-called Bohemian style beers. Yet that fame was soon to lead both the Czech Joint Stock Brewery and the Měšt'anský into conflict with a new and fast-growing international rival, an American company called Anheuser-Busch.

Trademark Battles in the 20th Century

German immigrants to the United States had been responsible for bringing over many beer recipes from the European continent, yet none proved as popular and enduring as those that originated in the Bohemia region. Among the newcomers to the United States was Adolphus Busch, who became the son-in-law of a struggling St. Louis brewer, Ebehard Anheuser, joining the business in 1957. Busch steered the Anheuser brewer toward the production of Bohemian-styled beers, and the business flourished. In 1876, Busch teamed up with another German immigrant, Carl Conrad, who had been working as a drink salesman, and the company began marketing its Bohemian lager under the Budweiser (which, in German, meant "from Budweis") brand name.

Conrad himself registered the Budweiser trademark in the United States in 1878, although A-B remained the beer brand's brewer. The new brand caught on quickly, leading the company to add other Bohemian brands, including Michelob, among others. In 1881, Conrad's company sold Anheuser-Busch the rights to its Budweiser trademark. Nonetheless, A-B's brand was not the only Budweiser available in the United States in the late 19th century. In addition to the Měšt'anský Budweiser, there were a number of others, including one brewed in Pennsylvania and another in Brooklyn, New York, the former of which continued production into the 1970s.

A-B, which through its aggressive marketing strategy had emerged as the United States' dominant brewer by 1900, went a step further, registering the Budweiser trademark as its own in 1907. This led A-B into direct conflict for the first time with both the Měšt'anský brewery and its Budweis/Budejovice hometown rival Český akciový pivovar. The three parties worked out an agreement in 1911, whereby A-B retained the right to use the Budweiser brand name in the U.S. market and elsewhere, with the exception of Europe, in exchange for a financial consideration. As part of that agreement, however, both Budweis breweries retained the right to market their beers using the Budweiser name worldwide. This agreement also allowed the company to market its beers in the United States, with the provision that it state clearly that the beer originated in Budweis/Budejovice, and not in the United States.

Following World War I, the town of Budweis officially adopted the Czech variant name Budejovice. Český akciový pivovar, which had suffered during the war due to a lack of ingredients and from being cut off from its export markets, once again resumed its exports, enabling the company to rebuild quickly in the postwar years. By the late 1920s, production had risen past prewar levels, and the company had completed a modernization and expansion of its production site, including sinking its first Artesian well in 1922. This well was followed by the sinking of two more wells by 1930, ensuring the company a good supply of clean water. In that year, the company registered its own trademark, Budvar.

Budvar, as the company came to be called, needed its expanded water supply for its growing production. The company had become especially successful on the export market, selling its beers throughout Europe and into the Middle East, Africa, and as far away as Japan. During the 1920s, the company added a number of new beer brands, including Český Budějovický granát, launched in 1922, a newly named Budweiser Bier in 1925, which was followed by Budbräu in 1934, and the Crystal beer brand in 1935, targeting the export market.

Key Dates:

1795: Měšt'anský pivovar (''Burghers' Brewery'') is founded in Budweis, in Bohemia (Czech Republic).

1872: Měšt'anský pivovar begins exports of its Budweiser brand to the United States.

1878: Carl Conrad registers U.S. trademark for Budweiser brand, which is brewed by Anheuser-Busch.

1895: Český akciový pivovar, or the Czech Joint Stock Brewery (Budvar), is founded in Budweis.

1911: Anheuser-Busch and Budvar sign their first agreement.

1922: Budvar expands and modernizes production, including sinking first of three Artesian wells.

1939: Second trademark agreement is signed by Budvar and Anheuser-Busch, barring Budvar from U.S. market and giving Anheuser-Busch the right to market Budweiser worldwide.

1948: Budvar is nationalized and absorbs Měšt'anský brewery.

1967: Name is officially changed to Budweiser Budvar, National Corporation.

1989: Collapse of Communist government in ''Velvet Revolution'' enables Budvar to resume expansion.

1994: Trademark ''truce'' between Anheuser-Busch and Budvar ends after Czech government refuses to allow U.S. company to acquire Budvar.

1996: Budvar expands domestically with opening of first retail outlets in Czech Republic.

1999: Company forms subsidiary partnership in Germany to support its exports to that country.

2001: Company launches subsidiary in the United Kingdom, company's second largest export market.

2003: The company successfully defends its right to use Budweiser and Bud trademarks in the United Kingdom.

The company formally adopted the Budvar name in 1936, becoming Budvar - Český akciový pivovar České Budějovice.

In the meantime, the Prohibition era had cut off the company from the U.S. market. The repeal of Prohibition, however, encouraged the company to resume exports to that country, and in 1937 Budvar registered a U.S. trademark, Imported Original Bohemian Budweiser Beer from Budweis City. Although the somewhat bulky name allowed Budvar to remain within the terms of the 1911 agreement with A-B, it quickly brought the two companies into new disputes.

By 1939, however, A-B had history on its side. As the Nazi government began claiming portions of the then Czechoslovakia as part of Germany itself, and following the Munich Agreement, which allowed the Germans to proceed with full annexation by the end of the year, Budvar came under increasing pressure from threats to confiscate its U.S. assets. As a result, Budvar was forced to agree to a new settlement with A-B, this time granting Anheuser-Busch the exclusive right to the Budweiser brand name in North America and the right to use it elsewhere in the world as well.

Budvar was taken over by the Nazis during the war, and exports were halted. Following the war, the company enjoyed a brief period as a private enterprise, but was soon after nationalized by the new Soviet-controlled Czech government. In 1948, Budvar then absorbed the Měšt'anský brewery, and its name was changed, to JihoČeské pivovary, národní podnik, or South Bohemian Breweries, National Corporation.

Under the Communist government, South Bohemian became one of three breweries picked to represent the country on the export market—virtually ending the brewery's domestic sales. In support of its export sales, the brewery launched an ambitious expansion program in 1964, designed to increase its production from 300,000 hectoliters to more than 830,000 upon completion in 1982. In 1967, the company was renamed Budweiser Budvar, National Corporation as work got underway. Yet the expansion stalled, and by 1982, production had barely climbed to 360,000 hectoliters. Nonetheless, Budvar continued to win its share of medals, including the Gold Medal in Leipzig in 1982, a Bronze Medal in England in 1985, and a Gold Medal in Paris in 1989.

Renewing Growth for the New Century

That year marked the end of Communist domination in Czechoslovakia (soon to separate into the Czech and Slovak republics) and the return to a free-market economy. While still a government-controlled business, Budvar began making fresh plans for expansion. Yet the company once again bumped up against Anheuser-Busch—except, by then, the St. Louis-based company had grown into the world's largest brewer, and its Budweiser brand, backed by one of the world's largest advertising juggernauts, had become the world's number one selling beer brand.

Litigation between the two companies had in fact resumed in the late 1970s, when both A-B and Budvar had begun expanding in the United Kingdom. The result of that litigation in 1984 led to a ruling that both companies were allowed to use the Budweiser trademark in the United Kingdom, a situation that was to prove unique in the world. Both companies appealed the decision, leading to a legal battle that would not be resolved until 2003, when Budvar received a ruling in its favor.

In the meantime, the collapse of Communism offered the prospects for a lasting truce, as the new Czech government indicated its willingness to privatize Budvar. Anheuser-Busch immediately began positioning itself as a candidate to take over its smaller rival, attempting to woo the Czech government by, among other initiatives, setting up a St. Louis Centre in Budějovice. The two sides agreed to a truce in their legal battles, starting in 1990. Yet popular support for maintaining Budvar's independence, including intervention from the United Kingdom's Campaign for Real Ale (which claimed that A-B would reduce the Budějovice site to little more than a museum) swayed the Czech government, which ruled against any sale to A-B. In response, A-B once again took up litigation.

Budvar, however, found support in the recently signed GATT agreement, also signed by the United States, which provided protection for local products and trademarks. From the mid-1990s, Budvar was increasingly successful in arguing that the Budweiser brand qualified as a locally based trademark, and, especially in many European markets, successfully established itself as the sole Budweiser in town.

By the beginning of the new century, Budweiser Budvar had imposed its brand on more than 60 countries worldwide. While exports remained a significant share of the group's sales, the domestic market became, for the first time in 60 years, the company's primary market. As production topped 1.3 million hectoliters per year, the domestic market had come to represent some two-thirds of the group's total sales. Supporting its Czech expansion, Budvar began opening its own retail outlets starting in 1996, with ten in operation at the beginning of the 2000s.

Budvar also took steps to expand its export business in 1999, setting up a partnership with its two main German distributors, to be named Budweiser Budvar Vertriebgesellschaft Deutschland and held at 70 percent by Budvar. That subsidiary supported the company's growth as a leading export brand in the world's second largest beer market. Its creation was followed by subsidiaries in the United Kingdom and Croatia as well. In 2003, the company's legal case was strengthened when it successfully defeated the latest attempt by Anheuser-Busch to claim sole ownership of the Bud and Budweiser trademarks in the United Kingdom.

Meanwhile, the company had marked a new historic moment in 2001 when it returned to the United States for the first time in nearly 70 years—marketing its beer under the name Czechvar to skirt continued trademark restrictions in that market. Although it appeared unlikely that Budweiser Budvar would be able to overturn brewing giant Anheuser Busch's hold on the Budweiser trademark on its home turf, many Americans welcomed the return of what many in the world consider the world's finest lager.

Principal Subsidiaries

Budweiser Budvar, d.o.o. (Croatia); Budweiser Budvar Vertriebgesellschaft Deutschland GmbH (Germany; 70%); Budweiser Budvar UK.

Principal Competitors

Altria Group Inc.; Philip Morris USA; Anheuser-Busch Companies Inc.; Groupe Danone; Kirin Brewery Company Ltd.; Madhvani Group; Asahi Breweries Ltd.; Interbrew SA/NV; Carlsberg A/S; Orkla ASA; Dr. August Oetker KG; Allied Domecq PLC.

Further Reading

"Budvar Wins Battle over Budweiser Name," *Independent*, July 9, 2003, p. 10.

Bull, Roger, "Hey Bud, Czechvar Is Good," *Florida Times Union*, October 17, 2002, p. C-5.

"Can They Be Buddies?" *Time International*, July 13, 1998, p. 58.

"It's My Brand, Bud," *Observer*, June 21, 1998, p. 8.

Koenig, Robert L., "Two Buds Too Diverse to Graft," *St. Louis Post-Dispatch*, October 20, 1996, p. 1E.

Lalor, Peter, "Czech Mate? No Way, Bud," *Daily Telegraph* (Australia), February 26, 2003, p. 50.

Stamborski, Al, "This Czechvar's for You," *St. Louis Post-Dispatch*, March 11, 2001, p. A2.

—M. L. Cohen

Campofrío Alimentación S.A

Avenida de Europa, 24
Parque Empresarial La Moraleja
28108 Madrid
Spain
Telephone: +34 91 484 2700
Fax: +34 91 661 5345
Web site: http://www.campofrio.es

Public Company
Incorporated: 1956
Employees: 9,037
Sales: EUR 1.42 billion ($1.4 billion) (2002)
Stock Exchanges: Madrid
Ticker Symbol: CPF
NAIC: 311612 Meat Processed from Carcasses; 311611
    Animal (Except Poultry) Slaughtering; 424470 Meat
    and Meat Product Merchant Wholesalers

Having long dominated its domestic market, Spain's Campofrío Alimentación S.A has set out to become one of the leading cured and processed meat companies in Europe. Campofrío produces a full range of deli meat products, including the Spanish ham favorite Serrano, as well as chorizo sausages, salami, and other cold cuts. The company also produces fresh and prepared foods for the restaurant and catering circuit. In addition to its own brand name, Campofrío has amassed a strong collection of brands, including longtime Spanish market rivals Oscar Mayer and Navidul Revilla; France's Montagne Noire; Poland's Morliny; and Russia's Kampomoc. Spain remains the company's primary market, at more than 68 percent of its sales of EUR 1.4 billion in 2002. Between its own brands and its private label production, Campofrío holds more than 20 percent of the Spanish cured and deli meats market. In addition, Campofrío has long pursued international growth, and has built up market leadership in Poland and France, and strong positions in Russia and Romania, with its sales and distribution network stretching throughout most of western and eastern Europe. The European Union countries accounted for nearly 11.5 percent of sales in 2002. Campofrío also operates internationally, balancing its 14 production plants in Spain with 12 plants in its European markets, including six in France. Hormel Foods of the United States holds a 21 percent stake in Campofrío; the founding Ballvé family, including CEO and Chairman Pedro Ballvé, hold 45 percent of the company, which is listed on the Madrid stock exchange's Mercado Continuo.

Slaughtering Origins in the 1950s

Campofrío Alimentación had its origins in the early 1950s, when José Luis Ballvé started a slaughtering business in the Spanish town of Burgos in 1952. By the end of the decade, however, Ballvé had begun to branch out, and in 1960 launched his own line of cured and processed meat products. Those products later became the company's specialty. Joining Ballvé in the family business was son Pedro José, born in 1954, who became president in 1978.

By then, the death of Francisco Franco and the opening of the Spanish economy presented new growth opportunities for the company. In 1978, Campofrío opened its capital to the United States' Beatrice Foods, which acquired a 50 percent stake in the small Spanish company. In exchange, however, Campofrío gained access to Beatrice Foods' technological superiority, as well as modern management, and organizational and marketing techniques.

Campofrío's partnership with Beatrice Foods enabled the company to rise quickly in the Spanish market, and by the end of the decade, the company had already gained a leading position in the domestic cured meats market. The death of José Luis Ballvé in 1985 spelled the beginning of a new era for the company. Now under the leadership of Pedro Ballvé, Campofrío sought to expand on its own, and began negotiations to regain the shares in the company held by Beatrice Foods.

That process was given a jump-start after Beatrice Foods was bought up in a leveraged buyout in 1987. That company's new owners soon reached an agreement to sell its 50 percent stake in Campofrío for $90 million. Ballvé regained control of Campofrío, backed by Banco Centrale, which took over 40 percent of Beatrice Food's former stake. A year later, Campofrío went public, listing 10 percent of its shares on the Madrid stock exchange.

Company Perspectives:

Campofrío is a customer-focused international foods and nutrition group with investments in three continents and manufacturing plants in 11 nations, reaching over 250 million consumers in over 40 countries worldwide. Campofrío is a company with a clearly global mission, growing both in size and quality, and equipped with the most up-to-date technology. Campofrío has created a solid business platform in the most important world markets, both in strong, consolidated economies and rapidly developing nations. Campofrío has adopted the Healthy Living philosophy as a lifestyle reflecting the key aspects of the Group: a continual search for healthy products providing maximum consumer satisfaction and ensuring an improvement in their quality of life. The Group pursues its business with this twin focus on health and food so that all of our activities always strive to strike a balance between the pleasure of eating well and the pleasure of eating healthy.

International Expansion in the 1990s

The younger Ballvé quickly showed his own entrepreneurial spirit and launched Campofrío on a new expansion phase. By the beginning of the 1990s Ballvé had succeeded in doubling the company's sales, which topped the equivalent of EUR 500 million in 1991, since taking over the reins from his father.

With market leadership assured at home, Ballvé turned his attention to building Campofrío into a global operation. Campofrío naturally turned to neighboring markets, opening its first foreign subsidiary for marketing and distributing its products in France in 1990. The following year, Campofrío moved into Portugal, launching a distribution subsidiary for that market.

Yet Ballvé had already spotted a new opportunity farther abroad. The collapse of the Soviet government promised a new and vast market for the company's meat products. In 1990, Campofrío became one of the first foreign companies to invest in Russia, setting up its first plant there. A year later, Campofrío formed a joint venture, CampoMos, with Moscow-based Mosmia Soprom, which had been given the beef supply contract supporting McDonald's Corporation's entry into Russia. Campofrío's own early entry into Russia—where processed foods had remained a scarcity throughout the Soviet era—enabled it to capture a leading share in the newly opened market. As Ballvé himself proudly told *International Management:* "Everyone knows our brand name in Moscow, like McDonald's."

Indeed, the company's Russian operations were to provide the motor for much of the profit and sales growth through the 1990s, and by the second half of the decade accounted for the largest part of the group's profits. Building on its success in Russia, the company established a second plant in Moscow in 1994. Initially, Campofrío's share of the CampoMos joint venture stood at 50 percent. By the end of the 1990s, however, Campofrío had increased its stake to more than 91 percent.

In the meantime, Campofrío continued its international expansion. In 1991, the company journeyed to the Philippines,

forming the 50–50 Campocarne joint venture in that country with San Miguel Corporation. The company then eyed expansion into the Latin American market, forming CampoAustral SA in Argentina. Campofrío's initial stake in that joint venture stood at just 25 percent, but was boosted to 40 percent by the end of the decade. The company then extended its South American operations with the opening of plants in the Dominican Republic and Bolivia.

Consolidating Leadership for the New Century

By 1996, Campofrío's sales had neared the equivalent of EUR 650 million. At the end of the year, the company found a new strategic partner in the United States' Hormel Foods Corp., then undergoing its own international expansion effort. In December 1996, Hormel acquired 21 percent of Campofrío from Banco Centrale. The move gave Campofrío access to the U.S. market as well as Hormel's marketing and technological expertise.

The economic crisis that swept through Russia in 1998 provided a new opportunity for Campofrío to step up its market share, which had already reached 20 percent in that country. At the same time, Campofrío began plans for expanding elsewhere in the Eastern European region. In April 1998, the company acquired nearly 80 percent of Romania's Tabco, then, at the end of the year, reached an agreement to acquire the controlling stake in Polish cured meats market leader Morliny SA.

Closer to home, the company began construction on a new production facility in Burgos that year. The following year, the company added production facilities in France through its acquisition of Gayraud Montagne Pyrénées, and its Montagne Noire brand. Campofrío also strengthened its operations in Portugal through its purchase of Fricarnes, the top brand in that country. Campofrío also attempted a diversification into pâtés and other prepared delicatessen items through its acquisition of Spanish group Delicass.

Yet Campofrío had already embarked on a drive to consolidate the Spanish cured meats sector and solidify its position as a domestic and European leader. In 1999, the company acquired Andalusia based Molina, then under liquidation proceedings, as part of the basis of a new subsidiary, Campocarne Andalusia.

In 2000, the United States' Sara Lee had been preparing an entry into the Spanish market, negotiating to acquire both of Campofrío's main rivals, Omsa, the Spanish Oscar Mayer branch, and Navidul. Yet Ballvé out-maneuvered the American food giant, and in May 2000 acquired 87 percent of Omsa for EUR 77 million. One month later, Ballvé completed its one-man consolidation of the Spanish cured meats sector when he reached an agreement to merge Campofrío with Navidul, in a deal worth some EUR 300 million.

The completion of the two acquisitions transformed Campofrío into one of Europe's largest cured meats companies. The purchases of Navidul and Omsa also shut out Sara Lee in its hopes to take market share from Campofrío on its home turf. At the end of 2002, Campofrío renamed its Campocarne subsidiary as Primayor, in order to integrate its newly acquired operations, as well as its fresh foods products. The company also decided to exit the pâtés market that year, selling off its Delicass subsidiary.

Key Dates:

1952: José Luis Ballvé founds Campofrío Alimentación in Burgos, Spain, as a slaughterhouse.

1960: Campofrío begins producing cured and processed meats.

1978: Ballvé sells 50 percent of company to Beatrice Foods International.

1985: Pedro Ballvé takes over company after his father's death.

1987: Ballvé regains control of Campofrío from Beatrice Foods.

1988: Campofrío goes public on Madrid stock exchange.

1990: Campofrío begins international expansion with subsidiary in France and opening of a plant in Moscow.

1991: Campofrío forms CampoMoc joint venture with Mosmia Soprom in Russia; launches subsidiary in Portugal; forms joint venture in the Philippines with San Miguel Corporation.

1993: Company enters Argentina through CampoAustral joint venture.

1996: Hormel acquires 21 percent of Campofrío.

1998: Company acquires Tabco in Romania and Morliny in Poland.

1999: Company acquires Montagne Noire brand in France; acquires Delicass to enter pâtés and prepared delicatessen foods sector (sold in 2002).

2000: Campofrío acquires majority of Omsa and merges with Navidul to solidify Spanish market leadership.

2001: Campofrío announces exit of Latin American and Asian markets to focus on European growth.

2002: Campofrío creates Primayor to take over former Campocarne subsidiary and integrate Omsa and Navidul operations.

2003: Company prepares to continue European expansion through acquisitions.

Campofrío's new dominance of the European market encouraged the company to focus its future expansion efforts in Western and Eastern Europe, and in 2001, the company announced its intention to sell off its South American holdings. At the same time, Campofrío sold its share of the Philippines joint venture to partner San Miguel.

By the end of 2003, Campofrío had completed its reorganization as a pan-European meat products company. The company's revenues now topped EUR 1.4 billion, and the company had succeeded in paying down much of the debt generated through the Omsa and Navidul acquisitions. Campofrío appeared in strong position to continue its international expansion into the new century.

Principal Subsidiaries

814 Americas INC (U.S.A.); Agrocarne S.A (Dominican Republic; 49%); Campoaustral S.A (Argentina; 40%); Campofrío Alimentación S.A.; Campofrío Montagne Noire S.A (France; 63%); CampoMos (Russia; 91%); Fricarnes S.A (Portugal; 80%); Morliny S.A (Poland; 98%); Navidul Extremadura S.A.; Omsa (80%); Primayor Alimentación Andalucía S.A.; Primayor Alimentación S.L.; Tabco Campofrío (Romania; 95%).

Principal Competitors

Ebro Puleva S.A.; Cooperativas Orensanas SCL; Corporacion Alimentaria Guissona; McDonald's Sistemas de Espana Inc.; Viscofan SA, Industria Navarra de Envolturas Celulosicas; Elpozo Alimentación S.A.; Casa Tarradellas S.A.; Grupo Navidul S.A.

Further Reading

''Campofrío Considers International Expansion,'' *Expansion,* August 23, 2003, p. 7.

Chapman, Peter, ''All the King's Men,'' *International Management,* June 1992, p. 50.

''Grupo Campofrío Becomes Leader in Polish Meat Sector,'' *Expansion*, November 19, 1998, p. 12.

''Pedro Ballvé, Président de Campofrío: Etre global est la seule voie de survie,'' *Actualités,* September 29, 2000.

''Spanish Meat Group Campofrío Alimentación Has Reported Satisfactory Results for 2002,'' *Food Engineering & Ingredients*, April 2003, p. 5.

White, David, ''Campofrío in Merger Plan with Navidul,'' *Financial Times,* June 3, 2000, p. 8.

—M. L. Cohen

Captain D's, LLC

1717 Elm Hill Pike, Suite A-1
Nashville, Tennessee 37210
U.S.A.
Telephone: (615) 231-2537
Toll Free: (800) 550-4877
Fax: (615) 231-2955
Web site: http://www.captainds.com

Limited Liability Company
Founded: 1969 as Mr. D's
Employees: 6,600
Sales: $300 million (2002 est.)
NAIC: 722211 Limited-Service Restaurants

Operating out of Nashville, Tennessee, Captain D's, LLC operates the Captain D's seafood restaurant chain, devoted to the "fast-casual" dining concept. The company owns and operates some 300 of the chain's more than 560 units, with the balance owned by franchisees. Captain D's restaurants are found in 22 states, mostly located in the South. In recent years the chain has established units at military bases, allowing Captain D's to go international with the 2003 opening of a restaurant on the Okinawa Air Force Base in Japan. Captain D's operates for lunch and dinner, its regular menu featuring a variety of fried, baked, and broiled fish and shrimp dishes, as well as seafood-stuffed crab shells and seasonal items. The chain also offers its Coastal Classic menu, which includes seafood recipes from across the country and such dishes as fried coastal flounder, fried gulf coast oysters, Southern style catfish, and shrimp scampi. Captain D's is a private company controlled by the investment group Lone Star Funds, following more than three decades under the ownership of Shoney's, Inc.

Tracing Company Origins to 1969 and Shoney's, Inc.

The origin of Captain D's is linked to Danner Foods, which merged with Shoney's, its longtime corporate parent. Shoney's was established in 1947 by Alex Schoenbaum, growing out of a single drive-in restaurant located in Charleston, West Virginia. In 1951 Schoenbaum began to open Big Boy restaurants as a franchisee, and two years later established his own restaurant concept, which as a result of an employee contest took on his nickname, Shoney's. Also during the 1950s another Big Boy franchisee, Nashville's Ray Danner, opened his first restaurant and soon assembled a sizable chain, which led to the 1968 formation of Danner Foods, Inc. to franchise Big Boy restaurants throughout the Southeast. In 1969 Danner went public. In that same year Danner created a fast-food seafood concept called Mr. D's, forerunner to Captain D's.

To manage the first Mr. D's, which opened in Donelson, Tennessee, Ray Danner tabbed David K. Wachtel, who would not only go on to head Shoney's but eventually run eight restaurant chains. Wachtel went to work for Danner as a teenager, washing dishes and busing tables at Danner's first Nashville restaurant. He worked at another Danner restaurant while attending the University of Tennessee-Knoxville. He began to study law, but left law school in 1965, moving back to Nashville to take a management position with Danner in 1968. Wachtel succeeded in establishing the Mr. D's seafood concept, and in 1974 it was renamed Captain D's. In the meantime, Danner and Schoenbaum merged their operations, in 1971 creating Shoney's Big Boy Enterprises, Inc. A year later it dropped Big Boy from its name, becoming Shoney's Enterprises, Inc., with Ray Danner taking over as CEO and chairman. The parent company of Captain D's was flying high in the mid-1970s, the most popular family restaurant in the Southeast. In 1976 it shortened its name to Shoney's, Inc., the same year Wachtel was named president. He succeeded Danner as CEO in 1981 as the company peaked. In addition to the Shoney's and Captain D's chains, the company's restaurants included Sailmaker and Fifth Quarter, as well as Kentucky Fried Chicken franchises. Tallied altogether, Shoney's was a billion-dollar-a-year business. Wachtel soon fell out with the autocratic Ray Danner, however, and left Shoney's in 1982.

For more than 20 years Captain D's deviated very little from the concept refined by Wachtel in the early 1970s. It competed with the likes of Long John Silver's and Arthur Treachers in the fast-food, deep-fried seafood category, a notch below the sit-down dining niche carved out by Red Lobster. The target customer was skewed toward a younger demographic, 18- to

49-year-olds. Cultural changes in the 1980s would have a significant impact on the fortunes of Captain D's. As the American people became more health-conscious during this period they began to eat more fish, a trend that benefited all seafood restaurants. Seafood consumption increased 25 percent over the course of the 1980s, peaking in 1989 with a rate of 15.9 pounds per capita. To take even greater advantage of this growing market, Captain D's introduced baked-fish items in the late 1980s. Moreover, the move decreased the chain's dependence on white fish, which starting in 1986 experienced drastic price swings. Captain D's was now able to explore alternative species. By the end of the decade, the chain totaled 610 units, of which 352 were company run. Chainwide revenues for fiscal 1989 were $400 million.

Falling Seafood Consumption in the 1990s

Entering the 1990s Captain D's looked to market to an older age group, 25 to 54 years of age. To further boost sales, the chain introduced drive-thru windows in 1990. But the start of the new decade proved to be difficult for the chain. Captain D's was not alone in its problems, as explained in a June 1991 *Restaurant Business* article that summarized prevailing conditions: "Seafood restaurants, especially chains, face tremendous challenges. Their biggest problem is not how to market seafood, but how to find supplies to meet rising demand. Dwindling supplies of some species and growing competition from overseas makes seafood a difficult commodity in which to deal. The expertise needed to handle a highly perishable product, the difficulty of marketing an expensive product in an era of falling menu prices, and reported safety concerns over contamination from natural toxins and polluted water are further complications." Primarily because of a rising cost in key species—cod, haddock, sole, and scallops—due to shortages, seafood restaurants were forced to raise prices, resulting in declining sales. In 1992 seafood consumption fell to 14.8 pounds per capita. Captain D's also faced a challenge from the other end of the price spectrum. If its price points were too low, customers began to question the quality and freshness of the fish. Management sought to find the right fit for the chain in the seafood category, eventually settling to be a notch above Long John Silver's but not quite aspiring to be Red Lobster. As a result of this repositioning, Captain D's was able to regain some lost ground. The company's corporate parent, in the meantime, was encountering problems of its own.

In the 25 years since launching Captain D's, Shoney's had diversified into other restaurant concepts, such as Pargo's and Lee's Famous Recipe. It also operated an institutional supplier, Mike Rose Foods, and even tried its hand at lodging. Shoney's also suffered a public relations nightmare when it was sued for racial discrimination by nine African American former employees, which culminated in a settlement payment of more than $100 million. With sales declining and burdened by excessive debt, Shoney's initiated a major restructuring plan in early

1995. The company sold off its Lee's Famous Recipe, Pargo, and Fifth Quarter restaurants, as well as Mike Rose Foods, retaining only the Shoney's and Captain D's chains. A number of top executives, including Shoney's Chairman and CEO Taylor Henry, were also ousted. In September 1995 the company merged with TPI Enterprises, its largest franchisee.

While Shoney's restaurants continued their slide, Captain D's enjoyed a run of several consecutive years of gains in same-store revenue. The chain, which peaked at nearly 650 restaurants in 1994, also closed some underperforming units to improve profitability. It was not until 1997, however, that Captain D's began to introduce the first significant changes to the chain's business model since the mid-1970s. An instrumental player was Captain D's current president and chief operating officer, Ronald E. Walker, who took over the presidency in 1996 and was well familiar with the operation after more than 15 years of service with Shoney's. He started out in the foodservice industry as an hourly employee at McDonald's, then in 1980 became a manager trainee with Shoney's and went on to serve in a wide range of jobs with Captain D's, including restaurant manager, franchise supervisor, field operations director, regional director, vice-president of company operations, vice-president of franchise operations, and executive vice-president.

The major thrust of the Captain D's overhaul was to position the chain in the "fast-casual" segment, to take advantage of the rising popularity in casual dining. The first visible step was a diversification of the menu, accomplished by the launch of Captain D's Coastal Classics menu, a rotating set of fresh seafood items with a regional emphasis. Another two years passed before management was ready to take the next step, the introduction of a prototype restaurant interior, which featured a dockside shack with a weathered look both outside and in, and a décor that included nautical bric-a-brac, softer lighting, and tables and chairs rather than plastic booths. The casual atmosphere was reinforced by the dress of crew members, who wore tropical print shirts, jeans, and baseball caps (an approach that had the added benefit of improving staff retention). The goal was to merge the speed of fast food with the comfortable dining experience of a full-service restaurant, without the need for servers. Moreover, the new Captain D's served beer and played light rock music instead of elevator music (another plus in staff retention) and, unlike most fast-food restaurants, began to accept credit cards.

By 2000 Captain D's was the strongest division of Shoney's, which initiated a financial restructuring that provided Captain D's with a $135 million line of credit and made the chain a stand-alone subsidiary. Shoney's was now in a position to explore a number of options with the business, including selling it. Because the Shoney's restaurant division was struggling, there was some speculation that Shoney's might actually choose to cast off its signature chain and concentrate on the more successful Captain D's. The parent corporation adopted a wait-and-see attitude and took steps to revitalize the Shoney's chain, including the closure of more than 70 company-owned restaurants.

Introducing the Compact Restaurant Prototype in 2001

Of concern for Captain D's was some erosion in store sales at company-owned units. At this stage, 354 of the chain's 565 units, about two-thirds, were company owned. In 2001 Captain D's initiated a push to increase franchising, as well as to pursue refranchising, with the hope of reversing the ratio of company-owned stores to franchised operations. Moreover, the chain looked to take advantage of its strong brand recognition in the Southeast and to open new units in overlooked markets in its 22-state area of operation. Management estimated that the Southeast alone could accommodate another 800 to 835 Captain D's restaurants. As part of its effort to expand into new and existing markets and to aid in its franchising plans, Captain D's introduced a new compact restaurant prototype in 2001. The first of these units opened in Rainbow City, Alabama, an end-cap property at a strip mall, which permitted the restaurant to operate a drive-thru window. Whereas a traditional 3,250-square-foot Captain D's was able to seat 128, the compact prototype, 1,800 square feet in size, could accommodate between 33 and 42 patrons. The smaller size allowed the chain to place new units where space was limited, either at in-line shopping centers or smaller freestanding retail sites. In addition, these units were cheaper and quicker to construct and needed less equipment than a traditional Captain D's restaurant—all of which translated into lower start-up costs for franchisees. The units maintained the fast-casual style of the dockside seafood shack of the larger restaurants, but relied on a more efficient kitchen layout and self-service beverage and condiment stations that allowed the smaller Captain D's to serve the same number of meals as the larger, traditional units but with less labor costs. Because the smaller format had limited seating, the floor design included a bar-height counter for single customers and, to prevent smaller parties from tying up larger tables, many four-seat tables were replaced with two-seat tables.

The smaller Captain D's format was ideally suited for a new potential growth area for the chain: military installations. In late 2001 the chain opened its first restaurant at a military location, and its first West Coast outlet, at the Travis Air Force Base in northern California. Some three years earlier the Army Air Force Exchange Service acquired worldwide franchising rights to Captain D's for all U.S. military installations. Because there were approximately 150 military exchange food courts around the world, this new avenue for growth held great potential for Captain D's. After setting up other domestic military units, in 2003 the chain opened its first international store on the Okinawa Air Force Base in Okinawa, Japan. This unit was also the chain's first military base restaurant offering sit-down and drive-thru service.

Ownership of Shoney's, Inc. changed hands in early 2003 when Lone Star Funds, a Dallas-based real estate-related investment group, agreed to pay approximately $20 million in cash and assume more than $250 million in corporate debt. As a result, Shoney's was taken private. Lone Star announced that it intended to operate both the Shoney's and Captain D's restaurant chains, putting an end, at least temporarily, to speculation that Captain D's might be spun off as a separate enterprise. Regardless, the future looked promising for Captain D's, due to the rising popularity of seafood restaurants in a nation that was becoming dominated by Baby Boomers entering their peak dining-out years who had a tendency to opt for seafood when eating away from home. Moreover, supply of suitable fish and stabilized pricing helped to fortify the category. With backing from Lone Star, Captain D's launched a major ad campaign to help the chain sustain its growth into the foreseeable future.

Principal Competitors

Darden Restaurants, Inc.; Long John Silver's; TruFoods Corporation.

Further Reading

Bertagnoli, Lisa, "Small Box, Big Design," *Chain Leader*, February 2002, p. 32.

Brumback, Nancy, "Net Worth," *Restaurant Business*, February 15, 2003, p. 41.

Forrester, Brian, "Captain D's Seafood Signs Up for U.S. Military Base Service," *Nashville Business Journal*, January 25, 2002, p. 5.

Peters, James, "Captain D's Plots Course for Franchise System Expansion," *Nation's Restaurant News*, February 19, 2001, p. 4.

——, "Shoney's Pending Buyer Eyes Franchising Growth," *Nation's Restaurant News*, February 4, 2002, p. 4.

Robinson, Fiona, "Ron Walker Spearheads Captain D's Turnaround," *Seafood Business*, September 2000, p. 44.

—Ed Dinger

Casino Guichard-Perrachon S.A.

24, rue de la Montat
42000 Saint-Etienne
France
Telephone: (+33) 4-77-45-31-31
Fax: (+33) 4-77-45-38-38
Web site: http://www.casino.fr

Public Company
Incorporated: 1898 as Société des Magasins du Casino
Employees: 206,000
Sales: EUR 22.86 billion ($22 billion) (2002)
Stock Exchanges: Euronext Paris
Ticker Symbol: CO
NAIC: 445110 Supermarkets and Other Grocery (Except
    Convenience) Stores; 551112 Offices of Other
    Holding Companies; 722110 Full-Service Restaurants

Casino Guichard-Perrachon S.A., or Groupe Casino, is one of France's largest retailers—battling it out with Carrefour and Auchan for the country's top spot—with an international network of more than 8,400 stores. France remains Casino's primary market, accounting for 77 percent of its 2002 sales of nearly EUR 23 billion. The company's French retail operations are separated into three primary categories: Hypermarkets, under the Géant name, with 286 stores in operation in 2003; Supermarkets, under the Casino, Leader Price, Franprix, Monoprix, and other names, with nearly 2,500 stores; Convenience stores, counting brands Petit Casino, Spar, Vival, Eco Service, and others; and Restaurants, primarily through the 240 Casino cafeterias. With further expansion limited in the mature and highly regulated French retail market, Casino has been making a push internationally. Present in the United States since the mid-1980s with the Smart & Final chain, Casino has expanded into South America, with operations in Argentina, Venezuela, Brazil, Mexico, and Colombia. The company is also present in Thailand, Taiwan, Vietnam, and Madagascar. In Europe, the company has built up a network of 11 hypermarkets in Poland, and, since 2002, has entered the Netherlands through its purchase of Laurus. Together, the company's international operations combine to produce 23 percent of the company's sales. Casino is majority controlled by Rallye SA, headed by Jean-Charles Naouri, which also controls the Go Sport, Athlete's Foot, and other retail chains. Rallye's share of Casino stands at nearly 51 percent, although its voting rights reach more than 63 percent.

Founding a Retail Empire in the 1860s

Casino's origins dated back to about 1860, when a grocery store was opened in Saint-Etienne, a city about 30 miles south of Lyon. It was named for the nearby Casino Lyrique, which had been closed in 1858 by the city fathers for "licentious spectacles." In 1864 the founder of Casino, a Monsieur Brechard, took as a partner Jean-Claude Perrachon, and the business became a general store. Perrachon's nephew Geoffroy Guichard later became partner of what became the Etablissements Guichard-Perrachon. In 1898 Guichard created the Société des Magasins du Casino and opened a second store in Veauche, about 12 miles to the south. To stock the stores it was necessary to build a warehouse in Saint-Etienne.

The father of eight children, Guichard was a paternalistic employer, and the company continues to give out scholarships to the descendants of his workers. Guichard also sponsored the city's museum of modern art and its soccer team, traditions the company maintains. In addition, Casino became manager of Saint-Etienne's museum of arts and industry in 1967.

Casino became a joint-stock company in 1900. Armed with an infusion of funds, it grew rapidly from this point. By the outbreak of World War I there were 215 branches, of which 56 were in Saint-Etienne alone. In 1919 a new factory replaced the existing facilities for making chocolate, confectioneries, and preserves. By 1922 warehouses also were located in Clermont-Ferrand, Lyon, Roanne, and Beaucaire, the latter to store wine. A soap factory and oil works were built in Marseille, and a perfume plant was opened in Saint-Etienne in 1922. Two more warehouses, at Chalon-sur-Saone and Avignon, opened in 1923. In 1934 a vast warehouse was established in Marseille to serve the entire southeast of France.

Post-World War II Expansion

On the eve of World War II Casino was by far the biggest holding company in southeastern France. Yet its greatest period of expansion was not to begin until 1960, when it opened its first supermarket in Grenoble. A warehouse for fresh produce was opened in Rhone a Grigny the following year. Its first cafeteria was introduced in Saint-Etienne in 1967. Casino entered the Paris region in 1970 by creating a subsidiary with the acronym SOMACA to operate the supermarkets of Saint-Denis and Bagneux. In the same year it absorbed a similar business in southwestern France, l'Epargne, into a new subsidiary named SABIM Sable.

Hypermarkets under the name Géant Casino were established during the early 1970s, first in Marseille, then in Saint-Etienne, Frejus, Montpellier, Bordeaux, and Nantes. The one in Saint-Etienne covered 10,842 square meters (116,702 square feet). In the early 1980s it had 45 different departments, 2,000 parking places, and a staff of 470, and was accompanied by an auto service station, a cafeteria, and a gallery of shops. Casino entered a new field in 1977 with the creation of S.A. CAR-FUEL, a subsidiary for the distribution of petroleum products. Between 1978 and 1980 Casino established SOMABRI, in collaboration with the Belgian group G.B., to operate hobby-and-garden centers. The one opened in Saint-Etienne in 1980 was offering 27,000 products two years later.

By 1981 Casino also had established the restaurant chains SARL, Stefany, and Caf'Casino and had taken a half interest in another, France Quick. SABIM operated slaughterhouses in Sable and Saint-Maixent. The industrial complex of Pont-de-l'Ane produced chocolates, confectioneries, and preserves, 85 percent for Casino's retail needs. There was a meatpacking plant at Saint-Priest and one for roasting meat at Marseille that not only satisfied Casino's needs but also exported products overseas. Three great bottling plants were located in Beaucaire, Lyon, and Clermont-Ferrand, and Casino began exporting two million bottles of wine a year to other European Community countries. SAIC was a building society managing thousands of dwellings. Finally, a fleet of trucks transported goods from Casino's 11 great warehouses.

Groupe Casino's presence in the United States dates from 1975, when it created Casino USA Inc. as a California-based subsidiary. By 1984 it was operating four Petit Casino retail stores and eight Café Casino French restaurants. In March 1984 Casino USA bought a controlling interest in Thriftimart Inc., owner of 86 Smart & Final Iris Co. cash-and-carry warehouses, for more than $15 million worth of Class B stock. Casino intended to use Thriftimart outlets to distribute its lines of jelly, jam, and bottled water. At the time of the deal, Smart & Final Iris specialized in discount volume sales of food and hardware

for bulk buyers and restaurants. Eventually, the deal had to be sweetened to avoid a lawsuit, so in the end Casino paid $116.7 million to acquire the company's Class A nonvoting shares of common stock as well.

The French parent saw a 10 percent increase in turnover in 1983 to FFr 157.9 million ($17.5 million), but this was accompanied by a decline of 2 percent in consolidated profits. However, Casino continued pursuing an aggressive acquisition program and in 1985 bought an 88 percent share of CEDIS, owner of hypermarkets, supermarkets, and smaller grocery stores. The transaction supplemented Casino's already strong presence in southern France and the Paris metropolitan area with CEDIS's base in eastern France, and added CEDIS's FFr 9 billion (about $977 million) in annual sales to Casino's FFr 23.5 billion (about $2.55 billion). Later in the year Casino entered into a joint venture with a subsidiary of the giant French oil company ELF-Aquitaine to create service stations, supermarkets, and fast-food outlets.

In 1986 Casino expanded further by acquiring a 46 percent interest in Paridoc and Giant supermarkets and a 99 percent interest in Etablissements Deloche, a wholesaler. In that year Groupe Casino was France's third largest food-distribution company, behind LeClerc and Carrefour. Its holdings in France consisted of 42 hypermarkets (16 under the Mammouth name of CEDIS) and 187 supermarkets, under the Casino, Suma, and Ravi names. In addition, there were 92 Smart & Final warehouses in the United States.

The company's activities in 1986 also included processed foods (12 percent of total sales) and restaurants and cafeterias (6 percent). The latter sector consisted of the restaurant chain Hippopotamus and the cafeteria chains O'Kitch and Quick, making Casino the largest food chain in France in number of meals served. Casino then sold Quick in 1993. American operations constituted another 6 percent of the company's volume, with food distribution accounting for the other 76 percent. Food processing declined to only 3 percent of revenues by 1993, while American revenues increased to nearly 8 percent of the total.

Merging Giants in the 1990s

Casino's acquisitions were part of the consolidation of the food industry taking place throughout France. The American-style hypermarket first made its appearance in France in 1963. By 1986 there were 645 of these giant stores, accounting for one-fourth of food revenues. Hypermarkets also saw a 10 percent annual gain in sales volume, compared to 2 percent for the industry as a whole. The big distributors expanded vertically as well as horizontally by absorbing suppliers.

In 1989 Casino stock reached a price level it would not attain again during the next four difficult years. Antoine Guichard announced in July 1990 that company employment would be cut by 1,450 before the end of 1992. Guichard explained that the company was being undercut by independent rivals offering lower prices because of their lower operating costs. He said the company would respond by renovating and remodeling its stores, and reorganizing the hypermarkets, supermarkets, and smaller food stores into separate and autonomous divisions. A new marketing division would be concerned with consumer relations, price, and the purchase and securing of provisions.

Key Dates:

1860: Grocery store opens in Saint-Etienne, near Lyon, taking its name for a closed casino.

1864: Jean-Claude Perrachon becomes partner in Casino store, later bringing in nephew Geoffroy Guichard as partner.

1898: Guichard founds Société des Magasins du Casino, and opens second store, and a warehouse.

1919: Company builds factory to make preserves, chocolates, and other confections.

1967: Company opens first Cafeteria in Saint-Etienne.

1970: Company enters Paris region through subsidiary SOMACA.

1970: Casino launches Géant hypermarket format.

1975: Company establishes Casino USA subsidiary.

1984: Company acquires Thriftimart, which controls Smart & Final stores.

1985: CEDIS hypermarket group is purchased.

1986: Casino acquires Etablissements Deloche, a wholesaler.

1990: Company sells its service stations to Shell France and Agip France; acquires La Ruche Meridionale.

1992: Rallye SA is acquired in exchange for 30 percent of Casino.

1996: Casino enters Poland with opening of first hypermarket.

1997: Rallye, with a friendly counteroffer, rescues Casino following hostile takeover bid by Promodes.

1998: Casino opens first Taiwan hypermarket; acquires cash and carry operation of US Grocers.

1999: Casino acquires 50 percent of Uruguay's Disco retail group and opens first Géant hypermarket in Montevideo.

2000: Company forms partnerships with Colombia's Exito and Brazil's CBM.

2001: Company acquires 100 Proxi convenience stores in France.

2003: Casino's total retail network tops 8,400 stores.

To cut its costs Casino sold its 172 service stations in December 1990 to Shell France and Agip France for FFr 660 million (about $131 million). However, Casino would continue to manage the stations under a 30-year contract. This transaction apparently was made to enable Casino to reduce its debt, which had grown to FFr 4.2 billion (about $840 million) after it had acquired La Ruche Meridionale, a supermarket company, earlier in the year.

In May 1989 Casino signed initial cooperation accords with Argyll Group PLC, owner of Safeway food stores in Great Britain, and Koninklijke Ahold N.V. of the Netherlands to form a combine. The accord called for the three food retailers to issue new shares that would give Argyll a 3.8 percent share in Ahold and a 3.4 percent stake in Casino, with Ahold and Casino in turn acquiring 1.5 percent of Argyll. The result was the European Retail Alliance (ERA), on which Antoine Guichard planned to base the company's future growth strategy. Looking toward the European Economic Union of 1993, Casino also bought 39 percent of an important Italian retailer, La Rinascente, in 1989.

Casino moved into second place among French food distributors by acquiring struggling rival Rallye S.A. in 1992, in exchange for new Casino shares representing more than 30 percent of the new ensemble. In so doing it acquired Rallye's 44 hypermarkets and 196 supermarkets—it also brought in financial wizard Jean-Charles Naouri.

Casino's expanded operations enabled it to increase sales to FFr 61.6 billion ($11.25 billion) in 1992 from FFr 40.6 billion in 1991, but profits fell from FFr 484 million to FFr 438 million ($80 million). Like other retailers, Casino was affected by stagnant consumer spending during a national economic recession that year. Rallye appeared to be a drag on the parent organization, its hypermarket sales falling 6 percent during the first four months of 1994 (while Casino's rose by 4.7 percent) and its supermarket sales dropping by 8 to 9 percent (while Casino's rose by 1 percent).

Through its subsidiary Casino USA, Groupe Casino had majority control of Smart & Final Inc., which operated 136 Smart & Final warehouse stores in the United States at the end of 1993. The number was scheduled to reach 149 by the end of 1994. More than half were leased from Casino Realty, with most of the rest subleased from Casino Realty or Casino USA. Among Smart & Final subsidiaries were Casino Frozen Foods Inc. and Casino American Food Services Inc. Under a joint venture with the Mexican retailer Central Detallista it was also to operate a chain of supermarkets in the southwestern United States and in Tijuana, Mexico, using the name Smart & Final. Two had opened by mid-1994, with a third scheduled for opening by the end of the year.

In order to accumulate money to remodel its French stores, Casino put Smart & Final Inc. up for sale in July 1993. Its Casino USA subsidiary held a 50.3 percent stake in the food chain, with a market value of about $178 million. The parent concern decided later that year not to sell, however, because in the words of Smart & Final's chairman, ''Groupe Casino is convinced the long-term value . . . is far in excess of the amount it might realize in the current weak market.'' During the first four months of 1994 Smart & Final's sales rose by 14 percent. Back at home, in 1995, Casino took a 65 percent share in the creation of a new group, Spar France, joining with IPAG, the owner of Spar International and French distribution group Mariault, to introduce the Spar convenience store format to France.

International Expansion for the New Century

The marriage of retailer Antoine Guichard and financier Jean-Charles Naouri had sparked skepticism by a number of observers. Yet the pair quickly developed a strong friendship and a complementary business relationship. Naouri, who, through investment vehicle Euris, had previously kept out of the actual operational end, soon developed an interest in Casino's day-to-day operations. When Guichard retired, Naouri took over as head of the Casino group, raising Rallye's stake in the company to 50 percent.

Naouri's financial background was crucial for Casino when the company found itself the target of a hostile takeover from rival retail group Promodes in 1997. Instead, Naouri and Rallye launched a friendly counteroffer, which was accepted by the

Guichard family. Naouri also set in place a new expansion drive for Casino in order to boost the company's value and thwart the Promodes offer. In 1997, Casino acquired French retail chains Franprix and Leader Price, then acquired Société Mariault, which operated a 600-store network of Spar, Vival, and Coccinelle convenience stores. By the end of the year, Rallye had successfully fought off Promodes to become Casino's majority shareholder. Promodes, licking its wounds, then hooked up with Carrefour, becoming the country's leading retailer—and one of the largest retail groups in the world.

Casino too had set its sights on further international expansion. In 1996, the company made its latest effort to expand beyond France, opening a first store in Poland. By 2003, the company had raised its total hypermarkets in Poland to 15. The company also introduced the Leader Price brand in Poland, starting with a first store in 2000. The deep discount supermarket chain grew especially strongly, topping 53 stores at the end of 2002, representing 20 percent of Casino's total sales in Poland.

Casino targeted growth in Asia as well, setting up a 50/50 partnership in 1996 with Taiwan's Dairy Farm International, in order to introduce the company's hypermarkets into that country. The partnership's first store opened in Taichung in 1998. The following year, Casino bought 66 percent of Thailand's Big C hypermarket group. Under Casino, Big C expanded rapidly, building a network of 20 hypermarkets by the end of 2002.

South America became another important expansion market for the company at the turn of the century, starting with a franchise agreement with Uruguay's Disco retail group. By 1999, Casino had acquired 50 percent of Disco, which opened its first Géant hypermarket in Montevideo in 1999. The company next partnered with Colombia's Exito group, acquiring 25 percent of that company in 2000 in order to participate in its expansion throughout Colombia, Venezuela, Equator, Bolivia, and Peru. Next, Casino turned to Brazil, reaching a similar partnership agreement with the CBD group (Companhia Brasileira de Distribuiçao), and its Extra, Pai de Açucar, Barateiro, and Eletro retail stores. With that agreement, Casino's direct and indirect holdings made it South America's second largest retail group.

In the United States, Casino had boosted its Smart & Final network with an agreement to acquire the cash and carry operations of United Grocers in 1998. That agreement added 39 new cash and carry stores on the West Coast. Back at home, the company merged its Auto Service operation into the Feu Vert

chain, an agreement that gave Casino a 38 percent stake in Feu Vert. In 2001, Casino extended its French retail network with the purchase of a 100-strong chain of Proxi convenience stores. The company also attempted to extend to the Internet, with the e-commerce site C-mes-courses. That service proved unprofitable, however, and was shut down by 2002.

By 2003, Casino had boosted its international sales share to 23 percent of its total revenues. Sales had neared EUR 23 billion, despite the difficult economic climate and a consumer spending slowdown in its core French market. The company remained one of the top French retail groups—fighting for the title among rivals Carrefour, LeClerc, and Auchan. It had also begun its assault on the global market, with plans to position itself among the world's major retail groups in the new century.

Principal Subsidiaries

Anfilco (50%); Asinco; Banque Groupe Casino (51%); Boidis; Casino Cafétéria; Casino Entreprise; Casino Service; Casino USA Inc.; Comacas; Dechrist Holding; Easydis; Feu Vert (38%); Géant Argentina; Gelase (Belgium); Immobilière Groupe Casino; Maruschka (Netherlands); Monoprix (49.35%); Nérée; Pachidis; Paglop; Plésia; Ségisor; Smilodon; Tevir; Tplm; Vindémia (33.34%).

Principal Competitors

Carrefour SA; Etab. E. LeClerc SA; Auchan SA; Intermarche SA.

Further Reading

"Casino Steps Up Expansion Pace," *MMR*, May 29, 2000, p. 12.
"Casino Top-Line Gains," *MMR*, February 24, 2003, p. 13.
Dowdell, Stephen, "Casino's Big Gamble," *Supermarket News*, April 1, 1991, pp. 1, 10–11.
Doyere, Josee, "Un [caddie] nomme desir," *Le Monde*, February 21, 1987, pp. 4–6.
Gardes, Gilbert, ed., *La ville des Saint-Etienne, Grand encyclopedie du Forez et des communes de la Loire*, Le Coteau: Editions Horvath, 1984, pp. 273–75, 298–305.
Shearlock, Peter, "High Rollers Hit Casino," *Banker*, October 1997, p. 20.

—Robert Halasz
—update: M.L. Cohen

CEMEX S.A. de C.V.

Avenida Constitución 444 Poniente
Apdo. Postal 392
64000 Monterrey, Nuevo León
Mexico
Telephone: (81) 8328-3000
Fax: (81) 8328-3188
Web site: http://www.cemex.com

Public Company
Incorporated: 1906 as Cementos Hidalgo
Employees: 26,452
Sales: 67.92 billion pesos ($6.54 billion) (2002)
Stock Exchanges: Bolsa Mexicana de Valores New York
Ticker Symbol: CEMEX CPO
NAIC: 327310 Cement Manufacturing; 327320 Ready-
   Mix Concrete Manufacturing; 551112 Offices of
   Other Holding Companies

CEMEX S.A. de C.V. (Cemex) is the third largest cement producer in the world, trailing only France's Lafarge S.A. and Switzerland's Holcim Ltd., and holds leading positions in cement in Mexico, the United States, Spain, Egypt, the Philippines, and a number of Latin American countries. Operating as a small regional player in Mexico for much of its history, Cemex embarked on an aggressive global expansion program in the early 1990s, completing a string of acquisitions in targeted markets. By the early 2000s, the company had amassed an impressive international portfolio of operations within more than 30 countries on four continents, with revenues breaking down as follows: 34 percent, Mexico; 24 percent, United States; 14 percent, Spain; 7 percent, Central America and the Caribbean; 4 percent, Venezuela; 3 percent, Colombia; 2 percent, Egypt; 2 percent, Philippines; and 10 percent, other countries. Cemex's primary markets are in countries with a great need for infrastructure and a growing demand for housing. In addition to cement, which comprises about 76 percent of revenues, the company also produces and distributes ready-mix concrete (21 percent) and clinker (3 percent), an intermediate cement product made from limestone, clay, and iron oxide. Cemex holds the distinction of being the world's largest trader of cement, based on its trade relations with more than 60 nations. Its more than 50 wholly owned cement plants worldwide have an annual capacity of 80.9 million metric tons, and the company has nearly 500 ready-mix concrete plants.

1906–89: From Local to Regional to Number One Cement Maker in Mexico

Cemex traces its origins to 1906, when Cementos Hidalgo was founded near Monterrey in northern Mexico; it began operating a cement plant with a capacity of 5,000 metric tons per year. In 1920 Lorenzo Zambrano established Cementos Portland Monterrey and began operating a 20,000-metric-ton cement plant in nearby Monterrey. Zambrano engineered the 1931 merger of these two companies, creating Cementos Mexicanos, later known as Cemex. The firm was headquartered in Monterrey, where its head offices remained through the early 2000s.

Cemex remained a small, local company for the next 35 years. It adopted a regional profile in 1966–67 when it acquired a plant in Mérida, Yucatán, from Cementos Maya and also constructed new plants in Ciudad Valles, San Luis Potosí; and Torreón, Coahuila. A national presence was gained in 1972–73 when Cemex installed new kilns at its plants in Mérida and Monterrey and acquired a plant in central Mexico. Then in 1976 the company was listed on the Mexican bolsa (stock exchange), and it also became the leading cement maker in Mexico by acquiring the three plants owned by Cementos Guadalajara. By the mid-1980s, Cemex had more than 15 million metric tons of annual production capacity.

Despite having operated successfully within Mexico for more than 70 years, Cemex saw its future as a cement supplier and distributor dim in the 1980s when the governments' relaxation of protectionist policies—which opened the market up to aggressively expanding multinational players—posed a considerable challenge to Cemex's market position. Fortunately for the company, the founder's grandson, also named Lorenzo Zambrano, a savvy, Stanford University-educated M.B.A., was named chairman and CEO in 1985. He had spent his teenage years at the Missouri Military Academy in Mexico, Missouri,

111

and later earned an industrial engineering degree from the Institute Tecnologico in Monterrey, Mexico's version of MIT, according to *Forbes* writer Claire Poole. In 1968 he returned to Monterrey after earning his M.B.A., and took a job with Cemex, where his uncle sat on the board, and proceeded to climb the corporate ladder for 18 years before becoming Cemex's CEO. Undaunted by the changing market climate, Zambrano began the implementation of an ambitious expansion plan, giving the company a near-monopoly in Mexico, where cement is the primary building material, beginning with the purchases of several smaller Mexican cement companies, including the 1987 purchase of Cementos Anahuac and the 1989 buyout of Cementos Tolteca, his biggest domestic competitor. Cemex ended the 1980s having secured domestic market share of 65 percent and having become one of the ten largest cement companies in the world. Cemex also diversified into other Mexican industries, such as tourism and hotels, but decided by the late 1980s to divest its non-cement holdings and concentrate on geographic diversification.

Gaining almost 5 percent of the U.S. cement market, Zambrano spent heavily to acquire marketing facilities all over the southwestern United States. Awakening to the Cemex threat, U.S. producers, including eight cement companies and two labor unions, filed an antidumping suit against Cemex, claiming "they had unfairly deflated cement prices and hurt the American companies' expansion plans in the Southwest and Florida," according to Poole. Zambrano was hit with a 58 percent countervailing duty when the International Trade Commission ruled that the U.S. producers had been hurt by the prices Cemex and other Mexican producers were charging—despite the fact that cement in Arizona and California was selling for the same price that Cemex charged. Zambrano reduced exports to the U.S. by 30 percent because the 58 percent import duty substantially affected Cemex profits. Zambrano held on to his U.S. market share in areas where the company could remain competitive due to higher prices. A GATT (General Agreement on Trade and Tariffs) later ruled that the antidumping duties levied by the U.S. Department of Commerce on imports of cement from Mexico were unfounded. Cemex's U.S. holdings, which were controlled through a subsidiary called Sunbelt Corporation, were augmented by the purchases of the Western U.S. affiliates of Blue Circle Industries and two Houston companies, Houston Shell & Concrete and Gulf Coast Cement. Because of the close proximity and language/cultural similarities, Cemex continued to develop ties within the mini-trade zone between northern

Mexico and southern Texas, California, Arizona, New Mexico, Kentucky, Florida, and even as far north as Minnesota.

Pouring Pesos into Mexican Infrastructure: Early 1990s

The economic situation was becoming more lucrative at home, where Mexico's president, Carlos Salinas de Gortari, a Harvard-educated political economist, initiated public works programs for infrastructure modernization, increasing the demand for cement, as well as increasing the government-set price for cement. The government gradually allowed cement prices to rise from $46 per ton to $72 per ton. The production costs of about $30 per ton at Cemex's Mexican plants were the lowest in North America. By 1990, the company reached sales of approximately $1.2 billion, and accounted for 66 percent of Mexico's cement market, gaining the attention of investors who also appreciated Cemex's operating margins: 27 percent versus 9 percent for U.S. rival Lafarge. Ten years after Mexico's debt crisis, the ratio of government debt to annual gross domestic product was down to about 40 percent, versus 60 percent in the United States. Zambrano was an outspoken proponent of the North American Free Trade Agreement (NAFTA), although he admitted that the opening of the Mexican economy would be damaging to many of their industries not well-prepared in the areas of managerial expertise, technology, and marketing. Cemex invested heavily in robots and computers, giving them a far-reaching efficiency edge. Their main competitor in Mexico was Aspasco, left with a 20 percent market share—a company controlled by Holderbank of Switzerland.

In 1992 Zambrano negotiated a bridge loan from Citicorp, among others, for the acquisition of majority holdings in the two largest Spanish cement companies—Valenciana and Sanson—spending $1.84 billion, and causing Cemex stock to plummet because of investors' fears that the company was expanding too rapidly. The move into Europe pitted Cemex against world leaders such as Switzerland's Holderbank and France's Lafarge Coppee. Zambrano told Joseph L. McCarthy in *Chief Executive*, "Every time we acquire a company, we are told that we paid too much, that we are buying at the wrong time, and that we are crazy. Our critics know a lot about Mexico, but not enough about the cement industry." Cemex had paid less than half of what Cemex's competitors Lafarge and Ciment Français (now part of Italcementi) paid for smaller Spanish cement companies in 1989. Critics worried that Cemex was taking on too much debt, and questioned whether or not the company had sufficient international management expertise. Cemex repaid a large portion of the loan by reselling nonstrategic assets in the Spanish cement companies. Justifying his ambitious expenditures, Zambrano explained to McCarthy, "We had to become one of the biggest global companies. If we didn't, someone undoubtedly would have acquired us." The two Spanish companies were combined into Valenciana de Cementos, becoming Spain's largest cement producer. In 1994 Valenciana's net profit jumped to $95.5 million, up from $37.7 million in 1993. Cemex operated ten plants, four grinding units, and 23 distribution terminals in Spain, both maritime and land-based. The *Economist* reported that Cemex almost doubled the operating margin of its Spanish plants by firing a third of its workers there, adding that the purchase enabled Cemex to by-

Key Dates:

1906: Cementos Hidalgo is established near Monterrey in northern Mexico and begins operating a cement plant.
1920: Lorenzo Zambrano opens a cement plant in Monterrey through his newly founded firm, Cementos Portland Monterrey.
1931: The two companies merge to form Cementos Mexicanos, later known as Cemex; firm is based in Monterrey.
1976: Cemex goes public; it becomes the largest cement maker in Mexico following the acquisition of Cementos Guadalajara's three plants.
1985: The founder's grandson, also named Lorenzo Zambrano, is named chairman and CEO; the new leader embarks on an ambitious program of expansion.
1989: Acquisition of Cementos Tolteca, the number two cement producer in Mexico, gives Cemex 65 percent of the Mexican market and makes it one of the ten largest cement companies in the world.
1992: The company buys the two largest cement companies in Spain, Valenciana and Sanson, for $1.84 billion.
1994: A controlling stake in Vencemos, the largest cement company in Venezuela, is acquired.
1997: Cemex makes its first direct investment in Asia, purchasing a 30 percent stake in Rizal Cement Company, Inc. of the Philippines.
1999: A majority stake in Assiut Cement Company, the leading cement maker in Egypt, is acquired.
2000: The second largest U.S. cement producer, Houston-based Southdown, Inc., is acquired for $2.63 billion.

pass antidumping duties imposed by the Bush administration to protect American cement producers, whose costs averaged a third more than Cemex's. Despite NAFTA, the Clinton administration maintained the duties (until a later ruling), which Cemex compensated for by exporting from duty-exempt Spain.

The company bought a cement plant located in New Braunfels, Texas, from Lafarge Corporation, which included four cement terminals and 52 percent of Parker Lafarge Inc., which was an aggregate plant producing an annual capacity of 820,000 metric tons. During this period Cemex had 18 cement production plants and 36 distribution terminals strategically located in Mexico and the United States. The company's first quarter 1994 American sales increased by 45 percent over the previous comparable quarter.

Mexico's economy began to decline and private investors were discouraged by the uprising in the south and the murder of the ruling party's candidate. Cemex's foreign operations gave the company a hedge against the weakening peso, down 7 percent against the dollar in the first half of 1994. The recession had the effect of paralyzing mortgage loans in Mexico, which in turn affected the housing sector and the demand for cement. Still, net sales dropped only 2.3 percent, offset somewhat by a decline in the costs of sales and operating expenses derived from lower

fuel and electric energy prices (a major expenditure in the cement industry), a decrease in personnel, and a 23 percent increase in worker productivity. To strengthen Cemex's presence in Latin America, Zambrano bought 60 percent of Vencemos, Venezuela's largest cement company, for $550 million, partly in preparation for export to places such as northern Brazil, Panama, and the Caribbean. In the Caribbean, Cemex completed negotiations for the acquisition of 50 percent of Scancem Industries, Ltd., a company that operated in five countries in the area. The transaction enabled the company to market half a million metric tons of cement to the region, accounting for approximately 50 percent of the imported cement consumption there. At a Panamanian government-held auction, Cemex was awarded Cementos Bayano of Panama, for a price of $60 million, furthering the consolidation of its Caribbean market. Cemex was pursuing its ambitious plan to provide raw materials for the large infrastructure projects developing in Spain, Asia, Africa, Europe, and other Latin markets. Within seven years the company had tripled its global production capacity.

Emerging Markets Throughout the 1990s

Chief Financial Officer Gustavo Caballero Guerrero told Victoria Griffith of *CFO Year* that "the company's main commitment is in emerging markets, and future purchases are likely to take place either in Asia or Latin America. Emerging markets have a number of advantages. First, they will grow much faster than the First World in the long run, and strong economic growth is essential in the cement market. Second, emerging markets view cement not as a commodity, like the First World, but as a brand-name product. It's much easier to differentiate ourselves in emerging markets from our competitors." Cemex established a sales office in Hong Kong, hoping to enter economies of scale necessary to beat its competitors, while also diversifying its sources of borrowing. Caballero explained that their financing of eurobonds, convertible bonds, and other sources of credit made raising money easier for Cemex than for other Mexican groups, but that financing is still expensive compared with international competitors. He admitted to one disadvantage of operating in Asia having to do with cultural and language differences, unlike their commonalities with Spain, the Latin countries, and the border with the United States, but acknowledged that Asia usually moved in different cycles from Latin America, which could be a significant overall market-equalizing factor. Cemex crossed a major milestone in 1995 when non-Mexican operations accounted for 51 percent of the company's $3 billion in annual sales, balancing declining cash flow from Mexican operations. In that year the company exported two million tons of cement products to Taiwan, Thailand, and Indonesia.

Into the 21st Century As Industry World Leader

Company officials credited Cemex's competitive abilities to its online information system. A network of satellite dishes, leased lines, and microwave communications linked all of the company's offices in Mexico and abroad. A Cemex competitor noted that their network is phenomenal, giving the company flexibility, for example, of where to bring in their product. Caballero told Jim Freer in *Latin Finance*, "Carrying our laptops is like carrying our telephones around. We do about 90 percent of our communications through e-mail," making global interactions instantly possible, and even acting to reduce the hierarchy, for example, because anyone could shoot off an e-mail to anyone else in the company. Cemex set the curve for Latin technology users, and attributed its successful global expansion efforts to its hands-on approach. Cemex was the only Mexican company named in *Computerworld*'s 1995 "Global 100" listing of the world's most outstanding users of information technology. A company official stated that he was surprised that Cemex's competitors have next to no computers. Cemex began by using technology to reduce costs and improve efficiencies, but improved on that functional view, and transformed the way it delivered to the market. Its system kept a constant log of the chemical composition of the cement it produced, of the reasons for kiln problems and shutdowns, and of the delivery routes of the company's trucks. Cemex's information technology department was maintained by a staff of 25, who worked with Cemtec, an engineering technology division to provide and develop information access. Gelacio Iniguez Jauregui, the company's director of information technology, told Freer that Cemex planned to continue to build on its record of developing information technology, "not just for the sake of having information, but for using it, sharing it, and providing access to it."

One of Zambrano's proudest achievements, according to Daniel Dombey, writing for *Industry Week,* was Cemex's Tepeaca complex—probably the most modern cement plant in the Americas, located two hours outside of Mexico City. Situated among green fields, the unassuming-looking plant screened out pollutants via bags of glass fiber that "filter out smoke before it reaches the open air; pollutants are gathered at 60 points throughout the complex," according to Dombey. Its emissions were far below legal requirements, attributable to a system financed by 10 percent of the total cost of the plant. With more capacity than any other kiln on the continent, Tepeaca supplied one-fifth of the Mexican market and was the lowest-cost cement producer in the world.

Having survived the worst recession in memory, Zambrano, while entrenched in Mexico, did not wish to place too much emphasis on operations there—it was foreign revenues that kept Cemex's top line growing during 1995–96, when Mexico's gross domestic product tumbled by more than 6 percent. Cemex's debt was at an enormous $4.8 billion, making it Latin America's biggest corporate debtor, restricting the company's cash flow. Nevertheless, Zambrano continued his dealmaking, purchasing Cementos Nacionales in the Dominican Republic in 1995 and controlling stakes in two Colombian cement makers, Cementos Diamante, S.A. and Industrias e Inversiones Samper, S.A., the following year. The addition of the latter two firms, which cost $700 million, gave Cemex a one-third share of the Colombian market and also made Cemex the third largest cement company in the world. Cementos Diamante was subsequently renamed Cemex Colombia, S.A., and in 1998 Samper was merged into that entity, creating the number two cement producer in the country. Colombia became a base for Cemex's penetration of the Caribbean market.

By the mid-1990s Cemex had built up a large presence in Asia as a cement trader, and in the final years of the decade it completed its first acquisitions there. Demand for cement was growing rapidly in the region, fed by a boom in construction.

Moreover, although the economic crisis that gripped the region in 1997 and 1998 put a hold on a number of construction projects, it also created opportunities as conglomerates began shedding noncore assets and governments began selling stakes in state-owned cement operations, opening the way for Cemex and other global competitors to enter these markets. The first such move for Cemex came in the Philippines, where the company spent about $70 million in 1997 for a 30 percent stake in Rizal Cement Company, Inc. Cemex then gained a controlling 70 percent interest in Rizal in November 1998 for an additional $130 million. In February 1999 APO Cement Corporation of the Philippines was acquired for $400 million, making Cemex the largest cement producer in that country. Indonesia was the next Asian market targeted for direct investment: Cemex acquired a 25 percent stake in the state-owned PT Semen Gresik, that nation's largest cement producer, for about $241 million.

To help raise financing for its growing presence in Asia, Cemex created an investment holding company called Cemex Asia Holdings Ltd. in 1999. That same year, the company continued to expand outside of Asia as well. In Latin America, it took a 12 percent interest in the largest cement producer in Chile, Cementos Bio Bio, S.A.; acquired 95 percent of Cementos del Pacífico, S.A., the leader in Costa Rica; and purchased two terminals in Haiti that supplied 70 percent of the cement to the Central American and Caribbean markets. The company made its first acquisition in the Middle East, paying the Egyptian government about $319 million for a 77 percent stake in Assiut Cement Company, and adding yet another national leader to the Cemex global portfolio; the stake in Assiut was increased to 90 percent in June 2000. Cemex ended the 1990s with net sales of $4.83 billion, a 12 percent increase over the previous year, and net income of $1.03 billion, a 22 percent jump.

Early 2000s: The Purchase of Southdown

In what turned out to be a foreshadowing of the next dramatic event in the company's history, Cemex's shares, which had been trading over the counter for some time as American depository receipts on the New York Stock Exchange (NYSE), received a full listing on the Big Board in September 1999. The NYSE listing was intended to provide Cemex with heightened visibility and financial transparency as well as offer investors increased access to the shares. Cemex's U.S. profile received a much larger boost, however, through the October 2000 acquisition of the second largest U.S. cement producer, Houston-based Southdown, Inc. Valued at $2.63 billion, this was the largest acquisition in company history. Southdown, which achieved 1999 sales of $1.3 billion, operated 12 cement plants and 45 distribution centers, mainly in the Southwest and Florida, through which it sold cement in 27 states. Southdown's plants had a production capacity of 11 million metric tons. The deal made Cemex the largest cement producer in North America. One of the key rationales for the acquisition was that it created a better balance between high-growth and mature markets in the Cemex portfolio. It also provided a measure of vindication for Cemex because Southdown was the company that had led the antidumping campaign against Cemex in the late 1980s. Southdown was merged into Cemex's existing U.S. business in March 2001, creating Cemex, Inc., which accounted for nearly 30 percent of the parent company's sales during that year.

Following its acquisition, Southdown received a postmerger treatment—known as the "Cemex Way"—given to all of Cemex's conquests. A "postmerger integration team" is quickly dispatched to analyze the acquired company, to identify ways to cut costs and reduce head count, and to harmonize the technical systems and management methods with those of Cemex—in fine detail. This somewhat authoritarian approach yielded substantial savings.

Cemex continued to invest heavily in technology in the late 1990s and early 2000s, staying on the cutting edge of information technology (IT). Because ready-mixed concrete has to be poured within 90 minutes of mixing, it is a major challenge to coordinate and properly time the movements of ready-mixed concrete trucks from the plants to construction sites. Cemex equipped every truck with a computer and a global positioning system receiver. By combining the positions of the trucks with the output at the plants and the orders from customers, Cemex was able to create a system that not only calculated which truck should go where but also enabled dispatchers to redirect the trucks en route. Truck productivity was thereby increased by as much as 35 percent. There were other IT initiatives as well. Miami-based CxNetworks was formed in September 2000 as a wholly owned, independently operated subsidiary to manage Cemex's various e-business efforts. Among these were Construmix, a construction industry online marketplace aimed at small and medium-sized contractors in Latin America; and Latinexus, an online exchange for indirect goods and services created in partnership with other leading companies in Mexico and Brazil.

In the wake of the blockbuster Southdown acquisition, Cemex once again focused on less-developed markets. In May 2001 the company gained a foothold in Thailand via the $73 million purchase of Saraburi Cement Company Ltd. (later renamed Cemex Thailand Co. Ltd.). Later that year Cemex attempted to take over one of the top three cement producers in Thailand, the debt-ridden TPI Polene PCL, but Cemex and the creditors of the ailing Thai firm were unable to reach an agreement. Cemex also ran into trouble in its attempt to acquire the Indonesian government's remaining 51 percent stake in Semen Gresik. The Padang people of West Sumatra protested the proposed foreign ownership of Semen Padang, a subsidiary of Semen Gresik. By late 2003 it appeared that Semen Padang would be spun off from its parent, perhaps finally clearing the way for Cemex to gain its long-sought-after controlling stake. In the meantime, the company encountered yet another setback for its expansion plans, this time in the Caribbean, when the shareholders of Trinidad Cement Limited (TCL) in July 2002 blocked a move by Cemex to acquire the 80 percent of TCL it did not already own. One month later, however, Cemex managed to enhance its Caribbean operations by way of a $180 million takeover of Puerto Rican Cement Company, Inc. That same month, the company purchased the 30 percent of the Philippines firm Rizal Cement it did not already own for $95 million. In December of that year, Rizal completed a merger with its subsidiary, Solid Cement Corporation, in which Solid was the surviving entity.

Cemex's global expansion program, concentrating in large part on developing markets, had clearly paid dividends by the early 2000s. Cemex was more profitable than either of its two big international rivals, Lafarge and Holcim, mostly because of its concentration on emerging markets that offered both long-term growth potential and high profit margins. Its longstanding commitment to IT investment also provided Cemex with a productivity edge. Critics of the company—as well as some financial institutions—consistently raised concerns over the company's massive debt load; long-term debt stood at $4.37 billion at the end of 2002. But Cemex continued to generate a steady flow of free cash with which it could keep this burden under control. Another potential concern for the future was the more limited acquisition opportunities—particularly in southeast Asia—that existed following the consolidation drive of the 1990s and early 2000s. Cemex had yet to directly penetrate either India or China, prompting some analysts to wonder whether Cemex was being too cautious about expanding into these two huge and potentially quite lucrative markets.

Principal Subsidiaries

CEMEX México, S.A. de C.V.; CEMEX España, S.A. (Spain; 99.5%); CEMEX Venezuela, S.A.C.A. (75.7%); CEMEX, Inc. (U.S.A.); Cementos del Pacífico, S.A. (Costa Rica; 98.4%); Assiut Cement Company (Egypt; 95.8%); CEMEX Colombia, S.A. (98.2%); Cemento Bayano, S.A. (Panama; 99.2%); Cementos Nacionales, S.A. (Dominican Republic; 99.9%); Puerto Rican Cement Company, Inc.; CEMEX Asia Holdings Ltd. (Singapore; 92.3%); Solid Cement Corporation (Philippines; 94.6%); APO Cement Corporation (Philippines; 99.9%); CEMEX Thailand Co. Ltd.; Latin Networks Holdings, B.V. (Netherlands).

Principal Competitors

Lafarge S.A.; Holcim Ltd.; Heidelberg Cement AG; Italcementi S.p.A.; Sociedad Cooperativa Cruz Azul; Dyckerhoff AG; Buzzi Unicem S.p.A.; Cimpor - Cimentos de Portugal SGPS, S.A.; Ash Grove Cement Company.

Further Reading

Barham, John, "An Intercontinental Mix," *Latin Finance,* April 2002, pp. 21–25.
Brown, Elicia, "Tolmex: Repaving Mexico's Roads," *Financial World,* July 23, 1991, pp. 18–21.
"Cementing Global Success," *Strategic Direct Investor,* March 2003, pp. 12–13.
"The Cemex Way," *Economist,* June 16, 2001.
"The Children with the Magic Powder," *Economist,* May 21, 1994, pp. 76–79.
Dombey, Daniel, "Well-Built Success," *Industry Week,* May 5, 1997, pp. 32–39.
Ellis, Junius, "Five Stocks to Buy on the World's Hottest Market," *Money,* September 1992, pp. 153–56.
Freer, Jim, "Check the Voltage, Please," *Latin Finance,* March 1996, p. 62.
Friedland, Jonathan, "Cemex Shares Make Debut on Big Board," *Wall Street Journal,* September 15, 1999, p. A26.
——, "Mexico's Cemex Wins Bet on Acquisitions," *Wall Street Journal,* April 30, 1998.
Fritsch, Peter, "Cemex Loves Its 'Ants' But Wants More," *Wall Street Journal,* October 2, 2000, p. A22.
——, "Hard Profits: A Cement Titan in Mexico Thrives by Selling to Poor," *Wall Street Journal,* April 22, 2002, p. A1.

Griffith, Victoria, "Not a Mexican Company," *Latin Finance,* September, 1995, pp. 24–26.

Hernandez, Janine, "Cementos Mexicanos," *Latin Finance,* July-August 1994, pp. 46–48.

Holland, Kelly, "Citicorp Leads 1.2 Billion Bridge Loan for Cemex," *American Banker,* August 14, 1992, pp. 1–2.

LaFranchi, Howard, "Concrete Can't Weigh Cemex Down," *Christian Science Monitor,* March 13, 1996, p. 9.

Lindquist, Diane, "From Cement to Services," *Chief Executive,* November 2002, pp. 48–50.

Luxner, Larry, "Taking the Plunge," *Pit and Quarry,* February 1996, pp. 26–29.

Mathias, Alex, "Cemex: Keeps on Growing from Strong Foundations," *Euromoney,* December 1998.

McCarthy, Joseph L., "Lorenzo Zambrano (CEO of Cementos Mexicanos)," *Chief Executive,* September 1993, p. 27.

Moreno, Jenalia, "Cemex Deal Laid Solid Foundation," *Houston Chronicle,* April 10, 2002.

Pandey, Umesh, "Mexico's Cemex Plans Investment Spree," *Asian Wall Street Journal,* August 9, 2001, p. 4.

Piggott, Charles, "Cemex's Stratospheric Rise," *Latin Finance,* March 2001, pp. 76–78, 80.

Piper, Mark, "Cemex Strengthens the Mix," *Latin Finance,* December 2000, p. 38.

Poole, Claire, "Cement Wars," *Forbes,* October 1, 1990, pp. 99–102.

Watson, Andrew, "Cement Empire Unshaken," *Business Mexico,* November 2001, p. 39.

Weeks, Scott, "Solid Sale: Cemex Converts in a Difficult Market," *Latin Finance,* November 1994, p. 68.

—Terri Mozzone-Burgman
—update: David E. Salamie

ChildrenFirst, Inc.

75 Federal Street, Lobby 4
Boston, Massachusetts 02110-1900
U.S.A.
Telephone: (617) 646-7000
Toll Free: (800) 244-5317
Fax: (617) 646-7070
Web site: http://www.childrenfirst.com

Private Company
Incorporated: 1992
Employees: 250
Sales: $30 million (2002 est.)
NAIC: 624410 Child Day Care Services

ChildrenFirst, Inc. is the national leader in the design and development of employer-sponsored backup childcare intended for working parents who need childcare on occasion, as a backup in case of an emergency or when children are on school vacation. The centers accept children from three months up to 13 years old and each child is allowed 20 visits per year; a reservation is required as each center holds a maximum number of children. ChildrenFirst owns and operates more than 30 backup childcare centers, primarily in urban centers conveniently located near client offices. ChildrenFirst facilities are located in Boston, New York City, Washington, D.C., Chicago, Houston, Minneapolis-St. Paul, Los Angeles, San Francisco, Toronto, and several other cities. ChildrenFirst cares for more than 45,000 children and serves more than 260 businesses, including prominent law firms; financial services companies; publishing houses; consumer product manufactures; and retailers. Most of ChildrenFirst's corporate clients share childcare backup centers through a consortium, with each company reserving a certain number of the available spaces for their employees. Larger clients can arrange for a dedicated center for the exclusive use of their employees. Employers provide backup childcare free or may require employees to make a co-payment, generally from $10 to $25 per child per visit.

All ChildrenFirst centers are accredited with the National Association for the Education of Young Children. Children-First's educational philosophy is concerned with age-appropriate learning activities and toys, so the company's centers provide children with a variety of options, such as books, materials for art, musical instruments, and computers. The company offers a high child-to-teacher ratio, from 8 to 10:1 for school age children and 1:1 for infants. ChildrenFirst hires only college-educated childcare professionals, with 90 percent holding a bachelor's degree and 40 percent holding a master's degree, and pays salaries above the industry average. ChildrenFirst's guiding principles for the care and education of children are patience, commitment, optimism, tolerance, and perseverance.

Founding the Company on Beliefs and Practical Research in 1992

Rosemary Jordano founded ChildrenFirst in 1992 based on two beliefs, that "each child is unique, precious, and unrepeatable," and that business can be an instrument for positive change, in this case the quality of children's care outside the home. Through the course of her education, obtaining a bachelor's degree in economics and psychology from Wesley College and a master's degree in developmental psychology from Oxford University in England, Jordano studied children in a variety of institutional settings. Dissatisfied with the quality of the environments and teachers and the level of investment in children, she entered Stanford University's M.B.A. program with the intention of developing a plan for a childcare business that would provide quality care and education in safe, stimulating surroundings. Returning to her native Massachusetts, Jordano worked in a Boston childcare center for three years before starting her own business.

Backup childcare itself originated during the late 1980s in a Washington, D.C. law firm where last-minute childcare needs interfered with work responsibilities during a busy time, requiring the firm to group children in a conference room under the care of paralegals. Because about 70 percent of childcare occurs in the home by a nanny or relative, attorneys sometimes found themselves without childcare when the caregiver became ill or took a vacation. With legal work being framed in billable hours, the impact of tardiness and absenteeism from the breakdown of childcare arrangements made apparent the need for a solution. In addition, backup child care developed as the num-

Company Perspectives:

At ChildrenFirst we believe that each child is unique, precious and unrepeatable and that every second of every day is a defining moment in the life of a child. Our dedicated team of professional educators and corporate staff work together with our community to reinforce this belief and to ensure that every child is safe, nurtured, respected and educated. The quality of care we provide to children is rooted in our safe and secure environments, educationally sound programs and especially our people.

ber of women in the workplace increased and men began to take more responsibility for the care of children.

In 1992 Jordano formed ChildrenFirst and assumed management of one of the country's first backup childcare centers, in operation since 1990 at Boston's largest law firm, Ropes & Gray, handling a maximum of 25 children per day. Originally, ChildrenFirst acted as a management company, but Jordano turned quickly toward ownership, funding the company's start-up with credit card debt. In 1992 ChildrenFirst earned revenues of $1 million and began to develop centers to serve corporate employers in New York and Boston.

Jordano promoted backup childcare to corporate employers, rather than to working parents, by introducing a new concept into the market, a consortium of businesses supporting one center. A location convenient to employees of several companies allowed for consortium participation. Not only did this structure provide low-cost backup childcare, it allowed small companies, with as few as 20 employees, to provide a valuable benefit to employees with children. Each company reserved a certain number of slots for its employees, paying less than $30,000 per slot annually.

ChildrenFirst launched the first consortium backup childcare center in 1993, serving law firms, financial services companies, and other businesses in downtown Boston. Three additional centers opened that year, another in Boston and two in New York City. The Manhattan locations involved a dedicated backup childcare center at a Wall Street investment firm and one in the New York Life Insurance building in Midtown, serving New York Life and other companies in the building.

Jordano addressed parental concern for the safety and security of children in urban locations by consulting with the heads of security at the company's first client companies. ChildrenFirst's strategy included a lack of signage that would indicate to the general public the presence of children and placement of the center in a discreet location. Frequent fire drills assured parents of the safety of children in the case of an emergency. ChildrenFirst equipped each center with a double-locked entrance and coded touch keypad entry as well as 24-hour video surveillance. To identify parents and children permitted into a center, security guards used a photo album containing a picture of each child and those allowed to take the child out of the center. For children's safety inside the center, each facility was designed to minimize risk and injury, with round wall edges, corner guards, and glass partitions for open viewing and hearing. Mirrors built into dia-

per-changing cabinets allowed staff to view the activity of children in the area behind them. Toys that children chewed were cleaned with a disinfectant before being returned to the toy box.

To fund further expansion, in 1994 Jordano raised $3 million in financing through her contacts from Stanford University. That year the company opened its first childcare center in Chicago's West Loop downtown, after the city council eliminated restrictive building codes that discouraged childcare centers from opening in the downtown area. ChildrenFirst opened in the financial district in downtown Los Angeles in 1995. New York Life led the formation of another consortium backup childcare center, this one opening in downtown San Francisco in 1996. By the end of 1997, ChildrenFirst operated 12 centers serving more than 150 companies and caring for more than 10,000 children. As the network of ChildrenFirst centers expanded, corporate clients found a variety of uses for the centers, such as to assist mothers in the transition from maternity leave, to provide temporary childcare for employees in the midst of relocation, and for employees who traveled to company offices in other cities.

The National Association for the Education of Young Children began to accredit backup childcare facilities in 1997. ChildrenFirst completed that process the following year; accreditation was awarded to all existing centers and new centers as they opened.

Late 1990s Growth in Backup Child Care

As backup childcare became known as an alternative to corporate-sponsored day care, the new niche in childcare attracted the attention of the news media. As leader of the new industry, ChildrenFirst received major media coverage. In 1996 *NBC News* did a story on the expansion of backup childcare with the spotlight on ChildrenFirst. The *Today Show* in 1998 focused on ChildrenFirst as well. Rosemary Jordano appeared on the CNNfn show *Business Unusual* in 1999 to discuss the benefits of backup childcare. In addition, Jordano actively participated in public forums on the childcare issue, most notably childcare conferences given by the Clinton White House.

New studies on the impact of parental responsibilities on employee productivity confirmed a need for backup childcare to support employees in sustaining a work-life balance. Parents reported a high level of satisfaction and security knowing their children would be well cared for if their regular caretaker was unavailable. From the perspective of business, sponsorship of backup childcare provided incentive for employee retention and improved productivity through lower absences and tardiness. Various studies showed that childcare-related absences cost businesses from $2,500 to $4,000 per employee per year. A 1998 study by the National Conference of State Legislatures found that 80 percent of working parents miss work five to eight times per year due to a last-minute breakdown in regular childcare arrangements. Catalyst research found childcare to be an important benefit for employee morale and retention. By 1998 more companies offered backup childcare than full-time day care as an employee benefit.

The presence of high-profile business and government leaders in attendance at the opening ceremonies of ChildrenFirst

Key Dates:

1992: Rosemary Jordano forms ChildrenFirst and begins management of backup childcare center.
1993: ChildrenFirst initiates first consortium of corporate sponsors for backup childcare; centers open in Boston and New York.
1998: Prominent business and government leaders attend opening of ChildrenFirst centers in New York and Chicago.
1999: First Lady Hillary Rodham Clinton visits the ChildrenFirst facility in Manhattan.
2000: With 22 centers in operation in seven cities, ChildrenFirst hosts its 250,000th child.
2001: The first international location opens in Toronto, Canada.
2003: The State of Minnesota gives ChildrenFirst the Working Family Support Award.

centers indicated the importance of backup childcare. In January 1998 ChildrenFirst opened a center in the Travelers Group headquarters in Manhattan, serving working parents at financial services companies Travelers Group and Salomon Smith Barney. The grand opening and a roundtable discussion on backup childcare was attended by Sanford I. Weill, chairman and CEO of Travelers Group, and Robert E. Rubin, U.S. Secretary of the Treasury, who attended as part of his research for the Treasury Department's Working Group on Child Care. When overflow demand at ChildrenFirst's downtown Chicago center required the company to open a second facility in April, the grand opening ceremony was attended by J. Michael Cook, chairman and CEO of Deloitte & Touche, Gary Grom, senior vice-president of Sara Lee Corporation, and former U.S. Secretary of Labor Lynn Martin.

Demand for backup childcare grew in Manhattan as existing centers filled to capacity. In January 1999 ChildrenFirst opened a new facility in Midtown Manhattan, serving 19 companies, including lead corporate sponsor The Seagram Company. ChildrenFirst opened a center on Fifth Avenue in the Fashion Center to serve a consortium of 34 companies, serving existing clients, such as Instinet Corporation and Avon Products, as well as new clients, such as Estée Lauder Cosmetics. First Lady Hillary Rodham Clinton visited the center in September 1999, a reflection of her activities advocating for the well-being of children. Rodham Clinton interacted with the children at the center, who gave her a handmade book that depicted their hopes for the millennium; the art project had become a tradition for new ChildrenFirst center openings. She participated in a roundtable discussion with Jordano and business leaders and parents of supporting companies.

Jordano found financial funding for continued expansion through Lazard Capital Partners and Carousel Capital, with a $16 million investment in 1999. New locations included the company's first center in Minneapolis, which opened in October. Located at Gaviidae Common downtown, the center served ten companies, including Dayton Hudson Corporation, American Express Financial Advisors, and Deloitte & Touche.

Two ChildrenFirst backup childcare centers opened in southern California in 2000. In February a center opened in Irvine, in Orange County, with Taco Bell Corporation as the lead business sponsor among 12 charter clients. In October ChildrenFirst opened a 3,000-square-foot facility in Burbank, with a capacity to care for 40 children per day. The site served several film studios and media companies, including Warner Brothers Studios, Universal Studios, Nickelodeon Animation Studios, and Viacom, Inc.

In June ChildrenFirst opened a center in The Condé Nast Building in Times Square, New York City. Jordano noted this as a commendable commitment to children on the part of Condé Nast Publishers and other companies given that space was especially costly in that area of Manhattan.

By the end of 2000 ChildrenFirst operated ten centers in Manhattan, one in Jersey City, three each in Boston, Chicago, and the greater Los Angeles area, and one each in Minneapolis and San Francisco. Future growth at ChildrenFirst was assured as a study by Work Family Directions found that for every dollar invested in backup childcare, a company garnered three to four dollars returned in productivity.

Early 2000s Expansion Serving New and Existing Clients and Markets

ChildrenFirst continued to expand with facilities in new and existing markets. Baker Botts, LLP, a leading international law firm, led the formation of a backup childcare consortium in downtown Houston, with the center opening in January 2001. The following March ChildrenFirst opened a center in Silicon Valley; the consortium of 18 charter members included the City of Palo Alto, ChildrenFirst's first municipal client. The 5,100-square-foot center supported care for 60 children daily. In May ChildrenFirst opened its fourth center in Boston, in the Back Bay area, providing another location for downtown clients and a new childcare opportunity for new clients there. The 3,500-square-foot center provided backup childcare for up to 40 children.

ChildrenFirst opened three centers in the Minneapolis-St. Paul metropolitan area in 2001, the company's fastest area of expansion and a model for growth elsewhere. In January a backup childcare facility opened in Woodbury, Minnesota, the company's first suburban center. The 3M Corporation led the consortium, reserving 12 of 43 childcare spaces available. A center sponsored by General Mills and other companies opened in Minnetonka, Minnesota, in July, with a capacity to care for 47 children. Another location in downtown Minneapolis opened in the new Target Corporation headquarters in December. With a capacity for 51 children, the 4,000-square-foot center supplemented space at the existing downtown center.

The company entered a new region with the October 2001 opening of a state-of-the-art backup childcare facility in downtown Washington, D.C. The 4,100-square-foot center provided care for up to 38 children per day. KPMG, one of the center's lead sponsors and an existing client in other cities, worked with ChildrenFirst to start the facility as part of a national network that would serve KPMG employees in major cities. A center of similar capacity opened at Tyson's Corner in nearby McClean, Virginia, in January 2002, the company's 30th location. The center served major legal firms and financial services companies, such as Freddie Mac. ChildrenFirst funded growth with the investment of $4.5 million from Suez Capital Partners II, LP.

Development of new childcare centers slowed in 2002 and 2003. ChildrenFirst opened its first international backup child care center in Toronto in August 2002, serving employees of CIBC. In late 2003 Lehman Brothers opened a center for the exclusive use of employees at its headquarters in New York City. ChildrenFirst initiated development for centers in Dallas, a new market for the company, and in Washington, D.C.

During this time ChildrenFirst focused on corporate management, expanding its executive team to address the growing demands of servicing more than 260 existing clients while courting prospective clients. Jordano took the position of chairman and promoted COO John Marvin, a successful entrepreneur who joined ChildrenFirst in 2000, to CEO. The company added a new position, executive vice-president of sales, client services, and marketing, hiring Amy Crawford for the position.

In recognition for her leadership in defining and promoting backup childcare, Jordano received several honors. American Women's Economic Development Corporation (AWED) named Jordano the 2003 Woman Entrepreneur of the Year, and the state of Minnesota gave ChildrenFirst its Working Family Support Award in October 2003 as part of its annual "Week of the Working Family" initiative to foster family health.

Principal Competitors

Bright Horizons Family Solutions; Caregivers on Call; Knowledge Beginnings Corporation; Lipton Corporate Child Care Centers, Inc.

Further Reading

Adams, Susan, "The Players in Backup Day Care: At Work," *Forbes,* January 11, 1999, p. 72.

"Child Care, City-Style," *Working Mother,* January 1997, p. 8.

Holland, Roberta, "Adventures in Babysitting: ChildrenFirst Provides Care When Regular Daycare Provider Cannot," *Boston Business Journal,* February 22, 1999.

Learner, Neal, "A Popular Perk for Parents: Backup Child Care," *Christian Science Monitor,* July 16, 2001.

Milligan, Amanda, "Backup Child Care Centers Help Parents Focus on Work," *Business Insurance,* May 4, 1998, p. 2.

——, "Child Care Centers Manage Risks Large and Small," *Business Insurance,* March 15, 1999, p. 1.

Moriarty, George, "Carousel Joins Lazard in ChildrenFirst Backing," *Buyouts,* October 11, 1999.

Neal, Victoria, Michelle Prather, and Karen E. Spaed, "Young Millionaires," *Entrepreneur,* November 1999.

"Oh, Baby! Now What?," *Workforce,* June 2000, p. 32.

Oster, Merrill, and Mike Hamel, *The Entrepreneur's Creed,* Nashville: Broadman & Holman Publishers, 2001.

Selix, Casey, "Child Care Company Offers Backup Plan for Minnesota Companies," *Saint Paul Pioneer Press,* January 23, 2001.

Sixel, L.M., "Houston-Area Companies Learn the Value of Providing Employees with Day Care," *Houston Chronicle,* December 17, 2000.

Song, Jason, "Center Watches Kids When Day Care Plans Fail," *Los Angeles Times,* October 31, 2000, p. 2.

—Mary Tradii

Citigroup Inc.

399 Park Avenue
New York, New York 10043-0001
U.S.A.
Telephone: (212) 559-1000
Toll Free: (800) 285-3000
Fax: (212) 793-3946
Web site: http://www.citigroup.com

Public Company
Incorporated: 1812 as the City Bank of New York
Employees: 255,000
Total Assets: $1.09 trillion (2002)
Stock Exchanges: New York Pacific Mexican
Ticker Symbol: C
NAIC: 522110 Commercial Banking; 522210 Credit Card Issuing; 522291 Consumer Lending; 522220 Sales Financing; 522320 Financial Transactions Processing, Reserve, and Clearing House Activities; 523110 Investment Banking and Securities Dealing; 523120 Securities Brokerage; 523991 Trust, Fiduciary, and Custody Activities; 524113 Direct Life Insurance Carriers; 525910 Open-End Investment Funds; 523920 Portfolio Management; 551111 Offices of Bank Holding Companies

The largest financial services company in the world, with assets in excess of $1 trillion, Citigroup Inc. is a product of the 1998 megamerger of banking behemoth Citicorp and non-banking financial services and insurance giant Travelers Group Inc. The company offers a wide range of financial services to both consumers and businesses, boasting around 200 million customer accounts in more than 100 countries. Retail banking operations include Citibank, which conducts business internationally with more than 1,700 branches and nearly 5,200 ATMs; and Grupo Financiero Banamex, S.A. de C.V., one of the largest banks in Mexico with a 1,400-branch network. Through Citi Cards and other subsidiaries, Citigroup is the largest issuer of credit cards in the world. Other major units include Primerica Financial Services, Inc., offering term life insurance and asset management to consumers; CitiFinancial, provider of consumer finance and community-based lending services in North America, Europe, and Japan; The Travelers Life and Annuity Company, specializing in life insurance and individual and group annuity products; Citigroup Global Markets, Inc., a leading investment bank and corporate advisory business; and Smith Barney, a major retail brokerage house and equity research unit.

Company Origins

Citicorp had its origin in the First Bank of the United States, founded in 1791. Colonel Samuel Osgood, the nation's first postmaster general and treasury commissioner, took over the New York branch of the failing First Bank and reorganized it as the City Bank of New York in 1812. Only two days after the bank received its charter, on June 16, 1812, war was declared with Britain. The war notwithstanding, the City Bank was for all intents and purposes a private treasury for a group of merchants. It conducted most of its business as a credit union and as a dealer in cotton, sugar, metals, and coal, and later acted as a shipping agent.

Following the financial panic of 1837, the bank came under the control of Moses Taylor, a merchant and industrialist who essentially turned it into his own personal bank. Nonetheless, under Taylor, City Bank established a comprehensive financial approach to business and adopted a strategy of maintaining a high proportion of liquid assets. Elected president of the bank in 1856, Taylor converted the bank's charter from a state one to a national one on July 17, 1865, at the close of the Civil War. Taking the name National City Bank of New York (NCB), the bank was thereafter permitted to perform certain official duties on behalf of the U.S. Treasury; it distributed the new uniform national currency and served as an agent for government bond sales.

Taylor was the treasurer of the company that laid the first transatlantic cable, which made international trade much more feasible. It was at this early stage that NCB adopted the eight-letter wire code address "Citibank." Taylor died in 1882 and was replaced as president by his son-in-law, Percy R. Pyne. Pyne died nine years later and was replaced by James Stillman.

Stillman believed that big businesses deserved a big bank capable of providing numerous special services as a professional business partner. After the panic of 1893, NCB, with

Company Perspectives:

We are an economic enterprise with . . . a relentless focus on growth, aiming to increase earnings by double digits on average; a global orientation, but with deep local roots in every market where we operate; a highly diversified base of earnings that enables us to prosper under difficult market conditions; capital employed in higher-margin businesses, each one of which is capable of profitable growth on a stand-alone basis; financial strength protected by financial discipline, enabling us to take risks commensurate with rewards to capture attractive opportunities; a close watch on our overhead costs, but with a willingness to invest prudently in our infrastructure—we spend money like it's our own; a focus on technological innovation, seamlessly delivering value to our customers across multiple platforms.

assets of $29.7 million, emerged as the largest bank in New York City, and the following year it became the largest bank in the United States. It accomplished this mainly through conservative banking practices, emphasizing low-risk lending in well-secured projects. The company's reputation for safety spread, attracting business from the largest U.S. corporations. The flood of new business permitted NCB to expand; in 1897 it purchased the Third National Bank of New York, bringing its assets to $113.8 million. That same year it also became the first big U.S. bank to open a foreign department.

Far from retiring or diminishing his influence within NCB, Stillman nonetheless began to prepare Frank A. Vanderlip to take over senior management duties. Stillman and Vanderlip, who was elected president of the bank in 1909, introduced many innovations in banking, including travelers' checks and investment services through a separate but affiliated subsidiary (federal laws prevented banks from engaging in direct investment, but made no provision for subsidiaries).

Expansion in the Early 20th Century

Beginning in the late 1800s, many U.S. businessmen began to invest heavily in agricultural and natural-resource projects in the relatively underdeveloped nations of South and Central America. But government regulations prevented federally chartered banks such as NCB from conducting business out of foreign branches. Vanderlip worked long and hard to change the government's policy and eventually won in 1913, when Congress passed the Federal Reserve Act. NCB established a branch office in Buenos Aires in 1914 and in 1915 gained an entire international banking network from London to Singapore when it purchased a controlling interest in the International Banking Corporation, which it gained complete ownership of in 1918.

In 1919 Frank Vanderlip resigned in frustration over his inability to secure a controlling interest in the company, and James A. Stillman, the son of the previous Stillman, became president. NCB reached $1 billion in assets, the first U.S. bank to do so. Charles E. Mitchell, Stillman's successor in 1921, completed much of what Vanderlip had begun, creating the nation's first full-service bank. Until this time national banks catered almost exclusively to the needs of corporations and

institutions, while savings banks handled the needs of individuals. But competition from other banks, and even corporate clients themselves, forced commercial banks to look elsewhere for sources of growth. Sensing an untapped wealth of business in personal banking, in 1921 NCB became the first major bank to offer interest on savings accounts, which it allowed individual customers to open with as little as a dollar. In 1928 Citibank began to offer personal consumer loans.

The bank also expanded during the 1920s, acquiring the Commercial Exchange Bank and the Second National Bank in 1921, the People's Trust Company of Brooklyn in 1926, and merging with the Farmers' Loan and Trust Company in 1929. By the end of the decade, the "Citibank" was the largest bank in the country, and through its affiliates, the National City Company and the City Bank Farmers' Trust Company, it was also one of the largest securities and trust firms.

Surviving the Great Depression

In October 1929 the stock market crash that led to the Great Depression caused an immediate liquidity crisis in the banking industry. In the ensuing months, thousands of banks were forced to close. NCB remained in business, however, mainly by virtue of its size and organization. But in 1933, at the height of the Depression, Congress passed the Glass-Steagall Act, which restricted the activities of banks by requiring the separation of investment and commercial banking. NCB was compelled to liquidate its securities affiliate and curtail its line of special financial products, eliminating many of the gains the bank had made in establishing itself as a flexible and competitive full-service bank.

James H. Perkins, who succeeded Mitchell as chairman in 1933, had the difficult task of rebuilding the bank's reputation and its business (it had fallen to number three). He instituted a defensive strategy, pledging to keep all domestic and foreign branches open and to eliminate as few staff members as possible. Perkins died in 1940, but his defensive policies were continued by his successor, Gordon Rentschler.

As a major U.S. bank, NCB was in many ways a resource for the government, which depended on private savings and bond sales to finance World War II. The bank followed its defensive strategy throughout the war, amassed a large government bond portfolio, and continued to stress its relationship with corporate clients. Unlike its competitors, NCB was so well placed in so many markets by the end of the war that it could devote its energy to winning new clients rather than entering new markets. Sixteen years after Black Tuesday, NCB had finally regained its momentum in the banking industry.

Innovation in the Mid-20th Century

The bank changed direction after the death of Gordon Rentschler in 1948 by moving more aggressively into corporate lending. In 1955, with assets of $6.8 billion, NCB acquired the First National Bank of New York and changed its name to the First National City Bank of New York (FNCB), or Citibank for short.

Citibank used its bond portfolio to finance its expansion in corporate lending, selling off bonds to make new loans. By 1957, however, the bank had just about depleted its bond reserve. Prevented by New Deal legislation from expanding its

Key Dates:

1812: Colonel Samuel Osgood takes over the New York branch of First Bank of the United States and reorganizes it as City Bank of New York.

1865: The bank converts to a national charter, adopting the name National City Bank of New York (NCB).

1897: NCB becomes the first major U.S. bank to open a foreign department.

1918: Foreign operations are enlarged through the purchase of International Banking Corporation.

1919: NCB is the first U.S. bank to reach $1 billion in assets.

1933: Passage of the Glass-Steagall Act forces NCB to divest its securities affiliate and greatly reduce its financial services offerings.

1955: NCB acquires the First National Bank of New York and changes its name to First National City Bank of New York.

1961: The bank invents a new product: the negotiable certificate of deposit (CD).

1962: The name of the bank is shortened to First National City Bank.

1965: The bank enters the credit card business.

1968: A one-bank holding company, First National City Corporation (FNCC), is created and becomes the parent of the bank.

1974: The name of the holding company is changed to Citicorp.

1976: First National City Bank is renamed Citibank, N.A.

1987: Citicorp sets aside a $3 billion reserve fund as a provision against potentially bad Third World loans and also posts a $1.2 billion loss for the year.

1991: Restructuring and other charges result in an $885 million loss for the third quarter, and company shareholders do not receive a quarterly dividend for the first time since 1813.

1998: Citicorp merges with financial services giant Travelers Group Inc. to form Citigroup Inc.

1999: Passage of the Financial Services Modernization Act, which does away with the regulation of Glass-Steagall, blesses the marriage of Citicorp and Travelers after the fact, meaning the firm can engage in both banking and insurance.

2000: Associates First Capital Corporation, a consumer finance company specializing in subprime loans, is acquired and merged into CitiFinancial.

2001: Citigroup acquires Grupo Financiero Banamex, a leading retail bank in Mexico.

2002: Citigroup spins off Travelers Property Casualty; the company becomes embroiled in scandals involving its equity research and investment banking operations as well as loans to Enron Corporation.

2003: The corporation agrees to pay $400 million to settle the equity research charges and $145.5 million to settle the Enron case.

---

business in private savings beyond New York City, Citibank had nowhere to turn for more funding. The squeeze on funds only became more acute until 1961, when the bank introduced a new and ingenious product: the negotiable certificate of deposit.

The "CD," as it was called, gave large depositors higher returns on their savings in exchange for restricted liquidity, and was intended to win business from higher-interest government bonds and commercial paper. The CD changed not only Citibank but the entire banking industry, which soon followed suit in offering CDs. The CD gave Citibank a way to expand its assets—but at the same time required it to streamline operations and manage risk more efficiently, because it had to pay a higher rate of interest to CD holders for the use of their funds.

The man behind the CD was not FNCB's president, George Moore, nor its chairman, James Rockefeller, but Walter B. Wriston, a highly unconventional vice-president. Wriston, a product of Wesleyan University and the Fletcher School, had worked his way up through the company's ranks since joining the bank in 1946. Having made a name for himself with the CD, Wriston was later given responsibility for revamping the company's management structure to eliminate the strains of Citibank's expansion. Like Vanderlip more than 50 years before, Wriston advocated a general decentralization of power to permit top executives to concentrate on longer-term strategic considerations.

In 1962 the bank's official name was changed to First National City Bank. Six years later, in an attempt to circumvent federal regulations restricting a bank's activities, Citibank created a one-bank holding company (a type of company the Bank Holding Company Act of 1956 had overlooked) to own the bank but also engage in lines of business the bank could not. The holding company was initially called First National City Corporation (FNCC). Within six months, Bank of America, Chase Manhattan, Manufacturers Hanover, Morgan Guaranty, and Chemical Bank had also created holding companies.

FNCC made no secret of its intention to expand, both operationally and geographically. In 1970 Congress—recognizing its error and concerned that one-bank holding companies would become too powerful—revised the Bank Holding Company Act of 1956 to prevent these companies from diversifying into traditionally "non-banking" activities.

Wriston, who was promoted to president in 1967 and to chairman in 1970, continued to press for the relaxation of banking laws. He oversaw Citibank's entry into the credit card business, and later directed a massive offer of Visa and MasterCharge cards to 26 million people across the nation. This move greatly upset other banks that also issued the cards, but succeeded in bringing Citibank millions of customers from outside New York state. The bank failed, however, to properly assess the risk involved. Of the five million people who responded to the offer, enough later defaulted to cost the corporation an estimated $200 million.

In an effort to gain wider consumer recognition, the holding company formally adopted Citicorp as its legal name in 1974, and in 1976 First National City Bank officially changed its name to Citibank, N.A. The "Citi" prefix was later added to a number of generic product names: Citicorp offered CitiCards, CitiOne unified statement accounts, and there were CitiTeller automatic teller machines and a host of other Citi-offerings.

Falling Fortunes in the 1970s and 1980s

Citicorp performed very well during the early 1970s, weathering the failure of the Penn Central railroad, the energy crisis, and a recession without serious setback. In 1975, however, the company's fortunes fell dramatically. Profits were erratic because of rapidly eroding economic conditions in Third World countries. Citicorp, awash in petrodollars in the 1970s, had lent heavily to these countries in the belief that they would experience high turnover and faced the possibility of heavy defaults resulting from poor growth rates. In addition, its Argentine deposits were nationalized in 1973, its interests in Nigeria had to be scaled back in 1976, and political agitation in Poland and Iran in 1979 precipitated unfavorable debt rescheduling in those countries. Shareholders soon became concerned that Citicorp, which conducted two-thirds of its business abroad, might face serious losses.

In its domestic operations, Citicorp suffered from a decision made during the early 1970s to expand in low-yielding, consumer-banking activities. Although New York usury laws placed a 12 percent ceiling on consumer loans, Citibank bet that interest rates would drop, leaving plenty of room to make a profit. But the oil shock following the revolution in Iran sent interest rates soaring in the opposite direction: Citicorp lost $450 million in 1980 alone. In addition, Citibank purchased $3 billion in government bonds at 11 percent, in the belief that interest rates would continue a decline begun during the summer of 1980. Again, the opposite happened. Interest on the money Citibank borrowed to purchase the bonds rose as high as 21 percent, and the bank lost another $50 million or more.

One investment that did not go awry, however, was the company's decision to invest $500 million on an elaborate automated teller network. Installed throughout its branches by 1978, the ATMs permitted depositors to withdraw money at any hour from hundreds of locations. Not only were labor costs reduced drastically, but by being first again, Citibank gained thousands of new customers attracted by the convenience of ATMs.

Citicorp raised the profitability of its commercial banking operations by deemphasizing interest rate-based income in favor of income from fees for services. Successful debt negotiations with developing countries cut losses on debts that would otherwise have gone into default. In addition, as a result of the 1967 Edge Act and special accommodations made by various states, Citicorp, until then an international giant known domestically only in New York state, was able to expand into several states during the 1980s. Beginning with mortgages and its credit card business, then savings and loans, and then banks, Citicorp established a presence in 39 states and the District of Columbia. Internationally, the company expanded its business into more than 90 countries. Some of this expansion was accomplished by purchasing existing banks outright.

Wriston, after 14 years as chairman of Citicorp, retired in 1984, shortly after the announcement that Citicorp would enter two new businesses: insurance and information. He was succeeded by John S. Reed, who had distinguished himself by returning the "individual" banking division to profitability.

In May 1987 Citibank finally admitted that its Third World loans could spell trouble and announced that it was setting aside a $3 billion reserve fund. Losses for 1987 totaled $1.2 billion, but future earnings were much more secure. Citibank's move forced its competitors to follow suit, something few of them were able to do as easily—Bank of America, for example, wound up selling assets to cover its reserve fund.

Reorganization and an Uneven Recovery in the Early to Mid-1990s

As Citicorp entered the 1990s, the United States' biggest bank faced perhaps its most challenging period since its founding. A faltering economy, coupled with unprofitable business loans—particularly in the commercial real estate market—led to serious financial difficulties that threatened the bank's existence. Year-end statistics for 1990 revealed a 20-year low for Citicorp's share price, which eventually fell to $8. Citicorp's ratio of core capital to total assets stood at 3.26 percent, considerably lower than the minimum 4 percent that regulators instituted as the standard requirement in 1992. The company was operating on an expenses-to-revenue ratio of 70 percent, which prompted immediate cost-cutting efforts in nearly all expendable (noncore) business operations. Third quarter financial statements for 1991 reflected the impact of restructuring charges, asset write-downs, and additions to reserves necessary for coverage of nonperforming loans: Citicorp reported an $885 million loss. For the first time since 1813, shareholders did not receive their 25 cents a share quarterly dividend. Citicorp was in desperate need of reorganization.

Chairman John Reed described this period of great instability as "tough, demanding," and a time of "turnaround." Widely viewed as a slow-moving and analytical visionary, Reed appeared to many to be unable to maneuver the ailing bank out of its mounting difficulties. Critics blamed Citicorp's loan crisis on Reed's efforts during the mid-1980s to expand in the international market and overextend credit to real estate developers, including Donald Trump. Reed silenced his critics, however, with the successful implementation of a two-year, five-point plan aimed at improving capital strength and operating earnings to offset future, but imminent, credit costs.

Of primary importance in the recovery process were cost-cutting measures, growth constraint, and disciplined expenses and credit quality—considered the control aspects of the banking industry. Staff cuts for the two-year restructuring period resulted in the layoff of more than 15,000 employees—including many in senior management positions. Expenses also were trimmed as Citicorp consolidated its U.S. mortgage service and insurance service operations, as well as its telecommunication resources.

Nearly half of Citicorp's third-quarter $885 million loss was affected by the write-down of its $400 million investment in Quotron Systems, Inc. Citicorp bought the stock quotation service for $680 million in 1986 at a time when the company was hoping to expand in the information business. Since the acquisition, Quotron had been losing contracts with major Wall Street firms such as Shearson Lehman and Merrill Lynch. Quotron Systems could not compete with the updated technology of its rival, Automatic Data Processing (ADP). In 1992 Citicorp sold two Quotron divisions to ADP, the leader in the computer services market.

To help raise the projected $4 billion to $5 billion in capital under the five-point plan, Citicorp sold its marginal operations in Austria, Italy, and France; abandoned its efforts in the United Kingdom; and offered $1.1 billion of preferred equity redemption cumulative stock (PERCS). An important factor in the company's recapitalization was investment by Saudi Prince al-Waleed bin Talal, who provided approximately $400 million of the $2.6 billion Citicorp raised in 1991 and 1992.

Although Citicorp relinquished some of its weaker holdings in Europe, it continued to expand and improve operations in the Asia/Pacific region. New branches were opened in Mexico, Brazil, Japan, Taiwan, South Korea, and Australia. Such selective investing produced growth in earnings of up to 30 percent. From September 1991 to September 1992, Citicorp obtained $371 million in net income from consumer banking in the developing world, exceeding earnings in the Japan, Europe, and North America (JENA) unit of global finance.

Citicorp continued its commitment to international core business, capital growth, and credit stability as it cautiously proceeded through a recovery period. Circumstances called for conservative action in the early 1990s to compensate for severe losses. In addition, Citicorp's freedom to make loans was abridged in 1992 when it was placed under regulatory supervision by the Federal Reserve Bank of New York.

Citicorp experienced losses in the value of its real estate holdings in the early 1990s. The company decided to hold on to the nonperforming property in the hopes an economic recovery would boost its value. However, Citicorp sold approximately 60 percent of its holdings in 1993 at a loss. Two years later the other 40 percent had recovered its value.

In 1996 a Citibank employee was accused of helping Raul Salinas, brother of Mexican President Carlos Salinas, sneak out of Mexico funds acquired by illegal means. Further embarrassment from Mexico ensued for Citicorp when its 1998 purchase of Banco Confia was linked to charges of laundering drug money. Domestically, Citicorp was faced with rising credit card write-offs as consumer bankruptcy increased in the late 1990s.

1998: Citicorp + Travelers = Citigroup

In 1998 Citicorp took the lead in mega-banking mergers by joining forces with Travelers Group Inc. Citigroup Inc., as the new entity was called, boasted assets of $698 billion. The merger created the largest financial services firm in the world, what the *Economist* called "a global financial supermarket." With little overlap in service offerings and two separate distribution networks, the two companies hoped to cross-sell to each other's customers. John Reed, chairman of Citicorp, and Sanford Weill, chairman of Travelers Group, agreed to run the new company together.

Despite the Glass-Steagall Act of 1933, which forbade banks from owning insurers and insurers from owning banks, the merger was approved by the Federal Reserve Board. Citigroup was required to sell off its insurance businesses, however, a ruling it hoped would be overridden with new legislation. It

stalled the sales while lobbying Congress to modernize the law. This tactic eventually succeeded with the passage of the Financial Services Modernization Act (FSMA), which was signed into law by President Bill Clinton in November 1999. With the longtime protections of Glass-Steagall now overturned, Citigroup became one of the first firms to qualify as a financial holding company under the FSMA, enabling it to continue to operate in both banking and insurance.

Shares of Citibank and Travelers Group shot up at the announcement of the merger, raising the combined value of the companies by $30 billion. The optimism waned in the months following the merger as cross-selling and creating economies of scale proved difficult to execute. With Travelers still struggling to integrate its recent purchase of Salomon Brothers into its own brokerage business (Smith Barney), the merger with Citibank did not proceed smoothly. Rather than cross-selling, the various subsidiaries and divisions moved to protect their own turf. One exception was subsidiary Primerica Financial Services, which sold a range of Travelers products to customers who took the company up on a free financial analysis.

The rift between Citibank and Travelers Group became apparent in late 1998 when Jamie Dimon, likely successor to Citibank's joint chairmen, Weill and Reed, abruptly quit. Employees divided along original company lines, with Citibank staff cheering the news as a victory for their man Reed over Weill, who had groomed Dimon to replace him at Travelers. Salomon employees, who had never been fully integrated into Travelers Group before the merger, showed their sympathy for Dimon with a standing ovation on their trading floor. Dimon's loss left a void in the company's leadership, especially because Weill and Reed were both nearing retirement age.

In 1999 Citibank announced a project to simplify its service offerings in an effort to reduce costs. As the bank had grown over the years, its complexity had multiplied to such mind-boggling dimensions that it needed 28 computer systems to handle its back-office records. As an example, Citibank offered 150,000 different kinds of checking accounts in 1999, with variations on how interest was calculated, what fees were charged, and so on. The goal of the new project was to cut complexity by 75 percent and eliminate at least 26 computer systems.

Meanwhile, the larger integration of Citicorp and Travelers resulted in restructuring charges of $1.3 billion and the elimination of more than 10,000 jobs from the workforce in 1998 and 1999. Continuing the branding of Citigroup's units with the "Citi" prefix, Commercial Credit, a consumer finance outfit that came from the Travelers side of the corporate tree, was rechristened CitiFinancial during 1999. Citibank Mortgage was similarly renamed CitiMortgage, Inc. in April 2000. The corporation's boardroom gained a big name in October 1999 when former Treasury Secretary Robert E. Rubin was named co-chairman. According to a *Business Week* article, Rubin, who had once been the CEO of Goldman Sachs, served as "a kind of roving corporate ambassador."

Major Acquisitions, Series of Scandals in the Early 2000s

In early 2000 Reed left the company, having lost a power struggle with Weill. The latter was now sole CEO. That April, Citigroup spent $2.4 billion to take full control of Travelers

Property Casualty Corp. In November the company paid $27 billion for Dallas-based Associates First Capital Corporation, a U.S.-based consumer finance firm specializing in the subprime segment of the credit market (which includes higher risk customers with prior credit problems or limited credit history); the acquired firm also had a large presence in Japan. Most of Associates was merged into CitiFinancial, which became the largest originator of home equity loans in the United States. Unfortunately, just months after the deal was consummated, the Federal Trade Commission (FTC) charged Citigroup with predatory lending in relation to what regulators considered to be deceptive marketing practices at Associates. In September 2002 Citigroup reached an agreement with FTC to settle the lawsuit whereby it would pay $240 million to the consumers affected by the allegedly deceptive practices—representing one of the largest consumer protection settlements in U.S. history.

The addition of Associates' Japanese consumer finance arm was part of a broader international drive by Citigroup to penetrate mid-level banking and finance markets abroad—Citibank having been content over the decades concentrating on the upper end. In Europe during 2001, Citigroup acquired the credit card unit of the U.K.-based Peoples Bank and 130-year-old Bank Handlowy, a retail bank in Poland with 80 branches. The corporation also spent $2.2 billion in January 2001 to purchase Schroders plc, a British investment bank. A further move into the Asian market came in April 2001 when Citigroup paid $800 million for a 15 percent stake in the Fubon Group, which operated five financial services companies in Taiwan; this was the largest-ever investment in that country's financial sector by a foreign firm. Closer to home, Citigroup completed its largest ever international acquisition in August 2001, laying out $6.26 billion in cash and a like amount in stock for Grupo Financiero Banamex-Accival (or ''Banacci''), one of the largest banks in Mexico, with more than 1,350 branches catering to middle class consumers and small businesses along with an investment bank and brokerage serving corporations and the more well-to-do. Citigroup's existing banking operations in Mexico were incorporated with those acquired under the Banamex name, creating the largest independent bank and brokerage in the country. Citigroup gained a listing on the Mexican stock exchange as a result of its takeover of Banamex, becoming the first foreign firm to do so.

Not neglecting the home market, Citigroup acquired the New York state–chartered European American Bank (EAB) from Netherlands-based ABN AMRO Bank N.V. for $1.6 billion in cash and the assumption of $350 million in EAB preferred stock. Completed in July 2001, the deal brought Citigroup an enhanced presence in the metropolitan New York and Long Island markets through EAB's 97 commercial banking branches, which were subsequently rebranded under the Citibank name. In November 2002 Citigroup paid about $5.8 billion for Golden State Bancorp, the parent of First Nationwide Mortgage and Cal Fed, the second largest thrift in the United States. Gained in this acquisition were 325 retail branches in California and Nevada, 1.5 million new banking customers, $25 billion in deposits, and $20 billion in loans that were added to the CitiMortgage portfolio.

The purchase of Golden State was funded in part from the spinoff of Travelers Property Casualty, a business that was considered more volatile and expected to grow more slowly than other Citigroup operations. In March 2002, 23.1 percent of the equity in the Travelers unit was sold to the public through an initial public offering (IPO) that raised more than $12 billion. Most of Citibank's remaining stake was distributed to shareholders in August of that year. Additional 2002 initiatives included the reorganization of the company's operations into a matrix-like structure encompassing nine product areas and six geographic regions; the start-up of retail banking operations in both China and Russia; and the formation of an alliance with Shanghai Pudong Development Bank to enter the emerging credit card market in China.

For Citigroup, however, the year 2002 is likely to be best remembered as the year of scandal. In addition to the Associates' deceptive marketing scandal, a number of state and federal investigations were launched into the questionable practices of the Salomon Smith Barney investment bank and equity research unit. Salomon's influential telecommunications analyst, Jack Grubman, was accused of hyping the stock of several firms whose shares later tanked, the firms having returned the favor by sending hundreds of millions of dollars in investment banking fees Salomon's way. Grubman resigned in disgrace in August 2002, but not before accepting a $33 million severance package. Weill himself was caught up in the scandal, when allegations were raised that he had tried to persuade Grubman to raise his rating on the stock of AT&T Corp., a firm for which Weill served as a director. In April 2003 Citigroup's Salomon (which by this time had dropped its scandal-associated name in favor of Citigroup Global Markets, Inc.) was part of a landmark $1.4 billion settlement between ten Wall Street firms and the New York Attorney General, the Securities and Exchange Commission (SEC), and other regulatory agencies. Citigroup agreed to pay $400 million in fines and payments—the largest amount paid by one firm. Grubman was fined $15 million and was barred from working in the securities industry for the rest of his life. Weill (along with other senior officers) was barred from speaking directly with Citigroup analysts on investment banking matters. The SEC also mandated the separation of investment banking and equity research operations—the building of a so-called Chinese wall—a move that Citigroup had already taken in creating a new and independent business unit called Smith Barney to be the corporation's retail brokerage house and equity research unit.

Citigroup also was embroiled in the huge Enron Corporation scandal. Both Citigroup and J.P. Morgan Chase & Co. were key Enron bankers and were involved in funding off-the-books ventures that played a central role in the alleged fraud that Enron executives had committed against the company's shareholders. The banks loaned billions of dollars to the Houston energy trading firm but structured the loans in such a way that the added debt was hidden from shareholders and in fact appeared to boost Enron's cash flow. In July 2003 Citigroup and J.P. Morgan reached an agreement with the SEC and others whereby they would pay a total of $305 million to settle the Enron case, with Citigroup's share being $145.5 million.

Despite these settlements, Citigroup still faced private and class-action lawsuits that had been filed on behalf of investors, bondholders, and others in relation to these scandals. In anticipation of the expected fines and anticipated settlement costs, the corporation had set aside $1.5 billion as a litigation reserve in

December 2002. Remarkably, Citigroup still managed to report record net income of $15.28 billion for the year. On the other hand, the scandals battered the corporation's stock, which fell about 25 percent for the year—a loss in market value of about $60 billion.

Although Citigroup's reputation had certainly been tarnished by the firm's involvement in the wave of corporate scandals that rocked the United States in the early 2000s, Weill tried to win the public relations battle by adopting reform measures ahead of the regulators and legislators. For example, Citigroup announced that at the beginning of 2003 it would begin expensing the cost of all stock options for employees, management, and board members, a move that many observers believed was necessary to provide a more accurate accounting of the finances of a company. In July 2003 Weill made headlines through a long-anticipated announcement: the tapping of a successor. Weill said that he would step down as CEO at the end of 2003, and Charles O. Prince was named to succeed him. Prince was a longtime Weill lieutenant who had been named COO in 2001 and later was placed in charge of the scandal-ridden investment bank. It also was announced that the head of the Citigroup consumer banking operation, Robert B. Willumstad, would succeed Prince as COO. Weill planned to stay on as chairman through early 2006. Meantime, two other July 2003 announcements signaled that Citigroup had weathered the scandal storm: the firm said that it would increase its dividend by 75 percent and that it would acquire the huge credit card business of Sears, Roebuck and Co. for about $3 billion.

Principal Subsidiaries

Citibank, N.A.; CitiFinancial; Citigroup Global Markets, Inc.; The Citigroup Private Bank; Primerica Financial Services, Inc.; The Travelers Life and Annuity Company; Grupo Financiero Banamex, S.A. de C.V. (Mexico).

Principal Operating Units

Global Consumer Group; Global Corporate and Investment Bank Group; Global Investment Management; Global Markets; Citigroup International.

Principal Competitors

J.P. Morgan Chase & Co.; Bank of America Corporation; Deutsche Bank AG; UBS AG; Merrill Lynch & Co., Inc.; The Goldman Sachs Group, Inc.; Credit Suisse Group.

Further Reading

Bianco, Anthony, and Heather Timmons, "Crisis at Citi," *Business Week*, September 6, 2002, pp. 34–38, 40, 42.

Bianco, Anthony, et al., "Citi's New Act," *Business Week*, July 28, 2003, pp. 30+.

Citibank, Nader and the Facts, New York: Citibank, 1974.

"Citicorp Battling Back," *Economist*, April 25, 1992, pp. 84, 86.

"Citigroup: Fall Guy," *Economist*, November 7, 1998.

Cleveland, Harold van B., and Thomas F. Huertas, *Citibank, 1812–1970*, Cambridge, Mass.: Harvard University Press, 1985.

Creswell, Julie, "Banks on the Hot Seat," *Fortune*, September 2, 2002, pp. 79–80, 82.

Egan, Jack, "The Fight to Stay on Top," *U.S. News and World Report*, December 30, 1991/January 6, 1992, pp. 70–71.

"Financial Mergers: Complex Equations," *Economist*, June 5, 1999.

Hutchison, Robert A., *Off the Books*, New York: William Morrow and Company, 1986.

Kadlec, Daniel, "Citi Slicker," *Time*, October 7, 2002, pp. 67+.

Langley, Monica, *Tearing Down the Walls: How Sandy Weill Fought His Way to the Top of the Financial World—and Then Nearly Lost It All*, New York: Simon & Schuster, 2003.

Lee, Peter, "Is Citi Back from the Dead?," *Euromoney*, December 1992, p. 30.

Leindorf, David, and Donald Etra, *Ralph Nader's Study Group Report on First National City Bank*, New York: Grossman, 1973.

Loomis, Carol J., "Citigroup: Scenes from a Merger," *Fortune*, January 11, 1999, pp. 76–78+.

——, "Sandy Weill's Monster," *Fortune*, April 16, 2001, pp. 106+.

——, "Whatever It Takes," *Fortune*, November 25, 2002, pp. 74+.

Meeham, John, and William Glasgall, "Citi's Nightmares Just Keep Getting Worse," *Business Week*, October 28, 1991, pp. 124–25.

Miller, Richard Bradford, *Citicorp: The Story of a Bank in Crisis*, New York: McGraw-Hill, 1993.

Miller, Suzanne, "Is Sandy Losing Focus?," *Banker*, September 2002, pp. 24–26, 28.

Pacelle, Mitchell, and Laurie P. Cohen, "J.P. Morgan, Citigroup Will Pay $305 Million to Settle Enron Case," *Wall Street Journal*, July 29, 2003, pp. A1, A2.

Pacelle, Mitchell, and Monica Langley, "Citigroup's Weill Taps a Top Aide As His Successor," *Wall Street Journal*, July 17, 2003, pp. A1, A6.

Prince, C.J., "The Dealmaker," *Chief Executive* (U.S.), July 2002, pp. 28+.

Silverman, Gary, et al., "Is This Marriage Working?," *Business Week*, June 7, 1999, pp. 127–34.

Stone, Amey, and Mike Brewster, *King of Capital: Sandy Weill and the Making of Citigroup*, New York: Wiley, 2002.

Thomas, Landon, Jr., "Citigroup's Chairman Is Barred from Direct Talks with Analysts," *New York Times*, April 29, 2003, p. C1.

Timmons, Heather, et al., "Citi's Sleepless Nights: The Bank Faces Lawsuits, Fines, and Closer Scrutiny," *Business Week*, August 5, 2002, pp. 42–43.

Timmons, Heather, Geri Smith, and Frederik Balfour, "Sandy Weill Wants the World," *Business Week*, June 4, 2001, pp. 88, 90.

"The Trials of Megabanks," *Economist*, October 31, 1998.

"Watch Out for the Egos," *Economist*, April 11, 1998.

Zweig, Phillip L., *Wriston: Walter Wriston, Citibank, and the Rise and Fall of American Financial Supremacy*, New York: Crown, 1995.

—Edna M. Hedblad
—updates: Susan Windisch Brown, David E. Salamie

Cognizant Technology Solutions Corporation

500 Glenpointe Centre West
Teaneck, New Jersey 07666
U.S.A.
Telephone: (201) 801-0233
Toll Free: (888) 937-3277
Fax: (201) 801-0243
Web site: http://www.cognizant.com

Public Company
Incorporated: 1994 as Dun & Bradstreet Satyam Software
Employees: 6,165
Sales: $229.1 million (2002)
Stock Exchanges: NASDAQ
Ticker Symbol: CTSH
NAIC: 541511 Custom Computer Programming Services

Cognizant Technology Solutions Corporation is a Teaneck, New Jersey-based company that employs an onsite/offshore development model to provide application maintenance services and enterprise consulting solutions to major corporations, primarily in the United States. Cognizant is one of the few companies that has found a way to take advantage of the large pool of English-speaking IT professionals produced in India, where approximately 80,000 programmers graduate each year from universities. Because these software professionals typically make around $15,000 a year, compared with $75,000 in the United States, Cognizant is able to offer considerable savings to its customers. The onsite/offshore model also allows the company to work 24 hours a day on a project. During the U.S. work day, Cognizant's onsite team meets with the customer to review the work their Indian colleagues completed the night before. Feedback is then available for the Indian programmers when they begin their day. A further advantage is that system work is done at a time when there is little network congestion. Moreover, cultural differences between the United States and India work in Cognizant's favor. In India, the position of software engineer is more prestigious, meaning that scores of talented people enter the field. Indians are also less individualistic than their American counterparts and more willing to adhere to a process, which is an important factor in making the onsite/offshore approach run smoothly. To provide security, the company runs background checks on overseas employees; to prevent theft of data, it provides only diskless personal computers. Cognizant operates 11 software development centers in India, as well as centers in Limerick, Ireland, and in Phoenix, Arizona. Sales offices are located in Atlanta, Chicago, Dallas, Minneapolis, Los Angeles, San Francisco, Toronto, London, and Frankfurt. With a focus on North American and European *Fortune* 1000 companies in the healthcare, financial services, and information fields, Cognizant boasts such major customers as AC Nielsen Corporation, The Dun & Bradstreet Corporation, First Data Corporation, and Metropolitan Life Insurance Company.

Forming the Company in 1994

The man behind the founding of Cognizant was Wijeyaraj (Kumar) Mahadeva, the company's current chairman and CEO. He was born in Sri Lanka, where his father was the head of the country's civil service. Mahadeva traveled abroad for his education, earning a master's degree in electrical engineering from the University of Cambridge in 1973. He then worked as a researcher at the British Broadcasting Corporation for three years before coming to the United States to continue his education at Harvard Business School, where he caught the eye of the consulting firm McKinsey & Co. He joined McKinsey in 1978 and over the next seven years was instrumental in building up the firm's technology practice. Looking back on his days as a consultant, Mahadeva told *Investor's Business Daily* in 2002, "I learned a lot at McKinsey, with its focus on client relationships and setting high standards for recruitment and staff development." According to McKinsey colleague Rajat Dupta, "Kumar was an absolute star who could deftly think through problems and articulate solutions." In 1985 Mahadeva accepted a position with AT&T Corp., a client adjusting to the court-ordered breakup that resulted in the divestiture of local telephone service and the creation of the seven "Baby Bells." AT&T, eager for new opportunities, was looking to take on IBM in the computer field. But Mahadeva soon grew disenchanted with the corporate politics that prevailed at AT&T and after four years left to take a job with Dun & Bradstreet Corporation (D&B), tabbed to head its entry into Asia. According to *Investor's Business Daily,* "Demand was weak for the busi-

Company Perspectives:

We provide application outsourcing services and enterprise consulting solutions to Fortune 500 and Blue Chip companies in the US and Europe. Leveraging a streamlined on-site/offshore development model, we can help your organization achieve a world-class level of technical excellence for less than half the cost of having the same work done by other e-business and outsourcing leaders.

ness research firm's service in the Asia Pacific region. Mahadeva, however, used the time there to watch and learn. What did he find? Low-cost software factories in India, where developers wrote computer code at a fraction of the cost in America. He recognized an opportunity. . . . The timing was ideal. Concerns were mounting at D&B about how to solve the pending Y2K computer crisis. At the same time, costs were coming way down for satellite bandwidth, making shared computer networks more cost-effective.'' He was able in 1994 to convince D&B to invest $2 million in a joint venture with Satyam, an Indian software outsourcing operation, which held a 24 percent interest in the start-up. The business was called Dun & Bradstreet Satyam Software, Cognizant's forefather.

Company Part of 1996 Spinoff

At first, the Indian subsidiary focused on large-scale full lifecycle software projects for such D&B businesses as AC Nielsen Co. and IMS Health. In November 1996 D&B spun off the unit along with Erisco, Inc.; IMS International Inc.; Nielsen Media Research; Pilot Software, Inc.; Sales Technologies, Inc.; and other assets to form a company named Cognizant Corporation. This move was part of a major restructuring of the parent corporation, which split into three major divisions: Dun & Bradstreet, AC Nielsen Consumer Products, and Cognizant Corporation. Three months later, Dun & Bradstreet Satyam changed its name to Cognizant Technology Solutions and began to function as a division of the newly formed Cognizant Corporation. It would now look to service companies outside of the D&B family, offering Y2K solutions as well as web page development. In July 1997 the subsidiary became wholly owned when the parent corporation bought Satyam's minority interest for $3.4 million. Because Cognizant lacked a reputation outside of D&B, it had some difficulty in attracting clients. Mahadeva fell back on his McKinsey experience and concentrated on customer satisfaction and the building of long-term relationships. Major signings for Y2K solutions included Northwest Airlines and Aetna Life Insurance Co. of Canada.

Mahadeva also proved to be adept at keeping Cognizant ahead of trends. Early in 1998, at a time when the Y2K business accounted for almost half of the company's revenues, he began to pull back Cognizant's exposure to the practice so that by the first quarter of 1999 Y2K work represented just 26 percent of revenues. According to a 1999 *Forbes* profile, ''Sensing that another consulting obsession was about to peak, Mahadeva kept clear of the $16.6 billion enterprise resource planning (ERP) software business—installing monolithic software packages that manage companies' backoffice functions. While other con-

sultants were raking in fat fees, Mahadeva steered Cognizant toward the more pedestrian chores of maintaining corporate software systems—fixing kinks in the code or extending the life of existing applications by adding new functions.'' Moreover, applications management was a business that would ''be around for as long as companies use computers.''

The parent company, Cognizant Corporation, underwent some structural changes in early 1998, dividing into two separate public companies as a way to help each unit maximize growth. Certain assets, including Cognizant Technology Solutions, were spun off to form IMS Health Incorporated. Cognizant Corporation and its remaining entities were renamed Nielsen Media Research. Several months later, in June 1998, IMS partially spun off Cognizant Technology Solutions and conducted an initial public offering (IPO) of stock. The timing proved to be less than ideal, as market conditions were poor for IPOs. As a result, Cognizant was only able to sell shares at $10, instead of the $11 to $13 the company and its underwriters had hoped it would fetch. The money was earmarked to pay off debt and finance the upgrading of offices in India, but in the end most of it was simply banked.

Mahadeva was named Cognizant's chairman and CEO in March 1998. He continued to display a creative and forward-looking mindset. According to a profile in the *Economic Times,* ''Another business model innovation the company came up with as early as 1998, when peers aligned themselves along geographies or technologies, Cognizant aligned itself along verticals. The results of early verticalisation is seen in the robust growth in each of the verticals that Cognizant focuses on—financial services, banking, insurance, healthcare, retail, manufacturing and logistics, and media and publishing. . . . The final distinction in strategy is in its listing destination. While its peers got listed in the geography they sourced from—that is India, Cognizant got listed in the geography they serviced, namely the US.''

In 2000 Cognizant looked to become involved in e-business, introducing a suite of services and offering to help customers build IT systems that it could then maintain on an outsourcing basis. The company also expressed interest in funding Internet start-ups in both the United States and India. When the Internet bubble burst and the tech sector in general suffered from the effects of a recession, Cognizant was nimble enough to stay afloat and actually maintain its growth. The cost savings that Cognizant could provide its customers through offshore centers made the company's services more attractive during lean economic times. Even following the terrorist attacks of September 11, 2001, corporations remained willing to have their IT services handled offshore by Cognizant and others. India's large pool of inexpensive IT talent was no longer a secret, but Cognizant was one of the few companies able to make the complicated onsite/offshore model run smoothly. Tensions between India and Pakistan over the Kashmir region that might lead to a military conflict between the two nuclear powers dampened investor enthusiasm and adversely impacted the price of the company's stock, but customers still did not pull back.

Rising Stock Prices in 2002

Because of its onsite/offshore arrangement, Cognizant was able to realize significant tax savings that also helped to improve profits during lean times. Wholly owned subsidiaries

Key Dates:

1994: The company is formed as a Dun & Bradstreet (D&B) in-house unit.
1996: D&B spins off the business as part of Cognizant Corporation.
1998: Parent Cognizant Corporation restructures, with Cognizant Technology now a public subsidiary of new parent IMS Health Incorporated.
2003: The company gains complete independence from IMS Health.

such as Cognizant's India operation were only obligated to pay taxes if they brought back profits to the United States. Instead the company invested the money to expand its overseas operations, initiating a $40 million project to build three development centers in India, large enough altogether to accommodate 6,000 employees. From October 2001 to October 2002, at a time when the stock market in general fared poorly, Cognizant saw the price of its stock increase by 170 percent. Nevertheless, some concerns began to creep in, as investors worried that most of Cognizant's business came from a handful of its pool of 105 customers and feared that Cognizant would face stiff new competition from both Indian service firms including Infosys Technologies and such industry giants as IBM and Accenture who were expanding their Indian operations. On the positive side, Cognizant had no debt and more than $100 million in the bank.

Cognizant posted revenues of $178 million in 2001 and $229 million in 2002. Estimates for 2003 topped $350 million. The company had always been accorded a great deal of latitude in how it conducted its business by parent corporation IMS, which opted to act more as a shareholder than an owner, and finally in 2003 Cognizant gained its complete independence following a split-off. To ensure its long-term freedom, Cognizant's board immediately instituted a poison pill provision to prevent unwanted takeover attempts.

Prospects appeared bright for the company, despite the threat of IBM and Accenture, which were clearly intent on aggressively challenging Cognizant. As a result, Cognizant was expected to maintain its business by lowering the price for its basic outsourcing work by some 5 percent over the next few years. As a counter, Cognizant looked to encroach on some of the territory of its large rivals and move into higher-end technology consulting. In this way, Cognizant would advise customers about how to improve their computer systems, which they would then maintain. Mahadeva told the *Economic Times* in June 2003, "We are looking at expanding our development

centres outside of India. We see strong demand for package implementation in areas such as SAP and PeopleSoft and we are looking at acquisitions in those areas. We are also looking for acquisitions in Europe." The company already had three acquisitions under its belt, all providing a positive effect. The June 2002 purchase of United Healthcare Ireland Limited assets added some 70 software professionals while increasing its international presences. Cognizant added another 300 software personnel when it acquired the American Express Travel-related Services account from Silverline Technologies, in the process bolstering its leading position in the financial services industry. It was through this transaction that Cognizant picked up its Phoenix development center. In 2003 Cognizant acquired Aces International Inc., a CRM company with a strong presence in healthcare, financial services, and telecommunications. According to the *Economic Times,* Cognizant believed that CRM capabilities would be the next wave of packaged software opportunity. Far from retreating, Cognizant was charging into the future, hoping to hire nearly 1,900 professionals in 2003, with perhaps as many as 400 in the United States. The global outsourcing business was by now a $550 billion industry and highly fragmented, with the largest five companies controlling less than 20 percent of the market. There was every reason to believe that ample opportunity existed for Cognizant to continue its impressive pattern of growth.

Principal Subsidiaries

Cognizant Technology Solutions U.S. Corporation; Cognizant Technology Solutions India Limited.

Principal Competitors

Accenture Ltd.; Infosys Technologies Limited; International Business Machines Corporation; Satyam Computer Services Limited; Wipro Limited.

Further Reading

Bonasia, J., "He Stays Cognizant of Clients' Success Strategy," *Investor's Business Daily,* December 18, 2002, p. A03.

Coleman, Murray, "Cognizant Expands Global Reach," *Investor's Business Daily,* October 12, 2001, p. A07.

Fleming, Eric, "Last Call," *Barron's,* October 7, 2002, p. T8.

Gold, Jacqueline S., "Globalization Gambit," *Institutional Investor,* August 2001, p. 22.

Rosa, Jerry, "International Man of Mystery," *Sm@rt Partner,* March 26, 2001, p. 56.

Sansoni, Silvia, "The Contrarian," *Forbes,* June 14, 1999, p. 172.

Shah, Kalpana, "From Low-Profile to Fast Growing," *Economic Times,* June 20, 2003.

—Ed Dinger

Condé Nast Publications, Inc.

4 Times Square
New York, New York 10036
U.S.A.
Telephone: (212) 286-2860
Fax: (212) 286-5960
Web site: http://www.condenet.com

Wholly Owned Subsidiary of Advance Publications Inc.
Incorporated: 1922
Employees: 10,000
Sales: $1.8 billion (2002 est.)
NAIC: 511120 Periodical Publishers

Condé Nast Publications, Inc. (CNP) was founded with a particular vision to serve various niche markets, and has done so with magazines devoted to many age groups, lifestyles, and appetites. While some have called this strategy pure genius, others have termed it pretentious. Nevertheless, the Condé Nast name stands for high-caliber periodicals devoted to their audiences, be they the cosmopolitan sophisticates who read *Vanity Fair, House & Garden, Condé Nast's Traveler,* or the *New Yorker*; the fashionistas who adore *Vogue* and *Glamour*; the young women devoted to *Teen Vogue, Mademoiselle, Bride's,* and *Modern Bride*; the gentlemen who buy *GQ* or *Wired*; or the epicureans who enjoy *Bon Appétit* and *Gourmet.* Beautiful, relevant, and sometimes irreverent, Condé Nast Publications has long set the standard for quality and attitude.

Coming on the Scene: Late 1800s to 1920s

The future success of Condé Nast's fashion-driven publications was mirrored and secured in part by the charm and polish of the man himself. His family, of mixed French and German stock, had settled for several generations in the United States. Born in 1873, Nast was strongly influenced by his aristocratic French mother, who infused him with the calculated manners and social restraint of high social circles. His father lived mostly abroad and died young, having much less, if any, influence on his son. As an adult, Nast was noted for his urbane persona.

Vogue magazine served as the early testing ground for what Nast called a "class publication" and he developed an entire business theory based on the belief that certain types of people, when offered a publication tailored to their class and particular needs, would then create a sizable and enduring market. *Vogue* was first published in 1892 as a weekly journal of society and fashion news interspersed with verse and lightly humorous drawings. Nast bought the magazine in 1909 with the intention of upgrading it and became its active owner and manager. He adhered to a strict "fixity of purpose" doctrine—always maintaining a firm vision of a publication's audience—in order to conserve the magazine's "pure class" standing. Fiction, for example, was not welcome in early *Vogue* even though Nast believed it might have increased circulation. Instead the magazine was carefully tailored to the expectations of its subscribers, down to the smallest details, from articles and photographs to page setup and advertising.

Nast's vision for *Vogue* made it a must-have for certain parts of society and it became the fashion bible of the times. The publisher next bought an interest in *House & Garden* in 1911. Four years later, Nast took *House & Garden* over completely and transformed the magazine from an architectural journal into an interior design authority. In 1914 Nast introduced *Vanity Fair,* a magazine that quickly set publishing standards in the world of arts, politics, sports, and high society. Under the editorship of Frank Crowninshield, *Vanity Fair* gained a reputation as a sophisticated and glamorous magazine infused with a lighthearted and often acerbic wit. In 1916, still flush with the success of *Vogue,* Nast took an unprecedented step and introduced an international edition for the United Kingdom called *British Vogue,* the first of many worldwide incarnations of the fashion magazine.

Nast also took steps to ensure quality production of his growing family of magazines. In 1921 he bought a small interest in Arbor Press of Greenwich, Connecticut. This facility eventually became the Condé Nast Press and was expanded and completely modernized to become one of the finest magazine manufacturing plants in the country. (The press was later closed in 1964 to make way for more centrally located sites capable of producing higher volume.)

A Changing of the Guard: 1930s to 1978

Despite the rigors of the Depression, CNP forged ahead with innovations in design and quality. Color photographs appeared within the pages of *Vogue, Vanity Fair,* and *House & Garden,*

Company Perspectives:

Home to many of the world's most celebrated magazines, Condé Nast Publications is committed to journalistic integrity, influential reporting and superior design. Each magazine features world-renowned editors, writers and photographers—an incredible stable of talent unmatched by any other publishing company.

and in 1932 the first color photograph appeared on the cover of *Vogue.* Although *Vogue* had continued to thrive since Nast acquired the fashion magazine, the lesser known though more highly evolved *Vanity Fair* struggled. In one of his few major errors in judgment, Nast decided to merge the two vastly different magazines in 1936, much to the chagrin of *Vanity Fair* editor Crowninshield. The combined periodical ran as *Vogue* and what was once *Vanity Fair* more or less vanished in *Vogue*'s fashion-dictated pages. In 1939, Nast introduced another magazine devoted to fashion and beauty, called *Glamour.* *Glamour* was the last publication Nast personally developed for the CNP collection; three years later, in 1942, Condé Nast died.

After Nast's death, his empire continued onward without much fanfare through the remainder of the 1940s. One major achievement of the time, however, was in international growth. Following the earlier success of the British version of *Vogue,* a French company was established to produce a French *Vogue.* By the end of the 1950s, however, CNP would change forever. In 1959, another man with set ideals of what publishing was and should be entered the picture. S.I. Newhouse, Sr., the renowned newspaper and media giant, purchased a controlling interest in the company and instituted a changing of the guard in senior administrative positions.

The same year Newhouse acquired CNP, the firm acquired Street & Smith Publications, Inc., which included titles such as *Mademoiselle* and several sports annuals such as *College Football, Pro Football, Baseball,* and *Pro and College/Prep Basketball.* In the early 1960s, CNP continued its international agenda with another *Vogue,* this time entering a partnership to produce an Italian version. Life within the Newhouse kingdom in the 1960s and early 1970s was marked by a period of acquisitions and the overhaul of existing publications rather than the creation of new publications in a highly competitive— and uncertain—publishing industry.

Father to Sons and Rampant Growth: 1979–89

Two decades after S.I. Newhouse, Sr., bought CNP, his death in 1979 passed management of the privately held empire, Advance Publications Inc., to his two sons. S.I. Newhouse, Jr., known as "Si," ran the magazine and book operations, while brother Donald Newhouse took charge of the newspaper and cable television operations. Following the transition, Si Newhouse purchased *Gentlemen's Quarterly* (*GQ*) from Esquire Inc. for CNP. Founded in 1928, *GQ* had once been a fashion booklet distributed in men's clothing stores but grew into a preeminent source for probing journalism, fiction, essays, and eclectic coverage of subjects from food to financial planning for its 25- to 39-year-old male audience.

The same year *GQ* came into the fold, CNP revisited its glory days by launching *Self* magazine, the first publication CNP had started from scratch since 1939's *Glamour. Self* became a popular sourcebook for women who were "reinventing almost every aspect of their lives from a health-aware, issue-oriented point of view," according to a CNP brochure. Offering information-packed, quick-read journalism to busy women, *Self*'s circulation was no less fast-paced: within 30 months of its launch, the magazine reached more than one million readers. Then adding to its diversity and transcontinental reach in 1982, CNP bought the *Tatler,* the British monthly magazine devoted to social news, the arts, features, and fashion.

Less than a year after taking on the impressive history of the *Tatler,* CNP made a comparable move in the United States by reviving *Vanity Fair,* which had disappeared after its merger with *Vogue* decades earlier. Amidst much fanfare in early 1983, CNP invested roughly $10 million toward strengthening the magazine editorially and getting it off to a powerful new start. Hoping to elevate *Vanity Fair* to its former status as a crown jewel of Condé Nast's "class" publications, CNP packed the lavish first reissue with an entire short novel by Gabriel Garcia Márquez, winner of the 1982 Nobel Prize for Literature. Its 290 glossy pages also included lively articles by Gore Vidal, paleontologist Stephen Jay Gould, and other gems to recapture what had once made it "America's most memorable magazine," according to critic and writer Cleveland Armory.

While *Vanity Fair* was underway, CNP also had acquired *Gourmet* magazine, the oldest and second largest of the four major American epicurean magazines. The company's appetite for growth was not sated, however, as CNP launched new premium magazines. In the fall of 1987 came *Condé Nast's Traveler,* a monthly magazine for affluent globetrotters, which incurred a startup cost of approximately $40 million.

Travel was not the only domain into which CNP ventured in the late 1980s. In early 1988 the publisher acquired *Details* magazine, an irreverent chronicle of Manhattan's downtown art, fashion, and club scene, and transformed it into a young men's fashion and lifestyle magazine. Later the same year CNP bought *Woman* magazine, an eight-year-old bimonthly with a circulation of 525,000, from Harris Publications. Less sophisticated than CNP's other women's magazines, the new magazine would steer into a previously uncharted niche market.

A New Era: 1990s

By the early 1990s CNP had not only expanded domestically but internationally as well, with foreign operations and subsidiaries in England, France, Italy, Germany, Australia, and Spain, and with licensee arrangements in Mexico, Brazil, and Japan. In addition, CNP's *Glamour* had become the largest-selling beauty/fashion/lifestyle magazine in the world. *Glamour* also had gained its share of critical recognition, winning the National Magazine Award for General Excellence in 1981 and 1992, among other distinctions.

Despite a growing slump in the magazine publishing industry, CNP started yet another glossy spread, *Allure,* in March 1991. Devoted entirely to beauty, *Allure* jumped from a starting circulation of 200,000 to reach 625,000 before its second anniversary, making it one of the fastest-growing magazines of its

Key Dates:

1873: Condé Nast is born.
1892: Fashion magazine *Vogue* is first published.
1909: Condé Nast buys *Vogue* and begins his publishing venture.
1911: Nast buys an interest in *House & Garden*.
1914: Nast launches *Vanity Fair* magazine.
1922: Condé Nast Publications (CNP) is incorporated.
1936: *Vogue* and *Vanity Fair* are merged.
1939: *Glamour* magazine debuts in the United States.
1942: Nast dies.
1959: S.I. Newhouse, Sr., newspaper magnate, buys CNP.
1979: Newhouse, Sr., dies and sons Si and Donald take over CNP and parent company Advance Publications Inc.
1983: *Vanity Fair* is reborn.
1988: CNP acquires *Details* magazine.
1993: CNP buys *Bon Appétit* and *Architectural Digest*; *House & Garden* is shuttered.
1995: *House & Garden* is relaunched for a younger female audience.
1999: New CNP headquarters at Times Square is completed, with a Frank Gehry cafeteria.
2001: CNP buys a majority stake in Ideas Publishing Group and launches *Lucky* shopping magazine.
2002: *Modern Bride* joins *Bride's* in the CNP bridal group.
2003: Plans for *Cargo*, the male version of *Lucky*, are announced.

time. With its unusual combination of high fashion and piquant journalism, *Allure* was nominated for a National Magazine Award in its first year.

Following its triumph with *Allure*, CNP acquired Knapp Communications in early 1993. Knapp published such prominent periodicals as *Architectural Digest* and *Bon Appétit*. *Architectural Digest* boasted sumptuous spreads on the homes of the rich and famous while *Bon Appétit*'s circulation of 1.2 million placed it in the top ranks of food magazines. Soon after CNP reacted to the "information highway" hype, buying a 15 percent interest (the remaining interest was bought in 1998) in *Wired*, the self-anointed "house organ of the digital revolution."

As CNP publications joined the digital age, the legendary Condé Nast culture—of high-brow literati and urbane tea-sippers—was undergoing changes of its own. CNP's quirky game of managerial musical chairs became more serious as several key directors stepped down from their long-held thrones. At the top of the hierarchy sat Alexander Liberman, who for more than 50 years had been the creative force, as editorial director, behind the entire group of magazines.

In April 1994 the 81-year-old Liberman was succeeded by 36-year-old James Truman, former editor of *Details* magazine, giving the media cause for lively speculation. New, young blood also found its way into the other key CNP post, as Steven T. Florio was named president effective June 1, 1994. Florio—who had served nine years as president and six years as CEO of the *New Yorker*—succeeded Bernard Leser, 68, a 34-year veteran of CNP and president since 1987. Florio took little time to start making changes; within a few months more than three-quarters of CNP's magazines had new publishers in place. The company also became more family-oriented, offering its employees flex-time and a backup childcare system at no cost (since CNP's workforce was made up of nearly 70 percent women, this was a major boon).

Next came a relaunch of the venerable *House & Garden,* on the shelf since *Bon Appétit* and *Architectural Digest* joined CNP. The new *House & Garden* was intended for a younger audience, primarily women in their 30s, who were looking for both a lifestyle and home decorating magazine. CNP also planned to take Italy by storm by securing the rights to the Italian version of its *Architectural Digest.* To keep up with evolving technology, CNP created CondeNet to design web sites for its magazines, beginning with *Condé Nast Traveler* and a gourmet web site called Epicurious featuring articles and information from *Bon Appétit* and *Gourmet* magazines.

The late 1990s marked further expansion abroad for CNP. In 1997 the firm established ties with South Africa to bring *House & Garden* to the country's readers, then worked out a deal with Japan's Nikkei to launch Japanese *Vogue* in early 1998. Stateside, CNP bought *Women's Sports & Fitness,* the magazine founded by tennis legend Billie Jean King, and it merged into *Condé Nast Sports for Women,* which had been introduced in late 1997. The revamped magazine, *Condé Nast Women's Sports & Fitness,* began publication in the fall with bimonthly editions.

Around the same time, CNP finalized its purchase of *Wired* magazine (rumored to be $75 million) and made plans to bring Newhouse's famed *New Yorker* magazine (bought in 1985 and run independently through Advance Publications) into the Condé Nast flock. For the *New Yorker,* placing it alongside CNP's other upscale publications seemed a logical move: not only would it be among urbane company but its new siblings were profitable while the *New Yorker* had been swimming in red ink. Although the *New Yorker* would still maintain its autonomy, CNP higher-ups believed the move would help the sophisticate regain its financial footing (which it did by 2002).

In 1999 the company entered discussions with Walt Disney to buy Fairchild Publications for $650 million. Fairchild, producer of periodicals *W, WWD, Los Angeles Magazine, Daily News Record, Footwear News, Jane,* and others, seemed to present a conflict of interest with CNP since the former's publications reported on the folks who filled the advertising pages of most CNP magazines. Rivals such as *Elle* and *Cosmopolitan,* on the other hand, filled Fairchild's ad pages and were reportedly loathe to put their dollars into a CNP-owned franchise. The situation was somewhat solved when CNP parent Advance Publications bought Fairchild in 1999.

Also in 1999, CNP finally moved into its new headquarters in revitalized Times Square. The 48-story building had been beset with problems since its original design was set forth, including construction accidents and several deaths. For the Condé Nast folks, however, their new offices were hip and ecologically correct, built by the "green" friendly Durst Organization, complete with a Frank Gehry-designed cafeteria.

A New Era: 2000 and Beyond

In 2000 CNP transferred *Details* magazine over to sibling Fairchild, then bought a majority stake in Ideas Publishing Group in 2001, which produced Spanish translations of major U.S. publications. At the top of CNP's wish list were Latin American versions of fashion titans *Glamour* and *Vogue,* and *Architectural Digest.* CNP bought the remaining interest in Ideas in early 2002, just as it expanded its lucrative bridal group with the acquisition of *Modern Bride,* the primary rival to *Bride's* magazine. The $52 million deal gave CNP a strong hold on the bridal market, with the two publications each producing six editions a year on a staggered schedule.

A shopping magazine called *Lucky* debuted in 2001, geared to young women. CNP believed the magazine was new in scope and coverage, offering readers something different from that contained in its other fashion, beauty, or lifestyle magazines. Initial sales were excellent, with *Lucky* living up to its name. In 2003 CNP took its most successful franchise, the esteemed *Vogue,* to a different audience by launching *Teen Vogue* in January. Despite weaker sales for such rival teen magazines as *Seventeen* and *Elle Girl,* CNP had high hopes for its fashion hybrid. The original *Vogue* itself was still going strong after a century in print, quietly increasing its circulation.

The venerable *GQ* (*Gentlemen's Quarterly*), unlike *Vogue,* was suffering sluggish ad sales and a drop in readership. To remedy the problems, Newhouse purged the magazine's staff and initiated a major makeover to appeal to a broader (read younger and hipper) spectrum of men, especially the ones who were buying the so-called "lad" magazine upstarts, including *Stuff, FHM,* and the more licentious and thriving *Maxim* and *Playboy.* The magazine also gained new exposure in the fall by teaming up with Spike TV (formerly TNN) to present the eighth annual *GQ's* Men of the Year awards.

New magazines set to launch included *Cargo,* masculine sibling to the successful shopping magazine *Lucky;* a U.K. launch for *Trash,* a joint venture with Ministry of Sound for an entertainment and lifestyle magazine (though its fate was uncertain); and an untitled art magazine appealing to the high-brow clientele of *Architectural Digest, Vanity Fair,* and *House & Garden* set to debut in 2004. Although CNP had changed a great deal from the days of its founder Condé Nast, the publishing firm had remained true to many of Nast's business doctrines concerning "class" publications and the people who bought them. Nast's visionary status, however, remained evident in the continued success of *Vogue, Glamour, Vanity Fair,* and *House & Garden.*

Principal Subsidiaries

Comaq Marketing Group LLC; Ideas Publishing Group.

Principal Competitors

Advanstar Communications, Inc.; Hachette Filipachi Médias; The Hearst Corporation; Time Inc.

Further Reading

A Brief History of the Condé Nast Publications, New York: CNP, 1993.

Caperton, Katie, "*Vogue* the Younger," *Folio: The Magazine for Magazine Management,* March 1, 2003.

Carmody, Deirdre, "At Condé Nast, Newhouse Maintains Loose Reins with a Tight Grip," *New York Times,* July 27, 1992, p. D6.

Carr, David, "Food and Design Magazines Are Bought by Condé Nast," *New York Times,* March 31, 1993, p. D1.

——, "Magazine Imitates a Catalogue and Has a Charmed Life So Far," *New York Times,* September 16, 2002, p. C1.

——, "New President of Condé Nast Predicts Clear Sailing Ahead," *New York Times,* December 19, 1994, p. D1.

Clark, Tim, "Year-Old *Wired* So Cool, It's Hot," *Advertising Age,* March 7, 1994, p. 10S.

Colford, Paul D., "Condé Nast Excels at Musical Chairs," *Newsday,* July 21, 1994, p. BO2.

"Condé Nast Acquires the Tatler," *New York Times,* April 6, 1982, p. D3.

Donaton, Scott, and Pat Sloan, "Florio Takes Charge at Condé Nast; New Generation Rises to Power," *Advertising Age,* January 17, 1994, p. 1.

Fine, Jon, "Condé Nast Plans High-End Art Title," *Advertising Age,* July 28, 2003, p. 3.

——, "The *New Yorker* Basks in Black Ink," *Advertising Age,* November 25, 2002, p. 39.

Garland, Madge, Review of *The Man Who Was Vogue: The Life and Times of Condé Nast, Financial Times,* September 11, 1982.

Granatstein, Lisa, "The Marrying Kind: After Decades of Competition *Bride's* and *Modern Bride* Are Together Under One Roof," *Mediaweek,* May 13, 2002, p. 46.

Huhn, Mary, "Condé Nast Warms Up to the Web," *Mediaweek,* April 24, 1995, p. 5.

Kerwin, Marie, "Fairchild Deal Presents Condé Nast Challenges," *Advertising Age,* August 23, 1999, p. 3.

"King James; At 36, James Truman Rules the Condé Nast Magazine Empire," *Los Angeles Times,* May 10, 1994, p. E1.

Lindsay, James, and Samantha Conti, "Do Men Read After Beer and Babes?," *WWD,* May 9, 2003, p. 12.

Marion, Don, "Condé Nast Buys Ideas Publishing," *South Florida Business Journal,* January 26, 2001, p. 14A.

McGee, Celia, "Condé Nast Completes Move to New York City's Times Square," *Knight-Ridder/Tribune Business News,* August 16, 1999.

"Resurrecting a Legend; Condé Nast Brings Back Vanity Fair—But Not Entirely to Life," *Time,* February 21, 1983, p. 62.

Salmans, Sandra, "Condé Nast Buying Gourmet Magazine," *New York Times,* September 28, 1983, p. D15.

Schnuer, Jenna, "Family Friendly Options Expand," *Folio: The Magazine for Magazine Management,* April 1, 1995, p. 22.

Seebohm, Caroline, *The Man Who Was Vogue: The Life and Times of Condé Nast,* London: Weidenfeld and Nicolson, 1982.

Smith, Liz, "Condé Nast's Hot Seat," *Newsday,* December 4, 1994, p. A11.

Vienne, Veronique, "Make It Right Then Toss It Away; An Inside View of Corporate Culture at Condé Nast," *Columbia Journalism Review,* July-August 1991, p. 28.

—Kerstan Cohen
—update: Nelson Rhodes

CONSOL Energy Inc.

Consol Plaza
1800 Washington Road
Pittsburgh, Pennsylvania 15241-1421
U.S.A.
Telephone: (412) 831-4000
Fax: (412) 831-4103
Web site: http://www.consolenergy.com

Public Company
Incorporated: 1991
Employees: 6,074
Sales: $2.14 billion (2002)
Stock Exchanges: New York
Ticker Symbol: CNX
NAIC: 212112 Bituminous Coal Underground Mining

Although essentially a coal mining company—one of the three largest in the United States—CONSOL Energy Inc. now positions itself as a multi-energy producer of coal, gas, and electricity. The Pittsburgh, Pennsylvania-based company owns some 4.3 billion tons of proven and probable coal reserves. Operating in seven states, it is the top U.S. producer of coal from underground mines, the leading operator of longwall mining systems, and the largest exporter of coal. In recent years CONSOL has taken steps to diversify, primarily through the exploitation of methane gas, a byproduct of coal mining, which the company captures and sells on the interstate pipeline system, and uses to fuel its own power generators. To support these efforts in methane gas, as well as to develop mining and pollution-control technologies, CONSOL maintains a private research and development facility. In addition, CONSOL distributes mining and industrial supplies through its Fairmont Supply subsidiary, while another subsidiary, CNX Land Resources Inc. owns timber and farming interests and is involved in commercial development projects. CONSOL is a public company; its largest shareholder is the German utility RWE AG with a stake of nearly 74 percent. In 2003 RWE announced that it was interested in selling at least a portion of its interest in the company.

Roots Stretching Back to Civil War Era

Consolidation Coal Company, the forefather of CONSOL Energy, was launched in 1860 when a number of small western Maryland mining companies merged their operations. The business was formally incorporated in 1864, and by 1927 Consol emerged as the nation's largest bituminous coal producer. In 1945 it merged with Pittsburgh Coal Company, resulting in the change of its base of operations to western Pennsylvania. Following World War II coal began to fall out of favor as a source for heating, especially in the Northeast, replaced by oil and cheap natural gas, which could now be delivered over a new nationwide pipeline system. In 1966 Continental Oil Co. (Conoco) acquired the company, a relationship that was ahead of its time. Consol was just the first of the major U.S. coal companies to be snapped up by oil interests in reaction to the emergence of OPEC in the 1970s and a dramatic increase in oil prices. Coal, which had powered the United States' rise as an industrial nation and faded in importance during the 20th century, now enjoyed a resurgence. Electricity producers signed 20-year-long contracts to ensure a steady supply of coal at a set price, which led to ramped up production in coal. By the mid-1970s Consol at its peak operated 56 mines and employed 19,000 miners, numbers that steadily receded over the next quarter of a century.

DuPont Acquisition of Consol As Part of 1981 Conoco Deal

In 1981 E.I. du Pont de Nemours & Company (DuPont) acquired Conoco Inc. and picked up the Consol business. DuPont, which split Conoco's oil and coal assets into separate subsidiaries, then sold some Pennsylvania mining interests to RWE. By the autumn of 1990 rumors were reported in the press that indicated RWE through its Rheinbraun subsidiary was interested in acquiring as much as half of Consol. Although a Rheinbraun spokesperson called such talk "fantasy," the speculation proved to be accurate. Several weeks later the two parties created a 50–50 joint venture, CONSOL Energy Inc., which was then incorporated in Delaware in January 1991. Rheinbraun contributed its 24 percent stake in two Consol mines and paid $890 million to DuPont. As a result, DuPont

Company Perspectives:

Through expansion and acquisitions, CONSOL Energy has evolved from a single-fuel mining company into a multienergy producer of coal, gas and electricity.

also was able to lower its exposure to the energy segment of its business, which in the previous year had accounted for almost half of its revenues and more than half of its net income.

For RWE, the CONSOL venture was one in a string of deals the giant German conglomerate had pulled off in recent years. They reflected a new aggressive spirit that was a major departure following decades of ultra-conservative management, during which it operated more like a public authority than a private business. Coal had been a major part of RWE business ever since it was formed in 1898 to generate electricity from coal in order to power the iron and steel industries and other companies that populated Germany's Ruhr Valley. In 1935 Germany parceled out its power market to major firms and granted RWE a virtual monopoly on electricity. Following World War II RWE grew with the recovering West German economy, emerging as the country's largest power company. With the fall of the Iron Curtain and the reunification of Germany in the 1980s, RWE faced a changed business climate, one that would increasingly require that it look beyond its home market for growth and compete on a European and global basis. A new head was installed, Friedhelm Gieske, who moved quickly to institute a policy of long-term growth, which in essence meant turning to the United States. The CONSOL joint venture was more than a mere effort at diversification: Because U.S. coal was cheaper than German coal, CONSOL represented an insurance policy to RWE, which if necessary could import American coal to fuel its German power plants.

With the rise of electricity deregulation in the 1990s, the coal industry faced a period of uncertainty as electric utilities took advantage of conditions to drive down the price of coal, which was in plentiful supply. Because it depended on utilities for 80 percent of its business, the coal industry possessed little leverage and found itself increasingly squeezed. CONSOL was fortunate to hold a number of long-term contracts that were priced well above the market rate, but they were scheduled to expire in the next few years, making it imperative that the company take steps to adjust to these new conditions. Investing in technology to keep down costs provided a much needed edge. CONSOL was especially committed to "longwall" mines, which according to a 1999 *Forbes* article, "Survival of the Fittest," are "straight seams that hold rectangular panels of coal, typically 1,000 feet by 10,000 feet or so and that can be mined by massive $30 million machinery systems designed to handle just this one kind of coal seam—from shaving the bitumen from the walls to loading onto conveyor belts, Consol's longwall mines cover hundreds of square miles in six states. Today, 46% of all underground coal in the U.S. is mined by longwall, and Consol produces over half of it. Consol's longwall output is 6.5 tons per man-hour, compared with an industry average of 4.9 tons for underground mine production." In order to gain this competitive advantage, CONSOL in 1998 invested

$35,000 per miner on machinery and equipment, 9 percent more than Arch Coal and 40 percent more than Peabody Group, CONSOL's leading rivals. CONSOL now operated 24 mines, compared with 56 mines in the mid-1970s, but managed to increase its output by 45 percent.

DuPont announced in April 1998 that it was adjusting its business mix to focus on its agricultural, biotechnology, and pharmaceutical business. As part of this restructuring it sold most of its holdings in CONSOL, leaving DuPont Energy with just a 6 percent interest in the coal business and RWE subsidiaries with a 94 percent share. To pay off DuPont, CONSOL took on $500 million in debt. In addition, in 1998 CONSOL paid $150 million to acquire Rochester & Pittsburgh Coal Company. To pay down some of the debt it incurred, CONSOL made a public offering of stock in April 1999, but the result was disappointing. The company had hoped to sell shares in the $18 to $21 range, which would have netted between $416 million and $479 million. With the stock market still caught up in the enthusiasm over dotcom issues, an old economy commodity such as coal received a cool reception. According to *Forbes,* when CONSOL's CEO conducted a road show for the offering, "investment bankers and fund managers looked at him as if he were peddling steam locomotives. Coal? Is there still a coal industry?" Indeed, the outlook for coal was not particularly bright at that moment. Warm weather resulted in a reduced demand for electricity, which hurt coal prices; the Asian economy was doing poorly; and coal was seen in a negative light by many who questioned the fuel's contribution to the greenhouse effect. When CONSOL held its offering it sold 22.6 million shares at $16 each, netting $343.5 million. At the end of the first day of trading on the New York Stock Exchange, CONSOL stock was valued at $14.25, a level at which it would remain for the next year. Because of pressure from shareholders urging increased profits, as well as to maintain competitiveness in the volatile coal industry, CONSOL took steps in early 2000 to cut costs by offering buyout packages to more than 1,000 employees in its headquarters, regional offices, and R&D facility.

CONSOL also placed greater emphasis on diversification, in particular the production of natural gas, a byproduct of coal mining, and electric generation. The thrust of the methane gas business is summarized in a 2002 *Pittsburgh Post-Gazette* profile of the company: "Before mining, companies drill vertical wells into coal seams as a safety precaution. At one time, the gas was burned off as a dangerous derivative of mining. Now it's captured and sold on the interstate pipeline system to electric generating plants and other consumers, as is the gas that escapes when controversial long-wall mining extracts underground coal." To fortify its position in natural gas, CONSOL in 2000 acquired the southwestern Virginia methane reserves and related facilities of MCN Energy Group Inc., paying approximately $160 million. Further strengthening its holdings in this region, CONSOL in 2001 spent another $158 million to acquire coalbed methane-gas production and pipeline assets from Conoco Inc. Subsidiary CNX Ventures in 2001 formed a joint venture with Allegheny Energy Supply Company to build an 88-megawatt, coalbed-methane-fueled power generating facility, which began operating in Virginia in 2002 using methane produced by CONSOL. Other diversification efforts included CNX Land Resources Inc., involved in timber and farming, and

Key Dates:

1860: Consolidation Coal Company is formed.
1945: The company merges with Pittsburgh Coal Company.
1966: Continental Oil Company acquires Consolidation.
1981: DuPont acquires the company.
1991: CONSOL Energy is formed as a joint venture between DuPont and RWE AG.
1999: CONSOL goes public and begins trading on the New York Stock Exchange.

CNX Marine Terminal Inc., a Baltimore general cargo and warehouse provider.

During this same period, CONSOL expanded its coal holdings. At the end of 2000 it acquired a 50 percent interest in Line Creek Mine, a Canadian operation, at a cost of more than $29 million. In 2001 CONSOL bought Windsor Coal Company, Southern Ohio Coal Company, and Central Ohio Coal Company from American Electric Power, followed by the $14 million purchase of a 50 percent interest in the Glennies Creek Mine, an Australian operation owned by AMCI, Inc. This property would be equipped with a longwall mining system to extract high-fluidity coking coal intended for steelmakers in the Pacific Rim region.

Strong Results in 2000–2001

In 2000 and 2001 CONSOL benefited from a spike in coal and natural gas prices, resulting in total revenues of $2.32 billion in 2000 and $2.36 billion in 2001. Net income during this period increased from $107 million in 2000 to $183.6 million in 2001. Some credit for these positive results was also due to CONSOL shutting down smaller, less efficient mines. But warmer than expected weather in the winter of 2001–2002 and the effects of an economy that lapsed into recession had an adverse impact on the balance sheet during the second half of 2001 and into 2002. Nevertheless, CONSOL was optimistic about the future. With George W. Bush assuming the presidency in 2001, CONSOL expected the new administration to be receptive to the ideas put forward by energy companies, especially fossil fuel producers. The company bolstered its one-man government affairs department by adding three more people, although management insisted that no matter who had been elected president the company needed more personnel in order to comply with regulations in new domestic and foreign mar-

kets. In truth, minor changes in government standards held the potential for significant financial rewards for heavily regulated industries including coal. By most accounts, the new administration in Washington was expected to help both the coal mining and nuclear power industries. Prospects for coal also received a boost following the California energy crisis and the resulting public perception that much more electricity needed to be generated in the United States. Because coal power plants operated around 70 percent of their rated output, they could increase production, and buy more coal, without much difficulty. Moreover, there was a chance that some utilities might construct new coal-fired plants.

In the meantime, CONSOL cut back production in 2002, achieved in large part by closing down seven mines that according to management had reached the end of their economic life. In 2002 CONSOL recorded revenues of $2.18 billion, a slight decline over the previous year, but income experienced a dramatic decline, falling to $11.7 million. In June 2003 RWE indicated that it was interested in selling some if not all of its stake in CONSOL, estimated to be worth about $1.25 billion. Whether the company would be sold, and when the economy would rebound, were unanswered questions. What was certain, however, was that CONSOL was well positioned for the long term, owning coal reserves that at current consumption rates could last for another two centuries.

Principal Subsidiaries

Consolidation Coal Company Inc.; CNX Ventures; Pocahontas Gas Partnership; Rochester & Pittsburgh Coal Company.

Principal Competitors

Arch Coal, Inc.; Massey Energy Company; Peabody Energy Corporation.

Further Reading

Androshick, Julie, "Survival of the Fittest," *Forbes,* September 20, 1999, p. 66.

Byrne, Harlan S., "New King Coal," *Barron's,* October 9, 2000, p. 23.

McKay, Jim, "German Firm to Take Control of Pennsylvania-Based Consol Energy," *Pittsburgh Post-Gazette,* September 18, 1998.

Reeves, Frank, "Consol Energy Boosts Natural Gas Production, Tries Power Generation," *Pittsburgh Post-Gazette,* April 24, 2002.

Roth, Terence, "Power House," *Wall Street Journal Europe,* April 8, 1991, p. 1.

—Ed Dinger

Coventry Health Care, Inc.

6705 Rockledge Drive, Suite 900
Bethesda, Maryland 20817
U.S.A.
Telephone: (301) 581-0600
Fax: (301) 493-0752
Web site: http://www.cvty.com

Public Company
Incorporated: 1986 as Coventry Corporation
Employees: 3,985
Sales: $3.6 billion (2002)
Stock Exchanges: New York
Ticker Symbol: CVH
NAIC: 621491 HMO Medical Centers

Coventry Health Care, Inc. is a managed healthcare company based in Bethesda, Maryland. The company operates in 14 midwestern, mid-Atlantic, and southeastern states, serving more than 2.1 million members enrolled in health plans under the names Coventry Health Care, Coventry Health and Life, Carelink Health Plans, Group Health Plan, HealthAmerica, HealthAssurance, HealthCare USA, Southern Health, and Well-Path. Coventry targets secondary markets that major health insurers ignore, and in recent years has fueled its growth by acquiring health plans owned by hospitals. By taking advantage of its medical claims and health provider networks, Coventry is able to make these plans more profitable. Unlike the major health insurers, Coventry will customize coverage for large employers looking to create self-insured plans. Coventry plans also include point of service, HMOs, PPOs, and Medicare and Medicaid products.

Coventry's Founder a 1960s Harvard Physics Student

Coventry Health Care was founded by Tennessee's current governor, Phil Bredesen, who grew up in a small town in upstate New York. In 1961 he entered Harvard University to study physics like his father, but before graduating decided that he was not suited for a career in the field. Instead he took a job as a computer programmer for Itek Corporation and also be-

came involved in politics. In 1970 he quit his job for an unsuccessful bid to become Massachusetts state senator. Bredesen then took a position with a pharmaceutical company, G.D. Searle & Co., and worked overseas, where he married Andrea Conte, a Searle's colleague who trained nurses how to use computers. While the couple was working in Saudi Arabia, Conte was offered a job as corporate nurse consultant by Nashville's Hospital Corporation of America. To join his wife in Nashville, Bredesen quit Searle and took a job negotiating management contracts with hospitals for Hospital Affiliates International. In 1980, with the birth of his son, Bredesen decided to strike out on his own and fulfill a dream of running his own business. With funding provided by four founders of Hospital Affiliates, he launched Healthplans, which later became known as HealthAmerica, a company that acquired and ran HMOs. The company grew rapidly and went public, but it ran into trouble in 1986 when the entire health insurance industry encountered a rough patch that sent stock prices tumbling. Although Bredesen wanted to ride out the downturn, the HealthAmerica founders, who maintained a controlling interest, insisted that he sell the company. In 1986 Bredesen found a buyer in Maxicare Health Plans Inc., pocketing $47 million for himself.

Formation of Coventry Corporation in 1986

Now wealthy, Bredesen in 1986 cofounded Coventry Corporation with Joseph P. Williams, former CFO of HealthAmerica. Williams served as CEO while Bredesen held the chairmanship, although he increasingly devoted his time to politics. He stepped down as chairman in 1990 but stayed on as a director. In 1987 he lost a runoff election to become mayor of Nashville, a post he won in a landslide in 1991. He was unsuccessful in his attempt to be governor in 1991, won a second term as Nashville's mayor, then in 2002 he tried for the governorship again. This time he won, and the New York native became Tennessee's 48th governor.

As Bredesen had done with HealthAmerica, Coventry looked to grow by external means. In 1987 it paid $23 million in cash plus stock to acquire American Service Life Insurance Company; American Service Underwriters, Inc.; American Service Telemarketing, Inc.; Private Enterprise Managements,

Inc.; as well as the assets of American Service underwriters. In 1988 Coventry completed two transactions. Paying nearly $1.5 million in cash, plus stock and other considerations, it acquired the Jess Jordan Agency. Coventry also picked up an 80 percent stake in Penn Group Corporation, a company newly formed to purchase Bredesen's original HMO, HealthAmerica Pennsylvania Inc., a health plan provider in Harrisburg and Pittsburgh, for $8 million. Coventry's largest deal in its early history was the 1990 $40 million cash and stock acquisition of Group Health Plan, Inc. To fund further growth Coventry made an initial public offering of stock in 1991.

Coventry adjusted its business mix in 1992 when management elected to discontinue the operations of American Service Company in order to focus on running HMOs. Coventry's plan was to view its current markets—Pittsburgh, central Pennsylvania (Harrisburg), and St. Louis—as hubs from which to expand the business. In this regard, Coventry acquired Healthpass, Inc., a provider organization affiliated with the Pennsylvania State University, located in central Pennsylvania, in a transaction valued at approximately $1.4 million. In the western part of the state, Coventry expanded through the acquisition of Riverside Health Plan, adding Beaver County, paying $3.9 million in debt and assuming liabilities in the $5 million range. From its St. Louis hub, Coventry also began to make inroads into southern Illinois. Although the company was interested in entering other markets, it was clearly focused on markets with no more than three million residents.

In the 1990s a large number of hospitals launched their own health plans and HMOs. By the middle of the decade they totaled nearly 3,300, but most proved to be money-losing ventures that hospitals were soon interested in unloading, thus providing a company like Coventry with ample acquisition targets and promising new markets to enter. In 1994 Coventry paid $50 million in cash to buy the remaining 20 percent interest it did not own of Penn Group Corporation. It also paid $3.7 million to acquire four physical group practices. In December 1994 Coventry used $75 million in stock to acquire Southern Health Management Corporation, based in Richmond, Virginia. Founded in 1984, the physician-owned HMO had 45,000 members in Richmond and central Virginia. As a result, Coventry gained a foothold in the southeastern market, with Richmond joining Pittsburgh, St. Louis, and Harrisburg as regional hubs. The company now boasted a total membership of 548,000. Coventry's balance sheet also reflected an upward trend. Revenues grew from $642 million in 1993 to nearly $777 million in 1994, with net income improving from $22 million to $29.3 million during the same period.

Coventry completed a major acquisition in July 1995 when it added Jacksonville, Florida-based HealthCare USA for $45 million in stock. HealthCare USA operated a 28,000-member Medicaid HMO in Jacksonville as well as Medicaid networks in St. Louis and Birmingham, Alabama, thereby adding the Medicaid risk product to Coventry's offerings and greatly extending the company's reach in the Southeast. Coventry began marketing its Medicaid product in the St. Louis and Missouri markets at the end of 1995 and rolled it out to western and central Pennsylvania in early 1996. By the end of 1996 Coventry had some 120,000 members enrolled in its Medicaid risk product.

Coventry suffered a major setback in 1995 when it lost two major accounts in the western Pennsylvania market and found itself saddled with excess capacity in 1996. Furthermore, in 1996 and into the early months of 1997 the company found that it had underpriced its health plans, while at the same time enrollments failed to keep pace with projections and administrative costs escalated. As a result, after barely breaking even the year before, Coventry posted a loss of more than $61.2 million in 1996, despite cracking the $1 billion mark in annual revenues. Much of the loss, some $40 million, was charges the company elected to take in order to increase its reserves and restructure its finances. The company took a number of steps to remedy the situation. It sold off a St. Louis-based dental insurance plan as well as nine medical centers in St. Louis to BJC Health System. The two parties then formed a ten-year strategic partnership that allowed Coventry to focus on marketing and management functions rather than the facilities themselves. Likewise, Coventry sold its group medical practices in Pittsburgh. Moreover, Coventry decided to close its Florida Medicaid HMO plan after attempts to sell the business proved unsuccessful. Due to its losses Coventry defaulted on some of its $90 million in debt, resulting in a restructuring of the covenants with bankers. A key to negotiating a one-year loan agreement that stabilized the company's finances was a letter of intent from investment firm E.M. Warburg, Pincus Ventures to invest $40 million in Coventry.

Coventry Merging with Principal Health Care in 1997

With its house in order, Coventry returned to profitability in 1997, earning nearly $12 million on revenues in excess of $1.22 billion. In November 1997 it merged with Principal Health Care, a managed care company that was enduring a plight similar to what Coventry had just overcome. The Bethesda, Maryland-based company, a subsidiary of Des Moines, Iowa-based Principal Financial Group, had lost more than $40 million in 1996 and during the first three quarters of 1997 lost some $15 million more. The $375 million stock swap, which closed in 1998, created a $2.4 billion company with 1.9 million members located in 18 markets. Coventry received a 60 percent ownership stake in the merged entity, which subsequently changed its name to Coventry Health Care. The company also decided to move its headquarters to Principal Health Care's offices in Bethesda. Bredesen expressed some displeasure over the change of address, although he said he understood the rationale. Because he could not spare the time to travel to Maryland for meetings he opted to resign from the Coventry board.

In 1998 Coventry completed a number of transactions to improve the company's fiscal health following the Principal

Health Care merger. Principal Health Care of Illinois was sold to First American Group for $4.3 million cash, and Principal Health Care of Florida Inc. was sold to Blue Cross Blue Shield of Florida, Inc. for $95 million in cash. In addition, in December 1998 Coventry acquired Healthcare America Plans, Inc., which was then merged with the operations of Principal Health Care of Kansas City, Inc. For the year, Coventry generated more than $2.1 billion in revenues. Although it posted a loss of $11.7 million, the company, after digesting the Principal Health Care merger, was clearly poised for strong growth.

Coventry was now able to grow aggressively via acquisitions; it was especially keen on buying and turning around unprofitable health plans that hospitals were increasingly looking to unload. In 1999 Coventry paid approximately $8.4 million to add Carelink Health Plans, serving West Virginia, and $1.8 million to acquire Kaiser Foundation Health Plan, serving North Carolina. In 2000, Coventry paid $3.9 million for PrimeONE, Inc., another West Virginia managed care company. It added to its St. Louis business by buying the 11,800-member Medicaid business of Prudential Health Care Plan at a cost of approximately $100 per member. Coventry also acquired Maxicare Louisiana, Inc. in a $3.5 million deal, and paid $21.2 million for WellPath Community Health Plans, a subsidiary of Duke University Health System. In addition in 2000 Warburg, Pincus invested $100 million in Coventry, giving the investment firm a stake of nearly 31 percent. For the year Coventry saw its revenues improve to more than $2.6 billion and net income grow to $61.3 million after sales of $2.16 billion and earnings of $43.4 million in 1999.

In 2001 Coventry added the commercial membership of Health Partners of the Midwest at a cost of $4.8 million. It also paid nearly $15 million to acquire Blue Ridge Health Alliance, Inc. and its QualChoice of Virginia Health Plan, Inc. subsidiary, which was primarily owned by the University of Virginia Medical Center. QualChoice was typical of the type of acquisition in which Coventry now specialized. Established in 1994 by the University of Virginia Medical Center, the HMO had lost $30 million, prompting the University of Virginia to put the business up for sale. Although its acquisition pace slackened somewhat, Coventry continued to supplement its holdings in 2002. It added New Alliance Health Plan of Erie, Pennsylvania. The 47,000-member health plan was the only employer-owned HMO in the country, having been taken over by businessman Joseph Prischak, owner of Plastek Group, a slate of plastics, toolmaking, and transportation companies. Coventry also acquired Mid American Health Partners Inc. in 2002, adding 121,400 HMO members in Missouri and Kansas.

Coventry saw revenues grow to $3.15 billion in 2001 and nearly $3.58 billion in 2002, while net income grew at an even more impressive rate, with $84.4 million recorded in 2001 and $145.6 million in 2002. It was clear that Coventry was a well-run company that had found its niche in the healthcare field and was well positioned for long-term success.

Principal Subsidiaries

HealthAmerica Pennsylvania, Inc.; Southern Health Services, Inc.; Carelink Health Plans, Inc.; HealthCare USA of Missouri, L.L.C.; Coventry Health Care Management Corporation; Healthcare America, Inc.; WellPath Community Health Plans, Inc.

Principal Competitors

Aetna Inc.; CIGNA Corporation; United Health Group Corporation.

Further Reading

Banstetter, Trebor, "Tennessee Health Care Firm's Profits, Shares Continue to Drop," *Nashville Banner,* February 25, 1997.

Jarboe, Kathleen Johnston, "Bethesda-Based Coventry Health Care Acquires Yet Another HMO," *Daily Record,* September 17, 2002, p. A3.

Lau, Gloria, "Coventry Health Care Inc.," *Investor's Business Daily,* June 11, 2003, p. A10.

Niedzielski, Joe, "Principal, Coventry Health Operations Wed," *National Underwriter,* November 10, 1997, p. 66.

Wissner, Sheila, "Tennessee Governor Candidate Profiles: Phil Bredesen, The Early Years," *Tennessean,* September 29, 2002.

—Ed Dinger

Credit Suisse Group

Paradeplatz 8
Post Office Box 1
8070 Zurich
Switzerland
Telephone: (01) 212 1616
Fax: (01) 333 2587
Web site: http://www.credit-suisse.com

Public Company
Incorporated: 1856 as Schweizerische Kreditanstalt
Employees: 72,501
Total Assets: SFr 1.02 trillion ($752.01 billion) (2003)
Stock Exchanges: Swiss Frankfurt New York
Ticker Symbol: CSGN
NAIC: 551111 Offices of Bank Holding Companies;
    522110 Commercial Banking; 522210 Credit Card
    Issuing; 522291 Consumer Lending; 522292 Real
    Estate Credit; 522293 International Trade Financing;
    523110 Investment Banking and Securities Dealing;
    523120 Securities Brokerage; 523920 Portfolio
    Management; 523930 Investment Advice; 523991
    Trust, Fiduciary, and Custody Services; 524113 Direct
    Life Insurance Carriers; 524114 Direct Health and
    Medical Insurance Carriers; 524126 Direct Property
    and Casualty Insurance Carriers; 525110 Pension
    Funds; 525910 Open-End Investment Funds

Credit Suisse Group, which began as a commercial bank in 1856, at a time when Switzerland was first embracing the industrial revolution, is Switzerland's second largest bank (behind UBS AG) and one of the top dozen or so financial services companies in the world. The group is organized into two business units: Credit Suisse Financial Services and Credit Suisse First Boston. The former, which serves individuals and small to medium-sized companies, provides banking, financial advisory, and asset management services, as well as life and non-life insurance and pension products from the Winterthur unit. The group's institutional, corporate, government, and very rich individual customers are served through the internationally active Credit Suisse First Boston, which provides a broad range of products and services, including investment banking, securities underwriting, financial advisory services, private equity investments, full-service brokerage, investment research, and asset management services. Summarizing its own history, the group claims to have "evolved from a Swiss bank with an international franchise into a global financial institution with a strong Swiss home market."

Quickly Becoming Switzerland's Largest Bank After 1856 Founding

In 1856 Switzerland's federal constitution was only eight years old and there was little industry in the country as the shift from an agricultural to an industrial economy had just begun. Alfred Escher, a young Zurich politician from a prominent local family, was making slow progress in his talks with foreign banks about ways to finance a proposed northeastern railway, so he decided to set up an independent bank in Zurich, putting SFr 3 million worth of shares on public offer. The response was overwhelming: he received SFr 218 million in subscriptions within three days, and Schweizerische Kreditanstalt opened for business on July 16. (The bank's German name translated literally as "Swiss Credit Institution," but it became known instead internationally as Credit Suisse.)

The American Civil War had a great impact on the emerging textile industry in Switzerland, which suffered when cotton prices collapsed after the war ended. Credit Suisse posted its first loss ever in 1867 and its last loss until the mid-1990s.

The growth of other industries in Switzerland and the continued expansion of the railroads provided ample opportunities for Credit Suisse to grow, however. The bank helped develop the Swiss monetary system and, by the end of the Franco-Prussian War in 1871, Credit Suisse was the largest bank in Switzerland.

Switzerland: Evolving into the Banking Capital of the World by World War I

The next 40 years, to the beginning of World War I, came to be known as the belle epoque for both the continent and for Credit Suisse. A number of significant changes occurred during this period, including the revision of the federal constitution in 1874 and the resulting political changes that eventually led to proportional representation in local and federal government; an increase in savings, which enabled the country to become an exporter of capital by the mid-1880s and reduce its reliance on foreign capital; and the introduction of electricity, the telephone, and the telegraph, all of which required large infusions of capital for construction of factories, power plants, and phone systems.

The founding of the Swiss National Bank in 1907 and the growth in foreign investment by Swiss banks sowed the seeds for Switzerland's eventual role as the banking capital of the world. Credit Suisse also branched out from Zurich during this period and had 13 different locations in Switzerland by the beginning of World War I; the bank's head count increased to more than 1,000. Credit Suisse had gained its first branch in 1905 when it took over the Basel branch of Oberrheinische Bank.

With the outbreak of World War I, foreign investment stopped completely. As investors in hostile countries returned Swiss securities, Credit Suisse played a crucial role in placing them on the Swiss market. Credit Suisse also had to defend the interests of Swiss investors abroad, a delicate matter during such a chaotic period.

After World War I, Credit Suisse continued financing the electrification of the country and, in response to a coal shortage, helped finance the national railroad's conversion to electricity in 1924. Foreign investment expanded rapidly during the 1920s, a period that came to a devastating end with the stock market crash in 1929.

The Great Depression led to cataclysmic changes in Europe, including the rise of nationalist thinking, the imposition of a range of trade barriers, including protective tariffs and import quotas, and other developments that resulted in lower production levels, less investment, and economic decline.

Increasing tensions in Europe led to Credit Suisse's emphasis on English-speaking companies, which resulted in the establishment of the Swiss-American Corporation in 1939 to focus on the securities business and the opening of Credit Suisse's first foreign branch in New York in 1940.

During World War II Credit Suisse extended large amounts of credit to Swiss authorities, who were owed more than SFr 1.7 billion by Germany by the end of the war. Despite the loss of

almost half of the company's employees to war-related service, Credit Suisse emerged from the conflagration financially sound and poised to capitalize on the impending economic upturn. Nevertheless, as the conduct of Credit Suisse and the other big Swiss banks during the Nazi era began to emerge in detail starting in the mid-1990s, it became clear that the bank was involved in a number of improper activities, including trading gold with Nazi Germany. The big banks also came under heavy criticism for the way they dealt with accounts that had been opened before 1945 by victims of the Holocaust—the so-called dormant accounts issue.

After the end of World War II, as normal banking activities resumed, reconstruction of the war-torn continent got underway and Credit Suisse again took up issuing paper for foreign debtors. At the same time, Credit Suisse expanded its services to its regular customers by developing new and different types of savings accounts and broadening into activities that were formerly handled by subsidiaries, such as issuing credit cards and providing consumer credit.

During the 1960s the bank also set up a farsighted business arrangement with White, Weld & Co., Inc., a leading American investment bank, that would eventually establish Credit Suisse's leading role in the Eurobond-issuing market and would ultimately lead to its relationship with the American investment bank First Boston. Cooperation with White Weld began in 1962 when Credit Suisse purchased the investment bank's Zurich subsidiary, White, Weld & Co. AG, which was subsequently renamed Clariden Finanz AG (and later still Clariden Bank). In 1970 Credit Suisse and White, Weld set up a holding company for Clariden called WW Trust. Four years later Credit Suisse became the largest shareholder in WW Trust, which was renamed Société anonyme financière du Crédit Suisse et de White Weld (CS&WW).

Foreign exchange dealings assumed greater importance during the 1960s, along with the precious metals markets. With the emergence of a free gold market in 1968, Credit Suisse became a major gold trading house and, through its acquisition of the precious metals refinery Valcambi S.A., in Ticino, a manufacturer of ingots and coins. By the turn of the decade, Credit Suisse had offices on every continent except Antarctica.

The 1970s brought the introduction of floating exchange rates and the subsequent devaluation of the dollar, a loss of investor confidence in the American market, and the oil crisis of 1973. The bank also experienced a major scandal in 1977 when authorities began investigating a fraudulent banking and foreign exchange trading scheme at the company's Chiasso branch involving more than $1.2 billion. The losses resulted in the resignation of several top executives and left Rainer Gut second in line; Gut became chairman in 1983 following the retirement of Otto Aeppli.

Major Changes Instilled by Rainer Gut During the 1980s

Gut, who was Swiss-born but trained in the United States, brought a measure of stateside savvy and aggressiveness to Credit Suisse. A former partner in New York's Lazard Freres, Gut shifted the company's focus from traditional Swiss banking practices, which emphasized security and caution, to world investment banking and money management.

Key Dates:

1856: Alfred Escher founds an independent bank in Zurich, Schweizerische Kreditanstalt, known internationally as Credit Suisse.
1905: The first branch opens in Basel.
1940: The first foreign branch opens in New York.
1962: Cooperation begins with White, Weld & Co., Inc., a leading American investment bank.
1977: Credit Suisse is rocked by the Chiasso affair, a major scandal involving fraudulent banking and foreign exchange trading at the bank's Chiasso branch.
1978: Following White, Weld's takeover by Merrill Lynch, Credit Suisse begins cooperating with U.S. investment bank First Boston Inc., particularly through the joint venture Financière Crédit Suisse-First Boston (CSFB).
1988: Credit Suisse and First Boston restructure their joint venture under a new company called CS First Boston, Inc.
1989: CS Holding becomes the publicly traded umbrella holding company for Credit Suisse, the group's stake in CS First Boston, and other group interests.
1990: Credit Suisse bails out troubled First Boston, pumping in $300 million in equity and gaining majority control of the firm.
1993: Swiss Volksbank, the nation's fourth largest bank, is acquired.
1994: The group enters into a strategic alliance with Swiss Re.
1995: The group enters into a strategic alliance with Winterthur Insurance, the number two Swiss-based insurance company.
1997: Major restructuring takes effect and includes the renaming of CS Holding as Credit Suisse Group and the merger of global investment banking operations under Credit Suisse First Boston; Winterthur is acquired and becomes a Credit Suisse Group operating unit.
2000: Donaldson, Lufkin & Jenrette, Inc., U.S.-based investment bank and asset management firm, is acquired.
2002: Travails at Winterthur and the scandal-plagued CSFB lead to a record net loss of SFr 3.31 billion ($2.12 billion).
2003: CSFB's Pershing unit and Winterthur's Churchill and Italian insurance operations are all divested.

By 1986 the bank's assets were $46 billion, and somewhere between $75 billion and $150 billion more were under active management by the bank—well ahead of the estimated $50 billion under the management of the leading American bank in the field, Citicorp. Under Gut, Credit Suisse was the first Swiss bank to acquire a bank in West Germany, Effectenbank, and it became one of only a handful of foreign operations doing trust banking in Japan.

In 1978 White, Weld was purchased by Merrill Lynch & Co. After Credit Suisse and Merrill Lynch failed to reach an agreement on a continued cooperation arrangement, Credit Suisse purchased Merrill Lynch's stake in CS&WW, increasing its interest to 76 percent. Still seeking to work with an established U.S. investment bank, Credit Suisse reached an agreement with New York-based First Boston Inc. whereby CS&WW was transformed into Financière Crédit Suisse - First Boston (CSFB), 46 percent owned by Credit Suisse, 31 percent by First Boston, and 23 percent by management and other shareholders. CSFB, in turn, took over a 25 percent interest in First Boston.

The terms under which CSFB was established caused the defection of CSFB Chairman and Chief Executive John Craven, who was replaced by Michael von Clemm. Although he was consistently pilloried as a bad manager and was eventually replaced as chief executive by Hans Ulrich Doerig from Credit Suisse, von Clemm was widely credited with helping the company achieve its undisputed dominance of the Eurobond market with innovative financing deals. He also oversaw, however, one of the greatest financial disasters in the company's history, a $150 million issue bought by the company in 1980. The deal eventually cost CSFB between $20 and $40 million, and the three years during which von Clemm managed the company were its least successful.

Four years later six executives, including three executive directors, left CSFB. The exodus coincided with the appointment of Jack Hennessey, formerly of First Boston, as chief executive to replace Doerig, who returned to Credit Suisse. A former assistant secretary of the treasury, Hennessey was brought in to reduce the friction and to assume management duties. Von Clemm remained as chairman. The problems were not over, however.

At the beginning of 1984, three CSFB executives defected to Merrill Lynch, taking seven others with them. Published accounts of the brouhaha suggested that the expansion of Deputy Chairman Hans-Joerg Rudloff's power base within the company offended a number of the executives, many of whom were accustomed to operating in a wide-open entrepreneurial environment. But the company was growing too large, and as senior executives tried to figure out how to manage CSFB, the infighting grew nastier; Rudloff was considered the consummate corporate infighter.

The final defection came in 1986 when von Clemm resigned quietly after 16 years with the company to devote more time to outside interests. Hennessey took over as chairman and chief executive.

At about the same time, full-service investment banking companies such as Salomon Brothers and Goldman Sachs, as well as Japanese and German concerns, started pushing their way into the Eurobond market. That forced CSFB to diversify into mergers and acquisitions, equity sales, and other specialties, as CSFB's share of the Eurobond market dropped from more than 16 percent to just more than 11 percent.

In addition, CSFB was encountering competition from, of all places, its own two parent companies, Credit Suisse and First Boston. As the need for better cooperation between family members became apparent, CSFB moved one of its New York executives to London to establish better relations. For a while things seemed to be working. One of the first joint ventures among the three companies involved a $4 billion bond floated by General Motors Acceptance Corporation. While First Boston was lead manager, Credit Suisse provided a letter of credit to back the notes and CSFB placed $400 million of the bonds in Europe.

The true survivor of CSFB remained Rudloff, who took the company into Amsterdam with a bank acquisition there in 1986, and then became a director and officer of Credit Suisse itself in early 1987. Rudloff's return to Switzerland was viewed by the staid Swiss banking establishment as a harbinger that the cozy days of gentlemanly Swiss banking had come to a close.

One result of the newly deregulated and ever-fluctuating markets of the 1980s was that the relationship among Switzerland's three major banks (which included Credit Suisse, Union Bank of Switzerland, and Swiss Bank Corporation), collectively known as "the syndicate," could no longer be so friendly. Once a fairly tightly knit trio, they adopted new guidelines giving each other flexibility to withdraw from deals with which the others were involved if they had doubts about the borrower and even to return up to 60 percent of their allocation of bonds after a deal was done.

Credit Suisse was characterized in the financial press as a lone wolf rather than a pack hunter sharing the spoils of its deals with other members of the syndicate, conduct that further indicated the end of an era in the Swiss banking industry. Some of the first signs of the new conditions came when restrictions on gray market trading (trading before the valuation date) were relaxed. Credit Suisse moved aggressively into this area of finance, one it had previously shunned. The other two major Swiss banks sat back and waited and watched. In any event, by the early 1990s the syndicate was history as Switzerland, like many other countries worldwide, continued to deregulate.

Meanwhile, the company was tainted by mid-1980s charges of laundering drug money from Turkey and Bulgaria. Although the company denied the charges and, technically, money laundering was not illegal unless the money was used to buy drugs, the stain remained.

Acquisitions, Restructurings, and Diversification Highlighting the 1990s

The stock market crash of 1987 hit CSFB and First Boston particularly hard. During the year that followed, CSFB's problems included an estimated $15 million loss on a 1987 debt swap with Italy. First Boston, meanwhile, suffered large losses from bad bridge loans for mergers and acquisitions. In 1988 Credit Suisse and First Boston restructured their troublesome marriage under a new company, CS First Boston, Inc. Two years later, Credit Suisse bailed out the still troubled First Boston by agreeing to pump $300 million in equity into the firm, increasing Credit Suisse's stake in First Boston to 64.2 percent and making the Swiss bank the first foreigner to own a Wall Street investment bank. Relations between Credit Suisse and First Boston managers remained strained during the early 1990s, as it was difficult to reconcile the more freewheeling style of First Boston with the more conservative (if aggressive for Switzerland) style of Credit Suisse.

Meanwhile, Credit Suisse had been reorganized in early 1989. CS Holding had been created as a sister company seven years earlier, mainly to hold the bank's interests in CSFB. In 1989 CS

Holding was transformed into an umbrella holding company, under which were placed Credit Suisse, the group's full-service bank in Switzerland; CS First Boston; Fides Holding, which specialized in trust business and management consulting in Switzerland; and the company's controlling stake in Electrowatt AG, the Swiss power utility. This simplification of what had been an extremely complex web of cross-holdings and sister firms cost the company about $80 million. The publicly traded shares in Credit Suisse were exchanged into shares in CS Holding.

Acquisitions and new growth areas were major themes of the 1990s for Credit Suisse. In April 1990 Bank Leu, Switzerland's sixth largest bank, was acquired in the first hostile takeover in Swiss banking. Bank Leu, which catered to the wealthy in Switzerland, became the centerpiece for Credit Suisse's private banking business, which also included Clariden Bank serving customers in North and South America, and the northern European activities of Bank Hofmann (which had been acquired in 1972).

In addition to private banking, Credit Suisse added another operating unit to its organization chart when it entered the insurance business, the first Swiss bank to do so, by establishing CS Life in October 1990. The group's involvement in insurance broadened in December 1994 when it entered into an alliance with Swiss Re, and in December 1995 when another alliance was formed, this one with Winterthur Insurance, the second largest Swiss-based insurance company.

In early 1993 Credit Suisse outbid Union Bank of Switzerland for the country's fourth largest bank, the troubled Swiss Volksbank, in a SFr 1.6 billion ($1.1 billion) deal. Over the next few years, Credit Suisse and Swiss Volksbank's network of domestic branches were reconciled. Meantime, in 1994, Credit Suisse acquired Neue Aargauer Bank, the largest regional bank in Switzerland. This acquisition gave Credit Suisse the largest branch network in the country and made it Switzerland's number one bank by market share—positions it would hold until the 1998 merger of Swiss Bank and Union Bank that formed UBS AG.

In 1994 the Fides trust business was placed within the Credit Suisse banking operation. A much more significant restructuring and a refocusing of the overall group began in 1996. Early in the year Credit Suisse discussed a merger with Union Bank, which would have created a Swiss banking giant. Instead, Credit Suisse decided to turn its attention away from Switzerland; rather than being a Swiss bank with significant international interests, the group decided to become a truly international banking and financial services power that happened to be based in Switzerland and had some core businesses there. Under the resulting reorganization, which took effect at the beginning of 1997 and was led by the newly appointed chief executive Lukas Mühlemann (who had been head of Swiss Re), CS Holding was renamed Credit Suisse Group. The company's operations were reorganized into a domestic banking unit called Credit Suisse, which represented a full merger of the operations of the old Credit Suisse and Swiss Volksbank; a private banking unit called Credit Suisse Private Banking, which included Bank Leu, Clariden Bank, Bank Hofmann, and other CS Holding private banks; Credit Suisse First Boston, which included a full merging of CS First Boston and CS Holding's other corporate banking operations; and Credit Suisse Asset Management. All units except for Credit Suisse were to operate on a worldwide basis. The restructuring also involved a workforce reduction of 15 percent, or 5,000 employees. Simultaneously, Credit Suisse made its first moves toward divesting its controlling stake in Electrowatt, which promised to focus the group further on its core financial services businesses. By 1998 the group had, in large part, completed this divestment, having retained only a 20 percent stake in Watt AG, the former energy division of Electrowatt.

About the same time that the company was being restructured for the 21st century, its activities—and those of the other "Big Three" Swiss banks—during World War II were being reexamined, with resulting negative publicity. Reports of the banks' financial dealings with Nazi Germany were published, and Jewish groups pushed for reclamation of money that had been placed into Swiss bank accounts before World War II by victims of the Holocaust. The Swiss banks were initially reluctant to cooperate with these efforts—in part because of their traditional secrecy—but the resulting worldwide outcry forced the banks to publish lists of people who owned dormant accounts that had been opened before 1945, accounts that contained a total of SFr 61.2 million ($41.3 million) in them. In early 1997, the Big Three banks agreed to set up a SFr 100 million ($70 million) humanitarian fund for the victims of the Holocaust. Then in August 1998, with state and local governments in the United States threatening sanctions against Credit Suisse Group and UBS, the two Swiss banking giants agreed to pay $1.25 billion to settle all the Holocaust-related class-action lawsuits that had been brought in the United States. Credit Suisse agreed to pay one-third of the total. Many Swiss criticized the deal as the result of the blackmailing of a smaller country by the United States.

In December 1997 Credit Suisse Group made a great leap forward in the insurance sector when it acquired Winterthur Insurance for about $9.51 billion. This move immediately vaulted Credit Suisse into the top ten financial services companies in the world, with total assets of about SFr 700 billion ($466 billion), which brought it close to the size of Europe's largest bank, Deutsche Bank AG. It also increased the group's assets under management to about SFr 700 billion ($466 billion), which ranked it third in the world, trailing only Fidelity Investments and AXA/UAP/Equitable. Winterthur was set up within the group umbrella as a fifth operating unit, and Credit Suisse's CS Life was integrated into Winterthur Life.

Credit Suisse First Boston also was bolstered through two late 1990s acquisitions. In 1997 the mergers and acquisitions, equity underwriting, equity trading, and equity research departments of Barclays de Zoete Wedd, the investment banking arm of the U.K.-based Barclays PLC, were acquired. The following year saw the purchase of the leading Brazilian investment bank, Banco de Investimentos Garantia S.A. In 1999 Credit Suisse Group acquired Warburg Pincus Asset Management, a unit of Warburg, Pincus & Co., for $650 million. The acquired unit became part of Credit Suisse Asset Management, which gained $22 billion in assets under management, including $10 billion in Warburg Pincus mutual funds.

The 1990s ended on a sour note for the group, and particularly for Credit Suisse First Boston. That unit had heavily involved itself in Russia in the postcommunist era, becoming the dominant dealer in Russian government bonds as well as a major lender to Russian companies and municipalities. When the Russian economic crisis erupted in 1998, CSFB had a huge exposure and ended up with a $1.3 billion loss from its activities in Russia, leading to a loss for the year of $154 million. In 1999 Japan's banking watchdog, the Financial Supervisory Agency, launched an investigation into Credit Suisse First Boston's sale of derivatives to Japanese banks and companies so that these firms could hide huge losses. Although technically legal, such practices were considered inappropriate under newly issued regulations. Credit Suisse admitted that some of its staff had obstructed the agency's investigation by shredding documents and hiding files. Japanese regulators subsequently revoked the license of the Japanese derivatives arm of CSFB.

Troubles in the New Millennium

In May 2000 Gut handed over the chairmanship to Mühlemann, who remained chief executive as well. Mühlemann engineered the second huge acquisition of his leadership reign in November of that year, acquiring Donaldson, Lufkin & Jenrette, Inc. (DLJ) for $12.36 billion. U.S.-based DLJ had both investment banking and asset management operations, and these were merged into CSFB and Credit Suisse Asset Management, respectively. The newly enlarged Credit Suisse First Boston ranked third globally in mergers and acquisitions advisory, fourth in equity underwriting, third in debt underwriting, and first in high-yield debt underwriting.

The acquisition of DLJ was poorly timed as it came right at the beginning of a major bear market. In addition to having to deal with the adverse market conditions, Credit Suisse First Boston was also at the very center of the Wall Street scandals that became regular headline-makers in the early 2000s. CSFB and other investment banks were accused of demanding kickbacks from their customers in exchange for shares in highly sought-after late 1990s technology IPOs. In January 2002 CSFB reached an agreement with U.S. regulators whereby it would pay $100 million in fines to settle these allegations. Frank Quattrone, the head of CSFB's technology underwriting group, was forced to resign from the company in March 2003, and one month later was charged with obstruction of justice for allegedly encouraging staffers to destroy e-mails at a time when he was aware that CSFB was under investigation. Then in April 2003 CSFB was part of a landmark $1.4 billion settlement between ten Wall Street firms and the New York Attorney General, the Securities and Exchange Commission, and other regulatory agencies. This deal settled a number of related allegations that had been raised against these financial firms, including that investment bankers had pressured research analysts to issue positive reports and that the analysts subsequently issued "worthless" stock recommendations even though they knew they were fraudulent. Credit Suisse First Boston's share of the settlement was $200 million in fines and penalties—an amount topped only by Citigroup Inc. Credit Suisse Group, meantime, took a pretax charge of SFr 700 million ($500 million) late in 2002 to cover damages from private lawsuits that were expected to be filed in connection with the CSFB scandals.

In mid-2001, as these scandals began unfolding and the red ink began to flow, the head of Credit Suisse First Boston, Allen D. Wheat, was relieved of his position and replaced by John J. Mack. Within two years of his appointment, Mack thoroughly overhauled what had become a bloated operation following the ill-advised acquisition of DLJ, cutting 10,000 jobs from the 27,500-person workforce and slashing costs by more than $3 billion. Part of the cost reductions came from a series of divestments that also helped to focus CSFB more on its core operations. Late in 2001 the unit's precious metals trading business and its Australian and New Zealand retail brokerages were sold off. In 2002 its U.K.-based online trading operation, DLJdirect Ltd., was sold to TD Waterhouse, and the sister operation in the United States, CSFBdirect, Inc., was sold to the Bank of Montreal. Then in May 2003 CSFB's Pershing unit, which provided financial services outsourcing solutions to broker-dealers and independent investment managers, was sold to the Bank of New York Company, Inc. for about $2.5 billion.

Meanwhile, the Credit Suisse Group was once again restructured in 2002. The structure was streamlined into two business units: Credit Suisse First Boston and Credit Suisse Financial Services. The latter encompassed private banking, corporate and retail banking, life insurance and pensions, and non-life insurance. In July 2002 Oswald J. Grübel, the former head of the group's successful private banking operation, was placed in charge of the financial services unit. Grübel was immediately faced with the challenge of dealing with Winterthur. The insurance unit had begun to lose money thanks to a steep decline in its investment income stemming from the collapsing stock markets. During 2002 Credit Suisse was forced to inject SFr 3.7 billion ($2.7 billion) into Winterthur to bolster its reserves. To effect a longer term repair to Winterthur's—and Credit Suisse's—capital base, several divestitures of insurance operations were completed. Two of the larger divestments occurred in later months of 2003: Winterthur's U.K. non-life insurer, Churchill Insurance Group plc, was sold to the Royal Bank of Scotland Group plc for about £1.2 billion; and Winterthur's Italian insurance operations were sold to Unipol, an Italian insurer, for EUR 1.46 billion ($1.7 billion).

The crises at both Credit Suisse First Boston and Winterthur resulted in a stunning net loss of SFr 3.31 billion ($2.12 billion)—making 2002 the worst year in company history. The stock of Credit Suisse Group fell sharply through most of 2002, with the company losing more than half of its market value over the course of the year. A recovery in the stock began late in the year following the announcement that Mühlemann—the person most closely associated with the ill-fated purchases of Winterthur and DLJ—would leave at the end of the year. Taking over as chairman at that time was Walter B. Kielholz, vice-chairman of Credit Suisse and also CEO of Swiss Re. The heads of the two operating units, Mack and Grübel, were named co-CEOs of the Credit Suisse Group.

Early results from 2003 pointed to a possible turnaround. Credit Suisse Group posted net profits of SFr 2 billion ($1.48 billion) for the first half of the year, compared with a net loss of SFr 211 million ($129 million) for the same period one year earlier. It was too early to tell, however, whether the scandals and acquisition headaches that had been dogging the group had been fully overcome.

Principal Subsidiaries

Bank Hofmann AG; Bank Leu AG; BGP Banca di Gestione Patrimoniale S.A.; Clariden Holding AG; Credit Suisse; Credit Suisse Fides; Credit Suisse First Boston; Credit Suisse First Boston (International) Holding AG; Credit Suisse Trust AG; Neue Aargauer Bank (98.6%); ''Winterthur'' Swiss Insurance Company; Winterthur Life; Credit Suisse Asset Management (Australia) Limited; DBV-Winterthur Versicherung AG (Germany); Winterthur Assicurazioni S.p.A. (Italy); Credit Suisse Trust and Banking Co. Ltd. (Japan); Credit Suisse Asset Management, Limited (U.K.); Credit Suisse First Boston (Europe) Limited (U.K.); JO Hambro Investment Management Limited (U.K.); Credit Suisse Asset Management LLC (U.S.A.); Credit Suisse First Boston LLC (U.S.A.); Credit Suisse First Boston (USA), Inc.; Frye-Louis Capital Management Holding Co., Inc. (U.S.A.).

Principal Operating Units

Credit Suisse Financial Services; Credit Suisse First Boston.

Principal Competitors

UBS AG; Citigroup Inc.; Deutsche Bank AG; The Royal Bank of Scotland Group plc; HSBC Holdings plc; Barclays PLC; Merrill Lynch & Co., Inc.; Goldman Sachs Group Inc; Morgan Stanley; Zurich Financial Services; Swiss Life Insurance and Pension Company.

Further Reading

Andrews, Edmund L., ''When the Sure-Footed Stumble: Swiss Banks Stagger After Several Investing Missteps,'' *New York Times*, October 23, 1998, p. C1.

Beckett, Paul, ''Credit Suisse and UBS Agree to Open 2.1 Million Holocaust-Era Accounts,'' *Wall Street Journal*, May 4, 2000, p. A12.

Cooper, Ron, ''Gut Instincts,'' *Forbes*, October 14, 1991, pp. 169–70.

——, ''Gut's Gang of Four,'' *Euromoney*, November 1990, p. 24.

Crabbe, Matthew, ''Gut's Secret Plan,'' *Euromoney*, January 1989, p. 38.

''Credit Suisse Restructures,'' *Banker*, August 1996, p. 5.

Fairlamb, David, ''On the Edge: Will a Radical New Strategy Save the Day for Credit Suisse's CEO?,'' *Business Week*, July 15, 2002, pp. 54–55.

Fairlamb, David, John Rossant, and Emily Thornton, ''This Bank Keeps Growing and Growing and . . . ,'' *Business Week*, September 11, 2000, p. 134.

Gasparino, Charles, ''Credit Suisse Agrees to Purchase Unit of Warburg Pincus for $650 Million,'' *Wall Street Journal*, February 16, 1999, p. B14.

''Gnomes at Play,'' *Economist*, July 6, 1996, pp. 61–62.

Grant, Linda, ''Will CS First Boston Ever Win?,'' *Fortune*, August 19, 1996, pp. 30, 34.

Greenhouse, Steven, ''Swiss Bank Turns Aggressive,'' *New York Times*, April 10, 1989, pp. D1, D2.

Hall, William, ''Swiss Business Star Stumbles at the Top,'' *Financial Times*, January 30, 2002, p. 13.

''In the Land of Milk and Honey,'' *Economist*, August 16, 1997, pp. 54+.

James, Jennie, ''How to Stop Sinking,'' *Time International*, November 25, 2002, p. 60.

Jung, Joseph, *From Schweizerische Kreditanstalt to Credit Suisse Group: The History of a Bank*, translated by James Knight, Zurich: Neue Zürcher Zeitung, 2000.

Jung, Joseph, ed., *Credit Suisse Group Banks in the Second World War: A Critical Review*, 2nd ed., translated by James Knight, Zurich: Neue Zürcher Zeitung, 2002.

"Knock, Knock," *Economist,* August 7, 1999, p. 63.

Langley, Alison, "Credit Suisse Reports Loss of $2 Billion," *New York Times,* February 26, 2003, p. W1.

——, "Credit Suisse Sets a Record with Its Loss of $1.4 Billion," *New York Times,* November 15, 2002, p. W1.

McGeary, Johanna, "Echoes of the Holocaust," *Time,* February 24, 1997, pp. 37–40.

McGeehan, Patrick, "Credit Suisse Shakes Up First Boston," *New York Times,* July 13, 2001, p. C1.

Muehring, Kevin, and Beth Selby, "Rainer Gut's Wall Street Headache," *Institutional Investor,* January 1991.

125th Anniversary of Credit Suisse: An Historical Survey, Zurich: Credit Suisse, 1981.

Rhoads, Christopher, and Margaret Studer, "Credit Suisse Plans to Buy Winterthur in Transaction Valued at $9.51 Billion," *Wall Street Journal,* August 12, 1997, pp. A3, A8.

Rodger, Ian, "The Enfant Terrible of Swiss Banking," *Financial Times,* January 9, 1993, p. 12.

Sellers, Patricia, "The Trials of Mack," *Fortune,* September 1, 2003, pp. 98+.

Shearlock, Peter, "Merger Will Create Powerful Force," *Banker,* October 2000, pp. 113–14.

Smith, Alison, "Rebranded Credit Suisse Thinks Global," *Financial Times,* January 20, 1997, p. 17.

Spiro, Leah Nathans, and John Templeman, "A Short Leash for First Boston," *Business Week,* November 26, 1990, p. 156.

Strom, Stephanie, "Japan Revokes Credit Suisse Unit's Banking License," *New York Times,* July 30, 1999, p. C6.

Studer, Margaret, "Credit Suisse Looks Ahead to Solving Antitrust Problems of Winterthur Deal," *Wall Street Journal,* August 18, 1997, p. A9.

"Swiss Banks Spat Over Mergers," *Banker,* May 1996, p. 4.

"Swiss Cure," *Economist,* January 9, 1993, p. 66.

"A Swiss Giant Limbers Up," *Economist,* September 22, 1990, pp. 88, 93–94.

"A Swiss Role," *Economist,* November 17, 1990, pp. 100, 106.

Tagliabue, John, "Taking the Challenge of Streamlining Credit Suisse," *New York Times,* November 29, 1996, pp. D9, D14.

"A Treaty in Store for CSFB," *Economist,* April 16, 1988, p. 91.

"Twin Peaks," *Economist,* September 28, 2002, p. 100.

Weberman, Ben, "A Gnome Named Gut," *Forbes,* September 22, 1986, p. 110.

Wicks, John, "Building Up a Big Bank: Credit Suisse CEO Robert Jeker Looks for Dynamic Growth in Financial Services," *swissBusiness,* November/December 1990, p. 6.

——, "Founding Father," *swissBusiness,* July/August 1991, p. 4.

—update: David E. Salamie

Delta and Pine Land Company

1 Cotton Row
Scott, Mississippi 38772
U.S.A.
Telephone: (662) 742-4000
Toll Free: (800) 511-7333
Fax: (662) 742-4196
Web site: http://www.deltaandpine.com

Public Company
Incorporated: 1919
Employees: 555
Sales: $257.80 million (2002)
Stock Exchanges: New York
Ticker Symbol: DLP
NAIC: 111920 Cotton Farming; 111110 Soybean Farming

Delta and Pine Land Company (D&PL) is the largest breeder, producer, and marketer of cottonseed in the United States. D&PL produces conventional cottonseed and cottonseeds genetically engineered as insecticides and herbicides. The company also produces soybean planting seeds containing a gene tolerant to herbicides. The company sells its products in more than a dozen countries, deriving the bulk of its international sales from Argentina, Australia, Brazil, China, South Africa, and Turkey.

Origins

D&PL's corporate roots in the area surrounding Scott, Mississippi, were planted by a group of businessmen in Manchester, England. The businessmen, owners of private textile mills in the region surrounding Manchester, wanted to secure a reliable supply of long staple cotton to feed their mills. The mill owners were part of the Fine Cotton Spinners and Doublers Association, the organization through which they created the predecessor to D&PL. In 1911, the Fine Cotton Spinners and Doublers Association purchased 38,000 acres in the area around Scott, a sparsely populated, rural area known as the Delta and Piney Woods region of Mississippi. The mill owners were forced to divide their property into three plantations. A Mississippi law passed in 1890 restricted farming operations by a single owner to no more than 12,500 acres. Consequently, the

Fine Cotton Spinners and Doublers Association formed three companies: The Mississippi Delta Planting Company, The Triumph Planting Company, and The Lake Vista Planting Company. The acreage around Scott was farmed by these three entities until the British mill owners were able to find a way to bring their property under the control of a single entity. In 1919, they discovered a dormant land company named Delta and Pine Land Company whose 1886 charter predated the law restricting farm ownership. By acquiring D&PL, the mill owners were able to operate their 38,000 acres under one company.

Although D&PL originally existed as a cotton producer, the company achieved its greatest success as a breeder of cotton planting seeds. D&PL developed into the largest such company in the United States, aided by the extensive plant breeding programs the company launched over the years. The company concentrated on producing varieties of cotton planting seed for cotton varieties grown in Arizona and east of Texas. Through its plant breeding programs, D&PL developed a gene pool capable of producing cotton varieties with superior traits that benefited both farmers and textile manufacturers. D&PL's cottonseeds could improve crop yields, a benefit to farmers, and the company's seeds could produce cotton with improved fiber characteristics, a benefit to textile manufacturers.

D&PL achieved its greatest success late in the 20th century when the company's financial might exponentially increased. Technological advancements, product diversification, and growth-minded management contributed greatly to the company's transformation. The new era of fast-paced growth began in 1978, when a group of U.S. owners led by Roger Malkin acquired D&PL. Under Malkin's leadership, D&PL made its first important diversification. In 1980, the company began marketing soybean planting seeds in the United States. The decade's most important achievement occurred later in the decade, once the company gained the executive who would lead it through its most prolific years of growth.

The Influence of Biotechnology in the 1990s

In 1988, a veteran of the agricultural seed business joined D&PL as executive vice-president. The arrival of Murray Robinson roughly coincided with the company's first concerted push overseas, a move that drew its impetus from Robinson. When Robinson joined D&PL, the company sold its cottonseed and soybean seed strictly to U.S. farmers. No one except the chief executive officer, he noted, had a passport. Robinson pushed for overseas expansion not long after joining D&PL, realizing, as he reflected in a June 11, 2001 interview with *Business Week,* that "for this company to grow long-term, it would have to participate globally."

Overseas sales eventually would account for a significant percentage of D&PL's financial growth, particularly during the late 1990s. Growth during the latter half of the 1990s also would be aided greatly by technological innovation, specifically by advancements in biotechnology. Although D&PL was one of the first seed suppliers to take full advantage of genetically altered seeds, the company did not develop the genetic material. Instead, the company had an invaluable partner, the giant chemicals, food ingredients, drug, and agricultural conglomerate, Monsanto Co. Based in St. Louis, Missouri, Monsanto already was deeply involved in the genetic engineering of food crops by the time D&PL was making its first steps overseas.

Plant science technology made its first leap forward in 1983, when Robert Fraley created the first genetically engineered plant, a petunia. From there, scientists in the biotechnology field went on to create genetically superior crops of corn, wheat, tomatoes, potatoes, and soybeans, among a host of other biotechnological improvements in the food supply. By the beginning of the 1990s, Monsanto was drawing attention for its work in developing pest-resistant cotton, particularly cotton that repelled bollworms and budworms. Every year, farmers in the United States used 100 million pounds of agricultural chemicals on their crops. Roughly 15 percent of the chemicals were used to kill insects, with cotton farmers ranking as the greatest users of insecticides, accounting for 40 percent of the total used on crops. Monsanto's efforts sought to reduce the use of insecticides by using a naturally occurring microbe found in soil called Bacillus thuringiensis, or B.t. B.t. produced a toxic protein lethal to budworms and bollworms, causing paralysis and death when ingested by the insect. Spraying B.t. on crops was not a viable option. The microbe washed away with rainfall and lost its insect-killing potential when exposed to sunlight, forcing Monsanto scientists to discover another way of incorporating B.t. into cotton. Researchers devised a way to take the protein gene from the microbe and insert it into the genetic structure of the cotton plant. Trials of Monsanto's genetically altered cottonseed proved successful in 1990, piquing interest. Monsanto awaited regulatory approval by the U.S. Environmental Protection Agency (EPA), hoping to begin marketing its development by 1995.

As the 1990s progressed, Monsanto became increasingly interested in biotechnology. Once a company whose mainstay business was in chemicals, the company sought to transform itself into a bioengineering concern with a focus on food and nutrition. Robert Shapiro, named chief executive officer and chairman of Monsanto in 1995, spearheaded the transformation, announcing the divestiture of the company's chemicals business and investing heavily in biotechnology interests. Shapiro's vision of Monsanto dovetailed nicely with D&PL's position as the nation's leading producer of cottonseed. In 1992, the complementary strategic orientations of the companies led to the first of several collaborative biotechnology licensing agreements. Under the terms of the agreements, D&PL was given the right to market Monsanto's B.t., or "Bollgard," gene technology. In March 1995, the two companies formed D&M International, LLC to introduce insect-resistant cotton planting seed in international markets. Later in the year, in October, the EPA completed its initial registration of the Bollgard gene technology, paving the way for commercial sales of cottonseed containing the Bollgard gene.

After years of waiting, D&PL commenced commercial sales in the United States of cotton planting seed containing Bollgard gene technology in 1996. D&PL was the only company licensed to market Monsanto's Bollgard gene technology. At this point, D&PL ranked as the largest breeder, producer, and marketer of cotton planting seed in the country, controlling roughly 40 percent of the market. The introduction of B.t. cotton strengthened an already strong company, capturing 13 percent of the U.S. cottonseed market within the first year of its introduction. D&PL's relationship with Monsanto grew in other directions as well, adding several more genetically altered products to its portfolio. In February 1996, the two companies executed what was called the Roundup Ready Gene License and Seed Agreement, giving D&PL another genetically altered cottonseed variety. Monsanto's Roundup Ready gene made cotton plants tolerant to contact with the company's most popular herbicide, Roundup. D&PL began marketing Roundup Ready cottonseeds in 1997, adding further luster to its financial growth.

By the fall of 1997, there was clear evidence of the gains achieved through D&PL's relationship with Monsanto. During the company's third fiscal quarter, sales rose 40 percent to $166 million in large part because of the success of the two Monsanto-developed products. The company's stock nearly doubled as well, jumping from a low of $20 per share in 1996 to $37.06 per share by September 1997. The year also saw the Monsanto-D&PL partnership produce a new product. In February, the two companies executed a Roundup Ready Soybean License agreement that enabled D&PL to begin marketing genetically altered soybean planting seeds. The following year, D&PL began selling cottonseed varieties containing both the Bollgard and Roundup Ready genes.

D&PL and Monsanto in the Late 1990s

The relationship between Monsanto and D&PL reached a significant juncture not long after the pair's collaboration on genetically altered seeds reached the market. In May 1998, the announcement was made that the two companies would merge, a deal that was valued initially at $1.8 billion. For 19 months, the proposed merger awaited approval by the U.S. Department of Justice. The months of waiting were in vain, as the merger collapsed, causing a furor that would drag on for months. In January 2000, roughly a month after withdrawing its filing seeking clearance from the Antitrust Division of the U.S.

Key Dates:

1911: The Fine Cotton Spinners and Doublers Association acquires 38,000 acres in the area surrounding Scott, Mississippi.
1919: The Delta and Pine Land Company (D&PL) is acquired, giving control of three plantations to a single entity.
1988: Murray Robinson joins D&PL as executive vice-president.
1995: D&M International, LLC is formed by Monsanto Co. and D&PL to market genetically altered cottonseed internationally.
1996: D&PL begins selling insect-resistant cottonseed in the United States.
1998: A merger between Monsanto and D&PL is announced.
1999: The merger with Monsanto collapses.
2000: Monsanto agrees to a $50 billion merger with Pharmacia & Upjohn Inc.; dissatisfied with an $81 million settlement it received after its own failed merger, D&PL files suit against Monsanto for $1 billion in damages.

Department of Justice for the D&PL merger, Monsanto agreed to a $50 billion merger, completed in March 2000, with Pharmacia & Upjohn Inc., igniting D&PL's furor. "For a year and a half, we exercised every reasonable effort and a tremendous amount of time, energy, and money to make this merger happen," a D&PL executive was quoted as saying in the January 24, 2000 issue of *Feedstuffs*. Monsanto paid D&PL the $81 million required by the merger agreement because it had terminated the contract, but D&PL wanted far more in compensation. The company filed a lawsuit against Monsanto in January 2000 demanding compensation for damaging its relationship with its customers and for the diversion of management's time. D&PL, in the January 24, 2000 issue of *Feedstuffs*, demanded "not less than $1 billion in compensatory damages, as well as punitive damages in an amount to be proved at trial."

In the wake of the litigious activity, D&PL and Monsanto continued to do business together. The benefits to each party were too great to sever all ties. By 2001, thanks to the affiliation between the two companies, D&PL enjoyed a stranglehold on the U.S. market for genetically altered cottonseed, controlling 85 percent of the market. The company's dominance in the U.S. market was impressive, but its progress overseas provided perhaps the most encouraging news as the 21st century began. Murray Robinson's vision of turning D&PL into a multinational concern had materialized, adding decided vigor to the company's financial health. D&PL sold its conventional and genetically altered cottonseeds in 16 foreign countries by the time the company's 90th anniversary arrived, gleaning the fruits of international expansion. By 2001, international sales accounted for 10 percent of the company's total revenues, and were increasing at a 35 percent annual clip. D&PL derived the majority of its international sales from countries where it maintained a presence, such as Argentina, Australia, Brazil, South Africa, Tur-

key, and China. For example, in China, the world's third largest cotton producer, D&PL's cottonseeds were used by more than one million farmers through joint venture companies in two of the country's 23 provinces. Thanks to the boost in sales provided by its involvement in foreign markets and to the advent of genetically altered seeds, the company recorded average annual sales growth of 20 percent between 1997 and 2000. Earnings recorded a decidedly more robust pace of growth, increasing at an average annual rate of 142 percent. Revenues by the end of 2000 reached more than $350 million. Before D&PL's genetically altered cottonseeds entered U.S. and foreign markets, annual revenues were $190 million.

D&PL's lawsuit against Monsanto extended into 2002. If successful in its court case, the company expected to make a tremendous financial gain; regardless of the court proceedings, however, D&PL presided as the country's preeminent producer of cottonseed. In the years ahead, D&PL promised to figure prominently in the biotechnology industry, its market position posing a formidable threat to other competitors. The company had secured control of the U.S. market, leaving it to apply the same tight grip on foreign markets.

Principal Subsidiaries

D&M International, LLC; Deltapine Australia Pty. Ltd.; D&PL South Africa, Inc.; Turk Deltapine, Inc.

Principal Competitors

Pioneer Hi-Bred International, Inc.; Savia, S.A. de C.V.; Syngenta AG.

Further Reading

Androshick, Julie, "Seeds of Doubt," *Forbes,* September 22, 1997, p. 268.
"D&PL: A Leader in the Cotton Revolution," *Agri Marketing,* September 2003, p. 46.
"DPL Acquires Remaining Interest in D&M International from Pharmacia," *Feedstuffs,* June 10, 2002, p. 23.
"DPL Announces Transition Plan," *Feedstuffs,* June 24, 2002, p. 6.
"DPL Realigns Management, Positions," *Feedstuffs,* September 10, 2001, p. 8.
"DPL Wins Favorable Opinions Against Monsanto," *Feedstuffs,* December 3, 2001, p. 8.
Hicks, Ed, "Delta Expands Scott Cotton Facility," *Memphis Business Journal,* November 23, 2001, p. 9.
Howie, Michael, "Delta Land & Pine Sues Monsanto for Breach of Contract," *Feedstuffs,* January 24, 2000, p. 5.
McDonald, Duff, "Ewe and Your Money: How to Profit from Discoveries," *Money,* April 1997, p. 71.
Northway, Wally, "D&PL Records Loss, Signs Deal," *Mississippi Business Journal,* January 13, 2003, p. 8.
Sewell, Tim, "Delta Land and Pine to Foster New Growth Through Reorganization into Divisions," *Memphis Business Journal,* April 7, 1997, p. 8.
Sikora, Martin, "Trying to Recoup the Cost of Lost Opportunities," *Mergers & Acquisitions Journal,* March 2000, p. 12.
Taylor, Gary, "Delta Rich Cotton Pickings," *Chemistry and Industry,* July 15, 2002, p. 9.
"This Cotton Is No Puffball," *Business Week,* June 11, 2001, p. 119.

—Jeffrey L. Covell

Deutsche Börse AG

Neue Börsenstraße 1
60487 Frankfurt/Main
Germany
Telephone: +49-69-2101-0
Fax: +49-69-2101-2005
Web site: http://www.deutsche-boerse.com

Public Company
Incorporated: 1993
Employees: 3,318
Sales: EUR 1.1 billion (2002)
Stock Exchanges: Frankfurt
Ticker Symbol: DB1
NAIC: 523210 Securities and Commodity Exchanges

Deutsche Börse AG operates a range of trading institutions out of Frankfurt, Germany's financial hub. It vies with the London Stock Exchange and Euronext, a French-Belgian-Dutch exchange, for control of Europe's capital markets. Deutsche Börse offers trading in cash securities on the Frankfurt Stock Exchange and trading in futures and options through the Eurex market, which it co-owns with the Swiss exchange. The company is notable for its use of technology, in particular the electronic trading platform Xetra, to achieve efficient trading. Deutsche Börse also offers settlement and clearing services through its subsidiary Clearstream and market information through the DAX index as well as through private information services for professional investors. Deutsche Börse's broad umbrella of services and vertically integrated structure allow it to play a part in nearly all stages of the trading process.

CEO Werner Seifert is credited with transforming the Frankfurt Exchange from a provincial market to a major player on the European stage. The Frankfurt Exchange most recently rose to prominence in the mid-1990s through a dynamic program of technological improvements, mergers, and partnerships. But Frankfurt's status as an international financial center has waxed and waned many times over the centuries since the exchange was founded in the 16th century.

From Medieval Market to Capital Source for Europe's Dynasties

Frankfurt has a long history as a center for trading and commerce. Emperor Ludwig the German gave the city the right to hold an annual fair back in the mid-ninth century, and after 1330 the city was allowed to hold a second fair in the spring as well. Frankfurt grew in importance as a regional center for trading in various commodities. In the early 16th century Martin Luther referred to the city as the "silver and gold hole" of the German Empire. Protestant merchants from France and the Netherlands came to Frankfurt to escape religious persecution and contributed to the establishment of wholesale commerce and banking institutions. People from all over Europe exchanged goods and money in Frankfurt. However, there was little trading in credit or currency beyond what was immediately related to commodity exchange.

The official founding of the Frankfurt Stock Exchange is generally considered to have occurred in 1585 when a group of merchants met at the fair and agreed on uniform exchange rates for the many different kinds of coins that came to the fair from surrounding regions. Up until that meeting, currency exchange was quite chaotic: exchange rates fluctuated arbitrarily and swindling and usury were common. Now that rates were agreed upon, trading in bills of exchange began as an activity separate from commodity trading.

For over a century, merchants met to set rates in an open field in front of the Frankfurt town hall. In 1694, the meetings moved to the Großer Braunfels building at Liebfrauenberg, one of the most important and spacious buildings in the city. The Exchange Rules and Regulations were enacted in 1682, creating an official structure for exchange activities.

Near the end of the 17th century, occasional trading in promissory notes and bonds began and non-merchants were now able to take part in exchange activities. In 1707 the directors of the Frankfurt Stock Exchange met and formed the Deputies of the Merchants as the official body representing trade in the city. In 1808 the Deputies were formed into the Chamber of Commerce and the stock exchange came under their umbrella as a public sector institution.

Company Perspectives:

Our mission is to improve the efficiency of markets. Our objective is to become the preeminent exchange organization. We will provide access to the most attractive securities and derivatives markets. Being the only fully integrated exchange organization worldwide, we offer a full range of trading, clearing, settlement, custody, information and infrastructure services at lowest costs. We will organize new markets and thereby improve their liquidity. We will provide first-class services targeted at intermediaries and vendors, investors and issuers worldwide. We initiate and support improvements of the regulatory framework and are open for valuable partnerships.

To achieve these goals we build on our uniquely skilled professionals and the power and reliability of our fully integrated electronic systems. Thus, we create superior shareholder value.

Trading in government bonds developed in the last decades of the 18th century. In 1779 the German Emperor in Vienna needed to borrow an unprecedented sum denominated in the millions. Bankhaus Bethmann arranged the loan by issuing fractional bonds to many small lenders, who then gained the right to share in some of the regular interest earnings. It soon became common to arrange large bond issues in Frankfurt on the precedent set by Bankhaus Bethmann.

Bankhaus Rothschild in Frankfurt became the leading capital intermediary for the European dynasties in the early 19th century. Frankfurt rivaled London and Paris as a center for international capital. In 1843 the exchange outgrew its meeting space and built a new headquarters, the Alte Börse or Old Stock Exchange, on the Paulsplatz. Before long, this building became cramped as well, so in 1879 the Exchange moved to a prestigious new building, the Neue Börse or New Stock Exchange.

With the advent of the Industrial Revolution, more and more companies realized it made sense to finance costly projects by issuing shares. The first company share traded in Frankfurt was a participating certificate in the Austrian National Bank issued in 1820. In general, however, Frankfurt shied away from share trading and remained involved mainly with secure government bonds and funds. While other European exchanges welcomed stock corporations, Frankfurt gained the reputation of "solid Frankfurt" and set the standard for both foreign and domestic bonds. The exchange expanded enormously in the mid-19th century. Frankfurt listed many U.S. bonds during the American Civil War and contributed significantly to the financing of the Union cause.

Frankfurt finally recognized the importance of share trading in the later 19th century. During the "Gründerjahre" boom of 1870–74 about 860 stock corporations were founded in Prussia alone. Meanwhile, Berlin had just become the capital of the new German Empire and was using its political importance to steal some of Frankfurt's financial clout. Frankfurt put up a fight, relying on its strong international contacts, but the city's financial leaders finally conceded that the exchange needed to move beyond its focus on bonds and government securities. Frankfurt

began campaigning to attract industry share listings and became a true stock exchange. The 1896 Stock Exchange Act established a uniform organization for Germany's exchanges, of which there were 29. Frankfurt was the second most prominent exchange in Germany after Berlin.

World Wars and Reconstruction

World War I severely damaged Frankfurt's standing as an international capital center. Germans sold their foreign shares and invested almost all capital in domestic government bonds. By the end of the war, Frankfurt had lost most of its international connections. Activity rebounded somewhat during the 1920s, but the worldwide financial crisis came in 1930, bringing runaway inflation and huge asset losses.

In 1933 the Nazis took over and centralized the nation's economic policy. The Frankfurt Stock Exchange was merged with the Mannheim Stock Exchange and the number of exchanges nationwide was reduced from 21 to nine. Under the stringent Nazi economic regime, free trade was suffocated. The majority of capital assets was directed to benefit the war economy. Frankfurt played only a minor role in financial transactions. The Neue Börse building was damaged in an allied air raid in 1944 and meetings had to be held in the basement.

After the collapse of the Nazi regime in 1945, the exchange closed for a few months and reopened in September. The Neue Börse was rebuilt. Frankfurt gradually came to play a major role in postwar reconstruction. In 1956 Germans were allowed to buy foreign securities once again and Frankfurt could reestablish some international connections. The Frankfurt exchange provided much of the capital for the "economic miracle" that made the Federal Republic of Germany a world leader economically. The Berlin exchange played a mostly ceremonial role at this time because of its awkward political situation. Frankfurt and Düsseldorf hosted the country's leading exchanges.

Reforming a Conservative Market: 1980s

After World War II Frankfurt once again became home to the nation's leading banks and financial institutions. But Germany's conservative financial culture kept the Frankfurt Stock Exchange from gaining much notice internationally. Much of Germany's postwar reconstruction was financed through close partnerships between banks and companies. Afraid of hostile takeovers, most companies preferred to raise capital through bonds or bank loans rather than share issues. Investors, in turn, put their money largely into bonds and savings accounts with predictable yields. Banks were the largest shareholders in the majority of companies; small investors were rare. An oft-quoted statistic was that the average German family spent more money annually on flowers than on shares.

In 1982 less than 500 companies were publicly listed in Germany. The election of the center-right candidate Helmut Kohl as Chancellor in 1982 triggered a rise in the market on expectations that he would implement business-friendly policies. Seventy companies went public between 1983 and 1987 and the Frankfurt Stock Exchange experienced a bull market through about 1986. Still, the exchange lacked volume and diversity compared to New York, Tokyo, or London.

Key Dates:

1585: Frankfurt merchants meet to establish uniform exchange rates.
1682: The Exchange Rules and Regulations are enacted, providing an official administration for the exchange.
1779: Bond trading develops when Bankhaus Bethmann arranges a loan for the Emperor.
1820: The Frankfurt exchange sells its first share in a stock corporation.
1843: The Frankfurt exchange builds its own headquarters, the Alte Börse.
1879: A new headquarters, the Neue Börse, is opened.
1933: The Nazis take power and Frankfurt's international financial connections are stifled.
1956: Germans are allowed to buy foreign securities again; Frankfurt helps finance postwar reconstruction.
1985: New legislation starts to make the Frankfurt exchange more efficient and more attractive to foreign investors.
1990: A German futures and options exchange, the Deutsche TerminBörse, is opened.
1993: Deutsche Börse is created as a holding company for the Frankfurt Stock Exchange and other entities; Werner Seifert becomes CEO.
1997: The Neuer Markt and the Xetra electronic trading system are introduced.
1998: The German and Swiss derivatives exchanges merge to form Eurex.
2000: A merger with the London stock exchange is announced but falls apart.
2001: Deutsche Börse completes an initial public offering.
2002: The Neuer Markt is shut down.

efforts played a role in the abolition of the stock exchange turnover tax starting in 1991.

The Frankfurt Stock Exchange survived crashes in October and November 1987 and increased its status as the nation's leading market. It accounted for 70 percent of share turnover in Germany in mid-1988, up from 50 percent a year before. In 1988 the exchange introduced the DAX, a blue-chip index for about 30 companies. The DAX replaced the FAZ index, published by the newspaper Frankfurter Allgemeine Zeitung, as the standard tool for tracking the stock market.

A prominent voice for change was Rolf Breuer, a director at Deutsche Bank. He told the *Economist* in 1989, "our stock-exchange structure is primitive, old-fashioned and customer-averse." In particular, he asserted the need for an international options and futures market in Frankfurt. Trading in derivatives was traditionally viewed as a slightly disreputable activity in Germany and as a result trading in options was hemmed in by legal restrictions. But by January 1990 the necessary legal changes had been made and the Deutsche TerminBörse (DTB) opened. The DTB was a screen-based futures and options exchange. Critics said that the electronic system would not work in hectic market conditions, but the DTB successfully handled 34.8 million contracts in 1992, up from 6.8 million in its first year of operation.

The Frankfurt Stock Exchange also advanced in its use of technology. The IBIS system was introduced in April 1991. IBIS was a screen-based interbank system offering quick access to prices on the most heavily traded stocks. After a year IBIS accounted for about a third of turnover in the 30 most frequently traded stocks. "Finanzplatz Deutschland," the ideal of Germany as a financial center for a unified Europe, was gradually taking shape.

A Unified Exchange: 1992–97

In 1992 the German finance ministry presented a plan expressing support for a single unified stock exchange in Germany and for increased transparency and regulation. The unified exchange came closer to reality with the creation of Deutsche Börse on January 1, 1993. Deutsche Börse was a holding company for the Frankfurt Stock Exchange, the derivatives market Deutsche TerminBörse and the settlements organization Kassenverein. The seven regional German exchanges owned a 10 percent share in the company but also continued an independent existence. Frankfurt-based banks and brokers owned the majority of the new entity. Rolf Breuer became chairman and Rudiger von Rosen, former managing director of the Frankfurt Stock Exchange, was named CEO.

The establishment of Deutsche Börse set a pattern of vertical integration for the Frankfurt exchange. As Breuer said in the *Financial Times* in 1993, "Right from the beginning of the process of placing an order, to the end where the order is wound up, the client need only deal with one organization. The whole process has been brought under one roof—for derivatives as well as for securities—something you don't find in London, Paris or New York." Frankfurt was also a leader in terms of technological sophistication and efficiency: trades were settled within 48 hours compared with up to three weeks in London.

By the mid-1980s financial leaders were taking a serious look at the need to rejuvenate share trading in Germany and win back the listings that were being lost to London and Paris. Trading in Germany remained confusing and expensive compared with other European exchanges. The eight regional German exchanges published different prices for the same shares. A stock market turnover tax made investing more expensive than in neighboring nations. The regulatory environment was simultaneously restrictive and permissive; government regulations limited the types of trades that could be carried out, companies were not required to disclose much financial information, and certain standard laws such as a prohibition on insider trading did not exist in Germany. Another drawback was that the exchange was only open for floor trading from 11:30 a.m. to 1:30 p.m. each day. Banks traded with each other after hours over the phone.

The Kohl regime responded to the concerns of financial reformers. In 1985 zero-coupon bonds and floating-rate notes were permitted. By 1987 foreign-owned banks were allowed to lead manage German bond issues and participate in government bond syndicates. The Federation of German Stock Exchanges, led by Rudiger von Rosen, was established in 1987 to represent the interests of the eight regional exchanges. The federation's

The exchange still faced its traditional chronic challenges, however: an underdeveloped investor culture in Germany and an inadequate regulatory regime that repulsed foreign investors. Breuer recruited a new CEO to bring a spirit of change to the Börse: Werner Seifert. Seifert was a Swiss national with a background at management consultant firm McKinsey & Co. He had no expertise in stock exchanges, but he had an aggressive approach that promised to shake up Germany's conservative financial culture. He disdained national loyalties and planned to pursue whatever route would achieve efficient capital markets and low-cost trades.

Frankfurt's regulatory regime finally caught up with contemporary standards when the Financial Markets Promotion Act was passed in 1994. Insider trading was now a crime for the first time. Interest in investing was still low, but the younger generation, which was poised to inherit significant amounts of money soon, had the potential to energize private investing. The Börse was hoping that the initial public offering (IPO) of Deutsche Telekom, scheduled for November 1996, would attract new investors. The IPO proved to be the second largest in the world, raising more than $13 billion. However, the company promised so many dividends and incentives that an investment in its stock was almost as secure as buying a bond. Still, the IPO was seen as a strong step toward the development of a stockholding culture in Germany.

Becoming an International Force: 1997–2003

Since taking over as CEO, Seifert had been laying the ground for technological improvements at Deutsche Börse and looking ahead to the planned introduction of the euro. His initiatives took off in 1997. In March of that year the Neuer Markt was established as a European alternative to the NASDAQ, intended to attract small companies in growth industries such as technology. Companies had to fulfill stringent requirements to be listed on the Neuer Markt, including providing quarterly reports and publishing accounts according to international standards. The new market took off with a flurry of IPOs and rapid share gains. It also attracted new investors to share trading. By 2001, over 20 percent of Germans owned equity funds and shares.

In November 1997 Deutsche Börse introduced Xetra, an electronic trading platform intended to replace IBIS. Seifert, a jazz enthusiast, composed and performed a song on piano to mark the occasion. Xetra automatically matched buyers and sellers of more heavily traded stocks. It cost less and was more transparent than floor trading.

With the introduction of the euro looming in 1999, financial analysts began speculating about the advent of a single pan-European trading system. Seifert worked to position Deutsche Börse as a leading player in any mergers and consolidations that might occur. In late 1997 the Börse launched a campaign to win back some of the futures trading that was dominated by London. The following year Deutsche Börse merged its derivatives subsidiary DTB with the Swiss derivatives exchange Soffex to create the Eurex exchange. In less than a year Eurex had attracted 95 percent of trading in Germany's Bund government bond futures back from Liffe, the London derivatives market. The move demonstrated for the first time that Frankfurt was able to challenge London's financial supremacy.

The developments of 1997 and 1998 put Frankfurt in a position to negotiate a partnership with the London Stock Exchange. In July 1998 the two exchanges announced their intention to create a common electronic trading platform for the top European stocks. Soon other European exchanges came on board, forming the eight-member European Exchange Alliance. But visions of a pan-European exchange proved to be difficult to achieve in reality. The various exchanges could not agree on whose trading technology to use and many of them still felt strong national loyalties. The alliance never achieved more than a few lukewarm agreements.

Mergers and takeovers became the preferred tool for working toward European consolidation. Deutsche Börse united its settlement and clearing unit with the Luxembourg-based Cedel in late 1999 to create Clearstream. The Börse was attracted by the efficient technology Cedel used in clearing. In March 2000 the Paris, Amsterdam, and Brussels exchanges merged into an entity known as Euronext, which became a strong rival to Deutsche Börse in the battle for control of Europe's capital markets. A few months later Deutsche Börse and the London Stock Exchange countered with their own merger plan. The two exchanges announced in May that they would combine to form the largest exchange in Europe, to be known as iX for International Exchange. It was a measure of how far the Frankfurt exchange had come that Deutsche Börse would control 50 percent of the merged entity and Werner Seifert would be CEO. But the deal fell apart suddenly in September when the London exchange announced it was withdrawing from the merger to concentrate on fending off a hostile bid that had just been launched by OM Gruppen, an exchange operator in Stockholm. The London-Frankfurt deal had been beset by difficulties well before it fell apart. The two sides never agreed to use a common regulatory system and traders on either side did not like the proposal of locating the blue-chip market in London and the growth market (Neuer Markt) in Frankfurt. Some also criticized Seifert's abrasive negotiating manner.

After the merger fell apart Deutsche Börse moved ahead with plans for a public listing. The company did not exclude the possibility of acquiring the London Exchange outright with the funds it would raise. The IPO occurred on February 5, 2001, and raised $930 million with a sale of 27 percent of Deutsche Börse's shares. For the time being, a union with the London Exchange remained on the back burner. Instead, Deutsche Börse used the capital from its share issue to acquire its partner's stake in the settlement firm Clearstream in April 2002. The acquisition allowed Deutsche Börse to further exploit synergies among its subsidiaries operating at various stages of the share trading process.

In the fall of 2002 Deutsche Börse announced that the Neuer Markt would be shut down. After a period of astounding growth the market had been hurt even more severely than its competitors when the technology boom fizzled. The value of companies listed had dropped more than 96 percent since the high in March 2000. In addition, several scandals had emerged in connection with the companies listed on the Neuer Markt. A new market segment known as the Prime Standard was created to carry on the stringent standards for corporate disclosure associated with the Neuer Markt.

After the economic slowdown that started in 2001, trading activity decreased and revenues from the trading of cash securities went down. The Eurex exchange, on the other hand, was bringing in large profits as investors sought to hedge their risk with derivative contracts. Deutsche Börse continued efforts to attract listings and cut the costs of trading. In March 2003 the company launched the TecDAX as a blue-chip index for technology shares. The company also created a central counterparty to act as a reliable intermediary in share trades. Deutsche Börse was also looking to establish an American presence and set up a partnership with the Chicago Board of Trade Clearing Corporation to lay the ground for launching a futures and options exchange in the United States. By 2003, Deutsche Börse had consolidated its position as one of the top exchange operators in Europe and was starting to extend its reach to other continents.

Principal Subsidiaries

Cedel International S.A. (Luxembourg); Clearstream International S.A. (Luxembourg); Filinks S.A.S. (France); Deutsche Börse Systems AF; Deutsche Börse Systems Inc. (U.S.A.); entory AG; Xlaunch AG; projects IT-ProjektBörse GmbH; Eurex Zurich AG (Switzerland; 49.97%); Eurex Frankfurt AG (49.97%); Eurex Clearing AG (49.97%); Deutsche Börse Computershare GmbH (51%); Infobolsa S.A. (Spain; 50%).

Principal Competitors

Euronext; London Stock Exchange Limited.

Further Reading

Andrews, Edmund L., "City of London (and Frankfurt)," *New York Times*, May 4, 2000, p. C1.
——, "London and Frankfurt Stock Exchanges Form Alliance," *New York Times*, July 8, 1998, p. D4.
Barber, Tony, "Borse's Innovative Chief Strikes the Right Note," *Financial Times (London)*, March 23, 1999, p. 4.
——, "Market Maestro: Man in the News Werner Seifert," *Financial Times (London)*, April 22, 2000, p. 17.
"Beating a Retreat," *Economist*, September 16, 2000.
Benoit, Bertrand, and Alex Skorecki, "Neuer Markt Closure," *Financial Times (London)*, September 27, 2002, p. 19.
Bowley, Graham, "Runaway Success Story," *Financial Times (London)*, June 24, 1998, p. 4.
Fairlamb, David, "Battle of the Bourses," *Business Week*, October 28, 2002, p. 68.
——, "Deutsche Borse Grows Rich—And Hungry," *Business Week*, February 19, 2001, p. 55.
——, "Slugfest Over Europe's Stock Exchanges," *Business Week*, November 19, 2001, p. 62.
"Finanzplatz Deutschland Sings to Big Bang's Tune," *Economist*, June 13, 1987, p. 83.
Fisher, Andrew, "Borse Bonus: A New German Market Is Aimed at Smaller, Rapid Growth Companies," *Financial Times (London)*, March 4, 1997, p. 12.
——, "Frankfurt Exchange Adds New Dimension," *Financial Times (London)*, November 28, 1997, p. 31.
"Frankfurt's Impatient Maestro," *Economist*, December 11, 1999.
"Germany Moves to Start Central Stock Exchange," *New York Times*, October 8, 1992, p. D2.
Greenhouse, Steven, "Stocks Fall Sharply Abroad," *New York Times*, November 11, 1987, p. D1.
Kent, C.H., *European Stock Exchange Handbook*, London: Noyes Data Corporation, 1973, pp. 179–81.
Landler, Mark, "German Technology Stock Market to Be Dissolved," *New York Times*, September 27, 2002, p. W1.
Luce, Ed, "A Dramatic and Unforeseen Coup," *Financial Times (London)*, October 25, 1999, p. 3.
"Plucked in Frankfurt," *Economist*, March 20, 1993, p. 82.
Simonian, Haig, "Better Trading Conditions Put Frankfurt First Among Equals," *Financial Post (Toronto)*, July 7, 1988, pp. 2–20.
Stevenson, Merril, "Finanzplatz Deutschland," *Economist*, December 16, 1989, p. 19.
Waller, David, "Germany Takes Stock," *Financial Times (London)*, May 7, 1993, p. 14.
——, "Survey of Germany," *Financial Times (London)*, October 26, 1992, p. 1.
Wassener, Bettina, "Doing Well in Troubled Times: Deutsche Borse," *Financial Times (London)*, June 10, 2003, p. 4.
"Werner Seifert," *Business Week*, June 19, 2000, p. 166.
"Werner's Silo," *Economist*, December 15, 2001.

—Sarah Ruth Lorenz

Dick's Sporting Goods, Inc.

200 Industry Drive
Pittsburgh, Pennsylvania 15275
U.S.A.
Telephone: (412) 809-0100
Fax: (412) 809-0724
Web site: http://www.dickssportinggoods.com

Public Company
Founded: 1948 as Dick's Clothing and Sporting Goods
Employees: 9,000
Sales: $1.05 billion (2002)
Stock Exchanges: New York
Ticker Symbol: DKS
NAIC: 451110 Sporting Goods Stores

Dick's Sporting Goods, Inc. is a chain of sporting goods superstores offering equipment for every kind of individual and team sport, as well as such outdoor activities as hunting, fishing, and hiking. The company also sells fitness equipment, and sports apparel and footwear. Within the large superstore format, a wide variety and availability of merchandise is displayed in distinct, easy to locate specialty stores-within-stores. Dick's supplies name brand merchandise from Nike, Adidas, Columbia Sportswear, and Calloway, as well as its private label brands, including Ativa apparel for women and Walter Hagen apparel for men. Dick's Sporting Goods stores provide patrons an opportunity to test equipment onsite, offering golf driving ranges, running tracks, and cement inline skating areas, for example. Dick's operates more than 135 stores located in two dozen states in the Northeast, Mid-Atlantic, South, and Midwest.

Making a Father and Son's Dreams Real

Richard "Dick" Stack founded Dick's Clothing and Sporting Goods in 1948 at the age of 18. The idea for the store arose while Stack was employed at an Army and Navy supply store in Binghamton, New York. The storeowner asked Stack if he thought the store should offer fishing gear. Stack did, and formulated a comprehensive merchandising plan on his own time, losing sleep for several nights. He was stunned to hear the storeowner's brutal rejection that Stack "would never make a good merchant." Stack sought solace from his grandmother who, upon hearing the story, took $300 in cash from her cookie jar and gave it to him, encouraging the pursuit of his dream. An avid fisherman, Stack used the money to open a small bait-and-tackle shop. A decade later, at the encouragement of his loyal patrons, Stack began to sell a broad spectrum of sporting goods.

Dick Stack's son Edward worked at the store as a teenager, but did not join the business until 1977, when his father's emergency heart surgery required the younger Stack to become involved. A certified public accountant at the time, Edward Stack was interested in expanding the business. A second store opened in Binghamton by the time the elder Stack retired in 1984. Edward Stack became president and CEO; he intended to transform the business into a large chain of superstores. By 1986 Dick's Clothing and Sporting Goods offered a complete line of sporting goods, including athletic apparel, footwear, and sports equipment. Dick's developed several private label brands: Adirondack Trading Company for casual clothing, Northeast Outfitters for hunting and work apparel and boots, DSX and DSXT for cycling apparel, and Steve Hill and Stone Hill Clubhouse for golf apparel and shoes.

The Dick's Clothing and Sporting Goods concept involved a warehouse size store, 35,000 to 45,000 square feet, with not only a wide selection of goods, but deep offerings within each category. With high sales volume Dick's offered merchandise at lower prices than its competitors. The big box exterior of the store was countered by a warm interior, with soft lighting and wood accents. The store itself encompassed many smaller specialty shops, with each main category organized as its own business and each with a distinctive atmosphere and identity, including signage, graphics, and colors. For instance, the Pro Shop offered golf merchandise in a wood paneled background while the Sportsman's Lodge displayed hunting and fishing merchandise in an artificial log cabin. The Dick's Outlet store-within-a-store offered clearance and closeout merchandise on basic display racks. Dick's offered patrons the opportunity to test the merchandise, placing a real running track in the shoe department, a driving range at the Pro Shop, and an archery range at the Sportsman's Lodge.

Company Perspectives:

Mission: To be the #1 sports and fitness specialty retailer for all athletes and outdoor enthusiasts through the relentless improvement of everything we do.

The expansion of Dick's as a chain of sporting goods stores started with the opening of two stores each in Syracuse and Rochester, New York. The company opened the first Buffalo area store, in Cheektowaga, in March 1992. Two stores opened in the Hartford, Connecticut area, followed by another store in western Massachusetts, and a store in Erie, Pennsylvania. The company's focus of growth involved small and medium-size cities, such as those in upstate New York, where the company opened stores in Albany in both 1993 and 1994.

The company relocated its headquarters to Pittsburgh in July 1994, coinciding with the opening of four stores in the area ranging in size from 32,000 square feet to 70,000 square feet. Stack chose Pittsburgh because of its access to airports and its national sports teams and as an area of extensive growth for the company, with a local population of outdoor enthusiasts. At the end of 1994, Dick's counted 22 stores in its chain in 11 markets in Pennsylvania, Connecticut, New York, and Massachusetts.

Growth accelerated in 1995 as Dick's opened several stores in major markets nearly simultaneously. The plan allowed for effective use of advertising dollars. That year the company opened six stores in the Cleveland, Ohio area, including one 60,000-square-foot store. Other stores in Ohio opened in Cincinnati and Youngstown. Dick's planned to open a total of 14 stores in Ohio, taking advantage of the vacuum created by the dissolution of Herman's World of Sports stores. Dick's opened three stores in the Baltimore area in October, including the 60,000-square-foot Hunt Valley store which acted as anchor store for the shopping mall. Dick's preferred shopping mall locations with larger stores, at 60,000 to 70,000 square feet, acting as anchors. Two additional stores opened in the Buffalo area and another two opened in Pittsburgh in 1995. Dick's funded expansion with private investment from Carrefour, a French retailer, and Donaldson, Lufkin and Jenrette, a New York underwriter.

The rapid pace of growth continued in 1996. The company opened four stores in the Philadelphia area, including one 70,000-square-foot store. Four stores opened in the Detroit suburbs, with additional stores in the planning stages. Other new stores were located in existing markets. By January 1997, Dick's operated 51 stores; industry insiders estimated company sales at $10 million to $12 million per store, in contrast to The Sports Authority, with sales of $7.7 million per store.

Midwest Expansion, Northeast Reinforcement: Late 1990s

Expansion continued at a steady pace during the late 1990s, with Dick's opening ten stores in 1997, nine in 1998, and 13 in 1999, for a total of 83 stores in operation at the end of 1999. Dick's continued to open stores in Pennsylvania, New York, Ohio, Delaware, and other Northeast markets. New markets in the Midwest included Lexington and Louisville, Kentucky; Clarksville, Indiana, near Louisville; and Champaign, Illinois.

At a new store in Columbia, Maryland, Nike introduced its new Women's Concept Shop, making Dick's the first sporting goods store to test the idea. The shop addressed the perception that athletic stores catered to men, though women accounted for half of shoppers at sporting goods stores, purchasing goods for their families as well as themselves. The Nike Women's Concept Shop attempted to address the needs of female athletes by expanding the selection of merchandise available to women.

In January 1999 Dick's successfully launched its Internet site on Super Bowl Sunday. The site was modeled on actual stores with merchandise organized in specialty shops. Customers could search by sport, brand, and price and ship to multiple addresses in one shopping trip by designating address book entries for each item purchased. The site performed well technologically and received positive consumer response in terms of interest and revenues, obtaining orders from all 50 states. During the first six months Dick's expanded the online product list to 34,000 units and the number of specialty shops from eight to 27. The company re-launched the web site in November, having changed the name of the company to Dick's Sporting Goods, and added name brand merchandise from Nike, Titleist, Adidas, North Face, and Columbia Sportswear. A $15 million promotional campaign supported the relaunch, offering coupons and seeking a national customer base with advertising on ESPN, CNN, and The Learning Channel.

In December 1999 *Chain Store Age Executive* named Edward Stack Retail Entrepreneur of the Year. With 83 stores in 15 states in the Northeast, Mid-Atlantic, and Midwest, Dick's Sporting Goods experienced a higher rate of merchandise turnover than the industry norm. The company reported $728.3 million in revenues for 1999, garnering a net income of $11.2 million.

To accommodate continued growth of the chain and the addition of online sales, Dick's opened a new $20 million distribution center in Pittsburgh in February 2000. The 383,000-square-foot facility provided space for double the capacity required by its existing stores. With 34 shipping and receiving doors, Dick's contracted with a trucking company to service distribution with 100 new drivers. Dick's implemented a rapid computer sorting system and, in 2001, a group of integrated merchandise management applications for state-of-the-art analytic reporting, promotional price management, and advanced allocation and planning.

The initial success of the company's web site stalled in 2000. First Dick's needed to change the web site address to dickssportinggoods.com because family Internet filters prevented access to the site. While the earlier advertising campaign succeeded in increasing traffic to the site, the coupons offered cut too deeply into profits. By April 2001 the company decided to abandon active management of the web site because it had become unprofitable. The company then outsourced handling of the site to Global Sports Interactive (GSI), which specialized in online retailing of sporting goods. Through a ten-year agreement Dick's licensed the company name to GSI in return for royalty payments on goods sold online; Dick's opted to receive stock in lieu of cash.

Key Dates:

1948: Dick Stack starts his own bait-and-tackle shop in Binghamton, New York.
1958: The small shop becomes a full-fledged sporting goods store, known as Dick's Clothing and Sporting Goods.
1984: After Dick Stack retires, his son Edward becomes CEO and president; plans expansion of sporting goods superstore concept.
1992: Dick's begins expansion outside Binghamton area.
1994: Dick's relocates to Pittsburgh; the company operates 22 stores in four states.
1996: Over 50 stores are in operation, generating an estimated $10 million in sales per store.
1999: *Chain Store Age Executive* names Edward Stack Retail Entrepreneur of the Year; company name is changed to Dick's Sporting Goods.
2001: Sales exceed $1 billion with more than 130 stores.
2002: Dick's Sporting Goods becomes a public company.

Venture Capital and Public Stock Offering Funding Growth: Early 2000s

With investment from Vulcan Northwest Venture Capital, Dick's accelerated its pace of growth, opening a total of 22 stores in 2000 and 20 stores in 2001. In addition to expansion in existing markets, Dick's extended its reach farther west, to Iowa, Wisconsin, and Missouri, and south, to North and South Carolina, Alabama, and Georgia. The company tended to locate stores in smaller cities, rather than the more competitive major metropolitan markets. For instance, Dick's chose to open a store in Macon, Georgia, rather than in the Atlanta area. Dick's clustered stores to make effective use of advertising spending. Dick's entered the Kansas City market in the fall of 2000 with a spectacular grand opening of five stores simultaneously on one Sunday. New specialty shop features included the provision of hunting and fishing licenses at the Sportsman's Lodge and a swing speed analyzer to assist customers in selecting golf clubs at the Pro Shop.

Dick's initiated a number of marketing initiatives to attract and retain customers. The "Scorecard" gave rebates to loyal customers based on their record of purchases; by August 2002 the company counted over one million participants. A new call service provided in-store telephone call boxes to request sales assistance from the fitting rooms. Dick's sought to serve families better by adding more children's merchandise and expanding the women's department to nearly triple the amount of equipment, apparel, and footwear. The company introduced casual footwear from Eastland, Clark's, and Columbia Sportswear. Dick's launched two new private label brands of apparel, Ativa for women and Walter Hagen for men.

In February 2002 Dick's opened a new store in the Pittsburgh area that would serve as a prototype for future stores. The two-story, 80,000-square-foot store featured 60-foot-high ceilings and red brick walls to mimic the feel of a sports stadium. The store refined all of the features of existing stores, such as well-defined specialty stores with unique signage. Televisions displayed instructional videos and sporting events relevant to that area of the store. The store incorporated a new emphasis on families, with lifestyle photography that featured kids, such as members of a little league team sitting in a dugout, and everyday athletes—not just celebrities—participating in sports and exercise. Also, old photographs of Dick Stack at the original Binghamton store were enlarged and displayed in the store.

Other new store openings in 2002 included the company's first Nebraska store, which opened in Omaha in May. A total of 15 new stores planned for 2002 included units in Wichita, Kansas; Lansing, Michigan; Worcester, Massachusetts; Normal, Illinois; and Evansville, Indiana. By the time of the company's initial offering of stock in October 2002, Dick's operated 134 stores in 24 states, including 20 each in New York and Ohio, 22 in Pennsylvania, six each in Maryland and New Jersey, seven in Michigan, and 13 in North Carolina. Additional stores were located in Tennessee, Vermont, West Virginia, and Virginia.

In October 2002 Dick's went public, offering 7.3 million shares of stock at $12.25 per share. Dick's attracted investors in a difficult market based on reported sales of $1.1 billion and net income of $23.5 million in the fiscal year ended February 2, 2002. In the prospectus Dick's presented the company as "the most profitable full-line sporting goods retailer as compared to the six largest full-line sporting goods retailers in the United States which are publicly traded. . . ." Shares offered directly by the company raised $27.9 million for debt repayment, new store openings, and working capital. Shortly after the initial public offering, Dick's opened stores in Barboursville, West Virginia, and Fredericksburg, Virginia. New stores were also under construction in Omaha and Wichita, with future plans involving expansion into Texas and Oklahoma markets.

Principal Competitors

Foot Locker, Inc.; Gart Sports Company; Galyan's Trading Company; Hibbett Sporting Goods, Inc.; The Sports Authority, Inc.; Wal-Mart Stores, Inc.

Further Reading

Carlton, Rachel, "Dick's Designs on the Future: The Newest Store from the Pittsburgh Powerhouse Shows Where the Chain, and Maybe the Industry, Are Headed," *Sporting Goods Business*, August 2002, p. 42.

Chamis, Eleni, "Dick's Sporting Goods Gets into Washington-Area Game," *Washington Business Journal*, November 9, 2001, p. 26.

"Dick's Clothing & Sporting Goods," *Chain Store Age Executive with Shopping Center Age*, March 1999, p. 162.

"Dick's Sporting Goods Balances Its Bad Timing for IPO with Positive Results," *Knight Ridder/Tribune Business News*, August 8, 2002.

"Dick's Sporting Goods IPO Shares Rise Despite Market Dip," *Knight Ridder/Tribune Business News*, October 17, 2002.

Elliott, Suzanne, "N.Y. Retailer Relocates HQ to Pittsburgh," *Pittsburgh Business Times*, February 7, 1994, p. 1.

Jenkins, Richard Dean, "The New Megastores," *Sporting Goods Business*, February 1995, p. 110.

Klein, Alec Matthew, "Dick's Sporting Goods Picks 3 Suburban Sites," *Baltimore Sun*, July 6, 1995, p. 10C.

Lindeman, Teresa F., "Findlay, Pa.-Based Sporting Goods Retailer Drops Online Operation," *Pittsburgh Post-Gazette*, February 22, 2001.

——, "Pittsburgh-Area Sporting Goods Store Changes Online Address," *Pittsburgh Post-Gazette*, November 24, 2000.

——, "Pittsburgh-Based Sporting Goods Retailer Says Warehouse Will Hire 400," *Pittsburgh Post-Gazette*, February 18, 2000.

Lubinger, Bill, "Dick's Sporting Goods Chain Plans 14 Ohio Stores," *Plain Dealer*, November 19, 1994, p. 1C.

McEvoy, Christopher, "See Dick's Run," *Sporting Goods Business*, July 1996, p. 92.

McMillin, Molly, "Sports Retailers Plan Second Location in Wichita, Kan.," *Wichita Eagle*, June 18, 2002.

Morris, Birkett. "Dick's Sporting Goods Pounces on Louisville Market," *Business First-Louisville,* March 22, 1999, p. 9.

"Retail Entrepreneurs of the Year: Edward Stack," *Chain Store Age Executive*, December 1999, p. 119.

Schenke, Jarred, "Dick's Sporting Goods Dips Toes in Georgia's Competitive Retail Market," *Pittsburgh Business Times*, July 27, 2001, p. 4.

Shim, Grace, "Sporting Goods Chains Are Preparing for Face-Off Store Openings," *Omaha World-Herald,* May 21, 2002, p. 1D.

Smith, Joyce, "Pittsburgh-Based Sporting Goods Chain Enters Kansas City, MO Market," *Kansas City Star,* September 29, 2000.

"Sporting Goods Chain to Open Locally," *Business First of Buffalo*, February 17, 1992, p. 3.

Troy, Mike, "Dick's Opens Five Midwest Stores," *DSN Retailing Today*, November 6, 2000, p. 1.

Wilson, Marianne, "Dick's: Where the Stadium Meets the Outdoors," *Chain Store Age Executive with Shopping Center Age*, June 1998, p. 114.

—Mary Tradii

Doman Industries Limited

435 Trunk Road
Duncan, British Columbia V9L 2P9
Canada
Telephone: (250) 748-3711
Fax: (250) 748-6045
Web site: http://www.domans.com

Public Company
Incorporated: 1955 as Doman's Lumber & Transport Ltd.
Employees: 2,400
Sales: US$402.7 million (2002)
Stock Exchanges: Toronto Vancouver
Ticker Symbol: DOM.A
NAIC: 321113 Sawmills

Doman Industries Limited is one of the largest forest products companies in Canada. Doman Industries is an integrated producer, involved in logging and sawmilling timber into lumber and wood chips. The company's activities also include manufacturing facilities that add value to wood-related products and facilities that produce dissolving sulphite pulp. Doman Industries ranks as the second largest coastal woodland operator in British Columbia. The company's products are sold in 30 countries.

Origins

The Doman family's involvement in the British Columbia, Canada, lumber business began at the dawn of the 20th century, although the first signs of a Doman lumber empire did not appear until the second half of the century. Not long after leaving his native India, Doman Singh bought a sawmill and lumber mill near Duncan, British Columbia. The purchase was made in 1905, but it would be another half-century before the Doman family included a genuine lumber baron. Doman Singh's grandson, Harbanse "Herb" Doman, became such a figure, eventually presiding over a C$1 billion business that ranked as one of the largest concerns of its type in Canada. Herb Doman's success was undeniable, but the enterprising family patriarch also made mistakes that steered his empire perilously close to bankruptcy.

Herb Doman, along with his brothers Ted and Gordon, started the Doman Lumber Company in 1953, incorporating the venture two years later. The brothers began by hauling and selling building supplies, two facets of Doman Industries that would help support the company for decades, but businesses it eventually exited. The building supply stores were replaced by a lumber wholesaling business in 1984. The trucking division evolved greatly from its modest beginnings, expanding throughout British Columbia and extending into Alberta and the Yukon, as well as into 11 western states in the United States. Despite its stature, the trucking business was sold at the end of 1990, by which time the Doman name had firmly implanted itself within the lumber business as representing a premier enterprise.

The development of Doman Industries' lumber business began a decade after the three Doman brothers founded their company. The Doman Lumber Company became Doman Industries in 1964, a name change that coincided with the company's debut as a public company, when it generated C$6 million in annual revenues. The year also marked the company's entry into the sawmilling and logging business, a move that initially involved four major sawmills on Vancouver Island. Doman Industries' first major sawmill, located at Ladysmith, became operational in 1967. The company's first sustained yield logging operation commenced in 1969, providing a supply of lumber for the Ladysmith facility and other sawmills to follow. In 1973, Doman Industries added a sawmill at Chemainus, by which point the company was selling 20 million board feet annually. The establishment of a facility at Chemainus was followed by a sawmill at Cowichan Bay in 1976 and another mill at Nanaimo in 1980.

By the end of the 1980s, Doman Industries had blossomed into a formidable lumber giant. Revenues neared C$700 million at the decade's conclusion, and Herb Doman ranked as aristocracy in the country's lumber industry, particularly in British Columbia where the company's Duncan headquarters was located. The company was at the top of its game at the end of the 1980s, but from that point forward its success began to slowly fade, leading to a wrenching saga of bad choices exacerbated by external forces that conspired to turn one of Canada's leading lumber companies into a floundering venture. The problems began in 1989.

Key Dates:

1953: The Doman Lumber Company is founded.
1964: Doman Industries Limited debuts as a publicly traded company.
1967: The company's first major sawmill becomes operational.
1989: Doman Industries increases its investment in Western Forest Products Ltd., thereby greatly increasing its debt.
1997: Doman Industries acquires Pacific Forest Products Ltd.
1999: Herb Doman is ordered by the British Columbia Securities Commission to vacate Doman Industries' presidential post for eight months.
2001: Rick Doman is appointed president.
2002: A restructuring plan is announced.

Hard Times in the 1990s

Of all the problems afflicting Doman Industries at the end of the 20th century, none delivered a more stinging blow than debt. The company's financial difficulties stemmed from its investment in Western Forest Products Ltd. (WFP), a joint venture company Doman Industries and two other British Columbia forest products companies formed in 1980. For C$420 million, the three companies acquired the British Columbia timber resources and manufacturing facilities belonging to a company named ITT Industries of Canada Limited. Included in the purchase were a dissolving sulphite pulp mill located at Port Alice, British Columbia, a pulp mill in Squamish, British Columbia, and three sawmills, as well as certain timber tenures. The problems associated with WFP did not emerge until 1989, when Doman Industries increased its ownership to 56.1 percent. Before increasing its investment in WFP, the company was virtually free of debt, but after securing control over WFP, Doman Industries was nearly $600 million in debt, putting the company in a hole it could not escape for more than the ensuing decade.

At roughly the same time the WFP investment became a ticking time bomb, Herb Doman found himself embroiled in controversy. In the fall of 1987, the U.S. forestry giant Louisiana-Pacific Corp. began accumulating shares of Doman Industries, a prelude to the Portland, Oregon-based company's offer of $12 per share for Doman Industries in October 1988. Louisiana later withdrew its offer to acquire Doman Industries, scuttling the C$250 million deal on November 4, 1988, a dark day in the history of Doman Industries. Herb Doman was accused of informing former British Columbia premier Bill Bennett and his brother, Russell Bennett, of the deal's collapse less than five minutes after it occurred. Within minutes, the Bennett brothers sold more than 500,000 Doman shares. The sale led to insider trading charges against Herb Doman and the Bennetts. The parties were acquitted in May 1989 by the British Columbia Provincial Court, but the British Columbia Securities Commission (BCSC) and the Ontario Securities Commission launched their own investigations. These investigations dragged on for years, providing an ugly backdrop to the company's increasingly damaging debt situation.

Doman Industries entered the 1990s saddled with debt and its founder and chairman facing a protracted legal struggle. Conditions in the new decade exacerbated the company's position, making for the most difficult period in Doman Industries' history. One individual keenly aware of Doman Industries' financial plight was Herb Doman's youngest child and only son, Jaspaul ''Rick'' Doman. Although he had preferred a career in finance, Rick Doman followed his father's wishes and joined the lumber industry at age 17, when he worked as an independent wholesale lumber seller. Rick Doman joined Doman Industries' board of directors in 1986, from which vantage he witnessed the company's decision to take on substantial debt in 1989. By 1994, his concerns about the company's financial position forced him to react. He persuaded his father to consider issuing corporate bonds in order to reduce debt, but his efforts failed. ''He just about threw me out of his offices,'' Rick Doman said, remembering his father's response in a March 2003 interview with *B.C. Business*. Rick Doman discussed his idea with his fellow board members, but the other directors dismissed his proposal. Rick Doman's struggle to have his warnings heeded had just begun.

As the mid-1990s approached, forces conspired against British Columbia lumber companies and against Doman Industries in particular. Part of Rick Doman's concern about his family's business was based on his perception of an emerging global lumber economy. In his mind, new competition for a company saddled with debt was one development Doman Industries could ill afford. Beginning around 1995, his fears became reality, as countries in central Europe and South America entered the market, offering their dry, relatively inexpensive, and market-specific lumber for sale. At roughly the same time, Herb Doman suffered a severe stroke in the summer of 1995 that left him partially paralyzed and unable to steward his company. For a six-month period, Rick Doman and Vice-President Jack Abercrombie led Doman Industries just as the new competition spawned by a global lumber market became perceptible to the Duncan-based company's business. With active control over the company, Rick Doman reiterated his growing concerns about the company's position, but he failed to gain the support of the board. According to Rick Doman, the board was convinced the company was merely experiencing a downturn in a historically cyclical business. ''The board's view was that things always get better,'' he said in his March 2003 interview with *B.C. Business*. ''And my view,'' he added, ''was that this time was different.''

During the latter part of the 1990s, Doman Industries' debt mounted, heightening the company's sensitivity to the impact of negative industry trends. Further, the company needed cash to maintain its operations, but the annual interest payments on the debt made capital improvements impossible. Doman Industries' facilities on the British Columbia coast, for instance, needed to be retooled for changing markets, but the company could do nothing. Meanwhile, Herb Doman's legal troubles were proving to be as persistent as the company's debt. In 1996, the BCSC found Herb Doman and the Bennetts guilty of insider trading, but an appeal to the Supreme Court of Canada was filed, ensuring that another round of debate awaited before the matter was resolved.

As Herb Doman's legal battle dragged on, the company completed another major acquisition and made another grievous error. In 1997, Doman Industries paid C$143.8 million for the operations of Pacific Forest Products Ltd. in British Columbia. The acquisition included three sawmills, woodland, and related operations that increased the company's annual fiber supply by roughly 80 percent. The acquisition was strategic and market-specific, reflective of management's decision to bolster its activities in the Japanese market. Yet the acquisition could not have been more ill-timed. Soon after the Pacific Forest purchase was completed, the Japanese economy deteriorated, plunging into an unprecedented recession that afflicted all of Asia. The Asian lumber market collapsed as a result. The Japanese market, which had been purchasing 2.3 billion board feet annually from British Columbia producers, was the first to succumb to the pernicious economic forces, delivering a heavy blow to Doman Industries.

Troubles in the Late 1990s

The problems plaguing Doman Industries were increasing, shaking the very foundation of the company. The company's debt, which had increased because of the Pacific Forest acquisition, neared a staggering C$1 billion by the end of the 1990s. Unfortunately for the company, the situation worsened as the new century neared. In 1999, all the appeals of Herb Doman's legal troubles were exhausted. The BCSC banned the Bennett brothers from trading in stocks for ten years and ordered Herb Doman to remove himself as Doman Industries' president for eight months.

As Doman Industries entered the 21st century, it was able to leave Herb Doman's legal troubles behind, but the resolution of the insider trading case was the only problem the company could count as part of the past. In 2000, the company's debt reached C$1 billion. At the beginning of the following year, when the company was on the verge of bankruptcy, Herb Doman suffered his second stroke and fell into a coma for several weeks. To Rick Doman's surprise, the company's board of directors asked him to replace his father as president. Although he had experienced years of frustration in dealing with the board, and earlier had decided to quit the board in the beginning of 2001, Rick Doman accepted the offer. In February 2001, Rick Doman was named president.

"I knew three things needed to be done immediately," Rick Doman said in his March 2003 interview with *B.C. Business.* "We had to reduce inventory, cut costs, and restructure the company." With Rick Doman at the helm, Doman Industries' C$340 million inventory was reduced by C$150 million. Costs were cut as well, but again Rick Doman found it difficult to convince the company's board to restructure. He was approached, in July 2001, by Tricap Restructuring Fund, a subsidiary of Ontario-based Brascan Corp., an investment conglomerate. Tricap wanted to assist in the company's recovery in exchange for equity. Rick Doman wanted to negotiate with Tricap, but Doman Industries' board was against exchanging debt for equity. Meanwhile, as the company's situation worsened, lumber industry developments worked against its favor. In March 2001, the softwood lumber agreement between Canada and the United States expired. In May 2002, the United States introduced a 27 percent tariff on Canadian softwood imports, which greatly impacted Doman Industries' business.

British Columbia generated half of the C$10 billion in Canadian lumber shipped into the United States annually. For its part, Doman Industries relied on the U.S. market for 65 percent of its business. Within one month, the introduction of the new tariff cost Doman Industries more than C$4 million.

Doman Industries' financial situation finally reached a point where some decisive action needed to be taken. After more than a decade of proceeding with a progressively worsening limp, the company was unable to make a $26 million interest payment in March 2002, two months before the 27 percent tariff was put into effect. In September 2002, after the Canadian federal government rejected a request for loan guarantees, the company missed a second interest payment. Rick Doman informed Doman Industries shareholders and bondholders that the company could not meet its debt obligations. At this point, Tricap returned its offer and finally the board relented. In November 2002, the company announced that a group of Doman Industries' unsecured bondholders, led by Tricap, had made a bid to become its owners in exchange for writing off $600 million of the debt.

The conclusion of Doman Industries' saga was not complete by the time the company celebrated its 50th anniversary. The restructuring agreement announced at the end of 2002 was later abandoned, having lost the support of bondholders. By August 2003, Rick Doman was talking with Cerberus Capital Management about a debt-refinancing deal, but nothing about the company's future was settled. A solution to the company's debt problem loomed as the company's most pressing issue. Whether or not Canada would lose one of its largest lumber concerns remained to be seen, as Doman Industries struggled mightily to unravel the web of problems spun during the 1990s.

Principal Subsidiaries

Doman Forest Products Limited; Western Pulp Limited Partnership; Western Forest Products Limited; Doman Log Supply Ltd.; Doman-Western Lumber Ltd.; Eacom Timber Sales Ltd.; Western Pulp Inc.

Principal Competitors

Deltic Timber Corporation; Hampton Affiliates; Plum Creek Timber Company, Inc.

Further Reading

"Doman Buys Pacific Forest Holdings," *Pulp & Paper,* February 1998, p. 23.
"Doman to Buy WFP Shares; Champion May Sell Plymills," *Forest Industries,* March-April 1992, p. 7.
Kershaw, Jim, "What Would You Have Done?," *BC Business,* November 1996, p. 26.
Paterson, Jody, "Fight to the Finish: Rick Doman's Battle to Save the Business That Bears His Family's Name," *BC Business,* March 2003, p. 44.
Schreiner, John, "Doman Is Poised for a Good Year," *Financial Post,* February 20, 1993, p. 26.
——, "No End in Sight to Bennett-Doman Insider Imbroglio," *Financial Post,* August 27, 1994, p. 14.

—Jeffrey L. Covell

Dorel Industries Inc.

1255 Greene Avenue, Suite 300
Westmount, Quebec H3Z 2A4
Canada
Telephone: (514) 323-5701
Fax: (514) 323-2030
Web site: http://www.dorel.com

Public Company
Incorporated: 1962 as Dorel Co., Ltd.
Employees: 3,600
Sales: $992.1 million (2002)
Stock Exchanges: NASDAQ Toronto
Ticker Symbols: DIIBF (NASDAQ) DII.B (Toronto)
NAIC: 337122 Nonupholstered Wood Household
    Furniture Manufacturing; 337124 Metal Household
    Furniture Manufacturing; 337214 Office Furniture
    (Except Wood) Manufacturing; 421210 Furniture
    Wholesalers; 337215 Showcase, Partition, Shelving,
    and Locker Manufacturing; 337121 Upholstered
    Household Furniture Manufacturing

Dorel Industries Inc. manufactures a broad range of juvenile furniture products, ready-to-assemble (RTA) furniture, and home furnishings, which it sells primarily through such mass merchants as Wal-Mart and Toys ''R'' Us, department stores, and specialty retailers. In addition to facilities in Canada and the United States, the company also has European operations. Dorel markets its ready-to-assemble furniture under the Ameriwood, Ridgewood, and Charleswood names; its juvenile products under the Cosco and Maxi-Miliaan names; and home furnishings under the Cosco and Sealy names.

The First 30 Years: A Family Business Growing Through Acquisitions

In 1962, Leo Schwartz founded Dorel Co. Ltd. in the basement of his home in Montreal, Quebec. Initially a small seller of crib mattresses, Schwartz by the 1970s had established a national sales network for his products. In 1987, Dorel merged with Ridgewood Industries Ltd., a wire-making company turned ready-to-assemble furniture maker, founded in 1969 by Schwartz's son, Martin, and his son-in-law. The merger completed, Dorel held its initial public offering, raising $9.4 million, which it put toward acquisitions, and changed its name to Dorel Industries Inc./Les Industries Dorel Inc.

Dorel made its first acquisition in 1988, purchasing Cosco, Inc., an American manufacturer of children's accessories and furniture. Cosco was three times the size of Dorel and had a distribution network that included clients such as Wal-Mart and Kmart. Despite the fact that Cosco was ailing, Dorel maintained production at Cosco's Columbus plant and raised its executives' salaries. Dorel also acquired Charleswood Corporation in 1990, another manufacturer of ready-to-assemble furniture and an apparently losing venture. Taking a different course than it had with Cosco, Dorel immediately cut Charleswood's staff in half and established new product lines for the company.

By 1990, Dorel's management consisted of Leo Schwartz, his three sons, Martin, Alan, and Jeffrey, and his son-in-law, Jeff Segal. Industry analysts considered the group a strong management team, capable of turning money-losing acquisitions into winners. Having weathered the Canada-U.S. Free Trade Agreement of 1989 and the devastating Canadian recession of 1990–91, which halved the ranks of Canada's furniture manufacturers, Dorel's management decided to become far more competitive and tackle the U.S. market. ''Free trade made us realize that we couldn't hide behind borders,'' Jeffrey Schwartz, one of Dorel's vice-presidents, told *Canadian Business* in 1998. ''In order to compete, we had to have world-class manufacturing facilities—and that's something we didn't have. . . .'' Management resolved to take a more active role in the operations of both its acquisitions, repositioning the top management at Charleswood and naming a new president for Cosco.

The company also engaged in several more acquisitions—companies that had overspent, were not efficient enough, and had the markets and relationships that Dorel did not have, according to Martin Schwartz, company president, in a 1992 *Canadian Business* article. In 1993, having purchased the assets of the Carol Anne furniture company, Dorel created Leadra Designs, a new Canadian division, to manufacture and distrib-

Key Dates:

1962: Leo Schwartz founds Dorel Co. Ltd.
1987: Company goes public and changes its name to Dorel Industries Inc./Les Industries Dorel Inc.
1988: Dorel acquires Cosco, Inc.
1990: Company acquires Charleswood Corporation; lists its shares on the Toronto Stock Exchange.
1991: Company holds a second public offering.
1992: Dorel acquires Infantino Inc.; Martin Schwartz assumes the position of head of the company.
1993: Dorel acquires Carol Anne Furniture Manufacturing Company Ltd. and then incorporates a new subsidiary, Leadra Design Inc., to continue Carol Anne operations.
1994: The company acquires Maxi Gerance B.V.
1998: Dorel acquires Ameriwood Industries International Corp. and Okla Homer Smith; the company begins trading on the NASDAQ and closes its Leadra unit.
2000: Company acquires Safety 1st, Inc. and sells Infantino, Inc.
2001: Dorel acquires Quint B.V. and closes its Okla Homer facility.

ute a line of mid-market bedroom sets, wall units, tables, and chairs. In 1994, it acquired Maxi-Miliaan and began to market the Maxi-Cosi brand of higher-end juvenile products.

These acquisitions provided Dorel not only with a broader line of products, but with a foothold in the United States and Europe; they transformed the company into an American corporation with a Canadian head office. Dorel also created Infantino Inc. in 1992, a California-based company that operated within its juvenile products division; it brought on line three new facilities as well: a new metal furniture manufacturing plant, a sewing facility, and a distribution center.

The Mid-1990s: Heavy Debt Load and Other Problems

Yet growth came at the expense of profits. Although sales quadrupled between 1988 and 1993 to reach $260 million, Dorel had accumulated an unhealthy amount of debt during its acquisition years. By 1994, the 2,500-employee company, ranked the 13th largest furniture manufacturer in North America by *Furniture Today*, carried a debt-load of $125 million. That same year it earned just $8 million in income on sales of $334 million.

The company faced another problem as well. Although Dorel exported to more than 40 countries by the early 1990s, 78 percent of its sales occurred in the United States in 1993, with only 17 percent in Canada and 5 percent internationally. More troublesome yet, Dorel was largely reliant on one client for distribution of its products; Wal-Mart booked 30 percent of its total sales.

To address this unhealthy balance, Dorel started shying away from acquisitions in 1995 to concentrate on building a more efficient and profitable set of consumer products businesses. It expanded its distribution through home centers, office superstores, and catalog merchants. In the second half of the 1990s, it began to produce futons for mass merchants, and in 1997, to manufacture and distribute futons under the Sealy brand name. The plan paid off, and Dorel doubled in size between 1995 and 1998. Its revenues in 1997 rose 25 percent to attain $532 million with earnings at $25 million. In 1998, sales increased another 44 percent to reach $767 million.

By 1998, the company was expanding rapidly in the ready-to-assemble furniture sector, growing both internally and by acquisition to become one of North America's top three or four RTA manufacturers in the lower end of the market. As a result, Dorel needed more production capacity. Once again turning to acquisition, it bought Okla Homer Smith, an American wood crib and dresser manufacturer, and Ameriwood Industries International Corp. in 1998. It also shut down its Leadra division,

which, according to the company, had never made any money. Further, it began to wean itself from dependence on Wal-Mart, winnowing total sales to the mass merchant from 56 percent to 50. The following year, Dorel expanded its ready-to-assemble plant in Ontario. Sales for 1999 continued to increase—30 percent over the previous year—to reach $642 million.

Increasing the Focus on Core Juvenile Products: Early 2000s

In 2000, Dorel made the decision to focus on its major brands and core juvenile products. The company embarked on a sweep of internal housekeeping to realize this decision, selling its Infantino unit to the division's existing management team. In its largest acquisition ever, it purchased Safety 1st, manufacturer of child-safety and other juvenile products, such as nursery monitors, booster seats, and bathtubs. Safety 1st was known widely for inventing the "Baby on Board" signs. Dorel combined Safety 1st with Cosco to form its new juvenile furnishings group. It also consolidated Ameriwood and Ridgewood under Ridgewood; this newly formed division focused on expanding into Japan and the United Kingdom. Lastly, Dorel signed a licensing agreement with Hasbro's Playskool brand in 2000. This agreement became the company's fourth such venture; it had earlier signed licensing agreements with Eddie Bauer, NASCAR, and Walt Disney.

Dorel continued its internal reorganization into the year 2001. Its growth strategy became one of concentrating on recession-resistant products with strong brand names and on intensive product development. It acquired Quint B.V., maker of Quinny brand strollers, which it integrated into Maxi-Miliaan's operations. In response to ongoing losses, the company closed its Okla Homer facility mid-year and began to outsource its major futon components, which it sold mainly to its large customers. It entered the North American tricycle market with a line of trikes and bikes made in China and marketed under the Safety 1st brand.

In 2002, Dorel turned its attention to increasing market share and brand recognition in Europe. It rolled out a new line of car seats and strollers for Europe's mass retailers under the Safety 1st and Safekid brands. Quint introduced a new stroller and travel system. The company acquired Ampa, which expanded its reach into France, Spain, Italy, and Portugal and further into the Netherlands, Germany, Britain, and Belgium. Revenue reached a new record of $992 million in 2002, up from $917 million in 2001—an accomplishment all the more impressive, according to Martin Schwartz, company head, ''in light of the continuing sluggish U.S. and European economies.''

Principal Subsidiaries

Ameriwood Industries; Ampa Group; Cosco, Inc.; Dorel Asia Ltd.; Dorel Financial Inc.; Dorel (U.K.) Limited; Dorel Home Products; Maxi-Miliaan B.V.; Ridgewood Industries.

Principal Competitors

Bush Industries, Inc.; Evenflo Companies, Inc.; Fischer Price Inc.; Newell Rubbermaid Inc.; O'Sullivan Industries Holdings, Inc.; Sauder Woodworking Co.

Further Reading

''Dorel Industries Inc. Maintains Focus on Recession-Resistant Products,'' *Market News Publishing*, May 31, 2002.

Hogarth, Don, ''Furniture Makers Feel Squeeze,'' *Financial Post (Toronto)*, April 16, 1990, p. 7.

Logie, Stuart, ''Expansion Plans: Weighing the Costs of Rapid Growth,'' *Canadian Business*, February 1990, p. 72.

Marks, Robert, ''Dorel Affecting U.S. RTA: Mass Merchants Eye Impact of Charleswood Buy,'' *HFD*, December 18, 1989, p. 21.

Millan, Luis, ''Some Assembly Required,'' *Canadian Business*, November 13, 1998, p. 102.

Schroeder, Angel, ''Dorel Industries to Acquire Safety 1st,'' *HFN*, May 1, 2000, p. 27.

—Carrie Rothburd

Dr. Reddy's Laboratories Ltd.

7-1-27, Ameerpet
Hyderabad, Andhra Pradesh 500 016
India
Telephone: 91-40-373-1946
Fax: 91-40-373-1955
Web site: http://www.drreddys.com

Public Company
Incorporated: 1984
Employees: 5,796
Sales: Rs 18.01 billion ($391.8 million) (2003)
Stock Exchanges: Bombay New York
Ticker Symbol: RDY
NAIC: 325412 Pharmaceutical Preparation Manufacturing

Dr. Reddy's Laboratories Ltd. is one of India's leading pharmaceutical companies with global ambitions. The company has departed from the Indian pharmaceutical market mainstream of copying patented drugs to pursue the development of its own—patentable—molecules. As such, the company has already achieved success with a number of promising antidiabetic molecules. At the same time, Dr. Reddy's is pursuing a share of the lucrative, but highly competitive, U.S. generics market, including the higher-margin "branded generic" market. Dr. Reddy's operates through several strategic business units, including: Branded Finished Dosages; Generic Finished Dosages; Bulk Actives; Custom Chemicals; Biotechnology; Diagnostics; Critical Care; and Discovery Research. A leader in its domestic market, the company is also active on the international scene, which accounted for 64 percent of the company's total sales of Rs 18 billion ($392 million) in 2003. North America contributed 32 percent of sales, while Russia added 28 percent. The rest of the company's international revenues were generated through the Asian, African, and South American markets. Dr. Reddy's is led by founder and Chairman Dr. Anji Reddy and CEO (and Reddy's son-in-law) G.V. Prasad. Dr. Reddy's Laboratories was the first Asian pharmaceutical company, excluding Japan, to list on the New York Stock Exchange.

Bulk Actives to Generics in the 1980s

In 1970, the Indian government, then led by Indira Ghandi, abrogated laws respecting international pharmaceutical patents. The move, meant to reduce the cost of providing healthcare to India's large and exceedingly poor population, had the effect of supercharging the country's pharmaceutical sector. With a long history in process chemistry, and a large and highly educated pool of scientists, the sector quickly became experts at reverse-engineering, and then copying, the drugs developed by the world's large multinationals.

The new industry quickly became one of the world's most energetic markets—by the 1990s, there were more than 20,000 companies operating in India's pharmaceuticals industry. Indian producers were able to produce drugs and their components for a fraction of the cost of their Western counterparts, and quickly found an enormous demand throughout the developing world. Yet the highly competitive domestic market, as well as the slender margins available from the copied—many would call them pirated—drugs forced the Indian companies to develop highly cost-effective manufacturing and marketing models.

Dr. Anji Reddy, the son of a well-to-do turmeric farmer in Andra Pradesh in the south of India, was one of the early entrants into the new and fast-growing market. Reddy traveled to Bombay to pursue pharmacology studies, then went on to earn a Ph.D. in chemical engineering. Reddy then went to work for state-owned pharmaceutical company IDPL. At the time IDPL had been reliant on Russian technology; yet the company quickly turned the tables, gaining expertise—and eventually providing that to Russia itself.

Reddy remained with IDPL into the early 1970s. The change of law and the rise of new opportunities in the pharmaceutical industry, however, encouraged him to set up his own business, and in the mid-1970s, Reddy founded a company for producing and selling bulk actives—the basic ingredients of drug compounds—to pharmaceutical manufacturers. Reddy's clientele soon featured a host of national and multinational companies, such as Burroughs Wellcome and others.

In the early 1980s, however, Reddy sought to aim higher and establish himself as a manufacturer of finished products. In

1984, Reddy founded Dr. Reddy's Laboratories, using $40,000 of his own, backed by a bank loan for $120,000. Reddy jumped into the market of producing copies, taking advantage of the 1970 law. As he told *Forbes:* "We are products of that. But for that, we wouldn't be here. It was good for the people of India, and it was good for this company."

Reddy's grew quickly, adding a large number of formulations, and achieving strong local success with its NISE range of painkillers. The company also had success with its copy of Bayer's antibiotic ciprofloxacin and, especially, with AstraZeneca's omeprazole, which, under the trade name Losec, had become the world's largest-selling drug. That drug provided fortune for Dr. Reddy's as well, as Reddy told the *Financial Times:* "After Astra, I think I must be the largest producer in the world."

Meanwhile, Reddy's took advantage of India's low wage and production costs to boost its production of bulk actives. By 1986, the company prepared to expand still further, and listed its stock on the Bombay exchange. In that year, also, the company began its first exports of bulk actives, including methyldopa.

The company achieved another crucial milestone in 1987 when it gained U.S. FDA approval for its ibuprofen formulation. That approval, which was coupled with the all-important FDA certification of its factory, marked the start of the company's international formulations exports.

In the meantime, Reddy's continued to develop its bulk actives business, becoming one of India's largest exporters of drug ingredients. In order to support that growth, the company made its first acquisition, of Benzex Laboratories Pvt. Ltd., a bulk actives specialist.

Risking on Research in the 1990s

By the early 1990s, Reddy's, like its Indian counterparts, boasted a wide range of "copied" drugs in its portfolio. International sales were also becoming an increasingly important part of the company's total revenues, a trend boosted by the company's entry into the Russian market in 1991. That country later grew into one of the company's primary export markets.

Reddy himself, however, by then joined by son-in-law and future CEO G.V. Prasad, recognized that continued pressure from multinational drug companies, with political backing from their domestic governments, coupled with India's desire to join the World Trade Organization, would eventually lead to the re-imposition of respect for international drug patents. At the same time, competition among Indian manufacturers—with as many as 100 companies producing knockoffs of the same drug preparation—had become increasingly heavy, making it harder to generate profits. Meanwhile, the restriction-free market in India had led to a mass exodus of the country's highly regarded researchers and scientists.

These factors led Dr. Reddy's to a dramatic strategic shift. In 1992, Reddy founded Dr. Reddy's Research Foundation and determined to lead his company through the transition from copier to pharmaceutical innovator. By 1993, the company's new research and development wing was operational, and it set to work performing "drug discovery" work in a variety of fields, including metabolic disorders, such as diabetes, and cancer treatments, among others.

Reddy's shift initially met with skepticism from the Indian community. As Reddy told the *Financial Times:* "I made a statement in Bangalore in 1993. I said: 'Don't think that because we don't have millions of dollars we cannot invent new drugs. Don't shy away from this.' But nobody had the conviction that an Indian company could discover anything."

Nonetheless, for its research and development effort, Reddy's adopted a standard practice among even the largest multinationals, that of developing "analogue" preparations of existing drugs. By slightly altering the composition of a molecule or preparation, Reddy would be able to present a new drug, which was sufficiently different chemically to achieve a separate patent.

The shift into research represented only one prong of Dr. Reddy's ambitions. In its determination to become a player in the global market, the company moved to end production of illegal copies and instead shift its operations to the manufacture of—legal—generic drugs. In 1994, the company placed a rights issue of $48 million in order to construct a new facility dedicated to producing generic drugs capable of meeting the legislative requirements of Western markets. The company also opened a U.S. subsidiary in New Jersey that year.

By 1995, Reddy's initial research and development efforts had already paid off, as the company filed its first patent application for a new and promising anti-diabetes formulation. The company successfully completed laboratory testing on the drug, an insulin sensitizer dubbed balaglitazone by 1997. Yet, lacking the funds to engage in its own clinical testing, the company placed the patent up for grabs, and licensed it to Novo Nordisk in 1997. This marked a first for an Indian-developed drug. The following year, Novo Nordisk acquired the license for Dr. Reddy's second insulin sensitizer, ragaglitazar.

Going Global in the 21th Century

The year 1997 marked a new era for Dr. Reddy's. In that year, the U.S. FDA adopted new rules, designed to encourage the growth of the generic drugs market in the United States, which provided a six-month exclusivity period for the first company to gain approval to market newly available drugs in a generic form. Dr. Reddy's decided to get in on the action—as an estimated $60 billion of drugs was expected to outgrow their patents over the next ten years—and in 1997 the company filed an abbreviated new drug application (ANDA, used for regis-

Key Dates:

1984: Dr. Anji Reddy founds Dr. Reddy's Laboratories, based on a bulk actives business he had founded in the 1970s, in order to extend into the production of drug formulations.
1986: Dr. Reddy's goes public on the Bombay stock exchange.
1988: The company acquires Benzex Laboratories in order to expand the bulk actives business.
1992: Dr. Reddy's Research Foundation is founded as part of the strategy to enter drug development.
1994: The company opens a subsidiary in the United States.
1995: The company files its first patent for an in-house developed drug.
1999: The company acquires American Remedies Ltd.
2000: The company acquires Cheminor Drugs Limited and becomes the third largest Indian drug company.
2001: The company lists shares on the New York Stock Exchange; a new research and development facility opens in Atlanta, Georgia.
2002: The company acquires BMS Laboratories Ltd. and its marketing and distribution subsidiary Meridian Healthcare Ltd. in the United Kingdom.
2003: The company gains tentative approval to market generic versions of Serzone, developed by Bristol Myers Squibb.

tering a drug in its generic formula) for a generic version of the popular anti-ulcer medication Zantac.

Buoyed by its early success, Dr. Reddy's moved to expand its operations at the turn of the century. In 1999, the company made a new acquisition, buying up American Remedies Limited, based in Chennai, boosting its formulations capacity. That year, also, the company set up a research and development subsidiary, Reddy US Therapeutics, in Atlanta, Georgia, placing part of its drug discovery effort closer to the U.S. market.

In 2000, the company made another important acquisition, this time of Cheminor Drugs Limited, which enabled Dr. Reddy's to claim the number three spot among Indian pharmaceutical companies. That year, the company launched the commercial distribution of its first generics in the United States. Back home, the company's research efforts had paid off with the filing of an Investigational New Drug Application for an anti-cancer molecule developed in the company's labs.

Dr. Reddy's global ambitions now took it to the New York Stock Exchange, where the company listed its stock in 2001, becoming the first Asian pharmaceutical company outside of Japan to do so. The company clearly revealed its ambitions, as Reddy told *Business Week:* "We want to be a truly innovative company discovering and marketing drugs the world over." That year, the company scored a new success in its research activities, licensing a second-generation anti-diabetic molecule to Novartis in a deal worth some $55 million. Meanwhile, on the generics front, the company was lifted when its application for a

40mg generic version of the popular anti-depressive Prozac was awarded a 180-day exclusivity period. That period generated some $56 million—nearly all profit—for the company.

By 2002, the Indian government had agreed to re-introduce patent enforcement in the pharmaceutical industry, starting in 2005. Although some observers questioned whether the company would maintain the political will to enforce the new rules, Dr. Reddy's emerged as one of only a handful of Indian companies capable of independent research. Indeed, the company had continued to build up its research capacity. In 2001, it had created a new subsidiary, Aurigene Discovery Technologies, dedicated to the biotechnology sector.

The year 2002 also marked the company's first overseas acquisition, when it paid £9 million to acquire the United Kingdom's BMS Laboratories Ltd. and its marketing and distribution subsidiary Meridian Healthcare Ltd. That purchase enabled the company to expand into the U.K.—and ultimately European—generics market.

At the end of 2002, Dr. Reddy's scored a new victory in the U.S. market, when it successfully defeated lawsuits lobbied by Pfizer to prevent the Indian company's marketing of its own variant of the pharmaceutical giant's Novasc. The company then began preparations to introduce its version of the drug in 2003. Yet the new compound was expected to mark a new step for the company, as it became determined to enter the higher-margin branded generics category.

Dr. Reddy's backed this change in strategy with a new portfolio of drugs, including the filing of an ANDA for fexofenadine HCI (better known as Allegra, from Aventis) in April 2003. In July of that year, the company scored a new victory when it was granted tentative FDA approval to develop and market generic versions of the Bristol Myers Squibb drug Serzone. Dr. Reddy's appeared well on its way to achieving its goal of becoming a global pharmaceutical company.

Principal Subsidiaries

Aurantis Farmaceutica Ltda (Brazil; 50%); Aurigene Discovery Technologies Inc. (U.S.A.); Aurigene Discovery Technologies Limited; Cheminor Drugs Limited; Compact Electric Limited; Dr. Reddy's Exports Limited (22%); Dr. Reddy's Farmaceutica Do Brazil Ltda.; Dr. Reddy's Laboratories (EU) Limited (U.K.); Dr. Reddy's Laboratories (Proprietary) (South Africa); Dr. Reddy's Laboratories (UK) Limited; Dr. Reddy's Laboratories Inc. (U.S.A.); DRL Investments Limited India; Kunshan Rotam Reddy Pharmaceutical Co. Limited (China; 51%); OOO JV Reddy Biomed Limited (Russia); Pathnet India Private Limited (49%); Reddy Antilles N.V. (Antilles); Reddy Cheminor S.A. (France); Reddy Netherlands B.V.; Reddy Pharmaceuticals Hong Kong Limited; Reddy Pharmaceuticals Singapore; Reddy US Therapeutics Inc.; Zenovus Biotech Limited.

Principal Competitors

RPG Enterprises; GlaxoSmithKline Consumer Healthcare Ltd.; East India Pharmaceutical Works Ltd.; Cipla Ltd.; Concept Pharmaceuticals Ltd.; Khandelwal Laboratories Ltd.; Dabur India Ltd.

Further Reading

"Coming at You, Merck," *Business Week,* April 9, 2001, p. 27.

Datta, Mrinalini, "Dr. Reddy Looks to the Next Level," *International Herald Tribune,* February 11, 2003, p. B4.

"Dr. Reddy's Lab: It's The People, Stupid," *Business Today,* September 1, 2002.

"Generic Genius," *Economist,* September 30, 2000, p. 66.

Merchant, Khozem, "Drugs Innovation Is Just What the Doctor Ordered," *Financial Times,* June 7, 2002, p. 28.

Pilling, David, "Doctor in Search of Patents," *Financial Times,* September 14, 1999, p. 8.

Slater, Joanna, and Gardiner Harris, "Legal Remedy," *Far Eastern Economic Review,* April 24, 2003.

Tanzer, Andrew, "Pill Factory to the World," *Forbes,* December 10, 2001, p. 70.

—M. L. Cohen

EGL, Inc.

Intercontinental Airport
15350 Vickery Drive
Houston, Texas 77032
U.S.A.
Telephone: (281) 618-3100
Toll Free: (800) 888-4949
Fax: (281) 618-3399
Web site: http://www.eaglegl.com

Public Company
Incorporated: 1984 as Eagle USA Airfreight
Employees: 8,700
Sales: $1.87 billion (2002)
Stock Exchanges: NASDAQ NMS
Ticker Symbol: EAGL
NAIC: 488510 Freight Transportation Arrangement

EGL, Inc. (doing business as EGL Eagle Global Logistics) is a leader in the international freight forwarding and logistics services market. The company has 400 facilities in 100 countries. EGL focuses on shipments larger than those sought by shipping companies and cargo airlines (more than 50 pounds). EGL keeps its costs low and investors happy by owning as few transportation assets as possible.

Air freight forwarding accounts for most of EGL's business; the company also books freight shipments on ships and trucks, and offers logistics and distribution services and customs brokering. Real time shipping data provides essential value for customers in a competitive business. EGL is one of the largest players in a highly fragmented industry. The company merged with Circle International in 2000, adding a huge international presence to one of the largest freight forwarders in the United States.

Founding of EGL: 1984

Company founder James R. Crane, who had been a baseball pitcher in college, earned a degree in industrial safety from Central Missouri State University in 1976. This led to a job evaluating commercial property for an insurance company, according to *Lloyd's List.* A high school friend then encouraged him to enter the freight forwarding business. Crane moved to Houston, where he worked for Northern Airfreight for a while before he was hired away by Ranger Airfreight.

Crane then founded Eagle USA Airfreight in Houston in March 1984 at the relatively young age of 30, with $10,000 borrowed from his sister. Crane told *Lloyd's List* Eagle made money in its first month; the start-up employed a sole receptionist, with Crane handling the loading and trucking himself. Crane would credit part of his success to an incentive-based pay structure for management. Constant monitoring of financial and operational data was also important, as was an aversion to debt.

Freight forwarders find space on commercial passenger and cargo airlines for their client's goods. Eagle specialized in loads weighing more than 70 pounds, diverting direct competition with Federal Express and United Parcel Service Inc. Eagle's average shipment weighed about 600 pounds, reported the *Journal of Commerce.* The Japanese-style zero inventory theories being popularized in U.S. manufacturing circles relied on efficient shipping and were a boon to the forwarding business.

According to one estimate, there were between 1,600 and 3,000 freight forwarders in the United States in the early 1990s. Eagle had five freight terminals by this time, expanding from Houston to Dallas, St. Louis, Atlanta, and Los Angeles. Revenues were $17.8 million in 1991.

According to the *Houston Chronicle,* the company landed its first *Fortune* 500 account, Compaq Computer Corp., in 1992. Other large customers were also computer makers, such as IBM and Packard Bell Electronics; retailer CompUSA was also a big client. Sales reached $47 million in fiscal 1993. The company grew very fast in the mid-1990s, and would triple revenues in just three years.

Going Public: 1995

Eagle went public on the NASDAQ in November 1995 (ticker symbol EUSA), raising $30 million. Proceeds were earmarked for building a new $4.5 million headquarters and distribution center and funding expansion. Founder James Crane owned two-thirds of the shares after the initial public offering.

Company Perspectives:

EGL, Inc. (EGL Eagle Global Logistics) has emerged as a leading global provider of supply chain solutions, demonstrating core competencies in transportation services, logistics management and information technology. Believing that these primary service components impact every stage of the supply chain, EGL utilizes its expertise and global infrastructure of approximately 400 offices and agents in more than 100 countries to establish a competitive advantage for the Company.

The framework of EGL's premiere non-asset-based business model consists of its international air and ocean freight forwarding, customs brokerage and related import/export services, North America expedited freight network, logistics and warehousing (including value-added distribution) and advanced information technology capabilities. Historically, transportation costs control a large percentage of the overall cost of supply chain expenses, and EGL's non-asset-based model combines the flexibility of traditional freight forwarding with multi-modal transportation without the fixed costs of owning and operating dedicated aircraft, truck fleets and ocean liners. Instead, the Company has cultivated dependable, cost-effective partnerships with suppliers that offer volume contracts to complement EGL's broad range of services.

Committed to operational excellence and superior customer service, EGL's network of global professionals remain focused on streamlining processes, improving information and providing supply and demand strategies that result in profitability for our large base of local, regional and multi-national customers. EGL maintains its loyal customer base by leveraging the collective knowledge and performance of each and every employee whose dedicated efforts result in total customer satisfaction.

Investors liked freight forwarders such as Eagle USA because, unlike transport companies, forwarders were not saddled with expensive assets to maintain and replace. Revenues were about $185 million in fiscal 1996, when the company had 1,000 employees. It operated at 50 terminals around the country, and was beginning to expand internationally. Eagle was also introducing its delivery trucks in more markets.

Computer manufacturers accounted for one-fifth of revenues, but the automotive industry was beginning to provide a significant amount of business. Eagle profited as Houston Intercontinental Airport challenged rival Miami as a Latin American gateway.

Eagle USA acquired S. Boardman, a London-based company, in 1998, thereby entering the international freight forwarding market. Eagle USA Airfreight acquired Eagle Transfer Inc., a similarly named but unrelated forwarder, later in the year. Eagle Transfer, which did business as Eagle Cos., had revenues of $19 million a year and 70 employees; it specialized in shipping to South America from its Miami base as well as Los Angeles. The acquisition gave Eagle USA a presence in Argentina, Brazil, and Chile for the first time. Eagle USA opened offices in Asia later in 1998.

In late 1999, Eagle USA acquired a couple of Canadian freight forwarders, Fastair Cargo Systems and CTI Canada, both privately owned and based in Toronto. EGL's revenues reached $638 million in 1999, when it handled 1.4 million shipments.

In October 1999, Eagle's USA Airfreight began doing business as EGL Eagle Global Logistics. The company's name was officially changed to EGL Inc. in February 2000. By this time, the company was leasing a dozen jet freighters of its own.

Acquisition of Circle International: 2000

EGL acquired Circle International Group Inc. in July 2000 in a $543 million stock swap. EGL shareholders owned 63 percent of shares after the deal; Circle shareholders owned 37 percent. There were a number of large mergers among forwarding and logistics businesses as consolidation swept the very fragmented industry. Mergers like that of EGL and Circle, which could provide customers with more global reach, were considered especially auspicious.

The combined companies had 1999 revenues of $1.4 billion and together employed 8,300 people in 400 facilities (300 of them from Circle) around the world. EGL, under CEO James Crane, had been aiming to increase its share of the growing international market for heavyweight cargo, reported the *Journal of Commerce*. Circle was much stronger internationally than EGL, which had served eight countries outside the United States. Circle operated in more than 100 countries, while EGL had become the largest American freight forwarder. Circle had few customers in common with EGL. Its main clients included Xerox Corp. and pharmaceutical giants Merck & Co. and SmithKline Beecham.

Circle had had trouble keeping its CEO position filled in the two years prior to the merger. James Crane filled the role at the merged company. EGL was considered to have better information systems at the time and a stronger, more entrepreneurial sales culture. After the merger closed on October 2, 2000, the Circle International name was phased out. Circle's San Francisco headquarters was closed; some of its employees there were transferred to Houston.

History of Circle International: 1898–2000

Circle International's origins can be traced back to 1898, when Fred Harper founded a customs brokerage in San Francisco. Its first business was importing art goods from the Orient. The Robinson family became involved in the business when their patriarch took an office job there after moving west from Kentucky.

The Robinsons acquired the firm for less than $15,000 in the early 1940s, reported *Forbes*, and the business was dubbed Harper, Robinson & Co. The firm had less than a dozen employees. As an agent for Pan American, the company expanded quickly in the Far East with the growth of the air freight business in the 1950s.

John Robinson succeeded his father as chairman of the company in 1963. Harper acquired New York-based Circle Airfreight Corp. during the year. The Harper Group came to be best

```
┌─────────────────────────────────────────────────┐
│                  Key Dates:                       │
│                                                   │
│ 1898:  Fred Harper launches customs brokerage in San │
│        Francisco.                                 │
│ 1963:  Harper acquires Circle Airfreight.        │
│ 1977:  Harper Group goes public.                 │
│ 1984:  James R. Crane founds Eagle USA Airfreight. │
│ 1989:  Harper's revenues are $400 million a year. │
│ 1995:  Eagle goes public.                        │
│ 2000:  Eagle acquires Circle International, changes name │
│        to EGL Inc.                               │
└─────────────────────────────────────────────────┘
```

known for this business. The 1960s marked the beginning of a period of international expansion. The company also expanded its diversity of services. In the 1980s, it maintained warehouses in Asia on behalf of Woolworth's.

Revenues were $40 million a year in 1976, producing profits of $3 million, reported *Forbes*. In June 1977, Harper Group became a public company. By the end of the 1980s, Harper was doing $400 million a year in business, and profits were up to $15 million. Harper employed 3,150 people in 280 offices in 42 countries around the world.

In 1988, Harper acquired Bowater Industries' freight forwarding unit for $9 million. Its 50 European branches had revenues of $85 million a year. Another significant acquisition of the late 1980s was Challenge Freight Services, a New Zealand-based specialist in perishables.

By 1993, the Harper Group was one of the top international freight forwarders in the United States, with 380 offices in 44 countries. The company developed a reputation for having the best information systems in the business.

Harper Group had 40 subsidiaries in the early 1990s, most trading under their original names. These included Max Gruenhut International, Inc. and Darrell J. Sekin and Co. (acquired in 1991). In January 1994, Gruenhut and the Circle Airfreight Corporation, Inc. were merged into Harper Robinson & Co., Inc., which was renamed Circle International, Inc. This merged with EGL, Inc. in 2000.

Beyond 2000

EGL acquired a 24.5 percent stake in charter operator Miami Air in the summer of 2000. Miami Air was converting its old fleet of eight Boeing 727s to freighters, while leasing Boeing 737s to carry passengers. It had revenues of $85.7 million in 1999. EGL leased a few of the freighters. EGL announced its first strategic alliance in November 2000, teaming with leading South American airline LanChile S.A.

EGL laid off 300 workers in January 2001, owing to a softer economy and disappointing earnings. The company also returned a couple of its leased aircraft. About 1,700 management employees took a week-long furlough in March, and another 400 layoffs were announced the next month.

EGL acquired Miami International Forwarders (MIF) in the spring of 2003. MIF had been founded in 1950 and specialized in serving the apparel industry in the Caribbean and Latin America. It had 275 employees and revenues of $23.6 million in 2002.

The U.S. occupation of Iraq kept EGL busy. The company chartered Ukrainian-made Antonov-124 freighters to keep up with demand, in addition to leasing space on two Air France 747 cargo flights a week on a Houston-Paris-Kuwait route. The rebuilding of Iraq was expected to create a demand for air freight at least until 2007.

Principal Subsidiaries

Circle International, Inc.

Principal Operating Units

Air Freight Forwarding Services; Domestic Local Delivery Services; Domestic Truck Brokerage Services; International Ocean Freight Forwarding and Consolidation; Customs Brokerage; Logistics and Other Services.

Principal Competitors

BAX Global, Inc.; DHL Danzas Air and Ocean; Expeditors International of Washington, Inc.; UPS Supply Chain Solutions; Menlo Worldwide Forwarding.

Further Reading

Armbruster, William, ''Circle International Shareholders Approve EGL Merger,'' *Journal of Commerce—JoC Online*, September 20, 2000.

——, ''EGL Adopts Poison Pill,'' *Journal of Commerce—JoC Online*, May 24, 2001.

——, ''EGL Acquires Miami International Forwarders,'' *Journal of Commerce—JoC Online*, April 1, 2003.

——, ''EGL Cuts 300 Jobs After Lower-Than-Expected Earnings Forecast,'' *Journal of Commerce—JoC Online*, January 24, 2001.

——, ''EGL Realigns US Sales, Expands DHL Alliance,'' *Journal of Commerce—JoC Online*, December 4, 2001.

——, ''LanChile, EGL Form Alliance,'' *Journal of Commerce—JoC Online*, November 15, 2000.

——, ''Not a Selling Point; Alliances Are Popular with Airlines But Low Among Forwarders' Priorities,'' *Journal of Commerce—JoC Week*, May 27, 2002, p. 22.

——, ''The Spoils of War; Capacity Tightens for Air-Cargo Carriers Even with Reconstruction of Iraq Just Getting Underway,'' *Journal of Commerce*, July 21, 2003, p. 22.

Boisseau, Charles, ''Eagle USA Airfreight Shares Fly High After Public Offering,'' *Houston Chronicle*, Bus. Sec., December 2, 1995, p. 2.

——, ''Houston Freight Forwarder Plans Public Offering of 2 Million Shares,'' *Journal of Commerce*, October 10, 1995, p. 2B.

Boisseau, Charles, and Ed Fletcher, ''And the Winners Are; 9 Local Firms Honored for Their Success,'' *Houston Chronicle*, Bus. Sec., July 2, 1996, p. 1.

''Eagle to Fly Under New Name: EGL,'' *Journal of Commerce*, February 24, 2000, p. 6.

Goldberg, Laura, ''Heavyweight in Freight; EGL to Fly Twice As High After Merger Completed,'' *Houston Chronicle*, Bus. Sec., August 18, 2000, p. 1.

Hailey, Roger, ''Crane Aims to Expand EGL and Boost Turnover to $2Bn,'' *Lloyd's List*, November 13, 2000, p. 7.

Hensel, Bill, Jr., "A Powerful Combination," *JoC Week,* July 17, 2000.

"Houston's Eagle USA to Buy Eagle Transfer," *Journal of Commerce,* January 7, 1998, p. 10A.

"International Air Freight Up in Houston; Total Cargo Moved Through 'Gateway' Doubled Since '87," *Journal of Commerce,* September 3, 1996, p. 4C.

Manolatos, Spyros, "The Power of Positive Imagery (Harper Group)," *Forbes,* April 16, 1990, p. 105.

Nelson, Eric, "John Robinson's Visionary Style Propels Harper Group's Growth," *San Francisco Business Times,* February 1, 1991, pp. 12+.

Putzger, Ian, "EGL Inc. to Buy Circle International," *Journal of Commerce—JoC Online,* July 5, 2000.

Sixel, L.M., "Furloughs Used Instead of Layoffs," *Houston Chronicle,* Bus. Sec., April 20, 2001, p. 1.

Tangeman, Nanci A., "The International Logistics of Freight Forwarding: Performance Measurement at the Harper Group," *National Productivity Review,* December 22, 1993, p. 107.

Watson, Lloyd, "New Team, New Image for Old-Line S.F. Firm," *San Francisco Chronicle,* July 22, 1987, p. 27.

"Young Freight-Forwarder Acquires Oldster," *Economist Intelligence Unit—ViewsWire,* July 26, 2000.

—Frederick C. Ingram

Emigrant Savings Bank

5 East 42nd Street
New York, New York 10017
U.S.A.
Telephone: (212) 850-4000
Toll Free: (888) 364-4726
Fax: (212) 850-4870
Web site: http://www.emigrant.com

Wholly Owned Subsidiary of Emigrant Bancorp Inc.
Incorporated: 1850 as Emigrant Industrial Savings Bank
Employees: 1,279
Total Assets: $9.73 billion (2002)
NAIC: 522110 Commercial Banking; 522291 Consumer
   Lending; 522310 Mortgage and Other Loan Brokers;
   551111 Offices of Bank Holding Companies

Emigrant Savings Bank is a savings bank chartered by the state of New York. In addition to providing its customers with a full range of traditional banking products, Emigrant offers life insurance, residential mortgages, commercial real estate loans, and business loans. Emigrant*Online* is the name of its web-based banking and bill-payment service. The bank is a subsidiary of a holding company, Emigrant Bancorp Inc.

Founding, Survival, and Growth: 1850–1970

The Irish Emigrant Society was founded in 1841 to aid immigrants to New York City from the Emerald Isle. At this time the average immigrant was arriving with only the equivalent of $8, and these newcomers were immediately set upon by boarding-house ''runners'' who steered them to dilapidated lodgings where they were charged excessive rates for rooms and baggage storage. The steady stream of Irish newcomers swelled to a torrent with the famine that followed the failure of the potato crop in 1846. Through its account with the Bank of Ireland, the Irish Emigrant Society sold bills of exchange which the immigrants bought with their wages to send home to their hard-pressed relatives, who remitted them for cash. This service forestalled swindlers who sold fraudulent drafts to immigrants.

With the support of Irish-born John Hughes, New York's first archbishop, 18 members of the society contributed $200 each to found the Emigrant Industrial Savings Bank in 1850. The bank opened for business at 51 Chambers Street, a squat clapboard building in downtown Manhattan. By the end of the year, the Emigrant Bank had nearly 300 customers, and by 1857, it was the city's seventh largest savings bank, with assets of $1.37 million. Bank deposits were invested in mortgage loans, with the first, at 7 percent, to a man who borrowed $6,000 in 1851 to buy three houses on a street corner of the Lower East Side. In 1852 the bank loaned Archbishop Hughes money to buy lots on a Fifth Avenue site—then far uptown—where St. Patrick's Cathedral now stands. Five years later, Emigrant bought shares offered by the Central Park Commission for the public park that bears this name.

Opening an account at the Emigrant Industrial Savings Bank was no easy task. To assure security, and often to compensate for the illiteracy of their clients, bank officers filled out responses to a lengthy questionnaire that included much personal information. The contents of these questionnaires are now stored in the New York Public Library. Since 80 percent of all early clients were Irish, these records are especially useful to Irish-Americans researching family history.

By keeping about half of its assets invested in government bonds and Treasury notes, the Emigrant Industrial Savings Bank avoided the ruin that beset many financial institutions and businesses in the second half of the 19th century. By 1900 it had more than $57 million in assets, and by 1925, with $290 million in assets, it was the largest savings bank in the United States. The original headquarters had been replaced and, since 1912, the Chambers Street site housed a 17-story building in the Beaux Arts style. The bank established its first branch in 1925, next to Grand Central Station in midtown Manhattan, which had replaced lower Manhattan as the commercial heart of the city. This branch moved to an East 42nd Street site close to Fifth Avenue in 1932. By this time the deposits of the midtown branch came to nearly one-third of the bank's total deposits of more than $400 million.

For a so-called thrift institution, Emigrant Industrial Savings Bank had unusual advice to offer during the Depression. In 1931 it urged its depositors to draw upon surplus savings for what a bank officer called "judicious spending" in order to spark a business revival by stimulating retail trade. This executive noted that the bank had received what he described to the *New York Times* as a "tide of commendation" from newspapers, firms, and individuals in every part of the nation during the three weeks since it issued its advice. He conceded, however, that bank deposits had continued to exceed withdrawals during this period.

Other banks were soon to receive so many withdrawal demands from depositors acting in a state of panic that they were unable to meet their commitments and had to suspend business or close for good. Conservatively managed Emigrant had no such problem. Although it failed to keep pace with the growth of some other savings banks, its assets more than doubled between 1925 and 1950. Emigrant opened another branch, in Manhattan's garment district, in 1953. In 1967 the bank dropped "Industrial" from its name and opened a midtown branch at Third Avenue and East 45th Street. Two years later, Emigrant moved its headquarters to a new 27-story building at 5 East 42nd Street. This also became the new location of its 42nd Street branch. The Chambers Street branch moved to nearby 281 Broadway at this time.

Major Changes: 1970–90

Emigrant Savings Bank was a survivor of the numerous mergers that characterized savings banks in the metropolitan New York area during the late 20th century. In 1970 Emigrant acquired the Queens-based City Savings and Loan Association. Nine years later it acquired Prudential Savings Bank, making it the fourth largest mutual savings bank in the state of New York and the fifth largest in the United States. The number of its offices in the city and Long Island now reached 32.

With their heavy investments in mortgage securities, U.S. savings banks found themselves badly squeezed by the high inflation of the 1970s and early 1980s. Depositors demanded, and received, interest rates far above what the banks were earning on their mortgage and bond investments. Emigrant lost $230 million between 1980 and 1984. In June 1982 a state official told a congressional committee that Emigrant, with assets of $3.1 billion, was in danger of failure by the end of the year if it did not receive federal assistance. Emigrant subsequently was one of several mutual savings banks allowed to issue net-worth certificates that then were purchased by the Federal Deposit Insurance Corp., which in turn issued promissory notes to the assisted institution. In mid-1985 Emigrant held $90 million in such certificates and would otherwise have had a negative net worth of $60.7 million.

Emigrant emerged from its difficulties at the end of 1986 by converting from a mutual to a stock savings bank, with the entire stock issued to real estate developers Seymour and Paul Milstein, who agreed to provide $90 million to the institution through their firm Milstein Properties Inc. Among the Milstein holdings in Manhattan were the Biltmore, Milford Plaza, and Roosevelt hotels, plus three large apartment buildings near Lincoln Center with a total of 1,964 units. For their money the Milsteins received a concern with 27 offices, 500,000 depositors, 70,000 borrowers, assets of $3.6 billion—and an operating profit, thanks to a turnaround in interest rates. The Milsteins agreed not to violate federal and state laws intended to prevent property developers from using thrift institutions to finance their own projects at favorable rates.

"Plain-Vanilla" Bank: 1990–2003

Many investment bankers expected the Milsteins to sell Emigrant for a quick profit. When they did not do so, the speculation was that the subsequent slump in the regional economy was making it hard for them to find a buyer. Another theory was that they were holding the institution to help their children establish careers in banking. In any case, the Milsteins invested another $50 million in the bank. Over the next five years Emigrant earned at least $30 million each year while, by contrast, savings banks as a group averaged a negative return on assets during this period. Emigrant's formula for success was to avoid construction loans, which turned sour during the 1990–91 recession. It also avoided junk bonds, speculative cooperative and condominium conversions, and highly leveraged transactions, choosing to remain what Emigrant Chairman and CEO Raymond V. O'Brien, Jr., called a "plain vanilla savings bank." Nonperforming loans—mostly mortgages for one- to four-family residences—came to only 2 percent in 1991.

In 1992 Emigrant, in a major expansion move, acquired troubled Dollar Dry Dock Bank for $34.9 million, thereby doubling its assets. Emigrant gained 20 branches by the purchase, some of which it sold, and some 1,200 employees, many of whom were dismissed. Dollar Dry Dock had fallen into trouble by making bad loans in commercial real estate. Its branches had been redesigned in the mid-1980s as one-stop providers of banking products, securities, insurance, foreign exchange, and even travel services, but O'Brien indicated that, like Emigrant's own branches, they would in future do little more than take deposits and underwrite residential mortgage loans. Emigrant did not make news again until 1999, when it established a $150 million fund, Emigrant Capital, to invest in emerging companies that typically do not qualify for bank loans. In 2001 the bank—somewhat belatedly—introduced EmigrantOnline, a free service enabling its customers to check their balances and statements by computer, transfer funds between accounts, make loan payments, and communicate with the bank through e-mail.

Of greater interest was the rift between Paul and Seymour Milstein that developed after the latter's son, Philip, was named president and chief executive officer of the bank and its holding company in 1993. According to a 2000 article by Alan Kline and Veronica Agosta of *American Banker,* a bank officer told this trade daily that at least six companies had considered acquiring Emigrant during the past few years, "and they were

Key Dates:

1850: Establishment of Emigrant Industrial Savings Bank to serve Irish immigrants.
1925: Manhattan-based Emigrant has grown into the largest savings bank in the United States.
1950: Assets have doubled since 1925.
1967: Emigrant drops ''Industrial'' from its name.
1969: The bank moves its headquarters uptown to 42nd Street.
1979: Acquisitions have made Emigrant the fifth largest U.S. mutual savings bank.
1986: Emigrant is acquired by real estate developers Seymour and Paul Milstein.
1992: Emigrant acquires financially troubled Dollar Dry Dock Bank.
2003: The two branches of the Milsteins agree to settle their family feud.

all turned back by the idea of the Milsteins being on their boards. They are constantly fighting. They are untrusted.''

Paul Milstein, along with his sons Howard and Edward, filed an unsuccessful lawsuit in 2000 seeking to remove Philip Milstein from his positions. The lawsuit contended that Howard Milstein had been appointed co-chief executive soon after 1993 but that Philip had undercut Howard's authority by refusing to call meetings that involved him and had not called a shareholders' meeting since 1996 in order to prevent a vote that might oust him. They also alleged that Philip Milstein had refused to consider converting Emigrant to a subchapter S corporation unless the shareholders agreed to make him president for life. They contended that such a conversion would have saved Emigrant about $50 million a year in federal taxes after banks and thrift institutions became eligible for such status in 1997, maintaining, ''In essence, Philip Milstein has hijacked Emigrant and is holding the institution . . . hostage to his demand for absolute and permanent control of Emigrant.'' Seymour Milstein died in 2001. The two branches of the family settled their feud in 2003. They agreed that Emigrant would be run by both until Paul's family bought out the interests of Seymour's family. The bank was valued at nearly $2 billion, and the Milsteins reportedly held 91 percent of the stock when Seymour died.

Emigrant Savings Bank, in 2002, had 12 branches in Manhattan, five in Brooklyn, five in Queens, three in the Bronx, eight on Long Island, and three in Westchester County. Its assets at the end of 2002 totaled $9.73 billion and its deposits, $5.05 billion. Its net income came to $114.22 million in 2002. Subsidiaries of the bank were engaged in activities such as offering residential and commercial mortgage loans and loans collateralized by multifamily and mixed-use properties, and financing for various business assets, focusing on equipment such as vehicles, aircraft, and construction and manufacturing equipment. A financial services agency of the bank was providing investment products (such as mutual funds) and life insurance.

Emigrant's primary deposit products were checking, savings, and term-certificate accounts, and its primary lending products were residential mortgage, commercial, and installment loans. It also offered personal loans, installment loans, safety deposit boxes, and credit cards. Most loans were secured by specific items of collateral, including business assets, consumer assets, and real estate. Commercial loans were expected to be repaid from cash flow from operations of businesses. Real-estate loans were secured by both residential and commercial real estate. Other financial instruments, which potentially represented concentrations of credit risk, included deposit accounts in other financial institutions and federal funds sold.

Principal Subsidiaries

American Property Financing, Inc.; Emigrant Business Credit Corp.; Emigrant Capital; Emigrant Funding Corp.; Emigrant Mortgage Company, Inc.

Principal Competitors

Apple Bank for Savings; Flushing Savings Bank; GreenPoint Bank; Independence Community Bank; Ridgewood Savings Bank.

Further Reading

Bagli, Charles V., ''Wealthy Real Estate Family Settles Decade-Long Feud,'' *New York Times,* April 16, 2003, p. D3.

Basch, Mark, ''Three NY Savings Banks Are About to Lose Their Liferaft,'' *American Banker,* September 6, 1985, pp. 3, 7.

Bennett, Robert A., ''Warning Issued on 2 Big Banks,'' *New York Times,* June 8, 1982, pp. D1, D11.

Berg, Eric N., ''Developers Acquire Emigrant Bank,'' *New York Times,* January 5, 1987, pp. D1, D6.

''Depositors Heed Advice on Spending,'' *New York Times,* September 8, 1931, p. 44.

''Emigrant Makes It Happen for Two Aspiring Bankers,'' *Newsday,* March 2, 1987, Part 3, p. 5.

Kline, Alan, ''N.Y.'s Emigrant Starting Capital Fund for Financing Small-Business Ventures,'' *American Banker,* August 6, 1999, p. 5.

Kline, Alan, and Veronica Agosta, ''Family Feud at N.Y.'s Emigrant,'' *American Banker,* May 2, 2000, pp. 1, 7.

McNatt, Robert, ''Thriftiest Thrives in Trying Bank Time,'' *Crain's New York Business,* March 2, 1992, pp. 1, 25.

''New Banking Quarters Ready,'' *New York Times,* November 13, 1932, Sec. 10–11, p. 1.

Pristin, Terry, ''Seymour Milstein, City Real Estate Magnate, Dies at 81,'' *New York Times,* October 31, 2001, p. A20.

Roosevelt, Phil, ''Emigrant: Cautious Lender, Bold Acquirer,'' *American Banker,* March 20, 1992, pp 1, 14.

Roth, Andrew, ''Emigrant: A Newcomer to Web Banking,'' *American Banker,* July 20, 2001, p. 18.

Song, Sora, ''A Rich History, *Community Banker,* July 2000, pp. 16 + .

—Robert Halasz

Engineered Support Systems, Inc.

Engineered Support Systems, Inc.

201 Evans Lane
St. Louis, Missouri 63121
U.S.A.
Telephone: (314) 553-4000
Fax: (314) 993-4615
Web site: http://www.engineeredsupport.com

Public Company
Incorporated: 1983
Employees: 2,412
Sales: $407.95 million (2002)
Stock Exchanges: NASDAQ
Ticker Symbol: EASI
NAIC: 333319 Other Commercial and Service Industry
Machinery Manufacturing; 333415 Air-Conditioning
and Warm Air Heating Equipment and Commercial
and Industrial Refrigeration Equipment
Manufacturing; 334511 Search, Detection, Navigation,
Guidance, Aeronautical, and Nautical System and
Instrument Manufacturing; 335312 Motor and
Generator Manufacturing

Engineered Support Systems, Inc. (ESSI) produces a number of items of specialized military gear. These include enclosed tent shelters to keep out biochemical hazards, HVAC systems and quiet generators, and the trailers used to ferry M-1 tanks to Baghdad.

CEO Gerald Daniels described the company's business as "sustainment"—giving troops the equipment and ground support they need to be deployed. As founder Michael Shanahan, Sr., puts it, "The military doesn't leave home without us." The U.S. government accounts for more than 90 percent of sales. "Acquisitions are a way of life for us," Daniels told the *St. Louis Business Journal* in 2003, and he set a goal of growing the company into a $1 billion business. ESSI's subsidiaries supply services as well as hardware. Through ESSIbuy.com, military personnel in the field can download manuals and order spare parts.

Origins

As the youngest of eight children of Irish immigrants, Michael F. Shanahan, Sr., learned the value of work early in life. Although only a "C" student, he confessed to the *St. Louis Post-Dispatch,* he eventually thrived and was able to give a great deal back to his community of St. Louis, helping out the local hockey team and supporting his alma mater, St. Louis University.

After launching his career with McDonnell Douglas Automation Co., Numerical Control Inc., and Cleveland Pneumatic Co., Shanahan cofounded Engineered Air Systems, Inc. (EAS) with Jerome V. LaBarbera. EAS was incorporated in Missouri on December 24, 1981. Shanahan served as the company's chairman and chief executive officer, and was also chairman of the St. Louis Blues Hockey Club. EAS acquired Allis-Chalmers Corporation's Defense Systems Division on March 30, 1982. In December 1983, Engineered Support Systems, Inc. (ESSI) was formed as a holding company for EAS. The company produced a variety of ground support equipment for the military, including nuclear, biological, and chemical defense systems; environmental control systems; and water and petroleum distribution systems.

Engineered Support Systems Inc. went public on the NASDAQ exchange on August 21, 1985, under the ticker symbol EASI. Revenues were $51 million in 1985; net income was about $2 million.

About 30 types of equipment produced by ESSI were used in the Persian Gulf War, including canisters in the famous Patriot missile. Water purification and laundry units were especially in demand. After the war, Pentagon cutbacks resulted in layoffs of 140 workers from a peak workforce of about 400. Sales were $67.7 million in 1991; they fell to $40.4 million in the fiscal year ended October 31, 1992, leading to a $239,000 loss.

Trying Commercial Plastics in 1993

After the post-Gulf War bust, ESSI went looking for commercial companies to acquire to bring it into new markets. According to the *St. Louis Post-Dispatch,* the company pored over 100 potential acquisitions in two years. In early 1993, it

Company Perspectives:

Engineered Support Systems' mission is clear—to continue delivering exceptional performance with our sound strategy of internal growth, selective acquisitions and differentiated technology. Our financial results clearly underscore this performance with seven consecutive years of record revenues and profits.

acquired Associated Products Inc., a plastics company based in Hot Springs, Arkansas, with sales of more than $20 million a year. Associated's two subsidiaries, Wycot Corp. and Life Time Faucets Inc., produced plastic television cabinets and plastic faucets, respectively.

Associated Products, renamed Engineered Specialty Plastics Inc., became the basis of ESSI's commercial division. Diversification came none too soon, as ESSI's defense revenues fell to $27.8 million in 1993. The plastics business contributed $14.4 million; ESSI was growing the business organically and through acquisitions and investing in increased capacity. ESSI achieved a profit of $520,000 in 1993.

It was the defense unit, rather than the commercial side, that saw the biggest growth in the mid-1990s, despite an overall decrease in military procurement in the United States. ESSI's earnings more than doubled in 1995, thanks in part to its military programs shifting from development to production phases. The commercial plastics business accounted for a third of ESSI's revenues of $65.5 million, but was barely profitable.

ESSI then shifted its acquisitions strategy to look for defense, rather than commercial, companies to acquire, particularly those whose skills it could tap in making its shelters, reported the *St. Louis Post-Dispatch*. The military support industry was ripe for consolidation, and ESSI aimed to be one of the survivors.

The defense slowdown of the early 1990s had one positive outcome for ESSI—it thinned the ranks of the competition. Later in the decade, the Department of Defense shifted more of the research and development burden to contractors like Engineered Support. Its products were typically unique, highly engineered, and often required hand assembly.

In 1996, EAS won a production contract for a new Kevlar-coated fabric shelter it had developed to protect Army troops from chemical or biological attack. The deal was worth at least $150 million and had a potential total value of more than $400 million.

In 1997, ESSI began developing a Humvee-mounted electronic targeting and communications system called STRIKER for the U.S. Army. It was in production within 18 months, with plans to complete 800 of the systems in ten years, a total value of more than $200 million.

Late 1990s Acquisitions Push

ESSI acquired four companies in 1998 and 1999, pushing its total revenues past $100 million. Nuclear Cooling, Inc., doing business as Marlo Coil, was acquired effective February 1, 1998. Marlo Coil produced HVAC systems for Navy and commercial use; it had revenues of about $26 million a year.

A major competitor, Keco Industries Inc., was acquired in June 1998. Keco operated a plant in Florence, Ohio, and had sales of $42 million a year. It produced HVAC equipment, water and fuel distribution systems, and shipping and storage containers.

In February 1999, ESSI announced the acquisition of Dynamics Corp. of America's fast-growing Fermont Division, which produced military generator sets. Fermont, formally named Engineered Electric Co., was based in Bridgeport, Connecticut, and had sales of $40 million a year. The $85 million acquisition of Systems & Electronics Inc. (SEI) in 1999 from Esco Corp. gave ESSI its largest facility, located in West Plains, Missouri.

ESSI grew rapidly because of acquisitions, tripling its sales in just a couple of years. Revenues were $361.5 million in 2000. ESSI had about 2,400 employees. The deployment of U.S. troops to Bosnia and numerous other trouble spots boosted the company's profile. Military procurement levels were rising again.

In February 2001, ESSI launched a web site, ESSIbuy.com, to sell spare parts and services. By going online with parts procurement, ESSI claimed to reduce the wait for some spare parts from months to days. Maintenance manuals could also be downloaded by military personnel in the field.

The September 11, 2001 terrorist attacks against the United States made defense stocks in demand again after a decade of uncertainty and downsizing following the end of the Cold War. ESSI supplied a variety of equipment to support U.S. troops in Afghanistan, from aircraft cargo loaders to quiet field generators.

Federal and state governments were expected to provide some demand for ESSI's unique product mix as the multibillion-dollar homeland security budget swelled. The potential civil defense applications of ESSI's biochemical protection shelters had already been discussed well before the terrorist attacks of September 11. ESSI ended 2001 with income of $18.6 million on $390.5 million in sales.

ESSI acquired Radian Inc., an Alexandria, Virginia-based engineering, logistics, and systems integration firm, for $42 million in May 2002. Radian had 400 employees and sales of more than $50 million a year.

Universal Power Systems, Inc. (UPSI) was acquired in June 2002. ESSI paid $5.5 million cash for the Chantilly, Virginia-based company, which had revenues of about $6 million a year. UPSI's uninterruptible power supply systems were in frontline service with a number of military branches, defense agencies, and remote industrial sites.

Net revenues increased 12 percent to $407.9 million in 2002 (nearly five times fiscal 1998 sales), while net earnings reached a record $23.5 million. During the year, ESSI closed its plant in Olivette, near St. Louis, Missouri, home to the Engineered Air Systems subsidiary. About 40 employees were laid off. EAS's administrative functions were transferred to ESSI's headquar-

Key Dates:

1981: Engineered Air Systems, Inc. (EAS) is founded.
1983: Engineered Support Systems, Inc. (ESSI) holding company is formed.
1985: ESSI goes public.
1997: The company launches a consolidation program.
1998: Marlo Coil, McIntyre Engineering, and Keco Industries are acquired.
1999: The Fermont Division of Dynamic Corp. of America and Systems & Electronics Inc. are acquired.
2002: The company acquires Radian, Universal Power Systems.
2003: Plastic Products is divested; TAMSCO, Engineered Environments is acquired.

ters in nearby Cool Valley, while production of shelters was transferred to ESSI's largest plant, in West Plains, Missouri. Another plant in Blue Ash, Ohio, was also closed, and its production transferred to a facility in Florence, Kentucky, along with the HVAC business from the Olivette plant. ESSI also maintained facilities in Hot Springs, Arkansas; Bridgeport, Connecticut; Sanford, Florida; and Bossier City, Louisiana. The Florida plant was closed in 2003.

New CEO in 2003

ESSI named Gerald (Jerry) Daniels its new chief executive officer and vice-chairman in April 2003. Daniels had been a captain in the Navy, and formerly led the Military Aircraft and Missile Systems unit of Boeing Co., and had also been an executive with McDonnell Douglas. He aimed to take ESSI to $1 billion in sales by partnering with prime defense contractors. Company cofounder and CEO since 1985, Michael Shanahan, Sr., continued as chairman.

The $66.5 million cash acquisition of Calverton, Maryland-based Technical & Management Services Corp. (TAMSCO) closed soon afterward. This pushed ESSI's 2003 revenues past $500 million. TAMSCO provided Internet and other communications services to Army and Air Force personnel in the field; it had revenues of about $115 million a year.

While it was consolidating its defense-related core, ESSI divested its marginally profitable plastic products business. Engineered Specialty Plastics Inc. and Lifetime Faucets Inc. were sold to a private equity group for $7.4 million in April 2003.

ESSI acquired Engineered Environments, Inc. (EEI), a maker of environmental control units for industry and the military, in September 2003. ESSI paid $15.5 million and paid off some of EEI's debts in the deal. Based in Cincinnati, EEI had 70 employees and 2002 revenues of $14.4 million, mostly from defense-related contracts.

Principal Subsidiaries

Engineered Air Systems, Inc. (EAS); Engineered Coil/Marlo Coil (MARLO); Engineered Electric/Fermont (FERMONT); Engineered Environments, Inc. (EEI); ESSIbuy.com (ESSIbuy); Keco Industries, Inc. (Keco); Radian Inc. (RADIAN); Systems & Electronics Inc. (SEI); Technical and Management Services Corporation (TAMSCO); Universal Power Systems, Inc. (UPSI).

Principal Divisions

Light Military Support Equipment; Heavy Military Support Equipment; Electronics & Automation Systems.

Principal Competitors

AAR Corp.; General Dynamics Corporation; Honeywell International.

Further Reading

Benesh, Peter, "A Match Made on the Battlefield; Defense Supplier Offers Equipment, Services to U.S. Troops Around Globe," *Investor's Business Daily,* September 29, 2003, p. B2.

Cancelada, Gregory, "Engineered Support Plans to Close Its Plant in Olivette; 120 Employees Will Lose Their Jobs As the Company Reduces Excess Capacity," *St. Louis Post-Dispatch,* July 18, 2002, p. C1.

Carey, Christopher, "Acquisition of Marlo Coil Will Expand Defense Unit's Business," *St. Louis Post-Dispatch,* February 12, 1998, p. B1.

——, "Defense Firm's Outlook Rosy," *St. Louis Post-Dispatch,* March 11, 1994, p. 9D.

——, "Engineered Support Closes ESCO Deal," *St. Louis Post-Dispatch,* October 2, 1999, p. 14.

——, "Engineered Support Suffers Growing Pains; Company Must Broaden Expertise, Shanahan Says," *St. Louis Post-Dispatch,* March 11, 1998, p. D2.

——, "Engineered Support Thriving on Defense," *St. Louis Post-Dispatch,* March 7, 1996, p. 3C.

——, "Engineered Support Will Try Out Its New Muscle; Shanahan Sees Strong Potential for Growth," *St. Louis Post-Dispatch,* March 9, 1999, p. C7.

——, "Shanahan's Other Team," *St. Louis Post-Dispatch,* May 14, 1995, p. E1.

——, "Special Shelters Mean Money; Engineered Support Gets Army Contract," *St. Louis Post-Dispatch,* October 11, 1996, p. 10C.

Droog, Pam, "2003 St. Louis Regional Advanced Manufacturing Award Winner: Engineered Support Systems Inc.," *St. Louis Commerce Magazine,* September 1, 2003, p. 62.

"Engineered Support Looks to Buy Radian," *St. Louis Business Journal,* March 4, 2002.

"Engineered Support Sells Plastics Unit to Private Equity Group," *St. Louis Business Journal,* April 21, 2003.

"Engineered Support to Close Fla. Plant, Move Production to Mo.," *St. Louis Business Journal,* March 31, 2003.

Goodman, Adam, "Engineered Support Expects More Orders; Pentagon, Foreign Nations Among Buyers," *St. Louis Post-Dispatch,* March 15, 1991, p. 3B.

——, "Engineered Support Layoffs Total 140," *St. Louis Post-Dispatch,* August 22, 1991, p. 1B.

——, "Engineered Support Looking to Diversify," *St. Louis Post-Dispatch,* March 13, 1992, p. 9D.

——, "Engineered Support Makes 1st Commercial Acquisition," *St. Louis Post-Dispatch,* January 3, 1993, p. 6B.

Majors, Dawn, "Q&A with Chairman of St. Louis-Based Engineered Support Systems," *St. Louis Post-Dispatch,* June 13, 2003.

Nicklaus, David, "Engineered Support Systems Lifts Stock Price Old-Fashioned Way: It Makes Money," *St. Louis Post-Dispatch,* July 28, 2001, p. 1.

——, ''Military Supplier Rides Winds of War,'' *St. Louis Post-Dispatch,* October 17, 2001, p. B1.

Romine, Joyce, ''2000 Entrepreneur of the Year Awards: Master—Michael F. Shanahan, Sr.,'' *St. Louis Commerce Magazine,* July 1, 2000, p. 24.

Song, Kyung M., ''Defense Firm Buys Competitor; Engineered Support Sees Higher Profit,'' *St. Louis Post-Dispatch,* May 19, 1998, p. C7.

Stuenkel, Gil, ''In Depth: Entrepreneur of the Year; Michael Shanahan Sr., Engineered Support Systems Inc.,'' *St. Louis Business Journal,* June 19, 2000.

Sybert, Laurie, ''Engineered's Daniels Converts Old Contacts into New Contracts,'' *St. Louis Business Journal,* September 22, 2003.

Tucci, Linda, ''They Keep Score, So Mike Shanahan Plays to Win,'' *St. Louis Post-Dispatch,* June 13, 2003, p. C5.

Wilson, Cynthia, ''Army Approves Production of St. Louis Company's Electronic Targeting System,'' *St. Louis Post-Dispatch,* November 21, 2000, p. B6.

——, ''Engineered Support Links Internet with the Battlefield; ESSIbuy.com Becomes a Storefront for Selling Spare Parts and Services,'' *St. Louis Post-Dispatch,* February 4, 2001, p. E1.

——, ''Engineered Support Looks for a Niche in Combating Terrorism,'' *St. Louis Post-Dispatch,* Business Plus Sec., April 8, 2002, p. 12.

——, ''Engineered Support Names Jerry Daniels Its New CEO; McDonnell Douglas, Boeing Vet Says He'll Aggressively Pursue $1 Billion in Sales,'' *St. Louis Post-Dispatch,* March 5, 2003, p. C1.

—Frederick C. Ingram

Enterprise Inns plc

3 Monkspath Hall Road
Solihull
West Midlands B90 4SJ
United Kingdom
Telephone: +44-121-733-7700
Fax: +44-121-733-6447
Web site: http://www.enterpriseinns.com

Public Company
Incorporated: 1991
Employees: 422
Sales: £368.9 million ($575.9 million) (2002)
Stock Exchanges: London
Ticker Symbol: ETI
NAIC: 722410 Drinking Places (Alcoholic Beverages);
    424820 Wine and Distilled Alcoholic Beverage
    Merchant Wholesalers; 531190 Lessors of Other Real
    Estate Property

Enterprise Inns plc is the United Kingdom's largest pub company, boasting a portfolio of more than 5,300 pubs across Great Britain. Unlike most of its competitors, Enterprise has long eschewed the managed pubs market and instead focuses on building up its estate of leased and tenanted pubs. Enterprise owns the properties and leases them to tenant-operators under a franchise-like arrangement in which Enterprise provides support services. In return, pub operators are required to purchase all of their beer and most of their other beverage needs from Enterprise. Some 75 percent of Enterprise's revenues, which neared £370 million ($576 million) in 2002, come from beverage sales; the remainder is generated by rents on its properties. This structure allows the company to maintain a relatively lean management organization; much of the company's management decisions are carried out through a team of district managers, each of whom oversees a group of 50 pubs in their region. As such, CEO Ted Tuppen, who formed the company in 1991, provides little day-to-day direction and instead concentrates on building the company's portfolio through an ambitious acquisition strategy—by early 2004, the company expects its portfolio

to soar past 9,000 pubs, giving the company control of some 15 percent of the total U.K. market.

Opportunistic Origins in the 1980s

Pubs in the United Kingdom had traditionally been controlled by the country's giant brewing groups. Yet in the late 1980s, the Tory government demanded limits placed on the brewing group's pub estates. As a result of the Beer Orders of 1989, which required that the brewers divest their excess properties before the end of 1992, some 11,000 pubs—of a total of more than 60,000—suddenly came onto the open market.

A number of entrepreneurs recognized the opportunity in building a new breed of pub-based businesses. One of these entrepreneurs was Ted Tuppen, then 38 years old. Tuppen had no prior experience in the pub or beverage industry, having initially worked as an accountant for KPMG in the 1970s, before going on to run an engineering company through most of the 1980s. Yet, as Tuppen told *Venture Magazine:* "Pubs which had previously not been available to outsiders suddenly became available in large quantities. It was a completely false market created by government interference, and it gave me the opportunity to start a new business—one in which I had no experience at all."

Yet Tuppen had begun building an experienced management team, including drinks industry veteran Michael Cottrell, who was named chairman of the company, and set about raising financing from venture capitalists. "It was opportunistic and it was easy to understand," Tuppen told *Venture.* "We were buying pubs that had been in the same format for 100 years; it wasn't introducing a new concept. We could predict trading patterns with a high degree of confidence."

In addition, under the previous "tied" owner-tenant relationship, breweries had no incentive to optimize a location's potential, where pubs served only a limited range of products produced by their owner-brewers. Under the Enterprise Inns business model, Tuppen promised to maximize the potential of its proposed assets, providing strong support services, including training programs, as well as expanded product lines. By the end of 1989, Tuppen had succeeded in raising £50 million.

Company Perspectives:

The Company continues to invest substantial capital, alongside our licensees, to further enhance the estate quality.

Enterprise Inns then began negotiating its first purchase, a process that resulted in the acquisition of 368 Midlands region-based pubs from the Bass brewery group (which later became Six Continents). The company then began negotiating wholesaling agreements with the country's major brewers, and by the middle of the decade had given its pub operators access to more than 30 brewers and some 90 percent of the United Kingdom's leading beer brands. Enterprise also worked toward improving its properties as well.

''We set about improving the fabric of our pubs: this is very subjective,'' Tuppen explained to *Venture*. ''It meant whatever was appropriate to that particular area. We have no desire to come up with a formulaic approach. We have improved the quality of our licensees through training and we have improved the quality of products offered.'' In this respect, Enterprise swam against the tide, as the U.K. pubs industry turned to a managed pub model, in which pubs—generally grouped into themed chains—were directly owned and managed by the pub company.

Nonetheless, Enterprise stuck to its tenanted concept and by 1994 the company was ready to begin its first expansion effort, the purchase of a package of 75 pubs from Allied Lyons, predecessor to Allied Domecq. That purchase was followed in early 1995 by the acquisition of 45 pubs from Whitbread.

In order to fuel further expansion, however, Enterprise had to look beyond its venture capital base. In November 1995, the company listed on the London Stock Exchange. The company's first purchase following the public offering was a modest one, adding ten properties from Greenalls.

Opportunity knocked again at the beginning of 1996, when Belgian brewing giant Interbrew decided to sell off its U.K. pub estate, John Labatt Retail. Enterprise stepped in, paying £61.5 million to acquire the 413-pub portfolio. The purchase placed the company on the pub map, enabling it to break out of its Midlands-region focus with a strong range of properties in the Southeast and London markets.

Building a ''Perfect'' Pub Giant for the New Century

That deal proved to be a turning point for the company, as it began to command new respect in the pub industry. As Tuppen said, ''We doubled our size and moved from being regional to national. It substantially changed the profile of our business. We began to develop our reputation as effective managers of a large pub estate and as canny acquirers.'' Enterprise also had begun to gain recognition for its commitment to a tenanted estate, particularly for its smaller properties where weekly revenues generated were not enough to justify the expense of direct management.

Tuppen began scouting for the next prospect, and in April 1997 announced that it had reached an agreement to acquire

Discovery Inns for the bargain price of £46 million. Formed from a spinoff of a number of former Whitbread-held pubs, the acquisition boosted Enterprise's portfolio by an additional 277 pubs located in Wales, the West Midlands, and the West Country. It also enabled Enterprise to renegotiate its supply contract with Whitbread, expanding its line of beers.

Enterprise turned to Whitbread directly in September 1997, paying £11 million for 94 pubs. The company also acquired eight more pubs that month from Southeast-based Pubmaster, paying less than £2 million. Yet Enterprise had already begun preparing a new large-scale deal, which culminated in February 1998 with the £48 million purchase of brewery and pubs group Gibbs Mew. Founded a century earlier, Gibbs Mew added 310 pubs to Enterprise's portfolio, which now climbed past 1,500 pubs. Enterprise then sold off Gibbs Mew's brewery and wholesale businesses, as well as a number of its underperforming pubs, raising some £20 million against its purchase price.

Setting itself a new goal of reaching 2,500 pubs by the end of the decade, Enterprise found its next acquisition target in October 1998, paying £37 million to acquire the 276-strong tenanted pub estate of Mayfair Taverns. The company then turned predator the following year, launching a hostile takeover of rival Century Inns in March 1999. That acquisition, at a cost of £78 million, added more than 500 new pubs to the company's estate. Soon after, Enterprise returned to Bass, paying £69 million—plus 20 managed pubs acquired from Century—in exchange for 217 tenanted pubs.

By the end of 1999, Enterprise had nearly succeeded in meeting its initial goal, with more than 2,400 pubs in its portfolio. The company nonetheless showed no signs of slowing down, announcing that its existing management structure was large enough to handle more than 3,000 pubs—and that it was willing to expand its estate to as many as 6,000 pubs.

The company slowed the pace of purchases through much of 2000, focusing instead on pruning its portfolio, selling off poor performers while spending some £50 million adding a number of individual properties. Nonetheless, the company made one major deal that year, paying Whitbread £110 million for 183 houses located primarily in Yorkshire and Lancashire. The company then generated some £50 million through the sale of 35 managed pubs acquired in that purchase.

Whitbread provided Enterprise with its next major acquisition the following year, when Enterprise agreed to pay £262.5 million to Morgan Grenfell—the Deutsche Bank arm that had taken over Whitbread's 3,000-strong pub portfolio—for a package of 439 managed pubs. These were then converted to the company's preferred tenanted pub format.

Meanwhile, Enterprise had partnered with Noble House Leisure, a themed bar and restaurant specialist, to take over 650 pubs from Scottish & Newcastle. Enterprise's share of that purchase added 432 houses to its portfolio, at a cost of £260 million. By the end of 2001, Enterprise had boosted its estate past 3,500 pubs.

Yet Tuppen's biggest deals were yet to come. In March 2002, Enterprise announced that it had formed a consortium, called the Unique Pub Company, to purchase the 4,000-strong

Key Dates:

1989: Ted Tuppen forms management team to found Enterprise Inns in order to acquire tenanted pubs.
1991: Enterprise buys 368 pubs from Bass.
1994: Enterprise buys 75 pubs from Allied Lyons.
1995: The company acquires 45 pubs from Whitbread; a public listing is made on the London stock exchange.
1996: The company acquires the 413-pub John Labatt portfolio from Interbrew.
1997: The company acquires Discovery Inns and buys 94 pubs from Whitbread.
1998: The company acquires Gibbs Mews, adding 310 pubs, and Mayfair Taverns, with 276 pubs.
1999: Century Inns undergoes a hostile takeover.
2000: The company acquires 183 pubs from Whitbread.
2001: The company acquires 439 pubs from Deutsche Bank's Morgan Grenfell and 430 pubs from Scottish & Newcastle.
2002: The company joins a consortium to acquire the 4,000-pub Unique Pub Company from Nomura; 1,869 pubs are acquired from Morgan Grenfell.
2003: Preparations begin to acquire full control of Unique Pub in 2004.

pub estate from Japan's Nomura for more than £2 billion. Enterprise's part in the consortium, which included as partners Cinven and Legal & General Ventures, stood at a little less than 17 percent; yet under the agreement Enterprise reserved the option to acquire the remaining 83 percent in 2004.

In the meantime, Enterprise immediately returned to the acquisition trail in April 2002, paying Morgan Grenfell £875 million to take over another 1,860 former Whitbread pub properties, which had been reformed a year earlier as Laurel Pub Holdings. That purchase propelled Enterprise into the leadership position among U.K. pub operators, boosting its portfolio to more than 5,000 pubs. At the same time, the company had nearly quadrupled its revenues in just four years, with sales at nearly £370 million in 2002.

With debt levels soaring to £1.6 million—more than its asset value—Enterprise cooled its acquisition drive in 2003, if only to prepare for its pending acquisition of the 4,000-strong Unique Pub group. As Tuppen explained to the *Birmingham Post:* "I'm going to have the whole issue of merging over 4,000 pubs with my existing 5,000 plus. To start getting a bit macho about it by snapping up everything that moves seems a bit silly."

In the meantime, industry developments appeared to be proving Tuppen right in his commitment to tenanted estates. With rising wages and other costs, and tightening government regulations, the managed pub concept had come under heavy pressure at the turn of the century. Enterprise, however, remained relatively protected from these issues. Indeed, as Tuppen boasted, "Enterprise is almost the perfect business, there is not a lot missing but I wouldn't be as pompous to say it was the perfect business. Over the next five years we are going to develop it into a top class estate. It's the perfect business concept but we don't do it all properly yet. We still have things to learn and get right."

Principal Subsidiaries

Enterprise Pubs Two Ltd.; Enterprise Pubs Four Ltd.; Enterprise Pubs Seven Ltd.; The Unique Pub Company (16.8%); Warwickshire Hotels Ltd. (50%).

Principal Competitors

Compass Group PLC; Whitbread PLC; Compass Roadside Ltd.; Punch Retail Ltd.; J D Wetherspoon PLC; Wolverhampton and Dudley Breweries PLC; Greene King PLC; Luminar PLC; Ascot PLC; SFI Group PLC.

Further Reading

Blackwell, David, "Acquisitions Drive Growth at Enterprise," *Financial Times,* November 24, 1999, p. 30.
Cole, Cheryl, "In a Changing World, This Enterprise Is Predictable," *Birmingham Post,* April 8, 2003, p. 23.
Cox, Stephen, "The Man Behind the Man Behind the Bar," *Observer,* May 3, 1998, p. B2.
Jones, Adam, "Enterprise Trying to Avoid Share Issue in £608m Deal," *Financial Times,* September 17, 2003, p. 27.
Reece, Damien, "Suppin' with Tuppen," *Daily Telegraph,* March 24, 2002.
Winn, Sheri, "The Spirit of Enterprise," *Venture Magazine,* June 2000.

—M. L. Cohen

Florida East Coast Industries, Inc.

One Malaga Street
P.O. Box 1048
St. Augustine, Florida 32085-1048
U.S.A.
Telephone: (904) 829-3421
Fax: (904) 826-2338
Web site: http://www.feci.com

Public Company
Incorporated: 1984
Employees: 834
Sales: $301.52 million (2002)
Stock Exchanges: New York
Ticker Symbol: FLA
NAIC: 482111 Line-Haul Railroads; 531210 Offices of
    Real Estate Agents and Brokers; 531312
    Nonresidential Property Managers; 233110 Land
    Subdivision and Land Development

Florida East Coast Industries, Inc. (FECI) is the holding company for the similarly named railroad as well as a major land development company. Florida East Coast Railway, L.L.C. (FECR) operates a rail service on 351 miles of track between Jacksonville and Miami. Observers have called FECR one of the best-run railroads in North America. Flagler Development Company owns and manages more than seven million square feet of commercial and industrial space, and about 5,000 acres of other Florida real estate. Formerly called Gran Central Corp., its name was changed in 2000 to reflect the legacy of company founder Henry Flagler.

Origins

The name of Henry Morrison Flagler looms large in the history of the commercial development of the state of Florida. Flagler was a cofounder of the Standard Oil Co. with John D. Rockefeller. He sold his 50 percent interest in Standard Oil for $50 million and headed to undeveloped Florida to start his next venture. He was able to buy land very cheap with the purpose of building resorts for his fellow millionaires.

On December 31, 1886, Flagler bought the Jacksonville, St. Augustine and Halifax River Railroad. This small operation was incorporated in 1892 and renamed the Florida East Coast Railway Company in September 1895.

Flagler acquired the railway in order to carry affluent tourists to the luxury vacation destinations he was developing along Florida's east coast, beginning with St. Augustine, which had only 4,000 permanent residents at the time. The railroad marketed these destinations under the slogan "Paradise Regained."

The railway ran to Palm Beach, site of Flagler's Poinciana Hotel, by 1894. A wealthy Miami landowner, Julia Tuttle, encouraged Flagler to continue laying rails further south. Passenger service from Jacksonville to Miami officially started on April 22, 1896, according to Seth Bramson's *Speedway to Sunshine: The Story of the Florida East Coast Railway*.

The railway grew along with the developments as far as Key West, requiring the spanning of 150 miles of open ocean. Historian Dan Gallagher called the building of the Key West Extension the second largest construction project in the world during the first decade of the 20th century. Contemporary critics called it "Flagler's Folly"; of 4,000 workers employed in building it, 160 died.

The extension officially opened on January 22, 1912, after five years of work and a year before Flagler died. Of the $41 million he had invested in Florida, Flagler had put $10 million into the Key West Extension and $18 million into the railroads, according to Fort Lauderdale journalist David Leon Chandler.

FECR's fortunes soared during the local real estate market boom in the 1920s. The railroad was used to transport building materials as well as passengers. Return trips provided transportation for Florida's abundant year-round produce.

The 1929 stock market crash dealt FECR a blow it would spend decades trying to overcome. The railway declared bankruptcy in 1931 and would spend the next 30 years in receivership. A hurricane on Labor Day, 1935, wiped out the Key West Extension. Rail all along the Atlantic Coast faced new competition from U.S. Highway 1, completed in 1938, which stretched from Maine to the Florida Keys.

FECR Exiting Receivership in 1961

FECR emerged from bankruptcy in 1961, controlled by the Alfred I. duPont estate, represented by eminent Florida businessman Ed Ball. However, it faced a number of serious problems. Ball found the railway overstaffed and encumbered by union regulations. Under Ball's leadership, the railway withdrew from labor negotiations in 1963 and replaced all striking workers. It would continue to operate that way for many years, at the same time increasing its frequencies from three trains a day each way between Jacksonville and Miami, to a dozen, while reducing the number of crew members on each train from 15 to two. The violent strike was called off in the early 1970s, and few original employees were rehired. The strike shut down passenger service on January 22, 1963. This resumed on August 2, 1965, though a lack of business killed the service on July 30, 1968. In the 1960s, the railway lost a significant amount of cargo business to the embargo on Cuba, at the same time as competition from a parallel railway (the origins of CSX Transportation), two new interstate highways, and a more efficient Intracoastal Waterway, reported the *Journal of Commerce.*

Other cost-cutting measures included truncating cabooses from trains and using longer-lasting concrete railway ties instead of wood ones. FECR began to show consistent profits in the mid-1970s. The Arab oil embargo of 1973 had prompted many truckers to have FECR carry their trailers south on flatbed cars. A local labor organization called the Florida Federation of Railroad Employees began representing FECR workers in 1977.

Reorganizing in 1984

FECR President Winfred L. Thornton was named chairman and CEO after the death of Ed Ball in 1981. The company underwent a restructuring three years later. Florida East Coast Industries, Inc. was formed as a holding company effective May 31, 1984. A new subsidiary, Commercial Realty & Development Co., was created to manage its 21,000 acres of property. The real estate arm was soon renamed Gran Central Corporation. It concentrated on developing commercial buildings. Operating revenues were $131.4 million in 1984; net income was $29 million.

The number of owner-operators plying their trade as truckers multiplied in the 1980s, and FECI itself owned two trucking subsidiaries: Florida East Coast Highway Dispatch, its delivery unit, and Florida Express Carriers, which operated to neighboring states.

FECI had estimated sales of $196 million in 1989. By this time, the real estate unit had built a million square feet of warehouse and office space, reported *Forbes.*

Transitions in the 1990s

In August 1992, Hurricane Andrew washed away the historic FECR depot building that had been a part of Homestead's Florida Pioneer Museum. FECR posted a profit of $24 million on sales of $184 million in 1992. It had 936 employees and 442 miles of track.

FECI acquired trucking company International Transit, Inc. (ITI) in 1995. Based in Cincinnati, Ohio, ITI had revenues of more than $21 million a year.

Norfolk Southern Corp., the fourth largest railway in the country, considered acquiring FECR after it was offered for sale in February 1996. The two already cooperated on some shipments; a buy would have extended Norfolk Southern's line past Jacksonville to Miami. This deal did not materialize, though, and FECR was taken off the market a few years later.

St. Joe Corp., a Jacksonville industrial conglomerate with interests in paper, real estate, transportation, and telecommunications owned 54 percent of FECR. A bid to acquire the remaining shares fell through over the issue of valuation. St. Joe then began to sell off its diversified holdings to concentrate on real estate development. It spun off its 54 percent interest in FECI in October 2000.

Forming a Telecom Unit in 1999

In May 1999, FECI created the Orlando-based telecommunications venture, FEC Telecom Inc., which was soon renamed EPIK Communications Incorporated. Telecom companies often looked to railways for rights-of-way to run their fiber-optic lines. FECI installed a 780-mile fiber-optic line connecting a handful of major cities in Florida, and had been leasing access to other telecoms since the early 1980s.

FECI got a new CEO in 2000, 20-year industry veteran Robert W. Anestis, who succeeded Carl Zellers, Jr. Anestis, from Connecticut, had been a financial consultant to the railroad industry.

In July 2000, FECI's commercial real estate unit, Gran Central Corporation, was renamed Flagler Development Company to reflect its connection with pioneering developer Henry Flagler. It then owned 55 buildings and about 19,000 acres of land, mostly in Jacksonville, Orlando, Fort Lauderdale, and Miami. Flagler, which employed fewer than two dozen people at the time, was moving into a new headquarters and opening offices in Fort Lauderdale and Orlando as its staff expanded. In September 2000, the company announced plans to borrow money for the first time in its history to fund the development of its 16 million square feet of space in Jacksonville, Orlando, Fort Lauderdale, and Miami, reported the *Business Journal of Jacksonville.* Flagler also was buying property for development in Tampa.

On October 10, 2000, Flagler Development was spun off from the St. Joe Corp., which had owned a 54 percent interest in it since 1961 and held contracts to manage Flagler's real estate; the last of these expired three years later. This brought Flagler into competition with the Codina Group, half owned by St. Joe, which was building an industrial park to rival Flagler's main development in Miami-Dade County. The Alfred I. duPont

Key Dates:

1886: On December 31, Henry Morrison Flagler, a co-founder of Standard Oil Co., buys the Jacksonville, St. Augustine and Halifax River Railroad.
1892: Company incorporates, adopting the name Florida East Coast Railway Company (FECR) three years later.
1931: FECR enters receivership.
1961: The duPont estate acquires a controlling interest in FECR.
1984: FECI is formed as a holding company for FECR and the real estate unit.
1999: A telecom unit is formed.
2002: The trucking and telecom units are divested.

Testamentary Trust remained the major shareholder in both FECI and St. Joe.

In 2000, Amtrak reached an agreement to use FECR's coastal tracks to begin a passenger service. Amtrak already operated on CSX's inland tracks, but there had been no passenger service down the coast since the late 1960s.

Exiting Telecom and Trucking in 2002

EPIK Communications Inc. proved a substantial drain on FECI's income, even as it extended its fiber-optic network throughout Florida and as far as Atlanta, Georgia. FECI sold EPIK to Palo Alto, California-based Odyssey Telecorp Inc. in December 2002. It also shut down its trucking operation.

FECI reported a net loss of $61 million on revenues of $247 million in 2001. Revenues rose to $301.5 million in 2002. The railroad accounted for $162 million of it. Land sales brought in $71 million.

Principal Subsidiaries

Flagler Development Company; Florida East Coast Railway, L.L.C.

Principal Divisions

Railway; Realty Operations; Land Sales.

Principal Competitors

Codina Group; CSX Transportation, Inc.; Echelon Development LLC.

Further Reading

"Amtrak Inks Deal to Run Train Service Down Florida's East Coast," *Miami Herald*, June 3, 2001.

Barker, Robert, "Will Florida East Coast Share the Wealth?," *Business Week*, July 21, 2003, p. 88.

Barton, Susanna, "FECI Borrows for First Time: Strategic Move," *Business Journal of Jacksonville*, September 11, 2000.

Basch, Mark, "Jacksonville, Fla.-Based Property Firm to Spin Off Stake in Rail Company," *Florida Times-Union*, October 28, 1999.

——, "Railroad, Real Estate Is the Main Focus of Florida East Coast Industries," *Florida Times-Union*, November 27, 2002.

——, "St. Augustine, Fla.-Based Florida East Coast Industries Remains Profitable," *Florida Times-Union*, May 31, 2002.

——, "Zellers Retires from CEO Job," *Florida Times-Union*, November 12, 1998, p. E1.

Beard, Alison, "Real Estate Gains Put Railroad Operators on Track for Profits," *Financial Times* (London), May 21, 2002, p. 31.

Bennett, Jane, "Flagler Flies Solo; St. Joe Spinoff Finds Own Identity," *Business Journal of Jacksonville*, June 17, 2002.

Bluhm, Donald, "A Homestead Attraction Gone But Others Remain," *Plain Dealer* (Cleveland, Ohio), June 27, 1993.

Bramson, Seth, *Speedway to Sunshine: The Story of the Florida East Coast Railway*, Erin, Ontario: Boston Mills Press, 1984, 2003.

Calnan, Christopher, "St. Augustine, Fla.-Based Firm Unloads Telecommunications Division," *Florida Times-Union*, December 5, 2002.

Campbell, Gordon, "Palm Beach Museum Was Home of Visionary," *Toronto Star*, November 5, 1988, p. F37.

Chandler, David Leon, *Henry Flagler*, New York: Macmillan, 1986.

——, "King Henry," *Sun Sentinel* (Fort Lauderdale), August 24, 1986, p. 7.

——, "The Man Who Built Florida," *Orlando Sentinel*, October 12, 1986, p. 9.

Cohen, Judy Radler, "Will Florida East Meet Its Mate?," *M&A Reporter*, February 23, 1998.

Dinsmore, Christopher, "Virginia's Norfolk Southern Corp. Considers Buying Florida Railroad," *Virginian-Pilot*, February 28, 1996.

Drummond, James, "Land Bank," *Forbes*, October 2, 1989, p. 266.

Dunlap, Craig, "Florida East Coast Keeps on Track," *Journal of Commerce*, September 15, 1986, p. 9A.

Finotti, John, "St. Joe Corp. Abandons Florida East Coast Railway Merger," *Florida Times-Union*, November 21, 1997.

Gallagher, Dan, *Florida's Great Ocean Railway: Building the Key West Extension*, Sarasota, Fla.: Pineapple Press, 2003.

"Henry Flagler's Railroad Built Florida Vacationland," *Plain Dealer* (Cleveland, Ohio), April 9, 1995, p. 5F.

Kaufman, Lawrence H., "Carl Zellers, New FEC President, to Keep Railroad on the Same Track," *Journal of Commerce*, July 20, 1992, p. 4B.

——, "Fla. Rail Takes on Truckers in Jacksonville-Miami Run," *Journal of Commerce*, June 17, 1993, p. 3B.

——, "Union Bids to Recapture Fla. Railway," *Journal of Commerce*, September 21, 1993, p. 1A.

Lunsford, Darcie, "Flagler Development Prepares for New Role," *South Florida Business Journal*, March 24, 2003.

Mann, Joseph, "Switch in Emphasis; Florida East Coast Industries Still Rides the Rails, But Also Looks to a Fiber-Optic Future That Stretches Beyond Its Home State," *Sun Sentinel* (Fort Lauderdale), August 27, 2000, p. 1F.

Rublin, Lauren R., "Sand and Muck: They're Paying Off for Ed Ball's Old Company," *Barron's*, November 28, 1988, pp. 13+.

Talley, Jim, "Railroad Finds No Uphill Grade When It Comes to Profits, Growth," *Sun Sentinel* (Fort Lauderdale), April 29, 1985.

Whitefield, Mimi, and Raul Rubiera, "Florida East Coast Industries Attempts to Parlay Property into More Profits," *Miami Herald*, March 31, 2002.

—Frederick C. Ingram

4Kids Entertainment Inc.

1414 Avenue of the Americas
New York, New York 10019
U.S.A.
Telephone: (212) 758-7666
Fax: (212) 754-7947
Web site: http://www.4KidsEntertainment.com

Public Company
Founded: 1970 as Leisure Concepts, Inc.
Employees: 185
Sales: $53.1 million (2002)
Stock Exchanges: New York
Ticker Symbol: KDE
NAIC: 512110 Motion Picture and Video Production;
    512191 Postproduction and Other Postproduction
    Services; 515120 Television Broadcasting; 517510
    Cable and Other Program Distribution

Little known until the late 1990s when Pokémon swept the planet, 4Kids Entertainment Inc. is the parent company of Leisure Concepts Inc., which was the sole licensing agent of the Pokémon phenomenon and rode an impressive wave of merchandising that extended from Nintendo's Game Boy to include a highly rated television series, two feature films, trading cards, action figures, apparel, home textiles, numerous book series, and even music. Yet Pokémon is not the only star of the 4Kids licensing stable, which includes Yu-Gi-Oh!, Teenage Mutant Ninja Turtles, the Hulk, Cabbage Patch Kids, Charlie Chan, a wide array of Nintendo characters and products, World Championship Wrestling, and Monster Jam truck rallies and toys.

In the Beginning: 1970s–80s

The sum of 4Kids Entertainment, Inc.'s parts is far less known than its components. Leisure Concepts, Inc. (LCI) was founded as an independent licensing agency in 1970 in New York City. The firm began making news in the 1980s through licensing actual people, a variety of products, and even concepts. LCI had numerous licensees, including "real" person Farrah Fawcett of *Charlie's Angels* fame, cartoon characters,

and a growing number of deals with television producers and toy manufacturers. In 1987 LCI took a chance on a futuristic movie project called *Star Wars,* from director George Lucas and with unheard of special effects by Industrial Light & Magic. When *Star Wars* became an enormous success, LCI reaped the rewards—orchestrating the kind of merchandising invasion considered commonplace today. Star Wars games, action figures, clothing, and trading cards were everywhere.

During 1987 LCI signed another licensing deal, this one with Nintendo of America, Inc. to market the software products that went along with its increasingly popular gaming systems. Nintendo had already introduced the *Legend of Zelda* for its home video game system, a software product that went on to sell more than one million copies during the year. In 1988 LCI hired Alfred Kahn, formerly of Coleco Industries, as its new chief executive. Kahn had already earned a reputation for marketing savvy, having acquired the licensing rights to an oddly-named bunch of dolls known as the Cabbage Patch Kids—which went on to conquer the United States and the world.

On the Verge: 1990s

With Kahn at its helm, LCI expanded its operations in the early 1990s by creating two new subsidiaries: The Summit Media Group, Inc. and 4Kids Productions, Inc. The former was established to handle syndication rights for various licensed products in both print and broadcast media, while the latter maintained a studio to buy and produce animated and live-action properties, which it then distributed to the television, home video, and theatrical markets.

Kahn and LCI turned in a new direction in the middle of the decade by launching the World Martial Arts Council (WMAC) and a new weekly television series, *WMAC Masters*, which brought together the world's most talented martial artists in a live-action format. Shannon Lee, daughter of martial arts champion Bruce Lee, lent considerable credibility to the show and its contestants by hosting. LCI hired Bandai American Incorporated to produce WMAC action figures and other merchandise.

LCI's lucrative licensing agreement with Nintendo continued to fuel its income as more and more kids bought gaming systems and Nintendo software. Next came the Game Boy, a hand-held portable gaming system that came with its own customized video games. In addition to the *Zelda* franchise, which had spawned a successful sequel, Nintendo had introduced *Mario Bros., Donkey Kong*, and in 1996 came a game about "pocket monsters" called *Pokémon*. The game consisted of catching unusually named creatures, taming them, and helping them "evolve" into stronger versions of themselves. *Pokémon*, previously introduced in Japan, became the must-have gaming cartridge of Game Boy players in the United States. LCI wasted no time in developing strategies to market the endearing *Pokémon* characters to youngsters everywhere.

As Pokémon mania began to take hold, LCI turned its attention to an entirely new area in 1987 when it agreed to handle licensing for the American Heart Association (AHA). The nonprofit AHA hired LCI to market its animated spokesperson, "Ticker," as a way to raise additional funds for the health organization. In turn, LCI merchandised Ticker to youngsters in a variety of products, from plush toys to apparel to books—all to promote cardio health.

By 1998 LCI had two revenue-producing television shows, *WMAC Masters* and *Pokémon*. Regarding the latter, LCI had also signed with Hasbro Inc. to produce plush toys, of which Pokémon character Pikachu (a bright yellow ratlike creature) was the most popular. An important milestone was also reached in children's television programming when the Toronto-based Nelvana signed a two-year contract with CBS to provide its morning television lineup. At the time, no television producer had been given exclusive rights to provide an entire block of children's programming. This would evolve in the coming years with LCI mastering the art of the deal. In the meantime, however, the company had reached total net revenues of just under $14.8 million for 1998, an increase of 46 percent over 1997's $10.1 million. Net income, however, rose significantly from 1997's $739,000 to $2.7 million.

LCI's fortunes changed exponentially in 1999. As the exclusive licensing agent for Nintendo, as well as other firms, LCI had both the notice and respect of the corporate world. Nintendo released the Nintendo 64 gaming system and a slew of Pokémon games to go with it, while LCI had inked a new deal linking monster truck promoter PACE Motor Sports and World Championship Wrestling (WCW). Additional Pokémon licensing included a three-year contract with Golden Books to produce 17 Pokémon books and an array of stickers and postcards for youngsters during the summer, just before the big screen debut of the first Pokémon movie by Warner Bros.

Pokémon mania hit a fever pitch with its characters gracing both the small and big screens, and a merchandising rollout unlike anything ever seen before. In its first day at theaters, *Pokémon* racked up $10 million in ticket sales and Warner Bros. completely ran out of the promotional trading cards it was distributing to early ticket buyers. By December, Golden Books had 30 million Pokémon titles in circulation, while Burger King's promotion of 100 million action figures and special gold-plated trading cards, placed in kids' meals, disappeared in a matter of weeks.

The hype fueled explosive growth for LCI and garnered it the top slot in *Fortune* magazine's "100 Fastest Growing Companies" in 1999. The company ended its remarkable year with net revenues of $60.5 million and net income of $23.7 million (up from 1998's $2.7 million).

Hitting the Jackpot: 2000s

The new century found LCI and its parent company, 4Kids Entertainment, Inc., switching from the NASDAQ market and joining the New York Stock Exchange. The firm's new ticker symbol was KDE and 4Kids was indeed riding high when it earned *Fortune*'s top slot on its 100 Fastest Growing Companies for 2000. The company's sales were just under $88 million, up more than 242 percent from the previous four quarters in 1999. According to *Variety* magazine, the Pokémon franchise had earned upwards of $16 billion worldwide since its original launch in Japan, and 4Kids, as the exclusive licensor for all things Pokémon, had racked up not only impressive sales but net income climbing to an all-time high of $38.8 million ($15 million higher than the last year). Knowing the Pokémon bubble would burst at some point, LCI continued to ink other licensing deals, including a new contract with Marvel Comics to market merchandise for its comic book properties such as X-Men, Incredible Hulk, and Fantastic Four.

During 2001 4Kids and LCI had several licensing properties gaining popularity, but not with the speed and impact of Pokémon. X-Men and Hulk projects were underway, while Cubix, an animated program about robots on the Kids' WB was gaining an audience. 4Kids scored a marketing coup when both McDonald's and Burger King were featuring its licensed products in their children's meals during the summer of 2001. Though the timing was unintentional, 4Kids had signed with Burger King to place its Cubix action figures in meals beginning the week of August 27th, while McDonald's was putting Mattel's Hot Wheels in Happy Meals with a special Monster Jam Trucks (licensed by 4Kids) placement to occur in August or September.

4Kids stock reached a high of $29.30 per share in the third quarter of 2001 due in large part to a successful bid to lease Fox television's "FoxBox" block of Saturday morning children's programming beginning in early 2002. 4Kids went up against Nickelodeon (of *Rugrats* fame), DIC Entertainment (known for its *Sonic the Hedgehog* and *Sabrina the Teenage Witch* series), Discovery Communications (purveyor of Animal Planet, TLC, and the Discovery channels), and Nelvana (Franklin the Turtle)—all of whom coveted the four-hour programming block. 4Kids won the $100 million four-year deal, yet it did not include old stalwart *Pokémon* or new phenom *Yu-Gi-Oh!*, which was promised to the Kids' WB.

Yu-Gi-Oh!, an animated series based on a Japanese comic book and card game, debuted on the Kids' WB in the fall of 2001. *Yu-Gi-Oh!* revolved around a boy who played a special card game and in doing so was able to transform himself into the "Master of Games" (a rough translation of the show's title) and

Key Dates:

1970: Leisure Concepts, Inc. (LCI) is incorporated in New York.

1987: LCI signs on to market *Star Wars* and inks a deal with Nintendo of America, Inc.

1988: Alfred Kahn joins LCI as chief executive officer.

1992: Two subsidiaries, Summit Media Group Inc. and 4Kids Productions, Inc., are formed.

1996: Nintendo debuts a new game for Game Boy called "Pokémon."

1998: Two LCI television shows gain considerable audiences: *WMAC Masters* and *Pokémon.*

1999: The Pokémon phenomenon takes the nation by storm.

2000: 4Kids Entertainment, Inc., parent company to LCI, goes public on the New York Stock Exchange.

2001: 4Kids bids on Fox television's "FoxBox" slot of children's programming and launches *Yu-Gi-Oh!* animated series.

2002: Two new subsidiaries are created: 4Kids Entertainment Music, Inc. and 4Kids Entertainment Home Video, Inc.

2003: 4Kids and the White House's Office of National Drug Control Policy team up, using the characters from the *Yu-Gi-Oh!* television series in a new stay-away-from-drugs campaign.

battle monsters. The show's targeted audience was older than its predecessor *Pokémon*'s, primarily due to the upstart's darker tone, elaborate plots, and scarier monster content. Like *Pokémon*, however, *Yu-Gi-Oh!* was already a hit when 4Kids became interested in the franchise's licensing rights. According to *Variety, Yu-Gi-Oh!* had racked up earnings of more than $2 billion in Asia by 2001 when 4Kids brought the animated series to the United States. While year-end net revenue for 4Kids fell from its all-time high in 2000, it was still a respectable $41.5 million in 2001. Net income came in at $12.2 million—and 4Kids believed its newest import would soon drive its sales to previous heights.

As Kahn envisioned, *Yu-Gi-Oh!* the television series attracted a growing audience of kids, mostly male, during its first six months. By April 2002 the show was no longer just on Saturdays but ran six mornings a week. Like *Pokémon, Yu-Gi-Oh!* spawned merchandise tie-ins such as action figures, trading cards, games, video games, apparel, lunch boxes, music, and even linens. Net revenues rose accordingly, up to $53.1 million, a $12 million leap from the previous year.

In early 2003 LCI and 4Kids resurrected the animated television series *Teenage Mutant Ninja Turtles* as well as a series version of *Back to the Future* into its Saturday morning FoxBox programming. Both 1980s favorites were revamped and updated to good results. 4Kids also lent its famous animated *Yu-Gi-Oh!* characters to the White House's Office of National Drug

Control Policy in a new anti-drug crusade called "Honor—My Anti-Drug." The new campaign was launched in July 2003 and featured special *Yu-Gi-Oh!* collectible stickers available through Blockbuster Entertainment video stores nationwide. Another deal came with the unusual pairing of *Yu-Gi-Oh!* characters and NASCAR, to create a *Yu-Gi-Oh!* paint scheme for car number 43 at the Talladega Superspeedway in a September 2003 race. The back of the Dodge car featured the *Yu-Gi-Oh!* famous line, "Let's Duel!"

4Kids Entertainment, parent to many subsidiaries, including marketing master Leisure Concepts Inc., continued to bring some of the world's most famous characters into the homes of mainstream Americans. Much of its success could be credited to Al Kahn, chairman and CEO, whose vision seemed to know no bounds. 4Kids had more than lived up to its name and would likely continue to do so in the years to come.

Principal Subsidiaries

4Kids Ad Sales, Inc.; 4Kids Entertainment Home Video, Inc.; 4Kids Entertainment Music, Inc.; 4Kids International, Ltd.; 4Kids Licensing, Inc.; 4Kids Productions, Inc.; 4Kids Technology, Inc.; Leisure Concepts, Inc.; Leisure Concepts International Inc.; The Summit Media Group, Inc.; Websites 4Kids, Inc.

Principal Competitors

DIC Entertainment; Discovery Communications; DreamWorks SKG; Nelvana; Nickelodeon; Walt Disney Company.

Further Reading

Bloom, David, "Pokémon Purveyor Has a Go at *Yu-Gi-Oh!*," *Variety,* March 18, 2002, p. 5.

Finnigan, David, "Burger King Gears Up 4Kids' Cubix," *Brandweek,* July 16, 2001, p. 6.

"Golden Inks Deal for Pokémon Titles," *Publisher's Weekly,* June 21, 1999, p. 13.

Kahn, Al, "Setting Your Own Course," *Playthings,* October 1995, p. 66.

"Monster Marketing: Pokémon Is White-Hot Now, but Will It Be Evergreen?," *Promo,* January 2000.

Reilly, Patrick, "LCI Expands Its Universe with Star Wars," *Crain's New York Business,* July 6, 1987, p. 10.

Schlosser, Joe, "Who'll Buy Fox's Kids?," *Broadcasting & Cable,* January 21, 2002, p. 20.

Schmuckler, Eric, "4Kids Expects Early Profits," *Mediaweek,* January 28, 2002, p. 6.

Schnuer, Jenna, "Alfred Kahn: Animé Star Has Winning Hand," *Advertising Age,* March 24, 2003, p. S6.

Waddell, Ray, "WCW & PACE Motor Sports Form Alliance," *Amusement,* June 14, 1999, p. 4.

Weiner, Daniel P., "Leisure Concepts, Inc.," *Fortune,* August 18, 1986, p. 62.

"What's Hot: Licensing with a Cause," *Discount Store News,* June 23, 1997, p. 105.

—Nelson Rhodes

Frederick's of Hollywood, Inc.

6608 Hollywood Boulevard
Los Angeles, California 90028-6208
U.S.A.
Telephone: (323) 466-5151
Toll Free: (800) 323-9525
Fax: (323) 962-9935
Web site: http://www.fredericks.com

Private Company
Incorporated: 1962
Employees: 1,600
Sales: $200 million (2002 est.)
NAIC: 448190 Other Clothing Stores; 454111 Electronic Shopping; 454113 Mail-Order Houses

Frederick's of Hollywood, Inc. is a leading U.S. intimate apparel retailer, with an emphasis on racier clothing and other items. Through about 160 mainly mall-based stores, a mail-order business, and an online shopping site, Frederick's sells lingerie, bras, and panties, as well as sportswear, dresses, swimwear, shoes, hosiery, accessories, and a line of menswear. Increasing competition from upstart lingerie retailer Victoria's Secret hurt the company throughout the 1990s, and Frederick's finally was forced to file for Chapter 11 bankruptcy protection in July 2000. Following a thorough restructuring, the firm emerged from bankruptcy in January 2003, majority owned by a consortium of creditors led by Crédit Agricole, a French investment bank. In an attempt to differentiate itself from Victoria's Secret and other competitors, Frederick's has repositioned its product line to appeal to younger women by returning to a racier image—but not to the raunchy image on which the company made its reputation.

Postwar Foundation

The company is named for its founder and longtime president Frederick Mellinger, who conceived of his lingerie business while serving in the armed forces during World War II. In 1946, after his discharge, Mellinger established a mail-order undergarment operation in New York City. Known as Freder-

ick's of Fifth Avenue, his shop offered racy black bras and panties embellished with lace and appliqués.

Mellinger took his fancy foundations to more permissive California in 1947, changing the name of the catalog business to Frederick's of Hollywood that same year. Tinseltown's glitz and glamour provided the perfect backdrop for the groundbreaking retailer, and a parade of starlets and models provided a ready customer base.

Mellinger, who came to be known as "Mr. Frederick" among his clientele, soon began to specialize in figure-enhancing foundations and accessories. He designed and began selling the first push-up bra, dubbed the "Rising Star," in 1948. Fanny pads, girdles, sky-high heeled shoes, hosiery, wigs, false eyelashes, even head pads to achieve the illusion of height—anything necessary to achieve "Frederick's figure balancing act"—followed in the years to come. The company even offered an inflatable bra that came complete with a "free straw." The catalogs and stores later added glamorous evening wear, much of it designed by Mr. Frederick himself. The garments featured daring necklines, high slits, and sheer fabrics intended to appeal to men as much as women. In fact, Mellinger once wrote that his goal was to offer "the most alluring, body-hugging, figure-enhancing outer fashions . . . always aimed at men."

Mr. Frederick opened his first retail store in California in 1952 and others soon followed. The flamboyant Art Deco flagship store soon became known as "the purple palace." Mellinger started advertising his catalog and garments in nationally circulated magazines using saucy tag lines such as "Fashions Change—But Sex Is Always in Style." It was Frederick's that brought French bikinis to the United States during the 1950s. After incorporating in 1962, Frederick's continued to expand its product offerings in the sexually permissive environment of the 1960s and 1970s. Soon pasties, anonymously written sexual guides, and other "sexually oriented non-apparel products" appeared in the catalogs.

Although Frederick's offered its stock to the public in 1972, the Mellinger family continued to control a majority of the company's stock through the early 1990s. By the end of the 1970s, the chain had expanded to more than 150 stores, ac-

Key Dates:

1946: Frederick Mellinger establishes a mail-order lingerie business in New York City called Frederick's of Fifth Avenue.
1947: Mellinger relocates the business to California, renaming it Frederick's of Hollywood.
1948: Mellinger designs and begins selling the first push-up bra, dubbed the "Rising Star."
1952: The first retail store opens in California.
1962: The company is incorporated as Frederick's of Hollywood, Inc.
1972: The company goes public, but the Mellinger family continues to own a majority stake.
1984: Frederick's suffers a net loss for the year, its first ever; Mellinger retires.
1985: George Townson is brought onboard as chairman and CEO and launches a "desleazification" of Frederick's.
1996: The company launches an online shopping site.
1997: Investment bank Knightsbridge Capital Corp. takes Frederick's private in a $66.6 million leveraged deal.
1999: Linda LoRe is named president and CEO.
2000: Knightsbridge sells the company to investment firm Wilshire Partners; burdened by debt, Frederick's files for Chapter 11 bankruptcy protection.
2003: The company emerges from bankruptcy under the majority ownership of a consortium of creditors led by Crédit Agricole, a French investment bank.

counting for over half of overall sales. The company enjoyed peak prosperity during the mid-1970s. Sales more than doubled, from $9.7 million in 1971 to $24 million in 1976, while net income tripled, from slightly less than $500,000 to $1.5 million. It was to be Frederick's highest-ever level of profitability, as a combination of societal changes and management problems converged on the lingerie retailer.

Americans' sexual mores and their tastes in lingerie grew increasingly conservative in the 1980s. The septuagenarian founder and his management team, however, were slow to realize these trends. (Unbeknownst to the board of directors, in fact, Mellinger was afflicted with Alzheimer's disease during this time.) While company sales rose from $39.3 million in 1981 to $45.3 million in 1984, net profits slid from a high of $2.2 million to $627,000. This dramatic decline in profitability was reflected in the company's eroding stock price, which dropped from $7 per share in mid-1983 to less than $2 by mid-1985. By the time Mellinger retired in September 1984, his company had experienced its first-ever loss, a $148,000 shortfall on sales of about $45 million. In 1985, *Forbes* magazine's Ellen Paris speculated that Frederick's dip into the red meant that sex must be "going out of style." Nevertheless, when Mellinger died in 1990 at the age of 76, he was praised as a brave pioneer of intimate fashions and groundbreaking foundations.

In May 1985, after a short period of leadership under interim managers, Frederick's board of directors hired former Carter Hawley Hale home furnishings division chief George Townson

to take the reins at Frederick's as chairman and CEO. Townson brought two decades of experience in mail-order retailing, although none of it was in apparel, let alone lingerie.

From Raunch to Romance in the Late 1980s

It did not take Townson long to pinpoint Frederick's problems. He later enumerated the shortcomings to *Direct Marketing*'s Mollie Neal: "Outdated business assumptions, deteriorating conditions of our stores, ineffective management, inadequate merchandising and financial reporting systems, a dwindling core customer base, more sophisticated competition, archaic structures and antiquated policies." The new CEO immediately mapped out a ten-year plan for what he called the "desleazification" of Frederick's.

Store renovations shunned the traditional garish purples and hot pinks for more subtle lavenders and mauves, while softer lighting and new carpeting in the stores made for a more romantic, less burlesque atmosphere. The high-profile, $300,000 renovation of the "purple palace" was a prime example of this physical repositioning. Not only did the company redecorate—including covering over the outrageous lavender facade with gray paint—but it also celebrated its heritage with the opening of the world's first Lingerie Museum, featuring some of Frederick's earliest designs as well as undergarments of the stars. Los Angeles Mayor Tom Bradley declared "Frederick's of Hollywood Day" on the occasion of the grand reopening, November 8, 1989. The vast majority (80 percent) of Frederick's nearly 200 stores had been redecorated by 1991.

CEO Townson hired marketing consultant Walter K. Levy to assess the company's product line and target audience. A new merchandising scheme emerged from his observations. Frederick's pared what had become an excessively broad and (in the eyes of many Americans) lewd line, dropping such items as explicit videos and bawdy games. Frederick's stores also stopped carrying certain lines of apparel and accessories, including wigs, sportswear, and swimwear (although these last two categories continued to be offered in mail-order catalogs). At the same time, the company expanded its loungewear and men's undergarment lines.

The revamp—or, as many company observers punned, "devamp"—of Frederick's of Hollywood catalogs also focused on bringing the publication out of the fringes and into the mainstream. Even into the 1980s, the catalogs had featured explicit black-and-white photos interspersed with exaggerated and cartoonish line drawings. The new catalogs featured heavier paper, a new logo and motto ("An Intimate Experience"), and tasteful color photographs of models wearing Frederick's lingerie. Although catalog sales slid by about 5 percent with the first new issue, they quickly began to recover, with sales and profits gaining by double-digit percentages in the latter years of the decade. Frederick's move away from mail-order's "red-light district" enabled it to buy mailing lists from catalogers who would have previously been embarrassed to be associated with the lingerie merchant. As a result, catalog circulation more than tripled from 7.5 million in 1985 to 26 million by 1990.

Behind the scenes, CEO Townson purged the executive ranks, bringing in 18 new managers within his first two years at the top. He also invested in new computer hardware, including cash registers and data processing equipment and software. Frederick's retail rebirth clearly followed the lead of upstart competitor Victoria's Secret, a subsidiary of The Limited Inc. By 1988, Victoria's Secret had more than triple the annual sales volume with about the same number of stores. But while Frederick's had shed much of its most explicit merchandise and imagery, the company still managed to maintain its "naughty" cachet. Townson reflected on this factor in a 1996 interview with Marianne Wilson of *Chain Store Age Executive* magazine, noting, "Generally speaking, Victoria's Secret is more mainstream and romantic. Frederick's is fun and sexy." The new CEO's turnaround was effective and quick. Frederick's sales more than doubled from $45.2 million in 1985 to $114.1 million in 1991 and profits burgeoned to a historic high of $5.2 million.

Furtive Growth in the Early 1990s

Sales increased from $117 million in fiscal 1992 to nearly $143 million in 1995, while profits declined from $5.1 million to a loss of $903,000 in 1994, then rebounded to $2.7 million in 1995. Townson blamed Frederick's difficulties on rising postage and paper costs, a generally soft retail environment, the severe recession in California (where the company had a heavy concentration of stores), and increasing competition. Indeed, Townson's 1995 letter to shareholders noted that "department stores, mass merchandisers and specialty stores have significantly expanded their intimate apparel lines." By this time, Victoria's Secret alone had $1.8 billion sales and 600 retail outlets.

In 1995 the company made its first international foray, circulating a holiday catalog in Canada. In 1996, the year the company celebrated its 50th anniversary, Frederick's rolled out a new store prototype. The new design was slightly more sophisticated than previous formats, aimed to be more customer friendly, and was nearly twice as large as the existing average outlet—2,300 square feet versus 1,200. The company also introduced a new cosmetics line, but it did not perform well and was soon abandoned. Late in 1996 the company launched its online shopping site, which generated more than $1 million in sales during its first year.

Going Private in the Late 1990s

In June 1996 the Mellinger family put its 50.2 percent stake in Frederick's up for sale. Frederick Mellinger's widow had died in 1993, and the family members were in need of cash to pay off estate taxes of between $11 million and $12 million that were coming due. This was not a propitious time for a sale, as the stock had fallen 78 percent over the previous three years, from $17.87 per share to $4. Following the company's announcement of a loss of $438,000 for the fiscal year ending in August 1996, the stock dipped below the $4 mark. It rebounded, however, after a strong earnings report of $2.9 million for the first half of fiscal 1997. This laid the groundwork for the board's approval in June 1997 of an offer from investment bank Knightsbridge Capital Corp. to pay $6.14 per share for all outstanding stock, translating into a $52.8 million deal. A brief takeover battle ensued, when Veritas Capital Inc., a merchant banker and private equity investment firm, made competing offers, first of $7 per share and finally of $9 per share. In late September, however, Knightsbridge prevailed with an in-

creased bid of $7.75 a share, or $66.6 million, for two main reasons: To pursue the higher bid from Veritas, Frederick's board would have had to pay Knightsbridge a $4.5 million termination fee, and Knightsbridge had already gained control of a majority of the shares, meaning that it could vote against any competing bids. A shareholder-led lawsuit to block the takeover was dismissed by a Delaware Court of Chancery.

Townson left the company following the takeover, and in December 1997 Frederick's of Hollywood hired its first female CEO. Terry W. Patterson came onboard having most recently served as head of Strauss Discount Auto. Knightsbridge executives felt someone outside the industry was needed to provide a fresh perspective. Patterson did indeed make some significant changes rather quickly, further eliminating some of the stores' and catalogs' sleazier elements and attempting to carry merchandise designed to appeal directly to women rather than to men buying for women. Her stint at the company was short-lived, however; Patterson was abruptly fired in March 1999 for reasons that were never fully disclosed, although it was later revealed that she had built up $22 million in excess inventory—a factor in Frederick's later bankruptcy. In July 1999 Linda LoRe, former president and CEO of upscale fragrance retailer Giorgio Beverly Hills, stepped in as president and CEO of Frederick's.

Reorganizing Under Bankruptcy Protection: Early 2000s

LoRe continued the "mainstreaming" of Frederick's that Patterson had begun, but the financial health of the company soon became the primary concern. In June 2000 Knightsbridge sold the company to Wilshire Partners, a private investment firm based in Newport Beach, California, for an undisclosed price. At this time Frederick's was sagging under the crushing weight of a $70 million debt load, most of which was a legacy of the Knightsbridge takeover, which was devised as a leveraged buyout. It was also losing its long-running battle with Victoria's Secret, whose sales neared the $3 billion mark by 1999—compared with Frederick's approximate revenues of $145 million. Therefore, Frederick's filed for Chapter 11 bankruptcy protection in July 2000 and secured new financing enabling it to maintain operations and continue to revamp its product lines and stores.

Cost-cutting came to the fore over the next few years, and during 2001 alone Frederick's reduced expenses by $6.5 million. Part of these savings came from the closure of more than 40 underperforming stores, bringing the total to around 160 by early 2003. LoRe and the other executives also used the bankruptcy as an opportunity to reposition the Frederick's brand. Knowing that they could not compete head on with the Victoria's Secret juggernaut, they pulled back on the softening of the company's image. At the same time, they had no desire to return to the raunchiness of Frederick's past. They settled for a middle ground, positioning the Frederick's brand, according to LoRe, quoted in *Women's Wear Daily,* as an "anti-establishment lingerie brand, an alternative brand that is playful, sexy, high quality and affordable." The company also began targeting a younger set of core customers—women in the 18- to 35-year-old age range—through such new products as the Get Cheeky line of boy-style cotton panties introduced in 2002. Also debuting were a new line of gift-packaged body care products called Boudoir Cafe and a fragrance line introduced in the fall of 2003.

Yet another new store format was unveiled that same year, a smaller 1,000-square-foot design that, according to *Women's Wear Daily*'s Kristin Young and Dan Burrows, "resemble[d] a jewel box with a boudoir-style interior decorated in cherry-wood paneling, red velvet drapes and leopard carpeting." The new format was to be rolled out very slowly as funds became available. Finally, Frederick's had traditionally used its catalogs as its main marketing tool, but the company launched an advertising campaign during the 2001 holiday season and continued to place ads thereafter—on bus shelters, on the radio, in print, but not yet on television.

In January 2003 Frederick's of Hollywood emerged from bankruptcy. As part of the reorganization plan, Wilshire Partners gave up its equity, and a consortium of creditors led by Crédit Agricole, a French investment bank, converted some of their debt into an 80 percent stake in the company. With liabilities of just $28.8 million, Frederick's exited Chapter 11 a much stronger company seemingly on the rebound. Observers saw some challenges in the company's future, however. Victoria's Secret also was targeting younger women, and several general apparel chains, such as Abercrombie & Fitch, Express, and the Gap, were launching their own lingerie lines. It also was reported that Crédit Agricole wanted to push for a sale of the company following the exit from bankruptcy, which added another element of uncertainty about Frederick's future course.

Principal Subsidiaries

FOH Stores; Hollywood Mail Order LLC.

Principal Competitors

Intimate Brands; Spiegel, Inc.; J.C. Penney Company.

Further Reading

Brookman, Faye, "Frederick's: Selling Beauty Along with Sex," *Women's Wear Daily*, August 30, 1996, p. 7.
Caminiti, Susan, "The Leading Man of Lingerie," *Fortune*, October 10, 1988, p. 163.
Cone, Edward F., "Skimpy Garments, Big Profits," *Forbes*, January 9, 1989, p. 12.
Cook, Dan, "Risque Business," *California Business*, May 1991, p. 21.
Dowling, Melissa, "Frederick's Gets Sold—Finally," *Catalog Age*, August 1997, p. 6.
Edelson, Sharon, "Getting More Intimate: 2 Key Lingerie Chains Focus on Manhattan," *Women's Wear Daily*, November 13, 1995, p. 1.
"Frederick's of Hollywood: A History, 1946–1996," Hollywood: Frederick's of Hollywood, 1996.
"Frederick's Year in Black," *Women's Wear Daily*, November 6, 1995, p. 16.
Ginsberg, Steve, "Frederick's of Hollywood: A New Image," *Women's Wear Daily*, March 10, 1988, p. I23.
Gill, Penny, "Desleazification Pays Off," *Stores*, May 1991, p. 44.
Gordon, Mitchell, "Frederick's of Hollywood Boasts Alluring Sales and Earnings Curve," *Barron's*, March 1, 1976, pp. 66–67.
Gottwald, Laura, and Janusz Gottwald, *Frederick's of Hollywood, 1947–1973: 26 Years of Mail Order Seduction*, New York: Drake Publishers, 1973.
Marlow, Michael, "Taming the Tease," *Women's Wear Daily*, July 8, 1991, p. 3.
Mathews, Anna Wilde, "Sagging Frederick's of Hollywood Looks Upmarket: Lingerie Maker Files to Revamp Under Bankruptcy Laws As Debt Crimps Operations," *Wall Street Journal*, July 11, 2000, p. B1.
Monget, Karyn, " 'Crushing' Debt Load Forcing Frederick's to File Chapter 11," *Women's Wear Daily*, July 11, 2000, p. 1.
——, "Frederick Mellinger Dead at 76; Rites Held," *Women's Wear Daily*, June 5, 1990, p. 14.
——, "Frederick's Gets Payoff from Its Cleaned-Up Act," *Women's Wear Daily*, January 18, 1990, p. 7.
——, "Frederick's Goes for Next Generation," *Women's Wear Daily*, June 16, 2003, p. 8.
——, "Perfumes to Panties: Linda LoRe Appointed CEO of Frederick's," *Women's Wear Daily*, June 21, 1999, p. 1.
Neal, Mollie, "Naughty to Nice," *Direct Marketing*, April 1990, p. 35.
Paris, Ellen, "Is Sex Going Out of Style?," *Forbes*, December 30, 1985, p. 94.
Rees, David, "Earnings Plunge Hits Frederick's Share Price Amid Upbeat Market," *Los Angeles Business Journal*, July 20, 1992, p. 7.
Robins, Cynthia, "It's Not Your Mother's Frederick's of Hollywood," *San Francisco Examiner*, March 28, 2000, p. C1.
Rozhon, Tracie, "A Lingerie Maker Returns to Its Racier Past," *New York Times*, October 25, 2002, p. C1.
Steinhauer, Jennifer, "What Becomes a Legend?: A New Executive Rethinks America's Lingerie Pioneer," *New York Times*, February 13, 1998, p. D1.
Wilson, Marianne, "Frederick's Looks to Future with Updated Design," *Chain Store Age Executive*, May 1996, pp. 116–17.
——, "The De-Sleazification of Frederick's," *Chain Store Age Executive*, September 1989, p. 94.
Young, Kristin, "Frederick's of Hollywood Files Reorganization Plan with Court," *Women's Wear Daily*, August 12, 2002, p. 3.
——, "Frederick's Undergoes Makeover," *Women's Wear Daily*, April 2, 2002, p. 2.
Young, Kristin, and Dan Burrows, "Frederick's Plan Approved by Court," *Women's Wear Daily*, December 23, 2002, p. 11.

—April Dougal Gasbarre
—update: David E. Salamie

FRIESLAND COBERCO
DAIRY FOODS

Friesland Coberco Dairy Foods Holding N.V.

Blankenstein 142
7940 AC Meppel
The Netherlands
Telephone: (+31) 522 276 276
Fax: (+31) 522 276 444
Web site: http://www.fcdf.com

Cooperative Company
Incorporated: 1997
Employees: 16,774
Sales: EUR 4.72 billion ($4.5 billion) (2002)
NAIC: 311511 Fluid Milk Manufacturing; 311512
Creamery Butter Manufacturing; 311514 Dry,
Condensed, and Evaporated Dairy Product
Manufacturing; 311520 Ice Cream and Frozen Dessert
Manufacturing; 424430 Dairy Products (Except Dried
or Canned) Merchant Wholesalers; 424490 Other
Grocery and Related Product Merchant Wholesalers;
311421 Fruit and Vegetable Canning

Friesland Coberco Dairy Foods Holding N.V. is one of the
world's largest dairy and foods products groups. Wholly owned
by Dutch farmers' cooperative Zuivelcooperatie De Seven Provincien UA—a grouping of 11,500 farmers that supplies most of
the company's fresh milk needs—Friesland Coberco produces a
full range of fresh and processed dairy products, including
cheese, butter, yogurt, and desserts, as well as fruit juices and
fruit-based beverages, food ingredients, and other prepared food
items. The Netherlands remains Friesland Coberco's largest
market, at 35 percent of its 2002 sales of EUR 4.7 billion ($4.5
billion), while the rest of Europe, including Eastern Europe,
added 33 percent to sales. Asia and Australia contributed 19
percent to sales, while Africa and the Middle East added 10
percent to revenues. The company's presence remains limited in
the Americas, which added just 3 percent to sales in 2002.
Friesland Coberco, formed in 1997, operates through 95
branches in more than 70 countries. In the early 2000s, the
company pared down its range of brand names, focusing on
Friesche Vlag, Frico Cheese, Dutch Lady, Appelsientje,

Chocomel, and others. The company also reorganized its operational structure, setting up nine primary divisions: Frico Cheese
(25 percent of sales); Friesland Dairy & Drinks (16 percent);
Friesland Consumer Products (15 percent); Friesche Vlag (8
percent); Friesland Coberco Butter Products (7 percent); Friesland Madibic Food Service (6 percent); Borculo Domo Ingredients (4 percent); Kievit (3 percent), and Friesland Asia Pacific
(15 percent). The latter division was formed with the specific
intent of expanding the company's activities in that region.

Merging a Dutch Dairy Giant in the 1990s

Friesland Coberco Dairy Foods was formed through the
merger of four Dutch dairy groups: the larger Friesland Dairy
Foods and Coberco, and the smaller Twee Provinciën and De
Zuid Oost-Hoek in 1997, one of the largest mergers in the
history of the Netherlands' dairy industry. The merger placed
Freisland Coberco under the ownership of the enlarged farmer
cooperative, Zuivelcooperatie De Seven Provincien UA, which
represented at the time more than 16,000 farmers—nearly half
the total number of dairy farmers in the Netherlands. These
farmers were guaranteed an outlet for their milk production, at
prices set each year by calculating the average milk price paid
by the global dairy industry.

Although created in the late 1990s, Friesland Coberco has
roots stretching back to the late 19th century, when a small
village-based dairy cooperative was founded in 1894. Friesland
Dairy Foods had long established itself as a leading dairy
products group both in the Netherlands and abroad—including
a subsidiary operation opened in Hong Kong in 1938 and
especially through the establishment of subsidiaries in the former Dutch colonial markets and elsewhere in the Asian Pacific
Region. Coberco, in the meantime, had grown into one of the
Netherlands' leading dairy and beverages groups, with a full
range of products, including fruit juices and other drinks. Both
companies had established strong brand names through the 20th
century, both in the Netherlands and abroad, including Friesche
Vlag, Coberco, Dutch Lady, Riedel, and others. The smaller
partners of the merger, Twee Provinciën and De Zuid Oost-
Hoek, had in the meantime specialized primarily in the production of cheeses.

Both Friesland and Coberco participated in the consolidation of the Dutch dairy sector, developing scale through mergers and acquisitions, especially in the second half of the 20th century. By the mid-1990s, the two companies were confronted not only with intensifying competition at home—notably from fellow Dutch dairy groups Nutricia and Campina—but internationally as well. The European market, which had dropped trade barriers among member countries in the early 1990s, presented not only new opportunities for growth, but also new perspectives in competition.

Merging Friesland and Coberco, and the addition of Twee Provinciën and De Zuid Oost-Hoek, created Europe's number three dairy company, behind Switzerland's Nestlé and France's Danone. The new company started out with revenues of more than NLG 9 billion ($4.4 billion) and more than 11,000 employees working at 18 production plants. Cheese production became the enlarged company's flagship product, and grew to represent some 25 percent of sales under the Frico Cheese banner. The company also included a strong fruit juice and fruit-based beverage unit, through former Coberco subsidiary Riedel. Founded in 1897, Riedel had developed a number of leading Dutch brands, including Appelsientje, Dubbelsientje, and others.

Friesland Coberco immediately set its sites on expansion on both the domestic and international fronts. Among the company's first acquisitions was milk-based food ingredients producer De Kievit, located in Meppel, in the Netherlands. Other Dutch purchases that year included cheese and dairy products wholesale and distribution operations, such as Kaashandel Tamminga, Kaashandel Culemborg, Kaashandel Schep, and KH de Jong's Exporthandel, as well as Frisian Protein Workum. At the same time, Friesland Coberco strengthened its position in the South American market with the establishment of Friesland Peru. Yet that operation quickly slipped into losses and was sold before the end of the following year.

In 1998, the company also extended its Asian operations, adding its first production facility in mainland China, in Tianjin,

controlled at 70 percent by Friesland Coberco. In 1999, the company boosted its Asian Pacific region operations with the acquisition of full control of Foremost Friesland, in Thailand. One of that country's leading dairy products groups, Foremost had long been held at some 75 percent by Friesland.

After completing its purchase of food ingredients group De Kievit (the acquisition had been held up by a mergers and monopolies commission review), Friesland Coberco prepared itself for a larger acquisition, that of the sales, marketing, and distribution operations of DSM Bakery Ingredients, which retained control of its production. The new addition, however, enabled Friesland Coberco to extend its distribution portfolio with DSM's line of confectionery items and ingredients.

In the meantime, Friesland Coberco had been integrating its operations. That process led to a streamlining of the company's brands portfolio. In 1999, the company merged the sales and marketing divisions of its Friesche Vlag and Coberco dairy products groups. Then, in 2000, the company dropped the Coberco brand in order to focus its efforts on promoting a single Friesche Vlag brand family. That year, also, the company revised its organizational structure into nine operating divisions—Frico Cheese; Friesland Dairy & Drinks; Friesland Consumer Products; Friesche Vlag; Friesland Coberco Butter Products; Friesland Madibic Food Service; Borculo Domo Ingredients; Kievit; and Friesland Asia Pacific. The last, newly created division emphasized Friesland Coberco's commitment to boosting its presence in the Asia Pacific—which, with the adoption of Western eating habits, represented one of the world's fastest-growing dairy markets at the turn of the century.

International Foods Group for the New Century

Another feature of Friesland Coberco's reorganization was a strategy of emphasizing higher value-added products, and especially processed foods and branded products. As part of this effort, the company acquired, in 2000, fresh juice producer Hoogsteeder Fresh Specialist, a small company set up in 1998, that boosted Friesland Coberco's Riedel juice unit. Yet Friesland Coberco's next large-scale acquisition came in 2001, when the company paid Royal Numico NLG 1.45 billion (EUR 700 million) to take over its Nutricia dairy foods division.

Founded in 1896, Nutricia had pioneered infant formula and other dietary dairy products in the Netherlands, starting with a license to produce formula using the Backhaus method. Exports had early on played a primary role in Nutricia's growth, starting as early as 1905. In the years following World War II, Nutricia's efforts went toward the development of so-called "scientific" products, ranging from infant formulas to dietary supplements for critically ill and other hospital patients. Yet Nutricia had also developed a number of strong dairy brands, including the highly popular Chocomel and Fristi brands.

Nutricia's international expansion stepped up in the 1980s, as the Netherlands began emphasizing breast-feeding over formula, and in 1981, the company acquired the United Kingdom's Cow and Gate. In the 1990s, Nutricia's international expansion led it to Eastern Europe, and especially to Hungary, which became a primary market for the company. In 1995, Nutricia acquired Germany's Milupa, gaining a place as one of Europe's

---

Key Dates:

1894: Predecessor to Friesland Dairy is founded.
1896: Nutricia is formed.
1897: Predecessor to Coberco is founded.
1997: Friesland Dairy and Coberco merge, together with Twee Provinciën and De Zuid Oost-Hoek, forming Friesland Coberco Dairy Foods Holding.
2000: Company announces reorganization and refocusing on limited range of value-added brands.
2001: Company acquires Nutricia from Royal Numico.
2002: Friesland purchases Romania-based Napolact and the Slovak Republic's Laktis-Zilinske-Mliekarne.
2003: Company sells bakery products division to CSM; sells NutriFit brand and Dairy to Weise.

---

leading infant formula groups. Soon after, Nutricia reorganized, placing its dairy operation under new parent Royal Numico—which then went on to refocus itself through the acquisitions of such companies as General Nutrition Companies, Rexall Sundown, and Enrich International.

Friesland Coberco's acquisition of Nutricia enabled it to claim the number two position among European dairy groups, and solidify its spot among the global top ten. It also gave the company a solid position in Eastern Europe. Meanwhile, the addition of Nutricia's strong brand lineup helped Friesland Coberco move closer to its goal of repositioning itself as a value-added producer. By the end of 2001, Friesland Coberco's sales had climbed to EUR 4.4 billion.

The year 2002 was marked primarily by the integration of the Nutricia operations, boosting the company's sales past EUR 4.7 billion by the end of the year. Friesland Coberco continued to make targeted acquisitions, however, such as its purchase of Transylvania, Romania-based Napolact, and the Slovak Republic's Laktis-Zilinske-Mliekarne. These acquisitions were followed by the purchase of assets from the recently bankrupted Swenty, a Dutch maker of cream and ice cream mix. Then, in October 2002, Friesland Coberco added to its share of the Greek and Balkan region market through the purchase of a factory in Patras, Greece.

By 2003, Friesland Coberco's transition to branded, high value-added products appeared well on its way, as its key drive brands grew to represent 42 percent of the group's total sales. The company continued in its reorganization that year, selling part of its bakery ingredients operations to CSM Bakery Sup-

plies Europe in June 2003. At the same time, the company sold off the DrinkFit brand and dairy in Schlüchtern, Germany, acquired through the Nutricia purchase. Sold to Germany's Klaus Weise, the move fit in with Friesland Coberco's transformation into a brand-driven, value-added global foods giant for the new century.

Principal Subsidiaries

Borculo Domo Ingredients; DrinkFit GmbH (Germany); Dutch Lady Milk Industries (Malaysia); Dutch Lady Vietnam; Foremost Friesland (Thailand); Frico Cheese; Frico Cheese Benelux; Frico Cheese Deutschland; Frico Cheese Export; Frico Cheese Handel; Frico Cheese Iberica (Spain); Frico France; Friesche Vlag; Friesland (Singapore); Friesland Asia Pacific; Friesland Coberco Butter Products; Friesland Coberco Corporate Research; Friesland Coberco Poeder Unit; Friesland Colombia; Friesland Consumer Products; Friesland Czech & Slovak Republic; Friesland Dairy & Drinks Benelux; Friesland Dairy & Drinks Central Europe (Hungary); Friesland Dairy & Drinks Group; Friesland Deutschland; Friesland Drinks; Friesland Export; Friesland Foods (Hong Kong); Friesland Foods (U.S.A.); Friesland Hellas (Greece); Friesland Hungary; Friesland Madibic Food Service (Belgium); Friesland Middle East (Saudi Arabia); Friesland Nutrition; Friesland Romania; Friesland Tianjin Dairy Foods (China); Friesland UK; Friesland West Africa; Frisian Flag Indonesia; K.H. de Jong's Exporthandel; Kievit; My Boy Taiwan; Riedel Drinks; West Africa Milk Company.

Principal Competitors

Kraft Foods Inc.; Dairy Farmers of America; Parmalat; Danone; MD Foods/Arla; Suiza Foods; Lactalis; Campina Melkunie.

Further Reading

"Dutch Dairy Industry Merger Will Be Europe's Third Biggest," *Europe Agri*, September 26, 1997.
Fenton, Susan, "Dutch Lady Milks High China Profits," *Window*, June 21, 1996.
"Friesland Coberco wil naar redivisie," *Reformatorisch Dagblad*, March 7, 2001.
"Minder winst en omzet voor Friesland Coberco," *Planeet.nl*, September 5, 2003.
"2000 a Vintage Year for Dutch Dairy Giant," *Dairy Industries International*, April 2001, p. 8.
Van de Web, Evert, "Brands Drive Success," *Dairy Industries International*, October 2002, p. 14.

—M. L. Cohen

General Maritime Corporation

35 West 56th Street
New York, New York 10049
U.S.A.
Telephone: (212) 763-5600
Fax: (212) 763-5602
Web site: http://www.generalmaritimecorp.com

Public Company
Incorporated: 1997 as General Maritime Ship Holdings
   Ltd.
Employees: 131
Sales: $226.4 million (2002)
Stock Exchanges: New York
Ticker Symbol: GMR
NAIC: 483111 Deep Sea Freight Transportation; 483211
   Inland Water Freight Transportation

General Maritime Corporation owns and operates a fleet of close to 50 mid-sized tankers, making it the world's second largest tanker company (based on cargo capacity). The firm contracts with client companies to transport crude oil, principally across the Atlantic. General Maritime serves major worldwide oil companies such as Chevron Corp., Exxon Mobil, Texaco, Phillips Petroleum, and the Citgo Petroleum Corp. Most of its ships are either Aframax or Suezmax tankers, which are medium-sized ships capable of serving most ports. General Maritime finds much of its business on the so-called spot market, where it picks up orders on short notice. General Maritime succeeds in this market because its fleet is primarily young—its ships are on average less than 12 years old—and so considered of high quality and safety. The company also arranges its tanker purchases so that most of its ships have one or two identical "sister ships" that can be used interchangeably. This gives General Maritime great flexibility in fulfilling orders. General Maritime is one of only a handful of publicly owned shipping companies. It is also a large player in a market still dominated by many small companies. The firm was founded by Peter Georgiopoulos, who owns approximately 10 percent of the company's stock.

A Varied Career Leading to Shipping by 1991

Peter Georgiopoulos was born circa 1961 and raised in New York City, where his father was a maritime lawyer. He attended Bronx Science High School, then went to Fordham University in New York, where he played football. He then took a master's degree in business administration from Tuck Business School at Dartmouth University. Georgiopoulos seemed to have grand dreams from early on. While still an undergraduate he was struck by a photograph in a design magazine of a certain antique bed, a luxury item that would have been out of place in a dormitory. He found a similar bed in a Greenwich Village antique dealer's shop, but was unable to purchase it. Years later, his stake in General Maritime worth an estimated $50 million, he was able to purchase the Renaissance Revival bed and pay a decorator to embellish his apartment with gilt furnishings, brocade upholstery, and original oil paintings.

Georgiopoulos's first job out of business school was with a Greek firm, Tsakos Shipping and Trading. Georgiopoulos worked in both the company's New York office and its headquarters in Piraeus, Greece. But during the mid-1980s, the shipping industry was in a downturn, and Georgiopoulos took what might have been a more glamorous job, with the investment firm Drexel Burnham Lambert. Drexel Burnham Lambert was a venerable Wall Street company that had been in something of a slump until it hired a young California native named Michael Milken. Milken is credited with more or less single-handedly building the high-yield bond market, dubbed by him the "junk bond" market, that fueled much of the corporate takeover frenzy of the 1980s. High-yield bonds give high returns because they are high risk. They are issued to companies that for various reasons are unable to secure investment-grade bonds. Drexel Burnham Lambert was the nexus of the junk bond market until the prosecution of Milken triggered a crash in the late 1980s. Drexel Burnham Lambert declared bankruptcy and dissolved in 1990.

With the decline of Drexel, Georgiopoulos moved to a Connecticut brokerage firm, Mallory Jones Lynch. But his education in junk bonds was evidently crucial to his later success. Much of the shipping industry is financed by sub-investment grade bonds, because the industry is typically extremely volatile and unpredictable. The shipping industry is also extremely capital-intensive, as shippers need to expend large amounts to upgrade their fleets or build more carriers. A few banks, such as the German bank Deutsche Schiffsbank, specialized in financing shippers, but other banks stayed away. Georgiopoulos became an expert both in high-yield bonds and in shipping companies, and his ability to finagle financing from wary investors became the key to his success. Georgiopoulos only stayed at Mallory Jones Lynch for a year and a half. Then in 1991, just before his 30th birthday, he started his own company, Maritime Equity Management.

Building the Company in the Early 1990s

Maritime Equity's office was at first just a desk Georgiopoulos rented out of a Manhattan office. But he had valuable contacts in the world of high-yield and hedge fund investing, former clients and business acquaintances who were used to taking some financial risk in order to reap potentially high rewards. Georgiopoulos put together a series of deals that were structured like real estate investment trusts, where several investors went in together on an asset, in this case shares in ships. Maritime Equity's first deal was to purchase half the equity in a Norwegian chemical tanker, the *Trollvan*. Over the next five years, Maritime Equity put together a dozen deals, sometimes bringing investors a return of 11 times their money. Sometimes the company bought equity in a ship at a discount, and then was able to force a sale at a favorable price. Maritime Equity also hung onto some assets, and by early 1997, the firm owned six ships.

That year, Georgiopoulos decided to move up. His expertise in the financing of shipping had been quite lucrative. But his goal now was to become a fleet owner. In 1997 he launched General Maritime Ship Holdings Ltd., a private company consisting of Maritime Equity's small fleet. He wanted to grow bigger fast, but even with his contacts it was difficult to break into the major leagues. Georgiopoulos contracted the management of his ships to Universe Tankships and traded on that company's reputation to wangle contracts with big oil companies. Universe Tankships was founded in 1947 by Daniel K. Ludwig, a self-educated Michigan native who became a billionaire by building bigger and bigger tankers. Ludwig was considered the father of the so-called supertanker, and his company had a formidable standing in the world of oil transportation. Georgiopoulos convinced some of Universe Tankships' executives to come work for him, and piggybacked his young company on the shoulders of the older one. According to an interview with *Forbes* magazine (September 29, 2003), when he went to speak to oil company executives about using General Maritime's ships, he told them, ''Basically, I'm Universe Tankships.'' Universe Tankships was known for the technical management of its ships, and evidently its name opened doors for

General Maritime. By 2000 the company had put together a fleet of 14 ships, all of the mid-sized tankers known as Suezmaxes and Aframaxes.

The General Maritime ships operated principally in what is known as the spot market. This means that instead of holding long-term contracts to move oil for certain customers, the ships would contract for specific trips, usually at short notice, and at wildly varying rates. In the 1970s, oil companies ran their own ships, but gradually the industry changed, and by the end of the century as much as 70 percent of oil transportation went to independent shippers. Many shippers held steady contracts. The spot market was potentially more lucrative, though it was extremely volatile. Rates on the spot market fluctuated according to decisions taken by OPEC (the Organization of Petroleum Exporting Countries) and due to other factors. Depending on the direction of the market, General Maritime could make or lose thousands of dollars per day per ship. For the most part, General Maritime did very well. ''We made a fortune,'' Georgiopoulos told *Forbes*. But in 1998 the spot market dropped, just after General Maritime had spent $160 million for four ships without long-term contracts. These ships began losing approximately $5,000 every single day, and General Maritime ended up being pressured by its lenders to recapitalize $20 million in loans. Eventually the company was bailed out by Oaktree Capital Management, an investment group that had faith in Georgiopoulos's ability to negotiate the ups and downs of the shipping industry for long-term gains.

General Maritime continued to grow after its 1998 debacle, while many competitors defaulted. The oil tanker industry was extremely fragmented, with hundreds of companies, most owning only a small number of tankers, continually bidding to move the millions of barrels of crude oil produced around the world each day. The years 1997 and 1998 were seen as boom years for tanker companies, and many shippers raised money with high-yield bond issues at that time. The decline in the spot market was a disaster for many of these companies, and in many cases the banks that had lent them money felt burned. According to an analysis in *Euromoney* (August 2003), a basic problem was that the shippers and their banks ''failed to understand each other's markets.'' This seemed to be where Georgiopoulos stood out from the crowd. He understood both the difficult financing that kept shippers going and the nuts and bolts of running a fleet. He also was able to convince investors like Oaktree that he knew what he was doing.

Over the next few years, the company tried to build its fleet more quickly with a large acquisition. Several potential deals fell through, however. General Maritime bid $400 million in 1999 to buy the Norwegian company Benor Tankers, only to pull out of the deal when Benor's ships proved to be of lower quality than expected. It also tried to buy another company, Bona Shipping, which went instead to a large competitor, Teekay Shipping Corp. But with smaller acquisitions here and there, General Maritime built up its fleet to almost 30 ships by the time it went public in 2001.

Public Company After 2001

Sales reached $72 million for General Maritime in 1999, with a loss of close to $5 million. The next year, the company brought

Key Dates:

1991: Georgiopoulos founds Maritime Equity Management.
1997: General Maritime is launched with six ships.
2001: The first public offering is made.
2003: The company buys the Metrostar fleet.

in $132 million, a significant jump, and earnings stood at $30 million. Such volatility was part of the shipping market, especially for a company like General Maritime, which derived as much as 80 percent of its business from the spot market. Georgiopoulos had long aimed to take the company public. Public companies are required to disclose a host of figures, including expenses and debt levels. Georgiopoulos was comfortable with exposing the intricacies of General Maritime's finances, feeling that it helped his big investors understand the business. General Maritime was listed on the New York Stock Exchange in April 2001. Hundreds of companies had gone public every year in the late 1990s and in 2000. When General Maritime debuted, it was only the 14th company that year to go public. But four of its competitors had already had their initial public offerings in 2001, and the oil industry was considered to be growing, while much of the rest of the economy stagnated. Consequently, General Maritime did very well, raising some $144 million as its shares sold near the top of their expected range.

General Maritime kept its expenses low. Georgiopoulos operated with such a small staff at his Manhattan office that he had to answer his own phone. General Maritime's fleet had a few distinct competitive advantages. For the most part, its ships were young—less than 12 years old, and so were considered safer and more reliable than older ships. In November 2002 the aging tanker *Prestige* spilled 70,000 tons of oil off the coast of Spain, which only pointed out the advantages of newer, smaller ships such as General Maritime's. The company also bought ships in pairs or triplets, which gave it more flexibility on the

spot market. It was able to substitute these sister ships for their siblings at short notice, since the ships were virtually identical, so General Maritime was able to respond quickly to its customers' demands.

In January 2003 General Maritime increased its fleet substantially when it spent $525 million for the 19-ship Greek firm Metrostar Management. The company took on heavy debt to swing the deal, but was able to pay it down very quickly. The purchase of Metrostar gave General Maritime access to the Black Sea for the first time, and it soon signed contracts to transport oil for the large Russian oil producer Lukoil. General Maritime posted record earnings for the first half of 2003, and expected to have a very good year. With the addition of Metrostar's ships to its fleet, General Maritime became the second largest tanker company in the world. This was a very rapid rise for the company, which had started only six years earlier with six ships.

Principal Subsidiaries

General Maritime Management LLC; United Overseas Tankers Ltd. (Greece).

Principal Competitors

Teekay Shipping Corporation; Stelmar Shipping Ltd.; Frontline Ltd.

Further Reading

Brown, Mark, *Euromoney*, August 2003, p. 52.
Gandel, Stephen, ''Launching City's First 2001 IPO a Slick Move for Tanker Owner,'' *Crain's New York Business*, March 19, 2001, p. 4.
Goldman, Lea, ''Buccaneer,'' *Forbes*, September 29, 2003, pp. 64–65.
Marcial, Gene G., ''General Maritime: Its Tanker Business Is Brisk,'' *Business Week*, August 11, 2003, p. 104.
Pittel, Christine, ''Gilt Trip,'' *House Beautiful*, December 2000, p. 106.
''A Portrait of the Owner As a Young Man,'' *Tanker Operator*, January/February 2003, p. 9.

—A. Woodward

Gerdau S.A.

Avenida Farrapos, 1811
90220-005 Porto Alegre
Rio Grande do Sul
Brazil
Telephone: (+55) 51-3323-2000
Fax: (+55) 51-3323-2080
Web site: http://www.gerdau.com.br

Public Company
Incorporated: 1901
Employees: 18,026
Sales: R 7.5 billion ($3.26 billion) (2002)
Stock Exchanges: Brazil New York
Ticker Symbol: GGB
NAIC: 331111 Iron and Steel Mills

A fast-rising star on the international steel market, Gerdau S.A. has long held the title of the leading producer of long steel products in Brazil and Latin America. The company is also among the top three Brazilian producers of crude steel, and also produces a range of specialty steels, principally for the automotive industry. Overall, Gerdau ranks among the top 25 global steel producers. Gerdau also manufactures a variety of finished products, including nails—the company's original product, a segment in which Gerdau is the world leader—wire, wire mesh, and wire fencing. Through subsidiary Comercial Gerdau, the company is also Brazil's leading distributor of flat steel products. Gerdau has long specialized in the operation of minimills, which use electric arc furnaces to produce steel from scrap and other metals. The company also operates a small number of traditional blast furnaces, which produce steel from raw iron ore, especially through its controlling stake in Açominos, acquired in 2002. Much of Gerdau's growth lies in a steady series of domestic and international acquisitions which had enabled it to build an international network of manufacturing facilities throughout South America and in Canada and the United States as well. In that latter market, the company controls 75 percent of AmeriSteel, based in Florida. That 1999 acquisition helped boost Gerdau's total production past seven million tons per year. Gerdau posted R 7.5 billion ($3.2 billion) in revenues in 2002. Listed on the Brazil and New York stock exchanges, the company remains firmly controlled by the founding Gerdau-Johannpeter family, who hold more than 70 percent of Gerdau's voting rights through the family holding company, Metalúrgica Gerdau.

Nailing the Brazilian Market: Early 20th Century

Johann Heinrich Kasper Gerdau, a native of Hamburg, Germany, immigrated to Brazil in 1869, and originally established himself as a trader, and then a merchant, founding a general store in Cachoeira do Sul. Around 1900, Gerdau, who had by then adopted the Brazilian first name Joao, moved to Porto Alegre. There, Gerdau entered a new business, buying up the nail factory Pontas de Paris in 1901. Gerdau's business interests also included furniture manufacture, through Gerdau Móveis.

Gerdau's son Hugo took over the nail operation in 1907. Educated in Europe, the younger Gerdau continued to make trips both to Europe and to the United States, returning to Brazil with new steelmaking techniques and production processes. In this way, Gerdau vastly improved the quality of nails available in Brazil, and before long the company became the country's leading nail producer, adding a second production facility in Passo Fundo in 1933. By the end of the 20th century, Pontas de Paris company had become the largest nail manufacturer in the world.

The Gerdau family continued to explore varied business interests. Hugo Gerdau, for example, was a founding partner in Companhia Geral de Industrias, which manufactured stoves under the Geral brand name. Gerdau also participated in the creation of what later became the Federaçao das Indústrias do Estado do Rio Grande do Sul (FIERGS, or the Federation of Industries of Rio Grande do Sul). Yet it was through Hugo's daughter's marriage that the company became one of Brazil's industrial giants.

Helda Gerdau married German-born Curt Johannpeter, who first came to Brazil as a branch inspector for Deutsche Bank's German Transatlantic Bank. Johannpeter joined the Gerdau family in the 1930s, then took over the leadership of the nail company in 1946. The company went public the following year, adopting the name Fábrica de Pregos Hugo Gerdau.

Faced with the shortage of raw materials in the aftermath of World War II, Johannpeter led Gerdau into steel production itself, thereby ensuring its nail operation's supply. In 1948, Gerdau bought Porto Alegre-based Siderúrgica Riograndense SA, which had been founded ten years earlier. By the late 1950s, steel production had grown into Gerdau's primary area of interest. In 1957, the company added a second mill, in Sapucaia do Sul. Four years later, the company added a continuous ingot casting unit, the first in Latin America, which enabled it to boost its production levels and the quality of its steel products.

A commitment to quality rapidly became a Gerdau hallmark, as the company set out to match European and North American quality standards. The company's growing influence in the domestic market, particularly with the construction of a new and modern nail production plant in Passo Fundo in 1961, forced Gerdau's suppliers to meet company-imposed standards of quality. Gerdau began adding computer technology in the mid-1960s, and in 1968 was one of the first in Brazil to incorporate computer-controlled production processes.

Domestic Steel Leader in the 1970s

Gerdau took Siderúrgica Riograndense public in 1966, although the group retained majority control over its growing steel operation. Gerdau then entered a period of domestic expansion and diversification. In 1967, the company acquired Sao Judas Tadeu Wire Factory, located in Sao Paulo, expanding to its own nail production and adding wire production facilities as well. In another diversification move, Gerdau purchased Indústria de Arames Sao Judas Tadeu S.A., also in Sao Paulo, in 1971. That company, which changed its name to Comercial Gerdau, became Brazil's largest distributor of long and flat steels, developing a national network of more than 60 branch offices.

Gerdau also stepped up its steel production at the end of the 1960s and into the 1970s. In 1969, the company acquired a steel producer in Recife, Siderúrgica Açonorte. Two years later, Gerdau formed a joint venture with August Thyssen Hüette, based in Germany, to build a new steel mill in Rio de Janeiro. That mill, called Cosiqua, developed into the largest long steel production facility in Latin America. Gerdau took full control of Cosiqua in 1979, then launched it as a public company in 1984.

In the meantime, Gerdau continued its Brazilian expansion, adding the Guaira mill, one of the first in the state of Paraná, in the south of the country, in 1971, then adding another steel producer, Comesa, in 1974. In the early 1980s, Gerdau built two new steel mills, Cearense, in Ceará, and Araucária, in Paraná.

Concurrent with the growth in the company's steel production was its diversification into related businesses. Such was the case with its participation in the creation of Seiva SA Florestas e Indústrias, and its acquisition of CIFSUL, which added a forestry component to the group in the early 1970s, ensuring its fuel supply. Gerdau had also pioneered the new "minimill" concept, utilizing electric arc furnaces rather than traditional blast furnaces. The minimills enabled steel companies to produce new steel products from scrap metals. The need for scrap in turn led Gerdau into that market, with the creation of Gerdau Metálicos in 1980. That company developed into the largest scrap collector, processor, and reseller in the Latin American market.

By the early 1980s, Gerdau had become Brazil's largest steel producer. Yet the company's nearly 50 percent market share left it little room for future expansion at home. At the same time, the company's focus on the domestic market left it highly exposed to fluctuations in the often volatile Brazilian market. The company, now under the leadership of Curt Johannpeter's four sons, Klaus, Germano, Jorge, and Frederico, decided to take the risk and expand onto the international market.

International Expansion in the 1990s

Although Gerdau's first purchase of a foreign company came in 1981, when it acquired Uruguay's Laisa steel mill, its true international growth started at the end of the 1980s, with the acquisition of Canada's Courtice Steel Inc. in 1989. Three years later, Gerdau added to its Latin American operations with the purchase of two Chilean steelmakers, Indac and Aza, which were consolidated into a single company, Gerdau Aza. In 1995, Gerdau returned to Canada, purchasing Manitoba Rolling Mills Inc., which was then renamed Gerdau MRM. Two years later, Gerdau entered Argentina, acquiring Sociedad Industrial Puntana SA, or SIPSA. The following year, Gerdau added a one-third stake in that country's Sipar Laminacion de Aceros as well.

Not all of Gerdau's growth occurred outside of Brazil during this period. Indeed, the company continued to expand its domestic operations throughout the early 1990s. Gerdau took advantage of the privatization drive of the Brazilian government, picking up a number of formerly state-controlled steel mills, including the Barao de Cacais mill in 1988, Usina Siderúrgica da Bahia S.A. in Usiba in 1989, and then Companhia Siderúrgica do Nordeste and Aços Finos Piratini S.A. in 1991. The last-named business, which focused on the specialty steels market, enabled Gerdau to add a range of high value-added products to its existing steel products lines.

Gerdau's acquisition drive moved to Divinópolis in 1994, where it bought German-controlled Korf GmbH and its steelworks Cia. Siderúrgica Pains S.A. That purchase subjected Gerdau to investigation by Brazil's mergers and monopolies body; Gerdau ultimately gained permission to proceed with the acquisition. Subsequently, Gerdau sold off the rest of the Korf operations and renamed the Pains mill Gerdau Divinópolis. Domestic expansion continued into the late 1990s with the purchase of a minority stake in semi-finished products group Açominos. Over the next several years, Gerdau increased its share of Açominos to nearly 37 percent in 1999, and finally to 87 percent in 2002, including more than 79 percent of voting rights.

By the mid-1990s, Gerdau had grown into an internationally operating group of more than 28 companies—including its own

Key Dates:

1901: Johann Heinrich Kasper (Joao) Gerdau acquires nail factory Pontas de Paris in Porto Alegre, Brazil.
1907: Son Hugo Gerdau takes over as head of nail factory.
1933: Company adds second nail production factory in Passo Fundo.
1946: Gerdau's son-in-law, Curt Johannpeter, assumes leadership of company and begins expansion into steelmaking.
1947: Company goes public as Fabrica de Pregos Hugo Gerdau.
1948: Company acquires first steel works in Riograndense.
1957: Gerdau expands Riograndense with second mill in Sapucaia do Sul.
1969: Gerdau acquires Açonorte steel works.
1971: Company builds Cosigua steel mill in joint venture with Germany's August Thyssen Hüette; acquires Comercial Gerdau distribution business; acquires Guaira steel mill.
1979: Company acquires full control of Cosigua, the largest long steel works in Latin America.
1981: Gerdau completes its first international acquisition, that of the Laisa steel mill in Uruguay.
1988: Company acquires Barao do Cocais steel mill.
1989: Company moves into Canada with acquisition of Courtice Steel in Ontario; acquires Usiba, in Bahia.
1992: Company acquires Indac and Aza in Chile; acquires Brazilian specialty steels producer Aços Finos Piratini.
1994: Company acquires Pains steel mill, which is renamed Gerdau Divinópolis.
1997: Company completes restructuring of operations under single entity, Gerdau S.A.; acquires minority stake in Açominos.
1999: Gerdau is listed on the New York Stock Exchange; acquires 75 percent of AmeriSteel in Florida; opens new steel mill in Chile.
2001: Gerdau begins construction of new steel plant in Aracariguama, scheduled to begin production as early as 2004.
2002: Company boosts stake in Açominos to more than 85 percent.

bank, launched in 1995 to provide financial services to its steel customers—and six publicly listed companies. In 1995, the company began a restructuring process in order to simplify its organizational structure. By 1997, Gerdau had completed the reorganization, merging its businesses into a single company, Gerdau S.A., listed on the Brazil stock exchange. Gerdau S.A. nonetheless remained under the control of the Gerdau family, whose members held more than 70 percent of the voting rights through their Metalúrgica Gerdau holding company. In 1999, Gerdau placed its stock on the New York Stock Exchange as well.

Despite its increasingly international operations, Gerdau remained a small player in the global steel market, ranked at the very bottom of the world's top 50 steel companies. Foreign sales represented just 10 percent of the group's total. In 1999, however, Gerdau took a leap into the big leagues when it paid Japan's Kyoei Steel $262 million to take over 75 percent of Florida-based AmeriSteel. The deal boosted Gerdau's total production past seven million tons per year, and transformed it into the second largest producer of concrete reinforcing bars. The addition of AmeriSteel allowed Gerdau to climb to the world's top 25 steel companies; it also shifted the balance of the group's geographic sales, as international revenues now reached 36 percent of the group's total.

Gerdau immediately began investing in its new U.S. business, pouring more than $340 million to expand production at AmeriSteel's four minimills by some 25 percent. At the same time, Gerdau's holding of AmeriSteel increased to 85 percent.

Gerdau's early internationalization was credited with helping the company bypass Brazil's economic crisis in the late 1990s. By the early 2000s, as the country's economy revived, Gerdau's good health placed it in a strong position to increase its clout in the domestic market. The company continued to invest in its home market, installing new rolling equipment at its Aços Finos Piratini unit to double its specialty steel capacity. The company also earmarked some $400 million for the construction of a new rebar plant in Sao Paulo. With a capacity of 1.1 million tons, the new plant was scheduled to begin operations as early as 2004.

After increasing its stake in Açominos past 85 percent in 2002, Gerdau began looking for further acquisitions. Yet the company remained focused on the Americas, judging European steel production as too expensive a market to enter, and the fast-growing Asian steel market as too culturally different. At the end of 2002, Gerdau found its next target, Toronto's Co-Steel, which merged into AmeriSteel in October of that year. The new unit was then renamed AmeriSteel Whitby. In 2003, Gerdau announced a plan to spend $60 million in order to integrate and improve its expanded North American operation. After more than 100 years, Gerdau appeared to have nailed down its place in the global steel market.

Principal Subsidiaries

Aceros Cox S.A. (Chile); Açominas Gerais S.A. (79%); Armafer Serviços de Construçao Ltda.; Gerdau AmeriSteel Corporation (Canada; 74%); Gerdau USA Inc.; AmeriSteel Corp. (U.S.A.; 74 85%); AmeriSteel Bright Bar Inc. (U.S.A.; 74%); Gerdau AmeriSteel MRM Special Sections Inc. (Canada; 74%); Gerdau AmeriSteel Cambridge Inc. (Canada; 74%); Gerdau AmeriSteel Perth Amboy Inc. (U.S.A.; 74%); Gerdau AmeriSteel Sayreville Inc. (U.S.A.; 74%); Gerdau Aza S.A. (Chile); Gerdau Internacional Emprendimentos Ltda. (Brazil); Gerdau GTL Spain S.L. (Spain); Gerdau Laisa S.A. (Uruguay); Seiva S.A. – Florestas e Indústrias.

Principal Competitors

Eclipse Foundries Ltd.; Panzhihua Iron and Steel Co.; Ishikawajima-Harima Heavy Industries Company Ltd.; C Grossmann

Eisen- u Stahlwerk AG; Benxi Iron and Steel Co.; Forjas de Santa Clara CA; Chongqing Special Steel Group Co.; Fiat S.p.A.; Xinyu Steel and Iron Plant General of Jiangxi; Krivorozhstal Krivoy Rog; Aceros Chile S.A.; Cargill Inc.; Ispat Karmet Steel Plant.

Further Reading

''Brazil's Gerdau—Who Dares Wins,'' *Economist,* September 23, 2000, p. 74.

Colitt, Raymond, ''Breaking from the Traditional Brazilian Mold,'' *Financial Times*, September 12, 2000, p. 12.

Kepp, Michael, ''Family Bonds, Global Vision Help Company Grow,'' *American Metal Market*, June 19, 2001, p. 16.

Kinch, Diana, ''Brazil's Gerdau Group Investing $60M in North American Units,'' *American Metal Market*, February 7, 2003, p. 5.

Romans, Christine, ''Gerdau Stays Top of Steel Distributors' List,'' *America's Intelligence Wire*, August 21, 2003.

—M. L. Cohen

Glanbia plc

Glanbia House
Kilkenny
Ireland
Telephone: (+353) 56-72200
Fax: (+353) 56-72222
Web site: http://www.glanbia.com

Public Company
Incorporated: 1997
Employees: 6,416
Sales: EUR 2.39 billion ($2.69 billion) (2002)
Stock Exchanges: Irish
Ticker Symbol: GLANBIA
NAIC: 311511 Fluid Milk Manufacturing; 311119 Other
   Animal Food Manufacturing; 311512 Creamery Butter
   Manufacturing; 311513 Cheese Manufacturing;
   311514 Dry, Condensed, and Evaporated Dairy
   Product Manufacturing; 311520 Ice Cream and Frozen
   Dessert Manufacturing; 311611 Animal (Except
   Poultry) Slaughtering; 325311 Nitrogenous Fertilizer
   Manufacturing; 424510 Grain and Field Bean
   Merchant Wholesalers

Glanbia plc is Ireland's top dairy foods producer and one of Europe's major dairy food groups, with a significant position in the U.S. cheese and food ingredients markets as well. Glanbia (Gaelic for ''pure food'') has repositioned itself to focus on two core businesses: dairy-based milk products, and the newly added Glanbia Nutritionals division, which specializes in producing nutritional foods. In the process, the company has sold off a number of operations, including its fresh milk and processed meat businesses. In 2003, the company announced its intention to exit the fresh meat business as well. In their place, Glanbia has sold a 49 percent stake in its Glanbia Cheese division to the United States' Leprino Foods Company, the world's leading manufacturer of mozzarella cheese, in exchange for access to Leprino's cheese-making technology. The deal positions Glanbia and the number one European producer of mozzarella cheese, itself one of the fastest-growing cheese segments. The company has also formed a joint venture with

Dairy Farmers of America and Selected Milk Producers to establish a new cheesemaking company—with an added goal to create nutritional and low-fat foods and drinks from whey, a byproduct of the cheese-making process. Fueling that effort was the group's announcement that it intends to expand its Idaho-based cheese manufacturing plant in 2003. In that year, the company took its first steps into the Latin American market, forming a joint venture with Uruguayan dairy coop Conaprole. Glanbia is traded on the Irish stock exchange, and is led by Managing Director John Moloney.

Emerging from Ireland's Dairy Consolidation in the 1960s

Dairy products have long formed the backbone of Ireland's agricultural sector. In the early 19th century, the country was among the world's largest producers of dairy products, and especially of butter, which was to remain a primary dairy end product into the 20th century. The invention of the centrifugal separator and its introduction into Ireland in the 1870s transformed the country's dairy sector, which had previously been operated by small, independent farmers. In order to support the cost of acquiring separators, dairy farmers grouped together and built centralized dairy processing facilities, which became known as ''creameries.''

Initially, creameries were privately held and operated. In the late 1880s, however, dairy farmers began adopting the cooperative format, often to enter into direct competition with the private creameries. The numbers of creameries increased dramatically by 1900, and by the eve of World War I, the country counted nearly 800 plants. The dairy market was unable to support such a large number, however, and the crisis in the country's agricultural market following the war led to a large number of creameries, and especially the more vulnerable, privately held creameries, to shut down.

Government policy intervened in the 1920s to consolidate the dairy market, and especially shift the sector away from privately held creameries, as the Dairy Disposal Company (DCC), established in 1927, began acquiring failing creameries. The government also put into place a number of measures designed to protect the domestic market from outside competi-

Company Perspectives:

Our Vision. Our Vision is to be the most relevant international player in cheese and nutrition.

tion. By the 1930s, the DCC had acquired nearly all of the private creameries, shutting down many of them, while directly controlling the remainder. The DCC had also taken over a large number of struggling cooperatives as well. In the years following World War II, the DCC had reduced the number of individual creameries under its control to just 17 large-scale facilities. At the same time, the number of cooperatives in Ireland had shrunk back to less than 220.

Butter remained the Irish dairy industry's core product, accounting for the vast majority of the creameries' production. The resulting skim milk was then sold at nominal cost to farmers, who used it to feed their livestock. Improvements in transportation, and especially the boom in the automotive sector in the postwar years, presented new growth opportunities, and the first diversification efforts appeared during this period. Among these was the establishment of a cheese plant in Limerick in the late 1940s, and, in 1951, the creation of a factory in Carrick-on-Suir. That facility, called Miloko, brought together nearly 40 cooperative creameries, together with English investors, to produce chocolate crumb, an important ingredient in chocolate preparations, for the English market.

In the early 1960s, the Irish government became determined to lower the trade barriers that had shielded the country's dairy industry. As part of the preparation for that event, the government set up the Irish Agricultural Organisation Society (IAOS), which in turn recommended a drastic consolidation of the sector, reducing the number of creameries in operation throughout the country to less than 20. That process, which involved merging the competing dairy cooperatives, was largely completed by the 1990s.

One of the first of the new, larger cooperatives to emerge was the Waterford Co-op, created in 1964 through the merger of the five Waterford-based cooperatives. The fact that the cooperatives were already neighbors, yet presented little in terms of overlap—and therefore were not direct competitors—allowed the merger process to proceed smoothly. Such was not the case in other regions, where large numbers of competing, and at times hostile, groups resisted amalgamation.

With its head start, Waterford was able to grow quickly and by 1966 the cooperative had already branched out with its first diversified product line, cheese production. Waterford stepped up its growth in the early 1970s, acquiring a number of other creameries. In 1973, the cooperative added a new product line, when it acquired the Irish license for the Yoplait product line. In support of that, Waterford built a new yogurt and fresh dairy processing center in Inch, in the county of Wexford. That plant was further expanded in 1978, while in that year Waterford built a new powdered milk plant at Dungarvan.

In the meantime, the group of cooperatives involved in the Miloko chocolate crumb factory sought to expand the facility's operation and also to diversify into other dairy categories. Yet the group met with resistance from its English investors, which preferred to rest with the chocolate crumb plant. In 1966, 25 of the cooperatives involved in the Miloko facilities agreed to join together to establish the Avonmore Creameries Federation. Backed by the British dairy giant Unigate, the new federation began construction of a dairy plant in Ballyragget with a capacity of 100,000 gallons of milk per day.

Avonmore originally focused on production of butter and powdered skim milk. The latter product helped transform the Irish dairy industry. By creating new value for skim milk itself, which previously had been considered as little more than a waste byproduct of butter production, the price of milk grew strongly, stimulating additional production. By 1969, the Ballyragget plant had reached full operating capacity. The following year, the group added casein, a product derived from milk powder, to its operations.

In 1973, and under the encouragement of the IAOS, 21 of the original 25 founding members of the federation agreed to a formal merger, creating Avonmore Farmers Ltd. The cooperative quickly began adding new product lines, starting with the purchase of a 40 percent share in the Roscrea Bacon Factory that same year. By the end of the decade, Avonmore had added other operations, including the 1977 purchase of feed producer Welfed. One year later, the cooperative bought back Unigate's stake in the Ballyragget facility. By the end of the decade, Avonmore's sales had topped £100 million.

International Expansion in the 1980s

Both Avonmore and Waterford expanded strongly into the 1980s. At home, both companies established leading brand names, while Waterford also enjoyed strong sales with its Yoplait franchise. The two cooperatives also continued to add product lines. Avonmore, for example, entered liquid milk production in 1981, a move that helped the company double its sales by 1983. Waterford in the meantime had completed construction of a new grain mill in Clonroche, the largest in Ireland. The Provender Mill, as it was called, produced grains for feed products.

The 1980s, however, marked a period of internationalization for both Avonmore and Waterford. The latter cooperative formed a new subsidiary, Waterford Foods International, in order to explore its international expansion opportunities, entering, among other markets, the United States with cheesemaking operations in Wisconsin. Avonmore followed suit, buying up plants in Wisconsin, Illinois, and Idaho in the late 1980s.

At the same time, both companies established international marketing operations. In Avonmore's case, the company's sales reached markets throughout Europe, and into Mexico, Japan, Korea, and Australia by the early 1990s. Avonmore continued its domestic expansion as well, acquiring several dairies, including Drogheda and Dundalk and Baileboro in 1986. In that year, Waterford enhanced its own European position with a joint venture agreement with the Netherlands' Wessanen to establish manufacturing operations in Ireland in order to produce continental cheese varieties for the European market.

Fueling their expansion, both Avonmore and Waterford went public in the 1980s. Avonmore went first, becoming Avonmore Foods Plc in 1987 with a listing on the Irish stock exchange.

Key Dates:

1951: Irish dairy cooperatives, in conjunction with British investors, found Miloko chocolate crumb ingredient plant in Carrick-on-Suir.

1964: Five Waterford-based dairy cooperatives merge to form the Waterford Cooperative.

1966: Twenty-five cooperatives involved in Miloko plant decide to form a new partnership, the Avonmore Creameries Federation, and build new plant in Ballyragget in partnership with England's Unigate.

1973: Most of the Avonmore Federation cooperatives formally merge into Avonmore.

1987: Avonmore goes public as Avonmore Foods Plc.

1988: Waterford goes public as Waterford Foods Plc.

1997: Avonmore and Waterford merge, forming Avonmore Waterford.

1999: Company changes name to Glanbia, meaning ''pure food'' in Gaelic.

2000: Company sells 49 percent stake in Glanbia Cheese to Leprino in exchange for cheesemaking technology.

2003: Glanbia forms joint venture with Dairy Farmers of America and Selected Milk Producers to build whey processing plant; forms joint venture with Conaprole (Uruguay) to enter Latin American market.

Waterford followed in 1988, changing its name to Waterford Foods Plc. Both groups remained majority controlled by the dairy farmers that had formed the original cooperatives.

With new access to capital, the companies began to acquire scale. Avonmore launched its U.S. expansion in 1989, spending some £20 million to establish its cheese manufacturing presence there. The company then bought up Ashmount Foods, a producer of meat products in Bradford, England, in 1990, paying £3 million.

Waterford's expansion included its 1989 purchase of a 50 percent stake in Premier Dairies, with Express Group Ireland, part of the Grand Met group, giving it a share in one of Ireland's major dairy brands. In 1991, Avonmore and Waterford nearly came together, launching merger talks to create an Irish super dairy group. Yet the two sides were unable to reach an agreement at that time.

A Merged Dairy Giant for the New Century

Instead, the two rivals continued making acquisitions. In 1992, Avonmore spent £11 million to acquire Churchfield/Tom Parker Dairies, further enhancing its profile in the British dairy market. One year later, Avonmore paid nearly £22 million for Perry Barr, part of the United Kingdom's Dairy Crest, run by Britain's Milk Marketing Board. That purchase helped push the company's revenues past the £1 billion mark and established it as a leading producer of dairy products for the Midlands and western England regions.

Waterford's acquisitions included the purchase of United Co-operative Dairies, based in Manchester, England, for £37.5 million. The following year, Waterford bought Express Group

from Grand Met, which, apart from giving it full control of Premier Dairies, also made it Ireland's leading dairy group. Another Waterford acquisition came in 1995 when it bought The Cheese Company, paying IR£125 million.

Yet Waterford's expansion came at a cost, as the group struggled to maintain profitability in the mid-1990s. By 1997, after Waterford posted a profit warning, the group once again found itself in merger talks with Avonmore. After rejecting an initial offer from Avonmore, for £280 million, Waterford agreed to Avonmore's next offer, for £377 million. The merged group, called Avonmore Waterford, not only became Ireland's largest dairy group, it also claimed a 10 percent share of the British milk market and a 20 percent share of the U.K. cheese market.

Avonmore Waterford began restructuring its operations, shutting down or selling off a number of plants and operations, including its Avonmore cheese plants in Wisconsin and Illinois, which were sold to Canada's Saputo Inc. in 1998. That year, the company sold off its fresh juice business, Waterford Juices, to Princes Ltd. for £14 million. The company's remaining operations were then placed under a new operating structure based on two primary dairy divisions, Consumer and Food Ingredients.

In February 1999, Avonmore Waterford changed its name, taking the Gaelic word for ''pure food'' as its own. Becoming Glanbia, the company now started a streamlining effort. In June 1999, the group sold off its U.K.-based fresh milk business to Express Dairies for £100 million. That same year, the company sold its Irish beef unit to DaWn Meat, for £110 million. These moves were made as part of the company's shift toward a focus on its growing food ingredients segment.

Glanbia achieved a new phase in its growth in 2000 when it signed an agreement with the United States' Leprino in which it transferred a 49 percent stake in its Glanbia Cheese division in exchange for Leprino's cheese technology. The deal made Glanbia the leading producer of mozzarella and pizza cheese—Leprino's specialty—in Europe. In the United States, Glanbia's operational focus switched to Idaho, where it began a large-scale expansion of its cheese production facility. That move also stepped up the group's production of cheese byproduct whey, which was fast becoming a highly sought after food ingredient. In 2003, the group created a joint venture with Dairy Farmers of America and Selected Milk Producers to build a new whey processing plant.

As Glanbia continued to refine its focus, targeting the new and fast-growing ''nutritional'' foods segment, the company began selling off its non-core segments, including its processed meat component, which was sold in 2002. In 2003, the company announced its intention to exit the fresh meat market as well. In the meantime, Glanbia sought new markets for expansion. In 2003, the company announced that it had reached an agreement with Uruguay's Conaprole cooperative to create and market dairy products for the Latin American market. Glanbia, already one of Europe's top dairy groups, now set its sights on joining the ranks of the global dairy giants.

Principal Subsidiaries

Glanbia Cheese UK; Glanbia Dairies Ireland; Glanbia Foods Inc. (U.S.A.); Glanbia Foods Ireland; Glanbia Foods UK;

Glanbia Ingredients Europe; Glanbia Meats Ireland; Glanbia Milk UK.

Principal Competitors

Nestlé Suisse S.A.; Kroger Co.; Publix Super Markets Inc.; Cirio S.p.A.; Co-operative Group CWS Ltd.; Dean Foods Co.; Southern Foods Group L.P.; Prairie Farms Dairy Inc.; Parmalat S.p.A.; Lactalis; Arla Foods amba; Friesland Coberco Dairy Foods Holding N.V.; Campina Melkunie UA.

Further Reading

Boyle, Pat, ''Modest Moloney Has Got the Right Ingredients for Glanbia,'' *Irish Independent*, August 31, 2002.

Breathnach, Proinnsias, ''The Evolution of the Spatial Structure of the Irish Dairy Processing Industry,'' Department of Geography, National University of Ireland, Maynooth.

Cope, Nigel, ''Glanbia Plans Glorious Future on Winning Whey,'' *Independent*, July 18, 2003, p. 21.

''Glanbia Starting to Get a Bigger Pizza the Action,'' *Journal*, August 28, 2003, p. 27.

Jenkins, William, ''Restructuring of Irish Dairy Co-operatives Since 1950: An Example from County Tipperary,'' Department of Geography, University College Dublin.

''New Glanbia Plan Would Replace 'Failed' Restructuring,'' *Irish Independent*, September 23, 2003.

Truman, Richard, ''Whey to Go for Glanbia,'' *Dairy Industries International*, April 2002, p. 18.

—M. L. Cohen

Golden Telecom, Inc.

1 Kozhevnichesky Proezd
115114 Moscow
Russia
Telephone: +7-501-797-9300
Fax: +7-095-797-9306
Web site: http://www.goldentelecom.ru

Public Company
Incorporated: 1999
Employees: 1,700
Sales: $198.7 million (2002)
Stock Exchanges: NASDAQ
Ticker Symbol: GLDN
NAIC: 517212 Cellular and Other Wireless
    Telecommunications

Golden Telecom, Inc. is one of the first foreign companies to provide telecommunications and Internet services in Russia and the Commonwealth of Independent States (CIS). Its roots go back to the late 1980s, when an American company began setting up data and voice links in joint ventures with partners in the Soviet Union. The American company, which became known as Global TeleSystems, Inc., eventually became a leading telecommunications provider across all of Europe. Golden Telecom was formed in 1999 when Global TeleSystems spun off its business activities in Russia and the CIS into a separate company. Although Golden Telecom is incorporated in Delaware and trades on the NAS-DAQ, it is majority-owned by Russian companies and all of its business dealings are in Russia and the CIS.

Golden Telecom is a market leader among the independent telecommunications companies that were set up shortly after the breakup of the Soviet Union to provide a more convenient and reliable alternative to the regular public telephone service. It offers a wide array of telecommunications-related services. The company has built its own alternative local access overlay networks, fiber optic and satellite networks in Russia and the CIS countries. Through this network, it is able to offer telephone, Internet, and data transmission services to corporate customers in Moscow, Kiev, St. Petersburg, Nizhny Novgorod,

and other population centers. It provides local, domestic long-distance, and international telephone services. Golden Telecom also offers dial-up Internet access to mass market consumers and operates several popular Russian-language web portals. In addition, the company is a leading cellular service provider in Kiev. Through acquisitions, it has furthered the consolidation of Russia's fragmented telecommunications sector.

Developing a Telecom Infrastructure in the 1990s

Golden Telecom's roots go back to 1983, when a nonprofit company known as San Francisco/Moscow Teleport, Inc. was set up to promote telecommunications connections with the U.S.S.R. In 1986 the company was incorporated as a for-profit corporation known as Global TeleSystems, Inc. That year it began offering data links between the U.S.S.R. and the United States. The company operated out of McLean, Virginia.

By the early 1990s Global TeleSystems was one of several Western companies that had set up telecommunications enterprises in Russia. Under state control, the country's existing network had failed to keep up with growing demand and technological advances. When the Soviet Union disintegrated in 1991, Russia was left with an inefficient and underdeveloped analog telephone system. The state Ministry of Communications transferred control of local access networks to 80 regional operators known as telcos, while a state-run enterprise known as Rostelecom took over the long-distance and international network. The small regional operators lacked the funds to update the country's overburdened infrastructure. Meanwhile, the gradually developing private business sector was demanding reliable local and long-distance telephone service as well as data connections. To spur investment, the Ministry of Communications issued licenses allowing domestic and foreign companies to construct their own overlay networks as an alternative to the traditional network. Private companies rushed in to provide up-to-date telecommunications services to the business customers who could afford to pay for them. Most of Global TeleSystems' early enterprises were set up as joint ventures with the entities that held licenses for network development.

Global TeleSystems set up two of its major ventures in 1990. Sovam Teleport was established to provide data transmission

Company Perspectives:

Golden Telecom anticipates strong growth in the next three to five years as the company expands with the expected strong growth of the Russian economy over the same period. Expanding demand from business customers for modern telecommunications services will drive the growth. Our main strategies are to: Pursue consolidation opportunities through acquisitions that will allow us to improve and expand our service offerings and maintain operational control. Increase market share by offering bundled data and voice services over an integrated network. Extend our leading position in high growth data and internet markets. Control operating costs and satisfy needs via network planning and optimization. Our network strategy includes building and owning our local exchange and customer access networks. Focus operating activities and capital investments opportunities in Moscow, Kiev, St. Petersburg, Nizhny Novgorod and other population centers in the CIS, where demand for our services is most heavily concentrated.

and Internet connections in Russia and the CIS. The company began offering local subscriber access to its networks in 1994 and eventually became a leading provider of business-to-business data connections. Another subsidiary, Sovintel, was founded in 1990 as an international long-distance carrier in a 50–50 joint venture with the state long-distance monopoly Rostelecom. Sovintel began building an alternative fixed-line network in Moscow and started offering international long-distance services in 1992. For the Russian partners in the enterprise, Sovintel represented a whole new way of operating a telecommunications business. Under the old system, customers had to write a letter to the phone company and go on a long waiting list to get a telephone. Now it was the other way around: the telecommunications company was pursuing customers, primarily in the private business sector. Alexander Vinogradov, who would eventually head Golden Telecom, said of his early years at Sovintel, ''We became students again. We were learning from our American partners, from our clients, from reading. We were finding ourselves in this world.''

In the mid-1990s Global TeleSystems expanded its offerings across Russia and in Moscow. The company TeleRoss was established in 1994 to provide domestic long-distance services via a satellite network. TeleCommunications of Moscow, or TCM, was set up that year to provide CLEC, or ''competitive local exchange carrier'' services. A CLEC network was an overlay network separate from and superior to the public network. In 1995 Global TeleSystems began offering cellular service on a small scale, and amassed shares in regional cellular networks through the holding company GTS Mobile Services. It also branched out to Kazakhstan, founding SA Telcom LLP as a partnership between Sovam Teleport and the Kazakh holding company Sary-Arka. Global TeleSystems reached the city of Nizhny Novgorod in 1996 when it set up a joint venture with Svyazinform Nizhny Region. A Ukrainian branch also was founded that year. At first the Ukrainian subsidiary provided only cellular service, but it soon began building a fiber optic network in Kiev in order to provide Internet and voice services.

By the end of 1997, Global TeleSystems had 3,160 dial-up Internet subscribers and 50 points of presence across Russia that could be used to access the Russia On-Line service that had been developed by the Sovam Teleport subsidiary. The TeleRoss subsidiary had amassed 50 percent ownership in 14 regional providers of domestic long-distance service. Net revenues from the CIS businesses in 1997 more than doubled from the year before to $27.2 million, but net losses for the past several years were in the millions of dollars.

Nevertheless, expansion continued at Global TeleSystems. The company acquired the ownership interest of its former partner in Sovam Teleport and also began acquiring full ownership of the regional telcos and converting them into branches of TeleRoss. Meanwhile, Global TeleSystems was focusing more and more attention on Western Europe, where the telecommunications market had just been deregulated. To generate funds for European expansion, Global TeleSystems went public on NASDAQ in February 1998. Billionaire George Soros held about 27 percent of the company. The proceeds from the initial public offering (IPO) supported acquisitions of major telecommunications operators across Europe, including Espirit Telecom, NetSource, and Omnicom. As a result, Global TeleSystems' Russia and CIS division accounted for only about 20 percent of revenues in 1999, down from 80 percent in 1997.

IPO and Acquisitions: 1999–2001

The relatively unstable ventures in Russia were now a liability with the potential to depress Global TeleSystems' share price and make it harder to borrow money for its activities in Western Europe. So the company decided to set up a separate legal entity for the Russia and CIS division. In June 1999 Golden Telecom Inc. was incorporated in Delaware and in September the company went public on NASDAQ. Stewart Reich, an American who had led Global TeleSystems' Russia and CIS division since 1997, became president and CEO of the new company. Global TeleSystems retained a ⅔ interest in Golden Telecom.

Golden Telecom's IPO, the first by a Russian company since the financial crisis in August 1998, was not viewed as a success. At the last minute, the company's underwriters decreased the estimated share price from $16 to $12 in an effort to generate greater investor interest. Nevertheless, Russia's unpredictable regulatory regime, President Boris Yeltsin's poor health, and the uncertainty of the upcoming Duma elections did not inspire investor confidence. The share price dropped to $8.56 later on the day of the IPO. Still, Golden Telecom came away with nearly $150 million in cash, including about $64 million from the share offering, a $50 million contribution from its parent company Global TeleSystems, and $30 from strategic investors including ING Barings and the Soros Fund.

By the end of 1999, confidence in Golden Telecom improved and the share price was more than $30. A minor scandal surfaced at the end of the year: The *New York Times* reported in December that sometime in the mid-1990s Global TeleSystems paid directors of the Moscow City Telephone Network $65 million for preferential treatment that would allow them to set up a premium telecommunications provider. Golden Telecom denied the allegations and the incident failed to have any lasting

Key Dates:

1983: San Francisco/Moscow Teleport, Inc. is set up as a nonprofit company.
1986: The company is incorporated as Global Tele-Systems, Inc., a for-profit corporation.
1990: Sovam Teleport and Sovintel are established to provide voice and data communication services in Russia.
1999: Global TeleSystems' Russia and CIS division becomes a separate company, Golden Telecom, and goes public on NASDAQ.
2000: Golden Telecom makes numerous acquisitions of Internet service providers and web properties.
2001: Alfa Group leads a consortium of Russian investors that purchases majority control in Golden Telecom.

effect. In 1999 both annual revenue and net loss attained new heights, reaching $97.9 million and $46.5 million, respectively.

Golden Telecom moved ahead with more acquisitions and consolidation. The data and Internet subsidiary Sovam Teleport had acquired Glasnet, a leading Russian Internet service provider, a few months before the IPO. In November 1999 Golden Telecom merged three of its subsidiaries in order to take advantage of operational and tax-related benefits: Sovam Teleport, the data and Internet division, and TCM, the CLEC services provider in Moscow, were combined into TeleRoss, the satellite communications operator.

A series of Internet-related acquisitions followed in 2000. Golden Telecom's web presence grew with the acquisition of the web sites Absolute Games and Referat.ru, Russia's number one educational site. This was followed by the $8.28 million purchase of IT INFOART STARS, an Internet portal that offered a wide variety of news and publication content, as well as the popular rating index 1000stars.ru. In August 2000 Golden Telecom completed one of the biggest deals yet in Russia's telecommunications sector when it bought the Agama family of web properties for $25 million. The purchase included the top bilingual search engine Aport and a popular entertainment portal known as Omen. With these acquisitions under its belt, Golden Telecom was able to roll out an enhanced version of its Russia-On-Line web portal in October 2000. No longer just a basic dial-up service, Golden Telecom now offered news, chat, games, shopping and search facilities. The company's goal was to become the dominant web portal in Russia.

Other acquisitions in 2000 extended Golden Telecom's reach as an Internet service provider. The company's Ukrainian subsidiary acquired its partner's interest in the data connections provider Sovam Teleport Kiev, so the company was able to offer both voice and data services in Kiev through one fully owned subsidiary. In April Golden Telecom bought a 51 percent share in KIS (Commercial Information Systems), an ISP that had been active in Nizhny Novgorod since 1992. CEO Stewart Reich told the *Moscow Times* in 2000 that, with only about 300,000 to 400,000 Internet subscribers in Russia, the country was far from hitting the Internet ceiling: "I don't even

believe we're at the start. The only barrier facing us is an overall domestic economic recovery. Once that happens, our products are available to everyone."

Reich hoped to enhance business-to-business services such as web hosting and design as well as mass market consumer services. One move in the "B2B" direction came in April 2000 when Golden Telecom acquired Fintek, a Moscow-based web design studio with expertise in advanced animation techniques and 3D imaging that could help shoppers preview goods on an e-commerce site.

By the end of 2000, Golden Telecom's data and Internet division had grown to rival the CLEC services division in terms of revenue generated. The company had 85,833 Internet subscribers and 132 points of presence across Russia. The following year Golden Telecom became the leading ISP in Russia with the acquisition of the Moscow-based ISP Cityline, with 62,000 subscribers, and the 51 percent acquisition of Uralrelcom, an ISP with 8,000 subscribers in the Ekaterinburg area.

Consolidating the Market As a Russian-Owned Company: 2001–03

In 2001 Golden Telecom became a truly Russian company when control moved into the hands of several large Russian investors. Since the fall of 2000, Golden Telecom's future had been uncertain, as its U.S.-based majority shareholder Global TeleSystems had indicated that it wished to get rid of its Russian assets and focus on Western Europe. The situation was resolved in May when the influential Russian conglomerate Alfa Group bought a 44 percent stake in Golden Telecom for $110 million. Although Alfa had no experience in the telecommunications industry, it had connections with bureaucrats in provincial areas that could help Golden Telecom extend its reach into the regions. Two other minority shareholders, Capital International and Barings Vostok, also purchased additional shares from Global TeleSystems at this time, leaving Global TeleSystems with an 11 percent stake in Golden Telecom. By the end of 2001, the company had sold its remaining stake to Golden Telecom and Barings Vostok. Observers agreed that it was advantageous for Golden Telecom to be a Russian company, since the Russian government had recently indicated that it was wary of foreign investment in telecommunications because of national security concerns. Now, with solid Russian credentials, Golden Telecom was free to pursue the full acquisition of the international long-distance carrier Sovintel, which it still operated as a joint partnership with the government concern Rostelecom.

Although the latest developments at Golden Telecom were promising, the company was still operating at a loss. In 2001 it lost $39 million on revenues of $140 million. Performance that year was hurt by lower-than-expected demand for advertising on the Russia-On-Line portal and by complications at the Ukrainian subsidiary that summer. The Ukrainian state phone monopoly Ukrtelekom had accused Golden Telecom (Ukraine) of using a deceptive call routing scheme to mask long-distance calls as local calls, thereby cheating the state company out of the fees that would normally have to be paid when Golden Telecom used state lines to route international calls to customers. Golden Telecom, in turn, had increased criticisms of the state organization in previous months for using unfair means to squeeze out smaller competitors. The dispute culminated in March 2002 when state prosecutors raided the Ukrainian subsidiary's offices. The General Director of Golden Telecom (Ukraine), Yury Bezborodov, subsequently stepped down and was replaced by Mladen Pejnovic, who pursued a compromise with the state entity.

In August 2001 Stewart Reich resigned and Alexander Vinogradov took over as president and CEO of Golden Telecom. Vinogradov had been working in the telecommunications industry since 1980. He joined Golden Telecom's Sovintel in 1991 and had served as general director of the subsidiary since 1995. As CEO, Vinogradov led Golden Telecom through another series of consolidations. In the summer of 2002 the company merged its operations in Nizhny Novgorod into a single entity that could provide both voice and data services, primarily to corporate customers. Golden Telecom had a 58 percent stake in the new entity, formed when TeleRoss Nizhny Novgorod and the Internet company KIS were merged into Agentstvo Delovoi Svyazi (ADS). Golden Telecom had acquired ADS, which operated a network infrastructure in Nizhny Novgorod, in September 2001.

In the fall of 2002 Golden Telecom completed the long-sought acquisition of international long-distance carrier and fixed-line operator Sovintel from its 50–50 state partner Rostelecom. Rostelecom received $52 million and a 15 percent share in Golden Telecom in the transaction. Sovintel was a profitable company that was expected to help Golden Telecom's balance sheet. In 2003, Golden Telecom's other main subsidiary, TeleRoss, was merged into Sovintel. With data and voice activities combined in a single entity, Golden Telecom would now be able to offer more integrated services to both businesses and consumers. Business services, at 54 percent, were by far the largest segment of Golden Telecom's operations, followed by services to other telecommunications operators at 33 percent, consumer services at 9 percent, and cellular services at 4 percent.

Golden Telecom reported its first profit in 2002. Net income was $29.8 million on revenues of $198.7 million. The trend continued into the first half of 2003, when the company reported a second quarter net profit of $11.9 million. The company continued an aggressive acquisition strategy. It purchased Sibchallenge Telecom, an ISP and alternative telephone provider in Krasnoyarsk, for $15 million. Golden Telecom also announced that it was in discussions with Norway's Telenor for one of its largest acquisitions yet. In exchange for a 19.5 percent stake in Golden Telecom, Telenor would give the company full ownership of its fixed-line operator Comincom, including the subsidiary Combellga. Telenor had acquired the companies from the Russian government in 2000 and was now willing to sell them in order to advance the consolidation of the market. Golden Telecom, meanwhile, stayed on the lookout for further acquisitions in its drive to become the dominant player in Russia's independent telecommunications market.

Principal Subsidiaries

TeleRoss LLC; ADS (58%); Golden Telecom LLC (Ukraine); GTS Mobile Services, Inc.; Cityline ZAO; Uralrelcom (51%).

Principal Divisions

CLEC Services; Data and Internet Services; Long Distance Services; Mobile Services.

Principal Competitors

Sistema Telecom; Moscow City Telephone Network; Metromedia International Group, Inc.; Ukrtelecom; Petersburg Telephone Network; Rostelecom; Equant; Ukrainian Mobile Communications.

Further Reading

Cattell, Brian, "Russian Phone Rollup Strikes Again," *Daily Deal,* August 21, 2003.

Chazan, Guy, "Companies: Golden Telecom Brings Acquisitions in Russia Together," *Wall Street Journal (Europe),* October 6, 2000, p. 4.

——, "Golden's Alfa Deal Will Help Its Fortunes," *Asian Wall Street Journal,* May 8, 2001, p. N2.

Heffernan, Patricia, "Banging the Drum for CIS Telecoms Provider," *Moscow Times,* March 21, 2000.

Knight, Jerry, "Global TeleSystems IPO Beats Expectations," *Washington Post,* February 6, 1998, p. G1.

——, "McLean Firm to Acquire Espirit Telecom," *Washington Post,* December 9, 1998, p. C15.

Koriukin, Kirill, "Moscow Firm Set for U.S. Float," *Moscow Times,* July 16, 1999.

Mcgee, Suzanne, "Russia's Golden Telecom Launches IPO, But the Issue Fails to Score Big Success," *Wall Street Journal,* October 1, 1999, p. 1.

Naumenko, Larisa, "Golden Chief Puts 20 Years' Experience to Work," *Moscow Times,* March 5, 2002.

Olearchyk, Roman, "Golden Telecom, Ukrtelekom in Talks," *Kyiv Post,* June 20, 2002.

Semenenko, Igor, "Golden Telecom Initial Public Offer Earns $64M," *Moscow Times,* October 5, 1999.

——, "Paper: Telecom Bosses Paid $65M Kickbacks," *Moscow Times,* December 29, 1999.

Shinkle, Kirk, "Golden Telecom Inc. Moscow, Russia; Big Cities Have Telecom Dialing for Rubles; Its Strategy? Buy, Buy, Buy," *Investor's Business Daily,* August 11, 2003, p. A05.

Wolfe, Elizabeth, "Alfa Buys 44% Stake in GTI for $110M," *Moscow Times,* April 3, 2001.

——, "Golden Buys 50% of Sovintel for $105M," *Moscow Times,* November 9, 2001.

—Sarah Ruth Lorenz

Grupo Leche Pascual S.A.

Avenida Manoteras 18
E-28050 Madrid
Spain
Telephone: (+34) 91-302-7686
Fax: (+34) 91-767-0983
Web site: http://www.lechepascual.es

Private Company
Incorporated: 1969 as Industrias Lacteas Pascual
Employees: 3,250
Sales: $955.3 million (2001)
NAIC: 311511 Fluid Milk Manufacturing; 311512
    Creamery Butter Manufacturing; 311514 Dry,
    Condensed, and Evaporated Dairy Product
    Manufacturing; 311520 Ice Cream and Frozen Dessert
    Manufacturing; 424430 Dairy Products (Except Dried
    or Canned) Merchant Wholesalers; 424490 Other
    Grocery and Related Product Merchant Wholesalers

Grupo Leche Pascual S.A. (also known as Leche Pascual Group) is one of Spain's leading producers of milk and dairy products, and is also a leading producer of bottled mineral water and fruit juices. The company is also extremely active on the export market, with sales in more than 60 countries worldwide—including the United States, where Leche Pascual became the first dairy products importer to receive the all-important ''Grade A'' certification. Leche Pascual's more than 300 products includes a range of fresh and UHT ''long-life'' milk products, butter, cream, yogurt, and other dairy items; bottled mineral water through its Bezoya, Cardó, and Zambra brands; fruit juices under its Zumosol brand; adult and children's cereals; egg products, including pasteurized liquid eggs; and pet foods, including feed products. The company also produces a variety of products for the restaurant, catering, and institutional food markets. In 2003, Leche Pascual sparked a great deal of controversy in its attempt to market a pasteurized, long-life desert product as yogurt—in the European Community, only yogurts containing live cultures are allowed to be marketed as such. The majority of the company's production takes place in nearly 20 Spanish production facilities; the company also operated production facilities in Portugal, France, and the United States. Spain remains the group's largest market, while its total European sales represent some 70 percent of overall sales of approximately EUR 1 billion. The Americas, including Puerto Rico, add 22 percent to annual sales. A private company, Leche Pascual remains wholly controlled by the founding Pascual family, and is led by CEO Tomás Pascual Gómez-Cuétara, son of the company's founder.

UHT Pioneer in the 1970s

As a child, Tomás Pascual, born in 1926, had helped out by delivering milk by donkey, before going to work at his father's bar. In 1969, Pascual took over the dairy cooperative in his home town of Aranda de Duero, in the Burgos district of Spain, which had opened in 1965. Initially known as Industrias Lacteas Pascual, or Pascual Dairy Industries, the company concentrated on the production of fresh milk and fresh milk products. By the end of its first year, the company's production had already reached 100,000 liters.

Pascual quickly revealed a flair for innovation—in 1973, the company became the first in Spain to produce UHT (ultra high-temperature) milk, which, packed in sterilized ''bricks'' had a shelf life of several months. The new sterilization procedure and packaging techniques enabled Pascual to begin selling its milk beyond its immediate area. By the following year, Pascual began to assert itself as a brand, changing the company's name to Leche Pascual S.A.

UHT milk quickly gained a majority share of the Spanish milk market—by the end of the century, more than 90 percent of all Spanish milk sales were of UHT milk, a figure emulated throughout much of Europe. Pascual differentiated itself early on by an insistence on high quality standards, even though the company was forced to charge higher prices for its products as a result. Yet Pascual proved a wily marketer, reportedly hiring groups of housewives to telephone storeowners asking why Leche Pascual products were not featured on their store shelves.

Over the next decades, Pascual began adding other products, starting in 1974 with the acquisition of Bezoya Mineral Water

Company Perspectives:

Leche Pascual Group's main activity is the packaging and preparation of milk, fruit juices, breakfast cereals, ultra-pasteurised liquid egg and omelettes, mineral water, as well as top-quality dairy products and the marketing of all these products.

Key Dates:

1965: Dairy cooperative is formed in Aranda de Duero, Spain.

1969: Tomás Pascual takes over dairy cooperative, founding Industrias Lacteas Pascual.

1973: Company becomes first to introduce ultra high-temperature (UHT) milk in Spain.

1974: Company changes name to Leche Pascual; acquires Bezoya Mineral Water.

1980: Leche Pascual launches first skim milk products in Spain.

1982: Company enters real estate and property development market.

1994: Company forms Pascual International and begins export operations; acquires dairy products packaging plant in Montauban, France.

1995: Leche Pascual builds new production facility for UHT yogurt.

1996: Company builds PET mineral water bottling plant; acquires 33.3 percent stake in new egg production business in Morocco.

1998: Company becomes first foreign company to receive Grade A classification for imported dairy products in the United States.

1999: Tomás Pascual turns over company leadership to son Tomás Pascual Gómez-Cuétara.

2000: Company undergoes restructuring, splitting off property development and real estate operations.

2001: Company acquires Naransur, a producer of orange juice.

2003: Company announces construction of EUR 30 million dairy process facility in Catalan region.

and the expansion into the bottled mineral water market. In 1980, the company added to its status of dairy products pioneer by becoming the first Spanish dairy company to produce skim milk. In 1985, the company added semi-skim milk as well. Then, in 1987, the company added a third major component with the launch of its own branded line of fruit juices, Zumosol. Pascual also expanded beyond its core food market, adding operations in the construction, property development, and real estate markets in the early 1980s. These activities, however, remained minor contributors to the group's overall sales; in 2000, the company restructured, separating its non-dairy businesses from its core Leche Pascual operation.

Diversification and Internationalization in the 1990s

The construction of a new production facility enabled Pascual to extend its offerings to include butter and cream products in 1989. The following year, the company purchased CEREX, giving it a facility for producing breakfast cereals in Vallodolid. Pascual quickly launched adult and children's breakfast cereals under its own brand name. In 1992, it began expanding the facility, investing some EUR 3.4 million during the 1990s.

Pascual added to its mineral water business as well, acquiring the Cardo Valley mineral water bottling plant in 1991, located in Tarragona. Two years later, Pascual built a new production facility in order to add another new product line, that of pasteurized liquid eggs. The company continued adding new products throughout the decade, including tortillas and pet foods. In 1993, the company added livestock feeds to its assortment, with the purchase of Pascual de Aranda SA.

Dairy products remained the company's core operation, however, accounting for 60 percent of sales. In 1994, the company began preparations to added another product line, acquiring the technology to produce UHT dessert products. In 1995, the company began construction of the first stage of a new production facility, which, completed in three stages by 1999, added such products as custards, rice puddings, and a UHT yogurt product.

Yet this last product brought the company a great deal of controversy—in Spain, as well as a number of other countries, products labeled as yogurt were required to contain live cultures. The production process for pasteurized yogurts, however, destroyed the cultures. Pascual began lobbying the Spanish government for a change in national legislation, and in 1998 the company was granted the right to launch its UHT yogurt on the Spanish market. Nonetheless, lobbying efforts by chief rival Danone, the world's largest dairy products company, and other Spanish yogurt producers, brought the issue to the European Community, which, in 2003, ruled against Pascual.

Despite the controversy at home, Pascual had in the meantime discovered a strong international market for its UHT yogurts, and in 1994, the company created a dedicated International Division to handle its growing export interests. By the beginning of the new century, Pascual had succeeded in developing export markets to more than 60 countries. Among these was France, which the company entered in 1994 through its acquisition from the French government of a dairy products packaging plant in Montauban.

In another international move, the company bought a 33.3 percent stake in the launch of an egg production facility in Rabat, Morocco, in 1996. That business began operations in 1998, with more than 150,000 laying hens. Part of the facility's egg production was directed at Pascual's new omelet preparation facility, which the company built at its home base of Aranda de Duero in 1996.

Pascual's international interests took on greater weight in the late 1990s when the company, seeking new outlets for its production, parlayed its long-held insistence on high-quality standards into an entry into the U.S. market. For this the company was required to receive Grade A certification, a status that no foreign company had yet achieved. In 1998, however, Pascual's efforts paid off, and the company became the first to import Grade A certified dairy products into the United States.

Pascual also stepped up its mineral water operations that year. After inaugurating a new PET bottling plant in 1996, the company expanded production with the acquisition of Zambra, located in Cordoba. That purchase added sales of more than 23 million liters of bottled water to the company's existing production.

Diversified Food Producer in the 2000s

By the late 1990s, Leche Pascual had grown into Spain's second largest milk companies, and one of the largest dairy products groups as well. In 1998, the company took a step closer to the lead with the acquisition of Morais SA, a dairy company that sold its milk products, including UHT milk, creams, milk powder, and concentrated milk under the Frixia and Pastoral brand names. Nonetheless, the company's growth was outpaced by chief rival Puleva, which captured the leading position at the beginning of the 2000s.

In 1999, company founder Tomás Pascual, then 73 years old, turned over control of the company to son Tomás Pascual Gómez-Cuétara. The following year, the group restructured, splitting off its property development and real estate wings, and creating a new holding company, Corporacion TIP. Under the new structure, Leche Pascual was transformed into a dedicated food products group. In its new form, the company began a strategy of targeting growth through mergers and acquisitions. The company's first purchase came in 2001, with the acquisition of orange juice maker Naransur.

The following year, however, the company attempted to add to its diversified line of food products. In March 2002, Pascual launched its own soft drink line, starting with a new brand, Euro Cola, meant to compete head-to-head with cola giants Coca Cola and Pepsi. In the meantime, the controversy surrounding Pascual's UHT yogurt came to a boiling point, resulting in a boycott against Pascual products in the Catalan region, the center of the country's yogurt production.

In response, Pascual announced that it would stop buying milk from Catalonian farmers, citing high transport costs needed to bring their milk to the company's facilities 300 kilometers away. Following the European parliament's decision to disallow classification of UHT products as yogurt, Pascual moved to placate Catalonian farmers, resuming milk purchases in the region. The company then went a step further, and in July 2003, announced its intention to invest some EUR 30 million to build a new dairy processing facility in the region. Despite the controversy, the Pascual brand remained one of the strongest in the Spanish market at the turn of the century.

Principal Subsidiaries

Pascual Dairy Inc. (U.S.A.).

Principal Competitors

Groupe Danone; Kraft Foods International, Inc.; Nestlé S.A.; Puleva SA.

Further Reading

Crawford, Leslie, ''Yogurt War Leaves a Sour Taste,'' *Financial Times*, March 12, 2003, p. 14.

Hemlock, Doreen, ''Spanish Milk Producer First to Meet US Standards,'' *Sun Sentinel*, September 11, 1999.

''Leche Pascual Enters Soft Drinks Segment,'' *Expansion*, March 5, 2002.

''Leche Pascual Invests 30m Euros in New Plant in Catalonia,'' *El Pais*, July 27, 2003, p. 9.

Nash, Elizabeth, ''Consumer Boycott of Milk Firm's 'Yoghurt' Keeps Food War Alive,'' *Independent*, March 22, 2003, p. 17.

—M. L. Cohen

Hanover Compressor Company

12001 N. Houston Rosslyn
Houston, Texas 77086
U.S.A.
Telephone: (281) 447-8787
Fax: (281) 447-0821
Web site: http://www.hanover-co.com

Public Company
Incorporated: 1990
Employees: 4,700
Sales: $1.0 billion (2002)
Stock Exchanges: New York
Ticker Symbol: HC
NAIC: 532412 Construction, Mining, and Forestry
   Machinery and Equipment Rental and Leasing

Hanover Compressor Company, based in Houston, Texas, provides natural gas compression services, operating the largest rental compression fleet in the industry, some 7,000 mobile units with a combined horsepower of 3.7 million. In addition, the company services the equipment, and also offers treatment services, compressor fabrication, production equipment fabrication, and measurement services. Although Hanover has a global reach, with operations on five continents, it operates primarily in the Western Hemisphere, but is stepping up its efforts to penetrate markets in Europe, Asia, and Australia.

Formation of Hanover Compressor Company: 1990

Compression is used to increase the pressure of natural gas in order to facilitate transit from the wellhead, through gathering pipelines and processing plants, to the main interstate pipelines. Natural gas reservoirs contain a sufficient level of pressure initially, but as the well is depleted it loses pressure until natural gas will no longer flow through the system on its own. As a result, compression equipment is used to more fully exploit the well. Two types of compressors are suitable for oilfield use: reciprocating and rotary. Both are cyclical in nature, taking in a certain quantity of gas, acting upon it, then discharging the compressed gas before repeating the process. A handful of

companies dominated the market for compression from the 1960s through the 1980s. Hanover Compressor emerged as a major player during the 1990s, but compression was in many ways an afterthought to the company's parent corporation Hanover Energy, which was primarily involved in the pipeline business in west Texas, as well as interests in gas marketing and exploration. By 1990 the company owned 17 compressors. Michael J. McGhan and other veterans of the compression business approached Hanover about managing their fleet of compressors and expanding the operation. McGhan, a teacher by education, had previously served as a sales manager for Energy Industries, Inc. In October 1990 Hanover Compressor was incorporated in Delaware. Two months later the four-employee venture added three major compressor rental companies located in Texas and Louisiana, offering equity stakes to acquire them.

Hanover quickly attracted major investors, such as GKH Partners, which included brothers Jay and Tom Pritzker, better known for their ownership of the Hyatt hotel chain, and Dan Lufkin, cofounder of Donaldson Lufkin & Jenrette. In May 1991 GKH acquired a controlling interest in Hanover. Later, the company attracted further investments from Western Resources Inc. and a group of investors that included former Treasury Secretary William E. Simon. In a short period of time it also became apparent to Hanover Energy's management that its fledgling compressor endeavor held the most potential of any of its businesses. The company decided to focus on compressors, and sold off its other energy interests to fund expansion. McGhan, who had been the subsidiary's chief operating officer, now became Hanover's CEO in October 1991.

Hanover formalized its compressor business in 1992, creating a common logo for its regional companies while standardizing operations. It also adopted a hub-and-spoke structure with larger regional companies serving as hubs for the organization. Michael W. O'Connor was brought in as chairman of the board, bringing with him more than 20 years of experience in the industry, serving as president of Gas Compressors Inc. from 1965 through 1986. To accelerate growth Hanover adopted an acquisition leaseback program. As had been the case with its initial acquisitions, the company gave equity stakes to executives of acquired companies. McGhan explained Hanover's reasoning

215

in a 1996 article in *Oil & Gas Investor:* "Bringing them in as partners was important because they are planners, thinkers and doers. They were ambassadors for us out in the field, building on decades-old relationships. We wanted to keep that local responsiveness." O'Connor added, "We left them running the businesses they had built with sweat equity—operations and customer relations were their concern. We brought the capital and marketing necessary to build the overall business."

Hanover enjoyed steady growth over the next three years. Sales improved from $33 million in 1992 to more than $56 million in 1994, while net income increased from $988,000 to $4.4 million during the same period. The company entered a new phase of growth in 1995 when it began an extended acquisition spree. In January Hanover acquired compressor rental assets from CBC Compression for $2.7 million in cash. A month later it completed two deals. First, it added 106 units with an aggregate of 14,190 horsepower from Gale Force Compression Services, Inc. for approximately $11.5 million in cash and stock. Hanover then bought the production equipment fabrication assets of Smith Industries, Inc. for $2.7 million in cash. The purpose of the latter deal was to take advantage of Smith's long-term relationships with customers in order to drum up further business when these companies were in the market for compression equipment.

Looking to Foreign Markets: Mid-1990s

Also during 1995 Hanover began to look overseas, a result of an increasing number of customers doing business internationally. Several of the acquisitions Hanover made in the second half of 1995 were predicated on the acquisition of overseas assets. One such deal was the $6.5 million cash and stock purchase of Proyetco Gas Natural, C.A., a Caracas, Venezuela, company. Late in 1995 Hanover also acquired a subsidiary of Western Resources, Astra Resources Compression, a $61.4 million deal, of which $55 million came in the form of stock. Astra brought with it major assets in Argentina, 145 compressors with nearly 104,000 horsepower, greatly bolstering Hanover's share of the Latin American market as well as adding a U.S. operation. Another important decision made in 1995 was to commit resources to the Gulf of Mexico, a region that most competing firms were exiting because it was considered both hazardous and dangerous. When that region enjoyed a boom over the next two years, Hanover was well positioned to reap the rewards. In addition, because wells in the Gulf were being depleted at an accelerated rate, the area would have an increasing need for compression services.

To fund its growth, Hanover was able in December 1995 to increase its line of revolving credit from $35 million to $90 million, backed by a group of bankers led by Chemical Bank. The company was also able to raise $21.6 million in a private placement of stock sold to some of its principal investors. Also in

December 1995 an even more significant source of funding, as well as an alliance was found, in Enron Corporation. At the time, at least, Enron appeared to be the ideal partner. Several years would elapse before Enron imploded, mired in fiscal scandal, and Hanover would find itself tarnished by its relationship to one of the most notorious corporate miscreants in American history. The first connection with Enron was forged in late December when Enron Capital & Trade Resources, the largest trader of natural gas in North America, bought $20 million in Hanover common stock and another $10 million in preferred. Moreover, it created a $100 million credit facility to fund Hanover's further expansion. The Enron alliance, according to Hanover officials, was expected to greatly help Hanover in its efforts to expand in both domestic and foreign markets. As Enron expanded globally, it would need compression services, and Hanover hoped to fill that need. Because of its 1995 acquisitions, Hanover, in terms of horsepower, possessed the second largest fleet in the rental compression industry, trailing only Tidewater, which the previous year had gained the top spot after picking up Halliburton's rental compression fleet. The rapid rise of Hanover was also reflected on the balance sheet. In 1995 revenues approached $96 million, coupled with a net profit of $5.6 million. A year later Hanover posted more than $136 million in revenues and a $10.4 million profit. In 1996 the company completed further acquisitions. On February 1, Hanover acquired compressor assets from New Prospect Drilling Company and Oxley Petroleum, paying $4.5 million in cash and another $225,000 in stock. Then in May 1996 Hanover paid nearly $2 million in cash for compressor units of Cactus Compression.

Going Public: 1997

Hanover went public in July 1997 and its stock began trading on the New York Stock Exchange. The company completed two further acquisitions during the course of the year. In September it paid nearly $6.3 million in cash for Wagner Equipment, Inc. and Gas Tech Compression Services, Inc. Two months later, Hanover paid $5.6 million for a 35 percent interest in Collicutt Mechanical Services, Ltd. Also in 1997 Hanover formed a joint venture with Enron in Venezuela to build and operate a gas compression project. For the year, Hanover recorded total revenues of nearly $198.8 million and net income of more than $18 million. Exceptional growth for the company continued in 1998, as sales approached $282 million and net income topped $30.3 million. A major strategic acquisition of the year was the purchase of the Packaged Power Systems Division of Waukesha-Pearce Industries Inc., a deal which included equipment and a lease/purchase agreement on a fabrication plant. Also in 1998, Hanover acquired Arkoma Compression Services, Inc. for $17.2 million in cash, and paid another $25.3 million to buy Eureka Energy Systems, Inc. In a lesser deal, Hanover bought a 10 percent interest in Cosacol for $2 million.

From 1999 to 2001, Hanover continued its impressive pattern of growth, completing a number of significant acquisitions that led to annual revenues topping the $1 billion mark and net income surpassing $72 million. The most important transactions occurred in 2001. The first was the $100 million stock transaction, plus the assumption of some $63 million in debt, that added OCE Compression Corporation. An even larger deal was completed in September 2001 when Hanover acquired the

Key Dates:

1990: Company is founded.
1996: Enron Corporation invests in Hanover.
1997: Company goes public.
2001: Schlumberger's natural gas compression business is acquired for $761 million.
2002: Shakeup in upper management occurs following accounting scandal.
2003: Landmark settlement ends shareholder suit.

natural gas compression businesses of New York energy services giant Schlumberger Ltd. for $761 million. Of that amount, $270 million was cash, $150 million in the form of a long-term subordinated note, and the balance in stock. As a result, Schlumberger gained a 10 percent stake in Hanover. Not only did the acquisition strengthen Hanover's business in the United States and Latin America, it helped the company to gain a presence in the Middle East, Africa, and Asia. The Schlumberger deal, however, would also mark a high point for the company, at least temporarily, as Hanover experienced a number of difficult months following the Enron debacle that unfolded in the final months of 2001.

At first, the price of Hanover's stock dropped merely because of the company's association with Enron, but in February 2002 the company was hit with a securities class-action lawsuit that alleged violations of accounting rules in order to inflate the price of Hanover stock. Matters soon worsened for management when it had to admit that it would be restating profits over the previous two years, reducing the number by $8.9 million. Moreover, the Securities and Exchange Commission (SEC) began to look into a joint venture with Global Energy involving a gas-processing joint venture in Nigeria. It was soon revealed that even though Hanover knew that Global had hit a snag with Royal Dutch/Shell about recovering natural gas from the project and that Hanover would not see any revenues until 2003, the company booked revenue based on the percentage of construction work completed. According to management, this was ''accepted accounting practice.'' In a matter of days, O'Connor resigned as chair, offering no reason, but remained as a director. He was replaced by Victor Grijalva, a retired vice-chairman of Schlumberger.

Hanover's accounting problems only worsened as 2002 continued. The company would end up restating results three times, so that it had to admit that every annual report had issued since going public was flawed. In the meantime, McGhan resigned along with COO Charles D. Erwin. Grijalva assumed the addi-

tional duties of CEO until another former Schlumberger executive, Chad Deaton, was named as a permanent replacement. Deaton took immediate steps to shore up Hanover's reputation, calling on 38 senior managers to sign disclosure statements that revealed some further transactions, completed in 1999, that might be deemed questionable. The amounts involved were negligible, but were pursued as part of an effort to reassure shareholders that the company had finally gotten to the bottom of its accounting irregularities. Nevertheless, in November 2002 the SEC launched a formal investigation of Hanover. At the same time, during the last quarter of 2002, the company restructured its senior management team and conducted a review of Hanover's business and decided to sell off non-oilfield power generation facilities and some used equipment business lines in order to focus on expanding the company's core compression operations. Late in 2002, Hanover announced it was laying off some 500 people around the world in keeping with its realignment.

As part of an effort to resolve its problems with the SEC, Hanover in 2003 agreed to what many considered was a groundbreaking settlement to a shareholder class-action lawsuit. Not only did management agree to pay approximately $65 million to wronged shareholders, it granted power to shareholders to appoint two independent directors. Moreover, Hanover became the first company to agree to rotate its outside audit firm every five years as part of the settlement. Calling the agreement a milestone for Hanover, CEO Deaton also maintained that it demonstrated a commitment to putting these issues to rest and returning the company's focus to growing its compression business.

Principal Subsidiaries

Hanover Compressed Natural Gas Services, LLC; Hanover Compressor Limited Partnership; Hanover Compressor Capital Trust.

Principal Competitors

Compressor Systems, Inc.; Enerflex Systems Ltd.; Universal Compression Holdings, Inc.

Further Reading

Antosh, Nelson, ''Hanover Settles Shareholder Suit,'' *Houston Chronicle,* May 14, 2003, p. 1.

Haines, Leslie, ''Shooting for the Moon,'' *Oil & Gas Investor,* July 1996, p. 41.

Mintz, Bill, ''Getting Bigger in Compression,'' *Houston Chronicle,* October 20, 1995.

Share, Jeff, ''Hanover Company Becomes Driving Force in Industry,'' *Pipeline and Gas Journal,* October 1999.

—Ed Dinger

Haskel International, Inc.

100 E. Graham Place
Burbank, California 91502
U.S.A.
Telephone: (818) 843-4000
Fax: (818) 556-2518
Web site: http://www.haskel.com

Private Company
Incorporated: 1952 as Haskel Engineering and Supply
    Company
Employees: 335
Sales: $55 million (2002 est.)
NAIC: 332919 Other Metal Valve and Pipe Fitting
    Manufacturing

Based in Burbank, California, Haskel International, Inc. is the global leader in the manufacture of hydraulic and pneumatic high-pressure pumping systems and accessories. The privately owned company draws its customers from a wide range of industries, including aerospace, automotive, defense, energy, and oil and gas. Haskel also operates through two subsidiaries: BuTech High Pressure Systems, makers of high pressure valves and fittings and Durameter, which manufactures a line of metering pumps. In addition to Burbank, North American operations are located in Williamsville, New York; Brea, California; and Erie, Pennsylvania. Internationally, Haskel maintains sales and marketing, distribution, and system assembly facilities in Australia, England, Scotland, France, Germany, Italy, The Netherlands, Singapore, and Spain.

Establishment of Haskel: 1946

Haskel grew out of Hayman Engineering, founded by engineer Richard L. Hayman. He teamed with Don W. Driskel to create Haskel Engineering and Supply Company in Burbank, California, in 1946. The ''Haskel'' name was coined by fusing the ''Ha'' from Hayman with the ''skel'' from Driskel. The name was retained in spite of Hayman buying out Driskel a year later. It was not until 1952 that Haskel was incorporated in California. In the beginning the company was involved in the design of hydrau-

lics and pneumatics, primarily to serve the aircraft industry, as well as for use in missiles and general engineering. A major step was the development of a patented nose wheel power steering and shimmy damping unit. The resulting growth to the company allowed Hayman to launch an industrial division, which began to distribute hydraulic and pneumatic equipment manufactured by third parties and later by Haskel itself.

In 1954 Haskel was a pioneer in the development of the first dry running hydraulically driven gas booster, which did not require lubrication for the compressor, used in missile technology with nitrogen and helium to pressures as high as 10,000 psi. Also during the 1950s, Haskel began to shift its attention from aircraft production activities in order to focus on the growing business of its industrial division. From 1958 to 1961 the company shifted its manufacturing efforts to licensees.

During the 1960s Haskel achieved a number of significant advances. In 1961 it launched a range of metal seals able to withstand the extreme temperatures of aircraft engines, a product line that would remain vital more than 40 years later. Another major development was the air-driven gas booster, introduced in 1963. This product line was supplemented with the introduction of air-driven liquid pumps, leading to the publication of the first liquid pump catalog in 1963.

Haskel added air pressure amplifiers in the 1970s. The company launched an international effort in 1978 with the acquisition of a 60 percent stake in U.K.-based Olin Energy Systems, Ltd., part of the Olin Matheson Group. The company subsequently changed its name to Haskel Energy Systems Limited, and the remaining 40 percent of the company was ultimately purchased by Haskel in 1983. The goal of the subsidiary was to distribute Haskel products throughout Europe and the Middle East. In 1984 Haskel Energy broadened its scope, opening an office in Aberdeen to serve the oil and gas industry. To better reflect the changing nature of the company, Haskel Engineering assumed the Haskel International name in 1986.

Death of Richard Hayman: 1991

Overseas expansion continued in 1991 when a controlling interest in its French distributor, General Pneumatic S.A., was

Company Perspectives:

Haskel International, Inc. is the world's leading manufacturer of hydraulically and pneumatically driven, high pressure systems and accessories. For nearly 60 years, the Company has been a recognized leader in high pressure technology.

acquired for approximately $1.6 million. All told, for more than 40 years Haskel enjoyed steady growth until shortly before Hayman's death in 1991, when decreasing sales combined with rising costs began to hurt the business. In an attempt to revive the flagging company and provide some diversification, management in November 1993 acquired M.G. Electronics, a Westlake Village, California, electronics parts distributor, paying $6 million in cash plus stock. Using a proprietary software system and telecommunications, MG was able to procure needed electronic components from anywhere in the world, especially integrated circuits, capacitors, transistors, and resistors. As part of the deal, which was completed in February 1994, MGE's president, Maury Friedman, was named Haskel's new president and chief executive officer. Friedman immediately launched an effort to restructure the company, firing some 50 workers. He also began implementing a growth strategy that called for the introduction of new industrial products as well as fresh applications for old product lines, and an aggressive move into emerging markets around the world. To help finance these changes, Friedman also prepared to take Haskel public. An initial public offering was completed in November 1994, and the company's stock, originally priced at $10 per share, began trading on the NASDAQ. A month later, the 44-year-old Friedman replaced A. Charles Wilson, 70, as chairman of the board. For the previous three years the company had been trending downward. Although sales increased from $35.5 million in 1992 to $41.4 million in 1994, net income steadily eroded, from $2.4 million in 1992 to $2.2 million in 1993, to just $3,000 in 1994.

In March 1995 Friedman reorganized Haskel's business within two new operating groups: the Industrial Products Group, to house the company's traditional pumping systems and accessories, and the Electronic Products Group, for the MGE operations in both the United States and the United Kingdom. Former Puroflow Inc. President Robert A. Smith was brought in to head the Industrial Products Group, reporting to Friedman who in addition would oversee the Electronics Products Group. Less than a month later Haskel underwent further management changes when the board eliminated the CEO position and replaced Friedman as chair with Edward Malkowicz. A Haskel director since December 1994, Malkowicz had previous executive experience at Turbo-tek International, Edwards Capital Corp., and Purex Industries. At the time he was elected chair, he was teaching business courses at Riverside Community College and Fullerton College. Now Friedman was on a par with Smith, both men reporting to Malkowicz. Haskel's balance sheet improved significantly, with revenues rising by nearly 25 percent to $51.7 million, while net income rebounded, topping $1 million. Nevertheless, the management arrangement proved short-lived. R. Malcolm Greaves was named president and CEO on February 14, 1996. A month later Friedman resigned. Greaves was well

seasoned, having been with Haskel since 1989. He held a number of top executive positions, including chief operating officer for Europe, the Middle East, India, and Africa.

Haskel looked to add to its international presence in its Industrial Products group. In 1995 it acquired the high-pressure pump distribution and systems fabrication division of Armaturenbau, GmbH, and opened Haskel Germany in Wesel, Germany, to provide sales, service, and system manufacture. A year later, an office was established in Zoetermeer, The Netherlands, named Haskel Benelux, to provide sales and service for Haskel's full line of high-pressure pumps, boosters, and systems. Haskel also supplemented its U.K. operation when Haskel Energy acquired Hydraulic Mobile Equipment Ltd., a Manchester, England-based company. At the same time, in 1996, the company's Electronic Products Group, which now contributed about one quarter of Haskel's revenues, was forced to close offices in the United Kingdom and Germany due to a drop in orders from computer and semiconductor manufacturers. In addition Haskel cut staff in its Westlake Village office. Meanwhile, domestically, the Industrial Products Group enjoyed strong growth in 1996, acquiring Hogan Fluid Power, a Houston-based company that supplied pumps and specialized systems for oil, gas, and fluid power applications. According to Greaves, the acquisition represented "an important strategic step in our efforts to expand our high-pressure system sales in the oil and gas business. Hogan's presence in the Gulf Coast region provides a direct foothold in the worldwide oil, gas and fluid power systems and service business, which industry sources estimate to be in excess of $150 million."

Sale of Electronic Products Group: 1997

Early in 1997 Haskel decided to put its electronic products business up for sale in order to focus on its core business of high-pressure technology. In September the unit was sold to an unnamed individual investor for an amount that was worth its net asset value. While the electronic products group was being divested in 1997, Industrial Products continued its expansion. Haskel established a sales office in Singapore to serve southeast Asia, a move which it soon supplemented with the establishment of a second Asian operation in Hong Kong, thus providing Haskel with the ability to grow in both the north and south Pacific Rim markets. Later in 1997 Haskel opened a sales, service, and systems facility in San Sebastian, Spain, a move that according to management provided an even stronger foothold in Europe and served to complement operations in the United Kingdom, France, Germany, and Holland. Haskel Energy also continued to grow via acquisition, acquiring Nanojet Engineering GmbH and Palpro Limited, which served the oil, gas, and petrochemical industries.

In 1998 Haskel expanded further in the Pacific region by completing the acquisition of two Australia-based companies, M.D.C., Pty. Ltd. and Hydraulics and Air. Pty. The businesses had served as exclusive distributors of Haskel products throughout the 1990s and combined for annual sales in the $2 million range. They now formed the basis of a company named Haskel Australasia, Pty. Ltd. Despite these positive developments, the price of Haskel stock languished in the marketplace and in the opinion of management was greatly undervalued. After going public at $10 a share, Haskel's stock peaked in September 1997

Key Dates:

1946: Company is founded by Richard Hayman and Don Driskel.
1952: Haskel Engineering and Supply Company is incorporated.
1986: Company changes name to Haskel International.
1991: Richard Hayman dies.
1994: Haskel goes public.
1999: Tinicum Capital takes company private.

at $16, but in early September 1998 fell to a two-year low of $6.625. Adverse investor reaction was due in part to the $7.5 million writeoff Haskel took in 1997, caused by the electronic division that had ultimately been cast off. Ironically, another major reason for investor reluctance was related to a significant economic downturn in Asia, a region which Haskel believed held great potential.

To enhance shareholder value, management decided in the fall of 1998 to engage investment banker Schroder & Co. to evaluate all strategic alternatives, including acquisitions, a buyout, or a merger. The company essentially put itself up for sale, but found no immediate suitors. In March 1999 Haskel management announced that once again it would become a private company. A group led by New York-based investment fund Tinicum Capital Partners LP agreed to pay $12.9 a share in cash, or approximately $72.8 million, to acquire Haskel. As a result of being taken private, Haskel no longer faced short-term earnings pressure and could better focus on long-term plans. In addition, according to CEO Greaves, "a number of costs will disappear."

Haskel completed one significant acquisition in 1999, picking up Erie, Pennsylvania-based BuTech, a 30-year-old company that had been a major supplier to Haskel of high pressure valves, fittings, and tubing. In 2001 the company made two significant developments. It opened an office in Italy for sales, service, and system manufacture. It also completed an acquisition, paying $3.75 million for Aqua Care Systems Inc., plus earnout payment of $1 million for the next two years, for Durameter Pump Company, Inc. The Angola, New York-based business designed, manufactured, and sold fluid handling and water purification systems and products. As part of the deal, Aqua Care retained the New York land and facilities, and Haskel moved the Durameter manufacturing and engineering operations to its Burbank headquarters.

In more recent developments, Haskel opened sales offices in China and United Arab Emirates in 2003.

Principal Subsidiaries

Haskel International, Inc.; BuTech High Pressure Systems; Haskel Energy Systems Ltd.; GermanyHaskel Hichdruck-Systeme GmbH; Haskel Benelux B.V.; Haskel Asia Pts. Ltd.; Haskel Australasia Pty. Ltd. (Australia).

Principal Competitors

SC Hydraulic Engineering; Schmidt Kranz & Company; Teledyne Technologies Incorporated.

Further Reading

Deady, Tim, "Changes at Haskel Industries Spark Rebound," *Los Angeles Business Journal,* January 1, 1996, p. 15.
"Haskel Has Over 55 Years Experience in the Hydraulic/Pneumatic Field," *Chemical Engineering,* July 1, 2001.
McNary, Dave, "Haskel Taking Offers, Gets None," *Daily News (Los Angeles),* October 31, 1998, p. B2.

—Ed Dinger

Hawk Corporation

200 Public Square, Suite 30-5000
Cleveland, Ohio 44114-2301
U.S.A.
Telephone: (216) 861-3553
Fax: (216) 861-4546
Web site: http://www.hawkcorp.com

Public Company
Incorporated: 1989 as The Hawk Group of Companies,
  Inc.
Employees: 1,680
Sales: $197.3 million (2002)
Stock Exchanges: New York
Ticker Symbol: HWK
NAIC: 551112 Offices of Other Holding Companies

Hawk Corporation is a Cleveland public company that manufactures specialized components across four product groups. The Wellman Products Group is a leading producer of friction-related assemblies used in the aerospace industry, trucks, motorcycles, mountain bikes, construction vehicles, agricultural vehicles, off-road vehicles, and industrial vehicles. Wellman products are distributed around the world and manufactured in plants located in North America, Europe, and China. Hawk's Precision Components Group manufactures advanced powder metal parts used in a wide range of applications: fluid power, trucks, home appliances, power tools, lawn and garden equipment, construction equipment, office equipment, and automotive products. Hawk's Motor Group supplies rotors for use in large and small household appliances as well as automated office machines. Finally, the Hawk Performance Group manufactures high-performance parts, such as gears, bearings, driveshafts, bellhousings, and starters for use in a variety of applications, including high-performance auto, severe-duty fleet, motor sports, emergency vehicles, light truck, motorcycle, snowmobile, and military.

Establishing Hawk in 1989

Hawk Corporation was founded in Cleveland in 1989 by Ronald E. Weinberg and Norman C. Harbert. Weinberg was born in Memphis, Tennessee, and educated at Harvard, where he earned a bachelor's degree in business and an M.B.A. from the Harvard Business School. He launched his career in New York City, first with the accounting firm of Arthur Andersen & Co. and later as an investment banker with Wertheim & Co. Weinberg had risen to the post of vice-president of corporate finance at Wertheim when in 1975 a Harvard classmate, Jeffrey Cole, head of National Corp., convinced him to strike out on his own, move to Cleveland, and start investing in companies. Weinberg helped to form Intercapco Inc., a venture capital company. Through Intercapco he became involved in the leveraged buyout of a local manufacturing company, Anderson International Corp. By default, Weinberg became the company's chief executive officer, which proved to be an unpleasant experience. Weinberg sold out in 1983 and started Collins & Weinberg to arrange acquisitions and provide management services. When partner Richard Collins left, the firm became known as Weinberg Capital Corp. Taking advantage of the contacts he made from his Wall Street days, Weinberg invested in a slate of companies, intentionally avoiding the assumption of majority control. One of his minority stakes was in *Cleveland Magazine*. When Gerald H. Gordon, the general manager of Sun Newspapers, a small independent chain, met with Weinberg to discuss his desire to buy *Cleveland Magazine*, they instead dwelled on the potential of Sun Newspapers. The two men became partners to purchase Sun Newspapers, with Weinberg supplying the financial expertise and Gordon tasked with running the operation. It was this type of delineation of roles that would later be employed at Hawk.

Representing Weinberg in the Sun transaction was a well-connected attorney named Byron Krantz. Weinberg and Krantz had become acquainted at a party shortly after Weinberg had moved to Cleveland and the two started doing business together. Two years after they completed the Sun deal, they were on a flight together when Weinberg told Krantz about a friend's idea. As Weinberg had done in publishing, his friend suggested he could find a partner with experience in manufacturing, roll up small manufacturers and create a major manufacturing company. Krantz immediately recommended that Weinberg meet with Norman Harbert, who had a wealth of manufacturing experience. Then the CEO of Warren, Ohio-based Ajax Magnethermic Corp., a heating equipment maker, and the owner and chairman of Maverick Tube Corp., Harbert also had 22 years of experience at Reliance Electric on his resume. Coincidentally, he was eager to move back to Cleveland and was looking for a business partner. He had a company lined up to buy but needed someone with financial experience to help him complete it. Krantz, who was a Maverick director, arranged a Sunday breakfast meeting. Weinberg and Harbert "hit it off immediately," according to Harbert, and they agreed to work together.

Friction Products: First Acquisition in 1981

The company in which Harbert was interested was Friction Products, a Medina, Ohio, company that made brake pads and discs for airliners and motorcycles, and transmission components for trucks, farm equipment, and construction equipment. It had a strong share of its niche market, a position that Weinberg preferred. They bought Friction Products, which they tucked into a corporation they formed: The Hawk Group of Companies, Inc. Hawk was drawn from their initials: "HA" from Harbert, "W" for Weinberg, plus "K" from Krantz, the man who had brought the partners together. At the same time, they bought a second business, Logan Metal Co., an Akron, Ohio, metal-stamping company. Harbert ran Hawk, while Weinberg scouted for complementary acquisitions in order to fulfill his dream of building a large manufacturing concern. A key tool to grow the business that Hawk employed from the outset was the issuance of stock options to middle management, in effect creating a entrepreneurial spirit in the company.

Over the next five years, Hawk grew "slow and steady"— in the words of Weinberg—with little equity and a modest amount of debt. The only expansion during this period was realized by internal means. Hawk Brake was established in Medina to produce high-performance, polymer-based brake materials. It was not until June 1994 that Hawk completed its third acquisition, buying Heisel Inc., located in Campbellsburg, Indiana. The company made parts from metal powders for use in the fluid power and hydraulics industries. With Heisel in the fold, Hawk topped the $100 million mark in annual revenues in 1994. An even more significant acquisition took place a year later, when in June 1995 Hawk paid $60 million in cash to MLC Corp. for S.K. Wellman Ltd., a deal that held the potential to double Hawk's annual sales overnight. The addition of Wellman was beneficial on a number of levels. Although Friction Products manufactured similar items, Wellman primarily served the industrial market while Friction Products concentrated on the aircraft industry. But because the manufacturing operations were the same, the two companies could trade off on capacity if needed. Both companies also had strong research and development efforts, which when integrated promised to generate even greater levels of innovation. Moreover, Wellman brought with it a European and Asian market presence that Friction Products lacked and could leverage to pursue overseas sales. One of Wellman's four plants, in fact, was located in

Italy. The other three were located in Ohio, Tennessee, and Ontario. In order to pull off the Wellman acquisition, Hawk relied on Weinberg's financial experience to refinance the Hawk slate of companies. Part of this effort included reincorporating in Delaware and formally bringing in the subsidiaries under an umbrella company. This move also set up Hawk to eventually make an initial public offering (IPO) of stock. A further step in this direction came in October 1996 when the company adopted its current name, Hawk Corporation.

Before going public, however, Hawk completed two more acquisitions. The first, the $12.1 million cash and stock purchase of Hutchinson Foundry Products company, closed in January 1997. Alton, Illinois-based Hutchinson was a rotor manufacturer. To fund the acquisition as well as to pay down debt, Hawk, prior to completing the deal, made a $100 million private bond offering and also secured a $25 million revolving line of credit through a subsidiary of one of the lead underwriters of the offering. In August 1997, Hawk completed its second acquisition of the year, paying $16.4 million in cash for Sinterley, Inc., a manufacturer of powder metal parts and powder metal products located in Solon Mills, Illinois.

Completing the IPO in May 1998

Hawk announced in November 1997 its intention to make an IPO of common stock. It planned to use part of the proceeds to redeem $30 million in 12 percent senior subordinated notes issued in 1995, and spend another $1.75 million to redeem 1,733 of more than 6,000 preferred shares outstanding. Management planned to reserve the balance of the funds for capital expenditures and future acquisitions. The offering was scheduled for January 1998, the same month that the Monica Lewinsky scandal rocked the Clinton administration and the entire nation. The uncertainty of the final outcome of the scandal, in turn, rattled the stock market. Hawk's IPO was postponed, in the hope that conditions would improve. The company tried again in May, following a grueling two-week road show that took company officials across the United States and to Europe to meet with prospective investors. The offering, lead-managed by Schroder & Co. along with co-managers Lehman Brothers and McDonald & Co. Securities Inc., was completed on May 12, 1998. Shares sold at $17. Had Hawk gone through with the IPO four months earlier, the stock would have likely been priced at $13 or $14. In the end the company netted $87.3 million. Now that Hawk was a public company, Weinberg and Harbert widened the level of management eligible for stock options. A month after its offering, Hawk completed another acquisition, paying $9.1 million in cash and other considerations for Clearfield Powdered Metals, Inc. Based in Clearfield, Pennsylvania, the company manufactured precision powder metal parts including bearings, bushings, sleeves, and washers, and structural parts such as cams, collars, and gears.

In the years prior to its IPO, Hawk had grown at a rapid clip, but starting in 1999, its first full year as a public company, it began to face some serious challenges that were the result of factors beyond management's control. Asian economies softened, while markets such as agriculture, mining, and construction experienced rough years. All of these factors hurt Hawk's business. Nevertheless, the company posted record results at the end of 1999, with revenues improving to $187.4

Key Dates:

1989: The company is formed.
1995: S.K. Wellman is acquired.
1996: The company assumes its current name.
1998: The company goes public.
1999: Allegheny Powder Metallurgy, Inc. and Quarter Master Industries, Inc. are acquired.
2000: Tex Racing Enterprises, Inc. and Net Shape Technologies LLC are acquired; the company is restructured into four business groups.
2001: Sales decline and the company posts a loss of $4.3 million; the domestic workforce is cut by 12 percent.

million. On the other hand, net income of $6.3 million was a 30.8 percent decrease over the previous year. Much of the gain in sales was due to a pair of acquisitions. In March 1999 Hawk purchased Allegheny Powder Metallurgy, Inc. for $14.5 million plus other considerations. The Falls Creek, Pennsylvania-based business sold its products mainly to the lawn and garden and automotive markets. A second acquisition was completed in October 1999, the $4.85 million purchase of Quarter Master Industries, Inc., makers of clutches and driveline components for high performance racing cars on both the NASCAR and Indy Racing League circuit. During 1999 Hawk also took steps to grow its business in new directions. Later in the year it opened a plant in Monterrey, Mexico, to produce aluminum die-cast rotors for the motor industry. The company also initiated plans to build a manufacturing plant in China. Another development of note in 1999 was the appointment of former congressman and football player Jack Kemp to the board of directors.

Despite challenging economic conditions, Hawk continued to record improved levels of revenues in 2000, up 7.8 percent to $202.3 million. Net income, however, continued to soften, falling to $5.8 million. Some of this drop was due to the start-up costs related to the recent opening of manufacturing facilities in China and Mexico. Management continued to look for strategic acquisitions, completing two deals during the course of the year. In November it closed on the purchase of Tex Racing Enterprises, Inc., a North Carolina company that manufactured transmissions and drive trains for racing cars. A month later, Hawk paid $480,000 in cash for Net Shape Technologies LLC, which specialized in the relatively new metal injection molding process to produce steel parts that did not require machining. As a result, significant savings could be realized, compared with components made in foundries or machine shops. Hawk had

been looking to become involved in this technology for several years and after reviewing a number of companies involved in it concluded that Net Shape possessed the best business plan management had seen. Because of Hawk's diverse number of companies, management in 2000 restructured the company into four business groups, each headed by a president responsible for its financial results.

Economic conditions in 2001 deteriorated enough that Hawk saw its sales decline to $184.4 million and the company posted a loss of $4.3 million. In the first several months of the year the commercial and general aviation markets were troubled, and the situation would only worsen following the terrorist attacks of September 11, 2001. There was also softening in the construction industry and agricultural market. Hawk was forced to cut costs, including the termination of 12 percent of its domestic workforce, some 150 jobs. Another challenging year followed, with Hawk recording a further loss of $18.2 million. Nevertheless, some aspects of the company managed to grow, such as the Wellman Products Group, which benefited from the introduction of new products, and Hawk Racing Group, which also thrived despite difficult economic conditions. In the early months of 2003 Hawk posted better than expected results, mostly due to sales realized through product innovation. But for the company to regain its earlier pattern of growth, and to entertain further acquisitions, it had to rely on the worldwide economy to show significant improvements.

Principal Subsidiaries

Friction Products Co.; S.K. Wellman Holdings, Inc.; Quarter Master Industries, Inc.

Principal Competitors

BorgWarner Inc.; Precision Castparts Corporation; Raytech Corporation.

Further Reading

Baird, Kristen, ''Hawk Completes $100 Million Offering,'' *Crain's Cleveland Business,* December 16, 1996, p. 2.

Klein, Dustin S., ''Anatomy of an IPO,'' *Crain's Cleveland Business,* September 1, 1999.

Mooney, Barbara, ''SunMedia Chief More Than Publishing Mogul,'' *Crain's Cleveland Business,* June 4, 1990, p. 3.

Shingler, Dan, ''Hawk Group Buys S.K. Wellman Ltd.,'' *Crain's Cleveland Business,* April 17, 1995, p. 1.

—Ed Dinger

Highveld Steel and Vanadium Corporation Limited

One Pretoria Main Road
P.O. Box 111
Mpumalanga
South Africa
Telephone: (+27) 1359-7011
Fax: +27 136903332
Web site: http://www.highveldsteel.co.za

Public Company
Incorporated: 1957 as Minerals Engineering Co.
Employees: 4,192
Sales: R 4.01 billion ($528.5 million) (2002)
Stock Exchanges: Johannesburg Frankfurt NASDAQ
Ticker Symbol: HSVLY (ADRs)
NAIC: 331221 Cold-Rolled Steel Shape Manufacturing;
    331111 Iron and Steel Mills; 331222 Steel Wire
    Drawing

Highveld Steel and Vanadium Corporation Limited is one of South Africa's leading vertically integrated producers of steel and steel products, including rolled and flat steel products, and a limited number of finished products, such as steel cages and other enclosures. Highveld is also one of the world's largest producers of vanadium, a rare, soft, corrosion-resistant metal used to strengthen steel. The company produces vanadium products, including vanadium pentoxide and trioxide, both for the export market and for its own production of vanadium steel alloys. Through its Transalloys division, Highveld also produces manganese alloys, most of which is sold as exports. The bulk of the company's production occurs at its main Witbank-region site in Mpumalanga. The company also operates a secondary site at Gauteng. Highveld also produces its own ore for its steel and other production from a mine in Mapochs. Steel and vanadium products represented 70 percent of the group's sales of R 4 billion ($528 million) in 2002, with ferro-alloys contributing 23 percent to sales. The company has been shedding noncore businesses, including its Columbus stainless steel joint venture in 2002 and its Rheem packaging subsidiary in

2003. Listed on the Johannesburg stock exchange, Highveld is held at more than 80 percent by the Anglo American Industrial Corporation.

An Anglo Alternative to Iscor in the 1950s

In the late 1950s, South Africa's steel industry remained dominated by the South African Iron and Steel Industrial Corporation, otherwise known as Iscor. Created by the South African government in the late 1920s in part to reduce the country's reliance on imported steel, Iscor remained a government holding. With the rise to political power of the Afrikaner-controlled National Party, Iscor, previously operated by the country's English-speaking community, came under the influence of the Afrikaner community, including the secretive Broederbond. Indeed, Iscor played a role in the development of the Apartheid state, providing the steel for the country's arms production after the voluntary boycott of arms imports in the early 1960s. At the same time, Iscor became a central part of the National Party's effort to redress the balance of economic power in South Africa as well, in a largely unsuccessful attempt to place more wealth in the Afrikaner community.

By the end of the 1950s, Iscor had nonetheless been successful in meeting some 70 percent of South Africa's domestic steel needs. This dominant position made entry into the country's steel market difficult, mostly because of Iscor's decidedly Afrikaner influence. During that decade, however, a number of companies, especially foreign businesses, had entered the South African steel and steel products market, in part to gain access to the country's vast mineral wealth.

Among these companies was Minerals Engineering Co. of South Africa. A subsidiary of Minerals Engineering of Colorado, controlled by the Rockefeller family, the new company set up a plant in Witbank in 1957 to produce vanadium pentoxide. Minerals Engineering Co. targeted its production at the U.S. market. At the time, use of vanadium remained somewhat limited to highly specialized products, such as high-speed steel tools and heat-treated engineering components. The relatively small market, coupled with high production costs, led to Minerals Engineering's decision to sell off the subsidiary by 1959.

Minerals Engineering turned to Anglo American Industrial Corporation, a British-controlled company that had established itself as one of South Africa's dominant mining companies, particularly through its Orange Free State gold mines. While that operation had become profitable by the late 1950s, difficult conditions in the gold market at the time made further mining investments in the country unattractive. Instead, Anglo American sought to diversify its South African holdings, targeting an entry into steel production.

Anglo American agreed to take over a two-thirds stake in Minerals Engineering in 1959, renaming it Transvaal Vanadium Co. The British-controlled company then began investigating methods for increasing its new subsidiary's profitability. A primary target for this goal involved finding a method of recovering and exploiting the iron content discarded as waste during the standard vanadium production process of the period. At the same time, Anglo American sought a more efficient method for extracting the vanadium from its titaniferous magnetite ore, which, with a high titanium content, was difficult to process using traditional blast furnace-based smelting methods.

In 1960, Anglo American formed a new company, Highveld Development Co., for the purpose of exploring a new smelting technique using a four-stage electrical process pioneered in the late 1940s and early 1950s. Highveld built a pilot plant and began carrying out experiments in 1961 and 1962, the successful outcome of which led Anglo American to propose to build a full-scale plant at Witbank. For this, Anglo American turned to Iscor, proposing to form a joint venture, together with outside capital from a foreign steel maker, to build and operate the new plant.

Iscor refused, driven in part by political motivations, as its Afrikaner leadership resented the incursion of English-dominated Anglo American on its operational territory, but also because Iscor itself had begun planning a large-scale expansion for the 1960s. Yet the discovery of new and more widely available methods for exploiting vanadium-based steel introduced an upswing in the market in 1964, and Anglo American decided to risk its own capital on the costly development of the Witbank plant. The move was described by CEO Harry Oppenheimer, an opponent to both the apartheid regime and the South African government's policies of nationalization of the country's industries, "a major single act of faith by private enterprise in the future of South Africa."

With no previous experience in steelmaking, Anglo American acquired outside expertise. In 1964, it bought South African steel producer Scaw Metals. Anglo American also formed a joint venture with Sweden's Avesta Jernverks AB, Transalloys

Proprietary Ltd., for the production of chromo-ferro alloys. Anglo American continued investing elsewhere in South Africa, buying stakes in a number of companies that were shortly to come under the control of the soon-to-be nationalized British Steel Corporation (BSC). In the meantime, the mining concern lined up financing for the project, some of which was raised in exchange for future equity in the Witbank company.

Construction began on the Witbank site, designed as a vanadium-based integrated iron and steel production facility in 1965. At the time the Highveld company was renamed Highveld Steel and Vanadium Corporation Limited. The following year, Anglo American acquired full control of Transvaal Vanadium, placing it under Highveld, where it became structured as the company's Vantra division. As construction proceeded, Anglo American began selling its future production, and by the time of the plant's completion in December 1968, Highveld held contracts for nearly all of its vanadium production through to the end of 1971.

By April 1969, the Witbank site was fully operational. In that year, also, Highveld went public on the Johannesburg stock exchange, in part to enable the project's financial backers to cash out on their investment. Nonetheless, Anglo American maintained control of the company, with more than 70 percent of Highveld's stock. Later, that stake was boosted past 80 percent.

In response to the launch of Highveld, Iscor began acquiring controlling stakes in engineering companies and other South African businesses that had previously been Iscor's exclusive steel customers. Among Iscor's targets were the South African subsidiaries of the new British Steel Corporation, created in 1967. BSC's holdings included full control of South Africa's second largest steel distributor, Baldwins, as well as major stakes in Stewarts & Lloyds, the country's leading maker of pipes and tubes, and Dorman Long, its largest structural engineering specialist.

Yet because Anglo American already held significant stakes in many of these companies, the three sides were forced into negotiations. A compromise was reached in 1970, with the creation of International Pipe & Steel Investments South Africa (Ipsa), which regrouped BSC's South African holdings. For Iscor, the compromise marked its success in controlling the English-speaking and foreign influences on the national steel market. For Highveld, it marked the start of a truce between itself and Iscor.

Toward Consolidation in the New Century

Highveld booked strong growth through the 1970s and 1980s. In 1976, the company acquired a 65 percent stake in Transalloys from its parent company. By 1985, Anglo American had transferred full control of the manganese alloys producer to Highveld. In that year, also, the company commissioned its second iron production facility.

The company continued to develop toward the end of the decade, particularly with the acquisition of Rand Carbide Ltd., also based in Witbank. Completed in 1978, the transaction gave Highveld access to Rand Carbide's 60 years of expertise in the production of ferrosilicon and other carbonaceous products.

Key Dates:

1957: Minerals Engineering Co. of South Africa is formed to produce vanadium pentoxide for the exports market.

1959: Anglo American acquires two-thirds stake of Minerals Engineering Co., which is renamed as Transvaal Vanadium Company.

1960: Highveld Development Co. is formed to build a pilot smelting facility using new electronic smelting techniques.

1964: Construction of Witbank integrated iron and steel facility begins.

1965: The company changes its name to Highveld Steel & Vanadium Corporation.

1966: Anglo American acquires full control of Transvaal Vanadium and transfers it to Highveld.

1968: The Witbank project is completed.

1969: Witbank enters full production and Highveld goes public.

1970: The formation of Ipsa leads to a truce between Iscor and Highveld.

1976: The company acquires 65 percent of Transalloys from Anglo American.

1978: The company acquires Rand Carbide and extends into ferrosilicon production.

1985: The company completes the acquisition of Transalloys; a second iron plant is commissioned; Rheem South Africa is acquired.

1991: The company initiates the creation of the Columbus Joint Venture and acquisition of Middelburg Steel & Alloys in a move to enter the stainless steel market.

1993: Rheem expands with a new aluminum can production plant.

1996: The new Columbus stainless steel plant begins production.

1998: Hochvanadium Holding AG is created in Austria.

2001: A joint venture is formed with Japan's Nippon Denko.

2002: The company sells Columbus in exchange for a stake in Spain's Acerinox.

2003: The company sells the Rheem packaging division to Coleus Packaging.

Highveld sought new diversification in the mid-1980s, particularly through its purchase of Rheem South Africa Ltd. in 1985. That purchase enabled the company to extend its steel production into finished products, including steel drums, pails, and related products. Later, in 1993, Highveld extended its Rheem subsidiary's operations with the construction of a plant dedicated to the production of aluminum cans.

By then, Highveld had already added another new product category, that of stainless steel. In 1991, the company formed a partnership with Samancor Ltd. to buy Middelburg Steel & Alloys Ltd. That company was then transformed into Columbus Stainless. In 1993, Highveld and Samancor sold a combined one-third share of Columbus to the South African government's Industrial Development Corporation. Highveld's own share of that company stood at 64 percent. Construction then began on a new stainless steel production plant, which was inaugurated in 1996.

With the completion of the new Columbus plant, South Africa became the world's number six producer of stainless steel. Columbus also quickly became an important source of revenues for Highveld, accounting for some one-third of the company's sales by 2001. Yet the collapse of the global market for stainless steel, linked with the Asian economic crisis in the second half of the decade, sent Columbus into a downward spiral. By the late 1990s, Columbus's losses had begun to drag Highveld into the red as well. The company and its partners began looking to offload the stainless steel business, and in 2001 agreed to sell Columbus to Spain's Acerinox in exchange for a stake in that company.

In the meantime, Highveld also had begun exiting its Rheem subsidiary, converting the aluminum can plant to steel production in 1999, then shutting the facility altogether in 2001. By 2003, Highveld had found a buyer for Rheem as well,

selling it to Coleus Packaging Ltd. for R 33 million in January of that year.

Steel prices, and Highveld's fortunes, began to rebound in the early 2000s. The creation of new trade barriers by the Bush administration, designed to protect the U.S. steel industry from foreign competition, had by then cut short the company's market there. Instead, Highveld formed a European trade subsidiary, Hochvanadium Holding AG in Austria in 1998. The company also reached a joint venture agreement with Japan's Nippon Denko in 2001, which involved moving the Japanese company's ferro-vanadium production to South Africa, giving Highveld increased access to that market.

The breakup of Iscor into separate steel and mining components in 2001 had sparked speculation of a coming consolidation of South Africa's steel industry. Highveld, held at more than 82 percent by Anglo American, appeared a likely target for a takeover offer by Iscor, which had evolved into one of the world's lowest-cost steel producers at the approach of the new century. In turn, Anglo American signaled its interest in eventually buying out Highveld's minority shareholders.

Toward the end of 2003, Iscor affirmed its desire for expansion, giving Highveld, and another South African-based steel company, Duferco, an ultimatum to reach an agreement on a takeover deal within a year—or lose out altogether. A takeover by Iscor, however, was likely to meet with tight scrutiny from the country's mergers and monopolies authority.

Meanwhile, Highveld had begun to benefit from the rising global steel and vanadium markets, despite the relative strength of the rand. At the same time, Highveld's stake in Acerinox—which had restored the Columbus facility to profitability—had also become an important part of the company's assets base, accounting for some half of its value. With revenues rising past R

4 billion ($585 million), Highveld appeared in a strong position to resist Iscor's takeover ambitions, at least for the near future.

Principal Subsidiaries

Lacerta Investment Holdings (Proprietary) Limited; Meehr Properties (Proprietary) Limited; Hochvanadium Holding AG (Austria); South Africa Japan Vanadium (Proprietary) Limited (50%).

Principal Competitors

Delta Steel Mill Co.; Laiwu Steel Corporation; Tangshan City Iron and Steel Grp Co.; Changcheng Special Steel Company Ltd.; Qingdao Iron and Steel General Corporation; Qiqihar Beiman Special Steel Corporation Ltd.; A H Al Zamil Group of Companies; Cathay Pacific Steel Corporation; Arcelor; Xilin Iron and Steel Co.

Further Reading

Cross, Tim, ''Afrikaner Nationalism, Anglo-American and Iscor: The Formation of the Highveld Steel & Vanadium Corporation, 1960–70,'' *Business History*, July 1994, p. 81.

Fraser, John, ''Move on Highveld or No Deal, Iscor Warns Anglo,'' *Business Day*, August 21, 2003, p. 1.

Lourens, Carli, ''Highveld Plans to Raise Export Volumes by As Much As 20%,'' *Business Day*, February 12, 2003, p. 15.

Marrs, Dave, ''Stainless Steel Exposure Adds Lustre to Highveld,'' *Business Day*, August 6, 2003, p. 10.

''Trevor Jones EC, Highveld Steel,'' *Africa News*, August 29, 2001.

—M. L. Cohen

HMV Group plc

Shelley House
2-4 York Rd.
Maidenhead
Berkshire SL6 1SR
United Kingdom
Telephone: (+44) 1628-818-300
Fax: (+44) 1628-818-301
Web site: http://www.hmv.co.uk

Public Company
Founded: 1921
Employees: 13,207
Sales: £1.71 billion ($2.74 billion) (2003)
Stock Exchanges: London
Ticker Symbol: HMV
NAIC: 451211 Book Stores; 451220 Prerecorded Tape,
Compact Disc and Record Stores; 551112 Offices of
Other Holding Companies

Having inherited its name from the famed "His Master's Voice" logo, featuring Nipper the dog, HMV Group plc is one of the United Kingdom's leading music, book, and entertainment media retailers, and a rising force on the global scene as well. Formed from the spinoff of HMV and Dillons bookstores from EMI, which were then merged with British bookseller leader Waterstone's, HMV Group operates more than 540 stores, including more than 340 HMV music stores, and nearly 200 Waterstone's bookstores. Together, the company's store network boasts more than 3.2 million square feet of selling space. HMV's music stores traditionally focus on music sales; DVDs, however, represent a rising proportion of the group's sales. At Waterstone's, the company has been accused, notably by former chairman and founder Tim Waterstone, of "dumbing down" selection to appeal to a broader market. The United Kingdom and Ireland remain HMV's primary markets, at more than 70 percent of sales and representing more than half of its music stores—including its Oxford Street superstore, the world's largest music store—and most of its bookstores. The

company nonetheless has a rising presence internationally, with strong markets in Canada and Japan, and stores in the United States, Germany, Hong Kong, Singapore, Australia, and elsewhere. HMV has also made the push into e-commerce, operating its own sites in North America, Japan, and Australia; Waterstone's online sales in the United Kingdom are carried out in conjunction with Amazon. HMV is traded on the London Stock Exchange; 80 percent of its shares are split evenly between former parent EMI and equity partner Advent Investors.

Single Store Origins in the 1920s

In 1921, The Gramophone Company, founded in 1897 to manufacture gramophones and to produce recordings for the machine, opened its first music retail store. Located on London's Oxford Street, where it remained for many years, the retail operation was launched under the auspices of British composer Edward Elgar. The retail store, the first in the world to offer listening booths, adopted the name HMV, after The Gramophone Company's famed "His Master's Voice" logo, itself patterned after a painting by Francis Barraud.

HMV remained a tiny part of the fast-growing EMI—formed in a 1931 merger between The Gramophone Company and Columbia Gramophone Company—which had grown to include U.S.-based Capital Records in the 1950s. Yet the explosion of record sales in the early 1960s, in part sparked by EMI's signing of the Beatles in 1962, introduced a new retail market for music sales. In 1966, EMI began to expand the HMV retail format, and by 1970, the company operated 15 stores.

The 1970s saw a period of rapid growth for the retail division, and by mid-decade, the company boasted 35 shops and gained a position as a leading music retailer in the United Kingdom. In the meantime, EMI had branched out into film production and diversified into other areas—one of the company's projects resulted in the invention of computer tomography imaging. Yet this latter endeavor had also played a part in EMI's financial difficulties at the end of the 1970s, resulting in the company's 1979 acquisition by diversified electronics and rental group Thorn Electrical Industries, founded in 1928. The resulting group was renamed Thorn EMI in 1980.

International Growth in the 1990s

HMV continued to grow throughout this period and in 1986, during a companywide restructuring, was recognized as one of Thorn EMI's core business areas and spun off from the recording company as a separate division under EMI Group. The new company was given the name of HMV Music Retailing, opening that same year its flagship store on Oxford Street, called the HMV Oxford Circus. The store, at 50,000 square feet of selling space, earned a place in the *Guinness Book of World Records* as the world's largest music store. The company's original Oxford Street store remained in operation, however.

As a full-fledged company within the EMI empire, HMV began its own quest for international expansion. In 1987, the company opened its first foreign store, in Mississauga, Ontario. The Canadian operation was a quick success, prompting the company to roll out its store format across the country. By the late 1990s, HMV Canada represented nearly 100 stores.

In 1990, HMV attempted to replicate its Canadian success in the United States, opening two stores that year in New York City. Yet HMV's effort to crack the U.S. market never neared the success of its Canadian counterpart, and the company's presence in the United States remained limited to less than 20 stores by the year 2000. Other markets proved equally elusive for the company, such as France, which it entered in the early 1990s, then quickly exited, and Germany.

More successful for the company were its excursions to the Asia Pacific, and especially to the Japanese market. Launched in Tokyo in 1990, the company's Japanese branch grew quickly, and, at 40 stores, claimed second place among international operations. Australia, Hong Kong, and, later, Singapore also provided profitable, if smaller markets for HMV.

Closer to home, HMV remained the leading dedicated music retailer in the United Kingdom and in Ireland. Yet the company's product mix was already beginning to shift, as it added video and then video game sections to capture a share of these rising markets. In 1995, however, the company gained a new branch when parent Thorn EMI added the Dillons bookstore chain. Founded by Una Dillon in 1936 as Dillons University Book Store, that chain had grown into a network of 75 stores throughout the United Kingdom. Dillons, placed under HMV, remained separated from HMV's music stores.

In another expansion move, HMV entered the music recording industry in 1995, when it released its first compact disc compilation. The disc, called HMV Classics, featured titles culled from the EMI catalog. HMV continued to add new titles in a similar vein through the 1990s, based on its access to EMI's strong backlist.

For years, rumors had circulated that HMV was slated to be spun off from Thorn EMI. Instead, in 1996, Thorn EMI itself split up, into its EMI music and retailing segment on the one hand, and its Thorn rentals business on the other. HMV remained an autonomous unit of EMI following the breakup. In 1998, however, the company was given new scope through the three-way merger between HMV, Dillons, and the fast-growing Waterstone's bookstore chain.

Music and Book Retail Leader in the 21st Century

By 1998, HMV had grown into an internationally operating chain of more than 270 music stores. Yet EMI, which had found itself among the smallest of the major labels, began a push to achieve scale in its recording and publishing operations, leading to its interest in spinning off HMV and Dillons. In the meantime, Waterstone's, founded by Tim Waterstone in 1982, then brought under the WH Smith retail umbrella, had developed into one of the United Kingdom's leading book chains, with an emphasis on so-called "high brow" and often hard-to-find books.

For the HMV spinoff, EMI created a 50–50 joint venture with private equity investment group Advent International, called HMV Media Group. That company then acquired both the HMV and Dillons chains from EMI, and, for £300 million, the Waterstone's chain from WH Smith. The Dillons chain was subsequently merged into Waterstone's, which became the brand for the entire book division. Tim Waterstone was named chairman of the new group, but CEO Alan Giles, formerly WH Smith's man in charge of Waterstone's, retained operational control.

While maintaining separate retail operations for its book and music stores, HMV nonetheless began imposing its own sales model on the Waterstone's chain, shedding some £15 million of slow-selling titles in a move to a more mid-market sales mix. The strategy appeared to backfire, as Waterstone's sales slumped in the new millennium, and new store openings were put on hold. It also led to charges that HMV was in the process of "dumbing down" Waterstone's, and to Tim Waterstone's resignation as company chairman in 2001. Waterstone then began lobbying to regain control of the bookstore.

In the meantime, HMV had discovered a new retail frontier, the Internet. In 1999, the company opened the first of four international e-commerce sites. HMV also began exploring other delivery formats for its music and books, such as online downloads and other digital delivery applications. Meanwhile, the company continued to expand its bricks-and-mortar chain, opening a new 66,000-square-foot flagship store in London's Piccadilly and adding new stores internationally. By 2003, the company operated more than 540 stores, including more than 340 HMV music stores.

A downturn in the music and book market at the beginning of the century had put plans to take the company public at the beginning of the new decade. In 2002, however, an upturn in sales, including growing profits at Waterstone's, brought the company to the London Stock Exchange. In that process, the

Key Dates:

1921: The Gramophone Company (later EMI) opens first HMV music store in Oxford Street under auspices of Edward Elgar.
1966: EMI begins expansion of HMV retail network.
1976: With 35 stores, HMV is leading music retailer in the United Kingdom.
1979: Thorn Electrical Industries acquires EMI, creating Thorn EMI in 1980.
1986: HMV becomes autonomous division under Thorn EMI; HMV begins international expansion with first store in Canada.
1990: HMV enters the United States, Japan, Australia, and later Hong Kong and Singapore.
1995: HMV releases first CD, using titles from EMI catalog; acquires Dillons bookstore chain.
1996: Thorn and EMI demerge; HMV remains part of EMI.
1998: EMI and Advent Investors create HMV Media Group joint venture, which then acquires HMV, Dillons and, from WH Smith, Waterstone's bookstore chain; Dillons is subsequently rebranded as Waterstone's.
1999: HMV Media launches first e-commerce site.
2002: HMV Media goes public on London Stock Exchange and changes name to HMV Group.
2003: Company opens first new Waterstone's in four years.

company simplified its name to HMV Group Plc. As a result of the offering, both EMI and Advent dropped back their shares in HMV to 40 percent.

Following the public offering, HMV began entertaining buyout offers for its Waterstone's chain, including a leveraged buyout led by Tim Waterstone. Yet, at the beginning of 2003, HMV ended sales talks, announcing its intention to retain the bookstore chain. Tim Waterstone, however, vowed to fight on in his attempt to regain control of the business he had founded more than 20 years earlier, telling the *Independent*: "We will come back and come back and come back again."

Despite its identification as a music specialist, HMV remained buoyed by the enormous success of DVD sales in the early 2000s—sales volumes leaped by more than 100 percent as DVD players became common home appliances. HMV itself claimed nearly 30 percent of the United Kingdom's DVD market by the end of 2003, and DVD sales had become a significant part of the group's sales—and profits. In the meantime, HMV renewed its commitment to building the Waterstone's bookstore chain, opening its first new store in nearly four years, and announcing plans to open at least nine more stores before the end of its 2004 calendar year. HMV Group had established itself as a major force in worldwide entertainment media sales.

Principal Subsidiaries

HMV Music Limited; HMV (IP) Limited; HMV USA LP; HMV Canada Inc; HMV Japan KK; HMV Hong Kong Limited; HMV Singapore Pte Limited; HMV Australia Pty Limited; HMV Tonträger GmbH (Germany); HMV Ireland Limited; Rustico Holdings Limited (Ireland); Waterstone's Booksellers Limited; Waterstone's Booksellers Amsterdam BV (Netherlands); Waterstone's Booksellers Belgium SA; Waterstone's Booksellers Ireland Limited.

Principal Competitors

Woolworths Ltd.; Borders Inc.; Blockbuster Inc.; Virgin Group Ltd.; Casa Paris S.A.; Musicland Stores Corp.; Trans World Entertainment Corp.; MTS Inc.; Shinseido Company Ltd.; Media Markt AG; Musimundo S.A.

Further Reading

Beavis, Simon, "Waterstone Vows to Fight on After Rebuff by HMV," *Independent*, January 31, 2003, p. 25.
Christman, Ed, "HMV Emerges As US Retail Force," *Billboard*, March 25, 1995, p. 1.
Ford, Jonathan, "HMV Media Set on Expansion," *Financial Times*, October 15, 1998, p. 28.
Kaiser, Kevin M.J., and Aris Stouraitis, "Reversing Corporate Diversification and the Use of the Proceeds from Asset Sales: The Case of Thorn EMI," *Financial Management*, Winter 2001, p. 63.
"The Lowdown: HMV's Master Won't Let the Record Get Stuck," *Independent Sunday*, February 23, 2003, p. 6.
Meads, Jeff Clark, "HMV's 75th Year Marked by Celebration, Expansion," *Billboard*, March 16, 1996, p. 1.
Milmo, Dan, "HMV Pins Hopes on Music and Swashbuckle," *Guardian*, September 30, 2003, p. 21.
Olins, Rufus, "HMV Chain Will Rock the World," *Sunday Times*, February 25, 1996, p. 1.
Rawsthorn, Alice, "Waterstone's, Dillons and HMV Bound in £800m Deal," *Financial Times*, February 26, 1998, p. 23.
Shah, Saeed, "HMV Takes Advantage of Retail Boom to Unveil £1bn Floatation," *Independent,* April 12, 2000, p. 21.
Smith, Alison, "HMV Shows Its Confidence in Waterstone's," *Financial Times*, September 29, 2003, p. 24.

—M. L. Cohen

HOK Group, Inc.

211 North Broadway, Suite 600
St. Louis, Missouri 63102
U.S.A.
Telephone: (314) 421-2000
Fax: (314) 421-6073
Web site: http://www.hok.com

Private Company
Incorporated: 1955 as Hellmuth, Obata and Kassabaum
Inc.
Employees: 2,000
Sales: $197 million (2002 est.)
NAIC: 541310 Architectural Services; 541330
Engineering Services

HOK Group, Inc. is one of the largest architectural and engineering firms in the United States, employing 1,600 professionals in offices located in North America, Latin America, Europe, and Asia. HOK's designs are visible in a number of different building types, ranging from airports and government buildings to sports complexes and transportation facilities. The firm provides design, engineering, interior design, program management, and planning services. HOK operates 12 offices in the United States, two offices in Canada, two offices in Europe, two offices in the Asia-Pacific region, and an office in Mexico City. Among the firm's most well known projects are Washington, D.C.'s National Air and Space Museum, Oriole Park at Camden Yards in Baltimore, Maryland, and the Moscone Convention Center in San Francisco, California.

Origins

HOK's longest-serving leader and its chief designer was cofounder Gyo Obata, a first-generation American whose career spanned more than a half-century. Obata was 18 years old in 1941 when the Japanese bombed Pearl Harbor, an act that provoked the United States' entry into World War II and ignited fear and suspicion toward Japanese nationals living in the United States and toward Americans of Japanese descent. When Pearl Harbor was bombed, Obata was studying architecture at California-Berkeley, where his father taught painting and enjoyed a distinguished reputation as an art professor. By the spring of 1942, an ugly chapter in U.S. history had begun. Internment camps were being opened, and the Obatas found themselves pulled by the tide of paranoia. The night before Obata's family was to be moved to a camp, his father sent him to St. Louis. In the thinking of the day, Japanese-Americans were perceived to pose less of a threat if they lived far inland, a mindset that enabled Obata to continue his studies in St. Louis. Obata studied under the renowned designer Eero Saarinen at Washington University, where he earned his master's degree in architecture. In 1945, Obata was drafted by the U.S. Army and sent to the Aleutian Islands.

After the war, Obata moved to Chicago and began his professional career as an architect. He was hired by a firm named Skidmore, Owings & Merrill, where he met Minoru Yamasaki, who would later design New York City's World Trade Center. Yamasaki became Obata's mentor and asked him to join his own firm. At Yamasaki's firm, Obata was introduced to George Hellmuth, one of the firm's partners. Obata and Hellmuth, striking a partnership that would last for decades, worked together in the early 1950s in St. Louis, where they collaborated on designing Lambert International Airport.

Hellmuth and Obata worked for Yamasaki's firm until the influential designer's health failed. The firm began to flounder without its leader, prompting Obata to start his own firm in St. Louis. He invited Hellmuth and a colleague named George Kassabaum to join him in his fledgling venture. The three principals opened their office in 1955, marking the founding date of Hellmuth, Obata + Kassabaum, or HOK.

Designing Its First Buildings: 1950s–70s

The new design firm started with 26 employees and the complementary talents of its three founders. The partners were well matched, each assuming a distinct role in the firm's operation. Kassabaum directed his energies toward project management. Obata focused on design. Hellmuth became the marketing expert, taking responsibility for HOK's most pressing need during its inaugural year. In search of the firm's first clients,

Hellmuth drove his car throughout rural Missouri and Illinois visiting school boards, the first type of client targeting by the design firm. At times, Hellmuth was forced to sell bags of charcoal from his farm to pay for gas—an indication of the modest means of HOK at its inception—but his junkets paid off. Hellmuth brought in $750,000 worth of business during his first year on the road. In 1955, the first HOK-designed building was erected, a public school in a St. Louis suburb.

HOK spent its first few years in business designing school buildings, establishing itself in the St. Louis market. The firm's turning point occurred during the early 1960s, when HOK first showed signs of becoming a designer of major projects. In 1961, the firm won its first major university commission, the Edwardsville campus of the University of Southern Illinois. The Edwardsville project set the company up for its next job, a defining point in the development of HOK and a seminal moment in Obata's career as a designer. In 1962, when HOK's net fees eclipsed $1 million for the first time, Obata designed a new chapel for Benedictine monks in St. Louis. The Priory Chapel, featuring parabolic arches, drew national recognition to Obata, whose design work earned the esteem of his colleagues and put the HOK name in the minds of prospective clients.

In the wake of the Priory Chapel project, HOK began to display its talents in a variety of directions, completing projects that carved a niche for the firm in several different design categories. The company also began to expand physically for the first time, making the 1960s a decade of significant importance for the blossoming firm. In 1964, HOK designed its first corporate building of national prominence, creating the IBM Labs in Los Gatos, California. During the year, the firm also designed the U.S. penitentiary in Marion, Illinois, the facility that replaced Alcatraz in the federal prison system. During the second half of the decade, the firm began opening satellite offices, situating itself near customers in high-growth markets. In 1966, HOK opened an office in San Francisco. In 1968, the firm opened an office in Washington, D.C. The following year, HOK opened an office in Dallas, Texas. HOK ended the decade by securing its first shopping mall projects. The firm designed Neiman Marcus in Houston in 1969, which led to the firm's design work on the Houston Galleria.

By the 1970s, HOK was on its way toward becoming the largest architectural and engineering firm in the United States. Mergers, landmark design projects, and leadership changes highlighted the decade's activities. In 1972, HOK designed the Dallas-Ft. Worth International Airport. The following year, the firm merged with Kahn-Jacobs, which enabled HOK to open an

office in New York City. HOK made business history two years later when it was awarded the largest single design project in the world at the time. In 1975, when the firm merged with Mills-Petticord and expanded its Washington, D.C., office, it won the bid for the $3.5 billion campus for King Saud University in Saudi Arabia. The massive project helped the firm exceed $15 million in net fees the following year, when it landed a prized contract that would put its work on display for millions of visitors. HOK, with Obata still functioning as the firm's lead designer, designed the National Air and Space Museum, destined to become the most popular of the Smithsonian institutions. In 1979, the year HOK designed the Cecil H. Green Library for Stanford University, Hellmuth retired. The departure of the firm's marketing expert prompted HOK to restructure its operations, giving it a new managerial organization for the 1980s.

Sports Facilities and International Expansion Fueling Growth in the Late 20th Century

One of the most prominent executives of the post-Hellmuth era was Jerry Sincoff, the future leader of HOK. Sincoff joined HOK in 1962 as a design and production architect and was named a principal of the firm in 1973. He played an instrumental part in the creation of one of HOK's most lucrative new business areas in the 1980s. He recruited several influential architects for a new HOK group originally named Sports Facilities Group but better known as HOK Sport + Venue + Event. The sports group was formed in 1983 with a staff of eight people, its creation occurring at roughly the same time the demand for new stadiums and arenas was exploding. Sincoff also spearheaded the firm's expansion overseas, which began in 1984 when HOK opened an office in Hong Kong. "He (Sincoff) is not only big on expanding internationally," a HOK executive explained in a December 2, 1991 interview with the *St. Louis Business Journal,* "he causes it to happen."

By the mid-1980s, HOK ranked as one of the largest architectural and engineering firms in the United States. The firm's design work on the Moscone Convention Center in San Francisco in 1981 and its design of the King Khaled International Airport in 1984 helped the firm eclipse $75 million in billings midway through the decade. Domestic expansion during the decade included the opening of an office in Kansas City and Los Angeles in 1983 and in Tampa in 1984. The first foray overseas with the Hong Kong office was followed by the opening of an office in London in 1988.

The 1980s were years of growth and change. George Kassabaum, HOK's project management guru, died in 1982, leaving Obata as the only founder still in control of the firm. As the 1990s began, Obata's influence over the company remained unchecked, but Sincoff took on an increasingly powerful role in the management of the firm. In 1990, he was named president of the firm, giving him the ability to express his penchant for international expansion. By the time Sincoff was named president, HOK had designed buildings in Indonesia, Singapore, Mexico, Malaysia, and elsewhere. New foreign office openings during the 1990s promised to increase HOK's international activities. In 1991, the firm opened an office in Tokyo, which was followed by the establishment of a series of satellite locations across the globe. In 1992, the firm opened an office in Berlin. The following year, it opened an office in Mexico City.

ers, 365 of whom were registered architects. During the year, the firm designed the Environmental Protection Agency's new headquarters in Washington, D.C. In the spring of 2002, HOK was awarded the coveted design contract for the new $939 million terminal at Indianapolis International Airport. Obata, spending 80 percent of his time on design, was busy creating the planned presidential library for Abraham Lincoln in Springfield, Illinois. In the years ahead, HOK promised to figure prominently in the design of major projects. As the firm neared its 50th anniversary, its legacy of success served as a seductive resume for the future, assuring that the HOK name would be behind numerous major construction projects in the 21st century.

Key Dates:

1955: Hellmuth, Obata + Kassabaum Inc. is formed.
1962: Gyo Obata designs the Priory Chapel in St. Louis.
1975: HOK wins a $3.5 billion contract for King Saud University in Saudi Arabia.
1976: HOK designs the National Air and Space Museum in Washington, D.C.
1984: The first international office, located in Hong Kong, opens.
1992: HOK-designed Oriole Park at Camden Yards in Baltimore, Maryland, opens.
2002: HOK designs the Environmental Protection Agency's headquarters in Washington, D.C.

Principal Subsidiaries

HOK Sport, Inc.

Principal Competitors

AEVOM Technology Corporation; M. Arthur Gensler Jr. & Associates, Inc.; URS Corporation.

In 1995, HOK offices debuted in Shanghai and Warsaw. In 1997, the firm opened offices in Toronto and Ottawa. In 1999, HOK opened an office in Brisbane, Australia.

HOK's projects during the 1990s solidified the firm's reputation as a prominent architectural and engineering firm capable of executing large-scale projects. The firm designed Oriole Park at Camden Yards in Baltimore, Maryland, home to Major League Baseball's Baltimore Orioles. The stadium was applauded for its architectural elegance, prompting other sports teams to marshal their forces for the construction of new stadiums and arenas. In the palpable surge of demand for new sports facilities, HOK was frequently turned to for assistance in designing stadiums and arenas. In the decade following the debut of Oriole Park, the firm designed the new baseball stadium in Cleveland, the Reliant Stadium, home of the National Football League's Houston Texans, and Heinz Field, where the National Football League's Pittsburgh Steelers played.

By the beginning of the 21st century, HOK stood as a venerated member of the global architectural community. The firm, according to *World Architecture,* ranked as the largest U.S.-based architectural firm and the second largest concern worldwide. In 2002, the company employed nearly 2,000 work-

Further Reading

Bochove, Danielle, ''China Stepping Stone for HOK Overseas,'' *St. Louis Business Journal,* July 24, 1995, p. 1A.
Craig, Bob, ''Architectural Vanguard,'' *Midwest Real Estate News,* February 2003, p. 12.
Dwyer, Joe, ''Orderly Succession Is Planned at HOK; Obata to Sell Out by June '93,'' *St. Louis Business Journal,* February 6, 1989, p. 1A.
Grone, Jack, ''Obata Still Devotes 80% of His Time to Design Work,'' *St. Louis Business Journal,* April 22, 1991, p. 14A.
——, ''Sincoff's Methodical Way Readies Him for HOK Helm,'' *St. Louis Business Journal,* December 2, 1991, p. 4A.
''HOK Evolves to Meet Changing Market Trends,'' *Building Design & Construction,* December 1994, p. 7.
Horwitz, Barbara, ''Only in America,'' *Building Design & Construction,* July 2002, p. 38.
McKenna, Jon, ''Big Architecture Firm Has New Atlanta Office,'' *Atlanta Business Chronicle,* August 5, 1994, p. 5B.
Tucci, Linda, ''Cards Ballpark Makes HOK Star Player Downtown,'' *St. Louis Business Journal,* June 22, 2001, p. 1.

—Jeffrey L. Covell

Hon Hai Precision Industry Co., Ltd.

2 Tzu Yu St.
Tu-Cheng City
Taipei
Taiwan
Telephone: (+886) 2-2268-3466
Fax: (+886) 2-2268-6204
Web site: http://www.foxconn.com

Public Company
Incorporated: 1974 as Hon Hai Plastics Corporation
Employees: 5,200
Sales: NT$245 billion (US$7.37 billion) (2002)
Stock Exchanges: Taiwan
NAIC: 334110 Computer and Peripheral Equipment
   Manufacturing; 334119 Other Computer Peripheral
   Equipment Manufacturing

Hon Hai Precision Industry Co., Ltd. is one of the world's leading manufacturers of computer connectors and components, as well as a major "barebones" desktop and notebook PC manufacturer working with many of the world's top tier computer brands and companies, including Apple, Dell, Compaq, Intel, and others. Operating internationally under the Foxconn name, Hon Hai has grown steadily through a combination of a willingness to invest heavily in order to adapt itself to its customers' demands; an early entry into the Chinese market, helping it maintain low production costs; and a diversification of its OEM-based product technologies, while avoiding the pursuit of the branded component market. Responding to the dropoff in the global computer market at the beginning of the 21st century, Hon Hai has extended its production to embrace new industries, notably the mobile telephone market. With the increasing use of computer and electronic technologies in modern automobiles, Hon Hai intends to enter that market as well. The company has also constructed a new plant in order to manufacture LCD screens for the computer, television, and other markets. Listed on the Taiwan stock exchange, Hon Hai has long distinguished itself by its discretion—some call it secrecy. The company remains led by founder, CEO, and Chairman Kuo Tai-ming. In

2002, the company's revenues reached NT$245 billion (US$7.4 billion)—a jump of nearly 70 percent over the previous year.

From Plastics to Connectors in the 1980s

Kuo Tai-ming (also known by the Westernized name Terry Kuo) had initially trained as a sailor, but decided instead to enter manufacturing in the early 1970s. In 1974, Kuo and brother Kuo Tai-chiang founded a small plastics company in Taipei's Tucheng industrial zone. The company, originally called Hon Hai Plastics Corporation, started out making plastic parts for black-and-white televisions. The company quickly added its own mold-making equipment, and in 1975 changed its name, to Hon Hai Industrial Corporation. Sales that year were just NT$16 million (less than US$500,000 at 2003 exchange rates).

Yet Kuo Tai-ming was committed to leading his company into Taiwan's major leagues. Indeed, Kuo would later claim not to have taken more than three days off at a time over the next nearly 30 years, working 15 hours per day, six days per week. As the famously reclusive Kuo told *Business Week* in a rare interview: You need real discipline. A leader shouldn't sleep more than his people; you should be the first one in, the last one out."

By the late 1970s, Kuo had already begun to develop an interest in a new market—that of the computer and electronics industries. If the basis of these industries remained for the time being in the United States and Europe, manufacturers had already begun to look to the Far East for the production of certain components—a trend that ultimately led to the rise of a number of Asian countries, and especially Taiwan as manufacturing centers for the computer industry.

Kuo quickly recognized the potential for producing computer components and led the company into developing its own range of products. At first, Kuo targeted the connectors market, and by 1981 Hon Hai, which adopted the name Foxconn for its international sales, had converted itself to a specialist subcontractor of connectors for the computer industry. Where other manufacturers focused on producing more high-profile components, Hon Hai concentrated its efforts on developing and producing the parts to connect the components together. In 1982, the company added a new product line—electric wire assembly.

Vision: From computer connectors, Foxconn has moved into communications connectors and connectors for consumer products. Similarly, from PC enclosures Foxconn has expanded into server enclosures and notebook enclosures. Stepping into the 21st century, Foxconn will continue to focus on three major business directions: computers, consumers, and communications. With a strong R&D capability and expertise in mold making and tooling, Foxconn is well equipped to meet any future challenges. Foxconn will continue to leverage on its strengths in global logistics to provide its customers with a fully integrated service. With sound management and clear business objectives, Foxconn is confident it will maintain solid growth in the future.

This was not the most exciting segment of the computer sector, yet it was perhaps the most universal, meeting the needs of the variety of computer formats and systems in existence at the time. Hon Hai's commitment to such low-profile segments enabled the company to grow strongly through the 1980s.

Kuo backed up his capacity to adapt to new markets with a willingness to invest in infrastructure. In 1983, for example, the company opened a new factory, also in Tucheng. The new facility enabled the company to step up both production and quality levels. Hon Hai now began targeting the world's emerging computer industry giants as customers. By the end of the decade, the company had already achieved a prominent place in the order books of many of the world's largest computer companies. The company's growth enabled it to adopt a policy of working closely with—and exclusively for—top tier companies. Unlike its competitors, however, Hon Hai made no effort to enter the branded market, contenting itself with an OEM role.

International Producer in the 1990s

Like many of the other rising Taiwanese computer manufacturers, Hon Hai at first gained an edge through its ability to churn out products at low prices compared to its Western competitors. Kuo recognized early on, however, that the strong growth in Taiwan's economy and the resulting rise in wages would cut into the company's ability to compete on price. In response, Kuo led Hon Hai to the Chinese mainland, becoming the first Taiwanese manufacturer to launch production on the continent in 1988.

Hon Hai went public in 1991, listing on the Taiwan stock exchange. Despite the public offering, the company, and Kuo, maintained their publicity-shy, almost secretive nature. While market observers complained about the group's lack of financial transparency, and particularly for leaving unclear the source of the group's profits, shareholders had little to complain about—within ten years, the group had become Taiwan's leading private sector computer company, with a market capitalization worth US$8 billion. Kuo's more than 25 percent stake in the company placed him among the world's 500 richest people.

The public offering enabled Hon Hai to begin a new era of expansion, with a focus particularly on the international manu-

facturing scene. The company moved to expand its fledgling mainland China operation with the construction of two new factories, in Shenzhen and Kunshan. Both factories launched production in 1993.

In 1994, Hon Hai added research and development sites in the United States and Japan. The move brought the company not only closer to these two primary computer markets, it also brought it closer to its main customers. Hon Hai, which traded as Foxconn overseas, showed itself a ready partner for the industry's major players, especially in its willingness to adapt to its customers' requirements—developing new products and entire product lines. For this effort, Hon Hai built up a strong team of more than 3,000 engineers and 100 Ph.D. holders.

Hon Hai's team of developers became one of the most dynamic in the Taiwanese high-tech sector, registering nearly 300 new patents in 1995 alone. By the beginning of the 2000s, the company had received more than 2,000 patents, many of which were developed in response to specific customer requests. Following its customers led the company into a variety of new markets, such as the launch of PC cases and enclosures production in 1996. By investing massively, the company entered its new area with a bang—within a year, Hon Hai counted among the world's largest PC case and enclosure groups, building "barebones" units for IBM, Dell, Apple, and Compaq, among others. Hon Hai had also by then become the world's leading maker of connectors for the computer industry.

As part of its new business, Hon Hai began preparing to move closer to its customers. In 1998, the company opened production facilities in England and Scotland. The following year, Hon Hai added manufacturing capacity in the United States, including an SMT production site in Houston, and in Ireland, where the group built a facility in direct support of the company's contract to supply enclosures for Dell's European PC operation. The group also joined in on the fast-rising notebook computer sector, launching a new subsidiary, Omni Switch Inc., in partnership with Quanta Computer Inc. and Inventec Corp. By the end of that year, the group's sales had topped NT$52 billion (US$1.5 billion).

Hon Hai's longstanding relationship with Apple brought it to the European continent in 2000, when the group constructed a factory in the Czech Republic in order to supply the barebones PCs for Apple's newest generation of iMac computers. Meanwhile, the company continued to expand its product range, adding motherboards for Intel—a move that included Hon Hai's takeover of Intel's manufacturing site in Puerto Rico. The company signed on another important client that year as well, when it agreed to produce components for Sony Corporation's Playstation 2 console.

Diversified Technology Group in the New Century

By the end of 2001, Hon Hai had already claimed the lead as the world's number one motherboard manufacturer. The company's revenues reflected the group's growth, soaring past US$4.5 billion and winning the group the position as Taiwan's leading private sector computer component manufacturer. By then, however, Hon Hai had already begun to take steps to ensure its growth streak would continue into the new century.

Key Dates:

1974: Kuo Tai-ming and his brother set up Hon Hai Plastics Corporation in Tucheng, Taiwan, to produce plastic components for black-and-white televisions.
1975: Company changes name to Hon Hai Industrial Corporation and begins development and production of molded parts.
1981: Company begins manufacturing connectors for computer industry.
1988: Company launches first manufacturing operations in mainland China.
1991: Hon Hai goes public on Taiwan stock exchange.
1994: Company opens research and development centers in Japan and the United States.
1996: Hon Hai begins production of PC cases, becoming world leader within one year.
1998: Hon Hai opens manufacturing facilities in Scotland and the United Kingdom.
1999: Company opens manufacturing plants in the United States and Ireland.
2000: Hon Hai opens factory in Czech Republic to produce iMac computers for Apple; takes over Intel's motherboard production facility in Puerto Rico.
2001: Hon Hai enters production of mobile telephone components.
2002: Hon Hai begins construction of new $1 billion facility in mainland China.
2003: Construction of new $1 billion LCD factory in Taiwan is undertaken; Motorola cell phone factory in Mexico is acquired.

As computer sales slowed at the beginning of decade, Hon Hai sought new areas for expansion, developing a "3C" strategy of developing computer, communications, and consumer appliance components.

The company launched the communications branch of its new strategy in 2001 by entering the mobile telephone market. By the beginning of 2002, the company had succeeded in winning a contract to supply components to cell phone leader Nokia. In that year, Hon Hai found its first target for the consumer appliance sector, launching a new, US$1 billion facility in Taiwan to produce LCD screens in August 2002. At the same time, Hon Hai announced construction of an industrial complex in China as well, expected to cost the group between US$700 million and US$1 billion.

As group sales rocketed past NT$245 billion (US$7.3 billion) in 2002, Hon Hai showed no signs of slowing down. In that year, the company received new orders from both Gateway and Apple that were expected to boost it to the top of the world's computer component suppliers. Hon Hai's mobile telephone operation also picked up steam, as the company announced its acquisition of Finland's Eimo Oy in September 2003. One month later, Hon Hai followed up that acquisition with an agreement to acquire Motorola's Mexico-based cellular phone manufacturing plant for US$18 million. The company also announced its plans to develop component manufacturing operations for the increasingly computer-laden automobile market. Former sailing student Kuo Tai-ming continued to lead his multinational components empire with a steady hand.

Principal Subsidiaries

Foxconn International, Inc.; Fox Semicon Integrated Tech Inc.; Foxteq Engineering; InnoLux Display Corp; Omni Switch Inc.

Principal Competitors

Acer Inc.; ASUSTeK Computer Inc.; Tatung Co.; Gigabyte Technology Company Ltd.; VIA Technologies Inc.; Ritek Corporate Sales; Advanced Application Technology Inc.; SerComm Corp.; Kouwell Electronics Corp.; Flextronics International Ltd.; Solectron Corporation; Sanmina-SCI Corporation.

Further Reading

Chin, Spencer, "Hon Hai Follows the Leaders," *EBN*, December 15, 2002, p. 16.
Flannery, Russell, "Out of the Limelight," *Forbes*, April 14, 2003, p. 44.
Hille, Kathrin, "Further Growth for Hon Hai Precision," *Financial Times*, September 1, 2003, p. 16.
"Hon Hai Lands NT$16 Bil Orders," *China Post*, September 7, 2003.
"Hon Hai Precision Remains Largest Private Maker in Taiwan in 2002," *Taiwan Economic News*, April 28, 2003.
"The King of Outsourcing," *Business Week*, July 8, 2002, p. 62.
Wang, Lisa, "Taiwan's Technology Leader Kuo Tai-ming," *Taiwan News*, June 2, 2001.

—M. L. Cohen

HVB Group

Am Tuckerpark
80538 Munich
Germany
Telephone: (89) 378-0
Fax: (89) 378-27784
Web site: http://www.hvbgroup.com

Public Company
Incorporated: 1869 as Bayerische Vereinsbank A.G.
Employees: 65,526
Total Assets: EUR 669.1 billion ($769.6 billion) (2003)
Stock Exchanges: Berlin Bremenk Düsseldorf Frankfurt
    Hamburg Hannover Munich Stuttgart XETRA
    Vienna Zurich Paris
Ticker Symbol: WKN 802200
NAIC: 551111 Offices of Bank Holding Companies;
    522110 Commercial Banking; 522291 Consumer
    Lending; 523110 Investment Banking and Securities
    Dealing; 523920 Portfolio Management; 523930
    Investment Advice; 523991 Trust, Fiduciary, and
    Custody Activities; 525910 Open-End Investment
    Funds

HVB Group not only ranks as the number two bank in Germany (behind Deutsche Bank AG) and the leading bank in its home base of Bavaria and in Austria (through its majority-owned subsidiary, Bank Austria Creditanstalt AG), it also has major presences throughout central and Eastern Europe, including in the five biggest nations in that region: the Czech Republic, Hungary, Poland, Slovakia, and Slovenia. Overall, it is one of the five largest banks in Europe. Its network of 2,100 branch offices serves more than 8.5 million customers in about 30 countries. The bank focuses primarily on individuals and midsized companies, offering deposit and lending services, private banking, asset management, mutual funds, investment banking, and corporate finance. HVB also has a substantial commercial real estate finance unit, but it is in the process of being spun off into a separate entity to be known as Hypo Real Estate Group.

HVB Group was created in 1998 through the merger of the two main Bavarian-based regional banks, Bayerische Vereinsbank A.G. and Bayerische Hypotheken- und Wechsel-Bank AG—rivals since their 19th-century foundings. The new super-regional bank was initially known as Bayerische Hypo- und Vereinsbank Aktiengesellschaft, before adopting the more internationally palatable HVB Group. Unlike Deutsche Bank, for example, HVB has kept its focus on its core market, dubbing itself ''the Bank in the Heart of Europe'' and largely resisting the allure of overseas adventures.

Early History of Bayerische Vereinsbank

Bayerische Vereinsbank A.G. traces its origins to 1869, when King Ludwig II of Bavaria granted a license to a consortium of private bankers to found a Munich-based commercial bank that would serve the needs of the growing Bavarian economy. Ludwig II is better known as a patron of the composer Richard Wagner and as the eccentric sovereign who dotted the Bavarian landscape with a series of fairy tale-like castles, so the bank was not his most colorful legacy but it did prove to be a lasting one.

In 1869 trade licenses and compulsory guild memberships were eliminated in Germany, opening up new entrepreneurial opportunities, and Bayerische Vereinsbank's initial mission was to encourage economic expansion. In 1870 it loaned money to the Bavarian Railway, and in 1871 it was granted the right to operate as a mortgage bank, issuing real estate loans and mortgage bonds. This last development transformed Bayerische Vereinsbank into an institution remarkably similar to Bayerische Hypotheken- und Wechsel-Bank (commonly known as Hypo-Bank), a mortgage bank established in 1835 by decree of Ludwig I of Bavaria. The rivalry between these two Bavarian banks intensified in 1899 when the Mortgage Banking Act forbade the further establishment of banks offering both mortgages and commercial loans, and it endured right up to their late-20th-century merger.

Bayerische Vereinsbank did not participate to any substantial degree in the German foreign banking boom of the late 19th century. It did loan money to the Austrian railway and underwrite securities issued by the Turkish government, but international business was left mostly to the large, Berlin-based Grossbanken that have always dominated the German banking industry.

Second-Tier Player in First Half of 20th Century

Indeed, the bank remained a relatively small institution into the 20th century. Although it had 15 branch offices at the beginning of World War I, the size of a bank's branch network was not the only measure of its importance. If the Grossbanken, such as Deutsche Bank and Dresdner Bank, occupied the first tier of German banking, then Bayerische Vereinsbank ranked in the middle of the second tier, with other large provincial banks such as Hypo-Bank and Barmer Bank. German finance had been moving toward ever greater centralization since the nation was united under Bismarck, with the Grossbanken wielding considerable power from their bases in Berlin. This trend continued through the economic crises that characterized the years following Germany's defeat in 1918, as struggling banks found that size often determined whether they survived or not.

Both during and after the war, the second-tier banks responded to this trend by joining each other in "community of interest" agreements, exchanging representatives from their boards of directors and operating in accord with each other. These agreements allowed the provincials to fend off takeovers from Berlin and preserve their independence. In the early 1920s, Bayerische Vereinsbank sought to consolidate its position by acquiring an interest in the small Berlin bank E.S. Friedman & Company and by allying itself with Bayerische Handelsbank AG. In 1922 it entered into a community of interest agreement with Mendelssohn & Company, a prestigious banking house based in Berlin and Amsterdam. Mendelssohn acquired an interest in Bayerische Vereinsbank and representation on its board of directors; Bayerische Vereinsbank justified the deal on the grounds that it would gain a valuable friend in Berlin without sacrificing autonomy.

Bayerische Vereinsbank prospered during the late 1920s; its capital grew from 21 million Reichsmarks in 1927 to 31.1 million in 1930, and its reserves grew from 9.3 million Reichsmarks to 13.8 million. Nonetheless, it remained somewhat smaller than rival Hypo-Bank in 1930 and considerably smaller than any of the Grossbanken.

Its lack of size and power relative to the Grossbanken should also be taken into account when considering the years of National Socialist rule. Virtually every major bank helped finance Germany's war effort to some degree until the German economy collapsed in 1944. When Allied occupation authorities investigated the extent to which the German business community had aided the Nazis, they found culpability among the Grossbanken, in part because their size and influence made their complete innocence inconceivable, but the investigation did not indicate that any of the second-tier banks were suspected of war crimes. Accordingly, in 1947, the occupation authorities decreed that the Grossbanken who survived the war should be broken up into smaller institutions, but smaller banks such as Bayerische Vereinsbank were not punished.

BV's Postwar Expansion

The bank emerged from the war with 52 branches. From there, it embarked on a course of expansion and internationalization that ensured it a position of prominence among West Germany's regional banks. In the 1950s, Bayerische Vereinsbank began to expand beyond its traditional base in Bavaria and to internationalize its business. It did so largely without opening foreign branches; it opened its first overseas representative office in Beirut in 1958, but eventually closed it. The bank did not venture abroad again until 1970, when offices were opened in Tokyo and Rio de Janeiro. It established a presence in the United States when its New York office opened on Madison Avenue in 1971; offices in Chicago, Los Angeles, Cleveland, and Atlanta appeared over the course of the decade. It also opened offices in Tehran (1971), Paris (1973), Johannesburg (1974), London (1976), Bahrain (1979), Hong Kong (1979), and Beijing (1986).

After the end of World War II, Bayerische Vereinsbank CEO Baron Hans Christof Freiherr von Tucher publicly suggested that his bank should merge with Hypo-Bank. The three surviving Grossbanken—Deutsche Bank, Dresdner Bank, and Commerzbank—had re-formed in 1958, just as large and influential as ever, to become West Germany's Big Three commercial banks. It was von Tucher's idea to merge Bavaria's two largest banks into an institution that could compete with them. Nothing came of his original proposal, but in 1969 Bayerische Vereinsbank and Hypo-Bank did begin merger talks. Negotiations continued for two years, then broke up when Hypo-Bank balked at the Bavarian state government's insistence the Bayerische Staatsbank, Bavaria's third largest bank, be included in the merger. In the aftermath of the failed merger, Bayerische Vereinsbank agreed to acquire Bayerische Staatsbank for DM 40 million—a bargain, because the latter's assets were valued at DM 5 billion.

In addition to its international expansion, Bayerische Vereinsbank produced a record of steady asset growth throughout the 1970s. In 1982 Wolfgang Graebner, a managing partner of Berliner Handels- und Frankfurter Bank, told *Euromoney*, "The BV bank is a conservative bank, and that's a genuine compliment. . . . They've achieved balance sheet growth instead of dramatic headlines; a smooth ride through troubled waters. That's what I call banking." In the late 1970s and early 1980s, an economic downturn and crises, such as the collapse of Bankhaus IG Herstatt and a sharp drop in Commerzbank's profits

Key Dates:

1835: Bayerische Hypotheken- und Wechsel-Bank AG (Hypo-Bank) is founded in Munich by decree of King Ludwig I of Bavaria.

1869: King Ludwig II of Bavaria grants a license to a consortium of private bankers to establish a Munich-based commercial bank, Bayerische Vereinsbank A.G. (BV).

1879: Hypo-Bank begins underwriting and securities trading.

1906: New regulatory laws force Hypo-Bank to spin off its insurance operations, creating the separate but wholly owned Bayerische Versicherungsbank AG.

Early 1920s: BV allies itself with Bayerische Handelsbank AG.

1921: Hypo-Bank enters into community of interest agreement with Barmer Bankverein and Allgemeine Deutsche Creditanstalt of Leipzig.

1922: BV enters into community of interest agreement with Mendelssohn & Company.

1923: Hypo-Bank sells its share in insurance subsidiary Bayerische Versicherungsbank.

1970: BV opens its first foreign representative offices in Tokyo and Rio de Janeiro.

1971: Bayerische Staatsbank AG, Bavaria's third largest bank, is acquired by BV.

1990: BV gains majority control of Hamburg-based Vereins- und Westbank AG.

1992: Majority stake in Schoeller & Co. Bank AG, an Austrian private bank, is secured by BV.

1994: Hypo-Bank launches Direkt Anlage Bank, the first discount telephone brokerage service in Germany.

1997: BV and Hypo-Bank announce that they will merge.

1998: Merger is consummated, creating Bayerische Hypo- und Vereinsbank AG, or HypoVereinsbank.

2000: Bank Austria Creditanstalt is acquired.

2002: HypoVereinsbank changes its name to HVB Group; records a net loss for the year; announces commercial real estate finance operations will be spun off as Hypo Real Estate Group.

2003: About one-quarter of Bank Austria Creditanstalt is sold through an initial public offering.

---

after a bad hunch on the direction of interest rates, sent shudders through the West German banking industry. But Bayerische Vereinsbank, thanks to what *Euromoney* called its ''pushy but conservative style,'' gained ground on Hypo-Bank and the Big Three. Depending on what statistical measure one used, Bayerische Vereinsbank either was very close to overtaking or had already overtaken Hypo-Bank as West Germany's fourth largest bank by 1982.

A contemporary trend in which Bayerische Vereinsbank did take part was the divestiture of business holdings. Public concern mounted during the 1970s over the influence that Germany's banks wielded in the commercial and industrial sectors through stock holdings and corporate directorships. To head off possible calls for nationalization, the banks began to sell off their portfolios. In 1982 Bayerische Vereinsbank sold its 36 percent interest in Hacker-Pschorr Brau, a Munich brewery, to local construction magnate Joseph Schoerghuber.

In 1985, however, the bank made a substantial investment in West Germany's defense industry. It bought a 5 percent interest in Messerschmidt-Boelkhow-Bloehm, becoming the first bank to ever hold an interest in the nation's premier aerospace concern. It then joined Messerschmidt and Dresdner Bank in a takeover bid for Krauss Maffei, manufacturer of the Leopard 2 main battle tank.

In the late 1980s Bayerische Vereinsbank continued to expand its international presence. In 1988 it acquired First National Bank of Chicago's branch offices in Milan and Rome. Then, in May 1989, it concluded a historic agreement with four other European banks—Italy's Banca Commerciale, Austria's Creditanstalt-Bankverein, France's Credit Lyonnais, and the Finnish bank Kansallis-Osake-Pankki—and the Soviet banks Vnesheconobank, Promstroybank, and Sberbank, to form the International Bank of Moscow. The bank constituted the first

joint banking venture between Western and Soviet institutions since the Revolution of 1917 and was intended to finance foreign trade and provide financial advice. By the end of the 1980s Bayerische Vereinsbank had also expanded into Eastern Europe by setting up cooperative arrangements with banks in Hungary and Bulgaria.

The Evolution of Vereinsbank into a European Superregional Bank, 1990s

In 1990 Albrecht Schmidt took over as chief executive, becoming the first non-Bavarian to head the bank. Schmidt engineered Bayerische Vereinsbank's shift from being a regional German bank to a superregional European bank—somewhat akin to the superregionals then being formed in the United States. Among the first moves was the securing of a presence throughout Germany. The bank had ended the 1980s with about 400 domestic branches, most of which were in Bavaria and the southwest. In 1990 Bayerische Vereinsbank increased its minority stake in Hamburg-based Vereins- und Westbank AG to 75 percent and began integrating the operations of this large northern German bank into its branch network. Following German reunification in 1990, the bank expanded rapidly into eastern Germany, operating nearly 80 branches there by 1994. And Bayerische Vereinsbank began filling in the one remaining hole in its German network by opening up new branches in the highly industrialized Ruhr area.

In addition to Germany, the bank's initial superregion also included Denmark, Austria, Switzerland, and the Czech Republic. In mid-1992 Schoeller & Co. Bank AG, one of the largest private banking groups in Austria with assets of about $2 billion, was acquired. Schoeller operated 13 branches throughout Austria, making Bayerische Vereinsbank the first German bank to have nationwide representation there. In 1993 Bayerische Vereinsbank opened a regional branch in Prague, and one year later the bank took full control of Bankhaus von Ernst & Cie. AG, an old Swiss private banking firm with branches in Bern, Zurich, Geneva, and London and assets totaling $1.2 billion.

During the mid-1990s both Bayerische Vereinsbank and Hypo-Bank outperformed the Big Three German banks because of the Bavaria-based banks' strong mortgage banking business. By 1995 Bayerische Vereinsbank ranked as the number four German bank with total assets of DM 320 billion ($229.2 billion). That year the bank raised about DM 1 billion ($731 million) through a rights issue to help fund further expansion of its activities at home and abroad. One area in which the bank was investing heavily was in new technology, spending DM 400 million on information technology alone during 1994. Bayerische Vereinsbank became the first German bank to introduce telephone banking nationwide, and it also launched an online banking service that enabled customers to access their accounts and make transactions via their home computers. In 1996 the bank introduced a new direct online bank called Advance Bank.

The bank also continued its international expansion. Its European superregion grew with the bank's entrance into Poland. It established a presence in Asia, opening a regional branch in Singapore in 1995 and an office in Shanghai, China, as well. Most surprisingly, Schmidt announced in November 1995 that Bayerische Vereinsbank had reached an agreement to acquire the U.S. brokerage firm Oppenheimer & Co. for about $400 million. Through this deal, the bank hoped to be able to offer its corporate customers, most of which were medium-sized companies, more investment banking services. But the proposed takeover ran afoul of U.S. regulatory acts, particularly the Glass-Steagall Act, which mandated the separation of commercial banking and securities underwriting. Thus to take over Oppenheimer, Bayerische Vereinsbank would have had to shutter its existing U.S. banking operations. It was willing to do so after acquiring Oppenheimer, but the U.S. Federal Reserve Board wanted the closure of the banking operations to come first, something that Bayerische Vereinsbank was unwilling to agree to. The deal was therefore scotched.

In July 1996 Deutsche Bank revealed that it had bought a 5 percent stake in Bayerische Vereinsbank. Speculation immediately became rife about a possible takeover of Vereinsbank by Deutsche, which by that point was the largest bank in Europe. Schmidt, however, used this potential prelude to a raid as a spur to engineer his own takeover, that of Hypo-Bank, finally bringing together the two longtime Bavarian rivals.

Early History of Bayerische Hypotheken- und Wechsel-Bank

Bayerische Hypotheken- und Wechsel-Bank AG was founded in 1835 by decree of King Ludwig I of Bavaria, who believed that his nation needed a new bank to increase the availability of credit and to stimulate the economy. His economic advisers decided that the new bank should be formed as a private company and, accordingly, Hypo-Bank's first share offering was made in December 1834. Hypo-Bank opened in October 1835 in the Preysing Palace in Munich, and two years later, it opened its first branch office, in the Bavarian city of Augsburg.

At its inception, Hypo-Bank's activities fell into three principal categories: mortgage banking, commercial banking, and

insurance. Deposits were not an important part of its business; they were, in fact, regarded as a potential capital drain. The bank's founding charter prohibited all forms of speculation, merchant banking, or investing in foreign securities. As the national bank of Bavaria, it had the exclusive privilege of issuing paper currency, but abandoned this practice in 1875 when the new Imperial Bank Law placed severe restrictions on issuing banks. The mortgage business was the bank's most popular activity from the outset. The introduction of mortgage bonds in 1864 added another popular and profitable dimension to its operations.

As an important part of the Bavarian economy, Hypo-Bank was vulnerable to the force of larger events. The political upheavals of 1848–49 threatened its securities business and prompted the bank to stop paying interest on its few deposits. It prospered, however, as a result of the Franco-Prussian War of 1870–71. It placed three million Gulden worth of war bonds at the outbreak of hostilities to support the imperial government's financial needs, and its commercial operations prospered during the economic boom that followed the German victory.

Hypo-Bank entered underwriting and securities trading in 1879 when it syndicated a Bavarian railroad bond worth 60 million Reichsmarks. It also began underwriting and dealing in foreign securities, although its 1879 annual report sought to reassure shareholders by emphasizing that the bank would touch only blue-chip issues. At first, it marketed only Austro-Hungarian, Russian, Romanian, and Bulgarian issues, but in 1889 it began marketing Asian, American, and Latin American securities in small quantities as well.

These latter developments came at a time when large German commercial banks were rapidly expanding their international operations. While Hypo-Bank was already a leading mortgage bank, its commercial banking department remained small compared to the Berlin-based Grossbanken. Nonetheless, it joined the big banks in founding the Deutsch-Asiatische Bank in Shanghai in 1889. It was also part of the Asiatische Konsortium, a famous group of German banks that cooperated with each other in loaning money to Asian nations.

Hypo-Bank began to outgrow its facilities in the Preysing Palace 50 years after its founding. During the 1880s the bank began purchasing houses around Munich and converting them into headquarters for its various divisions. A project converting its property on Theatinerstrasse into a new headquarters for the entire bank was proposed in 1893 and finished in 1898; this building was destroyed in World War II but Hypo-Bank's headquarters were rebuilt on the same site.

Surviving the Volatile First Half of the 20th Century

Hypo-Bank became Germany's leading mortgage banker when its volume of mortgage loans topped one billion Reichsmarks in 1908 and its total of mortgage bonds reached that level in 1909. But new imperial laws passed in 1906 regulating the insurance industry forced Hypo-Bank to spin off its insurance operations. The new insurance bank, which was named the Bayerische Versicherungsbank AG, nonetheless remained a wholly owned subsidiary of Hypo-Bank and inherited the Preysing Palace offices.

Despite its new stature, Hypo-Bank stayed a regional bank into the 20th century, while the Grossbanken grew ever larger and more powerful. As a result of this increasing centralization in the German banking industry, many smaller institutions were forced into alliances with the largest banks, surrendering their independence in exchange for the security that went with size. Hypo-Bank allied itself with both Dresdner Bank and Discontogesellschaft, but broke away in 1921 by entering a "community of interest" agreement with Barmer Bankverein and Allgemeine Deutsche Creditanstalt of Leipzig. Under the terms of the agreement, which was typical of provincial banks in the 1920s, the three institutions exchanged representatives from their boards of directors and agreed to coordinate their operations.

Of the years 1914–48, Hypo-Bank's official history says, "Business was at best difficult. . . . Success was measured simply in the ability to survive and assure long-term viability." After the outbreak of World War I, the bank's mortgage business benefited from money that flowed into agriculture from military purchases, but it suffered as the war hastened a crack in the urban real estate market. The bank continued to suffer as building activity, and the demand for mortgages, slackened during the war. Governmental decree also closed the stock market at the beginning of hostilities, limiting activity in the commercial sector. But the war did not stop Hypo-Bank's expansion; it purchased the Munich bank Fränkel & Selz in 1915, and in 1916 it bought the 50 percent of Nuremberg's Bayerische Disconto- und Wechsel-Bank it did not already own. It also expanded its branch network throughout Bavaria.

Hypo-Bank floundered along with the rest of the nation in the economic crises of the 1920s. Radical currency devaluation and skyrocketing inflation in 1922 and 1923 forced the bank to virtually shut down its mortgage business, as loans made under more favorable economic conditions were paid back in increasingly worthless paper currency. The Weimar government undertook currency reform in 1923, and the next year Hypo-Bank began to rebuild its mortgage business from scratch. Bank employees had to convert 73,000 old mortgages and 1.2 million mortgage bonds into the new currency, and the bank introduced gold-backed mortgages and bonds. Also in 1923, the bank suddenly sold all of its shares in its insurance subsidiary to the insurance concerns Münchner Rückversicherungsgesellschaft and Allianz Versicherung.

The economic crisis of 1928–29 that presaged the Great Depression in Germany hurt the bank's commercial department as rising deposits and declining demand for loans coupled to strain its resources. Economic conditions worsened in 1930 and all forms of commercial business declined significantly. In 1931, public panic reached its peak with a run on the nation's financial institutions, culminating in the closing of all banks and stock exchanges on July 14. As a result of the crisis, the bank was forced to reduce its annual dividends by 50 percent in 1933 and 1934. Nevertheless, its fortunes began to improve slightly in 1934. Although demand for credit was low, government rearmament and war financing stimulated the economy.

Hypo-Bank's official history is largely mute about the war years, saying only that the bank's mortgage business "continued to develop satisfactorily" until the economy collapsed in 1944, while deposits increased and commercial lending de-

clined. The Allied occupation authorities investigating the German banking industry after the war turned up evidence of possible war crimes principally among the Grossbanken; smaller institutions such as Hypo-Bank were seldom, if ever, mentioned in American newspaper accounts of the investigation. The years immediately following the war also proved painful for Hypo-Bank, as it had to write off mortgages on German property destroyed by the fighting, as well as those in Alsace-Lorraine and Soviet-occupied eastern Germany.

Postwar Expansion of Hypo-Bank

All of that began to change, however, on June 20, 1948, when the West German government enacted radical currency reform and began to rebuild its shattered economy. Aided by the Marshall Plan, economic conditions in the Bundesrepublik gradually approached a state of normalcy during the early years of the Cold War, and Hypo-Bank, riding the tide of increasing prosperity, could report in 1953 that its assets had reached DM 1 billion.

The 1950s for Hypo-Bank were marked by expansion and fundamental strengthening of its financial position. Its capital stock increased from DM 27 million in 1948 to DM 100 million in 1960, and its reserves went from nothing to DM 155 million in the same period. The bank's mortgage sector, its traditional mainstay, remained strong, but was surpassed in business volume by its general banking division. Hypo-Bank's workforce more than doubled, from 2,603 employees in 1948 to nearly 5,600 ten years later. It also began expanding beyond its geographic base in Bavaria, making business contacts in other German states as well as abroad. Nonetheless, *Euromoney* characterized Hypo-Bank's philosophy during these years as adhering to the old Bavarian proverb: "Bleib im Land und nähre dich redlich"—stay at home and live off the fat of the land.

Hypo-Bank continued to prosper and expand through the 1960s. In 1967, *Barron's* described it as one of three West German regional banks with more than $1 billion worth of assets, along with Bank für Gemeinwirtschaft and longtime Bavarian rival Bayerische Vereinsbank. In 1969 it began to negotiate a merger with Bayerische Vereinsbank that would have produced an institution large enough to rival the nation's Big Three commercial banks (Deutsche Bank, Dresdner Bank, and Commerzbank), but it broke off talks in 1971 when the Bavarian state government insisted that Bayerische Staatsbank be included. Also in 1969, it officially joined the trend among financial institutions worldwide by declaring that it would expand and diversify in order to keep up with its major competitors. Hypo-Bank opened 100 new branches between 1969 and 1975, including 37 outside Bavaria. It also internationalized its securities operations, entered the currency trading business, and loaned more money overseas. In 1972, it joined with Banque de Bruxelles, Algemene Bank Nederland, and Dresdner Bank to form ABD Securities Corporation in New York, offering securities and investment banking services to European investors interested in the United States.

This penchant for limiting risks through joint ventures also marked two of Hypo-Bank's other major enterprises during the 1970s. In 1972 it joined ABECOR (Associated Banks of Europe Corporation) along with its ABD Securities partners; Banque Nationale de Paris, Banca Nazionale de Lavoro, Barclays Bank,

Banque Internationale à Luxembourg, and Österreichische Länderbank later joined them. Despite early doubts from some observers, by 1983 ABECOR had 12,000 branches and $440 billion worth of assets. Hypo-Bank also joined 11 other European and Latin American banks to form the EuroLatin-American Bank in 1974.

Acquisitions and portfolio expansion also marked the bank's activities during this time. In 1971 Hypo-Bank purchased Westfalenbank of Bochum, and between 1968 and 1973, its stock holdings constituting a 10 percent or larger stake in a company increased from DM 148 million to DM 995 million. It made its most famous purchases in the brewery industry, including minority interests in Dortmunder-Union-Brauerei in 1969 and Löwenbräu in 1973. In the late 1970s, the bank began to sell off its industrial holdings amid mounting public concern over the power that West German banks were able to wield through their extensive stock portfolios and numerous company directorships. In 1982 Hypo-Bank began to concentrate instead on acquisition and expansion in finance, both foreign and domestic. In 1987 it bought a 15 percent interest in Italy's Banco Trento & Bolanzo. By the late 1980s Hypo-Bank ranked as the seventh largest bank in Germany and had been surpassed by Bayerische Vereinsbank as the largest Bavaria-based bank earlier in the decade.

Hypo-Bank's International Growth in the 1990s

Leading Hypo-Bank into the 1990s was Eberhard Martini, who had been named chairman in May 1988. Martini had two initial aims: transforming the bank's core property-lending business into a pan-European operation and diversifying into international asset management for private and institutional investors, including pension funds. By going after these two niches on a wider basis, Martini hoped to stop Hypo-Bank from being swallowed up by its ever larger rivals, both inside and outside of Germany. On the asset management side, Hypo-Bank bought a 50 percent stake in Foreign & Colonial Management Ltd., a London-based manager of international investment trusts, in 1989.

Following German reunification in 1990, Hypo-Bank moved aggressively into eastern Germany, opening up 23 branches and subbranches in 19 cities. The bank took an even more aggressive approach in funding real estate projects in eastern Germany—an expansion that would later come back to haunt Martini. Hypo-Bank was also quick to establish bank subsidiaries in the emerging Eastern European states. In 1992 Hypo-Bank CZ a.s. was set up in the Czech Republic. One year later came the creation of three more subsidiaries: Hypo-Bank Hungaria Rt., Hypo-Bank Polska S.A., and Hypo-Bank Slovakia a.s. In 1994 Hypo-Bank enlarged its pan-European network of property-lending operations by purchasing a 25 percent interest in Vienna-based Hypo-Bausparkasse Wien and by forming a Czech building society called Hypo Stavebni Sporiteina a.s. That same year, the bank launched Direkt Anlage Bank, the first discount telephone brokerage service in Germany, and opened representative offices in Beijing and Shanghai, China. In 1996 Hypo-Bank began installing bank branches in German supermarkets. The bank's asset management ambitions turned to the United States in 1996 when it entered into an alliance with Massachusetts Financial Services, a mutual fund company owned by Sun Life of Canada. By mid-1997, when the merger of Hypo-Bank and Bayerische

Vereinsbank was announced, Hypo-Bank had assets of DM 339 billion ($188 billion).

The Early, Troubled Years of HypoVereinsbank/HVB Group

By 1997 executives at Hypo-Bank were becoming concerned that Allianz, the huge Munich-based insurer, which had a 10 percent stake in Hypo-Bank, would pressure them into a merger with Dresdner Bank, which was also allied with Allianz. Meantime, Schmidt, over at Bayerische Vereinsbank, wanted to avoid a takeover by Deutsche Bank, which had bought a 5 percent stake in Vereinsbank in 1996. Schmidt approached Martini about a possible merger to stave off these unwanted advances, and a deal was soon struck and announced in July 1997. Although touted as a "merger of equals," the deal, as consummated in September 1998, really amounted to a Vereinsbank takeover of Hypo-Bank. Part of the unique structure of the deal involved Vereinsbank exchanging 19.3 million shares of Allianz stock for 45 percent of Hypo-Bank. Bavarian politicians, wishing to facilitate the creation of a Munich financial giant, declared the exchange of shares to be tax-free for shareholders (an incentive that was later outlawed). The politicians were also mollified by assurances that job cuts following in the wake of the merger—expected to total about 2,000 workers per year over a five-year period—would come from normal attrition and not the mass layoffs typical of a U.S.-style bank merger.

The merged entity, which was officially created on September 1, 1998, was called Bayerische Hypo- und Vereinsbank AG, or HypoVereinsbank. It ranked as the second largest bank in Germany, trailing only Deutsche Bank, with assets of about DM 800 million ($450 million), and had 40,000 employees. Given Vereinsbank's lead role in the merger, it was no surprise that Schmidt was named chairman of HypoVereinsbank; Martini took a spot on the supervisory board. HypoVereinsbank adopted Vereinsbank's strategy of being a superregional player in the European banking sector.

An unfortunate legacy from the Hypo-Bank side was that bank's reckless approach to funding real estate projects in eastern Germany in the early 1990s. By the late 1990s many of these loans had gone sour as the eastern boom went bust. In late 1997, during the period in which the Hypo-Bank-Vereinsbank merger was being consummated, Martini attempted to deal with the growing problem by setting aside a DM 1.5 billion ($840 million) provision to cover the bad real estate loans. But audits conducted in the immediate weeks following completion of the merger revealed this provision to be wholly inadequate. Schmidt announced in October 1998 that an additional DM 3.5 billion ($1.9 billion) provision was needed to cover the shaky Hypo-Bank loans. This led to a very public and lengthy battle between executives of the two predecessor banks; Martini and other Hypo-Bank executives contended that the problems had been exaggerated in an effort to force them from office. In October 1999, however, an independent audit supported the action taken by Schmidt, criticized Hypo-Bank for not recognizing the extent of the bad loans in 1997, and essentially declared Hypo-Bank's results for 1997 invalid. Martini and six other senior executives, all formerly of Hypo-Bank, resigned from HypoVereinsbank, leaving Schmidt and his followers from Vereinsbank firmly in charge.

Dealing with this scandal occupied much of the bank's attention, but integration efforts and some strategic deals did move forward. During 1998 and 1999, HypoVereinsbank purchased majority control of Bank Przemyslowo-Handlowy S.A. (BPH) of Poland. BPH was then enlarged in 1999 through the acquisition of Hypo-Bank Polska. Also during 1998 HVB Bank Czech Republic a.s. was created from the merger of Hypo-Bank's and Vereinsbank's subsidiaries in the Czech Republic.

During 2000 HypoVereinsbank acquired Bank Austria Creditanstalt, the largest bank in Austria, in a deal valued at about EUR 7.7 billion ($7.2 billion). The bank not only gained the number one position in Austria, it also secured Bank Austria's holdings in central and Eastern Europe. Among these was a majority stake in one of the largest banks in Poland, Powszechny Bank Kreditowy (PBK), which in 2001 was merged with BPH to form Bank Przemyslowo-Handlowy PBK S.A., which was the third largest bank in Poland—the largest market in Eastern Europe. The newly enlarged HypoVereinsbank had total assets of EUR 716.5 billion ($615 billion) by the end of 2000, making it the third largest bank in Europe.

During the early 2000s HypoVereinsbank was hit hard as weak economic growth depressed earnings. The bank responded in 2001 with a massive restructuring involving the closure of numerous branches and the elimination of more than 10,000 jobs—nearly 14 percent of the total payroll. Many of the job cuts were in Germany, but the bank also shed 4,000 jobs in Poland and 2,000 in Austria. The branch closures were made possible in part by customers' increased use of telephone and online banking services. HypoVereinsbank also began centering its asset management business around its Activest unit, which started to sell other companies' mutual funds. These developments made the Foreign & Colonial Management unit in the United Kingdom redundant, and it was sold to Eureko B.V., a European-wide insurance consortium. In a further retrenching move, HypoVereinsbank exited from the economically troubled country of Brazil in 2002, selling its 48 percent stake in Banco BBA-Creditanstalt S.A. to Brazil's Banco Itau S.A.

During 2002, a year in which HypoVereinsbank changed its name to the less German-sounding HVB Group, the bank had to take EUR 3.8 billion ($4.1 billion) in bad-loan provisions. These stemmed both from the continued hangover from Hypo-Bank's ill-advised eastern German loans of the 1990s and from the stagnant German economy of 2002, which led to record bankruptcies. The provisions resulted in a EUR 858 million ($917 million) net loss for HVB, forcing it to cancel its dividend.

At the beginning of 2003, HVB restructured its operations into three main operating units: Germany, Austria & Central and Eastern Europe (Austria/CEE), and Corporates & Markets. The Austria/CEE unit was led by Bank Austria Creditanstalt. A fourth unit comprising the bank's commercial real estate finance activities had been placed into discontinued operations during 2002, in advance of the 2003 spinoff of the unit into a separate entity to be known as Hypo Real Estate Group. Leading this restructuring was new chief executive Dieter Rampl, who in January 2003 was named to succeed Schmidt, who became chairman of the supervisory board. HVB also announced in early 2003 that in order to shore up its balance sheet it would dispose of EUR 100 billion in assets. The bank began

divesting nonstrategic holdings and selling off pieces of its huge investment portfolio. Proceeds of about EUR 1 billion were raised through the sale of about 25 percent of Bank Austria Creditanstalt, HVB's best-performing subsidiary, through an initial public offering on the Vienna stock exchange. HVB also sold Nuremberg-based norisbank, a consumer-finance unit, to DZ Bank for EUR 447 million ($500 million); and the Swiss private bank Bank von Ernst to the Royal Bank of Scotland plc for SFr 500 million ($381 million). In addition, in what promised to be an important streamlining of HVB's domestic operations, the bank announced in July 2003 that it would fully integrate the operations of Vereins- und Westbank, the group's retail banking unit for northern Germany, into its core German subsidiary, Bayerische Hypo- und Vereinsbank.

Principal Subsidiaries

GERMANY: Bayerische Hypo- und Vereinsbank AG; HVB Banque Luxembourg S.A.; Vereins- und Westbank AG (76.3%); Activest GmbH Marketing und Vertrieb; Activest Investmentgesellschaft mbH; Bankhaus Gebrüder Bethmann; Bankhaus Maffei & Co. KGaA; Bankhaus Neelmeyer AG; Bankhaus C.L. Seeliger (53.7%); DAB Bank AG (75.4%); FSB Fonds-ServiceBank GmbH (50%); H.F.S. Hypo-Fondsbeteiligungen für Sachwerte GmbH; HVB Leasing GmbH; Internationales Immobilien-Institut GmbH (94%); INDexCHANGE Investment AG (95.1%); Nordinvest Norddeutsche Investment-Gesellschaft mbH; Vereinsbank Victoria Bauspar Aktiengesellschaft (70%); Activest Investmentgesellschaft Luxembourg S.A.; Banco Inversión S.A. (Spain); direktanlage.at AG (Austria). AUSTRIA/CEE: Bank Austria Creditanstalt AG (77.5%); Asset Management GmbH (Austria); Bank Austria Creditanstalt d.d. (Slovenia; 77.5%); Bank Austria Creditanstalt Leasing GmbH (77.5%); Bankprivat AG (Austria); Bank Przemyslowo-Handlowy PBK S.A. (Poland; 71%); Capital Invest die Kapitalanlagegesellschaft der Bank Austria/Creditanstalt Gruppe GmbH (77.5%); Commercial Bank Biochim AD (Bulgaria; 99.7%); HVB Bank Croatia d.d. (80%); HVB Bank Czech Republic a.s.; HVB Bank Hungary Rt.; HVB Bank Romania S.A.; HVB Bank Slovakia a.s.; HVB Bank Yugoslavia A.D. (99%); Schoellerbank Aktiengesellschaft (Austria); Splitska Banka d.d. (Croatia; 90.1%). CORPORATES & MARKETS: Bayerische Hypo- und Vereinsbank AG; Bank Austria Creditanstalt AG (77.5%); HVB Banque Luxembourg S.A.; Vereins- und Westbank AG (76.3%); Bode Grabner Beye AG & Co. KG; Chemie Pensionsfonds AG; HVB Pensionsfonds AG; CA IB Corporate Finance Beratungs Gesellschaft m.b.H. (Austria); HVB Capital Asia Limited (Hong Kong); HVB Risk Management Products Inc. (U.S.A.); HVB Singapore Limited; HVB U.S. Finance Inc.; International Moscow Bank (Russia; 43.2%); Joint Stock Commercial Bank HVB Bank Ukraine (91.2%).

Principal Operating Units

Germany; Austria & Central and Eastern Europe; Corporates & Markets.

Principal Competitors

Deutsche Bank AG; Dresdner Bank AG; Commerzbank AG; DZ BANK Deutsche Zentral-Genossenschaftsbank Aktiegesellschaft; Westdeutsche Landesbank Girozentrale; Landesbank

Baden-Württemberg; Bayerische Landesbank Girozentrale; Bankgesellschaft Berlin AG.

Further Reading

"A Bavarian Botch-up," *Economist,* August 5, 2000, pp. 65–66.

"Bayerische Vereinsbank to Expand Its European Bank-Branch Network," *Wall Street Journal,* February 17, 1989.

"Beancounted Out," *Economist,* October 30, 1999, pp. 86–87.

"Built in Bavaria," *Economist,* July 26, 1997, p. 67.

Covill, Laura, "Bavarian Slow-Step," *Euromoney,* November 1997, p. 48.

Delamaide, Darrell, "Vereinsbank Starts to Drop Its Bayerische Label," *Euromoney,* January 1994, pp. 90–91.

Ewing, Jack, "Anatomy of a Tainted Merger," *Business Week,* April 12, 1999, pp. 54, 56.

Fairlamb, David, "Down for the Count: Will Bad Debt Crush Banking Giant HVB?," *Business Week,* January 20, 2003, p. 42.

Fisher, Andrew, "German Bank Shakes Off Attitudes of Old: Bayerische Vereinsbank Has Invested Heavily in New Technology," *Financial Times,* July 19, 1995, p. 20.

——, "German Banks Hope to Shake Off the Chill," *Financial Times,* December 20, 1994, p. 23.

A History of the Bayerische Hypotheken- und Wechsel-Bank, 1835–1985, Munich: Bayerische Hypotheken- und Wechsel-Bank, 1985.

"HVB Group to Restructure, Dispose of Eu100bn in Risk Assets," *Euroweek,* January 31, 2003, p. 8.

Morris, Jennifer, "The Grossbanken Have Nowhere Left to Hide," *Euromoney,* February 2002, pp. 52–57.

Rhoads, Christopher, "Bank Deal in Germany Is Nightmare," *Wall Street Journal,* May 6, 1999.

Roth, Terence, "West German Bank Plots Strategy for '90s," *Wall Street Journal,* August 14, 1989.

"Running Repairs," *Economist,* July 12, 2003, pp. 67–68.

Sesit, Michael, Greg Steinmetz, and Silvia Ascarelli, "Vereinsbank, Hypobank Set to Merge," *Wall Street Journal,* July 21, 1997, p. A3.

Shirreff, David, "Slugfest in Bavaria," *Euromoney,* December 1999, p. 87.

Siconolfi, Michael, "German Bank's Purchase of Oppenheimer Hits Unexpected Regulatory Roadblock," *Wall Street Journal,* December 14, 1995, p. C1.

Simonian, Haig, "BV Steps Forward in Modest Style," *Financial Times,* October 13, 1989, p. 33.

Walker, Marcus, "German Bank Focuses on the Unfashionable—Retail Accounts," *Wall Street Journal,* October 30, 2000, p. A26.

——, "No. 1 Bank in Austria Ties Knot: Germany's Hypo Forms Major Force in Central Europe," *Wall Street Journal,* July 24, 2000, p. A17.

Whale, P. Barrett, *Joint Stock Banking in Germany,* London: Fred Cass & Company, 1930.

—update: David E. Salamie

Irish Life & Permanent Plc

Irish Life Centre
Lower Abbey Street
Dublin, 1
Ireland
Telephone: +353 1 704-2000
Fax: +353 1 704-1900
Web site: http://www.irishlifepermanent.ie

Public Company
Incorporated: 1998
Employees: 5,294
Total Assets: $36.1 billion (2002)
Stock Exchanges: Irish
Ticker Symbol: IPM
NAIC: 522110 Commercial Banking; 522298 All Other
    Non-Depository Credit Intermediation; 524113 Direct
    Life Insurance Carriers

Irish Life & Permanent Plc (ILP) is the Republic of Ireland's third largest financial institution. The combination of Irish Life, Irish Permanent, and TSB Bank, ILP operates in both the insurance and retail banking markets. Irish Life carries out the group's insurance operations and is the country's number one provider of life insurance and pension plans, as well as other savings and investment products for the retail market and, through its Corporate Business Division, provides group pension and other insurance products to corporations and other groups and associations. Together, Irish Life's operations command a 20 percent share of its domestic market. Irish Life's retail insurance products are sold via the company's own direct sales force, other insurance intermediaries, and also through the branch network of ILP's banking arm, permanent tsb. Formed through the merger of Irish Permanent and TSB Bank, permanent tsb offers a full range of personal finance products and services, and is also the country's largest provider of home mortgages. The banking arm operates more than 110 branch offices and 65 agencies throughout the Republic of Ireland. ILP has reoriented its operations since the beginning of the 21st century, selling off its holdings in the United States, France, Hungary, and elsewhere to focus its growth on the Irish market. Listed on the Irish stock exchange, ILP is led by CEO David Went.

Financial Privatization in the 1990s

The three principal components of the future Irish Life & Permanent operated for much of their existence as government-run financial institutions. The oldest of the three, and the last to join the expanded bank and insurance group, was TSB Bank.

TSB's history stemmed back to the early 19th century and the founding of the first Irish Savings Bank in Waterford in 1816. Additional Irish Savings Banks were then founded, starting with a bank in Cork in 1917, and followed by banks in Limerick, Monaghan, and Dublin. The passage of the Savings Bank Act of 1863 placed the savings banks under government control and restricted their operations exclusively to savings accounts and services for more than a century.

These restrictions began to be lifted in the mid-1960s, starting with the first in a series of new legislation passed in 1965 enabling the country's savings banks to offer a more expanded range of financial products and services. Over the next two decades, the banks, which remained independent of each other, were empowered to offer loan and mortgage products, credit cards, foreign exchange, and other services.

The move toward a single TSB Bank began in the late 1970s, when the Irish Savings Banks in Dublin and Monaghan merged their operations. The Cork and Limerick banks followed suit in 1986, followed two years later by the Waterford bank, which merged into the larger Dublin bank. Last, the Irish Savings Banks came together when the Cork and Limerick banks merged with the Dublin branch of the United Kingdom's Trustee Savings Bank (later acquired by Lloyds to form Lloyds TSB) to form TSB Bank in 1992. The new larger bank operated as an unincorporated statutory entity under the oversight of the Irish government's Ministry of Finance.

By then, two other Irish financial institutions were in the process of evolving into publicly held, private sector businesses. Irish Permanent, the oldest of the two, had been set up in 1884 as a building society, in part a movement founded in the

19th century to provide housing for the growing U.K. working class. Irish Permanent Building Society took as its mandate to promote thrift and abstinence among its members.

In 1939, Irish Permanent took on a new managing director, Edmund Farrell, who transformed the building society into the largest mortgage lender in Ireland. Yet Farrell was said to have considered the building society as his own—and went so far as to appoint his own son as his successor. The younger Farrell served as the bank's managing director, until Roy Douglas, who had formerly worked with Ireland's two largest financial groups, Central Bank of Ireland and AIB, was appointed as the group's head. Under Douglas, Irish Permanent began to branch out from its traditional mortgage lending role, launching a new subsidiary in 1992, Irish Permanent Finance Limited, to offer personal and car loans.

Yet Douglas was hired for a more specific purpose—that of taking advantage of changes in the country's banking laws that allowed a building society to convert its status into that of a publicly owned bank. By 1993, Irish Permanent, which had grown to more than 145,000 members, began preparations for its public launch. During due diligence, however, the building society discovered a discrepancy in its books, leading to suspicions that Edmund Farrell, Jr., had used the building society's funds to finance the renovation of his family's mansion. The accusation, later settled out of court, eventually led to Farrell's ouster, and the public offering was completed in 1994.

Almost immediately afterward, Irish Permanent Plc, as the new bank was called, faced a threat to its existence after U.K. banking giant, and former building society, Abbey National bought a nearly 10 percent stake in its Irish counterpart. At the time, the move was widely viewed as the prelude to a full-scale takeover bid.

In the meantime, Irish Permanent began an effort to gain scale, buying Guinness & Mahon (Ireland) Ltd. in 1994 in order to add on that firm's private banking operation. The bank made a second purchase that year, adding Prudential Life of Ireland Ltd. Subsequently renamed as Irish Progressive Life Assurance Company, the acquisition added a life and pensions component to the bank.

Irish Permanent's interest in insurance products led the company to suggest a merger with another recent entrant into Ireland's publicly listed financial community, Irish Life, in 1996. Yet Irish Life, then under the lead of David Kingston, refused Irish Permanent's offer.

Douglas continued to seek new opportunities to build Irish Permanent, however. In 1997, as Irish Permanent's own fortunes rose with the buoyant Irish economy, Douglas reiterated the company's intention to expand as an Irish financial leader. This time, Douglas's target was TSB Bank, which was rumored

to be up for possible privatization before the end of the decade. As Douglas told the *Irish Times:* "It appears that TSB may be on the market in the not-too-distant future. We are interested. We believe the TSB and ourselves would be a strong business fit and a strong cultural fit."

Yet, before that event, Irish Permanent was given a new opportunity for Irish Life. When David Kingston retired, David Went, a somewhat flamboyant figure in the world of British banking who had previously worked at Ulster Bank before heading up British private banker Coutts, was installed as his replacement. Shortly after Went's appointment, he announced his intention to build Irish Life into one of the country's top-tier financial institutions. That announcement provided Douglas with the signal to make a new offer for a merger between Irish Life and Irish Permanent.

Irish Life had been formed in 1939 through the combination of nine insurance companies—five British and four Irish—that had been active in the Irish market. The Irish government, through the Ministry of Finance, held a share in the new insurance company, and by 1947 had gained control of 90 percent of Irish Life.

Irish Financial Mega-Merger for the New Century

Irish Life remained focused on its domestic market throughout the next decades, becoming the country's largest insurance provider. In the 1960s, however, Irish Life entered the U.K. market as well, opening the first of two branches in that country in 1966. Irish Life also gained its own banking arm, through a 25 percent stake in Irish Intercontinental Bank, which remained majority controlled by Belgium's Kredietbank. The state-owned company's international ambitions took on more steam in the 1980s, when it began entering a number of new markets, notably the United States, where it acquired Interstate Assurance Company in 1987. This move was followed by an entry into the Scandinavian and French markets at the beginning of the new decade.

By then, the Irish government was preparing to privatize a number of state-owned companies. Irish Life was earmarked as one of the first to be privatized, in large part to enable the company to accelerate its international expansion effort. In 1990, Irish Life was reorganized as a holding company and given the name Irish Life Plc. The following year, Irish Life was privatized, with a simultaneous listing on the London and Irish stock exchanges. The Irish government nonetheless retained a 34 percent stake in the company in order to shield it from potential takeovers.

Irish Life began making a series of acquisitions. In 1993, it picked up England's City of Westminster Assurance Company Ltd. (CWA), adding to its own British presence. Those operations were combined under the CWA umbrella in 1997. In the United States, Irish Life bought up that country's First Variable Life in 1994, then Guarantee Reserve in 1997. Irish Life also joined Kredietbank in a joint venture to acquire a 48 percent stake in Hungary's K&H Bank.

The arrival of David Went as head of Irish Life spelled the end of the company's international strategy, however. Judging that Irish Life had been unable to establish a solid presence on

Key Dates:

1816: Irish Savings Bank is founded in Waterford, followed by banks in Cork, Dublin, Limerick, and Monaghan.
1884: The Irish Permanent Building Society is founded in Dublin.
1939: Irish Life is created through the merger of nine British and Irish insurance companies.
1947: The Irish government gains 90 percent control of Irish Life.
1966: Irish Life adds a U.K. branch office.
1977: The Dublin and Monaghan banks merge.
1986: The Cork and Limerick banks merge.
1987: Irish Life acquires its first U.S. subsidiary, Interstate Assurance Company.
1999: Waterford bank is merged into Dublin bank.
1991: Irish Life is privatized and listed on the Irish and London exchanges.
1992: The completion of the amalgamation of Irish Savings Banks forms the state-controlled TSB Bank.
1994: Irish Permanent converts to public company status and lists on the Irish stock exchange.
1998: Irish Life and Irish Permanent agree to merge, creating Irish Life & Permanent Plc (ILP).
2000: ILP and TSB Bank agree to merge, creating permanent tsb as a banking subsidiary of ILP.
2001: ILP sells off most of its U.S. holdings as it refocuses on the Irish market.
2003: ILP completes its exit from the U.S. market with the sale of Guarantee Reserve Life Insurance Company.

the international market against the global industry's financial heavyweights, Went instead decided to refocus Irish Life on the domestic market. Irish Life began selling off its international holdings as Went announced his intention to transform the insurance company into one of Ireland's top financial firms.

That announcement provided Irish Permanent's Douglas with the opening to propose a new merger between his company and Went's, and by November 1998 the two sides had reached an agreement that, at a value of £2.8 billion, represented the country's largest ever merger. The new company, called Irish Life & Permanent (ILP), created Ireland's number three financial institution with a full range of banking and insurance products.

As it worked to complete its sell-off of its noncore holdings, ILP began looking for acquisitions to bolster its financial services operations. In 1999, the company acquired Dublin-based Woodchester Investment Brokers, which had been part of GE Capital. Much of the group's efforts over the next two years, however, went toward integrating the two rather different corporate cultures of its Irish Life and Irish Permanent wings.

By 2001, however, that integration was, in large part, complete. The company also took a big step toward its refocusing effort that year, when it sold Interstate Assurance and First Variable Life to Protective Life Insurance Company, based in Alabama. The deal resulted in a loss of some $70 million for the company.

Yet by then ILP had taken a major step forward in its "Irish First" strategy that year when it completed an agreement to acquire TSB Bank for EUR 430 million. The deal involved the merger of TSB into the Irish Permanent banking arm, creating a new Irish banking powerhouse, permanent tsb. The combined operation offered a banking network of more than 110 branches throughout the country, and gave ILP a 25 percent share of Ireland's mortgage market, and 20 percent of the country's insurance market.

ILP completed its exit from the U.S. market in 2003, when it sold its Guarantee Reserve Life Insurance unit to Reassure America Life, a branch of Swiss Re Life & Health America. In the meantime, ILP's domestic market continued to grow strongly, especially in the mortgage market. ILP also was boosted with the decision by a number of its competitors to end their free banking services, driving new customers to ILP's own free banking accounts. With its business building strongly, ILP began plans to challenge the country's state-owned banking leaders for the top spot in the new century.

Principal Subsidiaries

Capital Home Loans Limited (U.K.); City of Westminster Assurance Company Ltd. (U.K.); Cornmarket Investment Brokers Limited; Irish Life Assurance Plc; Irish Life International Limited; Irish Life Investment Managers Limited; Irish Permanent (IOM) Limited (Isle of Man); Irish Permanent Finance Limited; Irish Progressive Services International Ltd.

Principal Competitors

Barclays Bank PLC; AIB Group; Allied Irish Banks P.L.C.; Bank of Ireland; DePfa-Bank Europe PLC; Anglo Irish Bank Corporation PLC; Ulster Bank Ltd.; Bank of Scotland Ireland Ltd.; National Irish Bank Ltd.

Further Reading

Coyle, Dominic, "Irish Life & Permanent Introduces Free Banking As Rivals Withdraw Service," *Irish Times,* May 26, 2003, p. 18.
Creaton, Siobhan, "IL&P Agrees to Sell Last US Business for E112m," *Irish Times,* March 1, 2003, p. 17.
Fitzgerald, Kyran, "Irish Life & Permanent Merger with TSB to Create a Third Banking Force," *Irish Examiner,* December 6, 2000.
Fitzgibbon, Frank, "It's an Uphill Ride on the ILP Rollercoaster," *Sunday Times,* November 10, 2002, p. 10.
McCaffrey, Una, "Irish Life & Permanent Steals Show As Financials Progress," *Irish Times,* September 6, 2003, p. 16.
Miles, Richard, "Irish Bank and Insurer in Pounds 2.5bn Merger," *Times,* December 10, 1998, p. 28.

—M. L. Cohen

Johnson Controls, Inc.

5757 North Green Bay Avenue
Post Office Box 591
Milwaukee, Wisconsin 53201-0591
U.S.A.
Telephone: (414) 524-1200
Fax: (414) 524-2077
Web site: http://www.johnsoncontrols.com

Public Company
Incorporated: 1885 as Johnson Electric Service Company
Employees: 113,000
Sales: $22.65 billion (2003)
Stock Exchanges: New York
Ticker Symbol: JCI
NAIC: 335911 Storage Battery Manufacturing; 336322
Other Motor Vehicle Electrical and Electronic
Equipment Manufacturing; 336360 Motor Vehicle
Seating and Interior Trim Manufacturing; 336399 All
Other Motor Vehicle Parts Manufacturing; 333415
Air-Conditioning and Warm Air Heating Equipment
and Commercial and Industrial Refrigeration
Equipment Manufacturing; 334290 Other
Communications Equipment Manufacturing; 334512
Automatic Environmental Control Manufacturing for
Regulating Residential, Commercial, and Appliance
Use; 334513 Instruments and Related Product
Manufacturing for Measuring, Displaying, and
Controlling Industrial Process Variables; 334519
Other Measuring and Controlling Device
Manufacturing; 335314 Relay and Industrial Control
Manufacturing; 561210 Facilities Support Services

Johnson Controls, Inc. is a diversified company made up of two main business groups: automotive systems, including seating, overhead and instrument panels, floor consoles, door systems, engine electronics, and batteries; and building management and control systems. Johnson is the world's largest independent maker of automotive seating and interior systems, and is the leading supplier of automotive batteries for the original equipment and replacement markets in North America, South America, and Europe. The company is number one worldwide in building control systems, services, and integrated facility management, serving schools, hospitals, office buildings, airports, and other nonresidential buildings. The Automotive Systems Group generates nearly three-fourths of overall revenues, with the Controls Group responsible for the remainder. The percentage of sales generated outside North America has been on the rise, reaching about 40 percent. Over the course of more than a century, Johnson Controls has an impressive track record, including the consecutive payment of dividends since 1885 and 57 straight years of sales increases through 2003.

Origins in Control Devices

Warren Seymour Johnson was born in Rutland County, Vermont, and grew up in Wisconsin. Johnson worked as a printer, surveyor, schoolteacher, and school superintendent before he was appointed a professor at the State Normal School in Whitewater, Wisconsin, in 1876. He was known as a highly original teacher but Johnson's main interest was his laboratory, where he experimented in electrochemistry. In 1883 he produced the first Johnson System of Temperature Regulation, an electric thermostat system that he installed at the State Normal School.

When Johnson received a patent for the electric telethermoscope—the first room thermostat—he persuaded Milwaukee, Wisconsin, hotelier and heir to the Plankinton Packing Company, William Plankinton, to become his financial backer in producing the device. Their partnership, the Milwaukee Electric Manufacturing Company, allowed Johnson to resign his professorship so he could devote all his time to his inventions. Although retired from teaching, he would always be called "the Professor." On May 1, 1885, the company was reorganized as the Johnson Electric Service Company, a Wisconsin corporation, in Milwaukee. Plankinton became president and Johnson, vice-president and treasurer.

The professor continued to invent additional control devices, but he also designed products such as chandeliers, springless door locks, puncture-proof tires, thermometers, and a hose coupling for providing steam heat to passenger railcars. The creations for which the young company received the most recognition were the Professor's impressive tower clocks. He developed a system powered by air pressure that increased the reliability of such clocks. The company built its first big clock in 1895 for the Minneapolis courthouse and a year later built the clock for the Milwaukee City Hall tower. Johnson's largest tower clock was installed in the Philadelphia City Hall. A giant floral clock for the Saint Louis World's Fair in 1904 received international acclaim and enhanced the growing reputation of the company. The clocks' success helped prove the usefulness of the pneumatic operations the company was employing in its control applications.

At the Paris World's Fair of 1900, Johnson's wireless-communication exhibit won second prize. In the same competition Guglielmo Marconi, developer of the wireless telegraph, placed third. The professor, his sons, and inventor Charles Fortier began to test a variety of alloys in wireless sets. The men built a 115-foot tower several miles south of Milwaukee, but many attempts to transmit messages to the company's downtown factory were unsuccessful. Lee DeForest, whose audio tube would later provide the breakthrough for radio, also worked on the project.

Company directors elected Johnson president of the company in 1901, and a year later the firm's name was changed to Johnson Service Company. Even as president, Johnson was not able to convince the board to provide financial backing for his interest in establishing a national automobile company. Johnson saw the automobile as a way to ensure that the company was not completely dependent on temperature-regulating equipment. In 1907 he introduced a gasoline-powered engine. Johnson was the first to receive a U.S. contract to deliver mail with a horseless carriage. At the outset, according to an often-told story, the wary postmaster agreed to pay Johnson an amount equal to his horses' feed bills for the mail service. The company's failure to expand those automobile interests was a source of frustration to Johnson until his death in 1911. He had assigned more than 50 patents—most of them concerned with harnessing power generated by fluid, air, or steam pressure—to Johnson Service Company.

Harry W. Ellis was elected president in 1912. Ellis, who had been manager of the Chicago branch office, decided to concentrate on opportunities for growth in the controls field. He sold all of the company's other businesses, improved the efficiency of factory operations in Milwaukee, and introduced a modern accounting system.

In 1885, the year the company was incorporated, it had sold the rights to sell, install, and service its temperature-control-regulation systems to two firms. The firms did not perform up to expectations, but the situation was not changed for years. By 1912 Johnson had regained the rights to do business directly throughout the country and had established 18 U.S. branch offices, six Canadian offices, and direct agencies in Copenhagen, Berlin, Saint Petersburg, Manchester, and Warsaw.

Early 20th-Century Growth

The professor had insisted that only trained Johnson mechanics could install his company's devices and Ellis reinforced this policy. He insisted that the company was to serve not just as a producer of regulation equipment but as a single source for design, installation, and service. Johnson's temperature-control business expanded in tandem with the country's building boom. Skyscrapers became popular as structural steel replaced iron and other building systems were refined. During World War I, the company's temperature-control business was classified by the War Industry Board as nonessential to the war effort, because it was seen as a means of providing comfort. Johnson contracts dropped off as civilian construction was sharply reduced. The firm looked to government buildings for business and began seeking contracts to retrofit old buildings with new temperature-control systems.

In 1919 the company's new contracts exceeded $1 million. Although a business depression meant that few new office buildings were being constructed, movie theaters, department stores, and restaurants were introducing air-cooled interiors. By 1928 the company's new contracts passed the $4 million mark.

The Great Depression dealt a serious blow to the construction industry, and most new building-control installations in the 1930s aimed for economy. Projects in schools and government buildings that were assigned by the Public Works Administration also had fuel savings as a goal. Johnson's new Dual Thermostat, which allowed a building to save fuel by automatically lowering temperatures at times when the building was unoccupied, was in demand.

Joseph A. Cutler was elected president of the company in 1938. A former engineering professor at the University of Wisconsin, his presidency, like Ellis's, would last almost 25 years. Cutler oversaw the first public listing of Johnson's stock, which began trading over-the-counter on the NASDAQ in 1940.

After the United States entered World War II, Johnson was classified as part of an essential industry, evidence of the change in the way the public perceived building controls. Johnson's contributions to the war effort included installing temperature-and-humidity control systems in defense facilities and the engineering of special military products. The company also made leak detectors that were used to test barrage balloons used over

Key Dates:

1883: Professor Warren Johnson invents an electric thermostat system—the first room thermostat.
1885: Johnson forms Johnson Electric Service Company, based in Milwaukee, Wisconsin.
1895: The company builds its first tower clock for the Minneapolis courthouse.
1902: Company's name is changed to Johnson Service Company.
1912: Following Johnson's death, Harry W. Ellis is elected president and sells all the firm's operations except for the controls business.
1940: Johnson Service goes public with an over-the-counter listing on NASDAQ.
1956: Company begins building and installing pneumatic control centers.
1964: First foreign manufacturing plant is built in Italy.
1972: Johnson introduces the JC/80, the first minicomputer system that manages building controls.
1974: Company changes its name to Johnson Controls, Inc.
1978: To diversify, the company merges with Globe-Union Inc., the nation's largest maker of automotive batteries.

1985: Johnson Controls completes two major acquisitions: Hoover Universal, Inc., a major supplier of seating and plastic parts for automobiles and a new entrant in the plastic-container industry; and Ferro Manufacturing Corporation, supplier of automotive seating components and mechanisms.
1989: Pan Am World Services, Inc., provider of facility management services for military bases, airports, and space centers, is acquired.
1990: Metasys facility management system is introduced.
1995: Johnson acquires Roth Frères SA, a French supplier of automotive seating and interior systems.
1996: Company pays $1.3 billion for Holland, Michigan-based Prince Automotive, supplier of automotive interior systems and components.
1997: Plastic container division is sold to a unit of Viag Group AG for about $650 million.
1998: Johnson acquires Becker Group, Inc., a supplier of interior systems in both North America and Europe.
2001: France-based automotive electronics supplier Sagem SA is acquired.
2002: Johnson purchases the automotive battery business of Germany's Varta AG.

military installations, ships, and landing barges; developed the radiosonde to help combat pilots encountering unknown flying conditions to gather weather data; and manufactured echo boxes, devices that tested radar sets.

Post-World War II Boom

After World War II ended, civilian construction boomed and with it the company's new contracts. Along with this boom came a renewed interest in air conditioning. By 1949 the company's sales were $10 million.

In 1956 Johnson began to build and install pneumatic control centers that allowed a single building engineer to monitor panels displaying room temperatures, ventilating conditions, water temperatures, and the outdoor temperature. To ensure a steady and reliable source of customized control panels for these centers, Johnson purchased a panel-fabrication company in Oklahoma in 1960. Operations at company headquarters in Milwaukee were also expanding, so the company bought and eventually expanded an additional building there for its brass foundry, metal fabrications, assembly operations, and machining work.

Richard J. Murphy was elected company president in 1960, the year the company celebrated its 75th anniversary. Murphy had started with the company as a timekeeper in 1918 and had moved up through the ranks. Although his presidency lasted only six years, he was responsible for many innovations. Murphy established an international division, with subsidiaries in England, France, Australia, Belgium, Italy, and Switzerland. Each international office was managed as a virtually independent business, as were operations in the United States and Canada. In 1964 construction of the first foreign manufacturing plant began in Italy.

Since World War II, Johnson had enjoyed an excellent reputation for its work in atomic research plants and other installations requiring exceptional levels of reliability. In 1961 the Systems Engineering & Construction Division was established. It provided equipment for all 57 Air Force Titan II launch complexes and most other major missile programs. The National Aeronautics and Space Administration contracted with Johnson throughout the 1960s for mission-control instrumentation for the Apollo-Saturn program.

In 1962 Johnson, along with its main competitors Honeywell and Powers Regulator, were charged in a federal antitrust suit with price-fixing in the sale of pneumatic temperature control systems. The suit's resolution in a consent decree, coupled with new competitors entering the controls market, meant increasingly competitive bidding. Johnson occasionally won contracts on which it ended up making little or no profit.

Acquisitions in the 1960s

By the early 1960s it became apparent to Johnson management that electronics technology could be used to control all aspects of maintaining a building. To improve its in-house electronics capability, the company purchased the electronics division of Fischbach & Moore in 1963. Because of its increasing involvement in projects requiring exacting quality standards and high-quality components, Johnson acquired Associated Piping & Engineering Corporation and Western Piping and Engineering Company in 1966. The companies fabricated expansion joints and piping for nuclear and fossil fuel generating plants and many other industrial applications.

Fred L. Brengel became the sixth Johnson president in 1967. He had joined the company as a sales engineer in 1948 and served as manager of the Boston branch office and sales manager of the New England and Midwest regions before becoming vice-president and general sales manager in 1963.

The same year Brengel was elected president, Johnson introduced the T-6000, a solid-state, digital data logger that used "management by exception"—the system announced when its variables were outside specified limits so an engineer's attention was only called for when needed. The T-6000 not only performed heating, ventilating, and air conditioning functions, but also monitored fire and smoke detection, security, and emergency lighting systems.

Just a year after Brengel assumed the presidency, Johnson acquired Penn Controls, Inc., a 50-year-old company that manufactured controls for original equipment manufacturers (OEMs), distributors, and wholesalers. With its Penn acquisition, Johnson improved its competitive edge by having its own supply of electrical products for installation projects. Penn also had manufacturing plants and subsidiaries in Canada, the Netherlands, Argentina, and Japan, which helped Johnson expand its international markets. The year it acquired Penn, the company's sales rose about 20 percent, to $155 million.

Johnson introduced the JC/80, the industry's first minicomputer system that managed building controls, in 1972. One of the many advantages of the JC/80 was that operators of the system needed only a minimal amount of technical training. The JC/80, which could cut fuel requirements by as much as 30 percent, was introduced at the ideal time, just a year before international embargoes on oil would change the way people viewed energy consumption. Virtually overnight, people became interested in reducing energy costs.

The company adopted its present name—Johnson Controls, Inc.—in 1974. By 1977 it had captured approximately 35 percent of the estimated $600 million market for commercial-building control systems. It had 114 branch offices in the United States and Canada and more than 300 service centers, staffed by 10,000 engineers, architects, designers, and service technicians. In spite of a worldwide recession, the company's sales rose to almost $500 million that year.

Diversification into Batteries in 1978

Although Johnson fared well in the boom market for energy conservation products, new companies were beginning to crowd the building-controls field. To diversify, the company merged with Globe-Union Inc., the country's largest manufacturer of automotive batteries, in 1978.

Founded in Milwaukee in 1911, Globe Electric Company had as its original aim the fulfillment of the battery needs of streetcars, rural light plants, and switchboards. In 1925 Globe's treasurer, Chester O. Wanvig, entered an agreement with Sears, Roebuck and Co. President General Robert Wood to produce automobile replacement batteries for the company. Globe shareholders declined the opportunity and Wanvig organized the Union Battery Company to serve Sears. In 1929 Globe Electric and Union Battery consolidated, with Wanvig as president. By the late 1930s Globe-Union had ten manufacturing plants across the United States.

In the late 1950s Globe-Union invented the thin-wall polypropylene battery container, a major technological breakthrough that won the company a leadership position in the industry. The thickness of the battery walls was reduced and the container was lighter and stronger than hard-rubber cases. In 1967 Sears used this technology in its DieHard battery, made by Globe-Union. By 1971 Globe-Union had become the largest U.S. manufacturer of automotive replacement batteries, with its sales climbing past $100 million that year. The company turned to nonautomotive battery applications in 1972 when it formed an industrial products unit. One of its best-known creations was the Gel/Cell, a line of sealed, portable lead acid units for the standby power needs of security and telecommunications applications.

Johnson's merger with Globe-Union doubled its sales, broadened its financial base, and gave it leadership in a new field. Three years after the merger, sales surpassed $1 billion. In the early 1980s Johnson took the lead in developing controls for "intelligent buildings," which featured state-of-the-art technology to manage energy, comfort, and protection needs. Despite the entrance of many new companies into this sector, Johnson remained a leader in the field. In the latter part of 1989, Johnson announced a joint venture with Yokogawa Electric Corporation to manufacture control instrumentation and to integrate and service industrial automation systems for the North American market.

Acquisition of Hoover Industrial in 1985

Johnson greatly expanded its automotive business in 1985 when it acquired Hoover Universal, Inc., a major supplier of seating and plastic parts for automobiles and a new entrant in the plastic-container industry, for $219 million in cash and 6.3 million shares of common stock. Although company officials denied it, industry analysts speculated that the acquisition may have at least in part been an attempt to thwart a possible takeover by Miami financier Victor Posner. One of Posner's companies owned almost 20 percent of Johnson in 1985.

At the time of its purchase, Hoover was changing its emphasis from supplying seating components to building completely assembled automotive seating. The company had an excellent reputation for its just-in-time delivery system, which meant the company supplied its automotive customers with needed parts and components precisely when they needed them to avoid customer storage charges.

The same year it purchased Hoover, Johnson also acquired Ferro Manufacturing Corporation, a supplier of automotive seating components and mechanisms, for $98.3 million in cash. Hoover and Ferro units unrelated to Johnson's major businesses were sold shortly after the acquisitions were completed.

With its new components in place, Johnson became known as a parts supplier that could design, engineer, assemble, and deliver modular systems to their customers' plants "just-in-time." In addition to supplying components to the major domestic carmakers, Johnson also supplied several of the U.S. operations of Japanese auto manufacturers, including Toyota, Honda, and Nissan, and a Toyota-General Motors joint venture.

James H. Keyes was elected chief executive officer in 1988, after serving as president since 1986. A certified public accountant, he joined Johnson as an analyst in 1966 and held several key executive positions, including treasurer and chief operating officer.

Johnson expanded its plastics business in 1988 by acquiring Apple Container Corporation and the soft drink bottle operations of American National Can Company. In mid-1989 the company spent $166 million to purchase Pan Am World Services, Inc., a leading provider of high-tech and other facility-management services for military bases, airports, and space centers. This $167 million acquisition was intended to bolster Johnson's nascent business of providing engineering and protection services for commercial buildings.

Johnson's controls business had had an international presence, concentrated in Europe and the Far East, since the 1960s. During the mid-1980s Johnson also began to expand its plastic-container and seating businesses into Europe. This aggressive expansion was facilitated primarily through acquisitions. By 1990 Johnson claimed leadership positions in both markets.

In 1989, meanwhile, Johnson's battery group acquired Varta Ltd., the largest automotive-battery maker in Canada. That same year the battery division unveiled the EverStart, a new automotive battery that carried its own emergency backup power system. It was called the first real breakthrough in battery technology in decades.

Although there were rumors about possible takeovers of Johnson in the late 1980s, the company's management was committed to rebuffing all such attempts. President Keyes told *Forbes* in March 1989, ''It depends on whether you take a short-term view and want to improve returns immediately, or you take a long-term view and seek to maintain market leadership. We've chosen the latter approach.''

Automotive Systems Predominant in the 1990s

During the 1990s Johnson Controls' automotive businesses would become by far the company's most important business sector. The decade began, however, with the introduction of the Metasys facility management system. In development for three years at a cost close to $20 million, Metasys was a breakthrough system designed for buildings as small as 50,000 square feet and tied together the entire control system through a distributed computer-controlled network.

In 1991 Johnson acquired several European car seat component manufacturers, furthering its overseas expansion. That year also marked the company's involvement in a landmark sex discrimination lawsuit settled by the U.S. Supreme Court. During the 1980s Johnson Controls had switched from a voluntary to a mandatory policy barring women of childbearing age from jobs involving exposure to high levels of lead at its 15 car battery plants. The company was concerned that pregnant women exposed to a potentially harmful substance might sue if the exposure resulted in birth defects. The Supreme Court, however, in a 6–3 ruling, said that decisions about the welfare of future children ''must be left to the parents who conceive, bear, support, and raise them rather than to the employers who hire those parents.'' The Court ruled that Johnson Control's policy was discriminatory against women and therefore could not stand.

Of all of the company's diversified operations, its battery unit was the least profitable, partly because prices for batteries had not increased in a decade, and partly because the unit's

unionized plants had to compete with nonunion plants of other companies. In mid-1991 Johnson Controls attempted to sell the battery division but could not find a buyer. The unit was further battered when it lost its contract to supply DieHard batteries to Sears in late 1994. Since that time contracts were signed or renewed with such retailers as AutoZone and Wal-Mart, and the company also supplied the largest battery distributor in the nation, Interstate Battery System of America. In October 1997 a contract was signed to supply Sears with DieHard Gold batteries, the top of that product line. The battery unit also began to target overseas markets more aggressively, opening a plant in Mexico in 1994, forming a joint venture in China in 1996 to make batteries for Volkswagen, and creating another joint venture in 1997 with Varta Battery AG of Germany to make batteries in South America.

In the mid-1990s Johnson Controls made a number of significant acquisitions in the area of automotive systems that helped to greatly increase sales in the company's automotive segment—a 94 percent increase from 1995 to 1998 alone. In December 1995 Johnson spent $175–$200 million for a 75 percent interest in Roth Frères SA, a Strasbourg, France-based major supplier of seating and interior systems to the European auto industry. In October 1996 the company paid about $1.3 billion for the Prince Automotive unit of Prince Holding Corporation in the largest acquisition in Johnson Controls history. Based in Holland, Michigan, Prince Automotive brought to Johnson an innovative supplier of automotive interior systems and components, such as interior ceilings, overhead consoles and switches, door panels, armrests, and floor consoles. The addition of Prince meant that Johnson Controls could now make virtually all major interior auto components and could offer its customers complete seating systems.

Also in 1996 the company made a number of moves to expand in the Asia-Pacific region. A joint venture was formed in China with Beijing Automotive Industry Corp. to run a car seating and interior system factory in Beijing. Another joint venture was launched in India to supply seats and trim for Ford Escorts built there. In addition, Johnson Controls purchased Aldersons, a unit of Sydney, Australia-based Tutt Bryant Industries PLY Ltd. that supplied interior systems to Australia's four major automakers. For 1996, revenues exceeded the $10 billion mark for the first time.

To help pay down the heavy debt incurred by the purchase of Prince Automotive, Johnson Controls sold its plastic container division to Schmalbach-Lubeca AG/Continental Can Europe, a unit of German conglomerate Viag Group AG, for about $650 million in February 1997. That year also saw a major expansion of the company's automotive business in South America, where its number of plants increased from two to 11 during the year.

Joint ventures and acquisitions continued in 1998. In April the company announced the formation of a venture with Recaro North America Inc. (a unit of German seat manufacturer Recaro GmbH & Company) whereby Johnson Controls would supply brand-name specialty seats for the first time—under the Recaro brand. In July, Johnson acquired Sterling Heights, Michigan–based Becker Group, Inc., a supplier of interior systems in both North America and Europe, for $548 million and the assumption of $372 million in debt. The addition of Becker propelled Johnson Controls to the number one position in Europe in interior systems. The company soon divested two more noncore units to help pay down additional debt taken on to purchase Becker. The plastics machinery business was sold to Cincinnati Milacron Inc. for about $190 million in September 1998, and the industrial battery division was sold to C&D Technologies Inc. in March 1999 for approximately $135 million.

Meantime, John M. Barth, who had headed up the Automotive Systems Group, was named president and chief operating officer in September 1998, with Keyes remaining chairman and CEO. That month also saw Johnson form two joint ventures to make automotive batteries in Mexico and South America. Early in 1999 the corporation announced that it had regained its position as the sole supplier of batteries to Sears. On the controls side, the corporation spent about $41 million in November 1998 to buy Cardkey Systems, a maker of electronic access and security management systems based in Simi Valley, California. During 1999 the Automotive Systems Group began entering into partnerships with a host of electronics firms in order to start integrating electronics into every aspect of vehicle interiors. Early outcomes of these partnerships included integrated hands-free cellular car phone functions, in-car DVD players, and a computer-controlled seat that automatically adjusted several pressure points to combat driver fatigue.

Early 2000s and Beyond

From the late 1980s to the early 2000s, Johnson Controls' sales were increasingly coming from overseas markets in large part because of the international nature of the acquisitions at this time. Revenues stemming from outside North America increased from 30 to 40 percent during this period. The acquisitions made between 2000 and 2003 continued this trend. In October 2000 Johnson acquired its first major automotive asset in Asia by purchasing a controlling 90 percent stake in Ikeda Bussan Co. Ltd. for about $90 million. Ikeda was the primary supplier of automotive seating to Japanese automaker Nissan. Also in late 2000 Johnson acquired Gylling Optima Batteries AB, a Swedish maker of high-performance, leak-resistant lead-acid batteries marketed under the Optima brand name. This marked Johnson's first ownership of a battery brand as it had previously produced only original-equipment and private-label batteries. Another 2001 purchase was that of MC International, one of the leading providers of refrigeration and air-conditioning systems and services in Europe.

Johnson Controls significantly strengthened its automotive electronics capabilities via the October 2001 $435 million buyout of Sagem SA. Although Sagem's strength was in interior electronics, such as instrument panels, the French firm was also a supplier of fuel injectors and engine controllers—new areas for Johnson. A second deal was concluded that same month, the purchase of Hoppecke Automotive GmbH & Co. KG. Based in Germany, Hoppecke specialized in batteries designed for the emerging market in 36/42-volt automotive electrical systems, which promised to provide more power and to make cars weigh less—and thus get better mileage—because the wires in such systems can be smaller. The battery operations of Johnson received a further boost in October 2002 when the automotive battery division of Germany's Varta AG was acquired for about $310 million. The acquired business produced original equipment batteries for several European automakers and also made after-market batteries for a number of customers, including hypermarket chains and wholesalers.

This acquisition provided Johnson Controls with a leadership position in the European automotive battery market, ahead of arch-rival Exide Technologies.

In June 2002, meantime, workers at four Johnson Controls parts plants in the United States went on strike. The work stoppage lasted only two days, however, as Johnson's management agreed to give the workers higher wages and benefits and perhaps most importantly the right to organize workers at another 26 company plants in the United States that were suppliers to the Big Three U.S. automakers. Johnson's workforce had largely been nonunion, but the company believed that it had to become more of a unionized supplier in order to secure major outsourcing contracts from the Big Three—its three largest customers. The issue of outsourcing had become an increasingly contentious issue between these automakers and their largely unionized workforces.

For the fiscal year ending in September 2002, Johnson Controls' revenues surpassed $20 billion for the first time—representing a quadrupling of sales over a ten-year period—and its net income hit a record $600.5 million. At the end of that fiscal year, Barth was named president and CEO, with Keyes remaining chairman.

In July 2003 Johnson greatly bolstered its automotive electronics operations by acquiring Borg Instruments AG for EUR 117.5 million in cash. Based in Germany, Borg specialized in high-end instrument clusters and other information displays and was the producer of the Quo Vadis navigational system and an electronic parking assistance system that provided an electronic signal to a driver whose vehicle is about to bump another vehicle. That same month, the company announced that Keyes would retire at the end of 2003 and that Barth would take on the additional post of chairman. Keyes left behind a company with an enviable record of achievement, particularly during the uncertain political and economic climate of the early 2000s. With its fiscal 2003 results, Johnson Controls had achieved its 57th consecutive year of sales increases (reaching $22.65 billion), its 13th straight year of increased earnings ($682.9 million), and its 28th consecutive year of dividend increases. Over the previous ten years, sales had grown at an average annual rate of 14 percent, while net income had increased by 17 percent per year. The company had clearly been served well by its diversified operations in controls and automotive systems and by its ever growing capabilities within these two areas.

Principal Subsidiaries

Beijing Johnson Controls Co. Ltd. (China); Borg Instruments AG (Germany); Brookfield LePage Johnson Controls Facility Management Services, Ltd. (Canada); Building Services S.r.l. (Italy); Cointer S.r.l. (Italy); Comerit S.r.l. (Italy); Commerl S.r.l. (Italy); Controles Reynosa SA de CV (Mexico); Cybertron Systems Pty. Ltd. (South Africa); Ensamble de Interiores Automotrices, S. de R.L. de C.V. (Mexico); Hoover Universal, Inc.; Hyperion Corp.; Ikeda IOM Holdings (Malaysia); Intertec Systems, LLC; JCI Regelungstechnik GmbH (Germany); Johnson Control SpA (Italy); Johnson Controls & Summit Interiors Ltd. (Thailand); Johnson Controls (India) Private Limited (India); Johnson Controls (M) Sdn Bhd (Malaysia); Johnson Controls (S) Pte. Ltd. (Singapore); Johnson Controls (UK) Ltd.; Johnson Controls Alagon, S.A. (Spain); Johnson Controls Australia Pty. Ltd.; Johnson Controls Austria GmbH; Johnson Controls Automation Systems BV (Netherlands); Johnson Controls Automobilove Soucastky s.r.o. (Czech Republic); Johnson Controls Automotive (Belgium) NV; Johnson Controls Automotive (Pty) Ltd. (South Africa); Johnson Controls Automotive (UK) Ltd.; Johnson Controls Automotive Electronics SA (France); Johnson Controls Automotive France S.A.S.; Johnson Controls Automotive Mexico SA de CV; Johnson Controls Automotive NV (Belgium); Johnson Controls Automotive S.r.l. (Italy); Johnson Controls Automotive SA (France); Johnson Controls Automotive Spain S.A.; Johnson Controls Automotive Systems KK (Japan); Johnson Controls Automotive Systems SRL (Argentina); Johnson Controls Batterien GmbH & Co. KG (Germany); Johnson Controls Batterien Verwaltungsgesellschaft mbH (Germany); Johnson Controls Batteries (UK) Ltd.; Johnson Controls Batteries France SAS; Johnson Controls Battery Group, Inc.; Johnson Controls Battery Sweden Kommanditbolag (Sweden); Johnson Controls de Mexico SA de CV; Johnson Controls do Brasil Automotive Ltda. (Brazil); Johnson Controls Espana S.L. (Spain); Johnson Controls Eurosit SL (Spain); Johnson Controls France S.A.; Johnson Controls GmbH (Germany); Johnson Controls GmbH & Co. KG (Germany); Johnson Controls Headliner GmbH (Germany); Johnson Controls Holding Company, Inc.; Johnson Controls Holding SAS (France); Johnson Controls Hong Kong Ltd.; Johnson Controls IFM Phils Corp (Philippines); Johnson Controls II Assentos de Espuma, S.A. (Portugal); Johnson Controls Integrated Facility Management BV (Netherlands); Johnson Controls Interiors GmbH & Co. KG (Germany); Johnson Controls Interiors LLC; Johnson Controls International spol s.r.o. (Czech Republic); Johnson Controls International spol s.r.o. (Slovakia); Johnson Controls Investment Company, Inc.; Johnson Controls Investments (U.K.) Ltd.; Johnson Controls KK (Japan); Johnson Controls Ltd. (Canada); Johnson Controls Martorell, S.A. (Spain); Johnson Controls Nederland BV (Netherlands); Johnson Controls Norden AS (Norway); Johnson Controls Objekt Bochum GmbH & Co. KG (Germany); Johnson Controls Objekt Zwickau GmbH & Co. KG (Germany); Johnson Controls PanAmerica LLC; Johnson Controls Roth Frères Insitu Technologie GmbH & Co. KG (Germany); Johnson Controls Roth SAS (France); Johnson Controls SA/NV (Belgium); Johnson Controls Sachsen-Batterien Beteiligungs GmbH (Germany); Johnson Controls Sachsen-Batterien GmbH & Co. KG (Germany); Johnson Controls SRL (Italy); Johnson Controls Sweden AB; Johnson Controls Systems A.G. (Switzerland); Johnson Controls Technology Company; Johnson Controls Valladolid SAU (Spain); Johnson Controls World Services Inc.; MC International SA (France); Optima Batteries AB (Sweden); Optima Batteries, Inc.; Sicar BV (Netherlands); Sistemas Automotrice Summa SA de CV (Mexico); TechnoTrim, Inc.; Trim Masters Inc.; VARTA Automotive GmbH (Germany); VB Autobatterie GmbH (Germany; 80%).

Principal Operating Units

Automotive Systems Group; Controls Group.

Principal Competitors

Lear Corporation; Delphi Corporation; Faurecia SA; Intier Automotive Inc.; Visteon Corporation; Honeywell International Inc.; Siemens AG; Exide Technologies; East Penn Manufacturing Company, Inc.

Further Reading

Berss, Marcia, "Watizzit? Johnson Controls Is a Strange Mixture—Car Seats, Thermostats, Plastic Bottles, and Automobile Batteries. But It Works," *Forbes,* August 28, 1995, p. 100.
Byrne, Harlan S., "Johnson Controls: Back in Gear," *Barron's,* June 5, 2000, pp. 21–22.
——, "Johnson Controls: Strong Market Positions Help It Ride Out the Recession," *Barron's,* February 24, 1992, pp. 51–52.
Connole, Joe, "Johnson Controls to Storm into Europe," *Business Journal-Milwaukee,* May 16, 1988, pp. 1+.
Content, Tom, "Johnson Controls Buys French Unit: Deal Opens Door to Europe," *Milwaukee Journal Sentinel,* July 26, 2001, p. 1D.
——, "Johnson Controls Elevates Barth: Keyes to Remain Chairman As Part of Succession Plan," *Milwaukee Journal Sentinel,* July 25, 2002, p. 1D.
——, "Johnson Controls Plans to Boost Battery Power: Acquisition of German Firm to Bring Access to New Technology for Cars and Light Trucks," *Milwaukee Journal Sentinel,* August 24, 2001, p. 1D.
——, "Johnson Controls to Buy Varta Unit: Acquisition Would Boost Glendale Firm's Hold on Car Batteries in Europe," *Milwaukee Journal Sentinel,* August 7, 2002, p. 1D.
Dubashi, Jagannath, "Slump Control: Johnson Controls Thought One Good Deal Would Eliminate Two Pet Peeves," *Financial World,* May 29, 1990, p. 49.
Gallagher, Kathleen, "Johnson Controls in Driver's Seat with Diverse Sales," *Milwaukee Journal Sentinel,* August 19, 2001, p. 4D.
Gardner, Greg, "JCI Buys Itself a Prince," *Ward's Auto World,* August 1996, p. 35.
Gordon, Joanne, "Interior Motives: Johnson Controls Puts Spy Cameras in Cars—to Find Out What Features You Really Want," *Forbes,* September 2, 2002, pp. 74–75.
Lappen, Alyssa A., "Damn the Analysts, Full Speed Ahead," *Forbes,* March 20, 1989, pp. 171+.
Marsh, Peter, "A Sitting Target for Two Rivals," *Financial Times,* April 15, 1996, p. 10.
——, "Standing Up to Seating Challenge," *Financial Times,* February 23, 1998, p. FTS7.
Miller, James P., "Johnson Controls' Container Business Will Be Sold to Unit of Germany's Viag," *Wall Street Journal,* December 10, 1996, p. A3.
Right for the Times: Johnson Controls 100th Anniversary, Milwaukee, Wis.: Johnson Controls, Inc., 1985.
Rose, Robert L., "Johnson Controls Agrees to Purchase of Becker Group," *Wall Street Journal,* April 28, 1998, p. B22.
——, "Johnson Controls Gets a Big Boost from the Bottom," *Wall Street Journal,* February 3, 1997, p. B4.
——, "Johnson Controls Plans to Expand into Asia, Pacific," *Wall Street Journal,* September 26, 1996, p. B2.
——, "Johnson Controls to Buy Prince Unit As Car-Interior Industry Consolidates," *Wall Street Journal,* July 19, 1996, p. A3.
Rose, Robert L., and Robert L. Simison, "Johnson Controls and UAW Reach Pact," *Wall Street Journal,* February 21, 1997, pp. A3, A4.
Tetzell, Rick, "Mining Money in Mature Markets," *Fortune,* March 22, 1993, p. 77.
Wermiel, Stephen, "Justices Bar 'Fetal Protection' Policies," *Wall Street Journal,* March 21, 1991, pp. B1, B5.
Wiegner, Kathleen K., "Bright Spot," *Forbes,* July 5, 1982, pp. 175+.

—Mary Sue Mohnke
—update: David E. Salamie

The Laurel Pub Company Limited

Porter Tun House
500 Capability Green
Luton
Bedfordshire LU1 3LS
United Kingdom
Telephone: (+44) 07002-528735
Fax:
Web site: http://www.laurelpubco.com

Private Company
Incorporated: 2001
Employees: 11,000
Sales: £350 million ($560 million) (2002)
NAIC: 722410 Drinking Places (Alcoholic Beverages);
424820 Wine and Distilled Alcoholic Beverage
Merchant Wholesalers; 531190 Lessors of Other Real
Estate Property

The Laurel Pub Company Limited is one of the United Kingdom's top five operators of managed—as opposed to tenanted—pubs, with more than 650 pubs throughout the country under its control. Created in 2001 from the sale of former brewer Whitbread Plc's pub estate to German investment bank Morgan Grenfell Private Equity (which remains Laurel's owner), Laurel Pub is seeking a place among the survivors of the rapidly consolidating U.K. pub market. Yet the company's hopes for a place in the top three were dashed when it was dropped from the bidding for the more than 1,500-pub estate of Scottish & Newcastle Plc in October 2003. The failure to gain scale may make Laurel itself a vulnerable takeover target, if parent Morgan Grenfell seeks an early return on its investment. In the meantime, Laurel has been streamlining and redeveloping its own estate. In December 2002, the company sold nearly half of its pub estate in a sale-leaseback arrangement with London & Regional Properties, which freed up nearly £300 million for Laurel's investment and expansion effort. Laurel's pubs operate under five primary brands and formats: Hog's Head, Wayside, Champion, Town Traditional, and Tavern Venue. The company, led by former Bass executive Ian Payne, plans a public offering by 2005—if it avoids being swallowed by a larger rival.

Whitbread Pub Origins in the 19th Century

One of the most famous names in British brewing history, Whitbread—from which the Laurel Pub company was formed—traces its roots to the mid-18th century, when former brewing apprentice Samuel Whitbread acquired his own brewery in London in 1742. Whitbread's stout and porter appealed to London taste buds, and by the 1760s, the company owned two breweries and had become the second largest brewer in the city.

For over a century and a half, Whitbread focused on its brewing operation, supplying the large number of "free houses" in the London region. These pubs remained independent of the more than 100 brewers in the area (and many were brewers themselves), and were not restricted to sales of any particular brand. The 1880s, however, witnessed a sudden drop in demand for beer, placing a great number of pubs in financial distress. Eager to preserve their retail outlet, the country's brewers began buying up the struggling pubs, creating the so-called "tied house" system, in which pubs featured only the beers of their brewer owners. In turn, in order to finance these acquisitions, the brewers were forced to go public. Whitbread's turn at the stock market came in 1889.

Owning pubs, while giving brewers a guaranteed retail outlet, was not always profitable. Pricing pressures, and poorly managed pubs, coupled with recurring recessions, often transformed the tied houses into financial burdens for their brewer-owners. Whitbread faced the same cyclical difficulties, such as in 1900, when, as the result of attempts to boost profits by lowering prices, the company was forced to write off the property value of its tied houses. This move, however, was later credited with saving the company from financial ruin.

Beer consumption began to rise again in the early 1900s, and Whitbread's production increased accordingly. Yet on the eve of World War I, the British government imposed new and far higher license fees on the country's tied houses. Pubs once again became financial liabilities, and forced the closure and sale of many of the country's smaller breweries. In response, Whitbread stopped adding new tied houses, and instead focused its efforts on its bottled beer sales. First introduced in 1868, Whitbread's bottled beer had by then earned the company an international reputation. The successful expansion of the com-

Company Perspectives:

Our aim is to be the best pub and bar business in the UK. Our strategy is to grow the business both organically and by acquisition. Our investment programme combined with the commitment, quality and enthusiasm of more than 11,000 dedicated employees will make this happen.

pany's bottled beer business enabled it to reduce its reliance on sales within its tied houses.

Whitbread's pub estate stood at less than 100 through World War II. Indeed, the company's head, Francis Pelham Whitbread, who died in 1941, played a prominent role in opposing further development of the tied-house system, particularly in his position as chairman of the industry's Brewers Society.

The company's stance changed dramatically following World War II. Bombing raids had destroyed much of the company's brewery operations; however, the company's relatively strong financial position enabled it to rebuild—and embark on a modernization program in the 1950s.

Its brewing rivals had not fared as well, however, and, threatened for their survival, placed themselves under the protection of the "Whitbread Umbrella." Originally set up to enable the smaller brewers to join Whitbread's larger distribution network, the "umbrella" gradually turned into an acquisition program—between 1950 and 1971, Whitbread acquired some 26 brewers.

While many of these breweries were small, locally oriented affairs, a number of Whitbread's acquisitions brought the company larger regional and even national operations. The acquisition drive also enabled Whitbread to expand its network of tied houses to a national level. By the 1960s, the company's brewery acquisitions targeted more specifically those companies' pub portfolios. By the 1970s, the company operated more than 10,000 tied pubs.

A New Pub Company for the New Century

Yet the deep recession of the 1970s nearly brought Whitbread to bankruptcy. The harsh economic climate, coupled with a shift in the consumer beer market from traditional stouts, porters, and ales to lighter lagers, placed Whitbread under additional pressure. The company began to de-emphasize its reliance on brewery and pub operations during that decade, shutting down a number of breweries—including its original London-based brewery—consolidating production, and, especially, stepping up a diversification drive initially started in the 1960s.

Throughout the 1980s, Whitbread continued to redefine itself, adding a variety of entertainment, leisure, hotel, restaurant, and other operations. By the end of the decade, brewing and pub operations accounted for just a minor percentage of the company's total sales. Meanwhile, the British government's investigation of the monopolistic nature of the tied-house system led to the passage of the Beer Orders of 1989. Under this new legislation, restrictions were placed on the number of pubs brewers

were allowed to own. In Whitbread's case, it meant that the company would be forced to sell off, or lease out, nearly 2,300 pubs by 1992.

The Beer Orders created an entirely new industry in the United Kingdom, that of independently operating companies focused on pub ownership and/or management. Set up in large part through the raising of venture capital, the new companies, which included such names as Enterprise Inns, Punch Taverns, JD Wetherspoon, Luminar, and others, began vying for the pub estates of the country's brewery groups.

In 1990, Whitbread formed a new subsidiary, the Whitbread Beer Company, to take over its brewing, distribution, and marketing operations, as the company began withdrawing from much of its regional brewing assets. A second subsidiary, Whitbread Inns, was created to hold the 1,600 managed pubs the company intended to keep after complying with the Beer Orders. That process was completed within the government's deadline by the end of 1992.

Whitbread's transition into a restaurant, hotel, and leisure group continued through the 1990s, as the company continued to sell off pieces of its pub empire. In 1997, the company narrowed its pub focus, selling off houses that sold beer from other brewers. The company continued shifting its portfolio the following year, when it shed some 250 traditional-styled pubs. Nonetheless, the company had also continued to add new pubs, and by the late 1990s held some 3,000 managed and tenanted pubs. The latter represented more than two-thirds of the group's total pub portfolio.

In 1999, Whitbread made a last attempt to return to the top of the U.K. pub industry. In that year, the company reached an agreement, worth more than £2.8 billion, to acquire rival Allied Domecq's portfolio of more than 3,500 pubs, a move that would have required Whitbread to dispose of its brewery operation in compliance with the Beer Orders. Yet that deal was struck down by the country's Mergers and Monopolies Commission.

The failure to see the deal through led to the final phase in Whitbread's transition away from its roots in the brewing industry. In 2000, the company sold off the entirety of its brewing business to Belgium's Interbrew. The following year, the company put its fold of more than 3,000 pubs up for sale. In May 2001, Germany's Morgan Grenfell Private Equity, a unit of Deutsche Bank, agreed to pay more than £1.6 billion for the Whitbread estate.

Morgan Grenfell then set up a new company, the Laurel Pub Company, to operate its U.K. pub operation, placing former Bass executive Ian Payne in charge as CEO. Payne promptly moved to focus Laurel on the managed pub side, selling off the group's 2,300 tenanted pubs, including a package of nearly 1,900 pubs to tenanted pub specialist Enterprise Inns for nearly £900 million.

Laurel next began an investment program, installing a new state-of-the art EPOS (electronic point-of-sale) system across its entire 625-strong managed pub estate, at a cost of £15 million. The company also spent some £21 million refurbishing its pubs. Helping to fund this effort was the sale-leaseback agreement signed with real estate group London & Regional

Key Dates:

1742: Samuel Whitbread acquires first brewery in London, which later becomes one of the most prominent breweries in the United Kingdom.
1880s: Whitbread begins acquiring its first "tied houses," pubs owned by the brewer and selling its products.
1950s: Whitbread begins 20-year acquisition drive of breweries and their pub estates, building up a portfolio of more than 10,000 pubs by the 1970s.
1989: British government passes new Beer Orders that place restrictions on pub and brewery ownership by the country's national brewers; in response, Whitbread forms Whitbread Inns as a holding company for the pub estate it intends to keep.
1992: Whitbread completes disposal of more than 2,300 pubs in compliance with Beer Orders.
1999: After being barred from acquiring Allied Domecq's 3,500 pubs by the Mergers and Monopolies Commission, Whitbread announces its decision to exit the brewing and pub industries.
2001: Whitbread sells its 3,000-strong pub estate to Morgan Grenfell, part of Deutsche Bank, which sets up the Laurel Pub Company under Ian Payne; Laurel then sells 2,300 tenanted pubs to Enterprise Inns.
2002: Laurel sells freeholds on 280 pubs to London & Regional Properties in 60-year sale leaseback agreement.
2003: Laurel joins bidding war for 1,500 pubs of Scottish & Newcastle.

Properties Ltd. (L&R) at the end of 2002. Under that agreement, L&R acquired the freeholds to 280 of Laurel's pubs, collecting rents on the pubs, which remained managed by Laurel through 60-year leases, in a deal worth £318 million.

The U.K. pub industry underwent a rapid consolidation at the turn of the century, resulting in the creation of a small number of pub powerhouses, including Enterprise Inns, Punch Taverns, and others. Laurel attempted to join the race for scale with an interest in acquiring Mitchells & Butlers, the pubs group formed by the breakup of Six Continents (formerly Bass). The company renounced the attempt, however, balking at the £3 billion purchase price.

The consolidation of the industry took on new momentum in 2003, with the announcement by Scottish & Newcastle of its intention to sell off nearly 1,500 pubs. Laurel joined in the bidding war, teaming up with Japan's Nomura. Yet that pairing's bid failed to make the S&N shortlist. Instead, Laurel joined with investment group Cinven at the end of September to make a new offer. By the beginning of October, though, Laurel appeared to have once again lost out in the bid.

Laurel's failure to gain control of the S&N estate was seen as a signal that Laurel itself would become vulnerable to a takeover offer—the success of the S&N bid would have enabled Laurel to go public soon after, and allow the company's parent to cash out on its investment. With prospects of a public offering dimmed, observers now suggested that Morgan Grenfell would seek a return on its investment through an outright sale of Laurel. In the meantime, Laurel remained a valuable asset for its German parent, with sales topping £350 million and generating profits of £70 million in 2002.

Principal Operating Units

Pub Brands: Hog's Head; Wayside; Champion; Town Traditional; Tavern Venue.

Principal Competitors

Compass Group PLC; Enterprise Inns Plc; Compass Roadside Ltd.; Punch Retail Ltd.; JD Wetherspoon PLC; Wolverhampton and Dudley Breweries PLC; Greene King PLC; Luminar PLC; Ascot PLC; SFI Group PLC.

Further Reading

Barker, Sophie, "Payene Isn't Resting on His Laurels," *Sunday Telegraph*, June 1, 2003, p. 7.
Bridge, Sarah, "£320m Battle for Laurel Pubs," *Europe Intelligence*, October 6, 2002.
Buckley, Sophy, "M&B Escapes Laurel Interest," *Financial Times*, May 28, 2003, p. 24.
Clark, Andrew, "Last Orders for Whitbread Pubs," *Guardian*, March 21, 2001, p. 26.
Garrahan, Matthew, and Adam Jones, "Laurel and Cinven Team up for S&N Bid," *Financial Times*, September 30, 2003, p. 26.
Walsh, Dominic, "Laurel in £318m Leaseback Deal," *Times*, December 20, 2002, p. 27.

—M. L. Cohen

Li & Fung Limited

11/F LiFung Tower
888 Cheung Sha Wan Road
Kowloon, Hong Kong
People's Republic of China
Telephone: +852-2300-2300
Fax: +852-2300-2000
Web site: http://www.lifung.com

Public Company
Incorporated: 1937
Employees: 5,700
Sales: HK$37.28 billion (2002)
Stock Exchanges: Hong Kong
Ticker Symbol: 494
NAIC: 424310 Piece Goods, Notions and Other Dry
Goods Merchant Wholesalers; 423910 Sporting and
Recreational Goods and Supplies Merchant
Wholesalers; 423920 Toy and Hobby Goods and
Supplies Merchant Wholesalers

During the course of its nearly 100-year history, Hong Kong-based Li & Fung Limited has grown from a simple exporter to an expert in "global supply chain management." The company coordinates product design, raw material and factory sourcing, production management, and quality assurance for clients that have included The Limited, The Gap, Coca-Cola, and Kohl's Corporation. Li & Fung deals primarily with garments but is increasing its focus on promotional items, toys, sporting goods, and housewares.

When one of its clients needs a product, Li & Fung does much more than just find the lowest-price source. The company breaks apart the manufacturing process to find the best supplier for each stage of production. For example, if a client orders a polo shirt, Li & Fung might buy American cotton, have it knitted and dyed in China, and send it to Bangladesh for sewing. The company's 65 sourcing offices in 38 countries give it the global connections it needs to pull off this "borderless" manufacturing process.

Founded in 1906 as an exporter in Guangzhou, China, Li & Fung has survived World War II, China's move to Communism, and eventual reopening of China for trade. More recently, the company has adapted to the transition from a manufacturing to a service-based economy in Hong Kong and the emergence of the Internet. The company is now led by Victor and William Fung, the third generation of the Fung family to deal in exports. Li & Fung's flexibility and its expertise in East Asian and global manufacturing have allowed it to move beyond the role of a simple trading intermediary and develop a range of services that are still in demand in the 21st century.

Basic Exporting: Early 20th Century Through World War II

In 1906 Fung Pak-liu and Li To-ming founded an exporting company in the southern Chinese city of Guangzhou. The company was the first Chinese-owned exporter in a field controlled by foreign merchants. As a former teacher of English, Fung Pak-liu was able to act as an intermediary between Chinese-speaking factories and English-speaking buyers. He received a 15 percent commission for his interpreting services. In the first few years, Li & Fung dealt primarily in porcelain and silk, and later moved into bamboo and rattan ware, jade, ivory, handicrafts, and fireworks. The company came up with a new way to make fireworks in 1907, using a paper rather than a mud seal. The new product produced less dust and, because it was lighter, saved tariff costs since the U.S. import duty was based on weight. The design became the industry standard.

Because the river port in Guangzhou was too shallow for oceangoing clippers, the British colony of Hong Kong served as the deep water port for South China. So Fung Pak-liu's son Fung Hon-chu went to Hong Kong and established a branch to handle the shipping of goods. On December 28, 1937, Li & Fung was formally established as a limited company in Hong Kong.

World War II put a halt to trading for several years. Fung Pak-liu died in 1943 and control of the firm moved to the second generation. Li To-ming, who had been a silent partner, sold his shares to the Fung family in 1946. After the war, China became a Communist country and a flood of refugees came to Hong

Company Perspectives:

Global Supply Chain Management is our business. Working in partnership with our customers, we cater for their needs of competitive pricing, quality, on-time delivery, as well as ethical sourcing. We manage the logistics of producing and exporting goods across many producers and countries.

A one-stop-shop service—Small, dedicated teams of product specialists focus on the needs of particular customers and organize for them. We provide the convenience of a one-stop shop from product development, through production management, to customs clearance and delivery when required.

Kong. Li & Fung was now cut off from its factory sources in China and needed to find a new way of doing business. Fung Hon-chu reinvented Li & Fung as an exporter of the labor-intensive consumer goods that began being produced in Hong Kong during the postwar period. The company dealt in garments, toys, electronics, plastic flowers, and wigs. Its primary customers were retailers in the United States. As Hong Kong's manufacturing economy grew, Li & Fung grew with it.

The Third Generation: Modernization in the 1970s

Fung Hon-chu's sons Victor and William attended universities in the United States. The older son Victor attended the Massachusetts Institute of Technology, then got a Ph.D. in applied mathematics from Harvard, while his younger brother William studied computer science at Princeton and got his M.B.A. at Harvard Business School. The two might have pursued careers in the United States, but in 1972 their mother called and pleaded with them to come home and help their father so he would not have to work so hard. Having been exposed to Western business practices, the two were hesitant to go back to a traditional family-owned enterprise. "Trading is a sunset industry," their friends in the United States warned them. But their father suggested that they come back and show him how to run the business better. William returned in 1972 and Victor in 1974.

By the 1970s, competitive pressure was pushing Li & Fung's profit margins down to 5, or even 3, percent. Taiwan and Singapore had cheaper labor and were developing enough manufacturing capacity to vie with Hong Kong. Meanwhile, buyers were more inclined to bypass the middleman and deal directly with the manufacturer. If Li & Fung had nothing to offer beyond the ability to connect buyers with factories in Hong Kong, the company would have trouble surviving. Hong Kong as a whole was moving from a manufacturing to a predominantly service economy, and Li & Fung's best prospect was to find a way to make that transition itself.

The Fung brothers of the third generation brought a new perspective on the company's future, but they encountered a difficult environment for making drastic changes. Li & Fung was still run like a traditional patriarchal Chinese family conglomerate on the idea that the purpose of the company was to serve as the family's livelihood. More than 30 cousins had

stakes in the company and, even if they were not particularly skilled at business, they were hanging on to management positions in order to retain shareholder benefits. So William and Victor's first initiative was to convince their father to take the firm public. In 1973 Li & Fung was listed on the Hong Kong Stock Exchange in an issue that was oversubscribed 113 times. "It was the only way to get a lot of disgruntled relatives off our backs and attract professionals into management," William Fung told the *Far Eastern Economic Review* in 1992.

Now that the roles of ownership and management were separated, it was easier to make changes at the firm. The brothers established offices in Taiwan, Korea, and Singapore in order to diversify their manufacturing sources. As more and more East Asian countries industrialized, Li & Fung developed a buying network throughout the region. In 1979 China opened up for trade as well. Many Hong Kong manufacturers relocated to China, and China once again became a key sourcing point for Li & Fung as it had been in the first decades of the company's existence.

By expanding geographically, Li & Fung acquired broader regional expertise and a more substantial base of manufacturing contacts, and thus was able to offer its clients a more valuable service. For example, the company knew that Taiwan did better work with synthetic fabrics but Hong Kong was the best choice for cottons. Li & Fung was also well-practiced at negotiating the system of quotas that governed world textile trade and knew how to move orders between countries as quotas filled up. With expanded knowledge and resources, the company could expertly source large orders by putting together a package from the entire region.

From Middleman to Manager in the 1980s

Still, regional familiarity was a basic service without much potential to lift Li & Fung's profit margins out of the single digits. The company's trade margins were squeezed throughout the 1980s, exposing the need for a more sophisticated business strategy. The answer was to become more involved in the entire production planning process. The traditional way of operating was that a customer requested a specific product and Li & Fung found the best supplier. By the late 1980s, though, Li & Fung was offering a broader range of services. Once a company had an idea of the product it needed, it would send design sketches to Li & Fung. Li & Fung would find the right type of yarn and fabrics, create prototypes for the customer, set up contacts for each step of the supply process and develop a production schedule that covered the entire fashion season. Li & Fung was gradually making the transition from middleman to program manager.

The company also branched out into the area of retail in the mid-1980s. It acquired 50 percent shares in Circle K convenience stores and Toys 'R' Us chains in Hong Kong. In addition, Li & Fung established a venture capital enterprise in the United States in 1984, in part out of chagrin for not having taken advantage of an early chance to invest in its successful client The Gap, Inc. Known as LF International, the investment company's purpose was to identify companies that had good design ideas but could benefit from Li & Fung's experience in sourcing materials. LF International made modest investments in about four to five enterprises a year.

Key Dates:

1906: Fung Pak-liu and Li To-ming begin exporting jade and porcelain in Guangzhou, China.

1937: Li & Fung Limited is formally established in Hong Kong.

1949: When China turns Communist, Pak-liu's son Fung Hon-chu reinvents the company to export goods manufactured in Hong Kong.

1973: Hon-chu's sons William and Victor persuade him to list Li & Fung on the Hong Kong Stock Exchange; the Fung brothers institute a more modern management style.

1979: China opens up for trade, and Li & Fung develops a trading network throughout East Asia.

1989: The Fung brothers buy out family shares and take Li & Fung private in a management buyout.

1992: After being reorganized to focus on trade, the export division of Li & Fung is relisted.

1995: Li & Fung acquires the British trading company Inchcape Buying Services.

2001: The "dispersed manufacturing" approach has helped Li & Fung double profits twice over the previous six years.

In 1981 Victor Fung succeeded his father as managing director, but in 1986 he left the executive position to set up an investment bank. William Fung took over as managing director and Victor continued to guide the company as a nonexecutive chairman. William Fung saw the need for more changes at the firm but was hampered by the fact that 75 percent of Li & Fung was still held by a family trust. There were disagreements with the older generation, who remembered the difficult postwar transition, over whether Li & Fung should trust Communist China. To resolve the impasse, William and Victor formed a holding company, acquired the outstanding family shares, and privatized Li & Fung in a management buyout in 1989.

As a private company, Li & Fung had the flexibility to make drastic structural changes. William Fung refocused the company on its core trading business, selling off unrelated shipping, insurance, and real estate enterprises. He organized the company into two divisions: export trading and retail. Instead of assigning responsibilities by country, he organized services by customer. Each division was free to cross borders to find the best way to serve its client. For large clients like The Limited or Gymboree, an entire division at Li & Fung would devote itself to the product line and sourcing needs of one company.

By the beginning of the 1990s, the Fung brothers' changes were bearing fruit. Li & Fung was well established with 900 suppliers in the East Asia region in countries that included Indonesia, Singapore, South Korea, Taiwan, Thailand, and China. Retail clothing stores in the United States continued to be its major customers. The company began a period of exceptionally rapid growth in 1991, when net revenue grew 56 percent to HK$2.8 billion and net profit reached HK$86.9 million.

In order to acquire funds for further expansion, Li & Fung relisted its export trading division in 1992. The company issued 25 percent of its equity, raising HK$275 million. The now public trading division became known simply as Li & Fung Limited, while the retail division, with the profitable Toys 'R' Us and Circle K branch stores, remained a wholly owned subsidiary of the Li & Fung Group.

Borderless Manufacturing in the 1990s

After the public listing, Li & Fung's services evolved further toward truly borderless supply chain management. In a 1998 interview with the *Harvard Business Journal,* Victor Fung explained how Li & Fung reached the stage of "dispersed manufacturing." As manufacturing in Hong Kong became increasingly expensive, he said, almost all labor-intensive work moved across the border to China, while design, packaging, and other technically advanced manufacturing techniques were still done in Hong Kong. Eventually the whole East Asian region was pulled into the manufacturing process, depending on each country's particular industrial strengths. A garment labeled "Made in Thailand" might contain Korean yarn that was woven and dyed in Taiwan, sewn at five different factories in Thailand, and fitted with zippers made in China by a Japanese company. Li & Fung became expert at finding the best solution for each step in the manufacturing process. Fung told the *Journal,* "This is a new type of value added, a truly global product that has never been seen before . . . We're not asking which country can do the best job overall. Instead, we're pulling apart the value chain and optimizing each step—and we're doing it globally."

This global array of services supported rapid growth and acquisitions at Li & Fung throughout the 1990s. Net profit in 1993 reached HK$185 million on revenues of HK$5.38 billion. Then the firm nearly tripled its size with the HK$475 million acquisition of Inchcape Buying Services (also known as Dodwell) in 1995. Inchcape was a British trading company with a network of offices in India, Pakistan, Bangladesh, and Sri Lanka. The acquisition of Inchcape, with its European customer base and sourcing points across the Indian subcontinent, balanced Li & Fung's American customer base and East Asian sourcing network.

Now that growth had taken off, William Fung began using three-year plans to set ambitious growth targets. In 1998, despite some instability caused by the Asian financial crisis, the company achieved its goal of doubling profits from the 1995 level. Net profit reached HK$470 million on revenues of HK$14.3 billion, compared with HK$242 million and HK$9.21 billion in 1995, respectively.

In the following years Li & Fung continued to diversify geographically, moving into emerging centers of production in northern Africa such as Egypt, Tunisia, and Morocco. By 2000, the company was making an effort to move production closer to its North American and European end markets and began sourcing from factories in Central America, the Caribbean, and Turkey. Li & Fung also was courting new end markets with forays into Japan and Australia. Although the Fung brothers still took pride in their company's Chinese heritage, Li & Fung was becoming a multinational company with a workforce based in dozens of countries.

With the rise of the Internet in the late 1990s came predictions of a "frictionless economy" where companies would bypass middlemen like Li & Fung and buy all their parts online. Li & Fung, however, capitalized on the Internet to strengthen communications with customers and branch offices. In areas with less developed telecommunications, personal visits, phones, and faxes were still necessary to ensure that manufacturers delivered the product on time. Li & Fung's decades-long personal relationships with suppliers, as well as their practical expertise in things like textile quotas and quality assurance, kept their business relevant in the digital age.

In 1999 Li & Fung acquired the export trading firms Swire & Maclaine Limited and Camberley Enterprises Limited, adding to their U.S. and European customer base. The following year the company acquired Colby Group Holdings Limited, its main competitor, in a deal valued at almost HK$282 million. Revenue continued to grow, but 2001 net profit was hurt by the closing of an e-commerce venture in the United States known as StudioDirect. The company was set up in February of that year to let smaller enterprises build their own brands on a web site without having to place large orders. But the site failed to catch on, and Li & Fung shut down the venture after less than a year. The year 2001 marked the end of another three-year plan. The company announced that it had met its goal of doubling continuing operating profits over the period and reported 2001 net profits of HK$667 million on revenues of HK$33 billion.

Although Li & Fung was posting strong results, the company was vulnerable because nearly 80 percent of its revenue came from U.S. clothing retailers. The company began pursuing customers in the hard goods sector in order to develop a more balanced clientele. In 2002 Li & Fung landed a deal to make promotional items for Coca-Cola. That year it also acquired Janco Overseas Limited, a Hong-Kong based company that supplied nonfood hard goods to supermarkets in the United States and Canada. In 2002 hard goods accounted for 32 percent of Li & Fung's turnover. The company remained heavily focused on the United States, with North American customers contributing 76 percent of turnover.

Li & Fung got off to a slow start on the 2002–04 three-year plan due to an economic slowdown and the terrorist attacks of September 11, 2001, in the United States. The company was about half a year behind on its goal but was still optimistic that it would once again double continuing operating profits over the three-year period. Such feats were more difficult now that Li & Fung had grown to be a relatively large company. Yet whether or not the company was able to sustain the rapid growth of the

1990s, it had shown it had the flexibility to continue playing a key role in the global market of the 21st century.

Principal Subsidiaries

Basic & More Fashion Limited; Camberley Enterprises Limited; Colby International Limited; CS International Limited; Dodwell (Mauritius) Limited; Janco Overseas Limited; Li & Fung (Exports) Limited; Lloyd Textile Trading Limited; Maclaine Limited; Shiu Fung Fireworks Limited; Toy Island Manufacturing Company Limited; Verity Enterprises Limited; LF International Inc. (U.S.A.).

Principal Competitors

APL Logistics, Ltd.; William E. Connor & Associates, Ltd.

Further Reading

Balfour, Frank, "Stick to Knitting," *Far Eastern Economic Review,* June 18, 1992, pp. 80–81.
Biers, Dan, "The New Economy: Entrepreneurship—Li & Fung VC Arm Looks Past Darlings of New Economy," *Far Eastern Economic Review,* November 20, 2000, p. 30.
Chow, Lotte, "Li & Fung's Plan to Purchase Inchcape Unit Is Called Perfect Merger by Some Analysts," *Wall Street Journal (Europe),* May 10, 1995, p. 20.
Curry, Lynne, "Global Grasp," *Far Eastern Economic Review,* April 3, 1997, pp. 48–49.
Fokstuen, Anne, "Li & Fung Sails Steadily Despite Stormy Economic Times, *Asian Wall Street Journal,* March 9, 1998, p. 3.
——, "Tough Times Highlight Li & Fung Model," *Asian Wall Street Journal,* July 21, 1998, p. 6.
Glain, Steve, "Hong Kong Firm Trades on China Ties—Li & Fung's Planned Relisting Anticipates Steady Growth on Mainland," *Asian Wall Street Journal,* November 8, 1991, p. 1.
Hastings, Kirsti, "Hong Kong's Li & Fung Will Buy Colby Group," *Asian Wall Street Journal,* November 10, 2000, p. 16.
Holstein, William J., "Middleman Becomes Master: Wal-Mart Watch Out," *Chief Executive (U.S.),* October 2002, p. 53.
Lim, Wendy, "Li & Fung Net Falls 10% on Provision in U.S.," *Asian Wall Street Journal,* March 22, 2002, p. M3.
Magretta, Joan, "Fast, Global and Entrepreneurial: Supply Chain Management, Hong Kong Style," *Harvard Business Review,* September–October 1998, p. 102.
Tanzer, Andrew, "Stitches in Time," *Forbes,* September 6, 1999, p. 118.

—Sarah Ruth Lorenz

Liberty Mutual Holding Company

175 Berkeley Street
Boston, Massachusetts 02116-5066
U.S.A.
Telephone: (617) 357-9500
Fax: (617) 350-7648
Web site: http://www.libertymutual.com

Private Company
Incorporated: 1912 as Massachusetts Employees
    Insurance Association
Employees: 35,000
Total Assets: $55.87 billion (2002)
NAIC: 551112 Offices of Other Holding Companies

Liberty Mutual Holding Company is the holding company formed in 2002 by Liberty Mutual Insurance Company and affiliated companies as a way to better compete against stock-based insurers. The Boston-based company is composed of a diversified international group of insurance companies, ranked 129th on the 2003 *Fortune* 500 list of the largest U.S. corporations and boasting $56 billion in consolidated assets and $14.5 billion in consolidated revenue. The lion's share of the group's business is workers' compensation insurance, offered under several well-known brand names, such as Liberty Mutual and Wausau. Aside from offering insurance to businesses, Liberty Mutual also provides auto, home, life, and other insurance products to individuals in the United States and Canada. Liberty International offers insurance products around the world, including specialty casualty and casualty; marine, energy, and engineering insurance; and reinsurance. It is in the overseas markets that Liberty Mutual sees its greatest growth potential for the future.

Forming the Company in 1912

The history of Liberty Mutual is tied to the rise of workmen's compensation, now referred to as workers' compensation. According to scholars, the concept dates back as far as the days of Charlemagne, embodied in tribal laws. The first workers' compensation system was introduced in Germany in 1884, followed in 1897 by the first English Workmen's Compensation Act. In the United States some coverage was already being provided by private insurers, such as Lumbermen's Mutual Casualty Company, a Chicago firm devoted to lumberjacks. Early in the 20th century, workers' compensation laws were passed at both the state and federal level, which led to public backing for coverage. Maryland enacted a workers' compensation law as early as 1902, but two years later it was declared unconstitutional. The first law to pass muster in the United States was the Federal Employees Compensation Act of 1908. The first constitutional state law was passed in Wisconsin in 1911. Over the course of the next dozen years most of the states passed workers' compensation laws, although it would take until 1949 before the last state, Mississippi, enacted legislation.

In 1911 the Massachusetts Legislature passed a law mandating that employers provide workers' compensation. To meet this need, the forefather to Liberty Mutual was formed: The Massachusetts Employees Insurance Association (MEIA). It was formed by 15 executives as a mutual company, owned for the benefit of policyholders rather than stockholders, and began operations in Boston on July 1, 1912. From the beginning, the company took steps to provide safety measures for workers, not just provide payments once they were seriously injured or killed on the job. In 1912 some 20,000 U.S. workers lost their lives in accidents. The company advocated, and even helped to design, early machine guards to protect workers from such dangerous equipment as woodworking machinery, power presses, press brakes, milling machines, and drill presses. MEIA opened its first branch office in Springfield, Massachusetts, in 1914 and looked to diversify its offerings but was limited by law to liability coverage. Instead, it forged an alliance with the United Mutual Fire Insurance Company, a mutual fire insurance company chartered by Massachusetts in 1908. It would one day change its name to Liberty Mutual Fire Insurance and eventually become one of the components of Liberty Mutual Holding Company.

The Massachusetts Legislature passed new laws in 1915 that allowed MEIA to write all types of public liability insurance, resulting in the company issuing its first automobile policy. The following year further legislation permitted the company to do business outside of Massachusetts. Because of its growing range of activities, Massachusetts Employees Insurance Association was no longer a suitable name; thus in August 1917 the company changed its name to Liberty Mutual Insurance Company. In 1919 it launched its first advertising campaign. Liberty Mutual moved beyond the boundaries of the United States in 1925 when it began operating in Canada in conjunction with salespeople employed by the Rexall Drug Company, selling and servicing policies referred by the drug salespeople. In 1927 Liberty Mutual set up shop in Ontario, Canada at Rexall's headquarters. In the meantime, Liberty Mutual continued in its efforts to prevent workplace accidents. In 1921, at the height of the silent era of film, the company produced two safety films: *The Outlaw* and *The Hand of Fate*. It was estimated that more than 250,000 workers and plant managers viewed these films. On the automobile insurance side, Liberty Mutual in 1930 began distributing safety materials to high school students in drivers' education courses.

Becoming the Top Writer of Workers' Comp in the 1930s

Despite the difficulty of doing business during the Great Depression, Liberty Mutual was able to prosper in the 1930s. In 1936 it became the number one writer of workers' compensation insurance, the same year that it broke ground on a new headquarters in Boston. By the middle of the following year, Liberty Mutual was operating in all 48 states (some 20 years before the addition of Alaska and Hawaii). With the advent of World War II, Liberty Mutual became international in scope. To support the country's war effort, industry ramped up production and Liberty Mutual kept pace, providing workers' compensation coverage to customers' operations in both the United States and overseas, including such remote locations as Somaliland, Greenland, and Guam. Liberty personnel were captured by the Japanese army on Wake Island and in the Philippines and confined in prisoner of war camps for the duration of the war. It was also during World War II, as a response to the large number of seriously wounded soldiers returning home, that Liberty Mutual in 1943 launched an experimental rehabilitation center in Boston, with the goal of helping the injured to lead productive lives. The experiment quickly became a permanent feature of the workers' compensation field, during times of war and peace. Another Liberty Mutual innovation was introduced in 1943: the establishment of its Medical Advisors Network, a group of specialists available to review the cases of the seriously injured to help assure both workers and employers that a proper medical treatment plan was being pursued. Another advance attributed to Liberty Mutual during the 1940s was the development of the first escalator emergency shutoff switch, a device that would become a building code requirement for all U.S. escalators in 1960.

Liberty Mutual's commitment to safety was further reflected by the 1954 founding of a state-of-the-art laboratory, the Liberty Mutual Research Center in Hopkinton, Massachusetts. The Center became involved in a wide range of activities, including developing tests to determine fatigue caused by workplace activities and

creating an emergency assistance program for truck drivers. In 1957, at a time when 100 people were killed each day on U.S. highways, Liberty Mutual worked with Cornell University to create prototype "survival cars," featuring seat belts and headrests. These cars toured the country, seen by millions, and even made an appearance on the popular television game show *I've Got a Secret*. This Liberty Mutual initiative helped convince automakers to introduce a number of safety features that have become standard, such as collapsible steering columns and air bags, as well as headrests and safety belts. In addition, Liberty Mutual in 1964 opened the Skid Control School at Hopkinton to teach driver trainers how to control vehicles during skids and other emergency situations, techniques that they could then teach to commercial vehicle drivers. Liberty Mutual research center also worked with the Massachusetts Institute of Technology in the early 1960s to develop the Boston Elbow, the first battery-powered prosthetic elbow, which was a major improvement over the old harness and cable method that required a person to shrug to make the device operate. The Boston Elbow, now known as the Boston Digital Arm, used muscle signals from the surface of the skin to control the limb and allowed for a greater range of motion and the ability to lift much heavier weights. In addition, in the 1960s Liberty Mutual did pioneering research in the field of ergonomics, which would be influential in the safe-lifting criteria adopted by the National Institute of Occupational Safety and Health.

In 1964 Liberty Life Assurance Company of Boston was created to offer a full range of individual and group life insurance products. Liberty Mutual then became involved in the worldwide insurance market, establishing in 1967 Liberty International Insurance Agency, Inc., a wholly owned brokerage corporation that was able to accommodate the foreign insurance needs of American policyholders doing business in other countries, either by placing foreign insurance or through reinsurance. In 1973 Liberty Mutual opened its first wholly owned international office, located in London, to participate in the international reinsurance market. By now, Liberty Mutual had topped the $2 billion level in written premiums.

Developments in the 1980s included the establishment of The Back School at the company's Boston rehabilitation center. The program helped people learn how to live productive lives in spite of severe lower back pain. In the field of ergonomics, Liberty Mutual completed important cumulative trauma disorder research, simulating in the laboratory that kind of stress caused by such activities as repetitive assembly work, manual screw driving, and the use of pliers and knives. This work was then used to determine desirable wrist postures and grips, as well as establishing the maximum acceptable force for repetitive wrist motion. Of further note during the decade was the 1985 foundation of Liberty Financial Services, allowing the company to offer financial services. In that same year, Liberty Mutual launched a program to establish small local offices throughout the United States and Canada.

The 1990s proved to be a time of expansion and challenge for Liberty Mutual and the insurance industry as a whole. In 1993 the company established Liberty International Holdings, a venture that not only offered its health and safety services to foreign countries but also allowed it to underwrite commercial risks in international markets. In 1995 Liberty Financial was spun off as a public company, the same year that a new London

Key Dates:

1912: The company is formed as the Massachusetts Employees Insurance Association.
1917: The name is changed to Liberty Mutual Insurance Company.
1937: The company is operating in all 48 states.
1954: Liberty Mutual Research Center opens.
1972: The company tops the $2 billion mark in written premiums.
1985: Liberty Financial is established.
1998: An alliance is formed with Employers Insurance of Wausau.
2002: Shareholders approve the conversion plan, and Liberty Mutual Holding Company is formed.
2003: With an increasing emphasis on overseas expansion, the company acquires the Spanish operations of MetLife Inc.

subsidiary was formed, Liberty Reinsurance Co., to act as a global reinsurer. Liberty Mutual took other steps in the 1990s to bolster its international business. Through a series of acquisitions it gained a presence in Colombia, Hong Kong, the Philippines, and Singapore. On the domestic front, Liberty Mutual made a number of acquisitions to form its Regional Agency Markets organization. In 1998 it established an affiliation with Employers Insurance of Wausau that increased the number of Liberty Mutual's workers' compensation premiums by more than a third. Liberty Mutual's commitment to research also was reinforced during the decade with the establishment of the Center for Disability Research at the Hopkinton facility.

Many Mutuals Converting to Stock Ownership in the 1990s

Changes in the insurance industry during the 1990s began to have an impact on Liberty Mutual. Long-term changes undertaken by many mutual insurance companies came to fruition when a number of them decided to convert to stock ownership in order to gain stock as a currency to use in acquisitions and thereby achieve greater growth. In 1992 the Equitable Life Assurance Society converted, followed by State Mutual Life Assurance in 1995, and Farm Family Mutual Insurance and American Mutual Life Assurance in 1996. When giant Prudential Insurance Company decided to convert to stock ownership in 1998, the industry reached a tipping point and the other major players made plans to follow suit, all believing that they had no choice but to grow larger or face a slow death. Conversion plans used by mutual insurance companies fell under three general types. A ''full'' demutualization plan compensated policyholders with stock in the newly formed holding company or with cash, all insurance policies remaining in effect. A ''subscription rights demutualization'' conversion offered no compensation to policyholders other than the right to purchase stock in the new company before the general public. Under the final option, the insurer formed a holding company, which was owned by policyholders and controlled a majority stake in the insurance company, now its subsidiary.

Massachusetts passed a law in 1998 that permitted a mutual to adopt the mutual holding company structure. In 2000 Liberty Mutual announced that it planned to change its legal structure to a mutual holding company, citing the difficulty it had in acquiring other companies because of a limited access to capital. The idea was to create a three-tiered structure. Liberty Mutual Holding Company would stand on top, followed by a holding company—which had the potential of becoming a vehicle for a public equity offering for as much as 49 percent—and then at the base Liberty Mutual Insurance Company, Liberty Mutual Fire Insurance Company, and Employers Insurance of Wausau. Although management indicated that it had no immediate intention of taking the holding company public, opponents of the conversion quickly pointed out that in the event of an offering policyholders, while retaining majority control, were not in line to receive any compensation for the portion of the company sold off. Liberty Mutual was clearly not prepared for the political firestorm that grew out of this criticism. Massachusetts Democrats denounced the conversion and threatened to pass legislation to thwart Liberty Mutual's plan, urging instead that if the insurer wanted to become a public enterprise that it opt for a full conversion and fairly compensate its policyholders. Liberty Mutual fought back, even hinting that it might have to move out of the state if denied the right to reorganize. The company also faced a shareholders suit. In the end the suit was settled out of court and the conversion plan was presented to shareholders, who overwhelmingly approved it. In 2002 Liberty Mutual Holding Company was formed as part of the execution of the mutual holding company plan.

While the conversion was completed, Liberty Financial was sold as part of an effort to focus on the property and casualty insurance business. Perhaps of more importance was the company's increased emphasis on overseas expansion. In July 2003, Liberty Mutual acquired the Spanish operations of MetLife Inc. On that occasion, Liberty Mutual's CEO, Edmund F. Kelly, told the press, ''Business is going to be increasingly global. Either we expand internationally, or over time we become less important.''

Principal Subsidiaries

Liberty Mutual Fire Insurance Company; Liberty Mutual Insurance Company; Employers Insurance of Wausau.

Principal Competitors

The Allstate Corporation; Prudential Financial, Inc.; State Farm Insurance Companies.

Further Reading

Sclafane, Susanne, ''Liberty Mutual Sets Stage for MHC Structure,'' *National Underwriter Property & Casualty-Risk & Benefits Management,* September 25, 2000, p. 4.
——, ''Mass. Democrats Oppose Liberty Conversion,'' *National Underwriter Property & Casualty-Risk & Benefits Management,* January 29, 2001.
Walsh, Tom, ''Backlash Grows Against Liberty,'' *Boston Herald,* February 4, 2001, p. 31.
——, ''Taking Liberties? Foes Say Reorganization Is Unfair to Policyholders,'' *Boston Herald,* November 26, 2000, p. 31.

—Ed Dinger

Maidenform, Inc.

154 Avenue E
Bayonne, New Jersey 07002-4435
U.S.A.
Telephone: (201) 436-9200
Fax: (201) 436-8322
Web site: http://www.maidenform.com

Private Company
Incorporated: 1925 as Enid Manufacturing Company
Employees: 4,000
Sales: $250 million (2001 est.)
NAIC: 315231 Women's and Girls' Cut and Sew
    Lingerie, Loungewear, and Nightwear Manufacturing;
    448190 Other Clothing Stores; 454111 Electronic
    Shopping

Maidenform, Inc. is one of the nation's leading manufacturers of brassieres and other articles of women's intimate apparel. It was a pioneer in the development of brassieres and for many years produced and sold more bras than any other company. In addition to its flagship Maidenform brand, the company also markets Lilyette full-figure bras and Flexees shapewear. Maidenform's products are sold nationwide through department and discount stores, as well as directly from the company in its outlet stores and via the corporate web site. Known as the grande dame of the foundations industry, Maidenform was a family-owned and family-run company for 75 years before being forced to file for bankruptcy protection in July 1997. Two years later the company emerged from bankruptcy aided by the financial assistance of General Electric Capital Corporation, with Oaktree Capital Management, LLC, an investment firm specializing in troubled companies, holding a majority stake.

Maidenform to 1950

Ida Cohen came to the United States from what is now Belarus in 1905. She established a small dressmaker's shop in Hoboken, New Jersey, the following year and married William Rosenthal, a dress wholesaler and manufacturer, in 1907. She moved her shop to New York City in 1919 and three years later relocated on Manhattan's fashionable West 57th Street in partnership with an Englishwoman, Enid Bissett. The partners ran a custom dress business called Enid Frocks.

Mary Phelps Jacob (later known as Caresse Crosby) is credited with inventing the modern brassiere—free of bones and leaving the midriff bare—in 1913. The boyish silhouette favored in the 1920s required the bra to suppress, rather than enhance, the contours of the female bosom. Explaining the circumstances that led her into brassiere manufacturing, Mrs. Rosenthal later said, ''In those [flapper-era] days—it was a very sad story—women wore those flat things like bandages, towels with hooks in the back. Now in those days the cheapest dress we made was $125, and it just didn't fit right. So we made a little bra with two pockets. Not too accentuated, of course.''

William Rosenthal was an amateur sculptor. He improved his wife's brassiere, employing a fabric called swami, which was similar to soft nylon tricot. His bra also had an elastic center. At first this simple brassiere was built into the dresses that Mrs. Rosenthal and Mrs. Bissett created. But when clients began requesting separate bras, the partners started giving them away with each dress. This proved so successful that in 1922 they began manufacturing brassieres under the Maidenform (originally Maiden Form) name—the name chosen to contrast with the ''boyish form'' then in vogue—and within a few years left the dress business. In 1925 their company was incorporated as Enid Manufacturing Company, with capital of $4,500 provided by Mrs. Rosenthal, her husband, and Mrs. Bissett. Maidenform established its manufacturing operations in Bayonne, New Jersey, the following year. William Rosenthal, who became president of the company in 1927, took out many patents on brassiere design, including nursing, long-line, and full-figure bras and the first seamed uplift bra. Maidenform was credited with being the first to offer a truly fitted bra cup. Rosenthal also organized a production line, with one seamstress sewing backs, another making straps, and a third sewing together bra cups. His wife assumed charge of sales and financing. The success of the Maidenform brand led the company to change its name to Maidenform Brassiere Company in 1930.

By 1928 Maidenform was making nearly 500,000 brassieres a year. Sales declined only in the Great Depression year of 1932. During World War II the company also made parachutes, head nets, mosquito bars, mattress covers, and a brassiere-like nylon vest for carrying courier pigeons when they traveled with the armed forces, but it always received an allotment of cotton gingham for bras because, in Mrs. Rosenthal's words, "women workers who wore an uplift were less fatigued than others."

Maidenform at midcentury was selling more brassieres than any other U.S. company, with about 10 percent of the market, annual revenue of $14 million, and net profit of nearly $1 million. The 12 million bras it produced in 1950 came in 15 styles, each with more than 100 different combinations of size, cup size, color, and material. Even the simplest Maidenform brassiere consisted of at least 20 separate pieces, and a long-line model might have as many as 50. In addition to the Bayonne plant, Maidenform now was producing bras, bra pads, and garter belts at seven other factories in New Jersey and West Virginia. The company had 9,000 retail accounts selling its brassieres for between $1.25 and $5.

Adapting to the Marketplace: 1950s–70s

During the 1950s Maidenform's biggest seller became Chansonette, a pointy style. William Rosenthal died in 1958 and was succeeded by his widow as president, chairman, and chief executive officer of Maidenform. One year later, Rosenthal's son-in-law, Dr. Joseph A. Coleman, took over the presidency. In 1960, the same year that the company was renamed Maidenform, Inc., Rosenthal estimated that 30 percent of all U.S. women owned a Maidenform bra, and they were being sold in 115 other countries as well. That year the company, after taking in revenue of $34 million in 1959, continued to sell nearly 10 percent of all U.S. bras. By 1961 it also was selling swimsuits equipped with Maidenform bras.

Maidenform's profile in this period owed much to one of the most famous campaigns in advertising history, apparently prompted by the popularization of Freudian psychology in plays and movies of the 1940s. Between 1949 and 1969 the company launched 163 "dream sequence" print ads that showed a model wearing only a Maidenform bra above the waist. In the first one the copy read, "I dreamt I went shopping in my Maidenform bra," but from this prosaic start the campaign moved on to more adventurous activities, with the subject engaged in such dream pastimes as fighting a bull, hunting a tiger, addressing a jury, ascending a balloon, and floating down the Nile in a barge. The revolutionary Dream campaign ran through 1969.

By the mid-1960s Maidenform's annual revenue had reached an estimated $50 million to $55 million, but its well-known name had not kept Playtex, and perhaps Warnaco as well, from surging to the front in bra and girdle sales. Maidenform even briefly had to face competition from designer Rudi Gernreich's No Bra bra, although Ida Rosenthal warned that "after 35 a woman hasn't got the figure to wear nothing." Analysts said the company's conservative styles and reluctance to move heavily into television advertising had cost it sales. After Mrs. Rosenthal suffered a stroke in 1966, her daughter, Beatrice Coleman, became chairman of the company. Dr. Coleman, Beatrice's husband, became president but died two years later, whereupon Mrs. Coleman also assumed the presidency. Ida Rosenthal died in 1973 at the age of 87.

By 1970 Maidenform was making sportswear and lingerie as well as foundation garments. Its girdles and brassieres now also came in stretch materials such as Lycra. Annual sales had reached $65 million to $70 million, with the company's products sold to some 12,000 department and specialty stores through its own sales force. But by the mid-1970s Maidenform had fallen farther behind Playtex in brassiere sales, although the firm maintained it held the top spot in the contemporary segment, which was accounting for about one-quarter of the total market. Maidenform's contemporary bra line included No-Show Naturals, stretch-bra styles with a "softer, more natural frame than the traditional fortress-built bras," according to the company's vice-president for advertising.

Maidenform had annual revenue of about $100 million in 1980, more than 60 percent from brassiere sales. The company now had 14 factories, some of them abroad, making bras, panties, girdles, sleepwear, and swimwear, with some 10 to 15 percent of its production exported. During the late 1970s it continued to shift emphasis not only from cotton and nylon to stretch materials but also from basic white to a variety of colors. Maidenform introduced three coordinated bra and panty lines: stretch-lace Private Affairs and satin-and-lace Chantilly and Sweet Nothings, and successfully worked to place them in department store lingerie departments. Ten million Sweet Nothing bras had been sold by 1987, making it the industry's bestseller.

"Gradually we took a lesson from sportswear, and color and prettiness came in," Mrs. Coleman told a *New York Times* reporter in 1980. "Within the last five years, our production of white garments has shrunk to about half." She said the company had been profitable every year since its founding. Nevertheless, swimwear and sportswear, manufactured for Donald Brooks for about five years, proved unprofitable and eventually were dropped. The company also lost money on a short-lived jeans venture.

Advertising in the 1980s and 1990s

During the early 1970s Maidenform shifted 95 percent of its print-advertising dollars into television. Because TV stations would not show live models in their scanties, however, the company was reduced to unsatisfactory alternatives such as the 1976 "chorus line" theme that clad the dancers in top hat, vest, cuffs, and bra over leotards.

Maidenform then returned to relying on print ads. The campaign adopted in 1979 harkened back to the exhibitionist "dream" concept. Women were depicted parading in their underwear in public places such as a theater lobby, an antiques shop, and a basketball court—even descending from a helicopter with attaché case. One ad showed the model as a physician in a hospital, another in a train station with fully clothed men. The caption read: "The Maidenform woman. You never know where she'll turn up." Times had changed, however, and in 1981 and 1982 Women Against Pornography awarded the company a plastic pig for sexist advertising. Maidenform toned down the campaign in 1983, continuing to display models in the company's intimate apparel, but doing their fantasizing at home, with no men present.

In 1987 Maidenform introduced a TV ad campaign that, instead of displaying women wearing the company's products, featured leading men such as Omar Sharif, Michael York, Christopher Reeve, and Pierce Brosnan discussing lingerie. Feminists objected to what they regarded as the implication that women wear undergarments mainly for men, so in 1991 the company, to deplore sexism, showed images of a chick, tomato, fox, cat, and dog in one TV ad and stereotyped women like schoolmarms and strippers in another. But feminists said the campaign was actually promoting what it affected to deplore.

In 1997 Maidenform introduced an expensive new print-advertising campaign carrying the theme "Maidenform Unhooked" to promote a less formal, more contemporary image for the company's products. A number of women appeared in brassieres, alongside copy such as, "Most men don't notice my eyes are hazel" and "No one lays a hand on them without loving me first."

Falling into Bankruptcy in the 1990s

By 1989 Maidenform had dropped loungewear and sleepwear but was making lingerie items such as slips, petticoats, and camisoles. Garter belts had made a comeback, too. "They are a very hot item," Mrs. Coleman told a reporter. "I don't know what people do with them, but they are considered very sexy." The company also had introduced an Oscar de la Renta lingerie collection, consisting of about 30 daywear and foundation styles. In 1992 Maidenform acquired True Form Foundations Corp., a $40-million-a-year manufacturer of bodyshapers under the Flexees and Subtract names.

Mrs. Coleman died in 1990 and was succeeded as president by son-in-law Robert Brawer, husband of one of Coleman's two daughters, Catherine C. Brawer. Taking over as chairman was Coleman's other daughter, Elizabeth J. Coleman, an Atlanta lawyer. Maidenform's main factory remained in Bayonne, but there were five others in Puerto Rico, two each in Mexico and the Dominican Republic, one each in Costa Rica and Jamaica, and a cut-and-sew plant in Florida. A 250,000-square-foot distribution center was opened in Fayetteville, North Carolina, in 1992. Another distribution center was in Jacksonville, Florida. The company, which in 1985 also had opened a duty-free distribution and processing center in Shannon, Ireland, formed a European subsidiary in Hilden, Germany, in 1991. It closed a longtime production facility in Huntington, West Virginia, in 1992.

Maidenform began offering seamless bras in all its lines in 1994. That year it introduced a second Oscar de la Renta collection of bras and coordinated panties, aimed at younger customers. In 1995 the Maidenform name was added to a line of bras and coordinated panties under the Self Expressions label. The new line was aimed at mass merchandisers.

Brawer retired in 1995 and was succeeded as president and CEO by Elizabeth Coleman. That year the company acquired 92 percent of NCC Industries, Inc. from NCC's largest shareholder, German underwear manufacturer Triumph International Overseas Ltd., for $9.8 million in cash and 28.2 percent of Maidenform's common stock. NCC manufactured the Lilyette full-figured bra, a licensed line of Bill Blass bras and panties, and merchandise under the Minimizer and Reflections names. "It was a strategic acquisition for Maidenform," the new CEO told a reporter. "Our market is mostly for average to smaller sizes. And 35 percent of the bra market is full-figure." The purchase also added $126 million to Maidenform's annual sales, which were running close to $300 million. NCC's sales, however, came only to $99.8 million in 1996.

Coleman acknowledged in August 1996 that Maidenform had undergone "some cash-flow issues" earlier in the year. The company had, in 1995, entered into a revolving-credit arrangement for $120 million and had also taken out a $50 million term loan and issued $30 million in senior notes, pledging NCC's assets and stocks as collateral. At the end of 1996 its bank borrowings came to $171.2 million. A new agreement signed in December 1996 raised the revolving-credit line to $150 million. Maidenform lost money during both 1995 ($35.5 million) and 1996 ($75.5 million on sales of $396 million) and was reported to have defaulted from time to time on loan agreements during 1996. It also sold inventory below cost during the year in order to raise cash. VF Corporation, a $5-billion-a-year clothing manufacturer, signed a letter of intent in March 1997 to acquire Maidenform. Talks broke off, however, two weeks later.

In May 1997 Ted Stenger, a corporate turnaround expert, was hired as president to address the financial troubles as well as operational difficulties. Maidenform had run into difficulty integrating its two acquisitions and had fallen behind in tracking inventory and delivering it to stores. Stenger began restructuring Maidenform's operations, aiming to achieve annual savings of $40 million by consolidating the True Form and NCC subsidiaries into the parent company, reducing the company's three divisions into two, and slashing the product offerings to a tighter core of three main brands: Maidenform, Lilyette, and Flexees. But, saddled with $245.1 million in liabilities, and with its lenders unwilling to provide additional financing, Maidenform was forced to file for Chapter 11 bankruptcy protection in July 1997. By doing so, the company was able to continue the restructuring process backed by a $50 million infusion of debtor-in-possession financing.

In December 1997 management of Maidenform by the Rosenthal/Coleman family ended with the resignation of Elizabeth Coleman. Stenger took over the CEO responsibilities on an interim basis, while an entirely new board of directors was elected consisting of four outsiders and Stenger. That same month, the company launched a massive downsizing involving the closure of all of its facilities in Puerto Rico along with two of its three distribution centers—the ones in Cortland, New York, and Jacksonville. All domestic distribution would now be handled through the facility in North Carolina. These closures entailed the elimination of 1,200 jobs, or 18 percent of the workforce. Restructuring charges contributed to a loss of $111.6 million for 1997; revenues dropped 40 percent that year, to about $250 million, as a result of the operational difficulties and the cutbacks in the product lines. Maidenform abandoned most of its private-label business in order to focus on its core brands and also dropped the licensed Oscar de la Renta line. About 35 outlet stores were also shut down, leaving the company with 70.

Paul Mischinski replaced Stenger as CEO in March 1998. Mischinski, who was one of the new members of the Maidenform board, had spent more than a decade and a half in various executive positions at Sara Lee Corporation, including a three-year stint as the head of the Bali Company division. Also brought onboard as head of Maidenform Brands was another executive from an intimate apparel competitor, Maurice Reznik, who had been president of the Warner's division of the Warnaco Group, Inc. With the financial situation at the company stabilizing, the new leaders placed great emphasis on revitalizing the new product pipeline. Late in 1998 Maidenform introduced a line of convertible bras called Customize It by Maidenform, which could be worn three different ways; according to Reznik the new line received the biggest launch in company history.

Maidenform finally exited Chapter 11 status in July 1999, having secured $60 million in asset-based financing from General Electric Capital Corporation. The reorganization involved the conversion of debt into equity, and GE Capital thus gained a majority stake in Maidenform. But Oaktree Capital Management, LLC, an investment firm specializing in troubled companies, soon emerged as the majority owner.

A Firmer Foundation in the Early 2000s

Maidenform achieved an 11 percent increase in revenues in 2000 aided by new product launches. Shapewear was proving to be the biggest growth category, surging 35 percent in 2000 and 70 percent over a two-year period. The company also gained a modest boost in sales from the November 1999 relaunch of the company web site with the goal of offering consumers an improved shopping experience. Maidenform also had come a long way in fixing the problems in the supply chain. The sputtering economy and a weak retail climate provided the company with new challenges, but Maidenform secured a fresh infusion

of $82.5 million in cash and a $60 million revolving line of credit from Congress Financial, a unit of First Union Bank, in May 2001.

In August 2001 Thomas J. Ward succeeded Mischinski as president and CEO. Ward was the former president and COO of WestPoint Stevens Inc., a major producer of bed linens and bath towels. In January 2002 Maidenform introduced the One Fabulous Fit bra, which featured an ultrathin, stretch-foam style overlaid with very soft nylon and Lycra spandex. Later that year the company announced that it was boosting its annual ad spending to $6 million and would launch its first national advertising campaign in years in early 2003. This campaign centered around a new tag line, "This Is the One That Will Become Everyone's Favorite Bra." The new product got off to a very good start and soon became the top-selling bra in U.S. department stores.

Maidenform's future as an independent company remained very much in doubt throughout the post-bankruptcy period. Reports of talks with other companies interested in acquiring the firm and its three principal brands surfaced periodically, most often involving VF or Kellwood Company. Some observers speculated that a Kellwood-Maidenform deal would be ideal, given the former's strength in private-label clothing and the latter's strong branded business. Meantime, Maidenform continued to pursue new growth opportunities, announcing in April 2003 that it had signed four new licensing pacts involving sports and maternity bras, women's slippers, women's socks, and bra accessories.

Principal Competitors

Sara Lee Branded Apparel; VF Corporation; The Warnaco Group, Inc.; Intimate Brands.

Further Reading

Agovino, Theresa, "New Maidenform CEO Changing Firm's Shape," *Crain's New York Business,* May 20, 1991, pp. 3+.

Areddy, James T., "Maidenform, Run by Founding Family, Sells Image As Well As Intimate Apparel," *Wall Street Journal,* October 23, 1989.

Baltera, Lorraine, "Maidenform Goes on Stage for Dream Theme Revival," *Advertising Age,* April 26, 1976, p. 39.

Cook, Joan, "A Maidenform Dream Come True," *New York Times,* December 9, 1965, p. 62.

DesMarteau, Kathleen, "Maidenform Finds 'Bricks and Clicks' Balance," *Bobbin,* May 2000, pp. 12, 18.

Detman, Art, Jr., "Survival of the Fittest," *Sales Management,* June 1, 1966, pp. 43–44, 46, 48.

Dougherty, Philip H., "Advertising: Years of Maidenform Dreams," *New York Times,* September 10, 1967, Sec. 3, p. 16.

Elliott, Stuart, "Maidenform Aims for Soccer Moms and Just About Everyone Else," *New York Times,* March 12, 1997, p. D2.

Ettorre, Barbara, "The Maidenform Woman Returns," *New York Times,* June 1, 1980, Sec. 3, p. 3.

"Ida Rosenthal," *Time,* October 24, 1960, p. 92.

"Ida Rosenthal, Co-Founder of Maidenform, Dies," *New York Times,* March 30, 1973, p. 42.

Kanner, Bernice, "The Bra's Not for Burning," *New York,* December 12, 1983, pp. 26, 29–30.

——, "Sending Up the Bra," *New York,* December 17, 1990, p. 19.

King, Thomas R., "Maidenform Ads Focus on Stereotypes," *Wall Street Journal,* December 10, 1990, p. B6.

"Maidenform's Mrs. R.," *Fortune,* July 1950, pp. 75–76, 130, 132.

Monget, Karen, "Coleman: Keeping Maidenform Fit," *Women's Wear Daily,* August 5, 1996, pp. 14, 16.

——, "Maidenform Clinches Deal with Triumph for 92% of NCC," *Women's Wear Daily,* April 27, 1995, p. 2.

——, "Maidenform: Shaping Its Own Future," *Women's Wear Daily,* November 5, 1992, p. 8.

——, "Maidenform's Firmer Foundation," *Women's Wear Daily,* September 25, 2000, p. 16.

——, "Maidenform's New Foundation," *Women's Wear Daily,* March 18, 2002, p. 8.

——, "Maidenform: The Nightmare's Over," *Women's Wear Daily,* August 30, 1999, p. 16.

——, "VF Inks Letter of Intent to Acquire Maidenform," *Women's Wear Daily,* March 26, 1997, p. 2.

Monget, Karen, and Thomas J. Ryan, "Maidenform Files Chapter 11, Expects to Obtain $50M DIP," *Women's Wear Daily,* July 23, 1997, pp. 1+.

Morris, Michele, "The Mother Figure of Maidenform," *Working Woman,* April 1987, pp. 82, 86, 88.

Palumbo, Sandra, "Maidenform, Looking Back, Moving Forward," *Women's Wear Daily,* January 5, 1987, p. 14.

Ryan, Thomas J., "Maidenform Redux," *Women's Wear Daily,* July 27, 1998, p. 18B.

——, "$75.5 Million Loss in '96 Foreshadowed Maidenform's Chapter 11," *Women's Wear Daily,* July 28, 1997, pp. 1+.

Sacco, Joe, "Dreams for Sale: How the One for Maidenform Came True," *Advertising Age,* September 12, 1977, pp. 63–64.

Steinhauser, Jennifer, "Maidenform's Problems Reflect Industry Pitfalls," *New York Times,* July 24, 1997, pp. D1, D4.

—Robert Halasz
—update: David E. Salamie

Makita Corporation

3-11-8, Sumiyoshi-cho
Anjo, Aichi 446-8502
Japan
Telephone: (0566) 98-1711
Fax: (0566) 98-6021
Web site: http://www.makita.co.jp

Public Company
Incorporated: 1938 as Makita Electric Works, Ltd.
Employees: 8,344
Sales: ¥175.60 billion ($1.49 billion) (2003)
Stock Exchanges: Tokyo Nagoya Amsterdam
    NASDAQ
NAIC: 333991 Power-Driven Handtool Manufacturing;
    333210 Sawmill and Woodworking Machinery
    Manufacturing; 333112 Lawn and Garden Tractor and
    Home Lawn and Garden Equipment Manufacturing;
    333319 Other Commercial and Service Industry
    Machinery Manufacturing; 335212 Household
    Vacuum Cleaner Manufacturing; 335312 Motor and
    Generator Manufacturing; 811411 Home and Garden
    Equipment Repair and Maintenance

Makita Corporation is Japan's number one manufacturer and exporter of electric power tools. The company develops, manufactures, and distributes tools—more than 350 different products in all—in four areas. Makita's portable general purpose tools group, which accounted for more than 52 percent of 2003 revenues, encompasses drills, jackhammers, grinders, sanders, screwdrivers, and other construction equipment. The portable woodworking tools group includes saws, planers, routers, nailers, and other carpentry tools. It generated about 19 percent of sales in 2003. Stationary woodworking machines, including table saws, planer-joiners, and band saws, contributed just over 1 percent of sales. Though the company has traditionally targeted the professional user, Makita's distinctive turquoise tools increasingly appeal to the do-it-yourself market. Consumer tools include heavy-duty and household vacuums, chain saws, brush cutters, hedge trimmers, and blowers. These, along with

industrial-use dust collectors and generators, made up around 11 percent of annual revenues. Makita's parts and repair services were another important business area, contributing more than 16 percent of revenues in 2003.

Having launched multinational operations in 1970, Makita boasted more than 100 sales offices and 39 overseas subsidiaries in the early 2000s, selling its products in more than 100 countries around the world. Although North America was its oldest market and generated 26 percent of sales in 2003, Makita's largest foreign market was Europe, constituting just under 33 percent of sales. Approximately 22 percent of revenues originated within Japan itself, while Southeast Asia contributed almost 8 percent. Aiming to make its products as close to its customers as possible, Makita manufactures its power tools and other products at plants in Japan, Brazil, Canada, China, Germany, the United Kingdom, and the United States.

20th-Century Foundation and Development

The company traces its history to 1915 and the establishment of Makita Electric Works, a repair shop for electric tools and equipment in Nagoya, Japan, midway between Tokyo and Osaka. It was incorporated in 1938 as Makita Electric Works, Ltd. In April 1945, near the end of World War II, the plant was relocated to Sumiyoshi-cho in nearby Anjo City in an attempt to avoid damage from air raids. The company has been located in Anjo ever since.

But it was not until 1958 and the administration of President Juiro Goto that the company diversified into the manufacture of electric power tools. In January of that year, Makita began selling portable electric planers, the first such product in Japan. A 1962 public stock offering raised funds for the diversification program. By 1969—just over a decade later—Makita had leapfrogged to the top of the Japanese power tool market. The company credited its success in the domestic power tool market to high quality construction, pioneering research and development, and a unique system of direct distribution. Instead of relying on wholesalers to market its tools to retailers, Makita employed its own direct sales force. The close relationships engendered by this system gave the company insights into the needs of retailers as well as the end user, thereby fueling innovation.

With their brushed metal casings, the company's earliest tools looked bulky, heavy, and primitive by today's standards. Over the years, Makita traded metal casings for shock-resistant, turquoise plastic; added multi-speed motors and electronic controls; and developed a mind-numbing variety of accessories. Makita targeted professional tool users in the carpentry, construction, timber, and masonry trades with its powerful, durable equipment that often cost two to three times as much as a typical tool made for the consumer market. Focusing on the high end of the power tool industry mitigated price competition, thereby boosting profit margins substantially.

Overseas Expansion Beginning in 1970s

Realizing the limitations of the domestic market, Goto sought global expansion in the 1970s. Stock offerings in 1968 and 1970 generated a "war chest" that financed Makita's overseas campaign. The company employed a multinationalist strategy, establishing a new subsidiary in each target market. Makita set up a foothold in the United States first, in 1970. Within just four years, the company had operations in France, the United Kingdom, Australia, Canada, the Netherlands, and Italy. The late 1970s and early 1980s witnessed the creation of subsidiaries in Germany, Belgium, Brazil, Austria, and Singapore.

Makita used its comparatively low-cost production base to advantage in Europe and the United States. By the end of the 1970s, the company had captured almost one-fifth of the global professional tool market, nearly matching Black & Decker Corporation's market share. As an unidentified analyst told *Fortune*'s Bill Sapirito in 1984, "Basically, Makita had them by the you-know-whats and just said, 'Cough.'"

By this time, competition between Makita and U.S. industry leader Black & Decker had saturated that country's market for power tools to the point that sales growth appeared limited to replacements, parts, and trade-ups. In fact, manufacturer's sales slid 16 percent from 1980 to 1983. Fortunately, the development of cordless rechargeable power tools established a whole new avenue of growth. After ten years of research and development, Makita launched its first cordless tool, a drill, in 1978. Eliminating the cord freed the worker from the power source, but early cordless models had several limitations. They were often heavier and less powerful than their corded forebears, had very limited running time, and required long periods to recharge. Though these factors kept cordless tools out of many professionals' tool chests, they did appeal to the home handyman whose projects were less demanding. Improvements in battery technology throughout the late 20th century boosted power and running time while reducing recharging time. By the late 1980s, Makita's 9.6-volt family of cordless tools was beginning to find their way onto construction sites.

Establishment of Overseas Factories: 1980s

A variety of factors encouraged Makita to begin to establish manufacturing operations outside Japan during this period. Rising labor and production costs at home combined with a desire to minimize the effect of currency fluctuations and circumvent many trade restrictions while simultaneously reducing shipping expenses. Makita set up production facilities—dubbed "transplants" in business jargon—in Canada in 1980, Brazil in 1981, the United States in 1985, and the United Kingdom in 1991.

Makita also continued to expand its global presence throughout the late 1980s and 1990s, establishing sales, distribution, and service operations in Spain, Taiwan, Hong Kong, China, New Zealand, Poland, Mexico, the Czech Republic, Hungary, and Korea. The company augmented its manufacturing capabilities with the creation of plants in the United Kingdom (1989) and China (1993). By the end of 1997, the company's Chinese factory was churning out over 100,000 power tools each month. Makita also created the U.K.-based Makita International Europe Ltd. as a holding company for its burgeoning European operations.

New Products Driving Power Tool Market in 1990s

Makita pursued new product development in the 1990s, focusing on ergonomics as well as dust, sound, and vibration control. In 1991 the company bought into the market for gasoline-powered tools such as chainsaws via the acquisition of Germany's Sachs-Dolmar G.m.b.H., which was subsequently renamed Dolmar GmbH. Research and development costs averaged 1.7 percent of sales mid-decade, and totaled ¥2.7 billion ($21.4 million) in 1997. By that time, Makita held more than 150 patents worldwide and applications for hundreds more were pending. Some of the company's discoveries applied Makita's power tool know-how to home and garden appliances including cordless vacuum cleaners, rechargeable electric lawnmowers, remote-controlled drapery openers, and hedge trimmers. As Makita reached out to the consumer market, however, it had to take special care not to alienate its core constituency of professional tool buyers. The company launched two new lines of cordless tools powered by 12-volt and 14-volt battery systems in 1997 as well.

By the early 1990s, Makita had captured over 50 percent of the $400 million U.S. market for professional tools, far surpassing American power tool maker Black & Decker (B&D). But B&D moved to reclaim the segment in 1992, when it relaunched the DeWalt brand as its pro-tool standard-bearer. The construction-yellow competitor to Makita soon took the segment by storm. Such industry observers as *Fortune*'s Patricia Sellers characterized Makita as "complacent" in the face of this renewed competition.

In fact, Makita's strategy remained unchanged as the turn of the 21st century approached. Masahiko Goto, who had succeeded Juiro Goto as president in 1984, continued to lead Makita into the late 1990s. In his annual message for 1997, Goto expressed Makita's "aim to become a 'Strong Company'" by "developing products that accurately meet the needs of the market, increasing overseas production and further rationalizing production processes at its domestic production

Key Dates:

1915: Makita Electric Works is established in Nagoya, Japan, as a repair shop for electric tools and equipment.
1938: Company is incorporated as Makita Electric Works, Ltd.
1945: Company relocates to nearby Anjo City in an effort to avoid damage from World War II air raids.
1958: Under the administration of President Juiro Goto, Makita diversifies into the manufacture of electric power tools; a portable electric planer is the first such product.
1962: Company goes public to raise funds for the diversification effort.
1969: Makita attains the leading position in the Japanese power tool market.
1970: Overseas expansion begins with the establishment of a U.S. subsidiary.
1978: Company launches its first cordless product, a drill.
1980: First overseas factory is established in Canada.
1985: A U.S. manufacturing operation is created.
1991: Makita acquires Sachs-Dolmar, a German maker of gasoline-powered chain saws that is subsequently renamed Dolmar GmbH; Makita Corporation is adopted as the new company name.
1993: Makita sets up its first factory in China.
2001: Production begins at the company's second Chinese manufacturing plant.
2002: The Maktec line of low-cost, made-in-China power tools is introduced into Asian markets outside of Japan.

facilities, and strengthening its sales and distribution bases.'' This rather unimaginative plan did not serve Makita well in the 1990s.

Sales declined from ¥178.9 billion ($1.4 billion) in 1993 to less than ¥160 billion ($1.3 billion) in 1996 before recovering to ¥186.2 billion ($1.5 billion) in 1997. Net income fared worse, falling by more than 30 percent from ¥9.8 billion ($79 million) in 1993 to ¥6.7 billion ($54.4 million) in 1995, then rebounding somewhat to ¥8.1 billion ($65.4 million) by 1997.

Makita continued its struggles during the late 1990s, its difficulties compounded by the still stagnant Japanese economy, the economic turmoil that followed the Asian currency crises of 1997, and the sharp appreciation of the yen against both the dollar and the euro, which eroded the value of overseas sales in these regions. The company closed out the 1990s with rather dismal 2000 profits of ¥4.19 billion ($40.7 million) on revenues of ¥174.55 billion ($1.69 billion). Makita continued to expand its global network during this period, establishing subsidiaries in the United Arab Emirates, Argentina, Chile, Greece, and Romania. On the product development front, the company introduced the world's first cordless miter saw and also launched a line of 18-volt cordless power tools during 1999. Among the new products debuting the following year was a circular saw with an attached dust collector and also the world's

first line of cordless tools powered by nickel–metal hydride batteries. The latter were more environmentally friendly than the previously ubiquitous nickel-cadmium batteries, which contained cadmium, a heavy metal. By this time, the company had developed a recycling program that enabled customers to return their used batteries—both types—to any retailer within Makita's huge worldwide network.

Early 2000s: Struggling to Overcome Economic Turmoil and Heightened Competition

The uncertain economic and geopolitical situation that prevailed worldwide in the early 2000s made for a difficult operating environment for Makita. Net income dipped to a low of ¥133 million ($1 million) during 2002, a plunge of 94 percent from the previous year; part of the blame rested with weakness in global stock markets, which led to ¥2.74 billion ($20.6 million) in losses from securities held by Makita. The company also had to contend with an extremely competitive situation in the United States, where the aggressive entrance of low-priced products from China had cut its market share from 17 percent at the beginning of the 1990s to less than 10 percent a little more than a decade later. As a result, Makita's U.S. subsidiaries were operating in the red, and the company's North American subsidiaries reported operating losses of $16.5 million and $27.5 million in 2001 and 2002, respectively, before managing to eke out an operating profit of $2.3 million the next year.

Responding to these trends, Makita moved aggressively to cut manufacturing costs. In November 2000 a second manufacturing subsidiary was set up in China, and production began at this company in June 2002. Yet another Chinese subsidiary was established in March 2001 to handle the export of Chinese-made low-cost components to Makita's manufacturing plants around the world. By 2002, 28 percent of the company's production was being conducted in China. In a related development again aimed at countering the growing threat of Chinese power tool makers, Makita in the spring of 2002 began selling within Asian markets outside of Japan a new line of low-cost power tools under the brand name Maktec.

Elsewhere, Makita took further steps to enhance its global network of sales subsidiaries. In January 2001 a Miami, Florida-based subsidiary was created to handle sales to Central and South America as well as the Caribbean region. Two months later, Makita Oy was set up in Finland to facilitate sales in northern Europe, Russia, and the three Baltic nations.

While continuing to contend with the economic doldrums that were enduring in its home market, as well as the extremely competitive situation that existed in the power tools markets of North America, Europe, and Asia, Makita was taking aggressive action to cut fixed costs through restructuring efforts. The U.S. manufacturing and marketing operations were a prime target for action. During 2004 Makita reduced its U.S. warehouses from seven to four, and it also closed 20 of the 46 repair centers that it operated in that country, shifting the affected repair services to retail outlets. In the uncertain economic times of the new century, it was difficult to determine whether initiatives such as these would be enough to return Makita's profits to the levels achieved in the early to mid-1990s.

Principal Subsidiaries

Joyama Kaihatsu Ltd.; Makita Ichinomiya Corporation; Makita Herramientas Eléctricas de Argentina S.A.; Makita (Australia) Pty. Ltd.; Makita Werkzeug Gesellschaft m.b.H. (Austria); S.A. Makita N.V. (Belgium); Makita do Brasil Ferramentas Elétricas Ltda. (Brazil; 99.8%); Makita Canada Inc.; Makita Chile Ltda.; Makita (China) Co., Ltd.; Makita (Kunshan) Co., Ltd. (China); Makita Power Tools (HK) Ltd. (China); Makita France S.A. (55%); Dolmar GmbH (Germany); Makita Werkzeug GmbH (Germany); Makita S.p.A. (Italy); Makita Korea Co., Ltd.; Makita México, S.A. de C.V.; Euro Makita Corporation B.V. (Netherlands); Makita Benelux B.V. (Netherlands); Makita (New Zealand) Ltd.; Makita Singapore Pte. Ltd.; Makita, S.A. (Spain); Makita SA (Switzerland); Makita (Taiwan) Ltd.; Makita Gulf FZE (United Arab Emirates); Makita International Europe Ltd. (U.K.); Makita (U.K.) Ltd.; Makita Manufacturing Europe Ltd. (U.K.); Makita Corporation of America (U.S.A.); Makita U.S.A., Inc.

Principal Competitors

The Black & Decker Corporation; Ryobi, Ltd.; Hitachi Koki Co., Ltd.; The Stanley Works; Danaher Corporation; Robert Bosch GmbH; AB Electrolux; Cooper Industries, Ltd.; Stayer S.p.A.

Further Reading

Cory, James M., "Power Tools; Products and Prospects," *Chilton's Hardware Age,* June 1985, pp. 45–47.

"Electric Tool Industry Nearing Judgment Day," *Business Japan,* May 1987, pp. 45–46.

"Japan's Power Tool Industry," *Japan 21st,* June 1995, pp. 28–29.

Kansas, Dave, "Optimists Are Buzzing About Makita Turnaround," *Asian Wall Street Journal,* June 4, 1996, p. 13.

Kelly, Joseph M., "Cordless Tool Makers Power Up to Meet Market Demands," *Home Improvement Market,* September 1996, pp. 66–67.

——, "Power Tool Makers Battle in Court," *Home Improvement Market,* August 1996, p. 49.

Sapirito, Bill, "Black & Decker's Gamble on 'Globalization,'" *Fortune,* May 14, 1984, pp. 40–44.

Sellers, Patricia, "New Selling Tool: The Acura Concept," *Fortune,* February 24, 1992, pp. 88–89.

Smutko, Liz, "Building a Pro-Quality Niche," *Chilton's Hardware Age,* May 1994, pp. 59–61.

"Splinters," *Forbes,* June 6, 1983, p. 161.

—April Dougal Gasbarre
—update: David E. Salamie

The Manitowoc Company, Inc.

2400 South 44th Street
Post Office Box 66
Manitowoc, Wisconsin 54221-0066
U.S.A.
Telephone: (920) 684-4410
Fax: (920) 652-9778
Web site: http://www.manitowoc.com

Public Company
Incorporated: 1902 as Manitowoc Dry Dock Company
Employees: 7,800
Sales: $1.41 billion (2002)
Stock Exchanges: New York
Ticker Symbol: MTW
NAIC: 333120 Construction Machinery Manufacturing;
    333415 Air-Conditioning and Warm Air Heating
    Equipment and Commercial and Industrial
    Refrigeration Equipment Manufacturing; 333923
    Overhead Traveling Crane, Hoist, and Monorail
    System Manufacturing; 336611 Ship Building and
    Repairing

The Manitowoc Company, Inc. is a diversified manufacturer of cranes and related products, foodservice equipment, and ships. Its cranes operations, which contribute more than half of overall sales and which serve the heavy construction, energy, infrastructure, and other industries, lead the world in lattice-boom cranes, tower cranes, rough-terrain cranes, truck-mounted cranes, and boom trucks; Manitowoc also produces all-terrain cranes and aerial work platforms. The foodservice segment, accounting for about one-third of revenues, includes ice-making and beverage-dispensing machines, walk-in and reach-in refrigerators and freezers, and related products; industries served include the restaurant, hospitality, healthcare, convenience store, supermarket, soft-drink bottling and dispensing, and commercial ice service sectors. Manitowoc's marine operations, which generate about 16 percent of sales, are involved in building U.S. Coast Guard cutters, ferries, barges, and other vessels—both commercial and military—as well as the inspection, mainte-

nance, and repair of vessels. More than two-thirds of Manitowoc's revenues are generated in North America, about one-quarter in Europe, about 5 percent in Asia, and the remaining 3 percent elsewhere. Manitowoc started off in the early 20th century in shipbuilding, branched out into crane manufacturing in the 1920s, and in the 1940s entered the foodservice sector through the launch of freezer manufacturing. The company's more recent history is marked by several landmark acquisitions: Sturgeon Bay Shipbuilding and Dry Dock Company in 1968 (later renamed Bay Shipbuilding Company); The Shannon Group, Inc., a large manufacturer of commercial refrigerators and freezers, in 1995; Marinette Marine Corporation in 2000; the French firm Potain S.A. (renamed Potain SAS), the world's leading producer of tower cranes, in 2001; and Grove Worldwide, a global leader in mobile telescopic cranes, in 2002.

Early History

The founders of Manitowoc Company, Charles C. West and Elias Gunnell, originally worked for Chicago Ship Building Company in Chicago, Illinois. In 1899, however, when Chicago Ship Building was purchased by American Shipbuilding based in Cleveland, Ohio, the former firm was subsumed under the latter and lost its decision-making authority and engineering autonomy. Disappointed with the results of the purchase, West and Gunnell decided to buy a shipyard of their own. West, a marine engineer and naval architect, and Gunnell, an experienced shipbuilder, designer, and mechanic, reached the conclusion that their shipyard would build steel ships rather than the wooden ships commonly built at the turn of the century. Yet after consulting their acquaintances within the shipbuilding industry, the two entrepreneurs were convinced that the best plan of action was first to purchase a yard where wooden ship repairs could be done, because this would provide them with financial stability, and then, in due time, buy and install the necessary equipment for building steel ships.

The only shipyard for sale on the shores of Lake Michigan was located in Manitowoc, Wisconsin. Owned by brothers Henry and George Burger, the Manitowoc operation had grown large and lucrative from its extensive wooden ship repair business. Having found an acquisition that ideally suited their pur-

Company Perspectives:

Corporate Mission: Our mission is to continuously improve economic value for our shareholders.

Corporate Scope: The Manitowoc Company is a creator of market-leading engineered capital goods and support services for selected market segments, which today include Cranes and Related Products, Foodservice Equipment, and Marine. This is Manitowoc's strength.

Corporate Purpose: The centerpiece of our efforts will continue to be high-quality, customer-focused products and support services. Research, marketing, resources, manufacturing, support services, and all related elements will generally be product-oriented. The company will use this in evaluating and guiding its business units.

poses, West and Gunnell bought the Burger and Burger shipyard in 1902 for $110,000. Gunnell assumed the position of president and West became the general manager of the new Manitowoc Dry Dock Company. The first vessel launched by Manitowoc Dry Dock was the *Cheguamegon,* a wooden passenger steamer already under construction at the time of the purchase. By 1903, however, the company had contracted its first steel ship repair job, and by 1905 the firm had launched the passenger steamer *Maywood,* the first steel vessel built in the Manitowoc shipyard.

In 1904, Gunnell, West, and L. E. Geer, the secretary and treasurer of Manitowoc, had created a separate tool company to manufacture marine engines and other types of machinery necessary to outfit a ship. In 1905, Manitowoc purchased this company and incorporated it within its shipbuilding operations. In 1908, Manitowoc purchased Manitowoc Steam Boiler Works, a major manufacturer of marine boilers, pulp digesters, dryers, furnaces, ladles, vulcanizers, kilns, buoys, buckets, creosoting retorts, and tanks. These two acquisitions gave Manitowoc not only the ability to build new steel vessels but also the capability to completely equip them for operational service. With sales increasing and financial stability assured, to reflect a more modern image management decided to change the name of the firm—first to Manitowoc Shipbuilding and Dry Dock Company, in 1910, and then to simply Manitowoc Shipbuilding Company, in 1916.

During World War I the company grew dramatically. Although the war had started in 1914, the United States did not enter the hostilities in Europe until 1917. When Congress declared war on Germany in April 1917, however, the entire operations of Manitowoc were subsumed under the authority of the U.S. Shipping Board Emergency Fleet Corporation. The board immediately placed a large contract with Manitowoc for 3,500-ton freighters, and the company embarked on an extensive expansion program to fill this order. During the course of the war, Charles West was recruited by the U.S. Navy Bureau of Construction to supervise the construction of a Ford Motor Company shipbuilding plant in River Rouge, Michigan, near Ford's headquarters. For more than 18 months, West commuted from Manitowoc to Detroit and then back again to fulfill his duties to both companies. Before the war, Manitowoc turned

out an average of six ships per year. By the time the war ended in 1918, the company was capable of turning out 18 ships annually and had already made 33 3,500-ton freighters used during the war effort.

Unfortunately, when World War I ended the U.S. government canceled the remaining freighter contracts with Manitowoc. This loss of wartime revenue led to a postwar depression, not only for Manitowoc but also for the entire shipbuilding industry in the Great Lakes region. With its expanded capacity for shipbuilding, and numerous employees hired for the wartime production effort, West and Gunnell searched for new business that would compensate for the disappearance of government contracts. Luckily, the two men arranged for the company's shipbuilding plant to be converted into a railroad locomotive maintenance and repair shop. This kept the company barely solvent, with funds enough to pay employee wages, but it was clear that Manitowoc would have to undergo a transformation to survive.

In 1920, West and Gunnell came to a sharp disagreement as to the direction of the company. West was convinced that Manitowoc could survive only by implementing a broadly based diversification strategy. Gunnell, on the other hand, maintained that the company should continue to emphasize its shipbuilding capacity. Unable to reach a point of mutual agreement, the company was put up for sale. Interestingly enough, West made the only offer to purchase the firm. For a total of $410,000, West and Geer bought the company and renamed it the Manitowoc Shipbuilding Corporation. An immediate policy of diversification was established, including an expansion of the boiler works and new products for the machine shop. Because marine boilers were losing their popularity, the boiler works diversified into the manufacture of paper mill equipment, dryers for coal, rock, and clay, brewery tanks, air nozzles, and heating boilers. In 1925 the machine shop reached an agreement to manufacture Moore Speedcranes under the Moore patents. By 1928, Manitowoc had taken over the manufacture and sale of all of the crane models produced by the Roy and Charles Moore Crane Company. Of course, the diversification program did not mean that shipbuilding at the company was interrupted. During the 1920s, Manitowoc constructed its first self-unloading vessel, two carferries, five tugboats, four deck barges, two dipper dredges, two dump scows, two derrick scows, a floating dry dock, and the largest suction dredge in the world.

The Great Depression and World War II

With the stock market crash of 1929, the era of the Great Depression began in the United States. Manitowoc, like many other businesses during the time, was hard hit by the downward trend in business. Sales dropped precipitously from more than $4 million in 1931 to less than $500,000 by 1933. During the middle of the decade, the company operated at a net loss for four years in a row. Many employees were laid off, and those that remained were forced to take a reduction in their salaries. The company's shipbuilding business was severely affected by the Depression, and management was forced to rely more heavily on the crane business (now producing models under the Manitowoc name). During the 1930s, Manitowoc introduced an improved version of the Speedcrane and began a maintenance service to repair and keep cranes in first-class condition. Manitowoc cranes soon

Key Dates:

1902: Charles C. West and Elias Gunnell purchase the Burger and Burger shipyard in Manitowoc, Wisconsin, and rename it Manitowoc Dry Dock Company.

1905: The firm finishes work on its first steel-hulled vessel.

1910: The company changes its name to Manitowoc Shipbuilding and Dry Dock Company.

1916: The company name is shortened to Manitowoc Shipbuilding Company.

1920: West buys out the original shareholders and renames the company Manitowoc Shipbuilding Corporation.

1925: Manitowoc enters the crane business through an agreement to manufacture Moore Speedcranes.

1940: The U.S. Navy contracts the company to build ten submarines.

1945: Foodservice equipment enters the mix when Manitowoc begins manufacturing freezers.

1952: The increasingly diverse firm is renamed The Manitowoc Company, Inc.

1966: Manitowoc begins producing commercial ice-making machines.

1968: The company acquires Sturgeon Bay Shipbuilding and Dry Dock Company, merges its shipbuilding operations with those of this Sturgeon Bay, Wisconsin, firm, which is subsequently renamed Bay Shipbuilding Corporation.

1971: The company goes public through an IPO and is listed on NASDAQ.

1993: The company stock is shifted to the New York Stock Exchange.

1995: The Shannon Group, Inc., a major manufacturer of commercial refrigeration equipment, is acquired.

1997: The company acquires SerVend International, Inc., maker of ice and beverage dispensers.

2000: Manitowoc acquires Marinette Marine Corporation.

2001: French tower crane maker Potain is purchased.

2002: Mobile telescopic crane producer Grove Worldwide is acquired.

garnered a reputation for high quality within the industry and were purchased to help construct the Senate Office Building, the National Gallery of Art, the National Archives, and the Jefferson Memorial, all located in Washington, D.C.

In 1940, as the start of another world war became more evident to U.S. government officials, the Navy contracted Manitowoc to build ten submarines and provided the company with funds to make the necessary plant improvements and expansion. Although West hesitated because of his previous experience with U.S. government contracts, which left the company in dire financial straits after World War I, he reluctantly decided to engage in a comprehensive plant conversion. The increased capacity soon proved itself useful. Just one week after Pearl Harbor had been attacked by the Japanese, which initiated the American involvement in World War II, the company received an order from the U.S. Navy for immediate delivery of six

cranes for use in salvaging operations in the harbor. More than 58 cranes were made by the company for the Navy's Floating Dry Docks during the war, and 79 cranes and shovels were delivered to the U.S. Army.

Besides a huge order for submarine construction during the war, Manitowoc also built landing craft for use in both the Pacific and European theaters of operation. Extensive testing was conducted along the shores of Lake Michigan by company engineers, and design changes were made before actual production was begun. Manitowoc built a total of 1,465 landing craft, and received a presidential citation for the vehicle's performance during the Normandy landing in June 1944. In addition, by the end of the war the company had constructed 28 submarines for the U.S. Navy and had received the Navy "E" for excellence in production five times.

The Postwar Years

The immediate period after World War II brought the same problems that confronted the company after World War I: the necessary reorganization of the company and its manufacturing facilities to a peacetime economy. Unlike what happened the previous time, however, the U.S. Navy reimbursed Manitowoc for its wartime expenses and helped it to dismantle the Navy's portion of its shipbuilding operations. West, still in control of the company's direction, decided once again that diversification was the answer. Looking for products to manufacture that did not require significant capital investment, Manitowoc started making dry cleaning units and, in addition, freezers for Firestone and Westinghouse (production of the latter beginning in 1945). Soon the firm was making commercial frozen food cabinets used in supermarkets and restaurants and, by 1950, more than 50 percent of Manitowoc's equipment works was devoted to this business. In 1952 Manitowoc Shipbuilding Company was reorganized. To reflect its increasingly diverse operations, the company name was changed to The Manitowoc Company, Inc.; two chief units were made into subsidiaries— Manitowoc Shipbuilding, Inc. and Manitowoc Engineering Corporation (the cranes operation)—and a third, Manitowoc Equipment Works, became a division.

Manitowoc's shipbuilding operation was plagued by union strikes throughout the late 1940s but, with the end of the postwar recession in the marine industry, the firm reclaimed its role as a major shipbuilder and repair facility in the Great Lakes region. During the early 1950s, the company constructed the prototype of Nautilus, the country's first nuclear submarine. In addition, numerous commercial vessels were built during the decade, including the largest self-unloader on the Great Lakes, a coal hauler, the first diesel-powered carferry, and five crane barges. Charles West was particularly pleased to see his company survive the difficulties of the postwar period and, when he died in 1957, left behind what he considered to be a thriving firm with great potential for the future. The founder's son, John D. West, took over as president.

During the 1960s, Manitowoc continued to grow. The manufacture of dry cleaning units was expanded, as well as the production of freezers and frozen food cabinets. In 1966, the company introduced The Manitowoc Ice Dispenser, which quickly became very popular in both the hospital and lodging industries. Because shipbuilding at the time consisted mostly of smaller vessels such as dump scows and crane barges, management decided to combine its operations with another Great Lakes shipbuilding firm and relocate Manitowoc's shipbuilding operation to Sturgeon Bay, Wisconsin. In 1968, Manitowoc purchased all of the assets of the Sturgeon Bay Shipbuilding and Dry Dock Company and subsequently renamed its reorganized business the Bay Shipbuilding Corporation. This combination of both resources and facilities resulted in major contracts during the 1970s, including the first 1,000-foot ship, built to haul coal for Detroit Edison.

Growth and Transformation During the 1970s and 1980s

In addition to relocating and reorganizing its shipbuilding operation during the early 1970s—and also gaining a listing on NASDAQ through a 1971 initial public offering—the company divested its dry cleaning operation and sold off its freezer and frozen food cabinet business. The most successful and profitable product made by the company after World War II was its custom-built cranes. From the mid-1920s to 1945, management regarded the sale of its cranes as a fortuitous product of a necessary diversification program started after World War I. But after World War II, the demand for the company's cranes began to increase dramatically. In fact, during the 1950s and 1960s, Manitowoc was at the forefront of developing technological innovations to increase the quality of its cranes. The company was the first manufacturer to use T-1 high-strength steel in booms, design a controlled-torque converter for crane applications, and develop extendible crawlers. In 1967, Manitowoc engineers designed an assembly called the Ringer that doubled the lift capacity of any basic crane. By 1977, sales for Manitowoc cranes were reported at $146.5 million, whereas shipbuilding and repair revenues amounted to $73 million and ice cube maker sales totaled $14.4 million. In the late 1970s the company spent $35 million to build new manufacturing facilities for the Manitowoc Engineering and Manitowoc Equipment Works operations on a 100-acre site called SouthWorks located southwest of downtown Manitowoc.

John West remained CEO of Manitowoc through 1986 and chairman for most of the decade, but it was Ralph Helm who increasingly led the company during the 1980s, first as president and COO from 1981 through 1986 and then as president and CEO from 1986 to 1990. Helm had previously spent two decades at the Manitowoc Engineering crane subsidiary, helping increase sales there from $18 million in 1962 to more than $143 million by 1980.

During the 1980s, Manitowoc rode an economic roller coaster. The recession of the early 1980s, and the collapse of the petroleum boom, led to a dramatic plunge in Manitowoc's sales. The company's crane business fell flat, especially in the areas of large lift cranes used in the construction and offshore oil industries. The company's manufacture of ice-making machines for the foodservice, healthcare, and convenience store markets also took a nosedive, and shipbuilding at the Sturgeon Bay facility had to be abandoned altogether. By the end of the decade, conditions at Manitowoc had improved slightly. Manitowoc's crane business had benefited from the revival of offshore drilling in the Gulf of Mexico, and the company claimed that it was

the only manufacturer of large lift cranes left in the United States; all of the firm's competitors had either sold their holdings to foreign interests or gone out of business. The company's ice machine business replaced the crane business as Manitowoc's most profitable operation during the middle and late 1980s, and the Sturgeon Bay facility reported that it was one of only three remaining Great Lakes shipping repair and maintenance shops for the country's largest iron-ore carriers.

Shifting to More Modern Corporate Management: Early to Mid-1990s

In 1990 Fred M. Butler was named company president and CEO. Butler was a relative outsider, having joined the company as manager of administration only in 1988. Starting as an engineer, Butler had spent more than three decades moving up the ranks of a South San Francisco–based construction firm called Guy F. Atkinson Company. His perspective as an outsider is credited with shaking up a relatively moribund company and injecting it with a more modern operating philosophy.

During the early 1990s, Butler implemented a comprehensive cost-cutting and reorganization strategy, including a revamped marketing program that significantly enhanced Manitowoc's presence across the United States and in Europe. Modernization at the firm's large crane and boom-truck facilities increased production, and the introduction of new crane designs, especially the Model 888 crane with a 220-ton lift capacity, gained immediate market acceptance. At the same time, Bay Shipbuilding cut back on its shipbuilding operations but expanded its ship repair business to include two additional locations in the Great Lakes Region (in Toledo and Cleveland, Ohio) and, by the mid-1990s, operated more than 60 percent of all dry-dock footage on the Great Lakes. On the ice machine front, as part of Butler's drive to expand in the Asia-Pacific region, Manitowoc in 1994 entered into a joint venture to build ice machines with the Hangzhou Household Electric Appliance Industrial Corporation. The venture was based in the large city of Hangzhou, located about 100 miles southwest of Shanghai, China. Meantime, in 1993, Manitowoc's stock was shifted to the New York Stock Exchange to secure the broader exposure offered by that market.

Butler's most important move, however, was to persuade the company's traditionally conservative board of directors to direct some of Manitowoc's hoard of cash toward acquisitions. The company's first major acquisition came in November 1995, when The Shannon Group, Inc., a major manufacturer of commercial refrigeration equipment—particularly walk-in refrigerators and freezers—was purchased for $126 million. The purchase of Shannon turned Manitowoc into the largest supplier of commercial ice-cube machines and walk-in refrigerators in the world. The company now derived more than half of its revenues from foodservice equipment, with cranes and related products contributing 39 percent and shipbuilding/ship repair only 7 percent.

In 1996, when company sales surpassed the half-billion-dollar mark, Bay Shipbuilding lived up to its name for the first time in years when it completed construction of Integrity, a 460-foot integrated tug/barge. This was the first new Great Lakes vessel built since 1982. In 1997 the Equipment Works subsidiary, which specialized in ice-making machines, changed its name to the more descriptive Manitowoc Ice, Inc. This subsidiary was bolstered in October of that year through the $73 million purchase of Sellersburg, Indiana–based SerVand International, Inc., the third largest maker of ice and beverage dispensers in the United States. SerVand's major customers included fast-food restaurants, convenience stores, and soft drink bottlers.

Acquisitions Center Stage: Late 1990s and Early 2000s

A key figure in these two major foodservice acquisitions was Terry D. Growcock, who had joined the company in 1994 as head of Manitowoc's ice machine subsidiary. Having previously served in management positions at a variety of manufacturing companies, Growcock was soon promoted to head of Manitowoc's foodservice group in March 1995. When Butler retired as president and CEO in July 1998, Growcock was selected to succeed him, becoming the first company president to come through the foodservice side. Under his leadership, Manitowoc nearly tripled its 1997 revenues of $545.9 million by the year 2002, when sales hit $1.41 billion. Driving this growth was a string of acquisitions that Growcock engineered.

In 1998 Manitowoc gained a manufacturing presence in Europe with the acquisition of a 50 percent interest in Fabbrica Apparecchiature per la Produzione del Ghiaccio, S.r.l. (F.A.G.), an ice-machine firm based in Milan, Italy. The company also entered into a license agreement with Blue Star, an Indian company, to manufacture Kolpak walk-in refrigerators for sale in the Middle East and Asia. During 2000 Manitowoc purchased full control of its Chinese joint venture and also paid $21.2 million for Harford Duracool, LLC, a maker of walk-in refrigerators and freezers serving the U.S. East Coast.

The cranes business expanded as well. In November 1998 U.S. Truck Crane, Inc. (USTC) was bought for $51.5 million. Based in York, Pennsylvania, USTC produced boom trucks, rough-terrain forklifts, and other materials handling equipment. After another boom truck manufacturer, Pioneer Holdings LLC, was acquired in 2000, the company's three boom truck lines (the other being Manitex) were consolidated under a new brand, Manitowoc Boom Trucks. That same year, Manitowoc introduced the most popular crane in its history, the Model 999 lattice-boom crane, which could lift 275 tons. More than 80 of the units were sold within seven months of introduction.

Manitowoc's marine group nearly tripled its revenues through the $66.7 million purchase of Marinette Marine Corporation in November 2000. Based in Marinette, Wisconsin (just across Green Bay from Bay Shipbuilding's facility in Sturgeon Bay), the purchased shipyard, which specialized more in mid-sized research and military (particularly U.S. Coast Guard and U.S. Navy) vessels, was a good fit with Manitowoc's existing shipyards, which focused on commercial vessels. Manitowoc now operated more than 60 percent of the U.S. dry docks in the Great Lakes.

The company's appetite for growth increasing, Manitowoc next completed the two largest acquisitions in company history, both of crane companies. In May 2001 the firm laid out about $307 million in cash and assumed $138.8 million in debt for

Potain S.A. (later renamed Potain SAS). At the time a subsidiary of Groupe Legris Industries SA, Potain was headquartered near Lyon, France, and was a global leader in tower cranes for the building and construction industry. With annual sales of about $300 million, Potain operated eight manufacturing facilities in France, Germany, Italy, Portugal, and China, and distributed its cranes to more than 50 nations. The addition of Potain helped push Manitowoc's revenues past the $1 billion mark for the first time in 2001.

In August 2002 Manitowoc acquired Grove Worldwide for about $278 million. Grove, which had just emerged from bankruptcy, was one of the world's leading makers of mobile telescopic cranes. Its headquarters were in Shady Grove, Pennsylvania, and it had other plants in Germany and France. Grove also owned National Crane Corporation, a maker of boom trucks that competed directly with Manitowoc Boom Trucks. As a condition of approving the purchase of Grove, the U.S. Department of Justice stipulated that Manitowoc had to sell one of the two boom truck makers. The company elected to divest Manitowoc Boom Trucks, which was sold to Quantum Heavy Equipment LLC in early 2003. In another 2002 acquisition, Manitowoc purchased full control of its F.A.G. ice machine venture in Italy, which now operated as Manitowoc Foodservice Europe, S.r.l.

The two Crane purchases significantly expanded Manitowoc's presence overseas, with sales outside North America increasing from less than 6 percent in 2000 to more than 21 percent two years later. Nevertheless, this acquisition spree did not come without a price. Manitowoc posted a net loss of $20.5 million in 2002 thanks to $74 million in special charges, including costs incurred restructuring some of the crane and foodservice operations. The substantial expansion of the crane business, which now generated more than 60 percent of overall revenues, left Manitowoc dependent once again on a more cyclical business just as the global economy was struggling mightily. In mid-2003 Manitowoc warned that difficult market conditions and heightened competition were likely to translate into depressed earnings for the remainder of 2003 and into 2004 as well.

Principal Subsidiaries

CRANE GROUP: Grove Worldwide, Inc.; Manitowoc Cranes, Inc.; Manitowoc Potain Re-Manufacturing, Inc.; National Crane Corporation; Potain SAS (France). FOODSERVICE GROUP: Diversified Refrigeration, Inc.; Harford Duracool, LLC; Kyees Aluminum; Kolpak; Manitowoc Beverage Equipment, Inc.; Manitowoc Beverage Systems, Inc.; Manitowoc Foodservice Europe, S.r.l. (Italy); Manitowoc (Hangzhou) Refrigeration Co., Ltd. (China); Manitowoc Ice, Inc.; McCall Refrigeration. MARINE GROUP: Bay Shipbuilding Company; Cleveland Shiprepair Company; Marinette Marine Corporation; Toledo Shiprepair Company.

Principal Operating Units

Crane Group; Foodservice Group; Marine Group.

Principal Competitors

Terex Corporation; Hitachi, Ltd.; JLG Industries, Inc.; Sumitomo Corp.; Liebherr-International AG; Link-Belt Construction

Equipment Co.; Kobelco Construction Machinery Co.; Tadano, Ltd.; Manitex Inc.; Enodis plc; IMI Cornelius Group; Lancer Corporation; Hoshizaki America Inc.; Traulsen and Company Inc.; Nor-Lake Inc.; American Panel Corporation; Bollinger Shipyards, Inc.; Atlantic Marine, Inc.; Bender Shipbuilding and Repair Co., Inc.; Fraser Shipyards, Inc.; Friede Goldman Halter Inc.; Port Weller Dry Docks.

Further Reading

Byrne, Harlan S., "Manitowoc Company: Cost-Cutting Lays Ground for Earnings Rebound," *Barron's,* January 6, 1992, pp. 39–40.
——, "Manitowoc Company: From Cranes to Cold Cash, It Bucks Capital-Goods Trend," *Barron's,* November 12, 1990, pp. 41–42.
"CEO Interview: Terry Growcock," *Wall Street Transcript,* November 28, 2000.
Content, Thomas, "Manitowoc Picks Up Crane Maker," *Milwaukee Journal Sentinel,* March 19, 2002.
Doherty, Chuck, "Cranes Lifting Manitowoc to Higher Levels of Profit," *Milwaukee Sentinel,* August 14, 1990, Sec. 4, p. 1.
Gallun, Alby, "New CEO Cultivates Manitowoc Growth Plan," *Business Journal-Milwaukee,* December 4, 1998, pp. 26+.
Higgins, Terry, "Strategy Shows Upside for Manitowoc," *Business Journal-Milwaukee,* November 16, 1996, pp. 21+.
"Hoisting Job," *Forbes,* April 19, 1999, p. 152.
Krapf, David, "Inland Barge Construction Is Booming," *Journal of Commerce,* August 26, 1996, p. 8B.
"Manitowoc Expects to Close Grove Deal by June," *Cranes Today,* April 2002, p. 4.
Manitowoc: 75 Years of Growth and Diversification, 1902–1977, Manitowoc, Wis.: The Manitowoc Company, 1977.
Martin, Chuck, "Cranes Lift Firm's Hopes," *Milwaukee Journal,* January 26, 1992, p. D1.
Moore, Walt, "New Company, New Crane," *Construction Equipment,* October, 1994, p. 81.
Phalon, Richard, "Back in the Game," *Forbes,* December 5, 1994, pp. 58–60.
Prestegard, Steve, "Manitowoc Steers Toward Ice," *Marketplace Magazine* (Appleton, Wis.), April 30, 1996, p. 12.
Romell, Rick, "Manitowoc Co. to Buy Marinette Marine," *Milwaukee Journal Sentinel,* October 21, 2000.
Ryman, Richard, "Q&A: Manitowoc Co. CEO Talks About Company's Ability to Weather Recession," *Green Bay Press-Gazette,* December 23, 2001, p. E1.
Sandler, Larry, "Manitowoc Bids Adios to Mexico," *Milwaukee Sentinel,* November 11, 1993, p. 1D.
Voyage of Vision: The Manitowoc Company, A Century of Extraordinary Growth, Manitowoc, Wis.: The Manitowoc Company, 2002.

—Thomas Derdak
—update: David E. Salamie

Maverick Tube Corporation

16401 Swingley Ridge Road, Seventh Floor
Chesterfield, Missouri 63017
U.S.A.
Telephone: (636) 733-1600
Toll Free: (888) 628-8823
Fax: (636) 733-1670
Web site: http://www.maverick-tube.com

Public Company
Incorporated: 1978
Employees: 2,300
Sales: $453 million (2002 est.)
Stock Exchanges: New York
Ticker Symbol: MVK
NAIC: 331210 Iron and Steel Pipe and Tube
    Manufacturing from Purchased Steel

Maverick Tube Corporation is the largest North American producer of welded steel tubular products used by the oil industry. In industry parlance, Maverick makes "oil country tubular goods," or OCTG. While 70 percent of its revenue comes from the energy industry, Maverick also manufactures a variety of other tubing products. It makes tubing used in the construction and transportation industries, standard pipe and pipe piling, coiled tubing, umbilicals, and electrical conduits. The firm greatly expanded its North American market share in 2000 when it merged with a leading Canadian tube manufacturer, Prudential Steel Ltd. Maverick operates 24 production plants at nine locations in North America, including a huge state-of-the-art facility in Hickman, Arkansas. Maverick specializes in low-cost production, and it is known for using domestic steel. The company has suffered many ups and downs following sometimes abrupt swings in oil and gas production. But Maverick has grown steadily since its inception, both through acquisition and by adding on to existing facilities. The company began with a single Missouri mill, and by 2003 had the capacity to produce almost 2.1 million tons of pipe and tubing annually.

Jumping into the Oil Industry in the 1980s

Maverick Tube Corporation was founded in 1978 by Don Beattie, a mechanical engineer and successful Missouri businessman. Earlier, Beattie founded the Bull Moose Tube Company in 1962, in Wellston, Missouri. Bull Moose went through several owners after 1968, and became a leading North American tubing manufacturer. Beattie began Maverick with a single mill in Union, Missouri, which made mechanical tubing. Mechanical tubing is used in furniture, scaffolding, and in bicycle frames, as well as in other sports equipment. Beattie apparently chose the name Maverick to signify that his company would do things differently from the existing tubing companies found predominantly in the East. Specifically, he hoped the company would be more friendly to customers. After Maverick's first year, Beattie decided to move the company in a new direction. The oil and gas industry was booming, and Beattie converted the Union plant to make tubing for oil wells.

Beattie sold Maverick in 1981. For $15 million, the company became a subsidiary of San Diego-based Nucorp Energy Inc. Nucorp Energy began as a real estate investment company. In 1979 Nucorp was taken over by Richard L. Burns, a flamboyant executive who had previously headed an oil and coal company called R.L. Burns Corp. R.L. Burns had grown very quickly, raising money principally from Continental Illinois Bank & Trust Co., which lent it more than $100 million. Heavy debt and allegations of executive misconduct led R.L. Burns to the brink of bankruptcy by 1978. Burns left that company, which then changed its name to Pyro Energy Corporation, and began running Nucorp. Nucorp surged into the oil and gas industry, buying up more than 20 small oilfield equipment firms over the course of a few years. The company had sales of $38 million in 1979, the year Burns came in. By 1981, Nucorp posted sales of $416 million.

Nucorp left real estate for oil and gas at a time when the energy industry was undergoing an enormous expansion. Companies began investing heavily in domestic oil production in 1979, when the price of oil was rising. Companies that provided service and equipment to oil drillers faced a market that could gobble up whatever they could produce. Maverick Tube began

Company Perspectives:

Mission statement: To enhance shareholder value through the profitable manufacture and sale of high quality steel tubular goods. To deal fairly with our customers, vendors, and employees while being a good citizen to our communities. To achieve growth in sales and profits through expansion of our product offerings while being a low cost producer of those products we manufacture.

producing OCTG, as did hundreds of other small companies. According to *Business Week* (September 27, 1982), some 400 new oilfield service companies joined the industry group the International Association of Drilling Contractors between 1979 and 1981, providing a rough measure of how quickly the service industry grew in that short span. Nucorp rode the wave by buying up oilfield equipment makers, including Maverick Tube. Nucorp had no particular expertise in the oilfield service industry, but it was able to make money as long as the energy industry continued its upward climb. The company borrowed heavily to fund its acquisitions, and it piled up $525 million in debt by early 1982. That year the oil boom collapsed. Spending for oil and gas exploration dropped 25 percent, and the many companies that had worked around the clock to provide parts and equipment found themselves with warehouses full of excess inventory. Nucorp was not the only company caught by the sudden drop in oil exploration. Industry analysts had predicted a continued rise in the market for the next few years, and instead of a slowdown the market abruptly crashed. But Nucorp had such a high debt level that it could not survive. Profits had risen more than 200 percent in 1981 over the year previous, but the company racked up $42 million in losses over the first two quarters of 1982, then filed for bankruptcy.

Richard Burns left the company a few months before Nucorp filed for Chapter 11 (a bankruptcy proceeding that allows the company to continue to operate). The company was soon hit with allegations of misconduct, specifically that it had recorded revenue from sales that were only pending. The *Wall Street Journal* (July 5, 1983) called Nucorp "a corporate house of cards, shakily assembled on phony sales, questionable accounting and dubious claims about its oil reserves." Burns was convicted in 1985 of several charges brought against him by the Securities and Exchange Commission. Amidst all this mess, Maverick was apparently still operating profitably. But it had taken on debt through its parent company. The reorganization of the company under Chapter 11 found Maverick owing creditors $326 million. This was later reduced substantially, to only $22.8 million. Founder Don Beattie resigned from Maverick in 1983, and Jon Lloyd became president. Maverick managed to produce $100 million in sales for 1984, and it seemed to be doing the best among Nucorp's many subsidiaries. The company moved back into the southwestern and Rocky Mountain markets, areas it had fled after 1981, as business improved. Maverick at that time used exclusively domestic raw materials, and it was able to produce pipe at a low cost. The company's president declared that business for 1983 was outstanding, and it seemed that if it were not for Nucorp's troubles, Maverick would be getting

along just fine. Because Maverick was profitable, Nucorp was loathe to sell it, even as it divested itself of its other subsidiaries. Don Beattie expressed interest in buying back Maverick in 1984, but that deal did not come off. A total of 45 percent of Maverick's stock was owned by its creditor banks, and 55 percent by its other creditors.

Emerging from Bankruptcy in the Mid-1980s

In July 1984, Maverick Tube emerged from bankruptcy. It was the first Nucorp subsidiary to do so. In December 1985, the company severed its ties to Nucorp. As many as 20 different parties were interested in buying Maverick, which posted sales of $107 million for 1985. The company invested in new equipment, spending $150,000 to revamp machinery, and it began producing a new kind of steel pipe that was used for transporting crude oil above ground. Maverick lost money in the first quarter of 1986 as the oilfield services industry contracted again. Yet a Maverick board member told the *St. Louis Business Journal* (July 14, 1986) that the company was "doing quite well in a horrible market." The company benefited from being a low-cost producer, and it was able to use slack time to install new equipment and upgrade old machinery.

Maverick got new owners in 1987 when a management group bought out the company. The group paid approximately $15.5 million for the company, only a little more than what it sold for in 1981. Gregg Eisenberg became Maverick's new president in 1988. The oilfield services market seemed to be improving, and the company began to look for acquisitions. In the last month of 1989 Maverick bought the Conroe Pipe Co., in Conroe, Texas, for $11.5 million. The purchase of Conroe Pipe gave Maverick more production capacity, and also brought it into a new market, making larger diameter pipes that were used in deeper wells. Partially in order to pay off debt arising from the acquisition, Maverick held its first public stock offering soon after. Maverick debuted on the American Stock Exchange in March 1991. The company was still at the mercy, however, of sudden swings in the energy market. Maverick's stock went on sale at $13.50 and then rose to $16 a few weeks later. But before a month was up, the company had to announce a drop in its earnings. Sales fell by 25 percent in Maverick's first quarter as a public company, and it lost money. Maverick's stock dived to around $5. The company decided to relocate its Union, Missouri plant to new quarters in Hickman, Arkansas. With its stock price still greatly depressed, Maverick raised cash by selling a 5 percent interest in the company to a wealthy St. Louis family investment group.

Maverick hoped to diversify its product line in the early 1990s so it would be less vulnerable to the boom-and-bust cycles of the energy market. It hoped to buy an Oregon company in 1993 that made pipe for water and electrical transmission. But that sale did not come off. The company bought equipment in 1993 that would let it back into the structural tubing market, which it left in 1980 in favor of OCTG. The next year, Maverick moved its stock listing from the American Exchange to NASDAQ.

Maverick built a new mill at its site in Hickman, Arkansas, in 1994 and added a new product line, hollow structural sec-

Key Dates:

1978: The company is founded with one mill in Union, Missouri.
1981: The company is sold to Nucorp Energy Inc.
1982: The company declares bankruptcy as Nucorp goes under.
1984: The company emerges from bankruptcy.
1987: A management group buys the company.
1991: Maverick goes public.
2000: The company merges with Prudential Steel Ltd.

tions. The company's fate was still closely tied to the oil industry, however. The market for OCTG began to improve in the mid-1990s, and by 1997 Maverick was doing very well. The oil industry had finally used up equipment it had stockpiled in the early 1990s, and the demand for new pipe sent the price soaring. Maverick's stock price, which had long languished, suddenly climbed to more than $50 a share. Maverick's profit for 1997 was almost double that of the year previous. The company continued to look into new markets in the late 1990s. In 1999 it made another substantial investment in its Hickman plant, and added equipment to make certain large-diameter pipes.

Industry Leader in the 2000s

The big news in 2000 was Maverick's purchase of the Canadian company Prudential Steel Ltd. Prudential, based in Calgary, Alberta, was the second largest OCTG and line pipe producer in Canada. The combined company became the largest OCTG company in North America. The price was approximately $484 million, paid for with Maverick stock. The new company now had ten tube mills at five locations, and some 2,000 employees. While Maverick posted a third-quarter loss in 2000 due to expenses related to the merger, its sales increased substantially that year. As oil and natural gas prices went up, the company did very well. Sales for 2000 hit $560 million, with profits of $16.6 million. That year Maverick moved its stock listing from the NASDAQ exchange to the New York Stock Exchange.

The company took some time to adjust to the merger with its Canadian partner. In 2001 Maverick closed a plant in Longview, Washington, that it had acquired when it bought Prudential Steel. A Western steelmaker that had supplied the plant went out of business, making difficulties for Longview, so Maverick moved the plant's equipment to its large facility in Hickman, Arkansas. At the same time, Maverick bought up more tubing companies. In 2002 Maverick acquired Precision Tube Technology, a company that made coiled tubing and coiled line pipe. This broadened Maverick's product line. Also in 2002 Maverick purchased five pipe mills that had comprised the tube division of LTV Steel Corp., which went bankrupt. The LTV division made electrical conduit at five locations in the Midwest and South. Maverick spent approximately $120.2 million to acquire LTV's plants, which gave it another new market. LTV's electrical conduit, sold under the brand name Republic Conduit, controlled some 35 percent of the U.S. market.

Demand for natural gas increased in the United States in the early 2000s, stimulating new drilling in North America. Although Maverick had moved into several new product lines, it still made 70 percent of its revenue from energy-related tubing. More drilling and rising gas prices meant favorable conditions for Maverick, and the company expected increasing sales into the middle of the decade. Maverick made another key acquisition in 2003, picking up Houston-based SeaCat Corp., a manufacturer of coiled tubing that was used for undersea oil and gas rigs. By late 2003, the average daily rig count, a crucial indicator of oil industry growth, was up almost 30 percent compared with the same time a year earlier. Maverick expected a very good year, and sales were already up almost 100 percent. The company had been through many similar booms, and weathered the following busts as well. In the meantime it had grown from a small player into the industry leader.

Principal Subsidiaries

Prudential Steel Ltd. (Canada); Precision Tube Technology; Republic Conduit; SeaCat, LP.

Principal Competitors

LoneStar Technologies, Inc.; NS Group, Inc.

Further Reading

Bauman, Carry, "Weak Tech Takes Toll on Nasdaq; Transkaryotic, Maverick Tube Fall," *Wall Street Journal*, June 13, 2000, p. C10.

Beirne, Mike, "Maverick Mulls New Product," *American Metal Market*, December 3, 1993, p. 2.

Belsky, Gary, "Management to Bid for Maverick Tube's Assets," *St. Louis Business Journal*, January 6, 1986, p. 12A.

Brammer, Rhonda, "Blowing in the Wind," *Barron's*, October 28, 1991, pp. 10–11, 20.

Bryan-Low, Cassell, "Slump in Energy Stocks Triggers Buying," *Wall Street Journal*, October 3, 2001, p. C15.

Cohen, Laurie P., "If Bad News Hits a New Issue, Is It Underwriters' Fault?," *Wall Street Journal*, June 5, 1991, pp. C1, C10.

Desloge, Rick, "Maverick Tube's Profit Jumps, But Stock Slumps," *St. Louis Business Journal*, March 2, 2001, p. 5.

"Ex-Chief of Nucorp Convicted of Charges Brought by the SEC," *Wall Street Journal*, December 20, 1985, p. 5.

Frazier, Steve, "Financial Fiasco," *Wall Street Journal*, July 5, 1983, pp. 1, 15.

Fyhr, Magnus, "Maverick Tube Corporation," *Buyside*, April 2003, p. 72.

Hohl, Paul, "Management Group Buys Assets of Maverick Tube," *American Metal Market*, September 11, 1987, p. 2.

Lowes, Robert, "Maverick Tube Making Pipe to Carry Crude Oil," *St. Louis Business Journal*, July 14, 1986, p. 21A.

"Maverick Tube Posts $5.1M Loss," *American Metal Market*, November 1, 2000, p. 4.

"Maverick Tube to Buy Prudential Steel Ltd. in an All-Stock Deal," *Wall Street Journal*, June 12, 2000, p. A15.

Miller, Patricia, "Maverick Tube Plans $36 Million Public Offering," *St. Louis Business Journal*, October 29, 1990, p. 1A.

——, "Stupp Bros. Buys 5% Stake in Maverick," *St. Louis Business Journal*, July 20, 1992, p. 1.

"Nucorp Energy: Caught in Deep Debt When the Oil-Drilling Boom Collapsed," *Business Week*, August 23, 1982, p. 116.

"Nucorp Energy Trustee Will Seek Buyer, Abandon Proposal for Reorganization," *Wall Street Journal*, August 15, 1983, p. 4.

"Oil-Field Suppliers," *Business Week*, September 27, 1982, pp. 66–70.

Rhodin, Rebecca, ''Maverick Tube Moves Back into Southwest,'' *American Metal Market,* August 4, 1983, p. 8.

Robertson, Scott, ''Earnings Climb at Optimistic Maverick Tube,'' *American Metal Market,* July 18, 2003, p. 4.

Sacco, John E., ''Maverick to Buy Prudential Steel for $484M,'' *American Metal Market,* June 13, 2000, p. 1.

——, ''Maverick Tube Completes Buy of LTV Division,'' *American Metal Market,* January 3, 2003, p. 1.

——, ''Maverick Tube to Shut Longview Pipe Facility,'' *American Metal Market,* December 19, 2001, p. 1.

Sapino, Brenda, ''Maverick Producing New Pipe Products,'' *American Metal Market,* May 6, 1986, p. 11.

Tejada, Carlos, and Terzah Ewing, ''Profits Are Flowing for Makers of Oil-Field Equipment,'' *Wall Street Journal,* November 4, 1997, p. B4.

—A. Woodward

Medicis Pharmaceutical Corporation

8125 N. Hayden Road
Scottsdale, Arizona 85258-2463
U.S.A.
Telephone: (602) 808-8800
Fax: (602) 808-0822
Web site: http://www.medicis.com

Public Company
Incorporated: 1987 as Innovative Therapeutics Corp.
Employees: 279
Sales: $247.5 million (2003)
Stock Exchanges: New York
Ticker Symbol: MRX
NAIC: 325412 Pharmaceutical Preparation Manufacturing

Medicis Pharmaceutical Corporation is a Scottsdale, Arizona-based company that specializes in the sale of prescription and over-the-counter drugs used to fight acne, fungal infections, rosacea, hyperpigmentation, photoaging, psoriasis, eczema, skin and skin structure infections, seborrhea, and dermatitis. The company also sells an asthma drug and recently moved into the dermal aesthetic market. Medicis looks for niche opportunities in the dermatology field, acquiring the rights to drugs developed by major pharmaceuticals but which lack blockbuster potential. The company further divides its area of concentration by focusing on different aspects of a condition, such as acne, thus carving out niches within niches. Because Medicis is able to devote greater attention to the drugs, the major pharmaceuticals find it advantageous to sign over their rights, and because there are a small number of dermatologists to contact, Medicis is able to operate a lean sales force. The company also saves on manufacturing and research and development costs. Core Medicis brands include Dynacin, which treats moderate to severe acne; Loprox, a fungal and yeast infection treatment; Lustra, used to treat ultraviolet-induced skin discoloration; Omnicef, used to counteract skin and skin-structure infections; Oraped, used to treat children with acute asthma; Plexion, a treatment for acne rosacea; and Triaz, a prescription benzoyl peroxide skin cleaning product.

Company Founder Starting Career with Congress: 1970s

The driving force in the growth of Medicis was founder Jonah Shacknai. Born and raised in New York, Shacknai grew up planning to become an environmental activist, and as a consequence became interested in politics and civic affairs. While working on his undergraduate degree at Colgate University he received a fellowship with the U.S. Justice Department in 1977. After his six-month stint, he stayed in Washington, D.C., going to work for New York Congressman James Scheuer. In little more than two years he took over the running of the office, becoming the youngest chief of staff on Capitol Hill. At night he studied at Georgetown University, earning a law degree in 1982. Shacknai's legislative focus was his work on a subcommittee of the U.S. House of Representatives Committee on Science Technology, for which he became chief aide, involved in healthcare, consumer protection, and environment issues. As a result of his role in the drafting of all major legislation concerning food and drugs and healthcare research, Shacknai worked with a large number of pharmaceuticals. He put that experience to work in the private sector when in 1982 he became a partner in a Washington law firm, Royer, Shacknai & Mehle, which represented more than 30 pharmaceutical clients. Shacknai devoted most of his attention to Key Pharmaceuticals, eventually becoming an officer. After Key was sold in 1986 to Schering-Plough for $860 million, he became involved in the founding of Ivax Corp., which grew into the largest generic drug manufacturer in the world.

In a 1993 *Wall Street Transcript* interview, Shacknai revealed, "It occurred to me along the way that dermatology was really the place to be. It was more insulated from healthcare cost containment than any other field and medicine and pharmaceuticals in that the regulatory barriers to the introduction of new products were fewer. Finally, dermatologists are extremely receptive to new products. . . . The mixture of those factors was alluring to me, a $4 billion marketplace that is growing significantly each year and pleasant people to deal with and real market opportunities. I think that should be enough to attract any sensible business person."

Launching Medicis, Going Public, and Relocating: Late 1980s to Mid-1990s

Legally, Medicis dates back to the July 1987 incorporation of Innovative Therapeutics Corp., a company created to develop and market dermatological conditions. This entity was then merged with Medicis Corporation, established by Shacknai in July 1988 shortly after he quit his law practice. He became the company's chief executive officer and chairman. The company assumed the name Medicis Pharmaceutical Corporation a year later. For the first few years the company was run out of Washington, D.C., then relocated to New York City to be closer to Wall Street. In July 1989 Medicis obtained the rights to its first products, the Theraplex line of shampoos and moisturizers, used in the treatment of acne and eczema. Taking advantage of Shacknai's connections with IVAX, Medicis landed its next major acquisition one year later, acquiring from IVAX a worldwide license for Erythromycin 2% (marketed by Medicis as Terramycin Z) and Benzashave 5%, as well as other products.

As Medicis geared up, it lost more than $2.5 million during the first two years. In order to establish a dermatology sales force and launch a marketing campaign for several new products, pay off short-term debt, fund research and development, and add to its working capital, Medicis made an initial public offering of stock, which was completed in April 1990 and raised close to $7.4 million. Medicis was able to then move beyond the sale of shampoos and conditioners in 1991 with the establishment of its dermatological sales force and the launch of pharmaceutical products. The next major product acquisition came in 1992 when Medicis bought from SmithKline Beecham the Esoterica line of products, which included treatments for dry skin, sun screen protection, and fade creams for liver spots, freckles, and other minor discolorations. By now Medicis settled into a pattern of introducing a new product each year to spur growth. The product launch of 1993 was Dynacin, an acne drug employing the oral antibiotic minocycline. It would soon provide the lion's share of the company's revenues. Also in 1993 Medicis acquired a 75 percent interest in Genetic MediSyn Corp., a biotech that used anti-sense technology to treat acne, male pattern baldness, and excessive hair growth on women. Already at this early stage of its development, Medicis had a wealth of products. The challenge facing the company was how to strategically introduce them into the marketplace.

In the early 1990s, Medicis quickly moved toward profitability. Revenues grew from $7.7 million in fiscal 1992 to more than $17 million in 1994. During this period, the company posted net losses of $11.8 million in 1992 and $11.65 million in 1993 before achieving its first profitable year in 1994, recording more than $650,000. Sales topped $19 million in fiscal 1995 as profits

reached $1.6 million. It was also during 1995 that Shacknai decided to relocate the business, this time to Phoenix, Arizona. While the move lowered the company's overhead, it also deprived Medicis of what little notice it had received on Wall Street. For some time Shacknai had been disappointed in the low price of Medicis stock despite the company's impressive record. Concluding that the stock was depressed in large part because there were simply too many shares in circulation, he engineered a 1-for-14 reverse stock split. As a result, the price of Medicis shares rose from the 37 cents range to more than $5, which helped to reposition the stock. It was further helped in early 1996 when Shacknai was able to drum up interest from stock analysts. Over the course of the next several months, Medicis became an investor darling and the price of its stock soon topped the $30 mark, adjusted for a 3-for-2 split in 1997. On the product front, the company launched Triaz in 1996. For the year, Medicis saw its revenues grow by some 30 percent to $25.3 million, while net income soared to more than $7.8 million. Of some concern was the company's dependence on Dynacin products, which contributed 62 percent of the company's sales. Because of the success of Medicis with Dynacin it now faced competition from other minocycline-based treatments.

Medicis conducted another public offering of stock in 1997, this time raising more than $95 million. In 1997 the company acquired the Lidex and Synalar products from Syntex for $28 million in cash, plus subsequent payments that totaled another $3 million. Furthermore, in 1997 (fiscal 1998) Medicis paid $55 million for GenDerm Corporation, gaining its line of dermatological products. Also in 1997 Medicis introduced Dye-Free Dynacin. Despite this addition to the Dynacin line, the company actually reduced its dependence on Dynacin sales, which now accounted for half of fiscal 1997 revenues, totaling $41.2 million. Profits grew to $17.34 million.

Secondary Offering in 1998 Nets $210 Million

Medicis enjoyed a number of positive developments in 1998. In February it completed yet another public offering of stock, raising in excess of $210 million, earmarked to license or acquire new products, launch others, and expand marketing as well as research and development capabilities. In September Medicis reached a new level of prestige when shares began trading on the New York Stock Exchange. During the course of the year, Medicis received a patent for Triaz and introduced Lustra. It forged a collaboration with Abbott Laboratories and also bought the licensing rights to antifungal products from Hoechst Marion Roussel, Inc. The addition of such products as Loprox, Topicort, and A/T/S allowed Medicis to enter the $800 million antifungal market and bolster its position in the topical steroid market.

Medicis launched three products in fiscal 1999: Ovide, Lustra-AF, and Dynacin 75 mg (a version of the drug aimed at people who weigh 110–175 pounds). It also made an adjustment to its product mix, electing, in conjunction with its partner IMX Pharmaceuticals, to sell The Exorex Company and its line of over-the-counter psoriasis and eczema medications to Bioglan Pharma Plc for $40 million. The divestiture allowed Medicis to focus on other products that were more core to the company's future. Another development in fiscal 1999 was the $14.3 million

Key Dates:

1988: Jonah Shacknai founds Medicis and folds in Innovative Therapeutics Corp., founded a year earlier.
1990: Initial public offering is completed.
1993: Acne drug Dynacin is unveiled.
1995: Company moves to Phoenix.
1999: Company is listed on the New York Stock Exchange.
2002: Ascent Pediatrics is acquired for $60 million.

cash purchase of Ucyclyd Pharma, Inc. The Baltimore, Maryland-based pharmaceutical produced Buphenyl, the only approved drug substance for treatment of Urea Cycle Disorder, a rare genetic condition. Buphenyl had been classified by the Food and Drug Administration as an ''orphan drug.'' Because such medications treated diseases that occur in less than 200,000 cases, the FDA offered financial incentives to drug manufacturers for producing them. The Ucyclyd acquisition gave Medicis a toehold in the specialty niche orphan drug market.

In fiscal 2000 Medicis moved to a new 50,000-square-foot headquarters in Scottsdale, Arizona. It received a patent on Lustra Composition and launched Loprox Gel. In addition, Medicis acquired the Vectrin Product Line from Warner Chilcott. Vectrin is an antibiotic used to treat acne and other bacterial infections. Also in 2000 Medicis launched a skin care web site, www.sunandskin.com to promote skin care awareness. For fiscal 2000 Medicis recorded revenues of nearly $140 million and net income of approximately $43 million.

Medicis launched two new products in fiscal 2001: Plexion, a prescription skin cleanser for use in the treatment of acne rosacea, and Alustra, used in the treatment of ultraviolet-induced dyschromia and discoloration resulting from the use of oral contraceptives, pregnancy, hormone replacement therapy, or skin trauma. In 2001 Medicis also forged a development agreement with Corixa Corp. for the psoriasis drug PVAC, and licensed Omnicef, an antibiotic used to treat moderate skin infections and other conditions. Fiscal 2001 was another strong year for Medicis, which recorded sales of $167.8 million and net profits of more than $40.4 million, and fiscal 2002 would prove to be even stronger, as revenues improved to $212.8 million and net income grew by 25 percent, topping $50 million. Medicis launched Plexion SCT and established a strategic alliance with aaiPharma Inc. to develop and market an unspecified dermatological product. But the most important development of the year was the $60 million acquisition of Ascent Pediatrics Inc., a Massachusetts company that marketed a number of products for children, including asthma medication and antibiotics to treat ear infections. If certain milestones were met, the deal could be worth an additional $50 million over the next five years. Medicis also picked up Ascent's 70-member sales force and was optimis-

tic about selling many of its existing products, such as head-lice treatments, through Ascent's established pediatric sales channels. Another marketing development in 2002 was the hiring of Gerbir Snell/Weisheimer & Associates to create a direct-to-consumer marketing campaign for Lustra, used to treat sun-damaged skin. The effort targeted the Sun Belt and Gulf Coast. Direct-to-consumer marketing was a growing trend in the pharmaceutical industry, the result of the FDA easing up on advertising restrictions governing drug makers.

Despite difficult economic conditions, Medicis continued to prosper in fiscal 2003, increasing revenues to $247.5 million and recording net profits of more than $51.2 million. Moreover, the company was sitting on some $600 million in cash, a surprisingly large amount of money which could be used to make further acquisitions of companies and product lines. Shacknai maintained that Medicis was ''not the sort of company to make stupid acquisitions because there is money burning a hole in our pocket.'' A large portion of that money, some $160 million, would be spent on acquiring HA North America Sales AB, a subsidiary of a Swedish biotech, licensing the Restylane, Perlane, and Restylane Fine lines of dermal filler products. The deal was three years in the making. Shacknai called it ''the single largest business development opportunity ever presented to Medicis.'' The acquired products were injectable gels used to treat fine lines and wrinkles, shape facial contours, correct deep facial folds, and plump lips. The potential rewards for this entry in cosmetic dermatology were great. Because of the aging baby-boomer population, this practice was the fastest-growing segment of dermatology. Medicis had both the money and commitment to support a major move into the market, and there was every reason to believe that the company was on the cusp of experiencing even greater prosperity in the future.

Principal Subsidiaries

Medicis Dermatologies, Inc.; GenDerm Corporation; Ucyclyd Pharma, Inc.; Ascent Pediatric, Inc.

Principal Competitors

Allergan, Inc.; GlaxoSmithKline plc; Ortho-Neutrogena.

Further Reading

Abrahms, Doug, ''D.C. Cosmetic Company to Test Public Markets,'' *Washington Business Journal,* January 29, 1990, p. 11.
Elliott, Alan R., ''Medicis Pharmaceutical Corp.,'' *Investor's Business Daily,* November 14, 2000, p. A12.
Gianturco, Michael, ''The Acne Niche,'' *Forbes,* September 23, 1996, p. 212.
Gonzales, Angela, ''Success Requires Focus,'' *Business Journal—Serving Phoenix & The Valley of the Sun,* April 12, 1996, p. 24.
Mandell, Mel, ''Small Company Benefits from Corporate Castoffs,'' *D&B Reports,* September/October 1993, p. 50.

—Ed Dinger

Menasha Corporation

P.O. Box 367
Neenah, Wisconsin 54957-0367
U.S.A.
Telephone: (920) 751-1000
Fax: (920) 751-1236
Web site: http://www.menasha.com

Private Company
Incorporated: 1872 as Menasha Wooden Ware Company
Employees: 5,360
Sales: $1.03 billion (2002)
NAIC: 322130 Paperboard Mills; 322211 Corrugated and Solid Fiber Box Manufacturing; 322212 Folding Paperboard Box Manufacturing; 322299 All Other Converted Paper Product Manufacturing; 323119 Other Commercial Printing; 325211 Plastics Material and Resin Manufacturing; 326199 All Other Plastics Product Manufacturing

The third oldest privately held manufacturing company in the United States, Menasha Corporation is a holding company with four main subsidiaries: Menasha Packaging Company LLC, ORBIS Corporation, Poly Hi Solidur, Inc., and Promo Edge Company. Neenah, Wisconsin-based Menasha Packaging, the largest (more than half of sales) and oldest of the company's businesses, produces corrugated packaging, corrugated pallets, protective interior packaging, and folding cartons. It operates 25 plants in the Midwest, East, mid-South, and Southwest. Headquartered in Oconomowoc, Wisconsin, ORBIS is a producer of plastic returnable and reusable packaging that is used by a variety of customers to move products and materials through the supply chain. Poly Hi Solidur, based in Fort Wayne, Indiana, is a converter of plastic resins into engineered plastics with a wide range of uses; the company is the world's largest producer of semifinished ultra-high molecular weight polyethylene. Promo Edge, which operates out of Neenah and also Elk Grove Village, Illinois, is a major national designer and manufacturer of in-store promotional materials for consumer product firms. In addition to these four businesses,

Menasha also owns New Jersey Packaging Company, a Fairfield, New Jersey-based maker of pharmaceutical labels for both prescription and over-the-counter medications; and Hopkins, Minnesota-based Thermotech, which specializes in custom injection molding of precision plastic components.

From its 19th-century origins in woodenware production, Menasha shifted to paper-based packaging and material handling products in the 1920s and 1930s, earning its reputation as a "box maker." From the 1970s onward, active acquisitions resulted in rapid growth and diversification, carrying Menasha well beyond its original scope of interests in packaging and woodenware. By the early 2000s, the company employed close to 5,400 workers in 65 operations in the United States and nine other countries. Menasha remains majority owned by descendants of its founder, Elisha D. Smith, after more than 150 years of operation.

Early History: From Pails to Forest Products

Menasha's origins date back to entrepreneurial efforts of woodenware manufacturers in the mid-19th century Midwest. In 1849 a pail factory was founded in Menasha, Wisconsin. The undercapitalized venture—simply called the Pail Factory—was then sold to Elisha D. Smith for $1,200 in 1852. Under Smith's leadership, the venture survived the Panic of 1857, an economic crisis that bankrupted thousands of U.S. businesses, and expanded smartly during the Civil War, supplying pails and other wooden storage and shipping containers to the Union forces. By 1871 the Pail Factory had become the largest woodenware maker in the Midwest, with 250 employees manufacturing products ranging from pails to tubs, churns, measures, butter tubs, fish kits, kannikins, keelers, and clothespins.

Just one year later, however, post-Civil War inflation sent costs soaring faster than the factory's revenues, forcing the Pail Factory into receivership, $250,000 in debt. Smith's father-in-law, Spencer Mowry, provided the venture with an infusion of cash and reorganized it as Menasha Wooden Ware Company. It was incorporated under that same name on May 24, 1875. The original pail factory was destroyed by fire in 1878. Twelve years later, in 1890, the entire company was devastated by yet another fire, with only the Cooperage Shop escaping destruction. But quick reconstruction was followed by further expansion. In 1894 the founder's son, Charles R. Smith, merged the broom handle and barrel factory that he had founded with the Menasha Wooden Ware Company, creating the world's largest manufacturer of turned woodenware. By 1899, when the company founder died at age 72, Menasha Wooden Ware had annual revenues of $1 million and 1,000 people on the company payroll. Charles R. Smith was named to succeed his father, although he had in fact already been running the company for nearly a decade.

To provide vital raw materials as the company grew over time, Menasha began purchasing timberlands and related operations, first in Wisconsin, in 1900, and then—more importantly—in the Pacific Northwest, in 1903. By 1915, Menasha supplied 27 million feet of timber annually and was the United States' foremost producer of wooden food packaging in bulk. In 1929, with its plant in Tacoma, Washington, the company began production of wood flour, a powder made from spruce shavings that was used in explosives, plastic wood, and other products. In 1969 lumber products were further expanded as Menasha merged with the John Strange Paper Company, creating the Appleton Manufacturing Division and a majority interest in the Wisconsin Container Corporation, later to become Menasha's Solid Fibre Division. By 1980, wood fiber production—used primarily as industrial fillers and extenders in products such as plywood and molded plastics—had increased enough to warrant an additional wood fiber plant in Centralia, Washington, and the 1987 purchase of yet another plant in Marysville, Washington. Over time, Menasha would form its Forest Products Group specifically to develop its timber interests. By the early 1990s, its Land & Timber Division managed the corporation's 100,000 acres of timberlands in the Pacific Northwest alone, meeting worldwide timber needs. In addition, the Wood Fibre Division produced organic based wood flours.

Shifting to Corrugated Containers, 1920s

While timber development provided raw materials for woodenware and wood packaging, its uses changed toward paper production as Menasha moved into production of corrugated containers. In 1926 Menasha Wooden Ware was split into two separate but affiliated companies, the Menasha Wooden Ware Company, which owned a portfolio of stocks, and the Menasha Wooden Ware Corporation, which continued the manufacturing and marketing operations. (This arrangement lasted until 1981, when the investment company and the operating company were merged back together.) Accommodating changes in packaging technology, the latter organization pro-

duced Menasha's first corrugated containers in 1927. By 1935, corrugated containers had supplanted their wooden predecessors, and Menasha discontinued its line of barrels, converting woodworking plants to the manufacture of toys and juvenile furniture, a product line that would continue only until 1952. To supply its growing corrugated business with necessary raw materials, the corporation in 1939 acquired a 60 percent interest in the Otsego Falls Paper Company in Michigan; full ownership was gained 16 years later. The Otsego Falls mill formed the basis for Menasha's Paperboard Division. Its paper machines produced corrugating medium for several markets: the production of corrugated containers at Menasha's own container plants, outside sales, and trading in exchange for additional types of paperboard used but not manufactured by Menasha.

From the postwar era into the early 1960s, Menasha focused on expansion of its core business in corrugated containers and timber, acquiring and developing new facilities for corrugated medium, containers, plywood, wood fiber, and lumber. Major investments in the G.B. Lewis Company of Watertown, Wisconsin, led to Menasha's funding of that company's reorganization and Menasha's subsequent entry into plastic handling containers and other plastic products. With diminishing emphasis on woodenware products and increased diversity in the field of plastics, Menasha Wooden Ware Corporation changed its name to Menasha Corporation in 1962.

Corporate growth occasioned new emphasis on community services. In 1953 the Charles R. Smith Foundation—later renamed Menasha Corporation Foundation—was formed as an independent philanthropic organization funded by 1 percent of Menasha's pretax earnings. By the 1990s, the foundation provided substantial support for charitable, educational, health and welfare, cultural, and environmental projects and programs. In education, the foundation contributed to a wide variety of colleges and universities, in addition to sponsoring scholarship programs for its employees and other qualified students. At the University of Wisconsin-Stout and Oregon State University, the foundation also sponsored fellowships for select students studying packaging or forestry. Beneficiaries of health and welfare allocations included the United Way campaigns in communities where Menasha had plants, and various chapters of Special Olympics, hospitals, workshops for children with developmental disabilities, mental health centers, medical research appeals, and other concerns. The foundation also contributed to various cultural organizations, including the New Dramatists in New York City, Wisconsin Public Broadcasting, the Bergstrom-Mahler Museum in Neenah, Wisconsin, and the Oregon Coast Music Festival in Coos Bay, Oregon. Starting in the 1980s, the foundation increased contributions to environmental groups, including the Nature Conservancy, the Sigurd Olson Environmental Institute, the Ruffed Grouse Society, and the International Crane Foundation.

In the 1960s Menasha began a move toward packaging innovation and diversification that would position it as a main industry player by the 1990s. As part of a strategy to increase its share of the Midwest's corrugated market, the company in 1966 purchased a plant in Coloma, Michigan, from Twin Cities Container Corporation. In addition to expansion of existing container plants and paperboard operations, Menasha began production of multicolor corrugated containers, foreshadowing

Key Dates:

1849: A wooden pail factory is started in Menasha, Wisconsin.
1852: Elisha D. Smith buys the factory for $1,200.
1872: The venture is thrown into receivership; Smith's father-in-law provides an infusion of cash and reorganizes the venture as Menasha Wooden Ware Company.
1875: Company is incorporated.
1894: Merger with a broom handle and barrel factory formed by the founder's son makes Menasha the world's largest manufacturer of turned woodenware.
1903: Acquisition of timberlands in the Pacific Northwest begins.
1926: Company is reorganized into two separate but affiliated companies, Menasha Wooden Ware Company, which owns a portfolio of stocks, and Menasha Wooden Ware Corporation, which continues the manufacturing and marketing operations.
1927: With the woodenware business in decline, Menasha begins manufacturing corrugated containers.
1939: A majority interest in Otsego Falls Paper Company, maker of corrugating medium, is acquired.
1955: Menasha diversifies into plastics with the purchase of a 51 percent interest in G.B. Lewis Company, maker of plastic material handling containers.
1962: Company changes its name to Menasha Corporation.
1967: Corporate headquarters are relocated to Neenah, Wisconsin.
1971: Menasha acquires an interest in Poly Hi Inc., a leading manufacturer of ultra-high-density polyethylene.

1975: Menasha takes full control of G.B. Lewis, which is divided into two divisions: LEWISystems and Molded Products.
1977: Full ownership of Poly Hi is obtained.
1981: A paper mill, a box plant, and other facilities on West Coast are sold to Weyerhaeuser Company.
1985: Menasha acquires Mid America Tag & Label Co., which becomes the core of the company's promotional graphics business.
1993: Menasha takes over the U.S. operations of Solidur Deutschland GmbH, which are merged into Poly Hi to form Poly Hi Solidur.
1996: Several plastic returnable and reusable packaging product operations, including LEWISystems, are merged to form ORBIS; America Tag & Label and other promotional materials businesses are merged to form Promo Edge.
2000: The Material Handling Group, which includes ORBIS, is reorganized as a wholly owned Menasha Corporation subsidiary called Menasha Material Handling Corporation.
2001: Forest products business of Menasha is spun off into a separate company, Menasha Forest Products Corporation; Menasha Material Handling is renamed ORBIS Corporation; Menasha Corporation restructures into a holding company with four main subsidiaries: Menasha Packaging Company, ORBIS, Poly Hi Solidur, Inc., and Promo Edge Company.

future advances in graphics that would figure strongly a decade later. In 1967 new corporate offices were established in the town of Neenah, Wisconsin, replacing the former headquarters that had been destroyed by fire in 1964. Then, in 1968, the company purchased Vanant Packaging Corporation and developed its Sus-Rap Packaging operation, custom engineering and manufacturing interior protective packaging items to meet specific end-use requirements. Primary products of that line included Sus-Rap, Menasha Pads, and SuperFlute protective packaging. In 1969 a new wood flour plant was opened in Grants Pass, Oregon, and in 1972 the Hartford Container Company, of Hartford, Wisconsin, operator of a corrugated box plant, was acquired. Further expansion in packaging brought the 1977 purchase of a plant in Mt. Pleasant, Tennessee, and then the 1989 purchase of Colonial Container Company of Green Lake, Wisconsin, another producer of corrugated boxes.

Diversification into Plastics: 1950s

Just as changing packaging technologies had introduced corrugated containers to the woodenware arena in the 1930s, so the rise of plastics in the 1950s pushed Menasha to innovate and diversify in various areas of plastic manufacturing. In 1955 Menasha purchased a 51 percent interest in G.B. Lewis Company of Watertown, Wisconsin, which like Menasha had gotten its start in the 19th century as a woodenware maker and was in the midst of a shift in focus. Menasha's investment in the Lewis Company helped fund the latter's reorganization into a plastics company

and introduced Menasha to the field of plastic material handling containers for the first time. The Lewis Company and plastics in general would become keys to long-term growth and diversification. In 1973 Menasha Corporation assisted in the construction of two new G.B. Lewis company plants in Monticello and Manchester, Iowa. By 1975, G. B Lewis had been fully acquired, and Menasha formed the LEWISystems and Molded Products Divisions of its Plastics Group. Success of LEWISystems prompted the 1980 purchase of Dare Pafco Products Company of Urbana, Ohio, to increase that division's capacity.

In 1971, meantime, Menasha strengthened its profile in plastics by acquiring a one-third interest in Poly Hi Inc. of Fort Wayne, Indiana, a leading manufacturer of ultra-high-density polyethylene extruded products. Menasha gradually increased its investment in Poly Hi, taking full ownership of the company in 1977. As was the case with G.B. Lewis, the growth pattern at Poly Hi called for increased manufacturing capabilities, prompting the 1981 acquisition of Scranton Plastics Laminating Corporation of Scranton, Pennsylvania. Menasha's plastics operations expanded into reusable plastic and metal products with the 1984 acquisition of Traex Corporation of Dane, Wisconsin, specializing in such items as serving trays, dispensers for straws and condiments, tumblers, bus boxes, and ware-washing racks used in the foodservice industry worldwide.

Menasha's Plastics Group went international in 1985, when the corporation launched its first foreign joint venture with the

Japanese firm of Tsutsunaka Plastic Industry Co. Ltd. for the production of ultra-high-density polyethylene products. The joint venture's capital was set at ¥15 million, with projected sales of ¥1 billion for 1988. In 1987 Poly-Hi operations extended operations to Europe, with construction of a plant in Scunsthorpe, England. The following year, a precision injection molder of thermoplastics and engineered resins, Thermotech, was added to the Plastics Group. That division produced high performance plastic components for various applications including automotive, electrical/electronic appliances, and medical equipment.

Development of Promotional Graphics Operations: 1970s and 1980s

Menasha's developments in packaging and plastics were paralleled, and often supplemented, by innovations in graphics and promotional labeling. In 1977 the corporation acquired a graphics container plant in Roselle, New Jersey, which it then moved to South Brunswick, New Jersey. In 1982 Vinland Web-Print, a producer of web-printed paper and plastic film products, was also acquired. Construction of an additional graphics container plant was completed two years later, in Olive Branch, Mississippi. Expanding into identification and merchandising tags and labels, the corporation acquired Mid America Tag & Label Co. in 1985, followed by its 1986 acquisition of Murfin, Inc., a Columbus, Ohio, web-fed screen printer of label and identity products. With the 1987 acquisition of Neenah Printing, the corporation extended its graphics operations to a full range of printing services in commercial, business forms, and packaging applications, ranging from sample booklets to high image lithographic brochures. In 1989 the corporation added Labelcraft Corporation of Farmingdale, New Jersey, to its Mid America division, specializing in custom designed tags and pressure-sensitive labels. Production capacity for those items was further augmented by the 1990 purchase of Denney-Reyburn Co. of West Chester, Pennsylvania, and Tempe, Arizona. These investments quickly paid off, winning valuable accounts in the early 1990s. In 1991 a division of Mid America that served industrial customers was combined with the Denney-Reyburn plant in Arizona to form the Printed Systems Division.

Over the course of its business expansion, Menasha also developed a Material Handling Division to manufacture reusable plastic container systems including recycling containers, food handling products, small parts bins, work-in-process containers, Stack-N-Nest containers, distribution containers, and transport trays, among other products. In 1986 the corporation's Molded Products Division introduced plastic pallets designed to maximize warehouse inventory stacking and reduce work-in-progress inventories by virtue of their uniform weight. Their wooden predecessors had not only been costly to maintain, but could vary by several pounds in weight, resulting in inventory error of up to thousands of parts in lightweight merchandise. In 1991 similar plastic pallets, marketed as Convoy Opte-packs, were combined with reusable corrugated sidewalls to maximize carrying volume and strength.

Meanwhile, Menasha struggled throughout the 1970s to find a way to unlock some of the value of the company for its shareholders. The company paid very little in the way of a regular dividend, and because its stock was not publicly traded,

shareholders could not easily sell their stock. One solution was to take the company public, an idea proposed several times in the early 1970s but not acted upon. Menasha also pursued a number of mergers with other companies in the mid-1970s, including with Fibreboard Corporation, a leading West Coast paperboard producer, but the deals all fell apart for one reason or another. At this point, revenues were growing steadily, advancing for instance from $138 million in 1975 to $240 million in 1979, but earnings had stagnated at about $11 million. The company therefore found itself at the crossroads, and in the late 1970s considered a number of strategic courses. The one it settled upon called for the company to remain privately held and to adopt a more aggressive growth strategy for its existing businesses. In part to provide the shareholders with some liquidity, Menasha engineered the sale of its North Bend, Oregon, paper mill; its Anaheim, California, box plant; and secondary fiber facilities in Portland and Eugene, Oregon, to Weyerhaeuser Company for $68 million in stock. Menasha shareholders now held stock in Weyerhaeuser, a public company, which they could sell to raise cash if they so desired.

In response to heightened environmental concerns of the 1980s, Menasha took initiatives to literally clean up its act, along with its surroundings. In its "Environmental Mission Statement," the corporation noted that "environmental and industrial hygiene goals can and should be consistent with economic health." In 1989 negotiations were made with several discounters, including Wal-Mart, to provide products such as unbleached cellulose packing material that could replace bubble wrap; other products included recyclable shipping boxes, video cases, and other ecological alternatives.

1990s and Beyond, Transition to Holding Company Structure

In 1991 Menasha Corporation consolidated its developed industries into six primary business groups: Forest Products, Packaging, Promotional Graphics, Information Graphics, Plastics, and Material Handling. The Forest Products Group consisted of the Land and Timber division, Menasha Development, and Wood Fibre; Promotional Information Graphics Group consisted of Mid America, Murfin, Neenah Printing, and Printed Systems; the Packaging Group was made up of Menasha Packaging, Paperboard, and Color divisions; the Material Handling Group included Convoy, LEWISystems, and Special Products; and the Plastics Group combined Appleton Manufacturing, Molded Products, Thermotech, Traex, and Poly Hi. Such an operating structure divided the various divisions into working groups while permitting them to interrelate as working parts of an ever more diverse organization.

Menasha continued to grow in the early to mid-1990s. In 1991 Menasha Packaging was bolstered through the acquisition of North Star Container, Inc. which operated a box plant in Brooklyn Park, Minnesota. The following year a point-of-sale business was formed to sell promotional products produced by the Mid America, Neenah Printing, and Color Divisions (the latter division changed its name to DisplayOne in 1994 to reflect an increasing focus on point-of-purchase displays). Robert D. Bero, who had been vice-president of the plastics group, was named president and CEO in 1993. Also that year, Menasha acquired New Jersey Packaging Company, a producer of pressure-sensitive and heat-seal labels for the pharmaceutical and health-care industries. In another 1993 acquisition, Menasha took over the U.S. operations of Solidur Deutschland GmbH, the leading European producer of ultra-high molecular weight (UHMW) polyethylene; these operations were merged into Poly Hi to form Poly Hi Solidur. Four years later Solidur Deutschland itself was purchased and amalgamated with Poly Hi Solidur, which became the world's leading producer of UHMW.

The Material Handling Group was a particular focus for expansion in the mid-1990s. In 1993 DuraPAK was established as a supplier of reusable protective interior packaging, particularly for the automotive and electronics industries. LEWISystems expanded the following year through the opening of a new plant in Urbana, Ohio. Next, in 1995, Menasha acquired Donray Company of Mentor, Ohio, a producer of foam-cushioned packaging, including corrugated boxes with cushion inserts. Then in 1996, the company acquired Madison Heights, Michigan-based WolPac, Inc., which specialized in designing and engineering material handling systems for the automotive industry. This growth spurt was consolidated that same year with the creation of ORBIS, which combined the operations of LEWISystems, Convoy Plastic Pallets, DuraPAK, Donray, and WolPac, thereby providing customers with a one-stop source for plastic returnable and reusable packaging products and services. ORBIS further expanded its product portfolio via the 1997 introduction of the BulkPak line of plastic bulk containers for a wide variety of applications. A consolidation similar to the one that formed ORBIS occurred within Menasha's promotional materials operations. In 1996 America Tag & Label, DisplayOne, and the point-of-purchase business were merged to form Promo Edge.

In the meantime, Menasha Packaging continued its decades-long expansion. In 1995 Mid South Packaging of Cullman, Alabama, and Southwest Container Corporation of Phoenix, Arizona—both operators of corrugated container businesses—were acquired. During 1996 operations began at a corrugated sheet plant in Erie, Pennsylvania, and Middlefield Container Corporation of Middlefield, Ohio, was acquired. There was also one divestment of a noncore business by Menasha Corporation during this period. The Molded Products Division, which made such custom-molded products as plastic shells for lawnmowers and parts for buses, was sold to a private investment group.

In 1999 Menasha's board of directors made a strategic decision to further decentralize the company's structure. Differences over how this fundamental shift should be implemented led to Bero's departure from the company. Thomas J. Prosser, the board chairman, was named CEO on an interim basis, until the October 2000 appointment of Harold R. Smethills, Jr., to the position of president and CEO. Smethills, who had a background as a lawyer, banker, and corporate turnaround specialist, was brought onboard to implement the restructuring.

One of the first steps in the multiyear restructuring was the reorganization of the Material Handling Group into a wholly owned subsidiary called Menasha Material Handling Corporation. This subsidiary, created in 2000, was comprised of ORBIS, a division called Menasha Services that offered complete returnable packaging solutions to companies who elected to outsource this function, and subsidiary operations in Canada, Mexico, and Brazil. Menasha Packaging enlarged itself in 2000 through two acquisitions: Pittsburgh-based Package Products, Inc. and Pennsylvania Container Corporation, based in Latrobe, Pennsylvania. The former firm produced packaging and folding cartons used in supermarket in-store delis and bakeries, while the latter manufactured corrugated boards, sheets, and containers.

A major change in the company's portfolio of businesses occurred in 2001 when the forest products business of Menasha was spun off into a separate company, Menasha Forest Products Corporation. The descendants of Menasha Corporation's founder maintained majority control of both companies. Also in 2001, Menasha Material Handling was renamed ORBIS Corporation. Completing the restructuring, Menasha Corporation began operating in 2001 as a holding company with four main subsidiaries—Menasha Packaging Company, ORBIS, Poly Hi Solidur, Inc., and Promo Edge Company—and several investment companies either wholly or majority owned by Menasha: New Jersey Packaging, Menasha Printed Systems, Stratecom Graphics, Thermotech, and Traex. Menasha had thus shifted from a very centralized organizational structure to a decentralized one, with the holding company consisting of just a small staff focusing on overall strategic issues, and each subsidiary operating independently, better able to respond quickly to the needs of its particular market. Smethills hired a director for mergers and acquisitions to take the lead in seeking further growth opportunities for the subsidiaries. In addition, the company set up Menasha University to address its shortage of leaders, a heritage of the former centralized structure; this initiative offered a range of leadership and management training programs and courses to selective Menasha employees.

In the immediate aftermath of the restructuring, Menasha tightened its focus by divesting three of the businesses that had been placed into the "investment" category: Traex was sold to Libbey Inc. in December 2002, Menasha Printed Systems was sold to Kay Toledo Tag in August 2003, and Stratecom Graphics was sold to Cypress Multigraphics, Inc. in September 2003. Menasha also strengthened the remaining core through strategic, "bolt-on" acquisitions. ORBIS gained a plastic pallet manufacturer, Cookson Plastic Molding of Latham, New York, in October 2001, and then the following year, Nucon Corporation, which specialized in plastic pallets for the beverage industry, serving the U.S., European, and Mexican markets. Menasha Packaging bolstered its position in consumer packaging and point-of-purchase displays through two acquisitions: Philadelphia-based Triangle Container Corporation in December 2002 and United Packaging of Schaumburg, Illinois, in March 2003.

By the early 2000s, after more than 150 years as a privately held manufacturer, Menasha Corporation was a $1 billion company with a handful of strong subsidiary businesses. The company was still majority owned by descendants of Elisha D. Smith, but the top executives had all been nonfamily members since the early 1960s. Half of the members of the board of directors were descendants of Smith, however, and William A. Shepard, a great-great-grandson of Smith, served as president and CEO of Menasha Packaging, perhaps setting the stage for the future return of Smith family leadership at the 11th oldest private company in the United States.

Principal Subsidiaries

Menasha Packaging Company LLC; ORBIS Corporation; Poly Hi Solidur, Inc.; Promo Edge Company; New Jersey Packaging Company; Thermotech.

Principal Competitors

Smurfit-Stone Container Corporation; International Paper Company; Shorewood Packaging Corporation; Sonoco Products Company; Rock-Tenn Company; Longview Fibre Company.

Further Reading

Blodgett, Richard, *Menasha Corporation: An Odyssey of Five Generations,* Lyme, Conn.: Greenwich Publishing Group, 1999.

Cox, Jackie, "Automated Core Prep Systems Are Expanding into North American Mills," *American Papermaker,* October 1991, p. 22.

Dresang, Joel, "Menasha Chief Quits over Split with Board on Strategy," *Milwaukee Journal Sentinel,* July 13, 1999.

——, "New Leader Is on a Mission at Menasha Corp.," *Milwaukee Journal Sentinel,* July 29, 2001, p. 1D.

Dunn, Richard L., "Custom-Designed Plastic Pallets Reduce Costs, Errors," *Plant Engineering,* April 10, 1986, p. 58.

Geist, Al, "Logging Has Potential in Interior," *Alaska Journal of Commerce,* November 16, 1990, sec. 1, p. 7.

"Reputation, Not Ads, Woos Customers," *Discount Store News,* December 18, 1989, p. 213.

"Tsutsunaka to Sell Menasha Products," *Japan Economic Journal,* November 16, 1985, p. 21.

Whitehead, Sandra, "On the Prowl for Growth Opportunities," *Corporate Report Wisconsin,* January 1991, sec. 1, p. 10.

—Kerstan Cohen
—update: David E. Salamie

Mercury Interactive Corporation

1325 Borregas Avenue, Building A
Sunnyvale, California 94089
U.S.A.
Telephone: (408) 822-5200
Toll Free: (800) 837-8911
Fax: (408) 822-5300
Web site: http://www.mercuryinteractive.com

Public Company
Incorporated: 1989
Employees: 2,100
Sales: $400.1 million (2002)
Stock Exchanges: NASDAQ
Ticker Symbol: MERQ
NAIC: 511210 Software Publishers

Mercury Interactive Corporation helps corporate customers optimize the performance of their software applications. The company's software testing products detect flaws in software systems, enabling a customer to test realistic work scenarios automatically. Mercury's customers include Ford Motor Co., Sony Corporation, Barnes & Noble.com, Citibank, and Ameritrade. The company operates in 26 countries, ranking as one of the leaders in a fast-growing industry.

Origins

Mercury's formation in the late 1980s was the work of two Israeli entrepreneurs, Amnon Landan and Aryeh Finegold. The pair first met in 1985, four years before working together on the idea that gave birth to Mercury. Landan would serve as the junior partner of the collaborative effort. Although the older, more experienced Finegold spearheaded Mercury's formation, he eventually was succeeded in the company's guidance by Landan, who represented the principal figure behind the electric success of Mercury at the beginning of the 21st century.

Amnon Landan was raised in suburban Tel Aviv, the son of an engineer who also served as a career officer with the Israel Defense Forces. As required by Israeli law, Landan joined the army at age 18 in 1976, beginning his mandatory military service in a hotbed of hostilities. Landan, trained to be a paratrooper, was stationed in the region Israel etched out of Lebanon, an area that served as a buffer zone for the defense of Israel. Landan found himself thrust into intense action, required to make nightly helicopter drops and conduct covert searches for opposing forces. In this role, Landan excelled, rising quickly through the ranks of the Israel Defense Forces. His responsibilities increased and his ability to lead others became evident, giving him skills that would be called upon in his civil career as Mercury's leader. By the time he was 20 years old, Landan was leading a platoon of 25 soldiers, distinguishing himself as a commando. When he was 21 years old, Landan was put in charge of a company, responsible for leading 65 soldiers. After his obligatory four years of service, Landan was discharged from the Israel Defense Forces.

At the age of 22 in 1981, he embarked on a road trip with his future wife, driving across the United States in a battered Chevy Vega. The couple slept on a mattress in the back of the car, taking out the back seats to make room for their bed. During the trip, Landan stopped in the area that would later provide the fertile soil for the explosive growth of the nascent software industry. Landan's stop in California's Silicon Valley was symbolic, foreshadowing his return later and his eventual rise to become one of the region's most promising business leaders. In 1981, however, Landan was fresh out of the military without any advanced education.

After returning to Israel, Landan went back to school. He enrolled at the Technion-Israel Institute of Technology, an institution favorably compared to the esteemed Massachusetts Institute of Technology in the United States. Landan worked part-time as a software programmer to pay for his tuition and earned a bachelor's degree in computer science in 1985. Next, Landan was hired by an electronic design automation firm named Daisy Systems, a Mountain View, California-based company founded by Aryeh Finegold. Landan was hired to become part of the company's Israel-based research staff. Not long after joining the company, Landan was assigned to the company's U.S.-based research team and returned to Silicon Valley. He joined Daisy just as the company was reaching its peak, having grown from a startup concern in 1980 to a $122 million company in 1985. Quickly, however, the company's fortunes reversed, its success transmogrifying to despair as its technology aged. In mid-1986, Daisy's stock value plummeted, falling from $37 to $5 per share. In response, the company's board of directors removed Finegold.

Mercury Taking Shape in 1989

After the sudden collapse of Daisy, Finegold was appointed to a new executive position. He was picked to lead a new startup company called Ready Systems. Colleagues at Ready Systems encouraged Finegold to hire Landan as a programmer. After initially accepting Finegold's offer, Landan reneged. The two future partners next met at Daisy's 1989 annual meeting. At the time of their meeting, Finegold had already raised $5.5 million from venture capitalists who were compelled by his business plan. Aside from capital, Finegold needed expertise to make his plan work. He turned to Landan, explaining that he wanted to develop software that could assist in what soft engineers called "regression testing." Finegold described a product that would automate one of the most tedious aspects of passing a software product through the trying maturation from development to deployment, from creation to practical use. In the incremental process of developing new software applications, programmers had to retest any modified code, making sure that each change to the original code complied with specific requirements and that the viable parts of the original code remained untouched. Finegold hit upon a demand that was barely discernible during the late 1980s, but his vision would prove prescient. As the software industry experienced explosive growth during the next decade and the business world became increasingly dependent on the use of computers, Finegold's business plan became an instrumental component of keeping new software working at its optimal level. Landan agreed to join Finegold's new startup venture. Together, the pair worked to deliver Mercury's message to the business world.

Finegold and Landan began collaborating in 1989, working together to develop software and hardware tools that tested the compatibility of software and hardware manufactured by other companies. "Testing software systems is not rocket science," Landan remarked in a May 18, 1998 interview with *Forbes*. "In fact, it's boring," he said. "It's also been the first place to cut corners if deployment is behind schedule." Software applications often contained flaws in their code that manifested themselves once subjected to the rigors of practical use. To the user, glitches appeared, glitches that frustrated personal computer users and glitches that portended profound problems for corporate users. According to one consulting firm, Dennis, Massachusetts-based Standish Group International, seven of every ten new software systems failed in some way upon deployment. For companies that depended on software applications to effectively operate and manage their businesses—a dependence that applied to virtually every company in existence during the 1990s—the glitches and flaws were capable of bringing a business to its knees. Mercury presented itself as a source of salvation for corporate clientele, offering software that tested realistic work scenarios automatically.

When Landan first joined Finegold at the inception of Mercury, he began running one of two development groups based in Israel. Mercury began shipping its first software testing tools in 1991. The company generated its first profit two years later, the same year it converted to public ownership and the same year Landan left Israel and joined Finegold in Silicon Valley. Landan came to the United States in 1993 to run the company's operations, intending to stay for only a few years, but he spent the next six years in California working with Finegold to strengthen Mercury's market position. In 1995, he was named president of the company, assuming responsibility for worldwide sales and ensuring that the company did not overlook significant advancements in technology. During these pivotal years of growth in the software and computer industries, Mercury's products were certified as standard testing tools for major software producers such as PeopleSoft and Oracle.

Mercury in the Late 1990s

By 1998, the company was beginning to hit its stride financially, registering vigorous growth in a burgeoning industry. The testing software market generated $150 million worth of business in 1996, and was expected to be a $1.2 billion market by 2001. Mercury, which controlled more than one-third of the testing-tools market in 1998, stood to benefit substantially from the energetic growth of the industry. The company was recording a net profit margin of 16 percent by addressing the ever increasing needs of corporate customers. In 1998, for example, Mercury offered a software package that addressed problems stemming from Year 2000 issues, marketing TestSuite2000, which detected date-related glitches in software applications.

Mercury dominated its market largely because the company was able to nimbly respond to the increasing needs of potential customers. One market of great importance during the late 1990s was e-commerce, a sector that recorded phenomenal growth. Mercury developed a substantial position in the e-commerce sector during its 10th anniversary year, a milestone that also marked Finegold's exit from the company. When Finegold departed in 1999, Landan was appointed chairman of the board, taking resolute control over the company just as it began recording fast-paced growth. Much of the company's financial success was attributable to its development of e-commerce application-testing products. Within nine months in 1999, the revenue generated from Mercury's web-based business increased from 10 percent of sales to 70 percent of sales. The enormous growth of Mercury's Web-based business ignited the company's financial growth. Revenue, which totaled $77 million in 1997, swelled to $188 million in 1999.

By the beginning of the 21st century, Mercury was garnering praise for helping to develop a market vital to the success of software applications in the corporate world. In 2000, sales leaped 64 percent, reaching $307 million. During the year, the company ranked as one of *Fortune* magazine's 100 Fastest Growing Companies. *Barron's* magazine ranked Mercury ninth on its list of the best managed public companies. One of the

Key Dates:

1989: Mercury is founded.
1991: Mercury begins shipping its first products.
1993: Mercury converts to public ownership.
1995: Amnon Landan is appointed president.
1999: The development of web-based business spurs rapid growth.
2003: Mercury acquires Performant, Inc. and Kintana, Inc.

most astute decisions made by Landan during this period was to plough the company's profits back into research and development efforts. Landan's insistence on developing new growth engines for the company led to the creation of Topaz and ActiveWatch, two performance-monitoring products that cost $150 million to develop. By 2003, Topaz and ActiveWatch ranked among Mercury's fastest-growing products.

As Mercury's 15th anniversary approached, Landan continued to explore new business opportunities for the Sunnyvale, California-based company. New markets were penetrated by reinvesting profits and by acquiring companies that fleshed out the company's technological abilities. In the summer of 2003, the company completed two major acquisitions, adding assets that pushed the company's sales volume toward the $500 million mark. In May, Mercury acquired Performant, Inc., a Bellevue, Washington-based private firm equipped with technology that enabled users to diagnose and rectify software performance problems. In June, Mercury acquired Kintana, Inc., paying $225 million for the $44.5 million-in-sales company. Kintana, which also was based in Sunnyvale, developed software that helped companies prioritize the importance of technology projects. As the company plotted its future course, further acquisitions were expected. Other, larger software firms were increasing their interests in the lucrative testing-tools market, which portended increased competition for Landan's enterprise. In the years ahead, as the industry consolidated, Mercury's continued success depended on its ability to stay on the technological vanguard and beat back competition from well-financed concerns. With Landan at the helm, there was every expectation that the success of the first 15 years could be repeated in the years ahead.

Principal Subsidiaries

Freshwater Software, Inc.; Kintana, Inc.

Principal Competitors

Compuware Corporation; IBM Software; Segue Software, Inc.

Further Reading

Linsmayer, Anne, "Shake Those Bugs Out," *Forbes,* May 18, 1998, p. 198.
Shaw, Andy, "Taking Care of Business, with IT Leading the Way," *Computing Canada,* August 8, 2003, p. 13.
Silverstein, Roberta, "Mercury Rising to Internet Challenge," *Business Journal,* June 23, 2000, p. 10.
Upbin, Bruce, "Higher Ground," *Forbes,* October 27, 2003, p. 140.
——, "The Power of Technotype," *Forbes,* October 27, 2003, p. 146.

—Jeffrey L. Covell

Mitchells & Butlers PLC

27 Fleet Street
Birmingham B3 1JP
United Kingdom
Telephone: +44-870-609-3000
Fax: +44-121-233-2246
Web site: http://www.mbplc.com

Public Company
Incorporated: 2003
Employees: 38,747
Sales: $2.31 billion (2002)
Stock Exchanges: London New York
Ticker Symbol: MLB
NAIC: 722410 Drinking Places (Alcoholic Beverages)

Mitchells & Butlers PLC is one of the United Kingdom's largest operators of managed pubs, with more than 2,000 drinking and eating establishments located throughout the country. The company also operates a number of bars in Germany. Formed from the 2003 breakup of Six Continents Plc, which spun off its hotels business as International Hotel Group, Mitchells & Butlers revives one of the most venerable names in British drinking history. Yet the company is decidedly modern, managing a strong portfolio of branded and unbranded pubs and restaurants to appeal to nearly every consumer group and taste. Most of Mitchells & Butlers' pub brands were developed in-house, and include O'Neill's Irish bars; Flares 1970s theme bars; Scream, catering to university students; and Goose pubs, which also offer food. In addition to these pub brands, the company's portfolio includes Ye Olde Fighting Cocks, in St. Albans, one of the oldest pubs in Great Britain, the White Horse in London, and the Philharmonic in Liverpool. Mitchells & Butlers' restaurant division meanwhile operates under a number of brands as well, including All Bar One and Browns, and the Alex chain of brasserie bars in Germany. While these formats cater to the city center crowd, most of the company's restaurants target the suburban and rural markets, including Harvester flame grills; Toby Carvery for traditional foods; and Vintage Inns. Mitchells & Butlers is led by Chairman Roger Carr, and

CEO Tim Clarke, who held the same position at Six Continents. After losing out in its acquisition bid for the pub estate of chief rival Scottish & Newcastle, Mitchells & Butlers itself became widely viewed as a potential takeover target in September 2003.

Pouring British Pub History in the 18th Century

The Mitchells & Butlers entering the 21st century was the product of English pub and brewing history stretching back to the late 18th century through two main branches. The oldest of these began as a brewery founded by William Bass. Bass had run a business transporting ale for Burton brewer Benjamin Printon between London and Manchester, but sold that business to Matthew Pickford in 1877. Bass then set up his own brewery in Burton-on-Trent, a choice prompted in large part by the opening of the Trent & Mersey Canal that year.

Bass, like other Burton brewers of the era, originally focused his beer production on the export market, particularly to the Baltic region. This involvement with shipping led Bass to engage in a side business, importing lumber for sale in England. During the blockade of British ports in the early 1900s, however, Bass turned to supplying the London and Liverpool markets. Yet Bass continued to pursue other export markets, turning to India in the early part of the century. Bass and other Burton brewers developed new ale varieties for the new market, resulting in what became known as India Pale Ale.

The Bass brewery's true fame grew under Michael Bass, grandson of William, who took the brewery in 1827. Michael Bass correctly recognized the potential of the country's developing railway system—the company not only bought a stake in the Midland line, but also began construction of its own railway system. At 16 miles, the Bass railway grew to become the United Kingdom's largest private railway system. The company also built warehousing facilities in London's St. Pancras station, supporting its growing national and export business.

Burton's linkup to the country's national railway system in 1839 helped transform the company from a small-scale brewery into one of the world's largest and most renowned brewers. By the early 1880s, Bass's production topped one million barrels per year, and its sales neared £2.5 million per year. The com-

Company Perspectives:

Our strategy is to capitalise and build on our position as the leader in the managed pub and pub-restaurant sector in order to drive returns, cash generation, and long-term earnings growth to create value for shareholders.

We intend to implement this strategy by: owning and developing licensed properties with high AWT, maintaining high levels of amenity, service and value; evolving our retail brands and formats to gain market share and, as appropriate, creating new consumer offers; delivering high returns on incremental capital invested by developing prime sites into these brands and formats; and generating additional cost, margin and revenue benefits from unit, brand and corporate scale, to consolidate our leading position in the market.

pany was also the first English company to register its trademark, a red triangle, in 1876.

Bass initially avoided the "tied" house system, which linked pubs to brewers in exclusive contracts and had developed in England in the later part of the 19th century. Instead, the company favored working with wholesalers, which then in turn supplied to the country's growing numbers of pubs and bars. Yet by the end of the century, the tied house system had become dominant, while at the same the brewing industry had undergone a great deal of consolidation.

Finding itself barred from large numbers of the country's drinking establishments, Bass began merging with other brewers, such as Worthington & Company, also based in Burton, in 1926, adding their tied estates but generally shutting their breweries. By the end of the 1950s, Bass, by then known as Bass, Ratcliff & Gretton Ltd., had already become one of the country's largest brewing and pub companies, with a national network of more than 1,700 companies. In 1961, however, Bass took on an entirely new scale, linking up with regionally focused Mitchells & Butlers' 2,500 pubs to form Bass, Mitchells & Butlers Ltd.

Mitchells & Butlers had been among the large number of so-called "homebrew" pubs that had sprung up around England following the introduction of the Beerhouse Act of 1830 by the Duke of Wellington. Under the legislation—another attempt to steer drinkers away from gin—householders were allowed to sell beer from their premises. The new pub owners started out by brewing their own beer; yet the wide range of quality, including not only from pub to pub, but from batch to batch, as well as sanitary and other factors, encouraged the growth of dedicated visiting brewers.

In the meantime, a number of home brewers had begun to gain a reputation for the quality of their ales, and began to attract customers among other homebrew pubs. This new type of brewer developed into what became known as "common brewers" who supplied their own pubs and others in their region.

Among the more popular common brewers in the Birmingham region was Henry Mitchell, who had taken over his father's Crown Inn pub in Smethwick in 1861. The younger Mitchell

proved a master brewer, and by the middle of that decade was unable to meet the growing demand for his ales. In 1866, Mitchell built his first dedicated brewery, next to his pub. Yet demand continued to build, and in 1877 Mitchell acquired a 14-acre site in Cape Hill in order to build a larger brewery. Built over an artesian well, the new site opened in 1879. The brewery continued to expand, and in 1888, backed by financial partner Herbert Bainbridge, Mitchell incorporated the Cape Hill Brewery as a private company.

By then, a new trend was developing among Britain's pub and brewing companies, which had entered a rapid expansion and consolidation phase. A large number of brewing companies had become public companies, a trend launched by Guinness in the mid-1880s. The public companies used their financial might to buy up freehold pub estates. Yet passage of the Wine and Beerhouse Act in 1869, which drastically restricted the number of new pub licenses, caused property values of existing pub sites to soar. This situation encouraged the brewing companies to buy up their competitors in order to gain control of their pub sites. Other brewers began merging together in order to gain scale and protect themselves from the more aggressive, larger companies.

In 1898, Henry Mitchell agreed to merge his company with that of William Butler, whose Crown Brewery had grown into the region's second largest brewer and pub estate. Butler had come to Birmingham at the middle of the century and had worked as a bartender at the Crown Inn on Broad Street. In 1866, Butler used his savings to buy the London Works Tavern in Smethwick. By 1875, in partnership with his brother-in-law, Butler bought the Broad Street Crown Inn. It was there that Butler established the reputation of his ales, and Butler soon became a growing common brewer. Over the following decade, Butler bought up a strong pub estate as well.

Butler registered his company in 1895. Following the merger with Henry Mitchell, forming Mitchells & Butlers, the partners agreed to transfer their brewery operations to the larger Cape Hill site, which offered the company a better water supply and more room for expansion—by 1890, the partners had extended the Cape Hill site to 60 acres. The company also began acquiring other brewers in order to gain control of their pub estates. Such was the case in 1899 when they took control of the Vulcan Brewery, followed a year later by the purchase of James Evans Brewery.

National Brewery Powerhouse in the 1960s

Control of Mitchells & Butlers passed to the founders sons and, later, grandsons, after Butler's death in 1907 and Mitchell's death in 1914. The new owners continued to expand the company, buying up Alfred Cheshires Brewery Ltd. and its Windmill Brewery in 1913. That brewery was shut down the following year, however, as the company prepared to open a second brewery at the Cape Hill site, which was then extended by another 30 acres. Completed in 1914, the new No. 2 brewery offered a production capacity of 30,000 barrels per week.

The temperance movement gained strength through World War I, prompting new and more restrictive licensing legislation. One result of this trend was that brewing companies were

Key Dates:

1777: William Bass establishes a brewery in Burton-on-Trent.

1827: Bass's son Michael Bass takes over the brewery and develops it into one of the world's leading ale brands.

1861: Henry Mitchell takes over his father's Crown Inn pub in Smethwick.

1866: Mitchell builds a dedicated brewery next to his pub; William Butler buys London Works Tavern in Smethwick.

1875: Butler buys the Crown Inn in Birmingham.

1876: Bass becomes the first British company to register its trademark.

1877: Mitchell begins construction of Cape Hill Brewery, completed in 1879.

1898: Mitchell and Butler merge to form Mitchells & Butlers.

1961: A merger creates Bass, Mitchells & Butlers.

1967: The company merges with Charrington United to form Bass, Charrington, subsequently renamed as Bass Plc.

1969: Bass enters the hotel business with the creation of Crest Hotel group as part of the larger diversification effort.

1989: Beer Orders limits ownership of pubs by brewery groups.

1990: Bass completes the acquisition of Holiday Inn chain, becoming one of the world's leading hotel groups.

1994: The company begins developing and acquiring pub and bar brands, including O'Neill's Irish Pubs and All Bar One.

1995: An agreement to acquire the Carlsburg-Tetley brewing and pub group is rejected by the British government.

1999: The company buys 550 pubs from Allied Domecq as part of a repositioning of its pub portfolio.

2000: The company sells its Bass brewery operations and rights to the Bass name to Interbrew.

2001: The company is renamed as Six Continents Plc; the company sells 988 pubs to the Nomura group.

2003: Six Continents splits into InterContinental Hotels Group and Mitchells & Butlers, which is listed on the London Stock Exchange in April 2003.

---

granted a new suburban pub license only in return for the abandonment of several city center licenses. In response, pub owners began converting their existing city center sites. Mitchells & Butlers took advantage of this trend by launching a new generation of pub designs after the war, a precursor to the development of standardized bar brands at the end of the century.

Mitchells & Butlers grew strongly into the middle of the century. Acquisitions formed a part of the company's growth, including the purchase of Walsall's Highgate Brewery in 1939, a move that added nearly 40 new pubs to the company's growing estate. Takeovers enabled the company to expand beyond its Birmingham base following World War II, and included the purchases of Thatcher's Brewery in Newport in 1950, Darby's Brewery in West Bromwich in 1951, and Atkinsons Brewery in Aston and the Springfield Brewery in Wolverhampton in 1959.

The formation of Bass, Mitchells & Butlers in 1961 created a national brewery powerhouse, with one of the world's most famous beer brands and a portfolio of some 4,000 tied pubs and bars. Yet the company inaugurated a new era in British brewing history in 1967 when it merged with Charrington United Breweries. Backed by its Carling Black Label lager brand—a bestseller in the United Kingdom—Charrington United also managed an estate of more than 5,000 pubs.

The combined company, initially called Bass Charrington, now claimed a 25 percent share of the U.K. market. Renamed as Bass Plc, the company took the lead in the "new" U.K. brewery and pub market, which came to be dominated by just a handful of major groups by the 1980s.

A Return to Roots in the New Century

Bass had by then begun to diversify, starting with the founding of its own hotel chain, Crest Hotels, in 1969. A downturn in the pub market in the early 1980s led the company to sell off a number of its breweries and underperforming pubs. Instead, the company stepped up its hotel business and expanded into the international travel market as well. As part of that effort, Bass bought Horizon Travel, a vacation package and tour operator, in 1987.

The following year, Bass's hotel division took a big step forward when it purchased the Holiday Inn hotel chain, transforming Bass into one of the world's largest international groups. Meanwhile, Bass's diversification efforts had led it into such areas as bingo clubs, amusement game machines, and a national chain of betting parlors. These were sold off in the late 1990s, however.

The Beer Orders of 1989 created a new sea change in the British pub and brewing industry. The new legislation limited the number of tied pubs the dominant brewing groups were allowed to own. Bass, like the other major brewing groups, was forced to divest large swaths of its pub estates. The more than 10,000 pubs placed on the market created a new industry of businesses dedicated to pub and bar operations, which promptly began developing branded and themed bars, pubs, and restaurants for the regional and national markets.

Bass began developing its own portfolio of pub brands, such as the O'Neill's Irish bar concept, launched in Aberdeen in 1994, and the women-oriented All Bar One concept, which debuted in Surrey that same year. In addition to developing its own brands in-house, Bass made a series of acquisitions of existing pub, bar, and restaurant brands, such as the Harvester pub group acquired from Forte in 1995, Browns Restaurants, purchased in 1998, and, in that division's first international move, the Alex brasserie bar chain in Germany.

The following year, in a move to shift its pub portfolio, the company acquired 550 pubs from rival Allied Domecq. As a result of the reorganization of its pub portfolio, Bass, by then led by CEO Tim Clarke, was able to increase its AWT (average weekly take) from just £4,000 to an industry-leading £14,000. This success earned the company the Best Retail Company Award for 2001.

Bass also had been attempting to expand its brewing business internationally during the 1990s, including entries into the Czech Republic in 1993, and into China in 1995. Yet these efforts met with less than the hoped-for success. In the meantime, Bass had lost its lead in the U.K. market, when rival Scottish & Newcastle bought the Courage brewing group in 1995. Bass attempted to fight back, with an agreement to buy up the Carlsburg-Tetley brewery in the United Kingdom. But that purchase, despite being cleared by the Mergers and Monopolies Commission, was ultimately blocked by the U.K. government, which feared the emergence of a new brewing and pub giant.

In part in response to this rejection, Bass brought an era to an end in 2000 when it announced its decision to sell off its brewery arm to Belgium's Interbrew group. The purchase, for £2.3 billion ($3.46 billion), also included the rights to the Bass name. As a result, Bass renamed itself Six Continents Plc, in part to emphasize its shift in focus to its hotel division, in 2001.

Yet the Six Continents name was to prove short-lived. At the beginning of 2001, the group sold off 988 of its pubs to Japan's Nomura group for £625 million, in part to fuel an aggressive expansion of its hotel division. By the end of 2002, however, amid a slipping share price and growing shareholder discontent, Six Continents announced its intention to split itself in two, with its hotels business regrouped under the Intercontinental Hotels Group name. The pub and restaurant division was then spun off as publicly listed Mitchells & Butlers, in a move designed to revive the well-known name and present the company's solid link with its past.

The ''new'' Mitchells & Butlers debuted on the London Stock Exchange in April 2003, boasting sales of £1.5 billion and the country's largest portfolio of managed pubs. CEO Clarke next began to target further expansion—seen as a necessity in the rapidly consolidating pubs market at the dawn of the 21st century. After rejecting a takeover offer from investment group BC Partners, Clarke led the company into the bidding war for Scottish & Newcastle's 1,450-strong pub estate.

After failing in its £2.3 billion bid in August 2003, Mitchells & Butlers itself became the subject of takeover speculation. Industry observers suggested that whichever company succeeded in acquiring the Scottish & Newcastle estate would then go after Mitchells & Butlers in order to create a group capable of rivaling such fast-growing pub groups as Enterprise Inns. Mitchells & Butlers, however, shrugged off these suggestions. As the company told the *Mail on Sunday:* ''We are in a very good position at the moment. The S&N estate was a nice-to-have, not a must-have.'' With a name evoking more than 100 years of British drinking history, Mitchells & Butlers instead turned its focus toward charting a future as a dedicated pubs business.

Principal Operating Units

Bar and Restaurant Brands: All Bar One; Arena; Browns; Edward's; Ember Inns; Flares; Goose; Harvester; Innkeeper's Fayre; O'Neill's; Scream; Sizzling Pub Co.; Toby Carvery; Unbranded; Vintage Inns.

Principal Competitors

Diageo PLC; Compass Group PLC; Whitbread PLC; Enterprise Inns Plc; Punch Taverns PLC; Luminar PLC.

Further Reading

Bridge, Sarah, ''M&B Next in Line for a Takeover,'' *Mail on Sunday,* August 31, 2003, p. 8.

John, Peter, ''Mitchells & Butlers to Pay Back £400m,'' *Financial Times,* May 23, 2003, p. 25.

Mesure, Susie, ''Mitchells & Butlers Worth Supping,'' *Independent,* April 10, 2003, p. 13.

Reece, Damian, ''Clarke on a £2.3bn Pub Crawl,'' *Sunday Telegraph,* June 15, 2003.

—M. L. Cohen

Mobile TeleSystems OJSC

4 Marksistskaya Street
109147 Moscow
Russia
Telephone: (7) 095-766-0177
Fax: (7) 095-766-0100
Web site: http://www.mtsgsm.com

Public Company
Incorporated: 1993
Employees: 6,750
Sales: $1.36 billion (2002)
Stock Exchanges: New York
Ticker Symbol: MBT
NAIC: 513322 Cellular and Other Wireless
   Telecommunications

Mobile TeleSystems OJSC (MTS) provides cellular phone service to nearly 13 million subscribers in Russia and neighboring countries. The center of its operations is Moscow, where it shares the market with its major competitor, VimpelCom, and Sonic Duo, a recent arrival. However, acquisitions are helping MTS add to its subscriber base and establish a national footprint. The company holds licenses in most of Russia's 89 regions and operates in about half of them. In addition, its subsidiaries serve customers in the Ukraine and Belarus.

Established in 1993 as a joint venture between German and Russian companies, MTS was the first company in Moscow to offer service on the GSM (global system for mobile communications) standard. GSM eventually became the prevailing standard in the industry, helping MTS remain a market leader as the cellphone changed from an expensive status symbol for the rich to an accessible mass market product. The company has grown rapidly since its inception, negotiating cutthroat competition in a growing industry. MTS has been listed on the New York Stock Exchange since 2000. Principal shareholders are AFK Sistema, a Russian holding company with just over 50 percent, and T-Mobile, a subsidiary of Deutsche Telecom, with about 25 percent.

Origins

Russia seemed like an ideal market for cellular phones in the early 1990s. Fixed-line service was poor, and countless people were on waiting lists to get service set up by the government. Attracted by the potential of an untapped market, international companies brought their technical expertise to the private businesses and government organizations in Russia that had acquired licenses for cellular operations. Although the GSM standard was already the norm in Western Europe by 1991, the Russian cellphone industry operated on a number of different standards and frequencies in its early years. Analog standards such as NMT-450 (Nordic Mobile Telecommunications) and AMPS-800 (Advanced Mobile Phone Service) were cheaper than the digital GSM and required fewer base stations to cover a large area. The Russian government's policy was to license only one operator per standard in each region. The industry developed quickly and chaotically. By the mid-1990s, there were about 150 different operators nationwide, forming a patchy network of incompatible standards that forced users to switch phones or companies when traveling away from home.

The first cellular operator in Moscow was Moscow Cellular Communications, formed in 1992 when US West and Millicom International Cellular of Luxembourg teamed up with NMT-450 license holders. Later in 1992, a second company, AO VimpelCom, was founded by a Russian university professor, Dmitry Zimin, and entered the market on the AMPS standard. Mobile TeleSystems was created in 1993 when two German companies joined with several Russian telecommunications operators: DeTeMobil, a unit of Deutsche Telecom, held about 38 percent; the electronics manufacturer Siemens AG held about 10 percent; the Moscow City Telephone Network owned about 20 percent; and the remaining share was split among three smaller companies: ASVT, M-Bell, and TDSR.

MTS chose the GSM-900 standard for its operations, hoping that the advanced technology would give it a competitive advantage. GSM, a digital standard, was clearer, allowed for smaller handsets, and was more secure against pirating non-subscribers. Because it was already Europe's standard, GSM offered greater potential for international roaming. The digital technology also gave users access to services such as call waiting, voice-mail, call forwarding, and eventually more advanced services such as text messaging and Internet access. MTS debuted its product at the Expo Com '94 technology exhibition in Moscow in June 1994. The next month, it started operations on an experimental basis with 217 subscribers.

At the time, Moscow Cellular Communications was the market leader in Moscow with 6,000 subscribers, and VimpelCom was just getting started with several hundred customers. MTS stated that it would rely on superior technology rather than a price war to gain a foothold in the market. Nevertheless, when commercial operations began in late 1995, MTS claimed that its deal was better than the competition: tariffs of 56 cents a minute, a $100 monthly fee, and a $750 charge for the initial connection to the network. The deal was only slightly, if at all, better than alternative providers; the main cost advantage was that the Siemens phones available through MTS were less expensive than other options. In general, prices for cellular phone service in Russia were sky-high compared to Western Europe. Because Russia's middle class was small, companies had little to gain by offering more affordable rates.

Mikhail Smirnov became president and director of MTS in 1995. By the end of 1996, MTS had 19,000 subscribers and reported net revenues of $53.6 million. In 1997, the rival company VimpelCom, recognizing that GSM was the standard of the future, acquired a license for the GSM-1800 frequency. The former market dominator, Moscow Cellular Communications, remained on the outdated NMT-450 standard and gradually faded as a competitive threat. MTS and VimpelCom would share the largest piece of the Moscow market over the next several years.

Price Wars and Mass Market Competition in the Late 1990s

VimpelCom's competitive threat grew in 1998 when the government broke with its one-operator-per-frequency policy and issued VimpelCom a GSM-900 license. The lower frequency was more feasible operationally than the 1800 frequency. Smirnov protested the loss of his company's exclusive right to GSM, since Moscow was the only place where two licenses had been issued for the same frequency. Government officials claimed that First Deputy Prime Minister Boris Nemtsov helped VimpelCom get the license in exchange for financial assistance to the Russian Space Agency. MTS threatened to sue but did not. In September 1998, MTS acquired Rosico, a company with a license for the 1800 frequency, which solidified MTS's ability to offer competitive GSM service. By using two GSM frequencies, a company was less likely to overload its network.

By mid-1998, AFK Sistema, an investment vehicle owned by leaders in the Moscow government, had amassed a 47 percent share in MTS. Sistema also owned the Moscow city telephone network, which meant that MTS was able to pay lower interconnect fees. In early 1998, MTS was preparing to list on the New York Stock Exchange and had appointed Deutsche Bank and ING Barings as investment banking advisers. However, the August crash of the ruble put those plans on hold. In the wake of the economic crisis, nationwide cellphone use fell about 30 percent. The situation promised to winnow a fragmented and high-priced market down to the strongest contenders.

By the end of 1998, MTS had 114,000 subscribers and a 34 percent market share in Moscow. Early in 1999, MTS surpassed VimpelCom for the first time in terms of market share. MTS had cultivated a rich subscriber base and a reputation for better coverage in Moscow. Now, in tougher economic times, cellphone companies felt the necessity to lower their rates. They offered reduced tariffs to entice subscribers to "thaw out their cellphones." VimpelCom brought the price war to a new level in October 1999 with the introduction of its "phone in a box," the first cellphone package that was affordable for the general population. For only $49, Moscow residents could get a handset and a $10 prepaid phone card. The connection fee was waived. The package proved to be very popular, and many stores sold out within days. VimpelCom was selling the package at a loss, but the offer transformed cellphones from a luxury item to a mass market product.

MTS claimed not to be concerned with VimpelCom's move to grab market share. "We're interested in real subscribers, not inflated figures," said Igor Timofeyev, director of marketing at MTS. "Most of the people who bought these cheap phones can't afford the monthly upkeep and will stop using them within a couple of months." Nevertheless, MTS responded with some changes to make its package more attractive. It cut tariffs and handset prices and began selling prepaid cards in ticket booths of the Moscow Metro. Prepaid cards were a great step forward in convenience, especially since credit card and debit systems were underdeveloped in Russia. Before the advent of prepaid cards, customers had to stand in line for hours to pay bills at service centers. MTS's net income in 1999 was $85.7 million on revenues of $358.3 million.

New York Stock Exchange Debut: 2000

By mid-2000, MTS and VimpelCom each had about half a million subscribers. Plans for a public offering on the New York Stock Exchange were back on the table. The proceeds would be used to upgrade MTS's network, improve service in Moscow, expand into the regions and invest in new technology such as Internet access (WAP, or Wireless Application Protocol) and high-speed data transmission. The planned initial public offering (IPO), the first by a Russian company since the 1998 crash, was anticipated as an indicator of investor confidence in postcrash Russia. MTS's performance proved to be respectable. In May 2000, Mobile TeleSystems CJSC (closed joint stock company) merged with RTC OJSC, a company it had acquired in 1998, to form Mobile Telesystems OJSC (open joint stock company). On July 6, the company raised $305 million in an IPO of shares priced at $21.50 each, which set the value of the company at $2.1 billion. Although the IPO was risky, investors were reassured by the fact that MTS had a corporate governance

Key Dates:

1993: Mobile TeleSystems (MTS) is formed in a German-Russian partnership.
1995: Commercial operations begin in Moscow on the GSM standard.
1998: Rival VimpelCom acquires a GSM license; MTS has 114,000 subscribers.
1999: VimpelCom's "phone in a box" starts a price war.
2000: MTS debuts on the New York Stock Exchange; the company boasts 1.2 million subscribers.
2001: MTS begins expanding through regional and international acquisitions; the company now has 2.65 million subscribers.
2003: MTS purchases Ukrainian Mobile Communications; the number of the company's subscribers climbs to 12.8 million.

code, was able to provide GAAP accounting figures for its entire seven-year history, and that Deutsche Telecom was a major shareholder. MTS President Smirnov stated, "We took a risk. We had to overcome a big psychological barrier between us and western investors. Obviously, the greater expectation of stability under the new president [Vladimir Putin] helped."

Meanwhile, a new cellphone company was preparing to enter the market in Moscow. Sonic Duo, a company jointly controlled by the state-owned Svyazinvest and by Sonera of Finland, had been granted an operating license in May 2000, but no operating frequencies were available. In September 2000, Russia's Communications Ministry seized several 900 MHz channels from MTS and VimpelCom, intending to give them to Sonic Duo, but the action was annulled in the face of stockholder protests. In the summer of 2001, for reasons that the press could only speculate about, MTS handed over some unneeded radio frequencies to make space for a third operator. Sonic Duo launched in November 2001 on the GSM standard under the brand name Megafon. MTS and VimpelCom countered with expanded marketing campaigns and billing simplifications. By early 2003, Sonic Duo had acquired a 5 percent market share. At the end of 2000, MTS had 1.2 million subscribers and revenues of $535.7 million.

As cellphone technology advanced, MTS made sure it would be able to offer cutting-edge services. In 2000, the company had launched WAP service, which allowed subscribers to access e-mail or purchase goods online with their cellphones, but the feature was slow to catch on. As a result, MTS moved cautiously the next year in testing general packet radio service (GPRS), a technology that allowed for transmittal of broadband wireless data.

Expanding Through Acquisitions: 2001 and Beyond

A more reliable strategy for increased profits was expansion outside Moscow through acquisitions. MTS's goal was to create a single GSM network across Russia with seamless roaming. President Smirnov, quoted in the *Financial Times* in November 2001, said, "Our strategy is to become the first truly national

mobile cellular operator in Russia by integrating our regional networks into a single unified network, developing standardized tariffs, and deploying integrated nationwide customer service and billing systems." In May 2001, MTS purchased Telecom XXI, a company that held GSM licenses for ten regions in the northwest but had no subscribers. The acquisition would allow MTS to compete in the St. Petersburg market. Service was launched in December of that year with celebratory fireworks, and the company attracted 775,000 subscribers in its first year. In August 2001, MTS gained control of Telecom 900 Ltd., a company that held stakes in several smaller operators in the Ural, Siberian, and Far Eastern regions. The purchase won MTS another 117,000 subscribers. That fall, MTS beat out Russian, Austrian, and Saudi Arabian companies to win a tender for an operating license in Belarus. MTS formed a joint venture there known as Mobile Telesystems LLC but delayed starting work until the next year. Finally, the company also opened a network in Nizhny Novgorod, the provincial capital of the Volga region. This was the first GSM network in the city, and prospective customers lined up at the office door even before it opened.

Regional expansion looked ever more attractive as the market grew crowded in Moscow. Morgan Stanley reported in 2001 that only 1.5 percent of Russian regional residents had mobile phones, compared with 19.2 percent in Moscow. Although MTS had over half the Moscow market by the end of 2000, in September 2001 VimpelCom beat MTS in the number of new subscribers for the first time in nearly two years. VimpelCom had a new tariff system, so MTS responded with three new billing plans that offered lower per-minute rates and had lower monthly fees than the two plans previously available. In addition, an aggressive and, according to MTS, misleading marketing campaign by VimpelCom helped it continue to attract the majority of new subscribers. Net revenues at MTS continued to rise, but the average revenue per user was declining. At the end of 2001, MTS had 2.65 million subscribers and a $205.8 million profit on $893.2 million in revenues.

Further acquisitions helped MTS continue its growth in subscribers and revenues. In March 2002, the company bought a controlling share in OJSC Kuban, the top regional operator in Russia with several hundred thousand subscribers in the southern Black Sea region. In May 2002, MTS bought BM-Telekom, located in the Volga River republic of Bashkortostan. By this point, MTS was operating in 29 regions across Russia. Further acquisitions in 2002 included Mobicom-Barnaul in the Altai region, Dontelecom in the Rostov region, and Bit LLC, which had GSM licenses for four different regions. Late in 2002, MTS introduced the "Jeans" tariff plan aimed at low-spending cellphone users. By the end of the year, the company had 6.64 million subscribers.

The year 2003 started out on a sour note when a pirated CD containing personal data from MTS's customer database appeared for sale on the streets of Moscow. Similar leaks had occurred before at other companies. A company spokesperson suggested the data may have been sold by a low-level official at the Federal Security Service, since mobile phone operators were required to hand over customer information to that agency. MTS offered its subscribers personal identification numbers to prevent others from abusing their phone numbers.

Acquisitions continued in 2003. The most notable was the purchase of Ukrainian Mobile Communications in March. The company was the Ukraine's second largest mobile operator with 1.5 million subscribers. For MTS, the Ukraine presented a less stable business climate but lower operating expenses and greater potential for expansion. MTS also bought a controlling stake in Taif-Telcom, the largest operator in the Volga republic of Tatarstan. That spring, AFK Sistema also bought a 10 percent stake from Deutsche Telecom, which meant that Sistema had a controlling interest and MTS could be registered as an official Russian cellular company.

MTS's second quarter report for 2003 stated that the company had 12.8 million subscribers and net revenues over the first six months of $606 million. In August, Mikhail Smirnov's term as president expired and the board nominated Vassily Sidorov, a former director for finance and investments at Sistema-Telecom, as the new president. Sidorov announced that he would carry on the existing strategy at MTS, strengthening the company's position in its existing markets and expanding into new ones.

Principal Subsidiaries

Bit LLC; Telecom-900; Telecom XXI; BM-Telecom; MTS Barnaul; Dontelcom; MSS (83.5%) Kuban GSM (52.7%); JV UMC (83.7%); ReCom (53.9%); TAIF Telecom (51%); UDN-900 (51%); Mobile TeleSystems LLC (49%).

Principal Competitors

VimpelCom; Sonic Duo.

Further Reading

Aris, Ben, "Russia's Largest Cell Phone Operator Buys Stake in Ukraine Firm," *Sunday Business* (London), November 10, 2002.

Bershidsky, Leonid, "Phone JV Vows to Compete," *Moscow Times*, July 7, 1994.

Chazan, Guy, "Emerging Europe: Mobile TeleSystems Starts IPO Roadshow," *Wall Street Journal*, June 13, 2000, p. 35.

——, "Mobile TeleSystems Begins Trading in New York," *Wall Street Journal*, July 3, 2000, p. 15.

——, "Technology Journal: Russia's Latest Revolution Is Bringing Mobile-Phone Service to the Masses," *Wall Street Journal*, February 8, 2000. p. 30.

Farish, Robert, "MTS Joining Cellular Market," *Moscow Times*, June 4, 1994.

Fraser, Hugh, "From Russia with Love," *Institutional Investor International Edition*, January 2001, p. 66.

Gordeyev, Alexander, "Vimpelcom Attacked By Cell Phone Rival," *Moscow Times*, November 26, 1998.

"MTS Acquires Telecom 900 for $27 Million," *Russian Telecom*, September 2001, p. 4.

"MTS in New Regional Foray," *Russian Telecom*, October 2001, p. 4.

Musatov, Andrey, "MTS Shakes Up St. Pete Market," *Moscow Times*, August 7, 2001, p. 8.

Naumenko, Larisa, and Elizabeth Wolfe, "MTS Profits up As Megafon Arrives," *Moscow Times*, November 21, 2001, p. 9.

"Russia Annuls Order to Take Frequencies," *Wall Street Journal*, October 11, 2000, p. 6.

"Russia: Jeans Passes Million Mark," *IPR Strategic Business Information Database*, June 19, 2003.

"Russia: MTS Sees Profits Slide," *IPR Strategic Business Information Database*, April 23, 2002.

"Russian Mobile Operators Vow to Avoid Europe's 3G Mistakes," *Russian Telecom*, June 2001, p. 8.

Tavernise, Sabrina, "Personal Data Is Pirated from Russian Phone Files," *New York Times*, January 23, 2003, p. W1.

Taylor, Paul, "Home Growth Lifts Russian Mobile Operator Overseas," *Financial Times* (London), November 26, 2001, p. 23.

Warner, Tom, "MTS Forced to Suspend Takeover," *Financial Times* (London), January 22, 2003, p. 30.

Williamson, Elizabeth, "Russia's Patchwork of Operators and Systems Bogs Down the Market," *Wall Street Journal*, February 22, 1999, p. 14.

Wolfe, Elizabeth, "Sliding MTS Set to Hit St. Pete," *Moscow Times*, December 5, 2001.

—Sarah Ruth Lorenz

MYLAN LABORATORIES INC.

Mylan Laboratories Inc.

1500 Corporate Drive, Suite 400
Canonsburg, Pennsylvania 15317-8580
U.S.A.
Telephone: (724) 514-1800
Fax: (724) 514-1870
Web site: http://www.mylan.com

Public Company
Incorporated: 1961 as Milan Laboratories Inc.
Employees: 2,450
Sales: $1.27 billion (2002)
Stock Exchanges: New York
Ticker Symbol: MYL
NAIC: 325412 Pharmaceutical Preparation Manufacturing

Mylan Laboratories Inc. is one of the leading manufacturers of generic drugs in the United States. The firm produces and markets numerous generic and proprietary (brand-name) drugs, with the sale of generics providing 80 percent of total revenues. Mylan's generic operations are conducted through two principal subsidiaries, Mylan Pharmaceuticals Inc. and UDL Laboratories, Inc.; while the company's branded segment operates through Bertek Pharmaceuticals Inc. and Mylan Technologies Inc., with Bertek focusing on three therapeutic areas: dermatology, neurology, and cardiology. In addition, Mylan is involved in a 50–50 joint venture with Watson Pharmaceuticals, Inc. called Somerset Pharmaceuticals, Inc., whose single commercial product is Eldepryl, a treatment for Parkinson's disease. Mylan made its mark in the pharmaceutical industry as a manufacturer of generic drugs, or those pharmaceutical products no longer protected by patents. From the manufacture of generic drugs, the company branched out into brand-name pharmaceuticals, introducing its first proprietary drug, Maxzide, in 1984. Acquisitions completed from the late 1980s through the mid-1990s brought Mylan into other market niches, including anti-Parkinson's disease medications and transdermal drug delivery systems. During the early 2000s, the company's operations included research and development laboratories and manufacturing facilities in West Virginia, Puerto Rico, Texas, Vermont, and Illinois, and a distribution center in North Carolina.

Origins

Industry stalwart Mylan began business as a small, privately owned company in 1961. The company later earned accolades for its manufacturing speed and efficiency—two cornerstones of success in the generic drug business—but it began as an upstart distributor of pharmaceuticals based in the sleepy confines of White Sulphur Springs, West Virginia. Initially, the company operated under the name Milan Pharmaceuticals, Inc., drawing its corporate title from the name of one of the company's two founders, Milan Puskar, who directed the company's fortunes during two distinct eras in its history. Puskar, in his mid-20s when he founded Milan along with Don Panoz, an army buddy, scored his greatest success as a manufacturer of drugs but early on he subsisted exclusively by reselling drugs manufactured by other companies to pharmacies and doctors. The foray into manufacturing occurred four years after the company began business, and after two relocations of the company's headquarters. In 1963, Puskar moved his operations to Princeton, West Virginia, and then moved again two years later, settling in Morgantown, West Virginia. The move to Morgantown in 1965 occurred the same year the company began producing vitamins, the first product manufactured under the Milan banner.

Manufacturing in Morgantown picked up speed quickly following the company's debut as a vitamin producer. In 1966, Milan received approval from the Food and Drug Administration (FDA) to start manufacturing penicillin G tablets, the first in a long line of generic drugs the company would produce. Two years later, production activity in Morgantown was expanded when the FDA gave Milan the nod to produce the antibiotic tetracycline. By the following year—in 1969—Parke-Davis had begun purchasing the company's manufactured drugs, becoming the first major drug company signed up as a Milan customer. Over the course of the next several years the number of major drug companies who purchased Milan's products under private label increased, as did the number of FDA-approved drugs Milan manufactured, such as the addition of erythromycin in 1971 and ampicillin in 1973. What looked good on the outside, however, was not necessarily positive in Morgantown. Milan's roster of major customers was growing and the number of approved drugs manufactured by the company was increasing, but Puskar was unhappy, frustrated by the direction the company was taking. In 1972, after a management dispute, Puskar left the company he had cofounded 11 years earlier, ending the first chapter in the company's history and marking the beginning of a near disastrous period for the West Virginia pharmaceutical concern.

After Puskar's exit, Milan changed its name to Mylan Laboratories Inc. and converted to public ownership, debuting on the OTC (over-the-counter) market in February 1973. The years immediately following Puskar's resignation were difficult ones for the small but rapidly growing pharmaceutical manufacturer, years that evinced Puskar's perception that the company was headed in the wrong direction. When Roy McKnight, president of a manufacturer's representative company, joined Mylan's board of directors in late 1975 he discovered precisely how errant the company's course had been, portending Mylan "was facing imminent bankruptcy." Despite the company's early success in gaining FDA approval to manufacture drugs and the growing number of major drug firms who had signed on as customers, Mylan was in dire need of help. Inventories were overstated by $2 million, more than $400,000 was owed in back taxes, 320 production workers were on strike, and the company had a negative net worth of $900,000. The situation was grave, but McKnight, who had no previous experience in the drug industry prior to joining Mylan's board, could not muster sufficient support in finding a solution to the company's problems. Discouraged, he wrested control of the company, naming himself chairman and chief executive officer, and fired Mylan's president. For a replacement to the company's presidential post, McKnight chose Puskar, reinstating the company's founder to his creation.

New Management in 1976

McKnight and Puskar took the helm in early 1976 and immediately began to effect sweeping changes, resolving to concentrate on the manufacture of generic drugs. McKnight persuaded Mylan's bankers to extend additional credit to the company, trimmed the company's workforce by one-third, and spearheaded more aggressive marketing campaigns, vowing at the same time to discontinue the production of any drug that was unprofitable. One year later, the measures enacted by McKnight had proven effective. By 1977, Mylan was once again a profitable company. Mylan's stock began trading on NASDAQ in 1978.

During the years following Puskar's return and McKnight's arrival, Mylan recorded steady and encouraging growth, its operations leaner and more cost-efficient as a result of the lessons learned from the mistakes during the first half of the

1970s. The company used only four salespeople to sell commodity generic pharmaceuticals under their chemical names, marketing the drugs to bulk buyers such as drugstore chains, mail-order houses, and distributors. The company also moved heavily into producing and selling branded generics that were no longer covered by patents. In the business of producing such generic drugs, foresight, manufacturing speed, and manufacturing efficiency were key attributes for success, attributes Mylan exuded as it developed from a small pharmaceutical concern into one of the nation's dominant forces. Being the first to market a branded drug once its patent expired meant exponentially higher profits for a generic drug manufacturer. Once a patent expired, the generic equivalent was generally introduced at 70 percent of the price of the brand. As more and more generic manufacturers entered the fray, typically marketing as many as 12 generic equivalents for each branded drug, the price for the generics dropped, eventually bottoming out at 10 percent of the brand price. Consequently, the first to market a generic response earned the highest profits, while the latecomers earned only a fraction of the original yield for their efforts. Mylan, with its operating costs down and its efforts sharply focused on being the first to market, began to flourish in the race for supremacy in the discount market, ascending to the top of the industry in less than a decade.

First Proprietary Drug in 1984

Annual sales by the beginning of the 1980s eclipsed $30 million, and Mylan began to steel itself for its entry into a new, potentially lucrative area of the multibillion-dollar pharmaceutical industry. Development plans were underway by the beginning of the 1980s for Mylan's first proprietary drug, its first pharmaceutical product developed, manufactured, and marketed in-house. In 1984, after five years of clinical tests and a $5 million investment, Mylan introduced an antihypertensive called Maxzide, an achievement McKnight hailed as the "single most important event in Mylan's history." Lederle Laboratories was licensed to distribute the drug, which was expected to generate $100 million in sales by 1988, and tests were immediately underway to introduce another version of Maxzide. In 1988, after three years of clinical tests, the FDA approved half-strength Maxzide-25, giving the company another powerful revenue-generating engine.

As these first steps into proprietary drug production were being made, progress was being achieved on other fronts, as Mylan reigned as the leading independent drug manufacturer in the United States, a number one position first achieved in 1985. The following April the company's stock moved to the more prestigious New York Stock Exchange. Mylan's growing presence as a manufacturer necessitated the development of additional manufacturing facilities to complement its sole plant in Morgantown, which the company accomplished in 1987 when construction was completed for a new factory in Caguas, Puerto Rico. The company's first distribution center opened the following year in Greensboro, North Carolina.

As the 1980s drew to a close, McKnight and Puskar began an acquisition campaign aimed at developing a multifaceted Mylan with a greater, more well-rounded presence in the pharmaceutical industry. Much of the work toward this goal took place during the 1990s, when annual sales grew robustly, but before the 1980s were through Mylan completed a pivotal deal. In June

1989, the company acquired a 50 percent stake in Somerset Pharmaceuticals, Inc., the same month Somerset secured FDA approval to market a new medication for the treatment of Parkinson's disease called Eldepryl. Somerset was a joint venture with Bolar Pharmaceutical Co. Inc. (which changed its name to Circa Pharmaceuticals Inc. in 1993 and then was acquired by Watson Pharmaceuticals in 1995). Mylan's stock during the year provided an indication of the value of this acquisition, soaring 173 percent. Two years later, when annual sales topped the $100 million mark during the company's 30th anniversary year, Mylan completed another acquisition, merging with Sugar Land, Texas–based Dow B. Hickam Pharmaceuticals. A high-quality branded pharmaceutical company, Dow B. Hickam specialized in the manufacturing and marketing of wound and burn care pharmaceutical products, which added another quill to Mylan's quiver. The push to further broaden Mylan's arsenal of pharmaceutical goods continued in early 1993 when the company acquired St. Albans, Vermont–based Bertek, Incorporated, a manufacturer and innovator of transdermal (patch) drug delivery systems, for $39 million. The addition of Bertek gave Mylan five worldwide and seven domestic patents for transdermal drug delivery technology, the applications for which were expanding during the 1990s.

Meantime, Puskar and McKnight went public in 1989 with evidence of improprieties at the FDA's Generic Drug Division. This led to investigations by the Oversight and Investigations Committee of the U.S. House of Representatives, a U.S. Attorney, the U.S. Department of Health and Human Services, and the FDA itself. These probes found that some of Mylan's competitors had been involved in bribing and making payoffs to FDA employees, as well as faking test results. A number of generic drugs were pulled off the market by these companies as a result of the investigations and the resulting judicial action.

In late 1993, nine months after the Bertek acquisition was completed, Mylan employees were shocked to learn of the death of McKnight, who died suddenly of a heart attack on November 6. Three days later, Puskar was named chairman and CEO, assuming the posts vacated by McKnight and now wielding as much influence over the company as he had during its inaugural decade.

Growth Through Diversification in the 1990s

As the acquisitions were being completed during the early 1990s, annual sales rose sharply, leading to growth that quickly elevated Mylan's stature within the pharmaceutical industry. From $104 million in 1991, sales shot to $132 million in 1992, $212 million in 1993, and $252 million in 1994. Aside from broadening and deepening its involvement in the pharmaceutical industry through acquisitions, Mylan realized its animated growth by adhering to a philosophy of keeping manufacturing costs down and making sure to bring products to market quickly. The company used just three manufacturing processes for all 79 of its pharmaceutical products, enabling it to meet any order within five days. Further, its focus on research and development of branded drugs well before their patents expired often allowed the company to be the first on the market with the generic equivalent. In 1994, for instance, four of Mylan's six generic introductions were the first to market, giving the company hefty profit totals in comparison to the amount of revenue it generated. The company's introduction of cimetidine, a generic ulcer drug, in 1994, for example, held 39 percent of the market for all new cimetidine prescriptions in 1995.

As Puskar moved ahead with the strategy developed by McKnight and himself, he further penetrated the branded drug market, opting to fill niches deemed too small by the country's largest drug manufacturers. To give the company the manufacturing might to correspond to its growing presence, a third generic drug production facility was opened in Cidra, Puerto Rico, in late 1994, further bolstering the company's manufacturing capabilities in one of the havens of pharmaceutical production in the world. Sales catapulted in 1995, from $252 million to $396 million; net earnings also leaped, to $121 million, nearly twice the total of the previous year. The following year—in 1996—sales dipped to $393 million because of heightened generic drug competition, but to compensate for the depressed revenue total the company completed another acquisition, purchasing UDL Laboratories Inc., a supplier of unit-dose generic pharmaceuticals to the institutional and long-term care market, for about $47.5 million in stock.

As Mylan prepared to close out the decade and head into the 21st century, it occupied an enviable position in the pharmaceutical industry. Of all the pharmaceutical products produced by the company, 56 percent were ranked as the number one drug in their market and more than 70 percent were ranked either number one or number two. These percentage figures pointed to astute management and agile manufacturing abilities, qualities that promised to secure a leading market position in the future. The company's dedication to maintaining its position in the pharmaceutical industry was demonstrated in late 1996 when it opened a 150,000-square-foot research facility with bed space for 104 research subjects and two large laboratories.

Continuing its drive to increase participation in the branded drug segment, which offered higher profits than the generic sector, Mylan in August 1996 formed Bertek Pharmaceuticals Inc. as a subsidiary focusing on the development, manufacturing, and marketing of branded pharmaceuticals. This subsidiary combined the operations of Dow B. Hickam and the previous incarnation of Bertek. The next step in this effort came in October 1998, when Mylan purchased Penederm Inc., maker of branded dermatological creams and products, for about $200 million. Penederm was transformed into Bertek's Dermatology Division in August 1999.

Litigation at Center Stage: Late 1990s

Mylan became embroiled in litigation in the late 1990s over allegations that the company had attempted to corner the market on the raw materials used to make two anti-anxiety drugs, lorazepam and clorazepate. According to the Federal Trade Commission (FTC), which filed a suit against Mylan in December 1998, Mylan jacked up its prices on these drugs more than 3,000 percent after signing deals with its suppliers that allegedly locked out the firm's competitors. While the price increases certainly did take place, Mylan vehemently denied the other allegations and contended that it had done nothing wrong. The case was a major distraction for the company, and in the end, in July 2000, Mylan agreed to settle federal, state, and private lawsuits that were brought in connection with this matter. For the FTC, the $100 million that Mylan was required to pay the agency and 33 states was the largest monetary settlement in its history. Mylan, meanwhile, took a $147 million charge during the fiscal year ending in March 2001 to cover the payments that settled the various suits. It also agreed not to sign any more exclusive-supplier agreements. As a result of the charge, the firm posted net income that year of just $37.1 million, a 76 percent decline from the prior year's record total of $154.2 million. Revenues for 2001 reached a record $846.7 million.

Mylan was also involved in a number of other lawsuits during this period and into the early 2000s. Most of the suits involved other pharmaceutical companies, specifically brand-name drug firms who were increasingly filing suits and using other delaying tactics in order to maintain their rights to the exclusive marketing of their proprietary drugs for as long as possible. In one of the most noteworthy such cases, Mylan sued both Bristol-Myers Squibb Company and the FDA in late 2000 in its effort to begin selling a generic version of BuSpar, an anti-anxiety drug that had sales in excess of $600 million in 1999. In March 2001 a federal judge ruled in Mylan's favor, and the company immediately began selling the generic, buspirone, achieving $34 million in sales in just the first quarter on the market. The revenue boost that followed the introduction of buspirone helped push Mylan's revenues past the $1 billion mark during fiscal 2002. Mylan later received $35 million in damages from Bristol-Myers as part of the settlement of lawsuits that had been brought against that company because of the tactics it had used to try to keep the generic version off the market.

There were developments outside the courtroom during the early 2000s as well. In March 2001 Bertek Pharmaceuticals moved into brand-new headquarters in Research Triangle Park, North Carolina. Mylan itself relocated as well, shifting outside of Pittsburgh into that city's suburbs, specifically Canonsburg. In between, in September 2002, the company appointed a new CEO, Robert J. Coury. The new chief had been a strategic consultant to Mylan since 1995 and joined the company's board in early 2002, serving as vice-chairman. Puskar remained in his post as chairman. Mylan also continued to gain FDA approval for new products, including generic versions of such blockbuster drugs as the antidepressant Prozac (in 2002) and the gastrointestinal acid blocker Prilosec (2003). With patent protection on large numbers of top-selling branded drugs expected to expire over the next several years, and its proven ability to be the first or among the first to market with generic versions, Mylan Laboratories was positioned to be one of the main beneficiaries of this trend. One cloud on the company's horizon, however, was yet another lawsuit. In September 2003 the attorney general of Massachusetts filed suit against Mylan and 12 other pharmaceutical companies, accusing them of overcharging Medicaid plans as part of the practices they used to price generic drugs.

Principal Subsidiaries

Mylan Pharmaceuticals Inc.; Bertek Pharmaceuticals Inc.; UDL Laboratories, Inc.; Mylan Technologies Inc.

Principal Competitors

Teva Pharmaceutical Industries Limited; Watson Pharmaceuticals, Inc.; IVAX Corporation; Barr Laboratories, Inc.; Alpharma Inc.; Geneva Pharmaceuticals, Inc.

Further Reading

Angrist, Stanley W., ''The Good Samaritans,'' *Forbes,* December 6, 1982, pp. 122+.

Benson, Betsy, ''Mylan Sees Cure in Generic Scandal Fallout,'' *Pittsburgh Business Times,* October 9, 1989, p. 1.

''CEO Interview: Gary Sphar, Mylan Laboratories,'' *Wall Street Transcript,* August 26, 2002.

Davis, Christopher, ''Mylan Seeks Replacements from Outside,'' *Pittsburgh Business Times,* June 22, 2001, p. 3.

Drahuschak, Greg, ''Taking Stock: Mylan Labs Sets Pace for Local Market Index,'' *Pittsburgh Business Times,* January 8, 1990, p. 1.

''Drugs: Here Come the Sons of Valium,'' *Time,* September 16, 1985, p. 59.

Freudenheim, Milt, "Exposing the F.D.A.: Tiny Mylan Labs Hired a Private Eye and Shook Up the Generic Drug Industry," *New York Times,* September 10, 1989, p. F1.

Gaynor, Pamela, " 'I'm Not a John Wayne': New Mylan CEO Views Role As Building on Drug Maker's Strengths, Not Stirring Things Up," *Pittsburgh Post-Gazette,* December 3, 2002, p. C11.

——, "Mylan Builds $600 Million 'Kitty': Generic Drug Maker Looks for Acquisitions," *Pittsburgh Post-Gazette,* March 6, 2002, p. C1.

Lindeman, Teresa F., "Generic Anxiety: Fierce Competition Forced the Price of Lorazepam So Low It Cleared the Field for Mylan," *Pittsburgh Post-Gazette,* February 28, 1999, p. F1.

——, "Mylan to Pay $147 Million to Settle Suits on Price Hikes," *Pittsburgh Post-Gazette,* July 13, 2000, p. A1.

Marano, Ray, "Roy McKnight Still Standard-Bearer for Mylan Labs," *Pittsburgh Business Times,* May 10, 1993, p. 11.

"Mylan Is Glad It Opened This Can of Worms," *Business Week,* September 18, 1989, pp. 30+.

Novack, Janet, "Drug Abuse," *Forbes,* June 26, 1989, pp. 42+.

Oliver, Suzanne, "Make a Good Product," *Forbes,* August 14, 1995, p. 90.

Perine, Keith, "Mylan Labs May Face Antitrust Charges over Price Increases on Generic Drugs," *Wall Street Journal,* December 7, 1998, p. B4.

Schroeder, Michael, "Mylan to Pay $100 Million to Settle Price-Fix Case," *Wall Street Journal,* July 13, 2000, p. A4.

Stricharchuk, Gregory, "Bad Medicine: Drug Firm's Probe of the FDA Threatens Major Agency Scandal," *Wall Street Journal,* June 9, 1989, pp. A1+.

—Jeffrey L. Covell
—update: David E. Salamie

NewYork-Presbyterian Hospital

654 West 170th Street
New York, New York 10032
U.S.A.
Telephone: (212) 342-0932
Fax: (212) 342-0788
Web site: http://www.nyp.org

Unit of NewYork-Presbyterian Healthcare System, Inc.
Incorporated: 1996
Employees: 13,307
Operating Revenues: $1.85 billion (2002)
NAIC: 622110 General Medical and Surgical Hospitals

NewYork-Presbyterian Hospital is the biggest hospital in New York City. Its two medical centers, Columbia Presbyterian and NewYork Weill Cornell, are located on Manhattan's West Side and East Side, respectively. The medical colleges of Columbia University and Cornell University are the primary teaching affiliates of the two medical centers. NewYork-Presbyterian describes itself as "the world's first superhospital," with experts for every type of medical condition. It is ranked higher than any other hospital in the New York metropolitan area by the annual survey of *U.S. News & World Report.* The hospital and the two medical colleges are units of NewYork Healthcare System, Inc., a federation of hospitals, specialty institutes, and continuing care centers in the tristate area.

New York Hospital: 1771–1996

Chartered in 1771 to serve the infirm and poor, New York Hospital is the second oldest hospital in the United States. Established in lower Manhattan the following year, it was unable to function for many years, first because of the Revolutionary War and later because of a riot in opposition to the grave robbing used to procure specimens for autopsies. The hospital first opened to patients in 1791 and was, from its inception, closely linked to Columbia College's College of Physicians and Surgeons. It also received state support until 1866. During this period epidemics of such diseases as yellow fever, smallpox, cholera, and typhus were common problems. New York Hospital also treated the mentally ill in an 1808 building officially named the "Lunatick Asylum." This building quickly filled beyond capacity and the facility was moved uptown in 1821 and to White Plains in 1894.

New York Hospital had 500 beds in 1858. Its preeminence in surgery was put to the test during the Civil War, when it treated nearly 3,000 soldiers. After the main building was demolished in 1870, the hospital's governors decided to erect a new building on West 15th and 16th streets between Fifth and Sixth avenues. This structure opened in 1877. A nurses' home debuted in 1891 and a building for private patients in 1902. The administration building was rebuilt in 1891 to serve outpatients, among other uses. But the neighborhood of the second site of New York Hospital eventually was considered too congested, noisy, and pollution-ridden to be desirable. In 1924 philanthropist Payne Whitney bought a tract of land adjoining the East River between 68th and 70th streets and divided it between the hospital and Cornell University Medical College, which had become its affiliate in 1912. The block to the north was soon purchased as well. Whitney's will also left a trust fund of over $40 million for what became New York Hospital-Cornell Medical Center. Construction began in 1929, and the new medical center opened in 1932, with a 27-story central building for wards, private patients, and living quarters for the resident staff. Adjoining the main structure were buildings devoted to the medical college, the nurses' quarters, and clinics for women, children, and psychiatric patients. The Lying-In Hospital of New York also joined the complex.

Over the next 50 years, New York-Cornell pioneered in Pap tests, L-dopa drug treatment for Parkinson's disease, and the elimination of kidney stones without surgery. The burn center which opened in the 1970s was the largest in the nation. A center at 93rd Street and First Avenue provided service to the community, and special programs were directed toward the elderly, the poor, and teenage mothers. Beginning in 1984, however, New York Hospital's occupancy rate began falling behind that of other major teaching institutions on the East Side, although it had more beds than any other hospital in the city. In addition, the hospital's reputation was shaken by malpractice lawsuits arising from the unexpected deaths of two high-profile patients, one of them the artist Andy Warhol, who expired after routine gallbladder surgery in 1987.

When Dr. Samuel Skinner became chief executive of New York Hospital in 1987, the institution was losing about $1 million a week. A program of stringent cost-cutting, including streamlining accounts receivable and discharging patients to home healthcare or nursing homes when possible, helped put the institution in the black by 1993, when it recorded an estimated profit of $6 million. Still, it carried a heavy long-term debt and was committed to a six-year, $880 million expansion program, chiefly for the replacement of the aging central structure by the Greenberg Pavilion, jutting over the Franklin D. Roosevelt Drive to the East River. To increase the hospital's market share in patients, Skinner, in 1993, launched NYH Care Network Inc., a medical partnership of ten healthcare facilities in New York City's boroughs and neighboring Westchester County. This network included freestanding satellite centers and specialty arrangements with regional hospitals. After eliminating 150 more positions in 1995, which helped reduce the operating budget by 10 percent, New York Hospital recorded a profit of $13 million for the year.

Presbyterian Hospital and Columbia-Presbyterian Medical Center: 1868–1996

James Lenox founded Presbyterian Hospital in 1868 ''for the Poor of New York without regard to Race, Creed, or Color'' because his African American servant was refused admittance to several New York hospitals. The hospital opened in 1872 on the site he donated between Park and Madison avenues and East 70th and 71st streets. There were two main buildings, one for wards and private patients, the other for administration. A new building was erected in 1888 to serve as an outpatient dispensary. After the ward building was destroyed by fire in 1889, two new ones were built with a total of 349 beds. A nursing school was established in 1892. In 1911 Columbia University's College of Physicians and Surgeons was affiliated with Presbyterian, and plans were initiated to build a medical center for both. In 1922 Edward Harkness and his mother, Mrs. Stephen Harkness, donated a plot of 22 acres in Washington Heights, a rapidly developing middle-class neighborhood, between Broadway and Fort Washington Avenue and West 165th and 168th streets.

Construction of Columbia-Presbyterian Medical Center began in 1925 and was completed in 1927, with the centerpiece a 21-story building—the first skyscraper hospital—with 554 ward beds. It was connected to the west with the nine-story Harkness Pavilion for private patients. Both buildings made space for the Sloane Hospital for Women, which had served as a clinical hospital for Columbia's medical college, and for Sloane's accompanying outpatient Vanderbilt Clinic, which re-

ceived an eight-story building to the northeast. These and Babies' Hospital, psychiatric and neurological institutes, a urological clinic, the nursing school, and dental and public health schools all belonged to the medical center. Maxwell Hall, connected to the main hospital building to the north, housed the medical college. A building for an institute for ophthalmology opened in 1933. The city donated a tract in 1935 for a municipal health center, which opened in 1940. A city cancer hospital opened in 1950 and the New York Orthopaedical Hospital moved to the medical center the same year.

Columbia-Presbyterian was considered one of the finest and most prestigious institutions of its kind in the world. After World War II, however, its neighborhood began to fall into decay. Private patients started to gravitate to hospitals in better areas, while Presbyterian found itself called upon to serve increasing numbers of poor people as smaller hospitals in the community closed. The hospital lost $25 million between 1974 and 1976 as the proportion of indigent patients climbed from one-tenth to one-third over a 20-year span.

Instead of accepting a proposal to retrench, Presbyterian completed a new building for Babies' Hospital and committed $10 million to converting the open wards to semiprivate rooms with bathrooms, $5 million for a new obstetrics unit, $5 million for remodeling clinics, another $5 million for updating equipment, and $3 million for emergency rooms. Medical Center physicians with little responsibility for direct patient care were asked to think about what they could do to bring in patients themselves. The hospital began its first program to identify the medical needs of its neighborhood and committed itself to building the Allen Pavilion, a 300-bed community hospital in Inwood, just north of Washington Heights. Completed at a cost of about $100 million, it opened in 1988. Between 1980 and 1988 Presbyterian spent $105 million treating uninsured people.

The burden of shouldering a renovation program with huge cost overruns resulted in Presbyterian spending more than $250 million of its $300 million endowment to meet operating costs in the 1980s. Some 500 employees were dismissed between 1987 and 1989. Presbyterian lost $23 million in 1988 and perhaps twice that in 1989, including $30 million on its 135 clinics because Medicaid reimbursements were inadequate and many patients had no insurance at all. In early 1990 Presbyterian's embattled president, Dr. Thomas R. Harris, resigned under pressure.

An administrative reorganization, cost cutting, and higher reimbursement rates from the state cut Presbyterian's losses in 1990. The following year it completed, at a cost of $500 million, the Milstein Pavilion, a 745-bed facility facing the Hudson River that replaced the antiquated main building. During the next four years Presbyterian built several outpatient community clinics, opened a nurse-run clinic, built a regional network of six affiliated hospitals in the suburbs, and negotiated a managed-care agreement with Bronx Health Plan. It sponsored its own Medicaid health maintenance organization to serve its community, which was 40 percent Medicaid-eligible. But after a $50.9 million deficit in 1992, Presbyterian was in technical default of its mortgage. At one point it was days from closing, according to one account. Its chief, Dr. William Speck, eliminated nearly 800 jobs, refinanced the mortgage and short-term loans, and

Key Dates:

1771: New York Hospital is chartered as the second public hospital in the 13 colonies.

1868: Founding of Presbyterian Hospital on Manhattan's Upper East Side.

1911: Columbia University's College of Physicians and Surgeons becomes Presbyterian's affiliate.

1912: Cornell University Medical College becomes New York Hospital's affiliate.

1927: Completion of Columbia-Presbyterian Medical Center in upper Manhattan.

1932: New York Hospital-Cornell Medical Center opens on the Upper East Side.

1991: Milstein Pavilion replaces the main Columbia-Presbyterian building.

1996: Columbia-Presbyterian and New York-Cornell agree to merge.

1998: NewYork-Presbyterian Hospital is formed from this merger.

subcontracted many services, reducing the deficit to only $1.9 million in 1995.

NewYork-Presbyterian: 1996–2003

Both New York and Presbyterian were teaching hospitals facing the same basic problems: reduction of government support, loss of market share, excess capacity, too many specialists, and not enough primary-care practitioners. Merger negotiations between the two began in 1993 with the aim of saving $60 million by consolidating services. Completed in 1996, the agreement called for the establishment of NewYork-Presbyterian Healthcare System, Inc. with a 66-member board providing equal representation for both institutions. Skinner was named vice-chairman and chief executive officer, and Speck, president and chief operating officer. No corporate headquarters was created, and top executives shuttled the six miles between the two campuses. For legal and financial reasons, NewYork-Presbyterian Hospital was established as a separate corporation, but the Columbia and Cornell medical schools remained distinct. The merger did not go into effect until the beginning of 1998.

Columbia Presbyterian, in 1998, was in the midst of a ten-year, $1.13 billion construction and renovation of 4.27 million square feet of its complex, including the completion or near completion by the end of that year of a new diabetes center, storefront clinic, pediatric intensive care unit, eye clinic, and orthopaedic research center, and an expansion of the comprehensive cancer center. In addition, the New York State Psychiatric Institute was completed on the campus, and work on a new building for Babies' and Children's Hospital was underway. New York Hospital's Greenberg Pavilion was completed in 1997 at a cost of $810 million. NewYork-Presbyterian's mortgage debt now came to about $1 billion.

NewYork-Presbyterian board members soon grew concerned that the merger of the two institutions was proceeding too slowly, threatening the financial gains foreseen from consolidation. Although the Columbia and Cornell medical schools remained separate, their doctors founded a care unit that by the end of 1999 had contracted with 16 local HMOs, offering discounted fees for service. A few scattered programs were brought together, such as children's heart surgery. However, doctors were generally unwilling to give up power or cede any area of care to the other hospital, and there was little that could be done to make them yield. Often they were not even employed by the corporation but rather had admitting privileges and thus brought in patients—and therefore revenue.

NewYork-Presbyterian's profit fell from $10.4 million in 1997 to $2.5 million in 1998. It had been assumed that Speck would succeed Skinner as chief executive of the corporation when he stepped down in 1999, but as concern grew over the corporation's financial performance, board members questioned whether Speck's personality and managerial skills made him an appropriate choice. Before the end of the year Dr. Herbert Pardes, Columbia University's chief for health sciences, was appointed to the job. Pardes pledged to reconstitute the management team, boost efficiency, cooperation, and productivity, and make the institution friendly for patients and their families and congenial for doctors.

At the beginning of 2000 the NewYork-Presbyterian healthcare network consisted of 32 hospitals, five specialty institutes, 17 nursing homes, 11 home health agencies, and 103 satellite clinics and primary-care centers. That year NewYork-Presbyterian Hospital broke ground for a replacement for the Babies and Children's Hospital, which was to be renovated and turned into an outpatient center. In 2002 NewYork-Presbyterian won long-sought-after approval to build a $250 million biomedical research and cancer-treatment center on its White Plains campus.

NewYork-Presbyterian Hospital was the biggest one in the New York metropolitan area in 2002, with 2,369 certified beds, 96,423 inpatient discharges, 995,796 outpatient and emergency visits, and total revenues of $1.85 billion. The annual *U.S. News & World Report* survey of U.S. hospitals for 2003 ranked it 11th, higher than any other area hospital. NewYork-Presbyterian was considered especially strong in psychiatry (second), neurology and neurosurgery (fourth), and pediatrics (fourth). An annual survey published in *America's Top Doctors* named more physicians from NewYork-Presbyterian Hospital than from any other hospital in the nation.

Principal Competitors

Beth Israel Medical Center; Mount Sinai Medical Center; New York University Medical Center; St. Luke's-Roosevelt Hospital Center.

Further Reading

Agovino, Theresa, "City Hospitals Curing Many Financial Ills," *Crain's New York Business,* July 15, 1991, pp. 1, 22.

——, "Columbia-Presbyterian Begins Big Layoff," *Crain's New York Business,* February 6, 1989, p. 2.

——, "Embattled Hospital Chief Quits," *Crain's New York Business,* February 5, 1990, pp. 1, 25.

——, "N.Y. Hospital Cuts Deficit, Moves on to New Programs," *Crain's New York Business,* July 30, 1990, p. 5.

——, "N.Y. Hospital Runs to Staunch Flow of Red Ink," *Crain's New York Business,* August 29, 1988, pp. 1, 34.

"America's Best Hospitals," *U.S. News & World Report,* July 28–August 4, 2003, pp. 47–96.

Benson, Barbara, "How One Hospital Plans to Survive," *Crain's New York Business,* November 21, 1994, p. 20.

——, "NYP's Internal Medicine," *Crain's New York Business,* January 3, 2000, p. 19.

Brenner, Elsa, "NewYork-Presbyterian Wins Right to Develop Its Land," *New York Times,* August 17, 2002, Sec. 14 (Westchester), p. 3.

Dunlap, David W., "A Medical Center Works on Its Health," *New York Times,* October 4, 1998, Sec. 10, pp. 1, 24.

——, "NYH Builds Managed Care Sans HMO," *Crain's New York Business,* July 24, 1995, p. 9.

Farber, M.A., and Lawrence R. Altman, "A Great Hospital in Crisis," *New York Times Magazine,* January 24, 1988, pp. 14–17, 36, 40, 57.

Hopkins, A.A., "Hospital Luxury for Rich or Poor," *Scientific American,* December 1932, pp. 340–41.

Kamen, Robin, "New York Hospital Says: Bill, We Are Ready," *Crain's New York Business,* September 27, 1993, pp. 3, 52.

Kastor, John A., *Mergers of Teaching Hospitals,* Ann Arbor: University of Michigan Press, 2001, pp. 113–258.

Lamb, Albert R., *The Presbyterian Hospital and the Columbia-Presbyterian Medical Center 1868–1943,* New York: Columbia University Press, 1959.

Larrabee, Eric, *The Benevolent and Necessary Institution: The New York Hospital 1771–1971,* Garden City, N.Y.: Doubleday, 1971.

"Medical Center," *Fortune,* June 1944, pp. 148 +.

"New York's Academic Medicine World Goes Ape," *Modern Healthcare,* August 28, 1995, pp. 34–36, 40.

Rosenthal, Elisabeth, "2 More Hospitals Decide to Merge in New York City," *New York Times,* July 24, 1996, pp. A1, B3.

Steinhauser, Jennifer, "Hospital Mergers Stumbling As Marriages of Convenience," *New York Times,* March 14, 2001, pp. A1, B4.

——, "NewYork-Presbyterian Begins Work on Hospital for Children," *New York Times,* November 17, 2000, p. B2.

Sullivan, Ronald, "New York Hospitals Learning Economic Lessons," *New York Times,* August 7, 1978, pp. A1, B2.

Yalof, Ina, *Life and Death: The Story of a Hospital,* New York: Ballantine, 1988.

—Robert Halasz

Nidec Corporation

338 Kuzetonoshiro-cho, Minami-ku
Kyoto 601-8205
Japan
Telephone: +81-(075)-935-6140
Fax: +81-(075)-935-6141
Web site: http://www.nidec.co.jp

Public Company
Incorporated: 1973 as Nippon Densan Corp.
Employees: 33,331
Sales: ¥231.84 billion ($1.93 billion) (2003)
Stock Exchanges: Tokyo Osaka New York
Ticker Symbol: NJ
NAIC: 335312 Motor and Generator Manufacturing;
    333412 Industrial and Commercial Fan and Blower
    Manufacturing

Kyoto-based Nidec Corporation is the world's leading manufacturer of the tiny electric motors that power hard disk drives on personal computers and other digital electronics. The company supplies about two thirds of global demand for the so-called spindle motors that spin hard drives as data is recorded and retrieved. As hard drives begin to be incorporated into more and more devices, Nidec's motors are being used in products ranging from video game consoles to DVD recorders to car navigation systems. Nidec's precision products make use of "brushless DC motor" technology, which is quieter, more efficient, and longer-lasting than conventional brush DC motor technology. As applications for brushless DC motors expand beyond their use in hard drives, Nidec is making precision motors for a wider range of products including home appliances, office equipment, and power steering systems in cars. The company also makes fan motors used to dispel heat from computer chips as well as pivot assemblies for hard disk drives.

Since its founding in 1973, Nidec has grown rapidly through numerous mergers and acquisitions. The company's founder, CEO, and President Shigenobu Nagamori, is known for his competitive drive and his willingness to go against conventional

Japanese business practices. With more than three dozen subsidiaries, Nidec's production network stretches across Asia. The company has factories in China, Thailand, the Philippines, Indonesia, Singapore, and Vietnam, as well as in the United States. Nidec's research and development capabilities have helped it remain a leader in precision motor technology, enabling it to thrive amid the constantly advancing information technology industry.

Developing Markets for Precision Motors and Fans: 1973–88

In 1973 Shigenobu Nagamori was working for a precision machinery maker known as Yamashina Seiki when his boss called off development of the miniature motor project Nagamori was spearheading. Nagamori had been researching the development of precision motors since his high school days and was determined to pursue opportunities in the field. Consequently, he quit his job and, at the age of 28, started Nidec—originally known as Nippon Densan Corporation—from a small building behind his house in Kyoto. Three engineers from his former employer joined him. The four-person firm, with no startup capital except for Nagamori's life savings, began researching precision motors.

Nagamori had no success finding customers at the large electronics manufacturers in Japan. All they wanted to know "was how old I was and how many staff I employed," he told *Business Week* in May 1999. Nagamori lacked connections to Japan's large industrial groups, known as *keiretsu*, and in Japan's business climate small startup companies were only able to get subcontracts. Nagamori did not want to play second fiddle to anyone. Thus he set off for the United States, where he made cold calls to the companies he found in the Yellow Pages. He managed to set up a meeting at 3M headquarters in St. Paul, Minnesota, and won a contract worth $2,000. That contract grew into regular orders for precision motors that 3M used in high-speed cassette duplicators.

Soon after founding the company, Nagamori set an annual sales goal of ¥1 billion. His coworkers laughed, but the contracts gradually accumulated thanks to Nagamori's sales persistence and the quality of the company's product. IBM ordered

$1 million worth of disk drive motors in 1974. Contracts followed with Digital Equipment and other major U.S. corporations. Back in Kyoto, Nagamori had trouble getting credit for loans, so he invested his first profits into real estate which could be used as collateral. His employees were tempted to leave for more secure positions at larger companies, so he implemented stock options as a form of compensation—an unconventional approach for a Japanese firm.

The company established a factory in Kameoka City, Kyoto, in 1975 and a U.S. subsidiary, Nidec America Corp., in 1976. In 1978 a joint venture was set up with the U.S. fan manufacturer Torin Corp. to make axial fans for cooling of electronics. The company began full-scale production of axial fans using brushless DC technology in 1982. In 1984 Nidec gained full control of the fan manufacturing operation when it purchased the axial fan division of Torin Corp. Torin had been producing air blowers for over 100 years but became overwhelmed with red ink in the early 1980s. Nagamori promised to make the division profitable in three years. He put the former number two man, Thomas T. Keenan, in charge and asked him to follow a list of 117 points, such as the requirement that executives arrive at the office earlier than regular employees every day. Even though some of the requirements clashed with American culture, they were implemented and the division posted a $650,000 profit in 1987. Torin's precision fan technology was a good supplement to Nidec's precision motor technology. The company was rolled into Nidec America Corp. and became a research, development, and manufacturing center for many of Nidec's small motor products.

While the fan business began to take off in the 1980s, Nidec was also advancing in the hard drive motor business. A major breakthrough came in 1979 when the company became the first to successfully commercialize a spindle motor for an eight-inch hard disk drive. The product made the company a major player in the world computer market. In the past, hard drives were driven by belts attached to motors; Nidec's DC motor revolved the hard drive spindle directly and made possible the development of much smaller computers. Production of a 5.25-inch spindle motor began in 1981 and a 3.5-inch motor followed in 1985.

In 1988 Nidec went public with a listing on the Second Section of the Osaka Securities Exchange and on the Kyoto Stock Exchange. By this time, the company had established several manufacturing subsidiaries, including plants in Tottori and Okayama Prefectures in Japan. With over ¥25 billion in annual sales for 1988, the company had already surpassed the ¥1 billion and ¥10 billion sales goals set by Nagamori. His employees were not laughing at his next goal: ¥100 billion in sales by the company's 20-year anniversary in 1993.

Mergers, Acquisitions, and Offshore Subsidiaries: 1990s

Mergers, joint ventures, and acquisitions were the tools that drove Nidec's growth through the 1990s. With the 1989 purchase of Shinano Tokki Co. Ltd. from Teac Corporation, Nidec acquired one of the major world manufacturers of spindle motors for hard disk drives, with a factory in Nagano, Japan.

In 1989 the company entered the power supply market with the purchase of DC Pac Co., Ltd., followed by the 1991 acquisition of Power General Corporation, a Massachusetts-based manufacturer of power supply products. Nidec was hoping to increase its sales in this area. In 1993 Nidec acquired the power supply manufacturer Masaka Electronics Co. Ltd. The power supply units were merged into Nidec Power General Corp.

Nidec set up sales and procurement offices in Singapore, Taiwan, and Hong Kong in 1989, 1992, and 1993, respectively. The company also began locating factories outside of Japan to take advantage of cheaper labor. Nidec Electronics (Thailand) Co., Ltd. was established in 1990 and Nidec (Dalian) Ltd., in 1992. Nidec built a plant in the northern Chinese city of Dalian in 1994 in a joint venture with Koyo Seiko Co., Ltd., a leading Japanese manufacturer of bearings. The drive to move production offshore gained momentum in the mid-1990s as Nidec suffered from its exposure to exchange rate fluctuations. The company lost over ¥1.3 billion in the fiscal year ending March 1995 because of the strong yen. In the following years Nidec increasingly transferred production to plants in Thailand, Singapore, China, and the Philippines. The company established Nidec Philippines Corp. in late 1995 and invested ¥4.5 billion in a large plant there to make spindle motors for hard disk drives. As manufacturing jobs were transferred out of Japan, the domestic subsidiaries were converted into research and development centers.

Many of Nidec's major acquisitions in the 1990s targeted companies that were expected to create synergies with Nidec's existing operations. Nagamori's strategy was to seek out companies that had quality technology and potential for growth but were struggling financially. His view, as he told the *Nikkei Weekly* in 2002, was that nontechnical problems were easier to solve than technical deficiencies. "The biggest problem at a struggling company is not the ability of management and employees, but their morale," Nagamori explained. "We change the mindset of staff at acquired firms so they come to believe that posting red ink is a sin." Just as he had with Torin Corp. in the 1980s, Nagamori would revamp management at a newly acquired subsidiary and bring the company back into the black. Often Nidec would acquire a minority share, just enough to have a say in how things were run, and gradually gained full control of the company as its performance improved.

In 1995, for example, Nidec acquired a 36.5 percent stake in the struggling Japanese manufacturer Shimpo Industries Co. Shimpo made variable speed mechanisms for stepless automatic transmissions, and the acquisition was expected to improve Nidec's expertise in the area of midsize commercial use motors. The next year Shimpo absorbed Daisan Kogyo KK, a Japanese manufacturer of control equipment. The company, renamed Nidec-Shimpo Corporation, eventually became a wholly owned subsidiary of Nidec. Another acquisition in 1995 was Kyoritsu

Key Dates:

1973: Shigenobu Nagamori founds Nippon Densan in Kyoto to research precision motors.
1974: IBM orders $1 million worth of hard disk drive motors.
1976: Nidec America Corp. is founded.
1979: Nidec successfully commercializes a spindle motor for an eight-inch hard disk drive.
1984: Nidec purchases Torin Corp.'s fan manufacturing business.
1988: Nidec goes public on the Osaka Exchange.
1995: Currency exchange rate fluctuations spur Nidec to move more production offshore.
1998: Nidec achieves more than ¥100 billion in sales after a decade-long series of acquisitions.
2001: Nidec lists on the New York Stock Exchange.
2002: Nidec introduces a hard drive motor with "fluid dynamic bearings."

Machinery Co. Ltd., which made automated equipment for precision motor assembly lines. Nidec initially bought a 38.5 percent stake in the company, later gained control of 60 percent, and renamed the company Nidec Machinery Corporation.

Another major acquisition came in 1997 when Nidec bought 30 percent of Tosok Corporation from Nissan. Like Shimpo, Tosok made parts for continuous variable transmissions as well as other precision auto parts and machinery. In Nagamori's opinion, the company had languished under Nissan. He put it colorfully at a press conference in January 2000: "In the past an evil lord took all our money and discouraged our efforts to turn a profit." Nagamori discontinued Tosok's unprofitable products and moved production to Vietnam to cut costs. By 2000, the company was back in the black. Nidec gained majority control of the company in 1999. Other acquisitions in 1997 included Read Corporation, which made printed circuit boards and testing systems for computer displays, and Kyori Kogyo Co., Ltd., which made automatic presses and other types of industrial machinery. The companies were renamed Nidec-Read Corp. and Nidec-Kyori Corp.

In 1998 Nidec became the largest shareholder in Copal Co., a manufacturer of precision optical equipment and cell phone motors with factories in Malaysia and China. Nidec also established a joint venture, Shibaura Nidec Corp., with Toshiba Corp. and Shibaura Engineering to make precision motors for electric appliances and automobiles. Nidec pushed for extensive restructuring at the company, in which it had a 40 percent stake, and later acquired its partner's shares when profitability had improved. Through these two subsidiaries, Nidec established offshore plants in Malaysia, Thailand, the Philippines, and China. Nidec also opened a new $30 million plant in Singapore in 1998 for production of hard disk drive spindle motors and pivot assemblies.

New Technology, New Applications: 1998–2003

Nidec broke the ¥100 billion sales goal in 1998, when it reported net revenues of ¥115.7 billion and an after-tax profit of ¥6.33 billion. That year the company listed its stock on the First Section of the Osaka Securities Exchange and on the Tokyo Stock Exchange. The First Section was reserved for more prominent companies. But Nagamori, always striving to be number one, desired the prestige of being listed on the world's largest stock exchange. This goal was achieved on September 27, 2001, when Nidec debuted on the New York Stock Exchange, pushing ahead with a successful listing even though markets were still weak in the wake of the terrorist attacks several weeks earlier.

As a result of its numerous acquisitions, Nidec's sales more than doubled over two years to ¥249.2 billion in 2000. With its subsidiaries making a broader array of precision equipment, Nidec began to define its business sphere generally as "turning and moving" products. One activity, however, that did not fit into its business strategy was the power supply manufacturing capability it had acquired in the late 1980s and early 1990s. In 1997 Nidec sold a portion of its power supply subsidiary Nidec Power General Corp. to the Taiwanese power supply manufacturer Potrans Electronical Corp. In 2001 the remaining share was transferred to the Japanese Nipuron Corporation. Nidec completed its exit of the sector in 2002 when the American subsidiary sold its power supply division to Minneapolis-based Ault Incorporated.

Nidec had plenty to keep it busy in the area of brushless DC motor manufacturing. Although sales of personal computers were slowing worldwide, the use of hard drives in devices such as MP3 players, DVD recorders, and digital cameras was growing. Nidec also continued to acquire companies with expertise outside the traditional area of hard disk drive spindles. In late 1999 the company bought over 70 percent of Nemicon Corporation, which made electronic equipment such as optical rotary encoders and proximity sensors. In 2000 Nidec acquired Y-E Drive Corp., a maker of mid-size motors for industrial equipment and home appliances, and set up a joint venture with Johnson Electric of Hong Kong that gave them access to Johnson Electric's brush DC motor technology.

Meanwhile, Nidec kept pace with the latest developments in hard drive technology. A new technique known as "fluid dynamic bearings" was replacing the traditional bearing system in hard drives. Instead of metal ball bearings, the new technique used a thin layer of lubricant to separate rotating and nonrotating parts. Fluid bearings could spin faster than ball bearings while using less power, generating less friction, and standing up better to impacts. Nidec introduced a hard drive motor with fluid bearings in 2002 after spending $330 million on its development over four years. That year it also opened a factory to produce fluid dynamic bearings in Zhejiang, China, where some of its affiliates already operated. Another subsidiary, Nidec (Dongguan) Ltd., was set up to manufacture brushless DC motors in Guangdong Province in China.

Nidec celebrated its 30th anniversary in 2003 by moving into a new headquarters in Kyoto. The company also made yet another acquisition, buying a 40 percent share in Sankyo Seiki Manufacturing Co. Sankyo had been experiencing net losses in recent years and stood to benefit from Nidec's marketing capabilities, while Nidec was attracted to Sankyo's expertise in the manufacture of motors smaller than 1.8 inches. Although Nidec was an expert with 2.5 inch motors, it was not as strong in the production of the smaller motors that were increasingly used in portable electronic devices.

In 2003, Nidec was keeping pace with the latest hard drive technology while looking ahead to new applications for many different kinds of brushless DC motors. Automobiles became a huge potential market as power steering and braking systems began to be electrically operated. Nidec's efficient precision motors could also replace traditional motors in devices such as refrigerators, washing machines, and vacuum cleaners. Nidec's vision was to have its motors whirring quietly inside appliances, electronics, and automobiles around the world.

Principal Subsidiaries

Nidec Electronics (Thailand) Co., Ltd.; Nidec (Dalian) Limited; Nidec Singapore Pte. Ltd.; Nidec Philippines Corporation; Nidec Precision (Thailand) Co., Ltd.; Nidec Shibaura Corporation; Nidec Power Motor Corporation (78%); Nidec Nemicon Corporation (93.8%); Nidec-Kyori Corporation (69.2%); Nidec Machinery Corporation (60%); Nidec America Corporation; Nidec Taiwan Corporation; Nidec Electronics GmbH (Germany); Nidec (H.K.) Co., Ltd. (Hong Kong); P.T. Nidec Indonesia; Nidec Tosok Corporation (54.7%); Nidec-Shimpo Corporation; Nidec-Read Corporation (61.5%); Nidec Total Service Corporation (85.7%); Nidec (Zhejiang) Corporation (China); Nidec (Dongguan) Limited (China); Nidec (New Territories) Co., Ltd. (Hong Kong); Nidec System Engineering (Zhejiang) Corporation (China); Nidec (Shanghai) International Trading Co., Ltd.; Nidec Copal Corporation (46.7%); Nidec Copal Electronics Corporation (43.9%).

Principal Competitors

Matsushita Electric Industrial; Minebea Co.; Sankyo Seiki Manufacturing.

Further Reading

"Acquired Foreign Firms Face Special Challenges," *Japan Economic Journal*, August 22, 1987, p. 8.

"Ball Bearings Face Threat from Slick, New Challenger," *Nikkei Weekly (Japan)*, June 28, 1999, p. 8.

"Corporate Profile: Nippon Densan Listing," *Jiji Press Ticker Service*, November 4, 1988.

"Electronics: Nidec Buys Seagate Plant," *Bangkok Post*, November 7, 2000.

"End Run Around Japan Inc.," *Business Week*, May 31, 1999. p. 24.

"Japan's Nidec Buys Copal Shares from Fujitsu, Asahi Bank," *Asia Pulse*, February 23, 1998.

"Japan's Nidec to Buy 30 Pct Stake in Tosok Corp," *Asia Pulse*, February 25, 1997.

Kunii, Irene M., "Outsize Earnings from Tiny Motors," *Business Week*, July 22, 2002, p. 26.

"Mergers Drive Precision Motor Maker," *Nikkei Weekly (Japan)*, December 24, 2002.

"Nidec Posts Record Profits in FY '00, Expects Slowdown," *Jiji Press Ticker Service*, May 14, 2001.

"Nidec Taking over Sankyo Seiki for Small Motor Technology," *Nikkei Weekly (Japan)*, August 11, 2003.

"Nidec Targets 1 Trillion Yen in Sales in FY2010," *Nikkei Weekly (Japan)*, September 24, 2002.

"Nidec to Set up Motor-Making Unit in China," *Jiji*, February 6, 2002.

"Nidec to Set up Subsidiary in China to Make Small Motors," *Japan Economic Newswire*, April 22, 2002.

"Nidec Tosok Takes to New Regime," *Nikkei Weekly (Japan)*, January 10, 2000, p. 10.

"Nippon Densan to Gain Control of Shimpo Industries," *Japan Economic Newswire*, January 26, 1995.

Perng, Chee Jann, "Nidec to Pump $70m into the Region," *Straits Times (Singapore)*, September 25, 1998, p. 70.

Takeuchi, Yoshiharu, "Nippon Densan Heads Offshore to Cut Currency Risk," *Nikkei Weekly (Japan)*, October 28, 1996, p. 29.

Yamazaki, Atsuhiro, "Bearing Makers Scramble for China Foothold," *Nikkei Weekly*, May 30, 1994, p. 28.

—Sarah Ruth Lorenz

The Ohio Art Company

Post Office Box 111
Bryan, Ohio 43506-0111
U.S.A.
Telephone: (419) 636-3141
Fax: (419) 636-7614
Web site: http://www.world-of-toys.com

Public Company
Incorporated: 1930
Employees: 191
Sales: $38.99 million (2003)
Stock Exchanges: American
Ticker Symbol: OAR
NAIC: 339932 Game, Toy, and Children's Vehicle
　　Manufacturing; 332116 Metal Stamping; 336399 All
　　Other Motor Vehicle Parts Manufacturing

Headquartered in a small northwest Ohio town, The Ohio Art Company is best known for its classic drawing toy, the Etch A Sketch. In stark contrast to the faddish toys that crowded the toy market during the late 20th and early 21st centuries—as well as the increasing prevalence of toys featuring a licensed identity—the company's flagship product has endured more than 40 years, sold over 100 million units, and appealed to children in dozens of countries worldwide. About 25 percent of the firm's revenues are derived from the sale of writing and drawing toys. One of the oldest toymakers in the United States, Ohio Art produces about 50 toys in all, including the popular Betty Spaghetty line of dolls as well as water toys, children's drum sets, and sports sets. The company's slogan, "Making Creativity Fun," emphasizes its focus on art- and craft-oriented toys. Although toys generate the majority of Ohio Art's annual sales, the production and sale of custom metal lithography and molded plastic products, such as automobile trim, serving trays, and metal food containers, contribute more than one-third of revenues. After posting net losses in four out of five fiscal years from 1996 to 2000 thanks to a series of travails—and at times verging on bankruptcy—Ohio Art bounced back to profitability during fiscal 2002. The company remained vulnerable, however, because of its heavy reliance on two main toy lines, Etch A Sketch and Betty Spaghetty.

Early History: From Picture Frames to Lithographed Metal Toys

Ohio Art traces its history to the first decade of the 20th century, when Henry Simon Winzeler made a dramatic career change. Trained as a dentist, Winzeler opened a private practice in the tiny town of Archbold, Ohio, in 1900. Inspired by an oval mirror in his aunt's clothing store, Winzeler decided to start manufacturing oval picture frames. With $300 borrowed from friends, Winzeler made preparations to begin production in a rented hall. He sold the dental office in 1908 and opened a grocery, using the market's profits to buy equipment for the frame business. He continued to operate his "Hub Grocery" through early 1909.

Winzeler launched The Ohio Art Company in October 1908 with 15 employees. For the first two years, his oval metal frames were stamped in Toledo, then painted onsite in Archbold. In 1910 Winzeler bought his own stamping machine and consolidated production.

Sold primarily through the new breed of mass marketers such as Woolworth's, Kresge's, and Sears, Roebuck & Co., Ohio Art's framed pieces featured religious scenes, still lifes, and landscapes. Within just two years production had expanded to 20,000 units each day. The company's most popular view featured a pair of cupids, one asleep, one awake. The Cupid images were copyrighted by Taber-Prand Company, and Ohio Art paid a royalty on each set. Ohio Art's 75th anniversary publication noted that "Winzeler offered $100,000 for the rights to these pictures, but his offer was rejected. In 1938, Taber-Prand went into bankruptcy and Winzeler's son, Howie, bought the rights for $10." Company figures estimated that over 50 million of the cupid sets were sold, meaning that the decoration graced over one-half of all homes in the early 20th century.

Rising demand spurred moves to progressively larger plants, until Ohio Art moved to the town of Bryan and a specially built plant in 1915. The addition of lithography equipment that same year expanded the company's capabilities. Ohio Art diversified cautiously at first, lithographing wood-grain finishes on its traditional metal frames. This product line grew to include advertising signage and scale faces.

Ohio Art also expanded through acquisition during this period. The 1916 purchase of Chicago's Holabird Manufacturing Company broadened the product line to include glass-framed calendars featuring popular Ohio Art prints.

The onset of World War I in 1914 interrupted toy imports from Germany and afforded domestic toymakers the opportunity to fill the void. In 1917 Ohio Art acquired both the C.E. Carter Company's Erie toy plant and the Battle Creek Toy Manufacturing Company. During this period, Ohio Art began making the lithographed metal windmills, sand pails, toy cars, wagons, circus trains, spinning tops, and drum sets that would be mainstays throughout the 20th century. The company honed its lithography skills with the production of metal tea sets that featured detailed depictions of nursery rhymes, alphabets, animals, and children's stories.

In 1927 H.S. Winzeler retired from Ohio Art to concentrate on his West Coast businesses. Although Winzeler continued to own the company, Lachlan M. ("Mac") MacDonald succeeded Winzeler as president and directed Ohio Art's 1930 incorporation. About 20 percent of the company's equity was sold to the public at that time, but the Winzelers retained a controlling stake. Fifteen-year-old son Howard W. ("Howie") Winzeler started working part-time at Ohio Art in 1930 and joined the firm full-time three years later.

Ohio Art maintained its fiscal strength throughout the Great Depression and was even able to acquire several other companies hobbled by the crisis. In 1930 alone the company bought out four firms: Mutual Novelty Manufacturing Company in Chicago, a producer of artificial icicles for decorating Christmas trees; Veelo Manufacturing Company, maker of dolls and stuffed animals; Delta Products, a manufacturer of electric appliances and car parts; and Household Appliance Manufacturing Company, a maker of clothes dryers. Craftsman Studios, a manufacturer of brass and copper tableware, was acquired in 1931. Two printing companies, Kenyon Company, Inc., and Detroit Publishing Company, were purchased the following year. When H.S. Winzeler died in 1939 Howie was appointed to fill the vacant seat on the board of directors. By the end of the year, he had also advanced to vice-president.

During World War II, when virtually all domestic production was harnessed for the war effort, even toymakers such as Ohio Art were called upon to manufacture strategic products. The tiny northwest Ohio firm made parts for rockets, bombs, and aircraft throughout the war, and its contributions earned an "Excellence" award at war's end.

When Ohio Art resumed toymaking in the postwar era, it began using new plastics to make its traditional toys. Metal dollhouses featured plastic furniture, and tea sets, sand pails, and farm sets reappeared in plastic.

Enter the Etch A Sketch, 1960

H.W. Winzeler, who advanced to Ohio Art's presidency in 1953, encountered what would become the company's flagship product at a European toy fair in 1959. That was when France's Arthur Granjean pitched his "L'Ecran Magique" ("magic writer") to the chief executive officer. Winzeler was reluctant to pay the apparently steep price Granjean demanded to license the product but bought the rights after a second presentation later that year.

Renamed the Etch A Sketch, the toy featured a glass "window" enclosed in a red plastic frame. A combination of aluminum powder and plastic pellets inside the window made it look like a flat gray screen. Young sketchers could create line images by turning the white knobs on the left and right of the screen, which, by a series of internal strings and pulleys, controlled the horizontal and vertical movement of a stylus that scraped the aluminum powder from the back of the glass, leaving a thin black line. To erase a drawing and start over, the sketcher simply turned the toy on its face and shook, coating the glass with a new film of aluminum powder.

Ohio Art launched the toy in time for the 1960 holiday season and supported Etch A Sketch (which itself resembled a television) with its first televised advertising campaign. With seals of approval from *Good Housekeeping* and *Parents* magazines, the Etch A Sketch soon became a toy store mainstay. Sears, Roebuck & Co. alone sold ten million of the toys from 1960 to 1970.

Not content to rest, Ohio Art balanced the toy market's seasonally cyclical sales with the incorporation of Strydel, Inc., in 1962. Strydel applied Ohio Art's injection molding, lithography, and metal stamping capabilities to the production of metal and plastic industrial components such as auto trim, film canisters, and reproductions of classic metal signs and trays, mostly premiums for Coca-Cola. Ohio Art was eventually producing 500 lithographed designs. In 1968 Ohio Art acquired Trinc Company, a truck leasing firm formerly owned by Ohio Art executives, and a controlling interest in Emenee Corporation, a manufacturer of toy musical instruments.

Key Dates:

1908: In Archbold, Ohio, Henry Simon Winzeler founds The Ohio Art Company as a maker and seller of oval metal picture frames.

1915: Company is relocated to Bryan, Ohio, where it builds a new plant and also adds lithography equipment.

1917: Ohio Art ventures into toymaking through two acquisitions; company begins making lithographed metal toys and tea sets.

1930: Company incorporates and goes public, though the Winzelers retain a controlling stake.

1960: Ohio Art launches the Etch A Sketch during the holiday season.

1962: Strydel, Inc. is formed as a subsidiary focusing on custom metal lithography and molded plastic products.

1977: Winzeler family sells its controlling stake to William Casley Killgallon.

1978: The non-toy operations are consolidated within the Diversified Products Division.

1998: The Betty Spaghetty doll debuts.

2000: Ohio Art announces it will shift production of the Etch A Sketch from Ohio to China.

Shifting of Control to Killgallon Family in Late 1970s

The founding Winzeler family sold its controlling stake in Ohio Art to William Casley Killgallon in 1977. The Winzelers had drawn Killgallon from a rival toy company to become sales manager in 1955. He advanced to a seat on the board within two years and was elected president in 1966 and board chairman in 1978. William Killgallon was joined by his son Bill (William Carpenter) in 1968; Bill succeeded his father as president and chief executive officer in 1978 and was joined at the company by his brother, Martin ("Larry") Killgallon. They consolidated Ohio Art's peripheral businesses as the diversified Products Division in 1978.

Although Ohio Art had used licensed characters to make its products more attractive and recognizable to children and parents since the late 1920s, licensing efforts intensified dramatically during the 1980s. Ohio Art continued to license perennially popular Disney characters—even offering an Etch A Sketch in the shape of Mickey Mouse—as well as trendy animated figures such as Smurfs and Pac-Man. The company also introduced the Lil' Sport line of scaled-down basketball, baseball, and soccer toys during the late 1970s and early 1980s.

Ohio Art launched Etch A Sketch spinoffs during the 1980s, including plastic overlays with drawing games and puzzles, as well as travel and pocket Etch A Sketch models. The company's efforts to parlay its long-running (yet only moderately profitable) Etch A Sketch franchise culminated in the 1986 launch of the Etch A Sketch Animator. This electronic version of the classic toy could store several drawings at a time and play them back, effecting animation. At a retail price of about $50, the Animator was one of Ohio Art's most expensive offerings. The company's sales jumped 50 percent from about $31.3 million in 1985 to $47 million in 1986, and its profits quintupled to $2.5 million. Those high-flying results came back to earth in the ensuing years, however, when competition from video games battered Animator sales. Ohio Art lost $3 million in 1989 and 1990 and finally ceased production of the Animator.

In a more low-tech vein, Ohio Art launched a color Etch A Sketch in 1993 that used the traditional two-knob drawing method but featured six colors and produced a color copy of each drawing. In honor of the toy's 35th birthday in 1995, Ohio Art introduced pocket models in jewel tones.

Struggling for a Turnaround, 1990s and Early 2000s

Ironically, the recession of the early 1990s helped Ohio Art to a certain degree, as many of its toys retailed for less than $20 and thus appealed to budget-conscious parents. Art, craft, and educational toys offered to "Make Creativity Fun." Sales and profits peaked at $55.6 million and $3.4 million in 1992. However, as the United States slowly emerged from recession, Ohio Art's results headed downward again. Sales declined by over 25 percent to $41.1 million in 1994, and profits dropped by more than three-quarters to $824,000 during the same period. The Killgallons, who continued to own a controlling interest in the company, worked to regain Ohio Art's luster, reducing the workforce by about 15 percent, cutting inventory levels, and achieving efficiencies in administrative areas.

A turnaround would not come easily, however. Ohio Art saw its revenue increase to $47.4 million in 1995 thanks in large part to a jump in Etch A Sketch sales following the toy's inclusion in the hit animated film, *Toy Story.* Yet in 1996 revenues fell by 23 percent and the company slipped into the red, posting a $1.7 million loss, as a result of several factors, most notably the ending of a licensing deal with superstar Michael Jordan on its basketball games and the decision by two major retailers to discontinue carrying the pocket line. The loss widened to $5.1 million in 1997. A major factor was the first product recall in the company's history. That summer, Ohio Art had introduced its first water toy, Splash Off Water Rockets, but had to quickly initiate a voluntary recall when problems with the toy's material were discovered, problems that led to the cracking and breaking of seams.

Sales increased 27 percent in 1998, to $45.9 million, as the company scored a hit with its newly introduced Betty Spaghetty doll. Aimed at girls ages four and up, the small doll featured interchangeable limbs, spaghetti-like hair, and a variety of accessories, such as a cell phone, a laptop computer, and in-line skates, According to company President Martin Killgallon II, quoted in the *Cleveland Plain Dealer,* "She's funky. She's different. She's certainly not Barbie." Despite Betty's popularity, Ohio Art failed to post a profit in 1998, losing another $1.8 million, mainly because an unnamed "major retailer" abruptly canceled a $15.2 million toy order just before the holiday season. The company was left with a large amount of excess inventory and also was unable to cancel television advertising commitments that had been made in support of the holiday line.

In 1999 Ohio Art seemed on the verge of declaring bankruptcy. Its main lender, Fifth Third Bancorp, declared the company in default on a $17.7 million revolving loan because of the failure to meet the bank's standards of profitability and the necessary ratio of assets to liabilities. From May through September the company's stock was suspended from trading on the American Stock Exchange because Ohio Art had not filed its annual report for 1998. When the report was finally released in September, the auditors said that Ohio Art's finances raised "substantial doubt" about its ability to stay in business. As it searched for new financing, the company was able to fund its operations from its internal cash flow; aiding the company's survival was the release in 1999 of the smash-hit movie sequel *Toy Story 2*, which once again featured the Etch A Sketch. Despite its appearing onscreen for only about 30 seconds, the attendant free advertising helped boost sales of the drawing toy by 20 percent during the 1999 holiday season. Revenues for 1999 increased 16 percent, and Ohio Art even achieved a small profit of $356,000.

In April 2000 Ohio Art secured a new line of bank financing, bringing some stability to its financial picture. That year a major restructuring was launched in order to enhance the company's longer term viability. The goal was to reduce annual operating costs by $2.5 million by the fall of 2001. The most dramatic—and historic—change was the decision to shift production of the Etch A Sketch from Ohio to China, following a long line of other U.S. manufacturers who had made similar moves. The shift resulted in the elimination of 50 production jobs. For the year, Ohio Art posted its fourth loss in five years as revenues fell because of disappointing sales of the Betty Spaghetty line in the United States.

In 2001 Ohio Art recorded its highest profits ($3.1 million) in nearly a decade. Sales of Etch A Sketch were strong, and while the domestic performance of Betty Spaghetty continued to disappoint, the doll was scoring big in the European market. Ohio Art also managed to overcome the weak economic climate in the United States in late 2001 as well as the financial troubles at retailer Kmart Corporation, which abruptly canceled orders that holiday season.

Ohio Art's improving financial picture enabled the firm to begin investing in new products again. In early 2003 the company introduced a water gun called the A.R.M. 4000 XL, which it described as "the only water gun ergonomically designed to fit on the user's arm" (A.R.M. stood for "Aquatic Revenge Machine"). Hasbro, Inc. soon sued Ohio Art for patent infringement, claiming that the A.R.M. was too similar to Hasbro's Super Soaker water guns. In July 2003 a U.S. district judge dismissed the case, but Hasbro vowed to appeal. Meantime, it was reported in mid-2002 that Ohio Art was trying to sell its Strydel injection-molding subsidiary, hoping to use the proceeds to fund further toy development. Such a move might prove vital to Ohio Art's future as analysts consistently criticized the company's toy line as being too narrowly focused on just a few key products.

Principal Subsidiaries

Strydel, Inc.; Trinc Company.

Principal Competitors

Mattel, Inc.; Hasbro, Inc.; JAKKS Pacific, Inc.; Marvel Enterprises, Inc.

Further Reading

Brown, Paul, "Staying Power," *Forbes*, March 26, 1984, p. 186.

Chavez, Jon, "Dark Clouds Roll in Again for Ohio Art," *Toledo Blade*, November 10, 2002.

Cropper, Carol, "Etch a Mickey," *Forbes*, March 30, 1992, p. 14.

Flint, Troy, "Maker of Etch-A-Sketch Adjusting Financial Picture," *Cleveland Plain Dealer*, May 11, 1999, p. 1C.

Grimm, Matthew, "U.S. Toy Makers Invade the Eastern Bloc," *Adweek's Marketing Week*, June 4, 1990, p. 4.

"Lego Wars: A Christmas Tale," *Newsweek*, December 28, 1987, p. 40.

Melvin, Chuck, "Ohio Art Seeks Turnaround," *Cleveland Plain Dealer*, August 16, 1998, p. 2H.

Nibley, MaryBeth, "Ohio Art Co. Draws on Tradition," *Cleveland Plain Dealer*, December 26, 1989.

"Ohio Art Sparks Creativity with Its Scope Activity Toys," *Playthings*, February 1993, p. 140.

Salas, Teresa, "Manufacturers Plot to Tackle Toy Troubles," *Playthings*, February 1991, p. 66.

Sangiacomo, Mike, "Etch A Sketch Heads East: Toy's Made-in-Ohio Era Draws to a Close," *Cleveland Plain Dealer*, December 23, 2000, p. 1B.

Seewer, John, "Etch A Sketch Maker Shakes Up Classic Toy," *Grand Rapids (Mich.) Press*, November 23, 2001, p. D2.

A 75 Year Headstart on Tomorrow, 1908–1983: The Ohio Art Company, Bryan, Ohio: Ohio Art Company, 1983.

Slutsker, Gary, "Etch a Future," *Forbes*, March 23, 1987, p. 72.

—April Dougal Gasbarre
—update: David E. Salamie

OMI Corporation

1 Station Place
Stamford, Connecticut 06902
U.S.A.
Telephone: (203) 602-6700
Fax: (203) 602-6701
Web site: http://www.omicorp.com

Public Company
Incorporated: 1968 as Ogden Marine, Inc.
Employees: 48
Sales: $199.1 million (2002)
Stock Exchanges: New York
Ticker Symbol: OMM
NAIC: 483111 Deep Sea Freight Transportation

Operating out of Stamford, Connecticut, OMI Corporation owns and operates a fleet of 39 international crude oil and petroleum transport vessels, with another four new builds scheduled for delivery in 2004. Of those 39 ships, 23 are product carriers and 16 are crude oil tankers, at least half of the latter being double-hull Suezmax carriers (approximately 160,000 deadweight tons). The company also owns one massive, single-hull ULCC class tanker (approximately 322,000 deadweight tons). OMI makes its vessels available for charters on a time charter, bareboat, or voyage basis. Under a time charter basis, an OMI vessel is at the disposal of a customer for a specific period of time at a set price but it is operated by OMI. A bareboat arrangement gives customers possession of the vessel; customers are then responsible for the vessel's operation and management. Under a voyage, or "spot market," basis, OMI makes a vessel available for a single voyage at a price determined by current market conditions. While spot market arrangements have the potential to be quite lucrative, they are not without risk. In order to maintain some stability in cash flow in the highly cyclical shipping industry, OMI tries to strike a balance between spot and long-term chartering. OMI maintains one of the youngest fleets in the industry.

Founding the Company in 1968

The origins of OMI can be traced back to a shipping company named Oriental Exporters Inc. Assets of Oriental Exporters were sold to Ogden Marine, Inc., established as a Manhattan-based business in July 1968 by Ogden Corporation. One of the founders of Oriental Exporters, Michael Klebanoff, then became president of Ogden Marine in 1969. Over the next dozen years, Ogden Marine's parent company was involved in a variety of activities in addition to oil transport, which was actually a distant second in importance to shipbuilding. Some of Ogden's other businesses during this period included scrap and metal fabrication, leisure services, and a food products division that lost nearly $9 million in 1978 and another $10 million in 1979. Ogden was originally created in 1939 as a holding company for the reorganized Utilities Power & Light Corp. after its bankruptcy. In 1962 Ralph Ablon, who had married a woman set to inherit a controlling interest in an Ogden subsidiary, was named president and became instrumental in turning Ogden into a diverse conglomerate. Over the ensuing decades, Ogden entered and exited any number of businesses—childcare, building maintenance, electronics design, ferrous recycling, architectural design, and biomedical research—generally producing lackluster results for its shareholders.

Shipping, which had been in a slump in the 1970s, made a robust comeback in the 1980s, inducing Ogden Marine and others to bolster their fleets. In 1982 the subsidiary generated revenues of $226 million, a third of the parent company's turnover for the year, and recorded a net profit of $20.6 million. In September 1983 Ablon announced that it would spin off Ogden Marine to its shareholders on a one-for-one share exchange basis. Ogden at this stage was pursuing a services-oriented strategy, involved in businesses that were neither capital intensive, debt intensive, or cyclical in nature. Because shipping clearly did not fit this mold, management decided to divest itself of Ogden Marine and in the process removed more than $275 million in long-term debt from its balance sheet. In preparation for the spinoff, the subsidiary changed its name to OMI Corporation in December 1983, with the spinoff to Ogden shareholders completed on January 4, 1984. OMI stock then began to trade on the over-the-counter market, and two years later was listed on the NASDAQ. In 1989 OMI moved to the American Stock Exchange. At the time of the spinoff, OMI operated 29 oceangoing vessels totaling 1.78 million deadweight tons. They included 18 tankers, five bulk carriers, three car-bulk carriers, two liquefied petroleum gas vessels, and an ore-bulk-oil carrier.

Troubles Mounting in the Mid-1980s

Not only did OMI start off its existence as an independent company burdened with an excessive level of debt, its fleet was aging and would soon be in need of replacement. Moreover, there was an excess of capacity in the ocean shipping market and most of the company's fleet was scheduled to soon finish long-term charter agreements. It was unlikely that the deals would be renewed. OMI's troubles mounted in February 1986 when company President and CEO John J. Davin died in his sleep. But his successor, however unlikely a candidate, would prove to be the company's savior. In April 1986 47-year-old Jack Goldstein succeeded Davin, with Klebanoff serving as chairman. Goldstein, who earned an M.A. in economics at New York University, had no experience running a company, but knew the shipping industry after spending 15 years as the chief economist for Overseas Shipholding Group. According to a 1992 *Forbes* article, when Goldstein took over OMI, the "company was about to report a $27 million loss. And maybe worse. 'We had a company,' recalls Goldstein, 'close to bankruptcy.' " The company's banks informed him that OMI would be short of cash by $300 million within five years.

With OMI heavily in debt, Goldstein's first act was to issue nearly $55 million in new stock to retire some of the company's high-interest debt as well as to begin buying new replacement ships. He also brought some creativity to the shipping industry, in particular by forging joint ventures with foreign shipowners, which expanded OMI's fleet at a reasonable cost. Moreover, these joint ventures, in which OMI was a 49 percent owner, brought with them a tax benefit. In essence, OMI was able to invest pretax earnings to buy an interest in new ships. Derick Betts, a maritime tax lawyer, was quoted in a 1992 *Crain's New York Business* profile, maintaining, "Jack was really the first person in the industry to see the value of joint ventures. Before he did this, people in the shipping industry liked to hold on to their trade secrets. Jack pushed all that history aside. It was instrumental to OMI's turnaround." Goldstein told *Forbes,* "These joint ventures give us a worldwide reach that is unusual. We spread the risk, we stretch our capital, and we get expertise in areas where we may be weak."

Goldstein's expertise as an economist helped to make him a savvy trader. As explained by *Crain's,* "His forecasts helped OMI make a number of timely purchases, allowing the company to reap handsome profits off the sales of ships." One of his

first deals, in 1986, involved a three-year-old international tanker, the Settebello, which had never been paid for. According to *Forbes,* "Goldstein took her off the builder's hands for $15 million, about equal to the Settebello's scrap value. His timing was perfect. The shipping market was beginning to turn. Within two years Goldstein was able to sell a 51% interest in the ship to Norway's Bergesen group for $23 million." In 1990 Goldstein sold a tanker the company had on order from Mitsubishi Shipbuilding and turned a $15 million profit. A year later, he took delivery on another tanker, paying $33 million. After one voyage he was able to sell it for $47 million. Goldstein also proved adept at buying ships at reasonable prices.

Goldstein enjoyed mixed success in his attempts to diversify OMI beyond ocean shipping. Under his leadership, OMI paid $15 million for a 14 percent interest in Chiles Offshore Corp., an oil rig drilling company; bought an 88 percent interest in Petrolink, which unloaded oil from large tankers in the Gulf of Mexico; and bought a company that managed vessels for the U.S. Navy. OMI also became involved in the business of cleaning up oil spills. The Chiles investment was especially troublesome. "It's put a bit of a cloud over OMI," according to industry analysts James Winchester, as quoted by *Crain's.* Overall, however, Goldstein received high marks for the job he did in resurrecting OMI. In a matter of five years, OMI saw its revenues improve almost 65 percent to $284.8 million in 1991, while posting net earnings of nearly $30 million, a jump of 83 percent over the previous year. In 1992 OMI began trading on the New York Stock Exchange.

From 1988 until early in 1991, more of OMI's fleet was chartered for extended periods of time, providing a certain level of predictability. Yet in 1991, as many of OMI's charters expired, the rates for time charter agreements declined, forcing OMI to shift the vessels to the spot market, which because of a number of factors offered highly fluctuating rates. Demand for petroleum products was soft in the aftermath of the Persian Gulf War of 1991, a situation exacerbated by poor worldwide economic conditions. Moreover, a slate of new tankers came on line at the same time that oil demand dropped. The spot market rate for a tanker before the war was in the $28,000-a-day range, but when the market collapsed the rate fell below $10,000 a day.

Not only did OMI see its revenues reduced, it also faced higher operational costs due to new environmental laws and other regulatory changes that led to much higher insurance costs. Revenues for 1992 fell to $265.5 million and the company posted a loss of $11.4 million. Over the next two years, revenues stagnated and OMI lost an additional $8.7 million in 1993 and nearly $37.9 million in 1994. OMI lost another $31.9 million in 1995 on revenues of nearly $240 million before improving economic conditions brought with it improvement to the company's balance sheet.

Changing Course in the Mid-1990s

In November 1995 Klebanoff stepped down as chairman, although he remained a director and retained the title of chairman emeritus. Goldstein replaced him as chair, while COO Craig H. Stevenson, Jr., was named president. Stevenson came to OMI following a stint as president of Ocean Specialty Tankers Corp.

industry with content and services, in particular online chartering for the shipment of crude oil and petroleum products. But the core thrust of OMI remained the growth of its fleet of international oil tankers and product carriers. The company prospered in 2000 and 2001, posting net profits of $53 million and $82.3 million, before losing some momentum in 2002, when revenues declined by 5 percent and net income slumped to less than $15.5 million. The winter of 2003 proved to be especially lucrative to OMI, due to a number of factors. Cold weather, low oil inventories, and talk of war with Iraq all combined to spur demand for oil and allow OMI to increase day rates of its vessels. In the first quarter of 2003 alone, OMI earned $25.7 million, well above the company's profit for all of 2002.

OMI looked increasingly to the spot market to boost earnings, adopting an approach encapsulated by CEO and now Chairman Craig Stevenson: "We have a two-prong Strategy: to grab the maximum upside while making sure we cover our backsides." OMI appeared to be well positioned to take advantage of high future demand for tankers, which was expected to be dominated by one simple fact: while global consumption of oil was expected to grow by 1.2 percent to 2 percent per year, oil storage capacity would be unable to keep pace. As a result, the oil market would need to be replenished by tankers at an increasing rate, making OMI's prospects quite promising.

Principal Subsidiaries

Alma Shipping LLC; Ashley Shipping LLC; Delaware Shipping LLC; Elbe Shipping LLC; OMI Marine Services LLC.

Principal Competitors

Frontline Ltd.; Stelmar Shipping Ltd.; Teekay Shipping Corporation.

Further Reading

Cook, James, "Strong Hands at the Helm," *Forbes,* March 16, 1992, p. 74.
Dzikowski, Don, "OMI Moving Corporate Headquarters to Stamford," *Fairfield County Business Journal,* March 23, 1998, p. 12.
Leaner, Ellen, "Ogden's Next Trick," *CFO,* December 1996, p. 38.
Lubanko, Matthew, "For Stamford, Conn., Oil Shipper, It's Smooth Sailing," *Hartford Courant,* July 19, 2003, p. 1.
Temes, Judy, "Shipper's Keel Righted," *Crain's New York Business,* February 24, 1992, p. 3.

—Ed Dinger

Key Dates:

1968: Ogden Marine, Inc. is formed as a subsidiary by Ogden Corporation.
1983: Ogden Marine changes its name to OMI Corp.
1984: OMI is spun off by Ogden.
1986: Jack Goldstein is named chief executive.
1998: OMI is restructured as part of a merger with Marine Transport Lines.

After serving little more than a year as OMI's president, he succeeded Goldstein as CEO, effective January 1, 1997.

Although OMI returned to profitability, recording net earnings of $3.4 million in 1996 and $19.8 million in 1997, management decided that the company needed a course correction. Joint ventures had served OMI well for more than a decade, but now it was decided to concentrate on particular classes of vessels as well as to separate the U.S. operation from the international business. As a consequence, interests in joint ventures were reduced and a number of noncore vessels were sold. A key part of this shift in strategy involved the June 1998 merger with Marine Transport Lines, Inc., the oldest shipping company in the United States. A new OMI entity was then spun off, consisting solely of international assets, leaving Marine Transport with the U.S. flag vessels, the Gulf of Mexico oil unloading business, and OMI's ship management company. In this way, OMI could avoid paying U.S. corporate taxes and also garner the attention of foreign investors, who had previously been prevented from buying OMI's stock because of federal regulations. Moreover, the company overcame regulations that actually made it less profitable to enter an American port with a U.S.-owned vessel. OMI's revamped fleet consisted of 24 vessels, one of the most modern in the industry, with the average age of its ships less than eight years. As part of its restructuring OMI also moved the corporate headquarters from its Manhattan Park Avenue address to Stamford, Connecticut.

OMI took steps to sell stock to private investors and secure bank financing to support an expansion and upgrade of its fleet and thus become a premier product tanker company. In 1999 and 2000 it sold off its interests in several joint ventures, and then in 2001 it asked banks for $280 million to support a ten-ship building program. As larger, newer vessels entered the fleet, OMI sold off noncore ships, in the process further lowering the average age of its fleet. OMI dabbled in the Internet, forming SeaLogistics.com, which was intended to serve the shipping

OMNOVA Solutions Inc.

175 Ghent Road
Fairlawn, Ohio 44333-3300
U.S.A.
Telephone: (330) 869-4200
Fax: (330) 869-4288
Web site: http://www.omnova.com

Public Company
Incorporated: 1999
Employees: 2,400
Sales: $681.2 million (2002)
Stock Exchanges: New York
Ticker Symbol: OMN
NAIC: 325998 All Other Miscellaneous Chemical Product and Preparation Manufacturing

OMNOVA Solutions Inc. is a Fairlawn, Ohio, company comprised of two business segments: Decorative & Building Products and Performance Chemicals. The Decorative & Building Products segment includes four product categories. Commercial wallcoverings, accounting for nearly a third of the division's annual revenues, offers both decorative and protective wall surfacing products for such customers as hospitals, hotels, public and private offices, restaurants, schools, and stores. Coated fabrics products decorate and protect furniture at home and in the workplace as well as transportation seating. OMNOVA's decorative paper and vinyl laminates are used in a wide variety of applications, such as residential and office furniture, kitchen and bath cabinets, recreational vehicles, and floor and ceiling tile. The final product category of the Decorative & Building Products segment is commercial roofing, sold under the GenFlex brand and used in such structures as factories, government buildings, office complexes, restaurants, shopping malls, and stadiums. The Performance Chemicals business segment offers three product categories. Specialty chemicals are used in the manufacture of nonwoven products, such as diapers, engine filters, flooring and roofing mat, as well as plastic parts, tapes, tires, and textiles. OMNOVA's paper chemicals are used in the manufacture of a wide variety of papers used to produce maga-

zines and catalogs, as well as food cartons and packaging materials. Finally, the segment's carpet chemicals product category provides SB latex carpet backing adhesive used in the manufacture of both residential and commercial carpeting. OMNOVA is a public company trading on the New York Stock Exchange.

Lineage Dating Back to 1915

In 1999 OMNOVA was created as a spinoff from GenCorp, which grew out of the General Tire & Rubber Company, founded by William O'Neil, a former Firestone Company dealer who in 1911 quit to strike out on his own. His first business, Western Tire and Rubber, made tire repair materials in Kansas City. He relocated four years later to Akron, Ohio, which was quickly becoming the "Rubber Capital of the World," home to Goodyear, Goodrich, and Firestone, as well as General Tire. Akron was also where O'Neil's father, Michael O'Neil, owned a department store. Father and son launched General Tire to make repair materials but a year later, in 1916, it began to manufacture tires. General expanded over the next dozen years and although it controlled less than 2 percent of the tire market, concentrating on the higher-price range, by the start of the 1930s it was established enough to survive the Great Depression and complete a pair of acquisitions: Yale Tire and Rubber and India Tire and Rubber. It also began to diversify, turning at first to the ownership of radio stations.

General shifted to defense products during World War II, picking up Aerojet, a missile manufacturer which would become a major part of GenCorp. Because of natural rubber shortages caused by the war, General was also forced to become heavily involved in the production of synthetic rubber, which provided a natural bridge to the chemical industry. Before General's major push into performance chemicals, it made an acquisition that would form the basis of OMNOVA's Decorative & Building Products business segment. In 1945 it inherited a coated fabrics plant, located in Jeannette, Pennsylvania, after acquiring the Pennsylvania Rubber Company. In the postwar years General continued to diversify, creating an industrial products division to produce plastic and metal parts for electric appliances and aircraft. On the media side, General bought television stations in New York, Los Angeles, and Memphis, then acquired RKO Pictures from Howard Hughes to provide programming. The company also ramped up its production of synthetic rubber, which again became a necessity in the tire industry due to a shortage of natural rubber caused by the Korean War. In 1952 General laid the foundation for OMNOVA's Performance Chemicals business when its Mogadore, Ohio, factory began to manufacture styrene butadiene latex (SB latex), an emulsion polymer used to make paper, and SB vinyl pyridine latex, an adhesive used in the production of tire cords. When William O'Neil died in 1960, his sons took over General. During the 1960s the company bolstered its coated fabrics business by opening a plant in Columbus, Mississippi, adding a number of products. In the early 1970s the plant began to produce commercial wallcoverings. Also during the 1960s General's chemical segment added new products for the paper and carpet industries. Another aspect of what would become OMNOVA, the GenFlex roofing systems, began in 1980 with the introduction of a single-ply vinyl product line, which would eventually be followed by thermoplastic polyolefin and synthetic rubber membrane systems.

Formation of GenCorp: 1984

General underwent a number of changes in the 1980s, as its tire business began to erode at a rapid pace. The company was restructured in 1984 and GenCorp was created as a conglomerate to serve as a holding company for General's divisions now turned subsidiaries, which included Aerojet, RKO, and the tires, industrial products, and chemicals product lines. Later in the decade GenCorp began to shed assets, selling off its stake in Frontier Airlines, acquired by RKO in 1965, as well as RKO's television stations in Los Angeles and the New York market, RKO's radio station, and bottling interests owned by the subsidiary. Opting to focus on defense contracting and Aerojet, GenCorp also exited its original business, selling off its remaining tire operation to Continental AG of Germany in 1987.

In the 1990s GenCorp continued to grow the subsidiaries that would comprise OMNOVA's two business segments. In 1991 it acquired the wallcovering business of Canadian General Towers. The 1993 acquisition of Reneer Films Corporation from Goodyear broadened the company's vinyl and decorative laminate capabilities, resulting in GenCorp becoming North America's top maker of vinyl woodgrain laminates. Paper laminates were added in 1997 through the purchase of the Printworld business of Technographics, Inc., thereby giving GenCorp the ability to accomplish transfer printing for apparel and home furnishings. A year later the company bought the commercial wallcovering business of Walker Greenbank, based in the United Kingdom.

GenCorp's chemical product lines, in the meantime, were enhanced by the 1996 purchase of Morton International's Lytron plastic pigment product line used in the paper industry to enhance gloss brightness, opacity, and printability in paper and paperboard coatings. In 1988 GenCorp bought Goodyear's latex manufacturing plant located in Calhoun, Georgia. Also in 1998 it paid $108 million for Sequa Chemicals, the specialty chemicals units of Sequa Corporation. GenCorp completed two more acquisitions in 1999. The first added the U.S. acrylic emulsion polymer business of Germany-based PolymerLatex, a move that both strengthened the company's position in acrylic emulsions and also provided some market diversification. In addition, GenCorp bought the global latex floor care business of Morton International in 1999, a transaction that offered a number of benefits. Morton added a complementary product line with a new customer base and also provided a toehold in Europe and the Far East markets. Also of importance in 1999 was the establishment of a strategic alliance with PolymerLatex that benefited GenCorp's global paper customers.

Birth of OMNOVA: 1999

While many aspects of GenCorp enjoyed leading market positions and strong potential, it was difficult within the conglomerate structure for these interests to receive the kind of attention necessary in order to fully prosper. Moreover, investors had a difficult time assessing GenCorp and its diverse makeup. By the mid-1990s, mired in debt and troubled by environmental issues involving Aerojet, GenCorp was in need of new leadership at the top. It arrived in the form of John B. Yasinsky. After serving as a group president at Westinghouse Electric Corporation, he joined GenCorp in 1993, becoming president and chief operating officer. In 1994 he was named CEO and in March of the following year was also named chairman of the GenCorp board. Yasinsky was instrumental in turning around the troubled company. As a result, in 1999 GenCorp was secure enough that it could elect to shed its performance chemicals and decorative and building products interests by creating a tax-free spinoff. The hope was to unlock shareholder value in GenCorp's varied businesses as well as to provide the kind of focus that GenCorp had been unable to provide to these assets. GenCorp retained its aerospace, automotive, and pharmaceutical chemical businesses—and the GenCorp name. In order to be closer to its key asset, Aerojet, the much leaner company moved its headquarters to Sacramento, California.

The old GenCorp assets remained in Akron but assumed a new name: OMNOVA Solutions. "OMNOVA" was coined by fusing the Latin words "Omni" for "all" and "Nova" for "new." Not only was "all new" deemed fitting because the name represented a new start, but also because it connoted innovation, which was a major thrust of the newly independent company. Furthermore, "Solutions" was incorporated to indicate a commitment to customer satisfaction and a desire to forge long-term relationships. In addition to remaining in Ohio, Omnova also retained GenCorp's chief executive officer and chairman of the board, Yasinsky, to head the spinoff, which was completed on October 1, 1999. He guided OMNOVA as the company's CEO through its first year, and then in November 2000 turned over the post to President and COO Kevin McMullen. The 40-year-old McMullen came to GenCorp in 1996 after several years at General Electric, where he served stints as general manager for two separate divisions. McMullen became a vice-president of GenCorp Inc. and president of the Decorative & Building Products business unit.

For 1999, in the midst of the spinoff from GenCorp, OMNOVA recorded solid improvements over the previous year. Revenues grew by 23 percent to $767.4 million, due primarily to the acquisitions completed during the year. Both business segments posted significant gains, an 11 percent increase in sales for Decorative & Building Products and 44 percent for Performance Chemicals. The two OMNOVA segments combined to produce a net profit of $34.4 million. During this period the company also pursued what it called growth initiatives, achieved through joint ventures or strategic alliances. In 1999, for instance, the Decorative & Building Products segment formed a joint venture called Rayong with a Thailand-based decorative film and coated fabrics company as a way to expand into the Pacific Rim markets and also add new products for sale in North America and Europe. Another joint venture with similar goals was then established with a Shanghai, China-based maker of coated fabrics. OMNOVA in 2000 created Muraspec N.A. L.L.C. with partner Brewster Wallpaper Corp. in order to act as a national distributor for three OMNOVA-owned brands, plus decorative and functional wall surfacing products manufactured by outside firms.

The company's first full year after the spinoff from GenCorp, however, would not prove to be as successful as hoped. OMNOVA completed a minor acquisition, adding the specialty/textile coatings business of High Point Textile Auxiliaries, LLC for less than $1 million. But due to market softness and the rising costs of raw materials, the Decorative & Building Products segment decreased in sales by 3 percent over the previous year, leading to the elimination of 40 jobs in the division. Because Performance Chemicals grew by a modest 6 percent, OMNOVA recorded a slight gain in net sales over the previous year, totaling $773.3 million. Net income, on the other hand plummeted to $4.4 million. To help control costs, Performance Chemicals instituted a hiring freeze.

McMullen replaced Yasinsky as chairman in February 2001, but with the national economy beginning to sour OMNOVA

continued to slide during 2001. It made one acquisition, the $8.3 million purchase of product lines from Decorative Surfaces International, which helped somewhat, but the Decorative & Building Products segment still suffered a 3.2 percent decrease in revenues. As the main culprit, management pointed to poor market conditions in the United States and United Kingdom, which adversely impacted end-use markets. Performance Chemicals also experienced a 6.6 percent drop in sales over the previous year, attributed mostly to the poor economy. During the course of the year, OMNOVA took steps to rein in costs, closing a plant in North Carolina and laying off a number of workers companywide, totaling some 9 percent of its workforce. Nevertheless, OMNOVA saw its revenues decline to $737 million while recording a net loss of $6.7 million in 2001.

Business continued to deteriorate in both business segments in 2002. Net sales for Decorative & Building Products fell by 8.2 percent, due in large part to disappointing occupancy rates in the corporate and hospitality markets. Because of lower activity in commercial construction and refurbishment projects, roofing sales also suffered. Meanwhile, Performance Chemicals lost 6.7 percent of its business, again the result of a lackluster economy. Consequently, OMNOVA saw its net sales tumble to $681.2 million in fiscal 2002 while posting a net loss of $135.5 million. Business conditions continued to erode in 2003, matched by further layoffs and the elimination of some product lines.

Principal Subsidiaries

OMNOVA Services Inc.; OMNOVA Wallcovering (USA), Inc.; OMNOVA Wallcovering (UK), Limited.

Principal Divisions

Decorative & Building Products; Performance Chemicals.

Principal Competitors

The Dow Chemical Company; Johns Manville Corporation; RJF International Corporation.

Further Reading

Cimperman, Jennifer Scott, "In Need of a Fresh Coat," *Plain Dealer,* March 8, 2001, p. 1C.
Russell, Mark, "Fairlawn, Ohio-Based Chemical Company Omnova to Lay Off 25 Workers," *Akron Beacon Journal,* January 23, 2003.
——, "Fairlawn, Ohio-Based Chemical Firm Omnova to Cut 100 Jobs, Close Factory," *Akron Beacon Journal,* March 16, 2001.
Thompson, Richard, "Fairlawn, Ohio-Based Chemical Maker Names Spin-Off Company," *Akron Beacon Journal,* July 6, 1999.

—Ed Dinger

Onyx Acceptance Corporation

27051 Towne Centre Drive
Foothill Ranch, California 92610
U.S.A.
Telephone: (949) 465-3900
Fax: (949) 465-3530
Web site: http://www.onyxacceptance.com

Public Company
Incorporated: 1993
Employees: 968
Operating Revenues: $92.9 million (2002)
Stock Exchanges: NASDAQ
Ticker Symbol: ONYX
NAIC: 522291 Consumer Lending

Onyx Acceptance Corporation, a specialized consumer finance company, got off to a fast start in the mid-1990s but has threatened, at times, to stall. Engaged in the purchase, securitization, and servicing of motor vehicle retail installment contracts, Onyx works primarily with franchised automobile dealerships and focuses on the later model used car market. Onyx purchases the accounts receivables from the dealerships and then collects on the accounts. Unlike many competitors, Onyx has stuck with prime and near-prime consumers, not succumbing to the risky allure of the higher interest rates charged to subprime borrowers. To raise money to buy more accounts, Onyx stores up the assets it purchases and then spins them off as securities.

Start Your Engines: 1993–96

Auto finance executives eager to get in the race themselves revved up their engines and founded Onyx in 1993—most of top management had pulled away from Western Financial Savings Bank in Irvine, California. The six-person Orange County operation began the purchase, origination, and servicing of contracts in February 1994.

Running under the green flag, Onyx doubled the number of dealerships in its network during 1995. Total revenues climbed to $5.6 million, and the growth helped pare down the start-up company's losses. Plans were in the works to broaden its reach on the West Coast.

Onyx raised nearly $28.8 million in March 1996 when it sold 46 percent of the company to the public at the asking price of $11.50 per share. At least nine other auto finance companies had gone public during the past year, according to Knight Ridder.

When Brian McInnis resigned as CEO, in September 1996, John Hall succeeded him. The company the men helped found now operated in Washington, Arizona, and Nevada, as well as California. Eight regional offices served the company's customer base.

By this time, Onyx had completed its third asset-backed securitization. The automobile receivables the company bought were bundled together and then sold to raise funds. The $120 million transaction included loans originated outside California—a first in company history. "We were one of the few, if not the only company, who was able to go public with its securitization about nine months into our organization," Chief Financial Officer and Executive Vice-President Don Duffy told Asset Sales Report in 1999.

Onyx stayed the flow of red ink in 1996, recording a net profit instead of a net loss. Total revenues increased more than fourfold, to $25.2 million. An increase in the servicing portfolio helped the bottom line. Servicing income—the money earned on loans the company has securitized and sold—approximately doubled on the year. On the down side, delinquencies and loan losses jumped due to a rash of bad contracts out of its North Hollywood office. In response, Onyx began increasing its loan reserves. At the time, loan reserves were 2.17 percent of loan portfolio; the number increased to 3.68 percent by the end of 1997.

Avoiding Debris on the Track: 1997–98

The auto finance industry's image was tarnished from a string of unfavorable developments in early 1997. Jayhawk Acceptance Corp. in Dallas moved into bankruptcy protection, reeling from too many bad loans. Illinois-based Mercury Finance Corp. saw its stock plummet 86 percent in one day, following the report of accounting irregularities and a missing

Company Perspectives:

Onyx's prime and near-prime lending proficiency is the foundation for its contract purchasing, securitization and servicing operations. During its first nine years, Onyx has earned a reputation as a reliable and consistent source for dealers to effectively and competitively place their prime and near-prime auto buying customers.

accountant. The chairman of Ugly Duckling in Phoenix turned out to be a convicted felon, a revelation that came to light only after the company went public. Western Financial Services lost ground in the stock market as it reported a rise in uncollectable loans, according to a *Knight Ridder* article by Andre Mouchard.

Publicly traded companies, including Onyx, felt the reverberations. Trouble in the real estate industry also created ripples in the environment, causing investors to be more cautious with their money around subprime players in other industries.

In addition to falling stock prices, Onyx faced a possible weakening of the market for its asset-backed securities. Institutional investors, such as pension funds, were less likely to buy securities in a besieged industry. Onyx depended on the securities to bring in more capital for the purchase of additional loans from the auto dealerships.

Economic downturns also degraded the securities market: consumers were more likely to miss payments and drive down the value of the assets backing the securities. A rise in personal bankruptcies in the state of California did not bode well for the future, foreshadowing a possible upswing in losses and downturn in new business. Those companies with questionable underwriting practices were especially at risk when the economy soured.

Aware of the industry's vulnerabilities and seeing its own stock trading below its initial public offering, Onyx took measures to guard against an unwanted takeover. A "poison pill," giving shareholders preferred stock, was scheduled to go into effect if an investor accumulated a 15 percent stake in the company.

Although the company's total revenue climbed in 1997 to $36 million, net income fell. The decrease was attributed to increases in loan losses, loss reserves, and operating expenses. On the plus side, as others in the auto finance sector were showing flat or declining growth in loan volume during 1997, Onyx's volume climbed 89 percent.

In an effort to diversify, Onyx had begun exploring avenues for direct contact with consumers. Private party sales made up a significant segment of the used car market. To facilitate entry into this area Onyx looked into partnerships with other organizations, such as C.U. Acceptance Corp., which examined the records of consumers who had been turned down for loans by credit unions. Ultimately, Onyx would stick with its core dealership market.

Getting on the Map: 1999–2002

In order to fund the purchase of additional accounts receivable, Onyx itself took on debt. Credit deals in 1999 included

$150 million with Chase Manhattan Bank, $375 million with Triple-A One Funding, and $100 million with Merrill Lynch. According to *Loan Market Week*, "All three credits are warehouse facilities, meaning they are used to purchase assets that are stored up, or warehoused, before being spun off in an asset-backed securities deal."

The expansion drive brought Onyx recognition as one of the fastest growing companies in Orange County, California, and in the nation in 1999. Onyx had $1.5 billion of the $67 billion near-prime used car market that year.

Troubled by poor underwriting at times in the past, Onyx was now confident of the system it had in place. "Our credit people and the sales people work together as a team, and they're paid identically," said Duffy in *Asset Sales Report.* "And they're paid on the basis of their volume, and their yield, and the credit quality that comes from the audit processes. And we think that makes our underwriting process the best in the industry."

In 1999, net income rose by 61 percent to $9.8 million, and total revenue climbed 47 percent to $88.9 million, according to the *Orange County Register.* But, stock price had been sliding, hurt by rising interest rates. The Federal Reserve Board had been boosting interest rates to hold back inflation. Onyx raised its own rates to keep pace; some other lenders had not. Fears of increased loan delinquencies also had depressed stock price. In early March 2000, Onyx slid to around $5 per share, off 44 percent from its July 1999 trading price of about $9 per share.

At the beginning of May 2000, Onyx operated 17 auto finance centers: five in California and one each in Arizona, Washington, Nevada, Florida, Illinois, Georgia, Michigan, New Jersey, North Carolina, Virginia, Pennsylvania, and Texas. An 18th auto finance center opened later in the month in the metropolitan Boston area and an account servicing center, and its 19th auto finance center opened in St. Louis in June. Also in June 2000, the board authorized the company to begin a stock repurchase program. The company considered its stock to be undervalued.

Net income and earnings per diluted share slid in 2001 as compared with 2000, hurt by the national economic slowdown following the September 11 attacks on the United States. The U.S. economy and the used car market remained troubled into 2002. Onyx concentrated on maintaining credit quality and improving operating efficiencies, and proceeded to produce a seventh straight year of profitability.

Continuing the Race: 2003 and Beyond

Overall, Onyx had purchased and securitized more than $9.2 billion in auto contracts by May 2003. The company's auto dealer base numbered 11,000: 90 percent franchised and 10 percent independent. Its finance centers served most areas of the country, particularly targeting those areas with a high concentration of dealerships. Onyx worked with dealers in 36 of the 50 states.

The company's future hinged on a number of risk factors, including competition within the industry, economic conditions, and availability of capital. Among its competitors were captive finance affiliates of major auto manufacturers, banks, independent finance companies, credit unions, and leasing com-

---

Key Dates:

1993: The company is formed by a group of executives experienced in auto finance.
1994: The company begins purchasing, originating, and servicing auto contracts.
1996: Public trading of stock begins.
1997: The company survives a dramatic scale-back of the auto lender industry.
2000: The company is cited as one of the nation's fastest growing companies.
2003: The company enjoys its seventh consecutive year of profitability.

panies. Some of these competitors surpassed Onyx in terms of financial resources, longevity of relationships with dealerships, and range of financing or services. Onyx, in turn, emphasized its superior level of service to dealerships and their customers.

The economy continued to be unsettled into 2003. The deficit was on the rise due to mounting war-against-terror costs, and domestic unemployment rates remained elevated. Onyx planned to introduce a product targeting high-end prime customers and to enter the New York and Ohio markets.

To raise additional funds, Onyx added another route: renewable, unsecured, subordinate notes offered directly to consumers. Investors in the bonds could reap high yields, but only by accepting a high level of risk. The venture was not unlike the auto finance industry, which had fallen from about 30 publicly traded companies in 1996 to five in 2003.

Principal Competitors

Ford Motor Credit; General Motors Acceptance Corporation; Toyota Motor Credit.

Further Reading

Gregory, Michael, "Onyx Grows, Focusing on Superior Product," *Asset Sales Report,* November 15, 1999.

Lubanko, Matthew, "The Hartford Courant, Conn., Money Talk Column," *Knight Ridder/Tribune Business News,* May 18, 2003.

McCabe, Diana, "The Fast Lane Beckons to Auto Lender Onyx," *Orange County Register,* March 5, 2000.

Mouchard, Andre, "Auto Finance Industry Undergoes Tumultuous Period, *Knight-Ridder/Tribune Business News,* February 16, 1997.

——, "Onyx Acceptance Corp. Raises $28.8 Million in Public Offering," *Knight Ridder/Tribune Business News,* March 26, 1996.

"New $150 MLN Deal Meets Onyx Capacity Needs," *Loan Market Week,* September 6, 1999, p. 7.

Rechtin, Mark, "Near-Prime Player Remains Strong," *Automotive News,* March 27, 2000.

Smith, Elliot Blair, "Orange County, Calif., Auto Finance Company Makes Anti-Takeover Move," *Knight Ridder/Tribune Business News,* July 10, 1997.

—Kathleen Peippo

Perrigo Company

515 Eastern Avenue
Allegan, Michigan 49010-9070
U.S.A.
Telephone: (269) 673-8451
Toll Free: (800) 253-3606
Fax: (269) 673-7535
Web site: http://www.perrigo.com

Public Company
Incorporated: 1892
Employees: 3,983
Sales: $826.0 million (2003)
Stock Exchanges: NASDAQ
Ticker Symbol: PRGO
NAIC: 325412 Pharmaceutical Preparation
    Manufacturing; 325413 In-Vitro Diagnostic Substance
    Manufacturing

Perrigo Company is the largest manufacturer of over-the-counter (OTC) pharmaceuticals and nutritional products for store brands in the United States. The company estimates that it holds more than 50 percent of the store brand market. Perrigo produces more than 30 billion pills per year and manufactures about 1,200 products. Most of these are pharmaceuticals—such as analgesics, cough and cold remedies, and gastrointestinal and feminine hygiene products—which account for about four-fifths of the company's sales. Perrigo ranks as the largest producer of aspirin in the United States. The remaining 20 percent of revenues come from the sale of nutritional products, including vitamins and nutritional supplements and drinks. Perrigo supplies 300 different retailers with these products under the retailer's own label so that they can be promoted as house brands. These customers include major drugstore chains (CVS, Eckerd, Walgreens), grocery chains (Albertson's, Kroger, Safeway), mass discounters (Kmart, Target, Wal-Mart), and major wholesalers (McKesson, Supervalu). Perhaps not surprisingly, the largest Perrigo customer by far is retailing giant Wal-Mart, which accounted for 27 percent of net sales for fiscal 2003. The company also markets certain products under its own brand name, Good

Sense, although such products account for only a small percentage of sales. Two non-U.S. subsidiaries generate a little more than 9 percent of revenues. Wrafton Laboratories Ltd. supplies store brand products to major grocery and drug retailers in the United Kingdom, while the Mexican firm Química y Farmacia, S.A. de C.V. produces mainly OTC and prescription pharmaceuticals for retail, wholesale, and government customers. Perrigo Company operates 11 manufacturing plants in Michigan, South Carolina, Mexico, and the United Kingdom. Perrigo has enjoyed nearly continuous growth since the end of World War II. This growth can be partly attributed to the mass acceptance of generic and store brand pharmaceutical products.

Early Years

The company was founded by Luther and Charles Perrigo in 1887. The Perrigo brothers had moved to Allegan County, Michigan, a few years earlier from New York. Once in Michigan the brothers established a modest business. Luther Perrigo ran a country general store and apple drying business, while Charles helped with sales. Luther decided to package generic home remedies and sell them to other small country stores like his own. The first packaging plant for these medicines was run out of Charles Perrigo's home, but Charles soon moved to Ohio, leaving the business entirely to his brother. Luther became president of the firm when it incorporated in 1892. Perrigo remained a family-owned business for 90 years. Five of the company's seven presidents were descendants of Luther Perrigo, who died in 1902. His son Harry became president at that time, holding the position for the next 49 years.

During the 1920s the company turned to the private label concept in order to build customer loyalty. Stores ordering a certain minimum number could have their own names imprinted on the labels. Products of the era that were the subject of such deals included aspirin, bay rum, epsom salts, sweet oil, and zinc oxide. In the mid-1930s Perrigo gained its first major private label customer, the K & W group, a buying organization that evolved into the People's Drug Store chain. The second such customer was Sam's, a major Detroit area drug chain. At the same time the company's customer base was shifting from small general stores to large regional and national drug chains.

Post–World War II Shift from Packager to Manufacturer

Harry Perrigo turned over the reins to his brother Ray in 1951. It was in the 1950s that the company, while still under the leadership of Ray Perrigo and future President William L. Tripp, Sr., made a crucial decision. Perrigo shifted its focus from that of a repackager of generic drugs to a manufacturer of quality drugs and beauty aids.

William L. Tripp, one of Luther Perrigo's grandchildren, became president in 1967. During Tripp's tenure as president the company began to reap the rewards of the change from repackager to manufacturer. The company's income and the number of Perrigo employees quadrupled. When Tripp died in 1969 his son Bill Tripp, Jr., took over the presidency. During the 1970s Perrigo's base of customers expanded with the addition of grocery chains and mass merchandisers to the core drugstore chains. By the time of his death in a boating accident in 1980 at the age of 45, Perrigo was the leading private label manufacturer of health and beauty products in the United States. William C. Swaney had been named president of the company two years before the accident, becoming the first leader of the company who was not a member of the Perrigo family.

End of Family Ownership: Early 1980s

Swaney's presidency lasted from 1978 until 1983. In those five years Perrigo sales tripled and the company became a much larger operation all around. Swaney acquired new companies, set up distribution centers in three states, and expanded and refurbished existing plants. Before leaving as president Swaney oversaw the sale of the company from the Perrigo family to the management. After almost 100 years of family operation the company was sold.

Michael Jandernoa, who had joined the company in 1979 as vice-president for finance, became the seventh president of Perrigo in 1984, while Swaney took over as chairman of the board and CEO. Swaney instituted a style of management at Perrigo that his successor Jandernoa admitted he probably would have tried to block had he been in a position to do so at the time. Yet Jandernoa came to appreciate the open style of administration that Swaney initiated. The company contended that the different disciplines interacted in the decision-making process much more than in traditional American businesses.

Part of the Grow Group, 1986–88

Jandernoa continued the policy of expansion started by Swaney. Perrigo acquired Bell Pharmacal Labs of South Caro-

lina in 1984. Early in the Jandernoa presidency, however, the board of directors began entertaining offers from larger companies that might want to acquire Perrigo itself. In 1986 Perrigo became the largest single company in Grow Group, Inc., a publicly held group of 23 manufacturing companies that bought Perrigo for $45 million. Jandernoa was named CEO of Perrigo; he continued to serve as president. Perrigo represented about a third of Grow Group. As the largest component in a conglomerate with access to funds through the New York Stock Exchange, Perrigo was able to raise new funds for more expansion.

Perrigo celebrated the company's centenary with two ambitious building projects. It built a $1.5 million plant for the manufacture of effervescent tablets and a $3.5 million graphics art complex to house all of the company's printing needs. Because Perrigo supplied many different retailers with the same house brand product, their printing facilities were an important part of their production system. The graphics and printing department employed about 290 people and produced almost 70 percent of the company's labels and 44 percent of their cartons in the early 1990s. The construction of the graphics department, coupled with other expenses, totaled approximately $12.6 million in outlays to the company's printing and graphics department since the Grow purchase in 1986.

Back to Management Ownership and Then Taken Public: Late 1980s to Early 1990s

After only two years as a part of Grow Group, however, Perrigo was sold back to its management in 1988 in a $106 million deal. That year the company posted sales of $146 million, but by 1994 company sales had ballooned to $669 million. Three years after the sale by Grow to Perrigo management, Jandernoa took the company public. The stock proved popular, though the value fell and rose significantly over time. The market value of the company in July 1994 based on a closing price of $14 a share was $1 billion, for instance. But this price was down from a value of $32 a share in January 1994.

The drop in the value of Perrigo shares was attributed to a drop in sales growth. The company, in fact, had another year of record sales and continued to expand, but stock speculators felt that the market had overreacted to the Perrigo stock offering and had inflated the value beyond its true market worth. Some analysts predicted that the drop in growth was a sign that the national brands would win back bargain-hunting customers in a healthy economy.

Other problems that Perrigo faced in its competition with national brands in the early 1990s concerned finding the right price range for its products. While Perrigo had long wielded its ability to offer lower prices than national brand competitors, sometimes the price difference could be so dramatic—more than 50 percent in some cases—that it could have a reverse effect on the consumer. The consumer weighed the relative cost savings with a judgment on efficacy equivalence. If the price difference was too dramatic, some observers contended, the consumer became suspicious of the Perrigo brand and turned to the national brand. Perrigo therefore developed a system whereby some of the money that it saved from advertising was spent on market research to determine exactly how its products were accepted by the consumer, which products were worth

Key Dates:

1887: Luther and Charles Perrigo begin packaging generic home remedies and selling them at their own and to other general stores.
1892: Company is incorporated.
1920s: Perrigo begins offering private label products.
1930s: Customer base begins to shift from general stores to large regional and national drug chains.
1950s: Company shifts from a repackager of generic drugs to a manufacturer of quality drugs and beauty aids.
1970s: Grocery chains and mass merchandisers are added to the customer base.
1980: Perrigo is now the nation's largest private label manufacturer of health and beauty products.
Early 1980s: Perrigo family ownership ends with the sale of the company to management.
1986: Company is sold to Grow Group, Inc. for $45 million.
1988: Grow Group sells the company back to management for $106 million.
1991: Perrigo is taken public.
1997: Controlling stake in Mexican pharmaceutical firm Química y Farmacia, S.A. de C.V. is acquired.
1998: Perrigo posts a net loss of $51.6 million thanks to a restructuring of its personal care business.
1999: The personal care business is divested to focus the company on OTC drugs and nutritional products.
2001: Perrigo acquires Wrafton Laboratories Ltd., a U.K. maker of store brand pharmaceuticals.

developing, and which had limited potential because of brand allegiance.

One reason for Perrigo's enormous dominance over the store brand market was its ability to work closely with retailers to promote consumer allegiance to store brands. Beginning in the 1980s Perrigo began a major campaign to help retailers design labels, manage inventory, and develop promotions. Perrigo used its house printing and graphics department to ensure accuracy and reliability in labeling and packaging, permitting rapid new product introductions. Perrigo also enjoyed an advantage over many of its competitors because retail stores had a real incentive to give Perrigo's product prominence on their shelves. Profit margins for store brand products were considerably greater than for national brands. The store's public image could be enhanced as well, provided the product sold under their name was satisfactory.

Most of Perrigo's products were packaged to be readily identifiable with the national brand equivalents. There was a fine line between taking advantage of the competitor's advertising and carving out a niche that was independently recognized by the consumer. The *OTC Market Report* disclosed in 1995 that the company was threatened with lawsuits "once or twice a year," but the vast majority of them were settled in a short period of time. Most of the disputes focused on product dress rather than the actual content of the product. While Perrigo management had become accustomed to lawsuits from competi-

tor companies, in July 1994 Perrigo found itself faced with a lawsuit from closer to home. Its former parent company, Grow Group, filed suit against the company. The Grow Group, valued at less than half of Perrigo, demanded the return of Perrigo stock or a sizable settlement in lieu thereof. Grow claimed that Perrigo management did not act in good faith at the time of the 1988 sale, particularly alleging that they did not reveal a pending agreement to supply products to Wal-Mart, and asked for $2 billion in actual damages and $2 billion in punitive damages. Perrigo contended that the suit was wholly without merit.

One of the company's strengths was that it faced little legitimate competition. In December 1994 the company purchased Vi-Jon Laboratories, Inc., a leading manufacturer of store brand personal care products, thereby expanding Perrigo's sales and eliminating a potential competitor at the same time. The purchase price was about $33 million. A similar acquisition occurred earlier, in January 1992, when Cumberland-Swan, Inc., a Tennessee-based maker of store brand personal care products and vitamins, was bought for $35 million.

As the patents on dozens of major prescription drugs began to run out in the mid-1990s, Perrigo began to aggressively go after these lucrative new sources of revenue. Once a prescription drug was reclassified as OTC, the patent holder had two years of exclusivity. At that point generic versions of brand-name OTC products could be produced. An example of this process was Tavist-D, a decongestant and antihistamine that switched from prescription-only to OTC status in 1992. Two years later, Perrigo reached an agreement with the drug's maker, Sandoz Pharmaceuticals Corp., to begin making a store brand version of Tavist-D in 1995. In subsequent years, Perrigo increasingly turned to such joint ventures to develop new products.

Also in the mid-1990s, Perrigo began looking to the international market for growth, forming subsidiary Perrigo International, Inc. to lead this effort. Among the initially targeted countries were Canada, Japan, Mexico, and Russia.

Late 1990s Travails

With the Grow Group lawsuit still pending, Perrigo received another legal headache in early 1995 when it was the subject of a class-action lawsuit initiated by shareholders. The investors had purchased company stock through an October 1993 secondary offering, in which mostly shares held by company officials were sold. Only a few months later the stock price plunged after its stellar earnings growth began to fade. The plaintiffs claimed that company officials inflated the stock's offering price by withholding critical information indicating potential problems facing Perrigo. By the late 1990s, however, both this suit and the one brought by the Grow Group had been dismissed, but not before Perrigo had spent about $27 million defending itself against the suits, which also served as a major distraction.

Revenue growth slowed and profits fell in both fiscal 1995 and 1996 thanks to a number of factors: stiffer competition, including surging sales of the pain reliever Aleve, which switched to OTC status in 1994 and cut into Perrigo's analgesic sales; difficulties with the personal care product lines that had been acquired from Vi-Jon Laboratories; and two unusually weak cold and flu seasons in a row. Perrigo responded in June

1995 with a restructuring involving 180 job cuts, a reduction in distribution centers from seven to four, and a merger of sales and marketing functions across all of the company's product lines.

Results for fiscal 1997 were better with both revenues and profits on the upswing. Aiding this performance was the launch of additional store brand products for former prescription drugs that had switched to OTC status. These included Aleve and the hair-restoration product Rogaine. In late 1997 Perrigo purchased an 88 percent stake in Química y Farmacia, S.A. de C.V. (Quífa) for $17 million. Based in Monterrey, Mexico, Quífa was a producer of both OTC and prescription products. The purchase provided Perrigo with its first manufacturing capacity outside of the United States.

Perrigo also spent $14 million to acquire a minority stake in Sagmel, Inc., the biggest distributor of pharmaceutical products in Russia and the Ukraine, in 1997. This move soon turned disastrous, however, when the Russian economic crisis erupted, and the subsequent devaluation of the ruble cost the company millions—and ended its Russian venture. Compounding the company's difficulties was the continuing poor performance of its personal care business. In June 1998 Perrigo announced that it would sell this unit, which included baby care items, toothpaste, deodorants, and other products, in order to focus on its higher-margin OTC drug and nutritional product lines. Two plants in California and Missouri were closed, eliminating about 160 jobs from the workforce, and an $86.9 million restructuring charge was taken, resulting in a net loss for the year of $51.6 million.

Yet more difficulties cropped up following the extremely botched implementation of a new companywide computer system. Installation of the system began in September 1998, and it would take 18 months before all of the problems were ironed out. Perrigo suffered tens of millions of dollars in lost revenues because products could not be shipped to its customers. New product development was largely put on hold as company officials had to concentrate on the computer fiasco. The company did manage to sell its personal care business, offloading it in August 1999 to a Nashville investor group calling itself Cumberland Swan Holdings Inc. A further cost-cutting move in 1999 involved the elimination of another 130 jobs from the company payroll, a measure aimed at saving as much as $6 million a year.

Effecting a Turnaround Under New Leadership in the Early 2000s

In May 2000 David T. Gibbons was brought onboard as president and CEO; Jandernoa remained chairman. Reputed to be a turnaround artist, Gibbons had more than three decades of experience at two major consumer goods companies, Minnesota Mining & Manufacturing Company and Rubbermaid Incorporated. Gibbons joined Perrigo at a particularly dark time; investors had pummeled the stock, sending it down to just over $5 per share.

Within months of taking his post, the new leader had to grapple with two more challenges. In August 2000 the Food and Drug Administration (FDA) issued a warning letter to the company because it had mislabeled 500-mg acetaminophen as 200-mg ibuprofen. Perrigo voluntarily stopped production of the product, and the FDA said that it would not approve any new Perrigo products until the quality-control issue was fixed. Gibbons soon had 130 people working on this issue, and when the FDA revisited the plant in question in May 2001, it received a clean bill of health. The company was then able within the next couple of months to rush to market two new products, private-label versions of Pepcid AC, an acid reducer, and Advil Cold and Sinus. Perrigo was now placing an increasing emphasis on being the first to market, particularly with products switching from prescription to OTC status, because a new FDA incentive gave the first to market with such a "switch" drug a 180-day period of exclusivity before competitors could join the fray—a keen advantage. In the early 2000s, Perrigo succeeded in being first to market on 80 percent of the switch products it sold; in fact, with one-third of such products, Perrigo remained the only supplier of a store brand equivalent.

In November 2000, meanwhile, the FDA recommended that phenylpropanolamine (PPA), a key ingredient in many cough and cold remedies, no longer be considered safe because it was believed to cause hemorrhagic stroke. Perrigo used PPA in ten of its product formulas, resulting in a huge recall that cost the company about $21 million. Despite these latest difficulties, Perrigo managed to achieve a profit of $27.7 million in fiscal 2001, which was a 43 percent increase over the prior year. In June 2001, at the end of that fiscal year, Perrigo paid $44 million to acquire Wrafton Laboratories Ltd., a manufacturer of store brand products for grocery and pharmacy retailers in the United Kingdom.

During fiscal 2002 and 2003 Perrigo achieved steadily increasing profits and made numerous new product introductions. In fiscal 2002 these included store brand equivalents of Excedrin Migraine and Centrum Performance, a multivitamin. Perrigo that year began an expansion of its research and development lab in Allegan to bolster its ability to develop new products. In addition, the Mexican subsidiary Quífa, now wholly owned by Perrigo, was restructured in order to build its store brand business and deemphasize its prescription drug activities. In January 2003 Perrigo's recovery had proceeded to the point where it could count on ongoing cash flow—and could begin paying a dividend for the first time. That same month, the company signed an agreement with Andrx Corporation whereby Andrx would manufacture and Perrigo would package and resell several versions of Claritin. A blockbuster as a prescription allergy drug, Claritin was the latest brand-name drug to make the switch to an OTC product—and it was potentially one of the most lucrative for the likes of Perrigo. In June 2003 the company began shipping a store brand version of Claritin-D 24 Hour. Two months later, Gibbons was rewarded for his turnaround efforts by being named to the additional post of chairman; Jandernoa relinquished the post but remained on the board of directors. A newly confident Perrigo also announced at this same time that it would spend $5 million to $7 million over the following year in an attempt to capture a share of the rapidly growing generic prescription drug market. It appeared that a resurgently formidable player in the pharmaceutical industry—the undisputed leader in the store brand OTC sector—was about to take on some new competition.

Principal Subsidiaries

L. Perrigo Company; Perrigo Company of South Carolina, Inc.; Perrigo de México S.A. de C.V.; Química y Farmacia, S.A. de C.V. (Mexico); Wrafton Laboratories Ltd. (U.K.).

Principal Competitors

Johnson & Johnson; Novartis AG; Bayer AG; Pfizer Inc.; Wyeth; GlaxoSmithKline plc; Alpharma Inc.; Bristol-Myers Squibb Company; Johnson & Johnson - Merck Consumer Pharmaceuticals Co.; Leiner Health Products LLC; Schering-Plough Corporation.

Further Reading

Benson, Tracy, "Industry's Unsung Heroes: Michael Jandernoa," *Industry Week,* December 7, 1992, pp. 31–32.

Brammer, Rhonda, "The Right Medicine," *Barron's,* May 27, 2002, p. 26.

Couretas, John, "Perrigo Flies High with Humble Products," *Grand Rapids (Mich.) Press,* March 29, 1992, p. D1.

Crawley, Nancy, " 'It's Tough to Knock Us Off the Shelf,' Perrigo Shows," *Grand Rapids (Mich.) Press,* June 10, 2001, p. G1.

Czurak, David, "Judge Tosses Suit Brought by Former Perrigo Owner," *Grand Rapids (Mich.) Business Journal,* June 29, 1998, p. 8.

Geer, John F., Jr., "The Private-Label Hoax," *Financial World,* October 10, 1995, pp. 34, 36.

Gold, Howard R., "High Priced Brand?," *Barron's,* January 31, 1994, pp. 36–37.

Kirkbride, Rob, "Perrigo Counts on Prescriptions for Healthy Growth," *Grand Rapids (Mich.) Press,* August 12, 2003, p. A13.

Lane, Amy, "Pushing Perrigo Overseas," *Crain's Detroit Business,* March 18, 1996, p. I4.

Liscio, John, "No Go for Perrigo," *Barron's,* March 21, 1994, pp. 14–15.

Morris, Kathleen, "No-Name Power," *Financial World,* March 16, 1993, pp. 28–33.

"Perrigo Profile," *OTC Market Report,* January 1994, pp. 1–6.

Prince, Ted, "Plagiarism-Driven Business Strategy," *Journal of Business Strategy,* September/October 1993, pp. 16–17.

Radigan, Mary, and Barbara Wieland, "Drug Recall Will Cost Perrigo $15 Million," *Grand Rapids (Mich.) Press,* November 8, 2000, p. C6.

Rohan, Barry, "Pain into Profit," *Detroit Free Press,* January 20, 1993, p. 1E.

Sabo, Mary Ann, "Perrigo Dumps Personal Care Business, Shuts Plants," *Grand Rapids (Mich.) Press,* June 30, 1998, p. B5.

Shellum, Bernie, "Perrigo Is Sued by Former Owner," *Detroit Free Press,* July 29, 1994, p. 2E.

Stern, Gabriella, "Cheap Imitation: Perrigo's Knockoffs of Name-Brand Drugs Turn into Big Sellers," *Wall Street Journal,* July 15, 1993, p. A1.

Whisenhunt, Eric, "Wall Street's Loss, Perrigo's Gain," *Michigan Business,* September 1988, p. 21.

Wieland, Barbara, "No More Bitter Pills? New CEO Confident He Has Prescription for Turning Perrigo Around," *Grand Rapids (Mich.) Press,* October 1, 2000, p. B1.

——, "Perrigo Hires New CEO, President," *Grand Rapids (Mich.) Press,* April 21, 2000, p. A10.

Wieland, Barbara, and Chris Knape, "Claritin Call: Perrigo Cannot Wait to Offer a Generic Equivalent," *Grand Rapids (Mich.) Press,* November 10, 2002, p. E1.

—Donald C. McManus and Hilary Gopnik
—update: David E. Salamie

Pioneer Natural Resources Company

5205 N. O'Connor Boulevard, Suite 1400
Irving, Texas 75039
U.S.A.
Telephone: (972) 444-9001
Fax: (972) 969-3576
Web site: http://www.pioneernrc.com

Public Company
Incorporated: 1997
Employees: 979
Sales: $717.4 million (2002)
Stock Exchanges: New York
Ticker Symbol: PXD
NAIC: 211111 Crude Petroleum and Natural Gas
        Extraction

Pioneer Natural Resources Company is a gas and oil exploration, development, and production company, with onshore and offshore properties in the United States, Canada, Argentina, South Africa, Tunisia, and Gabon. Domestic properties include the West Panhandle gas field and Spraberry Trend oilfield, both in Texas and the Hugoton gas field in southwestern Kansas; gas processing facilities are located in Fain, Texas, and in Satana, Kansas. Pioneer owns and operates the Falcon gas fields in the Gulf of Mexico, southeast of Corpus Christi, and holds a working interest in several offshore exploration and development projects in the deepwater Gulf, including Devils Tower oilfield, southeast of New Orleans. On Alaska's North Slope, Pioneer holds an interest in ten oil development sites on the Kuparuk River field. The producing Chinchaga gas field in northeast British Columbia, Canada, includes gas processing facilities and a pipeline. International interests include the Sable oilfield in shallow water offshore South Africa, the Adam oilfield onshore in Tunisia, and exploration and development properties in Gabon. Producing and development properties in Argentina are located in the Tierra del Fuego and Neuquen Basin and produce oil, gas, and natural gas liquids. As of December 31, 2002, Pioneer held proved reserves of 737.7 MBOE (million barrels of oil equivalent), equivalent to 380.8 million barrels of oil and natural gas liquids and 2.1 billion cubic feet of natural gas. Mid-continent properties in Texas and Kansas accounted for approximately two-thirds of proved reserves.

1997 Merger Creating Growth-Driven Company

Pioneer Natural Resources Company formed in April 1997 through the merger of Parker & Parsley Petroleum Company and Mesa, Inc., companies whose histories in the oil and gas industry trace back to the 1950s and 1970s, respectively. Mesa CEO Jon Brumley initiated the merger after Richard Rainwater, a wealthy investor who saved Mesa from bankruptcy in 1996, hired Brumley for the purpose of helping Mesa grow beyond its debt-ridden state. Brumley found an interest and a good strategic fit in Parker & Parsley. Upon shareholder approval in August, Pioneer opened on the New York Stock Exchange at slightly more than $37 per share. Parker & Parsley Chairman Scott Sheffield took the positions of president and CEO and Brumley became chairman.

The merger formed the third largest independent oil and gas exploration and production company at that time. The new company owned proved reserves of 611 MBOE, primarily located in the West Panhandle and Hugoton gas fields and the Spraberry Trend oilfield. These long-lived resources provided a dependable base of low-risk revenues that could be invested to expand the company. Pioneer planned to increase development and production in these areas, including 600 development wells in Spraberry Trend. Pioneer also planned exploration and development in 200 locations at the Greenhill Petroleum properties in the Gulf of Mexico just purchased by Mesa. Pioneer's goal was to double its growth over five years, primarily through acquisition, seeking opportunities in the East Texas basin, the Rocky Mountain region, and Canada. The company prepared to increase exploration as well, by expanding its team of geoscientists, particularly with expertise in deepwater exploration.

Seeking to improve the company's cash flow, Pioneer expanded immediately through two acquisitions. In September Pioneer announced an agreement to acquire Chauvco Resources Ltd., of Calgary, Alberta, involving properties in western Canada and Argentina with 153 million proven BOE of gas and oil properties and a backlog of 1,700 drilling locations. The $1.2 billion stock transaction involved a stock exchange valued at

Company Perspectives:

"We have the right strategy, the financial strength and the organizational agility to sustain an aggressive pace. Our strategy for growth combines selective investment in exploration balanced with aggressive development in our core areas and complementary acquisitions."
—Scott D. Sheffield, chairman, president, and CEO

$975 million and $220 million in assumed debt. In October Pioneer announced that it would acquire assets in East Texas Permian Basin from subsidiaries of Belgium's Electrafina, for $157 million in cash and stock. Pioneer obtained producing wells, land, seismic data and royalties, and a gathering system, pipeline, and gas processing plant. Pioneer became one of the largest holders of acreage in the East Texas basin, with assets producing 25 MMcfd (million cubic feet per day) of gas.

To fund acquisitions and maintain cash flow Pioneer sold several properties that no longer fit with the company's goals. Pioneer sold properties in the Permian Basin of West Texas for $55 million in cash and properties in Oklahoma, the Texas Panhandle, and along the Gulf of Mexico in Texas and Louisiana for $50 million. The company placed for sale another 425 properties originally owned by Parker & Parsley, accounting for 95 percent of domestic fields but only 15 percent of cash flow. After divestments and acquisitions Pioneer held 762 BOE proved reserves at the end of 1997, equal to 384 million barrels of crude oil and natural gas liquids and 2.3 trillion cubic feet of natural gas.

Oversupply of Gas and Oil Constricting Revenues in the Company's First Year

Pioneer's pursuit of growth encountered major difficulties when gas and oil prices declined significantly in late 1997, decreasing the value of certain reserves and forcing the company to sell many properties. In the fourth quarter Pioneer took a noncash write-down of $863 million on certain reserves, resulting in a loss of $890.7 million on revenues of $546 million in 1997. As prices continued to decline in 1998, to as low as $10 per barrel of oil, Pioneer reduced its 1998 capital budget from $600 million to $480 million, allocating $265 million to develop producing wells, $115 million for exploration, and $60 million in property acquisitions. Other cost reduction activities included consolidation of administration activities to the Irving, Texas headquarters and closure of the Corpus Christi, Texas office, eliminating 200 staff positions. In 1999 the company closed offices in Houston and Oklahoma City, eliminating an additional 150 jobs.

Pioneer's new emphasis on exploration resulted in significant oil and gas discoveries in 1998 and 1999. Using the latest 3-D seismic imaging technology, Pioneer made a significant discovery at the Greenhill properties along the Gulf coast off Louisiana, which tested at 3,000 Bbl/d (barrels per day) of oil and 7 MMcfd of gas. Through a joint venture with state-owned Soeker Exploration & Production Pty., Ltd., in which Pioneer owned a 49 percent interest, the company made the Sable oil discovery in shallow water offshore South Africa in June 1998. In the deepwater Gulf, a joint venture made the March 1999

Aconcagua discovery in a lease property known as Mississippi Canyon Block 35, in which Pioneer owned a 25 percent interest. Exploration continued in South Africa, Gabon, Argentina, and gas fields in Canada.

For 1999, the $300 million capital budget was cut further as low gas and oil prices averaging $15.36 Bbl oil hindered cash flow. In April 1999 Pioneer halted plans for exploratory drilling at offshore sites in South Africa and the U.S. Gulf Coast Transition Zone. Exploration continued in both the deepwater Gulf and onshore wells in Louisiana and Texas. Pioneer also allocated $100 million to develop gas wells in Canada, Argentina, and the U.S. mainland.

To service a high level of debt Pioneer divested properties in 1999, including many along the Gulf Coast, for a total of $410 million. In May the company sold a package of 400 domestic oilfields to Prize Energy, formed by executives and directors of Pioneer who resigned their positions to lead the new company. Pioneer received $215 million in cash and $30 million in stock from Prize. Pioneer sold additional properties through ten separate deals for a total of $105 million. The largest sale, at $62.3 million, involved natural gas properties in South Texas. The company sold noncore Canadian properties and the West Texas field, but kept its northeast British Columbia property, the Chinchaga gas field, where a gas pipeline was under construction.

The sale of property resulted in a profit for the third quarter of 1999, but Pioneer ended the year with a loss of $22.5 million on revenues of $644.6 million. While revenues represented a 9 percent decline from 1998, these were derived from fewer working assets, as Pioneer had become a more streamlined company. The average cost of production per BOE had declined from $2.40 in 1998 to $2.11 in 1999.

Pioneer's capital investment focused on opportunities that would provide long-term reserves. In November 1999 Pioneer acquired two properties in Argentina's Neuquen Basin for $40 million, involving eight blocks over 230,000 acres. The properties held net proven reserves of 7.7 million BOE with existing wells producing 2,000 Bbl/d and 9 MMcfd. Pioneer planned to invest $1.2 billion during the course of 17-year concession contracts. Exploration at the new property procured a discovery with the first well in the Al Sur de la Dorsal Block in February 2000.

Pioneer continued to improve its operating cash flow in 2000, selling shares of Prize Energy for $18.6 million in March 2000. The company divested $102.7 million in nonaffiliated entity and noncore domestic properties located in Oklahoma, Louisiana, and New Mexico. The company sought funding through the issuance of $400 million in ten-year bonds, but stopped the plan when interest lagged. Oil and gas prices continued to rise during 2000, however, allowing Pioneer to improve its balance sheet without the bonds and to expand its holdings through incremental increases in existing interests.

In late 2000 Pioneer invested a total of $38 million in development properties, notably in the deepwater Gulf of Mexico discoveries and Chinchaga gas fields. For $23 million the company acquired 12 nonproducing blocks in the Gulf of Mexico, including a 33.3 percent interest in the Camden Hills gas discovery in Mississippi Canyon, for a total 18 percent interest in the Canyon Express development project where the

Aconcagua discovery is located. Pioneer increased to 20 percent its interest in the Devil's Tower oil discovery in Mississippi Canyon. Pioneer became sole owner of the Chinchaga gas field in British Columbia, acquiring the remaining 13 percent interest in that property. The company planned 70 extension and infill wells at Chinchaga over the next three drilling seasons.

During 2000, Pioneer became a profitable company. Although the company's producing assets had declined significantly, higher gas and oil prices offset the changes. Revenues of $852.7 million and net profit of $152.2 million originated from 4,717 gross productive wells (gross wells in which the company owns a working interest; 2,970 net wells based on percentage of ownership), compared with $711.5 million in 1998 revenues from 13,184 gross productive wells (7,378 net). On average across all geographic regions, oil prices rose from $13.00 Bbl in 1998 to $24.01 Bbl, and natural gas liquids prices rose from $8.90 Bbl to $20.27 Bbl; gas prices rose from $1.80 Mcf (thousand cubic feet) to $2.81 Mcf. Overall production declined across geographic region and type of mineral, with a significant decline in oil and gas production in the United States and in gas production in Canada. In Argentina gas production increased by more than one-third over those three years, however.

Pioneer prepared for long-term growth through exploration and development. Of 1,168 gross development and exploratory wells drilled from 1998 to 2000 (852.8 wells net), 92 percent was successfully completed as productive. As immediate demand and commodity prices rose, Pioneer increased production and development. In 2000 Pioneer put 86 oil wells into production at Spraberry Trend and 51 gas wells at the West Panhandle field, and two development wells were completed at the Hugoton field in 2000. In Canada 17 of 21 development wells and 12 of 14 development wells were successfully completed. In Argentina, 28 of 30 development well and 38 of 54 exploratory wells were successfully completed. At the end of fiscal 2000 Pioneer reported proved reserves of 87.2 Mbls of oil and natural gas liquids and 419.6 billion cubic feet of natural gas.

Early 2000s: Consolidating Assets and Developing New Discoveries

As Pioneer returned to profitability, the company increased its 2001 capital budget by 28 percent to $430 million. The company allocated $115 million for international exploration and development projects and $315 million for domestic projects, the latter involving $244 million for development at low-risk, long-lived domestic fields and $74.5 million for exploration and development projects in the deepwater Gulf. Funds applied to development included new discovery sites scheduled to become productive in 2002 and 2003. Pioneer expected its hedging contracts to produce more cash flow than the capital budget required, allowing the company to apply excess funds to debt reduction, stock repurchase, core area acquisitions, and further development. With the help of higher oil and natural gas prices the company reduced its debt from $1.6 billion to $700 million during the second quarter 2001.

Pioneer's exploration activities procured several new discoveries in 2001. Overseas, Pioneer was successful in finding significant oil and gas in the Boomslang prospect south of Mossel Bay, South Africa. Pioneer owned a 49 percent working interest in the joint venture with the state-owned Soeker. In May Pioneer made a discovery in Gabon at Olowi block in offshore West Africa, a wholly owned working interest. Deepwater Gulf of Mexico exploration resulted in the Falcon discovery in April and the Ozona Deep discovery in October, with Pioneer owning a 45 percent interest and a 32 percent interest in the properties, respectively. The Ozona Deep discovery represented the company's 13th successful discovery of 17 exploration wells drilled in the Gulf of Mexico since 1998. Exploration of deepwater locations resulted in a discovery at the Turnberry prospect as well, where Pioneer owned a 40 percent working interest.

In 2001 Argentina acquired or increased to 100 percent its interests in four properties in the Neuquen Basin. The Anticlinal Campamento block included a newly developed field producing 7 Mcbd of gas and the Cerro Vagon block where several discoveries would be further appraised. Construction projects involved production facilities and a pipeline for Loma Negra Norte field and an NGL extraction facility (for recovering ethane, propane, butane, and other sales quality gases) at the Loma Negra gas complex. Construction completed on a dehydration plan and an eight-mile pipeline allowed production to begin at the Lago Fuego block in Tierra del Fuego, extracting 200 Bbls of natural gas liquids per day and 7 MMcfd of natural gas.

Pioneer completed the merger of 42 Parker & Parsley Limited Partnerships, involving privately and publicly owned stock. Shareholders approved the merger in December 2001; four partnerships, however, did not approve the merger and remained partially owned subsidiaries of the company. Pioneer issued $99.2 million in a stock exchange. Aggregate reserves of the partnerships involved 29 million BOE of gas and oil reserves, including the dependable Spraberry Trend. In other business, Pioneer increased its interests in the Aconcagua field and Canyon Express pipeline project, to 37.5 percent and 23.5 percent, respectively, for $25.5 million.

In the spring of 2002 Pioneer offered 11 million new shares of stock at $21.40 per share, netting $235 million to fund $193 million in acquisitions. In addition, the company sold $150 million in senior notes to refinance debt. Acquisitions involved increasing the company's working interest in several development projects. Pioneer acquired a 25 percent interest in the Falcon field, increasing its interest to 75 percent; the project became the first deepwater Gulf project for Pioneer to operate. Pioneer acquired an additional 25 percent working increase in 11 blocks in the vicinity of the Falcon field, as well as a 100 percent interest for ten development blocks in the area. In addition, Pioneer became the sole owner of field and gathering systems at the West Panhandle gas field.

With a capital budget of $425 million in 2002, Pioneer prepared to exploit its discoveries with several projects in development for initial production in 2002 and 2003. Development of discoveries in the deepwater Gulf involved the Falcon and Devil's Tower discoveries, with production expected to begin in 2003 and 2004, respectively. The Sable oil well development project began in late 2001, with initial production slated to begin within 12 to 18 months. Gas production began at the Camden Hills discoveries at Canyon Express in September 2002, extracting 110 to 120 MMcfd of gas with prices rising to new highs. During 2002 Pioneer placed 89 new wells on production at the Spraberry Trend and 40 wells at West Panhandle and began evaluation of new development sites at Hugoton.

In September 2002 Pioneer found oil in Tunisia's Ghadames Basin, where the company owned a 40 percent working interest. The primary zone at Adam 1 well tested at 3,500 Bbl/d. Through use of nearby production facilities development of the well progressed quickly and production began in May 2003, with first sales expected by the end of the year. Pioneer continued development and exploration in the Adam concession as well as exploration in the Anaquid permit, the latter operated by Anadarko.

Progress in other international locations involved renegotiation of Pioneer's exploration interests in Gabon and initial production at the Sable field, after some delays due to problems with leased equipment, in late 2003. In Argentina's Neuquen province a $23 million liquefied petroleum gas plant began production. Pioneer concentrated activities on extension and development wells in the oil reserves in the Neuquen Basin.

The company acquired a 70 percent working interest in oil exploration on Alaska's North Slope. Pioneer operated ten leases covering 14,000 acres in the Kuparuk River field for its partner Armstrong Resources. In early 2003 the company drilled three exploration wells in NW Kuparuk, testing for possible extension wells in shallow waters offshore. Potential production at the Kuparuk prospects was estimated at one half billion BOE, with production expected to begin in 2005, increasing to 50,000 to 75,000 barrels of oil per day by 2008.

Pioneer acquired full interest in 32 blocks at the Falcon discovery area in June 2003 for $113 million cash. The acquisitions included the Harrier field, a satellite discovery made in early 2003. Production began at Falcon in April and tie-back production from the Harrier field was expected to be completed in early 2004. Pioneer estimated that together the Falcon and Harrier wells would produce 275 MMcfd in gas. Exploration procured two additional discoveries, the Tomahawk prospect and the Raptor field, in August and September, respectively. Pioneer planned to tie-back the Tomahawk and Raptor wells to Falcon platform for production in 2004. The tie-back system provided a cost-efficient method of expanding production and the Falcon facility accommodated up to 400 MMcfd.

Principal Subsidiaries

Pioneer Natural Gas Company; Pioneer Natural Resources Alaska, Inc.; Pioneer Natural Resources (Argentina) S.A.; Pioneer Natural Resources (Tierra Del Fuego) S.A.; Pioneer Natural Resources Canada, Inc.; Pioneer Natural Resources South Africa Limited; Pioneer Natural Resources Tunisia Ltd.; Pioneer Natural Resources USA, Inc.; Pioneer Resources Gabon-Olowi, Ltd.; Westpan Resources Company.

Principal Competitors

Apache Corporation; BP plc; Chesapeake Energy Corporation.

Further Reading

Brocato, Bill, ''New 'Mega-independent' Pioneer Looks to Exploration for Next Growth Phase,'' *Oil and Gas Journal,* July 27, 1998, p. 31.

Broyles, Karen, ''Pioneer Sets Spending for 1998 at $600 Million, Announces Asset Sales,'' *Oil Daily,* November 17, 1997, p. 10.

Cawley, Rusty, ''Pioneer Moves to Cut Its Bank Debt in Half,'' *Dallas Business Journal,* March 31, 2000, p. 8.

Collin, Jane, ''Pioneer Makes Debut As No. 3 Independent,'' *Oil Daily,* August 11, 1997, p. 9.

——, ''Pioneer to Add East Texas Assets to Portfolio,'' *Oil Daily,* October 28, 1997, p. 5.

Fletcher, Sam, ''Pioneer Buys Stakes in Argentine Properties,'' *Oil Daily,* November 24, 1999.

——, ''Pioneer Nets $105 Million As It Inks 10 Deals for Spin-offs in Canada, Texas,'' *Oil Daily,* June 17, 1999, p. FAUL99168008.

''Interview with Scott D. Sheffield, Chairman, President and CEO of Pioneer Natural Resources Co.,'' *Oil and Gas Investor,* October 2001, p. 1S19.

Mack, Toni, ''Staying at Home,'' *Forbes,* October 26, 1992, p. 47.

''Mesa Stockholders OK Proposal Giving Control to Rainwater,'' *Oil Daily,* June 26, 1996, p. 5.

Nulty, Peter, ''Boone Pickens, Company Hunter,'' *Fortune,* December 26, 1983, p. 54.

Pillar, Dan, ''Fort Worth, Texas-Based Pioneer Natural Resources Buying Canadian Oil Firm,'' *Knight Ridder/Tribune Business News,* September 4, 1997.

''Pioneer Announces Series of Exploration Successes,'' *Canadian Corporate News,* April 25, 2001.

''Pioneer Announces 2001 Capital Budget,'' *Canadian Corporate News,* January 9, 2001.

''Pioneer Makes Gulf Gas Discovery,'' *Oil Daily,* August 19, 2003.

''Pioneer Makes Raptor Find,'' *Oil Daily,* September 18, 2003.

''Pioneer Makes 3 Deals to Acquire Properties,'' *Oil Daily,* October 24, 2000.

''Pioneer Natural Resources Co., Dallas, Has Acquired the Remaining Interest in 32 Blocks in the Falcon Area in the Deepwater Gulf of Mexico,'' *Oil and Gas Investor,* June 2003, p. 68.

''Pioneer Natural Resources Co./Irving, Texas Fuel Search Takes Patience, But Payoff Is Huge,'' *Investor's Business Daily,* June 14, 2001, p. A12.

''Pioneer Natural Resources Co. – Receives Limited Partners' Approval to Merge 42 Parker & Parsley – Limited Partnerships,'' *Market News Publishing,* December 21, 2001.

''Pioneer Natural Resources Co. – Test Results of Boomslang Discovery in South Africa,'' *Market News Publishing,* June 8, 2001.

''Pioneer Natural Resources Co. – 2002 Capital Budget; Expects Production to Increase 45–50%—by Early 2003; Provides Update on Hedging Program,'' *Market News Publishing,* December 12, 2001.

''Pioneer Natural Resources Co. – Updates Activity in Argentina,'' *Market News Publishing,* July 27, 2001.

"Pioneer Sanctions Development of Devils Tower Field, Updates Deepwater Activity," *Canadian Corporate News,* June 20, 2001.

"Pioneer Stakes Its Claim," *Petroleum Economist,* July 2000, p. 43.

"Pioneer to Cut 15% of Workers, Close Offices in Houston, Oklahoma," *Oil Daily,* November 13, 1998.

"Pioneer to Issue New Shares to Pay for $193 Million," *Oil Daily,* April 10, 2002.

Shook, Barbara, "Pioneer Finally Finds Buyer for Properties," *Oil Daily,* May 18, 1999.

——, "Pioneer's Leadership Grooming Offspring to Begin Life As Aggressive, Growing Firm," *Oil Daily,* April 10, 1997, p. 1.

Shook, Barbara, and Karen Broyles, "Pioneer Write-Down Creates $900 Million Loss," *Oil Daily,* February 11, 1998, p. 1.

—Mary Tradii

Regal Entertainment Group

9110 East Nichols Avenue, Suite 200
Englewood, Colorado 80112
U.S.A.
Telephone: (303) 792-3600
Fax: (303) 792-8221
Web site: http://www.regalcinemas.com

Public Company
Incorporated: 2002
Employees: 22,727
Sales: $2.14 billion (2002)
Stock Exchanges: New York
Ticker Symbol: RGC
NAIC: 512131 Motion Picture Theaters, Except Drive-In

Regal Entertainment Group is the largest movie theater chain in the world. The company operates 6,119 screens in 562 theaters in 39 states, controlling roughly 16 percent of all of the screens in the United States. Nearly twice as big as it closest rival, Regal Entertainment is controlled by Philip Anschutz, a highly successful businessman who is estimated to be one of the five wealthiest individuals in the world.

Founder's Background

Regal Entertainment was created from the ashes of three broken-down companies, which were merged in 2002 to create the world's largest chain of movie theaters. Although two of the three merged companies were veteran concerns, each operating for more than a half-century before their financial collapse, the story of Regal Entertainment's formation drew its plot from the life of the individual who orchestrated the 2002 merger. The figure behind the scenes was Philip F. Anschutz, reputed to be one of the five wealthiest individuals in the world. Anschutz represented a rare breed of business tycoon, a man able to cultivate a vast fortune in not only one business, but in an impressive spectrum of businesses. His success in one industry was parlayed into success in another industry, with Anschutz proving himself to be a shrewd, patient, and opportunistic businessperson. Anschutz built a vast and diverse business empire, one that eventually set its sights on the motion picture exhibition industry and pounced, adding the largest chain of movie theaters as the new jewel of Anschutz's holdings. Regal Entertainment began as a $2 billion company, but the resources and business acumen needed for its creation were developed throughout Anschutz's career.

Philip Anschutz was born in Russell, Kansas. After moving to Hays, Kansas, his family settled in Wichita, where Anschutz attended high school and where his father operated an oil exploration business named Circle A Drilling. Anschutz earned a finance degree in 1961 from the University of Kansas and prepared for a career in law, but just before he was scheduled to attend law school at the University of Virginia he balked. He decided to join his father's oil company instead and spent the next four years drilling, buying and selling oil leases, and overseeing seismic tests. After a four-year stint with his father, Anschutz decided to start his own oil business. During the next ten years, Anschutz acquired oil fields in Montana, Texas, Colorado, and Wyoming, a period in which he displayed his skill at overcoming major obstacles and emerging victorious.

Anschutz's first foray into the entrepreneurial world nearly met with disaster. In 1967, not long after leaving his father's company, Anschutz received a telephone call informing him one of his exploratory wells had exploded. He chartered a plane to the site, located in Gillette, Wyoming, to check on the damage. Standing ankle-deep in crude oil, with natural gas permeating the air, Anschutz saw the crisis firsthand and ordered that the well be capped. He also sensed that he was standing atop substantial stores of crude oil and natural gas. Before others learned of his gushing well, Anschutz purchased several oil leases in the surrounding region. Strapped for cash, he purchased the leases on 30 days' credit, then returned to Denver thinking that the problem had been resolved. When he turned on the television back at home in Denver the next day, Anschutz heard disturbing news. A massive oil fire was raging in Gillette, Wyoming. He flew back to Gillette, where the devastation on display spelled his ruin. The cost of fighting the fire and the impending payment for the leases he had acquired the day before promised to force Anschutz into bankruptcy. His predicament was grave, but Anschutz rallied. He learned that

Universal Studios was making a film based on famed oil-field fighter Red Adair, presumably from Adair himself, who had agreed to snuff the flames in Gillette. Anschutz reached an agreement with Universal Studios that let the film studio film on his land in exchange for a $100,000 fee. The footage was used in the 1968 film *Hellfighters,* starring John Wayne.

Anschutz continued to invest in the oil business throughout the 1970s and into the 1980s. He also demonstrated his penchant for diversifying his business interests—''Phil had a philosophy that you had to have a lot going on, because not all things would work out,'' a colleague noted in a September 6, 1999 interview with *Fortune.* Anschutz purchased uranium and coal mines, he bought cattle ranches and vegetable farms, and he founded an oil and metals commodity trading company. Meanwhile, his oil exploration business experienced its vicissitudes. At one point, he drilled 30 dry holes in a row. Eventually, however, his persistence paid off. He purchased a farm in northern Utah in an area already explored by oil companies. Anschutz purchased the property anyway because during the late 1970s new seismic technology had been developed that offered hope of discovering oil. Anschutz took a look where others had already explored and discovered a billion-barrel pocket of oil one mile down, a find that ranked as one of the largest U.S. oil discoveries since Prudhoe Bay in Alaska in 1968. In 1982, just before oil prices collapsed, Anschutz sold half his stake in the northern Utah field to Mobil Oil, gaining $500 million from the sale.

The sale to Mobil made Anschutz immensely wealthy, giving him the financial might to pursue other business interests. ''He wanted to get away from too much oil and gas,'' a business associate explained in a September 6, 1999 article in *Fortune.* ''He wanted to do some wheeling and dealing,'' the colleague added. Anschutz opted for railroads, acquiring Denver & Rio Grande Western railroad in 1984. Not long after acquiring the midsized railroad, he learned of a proposed merger between two nearby railroads that threatened the future of his newly acquired railroad. When federal government regulators ordered that one of the two railroads be sold, Anschutz swooped in, acquiring San Francisco-based Southern Pacific. He merged Southern Pacific and Denver & Rio Grande, eventually selling the line to Union Pacific Corp. for $5.4 billion, which netted more than $1 billion on his initial outlay.

Anschutz's involvement in the railroad business facilitated his next great investment, an impressive foray into telecommu-

nications. Southern Pacific, which remained with Anschutz until 1996, had a small division named SP Telecom that installed fiber optic cable along its track for itself and other telephone companies. Under Anschutz's directions, SP Telecom was given access to an unprecedented amount of capital, money that would be used to lay specially switched networks of large capacity. Anschutz envisioned the need for packet switching, which carried digital data with far greater efficiency than conventional networks. In 1995, a year before selling Southern Pacific, Anschutz separated SP Telecom from the railroad and merged it with another company, a Dallas-based digital microwave company named Qwest, acquired by Anschutz in 1995. He merged the two companies to form Qwest Communications. Qwest, after installing 18,500 miles of fiber through 150 cities, developed into a leader in the telecommunications industry. When Qwest merged with U.S. West in 2000, the transaction increased Anschutz's net worth to an estimated $16.5 billion.

Anschutz used his considerable wealth to invest in a number of different directions. During the mid-1990s, he invested in Major League Soccer (MLS), purchasing four MLS franchises. He became a majority owner of the Staples Center in Los Angeles. He also purchased substantial stakes in the facility's occupants, taking on large interests in professional sports teams such as the National Basketball Association's Los Angeles Lakers and the National Hockey League's Los Angeles Kings. During the late 1990s, Anschutz's acquisitive eye also turned to the movie theater industry, his interest piqued by the impending collapse of a host of the industry's major operators.

2001: The Formation of Regal Entertainment

During the late 1990s, the business of operating a chain of movie theaters was fraught with difficulty. To stay ahead of competitors, major chains were borrowing heavily to expand and upgrade their operations. Movie theater chains were expanding at a rapid rate, hoping to drive one another out of business by erecting more screens and designing grander facilities than any other operator. The frenzied trend toward expansion led to overcapacity. Soon, there were not enough patrons to fill the hundreds of thousands of new stadium-style seats that were in existence. Saddled with high-interest payments on the debt accumulated during the expansion spree, the chains became financially distressed. Financial failure replaced frenzied expansion as the new industry trend, resulting in an alarming number of bankruptcies. In 2001 alone, six movie theater chains declared bankruptcy. Of those six, there were three companies that attracted Anschutz's attention: Regal Cinemas Inc., United Artists Theatre Company, and Edwards Theatres Circuit Inc. Combined, the three operators had invested approximately $1.9 billion in expansion and upgrades during the last several years of the 1990s. By the beginning of the 21st century, the companies were financially exhausted from the race to drive out competitors.

Anschutz orchestrated his three-pronged attack on the movie theater industry in 2001, negotiating, at roughly the same time, the three deals that would lead to Regal Entertainment's formation. He completed his first deal in January 2001, when he acquired a majority stake in United Artists, which was two months away from finishing its bankruptcy proceedings. Founded in 1926 by shareholders that included Mary Pickford, Douglas Fairbanks, and Sam Goldwyn, United Artists operated

Key Dates:

1926: United Artists is founded.
1930: Edwards Theatres opens for business.
1989: Regal Cinemas is founded.
2001: Regal Cinemas, Edwards Theatres, and United Artists file for bankruptcy; Philip Anschutz acquires a majority stake in United Artists in January; Anschutz and Oaktree Capital Management reach an agreement to acquire Edwards Theatres by the summer; Anschutz reaches an agreement to acquire Regal Cinemas in the fall.
2002: Regal Entertainment completes its initial public offering of stock in May.

205 theaters housing 1,573 screens. Anschutz acquired United Artists on his own; his next acquisition saw him partner with Oaktree Capital Management, a distressed-debt specialist. The two parties began negotiations to acquire Edwards Theatres, the smallest of the three companies that would form Regal Entertainment. A family-owned business in operation for more than 70 years, Edwards Theatres ranked as the largest movie theater chain in California, controlling 59 theaters with 690 screens. By mid-2001, Anschutz and Oaktree had agreed to pay $56 million to take control of Edwards Theatres, which emerged from bankruptcy in September 2001. Meanwhile, Anschutz was in the midst of negotiations to purchase the largest of his acquisition targets, Knoxville, Tennessee-based Regal Cinemas.

Regal Cinemas ranked as the largest movie theater chain in the United States at the time of Anschutz's interest. The company began as a private concern in 1989 before converting to public ownership in 1993. In 1998, the company was taken private again in a $1.05 billion leveraged buyout led by Kohlberg, Kravis, Roberts & Co. and Hicks, Muse, Tate & Furst. Regal Cinemas, like a number of movie theater chains, fell victim to the financial strains of overexpansion, slipped into bankruptcy, and left its joint venture owners with little hope of making a profit on their 1998 investment. In September 2001, Regal Cinemas' management endorsed a $1.25 billion reorganization proposal that gave Anschutz control over the nation's largest movie theater chain. Regal operated 304 theaters housing 3,898 screens.

Regal Entertainment's 2002 Public Debut

Anschutz combined the three companies to form Regal Entertainment, a company led by co-chief executive officers and vice-chairmen Michael Hall, the former head of Regal Cinemas, and Kurt Hall, president of United Artists. Anschutz served as non-executive chairman of Regal Entertainment. Because of the reorganizations each of the three components of Regal Entertainment were forced to undergo, the assets supporting the three entities were in better shape than before filing for Chapter 11 protection. During the process of reorganization, the movie theater chains were able to extricate themselves from bad leases and to shed underperforming locations. The process created leaner, stronger companies whose union resulted in by far the largest movie theater chain in the world. Regal Entertain-

ment, as it started out, operated 561 theaters and 5,885 screens located in 36 states. The company was nearly twice as large as its closest competitor, Kansas City, Missouri-based AMC Entertainment.

Anschutz aspired not only to own the nation's largest chain, but also to leverage his market dominance for what he termed "high-margin ancillary businesses such as advertising," according to Securities and Exchange Commission documents filed by the company. Anschutz planned to use his myriad screens to create a digitally wired network that could display an unprecedented amount of advertising. "Research," Kurt Hall said in a June 10, 2002 interview with *Forbes*, "shows lots of people are in their seats 15 minutes or so before the show. We can maximize the value of those spaces." In addition to his position as Regal Entertainment's co-chief executive officer, Hall also headed Regal CineMedia, the entity through which Anschutz planned to deliver his vision of movie theaters as locations capable of showing more than films. Regal CineMedia began building a $70 million network, dubbed the "Digital Content Network," of more than 400 theaters, representing roughly 4,900 screens, that were capable of receiving, storing, and digitally projecting alternative content. The content ranged from advertising, to live MLS games, to corporate presentations displayed to workers gathered in one of Anschutz's movie theaters.

Anschutz filed for Regal Entertainment's initial public offering (IPO) of stock in March 2002. In May 2002, the company completed its IPO, beating the expected offering price of between $16 and $18 per share. Investors purchased 18 million shares at $19 apiece.

As Regal Entertainment prepared for its future, the company stood as a powerful tool for Anschutz to enact his vision. Completion of the Digital Content Network was expected in March 2004, an entity that one analyst predicted would generate between $90 million and $100 million in annual advertising revenue. The idea of using movie theaters as more than spaces to project films promised to add to the already considerable might of Regal Entertainment. The company dominated its industry and it was supported by a veteran visionary whose business skill was legendary. With Anschutz at the helm, there were few observers who could question the future success of Regal Entertainment, a genuine industry behemoth.

Principal Subsidiaries

Regal Entertainment Holdings, Inc.; Regal Cinemas Corporation; United Artists Theatre Company; Regal Cinemas, Inc.; Edwards Theatres, Inc.; Regal CineMedia Corporation.

Principal Competitors

AMC Entertainment Inc.; Cinemark, Inc.; Loews Cineplex Entertainment Corporation.

Further Reading

"Anschutz Looking at Chain," *Denver Business Journal*, January 12, 2001, p. 6A.
"Anschutz Taking Over Edwards," *Los Angeles Business Journal*, June 4, 2001, p. 29.

Carey, David, ''Anschutz, Oaktree Consolidate Control of Regal Cinemas,'' *Daily Deal,* May 29, 2001, p. 34.

''Coming Distractions,'' *Forbes,* June 10, 2002, p. 50.

DiOrio, Carl, ''Anschutz in Regal Spot,'' *Variety,* April 2, 2001, p. 12.

——, ''Anschutz Wires Circuits,'' *Variety,* September 10, 2001, p. 3.

Harrington, Ann, ''Billionaire Next Door,'' *Fortune,* September 6, 1999, p. 139.

Fugazy, Danielle, ''Regal Entertainment Gets Ready for the Show,'' *IPO Reporter,* March 18, 2002.

Rebchook, John, ''King of the Silver Screen Anschutz Unveils World's Largest Chain of Theaters,'' *Rocky Mountain News,* March 12, 2002, p. 1B.

Storch, Charles, ''Regal Entertainment Group Looks to Alternative Content Delivered Digitally,'' *Knight Ridder/Tribune Business News,* July 1, 2003.

''Theater Chain Reprieve,'' *Los Angeles Business Journal,* May 14, 2001, p. 38.

Westergaard, Neil, ''What's Anschutz Up to Now?,'' *Denver Business Journal,* March 2, 2001, p. 54A.

—Jeffrey L. Covell

RE/MAX International, Inc.

8390 East Crescent Parkway, Suite 500/600
Greenwood Village, Colorado 80111
U.S.A.
Telephone: (303) 770-5531
Toll Free: (800) 525-7452
Fax: (303) 796-3599
Web site: http://www.remax.com

Private Company
Incorporated: 1973
Employees: 83,000
Sales: $3 billion (2002 est.)
NAIC: 531210 Offices of Real Estate Agents and Brokers

RE/MAX International, Inc. is one of the largest real estate companies in the world. RE/MAX specializes in residential real estate transactions, operating a franchise network comprising more than 4,600 offices located in 44 countries. RE/MAX sales agents receive 100 percent of the commission on their home sales rather than the traditional 50 percent received by agents working in conventional brokerage firms. The company's compensation system attracts top selling agents whose earnings are sufficient to pay for monthly franchise fees and other overhead expenses.

Origins

Dave Liniger's entrepreneurial career sent a shock wave of change throughout the real estate industry, but it began as a near failure, making for one of the most triumphant comeback stories in the history of late 20th-century business. Liniger grew up in Marion, Indiana, and attended the University of Indiana before dropping out of college. He joined the Air Force, which stationed him in Phoenix, Arizona, the birthplace of the real estate concept that Liniger would use to create a multibillion-dollar enterprise. Liniger's introduction to the real estate business occurred while he was in the Air Force. At age 19, he bought a house in Tucson, Arizona, remodeled it, and sold it for a $4,000 profit. Encouraged by his success, Liniger threw himself into his new line of work, using his salary from the military as down payments for properties and remodeling them for a profit. By the time he was 24, Liniger owned 20 single-family homes.

After securing his real estate license, Liniger joined a brokerage firm in Phoenix. He flourished as a sales representative, becoming the firm's top sales agent. Next, he moved to another Phoenix brokerage firm, a move critical to the future success of RE/MAX. Although Liniger spent only three months at his second Phoenix brokerage firm, it was there that he learned of the 100 percent commission concept. At a conventional brokerage firm, sales agents split their commission on sales with the brokerage's owner, who paid for rent, advertising, and other overhead expenses. At the Phoenix brokerage where Linger worked, sales agents received the entire commission and paid the office's overhead expenses together. It was a compensation system that placed greater financial responsibilities on the sales agents, but one that allowed top sales agents to garner a greater share of the profits produced from property sales.

After his three-month stint in Phoenix, Liniger moved to Denver, Colorado, arriving in October 1971. The sales skills he demonstrated in Phoenix rose to the fore in Denver, where Liniger excelled as a real estate agent and quickly established himself as a multimillion-dollar salesman. Liniger enjoyed resounding financial success in Denver, but after having experienced the rewards of the 100 percent commission concept, he disliked giving away 50 percent of his commission. Liniger's frustration spurred his desire to start his own company, one based on the concept under which he had worked in Phoenix. The 100 percent commission model was suited perfectly for sales agents of Liniger's caliber. Part-time agents, or those who recorded fewer sales, could not afford to pay for their own overhead expenses. The 100 percent commission system favored those at the top of their profession, the superstars of real estate sales. To make his entrepreneurial venture work, Liniger needed real estate agents modeled after himself, a legion of top-rated sales representatives who would inject the vigor his fledgling company would need to succeed. Theoretically, Liniger's business model promised success, but the practical application of the 100 percent commission system under Liniger's direction floundered profoundly at its start.

Liniger needed money to start his business, a company he named RE/MAX—an acronym for "real estate maximums." To obtain the financing, Liniger relied on his sales skills, acting

Company Perspectives:

Deciding to sell or buy a home is a big step. To make sure it's a step in the right direction choose the person best qualified to handle your real estate needs: a RE/MAX Sales Associate.

Averaging three times the production and more advanced industry education than other agents, RE/MAX Associates are truly "The Real Estate Leaders" in quality customer service.

as a pitchman for the lucrative potential of a nationwide real estate business predicated on the 100 percent commission model. Liniger convinced five Denver developers to invest $300,000 in his venture. Once he had their word that the money would be available, Liniger contacted a local personnel office to help him find his first employee. By his own admission, he lacked marketing experience and the ability to turn his venture into a nationwide business without help. The personnel office sent him a dozen candidates and Liniger rejected each one. The personnel office sent him a dozen more candidates and, again, Liniger rejected each one. Liniger interviewed still more applicants before he was satisfied. The 28th applicant was his future wife Gail, who was hired as RE/MAX's executive secretary. A St. Louis native, she had received a marketing degree from Southern Illinois University, which landed her a job at Ralston Purina Company, where she served as a customer service supervisor for five years before meeting Liniger. The pair, occupying an office in Denver, set out in 1973 to make RE/MAX a reality.

Troubles from the Start: RE/MAX in the Early 1970s

The business started promisingly, with David and Gail Liniger proving to be an energetic force. They opened eight offices in one month, but the company soon was beset by the first of numerous difficulties. The Arab oil embargo delivered a severe blow to Denver's real estate market in the fall of 1973, prompting Liniger's financial backers to withdraw their promise of $300,000. The developers found themselves strapped for cash by the collapse of the Denver real estate market, and Liniger found himself with eight real estate offices under his control and no money to sustain operations. Further, his business model depended on recruiting the region's most successful agents, which Liniger had failed to do. "We interviewed 204 agents the first month that we were trying to kick RE/MAX off," he explained in an April 1990 interview with *Nation's Business*. "But only four agents signed up—and they weren't the four best ones." Not surprisingly, those agents who were the market leaders in their profession were unwilling to uproot themselves and join an upstart brokerage. Before long, RE/MAX was incurring $30,000 to $40,000 a month in negative cash flow. From there, the situation worsened.

Liniger's debt mounted, leaving RE/MAX teetering on the brink of collapse. He was unable to pay quarterly federal withholding taxes, which prompted the Internal Revenue Service (IRS) to padlock all of the company's offices. Liniger prevailed in convincing the IRS that the only way the government could hope to get its money was to unlock his offices, but government

officials were not the only ones demanding payment. The company was inundated with calls, as its debt reached $780,000. Creditors were demanding payment, but Gail Liniger was able to stave off their pleas for money while David Liniger worked furiously to recruit agents. By the end of the company's first year, the Linigers had 21 sales agents under their employ.

The couple's eventual success in recruiting a small number of top-selling sales representatives yielded a sense of stability, but also created its own problems. Denver brokerage firms eyed RE/MAX warily, becoming increasingly worried about the emergence of a new compensation scheme that threatened to seduce their best employees into leaving. Against the backdrop of this reputed fear, RE/MAX was beset by a flurry of damaging rumors. The company was accused of engaging in illegal stock offerings, that its sales agents were illegally dealing in government-backed mortgages, and that Liniger was using home buyers' escrow accounts to pay for existing bills. Before long, RE/MAX found itself the object of intense scrutiny. The Federal Bureau of Investigation and the Securities and Exchange Commission launched concurrent investigations into RE/MAX's practices. The state Real Estate Commission conducted its own investigation, dispatching auditors once a week for six months to examine RE/MAX's books related to escrow accounts. Each investigation failed to find any wrongdoing, but the company could ill-afford the negative publicity.

RE/MAX's arduous start tested the perseverance of the Linigers. The troubles also forced David Liniger to make one important alteration to his original plans for expansion. From the start, he wanted to create a nationwide network of RE/MAX offices that he alone owned. Financial constraints, however, led him to embrace a new mode of expansion: franchising the RE/MAX concept. Initially, Liniger's attempt to franchise the 100 percent commission concept failed; yet another problematic start endured by RE/MAX. Liniger tried to convince independent brokers to convert their offices to RE/MAX offices, but most agents were unable to pay for the monthly franchise fee and overhead payments. His attempts to expand failed until 1977, when he tried a new strategy. Liniger began selling franchises to entrepreneurial brokers who started their RE/MAX offices from the ground up. The strategy worked, as the company recruited 316 agents in 1977, nearly twice the number of agents who had joined RE/MAX during the previous four years. In an April 1990 interview with *Nation's Business*, Liniger explained the turnaround in the company's fortunes: "Our cash flow exploded, we took over the Denver market, we paid off our debts, and the rest is history."

After years of struggle, the RE/MAX concept began to demonstrate tremendous market strength and acceptance. Expansion carried the RE/MAX name across the nation, as the company built up its presence in cities such as Chicago, Dallas, and Atlanta. In 1980, RE/MAX expanded into Canada for the first time and quickly recorded astounding success. By 1986, the company dominated the Canadian residential real estate market, part of a systemwide network consisting of 11,500 agents.

By the end of the 1980s, RE/MAX stood as a towering real estate giant. The company had passed Coldwell Banker in the industry rankings, trailing only Century 21, the largest broker of residential properties in North America. As the 1990s began,

```
┌─────────────────────────────────────────────────┐
│              Key Dates:                           │
│                                                   │
│ 1973:  David Liniger opens the first RE/MAX office in │
│        Denver, Colorado.                          │
│ 1977:  A new franchise strategy spurs growth.     │
│ 1980:  RE/MAX expands into Canada.                │
│ 1991:  RE/MAX enters the Caribbean Basin.         │
│ 1995:  RE/MAX expands into Africa and Europe.     │
│ 1997:  RE/MAX sales agents record more than one million │
│        transactions, the most recorded by any real estate │
│        network.                                   │
│ 2003:  The network of RE/MAX sales agents includes │
│        more than 80,000 representatives.          │
└─────────────────────────────────────────────────┘
```

Liniger's prognostications of RE/MAX's potential growth typified the confidence exuding from the company's management. Liniger predicted his company would not stop growing until there were 80,000 RE/MAX sales representatives working in the United States, at which point, he estimated, his company would account for 35 percent of all residential real estate transactions in the country.

International Expansion in the 1990s

During the 1990s, RE/MAX expanded aggressively, as the company completed its first 25 years of existence. In 1993, after several years of negotiations, the company made a bold move overseas. RE/MAX signed an agreement for offices to be opened in 28 European countries and in Israel. First, the company expanded into Austria, Israel, and Holland, with its second wave of expansion targeted at England, France, Germany, and Spain. At roughly the same time, the company began forging agreements for its Pacific operation, with Japan, Korea, and Thailand slated for penetration.

RE/MAX celebrated its 25th anniversary in 1998 as a formidable competitor in the global residential real estate industry. International expansion, which began in earnest in 1995, had extended the company's presence into the United Kingdom, Mexico, Australia, Turkey, South Africa, Singapore, Israel, and the Caribbean. Systemwide, there were 2,883 franchises operating in 22 countries. Sales agents, who had been difficult to recruit a quarter-century earlier, flocked to the "real estate max-

imums" concept, numbering more than 50,000 by 1998. The ranks of RE/MAX sales representatives constituted the upper tier of real estate agents, a body whose level of success far outstripped the performance of its peers. In 1998, the typical RE/MAX agent earned nearly $80,000 in gross personal income, more than three times the industry median income.

As RE/MAX entered the 21st century, the company's expansion continued, creating a massive franchise network that spread across the globe. By 2001, the company's largest overseas operations were in Spain and South Africa, but the company also enjoyed success in a host of other regions, including the Middle East, where there were 77 offices and 405 agents in Israel and Turkey, and in Australia, home to 53 offices and 247 agents. By 2003, the entire RE/MAX network included more than 4,600 offices in 44 countries, with more than 80,000 sales agents working under the "real estate maximums" concept. In the years ahead, the company's redoubtable domestic strength and its growing international presence promised to ensure that the RE/MAX name would remain a leading force in the industry.

Principal Subsidiaries

RE/MAX of New York.

Principal Competitors

Century 21 Real Estate Corporation; Coldwell Banker Real Estate Corporation; Prudential Financial, Inc.

Further Reading

Buss, Dale, "Success from the Ground Up," *Brandweek,* June 16, 2003, p. 21.

Flass, Rebecca, "Re/Max Wants More Personality," *ADWEEK,* March 17, 2003, p. 14.

McCrerey, Linda, "Re/Max Celebrates 25 Years," *Colorado Business Magazine,* January 1998, p. 16.

Moore, Paula, "The Re/Max Revolution," *Denver Business Journal,* January 28, 1994, p. B17.

Taylor, Mike, "Re/Max Worldwide," *ColoradoBiz,* October 2001, p. 18.

Wells, Garrison, "Re/Maxed," *Colorado Business Magazine,* November 1994, p. 92.

—Jeffrey L. Covell

ROCK-TENN COMPANY

Rock-Tenn Company

504 Thrasher Street
Norcross, Georgia 30071-1967
U.S.A.
Telephone: (770) 448-2193
Fax: (770) 263-4483
Web site: http://www.rocktenn.com

Public Company
Incorporated: 1973
Employees: 8,418
Sales: $1.44 billion (2002)
Stock Exchanges: New York
Ticker Symbol: RKT
NAIC: 322130 Paperboard Mills; 322211 Corrugated and
    Solid Fiber Boxes Manufacturing; 322212 Folding
    Paperboard Box Manufacturing; 322226 Surface-
    Coated Paperboard Manufacturing; 326199 All Other
    Plastics Product Manufacturing

Rock-Tenn Company is one of the largest U.S. manufacturers of 100 percent recycled paperboard, a product made from recovered wastepaper that the company also converts into packaging products. These converted products include folding cartons for food, paper goods, health and beauty items, clothing, and other products (with cartons accounting for 41.5 percent of overall revenues in 2002); solid-fiber partitions used in the interiors of packaging of such items as glass containers (through RTS Packaging, LLC, a venture 65 percent owned by Rock-Tenn); and laminated paperboard for book covers, furniture, and other products. In the early 2000s Rock-Tenn was using about 30 percent of its paperboard production to make its own paperboard products. In addition to these more traditional activities of the company, Rock-Tenn has also begun to focus on the manufacture of merchandising displays, quickly becoming the leading North American producer of point-of-purchase displays. Another high-growth area for the company is the production of plastic packaging products, including custom thermoformed plastic packaging for food, foodservice, and consumer products. Rock-Tenn operates 12 paperboard mills and 65 converting facilities in 24 states, Canada, Mexico, and Chile. Less than 6 percent of 2002 revenues was generated outside the United States. Long a privately held company, Rock-Tenn made its first public offering of stock in 1994.

Background on the Predecessor Companies

Rock-Tenn Company was formed in 1973, the product of a merger between Tennessee Paper Mills Inc. and Rock City Packaging, Inc. Its origins date back to 1898, when the Rock City Box Company of Nashville, Tennessee, was founded. Among its customers in the mid-1940s were a local boot factory, a local candy manufacturer, a hosiery company, and several shirt manufacturers. The owners, Joe McHenry and A.E. Saxon, who also operated several other business ventures, wanted to sell out and retire. Rock City was attractive to Arthur Newth Morris, owner of the Southern Box Company, not least for its bank account of $60,000. Morris purchased the company in 1944 for $200,000, making a cash down payment of $50,000.

The 25-year-old Morris had been a printer and part-time Presbyterian minister when he went to work in 1926 for Edwin J. Schoettle, a Philadelphia industrialist who owned a group of box and printing companies that bore his name. For a monthly salary of $350 Morris was expected to manage several hundred employees, some of them more than twice his age. He also traveled along the eastern seaboard, explaining to meatpackers his discovery that they could avoid shrinkage of their hot dogs by putting them in Schoettle's boxes instead of stringing them up like bananas.

By 1935 Morris was making a salary on which he could comfortably support his wife and four children, but he wanted to go into business for himself. Armed with life savings of $5,000 and a $7,500 investment by his boss, he moved to Baltimore. There he managed the J.E. Smith Box & Printing Co. during the day, while running the Southern Box Company, a company he founded in 1936, at night. Using Smith's presses, die-cutters, and other boxmaking equipment during the evening, Morris began servicing two anchor customers who knew him from his Philadelphia days.

Only six months after Morris had left Philadelphia, Schoettle came to Baltimore to offer him a promotion and a $25,000 salary. When Morris refused, Schoettle offered to sell Morris his own majority share of Southern Box for $25,000. A bank

Company Perspectives:

Rock-Tenn provides superior marketing and packaging solutions to consumer product companies at very low costs. We attract capable, highly motivated people who seek an opportunity to apply their talents to build a great company. We are committed to relentless performance and: exceeding our customers' expectations every time; creating long-term shareholder value; encouraging and rewarding employee excellence.

loan to Morris made the deal possible. He moved to new quarters for $200 a month, left day-to-day management to one of his employees, and devoted himself to finding new accounts. In its first year the company made a few thousand dollars on sales of $60,000.

By 1942 Morris was doing well enough to open a corrugated box plant and to buy another Baltimore enterprise, the King Folding Box Co., where he installed a corrugated sheet cutter. Morris sold corrugated partitions to major glass companies, which needed them to separate the bottles and glasses they shipped. The following year the name of his enterprise was changed to Newth Morris Box Company. In 1944 another branch was opened in Jacksonville, Florida, where the company produced cardboard anti-radar devices for World War II American troops and popcorn boxes for movie theater owners. Following Morris's purchase of Rock City Box Co. that same year, he changed the name of Newth Morris Box Co. to Rock City Box Sales Company.

Morris's purchase of Rock City Box Co. put him in contact with one of its suppliers and his future merger partner: Tennessee Paper Mills. A.L. Tomlinson and John Stagmaier, two of Tennessee Paper's three founders, were Athens, Tennessee, businessmen who already owned box factories. The company's third founder was A.M. Sheperd of Vincennes, Indiana, a boxboard manufacturer. Tennessee Paper Mills was incorporated in 1917 with Stagmaier as president, Tomlinson as vice-president, and Sheperd as general manager. With $300,000 raised from stock offerings, the three men established a paperboard factory in Chattanooga, where operation began in July 1918. By the end of the year the new company had made a handsome net profit of $23,367 on sales of $165,799.

Although the founders originally planned to make board from wheat straw, they turned instead to wastepaper as the primary raw material; thus Tennessee Paper became the first recycled paperboard mill in the South. To reduce its electric bill, the company installed its own steam generating plant in 1926. Paperboard production averaged 20 tons a day in the early years, reaching an average of 56.77 tons in 1930, the same year that the company produced a record 15,557 tons of product. This figure would not be matched for some time because of the Great Depression; production dropped to 11,995 tons in 1934. The company remained profitable, however, although only modestly so. As the nation's economy slowly recovered, Tennessee Paper's volume of business increased to meet renewed demand. During 1939 the factory operated at 85 percent capacity, compared with the industry average of 71 percent. In 1941 it

operated a record 305 days. Sales volume exceeded $1.7 million in 1945. A second papermaking machine doubled the mill's capacity in 1949.

Beginning in 1954, however, Tennessee Paper began losing customers to companies manufacturing lower-cost folding cartons and corrugated and plastic containers. The trend in the business was toward vertical integration. Many paperboard companies acquired—or merged with—their customers. Typically profits were made at the mill level, by selling boxes virtually at cost. The effect on boxmakers was so severe that by 1957 Tennessee Paper was extending credit and loans to its customers in order to keep their accounts.

One of these customers was Rock City. Its consumption of Tennessee Paper's board grew from about 1,000 tons in 1944 to about 37,000 tons in 1972, when it took 44 percent of Tennessee Paper's total boxboard production. Between 1965 and 1968 Tennessee Paper bought 29.5 percent of Rock City's common stock, preparing the way for the eventual merger of the two companies. By then Rock City owed Tennessee Paper more than $4 million in loans.

Morris's burgeoning industrial empire grew both by acquisitions and by establishing new companies. Among the former was the Parks Box & Printing Co., located on a leased 11-acre tract in Norcross, Georgia. This land was purchased in 1957 and gradually became the focal point for management of all the Morris companies. A new 30,000-square-foot warehouse was added to the Norcross facility in 1960.

Each of the Morris companies operated as a separate and virtually autonomous profit center. Rock City opened not only small set-up and folding carton plants but also facilities in Livingston and Milan, Tennessee, to meet the packaging needs of shirtmakers. A set-up box division was established in 1955. Rock City Waste Paper Co. collected, sorted, and baled wastepaper for sale to paper mills. Other Morris companies and plants sprouted throughout the South. Sales grew from $8 million in 1959 to $12.9 million in 1967, when all the companies were consolidated into Rock City Packaging, Inc. Morris became chairman of the board and a son-in-law, Worley Brown, became president. Sales volume reached $23 million in 1972.

Meanwhile, in order to meet the competition, Tennessee Paper began buying customers to assure continued markets for its paperboard products. In 1964 it acquired Knoxville Paper Box Co., Inc., a manufacturer of folding and set-up boxes, for about $1 million. In 1969 Tennessee Paper acquired wastepaper factories in Knoxville and Atlanta, and in 1972 it built another wastepaper plant in Chattanooga.

Formation of Rock-Tenn in 1973

The merger of Rock City Packaging and Tennessee Paper Mills in 1973 gave Morris, Brown, and others who held stock in the former companies a controlling interest in the new corporation, Rock-Tenn Company. Most Tennessee Paper common stockholders received preferred stock in the new company that earned them triple the dividends they had been receiving. Some shareholders, however, opted for cash instead. The president of Tennessee Paper, W. Max Finley, and his immediate family, received common stock in the new company. Finley was elected

Key Dates:

1898: Rock City Box Company is founded in Nashville, Tennessee.
1917: Three partners form Tennessee Paper Mills, Inc., establishing in Chattanooga the first recycled paperboard mill in the South.
1936: Arthur Newth Morris founds Southern Box Company in Baltimore.
1943: Morris changes the name of his company to the Newth Morris Box Company.
1944: Morris purchases Rock City Box Co. and changes the name of his other company to Rock City Box Sales Company.
1967: The various companies owned by Morris are consolidated into Rock City Packaging, Inc.
1973: Tennessee Paper Mills and Rock City Packaging merge to form Rock-Tenn Company, based in Norcross, Georgia.
1983: The company acquires 11 plants from Clevepak Corporation.
1993: The Canadian firm Les Industries Ling is acquired.
1994: Alliance Display and Packaging, maker of corrugated displays, is purchased; Rock-Tenn goes public.
1997: Waldorf Corporation, producer of folding cartons and recycled paperboard, is acquired; Rock-Tenn and Sonoco Products Company merge their fiber partition operations into a joint venture called RTS Packaging, LLC.
2003: The company acquires Cartem Wilco Group Inc., a Canadian firm specializing in pharmaceutical and health and beauty packaging.

chairman of the board and Brown became president and chief executive officer.

Reorganization did nothing to slow down expansion. The Crescent Box & Printing Co. of Tullahoma, Tennessee, was acquired in 1973 and Clevepak Corporation's Conway, Arkansas, folding carton plant in 1974. By 1976 the company had 29 divisions. Sales in 1974, the first fiscal year after the merger, reached $47.7 million. In 1978 Bradley Currey, Jr., a veteran officer of the Trust Company of Georgia who had helped effect the merger, became president and chief operating officer of Rock-Tenn. Brown became chairman of the board while remaining chief executive officer. Finley moved to senior chairman of the board. Morris remained chairman of the executive committee until his death in January 1985. Currey later became Rock-Tenn's chairman (in 1993) and CEO (in 1989) as well as its president.

Acquisition-Fueled Growth in the 1980s and 1990s

In 1982 Rock-Tenn's sales volume reached $133 million and its production of recycled paperboard peaked at 180,000 tons, most of which it used itself in the manufacture of folding cartons and containers and corrugated boxes. Its many customers included Coca-Cola, DuPont, and Kentucky Fried Chicken, which it serviced from facilities in Alabama, Arkansas, Georgia, Maryland, Massachusetts, North Carolina, Ohio, Tennessee, and

Texas with a workforce of 1,700 people. In a 1983 *Atlanta Constitution* interview, Currey attributed the decade-old company's growth to "luck, chance, and circumstance . . . but the success of any company depends on its people." He added that the company had gone to great lengths "to make sure the workers know that we care"—a group of senior executives took a month each year to travel to each of the company's facilities in order to talk to employees and present service awards.

Rock-Tenn made its biggest acquisition yet in 1983, when it paid $40 million to buy 11 Clevepak Corporation plants, seven of which were making partitions to protect glass and plastic containers. Currey said the acquisition would allow Rock-Tenn to capture about one-fourth of the partition market, raise annual revenue to more than $200 million, and increase production of recycled paperboard to 235,000 tons. In 1989 net sales had reached $515.9 million, and net income was $31.1 million. The following year the company dedicated to Chairman of the Board Finley a 33,000-square-foot office building behind its headquarters in Norcross.

In 1990 Rock-Tenn acquired Allforms Packaging Corp. of Long Island and Box Innards Inc. of Orange, California. The next year it purchased the former Specialty Paperboard Inc. mill in Sheldon Springs, Vermont, and Ellis Paperboard Products Inc. of Scarborough, Maine, a manufacturer of folding cartons and solid-fiber partitions. The Ellis purchase included its Canadian subsidiary, Dominion Paperboard Products Ltd. With these additions Rock-Tenn controlled 60 manufacturing and distribution operations, including eight mills with a total annual production capacity of 607,000 tons of recycled paperboard products. Rock-Tenn now ranked sixth among U.S. producers of recycled paperboard, with market share of 5.7 percent.

Net sales rose from $564.1 million in 1991, ending September 30, 1991, to $655.5 million in 1992, but dipped to $650.7 million in 1993. Net income rose from $25 million in 1991 to $33.2 million in 1992 before dipping to $25.5 million in 1993. The 1993 figure included unusual after-tax expenses of $5.8 million. Production in 1994 was 700,000 tons of recycled paperboard, of which 182,000 tons was clay-coated recycled paperboard.

The first public offering of Rock-Tenn stock, amounting to about 14 percent of the shares outstanding, was made in March 1994. A handful of shareholders offered about 3.6 million shares of Class A common stock, while the company itself offered about 900,000 shares. An analysis in *Barron's* described Rock-Tenn's balance sheet as "attractive" and said the company was "more soundly financed than many in its field," noting that long-term debt of $51.6 million was only one year's cash flow. Although calling the offering somewhat pricey at $16.50 a share, it noted that "Rock-Tenn's emphasis on recycling makes it well-suited to customers wishing to appear environmentally responsible, and could also prove profitable if use of woodlands is restricted." Officers and directors of Rock-Tenn still controlled about 71 percent of the combined voting power of Class A and B common stock after the offering.

In December 1993 Rock-Tenn paid $35 million for Les Industries Ling, a Canadian company that used recycled paperboard to make folding cartons. The newly acquired plant, which was to serve as the principal supplier of recycled clay-coated paperboard for Rock-Tenn's Vermont mill, became the company's second largest folding carton facility. A year later, Rock-Tenn agreed to acquire Olympic Packaging, an Illinois-based manufacturer of folding cartons, and Alliance Display and Packaging Co. of Winston-Salem, North Carolina, maker of corrugated displays. The purchases, which boosted Rock-Tenn's acquisitions of manufacturing operations to 17 in a decade, cost about $75 million.

By the middle of the 1990s, Rock-Tenn had 59 facilities in 19 states and Canada. Net sales reached $705.8 million during 1994, constituting an 11.8 percent compounded annual growth rate for the past decade. Net income came to a record $37.5 million. Late in 1995 COO Jay Shuster was named president of Rock-Tenn, with Currey retaining the posts of chairman and CEO.

In January 1997 Rock-Tenn consummated the largest acquisition in its history, purchasing Waldorf Corporation for $239 million in cash and the assumption of $170 million in debt. Based in St. Paul, Minnesota, Waldorf operated six folding carton plants and three paperboard mills in Illinois, Massachusetts, Michigan, Minnesota, North Carolina, and Wisconsin; the firm had revenues of $377 million during 1996. The acquisition propelled Rock-Tenn into the number two position among producers of folding cartons in North America and also made the company the leading manufacturer of recycled paperboard in the United States. Rock-Tenn followed up with two smaller deals in mid-1997, adding Wright City, Missouri–based Rite Paper Products, Inc., a producer of laminated recycled paperboard products primarily for the furniture industry, and the Davey Company, a manufacturer of high-density recycled paperboard mainly used in book covers and binders that operated mills in Aurora, Illinois, and Jersey City, New Jersey. Also in 1997, Rock-Tenn and Sonoco Products Company created a fiber partition joint venture called RTS Packaging, LLC, with Rock-Tenn holding a 65 percent stake and Sonoco the remaining 35 percent. The venture combined Rock-Tenn's eight partition plants with the seven that had been owned by Sonoco.

Although the purchase of Waldorf pushed Rock-Tenn's revenues past the $1 billion mark for the first time in 1997, difficulties in the integration process resulted in a depressed profit figure of $16.1 million. Some of the profit shortfall was attributable to costs stemming from plant closings, and the company closed additional plants in the next two fiscal years as profit levels recovered somewhat.

Increasing Focus on Packaging and Merchandising Displays: Early 2000s

In October 1999 Rock-Tenn went outside its ranks for a new CEO, hiring James A. Rubright, who had previously been the head of the pipeline group and energy services business of Sonat, Inc. Currey handed over the chairmanship to Rubright as well in January 2000. Later in 2000, Shuster, having been passed over for the CEO position, left the company. Rubright accelerated the pace of restructuring at Rock-Tenn through the closure of a number of underperforming plants. He also shifted the company's emphasis away from the slow-growing recycled paperboard side and toward the areas with higher growth potential: the folding carton and plastics packaging businesses, as well as the

burgeoning merchandising display operation, which by the early 2000s was the U.S. leader in point-of-purchase displays.

During 2000, Rock-Tenn closed one laminated paperboard products plant and three folding carton plants, resulting in 550 employee terminations and charges of $61.1 million—and a net loss for the year of $15.9 million. Seven more plants were shuttered over the next three years, resulting in the loss of 450 more jobs and an additional $19 million in charges. Meantime, in February 2000 the company formed a joint venture with Lafarge Corporation called Seven Hills Paperboard, LLC, which was charged with producing gypsum paperboard liner for the U.S. drywall manufacturing plants of Lafarge. Rock-Tenn owned 49 percent of the venture. Rock-Tenn also beefed up its merchandising display business, its fastest growing segment, through two acquisitions costing a total of $25.4 million. In November 2001 Advertising Display Company, a producer of both temporary and permanent point-of-purchase displays, was acquired. In March of the following year Rock-Tenn bought Athena Industries, Inc., a Burr Ridge, Illinois, manufacturer of permanent point-of-purchase displays, with an emphasis on wire displays. Acquisition activity continued in 2003 with the purchase of Cartem Wilco Group Inc., a privately held Canadian maker of folding cartons and specialty packaging, for $65.3 million. The deal accelerated Rock-Tenn's expansion into the growing pharmaceutical and health and beauty packaging market. Cartem Wilco, which operated plants in Montreal and Quebec City, also produced folding cartons for food packaging and consumer products. In August 2003 Rock-Tenn paid about $16 million for Pacific Coast Packaging Corp., located in Kerman, California. Rock-Tenn secured its first folding carton operation on the West Coast through this acquisition, gaining a manufacturer of folding cartons for the fast-food, in-store deli, and gift box markets.

Principal Subsidiaries

Concord Industries, Inc.; Rock-Tenn Company, Mill Division, Inc.; Rock-Tenn Company of Arkansas; Rock-Tenn Company of California, Inc.; Rock-Tenn Company of Illinois, Inc.; Rock-Tenn Company of Texas; Rock-Tenn Converting Company; RTS Packaging, LLC (65%); Seven Hills Paperboard, LLC (49%); Waldorf Corporation; Dominion Paperboard Products, Ltd. (Canada); Ling Industries, Inc. (Canada).

Principal Divisions

Alliance Display Division; Coated Paperboard Division; Corrugated Division; Folding Carton Division; Laminated Paperboard Products Division; Plastic Packaging Division; Recycled Fiber Division; Specialty Paperboard Division.

Principal Competitors

Smurfit-Stone Container Corporation; Shorewood Packaging Corporation; Sonoco Products Company; Stora Enso North America Corporation; Temple-Inland Inc.

Further Reading

Ceron, Gaston F., ''Rock-Tenn Aims to Increase Its Earnings by Cost-Cutting After Two Tough Years,'' *Wall Street Journal,* December 7, 1998, p. B7E.

Cochran, Thomas N., "Offerings in the Offing," *Barron's,* February 21, 1994, p. 50.

"Company Interview: Rock-Tenn Company," *Wall Street Transcript,* December 2, 2002.

Fernandez, Don, "Rock-Tenn Co. to Close Carton Plant in Norcross," *Atlanta Journal-Constitution,* April 29, 2000, p. J1.

Harte, Susan, "Rock-Tenn Plans Another Acquisition," *Atlanta Constitution,* December 16, 1994, p. G2.

——, "Rock-Tenn's Public Stock Offering Finances Expansion, Acquisitions," *Atlanta Constitution,* December 1, 1994, p. F7.

Herndon, Keith, "Rock-Tenn Seeks Knockout Punch," *Atlanta Constitution,* July 11, 1983, p. C12.

Mitchell, Cynthia, "Rock-Tenn Announces Acquisition," *Atlanta Journal and Constitution,* December 21, 1996, p. E1.

Paul, Peralte C., "Carton Maker Rock-Tenn to Close Third Plant This Year," *Atlanta Journal-Constitution,* July 22, 2000, p. F4.

"Rock-Tenn Agreement to Purchase Waldorf," *Pulp and Paper,* February 1997, p. 23.

The Rock-Tenn Story, Norcross, Ga.: Rock-Tenn Company, n.d.

"Rock-Tenn to Make Key Acquisitions," *Pulp and Paper,* July 1997, p. 25.

—Robert Halasz
—update: David E. Salamie

SABMiller plc

One Stanhope Gate
London W1K 1AF
United Kingdom
Telephone: (20) 7659-0100
Fax: (20) 7659-0111
Web site: http://www.sabmiller.com

Public Company
Incorporated: 1895 as The South African Breweries
     Limited
Employees: 42,402
Sales: $9.11 billion (2003)
Stock Exchanges: London Johannesburg
Ticker Symbol: SAB.L
NAIC: 312120 Breweries; 551112 Offices of Other
     Holding Companies; 312111 Soft Drink
     Manufacturing

SABMiller plc ranks as the world's second largest brewer in terms of volume, trailing only Anheuser-Busch Companies, Inc. Although now based in London, the company owns no breweries in the United Kingdom. Its true home country is South Africa, where The South African Breweries Limited (SAB) was founded in 1895 and where SABMiller today holds an impressive 98 percent share of the beer market. The firm operates seven breweries in South Africa, where it sells 14 brands of beer, including local lager Castle (the best-selling beer in Africa), SABMiller import brands Pilsner Urquell and Miller Genuine Draft, and one foreign brand brewed under license—Amstel. The company also maintains a major presence in the South African soft drink market through a 74 percent interest in Amalgamated Beverage Industries Ltd., the country's largest bottler and distributor of the Coca-Cola line of products, and full ownership of Appletiser South Africa (Pty.) Ltd., a producer of nonalcoholic sparkling fruit juices. In addition, SABMiller owns a 30 percent stake in Distell Group Ltd., the leading distributor of wines and spirits in South Africa, and 49 percent of Tsogo Sun Holdings (Pty.) Ltd., an operator of hotels and casinos in southern Africa.

South African Breweries embarked on an aggressive program of overseas expansion in the post-apartheid era, initially concentrating on the emerging markets of sub-Saharan Africa, central Europe (first entered in 1993, in Hungary), China (1994), India (2000), and Central America (2001). By the early 2000s SAB was the number two brewer in China and produced two-thirds of all beer in Africa. In July 2002 SAB acquired Miller Brewing Company, the number two U.S. beer producer, and renamed itself SABMiller plc. This move into the developed world was followed by a second, the June 2003 purchase of majority control of Birra Peroni S.p.A., Italy's second largest brewer. Via this acquisition spree, SABMiller had by late 2003 amassed a total of 115 breweries in about two dozen countries on four continents.

The history of SAB is in many ways the history of the South African brewing industry, most notably through the government-ordered merger of the largest breweries in 1956. The company's history was also greatly influenced by the apartheid system and its effect on the domestic economy, on domestic firms, and on foreign investment in South Africa.

Early History

The discovery of gold on the Witwatersrand (a region encompassing Johannesburg) in 1875 brought large numbers of prospectors to South Africa. Small outposts for white settlers were transformed into busy cities with new industries. Several brewmasters, most with little experience, began to produce a variety of beers that immediately gained popularity with the settlers.

In 1889 a British sailor named Frederick Mead left his ship in Durban and took a job working in the canteen of a local army garrison at Fort Napier. While there, Mead, who was only 20, became acquainted with a businessman in Pietermaritzburg named George Raw. Neither of them knew anything about brewing, but they persuaded the local residents to help establish the Natal Brewery Syndicate. After purchasing a factory site, Frederick Mead returned to England to procure machinery and raise capital. In need of brewing expertise, Mead approached W.H. Hackblock, head of Morgan's Brewery in Norwich. The two men became friends and Hackblock agreed to serve as chairman of Mead's company, which was registered in 1890 as the Natal Brewery Syndicate (South East Africa) Limited. The company brewed its first beer in July 1891.

Mead remained interested in establishing a brewery in the rapidly growing Witwatersrand. In 1892 he purchased the Castle Brewery in Johannesburg from its proprietor Charles Glass. The expansion of this facility, however, was beyond the means of the Natal Brewery Syndicate, and Mead returned to England to attract new investors. In the final arrangement, Mead formed another larger company based in London called The South African United Breweries. This company took over the operations of both the Natal Brewery Syndicate and the Castle Brewery.

After construction of the new Castle Brewery, South African United Breweries made additional share offerings which were purchased by South Africa's largest investment houses. Subsequent growth precipitated a restructuring of the company and reincorporation in London on May 15, 1895, as The South African Breweries Limited.

In 1896 South African Breweries purchased its first boarding houses. That same year, Frederick Mead moved to England for health reasons but continued to occupy a seat on the board of directors and frequently returned to South Africa. From London, Mead directed the purchase of machinery for brewing lager beer from the Pfaudler Vacuum Company in the United States. Patent restrictions and mechanical difficulties delayed production of Castle lager until 1898. The beer gained such widespread popularity that competing breweries rushed to introduce their own lagers.

South African Breweries, or SAB, was listed on the London Stock Exchange in 1895 and two years later became the first industrial company to be listed on the Johannesburg Stock Exchange. Through these listings SAB had greater access to additional investor capital.

On October 11, 1899, a war broke out between British colonial forces and Dutch and Huguenot settlers known as Boers. The war drove residents of Johannesburg out of the city and forced the Castle Brewery to close for almost a year. When British troops recovered the area, the brewery had sustained little or no damage. British authorities regarded the plant as an essential industry and encouraged the company to resume production in August 1900. Disrupted supply lines caused shortages of yeast and other raw materials, but within a year production had returned to full capacity.

The Boer War ended in 1902 but was followed by a severe economic depression. The brewing industry was not as adversely affected as others, however, and SAB was able to continue its expansion across southern Africa. The company acquired the Durban Breweries and Distillers company, and established a new plant at Bloemfontein. SAB purchased Morgan's Brewery in Port Elizabeth in 1906 and, five years later, acquired another brewery in Salisbury, Rhodesia (now Harare, Zimbabwe). At its northernmost point, SAB established a brewery at Ndola, northern Rhodesia (now Zambia).

W.H. Hackblock died in 1907 and was succeeded as chairman by Sydney Chambers. In 1912 Chambers led the company into an innovative arrangement with its competitor, Ohlsson's Brewery, to cultivate hops jointly at a site near the city of George, midway between Port Elizabeth and Cape Town. A joint subsidiary called Union Hop Growers spent many years developing new hybrids, which delayed the first commercial use of South African-grown hops until 1920.

Diversified into Bottles, Lodging, and Mineral Water in Early 20th Century

After Frederick Mead died in August 1915, John Stroyan, who succeeded Sydney Chambers a few months earlier, became the most important figure in SAB management. Stroyan faced a serious challenge the following year when hostilities during World War I interrupted the supply of bottles to South Africa. SAB decided to establish its own bottle-making plants in 1917. Actual production, however, did not begin until 1919, the year the war ended.

Another economic depression beset South Africa after World War I, but steady growth in the demand for beer reduced many of the detrimental effects of the depression. SAB was financially strong enough in 1921 to purchase the Grand Hotel in Cape Town, an important addition to the company's lodging business. SAB gained an interest in the mineral water business in 1925, when it purchased a substantial interest in the Schweppes Company.

The Great Depression of the early 1930s had little effect on the South African brewing industry; SAB continued to expand its operations and improve its facilities. The company's biggest problems were shortages of labor and capital. The Spanish Civil War and rising political tensions in Europe during the mid- and late 1930s caused a disruption in the supply of cork to South Africa. Faced with a severe shortage of cork seals for its beer, SAB developed a method of recycling old cork until a new supplier of cork could be found.

Castle Beer accompanied South African soldiers to the East African and Mediterranean theaters of World War II, but apart from its involvement in Europe, South Africa was relatively unaffected by World War II. When hostilities ended in 1945, SAB turned its attention to further modernization and expansion. Arthur Griffith-Boscawen, who had succeeded John Stroyan as chairman in 1940, died in 1946, and was replaced by John Stroyan's son, Captain John R.A. Stroyan. Under the leadership of the younger Stroyan, SAB concentrated on the establishment of a South African barley industry as an extension of the joint agricultural project it operated with Ohlsson's.

Key Dates:

1895: The South African Breweries Limited (SAB) is incorporated in London, with a listing on the London Stock Exchange and ownership of Castle Brewery in Johannesburg, South Africa.

1897: SAB becomes the first industrial company to be listed on the Johannesburg Stock Exchange.

1898: Company begins producing Castle lager, which becomes a phenomenal success.

1899: The outbreak of the Boer War forces Castle Brewery to close for nearly a year.

1925: Company diversifies into soft drinks, buying a stake in the Schweppes Company.

1950: The head office is moved from London to Johannesburg.

1956: SAB acquires Ohlsson's Cape Breweries and United Breweries, thereby uniting the three largest South African brewing companies and gaining 90 percent of the domestic market.

1970: SAB is reincorporated in South Africa.

1977: Company takes control of Amalgamated Beverage Industries Ltd., a Coca-Cola bottler in South Africa.

1979: SAB acquires the beer interests of the Rembrandt Group—giving it nearly 99 percent of the South African market—and turns over its wine and spirits operation to an independent subsidiary in which it owned a 30 percent interest; 49 percent stake is taken in Appletiser South Africa (Pty.) Ltd., a producer of fruit drinks.

1990: Dismantling of apartheid begins.

1993: International expansion into emerging markets begins with the purchase of majority control of Dreher Breweries, the largest brewer in Hungary.

1994: SAB enters the Chinese beer market through a joint venture with China Resources Enterprise Limited.

1997: Two-year program of divesting noncore assets begins.

1999: SAB relocates headquarters to London, reincorporates as South African Breweries plc; divestment program reduces interests to beer, soft drinks, wine and spirits, and hotels and gaming.

2000: Company buys its first brewery in India.

2001: SAB enters Central American market through purchase of Honduran beverage company and creation of a joint venture, BevCo Ltd., with a prominent family in El Salvador.

2002: SAB acquires Miller Brewing Company, the number two U.S. beer maker, from Philip Morris Companies Inc. for $3.48 billion in stock; company renames itself SABMiller plc.

2003: Company makes its first major investment in Western Europe, purchasing a 60 percent stake in Birra Peroni S.p.A., Italy's number two brewer.

Takeover of Ohlsson's and United Breweries in 1956

South African Breweries entered a new stage of its development in 1950. That year, in the midst of a large corporate modernization program, SAB decided to move its head office from London to Johannesburg. In 1951 the company acquired the Hotel Victoria in Johannesburg, and a second brewery in Salisbury. Captain Stroyan retired the following year and returned to England. His successor, a talented barrister named J.K. Cockburn Millar, died after only four months in office, and was replaced by a solicitor, S.J. Constance.

After producing nothing but beer for more than 60 years, SAB began to introduce a range of liquor products. The incentive to diversify was provided by increased taxes on beer. Consumption of beer in South Africa fell for the first time on record and showed every indication of further decline.

Officials of the three largest brewing companies in South Africa, SAB, Ohlsson's Cape Breweries, and United Breweries, met on several occasions in London and Johannesburg to discuss the viability of competition under deteriorating market conditions. In 1956 these officials decided that the three companies should merge their operations into one large brewing concern. SAB acquired all the shares of Ohlsson's and United Breweries, thus retaining the South African Breweries name. B.C. Smither of Ohlsson's and M.W.J. Bull of United Breweries joined the SAB board of directors.

Although the new company controlled 90 percent of the market for beer in South Africa, antiquated production facilities narrowed profit margins. In response, company activities were centralized in the Transvaal and the Western Province, areas where the three companies had previously competed. In addition, the old Castle Brewery in Johannesburg was closed in 1958. After succeeding Constance as chairman in 1959, M.W.J. Bull initiated a further diversification into wines and spirits. In 1960 SAB acquired the Stellenbosch Farmers Winery and later added Monis Wineries. Bull retired at the end of 1964 and was replaced by Dr. Frans J.C. Cronje, an economist and lawyer with substantial experience in government.

The company encountered a severe financial crisis in 1966 when Whitbread and Heineken entered the South African beer market. The most damaging market developments, however, came from government quarters as successive increases in excise duties made beer the most heavily taxed beverage per serving. Consumers began to abandon beer for wine and sorghum beer. SAB was able to reduce the effect of this crisis by increased sales of products from the Stellenbosch winery.

South African Breweries CEO Ted Sceales was instrumental in the creation in 1966 of a new subsidiary called Barsab Investment Trust, jointly held by SAB and Thomas Barlow & Sons Ltd. (later Barlow Rand), the rapidly expanding mining services group. Barsab permitted SAB and Barlow to invest in each other and pool their managerial and administrative resources. It also provided SAB with the resources needed to adapt to rapidly changing market conditions. Sceales died following an auto accident in 1967, but the success of Barsab continued under the new chief executive, Dick Goss.

South African Breweries first attempted to move its legal domicile from Britain to South Africa in 1950, but was prevented from doing so by complex tax obligations to the British government. Consequently, SAB, which still derived about one-third of its income from investments in Rhodesia and Zambia, was bound to observe the British trade embargo against Rhodesia in 1967.

Reincorporated in South Africa in 1970

Parliamentary motions to permit the reincorporation of SAB in South Africa were initiated in 1968. These motions, however, did not gain approval until March 17, 1970. On May 26, 1970, after 75 years as an English company, SAB became a de jure South African company.

During the mid- to late 1960s SAB began brewing a number of new beers—some under license from foreign brewers—including Guinness, Amstel, Carling Black Label, and Rogue. The company also acquired the Old Dutch and Stag brands, as well as Whitbread in South Africa. While sales of wine and spirits continued to rise, SAB sold a number of its liquor-oriented hotels, and reorganized those that remained under a new subsidiary called the Southern Sun Hotel Corporation. Southern Sun, which operated 50 hotels in South Africa, was formed by the merger in 1969 of the existing SAB hotel interests with those of the Sol Kerzner family.

The South African government barred SAB from further investment in the liquor industry and limited its ability to invest overseas. The company then made several attempts to diversify its operations. In 1972 SAB and Barlow Rand decided to alter their collaboration and dissolve Barsab. As a result, two former Barsab holdings, the Shoe Corporation, and Afcol, South Africa's largest furniture manufacturer, came under SAB control. The following year, SAB acquired OK Bazaars, a large discount department store chain. Certain other investments were disposed of, however, including ventures in banking and food products.

Several brewing interests attempted to challenge SAB's dominant position in the South African market. Various German interests set up breweries in Botswana and Swaziland in a failed attempt to gain a foothold in South Africa. Louis Luyt, a South African entrepreneur, also failed, and sold his breweries to the Rembrandt Group in 1973. The Luyt breweries, which formed the core of Rembrandt's alcoholic beverage group, were later incorporated as Intercontinental Breweries. Determined to succeed, Rembrandt's chairman, Dr. Anton Rupert, committed his company to a scheme of competition based on control of liquor retail outlets. In 1978 Rembrandt acquired a 49 percent share of Gilbey's, the third largest liquor group in South Africa. The addition of Gilbey's 100 retail outlets gave Rembrandt access to a total of 450 stores. South African Breweries responded by acquiring Union Wine, an independent liquor retailer with 24 hotels and over 50 retail outlets.

Once again, market conditions were not conducive to competition. The government, therefore, proposed a rationalization program in which SAB would take over Rembrandt's brewing interests—giving it nearly a 99 percent market share in South Africa—and turn over its wine and spirits operations to an independent subsidiary called Cape Wine and Distillers. The program, executed in November 1979, also called for Rembrandt to turn over its Oude Meester wine and spirits operations to Cape Wines, in which SAB, Rembrandt, and the KWV wine

growers cooperative each owned a 30 percent interest. The remaining 10 percent interest was sold to private investors. Also in 1979 SAB gained a 49 percent stake in Appletiser South Africa (Pty.) Ltd., a producer of nonalcoholic sparkling fruit juices; full control of Appletiser was gained three years later.

Government Restrictions Leading to More Diversification: 1980s and Early 1990s

By the early 1980s the South African government's system of racial separation (apartheid) and deteriorating social conditions for blacks had become international issues. Many business leaders openly called for change, but the government still prevented companies such as SAB from transferring capital out of South Africa through foreign investments. Often these companies had little choice but to reinvest their surplus capital in South African ventures, which in turn gave them a more crucial interest in the resolution of social and human rights problems within South Africa.

Many foreign-owned companies, which faced fewer restrictions on divestment, sold their South African subsidiaries and closed their offices in South Africa. This trend made acquisitions by South African companies easier. SAB had taken over control of Amalgamated Beverage Industries Ltd., a Coca-Cola bottler, from the Coca-Cola Company in 1977, and later added several clothing retailers, including Scotts Stores (acquired in 1981) and the Edgars chain (added in 1982). A government order in 1979 for SAB to sell its Solly Kramer retail liquor stores was completed in 1986, five years before its deadline. Also in 1986 SAB established a joint venture with Ceres Fruit Juices to sell leading noncarbonated juice brands Ceres, Liquifruit, and Fruitee.

In 1987 Murray B. Hofmeyer succeeded Cronje as chairman. Hofmeyer and his successor, Meyer Kahn, continued to diversify through acquisition, adding Lion Match Company, the leading manufacturer of safety matches in Africa, in 1987; Da Gama Textiles Company, a leading South African textile manufacturer, in 1989; and the Plate Glass Group, a manufacturer of glass and board products, in 1992.

International Expansion in the Post-Apartheid Era

The dismantling of apartheid finally began in 1990, with the unbanning of opposition political parties, including the African National Congress (ANC), and the release of political prisoners, including Nelson Mandela. Major political changes rapidly followed. In 1991 the remaining apartheid laws were repealed. In 1992, an all-white referendum approved a new constitution that would lead to eventual free elections. Finally, in 1994, the first nationwide free elections were held and were won by the ANC, with Mandela elected president.

SAB—acting largely out of self-interest given that 85 percent of the beer in South Africa was purchased by blacks—was well out in front of the political changes as it had begun to hire blacks in the early 1980s. By 1985, 28 percent of salaried employees were black, a figure that rose to 48 percent by 1994. Nevertheless, the threat of a government-forced breakup of SAB's beer monopoly hung over the company following the end of apartheid.

Partly in response to this threat, and partly in response to the loosening of laws regarding foreign investment, the Kahn-led South African Breweries aggressively expanded outside its home country starting in 1993. That year, SAB spent $50 million for an 80 percent stake in Hungary's largest brewer, Dreher Breweries, the first of a series of moves into the emerging markets of central Europe. From 1995 to 1997 the company gained joint control of two of the largest breweries in Poland, Lech Brewery and Tyskie Brewery, as well as three breweries in Romania and one in Slovakia. In 1994 SAB created a joint venture with Hong Kong-based China Resources Enterprise Limited; by early 1998 this joint venture had gained majority control of five breweries in China. A third area of foreign growth for SAB was in sub-Saharan Africa, where management control was gained of breweries in Botswana, Swaziland, Lesotho, Zambia, Tanzania, Mozambique, Ghana, Kenya, Ethiopia, Zimbabwe, and Uganda during this period.

In August 1997 Kahn was appointed chief executive of the South African police service, becoming the first civilian to hold the post. The outspoken Kahn, who had been vocal in calling for the rapid liberalization of the economy and for a restoration of law and order, was made responsible for cracking down on a national crime epidemic. Taking over as acting chairman of SAB was Cyril Ramaphosa, South Africa's most prominent black capitalist and a former militant trade unionist.

By this time, South African Breweries was the world's fourth largest brewer and had a rapidly expanding international brewing empire. The company was now free to unload its noncore businesses in order to concentrate more closely on brewing and its other beverage operations. Under Ramaphosa, it did just that. From late 1997 through early 1999 SAB divested its holdings in OK Bazaars, Afcol, Da Gama Textiles, Edgars, Lion Match, and Conshu Holdings, a footwear maker. With the mid-1999 sale of Plate Glass, SAB had trimmed its holdings down to beer, soft drinks, wine and liquor, and hotels and gaming.

The year 1999 was a pivotal year in SAB's history for a host of other reasons as well. Seeking access to capital markets better endowed that those at home, the company in early 1999 shifted its headquarters back to London—reincorporating itself as South African Breweries plc—and moved its primary stock exchange listing from Johannesburg to London, retaining the former as a secondary listing. As part of its London listing, it raised £300 million to fund further international expansion. There were also changes on the management front. Kahn returned to the chairmanship, his two-and-a-half-year stint at the police service complete; Ramaphosa remained on the board as a director. In addition, Graham Mackey, who had served as group managing director since 1997, was named chief executive in early 1999. On the international front, SAB acquired a stake in a sixth Chinese brewery in 1999 and began producing beer in Russia at Kaluga Brewing Company, which had been acquired the previous year. SAB's two Polish breweries, Lech and Tyskie, were merged to form Kompania Piwowarska S.A. The most important brewery transaction that year, however, occurred in October, when SAB acquired from Nomura International plc for $321 million a controlling interest in Pilsner Urquell and Radegast, two brewers in the Czech Republic that combined comprised the leader (with a 44 percent market share) in a nation whose citizens consumed more beer per capita than

anyone else in the world. The crown jewel of this deal was the Pilsner Urquell brand, the most famous Czech beer and the original pilsner, first produced at a brewery in Pilsen in 1842. SAB began laying plans to make Pilsner Urquell the company's flagship brand outside of Africa and to seek entrée into developed markets through the export of this brand. Via this acquisition, South African Breweries became the leader of the central European beer market and jumped into third place among global brewing titans.

Moving into the Developed World As SABMiller, Early 2000s

SAB's drive into emerging markets continued in the early 2000s. South African Breweries entered the Indian beer market for the first time in 2000, taking a majority stake in Narang Breweries. Control of two more Indian brewers, Mysore Breweries and Rochees Breweries, was purchased the following year. In April 2001 SAB and the Castel group, the two largest beverage companies on the African continent, entered into a strategic alliance whereby SAB exchanged a 38 percent interest in its African division (excluding South Africa) for a 20 percent stake in Castel's beer business. SAB thus gained a share of a wider array of African breweries, and the two partners also agreed to seek investments in new African markets via 50–50 joint ventures. Also in 2001 SAB entered into a new joint venture in China with the Sichuan Blue Sword Breweries Group, which owned ten breweries in Sichuan province. SAB now had interests in more than two dozen Chinese breweries and had positioned itself as that nation's number two brewer, trailing only Tsingtao. Yet another development in 2001 was that South African Breweries became the first international brewer to enter the Central American market. In November the company acquired a 97 percent stake in Cervecería Hondureña, S.A., the sole brewer and the largest bottler of soft drinks (Coca-Cola) in Honduras, from the Dole Food Company Inc. for $537 million. Simultaneously, SAB and the prominent Meza family of El Salvador created a joint venture called BevCo Ltd. to which SAB contributed its new Honduran holding and the Meza family contributed the bulk of its brewing, soft drink, and bottled water businesses in El Salvador.

By fiscal 2002, just eight years after its first brewing acquisition outside of Africa, 55 percent of SAB's $4.36 billion in revenues were derived from its non–South African operations. This figure would shoot up to an even more remarkable 75 percent just one year later following the company's boldest move yet—its takeover of Miller Brewing Company, the number two beer maker in the world's largest beer market, the United States, whose main brands included Miller Genuine Draft, Miller High Life, Miller Lite, and Milwaukee's Best. Consummated in July 2002, the deal consisted of a stock swap with Miller's owner, Philip Morris Companies Inc., that was valued at $3.48 billion. SAB additionally absorbed $2 billion in Miller debt. Upon completion of the acquisition, SAB changed its name to SABMiller plc and was now the world's number two brewer, behind only Anheuser-Busch. Philip Morris (which changed its name to Altria Group, Inc. in 2003) became the biggest SABMiller shareholder with a 36 percent economic interest and 25 percent of the voting rights (the total at which it was capped) and also gained three seats on the SABMiller board. Miller had recorded 2001 revenues of $4.24 billion but had for some time been losing market share to the number one and number three U.S. players, Anheuser-Busch and Adolph Coors Company, respectively. SABMiller took immediate action to try to reverse Miller's fortunes, announcing that one of Miller's nine U.S. breweries would be closed, and bringing in a new CEO for Miller, Norman Adami, who had headed up the South African brewery operations of SABMiller.

In March 2003, in a further pullback from noncore operations, SABMiller moved its entire hotel and gaming interests into a new company called Tsogo Sun Holdings (Pty.) Ltd., which was to be majority controlled by black empowerment company Tsogo Investments. SABMiller held an initial 49 percent interest in the new company but said that it intended to continue to reduce its hospitality holdings. Despite having just completed the Miller acquisition, the company did not shy away from making additional purchases and deals. Early in 2003 Browar Dojlidy, a brewer in northeastern Poland, was acquired for $38 million. In June SABMiller made its first major investment in Western Europe, buying a 60 percent stake in Birra Peroni S.p.A., the number two brewing company in Italy, for EUR 246 million ($279 million). Later in 2003 Peroni ended its licensed brewing and selling of the Budweiser brand in Italy and instead started import sales of Miller Genuine Draft. Similar synergies between SABMiller's increasingly global operations were being implemented, such as the launch of Pilsner Urquell and Miller Genuine Draft in South Africa in early 2003 and the introduction of Miller Genuine Draft into several more European countries, including Russia, Romania, the Czech Republic, and Poland. Over in Asia, SABMiller consolidated its operations in India under Mysore Breweries; the operations of Mysore were then consolidated with the brewing operations of Shaw Wallace and Company Limited, the second largest brewing group in India, to form a joint venture called Shaw Wallace Breweries Limited, 50 percent owned by Mysore. This deal cost SABMiller $132.8 million. The firm spent an additional HK$675 million ($87 million) for a 29.6 percent stake in Harbin Group Limited, China's fourth largest brewer and the leader in that country's northeastern region.

The SABMiller of the early 21st century, a globally active company with a sharp focus on beverages—mainly beer—was a far different company from the apartheid-era SAB, which was centered largely in South Africa where it had diversified interests. SABMiller had been built through a bold yet focused program of international expansion. It faced a real challenge, however, in turning around Miller Brewing, a process that Mackey said in late 2002 could take two to three years. In addition to attempting to make Miller Genuine Draft an international premium brand and launching new advertising campaigns in the United States, the new owners of Miller also planned to prune the more than 57 brands in the Miller portfolio, focusing more on the higher end of the market. SABMiller's bold moves, though clearly not yet fully realized, had the potential for a huge payoff.

Principal Subsidiaries

CENTRAL ADMINISTRATION: SABMiller Finance B.V. (Netherlands); SABSA Holdings (Pty.) Ltd.; SABMiller Africa and Asia B.V. (Netherlands). MILLER—US OPERATIONS: Miller Brewing Company (U.S.A.); Foster's USA, LLC (50%); Jacob Leinenkugel Brewing Co., Inc. (U.S.A.). CENTRAL

AMERICAN OPERATIONS: BevCo Ltd. (British Virgin Islands; 58%); Cervecería Hondureña, S.A. (Honduras; 58%); Industrias La Constancia, S.A. (El Salvador; 58%); La Constancia, S.A. (El Salvador; 58%); Embotelladora Salvadoreña, S.A. (El Salvador; 58%); Industrias Cristal, S.A. (El Salvador; 58%). EUROPEAN OPERATIONS: SABMiller Europe B.V. (Netherlands); Birra Peroni S.p.A. (Italy; 60%); Compania de Bere Romania (97%); Compania Cervecera de Canarias S.A. (Spain; 51%); Dreher Sörgyárak Rt. (Hungary; 99%); Kaluga Brewery Company OOO (Russia); Kompania Piwowarska S.A. (Poland; 72%); Pivovar Šariš AS (Slovakia); Plzeňský Prazdroj S.A. (Czech Republic; 97%). AFRICAN OPERATIONS: SABMiller Africa B.V. (Netherlands; 62%); SABMiller Botswana B.V. (Netherlands; 62%); Accra Brewery Ltd. (Ghana; 43%); Botswana Breweries (Pty.) Ltd. (29%); Cervejas de Moçambique SARL (Mozambique; 43%); Coca-Cola Bottling Luanda Ltd. (Angola; 28%); Coca-Cola Bottling Sul de Angola SARL (37%); Chibuku Products Ltd. (Malawi; 31%); Kgalagadi Breweries (Pty.) Ltd. (Botswana; 29%); Lesotho Brewing Company (Pty.) Ltd. (Lesotho; 24%); National Breweries plc (Zambia; 43%); Nile Breweries Ltd. (Uganda; 59%); Swaziland Brewers Ltd. (37%); Tanzania Breweries Ltd. (33%); Zambian Breweries plc (53%). ASIAN OPERATIONS: SABMiller Asia B.V. (Netherlands); Mysore Breweries Ltd. (India; 83%); Narang Breweries (Pvt.) Ltd. (India; 85%); Rochees Breweries Ltd. (India; 81%). BEER SOUTH AFRICA: The South African Breweries Ltd.; South African Breweries Hop Farms (Pty.) Ltd.; Southern Associated Maltsters (Pty.) Ltd. OTHER BEVERAGE INTERESTS: Other Beverage Interests (Pty.) Ltd.; Amalgamated Beverage Industries Ltd. (74%); Appletiser South Africa (Pty.) Ltd.

Principal Competitors

Adolph Coors Co.; Anheuser-Busch Companies, Inc.; Heineken N.V.; Interbrew S.A.; Carlsberg A/S; Companhia de Bebidas das Américas.

Further Reading

Anderson, Robert, and John Willman, "SAB Buys Czech Republic's Largest Brewer," *Financial Times,* October 8, 1999, p. 23.

Ashurst, Mark, "Breweries Chief to Head SA Crackdown on Crime," *Financial Times,* May 26, 1997, p. 22.

"Big Lion, Small Cage," *Economist,* August 12, 2000, p. 56.

Bilefsky, Dan, "Miller Beer Aims to Be Icon in Europe," *Wall Street Journal,* June 13, 2003, p. B7.

Block, Robert, "South Africa's Corporate Exodus Picks Up: A Big Brewer Announces It Is Moving to London," *Wall Street Journal,* December 7, 1998, p. A26.

Bobinski, Christopher, and Roderick Oram, "South African Breweries in Polish Acquisition," *Financial Times,* October 2, 1996, p. 24.

Branch, Shelly, "Ailing Miller Will Be Big Concern for New Philip Morris Chief," *Wall Street Journal,* January 30, 2002, p. B1.

Fairclough, Gordon, "Philip Morris to Sell Miller to SAB," *Wall Street Journal,* May 30, 2002, p. A3.

Fridjhon, Michael, and Andy Murray, *Conspiracy of Giants: The South African Liquor Industry,* Johannesburg: D. Stein, 1986.

Grey, Sarah, "No Small Beer from This SA Giant," *Accountancy,* November 1997, pp. 26–27.

Hawthorne, Peter, and Jan Stojaspal, "They Just Get Lager and Lager," *Time International,* December 20, 1999, p. 45.

Jones, Adam, "Brewer's Head Promises to Pull No Punches," *Financial Times,* November 22, 2002, p. 28.

Jones, Adam, and Lisa Urquhart, "SABMiller Takes Control of Birra Peroni," *Financial Times,* May 15, 2003, p. 20.

Kaplan, Andrew, "South African Time," *Beverage World,* July 15, 2002, pp. 11–12.

Kapner, Suzanne, "A Niche Brewer Is Making Waves," *New York Times,* December 4, 2001, p. W1.

Koppisch, John, Gerry Khermouch, and Kerry Capell, "It's Miller Time in Johannesburg," *Business Week,* April 22, 2002, p. 52.

la Hausse, Paul, *Brewers, Beerhalls, and Boycotts: A History of Liquor in South Africa,* Johannesburg: Ravan Press, 1988.

Lenzner, Robert, "Empowerment: South Africa's Most Visible Black Capitalist Was Formerly Its Most Militant Union Leader," *Forbes,* August 25, 1997, p. 47.

"Lion of Africa, Brewer to the People," *Economist,* September 9, 1995, p. 72.

Mallet, Victor, "SA Breweries Set to Unbundle Non-Core Assets," *Financial Times,* March 25, 1998, p. 44.

Martin, Peter, "Selling Old Beer in New Bottles," *Financial Times,* June 4, 2002, p. 17.

McNeil, Donald G., Jr., "In South African Beer, Forget Market 'Share,' " *New York Times,* August 27, 1997, pp. D1, D4.

McSheehy, Will, "The Best Brewing Strategy in the World—Probably," *Strategic Direct Investor,* January/February 2002, pp. 8–11.

Pringle, David, "Miller Deal Brings Stability to SAB," *Wall Street Journal,* May 31, 2002, p. B6.

"Rand Illusion: Africa's Largest Brewer Is Looking to China and Other Emerging Markets for Growth," *Institutional Investor,* April 2002, pp. 23–24.

Ross, Priscella, "SA Breweries Moves into Ethiopia, Uganda," *African Business,* December 1997, p. 28.

Simon, Bernard, "An Old School Brewer for Miller," *New York Times,* February 2, 2003, sec. 3, p. 2.

The South African Breweries Limited: 100 Year Commemorative Brochure, Johannesburg: South African Breweries Limited, c. 1995.

"Trouble Brewing for the ANC," *Economist,* May 21, 1994, pp. 70, 73.

"Under the Froth: South Africa's Beer Wars," *Economist,* February 8, 1997, p. 73.

Willman, John, and Robert Anderson, "SAB Is Prepared for More Beer and Scuffles," *Financial Times,* October 8, 1999, p. 26.

—update: David E. Salamie

Sadia S.A.

Rua Fortunato Ferraz, 659
Vila Anastácio
05093-901 Sao Paulo
Brazil
Telephone: (+55) 11-3649-3552
Fax: (+55) 11-3649-1785
Web site: http://www.sadia.com

Public Company
Incorporated: 1971 as Sadia Concórdia S.A. Indústria e
    Comércio
Employees: 32,184
Sales: R 4.69 billion ($1.18 billion) (2002)
Stock Exchanges: Brazil New York
Ticker Symbol: SDA
NAIC: 311611 Animal (Except Poultry) Slaughtering;
    311119 Other Animal Food Manufacturing; 311211
    Flour Milling; 311612 Meat Processed from
    Carcasses; 311615 Poultry Processing

Sadia S.A. is one of Brazil's leading food processing companies and the country's top producer in a number of food categories, including domestic poultry and pork, and poultry exports—the company ships to more than 50 countries worldwide, and counts among its customers such food chains as Arby's, McDonald's, and others. It is also one of the largest poultry brands in the Middle East, for which it operates special Halal-certified slaughterhouses in Brazil. Altogether, exports represented 42 percent of Sadia's nearly R 4.7 billion ($1.2 billion) in revenues in 2002. Sadia is a vertically integrated food producer, forming long-term and exclusive contracts with more than 9,000 Brazilian farmer-suppliers. The company operates 12 production plants throughout Brazil, processing more than 850,000 tons of poultry and 350,000 tons of pork each year, as well as pasta, margarine, and dessert and dairy products, the latter under the Miss Daisy brand. Since the 1990s, Sadia has emphasized a transition toward value-added processed foods, including frankfurters, sausages, and its own lines of ready-cook meals. Sadia (the name means ''Healthy'' in Portuguese) is listed on the Brazil stock exchange and trades its

ADRs on the New York Stock exchange as well. The company remains controlled by the founding Fontana family, represented by Chairman Luiz F. Furlan and CEO Walter Fontana Filho.

Healthy Beginnings in the 1940s

Attilio Fontana, son of Italian immigrants, began his professional career as a grocer. Yet Fontana also operated a small side business selling livestock, and it was this activity that brought him in contact with the owners of a grain mill and meat-packing plant in the town of Concordia, in Brazil's southern state of Santa Catarina. The owners of the plant, who had begun constructing a cold-room facility in the early 1940s, had fallen into financial difficulties and approached Fontana with the offer to sell him half of the business. Fontana agreed, and took over the direction of the slaughterhouse as well. Just one year later, Fontana bought out the original owners, and changed the company's name to Sadia—adding the ''dia'' from Concordia to SA (the equivalent to ''Inc.'') to produce the Portuguese word for ''healthy.''

Sadia started small, milling flour and wheat bran. Fontana reinvested those earnings and soon after was able to complete construction of the unfinished cold storage room. Sadia began processing pork, and by 1946, the company production topped 100 head per day. To its grain sales, Sadia now added a variety of pork cuts and other finished pork products, including lard, sausages, ham, salami, and other cured meats. Fontana, joined by son Omar, had already begun to think on a national level, and in 1947 the company opened its first sales office, in Sao Paulo.

If Concordia and the surrounding region became one of the fastest-growing economic areas of Brazil, in the early 1950s the region remained remote and difficult to access. Transporting goods was hampered by a poorly developed road network. In response, Omar Fontana launched a new venture, leasing an airplane from the Brazilian airline Panair and beginning air transports of Sadia's products to Sao Paulo in 1952. The move enabled Sadia to expand its distribution, and notably of its fresh meats. In 1953, the company adopted the highly popular motto: ''Pelo ar Para Seu Lar'' (translatable as ''From the Air to Your Lair''). Omar Fontana later expanded the group's air transport operation, which grew into the Transbrasil airline.

In 1953, Sadia also opened its first new meat processing plant, in Sao Paulo. The company then began expanding its commercial operation, opening sales and distribution centers in Bauru, Campinas, Ribeirao Preto, and Rio de Janeiro. Sadia also expanded its product line, adding chicken processing in 1956.

In order to ensure its livestock supply, and to guarantee quality standards, Sadia developed its own vertical integration model, based on partnerships with livestock producers. Launched in 1961, the program later grew to include more than 9,000 farmers in Brazil, who, in exchange for meeting Sadia's quality standards, received feed and technical assistance, and a steady sales outlet.

Sadia expanded again in 1964, founding Frigobrás - Companhia Brasileira de Frigoríficos, a cold storage food processing specialist that enabled the company to enter the branded processed and frozen meats market. Sadia launched a number of product lines, including, in 1969, its highly successful hamburger.

Growth and Diversification in the 1970s

Sadia continued to diversify its product offerings, testing turkey products in the 1960s, before rolling out its own range of fresh and processed turkey meats in early 1973. In the mid-1960s, Sadia also began its first export operations. Then in 1967, it added beef slaughtering and processing. In that same year, the company created a dedicated sales and marketing unit, Sadia Comercial Ltda., which took over its growing network of sales offices. By then, the company had opened offices in Porto Alegre, Erechim, Porto Uniao, Blumenau, Foz do Iguaçu, Curitiba, Londrina, Belo Horizonte, and Brasília.

Sadia's strong growth through the 1960s and its plans for future expansion brought it to the stock market in 1971, when it listed its stock on the Sao Paulo exchange. At that time, the company changed its name to Sadia Concórdia S.A. Indústria e Comércio. Yet Sadia remained controlled by the Fontana family, which held a majority of the company's voting rights.

Sadia's expansion continued through the 1970s and into the 1980s, as the company acquired a number of new meatpacking plants around the country. The company also opened plants in Toledo and Dois Vizinhos. In 1978, Sadia created its own research and development laboratory, Sadia Agropastoril. The following year, the company opened a new production plant in Rio de Janeiro. That same year, it acquired a soy milling and oil operation in Joaçba.

In the 1970s, Sadia stepped up its export operations, and especially, starting in 1975, sales of frozen chickens to the Middle East. For this effort, the company readily adapted itself, adding Halal-certified slaughtering facilities and developing chickens specifically for Middle Eastern tastes—which favored a smaller, single serving-sized bird. In this way, Sadia—which enjoyed the added benefit that its name closely resembled the Arabic word for "happiness"—quickly became the second largest poultry brand in the region. Sadia also enjoyed strong penetration into the European and U.S. markets, particularly through its pork and beef exports.

With its domestic profits eaten up by the hyper-inflation and uncertain currencies of the 1980s, Sadia focused on stepping up its export sales—a more reliable source of profits for the company. Sadia set up a dedicated international sales subsidiary, Sadia Trading, which enabled it to enter a number of new markets, and especially the Far East. Those regions, and particularly Japan, Hong Kong, and China, presented a similar profile to the Brazilian market, where rising spending power encouraged consumers to shift from largely grain-based diets to protein-heavy eating habits. Closer to home, the company shifted into neighboring Latin American markets, including Argentina, where the company began distributing its products in 1992. Yet the Middle East remained the group's strongest foreign market.

Supporting its growing markets, both at home and abroad, Sadia opened a series of new production facilities, including a soy processing center in Paranaguá in 1983 and another in Rondonópolis in 1986; a beef plant in Barra do Garças in 1985 and two more, in Andradina and Araçatuba in 1989. By then, the company had also opened a new pork packing plant in Três Passos in 1985.

Leading the Domestic Market in the New Century

Attilio Fontana died in 1989, leaving behind a sprawling empire of more than 20 companies. By then, Sadia's sales had topped $1 billion, and the company had succeeded in establishing itself among the leaders in the Brazilian food production market and particularly as the country's leading food exporter. The Sadia family, which by then was represented by seven—at times, squabbling—branches, chose Fontana's grandson Luiz Furlan to lead the company into the new century.

The introduction of the Real Plan inaugurated a new era in the Brazilian economy. With a new, more stable Real—the Brazilian currency—the domestic market entered a new era of fast growth. The stability of the market led Sadia to focus more of its efforts on domestic expansion, and into the mid-1990s, its exports levels actually dropped off somewhat in favor of sales at home. At the same time, the new access to foreign capital encouraged the company to expand rapidly—taking on a high foreign debt load. Unlike many of its competitors, however, Sadia recognized the risk in time, and began cutting its dollar debt, shielding the company from the worse effects of the country's economic slump in the late 1990s.

Sadia was not alone in its domestic expansion—indeed, competition among Brazil's food producers intensified during the 1990s, slashing into the company's margins. In response, Sadia began a cost-cutting effort, including the shedding of some one-third of its payroll, that enabled it to become one of the lowest-cost producers not only at home, but abroad as well.

Key Dates:

1942: Attilio Fontana acquires 50 percent of small grain mill in Concordia, Brazil.
1944: Fontana buys other half of business, which he re-names Sadia.
1946: Sadia enters pork slaughtering and processing.
1951: Sales office opens in Sao Paulo.
1953: Shipments begin by air, a move that leads to creation of Transbrasil airline; meat processing plant opens in Sao Paulo.
1956: Chicken slaughtering begins.
1961: Vertical integration is introduced through contract partnerships with farmers.
1964: Frigobras, a cold storage and frozen meats specialist, is founded.
1971: Sadia goes public and changes its name to Sadia Concórdia S.A. Indústria e Comércio.
1973: Company begins turkey meat production.
1975: Exports begin to Middle East, which becomes the company's largest export market.
1979: Acquisition of soy milling and oil operation is completed.
1989: Attilio Fontana dies and grandson Luiz Furlan takes over as head of the now $1 billion company.
1992: Sadia enters Argentina as part of South American expansion.
1997: Sadia restructures, expanding its processed foods operations, and selling off soybean and beef businesses.
1999: Frozen desserts brand Miss Daisy and pork and poultry products producer Rezende are acquired.
2000: Sadia forms Concordia Foods Ltd. joint venture in United Kingdom with Cargill Foods.
2001: Company forms BRF International export joint venture with Perdigao, but exits partnership the following year.
2002: Sadia creates Apprimus foodservice joint venture with Accor and Grupo Martins.
2003: After exiting Argentina market, Sadia announces plans to reenter Argentina; launches new ice cream line under Miss Daisy brand.

Another feature of the cost-cutting effort was the streamlining of the company's organizational structure, which ultimately resulted in the creation of a single group, Sadia S.A.

Sadia's restructuring continued into the late 1990s. On the one hand, the company streamlined its focus into the pork, poultry, and processed foods segments. As part of that effort, the company sold off its noncore operations, including its soybean processing wing, which was acquired by Archer Daniels Midland at the end of 1997 for $165 million. The company also sold its 12 grain storage and distribution centers, exiting that market as well.

Instead, Sadia concentrated its effort on expanding its range of value-added food products, including new lines of ready-to-eat and frozen meals. As such, the company's processed foods division became its fastest-growing in the early 2000s. Between 1999 and 2001 alone, Sadia launched more than 250 different products. As part of its new focus on value-added foods, Sadia made two important acquisitions during this period, buying the Miss Daisy line of frozen desserts and the poultry and pork producer Granja Rezende, with that company's strong line of branded products.

With competition growing in Brazil—particularly following the entrance of Italy's Parmalat and France's Doux—Sadia's export operations, now filled out with its processed foods lines, once again became the company's motor of growth. Exports showed a steady rise at the turn of the century, building from less than 27 percent of sales in 2000 to more than 42 percent of total group revenues in 2002. Aiding this effort were a number of partnerships, such as the creation in 2000 of U.K.-based Concordia Foods Limited in a joint venture with Cargill, which began supplying chicken for the McDonald's network in the United Kingdom.

Sadia stepped up its international stature in 2001 when it listed its shares as ADRs on the New York Stock Exchange. That year, also, the company joined with chief Brazilian rival Perdigao to create the export group BRF International Foods with the aim of developing markets in Russia and Eastern Europe and elsewhere. That partnership proved short-lived, however, and Perdigao took full control of BRF the following year.

A more fruitful partnership came when Sadia joined with France's Accor Group and Brazilian wholesale group Grupo Martins to establish Apprimus. That operation gave Sadia an entrance into the foodservice sector. Also in 2002, Sadia established a new Austrian subsidiary, Sadia GmbH, in order to enhance its exports to the European Community markets.

After abandoning Argentina in 2002, amidst that country's economic crisis, Sadia announced its intention to re-enter that market in 2003. Meanwhile, at home, Sadia prepared to launch a new product line, ice cream, under its Miss Daisy brand. The move marked a new highlight in Sadia's transition from pork and poultry specialist into a global branded food products group for the new century.

Principal Subsidiaries

Churrasq. Beijing (China; 50%); Concórdia Foods Ltd. (U.K.; 50%); Concórdia S.A.; Concórdia S.A. (Grand Cayman); EzFood Serviços S.A. (aka Apprimus; 33.33%); Laxness F.C.P.A.Lda.; Rezende Mkt. e Comunic. Ltda.; Rezende Oleo Ltda.; Sadia Argentina; Sadia Chile (60%); Sadia Europe Ltd. (U.K.); Sadia G.M.B.H. (Austria); Sadia Internatlional Ltd.; Sadia Itália; Sadia Uruguay.

Principal Competitors

Cargill Inc.; Tyson Foods Inc.; ConAgra Foods Inc.; Smithfield Foods Inc.; Orkla ASA; Hillsdown Holdings Ltd.; Nutreco Holding NV; Alfa S.A. de C.V; QP Corp.; Maple Leaf Foods Inc.; ContiGroup Companies Inc.; Protinal/Proagro CA; Keystone Foods L.L.C.; Perdue Farms Inc.; Perdigao SA.

Further Reading

''All Clucked Up,'' *Economist*, April 4, 1998.

Barbaro, Michael, and Steven Gray, ''Sadia Plans Return to Argentina,'' *America's Intelligence Wire*, September 19, 2003.

Colitt, Raymond, ''Business As Usual in a Financial Crisis,'' *Financial Times*, September 5, 2002, p. 13.

Millman, Joel, ''We Drove Our Exports Home,'' *Forbes*, December 18, 1995, p. 190.

Ogier, Thierry, ''Playing Chicken,'' *Latin Trade*, June 1999, p. 70.

Sadia's 50th Anniversary: Writing Its Own History, Sao Paulo: Sadia S.A., 1994.

—M. L. Cohen

Saputo Inc.

6869 Métropolitain Blvd. East
Saint-Léonard, Quebec H1P 1X8
Canada
Telephone: (514) 328-6662
Fax: (514) 328-3364
Web site: http://www.saputo.com

Public Company
Incorporated: 1954
Employees: 7,000
Sales: C$3.39 billion (US$2.3 billion) (2003)
Stock Exchanges: Toronto
Ticker Symbol: SAP
NAIC: 422430 Dairy Product (Except Dried or Canned)
 Wholesalers

Quebec's Saputo Inc. is Canada's number one dairy group, and, through a series of acquisitions in the late 1990s and early 2000s, has joined the top five North American dairy processors. Saputo has also taken its first steps on the global market, announcing its acquisition of Molfino, in Argentina, in October 2003. In addition to its flagship line of mozzarella cheeses, Saputo produces a wide variety of natural and specialty cheeses, including provolone, ricotta, cheddar, blue cheese, brie, camembert, and others. The company also boasts an array of brand names, ranging from its own Saputo brand, to Stella, Frigo, Dragone, Armstrong, Caron, and Cayer. A strong proportion of the group's sales come through industrial and foodservice channels. In addition to its core cheeses, Saputo, through its Dairyland, Baxter, and Nutrilait brands, is also Canada's leading producer of fresh milk, cream, butter, and other non-cheese dairy foods. The company operates through four primary divisions: Cheese (Canada), Cheese (USA), Milk, which is focused on the Canadian market, and Bakery. This latter, the company's smallest at less than 5 percent of sales, encompasses the Vachon brand, and includes such beloved Canadian snacks as Jos. Louis, Hop & Go!, Ah Caramel, and Passion Flakie. Listed on the Toronto stock exchange, Saputo remains controlled at 60 percent by the founding Saputo family, including Chairman Lino Saputo

and his son and company CEO Lino Saputo, Jr. In 2003, the company posted sales of C$3.4 billion (US$2.3 billion).

Sicilian Success Story in the 1950s

Sicilian native and master cheesemaker Giuseppe Saputo arrived in Montreal in the early 1950s and began working as a laborer. By 1952, Saputo had earned enough to bring over his wife, Maria, and their eight children. Among them was fourth child, Emanuele, more familiarly known as Lino, who at 17 years old had just completed his high school education. In 1954 Lino, fearing that his father was losing his dignity as a laborer, encouraged him to set up a small cheesemaking operation in order to produce mozzarella cheese for the city's Italian community. As Lino told the *Financial Post:* "I knew he could do much better for himself, so with $500 I'd saved we started making cheese in a corner we rented at a downtown cheese factory."

The Saputo family's initial production was limited to just ten kilos (22 pounds) per day. Lino himself took charge of delivery, using his bicycle. Within a few months, however, the family bought its first truck, and by 1957, demand for the Saputo family's cheese had grown so strongly that the family established its own factory, in the Montreal suburb of St. Leonard.

By the end of the 1960s, Saputo's sales had spread beyond Quebec, into Ontario and the Maritimes regions, although the bulk of the company's production remained targeted at the Montreal market. In order to support its expansion, Saputo began acquiring a number of Quebec dairies in the 1970s. By then, Lino Saputo had taken over as president and chairman of the company, after Giuseppe Saputo retired in 1969.

The company continued expanding nationally, adding operations in Manitoba and New Brunswick. By the end of the 1970s, Saputo had already become Canada's leading producer of mozzarella, eventually capturing more than one-third of the market. This position was supported by the company's 1981 purchase of a cheesemaking facility in Ontario. At the same time, Saputo built a new factory for itself in Mont Laurier to support its growth in its home Quebec region. In 1984, the company bought a new facility in Saint-Hyacinthe specialized in converting liquid whey—a byproduct of the company's cheesemaking operations—into whey proteins and lactose used by the food industry.

U.S. Entry in the 1990s

Saputo had long sought an entry into the U.S. market; yet that expansion was haunted by an incident in the early 1960s. In 1964, New York mafia boss Joseph Bonanno had attempted to gain Canadian citizenship in order to avoid U.S. prosecution, and to this end convinced Giuseppe Saputo to sell him a part of the family's business. Yet the Saputo family claimed that they had been unaware of Bonanno's reputation, and canceled the deal as soon as they learned of Bonanno's mafia connections. Nonetheless, the family company long lived under the shadow of its purported link to Bonanno—the company was even raided in 1972 by Montreal police. The police found no evidence of a mob connection, however. As Lino Saputo told *Maclean's:* "I can tell you, I've worked honestly all my life."

By the late 1980s, Saputo was ready to enter the United States. In 1988, the company made its first acquisitions in its southern neighbor, buying up cheesemaking factory in Vermont and Jefferson Cheese, located in Hancock, Maryland. Yet Canada remained the company's primary focus into the early 1990s, where the company backed up its domestic operations with the opening of a new headquarters, production, and distribution facility in its Saint-Leonard home.

Mozzarella remained the company's core product line into the mid-1990s as well. Still, as it faced the new century—and the coming end to trade barriers set up by the Canadian government to protect the country's dairy industry—Saputo launched a new, more aggressive expansion strategy.

In 1996, the company bought Fromages Caron, based in Beloeil, Quebec, giving it a new distribution arm specializing in imported cheese specialties, and especially French cheeses such as brie and camembert. The following year, however, marked still more significant changes for the company.

Saputo's next acquisition target was Canada's Ault Foods, a maker of cheese and butter, that had sold its fresh dairy business the previous year. However, Saputo's C$360 million bid was rejected as too low by Ault, which accepted an offer by Italy's Parmalat instead. In response, Saputo turned to a new market altogether, buying up Crémerie des Trois Rivières, also based in Quebec. That acquisition enabled Saputo to extend its operations into the fresh dairy, including liquid milk, and frozen dairy markets.

Saputo's thrust, nonetheless, remained its core cheesemaking operations. After being thwarted in a second attempt to

acquire a Canadian company, the company turned its acquisitive eye on the U.S. market. At the end of 1997, the company reached an agreement to acquire Illinois-based Stella Foods from Bass Brothers unit Specialty Foods Corporation for C$563 million. In order to pay for the acquisition, Saputo went public as Saputo Group Inc. on the Toronto stock exchange in October, in what was one of the country's most successful initial public offerings of the year. As a result, the Saputo family reduced its stake in the company to just 70 percent. In the process, however, Lino Saputo became one of Canada's wealthiest men.

Going Global for the New Century

The acquisition of Stella Foods not only gave Saputo a range of new brand names, including Stella, Frigo, Dragone, and others, it also tripled Saputo in size—pushing sales past C$1.5 billion and giving the company a place among the United States' leading cheesemakers, with a 9 percent market share.

Saputo's drive to solidify its position as one of North America's leading dairy products companies brought it to the U.S. cheesemaking capital of Wisconsin with the purchase of Avonmore Cheese Inc. and Waterford Food Products, formerly part of Ireland's Avonmore Waterford Group (later Glanbia plc). The purchase, for US$36 million, yielded more than US$180 million in new revenues, boosted Saputo's Italian cheese production, and added food ingredient production operations, including powdered and condensed milk products. Saputo continued its acquisition campaign in 1998, buying Riverside Cheese and Butter, based in Trenton, Ontario, and Bari Cheese Ltd., an Italian specialty cheese producer based in Vancouver.

Saputo began looking for new acquisitions in 1999, with a particular interest in consolidating its share of the U.S. mozzarella market—that cheese segment had become particularly attractive, due to the increasing popularity of pizza, and also to the growing tendency for time-pressed consumers to turn to frozen and other prepared foods, including pizza and lasagna.

Nonetheless, Saputo's next acquisition took it into a new product category altogether. Backed by the SGF (Société Generale de Financement du Quebec), Saputo played the role of white knight when it agreed to acquire Quebec-based Culinar Inc. for C$282 million, beating out a rival offer from Interstate Bakeries, controlled by Ralston Purina. The Culinar acquisition gave Saputo its first taste of baked goods, including leading Canadian brand Vachon. The deal also added another C$315 million to Saputo's annual sales.

At the same time, Saputo, which had earned itself the nickname as the "Mozzarella King" because of its nearly 40 percent share of the Canadian market, continued to broaden its offerings beyond that core product line. In January 2000, the company took a step in that direction by paying C$20 million to acquire Quebec's Cayer-JCB in order to access that company's expertise in the production of European-style cheeses, including havarti, brie, feta, and goat cheeses.

In 2001, the company's milk division acquired another scale altogether when Saputo purchased former dairy cooperative Dairyworld Foods, based in Vancouver, for C$400 million. That deal boosted the company's revenues past C$3 billion, making it the fifth largest dairy group in North America. Soon

Key Dates:

1954: Lino Saputo and parents Giuseppe and Maria Saputo begin making mozzarella cheese in Montreal in space rented in a local cheese factory.

1957: Saputo opens its first company-owned cheese factory in Saint Leonard, a Montreal suburb.

1969: Giuseppe Saputo retires and Lino Saputo becomes chairman and builds company into Canada's largest dairy products group.

1981: After expanding by acquiring a number of dairies in Quebec, Saputo buys a cheese plant in Ontario.

1984: Company acquires plant to process whey protein, lactose, and other food ingredients from liquid whey byproducts.

1988: Saputo enters U.S. market with purchase of facility in Vermont and cheesemaker in Maryland.

1996: Saputo acquires Fromages Caron in Quebec, adding that company's cheese import and distribution business.

1997: Company enters liquid milk and ice cream markets with purchase of Crémerie des Trois Rivières; goes public with listing on Toronto exchange; triples in size through purchase of U.S.-based Stella Foods.

1998: Company acquires Wisconsin cheese operations from Avonmore Waterford; acquires Vancouver's Bari Cheese.

1999: Saputo buys Culinar, the leading maker of snack cakes and other baked goods in Canada.

2000: Company acquires European cheese specialist Cayer-JCB.

2001: Company acquires Dairyworld Foods to become leading dairy products group in Canada; restructures into four primary divisions.

2003: Saputo moves onto global cheese market through acquisition of Molfino Hermanos, the third largest dairy products group in Argentina.

after that deal, the company found a home for the cookie, bread, and soup operations acquired with Culinar in family-owned Dare Foods Inc. In exchange, Saputo gained a 20 percent stake in Dare.

Saputo restructured in 2001, creating four operating divisions, Cheese (Canada), Cheese (USA), Milk, and Bakery, to reflect its expanded organization. By then, the company had already simplified its name to Saputo Inc., in a move to highlight its unified status.

Saputo's external expansion slowed down a bit in 2002, as it moved to integrate its newly acquired operations. Nonetheless, the company completed the purchase of a new mozzarella and provolone processing plant in Pennsylvania from ConAgra that year. The company returned to ConAgra in 2003, buying up the Treasure Cave and Nauvoo brands from ConAgra. That purchase gave Saputo a leading share of the North American blue cheese market.

At this time, Lino Saputo announced his intention to retire in 2004, and his decision to turn over the chairman and CEO positions of the company to son Lino, Jr., who had been serving as CEO of the company's Cheese USA division. Yet the elder Saputo had not finished guiding the company's expansion. In October 2003, the company signaled the start of a new direction when it announced an agreement to acquire the third largest dairy producer in Argentina, Molfino Hermanos SA, for US$51 million. The acquisition represented Saputo Inc.'s first step on its next frontier—that of the global dairy products industry.

Principal Subsidiaries

Saputo Cheese USA Inc.

Principal Divisions

Cheese (Canada); Cheese (USA); Milk; Bakery.

Principal Competitors

Kraft Foods Inc.; Leprino Foods Company; Parmalat North America.

Further Reading

Branswell, Brenda, "A Big Cheese Gets Bigger," *Maclean's*, March 12, 2001, p. 38.

Gibbens, Robert, "Saputo Put in Long Years to Have His Jos. Louis: It Took a Mere 45 Years to Make Saputo One of Quebec's Richest Men," *Financial Post*, August 5, 1999, p. 6.

Kohane, Jack, "The Big Cheese," *Food in Canada*, April 2000, p. 20.

"Saputo Founder to Retire," *Dairy Foods*, September 2003, p. 10.

"Saputo Gains Foothold for Export Strategy: Expands into Argentina," *Financial Post,* October 3, 2003.

"Saputo on the Prowl for Acquisitions in the US," *Food Institute Report*, August 19, 2002, p. 6.

—M. L. Cohen

Schlumberger

Schlumberger Limited

153 East 53rd Street
57th Floor
New York, New York 10022-4624
U.S.A.
Telephone: (212) 350-9400
Toll Free: (800) 997-5299
Fax: (212) 350-9457
Web site: http://www.slb.com

Public Company
Incorporated: 1956
Employees: 78,000
Sales: $13.47 billion (2002)
Stock Exchanges: New York Paris Amsterdam London
   Swiss
Ticker Symbol: SLB
NAIC: 213111 Drilling Oil and Gas Wells; 213112
   Support Activities for Oil and Gas Operations;
   333132 Oil and Gas Field Machinery and Equipment
   Manufacturing

As oil is explored for and developed all around the world, so is Schlumberger Limited providing a range of oilfield services and products spanning the entire reservoir life cycle. Among these activities are seismic surveying (through the 70-percent-Schlumberger-owned WesternGeco joint venture with Baker Hughes Incorporated), wireline logging (a company invention dating from 1927), directional drilling, measurements while drilling, well services from construction through completion, and integrated project management. Through 28 service regions, the firm's oilfield services operations serve customers in 100 countries. Nearly 70 percent, or $9.35 billion, of the company's 2002 revenues were generated by these services. Beyond these operations, Schlumberger (pronounced shlum-ber-jay) in the early 2000s also operated SchlumbergerSema, a unit that provided information technology consulting, systems integration, and network and infrastructure services to the energy and other industries. The company, however, announced in September 2003 that it would sell the bulk of this unit to Atos Origin

SA. Also designated for divestment is a unit called Axalto, which specializes in smart cards and point-of-sale terminals.

Founding an "Electrical Prospecting" Firm in 1919

Schlumberger was the creation of two brothers of that name, Conrad, born in 1878, and Marcel, younger by six years. Rooted in the Alsace region of France, the Schlumberger family had made its mark in both politics and business; the Schlumberger brothers' great-grandfather served as prime minister under Louis Philippe (the king of France from 1830 to 1848) and their father, Paul Schlumberger, later amassed a fortune in the textile industry. Conrad Schlumberger early displayed a genius for science and, by 1907, had become a professor of physics at the École des Mines, while his brother Marcel pursued mechanical engineering and business. Conrad became interested in the electrical resistance generated by different types of rock formation and was soon testing his results on the family's summer estate in Normandy. In 1914 Conrad successfully completed the first commercial application of this technique, locating a body of copper ore for a client in Serbia. World War I brought all experimentation to a halt, but in 1919 Conrad and Marcel Schlumberger set up a modest business in Paris to pursue the further evolution of electrical prospecting, as it was called.

At this point the brothers received crucial financial backing from their father, who made it clear that he considered their work a type of scientific inquiry, and only secondarily a means to monetary rewards. This scientific bias has remained strong at Schlumberger, which has always depended on its technological superiority. Bolstered by this aid, which eventually reached FFr 500,000, Conrad resigned from his teaching position in 1923 to devote his energy to the new company, which was named Société de Prospection électrique in 1926. Also in 1923, the brothers received their first order from an oil company, resulting in the successful mapping of an oil-rich salt dome in Romania.

A few years later the Pechelbronn Oil Company of France asked the Schlumbergers to make such measurements not from ground level, but from the interior of an already drilled borehole. Conrad asked Henri Doll, his son-in-law and longtime technical supervisor, to design the necessary equipment, and in September 1927 the men compiled the first "wireline log" by lowering an electrical recording device down a Pechelbronn oil well and measuring the resistance every few feet. The results were accurate, meaning that oil deposits could now be located and measured without resorting to expensive and time-consuming mechanical coring.

The world did not immediately beat a path to the Schlumberger door, however. By the time logging teams had been sent to Venezuela, the United States, and the Soviet Union, the Great Depression had taken hold, and drilling activity had come to a virtual halt. The Venezuelan tests went so well that Royal Dutch Shell became interested and ordered additional work to be done in Romania, Sumatra, and Trinidad. Furthermore, the Soviet Union proceeded with its drilling in the Baku oil fields regardless of the Depression, and there the Schlumbergers landed sufficient orders to get them through the first lean years. An ardent socialist, Conrad Schlumberger was pleased to do business in Soviet Russia.

Successfully Expanding into U.S. Market in 1932

The young company's biggest break came with its introduction to the U.S. market in 1932, when Shell asked it to run logs in California and on the Texas gulf coast. These again proved successful and Schlumberger was soon picking up business among the many wildcatters in Texas and Oklahoma. In 1934 the brothers founded Schlumberger Well Surveying Corporation in Houston, Texas, to meet the growing demand for their services, and this U.S. division soon became the largest and most profitable of the parent company's worldwide businesses.

Once underway, Schlumberger expanded rapidly, despite the Depression. The brothers had a long technological lead on any would-be competitors, an advantage the company has maintained to this day by consistently hiring top engineering talent and spending liberally on research and development. In addition, Schlumberger remained very much a family organization, with the resulting high degree of trust and unity helping to keep employees motivated and loyal. This became of greater importance after the death, in 1936, of Conrad Schlumberger. Marcel Schlumberger assumed control of a burgeoning business, which was already doing more than 1,000 logs a month in North America alone, but he soon had help from other members of the extended family.

As world depression gave way to World War II and France was overcome by Germany, Marcel Schlumberger worked with Jean de Ménil to move the corporation from Paris to Trinidad. De Ménil, the husband of Conrad Schlumberger's daughter Dominique, was a banker who became head of Schlumberger's financial affairs in 1939. De Ménil is generally credited with managing the move to Trinidad. De Ménil remained overseas and eventually became head of Schlumberger's South American and Middle Eastern businesses, operating out of the Houston office.

Although information is sparse, it is clear that the war was not good for Schlumberger's business. It was necessary to retreat before the Nazi advance, and the war effectively scattered key members of the Schlumberger family. Doll, the company's top technician, fled to Connecticut, where he formed a company called Electro-Mechanical Research that went on to do important work for the Allied war effort. Schlumberger eventually bought out Electro-Mechanical, and Doll emerged as the head of all technical research for Schlumberger worldwide. On the other side of the Atlantic Ocean, Marcel's son-in-law René Seydoux spent two years as a German prisoner of war before assuming control of all European operations. In Houston Pierre Schlumberger, Marcel's son and the only male heir of either of the founders, began to rebuild the U.S. business in 1946 and guided it back to a position of leadership.

Thus fragmented by war, the Schlumberger family was held together largely by Marcel, whose devotion to the business became legendary. In 1940, when it was clear that France would soon fall and many thought that the Schlumbergers would be ruined, Marcel Schlumberger was offered $10 million for his business by the head of rival Halliburton Oil. It is said that Marcel did not even respond to the suggestion, but instead showed his guest to the door.

When Marcel Schlumberger died in 1953, the remaining Schlumbergers were unable to decide on a successor. The firm was left divided, roughly between Doll, who controlled technical research; de Ménil, who controlled the business in South America and the Middle East; Seydoux, who controlled the company's European business; and Pierre Schlumberger, who ran the company's U.S. operations.

Incorporated in the Netherlands Antilles in 1956

Pierre Schlumberger, the natural candidate to follow his father as president, strongly favored incorporating the company and selling stock to raise capital needed to take advantage of the booming postwar economy. Other family members resisted the idea, fearing a loss of both control and quality, but in 1956 Schlumberger Limited was formed in Curaçao, Netherlands Antilles. That location was chosen for tax purposes. Pierre became president and Henri Doll was named chairman.

The new corporation was headquartered in Houston. It remained under family control, as it did for many more years, but it began to sell stock, and the fresh capital allowed Schlumberger to expand rapidly at a time when postwar U.S. oil drilling was at its peak. As the undisputed technical leader in the field, Schlumberger charged what it pleased, and when the initial financial statements were made public in 1958 they showed a first year profit of $12.2 million.

Key Dates:

1919: Brothers Conrad and Marcel Schlumberger set up a business in France specializing in "electrical prospecting."

1923: The brothers receive their first order from an oil company, mapping an oil-rich salt dome in Romania.

1926: Their business begins operating as Société de Prospection électrique.

1927: The company completes the first "wireline log" on an oil well in Pechelbronn, France.

1934: The brothers open a U.S. division based in Houston that soon becomes the company's largest and most profitable business.

1936: Conrad dies, and Marcel assumes control of the firm.

1940: As Germany conquers France, the company's headquarters are moved from Paris to Trinidad.

1953: Marcel Schlumberger dies, leaving a firm divided.

1956: Company is incorporated in the Netherlands Antilles as Schlumberger Limited, with headquarters in Houston; Pierre Schlumberger, son of Marcel, serves as president; the firm soon goes public.

1960: Company forms a joint venture, Dowell Schlumberger, with Dow Chemical to provide oil-well completion services.

1961: Schlumberger acquires Daystrom, a maker of electronic instruments, mainly military.

1965: Jean Riboud succeeds Pierre Schlumberger as company president; headquarters are relocated to New York City.

1970: Compagnie de Compteurs, French maker of utility meters, is acquired.

1979: Drive into electronics continues with acquisition of Fairchild Camera and Instrument Corporation.

1985: Schlumberger pays $1 billion for SEDCO, a large drilling company.

1986: Oil glut leads to the firm's first loss ($1.6 billion) since incorporation; Euan Baird, a Scottish geophysicist, becomes the first non-Frenchman to head the company; Schlumberger enters the seismic data field via acquisition of 50 percent of GECO of Norway.

1987: Schlumberger sells the money-losing Fairchild at a loss of $220 million.

1992: GeoQuest Systems, Inc. is acquired.

1993: Company buys out its partner Dow in the Dowell Schlumberger joint venture.

1998: Schlumberger acquires Camco International Inc.

1999: The company joins with Smith International Inc. in a drilling fluids joint venture, M-I; Schlumberger's offshore contract drilling unit, Sedco Forex, is spun off to shareholders and then merged into Transocean Offshore Inc., creating Transocean Sedco Forex Inc.

2000: Schlumberger and Baker Hughes Incorporated combine their seismic units into a joint venture, WesternGeco.

2001: Information technology concern Sema plc is acquired; Sema is integrated with several existing information technology businesses to form SchlumbergerSema.

2002: More than $3 billion in charges—mainly related to a writedown in the value of SchlumbergerSema—leads to a net loss of $2.32 billion.

2003: Baird resigns and is succeeded by Andrew Gould, who refocuses on oilfield services; company reaches an agreement to sell most of SchlumbergerSema to Atos Origin SA.

The next 25 years may someday be thought of as the company's golden age. By carefully managing the high profits earned by its wireline business, Schlumberger diversified slowly into a number of related fields, giving each acquisition the time and resources needed to make it healthy. Aside from a pair of French electronics firms, the company's first significant purchase was the 1959 acquisition of Forages et Exploitations Pétrolières (Forex), a French oil drilling company. A complementary deal was the 1960 formation of Dowell Schlumberger, a joint venture with Dow Chemical to provide oil well completion services such as cementing and flow stimulation. Schlumberger was now a complete oil services company, able to set up drilling operations anywhere in the world.

As oil drilling gradually fell from its 1957 peak, Pierre Schlumberger and his advisers thought it prudent to expand further into the electronics field. This was a natural extension, as Schlumberger had always used sophisticated electrical monitoring devices and was at home in the electronics field. Accordingly, the firm made a major acquisition in 1961 when it swapped stock with Daystrom, a manufacturer of various electronic instruments primarily for military use. With $90 million in sales, Daystrom was nearly as large as Schlumberger ($130 million), but did not turn a profit for several years after. The parent company pursued many other electronics concerns, eventually absorbing 11 French companies and several in England and the United States. Most of the newcomers required years of work before paying dividends; in 1966, for example, 42 percent of Schlumberger's $343 million in sales was generated by the electronics division, whose operating deficit held down overall corporate profit to $28 million.

After a few wobbly years in the early 1960s, the Schlumberger board of directors decided that Pierre Schlumberger should step down as president. Promoted to his place in 1965 was Jean Riboud, a longtime friend of the Schlumbergers, particularly Marcel. Riboud guided Schlumberger for the next 20 years, during which time the company's net income and worldwide reputation rose with equal regularity.

Riboud immediately moved corporate headquarters from Houston to New York City and reorganized the now diffuse company on the basis of product lines rather than geography. In 1970 Riboud further diversified the Schlumberger portfolio with the $79 million purchase of Compagnie de Compteurs, an aging French manufacturer of utility meters, which also took a few years to become profitable. By 1980 it had made Schlumberger the largest meter manufacturer in the world and formed the heart of one of the company's four divisions.

The 1973 OPEC oil embargo spurred a massive worldwide increase in oil exploration and drilling, with Schlumberger positioned to benefit from every new well. Its wireline services helped to find new oil, Forex-Neptune drilled the wells, and Dowell Schlumberger kept them pumping. In the space of five years Schlumberger's sales jumped from 1972's $812 million to a robust $2.2 billion in 1977, with profit exceeding $400 million in 1977. Schlumberger earned spectacular profits by delivering a superior and much needed product.

Unwise Acquisitions, Oil Glut Leading to Lower Profits: 1980s

The boom years at Schlumberger reached their peak in 1982. At that time the company had sales of $6.3 billion and profits of $1.35 billion, a staggering 21 percent ratio that made Schlumberger the most profitable of the world's 1,000 largest corporations. The firm's hold on the wireline logging business rivaled that of IBM's in computers, with seven out of every ten logs in the world taken by Schlumberger. Its drilling operation was the world's largest, and it produced more utility meters than anyone else.

As 1982 drew to an end, however, a close observer would have noticed that Schlumberger's quarterly profits were slipping, and they continued to do so as a world recession and greater oil conservation combined to put the brakes on oil exploration. In addition, Chairman Riboud had made a tactical mistake, and he was about to make a second. In 1979 Riboud paid $425 million to buy the leading American semiconductor manufacturer, Fairchild Camera and Instrument Corporation. Schlumberger hoped that Fairchild's technical expertise would help keep it ahead of the pack in its various fields, but the move was a failure from the beginning. Fairchild lost money and drained valuable research and development dollars from the rest of Schlumberger; the parent company was forced to write off much of Fairchild's assets and sell the rest to National Semiconductor in 1987, at a loss of $220 million.

Schlumberger's, and Riboud's, second mistake came in 1985, when it paid $1 billion for SEDCO, another enormous drilling company. Riboud apparently assumed that the oil glut would soon turn around; it did not. Riboud died in 1985 and was succeeded by Michel Vaillaud, who was ousted the following year by the board of directors, during a year that turned out to be the first one in which Schlumberger posted a loss ($1.6 billion) since incorporation. Next in the chairman's seat came 30-year Schlumberger veteran Euan Baird, a Scottish geophysicist and the first non-Frenchman in history to run the company.

Baird-Led Turnaround, Late 1980s Through Mid-1990s

As the oil glut continued, Baird quickly moved to turn the company around by refocusing on the core oil field services and measurement and systems business groups. In addition to selling Fairchild, other noncore businesses were divested. Schlumberger also underwent a restructuring to cut costs and become more cost-effective to survive in the difficult economic environment.

At the same time Baird was creating a leaner Schlumberger, he also invested heavily in research and development to keep the company at the technological forefront. From 1987 into the early 1990s, research and development spending was 37 percent higher than before Baird took over. The result was successful innovations, such as EB-Clean and Maxis.

EB-Clean, introduced in 1990, was an additive used in a well bore to enlarge cracks. After it drained away, more oil and gas was able to flow through the now larger cracks. The additive was developed by the joint venture Dowell Schlumberger, which Schlumberger later owned outright when it bought Dow's half-interest in 1993 for $800 million in cash and warrants.

Maxis, also developed in the early 1990s, was a premium imaging system that provided much clearer, more detailed, and faster evaluations of potential well sites than previous systems had done. When rival Western Atlas introduced a competitive system, Schlumberger was ready with a new Maxis Express unit that was smaller and 50 percent cheaper to operate.

In addition to new product development, Baird also actively sought out acquisitions to enhance Schlumberger's oil field services core. Soon after becoming chairman, Baird moved the company into a new area of oil field services, seismic data, which involved using and measuring sound waves bounced off the earth's surface to search for oil-bearing formations. In 1986 a 50 percent interest in the Norwegian firm GECO, one of the world's top seismic companies, was acquired; the remaining 50 percent was bought two years later. In 1991 Schlumberger acquired 51 percent of Prakla Seismos, a leader in onshore seismic operations, from the German government. In 1992 Seismograph Service Limited was purchased from Raytheon Company. The following year, Schlumberger purchased the remaining 49 percent of Prakla. All of the company's seismic operations were then combined within a Geco-Prakla division. The seismic area proved to be highly competitive and not immediately profitable, but by 1995 Schlumberger's focus on improvements to seismic technology had begun to pay off.

Another important acquisition came in 1992 when GeoQuest Systems, Inc. was purchased, also from Raytheon. GeoQuest specialized in computing and information technology services geared to hydrocarbon exploration and production. In late 1994 Schlumberger formed a joint venture, Omnes, with Cable & Wireless plc to provide communications and information technology systems for oil, gas, and other companies with operations in remote areas.

By the mid-1990s, it was increasingly clear that Baird had successfully turned Schlumberger around from that bleak year of 1986. In 1994 and 1995, the company achieved revenue of $6.7 billion and $7.6 billion, respectively, and net income of $536.1 million and $649.2 million, respectively. Schlumberger's wireline testing services remained the industry's unchallenged leader, and its growing stable of electronic subsidiaries was helping to keep the company at the forefront of technical innovation.

Acquisitions, Joint Ventures, and Divestments: Late 1990s and Early 2000s

Schlumberger rode the peak of the latest oil industry cyclical upturn to record results in 1997 of $10.65 billion in revenues and profits of $1.3 billion. But in 1998, even though revenues inched slightly higher, profits fell nearly 22 percent as the industry went into another tailspin. Demand for oilfield services declined sharply during the second half of 1998 as a result of the combined effects of the Asian economic crisis, tropical storms, and slumping oil prices. Schlumberger quickly cut costs, axing more than 10,000 workers from the payroll from mid-1998 to mid-1999. The corporation achieved just $366.7 million in net income on revenues of $8.39 billion in 1999.

In the meantime, consolidation in the oil-services field was continuing apace, with Halliburton Company acquiring Dresser Industries, Inc. and Baker Hughes acquiring Western Atlas Inc., both in 1998. Schlumberger engineered a large takeover of its own that year, buying out Camco International Inc. in August in a stock swap valued at $2.2 billion. Schlumberger also assumed $160 million of Camco debt. The purchase of Houston-based Camco, which had 1997 revenues of $913.9 million, filled a hole in Schlumberger's array of services—the high-end of the oil well completions business, which centered around building wells and readying them for production.

In another industry trend during this period, oil-services firms were forming a variety of joint ventures, and Schlumberger was a player here as well. In July 1999 Schlumberger merged its non-U.S. drilling fluid operations with the M-I unit of Smith International Inc., forming a new M-I joint venture, 40 percent owned by Schlumberger and 60 percent owned by its new partner. In addition to its contribution of assets, Schlumberger also injected $325 million into the venture. Just a couple of weeks after the deal's completion was announced, however, the U.S. Justice Department filed a petition in a U.S. district court accusing the two companies of a criminal violation of antitrust law. The government alleged that the new joint venture violated a 1994 consent decree that specifically barred Smith from combining M-I with the drilling fluid operations of Schlumberger and several other firms. In December 1999 a federal judge found Schlumberger and Smith guilty of criminal contempt, assessing each a fine of $750,000 and five years of probation. The firms also reached an agreement with the Justice Department whereby they would pay a $13.1 million civil penalty and would be able to continue operating the M-I joint venture.

Schlumberger next divested its offshore contract drilling business, Sedco Forex, in December 1999. This unit was first spun off to Schlumberger shareholders and then merged into Transocean Offshore Inc., creating Transocean Sedco Forex Inc. In November 2000 yet another joint venture was created. Schlumberger and Baker Hughes combined their seismic businesses, Geco-Prakla and Western Geophysical, respectively—the two largest seismic firms in the world—into a joint venture called WesternGeco. Schlumberger paid Baker Hughes $500 million as part of the transaction, which resulted in the former company taking a 70 percent stake and the latter a 30 percent stake.

Schlumberger's focus on technical innovation throughout its history naturally led the firm into the information technology field, and the firm had made some notable achievements, despite having never quite lived down its disastrous purchase of Fairchild. It had been one of the first commercial users of the ARPAnet (the precursor to the Internet) and had presciently registered the domain name slb.com in 1987, years before the World Wide Web had achieved any sort of critical mass. One of

Schlumberger's least-known achievements was its development of smart cards, which grew out of technology that the company had developed for oil wells. A smart card was similar to a credit card but had a computer chip embedded into it and a variety of applications. By the early 2000s they had become quite popular in Europe but were slow to catch on in the United States. Schlumberger bolstered its operations in this area in March 2001 by purchasing the smart-card unit of France's Groupe Bull S.A. for $313 million. In a much more ambitious foray into information technology, Schlumberger spent $5.19 billion to acquire Sema plc, an Anglo-French systems integration, consulting, and outsourcing firm, in April 2001. Sema's customers centered around the telecommunications, energy, transportation, and finance sectors. Its operations were integrated with several of Schlumberger's information technology units to form SchlumbergerSema.

By 2002, however, the Sema acquisition was already being viewed internally as a disappointment and externally as another huge mistake. The collapse of the technology and telecommunications sectors sharply reduced the value of SchlumbergerSema, and under new accounting guidelines related to the impairment of goodwill, Schlumberger was forced to take a charge of $2.64 billion to reflect the lower value of the unit. Additional charges of $587 million were also taken in 2002, most of which were tied to restructurings of SchlumbergerSema and the WesternGeco joint venture. About 1,200 WesternGeco employees lost their jobs as the company closed down the venture's land-mapping operations amid the start of another drilling downturn. At SchlumbergerSema, meantime, the businesses that revolved around products rather than services—including the smart cards, point-of-sale terminals, and utility meters units—were separated from the unit, which also began to focus more narrowly on services oriented to the global energy industry. This restructuring involved an additional 3,300 job cuts. The charges resulted in a net loss for 2002 of $2.32 billion on revenues of $13.47 billion. In December of that year, Schlumberger sold Reed Hycalog, a maker of drill bits that had been inherited from Camco, to Grant Prideco for $362 million in cash and stock.

In February 2003 Baird resigned and was succeeded as chairman and CEO by Andrew Gould. The new chief, who had headed up the firm's oilfield services operations from 1999 to 2002 before being named president and chief operating officer, quickly began refocusing Schlumberger on its core business. During 2003 the corporation's semiconductor-testing and electricity meters businesses were divested, and the smart-card unit was renamed Axalto in preparation for a sale or spinoff during 2004. Most importantly, the company announced in September 2003 that it had reached an agreement to sell most of SchlumbergerSema to Atos Origin SA for EUR 1.3 billion (US$1.5 billion) in cash and shares. Of the retained Sema operations, all except one were slated to be separately divested; the exception, the information technology business focusing on the upstream oil and gas market, was merged into the existing Schlumberger Information Solutions segment, which was already an integral part of the firm's core oilfield services operations. Once it was able to complete the divestments—and rid itself of what many analysts considered unnecessary distractions—Schlumberger seemed likely to become an even stronger player in the oilfield services sector.

Principal Subsidiaries

Schlumberger B.V. (Netherlands); Schlumberger Canada Limited; Schlumberger GmbH (Germany); Schlumberger SA (France); Services Petroliers Schlumberger (France); WesternGeco B.V. (Netherlands; 70%); WesternGeco A.S. (Norway); Schlumberger Offshore Services N.V. (Limited) (Netherlands Antilles); Schlumberger Antilles N.V. (Netherlands Antilles); Schlumberger Overseas, S.A. (Panama); MC&C Holdings Limited, (British Virgin Islands); Schlumberger Plc (U.K.); Schlumberger Evaluation and Production Services (UK) Limited; WesternGeco Limited (U.K.; 70%); Schlumberger Oilfield Holdings Limited (British Virgin Islands); Anadrill Holdings Limited (British Virgin Islands); Dowell Schlumberger Corporation (British Virgin Islands); Schlumberger Holdings Limited (British Virgin Islands); Schlumberger Middle East S.A. (Panama); Schlumberger Seaco, Inc. (Panama); Schlumberger Surenco, S.A. (Panama); WesternGeco Seismic Holdings Limited (British Virgin Islands; 70%); Schlumberger Technology Corporation; WesternGeco L.L.C. (70%).

Principal Competitors

Halliburton Company; Baker Hughes Incorporated; Weatherford International Ltd.; BJ Services Company; Smith International, Inc.

Further Reading

Allaud, Louis, *Schlumberger: The History of a Technique,* New York: Wiley, 1977.

Antosh, Nelson, "Seismic Handshake Deal," *Houston Chronicle,* June 1, 2000.

Auletta, Ken, *The Art of Corporate Success: The Story of Schlumberger,* New York: Penguin Books, 1984.

Barrionuevo, Alexei, "Schlumberger to Find Out If Oil and High Tech Mix," *Wall Street Journal,* February 15, 2001, p. B4.

——, "Schlumberger to Take Charges, Cut 3,300 Jobs," *Wall Street Journal,* December 11, 2002, p. A6.

Brown, Stanley H., "It's a "Slumber-Jay" and It's a Money Gusher," *Fortune,* September 1973.

Coffman, Peter, "The Data-Centric Corporation: Schlumberger in the 21st Century," *Oil and Gas Journal,* Fall 2000, p. 8.

Davis, Michael, "Smith, Schlumberger Hit with Fines," *Houston Chronicle,* December 10, 1999.

DeFotis, Dimitra, "Good As Gould?: New CEO May Get Schlumberger Back on Track," *Barron's,* February 10, 2003, p. T6.

Delaney, Kevin J., and Alexei Barrionuevo, "Atos to Acquire Schlumberger Unit," *Wall Street Journal,* September 23, 2003, p. B5.

Doherty, Jacqueline, "Here's One Slick Oil Outfit," *Barron's,* November 2, 1998, pp. 19, 21.

Dunham, Kemba, "Schlumberger to Buy Camco International," *Wall Street Journal,* June 22, 1998, p. A3.

Hager, Bruce, "How Euan Baird Is Pumping Life Back into Schlumberger," *Business Week,* July 9, 1990, pp. 52–53.

Headden, Susan, "Drilling Deep for Dollars: Oil Services Giant Schlumberger Uses New Technology to Coax Out Crude," *U.S. News & World Report,* July 10, 1995, pp. 40–41.

Lubove, Seth, "Do Oil and Data Mix?," *Forbes,* March 18, 2002, pp. 76–78.

McWilliams, Gary, "Schlumberger Digs Deeper," *Business Week,* July 27, 1998, pp. 48–49.

Pringle, David, "Schlumberger to Buy Sema for $5.2 Billion," *Wall Street Journal,* February 13, 2001, p. A21.

Reingold, Jennifer, "Reading the Rock: Schlumberger Outmaneuvers Its Competition to Keep the Lead in Oil Field Services," *Financial World,* March 15, 1994, pp. 26–27.

Santos, Karen, "Schlumberger Fills in Holes: Camco Sells for $3 Billion," *Houston Chronicle,* June 20, 1998.

Schlumberger: The First Years, New York: Schlumberger Limited, 1979.

"Schlumberger, Baker Hughes Combine Seismic Units," *Oil and Gas Journal,* June 12, 2000, p. 28.

Tejada, Carlos, "Schlumberger's Sedco and Transocean to Merge," *Wall Street Journal,* July 13, 1999, p. A3.

"This Is Schlumberger," New York: Schlumberger Limited, 1988.

Toal, Brian A., "The Path to Profits: Schlumberger Ltd.'s Oilfield Services Group Is Integrating New Technologies and Services to Fit Client Needs," *Oil and Gas Investor,* December 1993, pp. 60–63.

Walsh, Jennifer, and L.M. Sixel, "Smith, Schlumberger Facing Charges," *Houston Chronicle,* July 28, 1999.

—Jonathan Martin
—update: David E. Salamie

Showa Shell Sekiyu K.K.

Daiba Frontier Building
2-3-2 Daiba
Minato-ku
Tokyo 135-8074
Japan
Telephone: (03) 5531-5591
Fax: (03) 5531-5598
Web site: http://www.showa-shell.co.jp

Public Subsidiary (50 Percent Owned by Royal Dutch/ Shell Group)
Incorporated: 1942 as Showa Oil Co., Ltd.
Employees: 1,122
Sales: ¥1.62 trillion ($13.65 billion) (2002)
Stock Exchanges: Tokyo Osaka Nagoya Fukuoka Sapporo
Ticker Symbol: 5002
NAIC: 324110 Petroleum Refineries; 324121 Asphalt Paving Mixture and Block Manufacturing; 324191 Petroleum Lubricating Oil and Grease Manufacturing; 422710 Petroleum Bulk Stations and Terminals; Petroleum and Petroleum Products Wholesalers (Except Bulk Stations and Terminals); 447110 Gasoline Stations with Convenience Stores; 447190 Other Gasoline Stations; 454311 Heating Oil Dealers; 454312 Liquefied Petroleum Gas (Bottled Gas) Dealers

Showa Shell Sekiyu K.K. is one of Japan's leading oil refiners and distributors of petroleum products. The company is part of the Royal Dutch/Shell Group, which holds a 50 percent stake in Showa Shell. The company's main petroleum products include gasoline, diesel fuel, fuel oil, kerosene, jet fuel, naphtha, liquefied petroleum gas, lubricants, and asphalt. It controls three crude oil refineries in Japan through three affiliated companies: Showa Yokkaichi Sekiyu Co., Ltd. (refinery in Yokkaichi), Toa Oil Co., Ltd. (Keihin), and Seibu Oil Co., Ltd. (Yamaguchi); collectively, these refineries have a daily capacity of about 515,000 barrels. Two plants manufacture lubricants in

Yokohama and Kobe, and the company also maintains a petroleum import terminal in Niigata. Showa Shell operates approximately 5,200 gasoline service stations in Japan—garnering a 13.5 percent share of the domestic gasoline market in 2002—and also is engaged in the direct sale of various petroleum products to manufacturing firms, power companies, construction firms, and others. The company has entered into alliances and joint ventures with Japan Energy Corporation whereby the two firms cooperate in certain aspects of their refining and distribution operations. Showa Shell has further interests in the alternative energy sector, principally solar power generation systems and fuel cells. Showa Shell Sekiyu was formed through the 1985 merger of two oil companies, Showa Oil Co., Ltd. and Shell Sekiyu K.K. The two companies had had close ties ever since the close of World War II.

Early History

Petroleum was not commonly used in Japan until after 1868, when Japan opened its commerce to Western markets. Until that time, domestically mined coal was used for heating and energy. Though some oilfields were discovered in Japan, from the 1880s through World War II the Japanese oil market was dominated by two foreign organizations, Standard Oil and Royal Dutch/Shell. These groups, already operating on a global scale, were able to flood the Japanese market with cheap imported oil.

With Japan's military and industrial buildup in the years preceding World War II, petroleum came to be important to the country's economy. Jet fuel in particular was crucial to the success of the Japanese air force. Tokyo-based Showa Oil Co., Ltd. was established during the war, in 1942, from the merger of three smaller oil companies, Hayama Oil, Asahi Oil, and Niitsu Oil.

Shell Sekiyu was begun around 1876 in Yokohama by Samuel Samuel & Co., a forerunner of the Shell Group. In 1900 the company was incorporated as the Rising Sun Petroleum Company, to handle escalating petroleum imports.

Prior to World War II, oil production had never really been enough to support the industrializing nation. In addition, bombing during the war had decimated the company's physical plants. After the war occupation forces refused to allow the Japanese

Company Perspectives:

Showa Shell has a unique corporate culture that features the best of both Japanese and Western management practices. While working to accurately grasp the needs of local customers, we are quickly and boldly taking on the challenges of the changing roles required of today's companies. This hybrid business style has enabled us to lead the Japanese oil industry in corporate reforms. As a member of the Royal Dutch/Shell Group, a multinational corporation operating in more than 100 countries, the Showa Shell Group benefits from its shared technologies, expertise and data, and continues to move forward with industry-leading structural reforms in order to remain highly competitive in today's deregulated, international energy market.

refining industry to start up until 1949. At that time joint operation with a foreign company was the most effective way to revive the almost dead petroleum industry, and Showa Oil signed an operating agreement with Royal Dutch/Shell in 1949. Shell Sekiyu did the same a year later. The U.S. occupation forces encouraged these mergers. In 1951 the ties between Showa Oil and Royal Dutch/Shell deepened when the latter began making equity investments in Showa, eventually gaining a 50 percent stake. Shell Sekiyu remained 100 percent owned by Royal Dutch.

Building Refinery Capacity in the Postwar Era

In the 1950s Showa Oil and Shell Sekiyu were among several foreign-owned companies that dominated the Japanese petroleum market, focusing on rebuilding and expanding their refineries. Like most Japanese oil companies at that time, the Shell companies were not interested in exploration but in importing crude. The crude was refined, marketed, and distributed in Japan. In 1949 Showa Oil's Kawasaki refinery could handle 6,000 barrels of crude per day but capacity increased to 102,000 barrels per day by 1965. At the same time Shell Sekiyu had the capacity to refine 180,000 barrels per day. Most of the crude oil was imported from the Persian Gulf countries.

The tremendous buildup of the Shell affiliates' refining capacities was made possible without government loans, and with minimal government regulation. In the early 1960s, however, Japan's Ministry of International Trade and Industry (MITI) took an increasingly large role in the oil industry, in some ways working against Showa and other foreign-owned companies. The Petroleum Industry Law was enacted in 1962, which favored the development of domestically owned oil companies; the law also assigned to MITI a permanent supervisory role over the future development of the petroleum industry. The Japanese government wanted to avoid control of the oil industry by international oil companies, as had been the case before the war, and used its regulatory forces to ensure that domestic companies got favorable positions in the booming petroleum market. Around this time, Showa and Shell Sekiyu supplied roughly 12 percent of the Japanese oil market. Foreign-owned companies combined controlled roughly 80 percent of Japan's oil market, of which the Shell group was the third largest. MITI's aim was to approximate an even split between the international and domestic

companies' shares of the market. MITI achieved this desired balance over the next ten years, without adversely affecting Showa Oil or Shell Sekiyu. The new government regulations directly or indirectly shaped the business strategies of the Shell companies in the years to come.

An overall effect of the 1962 regulatory act was to increase competition among all the companies dealing in the Japanese oil market. MITI actively encouraged mergers between smaller domestic companies so they could rival the larger, older, foreign-affiliated firms such as Showa. The major *zaibatsu* established banking and corporate dynasties such as Mitsui, Sumitomo, and Mitsubishi, and plunged into the oil business around the end of the 1950s. With longstanding political and economic power in Japan, these groups did not take long to come to the fore of the petroleum industry. The Japanese oil market became more competitive because the major companies were for the most part caught up to each other technologically. Japanese engineers, sponsored by MITI, were working diligently to master and improve petrochemical technology. As long as the price of imported crude remained stable, the competitive edge in the domestic market would go to the company with the most efficient, low-cost refining technology.

The powerful backing of Royal Dutch/Shell propelled Showa Oil and Shell Sekiyu through the first decade of MITI's regulation. In addition, Royal Dutch/Shell had sources for crude oil in all parts of the globe. Foreign-affiliated firms still had advantages, particularly in international contract negotiations. The newer Japanese companies had little experience in negotiating drilling and exploration rights. Experts in Japan and abroad agreed that the new Japanese companies were not yet ready to take a major position in the world oil scene.

In the early 1970s, with rising political tensions in the Middle East, finding new sources of crude became important to the stability of the oil industry. By comparison with the other major international oil firms, Royal Dutch/Shell was considered short on crude oil. Its historical position as one of the two or three largest international oil companies was based on its efficient refining and marketing and long-range planning. Well before the 1973 OPEC embargo, the Shell companies were looking for oil sources outside the Middle East. Showa Oil began to seek out joint refining ventures abroad at the same time.

In 1975 Showa made an agreement with Algeria's National Hydrocarbon Corporation to provide technical assistance for the design and operation of two new oil refineries. Royal Dutch/Shell discovered a large natural gas field off Australia's northwest shelf around the same time; that gas was intended for marketing in Japan. Royal Dutch/Shell discovered the gigantic North Sea gas field in 1979, which improved the Shell affiliates' position considerably.

In the same year as the North Sea discovery, Showa Oil acquired a 25 percent interest in another Japanese company, Toa Oil Co., Ltd., which interest was formerly held by C. Itoh, a Japanese holding company. In addition to operating a refinery in Keihin, Toa Oil had valuable contracts to import and wholesale 230,000 barrels of oil daily through direct purchases; Toa could buy this oil directly from the oilfield, without any international oil company intermediary. MITI had encouraged the domestic

Key Dates:

c. 1876: Forerunner of Shell Sekiyu is founded in Yokohama by Samuel Samuel & Co., a forerunner of Shell.

1900: Yokohama firm is incorporated as Rising Sun Petroleum Company.

1942: Tokyo-based Showa Oil Co., Ltd. is established from the merger of three oil companies, Hayama Oil, Asahi Oil, and Niitsu Oil.

1949: Showa Oil signs an operating agreement with Royal Dutch/Shell.

1951: Royal Dutch/Shell begins making equity investments in Showa Oil, eventually gaining a 50 percent stake.

1979: Showa Oil buys 25 percent stake in Toa Oil Co., Ltd.

1985: Showa Oil and Shell Sekiyu merge to form Showa Shell Sekiyu K.K., which is 50 percent owned by Royal Dutch/Shell.

1993: Company loses ¥166.3 billion from $6.4 billion worth of speculative foreign-exchange contracts.

1996: Deregulation of Japan's oil industry begins; Showa Shell launches a multiyear restructuring program to adapt to the new environment.

oil companies to make direct purchase contracts. Though C. Itoh initiated the sale of Toa to Showa, MITI was disturbed by the transaction. The domestic company would lose its direct purchase contracts to the foreign-affiliated Showa, shifting the balance within the Japanese oil industry to foreign affiliates. The market split between the foreign and domestic groups was very nearly 50–50 before the Toa sale, and MITI wanted to maintain this even split or tip it in favor of the domestic companies. In this case, however, the industry went against the regulators' wishes.

Following the acquisition of Toa, Showa strengthened its ties with Kuwait. In 1980 the Kuwaiti government agreed to export 30,000 more barrels of crude oil per day to Showa Oil. Showa's efforts to secure a variety of sources for crude oil were generally successful in the 1970s. In the 1980s Showa found its profits still too closely tied to the fluctuations in the price of crude. In 1981 the company posted a loss of ¥21.2 billion. The next year, Showa showed a profit of ¥1.2 billion. In spite of highly sophisticated refining and marketing techniques, the company could do little to control the swings of the world's crude oil markets. Showa began to diversify its product line, and in the 1980s built and bought office buildings and apartment houses, to gain rental income. Showa also invested in rental car and travel businesses.

Formation of Showa Shell Sekiyu: 1985

Showa Oil and Shell Sekiyu formally merged in 1985. They had had a close operating relationship through most of their history. The merger made them equal partners in the new corporation, Showa Shell Sekiyu K.K. Royal Dutch/Shell retained a 50 percent interest in the new company. The merger streamlined

the Shell affiliates' operations and made management more efficient and cost-effective. Tokio Nagayama was named chairman of Showa Shell, having served for 17 years as president of Showa Oil, earning the nickname the "Emperor."

Despite the company's ventures into non-oil areas, including the 1987 launch of a computer software company, Computer Plaza K.K., Showa Shell Sekiyu's focus remained on oil. Exploration was still very much a part of the company's interests. For example, in 1990 the company bought a 20 percent interest in the development rights to inland oil concessions in Myanmar. Two years later Showa Shell took a stake in exploration blocks off the southwestern coast of Vietnam. By this time, Nagayama had retired, and Kiyoshi Takahashi had taken over as chairman, with Takeshi Henmi serving as president.

The two leaders, however, resigned in August 1993 to take responsibility for a huge loss that Showa Shell had incurred on foreign-exchange futures contracts. The company had revealed in February of that year that it had an unrealized loss of ¥125 billion ($1.05 billion) stemming from $6.4 billion worth of speculative foreign-exchange contracts involving bets on the value of the dollar versus the yen. The loss later ballooned to ¥166.3 billion because of further declines in the U.S. currency's value. As it wrote off these losses over the next couple of years, Showa Shell compensated by raising cash through the sale of securities and property.

Restructuring Following Deregulation, Late 1990s and Beyond

The Japanese oil industry entered a new, more highly competitive era in the late 1990s as a result of deregulatory moves initiated by the government. In April 1996 a law limiting oil imports to 29 refiners and distributors was repealed, opening the door for supermarkets, trading companies, and even farm cooperatives to begin importing petroleum products for direct distribution in Japan. Further roiling the industry was the late 1990s introduction of self-service gasoline stations in the Japanese market for the first time, after they had long been banned because of an arcane fire regulation.

Even before the deregulation began, Showa Shell launched an aggressive, multiyear program of restructuring to retain its competitiveness in the new environment. An ambitious cost-cutting effort gradually reduced the corporation's annual operating costs by ¥111.2 billion ($937 million) by 2002. During this period the workforce was cut in half mainly through attrition and voluntary retirement programs. The new competition resulted in lower gas prices at the pump, leading in turn to many gas stations no longer being profitable. Showa Shell, along with the other Japanese refiners, began shuttering underperforming outlets. Between 1996 and 2002, Showa Shell reduced the number of stations in its network by nearly 2,000. The company also joined in on the self-service revolution, opening its first such stations in 1999 and operating nearly 200 of the cheaper-to-operate outlets by 2002. In 1999 Showa Shell also closed down one of its four refineries, the one in Niigata, which had a daily capacity of 40,000 barrels. In addition to the cost-containment efforts, Showa Shell also strengthened its balance sheet, reducing its interest-bearing debt from ¥439.8 billion in 1996 to ¥150.5 billion in 2002.

In another key move during this period, Showa Shell began concentrating on the downstream side of the oil business, that is, refining and distribution. The company gradually dissolved and liquidated its oil-field development projects, finally shutting down its remaining upstream subsidiaries in the early 2000s. Eventually, therefore, the company began relying fully on imports from other firms to supply its refineries, and increasingly it derived its crude oil from companies within the Royal Dutch/ Shell Group—nearly 50 percent of the total by 2001.

The new competitive environment, coupled with overcapacity within Japan in both refining and distribution, brought about pressure for consolidation within the oil industry. For instance, Nippon Oil Company, Limited bought Mitsubishi Oil Co., Ltd. in 1999, and Tonen Corporation merged with General Sekiyu K.K. to form TonenGeneral Sekiyu K.K. the following year. For its part, Showa Shell in 1997–98 had discussed a merger of its refinery operations with those of Mitsubishi Oil, but the latter firm called off the talks. In the early 2000s, however, Showa Shell succeeded in creating several alliances and joint ventures with Japan Energy Corporation through which the two firms began cooperating in various areas of refining and distribution. Showa Shell was simultaneously pursuing a greater focus on more profitable value-added products. In March 2002 the company launched Shell Pura in the Tokyo metropolitan area, touting the new product as a high-octane "environmentally friendly," "engine-cleansing" gasoline; it was formulated to remove deposits from automobile engines, thereby improving performance and reducing the emission of harmful pollutants. Following its successful Tokyo introduction, Shell Pura began to be rolled out to other areas.

Heading up Showa Shell in the early 2000s was Haruyuki Niimi. In March 2002 John S. Mills was promoted from vice-president to president and chief operating officer, with Niimi remaining chairman and CEO. Mills became the first foreign national to occupy the presidency at Showa Shell Sekiyu, and he was expected to promote closer ties with the Royal Dutch/ Shell Group. Showa Shell had positioned itself through its thorough post-deregulation restructuring as one of the most financially sound of the major Japanese oil industry players. The company seemed poised to survive another round of industry realignments that many analysts were anticipating.

Principal Subsidiaries

Showa Yokkaichi Sekiyu Co., Ltd. (75%); Toa Oil Co., Ltd. (37.4%); Seibu Oil Co., Ltd. (24.5%); Showa Shell Sempaku K.K.; Hiewa Kisen Kaisha, Ltd.; Japan Oil Network Co., Ltd. (49%); JLS Corporation (50%); Niigata Joint Oil Stockpiling Co., Ltd. (28%); East Ogishima Oil Terminal K.K. (70%); Hokkaido Joint Oil Stockpiling Co., Ltd. (10%); Oita L.P.G. Joint Stockpiling Co., Ltd. (15%); Shoseki Engineering & Construction Co., Ltd.; Red and Yellow Co., Ltd.; Nippon Grease Co., Ltd. (99.3%); Rekisei Kagaku K.K.; Showa Solar Energy K.K. (75%); K.K. SVC Tokyo; Shoseki Kako K.K.; Shoseki Gas K.K.; K.K. Rising Sun; Sallis Co., Ltd.; Kyoto Sky Parking K.K.; K.K. Creco.

Principal Competitors

Nippon Oil Corporation; Idemitsu Kosan Co., Ltd.; Cosmo Oil Company, Limited; TonenGeneral Sekiyu K.K.

Further Reading

Ando, Mayumi, "Slick Moves Fuel Financial Strength," *Nikkei Weekly,* September 9, 2002.

"Competitive Pressures Fuel Oil Refiners' Move to Combine," *Nikkei Weekly,* February 24, 1997.

Dawkins, William, "Fueling Japan's Petrol Price War," *Financial Times,* December 14, 1995, p. 30.

Friedland, Jonathan, "Shell-Shocked in Japan," *Far Eastern Economic Review,* March 4, 1993, p. 58.

Harney, Alexandra, "Showa Shell to Cut Costs with Refinery Closure," *Financial Times,* July 16, 1998, p. 41.

Ikeya, Akira, and Hiroshi Toyofuku, "Showa Shell Execs to Resign over Losses," *Nikkei Weekly,* March 1, 1993.

"Japan: Today and Tomorrow," *Oil and Gas Journal,* May 31, 1965.

Nakamoto, Michiyo, "Tremors Follow Showa Shell's Futures Shock," *Financial Times,* February 23, 1993, p. 26.

Nakamoto, Michiyo, and Deborah Hargreaves, "Top Two at Showa Shell to Quit over Losses," *Financial Times,* February 26, 1993, p. 29.

"Shell's Foreign Exchange Disaster," *Economist,* February 27, 1993.

Vernon, Raymond, *Two Hungry Giants: The United States and Japan in the Quest for Oil and Ores*, Cambridge, Mass.: Harvard University Press, 1983.

Watanabe, Mika, "Japan Energy and Showa Shell Face Hurdles As New Partners," *Asian Wall Street Journal,* March 20, 2000, p. 22.

——, "Showa Shell Hopes Restructuring Will Prevent a Japanese Oil Glut," *Asian Wall Street Journal,* August 6, 1998, p. 23.

Yoshino, M.Y., *Japan's Multinational Enterprises*, Cambridge, Mass.: Harvard University Press, 1976.

—Angela Woodward
—update: David E. Salamie

Smith International, Inc.

411 North Sam Houston Parkway, Suite 600
Houston, Texas 77060-3545
U.S.A.
Telephone: (281) 443-3370
Toll Free: (800) 877-6484
Fax: (281) 233-5199
Web site: http://www.smith.com

Public Company
Incorporated: 1937 as H.C. Smith Oil Tool Company
Employees: 11,165
Sales: $3.17 billion (2002)
Stock Exchanges: New York Pacific
Ticker Symbol: SII
NAIC: 213111 Drilling Oil and Gas Wells; 213112
    Support Activities for Oil and Gas Field Operations;
    333132 Oil and Gas Field Machinery and Equipment
    Manufacturing; 333999 All Other Miscellaneous
    General Purpose Machinery Manufacturing; 325998
    All Other Miscellaneous Chemical Product and
    Preparation Manufacturing

Smith International, Inc. is a leading global supplier of products and services for the oil and gas and petrochemical industries. Smith International operates through four business units: M-I (49 percent of 2002 revenues), Wilson (28 percent), Smith Services (13 percent), and Smith Bits (10 percent). M-I specializes in drilling fluids and systems as well as equipment used in drilling to control solids, manage pressure, and handle waste; this joint venture is 60 percent owned by Smith International and 40 percent by Schlumberger Limited. Wilson is a distributor of a variety of products mainly used in the petroleum and mining industries and also provides supply-chain management services within these and other fields. Smith Services provides drilling, fishing, and completion products and services to the oil and gas drilling industry. Smith Bits designs, manufactures, and markets highly engineered drill bits mainly used to drill oil and natural gas wells. These units operate from more than 400 locations worldwide, and more than half of the com-

pany's revenues originate outside the United States. After filing for protection under Chapter 11 of the U.S. Bankruptcy Code in early 1986, and then emerging out of bankruptcy reorganized and restructured in late 1987, Smith spent several years consolidating its businesses before embarking on a ten-year spree of acquisitions in late 1993 that resulted in a remarkable increase in revenues from $220.7 million to $3.17 billion.

Early History

The historical roots of Houston, Texas-based Smith International originate in southern California, where the founder of the company, Herman C. Smith, resided and where the company maintained its corporate offices for most of the 20th century. The chain of events that led up to the creation of Smith International began in 1902, when Herman Smith opened a blacksmith shop in Whittier, California. Later that same year, oil was discovered in the area, a defining and auspicious discovery for Smith International and an event to be heralded by the 20-year-old Smith and his infant blacksmith shop. The arrival of oil rigs and attendant oil workers provided a welcome infusion of business for Smith's shop, keeping the young blacksmith busy sharpening the oilmen's drill bits and providing a steady source of cash. For years, Smith kept the area's drill bits sharp and repaired other tools used in drilling for oil, developing a relationship with the oil drillers who frequented his shop that gradually led Smith in a new business direction and formed the foundation for Smith International.

By listening to oil drillers discuss the shortcomings of the tools of their trade and by eliciting their suggestions for improvements, Smith developed an expertise that set him apart from the typical blacksmith and, over time, distinguished his shop as a haven for oil drillers and their equipment. Using the information he had gleaned from oil drillers, Smith began making unique adjustments to the tools brought into his shop and he began developing new tools. By the 1920s, Smith's business, which had been named H.C. Smith Manufacturing Company, subsisted on re-working fishtail bits and modifying oil tools as its mainstay business, having secured a place for itself in the California oil and gas industry by staying attuned to the peculiar needs of its customers. The business of H.C. Smith Manufacturing Company, however, would not be inherited by

Smith International, despite logical inferences to the contrary. In the history of Smith International, the three decades Smith spent in building H.C. Smith Manufacturing Company represented a proving ground for the establishment of the company that would eventually become one of the world's largest suppliers of drill bits and other oilfield products to the global oil and gas industry. For Smith International, the history of H.C. Smith Manufacturing Company was merely the prelude to its distinct genesis and the decades of development to follow.

The cause for the interruption was attributable solely to Herman Smith, who, by the late 1920s, had decided it was time to retire. In 1929, at age 47, Smith sold the business he had created over the previous 27 years to Globe Oil Tools, then settled into retirement and ended his working days in the oil and gas industry. As it turned out, however, Smith's departure from the oil and gas industry did not mark the beginning of his retirement, but rather the start of a seven-year hiatus. Unable to enjoy the vicissitudes of retirement, Smith returned to action in the business world when he purchased Allen Brothers Oil Tools in 1936 and then the following year renamed the company H.C. Smith Oil Tool Company, the earliest predecessor to Smith International.

Emergence of Smith International, 1960s

Once back in business, Smith set to work building an enterprise that would make his name internationally recognized decades after his death, leaving a lasting vestige to his efforts in creating H.C. Smith Manufacturing Company and H.C. Smith Oil Tool Company. The H.C. Smith Oil Tool Company corporate title was retained until 1959, when the company went public and changed its name to Smith Tool Co. The following year a parent organization, Smith Industries International, Inc., was formed to facilitate expansion both domestically and abroad in the coming decade, which the company accomplished at a 15 percent rate during the 1960s. By the end of the 1960s, yet another name change was in the offing, occurring in 1969 when "Industries" was dropped from the corporate title and Smith International, Inc. was adopted as the company's official name. As Smith International, Inc., the company would record its most prolific growth, rising to become an international giant in the oil and gas equipment industry, and, under the same corporate banner, the company also would struggle through its most tortuous years, teetering on the brink of failure.

By the beginning of the 1970s, Smith International had established itself as a leading manufacturer of drilling equipment for natural resource development, its broad line of drilling equipment used by companies involved in developing oil, gas, minerals, and water. Supported by a well-established overseas business, which generated nearly 40 percent of the company's total annual sales, Smith International had grown to become a roughly $100-million-a-year concern by the early 1970s, deriving three-quarters of its sales from its involvement in oil and gas markets. In the decade ahead, Smith International would register its most prodigious success, outdistancing its competitors to leap to the top tier of its industry, ranking, by the beginning of the 1980s, as the second largest drill-bit manufacturer in the world, trailing only Hughes Tool Company. Through internal growth, astute acquisitions, and international and domestic expansion, annual sales for the company soared exponentially, swelling to $1.2 billion by the beginning of the 1980s, while earnings followed suit, jumping to $133 million, more than the company had collected in sales a decade earlier.

Near-Fatal Developments in the 1980s

Despite the impressive financial figures posted by the company, the early 1980s marked the beginning of what could have been the end for Smith International, as the demand for oil rigs shuddered to a halt in the face of declining oil prices. Heavily dependent on the fortunes of the oil and gas industry, Smith International began to suffer from the repercussive effects of anemic drilling activity, not the first time the company's business had faltered in its nearly 50 years of existence in the frequently capricious oil market. Periods of market stagnation had pocked Smith International's financial performance throughout its history, but the effects of widespread depressed oil activity were exacerbated by other negative developments peculiar to Smith International, which would leave the company perilously close to complete collapse.

The first of the negative developments to compound the severity of pervasive depressed oil drilling activities was Smith International's ill-conceived, ill-timed attempt to take control of Gearhart Industries, Inc., an oilfield services company that specialized in sophisticated wireline, measurement-while-drilling services. In November 1983, as the oil industry continued its retrogressive slide, Smith International paid more than $100 million for General Electric Company's 23 percent stake in Gearhart, a move welcomed by Gearhart's founder, Marvin Gearhart, because it staved off General Electric's attempt to purchase his company. Marvin Gearhart's ire was raised, however, when Smith International increased its holding in Gearhart Industries to 33 percent, then announced it intended to acquire 56 percent of the wireline services firm. Marvin Gearhart vehemently opposed Smith International's tender offer and did everything in his power to thwart such a transaction from being completed, touching off a squabble between the two companies that, in the end, left Marvin Gearhart victorious in his attempt to keep his unwanted suitor at arm's length and saddled Smith International with enormous debt.

When the dust had settled from Smith International's failed attempt to acquire control of Gearhart Industries' sophisticated "downhole" measuring technology, the losses amounted to well over $150 million. Smith International withdrew its bid in March 1985, by which time the company had spent $165 million in trying to buy Gearhart Industries. The stock Smith International had acquired was sold for $80 million, but the company took an $85 million charge against working capital after selling its Gearhart Industries holdings, giving it a cumbersome burden to carry in the depressed economic times within the oil industry. By mid-1985, the combined effects of a laggard economic climate and the losses incurred from the failed Gear-

Key Dates:

1902: Herman C. Smith opens a blacksmith shop in Whittier, California; oil drillers soon develop into his main customers, with Smith sharpening their drill bits and repairing oil drilling tools.

1920s: Smith's company, now known as H.C. Smith Manufacturing Company, focuses on re-working fishtail bits and modifying oil tools.

1929: Herman Smith decides to retire and sells his business to Globe Oil Tools.

1936: Smith comes out of retirement to acquire Allen Brothers Oil Tools.

1937: Smith renames the company H.C. Smith Oil Tool Company.

1959: Company goes public as Smith Tool Co.

1960: To facilitate expansion, a parent company called Smith Industries International, Inc. is created.

1969: Company shortens its name to Smith International, Inc.

1983: Smith International acquires a minority stake in Gearhart Industries, Inc., a specialist in wireline, measurement-while-drilling services; Smith soon launches a takeover bid of Gearhart.

1985: Smith is forced to withdraw its bid for Gearhart, having spent $165 million trying to buy it.

1986: A federal court orders the company to pay Hughes Tool Company $205.4 million for infringement upon Hughes's patent for an "O-ring seal" rock bit; Smith International is forced to file for Chapter 11 bankruptcy protection.

1987: Having divested noncore businesses and reined in costs, Smith emerges from bankruptcy in December.

1989: Corporate headquarters are relocated from California to Houston, Texas.

1990: A proposed merger with Dresser Industries, Inc. falls through.

1993: Smith's directional drilling business is sold to Halliburton Company for $270 million.

1994: Smith acquires Dresser's 64 percent interest in M-I Drilling Fluids Co.; company reorganizes into three operating divisions: Smith Drill Bits, Smith Drilling and Completion Services, and M-I Drilling Fluids.

1996: M-I acquires Anchor Drilling Fluids.

1998: Company acquires Wilson Industries, Inc., distributor of oil and gas equipment, for $454 million in stock, and also buys Halliburton's 36 percent stake in M-I for $265 million.

1999: New M-I joint venture is formed that includes the non-U.S. operations of Schlumberger's Dowell unit; Schlumberger, which pays Smith $280 million as part of the deal, owns 40 percent of M-I, Smith owns 60 percent.

---

hart Industries acquisition had thrust Smith International into a precarious position, forcing it to close plants, lay off more than half of its 14,000 employees, and cease production of certain products. Annual sales, which had stood at $1.2 billion in 1981, plummeted to $747 million in 1984. Earnings took a more precipitous plunge, dropping from $133 million in 1981 to a loss of $65 million in 1984. By all accounts, the early 1980s had been disastrous years for the company, but the worst was yet to come. The "St. Valentine's Day Massacre," as a Smith International chief financial officer dubbed it, was looming ahead, and its arrival would deliver a near fatal blow to Smith International.

The company was still contending with the difficulties caused by its declining business and the Gearhart Industries imbroglio when, on February 14, 1986, the Federal District Court for the Central District of California issued a ruling that rocked all those at Smith International. The judgment by the court marked the culmination of a lawsuit originally filed by Smith International against Hughes Tool in 1974, a lawsuit Smith International would later regret having filed. By the end of the protracted legal dispute over patents, Smith International was found to be the culprit and was ordered to pay what ended up being $205.4 million for its infringement upon Hughes Tool's patent for an "O-ring seal" rock bit. Combined with Smith International's other losses, the ruling handed down by the court represented the third devastating strike incurred by the company, the meting of a "triple whammy" as one industry observer phrased it, and Smith International reeled from the successive blows, leading a host of bankers and analysts to predict that Smith International would either be sold or forced into Chapter 11 bankruptcy.

On the heels of the judgment against Smith International, immediate steps were taken to salvage the company, leading to what one analyst referred to as the company's "weekend bloodbath." Smith International laid off 32 vice-presidents, consolidated several divisions, and announced it would lay off as many as 2,000 employees, but by the first week of March 1986 there was nothing left to do but seek protection under Chapter 11 of the U.S. Bankruptcy Code.

While under Chapter 11, Smith International divested its noncore businesses, retaining only its tool manufacturing and drilling divisions to carry the company forward. Its corporate office building in Newport Beach, California, was sold as well as a plant in Irvine, California, giving the company $46 million to go along with the $200 million raised through its divestiture of noncore businesses. The company also reached a settlement with Hughes Tool over the patent dispute, paying that firm $95 million. Smith International's headquarters were relocated to a one-story industrial building next to its primary plant in Irvine, as consolidation and cost-cutting reigned during the company's nearly two-year-long battle to reorganize while in bankruptcy.

In December 1987 Smith International emerged from under the protective umbrella of bankruptcy, coming out of a year in which the company recorded $264.4 million in sales and registered a $26.1 million loss in earnings. Smith International was a shadow of its former self, but what remained was lean and, despite the loss recorded in 1987, capable of generating positive gains for the company. Over the course of the following year, a vibrant company began to emerge, buoyed by its continued investment in research that provided Smith International with a range of new, high-technology drilling products. Net productivity per employee during 1988 stood at $126,000, an all-time high, fueling hopes that the company had begun to wrest free from the debilitating first half of the decade.

In 1989 Smith International closed its sprawling 638,000-square-foot Irvine, California production facility, then consolidated all petroleum and mining-bit operations into its 169,000-square-foot manufacturing plant in Ponca City, Oklahoma. The company's headquarters moved as well, relocating from Irvine to Houston, Texas, where Smith International's management could superintend a company that had dramatically ameliorated its ability to compete as an oil and gas equipment and services firm. In March 1989 Doug Rock was named president and CEO. Rock, a chemist by training, had joined Smith in 1974 as a computer systems expert, working his way up through the ranks over the next 15 years.

Fueling Growth Through Acquisitions, 1990s and Early 2000s

Smith International entered the 1990s as a company well-positioned in the high-technology drilling market, where demand was high for its heavy investment in products such as "steerable systems," or devices patterned after aerospace guidance systems that allowed oil workers to drill in different directions from a single site. In 1990 a proposed merger between Dresser Industries, Inc. and Smith International fell through when Dresser Industries backed out of the deal citing potential antitrust problems with the U.S. Justice Department.

The corporation faced more litigation when a federal lawsuit was filed accusing Smith International, Baker Hughes Incorporated (the product of the 1987 merger of Hughes Tool and Baker International Corporation), Camco International, and Dresser Industries of fixing prices of drill bits from 1986 through 1992. Although Smith vehemently denied any wrongdoing, it agreed to settle the suit in 1993 because the other three defendant companies had done so. Smith agreed to pay a $200,000 fine to settle the criminal suit and $19 million to settle a civil suit brought by customers.

By 1993 directional drilling technology was emerging as a key drilling innovation. Smith International's operations in this sector accounted for more than 40 percent of the company's revenues, but Smith was at a competitive disadvantage because two much larger firms, Halliburton Company and Baker Hughes, were furiously pumping money into their directional drilling units. Rock decided the time was right to exit the business, and in March 1993 he sold it to Halliburton for $270 million in Halliburton stock.

The proceeds from this divestment were earmarked to develop a new niche for Smith International—drilling fluids and other well completion services—and to restore some of the magnitude lost during the previous decade. On February 28, 1994, eight years and two weeks after the bleakest day in Smith International's history, the company acquired Dresser's 64 percent interest in M-I Drilling Fluids Co., a $160 million acquisition that ranked as the largest in company history. It also provided a tremendous boost to Smith International's stature as a competitor in the oil and gas equipment and services industry.

Houston-based M-Drilling was a joint venture with Halliburton, which owned 36 percent of the venture. It specialized in drilling and completion fluids and systems, solids-control equipment, and waste management services for the oil and gas drilling industry. In drilling, fluids and muds were used for such procedures as cooling drill bits, lubricating drill pipes, flushing out rock cuttings, and balancing pressure in wells. Concurrent with the acquisition, Smith International reorganized into three operating divisions: Smith Drill Bits, Smith Drilling and Completion Services, and M-I Drilling Fluids. In the wake of the purchase of M-I Drilling, Smith International's revenues leaped to $653.9 million from the $220 million generated in 1993, while gross earnings doubled.

Over the next ten years, Smith International completed more than 40 acquisitions to strengthen its existing operations and diversify into related areas. In June 1996 M-I became the largest firm in the worldwide drilling fluids industry by acquiring Anchor Drilling Fluids, A.S. from Norway's Transocean A.S. for $114.7 million in cash and assumed debt. Anchor was particularly attractive because of its strong presence in the North Sea and Malaysia, where M-I had less of a presence. To pass antitrust muster with the U.S. Justice Department, M-I had to sell Anchor's U.S. operations, which were subsequently sold to Jordan Drilling Fluids. Of the several other acquisitions completed by M-I from 1996 to 1998, two were especially noteworthy. In October 1997 M-I spent $17.3 million for Calgary-based Fleming Oilfield Services, Ltd., a provider of drilling fluid products and services to the Canadian oil and gas industry. Then in May 1998 Safeguard Disposal Systems, Inc., of Lafayette, Louisiana, was bought for $42.7 million in stock and cash. Safeguard specialized in the rental of waste management systems used in petroleum drilling. Meanwhile, Halliburton reached an agreement in early 1998 on a merger with Dresser Industries. To gain approval for this deal from the Justice Department, Halliburton had to divest its 36 percent stake in M-I. In August of that year, Halliburton sold the stake to Smith International for $265 million, giving Smith full control of M-I.

During this same period, Smith Drilling and Completions made its own string of acquisitions. Among these were the October 1996 purchase of The Red Baron (Oil Tools Rental) Ltd. for about $40.3 million and the April 1997 buyout of Tri-Tech Fishing Services, L.L.C. for approximately $20.4 million. Based in Aberdeen, Scotland, Red Baron supplied fishing and other downhole remedial products and services to oil and gas drillers in the North Sea, the Middle East, and Southeast Asia. Tri-Tech, operating out of Lafayette, Louisiana, had an operational profile similar to that of Red Baron, but it was active in the U.S. Gulf Coast region. The Smith Drilling and Completions unit was renamed simply Smith Services in August 1999.

Smith International ventured into a new field in April 1998 through a merger with Wilson Industries, Inc. in a stock swap valued at about $454 million. Wilson, a private company based in Houston, was a distributor of pipe, valves, and other miscellaneous supplies to the oil and gas industry. Wilson became one of Smith International's main operating units.

Smith saw its revenues surge past the $2 billion mark in 1998 thanks to its string of acquisitions. But the oil industry went into another cyclical downturn, leading to a net loss of

$16.1 million in the final quarter of the year and full-year earnings of just $34.1 million, down from the 1997 total of $102.4 million. The company moved quickly to control costs, cutting its workforce from 9,100 in March 1998 to 6,300 in mid-1999. Revenues for 1999 fell about 15 percent, to $1.81 billion, but profits rebounded to $56.7 million.

In July 1999 Smith combined its M-I unit with the non-U.S. drilling fluid operations of Schlumberger's Dowell unit into a new M-I joint venture, 60 percent owned by Smith and 40 percent by its new partner. In addition to its contribution of assets, Schlumberger also paid Smith $280 million in cash. Just a couple of weeks after the deal's completion was announced, however, the U.S. Justice Department filed a petition in a U.S. district court accusing the two companies of a criminal violation of antitrust law. The government alleged that the new joint venture violated a 1994 consent decree that specifically barred Smith from combining M-I with the drilling fluid operations of Schlumberger and several other firms. In December 1999 a federal judge found Smith and Schlumberger guilty of criminal contempt, assessing each a fine of $750,000 and five years of probation. The firms also reached an agreement with the Justice Department whereby they would pay a $13.1 million civil penalty and would be able to continue operating the M-I joint venture.

With this legal distraction behind it, Smith International continued to seek growth via the acquisition route. Several deals involved M-I. In December 2000 M-I acquired Emerson's Sweco Division, a producer of specialty screen and separation equipment for oilfield applications, for $75 million. The oilfield and industrial screen operations of Madison Filter Belgium S.A. were acquired in October 2001 for $93.5 million. In January 2003 M-I paid about EUR 76 million for the oilfield chemical business of Finland-based Dynea International. Wilson, meantime, was bolstered through the January 2001, $41.1 million acquisition of Van Leeuwen Pipe and Tube Corporation, a Houston-based distributor of pipe, valves, and fittings to the refining, petrochemical, and power generation industries.

Smith International posted record revenues and net income in 2001 of $3.55 billion and $152.1 million, respectively. Yet another cyclical downturn in exploration and production hit the firm's results the following year, however, with revenues falling 11 percent and profits plunging 39 percent. Despite such inevitable setbacks, Smith seemed certain to remain one of the key players in the global oilfield products and services industry.

Principal Subsidiaries

S.I. Nederland B.V. (Netherlands); Smith (Bermuda) Ltd.; Smith International Acquisition Corp.; Smith International Australia (Pty) Ltd.; Smith International Canada Ltd.; Smith International do Brasil Ltda. (Brazil); Smith International Deutschland GmbH (Germany); Smith International Development

Corporation (Panama); Smith International Inc., S.A. (Argentina); Smith International Italia, S.p.A. (Italy); Smith International (North Sea) Ltd. (Scotland); Smith Internacional de Venezuela, C.A.; Wilhold, Inc.

Principal Operating Units

M-I (60%); Smith Bits; Smith Services; Wilson.

Principal Competitors

Halliburton Company; Baker Hughes Incorporated; Schlumberger Limited; Weatherford International Ltd.; BJ Services Company; Varco International, Inc.; Tetra Technologies, Inc.; Ambar, Inc.; Grant Prideco, Inc.; Ondeo Nalco Energy Services L.P.; Champion Technologies, Inc.; TIW Corporation; National-Oilwell Inc.; Redman Pipe and Supply Company; Derrick Corporation; McJunkin Corporation; W.W. Grainger, Inc.; Hagemeyer N.V.

Further Reading

"Another Setback for Smith," *Business Week,* March 3, 1986, p. 46.

Antosh, Nelson, "M-I Getting an Anchor in the Mud," *Houston Chronicle,* December 12, 1995.

Carson, Teresa, "Smith International: When a Takeover Try Goes Bust," *Business Week,* April 1, 1985, p. 65.

Davis, Michael, "Smith, Schlumberger Hit with Fines," *Houston Chronicle,* December 10, 1999.

De Rouffignac, Ann, "Rock on a Roll," *Houston Business Journal,* October 17, 1997, p. 12A.

Durgin, Hillary, "Purchase Puts Smith in New Fields: Wilson Industries Sold for $454 Million in Stock," *Houston Chronicle,* January 21, 1998.

——, "Smith Cut 900 Jobs in Quarter," *Houston Chronicle,* October 20, 1998.

Francis, Robert, "Smith Int'l Lays Off 32 VPs, Consolidates Some Divisions," *American Metal Market,* March 3, 1986, p. 4.

Ivanovich, David, "Smith International's Choice to Swim Against the Flow Proves to Be a Winning Strategy for Houston Drill Bit Company," *Houston Chronicle,* May 19, 1996.

Jaffe, Thomas, "Someone's Knocking," *Forbes,* May 7, 1984, p. 213.

Kindel, Stephen, "Mission Mistaken," *Financial World,* May 31, 1988, p. 16.

Klinkerman, Steve, "Marvin Gearhart Has Won His Independence—But Not Much Else," *Business Week,* April 1, 1985, p. 64.

Koprowski, Gene, "New Zealand Financier Wants Control of Smith," *Metalworking News,* June 5, 1989, p. 6.

Pybus, Kenneth R., "Revenues Rise After Largest Buy in Smith International's History," *Houston Business Journal,* June 9, 1995, p. 22B.

Walsh, Jennifer, and L.M. Sixel, "Smith, Schlumberger Facing Charges," *Houston Chronicle,* July 28, 1999.

—Jeffrey L. Covell
—update: David E. Salamie

Specialty Products & Insulation Co.

1097 Commercial Avenue
East Petersburg, Pennsylvania 17520-0576
U.S.A.
Telephone: (717) 569-3900
Toll Free: (800) 788-7764
Fax: (717) 519-4046
Web site: http://www.spi-co.com

Private Company
Incorporated: 1982
Employees: 500
Sales: $150 million (2002 est.)
NAIC: 235420 Drywall, Plastering, Acoustical, and
    Insulation Contractors

Specialty Products & Insulation Co. (SPI) is a privately owned company located near Lancaster, Pennsylvania. Through a number of subsidiaries, it fabricates and distributes mechanical, industrial, commercial, building, metal building, and HVAC insulation systems; passive fire protection systems; architectural/acoustical ceiling, wall, and flooring systems; and other specialty products. In addition, SPI offers specialty services such as energy audits, estimating, laser leveling and alignment equipment, material management, product training and installation seminars, and recycling/disposal programs. Domestically, the company maintains 70 facilities located strategically in 25 states, and it is able to export its products through a number of ports, including Baltimore, Boston, Charleston, Ft. Lauderdale, Houston, Jacksonville, Miami, New Orleans, New York, Philadelphia, Portland, San Francisco, and Seattle. SPI is also capable of serving its customers by importing products from overseas manufacturers.

Company Origins Dating Back to the Civil War Era

The foundation of SPI is very much tied to the history of Armstrong World Industries and the cork business. The founder of the Armstrong empire was Thomas Morton Armstrong, a Pennsylvania native whose parents immigrated to the United States from Londonderry, Ireland. As a young man Armstrong

worked as a shipping clerk for bottle maker Williams McCully & Co. By the time he was 24, in 1860, he was able to save enough money to invest $300 and buy into a two-man cork cutting shop owned by John O. Glass in Pittsburgh, Pennsylvania. Armstrong's brother would buy out Glass in 1864, and the business became known as Armstrong, Brother & Company. During this period, the main business for cork cutters, as Armstrong well knew from his days at McCully & Co., was to supply cork stoppers for bottles. The material was supplied by the bark of cork trees, imported from Portugal, Spain, and northern Africa, and was cut by hand until the process was automated in 1862. Like many businessmen, Armstrong greatly benefited from the Civil War, during which his cork company earned a solid reputation for supplying stoppers for the Union Army. Unlike many businessman of the period, who sold shoddy goods at exorbitant prices, Armstrong earned high regard for meeting its obligations at contracted prices. The company was also innovative in the way it stamped ''Armstrong'' on its corks and offered a written guarantee concerning the quality of the product. Following the war Armstrong landed the business of a major New York drug firm, a deal that was instrumental in establishing the company as a national concern. In 1878 Armstrong established an international presence when it began to process corkwood in Spain and directly import to the United States. In the 1890s Armstrong became the world's largest cork company. It also purchased the Lancaster Cork Works in southeastern Pennsylvania, which the company's headquarters would relocate in 1929.

Because other materials challenged cork in the beverage-bottling business, Armstrong found other uses for cork in the 1890s, including insulation and gaskets. The company also became involved in the linoleum floor covering business. Linoleum, invented in England in 1863 by Frederick Walton, was pressed from a blend of cork flour, mineral fillers, and linseed oil under high temperatures and then colored. A linoleum plant was built in Lancaster and in 1909 Armstrong began to market its linoleum. It was through linoleum that Armstrong evolved into a company devoted to a wide variety of floor coverings and other home products. As part of its push for diversification in the early 1900s Armstrong also entered the contracting business, installing cork insulation in commercial refrigeration systems—taking further advantage of cork's versatility. Because of cork's cellular structure it trapped small pockets of air, making it an excellent insulating material and a popular lining for ice houses, steam pipes, and homes. It could also be shaped without loss of its properties, thus it could serve as a natural gasket for machine parts.

Formation of Armstrong Contracting and Supply Corporation in 1957

Synthetic materials and chemicals replaced cork as Armstrong's primary raw material during the 1950s, accelerating the move into diverse product lines. In 1957 Armstrong packaged its insulation and contracting and distribution businesses into a subsidiary it named Armstrong Contracting and Supply Corporation, which was later renamed ACandS, Inc. By the end of the decade, 60 percent of sales were attributed to building materials, with industrial specialties and packaging accounting for 20 percent each. In the mid-1960s Armstrong became involved in carpeting and with the promotion of flooring executive James H. Binns to the presidency in 1968, the company moved even further away from its traditional businesses. The interior furnishings market was thriving at this time, prompting Binns to pursue an "interior world" concept for the company. During the next few years Armstrong sold off businesses that accounted for about 25 percent of its $500 million in annual sales. Because ACandS no longer fit into the parent company's vision for the future, its employees approached Armstrong's management about buying the subsidiary. Armstrong agreed and in 1969 a group of management investors created a holding company named North Lime Corp., an allusion to the Lancaster address of the business. It sold shares priced at $1.19 each to 31 investors, comprised almost entirely of existing or retired ACandS executives. North Lime then bought the outstanding capital stock of ACandS. A year later all salaried employees were given the chance to buy stock at $2.50 per share. Heading the new company was James W. Liddell, who was instrumental in the rise of both North Lime and, ultimately, SPI. He also provided the inspiration for a new name for North Lime, Irex Corporation, an allusion to a submarine he served on during World War II.

Despite poor economic conditions of the 1970s, over the next dozen years Irex not only managed to survive, it expanded beyond its ACandS holdings, so that by the early 1980s it was one of the country's leading commercial and industrial insulation and specialty contractors. By this point the mechanical insulation industry was undergoing a number of changes: many smaller contractors were entering the market while at the same time manufacturers were choosing to focus on the manufacturing operations and paying less attention to distribution. Irex recognized that there was a need and an opportunity to establish an independent distribution company to service the mechanical, HVAC, industrial, and commercial insulation industries.

In 1982 Irex executives Alexander V. Stoycos and W. Kirk Liddell cofounded SPI. Liddell was the son of Irex's original president. Born and raised in Lancaster, he had planned a career in government administration rather than to follow in his father's footsteps. After earning an economics degree from Princeton as well as an M.B.A. and law degree from the University of Chicago, Liddell was working for the Washington, D.C. law firm of Covington and Burling in 1980 when he decided to move back to Lancaster and take a position as Irex's general counsel. After cofounding SPI, Liddell was named Irex's chief executive officer in 1984 while Stoycos stayed on to head SPI. From the outset the goal of SPI's founders was to create a business that would one day be large enough to stand on its own. Their belief that a pure distribution business would replace the distribution operations of manufacturers and contractors was borne out by the growth of the company in the ensuing years. SPI expanded both through internal means and by acquisition. It also maintained ties with its ancestral roots, becoming a top-three distributor of Armstrong's commercial ceilings. The two companies worked closely together to determine the best way to sell more Armstrong products.

In the early 1990s SPI enjoyed an accelerated rate of growth. From 1992 to 1997 the company saw its annual revenues double to $158 million while operating profits tripled. Also in 1997, SPI surpassed the combined sales of Irex's three other subsidiaries, all specialty contractors. SPI was now large enough and established in the marketplace to fulfill the dream of its founders and become a stand-alone company. Unfortunately for Stoycos, his health was failing and in May 1997 he died. According to the *Lancaster New Era,* "Liddell drew some comfort from the fact that, in one of his last conversations with Stoycos, he informed Stoycos that plans to spin off SPI were being developed. 'He was very, very pleased to know,' Liddell said." He also told the *New Era,* "Irex's plan is a vote of confidence in the management of SPI." There were also very practical reasons for the spinoff. According to Liddell, "Contracting and distribution are very different. SPI requires a lot of growth capital. By putting SPI out on its own, it (can) raise money to acquire additional distribution businesses." Moreover, he maintained, "SPI's industry is consolidating right now, and SPI has the opportunity to be the leading consolidator, because of its market position and its reputation." Making SPI independent was also good for Irex's contracting businesses, which competed with a large number of SPI's customers. In addition, the contracting and distribution segments of Irex were often at odds in their needs, whether it be computers or the need for capital. "We'll no longer have to do things that fit both businesses."

Taking over as president of SPI following the death of Stoycos was Ronald L. King, who brought with him some 35 years of experience in the insulation, asbestos, and safety industries. Before joining SPI in 1993 he served as a vice-president and general manager at a major insulation contractor. Following the announcement that SPI would be spun off, King told the *New Era,* "Our whole theme is to leverage our business to provide unequaled customer service, continue to drive costs out of the system and create an environment where innovative and challenged people want to come to work."

The drive to make SPI a major industry consolidator was launched well before the spinoff was finalized. In November

Key Dates:

1860: Thomas Morton Armstrong becomes involved in cork business.
1957: Armstrong forms Armstrong Contracting and Supply Corporation.
1969: Armstrong Contracting is sold to an employee-led group, becoming part of Irex Corporation.
1982: Irex forms distributing subsidiary Specialty Products & Insulation Co. (SPI).
1998: Irex spins off SPI.

1997 SPI acquired Richlar Industries, an upstate New York company that served air conditioning and heating manufacturers, packaging, specialty wholesale, and retail customers. Richlar specialized in precision die cutting, lamination, specialty fabrication, and material conversion (such as rubber, fiberglass, elastomeric, and polyethylene) to customer specifications. In December 1997 SPI added Construction Systems, whose specialty products included acoustical systems and such architectural products as drywall and metal studs. In March 1998 SPI acquired Extol, a Texas insulation fabrication house and distributor serving the Gulf Coast as well as international customers.

Canceling the 1998 IPO

Following Irex's January 1998 announcement that it would spin off its distribution subsidiary, SPI filed paperwork with the SEC on April 10 in order to conduct an initial public offering (IPO) of stock. The plan was to sell two million shares of common stock, priced between $10 and $12 per share. The offering was to take place in June but poor market conditions for small-cap companies resulted in a postponement and eventually a cancellation. Instead, in October 1998 Irex and SPI worked out another way to spin off the business and enjoy an infusion of cash. The revised plan called for Irex shareholders to receive one share of SPI stock for every 50 shares of Irex stock they owned. In addition, a New York City private equity firm, Evercore Capital Partners, agreed to purchase $15.4 million of common stock and $3.5 million of subordinated debt, resulting in Evercore owning a 45 percent stake in SPI. In addition, Evercore made a commitment to invest as much as $20 million in financing through subordinated debt to pay for further SPI acquisitions over the next three years. SPI also retained the ability to offer an IPO at a later date. According to CEO King, "This transaction greatly enhances SPI's financial strength and, in my opinion, is a better result than we would have gotten from the IPO."

SPI completed three more acquisitions in 1998. In May it added Presnell Insulation, a southeastern group of fabrication houses. SPI bought Paragon Pacific Insulation (the company's only formal subsidiary). Paragon distributed insulation products to commercial and industrial customers in the Northwest. In December 1998 SPI closed on two deals, picking up Chem-

power, a distribution/fabrication business serving the Ohio and West Virginia Valley markets, and Acoustical Supply Corporation, distributors of architectural, acoustical, and specialty products in mid-Atlantic markets.

In 1999 and 2000 SPI acquired seven more businesses. In May 1999 Acoustical & Interior Distributors was bought, adding to SPI's capacity to service the midwestern commercial building industry. A month later SPI closed on the purchase of Pamrod Products Company, maker of insulation vessel head products. SPI completed four acquisitions in August 1999. The first, Goodwin Insulation Distributors, served the commercial and industrial customers in New England. The second, House of Ladders, offered some diversity to SPI. The specialty distributor provided a broad range of ladder products, including step ladders, extension ladders, work stands, trestle ladders, and ladder jackets. SPI also added Abacus, Inc., a wholesale distributor of acoustical ceiling systems and commercial building materials in the Atlanta and northern Georgia market. Finally in August, SPI picked up International Technifab, a mechanical and building insulation distributor and fabricator, serving the Mountain States Region. In March 2000 SPI acquired Alpha Sales & Contracting, serving commercial and industrial customers in Oklahoma and Kansas.

As a private company, SPI had no incentive to reveal how well it was able to assimilate its slate of acquisitions or how well it was doing financially. Neither did SPI feel the need to promote itself in the press, relying instead on a longstanding reputation for excellence to maintain a leading position in its industry. With the advent of difficult business conditions in the new century, SPI ceased its buying spree and waited for better economic times to emerge. Despite the lack of forthcoming information on the company's finances, there was every reason to believe that SPI would remain a healthy and viable concern.

Principal Subsidiaries

Paragon Industries, Inc.

Principal Competitors

Guardian Building Products; Johns Manville Corporation.

Further Reading

Hanson, Joyce, "Irex Corp. Spins Off Subsidiary," *Central Penn Business Journal,* March 12, 1999, p. 1.
Mekeel, Tim, "'It's Able to Function on Its Own,'" *Lancaster New Era,* February 12, 1998, p. B5.
Reiff, Annette, "International Irex Calls Lancaster Home," *Central Penn Business Journal,* January 31, 1997, p. 12.
Rohland, Pamela, "Top Fifty Fastest Growing Companies: Specialty Products & Insulation Co. #14," *Central Penn Business Journal,* October 9, 1998, p. S14.

—Ed Dinger

spirax/sarco

Spirax-Sarco Engineering plc

Charlton House
Cirencester Rd.
Cheltenham, Gloucestershire GL53 8ER
United Kingdom
Telephone: (+44) 1242-521361
Fax: (+44) 1242-581470
Web site: http://www.spiraxsarcoengineering.com

Public Company
Incorporated: 1952 as Spirax-Sarco Ltd.
Employees: 3,998
Sales: £296.4 million ($492.9 million) (2002)
Stock Exchanges: London
Ticker Symbol: SPX
NAIC: 332911 Industrial Valve Manufacturing; 332912
    Fluid Power Valve and Hose Fitting Manufacturing;
    332919 Other Metal Valve and Pipe Fitting
    Manufacturing; 333911 Pump and Pumping
    Equipment Manufacturing; 333912 Air and Gas
    Compressor Manufacturing; 333913 Measuring and
    Dispensing Pump Manufacturing; 333996 Fluid Power
    Pump and Motor Manufacturing

Spirax-Sarco Engineering plc is the world's leading manufacturer of steam traps, the number one producer of peristaltic pumps (through subsidiary Watson-Marlow Bredel) and a leading manufacturer of flowmeters, temperature and pressure controls, and other apparatus and equipment used for controlling steam. Spirax-Sarco's products are used in virtually every industry, with applications including heating and air-conditioning systems; oil refinery and chemical processing; in the pharmaceutical and foods industries, and for the manufacture of plastics, textiles, and other materials. Spirax-Sarco encompasses seven manufacturing facilities worldwide, although its primary manufacturing operations take place in its Cheltenham, England home. The company is present in 32 countries, through 42 sales offices. Exports have long accounted for the majority of the group's sales, and represented some 80 percent of 2002 revenues of nearly £300 million. Spirax-Sarco has continued to make small acquisitions in the 2000s, such as its 2002 purchases

of Australia-based Marford Engineering, a specialist in water treatment systems, and Italy's AMPE, which makes pneumatic and electronic instruments and actuators. The company has also boosted its international sales network. Quoted on the London Stock Exchange since the late 1950s, Spirax-Sarco is led by CEO Marcus Steel.

Building up Steam in the 19th Century

The Industrial Revolution and the adaptation of steam power to a variety of industrial uses opened up vast areas of entrepreneurial development, as steady advances in technology required new engineering solutions and products. The use of steam—a powerful, clean source of heat—introduced a need for a device to drain off water condensation while retaining the steam itself. The resulting device was called the steam trap, and one of the earliest manufacturers was a British firm called Sanders, Rehders & Co. That company was formed to make and sell steam traps and other steam power-related parts, devices, and equipment in London in 1888.

Sarco (from Sanders Rehders & Co.), as the company and its products became known, developed into a leading engineered steam products group. In 1908, the company set up a sales office in New York City, sending Clement Wells there as the company's representative. Sarco quickly developed into a full-fledged company; when imports of steam traps became too expensive during and after World War I, Wells transformed Sarco Inc. into a manufacturing operation, opening a plant in Allentown, Pennsylvania. Wells then extended the company's production to include thermostats and other temperature regulators, all the while sticking to the company's focus on steam.

Before long, Sarco U.S. became a primary manufacturer of Sarco-branded steam traps and apparatus, starting export operations to the European continent—and to the United Kingdom. Sanders, Rehders by this time had reduced its role to that of a selling agent for Sarco products, changing its name to Sarco Thermostats and moving to Cheltenham. At the same time, Sarco opened its first foreign subsidiary, in Toronto, Canada, in 1926. That company was led by Eric Wells, brother of Clement Wells. At first operated as a sales office, the Canadian business set up its own manufacturing facility in Clairmont, Ontario, in 1941.

Company Perspectives:

MISSION STATEMENT: To profitably supply world class products, services and expertise to ensure our customers optimize energy usage and maximize process efficiency in steam and condensate systems. VISION STATEMENT: To be the USA's leading supplier of steam system solutions by being market driven, providing excellent quality and promoting productivity in a work culture of high performance, involvement, respect and equity.

The Depression once again made foreign shipments too costly—this time, however, its was the U.S.-based business that sought a manufacturing partner overseas. In 1932, HA Smith and others, including later company Chairman Lionel Northcroft, established a new business in London to manufacture the Sarco steam traps, but under a different brand name: Spirax.

The Spirax Manufacturing Co. remained in London for the first half of the 1930s, then, after acquiring Sarco Thermostats, moved to Cheltenham in 1937. That purchase gave the company the right to use the Sarco brand name as well. In the years leading up to World War II, the British company acquired a second branded line of steam traps, Ogden, after purchasing the English company Ogden & Cunliffe. By then, Spirax had been granted the rights to trade in the United Kingdom (excepting Canada), Ireland, Denmark, Holland, Portugal, Sweden, and Norway, while the U.S.-based Sarco reserved the rest of the world's market for itself.

In 1952, Spirax bought Sarco Co.'s remaining U.K. interests (a process completed the following year) and renamed itself Spirax-Sarco Ltd. At that time, a new U.S.-based company was formed, Sarco International Corporation of New York, or Simco, which acquired the Sarco steam trap rights outside of North America. Simco opened two new European businesses, Sarco Appareils pour la Vapeur, in Paris, taking a 49 percent stake, and a sales office in Belgium, established in 1952. Two years later the company launched a manufacturing operation in Konstanz, Germany, Sarco GmbH, a joint venture in which Simco controlled slightly more than 50 percent.

Spirax-Sarco took over Simco in 1957, gaining worldwide rights to the Sarco steam trap brand—other than the United States and Canada. These markets stayed under the control of what remained of Sarco Co., which became a subsidiary of White Consolidated.

Building Steam Internationally in the 1970s

Spirax-Sarco acquired two other Cheltenham-based companies in 1957, John Such & Sons and Heat Transfer Ltd., in a move to diversify its product range. John Such, founded in 1909, manufactured tools, jigs, and other engineering equipment and tools. John Such also manufactured heat exchangers designed and distributed by Heat Transfer Ltd., which had been set up just one year earlier. The two acquisitions enabled Spirax-Sarco to expand its manufacturing base, adding some 20,000 square feet to reach a total of 50,000 square feet of production space.

Spirax-Sarco went public as Spirax-Sarco Engineering Ltd. in 1959. That year, HA Smith retired, and Northcroft took over as chairman. The company took advantage of its worldwide rights to the Sarco brand, establishing manufacturing operations in Argentina, Sweden, Mexico, and Italy, then forming a joint venture to enter India in 1959 and establishing a new subsidiary, Sarco Sul Americana, in Brazil the following year.

Over the next decades, Spirax-Sarco continued its growth, through both acquisitions and international expansion. Acquisitions helped the company diversify its product range, such as its purchase of Bir-Vac Ltd. in 1961, adding a line of industrial and special-purpose vacuum equipment. In other areas, Spirax-Sarco started up its own businesses, such as the launch of Theta Controls Ltd. in 1963, adding electronic thermostats for the residential market.

Among the most significant acquisitions made by the company was that of Drayton Controls Ltd. in 1963. That purchase doubled the company in size and extended its operations into such product ranges as filled thermostatic systems; domestic, commercial and industrial controls; and advanced sterilizing equipment and other hospital equipment. The company in the meantime continued its international expansion, adding subsidiaries in the Netherlands, Austria, and Singapore. In 1972, Spirax-Sarco added an Australian component, soon followed by operations in New Zealand as well. Spirax-Sarco then entered the Japanese market in 1973. Later, Spirax-Sarco's presence in Asia expanded to include China, Taiwan, Malaysia, Thailand, Korea, and other markets.

Spirax-Sarco at last acquired the rights to the United States and Canada when it paid White Consolidated $29.9 million to acquire Sarco Co. With full control of the Sarco brand, Spirax-Sarco continued its expansion through the rest of the decade, establishing itself as the world's preeminent maker of steam traps. By the end of the decade, Spirax-Sarco had become a truly international company, posting more than 75 percent of its sales overseas. Spirax-Sarco was also eminently profitable—in 1990, the company celebrated its 22nd consecutive year of profit growth, a record Spirax-Sarco maintained throughout much of the economic uncertainty of the early 1990s.

Steaming Ahead in the New Century

At the beginning of the 1990s, Spirax-Sarco made a new move to diversify and expand its operations. In 1990, the company paid £15.3 million to pharmaceutical group Smith & Nephew for Watson-Marlow. Founded in Buckinghamshire in 1956, Watson-Marlow had been a pioneer in developing pumps based on the peristaltic system for the hospital market, leading to its acquisition by Smith Nephew in 1977. Over the next decade, Watson-Marlow began expanding beyond the medical applications into a variety of markets—many of which were shared with Spirax-Sarco—although maintaining a specialty of small-scale pumps.

In 1997, Spirax-Sarco stepped up its peristaltic pumps presence when, through Watson-Marlow, it acquired Netherlands-based Bredel Holdings. Where Watson-Marlow specialized in smaller pumps, Bredel's specialty lay in larger pumps. The resulting business gave Spirax-Sarco the world leadership in the manufacture of peristaltic pump systems. Watson-Marlow and

Key Dates:

1888: Sanders, Rehders & Co. (Sarco) starts operations in London selling steam traps.

1908: New York office opens and begins selling "Sarco" steam traps.

1926: Company establishes Canadian subsidiary, which adds manufacturing capacity in 1941.

1932: Spirax is created to manufacture Sarco steam traps in United Kingdom under Spirax brand name.

1952: Spirax acquires U.K. Sarco branches and becomes Spirax-Sarco; Sarco International (Simco) is established by Sarco Co., which operates independently in North America until 1983.

1957: Spirax-Sarco acquires Simco.

1959: Spirax-Sarco goes public as Spirax-Sarco Engineering.

1963: Company acquires Drayton Controls Ltd., doubling in size and diversifying its product line.

1972: Company enters Australia market as part of internationalization drive.

1973: Company enters Japan with opening of sales office.

1983: Spirax-Sarco acquires Sarco Co. from White Consolidated, gaining access to North American markets.

1990: Watson-Marlow is acquired from Smith & Nephew, adding peristaltic pumps line.

1997: Company purchases Bredel, becoming world's leading supplier of peristaltic pumps.

1998: U.S. manufacturing plant is moved to South Carolina.

2003: South African Watson-Marlow distribution business is acquired.

Bredel were formally merged into a single company, Watson-Marlow-Bredel, in 2000.

By then, Spirax-Sarco had been forced to overcome a bump in the late 1990s, after the company shut down its Allentown plant and moved its U.S. manufacturing operations to South Carolina. The company had underestimated the cost of moving, especially training costs after a majority of its former Pennsylvania workers refused to relocate with the rest of the company.

Despite this episode, Spirax-Sarco continued its slow but steady growth, making a series of acquisitions at the turn of the century. In 1998, the company moved into Spain, buying the safety valve operation of Especialidades Hydra, based in Barcelona, for £3.1 million. In 2000, the company added M&M International, based in Italy, paying £6.8 million for its solenoid and piston-activated valve manufacturing operation. The company returned to Italy at the end of 2002 when it acquired Milan-based AMPE, a maker of pneumatic and electronic instrumentation and actuators. By then, the company had expanded its Australian subsidiary as well, acquiring Marford Engineering for £1 million, based in Brisbane.

By 2003, Spirax-Sarco's sales neared £300 million, and the company had established clear leadership in two core product categories. The company remained committed to expansion, both internationally and organically. In 2003, it bought its South African peristaltic pumps distributorship from that country's Walter Becker, for £1.3 million. At the same time, the company announced its plans to spend £250,000 to expand Watson-Marlow-Bredel's production capacity by 2004. Spirax-Sarco seemed far from losing steam as it entered the new century.

Principal Subsidiaries

Spirax-Sarco Engineering plc (Germany); AMPE S.r.l. (Italy); Bredel Hose Pumps B.V. (Netherlands); Especialidades Hydra S.L. (Spain); Hygromatik Lt. A. GmbH (Germany); M&M Iberica S.L. (Spain; 67%); M&M International S.r.l. (Italy); Sarco International, Corp. (U.S.A.); Spirax Oy (Finland); Spirax-Sarco (Thailand) Ltd.; Spirax-Sarco Canada Ltd.; Spirax-Sarco Co. Ltd. (Taiwan); Spirax-Sarco Engineering (China) Ltd.; Spirax-Sarco Equip. Ind. Lda. (Portugal); Spirax-Sarco GmbH (Austria); Spirax-Sarco Ind. e Com. Ltda. (Brazil); Spirax-Sarco Ltd. (New Zealand); Spirax-Sarco S.A. (Spain; 95.1%); Spirax-Sarco S.A. (Argentina); Spirax-Sarco Sp. z o.o. (Poland); Spirax-Sarco spol. s r.o. (Czech Republic); Spirax-Sarco, Inc. (U.S.A.); Spirax-Sarco (Korea) Ltd. (97.5%); Spirax-Sarco (Private) Ltd. (Singapore); Spirax-Sarco A.B. (Sweden); Spirax-Sarco A.G. (Switzerland); Spirax-Sarco Engineering B.V. (Netherlands); Spirax-Sarco Engineering S.L. (Spain); Spirax-Sarco GmbH (Germany); Spirax-Sarco Investments B.V. (Netherlands); Spirax-Sarco Investments Ltd.; Spirax-Sarco Ltd.; Spirax-Sarco Ltd. (Denmark); Spirax-Sarco Ltd. (Norway); Spirax-Sarco Mexicana S.A. (49%); Spirax-Sarco N.V. (Belgium); Spirax-Sarco Overseas Ltd.; Spirax-Sarco Pty. Ltd. (Australia); Spirax-Sarco S.A. (France); Spirax-Sarco S.r.l. (Italy); Spirax-Sarco Sdn. Bhd. (Malaysia); Spirax-Sarco South Africa (Pty.) Ltd.; Watson-Marlow B.V. (Netherlands); Watson-Marlow Bredel Holdings B.V. (Netherlands); Watson-Marlow GmbH (Germany); Watson-Marlow Ltd.; Watson-Marlow N.V. (Belgium); Watson-Marlow S.A. (France); Watson-Marlow S.r.l. (Italy); Watson-Marlow, Inc. (U.S.A.); WM Alitea A.B. (Sweden).

Principal Competitors

ZF Friedrichshafen AG; KSB Bombas Hidraulicas S.A.; Parker Hannifin Corp.; Rinar Joint Stock Co.; Dalenergomash Joint Stock Co.; Wuzhong Instrument Company Ltd.; Burkert GmbH und Co. Fluid Control Systems KG; Tomkins PLC; Flowserve Corp.

Further Reading

Brun-Rovet, Marianne, "Asian Markets Buoy Spirax," *Financial Times*, March 11, 2003, p. 22.

Davouid, Salamander, "Spirax-Sarco Boosted by Asian Revival," *Financial Times*, September 12, 2003, p. 30.

Ford, Jonathan, "Spirax Makes Headway in 'Demanding' Markets," *Financial Times*, March 17, 1998, p. 30.

Harney, Alexandra, "Spirax-Sarco Cautious amid Clouded Outlook," *Financial Times*, March 12, 2002, p. 29.

"Steam Power Keeps Spirax Ticking," *Independent*, March 11, 2003, p. 22.

Tyler, Richard, "Spirax Keeps Spiralling Upwards," *Birmingham Post*, March 11, 2003, p. 19.

—M. L. Cohen

STINNES
Logistics

Stinnes AG

Leipziger Platz 9
10117 Berlin
Germany
Telephone: +30 297-54021
Fax: +30 297-54029
Web site: http://www.stinnes.de

Wholly Owned Subsidiary of Deutsche Bahn AG
Incorporated: 1902 as Hugo Stinnes GmbH
Employees: 44,320
Sales: DM 13.37 billion ($14.02 billion) (2002)
NAIC: 541614 Process, Physical Distribution, and
   Logistics Consulting Services; 481212 Nonscheduled
   Chartered Freight Air Transportation; 483111 Deep
   Sea Freight Transportation; 483211 Inland Water
   Freight Transportation; 484110 General Freight
   Trucking, Local; 484112 General Freight Trucking,
   Long-Distance; 488310 Port and Harbor Operations;
   488510 Freight Transportation Arrangement; 493110
   General Warehousing and Storage; 493120
   Refrigerated Warehousing and Storage

Following its acquisition in 2002 by rail operator Deutsche Bahn AG, Stinnes AG has been repositioned as the lead company for all of the Deutsche Bahn Group's transportation and logistics operations. Stinnes offers a complete and integrated range of logistics services running from procurement through transport and on to distribution. These operations involve a full array of trucking, rail, and multimodal transportation services, air and sea freight services, and global supply chain management and warehousing services. Following the takeover by Deutsche Bahn, Stinnes announced that it would sell off its two main nontransportation companies, Brenntag AG, a distributor of chemicals, and Stinnes Interfer AG, a distributor of steel products and raw materials.

Early History

Stinnes AG has deep roots in modern German history. The company's founder, Mathias Stinnes, was born in Mülheim in the Ruhr valley during the time of the French Revolution, when the German states were heavily fragmented and decentralized. It is all the more amazing that entrepreneurship could succeed in an area of Europe where innumerable regional interests competed against one another. Added to this politically and economically unstable environment were the numerous invasions of the Napoleonic armies that devastated the very region in which Mathias Stinnes was born.

One of many children of a poor bargeman and his wife, Mathias was affected deeply by the winds of change buffeting him and his generation. The democratic ideas of the French Revolution and Napoleon's forced and short-lived consolidation of the German states signaled change. The legacy of that brief union was not lost on the diplomats gathered at the 1815 Congress of Vienna, who issued a call for a voluntary lifting of trade restrictions on the Rhine, the longest river in western Europe, of which the Ruhr is a tributary.

With so much change in the air, Mathias Stinnes and his two brothers did not follow in their father's footsteps, as generations before them had. Instead of remaining poor laborers, they opted to hire laborers and go into business for themselves. In 1808 Mathias Stinnes, with the help of his brothers, set up his own company, named after himself as elder brother, that hauled goods and raw materials on a boat via the Ruhr.

Stinnes's business grew, despite the community's deep-rooted distrust of someone who chose to strike out on a path different from his forefathers. When Mathias died in 1845, his steamboats plied the Ruhr, and he had become the largest private owner of inland shipping in the fragmented German states. Unusual for that day and age, he branched out into other businesses: the Ruhr area was rich in coal, and by the time he died, the Mathias Stinnes company owned shares in 36 mines, four of which his firm had built. Stinnes's traditional lines of business—trading in raw materials and transportation on inland waterways—were well established by the 1840s.

Mathias's sons took over the family enterprise in turn, each one dying at a young age. Despite the succession of political crises in Germany occasioned by wars of unification as well as the rise of an organized labor movement, the Stinnes firm continued to expand. In 1908, 100 years after the company was founded, it possessed 21 tugs and nine of its own ports along

Company Perspectives:

Both Stinnes and Deutsche Bahn's freight services have long been doing business in logistics—day in, day out. Together under a single roof, we are now set to become an international leader in logistics services provision. Our solutions are as individual as our customers. We possess the know-how and the technology, and we know the sector. For our customers, the all-round competence we continuously provide enhances their competitive edge. And we keep the needs of the environment in mind—always. With our integrated multi-modal transportation networks, we have optimal ways of conserving resources.

with their storage facilities and owned and controlled five mines. By then, however, a new company had arisen that in time would engulf the old Mathias Stinnes firm.

Hugo Stinnes, grandson of Mathias Stinnes, was born in 1870. Dissatisfied with the traditional family business, the 21-year-old Hugo persuaded his mother to sell her ownership in the firm and to lend him 50,000 gold marks to start up his own business, which he founded in 1892 and then incorporated in 1902 as Hugo Stinnes GmbH in Mülheim. He still retained technical management of the Mathias Stinnes mines, however, and gradually the two companies became indistinguishable.

Hugo Stinnes was a dynamic, forceful, and imaginative entrepreneur whose horizons stretched well beyond the traditional family enterprises and the customary way of doing things. His original business—coal mining and transportation—was what he knew best; from there, however, he went on to found the biggest business empire that Germany, unified into a centralized state in 1871, had ever seen.

Even the coal business would change under the farsighted entrepreneur: in the years before World War I, Hugo Stinnes entered into a partnership with the much older August Thyssen. Together, the two established the Mülheimer Bergwerksverein, which took over used mines and made a profit out of them. Soon Hugo Stinnes's firm had branches of its coal business in Great Britain, Italy, and Russia. He entered the shipping business on his own, and his fleets competed with and would eventually absorb the family fleets. He experimented with recycling gas from coke furnaces and became the foremost promoter of electricity in Germany. Hugo Stinnes tirelessly expanded into new business arenas, not for the mere sake of expansion, but to integrate all of his businesses "vertically," a feat that he would not fully accomplish until after World War I.

War Years

Despite the shortages of various raw materials because of the Allied blockade of Germany's ports, Hugo Stinnes GmbH emerged unscathed from the war and with an even bigger portfolio. With the Kaiser in exile and a new democratic government in place, Hugo Stinnes became a member of the Reichstag and thus politically influential. The French occupation of the Ruhr valley, where many of Stinnes's assets, especially mines, were located, convinced him that vertical integra-

tion of his business, from raw materials to the finished product—including transporting the finished product and controlling the sources of energy in Germany to complete this process—must be accelerated.

A veritable frenzy of expansion followed, in the course of which Stinnes established a partnership with Stahlwerk Breuningshaus steelworks and proceeded to purchase companies that would fully complement this line of business, such as rolling mills, rivet and wire works, a machine tool factory, and other related companies. In 1920 Hugo Stinnes acquired a mining and foundry business that employed 18,000 workers and joined with Germany's largest manufacturer of electrical equipment and appliances, Siemens, to enter that line of business in a partnership. Interested in new energy sources, especially petroleum, Hugo Stinnes's firm began acquiring oil wells abroad, along with refineries and the ocean vessels necessary for conveying the precious fuel. Shipping and transportation companies were purchased as a matter of course, and with Hugo Stinnes's increasing involvement in politics, his business interests turned to newspaper presses, publishing houses, and printing establishments, which his firm acquired in short order. Helping this process of acquisition was the cataclysmic German inflation of the early 1920s; property could be bought for almost nothing.

At the time of his premature death in 1924, not only was Hugo Stinnes Germany's most influential and powerful industrialist, but he was also the owner of the largest firm (in terms of assets and revenues) in the country. Hugo Stinnes GmbH consisted of more than 4,500 businesses and employed more than 600,000 workers.

A year and a half after Hugo Stinnes's death, the company was on the brink of ruin. Profligate sons succeeded him and competed against each other; banks recalled their loans, and finally, son Hugo, Jr., sold half of the company's shares to two American banks in return for a huge loan. Much of the company's assets and property were destroyed during the succeeding war years; immediately afterward, the Stinnes firm reverted to the control of the Allied occupation authorities. Half of the firm was still owned by banks in the United States.

The Hugo Stinnes company probably would have gone under, its stock sold to the highest bidder—most likely to a foreign company—without the intervention of Heinz P. Kemper. Because he had no Nazi party affiliation during World War II and had for many years directed an American subsidiary in Germany, the American occupation authority selected him to head Stinnes. As its director, Kemper dismissed Hugo Stinnes, Jr., from the helm, thereby ending the Stinnes family's connection to that firm.

Postwar Reorganization

Reviving the company and returning it to prosperity was nearly impossible, especially because its assets were spread throughout Germany and British and French authorities were far less friendly and compromising than the Americans. There was also the urgent matter of repurchasing the half of Stinnes still under American ownership, because the Americans were in a position to make a takeover bid for the other half. Unfortunately, Stinnes's finances were in turmoil, and there was no money for repurchase.

Key Dates:

1808: Mathias Stinnes sets up a shipping and coal trading company in Mülheim in Germany's Ruhr valley.

1892: Hugo Stinnes, grandson of Mathias Stinnes, founds his own coal trading and transportation company, also based in Mülheim.

1902: Hugo Stinnes GmbH is incorporated; this company gradually absorbs the operations of the other Stinnes family firm.

1924: Hugo Stinnes dies, leaving behind Germany's largest firm, consisting of more than 4,500 businesses and employing more than 600,000 workers.

1925–26: Hugo Stinnes's sons quickly run the company to the brink of ruin; son Hugo, Jr., sells half of the company to two U.S. banks.

1947: Allied authorities appoint Heinz P. Kemper to head Stinnes; Kemper fires Hugo Stinnes, Jr., thus ending the involvement of the Stinnes family in the firm.

1956: After the U.S. banks announce their plan to sell their stake in the company, Kemper, with the help of Konrad Adenauer, the German chancellor, and a consortium of German banks, succeeds in making Stinnes once more a wholly German-owned company.

1961: The company is reorganized under the newly formed Hugo Stinnes AG.

1964: Petrochemical firm Brenntag is acquired.

1965: German conglomerate Veba AG acquires 95 percent of Stinnes, turning it into a subsidiary; Stinnes sells its glassworks, coal mines, and chemical company to Veba in exchange for a major Veba barge line.

1979: The name of the firm is changed to Stinnes AG.

1991: Transportation and logistics company Schenker is acquired.

1992: Veba acquires the 5 percent of Stinnes it does not already own.

1997: Veba announces that it will sell a minority stake in Stinnes through an initial public offering (IPO), slated for 1998, and eventually divest its entire interest in the company; the IPO is delayed until 1999.

1999: Schenker takes over the Swedish transportation and logistics company, BTL AB; Veba sells a 34.5 percent stake in Stinnes to the public.

2000: Veba merges with Viag AG to form E.ON AG; Brenntag acquires Holland Chemical International, becoming the largest chemical distributor in the world.

2002: Deutsche Bahn offers to pay DM 2.5 billion for Stinnes; following E.ON's agreement to the offer, Deutsche Bahn holds nearly all of the shares by October.

2003: Deutsche Bahn gains the remaining Stinnes shares, making it a wholly owned subsidiary; efforts to sell Stinnes's Brenntag subsidiary and its steel product and raw materials distribution businesses are underway; Stinnes's headquarters are relocated to Berlin.

The firm began to slowly recoup some of its losses and show a profit, thanks in part to the reform of German currency in 1948 and to the formation of the West German state, or Federal Republic of Germany, in 1949. The company was hardly out of deep water, however. The U.S. government informed Kemper in the mid-1950s that Stinnes stock held by U.S. banks would be sold to the highest bidder and Germans would be excluded from bidding. Desperate to save the company, Kemper turned to the German government in Bonn for help. Chancellor Konrad Adenauer gave Kemper a sympathetic hearing. Adenauer in turn had a friendly relationship with U.S. President Dwight D. Eisenhower, who was able to pull enough strings to allow the Germans to participate in bidding for their own stock. The Stinnes company, however, did not possess the required capital—DM 100 million—the likely price of repurchasing the stock. Hence, the German government intervened once more; Finance Minister Ludwig Erhard worked to set up a consortium of German banks that could provide the necessary loan, all of which would have to be repaid to the last pfennig. In the United States, Kemper successfully outbid his competitors, including some of the most powerful firms in the Common Market, and the Hugo Stinnes firm, as of 1956, was once more a wholly German-owned company. It was reorganized under the newly formed Hugo Stinnes AG in 1961.

Growth in the 1970s and After

The Marshall Plan for the resurrection of the German economy as well as the economic benefits of West German unification laid the foundations of the German "economic miracle." The Hugo Stinnes company once again became one of Germany's largest transportation and raw material supply companies, with sales in the multibillion-dollar range by the early 1970s. In 1976 the company's name was changed to Stinnes AG, in recognition of the fact that the firm was no longer in the hands of the Hugo Stinnes family and as a reflection of the traditions of both Mathias Stinnes, the founder, and Hugo Stinnes, the daring entrepreneur. By then, Stinnes AG had joined the Veba AG group of companies, Germany's largest firm. In 1965 Veba AG had bought 95 percent of Stinnes stock, thus turning the company into a subsidiary. By becoming part of this holding company, Stinnes turned into the biggest transportation company in West Germany, because Veba AG sold one of its largest barge lines to Stinnes in return for the Stinnes glassworks, the company's coal mines, and the chemical firm Chemiewerk Ruhroel.

By the early 1990s Stinnes AG had become a multibillion-dollar company, operating the largest transportation network in Europe and also serving as the owner of Brenntag AG, the largest supplier of petrochemicals on the continent. (Interestingly, Brenntag had been owned by the Stinnes family from 1937 to 1964, when it was purchased by Hugo Stinnes AG.) Still headquartered in Mathias Stinnes's hometown of Mülheim on the Ruhr, Stinnes had branched out into every continent on the globe and into every country in Europe, including Eastern Europe and Russia. In the early 1990s Stinnes consisted of a multitude of major companies, most of which concentrated on three business operations: trading in raw materials, distribution, and transportation. Two-thirds of Stinnes's revenues were derived from foreign markets, and one-third of its greater than 35,000-member workforce was employed by Stinnes businesses outside of Germany.

In the early 1990s Europe's biggest transportation (in terms of land traffic) network was the Schenker Eurocargo group, which merged with Stinnes in 1991. (Schenker had previously been owned by Deutsche Bundesbahn, the West German railway operator that merged with its East German counterpart, Deutsche Reichsban in 1994, forming Deutsche Bahn AG.) A fleet of trucks and other conveyances—including railroads—transported merchandise throughout Europe, including Eastern Europe. Schenker-Rhenus AG, along with its subsidiaries, employed a total of 20,000 people and was without doubt Stinnes's largest component. Stinnes's Schenker International division was a major air and sea transporter of freight and operated 14 travel agencies as well. In the trading division, Stinnes Intercarbon was the top supplier and marketer in Europe of coal and its byproducts. Also in the trading division, the Stinnes firm Frank & Schulte GmbH processed and supplied ores, minerals, and metals to anywhere in the world via its 20 subsidiaries. In the distribution segment, consisting of approximately six major companies, Brenntag AG was the number one supplier of industrial chemicals to chemical manufacturers and the cosmetics industry throughout Europe. An increasingly important segment of Stinnes business was the service sector, especially home improvement chain stores. A small but important enterprise was the replacement tire market operated by Stinnes Reifendienst, which held the number one market position in Germany; this Stinnes division also owned more than 200 service stations throughout Germany, The Netherlands, Switzerland, Austria, and Alsace.

After the unification of East and West Germany, Stinnes, unlike many former West German companies, was in the forefront of investment and expansion into the former German Democratic Republic. Stinnes was also one of the first West German companies to establish corporate branch offices in the East German states and to establish major delivery routes into and out of those states. Brenntag AG opened a major distribution center in Magdeburg in former East Germany and quickly established branches of the firm throughout eastern Germany. Shortly after unification in the fall of 1991, Stinnes's earnings from eastern Germany alone totaled DM 1.5 billion—more than $1 billion.

So hungry was the Eastern European population—which for decades lived under restrictive communist governments—for Western goods in the early 1990s, that Stinnes was fortunate to have cultivated strong economic ties long before the fall of communism in Eastern Europe and Russia. For one thing, the opening up of the East led to new raw material sources for Stinnes, the largest supplier of raw materials in Europe. Because of this, the Stinnes division Frank & Schulte had a year of record profits during the period of slow worldwide growth in 1991. Ores, minerals, and alloys were increasingly being obtained by Frank & Schulte from its Eastern European markets, which represented the best opportunity for growth for that company. Brenntag opened an important branch in Warsaw and offices in Prague and Moscow, only the beginning of its full penetration of the Eastern European market. The majority of Stinnes's divisions were racing to develop or extend their business in the east, including Russia, where the future of the vast Stinnes firm seemed to lie. Meanwhile, in 1992, Veba acquired the remaining 5 percent of Stinnes it did not already own, and the company's stock was taken off the stock exchange.

Focusing on Distribution and Logistics in the Late 1990s

According to a past chairman of Stinnes AG, Guenter Winkelmann, the company could not exist without international markets. For this reason, Stinnes was particularly affected by the recession in North America, Australia, and Great Britain in the early 1990s. A more embarrassing setback came to the company in 1994, when it was revealed in the leading German newspaper *Die Welt* that a manager at Stinnes had embezzled millions of Deutschemarks from the company, through systematic fraud at one of the company's insurance subsidiaries. The manager, Baerbel Ruske, had been in charge of Hamburger Hof, an insurer that had prospered after reunification by doing brisk business in eastern Germany. Hamburger Hof had issued insurance policies on an estimated half million East German residences. Commissions on these policies were evidently siphoned into Ruske's account, and he was said to have come away with 11.9 million marks before being caught. Initial reports stated that Ruske's depredations would cost Stinnes six million marks, though Stinnes Chairman Hans-Juergen Knauer later amended the figure significantly downward, to only 800,000 marks.

By 1995 Stinnes was already Germany's largest independent steel trader; the company boosted its status even more with the acquisition of Krupp Hoesch Stahlhandel, a unit of Krupp AG. The Stinnes subsidiary Stinnes Interfer bought the unit. Krupp Hoesch Stahlhandel operated a network of six steel trading facilities, mostly in northern Germany. Its sale took its parent, Krupp AG, out of steel trading altogether. That company had complained that the business was becoming too consolidated, with large companies such as Stinnes Interfer making it difficult for the small Krupp unit to compete. After the acquisition, Stinnes Interfer was a giant, with a network of 37 steel trading branches and 1,500 employees.

As the company was growing in steel, it trimmed other areas. In 1997 Stinnes shed its hard-coal trading business. The sale of the business went 50 percent to a German company, Rheinbraun Brennstoff GmbH, and 50 percent to the Dutch SHV Energy NV. Also divested in 1997 were the company's service stations. Further cuts in Stinnes's business were announced in December 1997, when parent company Veba AG announced that it would sell about half of Stinnes.

Veba AG had been working hard to cut costs in the mid-1990s and next decided to concentrate its energies on fewer businesses. The massive conglomerate was characterized as a diversified utility company, and it controlled many municipal electrical utilities. But like its subsidiary Stinnes, it was involved in hundreds of businesses and its corporate structure was unwieldy. At the end of 1997, Veba AG announced that it would step back from direct management of Stinnes by floating up to 49 percent of its subsidiary on the stock market in late 1998. At that time Stinnes AG accounted for almost a third of its parent's annual sales. The divestment of the subsidiary would not only give Veba AG a massive infusion of cash, but Stinnes would be able to fund its own growth and expansion. With the announcement of the sale, Stinnes also said it would give up its recycling business, its inland shipping, and direct control of its tire service businesses and do-it-yourself construction outlets. Stinnes's three core areas were to be chemical distribution, land transport, and trading in building materials and air freight.

Stinnes proceeded to sell its Rhenus recycling division, the inland waterway shipping operation of RS Partnership, and a German seaport company called Midgard to Rethmann AG early in 1998. Later in the year Stinnes's home improvement retailing operations in Germany and Poland were divested. In November 1998 the company's chief executive, Erhard Meyer-Galow, was fired by the boards of Veba and Stinnes when he refused to back down from plans to complete a $591.9 million hostile takeover of a foreign public company prior to the pending initial public offering (IPO). Wulf H. Bernotat was appointed as the new chairman.

In 1997 Stinnes had acquired a shareholding in BTL AB of Sweden. The following year Schenker and BTL began coordinating their land-transport operations in Europe under the Schenker-BTL name. Then in 1999 Schenker completed a takeover of BTL, making Schenker-BTL one of the largest transportation and logistics companies in Europe.

The public offering of Stinnes stock, originally scheduled for 1998, was delayed until June 1999. Even then a lukewarm response from investors forced Veba to sell only a 34.5 percent stake rather than 49 percent. About 22.8 million shares were sold at DM 14.50 per share, raising about DM 330.6 million. Later in 1999, Veba announced plans to merge with Viag AG; the creation in 2000 of the resulting energy giant, which adopted the name E.ON AG, confirmed Veba's plan to completely divest what were now considered the noncore operations of Stinnes. Also in 1999, Schenker expanded its Asian operations by forming a strategic alliance with Seino Transportation Co., Ltd., a major Japanese logistics firm. Brenntag acquired the Vienna-based Neuber Group from Degussa-Hüls AG, gaining the leading distributor of chemicals in both Austria and Poland and major operations in Croatia, the Czech Republic, Hungary, and Slovakia as well.

Shift of Control from E.ON to Deutsche Bahn in the Early 2000s

In the wake of the IPO, Stinnes made further divestments in order to focus more keenly on its core areas. In 2000 the company sold its retail tire service business and its building materials distribution operation. Stinnes had now slimmed down to three principal operations: transportation and logistics firm Schenker, chemical distributor Brenntag, and steel and raw materials distributor Stinnes Interfer. During 2000 the company launched an ambitious e-commerce strategy across all its businesses, aiming to generate $1 billion in additional revenues within five years. Although the disappointing initial results placed the attainment of this goal in serious doubt, Stinnes quickly set itself up as a logistics partner for several Internet marketplaces. Meantime, Schenker joined with Deutsche Bahn in 2000 to establish a joint venture called Railog focusing on rail-related logistics services. Brenntag became the largest chemical distributor in the world in November 2000 when it acquired Holland Chemical International (HCI), which had ranked fifth, for DM 288 million in cash and the assumption of DM 257 million in debt. The addition of HCI made Brenntag the market leader in Scandinavia and Latin America, two regions where it had not previously been active, reinforced its leading positions in both central and Eastern Europe, and made it the number three player in the U.S. market.

In 2001 Schenker-BTL and Schenker International were merged to form Schenker Deutschland AG. Further expansion in Asia was also on the agenda. Having previously operated in China since the 1970s through representative offices, Schenker established its first subsidiary in that emerging economic power during 2001. The following year Schenker entered into a joint venture with the Beijing International Technology Cooperation Center. Named Schenker BITCC Logistics (Beijing) Co. Ltd., the venture began constructing a state-of-the-art multifunctional logistics center near the Beijing airport. Also in 2002 Schenker and Seino Transportation merged their air and sea freight operations in Japan into the joint venture Schenker-Seino Co. Ltd., with Schenker holding a 60 percent stake.

During 2002 the desire of E.ON to speed up its divestment of Stinnes—a desire heightened by the company's drive to take over natural gas distributor Ruhrgas AG—combined with Deutsche Bahn's interest in bolstering its cargo and logistics operations to effect another change in ownership for Stinnes. In July, Deutsche Bahn announced that it would acquire Stinnes for DM 2.5 billion ($2.45 billion), or DM 32.75 per share. E.ON agreed to the takeover, and by October nearly all of the holders of the publicly traded interest had cashed in their shares. In May 2003 Deutsche Bahn gained the remaining shares, Stinnes became a wholly owned subsidiary of the German railway giant, and the company's stock was delisted.

Under its new ownership, Stinnes became the freight transportation and logistics holding company of Deutsche Bahn, with Schenker continuing to serve as the rail freight forwarding and logistics arm of Stinnes. Replacing Bernotat as chief executive of Stinnes was Bernd Malmström, who had been the head of DB Cargo, one of Deutsche Bahn's rail carriers. Schenker was already being expanded by early 2003, when the company acquired Joyau, one of the leading providers of logistics services in France with revenues of about DM 250 million. Deutsche Bahn also announced that it intended to sell Stinnes's nontransportation companies, Brenntag and Stinnes Interfer. In March 2003 the raw materials businesses of Stinnes Interfer, including Frank & Schulte and Fergusson, Wild & Co. Ltd., were sold to Swedish iron ore company LKAB. This left the steel logistics operations of Stinnes Interfer still to be sold off. By July 2003, meanwhile, Deutsche Bahn had narrowed the field of potential bidders for Brenntag to four, all of which were private equity capital companies, two American and two British. Stinnes was also busy making plans for a late 2003 relocation of the head office from Mülheim to Berlin, where Deutsche Bahn was based.

Principal Subsidiaries

Schenker Aktiengesellschaft; Schenker Deutschland AG; Stinnes Intertec GmbH; Inter-Union Technohandel GmbH;

Brenntag AG; Brenntag GmbH; Brenntag International Chemicals GmbH; Stinnes Interfer AG; Stinnes Stahl GmbH; Walter Patz GmbH; Stahlex GmbH.

Principal Competitors

Deutsche Post AG; Exel plc; Kühne & Nagel International AG; Hays plc.

Further Reading

Atkins, Ralph, "Stinnes Puts Its Weight into Listing: German Group Is Putting Its Faith in the Heavy Logistics Market," *Financial Times,* May 31, 1999, p. 21.

Burgert, Philip, "Krupp Sells Unit, Exits Steel Trading," *American Metal Market,* October 2, 1996, p. 2.

The Making of a Business Empire; 175 Years of Stinnes; Portrait of a German Company, Econ Verlag, 1983.

Needham, Paul, "Logistics Is Now for Railroads," *Journal of Commerce Week,* July 15–21, 2002, pp. 26–27.

Norman, Peter, "Veba Shake-Up Includes Stinnes IPO," *Financial Times,* December 5, 1997, p. 26.

Parker, John, "Geared for Growth," *Traffic World,* June 25, 2001, pp. 20–21.

——, "Old Dog's New Tricks," *Traffic World,* June 19, 2000, pp. 17–18.

"People in Finance: Hugo Stinnes," *Banker,* October 1982, pp. 74–75.

Rosa, Virginia, "Stinnes Float May Need Buoy in Sea of IPOs," *Wall Street Journal Europe,* June 10, 1999, p. 13.

Stinnes, Edmund Hugo, *A Genius in Chaotic Times: Edmund H. Stinnes on His Father, Hugo Stinnes (1870–1924),* Bern: E.H. Stinnes, 1979.

Young, Ian, "Brenntag Enters the U.S. Top Three," *Chemical Week,* April 25, 2001, pp. 26–28.

——, "Brenntag Shifts Up a Gear," *Chemical Week,* August 16, 2000, pp. 50–51.

——, "Stinnes Agrarchemie Builds Five Centers," *Chemical Week,* February 3, 1993, p. 13.

—Sina Dubovoj
—updates: A. Woodward, David E. Salamie

Suzuki Motor Corporation

300, Takatsuka-cho
Hamamatsu-shi
Shizuoka 432-8611
Japan
Telephone: (53) 440-2061
Fax: (53) 440-2776
Web site: http://www.globalsuzuki.com

Public Company
Incorporated: 1920 as Suzuki Loom Manufacturing
    Company
Employees: 13,920
Sales: ¥2.02 trillion ($16.77 billion) (2003)
Stock Exchanges: Tokyo Osaka Nagoya
Ticker Symbol: 7269
NAIC: 336111 Automobile Manufacturing; 336211 Motor
    Vehicle Body Manufacturing; 336300 Motor Vehicle
    Parts Manufacturing; 336991 Motorcycle, Bicycle,
    and Parts Manufacturing; 333618 Other Engine
    Equipment Manufacturing

Suzuki Motor Corporation is Japan's fourth largest automaker (trailing Toyota Motor Corporation, Nissan Motor Co., Ltd., and Honda Motor Co., Ltd.), marketing its vehicles in more than 190 countries around the world. During fiscal 2003 the company sold about 1.8 million automobiles, with slightly less than half of the sales occurring outside of Japan. Suzuki is best known in the United States and Europe as a manufacturer of small, fuel-efficient cars and sport-utility vehicles, as well as powerful motorcycles, although it moved into the midsize car sector during the 2004 model year with the introduction of the Verona. In its home market of Japan, however, the company is the leading maker of "minicars"—a classification almost unknown outside Japan. These tiny automobiles—smaller than American subcompact models—are popular because of the tremendous overcrowding in Japanese cities, where since the early 1990s a larger car cannot be purchased legally until the owner can show proof that he or she has a parking spot. In the market for two-wheeled vehicles, approximately 80 percent of Suzuki's domes-

tic output is mopeds, or motor-driven bicycles; overall, Suzuki holds the number three position in the Japanese motorcycle market, behind Honda and Yamaha Motor Co., Ltd. The company also makes marine outboard motors, generators, and water pumps. In addition, through its network of foreign assembly plants, Suzuki is adept at turning out millions of car parts.

Suzuki's growth has been predicated on its distinctive domestic and international strategies. Domestically, the company owes its success to its high-quality engines, around which it designs a wide variety of vehicles for special or emerging niche markets. Internationally, Suzuki has traditionally targeted developing countries with growing populations, including Cambodia, India, China, Hungary, Indonesia, and Pakistan. Suzuki's policy in these markets is to find a local partner to sell simple, more affordable vehicles, taking advantage of the small margins on huge volumes of sales. Suzuki is also involved in a long-standing alliance with General Motors Corporation (GM), with Suzuki acting as a key component in GM's network of alliances with Asian automakers; GM holds a 20 percent stake in Suzuki. As part of this alliance, Suzuki has taken a 15 percent stake in South Korean automaker GM Daewoo Auto & Technology, the former Daewoo Motor Company. Suzuki also holds majority control of automakers Maruti Udyog Ltd. of India and P.T. Indomobil Suzuki International in Indonesia. In the U.S. market, Suzuki's strategy is an extension of its domestic plan. While the major automakers battle for leadership in mass markets, Suzuki excels in the quirky niches between jeep and sport-utility vehicle and between compact and subcompact.

Early 20th-Century Founding

Suzuki Motor Corporation was founded by Michio Suzuki in 1909 as a manufacturer of weaving machines. From its base in Hamamatsu, the Suzuki Loom Works, as it was then known, supplied weaving equipment to hundreds of small fabrics manufacturers in and between Tokyo, Yokohama, and Nagoya. At the time, textile manufacturing was one of Japan's biggest industries. It provided a growing and stable market for the Suzuki enterprise. In 1920 Michio Suzuki took his company public and named the new firm Suzuki Loom Manufacturing Company.

Suzuki continued to manufacture weaving machines exclusively throughout the 1920s and until the mid-1930s. At that time a militarist clique gained control of the government and began a massive mobilization program called the "quasi-war economy." Companies throughout the country were asked to begin planning for a conversion to armaments manufacturing. Suzuki was an especially attractive supplier because it was in the business of equipping other factories. In addition, the company was located far away from major industrial centers that would become primary bombing targets.

By 1937 Suzuki had begun production of a variety of war-related materials, which may have included vehicle parts, gun assemblies, and armor. For its part in Japan's World War II effort, Suzuki, like thousands of other companies, was requisitioned for war production and probably had no intention of becoming a manufacturer of military implements. Nevertheless, the company continued to manufacture weaving machines for the duration of the war. Fortunately, the Suzuki factory and the city of Hamamatsu escaped the ravages of U.S. bombing campaigns. The company was capable of resuming production after the war, but the economy and supply networks were in ruins.

New Directions After World War II

Suzuki reestablished production of textile manufacturing equipment soon after World War II. Japan, however, was so impoverished that there was little demand for new woven products. As a result, few companies could afford to purchase new looms. By 1947 the pace of investment continued to be slow, prompting Suzuki to make a major change in its business. That year the company moved to a new headquarters building and, relying on the manufacturing experience it had gained during the war, began design work on motorized vehicles. The prospects were favorable; Japan was a nation of nearly 100 million people, nearly all of whom lacked access to basic transportation.

The heart of the new Suzuki product line was a small 36cc engine that could be used to motorize bicycles. Production of the moped, called the Power Free, began in 1952, prompting Suzuki to abandon weaving equipment entirely. In conjunction with the introduction of the new product line, the company changed its name to Suzuki Motor Co., Ltd. in 1954, the same year it introduced its first motorcycle, the Colleda. Later in 1954, Suzuki graduated from two-wheeled vehicles to a lightweight passenger sedan called the Suzulight, powered by a 360cc engine. In the process, Suzuki gained valuable experience in developing larger internal combustion engines, vehicle frames, gear systems, and steering mechanisms. In 1958 Suzuki developed an improved moped, named the Suzumoped. The following year it began production of a revolutionary delivery van, much smaller than conventional delivery trucks then in use and more appropriately suited to many motorized businesses.

Suzuki banked on the fact that, as its customers' operations grew, so would their needs. Therefore, it would be pointless for the company to squander hard-won loyalty by neglecting to offer its customers a properly diverse product line. Having gained an important foothold in various sectors of the Japanese vehicle market, Suzuki cleverly used these beachheads for further expansion. The popular delivery van of 1959 convinced the company to develop a light truck, called the Suzulight Carry FB, in 1961.

The single event that gained Suzuki its greatest international recognition, however, occurred the following year, when a Suzuki motorcycle won the 50cc-class Isle of Man race. It was the first of many victories for Suzuki motorcycles, victories that firmly established the previously unknown company model as a world leader. By 1970, demand for more powerful motorcycles would prompt Suzuki to develop its first line of four-stroke engine motorcycles. This preserved Suzuki's position of leadership in the market.

Exporting and Diversifying: 1960s–70s

Suzuki had difficulty expanding into domestic automobile markets that were dominated by Toyota, Honda, and Nissan. As a result, it was unable to develop a more sophisticated product line. In its search for growth, Suzuki turned instead to export markets that were in the same economic condition Japan had been in 10 or 15 years earlier. The most promising market was Thailand, a country that historically had close ties with Japan. In 1967 Suzuki established a factory in Thailand to assemble a variety of vehicles whose parts were made in Japan. By providing local employment and inviting Thai investment in the venture, Suzuki skirted import restrictions that locked out other manufacturers. Later, Suzuki duplicated the export development formula in Indonesia and the Philippines.

Still unable to reach sales goals for domestic vehicles, however, Suzuki began a diversification campaign. The company's small engines were fitted to electrical generators, yielding an entirely new line of portable power sources. In 1965 Suzuki expanded into outboard motors for boats. In addition, the company dabbled in housing, an initially successful but short-lived venture.

The 1973 Organization of Petroleum Exporting Countries (OPEC) oil embargo drastically changed the automobile market. Faced with skyrocketing fuel prices, consumers showed interest in more efficient cars. But while Suzuki's little cars and trucks sipped gasoline, they were underpowered when compared with competing models from Japan's big three. The company's domestic auto sales slid further during a 1974 recession resulting from the oil crisis. That year, total sales of minicars—Suzuki's prime automobile segment—fell by more than 65 percent from 1970.

Suzuki began a major export campaign soon afterward, commencing full motorcycle production in Thailand, Indonesia, and Taiwan. In addition, it sent automobiles to the United States for

Key Dates:

1909: Michio Suzuki founds Suzuki Loom Works, a manufacturer of weaving machines.

1920: The company is taken public as Suzuki Loom Manufacturing Company.

1952: Shift to motorized vehicles begins with the introduction of the Power Free moped.

1954: The company name is changed to Suzuki Motor Co., Ltd.

1955: The first motorcycle, the Colleda, debuts; Suzuki introduces the Suzulight, a lightweight passenger car.

1961: The company makes its first light truck, the Suzulight Carry FB.

1967: The first overseas assembly plant is established in Thailand.

1981: Suzuki enters into a marketing and production alliance with General Motors (GM), which purchases a 3 percent stake in Suzuki.

1985: Suzuki introduces the Samurai, the first compact sport-utility vehicle, to the U.S. market.

1986: American Suzuki Motor Corp. is established as a U.S. holding company subsidiary.

1988: *Consumer Reports* declares the Samurai unsafe because of an alleged propensity to roll over; sales of the Samurai plunge.

1990: The company changes its name to Suzuki Motor Corporation.

1993: The Wagon R miniwagon is introduced into the Japanese market.

1997: The Wagon R becomes the top-selling vehicle in Japan, posting sales of nearly 250,000 units.

1998: GM and Suzuki agree to jointly develop subcompact cars in Europe, and GM increases its stake in Suzuki to 10 percent.

2001: Ties between GM Suzuki deepen: GM increases its stake in Suzuki to 20 percent, and the two companies begin marketing the codeveloped Chevrolet Cruze, which is manufactured by Suzuki in Japan; Suzuki enters into an agreement with Kawasaki Heavy Industries to begin joint development of motorcycles.

2002: Suzuki takes over majority control of two former overseas joint ventures: Maruti Udyog in India and P.T. Indomobil Suzuki International in Indonesia; the company takes a 15 percent stake in GM Daewoo Auto & Technology, the GM-formed successor company to bankrupt South Korean automaker Daewoo Motor.

the first time. The product was a bit unusual in the U.S. market, where the roads were dominated by enormous, heavy cars. Suzukis were introduced in the United States in small numbers but were refreshingly fuel-efficient, capable of using one-third to one-half as much gasoline as some American models. Suzuki, however, entered the U.S. market well behind Toyota, Honda, Nissan, and even Mazda and Subaru. Furthermore, by 1978, fuel prices had fallen, and demand for Suzuki's "economy cars" was evaporating. Oil prices would shoot up again briefly in 1979, following the Iranian Revolution, but by then many of Suzuki's most promising markets had enacted tough laws restricting imports from Japan.

1970s–80s: Forging Partnerships

Returning to the development strategy it had begun in Thailand in 1967, Suzuki negotiated a number of foreign investment deals, agreeing to locate production facilities in several countries in return for access to their markets. In 1982 the company established a Pakistani production firm called PACO and a similar operation in India called Maruti Udyog Ltd., which was a joint venture with the Indian government. Suzuki also established a partnership in Spain with Land Rover, known as Land Rover Santana S.A. Two years later Suzuki set up new marketing operations in New Zealand and France.

In the United States, Suzuki's largest market outside Japan, the company signed a series of marketing and production contracts with General Motors and rival Isuzu Motors, Ltd. in 1981 (the latter two companies were already affiliated, with GM holding a 34 percent stake in Isuzu). As part of the deal, GM purchased a 3 percent interest in Suzuki. The companies planned to share production facilities and handle marketing of

each other's products. In 1983 Suzuki began production of its Swift subcompact, selling the cars through GM as the Chevy Sprint and later as the Geo Metro. Another result of Suzuki's arrangements with GM was the creation of a joint subsidiary in Canada, called CAMI Automotive Inc., in 1986. This plant went into production in 1989, manufacturing Sprints, Metros, and Suzuki Sidekicks (also marketed as Geo Trackers).

While Suzuki's joint venture with GM was off to a good start, Suzuki had considerably more trouble of its own. In 1985 it had begun importing the Samurai, the first compact sport-utility vehicle (SUV) sold in the United States (that term had not yet been coined, however, so the Samurai was called a "multipurpose vehicle"). One year later the company established American Suzuki Motor Corp. as a U.S. holding company subsidiary at Brea, California. U.S. sales of the Samurai surged to 83,334 by 1987, but one year later *Consumer Reports* declared that the Samurai was an unsafe vehicle. Specifically, the magazine noted that the Samurai's high center of gravity could cause it to flip over while negotiating turns even at low speeds. Suzuki launched its own investigation and took remedial measures, but the damage had already been done; sales plunged 31 percent in 1988, bottoming out at just 13,979 units by 1990. Worse for Suzuki, the company's entire U.S. executive team resigned—a gesture of atonement that was misinterpreted as an abandonment of the company's commitment to the product and to the U.S. market in general. The Samurai meantime received a clean bill of health from the National Highway Traffic Safety Administration, which conducted an investigation of the vehicle and found it no more prone to roll over than other light-duty vehicles.

Domestically, Suzuki developed several new models during the 1980s, including the Cultus subcompact in 1983 and the four-wheel-drive Escudo in 1988. Also in 1988, Suzuki agreed to handle sales of Peugeot automobiles in Japan. The following year, the company rolled out the Cultus Esteem, which shared the same 1600cc engine as the Escudo. Also shoring up revenues were motorcycle sales, which were recovering by 1990, following a decline that had begun in 1982.

With the Samurai debacle mostly behind it, Suzuki initiated a subtle campaign to reestablish the vehicle's promising U.S. franchise. The high-riding Samurai was popular with younger adults who favored a more rugged jeep-like buggy that was impervious to off-road obstacles. Above all, it was fun to drive and distinctive in appearance.

Suzuki also continued its push at globalization, opening a plant in Great Britain in 1986 that turned out 15,000 microvans annually. The company established a partnership with the Egyptian company Modern Motors SAE, called Suzuki Egypt SAE, to build compact cars and the Super Carry truck and van line in that country. Suzuki licensed manufacture of its Swift/Forsa model through Colmotores SA in Columbia. The Pakistani venture also was expanded to include automobile manufacture under a new company, Pak Suzuki Motor Company, Ltd. In April 1991 Suzuki established a joint venture with C. Itoh, the start-up Hungarian auto manufacturer Autokonzern RT, and the International Finance Corporation. The enterprise, called Magyar Suzuki Corporation, began production of the Suzuki Swift in Hungary the following year. In addition to putting up $230 million in capital for the new company, Suzuki flew each of its Hungarian workers to Japan for training in its production methods.

Meantime, in 1990, Suzuki Motor Company adopted the more international name Suzuki Motor Corporation. During this time, the company suffered reverses in its largest enterprise, midget cars with engines under 550cc. This was due to two factors: new laws that extended parking restrictions to cars of that class and a worsening recession in Japan. Suzuki's losses were partially offset by an increase in motorcycle sales, but because revenues from auto manufacturing were nearly five times greater than motorcycle sales, the company's overall growth rate slowed substantially.

A promising area for Suzuki was its place under the corporate umbrella of General Motors' international ventures. Through teaming agreements, Suzuki was designated GM's *de facto* small car division, developing automobiles for the American company under the Geo nameplate. Elsewhere in Suzuki's U.S. business, sales of the Samurai recovered to 20,000 in 1992 but they never again approached the level achieved in 1987, and the Samurai model ceased production in 1996. Suzuki continued to produce the Sidekick, however, and in 1995 the company introduced the mini sport-utility vehicle, the X-90. With engines, suspensions, and four-wheel-drive options similar to the two-door Sidekick, the two-seat X-90 combined off-road capabilities with carlike, commuter-friendly features.

Exploiting Niche Markets in the 1990s

Globally, Suzuki continued to seek out countries with emerging markets and large populations. Its joint ventures with the governments of Pakistan, Hungary, Egypt, and Columbia

had been low-risk and cost-effective means of expansion. The company stepped up that same successful strategy in the early to mid-1990s in India and China. Having begun a joint venture with the Indian government-controlled Maruti Udyog in 1982, Suzuki increased its equity hold to 50 percent in 1992 and raised that company's capacity to 200,000 units in 1994. By 1998 the Suzuki-Maruti venture held 80 percent of the Indian automobile market. In China, Suzuki built on a licensing agreement with the government in 1993 to become the first Japanese company to invest in a Chinese automobile manufacturing venture.

In the mid-1990s Suzuki introduced two successful products to the Japanese market: the Wagon R miniwagon, which debuted in 1993, and the Alto van, which was introduced one year later with a $5,000 price tag that made it the least expensive automobile in the country. Also during this time, however, Suzuki's problems with the Samurai returned to haunt the company. In 1995 the U.S. courts awarded $90 million to a woman who was paralyzed as the result of a Samurai rollover accident. Suzuki responded by suing the Consumers Union, the publisher of *Consumer Reports,* in 1996. The company claimed that the Consumers Union had purposely manipulated the test in 1988 to ensure that the Samurai failed the short-course maneuvering portion.

As Suzuki approached the 21st century, it remained primarily a niche manufacturer. The company derived about 70 percent of its income from sales of automobiles, including the Cervo, Alto, and Swift car models; the Carry van; and the sport-utility vehicles Samurai and the Escudo, which was sold in the United States as the Sidekick. In 1998 the company introduced a compact SUV called the Jimny Wide. Hoping to sell 2,000 of the 1,300cc-powered vehicles a month in Japan, Suzuki planned to begin exporting the vehicle in mid-1998.

Moreover, in the late 1990s, Suzuki remained Japan's leading minicar manufacturer, a position it had held for almost 25 years. Motorcycles, which ranged from 50cc scooters to 1100cc touring bikes, represented approximately 15 percent of Suzuki's business. In addition, outboard motors contributed 3 percent of Suzuki Motor Corporation sales.

The company sold approximately two million vehicles in 1997, including nearly 250,000 Wagon R miniwagons, which made that model the top-selling vehicle in Japan. The Wagon R maintained that position through 2000. Suzuki had hoped to increase the number of vehicles sold per year to 2.5 million by 2000, but the economic turmoil in Asia in 1997 and 1998 derailed these plans. The economic crisis seriously affected several markets in which Suzuki had major operations, including Indonesia, Thailand, and the Philippines.

In the U.S. market in the late 1990s, both the Sidekick and the X-90 ended their production runs. The Sidekick had been more successful than the whimsical X-90, which simply never caught on, but the Vitara (marketed in Japan as the Escudo) replaced the Sidekick as Suzuki's compact SUV in the United States in 1998. At the same time, Suzuki introduced a beefed-up version of the Vitara, the Grand Vitara (the Grand Escudo in Japan), which was the first small SUV to feature a V-6 engine. To support the new models, Suzuki significantly increased its network of U.S. dealerships.

Increasing Ties with GM in the Early 21st Century

Spurred in part by the 1998 creation of DaimlerChrysler AG, which shook up the global auto industry, GM and Suzuki strengthened their relationship. In 1998 the companies agreed to jointly develop subcompact cars for the European market, and GM spent about $318 million to increase its stake in Suzuki to 10 percent. Early in 2000 their jointly developed European car, the Suzuki Wagon R + /Opel Agila, began coming off assembly lines in Hungary (through Magyar Suzuki) and Poland (through an Opel plant—Adam Opel AG being a GM subsidiary). The partners were also active on the South American continent: In April 2000 production of the Grand Vitara began at General Motors de Argentina S.A. The companies also were collaborating in Colombia, Ecuador, and Venezuela.

In June 2000 Osamu Suzuki, who had served as president of Suzuki Motor since June 1978, became chairman and CEO of the company. The longtime leader, who had married a granddaughter of the company founder and took his wife's family name, had built Suzuki into a global powerhouse through his consistent focus on small cars, cost-containment, and conservative fiscal practices, as well as an aggressive approach to expanding into developing markets. Taking over as president and COO was Masao Toda, who had been a vice-president in charge of technology, manufacturing, and purchasing. Toda remained president until April 2003, when he stepped down for health reasons and was replaced by Hiroshi Tsuda, a senior managing director.

Suzuki and GM strengthened their alliance in September 2000, placing further emphasis on Suzuki's position as GM's small-car partner. GM subsequently injected about $600 million into Suzuki in January 2001 to increase its stake to 20 percent. As part of the deal, GM Chairman John F. Smith, Jr., gained a seat on the Suzuki board, becoming the first outsider to hold such a position. Part of the money invested into Suzuki went toward the start-up of production in Japan of a new jointly developed all-wheel-drive compact car, the Chevrolet Cruze. Japanese sales of the Cruze began in October 2001, and then exports of the vehicle to Australia began in April 2002 where it was sold as the Holden Cruze by a GM subsidiary, Holden, Ltd.

On the motorcycle front, meanwhile, Suzuki and the other ''Big Four'' Japanese motorcycle makers (the others being Honda, Yamaha, and Kawasaki Heavy Industries, Ltd.) had for years faced heightened competition from newly insurgent European and U.S. manufacturers as well as from Chinese companies making pirated copies of their machines. Responding to such threats, Suzuki and Kawasaki announced in August 2001 that they had entered into a cooperation agreement whereby they would jointly develop new motorcycle models and would unify their parts procurement and production operations to cut costs. In an unrelated development, Suzuki in May 2002 began manufacturing products in the United States for the first time when a plant in Rome, Georgia, run by U.S. subsidiary Suzuki Manufacturing of America Corporation began turning out all-terrain vehicles (ATVs).

Also during 2002 Suzuki converted two of its key overseas production joint ventures—Maruti Udyog in India and P.T. Indomobil Suzuki International in Indonesia—into consolidated subsidiaries by acquiring majority control of the ventures.

Suzuki now held a 54.2 percent stake in Maruti Udyog and 90 percent of Indomobil Suzuki. In July 2003 the Indian government sold 25 percent of its remaining interest in Maruti Udyog to the public through an initial public offering (IPO).

As part of GM's 2002 takeover of the remnants of the bankrupt Daewoo Motor Company of South Korea, Suzuki laid out $89 million for a 15 percent stake in GM Daewoo Auto & Technology, the South Korean company that GM formed as a successor to Daewoo Motor. The first outcome of this new alliance was the introduction of two new Suzuki models into the U.S. market in the fall of 2003, both of which were rebadged Daewoo models. The Verona, a five-passenger sedan competing directly against such top-sellers as the Toyota Camry and Honda Accord, marked Suzuki's entrée into the midsize segment of the car market, while the Forenza was marketed as a ''premium'' compact sedan. These vehicles were the first of nine new vehicles that Suzuki planned to introduce into the U.S. market over a five-year period, during which time the firm aimed to roughly triple its U.S. sales from the 68,000 it sold in 2002 to 200,000 by 2007. Meantime, plans were being made for Suzuki to begin selling GM Daewoo models in Japan under the Chevrolet brand in either late 2003 or early 2004.

At the same time that Suzuki was attempting to triple its U.S. sales, its legal battle against Consumers Union continued. By 2002 the ruling that had awarded $90 million to a woman paralyzed in a Samurai rollover accident had been overturned. Suzuki's lawsuit against Consumers Union was dismissed in 2000, but Suzuki won an appeal to a U.S. Court of Appeals, which in 2002 ordered the case to trial. Consumers Union then filed an appeal to the U.S. Supreme Court.

Principal Subsidiaries

Bell Art Co., Ltd.; Enshu Seiko Co., Ltd.; Hamamatsu Pipe Co., Ltd.; Snic Co., Ltd.; S. Tech Co., Ltd.; Suzuki Akita Auto Parts Mfg. Co., Ltd.; Suzuki Business Co., Ltd.; Suzuki Hamamatsu Auto Parts Mfg. Co., Ltd.; Suzuki Marin Co., Ltd.; Suzuki Nousei Center Co., Ltd.; Suzuki Precision Industries Co., Ltd.; Suzuki Toyama Auto Parts Mfg. Co., Ltd.; Suzuki Transportation and Packaging Co., Ltd.; Suzuki Works Techno Ltd.; Suzuki Australia Pty. Ltd.; Suzuki Austria Automobil Handels G.m.b.H.; Cambodia Suzuki Motor Co., Ltd.; Suzuki Canada Inc.; Suzuki Motor de Colombia S.A.; Suzuki France S.A.; Suzuki International Europe GmbH (Germany); Magyar Suzuki Corporation (Hungary); Maruti Udyog Ltd. (India; 54.2%); P.T. Indomobil Suzuki International (Indonesia; 90%); Suzuki Italia S.p.A. (Italy); Myanmar Suzuki Motor Co., Ltd.; Suzuki New Zealand Ltd.; Pak Suzuki Motor Co., Ltd. (Pakistan); Suzuki Motorcycles Pakistan Ltd.; Suzuki Philippines Inc.; Suzuki Motor Poland Ltd.; Suzuki Auto Madrid S.A. (Spain); Suzuki Motor España, S.A. (Spain); Thai Suzuki Motor Co., Ltd. (Thailand); Thai Suzuki Trading Co., Ltd. (Thailand); Suzuki GB PLC (U.K.); American Suzuki Motor Corporation (U.S.A.); Suzuki Manufacturing of America Corporation (U.S.A.).

Principal Competitors

Toyota Motor Corporation; Nissan Motor Co., Ltd.; Honda Motor Co., Ltd.; Mitsubishi Motors Corporation; Mazda Motor

Corporation; Yamaha Motor Co., Ltd.; Ford Motor Company; DaimlerChrysler AG; Hyundai Motor Company.

Further Reading

Bedard, Patrick, "The Next Big Thing," *Car and Driver,* May 1995, pp. 52–56.

"Cars Are a Sideline for Suzuki; Sport-Utes Carry the Load," *Automotive News,* April 29, 1996, pp. S72+.

Eisenstodt, Gale, "A Four Billion People Market," *Forbes,* September 27, 1993, pp. 48–49.

Finlay, Steve, "Suzuki Gets Aggressive," *Ward's Auto World,* May 1998, p. 174.

Friedland, Jonathan, "Mini Miracle: Suzuki Holds Its Own While Other Carmakers Suffer," *Far Eastern Economic Review,* April 28, 1994, p. 76.

Miller, Karen Lowry, "Why the Road Less Traveled Suits Suzuki," *Business Week,* June 15, 1992, p. 126E.

Reitman, Valerie, "Frugal Head of Suzuki Drives Markets in Asia," *Wall Street Journal,* February 26, 1998.

Treece, James B., "GM, Suzuki Zero in on Developing Markets," *Automotive News,* September 21, 1998, p. 3.

White, Gregory L., and Norihiko Shirouzu, *Wall Street Journal,* September 14, 2000, p. A3.

—John Simley
—updates: Susan Windisch Brown, David E. Salamie

Telcordia Technologies, Inc.

445 South Street
Morristown, New Jersey 07960-6438
U.S.A.
Telephone: (973) 829-2000
Fax: (973) 829-3172
Web site: http://www.telcordia.com

Wholly Owned Subsidiary of Science Applications
International Corporation
Incorporated: 1984
Employees: 5,000
Sales: $1.08 billion (2003)
NAIC: 517110 Wired Telecommunications Carriers

Telcordia Technologies, Inc., based in Morristown, New Jersey, is the former research unit of the Baby Bells, the seven regional telephone companies that resulted from the breakup of AT&T. Although it is now owned by San Diego-based Science Applications International Corporation (SAIC), Telcordia continues to serve many of its erstwhile owners as well as other telecommunications customers. The company is involved in network systems, operations support systems, and business support systems, serving both wireline and wireless service providers as well as cable operators. Telcordia is little known by the general population, but its products and services are widespread. It is estimated that 80 percent of all U.S. telecommunications networks rely on Telcordia software. The company holds hundreds of significant patents, many connected to such broadband data communications technologies as ASDL, ATM, ISDN, Frame Relay, SONET, and video-on-demand. Through a wholly owned subsidiary, Telcordia Venture Capital Corporation, the company is able to spin off start-up companies to take full advantage of Telcordia's intellectual property.

Forming in the Wake of the 1984 AT&T Breakup

The origins of Telcordia can be traced back to the invention of the telephone, Alexander Graham Bell, and the American Bell Telephone Company that was created to exploit the device. In 1885 American Telephone and Telegraph Company was created as a subsidiary to build and operate the first long distance telephone network. AT&T became the parent company of the Bell System, which had a monopoly on telephone service in the United States, and eventually grew into the largest corporation in the world. Advances in technology made it possible for competitors to emerge, especially in general long distance, so that by the 1970s the U.S. government concluded that it was in the best interests of the public that the power of AT&T be curtailed. In 1974 the Justice Department filed an antitrust lawsuit against the company, a case so complicated and heavily litigated that the pretrial discovery process dragged on for more than six years. With U.S. District Court Judge Harold H. Greene presiding, the trial commenced in 1981. After a year the two parties announced they had reached a settlement, but another six months would pass before Judge Greene accepted the concept of AT&T dividing itself into local telephone companies, and an additional year before he issued a Modification of Final Judgment (MFJ). In August 1982 AT&T agreed to his conditions calling for AT&T to be split into eight separate companies: the new AT&T, devoted to long distance service, and seven regional Bell operating companies offering local service. The so-called Baby Bells were Ameritech, NYNEX, Bell Atlantic, Pacific Telesis, Bell South, US West, and Southwestern Bell. The divestiture took place on January 1, 1984. As part of the AT&T breakup, Judge Greene allowed AT&T to retain much of its world-renowned research unit, Bell Labs, and also mandated that because of national security and emergency preparedness, the new regional Bells were required to create a common research and development operation. Originally called the Central Service Organization, this new lab became known as Bell Communications Research Inc., a name soon shortened to Bellcore—and ultimately Telcordia.

The scope of Bellcore's business was spelled out in detail by Greene's MFJ. It was forbidden to manufacture or even design equipment, nor could it certify that equipment designed and manufactured by outside companies was acceptable to the regional Bells. At best, Bellcore could produce prototypes for its collection of captive customers. Essentially by default, Bellcore was devoted to the creation of intellectual property, in particular the software that supported the exchange access operations of the Baby Bells, as well as various administrative, reporting, and gateway applications. The seven regional telephone companies were mandated to financially support the activities of Bellcore, each signing a five-year contract in a relationship that required advance notification before cancellation. But the amount of support varied between the seven, who were given the option to select the research projects in which they were interested. Work mandated by the MFJ was termed ''core research,'' amounting to about 40 percent of the lab's activities, with the balance referred to as ''client programs.''

The bulk of Bellcore's personnel, some 4,000, was drawn from the ranks of Bell Labs. Rumors circulated in telecommunications circles that the ex-Bell Lab scientists and engineers were involuntarily transferred to Bellcore and were essentially unwanted Bell castoffs, but in truth these people were volunteers. According to Irwin Dorros, a Bell Labs technical chief who took a top position at Bellcore, ''It was the pioneering types who wanted to go into this thing called Bellcore, so we got some really go-getter people.'' It did not take long, however, before many of these enterprising employees grew frustrated with life at Bellcore. Scientific curiosity was artificially limited by Judge Greene's strictures, prompting an in-house joke that if lab personnel made a prototype look too good they could get in trouble with Judge Greene. In addition, the regional Bells were not overly enthusiastic in their support for Bellcore. The common R&D unit was originally seen as an important tool for the Baby Bells to ward off potential competitors in local telephone service, but in short order the regional telephone companies began to see each other as competitors and took steps to establish their own labs. Within two years rumors began to circulate that some of the regional Bells might withdraw from Bellcore.

Among the Baby Bells, US West proved to be, in the words of *Forbes,* ''the cowboy in the group.'' It served formal notice that it would sever its relationship with Bellcore when its funding commitment expired in 1990, and it planned to sell its one-seventh equity interest in the R&D unit. ''As it turned out,'' according to *Forbes,* ''US West's threat amounted to nothing more than a temper tantrum designed to get the Bellcore board to change some of its rules.'' In particular, Bellcore agreed to do private work for individual regional Bells. Previously, Bellcore would have allowed its other six owners an opportunity to participate at any time during development. Under the new conditions such proprietary work would be kept under wraps for two years before being shared with the Bell siblings. In addition, Bellcore cut back some layers of bureaucracy. Instead of 100 groups overseeing a core research project, now just five fulfilled the same function. The company also took steps to offer some customer care to the regional telephone companies, sending out teams to receive feedback.

In the early years of its existence, Bellcore achieved a number of advances in such areas as superconductors and ISDN, but it continued to come up short in customer service. A study the company conducted in 1993 revealed that it had a customer satisfaction rating of only 71 percent. Over the next couple of years, Bellcore took steps to rectify that shortcoming and made some improvements, but by the mid-1990s it was apparent that the original conceit for the business was simply not viable. To ensure secrecy, the regional Bells increasingly turned to telephone equipment manufacturers and others to conduct proprietary work. Moreover, they built up their own research units, often raiding Bellcore for key personnel.

Up for Sale in 1995

In April 1995 the Baby Bells announced that they planned to sell Bellcore, maintaining that the jointly owned business ''no longer makes sense.'' As a result, Morgan Stanley Inc. was retained to sort through the available options, which included an outright sale of the entire business, the selling of a major interest, or a public offering. The matter lingered for the next 18 months, with a number of companies rumored to be potential buyers, including Electronic Data Systems Corp. and IBM. Finally, in November 1996 an agreement was announced that Bellcore would be sold for some $700 million to Science Applications International Corp.. What SAIC was getting, according to Bellcore's CEO, was a $650 million-a-year software business and a $350 million-a-year professional services business. The approval process for the deal was arduous, passing muster with seven owners and nine state regulatory agencies, so that the sale was not completed until November 1997.

SAIC was founded in 1969 by Dr. J. Robert Beyster, a physicist who worked at Los Alamos National Laboratory during the 1950s before going to work for General Atomics (GA) in San Diego. When GA was sold to Gulf Oil in 1968 and underwent a change in management, Beyster became disenchanted with the company's move away from small research projects, opting instead to focus on the manufacture of large nuclear reactors. Over the years, a number of his colleagues had left to launch start-up companies, and now in his early 40s Beyster decided to join their ranks. He established SAIC as a research and engineering firm, a key element of which was his insistence on making the company employee-owned and sharing the rewards on an equitable basis. To many, Beyster's employee-ownership ideas were little more than a hobby horse and an indication that he simply did not care to make money. By handsomely rewarding employees for generating new business, however, Beyster in effect bred a host of aspiring entrepreneurs. By the time it acquired Telcordia, SAIC was a government contractor, primarily involved in defense, generating more than $2.1 billion in annual revenues. Telcordia's expertise in telecommunications presented SAIC with new areas for growth in the private sector.

A condition of the sale called for Bellcore to drop ''Bell'' from its name. The New York consulting firm of Lister Butler was hired to help in the process of coining a new name for the company. In the end, a hybrid was formed out of employee suggestions. The ''Tel'' for Telcordia referred to telecommunications, while ''cordia'' was to connote accord with the company's customers. No matter what the company hoped to con-

Key Dates:

1982: AT&T agrees to court-ordered split into the new AT&T, devoted to long distance, and seven regional Bell operating companies.
1984: Bellcore is formed as a research unit for seven regional Bells.
1995: The regional Bells decide to sell Bellcore.
1997: Science Applications International Corporation acquires the business.
1999: Bellcore changes its name to Telcordia.
2002: Matthew J. Desch is named chief executive officer.

vey through its new name, of more importance to the future of the company, now free from the ownership of the Baby Bells, was how it adapted to its new free-agent status and how successfully it was able to market its services. In the wake of the name change, Telcordia introduced a suite of products called Next Generation Networks that allowed telephone carriers to integrate voice, video, and data services. The company was banking that the telecommunications industry would continue to experience deregulation, and also that circuit-based architectures would give way to packet-based architectures.

Matthew Desch Becoming CEO in 2002

What Telcordia did not anticipate was the meltdown of the entire telecommunications industry at the start of the new century and a severe downturn in the economy that resulted in major cutbacks in equipment sales and telecommunications services in the corporate world. In 2001 Telcordia suffered a major setback when Sprint terminated its On-Demand Network project, a long-term effort to integrate voice and data. Subsequently, Telcordia slashed its head count, eliminating 2,000 employees from a workforce that at its peak numbered 7,000. In 2002 these cuts were matched with changes at the top. Jerry Roberto, a board member and group president, retired, followed by the ouster of Chief Operating Officer Harold Smith and Chief Executive Officer Richard Smith, Jr., who had headed Telcordia for five years. In July 2002 Matthew J. Desch was named the company's new CEO. Desch received a B.S. in Computer Science from The Ohio State University and worked on assignment at Bell Labs, where he was initially involved in software development and was later transferred to Chicago to work in large-scale systems software development. Desch then returned to school, earning an M.B.A. from the University of Chicago in 1987. He returned to Bell Labs, but was dissatisfied with the available assignments following the AT&T breakup. In 1991 he went to work for Northern Telecom to head product management for a new wireless division, and over the next

dozen years held a number of senior management positions at Nortel Networks. Serving as president from 1996 to 1999, he was instrumental in growing Nortel's Wireless Solutions division from $1 billion a year in revenues to more than $4.5 billion.

Desch took over a company in Telcordia that was having difficulty changing directions. It was still struggling to shed a prevailing image that it was so devoted to pure research that the customer was regarded as a nuisance. In the meantime, the competition was decidedly customer-oriented. Moreover, Telcordia also had lost touch with the new directions taken by the telecom industry. It was predominantly a North American wireline company and was only taking the initial and necessary steps to recast itself as a global multi-service company. The choice of Desch, with his extensive background in wireless, was a sure indication that the company was committed to this change in business focus. Desch quickly moved to restructure the organization, eliminating some 500 employees, half at the management level, and bringing in outsiders to assume key management positions. As part of the makeover Desch put all software developers in one unit, thereby altering the company's traditional centers of decision making and aiding in changing Telcordia's focus to sales and the company's customers. Desch also made it clear that going forward Telcordia was going to emphasize wireless and cable, and look more to overseas growth. He even indicated that he might rebrand the business, which received little value from the Telcordia name.

Principal Subsidiaries

Telcordia Venture Capital Corporation.

Principal Competitors

Amdocs Limited; Lucent Technologies Inc.; Nortel Networks Corporation.

Further Reading

Bernier, Paula, "Telcordia's Dramatic Transformation," *XCHANGE,* April 2003.
Howe, Charles L., "Bellcore Struggles to Prove Itself, Despite Critics," *Data Communications,* November 1, 1986, p. 78.
Mitchell, Jim, "Bellcore Blazes New Trails in Research for Former AT&T Units," *Dallas Morning News,* May 10, 1986, p. 1G.
Roberts, Johnnie L., "Growing Competition Among Regionals Is Changing for Whom This Bell Tolls," *Wall Street Journal,* April 8, 1987, p. 1.
——, "U.S. West May End Its Role in Bellcore," *Wall Street Journal,* January 14, 1987, p. 1.
Siwolop, Sana, "The Stepchild," *Financial World,* October 16, 1990, p. 60.

—Ed Dinger

Universal Compression, Inc.

4440 Brittmoore Road
Houston, Texas 77041
U.S.A.
Telephone: (713) 466-4103
Toll Free: (800) 234-4650
Fax: (713) 466-6574
Web site: http://www.universalcompression.com

Public Company
Incorporated: 1954 as South Coast Gas Company
Employees: 2,280
Sales: $625.22 million (2003)
Stock Exchanges: New York
Ticker Symbol: UCO
NAIC: 532490 Other Commercial and Industrial
Machinery and Equipment Rental and Leasing

Universal Compression, Inc. rents, maintains, and operates a fleet of compressors used to pressurize natural gas pipelines. It owns one of the largest rental fleets in the United States, and has been developing its international business in Argentina, Venezuela, Canada, and the Pacific Rim. International operations accounted for 28 percent of revenues in 2003.

Compression equipment is used to boost the pressure of natural gas as it is being gathered, processed, and distributed. Universal Compression has grown to a leading position in the rental market for compression equipment in part through acquiring a series of related businesses over the years. In early 2003, Universal's compressor fleet numbered 7,400 units providing 2.3 million horsepower. The individual compressors ranged in size from 100 to 5,000 horsepower, allowing Universal to serve a wide spectrum of users.

Origins of Tidewater Compression Services

Tidewater Inc.'s origins date back to the South Coast Gas Company, formed in 1954. Tidewater had the world's largest fleet of vessels dedicated to supporting the offshore oil industry. By the late 1980s, the company's compression business was worth $50 million a year. At this time, Minstar Inc., a group led by a Minneapolis investor, launched an unsuccessful takeover bid for Tidewater Inc. After that failed, Minstar offered to buy Tidewater's compression business alone, also without success.

Compressors are a requirement for gathering and moving natural gas through pipelines; more compressors are needed as the pressure falls in aging wells. In the early 1990s, more natural gas producers began turning to rental companies to meet their compression needs. According to Universal Compression's prospectus, these companies accounted for one-quarter of the natural gas field compression market in 1996. Most natural gas producers, transporters, and processors owned their own equipment, though the rental market expanded at a rate of 8 percent a year in the 1990s.

A couple of small acquisitions were made in the summer of 1993. Tidewater bought Santa Fe, Texas-based Allison Production Services' 26 compressors and acquired a fleet numbering 113 units from BJC Operating Co. of Shreveport, Louisiana. This brought Tidewater's fleet to 954 units.

Tidewater acquired Halliburton Compression Service for $205 million in 1994. The Halliburton business had revenues of $50 million a year in North America. Soon after, Brazos Gas Compressing Company was added. The two purchases together added 287,000 horsepower to the fleet, bringing its total to 480,000 horsepower. This gave TCS the largest rental fleet of natural gas compressors in the United States. Tidewater then spent a couple of years consolidating these acquisitions and improving utilization rates of the acquired companies in line with its own.

TCS posted net income of $7.8 million on revenues of $113.9 million in the fiscal year ended March 31, 1997. In 1997, Tidewater decided to sell off subsidiary Tidewater Compression Services (TCS) in order to focus on its much larger marine support business. It boasted the world's largest fleet of offshore oil service vessels, 750 in all. TCS accounted for only about a seventh of Tidewater Inc.'s total revenues.

1998 Formation of the Company Followed by Public Offering in 2000

Castle Harlan, a New York merchant bank, formed TW Acquisition Corporation on December 12, 1997, to acquire

Key Dates:

1954:	South Coast Gas Company is founded.
1968:	Tidewater, Inc. acquires South Coast Gas.
1994:	Halliburton and Brazos compression businesses are acquired.
1998:	Universal Compression is formed; the company buys Tidewater Compression Services.
2000:	Universal Compression goes public on the New York Stock Exchange.
2001	Weatherford Global Compression Services and others are acquired.

Tidewater Compression Services, Inc. After the $350 million acquisition, completed on February 20, 1998, TCS was merged with TW Acquisition Corporation and renamed Universal Compression, Inc.

In the fiscal year ended March 31, 1998, revenues for the business slipped to $108.8 million and the company recorded a net loss of $3.2 million. The company owned one of the largest rental fleets in the United States, and was developing its international business in Argentina, Venezuela, Canada, and the Pacific Rim. As of June 1998, Universal Compression had 37 units providing 21,000 horsepower deployed in the markets. Its total fleet consisted of 2,700 units providing 512,000 horsepower. The company had more than 500 customers.

Universal posted a net loss of $2.4 million on sales of $129.5 million in the fiscal year ended March 31, 1999. Soon, it was looking to raise new capital to pay down some of its debt, which then amounted to about $350 million. The market for compressor-related stocks was good in 2000, reported the *Houston Business Journal.*

Universal Compression completed an initial public offering (IPO) on the New York Stock Exchange in June 2000. Universal raised $154 million in the IPO.

In September 2000, Universal Compression acquired Gas Compression Services Inc. (GCSI) for $12 million in cash and $46 million in Universal stock, plus $53 million in assumed debt and operating leases. GCSI was based in Traverse City, Michigan.

More Acquisitions in 2001

Two more companies were acquired in February 2001: Weatherford Global Compression Services, L.P. and ISS Compression, Inc, the parent of IEW Compression, Inc. The purchase of Weatherford International Ltd.'s compression business doubled Universal's size, adding 950,000 horsepower to the fleet, making it the second largest oilfield compression company after Hanover Compressor of Houston. As a result of the deal, Weatherford International gained a 48 percent holding in Universal, worth $412 million, making it Universal's majority shareholder.

Universal paid $15 million cash for IEW, which had revenues of about $19.5 million a year. IEW brought Universal a strong presence in the Gulf of Mexico. Universal paid $707.3

million in stock and assumed debt for the Weatherford unit, which took the company into Canada.

Tulsa, Oklahoma-based KCI Inc. was acquired in July 2001 for $98.7 million in cash, stock, and assumed debt. Universal had previously been focused on the field side of the natural gas business; KCI was much stronger on the pipeline side, reported the *Houston Chronicle.* July 2001 also saw the purchase of Louisiana Compressor Maintenance Co. Inc. (LCM) and LCM Turbo. Universal paid $25 million for LCM. Technical Compression Services, Inc. was added in October 2001. After Hanover Compressor bought out the Schlumberger natural gas businesses in 2001, Universal and its Houston-area rival together controlled 85 percent of the natural gas compression business, reported the *Houston Chronicle.*

Universal was affected by something of an industry downturn in 2001 and 2002, due to the Enron scandal and a slow economy. Its services remained in demand, however, even when fewer natural gas rigs were being developed, since older wells required more compressors.

Universal operated the second largest domestic fleet of natural gas compressors. Its 6,900 units totaled two million horsepower. Besides renting compression equipment, Universal had two divisions to fabricate and service it. The fabrication division, which employed about 100 people, was moved from Tulsa to Houston in the spring of 2003. The rental business was divided into domestic and international divisions. These accounted for a little more than half of sales, but 81 percent of gross profit, reported *Investor's Business Daily* in 2002. Net income rose 32 percent to $33.5 million in the fiscal year ended March 31, 2003, on sales of $625.2 million, up 8 percent.

Principal Subsidiaries

BRL Universal Equipment 2001 A, L.P.; BRL Universal Compression Funding I 2002, L.P.; Compression Services de Mexico, S.A. de C.V.; Compression Systems International, Inc.; Enterra Compression Investment Company; PT Universal Compression Indonesia; UCO Compression Holding, L.L.C.; UCO Compression LLC; UCO Compression 2002 L.L.C.; Universal Compression Argentina, S.A.; Universal Compression (Australia) Pty, Ltd.; Universal Compression B.V. (Netherlands); Universal Compression (Canada) Holdings, Ltd.; Universal Compression Canada, Ltd.; Universal Compression of Colombia, Ltd. (Cayman Islands); Universal Compression Company, L.P.; Universal Compression Finance Company,

Ltd. (Barbados); Universal Compression, Inc.; Universal Compression LTDA (Brazil); Universal Compression International, Inc.; Universal Compression International, Ltd. (Cayman Islands); Universal Compression de Mexico, S.A. de C.V.; Universal Compression (Ontario), Ltd. (British Virgin Islands); Universal Compression del Peru, S.R.L.; Universal Compression Services, L.P.; Universal Compression Services de Venezuela, C.A.; Universal Compression (Thailand), Ltd.; Universal Compression de Venezuela Unicom, C.A.; Uniwhale Ltd. (Cayman Islands); Uniwhale de Colombia E.U.

Principal Divisions

Domestic Contract Compression; International Contract Compression; Fabrication; Aftermarket Services.

Principal Competitors

Compressor Systems, Inc.; Hanover Compressor Company; J-W Operating Company.

Further Reading

Darmin, Jennifer, "Universal Compression Launches Bid to Raise $172.5 Million in IPO," *Houston Business Journal,* April 17, 2000.

Davis, Michael, "Castle Harlan to Buy Tidewater Gas Business," *Houston Chronicle,* Bus. Sec., December 20, 1997, p. 2.

——, "Chronicle 100 Energy—Oil and Gas: Five Local Energy-Related Stocks Go Great Guns; But 2 Biotech Companies, Caught in Tech Morass, Have a Tougher Time," *Houston Chronicle,* May 20, 2001, p. 16.

——, "Deal Would Compress Companies; Weatherford to Buy Stake in Universal," *Houston Chronicle,* Bus. Sec., October 25, 2000, p. 1.

——, "Houston-Area Firm to Buy Natural Gas Compression Holdings," *Houston Chronicle,* June 29, 2001.

"Gas Compression Services Being Bought by a Rival," *New York Times,* August 8, 2000, p. C4.

"GE Unit Acquires U.S. Weatherford's Gas Compressor Unit Gemini," *AFX European Focus,* December 22, 1999.

Judice, Mary, "Castle Harlan to Buy Tidewater Inc.'s Compression Business for $360 Million," *Times-Picayune* (New Orleans), December 19, 1997, p. C2.

Lemons, Deidra M., "Compression Firm Adds Tulsa, Okla., Company to Its Acquisitions," *Houston Chronicle,* May 30, 2001.

McKanic, Patricia Ann, "Tidewater Bid Led by Jacobs Is Called Off," *Wall Street Journal,* May 9, 1999, p. 1.

"Texas Firm Buying Out KCI Inc.," *Tulsa World,* May 30, 2001, p. 1.

"Tidewater Boosts Compressor Fleet," *Times-Picayune* (New Orleans), August 3, 1993, p. C10.

"Tidewater Buys Halliburton Compression Unit," *Lloyd's List,* December 3, 1994, p. 2.

"Tidewater Inc. Holder Seeks Auction Process in Sale of Any Assets," *Wall Street Journal,* May 16, 1989, p. 1.

"Tidewater Says It May Sell Compression Operation," *New York Times,* August 22, 1997, p. D3.

"UCO Agrees to Buy Louisiana Compressor Maintenance for $25 Million," *Petroleum Finance Week,* June 25, 2001.

"Universal Compression Announces an IPO of 7 Million Common Shares," *Petroleum Finance Week,* May 29, 2000.

"Universal Compression Holdings Moves 100 Tulsa Jobs to Houston," *Journal Record* (Oklahoma City), April 30, 2003.

Walsh, Andrew, "Centillium IPO Gains More Than 20%," *Daily Deal,* May 24, 2000.

Woodard, Chris, "Universal Compression Holdings Inc.; Houston, Texas; Trends, Purchases Rev Up Business Here," *Investor's Business Daily,* February 6, 2002, p. A8.

—Frederick C. Ingram

Universal Forest Products

Universal Forest Products, Inc.

2801 East Beltline, NE
Grand Rapids, Michigan 49525-9680
U.S.A.
Telephone: (616) 364-6161
Fax: (616) 361-7534
Web site: http://www.ufpi.com

Public Company
Incorporated: 1955 as The Universal Companies, Inc.
Employees: 7,000
Sales: $1.64 billion (2002)
Stock Exchanges: NASDAQ
Ticker Symbol: UFPI
NAIC: 321113 Sawmills; 321114 Wood Preservation;
321213 Engineered Wood Member (Except Truss)
Manufacturing; 321214 Truss Manufacturing; 326199
All Other Plastics Product Manufacturing; 421310
Lumber, Plywood, Millwork, and Wood Panel
Wholesalers

Universal Forest Products, Inc. manufactures, treats, distributes, and installs lumber, composite, plastic, and other building products for the do-it-yourself/retail (46 percent of 2002 sales), site-built construction (20 percent), manufactured housing (18 percent), and industrial (16 percent) markets. The largest producer of pressure-treated lumber in the United States, the company is also North America's leading manufacturer of engineered roof trusses for the manufactured housing market. Other major product lines include dimension lumber and value-added lumber products such as lattice, fence panels, deck components, and various kits for individual home renovation projects. With 90 manufacturing, treating, and distribution plants in the United States, Canada, and Mexico, Universal serves more than 7,000 customers; it has one major customer, however: home improvement retailer The Home Depot, Inc. accounts for about 30 percent of overall revenues.

Early History

Universal Forest Products was established in 1955 as The Universal Companies, Inc. to distribute lumber to the burgeoning postwar mobile home manufacturing industry. In its early years, the company's major stockholder, William F. Grant, also served as its only salesperson. Universal initially relied solely on the railway system to distribute the lumber it sold. But as the country's railway system began to decline in the 1960s, and demand for the company's product increased, Universal sought to gain greater control of its distribution process. Toward that end, in 1970, the company purchased the assets of a component yard in Thomasville, Georgia (later moved to Moultrie, Georgia); the following year, the company acquired a second component yard, in Pennsylvania. The establishment of such distribution centers was part of a plan to meet the demand for lumber wherever it most frequently arose; the company therefore became less dependent on the railway system and was able to pass on its rail service savings to the customer. After the success of the first two component plants, others were opened in Florida and North Carolina, and Universal made its first direct business acquisition, Lumber Specialties of Granger, Indiana, in 1973.

In 1971 Universal reported sales of $12 million. That year, company Vice-President Peter F. Secchia, who had joined Universal upon graduation from Michigan State University in 1962, purchased a controlling share of the company. Soon thereafter, Secchia initiated a plan that would allow salaried employees to share in the equity of the corporation; by 1994, employees owned approximately 18 percent of Universal. Secchia also introduced a policy of remanufacturing Universal's inventory as supply needs changed.

Expansion continued through the 1970s, and, by 1983, a reorganization along geographic lines became necessary. The new Universal divisions oversaw manufacturing and distribution in the Atlantic, Midwest, Northeast, Southeast, and Southwest. Affiliate companies, such as Lumber Specialties, also adopted the name of the parent company in hopes of enhancing Universal's national presence and public recognition.

Company Perspectives:

Universal participates in markets offering strong growth potential and complementary characteristics. A number of factors drive Universal's growth: The diversity of its markets gives Universal's business a cushion against economic uncertainty through a balance of counter-cyclical, non-cyclical and somewhat cyclical markets. Consolidation among customers in all of Universal's markets has created a need for suppliers with national distribution capabilities to fulfill the requirements of the remaining dominant customers. As the largest supplier to its markets, Universal has a strong competitive advantage. A growing need for value-added products and engineered components in all markets is driving profitability for Universal due to higher profit margins generated by these products.

In 1977, meantime, Secchia merged his private restaurant holdings into Universal Companies. In 1986, however, he sold those that had liquor licenses, and in 1994 he spun off what remained of the restaurant group into a separate company called River City Foods.

Diversifying and Entering New Markets, Late 1970s Through Late 1980s

The U.S. market for manufactured housing units experienced substantial declines during the 1980s. In an effort to offset similar declines in the company's growth rate, Universal began to offer a more varied array of manufactured products, including re-graded items, mixed loads of lumber, particle board, and plywood. Moreover, a research and development department was introduced, comprised of a full-time engineering staff.

Also during this time, Universal entered the wood treating business, representing an investment that fortuitously coincided with the rise of the do-it-yourself (DIY) market. The DIY revolution, beginning in the 1980s, had a profound effect on the lumber industry, as smaller lumber yards were replaced by huge retail warehouses, including The Home Depot and Lowe's Companies, Inc., catering to individual home renovation projects. Universal's distribution network proved well suited to this change in the industry. Universal first began producing pressure-treated lumber in 1978 at its plant in Auburndale, Florida. (Pressure-treated wood, most commonly treated with chromated copper arsenate [CCA], offered protection from damage by insects, moisture, and fungi in outdoor applications.) Several more such operations were soon either opened or acquired.

Manufactured housing, which had represented 90 percent of Universal's sales in the late 1970s, was responsible for only 35 percent of sales in 1985. By 1989, Universal had become the nation's largest producer of CCA-preserved lumber. Over the next five years, the company established 15 treating plants and planned for two more. With 28 locations in 18 states and two in Canada, Universal focused on guaranteeing customers stock availability, which smaller suppliers often could not supply.

Seeking to never let a customer down by not having available product, Universal also remained committed to curbing the financial loss involved in overstocking merchandise.

In 1989, President George Bush appointed Universal board Chairman and CEO Peter Secchia as U.S. Ambassador to Italy. Secchia, the son of Italian immigrants, had a long association with the National Italian-American Foundation. He had also been active in Republican politics in the Midwest, acting as vice-chairman of the Republican National Committee for the 13 states of the Midwest and campaigning for George Bush during the 1988 elections. Universal President Bill Currie, hired by Secchia in 1972, replaced Secchia during his tenure as U.S. Ambassador to Italy. After President Bush was defeated in the 1992 election, Secchia's tenure as ambassador came to an end, and he returned as chairperson of Universal.

Higher Profile As Public Company: Early 1990s

Under the Clinton administration, Universal and others in the lumber industry faced stricter limitations on annual timber harvests. The short-term effect of Clinton's environmental policy actually helped companies with large inventories, such as Universal, by creating a temporary shortage in the lumber industry that prompted a sharp rise in prices. Moreover, unusually wet conditions in the country's forests during this time, as well as a public debate over the effects of logging on the preservation of the spotted owl, inflated lumber prices further. Nevertheless, the long-term effects of Clinton's policy were regarded as potentially harmful to the lumber industry. In May 1993, an inevitable dip in lumber prices occurred.

Meanwhile Universal continued to grow, making new acquisitions of smaller companies that were less well positioned to adjust to the changing lumber industry. Although growth through acquisitions clearly became an important part of Universal's strategy for the 1990s, Secchia preferred to downplay this aspect of their business plan. In a 1993 article in the *Grand Rapids Business Journal,* for which he was questioned about the aggressiveness of the company's acquisition strategy, Secchia commented, "I'm very reticent about that because some of our acquisitions have not been that successful."

Between 1992 and 1993, Universal had a remarkable 43 percent rise in sales from $449.5 million to $643 million. During this time, Universal acquired Chesapeake Wood Treating Co., a division of Chesapeake Corp., a deal that included five wood treatment plants. With $90 million in sales in 1991, Chesapeake Wood Treating Co. accounted for approximately 10 percent of Chesapeake Corp.'s consolidated net sales. The acquisition was the largest in Universal's history, and it came just one month before the company went public.

Universal's exceptional gains, as well as the return of Secchia as chairperson, boosted investor confidence in Universal. The company went public in November 1993, offering 5.2 million shares of common stock at $7 per share, and gaining approximately $33.4 million from its initial public offering (IPO) on the NASDAQ. These funds were used to reduce notes payable to banks and to invest in new machinery connected with the acquisition of Chesapeake. Also in November 1993 Universal Companies merged with its wholly owned subsidiary Universal Forest Products, Inc., and the parent company adopted that subsidiary's name.

Pursuing the Site-Built Construction Truss Market, Late 1990s

In the next few years after the IPO, Universal steadily expanded, opening new treating and distribution centers in Hamilton, Ohio; and Harrisonville, Missouri, as well as a manufacturing and distribution facility in Rockwood, Tennessee. By 1996 revenues reached $867.7 million, and then sales topped the $1 billion mark the following year.

During the last years of the 1990s Universal completed a string of acquisitions aimed at building up a national leadership position in the manufacturing of trusses for the residential site-built construction market. (Trusses are the wooden skeletons of walls, roofs, and floors that are built in a factory for delivery to a construction site; a builder can use roof trusses, for example, instead of building a roof from scratch.) Universal was already the nation's leading supplier of trusses for manufactured homes, a position bolstered in October 1996 when Universal paid nearly $11 million for Hi-Tek Forest Products, Inc., a maker of floor and roof trusses with operations in Idaho, Oregon, and California. Between September 1997 and November 1998 the company went after the site-built construction market in earnest, acquiring six suppliers of trusses, two of which were particularly significant. In March 1998 Shoffner Industries, Inc. was purchased for $90 million in cash and stock—the company's biggest acquisition yet. Shoffner, based in Burlington, North Carolina, operated 14 truss factories in seven states in the Southeast and had 1997 sales of $90.2 million. Universal paid

$27 million in cash for Lafayette, Colorado-based Advanced Component Systems, Inc. (ACS), a $40 million per year maker of engineered trusses and building components. ACS's importance lay in its position as a top supplier to home builders in the rapidly growing Denver market.

Universal had thus established itself as a major player in three separate markets—retail DIY, manufactured housing, and site-built construction—but there was a fourth area that the firm's leaders targeted as well: the industrial sector. Here, the company concentrated on packaging, specifically pallets and crates, which could be made from lower grade lumber that might otherwise be considered waste. Universal, by entering the packaging field, could make more products out of the same amount of wood that it received from its suppliers, thereby lowering its overall material costs. Two packaging firms were bought during the first half of 1998: Industrial Lumber Company, Inc. of Newark, California, a distributor of low-grade cut lumber for packaging; and Atlantic General Packaging, Inc. of Warrenton, North Carolina, a producer of specialty wood packaging products. Through these and other acquisitions, Universal Forest Products saw the portion of its sales deriving from the manufactured housing and retail DIY markets fall from 89 percent in 1996 to 77 percent two years later.

There was a transnational geographic component to the corporation's expansion during this period as well. In November 1998 Universal acquired a 59 percent stake in Nascor Incorporated of Calgary, Alberta, a producer of trusses, pre-insulated wall panels, and another value-added lumber product, I-joists. One month later the company bought a 45 percent interest in Pino Exporta (later renamed Pinelli Universal, S. de R.L. de C.V.). Based in Durango, Mexico, Pino Exporta operated a molding and cut stock manufacturing plant.

During 1999 Universal and its subsidiaries concentrated more on organic growth than acquisitions. For instance, ACS opened a new facility in Denver to manufacture roof trusses and wall panels. Shoffner increased its capacity to produce I-joists, roof trusses, floor trusses, and wall panels by opening new plants in Hohenwald, Tennessee; and Liberty, North Carolina. Revenues reached $1.44 billion by 1999, nearly doubling the same figure from 1995; during that same time span, net income jumped from $14.1 million to $31.4 million.

Early 2000s and Beyond

The rockier economic times of the new century provided a test for Universal's multimarket strategy. During 2000, for instance, the manufactured housing market went into a serious slump, and lumber prices dropped to an eight-year low. Nevertheless, Universal was able to compensate to a degree by increasing its DIY sales, particularly to key customer The Home Depot, and by shifting production capacity into packaging products, the sales of which grew 5 percent. Universal was in this manner able to achieve the same profit margin as in 1999, while both revenues and net income fell only slightly. There was also one major acquisition in 2000, the $29.4 million purchase of Gang-Nail Components, Inc., a producer of engineered roof trusses for site-built housing headquartered in Fontana, California—marking Universal's entrance into the southern California market.

Another development in the early 2000s saw Universal move into the installation side of the business. During early 2001 the company acquired D&R Framing Contractors, which was based in Englewood, Colorado, and provided framing services to Colorado home builders. In other 2001 acquisitions, Universal bought: the Sunbelt Wood Components Division of the bankrupt Kevco, Inc., thereby gaining its largest competitor in the manufactured housing industry and four plants in North Carolina, Alabama, Georgia, and Arizona; two facilities of Superior Truss in Syracuse, Indiana, and Minneota, Minnesota, serving the site-built construction market; and another player in the site-built sector, P&R Truss Company, Inc., operator of four plants in New York.

By 2002 revenues at Universal Forest Products had reached $1.64 billion—an impressive figure though far short of the goal of $2 billion set five years earlier. The company blamed this failure on the troubled economic times. During 2002 Universal moved into the site-built truss market in northern California by buying certain assets of Modesta-based TopLine Building Products. It also opened a new plant in southwest Michigan where roof trusses, wall panels, and floor systems began to be assembled. This plant replaced two existing plants in nearby Indiana. Surprisingly, this was the firm's first production facility in its home state; Universal had been founded in Grand Rapids and had remained headquartered there ever since because its top managers hailed from the area and had no desire to relocate. Secchia remained one of these managers until the end of 2002 when, having reached the company's mandatory retirement age of 65, he retired from active employment, though he stayed on the board as "nonemployee chairman." In advance of his retirement, Secchia sold back to Universal two million shares of company stock held by Secchia and his family, at $18 per share, a transaction completed late in 2001.

Also in 2002 the company bought the assets of Inno-Tech Plastics, Inc., thereby entering the wood alternative market. The deal enabled Universal to begin selling decking and molding products made from extruded thermoplastic polystyrene resin. Such plastic alternatives to wood were becoming increasingly popular, despite their higher price tags, because of the decreased need for maintenance and because such products were less susceptible to warping than wood. Also fueling the demand were the concerns of a growing number of consumers regarding CCA-treated lumber. Although Universal and other producers of such lumber insisted that the wood was safe, environmental groups contended that the CCA preservative, which contains arsenic, could leach from wood as it ages and pose a cancer threat to people coming into contact with it. Lawsuits began to be filed on behalf of homeowners contending that CCA-treated lumber was an inherently defective product, and Universal, as the nation's leading producer of CCA lumber, was front and center in these suits. Despite their protests about the product's safety, Universal and other CCA lumber producers reached an agreement with the U.S. Environmental Protection Agency in February 2002 wherein they voluntarily agreed to stop producing the product. Universal began converting its 24 wood preservation plants to a new preservative, ammoniacal copper quat (ACQ), that does not contain either arsenic or chromium, another potentially hazardous chemical used in CCA. Each plant's conversion cost between $50,000 and $100,000, and by late 2003 most of the overhauls had been completed.

By late 2003, Universal Forest Products was on its way to another record year, boosted by a strong construction market. Over the previous ten years, the company's revenues had been increasing by an average of nearly 14 percent per year, and its consistent profitability during this period proved the worthiness of its strategy of targeting four different markets. Through its organic and acquisition-driven growth, Universal had developed into a national supplier and had been a key consolidator within what had been a fragmented industry. Also boding well for the future was Universal's seasoned senior management team and the firm's reputation for adapting to changes in the lumber market.

Principal Subsidiaries

Advanced Component Systems LLC; Consolidated Building Components, Inc.; D&R Framing Contractors (50%); ECJW Holdings Ltd. (Canada); Euro-Pacific Building Materials, Inc.; Nascor Incorporated (Canada; 57%); Nascor Structures, Inc.; Pinelli Universal, S. de R.L. de C.V. (Mexico; 50%); Shoffner Holding Company, Inc.; Syracuse Real Estate, L.L.C.; Tresstar, LLC; UFP Framing LLC; UFP Insurance Ltd. (Bermuda); UFP Real Estate, Inc.; UFP Transportation, Inc.; UFP Ventures, Inc.; UFP Ventures II, Inc.; Universal Consumer Products, Inc.; Universal Forest Products Canada Limited Partnership; Universal Forest Products Eastern Division, Inc.; Universal Forest Products Foundation; Universal Forest Products Holding Company, Inc.; Universal Forest Products Mexico Holdings, S. de R.L. de C.V. (Mexico); Universal Forest Products Nova Scotia ULC (Canada); Universal Forest Products of Canada, Inc.; Universal Forest Products of Modesto L.L.C.; Universal Forest Products Reclamation Center, Inc.; Universal Forest Products Shoffner LLC; Universal Forest Products Texas Limited Partnership; Universal Forest Products Western Division, Inc.; Universal Truss, Inc.; Western Building Professionals, LLC; Western Building Professionals of California, Inc.; Western Building Professionals of California II Limited Partnership.

Principal Competitors

Georgia-Pacific Corporation; Weyerhaeuser Company; Hampton Affiliates; Fletcher Challenge Forests Limited; Simpson Investment Company.

Further Reading

Blake, Laura, "Lumber Prices Dip," *Grand Rapids (Mich.) Business Journal,* May 17, 1993, p. 1.
Boyer, Kerry, "Universal Forest Opening Lumber Plant in Hamilton," *Greater Cincinnati Business Record,* August 2, 1993, p. 4.
Calabrese, Dan, "Secchia May Take Universal Public," *Grand Rapids (Mich.) Business Journal,* August 2, 1993, p. 1.
——, "Universal Focus Is on Growth," *Grand Rapids (Mich.) Business Journal,* January 3, 1995, p. B5.
——, "Universal's IPO Move Shows Initial Promise," *Grand Rapids (Mich.) Business Journal,* November 22, 1993, p. 6.
Czurak, David, "UFPI Planning Debut for New Product Line," *Grand Rapids (Mich.) Business Journal,* April 22, 2002, p. B7.
——, "Universal Building Momentum," *Grand Rapids (Mich.) Business Journal,* November 20, 2000, p. 1.
Emrich, Anne Bond, "Secchia Family Sells Two Million Shares Back to Universal," *Grand Rapids (Mich.) Business Journal,* November 19, 2001, p. 1.

——, "UFPI Chairman to Sell Portion of Shares in Advance of Retirement," *Grand Rapids (Mich.) Business Journal,* September 10, 2001, p. 3.

——, "Universal Thrives Despite Conditions," *Grand Rapids (Mich.) Business Journal,* April 23, 2001, p. 3.

Gonzalez, Jason, "Universal Forest: Wood Products Giant Wants to Lead with Four-Part Strategy," *National Home Center News,* March 22, 1999, pp. 28, 30–31.

Knape, Chris, "Universal Forest Products Defends Treated Lumber As EPA Assesses the Arsenic Risk to Consumers," *Grand Rapids (Mich.) Press,* September 21, 2003, p. E1.

La Franco, Robert, "Forest Products and Packaging," *Forbes,* January 3, 1994.

Lane, Amy, "State Firm Pushes Across Borders, but Carefully," *Crain's Detroit Business,* March 17, 1997, p. I2.

"A Living Story: How Universal Forest Products Rose to Its Current Prominence in the DIY Market," Grand Rapids, Mich.: Universal Forest Products, 1992.

Longcore, Kathleen, "Out of the Woods: Universal Forest Products Is Coming of Age," *Grand Rapids (Mich.) Press,* March 10, 1996, p. F1.

Turner, Mike, "New Universal Chief Harbors Presidential Ambitions," *Grand Rapids (Mich.) Business Journal,* July 17, 1989, p. 3.

—Hilary Gopnik and Donald Cameron McManus
—update: David E. Salamie

WestCoast Hospitality Corporation

201 W. North River Drive, Suite 100
Spokane, Washington 99201-2293
U.S.A.
Telephone: (509) 459-6200
Fax: (509) 325-7324
Web site: http://www.westcoasthotels.com

Public Company
Incorporated: 1997 as Cavanaughs Hospitality
   Corporation
Employees: 4,400
Sales: $194.2 million (2002)
Stock Exchanges: New York
Ticker Symbol: WEH
NAIC: 721110 Hotels (Except Casino Hotels) and Motels

WestCoast Hospitality Corporation is a public company located in Spokane, Washington, primarily devoted to the hotel business. The company has an ownership interest, manages, or franchises some 90 hotels under the "WestCoast" or "Red Lion" brand names, located in 16 states: Alaska, Arizona, California, Colorado, Hawaii, Idaho, Minnesota, Missouri, Montana, Nebraska, Nevada, Oregon, Texas, Utah, Washington, and Wyoming. WestCoast also owns TicketsWest, a computerized ticketing operation serving nine states and British Columbia through ticketing outlets, toll-free telephone numbers, and via the Internet. In addition, TicketsWest arranges for the presentation of touring Broadway shows and other entertainment event productions, primarily as a way to provide synergy with the company's hotels. Finally, WestCoast maintains a real estate division, which formed the basis for this family-run business. Donald Barbieri serves as chairman, while brothers Richard and Thomas, and their brother-in-law David M. Bell, also work for the company that for many years was headed by their father, Lou Barbieri.

Roots of Company Date to 1937

The son of Italian immigrant homesteaders, Lou Barbieri was born in DeSmet, Idaho, in 1915. Despite their limited resources, his parents were able to send him to Gonzaga University in Spokane where he received a business degree in 1937 and a law degree in 1940. Deciding to stay in Spokane, Barbieri accepted a position with a local bank, Washington Trust Bank, working for its property management division, which had been founded in 1937 and run by a man named Frank Goodale, who served as a mentor to Barbieri. In 1944 Goodale bought the business and Barbieri stayed on. In 1955 he became Goodale's partner and the business became known as Goodale & Barbieri Companies. Although he bought out Goodale in 1959, Barbieri retained the company name. Primarily a manager of apartment properties, Goodale & Barbieri was just a six-person operation when Barbieri gained sole ownership.

In 1969, upon graduation from college, Donald Barbieri went to work for his father at Goodale & Barbieri. It was during his college days that Donald Barbieri became committed to the development of quality low-income and senior housing, a passion that his father shared, so that despite the limited profits involved, affordable housing became a focus of the family company. It took advantage of newly passed federal housing legislation and worked with nonprofit sponsors including the Episcopal Diocese and Catholic Charities. Civic-minded, the elder Barbieri also helped to bring the World's Fair to Spokane in 1974, an event that also marked the entry of Goodale & Barbieri into the hotel business.

Hotel Business Dates to 1975

To provide lodging for the exposition, Goodale & Barbieri built the downtown Spokane Sheraton, a move that spurred the company to become further involved in the hospitality business. In 1975 the company joined forces with Burlington Northern Land Development to build the Cavanaughs River Inn in Spokane, utilizing an old railroad coal yard that had once served the Burlington Northern Railroad. Don Barbieri was instrumental in the diversification of Goodale & Barbieri, and in 1978 he became chief executive officer, succeeding his father, who retained the chairmanship. Other family members also became involved in the business. Thomas M. Barbieri started out in 1979 serving as the general manager of Cavanaughs River Inn. Richard L. Barbieri, an attorney, became a director of the

Company Perspectives:

WestCoast Hospitality Corporation provides a commitment of care, comfort & value and takes a leadership position in our communities, which will promote repeat business, profitability and future company growth.

company in 1978, and from that year until 1995 served as outside counsel and secretary of the company, while practicing law for two area firms. He became general counsel for Goodale & Barbieri and a senior vice-president of the company in 1997. In addition, brother-in-law David M. Bell, a trained engineer, joined the company in 1984 and became a vice-president involved in a number of development projects.

Goodale & Barbieri added another hotel in 1978, the 245-room Cavanaughs at Columbia Center in Kennewick, Washington. In 1980 the company took the next step in its move into the hospitality industry by establishing its proprietary Cavanaughs brand name. During the 1980s two more hotels were added to the portfolio: in 1983 the 402-room Cavanaughs Inn at the Park in Spokane; and in 1986 the 132-room Cavanaughs at Kalispell Center, located in Kalispell, Montana. Also in the 1980s the company built Cavanaughs Motor Inn in Moscow, Idaho. In the meantime, Goodale & Barbieri continued its property management business as well as a commitment to low-income and senior housing. In 1988, however, the company built a slightly different kind of senior project, the 105-unit Rockwood Lane Retirement Community, which catered to middle- and upper-income retirees.

Also during the 1980s Goodale & Barbieri became involved in the computerized event ticketing business. The motivation behind this move was a decision by a touring Broadway production of *Cats* to bypass Spokane because the city had a population of only 175,000. City officials asked Goodale & Barbieri if it could help and the company arranged with the New York producers to underwrite the show's appearance in Spokane. Goodale & Barbieri then created a Broadway series around that anchor event. To sell tickets for the series, the company in 1987 created G&B Select-A-Seat, and was awarded the event ticketing contract from the city of Spokane, which was looking for an alternative to Ticketmaster. While ensuring that Spokane would not be left out of major entertainment events and offering an alternative to Ticketmaster, Goodale & Barbieri also saw event underwriting and ticketing as a potential benefit to the company's hotel business, because entertainment packages could be marketed in connection with its Cavanaughs hotels.

In the 1990s Goodale & Barbieri enjoyed a period of exceptional growth. In the hotel business, the company added two properties in 1991: Cavanaughs Fourth Avenue, a 153-unit Spokane hotel, and the Yakima Towne Plaza, a 155-unit hotel in Yakima, Washington, which was subsequently renamed Cavanaughs at Yakima Center. While two properties were added to the Cavanaughs chain in 1991, one was sold off. The Moscow Motor Inn became expendable when its market became saturated with lodging. The University of Idaho acquired the property and converted it into student housing. Through the Yakima purchase,

Goodale & Barbieri also became involved in the catering business. In early 1992 the company formed a contract foodservices division, which management considered to be a natural outgrowth of its expanding hospitality business. It also delved into some side areas. Goodale & Barbieri acquired a historic dairy, Broadview Diary, located in downtown Spokane, around which it created a food processing division. In the mid-1990s the company launched a retail division and acquired a 50 percent interest in Moose Lake Co., a northwestern outdoor experience store, with outlets in Spokane and Kalispell.

The mid-1990s marked a turning point for Goodale & Barbieri. Don Barbieri added the chairmanship to his role as CEO and set an aggressive goal to double the size of the business within ten years, primarily by moving into Seattle and other markets situated along the Interstate 5 corridor. The first step in this plan was achieved in May 1996 when Goodale & Barbieri opened its first Seattle hotel, Cavanaughs on Fifth Avenue, a conversion of a former U.S. Bank building. Only two floors of the 300-unit hotel were opened at first, but by the fall of 1996 all 16 floors were converted and available to be booked. The property was centrally located, close to Seattle's theater community and trendy restaurants. Although the renovation did not save money over new construction, it allowed Goodale & Barbieri to open a facility in less than a year, as opposed to five years if it had been required to go through the normal permit and construction process. Moreover, by utilizing an existing structure, the hotel was exempt from height-control limitations placed on the neighborhood. While new buildings were limited to 85 feet, Cavanaughs on Fifth Avenue stood 250 feet high, able to offer panoramic views of Puget Sound. In addition, because Goodale & Barbieri was able to make use of an empty building, the project was a welcome addition to local efforts to revitalize the neighborhood.

In July 1997 Goodale & Barbieri marked another, and sadder, milestone when at the age of 82 Lou Barbieri died after undergoing kidney dialysis treatment at a Spokane hospital. He left a wife, seven children, and scores of grandchildren and great-grandchildren. His son, Don, told the press, "He always taught us to follow our own passion. It was a good lesson. Every day is a gift. Live it to the fullest. At age 82 he was doing that."

Goodale & Barbieri added another Yakima hotel in 1997, the 172-unit Cavanaughs Gateway Hotel. The company also bolstered its management business by taking over the property management portfolio of R.W. Robideaux and Co., a Spokane competitor, consisting of some office, medical, retail, shopping center, and residential properties in eastern Washington and northern Idaho. But the major focus going forward was clearly on the hotel division. The Barbieri family believed that the Northwest had developed into a strong economic region and that the time had come for a major hotel brand to emerge from the area, and they were determined to make Cavanaughs that brand. In the early weeks of 1998, Goodale & Barbieri added five hotels to its portfolio, including the 167-unit Templins Resorts in Post Falls, Idaho; the 142-unit West Bank Holiday Inn in Idaho Falls, Idaho; the 342-unit Ridpath Hotel in Spokane; the 220-unit Best Western Outlaw Inn in Kalispell, Montana; and the 123-unit Hallmark Inn in Hillsboro, Oregon. Some of these acquisitions were contingent upon Goodale & Barbieri's success in completing a public offering of stock, the

---

Key Dates:

1937: The company is launched as the property management division of a bank.
1944: Frank Goodale buys the business.
1955: Lou Barbieri becomes a partner of the company.
1959: Barbieri buys out Goodale.
1975: The company builds its first hotel.
1997: The company goes public.
1999: WestCoast Hotels is acquired.
2001: The Red Lion hotel chain is acquired.

---

proceeds of which the company hoped to use to pay down debt and fuel even further expansion.

Going Public in 1998

In preparation for going public, the company had already changed its name to Cavanaughs Hospitality Corporation in October 1997. Following a month-long road show, the initial public offering (IPO) was completed in April 1998, raising $89 million. A month later Cavanaughs added another hotel to the fold, paying $31.6 million for the 393-unit Olympus Hotel and Conference Center in Salt Lake City, Utah. In August 1998 the company continued its acquisition spree, buying four hotels from Sunston Hotel Investors, Inc. for $30.3 million: the 238-unit Boise Park Suite Hotel in Boise, Idaho; the 112-unit Canyon Springs Park Hotel in Twins Falls, Idaho; the 152-unit Pocatello Park Hotel and Convention Center in Pocatello, Idaho; and the 149-unit Colonial Inn in Helena, Montana. At the close of the year, Cavanaughs made one more purchase, picking up the 177-unit Olympia Holiday Inn in Olympia, Washington. With the completion of this deal, the Cavanaughs chain consisted of 19 hotels and 3,933 rooms, as well as 47 restaurants and lounges and 196,900 square feet of meeting space.

Along with the growth of its hotel portfolio, Cavanaughs bolstered its entertainment business. The company's New Millennium Series, which had offered 27 performances of Broadway shows in 1998, grew to 70 performances in 1999. Cavanaughs also decided in 1999 to merge its entertainment division with its computerized event ticketing service, creating a new operating division called TicketsWest.com, which had the capability to allow patrons to purchase travel services (both airline and car rental), lodging, and entertainment tickets through a single source. Cavanaughs quickly moved to bolster the unit by acquiring Portland-based Oregon Ticket Company, operating under the Fastixx name in 93 outlets located in a territory that stretched from California to Canada. Many of the outlets were housed in supermarkets owned by The Kroger Company, the largest grocery retailer in the United States. TicketWest.com struck a subsequent arrangement with a subsidiary of Kroger to establish outlets in Colorado supermarkets to sell ski lift tickets.

The most important development for Cavanaughs in 1999, however, came late in the year when it acquired Seattle-based WestCoast Hotels, a larger rival in the region. The total purchase of $45.5 million included $21.4 million in cash and the

assumption of $17.2 million in debt and other liabilities. WestCoast had a deep history, established in 1910 as Vance Hotels. In 1987 Vance became WestCoast Hotels and began a rapid expansion, primarily achieved through franchising and management agreements. The WestCoast acquisition added 46 hotels to Cavanaughs' portfolio, but, more important, gave the company a presence in first tier cities along the Interstate 5 corridor. Management believed that the WestCoast brand was more descriptive of the chain than Cavanaughs—a name that Goodale & Barbieri had difficulty selling to Wall Street during its IPO. The company quickly moved to rebrand existing Cavanaughs hotels, and then in February 2000 renamed the corporation WestCoast Hospitality Corporation.

To further the company's growth, management sought more management and franchising arrangements, with the goal of expanding the WestCoast chain to 100 hotels in the next five years. To help fund this plan the company in 2001 sought to divest some $70 million in noncore assets. It also expanded on a franchising and branding effort initiated two years earlier, now looking to establish as many full-service hotel franchise operations as possible in a territory that ranged from the Mississippi River to the Pacific Ocean. This effort was greatly enhanced by the $52 million cash and stock purchase of the Red Lion hotel chain, adding 41 properties. The Red Lion brand was established in the 1960s and peaked at 59 hotels in 1996 when it was acquired by Doubletree. Over the next several years, the chain shed hotels as ownership changed hands to Promus Hotel Corp., and then Hilton Hotels Corp. Because the Red Lion name was well established in certain markets, WestCoast decided to rebrand a number of hotels under the Red Lion name. The brand also proved helpful in WestCoast's franchising efforts.

As was the case with the lodging industry in general, WestCoast suffered a downturn in business due to a slowing economy and the adverse impact the terrorist attacks of September 11, 2001, had on travel. Nevertheless, WestCoast fared better than most of its competitors and was very much a company on the rise. It would carry on, however, with a new chief executive officer. In April 2003 Don Barbieri stepped down, turning over the CEO position to longtime Chief Financial Officer Art Coffey. Barbieri remained as chairman. While there was a belief expressed in some quarters that what WestCoast needed to take it to the next level was an experienced outsider with a reputation, other observers hailed the choice, believing that Coffey was up to the task of growing WestCoast despite poor economic conditions.

Principal Subsidiaries

Red Lion Hotels, Inc.; TicketsWest.com; WestCoast Hotels, Inc.

Principal Competitors

Best Western International Inc.; InterContinental Hotels Group PLC; Starwood Hotels & Resorts Worldwide, Inc.

Further Reading

Denne, Lorraine, ''Eastern Exposure,'' *Puget Sound Business Journal*, June 24, 1991, p. 41.

Harrell, Lisa, "WestCoast Readies to Expand," *Journal of Business,* May 31, 2001, p. A1.

Jacquette, Leslee, "Small Chain Establishes Position in Seattle," *Hotel & Motel Management,* September 16, 1996, p. 6.

Mayne, Jack, "WestCoast Hospitality Meets Expansion Goals," *Puget Sound Business Journal,* April 13, 2001, p. 18A.

Murphey, Michael, "Goodale & Barbieri Looks West for Room to Grow," *Puget Sound Business Journal,* August 2, 1996, p. 19.

Smith, Rob, "Purchase Gives Hospitality Firm Rooms for Growth," *Puget Sound Business Journal,* June 2, 2000, p. 37.

—Ed Dinger

Whirlpool Corporation

2000 North M-63
Benton Harbor, Michigan 49022-2692
U.S.A.
Telephone: (269) 926-5000
Toll Free: (800) 253-1301
Fax: (269) 923-5443
Web site: http://www.whirlpoolcorp.com

Public Company
Incorporated: 1929 as Nineteen Hundred Corporation
Employees: 68,272
Sales: $11.02 billion (2002)
Stock Exchanges: New York Chicago
Ticker Symbol: WHR
NAIC: 333415 Air-Conditioning and Warm Air Heating
    Equipment and Commercial and Industrial
    Refrigeration Equipment Manufacturing; 335211
    Electric Housewares and Household Fan
    Manufacturing; 335221 Household Cooking Appliance
    Manufacturing; 335222 Household Refrigerator and
    Home Freezer Manufacturing; 335224 Household
    Laundry Equipment Manufacturing; 335228 Other
    Major Household Appliance Manufacturing

From its beginning as a manufacturer of electrically powered clothes washers, Whirlpool Corporation has become the world's leading producer of major household appliances. Its main products include home laundry equipment, dishwashers, refrigerators, freezers, ovens, ranges, room air conditioners, and mixers and other small household appliances. The company's appliances are sold in more than 170 countries worldwide under such brand names as Whirlpool, KitchenAid, Roper, Estate, Bauknecht, Ignis, Laden, Polar, Brastemp, Consul, and Eslabon de Lujo. Whirlpool is a major supplier of appliances to Sears, Roebuck and Co., which accounts for about one-fifth of Whirlpool's net sales; these include Whirlpool-made products marketed under Sears' Kenmore brand, as well as Whirlpool and KitchenAid brand products. The corporation has 47 manufacturing locations, ten of which are in the United States; the remainder are in Canada, Mexico, France, Germany, Italy, Poland, Slovakia, South Africa, Sweden, Brazil, China, and India. Two-thirds of sales are generated in North America, 20 percent in Europe, and 11 percent in Latin America.

Washing Machine Beginnings

The company that preceded Whirlpool was founded in 1911 by Lou Upton and his uncle, Emory Upton, who lent their family name to the machine shop they opened in St. Joseph, Michigan. Lou Upton, a life insurance salesman, had recently lost his investment in a small appliance dealership that had failed. In an attempt to compensate Upton for his loss, the dealer gave him the patent for a manually operated clothes washer. Emory Upton was able to outfit the machine with an electric motor, and—with a $5,000 stake from L.C. Bassford, a Chicago retailing executive—the Upton Machine Company began producing electric wringer washers. The company soon snared its first customer, the Federal Electric division of Chicago-based Commonwealth Edison.

The relationship lasted three years, until Federal Electric began manufacturing its own washers. Although losing this customer was a major blow, the company stayed afloat by manufacturing toys, camping equipment, and automobile accessories until it rebounded in 1916 with an agreement to produce two types of wringer washers for Sears, Roebuck and Co., which at that time operated exclusively through mail order. Sales of Upton's washers through the Sears catalog (under the Allen trade name) grew rapidly during and after World War I. In order to avoid total dependence on the Sears account, however, Upton also launched a washer under its own brand name in the early 1920s.

During the 1920s, Sears's expansion into retailing and its selection of Upton as its sole supplier of washing machines forced the company to find a way to increase its manufacturing capacity and distribution efficiency. This was accomplished through a merger, in 1929, with the Nineteen Hundred Washer Company of Binghamton, New York. The post-merger company, known as the Nineteen Hundred Corporation, survived the Great Depression without any lasting damage and even expanded and modernized its production facilities during this time to handle increasing sales volume.

Company Perspectives:

At Whirlpool, we believe that innovative thinking comes from anyone and anywhere within our company. That's why, in 1999, we launched a worldwide effort to instill innovation as a core competency throughout our organization. Since then, Whirlpool people worldwide have participated in and contributed to innovation-related activities that have resulted in new ideas, products and services that deliver real value to our consumers in ways never before seen in either our company or our industry.

Innovation is Whirlpool Corporation's differentiating strategy, one we believe provides us with a significant competitive advantage. Innovation also brings us closer to our consumers and enables us to meet their unmet needs.

During World War II the company manufactured weapons parts and related products needed for the war effort. The company also focused on the development of an automatic, spinner-type washer during the 1940s. This machine, nicknamed the "Jeep," was introduced by Sears in 1947 under that company's Kenmore brand name, and then under Nineteen Hundred's own newly introduced Whirlpool brand one year later.

In 1949 Elisha "Bud" Gray II succeeded retiring Lou Upton as president and led the company through the postwar period, which was characterized by heavy consumer demand for convenience products. The Nineteen Hundred Corporation aggressively launched a complete line of Whirlpool home laundry appliances, including wringer and automatic clothes washers, electric and automatic clothes dryers, and irons. In 1950 the company changed its name to Whirlpool Corporation.

Diversifying the Product Line: 1950s–60s

Although sales continued to climb, it became clear by the mid-1950s that the company's emphasis on laundry equipment made it vulnerable to increasing competition from more diversified manufacturers. In 1955 Whirlpool merged with the Seeger Refrigerator Company and added a line of refrigerators. The company also began to make air conditioners and cooking-range products in 1955. The two lines had formerly been produced by Radio Corporation of America (RCA), and were marketed under the RCA-Whirlpool name. The company itself operated under the name of Whirlpool-Seeger Corporation until 1957. Between 1955 and 1957 the company introduced its first full line of home appliances under the RCA-Whirlpool brand. The line consisted of 12 types of machines and 150 models. The 1957 merger with Chicago's Birtman Electric Company brought a vacuum cleaner line under Whirlpool's expanding product umbrella.

As its product line grew, Whirlpool's network of independent dealers and distributors assumed an increasingly important role in the company's marketing and sales efforts. A subsidiary called Appliance Buyers Credit Corporation was formed in 1957 to provide financing to these distributors and to help strengthen Whirlpool's position as an industry leader. In 1958 the company broadened its reach beyond the United States by initiating the first of several acquisitions of major Brazilian appliance manufacturers, taking a stake in Brasmotor S.A.

Intensifying consumerism in the 1960s created growing pressure on appliance manufacturers to offer better quality and service. As a result, Whirlpool launched new support services, as well as a continuing stream of new products, such as the home trash compactor. Its toll-free Cool Line service enabled Whirlpool appliance owners to obtain immediate information on such subjects as installation and repair. At the same time, however, price reductions, caused by the softening demand for appliances, and growing competition led the company to institute a series of measures designed to streamline production and decrease manufacturing costs. Because the Whirlpool name itself had gained wide acceptance, the company also reached a friendly agreement with RCA during the mid-1960s to drop RCA's brand name from the company's products.

Further attempts to diversify yielded mixed results. The company's purchase of Heil-Quaker Corporation in 1964 enlarged Whirlpool's scope beyond consumer appliances to central heating and cooling equipment. But this subsidiary was sold to Inter-City Gas Corporation of Canada in 1986 as Whirlpool refocused its attention on home appliances. Its 1966 entry into the consumer electronics market with the acquisition of Warwick Electronics ended in failure ten years later, at which time the business was sold to Sanyo Electric Company. To close out the decade, the company penetrated the Canadian market for the first time with its 1969 purchase of a 33 percent stake in John Inglis Co. Ltd., a home appliance manufacturer. This company was renamed Inglis Limited in 1973, and Whirlpool increased its ownership interest to majority status in 1985; Inglis served as Whirlpool's Canadian arm.

Negotiating the Economic Uncertainties of the 1970s

Continued emphasis on consumerism combined with the 1973 energy crisis, a slump in the housing industry, and an economic recession increased pressure on the appliance industry to produce more energy-efficient products and to improve manufacturing efficiency. Faced with sluggish retail sales, Whirlpool dealers and Sears, still the company's largest customer, liquidated their inventories, a move that forced Whirlpool to lay off over one-third of its workforce. A 1974 strike at its Evansville, Indiana, plant, which produced refrigeration and air conditioning equipment, further tested the company's ability to weather the downturn in the appliance market. Although the strike ended after four months, the plant's compressor facilities closed permanently in 1983 as part of a companywide initiative to reduce manufacturing costs. These developments stood in marked contrast to the period between 1967 and 1973, when manufacturers had built, delivered, and sold one appliance every 3.2 seconds.

By 1977 the market cycled upward, and Whirlpool and its competitors were again experiencing strong demand for labor-saving devices from first-time buyers of the postwar generation, from households replacing existing appliances, and from the military post exchanges with which the company had established a buying arrangement in 1967. As Whirlpool grew, however, traditional appliance retailers struggled against the increasing sales strength of mass merchandisers.

Key Dates:

1911: Lou Upton and his uncle, Emory Upton, found Upton Machine Company in St. Joseph, Michigan, to begin producing electric wringer washers.

1916: Upton begins making washers for Sears, Roebuck and Co., which markets them under the Allen trade name.

1929: Manufacturing capacity is increased through a merger with the Nineteen Hundred Washer Company of Binghamton, New York, forming Nineteen Hundred Corporation.

1947: Company introduces the first automatic, spinner-type washer under Sears' Kenmore brand.

1948: Sale of Whirlpool brand washers begins.

1950: Company adds automatic dryers to its product line and changes its name to Whirlpool Corporation.

1955: Whirlpool gains line of refrigerators via merger with Seeger Refrigerator Company and changes its name to Whirlpool-Seeger Corporation; company acquires air conditioner and cooking range lines of Radio Corporation of America (RCA), which are marketed under the RCA-Whirlpool name until the mid-1960s.

1957: Company changes its name back to Whirlpool Corporation.

1958: In its first move outside the United States, Whirlpool buys a stake in Brasmotor S.A., a major Brazilian appliance maker.

1969: Whirlpool takes a 33 percent stake in John Inglis Co. Ltd., entering the Canadian home appliance market.

1986: Company acquires the KitchenAid division of Hobart Corporation.

1989: Whirlpool secures the rights to the Roper brand name; it joins with the Dutch company N.V. Philips to establish Whirlpool Europe B.V., a joint venture through which Whirlpool will market a full line of major home appliances in Europe.

1991: Whirlpool buys out its European partner, taking full control of Whirlpool Europe.

1997: Company launches a global restructuring involving the elimination of 4,700 jobs, the closure of plants and other facilities, and a charge of $350 million.

2000: Another major restructuring is launched that includes more than 7,000 job cuts and $373 million in charges over the following two years.

Whirlpool's progress during the 1970s was guided by Chairman John H. Platts, who had started his career with the company in 1941 on the assembly line and was hand-picked to succeed Elisha Gray II in 1971. Improvement of products for residential use remained an important priority for Whirlpool during this period. In 1977 it introduced the first automatic clothes washer with solid-state electronic controls and a line of microwave ovens. The company had originally entered the microwave market in the late 1950s and quickly withdrew because of limited potential.

A move toward vertical integration was also initiated in 1977, when the company started producing its own appliance motors to reduce its dependence on outside suppliers. One of Whirlpool's few failures during the decade involved the launch of a commercial ice-making system for use in hotels and motels and by food purveyors. The product never met sales goals and the business was sold in 1982.

1980s: Adding the KitchenAid and Roper Brands, Penetrating Europe

In 1980 Whirlpool was found guilty of discrimination in a suit brought by the Department of Labor, alleging that Whirlpool had taken inappropriate disciplinary action against two employees who had refused to perform what they considered to be hazardous work in the company's Marion, Ohio, plant. After several years of litigation, the U.S. Supreme Court ruled in the employees' favor, stating that the act of placing letters of reprimand in their personnel files was discriminatory.

Upon Platts's retirement in November 1982, Vice-Chairman Jack D. Sparks became chairman and CEO, and set about broadening the company's focus. Sparks's sales and marketing experience was felt important as Whirlpool faced an environment of increasing foreign competition in the United States, industry consolidation, and changing consumer preferences. Under Sparks's leadership, Whirlpool embarked upon a major capital spending program to increase manufacturing productivity and instituted a five-year plan to address industry trends.

One result of this planning process was the expansion of the company's product line beyond appliances and into related consumer durable goods. In 1985 Whirlpool entered the lucrative kitchen-cabinet market by acquiring Mastercraft Industries Corporation, followed by the purchase of another cabinet manufacturer, St. Charles Manufacturing Company, the next year. The cabinet business did not produce the hoped for results—Whirlpool was unable to capture a satisfactory share of the residential-construction market—and the cabinet operation was sold in 1989.

Sparks also oversaw the acquisition of the KitchenAid division of Hobart Corporation, which added a popular line of higher-priced dishwashers, ovens, and other kitchen appliances to the Whirlpool product line. Initiated in 1985, the transaction's completion was delayed for a year as White Consolidated Industries alleged antitrust violations. White's suit eventually proved unsuccessful and the acquisition was finalized in 1986.

Sparks also emphasized growth in the company's international markets and formed Whirlpool Trading Company in 1984, to explore overseas opportunities. Two years later the company attempted to forge a joint venture with Dutch company N.V. Philips to manufacture and market household appliances overseas. The project fell through because of unstable currency and market conditions.

In 1987 David R. Whitwam, succeeding Jack Sparks as president and CEO, took over the direction and implementation of the company's five-year global strategy. The company continued to focus on increasing manufacturing productivity and reducing costs, while applying new technology to appliance production. Whirlpool contracted with McDonnell Douglas Astronautics Company to develop prototypes of appliances for use in U.S. space stations. Also in 1987 Whirlpool and Sundaram-Clayton Limited of Madras, India, formed a joint venture called TVS Whirlpool Limited to make compact washing machines for the Indian market. One year later, Whirlpool entered the Mexican appliance market through the formation of Vitromatic, S.A. de C.V., a joint venture with Vitro S.A., a glass manufacturer based in Monterrey.

Until 1988 the company operated under a centralized structure, with decision-making concentrated at the senior management level. In 1988 Whirlpool reorganized its activities into seven units in order to maximize efficiency and market responsiveness. These units were: the Kenmore, KitchenAid, and Whirlpool appliance groups; Whirlpool International; Inglis Limited; Whirlpool Finance Corporation; and the company's export group.

Shortly thereafter, the company attempted to acquire Roper Corporation, another major manufacturer and supplier of appliances to Sears. This move was made to strengthen Whirlpool's cooking-appliance product line with electric and gas ranges and open new opportunities in the outdoor-equipment market Roper served with its lawn mowers and garden tractors. The Roper purchase was stymied, however, by General Electric Company (GE), which alleged that Roper had not solicited competitive bids upon receiving the Whirlpool offer as it was required to do by the Securities and Exchange Commission. As the controversy intensified, Whirlpool withdrew its tender offer and reached a settlement with GE in 1989 in which GE would acquire Roper's manufacturing facilities while Whirlpool would obtain the rights to the Roper name. The rivals also forged a two-year agreement under which GE would supply Whirlpool with appliance motors and gas and electric ranges. Meantime, the addition of Roper provided the company with a three-tier brand structure in North America consisting of the high-end KitchenAid, the popular-priced Whirlpool, and the value-priced Roper.

In 1989 the company successfully revived its proposed joint venture with N.V. Philips. This effort was spurred primarily by Whirlpool's desire to participate in the post-1992 European market for home appliances. The ensuing agreement cleared the way for Whirlpool to market a full line of major home appliances in Europe through a joint venture called Whirlpool Europe B.V. Philips's appliances were more appropriately designed for European customers than Whirlpool's models. The Whirlpool name was added to the Philips product line to strengthen recognition in the European market. By the end of the 1980s, Whirlpool's initiatives at home and abroad had paid off in the form of revenues in excess of $6 billion, more than tripling the 1978 total of $2 billion.

Global Ambitions in the 1990s

Whirlpool's initiatives in Europe reflected the company's aggressive international strategy, which earned it a reputation as one of the most globally diversified companies in the world during the early 1990s. Indeed, during this period Whirlpool expanded its overseas operations at a steady pace and lengthened its lead as the largest producer of appliances in the world. By late 1994, Whirlpool was manufacturing in 11 countries and marketing its products under ten brand names in 120 nations. The company enjoyed hefty sales gains in its giant European market in the early and mid-1990s, particularly following Whirlpool's mid-1991 buyout of its European joint venture partner in a $600 million deal. Further European growth came via an expansion into the newly opened markets of central and eastern Europe, with the first ventures centering on Hungary and Slovakia; later in the decade, the firm moved into Poland, the Czech Republic, Romania, Bulgaria, and Russia. Whirlpool, however, was pinning its hopes for greatest growth on Asia, to which it shipped 700,000 units in 1994. Similarly, sales in Latin America leapt 40 percent in 1994.

Besides surging global sales, Whirlpool worked to improve its operations in the flattening North American appliance market by restructuring. In 1994 it announced plans to cut about 9 percent of its global workforce, primarily through plant closures in Canada and the United States. A $250 million restructuring charge cut 1994 profits by 32 percent, to about $158 million. During the same year, though, Whirlpool's total revenues jumped more than 8 percent.

During the mid-1990s Whirlpool made a big push into Asia, forming several joint ventures in China and India. In 1994 the company had gained control of Kelvinator of India, Ltd., which it merged two years later with another majority-owned Indian firm, Whirlpool Washing Machines Limited, to form Whirlpool of India. Asia nonetheless accounted for only 6 percent of the 1996 revenues of $8.5 billion, and the ventures in this region were yet to be profitable. The firm lost $70 million in Asia that year. Late in 1997, as part of a global restructuring effort, Whirlpool announced that it was pulling out of two money-losing joint ventures in China. The company's European push had also been less than fully successful. It had proved very difficult to establish the Whirlpool brand on that continent, where there was stiff competition from entrenched players and where appliance manufacturers had to cater to specific demands of customers from a wide variety of cultures—a key contrast to the largely homogenous U.S. market. This was a lesson that Maytag Corporation, one of Whirlpool's main U.S. rivals, had already learned, having abandoned the European market in 1995 after encountering its own problems there. Although Whirlpool stayed the course in Europe, its operations there were thoroughly overhauled as part of the restructuring launched in late 1997. This restructuring involved the elimination of about 4,700 positions (about 10 percent of the payroll), mainly in Europe and Asia, the shuttering of various manufacturing and service facilities, and a $350 million charge that led to a net loss for the year of $15 million. Whirlpool also announced that it would sell its consumer-financing unit, Whirlpool Finance Corporation, to Transamerica Corporation for $1.35 billion.

By the late 1990s the European operations had been successfully turned around and returned to profitability. Leading the effort as head of Whirlpool Europe was Jeff M. Fettig, who was rewarded for his efforts by being named president and chief operating officer of Whirlpool Corporation in June 1999. Whitwam, who had been named chairman in 1992, remained

CEO. Whirlpool ended the decade with record 1999 revenues of $10.51 billion and record net earnings of $347 million. More than 40 percent of the revenues and 30 percent of the profits originated outside of North America.

Developments in the Early 2000s

Whirlpool continued its international expansion efforts in the early 2000s. In January 2000 the firm spent $283 million to increase its equity interests in its two key Brazilian subsidiaries, Brasmotor S.A. and Multibrás S.A. Eletrodomésticos, to 94 percent. Whirlpool gained full ownership of the Mexican venture Vitromatic in a July 2002 transaction involving $151 million in cash and the assumption of $143 million in debt. Vitromatic was subsequently renamed Whirlpool Mexico, S.A. de C.V. Over in Europe, a 95 percent interest in Polar S.A., a leading maker of home appliances in Poland, was acquired for $48 million in cash and assumed debt. In August 2003 Whirlpool entered into a global strategic alliance with Fisher & Paykel Appliances, a major New Zealand-based home appliance maker. The alliance was set up to market existing appliances as well as develop new ones.

The global economic downturn of this period had a significant negative impact on the major appliance industry, prompting Whirlpool to begin another major global restructuring in late 2000. Much of the restructuring involved the corporation's European operations, which remained less profitable than those in North America. Over the next two years, Whirlpool eliminated more than 7,000 positions, paring the workforce by more than 10 percent. It aimed to achieve annual savings of $200 million by boosting cost-effectiveness worldwide. Restructuring charges totaled $273 million in 2001 and 2002. Whirlpool incurred additional extraordinary expenses from two recalls. Certain dishwasher models were recalled in 2000 because some had been catching fire. Then in October 2001 Whirlpool issued the largest recall in its history. Some 1.8 million microwave ovens were recalled because they could catch fire. Whirlpool set aside $300 million to handle the problem. The company barely eked out a profit of $21 million in 2001, before posting a net loss of $394 million in 2002 on record revenues of $11.02 billion. The 2002 loss, however, resulted from implementation of a change in accounting principles relating to goodwill impairment. Whirlpool took an aftertax charge of $613 million in implementing this change.

As it moved through the difficult times that the new century brought, Whirlpool worked aggressively to develop successful new products. During 2002 the Whirlpool Duet washer and dryer were introduced, with the washer featuring 60 percent more capacity than standard front-load washers. Also introduced that year were the KitchenAid Briva in-sink dishwasher and the Whirlpool Polara refrigerated range, which was the first range to combine both cooking and refrigeration functions. But Whirlpool was also moving beyond the kitchen and the laundry room. New products in 2002 also included the company's first line of jetted baths as well as the Gladiator GarageWorks line of organizing products for the garage. Whirlpool's core, however, remained its lines of major home appliances, and its continued innovation in that area promised to keep the company in the lead of the global appliance market.

Principal Subsidiaries

Empreso Brasileira de Compressores S.A. (Brazil; 94%); Multibrás S.A. Eletrodomésticos (Brazil; 94%); Whirlpool Canada Inc.; Whirlpool do Brasil Ltda. (Brazil); Whirlpool Europe B.V. (Netherlands); Whirlpool Financial Corporation; Whirlpool Mexico, S.A. de C.V.; Whirlpool Patents Company; Whirlpool Properties, Inc.

Principal Operating Units

Whirlpool North America; Whirlpool Europe; Whirlpool Latin America; Whirlpool Asia.

Principal Competitors

GE Consumer Products; Maytag Corporation; AB Electrolux; BSH Bosch und Siemens Hausgeräte GmbH; Merloni Elettrodomestici S.p.A.; El.Fi Elettrofinanziaria S.p.A.

Further Reading

Bary, Andrew, "Unbalanced Spin," *Barron's,* August 14, 2000, pp. 18, 20.

Beatty, Gerry, "Breaking Away: Whirlpool Realigns to Spur Impulse Purchases of Major Appliances," *HFD—The Weekly Home Furnishings Newspaper,* November 23, 1992, pp. 58+.

Benway, Susan Duffy, "Giving Growth a Tumble: Whirlpool Pushes Expansion," *Barron's,* February 10, 1986, pp. 32+.

Berss, Marcia, "Whirlpool's Bloody Nose," *Forbes,* March 11, 1996, pp. 90+.

DuPont, Ted, "Whirlpool's New World," *HFD—The Weekly Home Furnishings Newspaper,* July 6, 1987, pp. 1+.

Hussey, Allan F., "No Dry Cycle: Despite Recent Slump, Whirlpool Boasts String of Record Profits," *Barron's,* April 2, 1984, pp. 55+.

"Innovation Runs Rampant in Benton Harbor," *Appliance,* October 2002, pp. 54–55.

Jancsurak, Joe, "Whirlpool: U.S. Leader Pursues Global Blueprint," *Appliance Manufacturer,* February 1997, p. G21.

Johnson, Robert, and Matthew Winkler, "Venture Is Set by Whirlpool and N.V. Philips," *Wall Street Journal,* August 19, 1988.

Kindel, Stephen, "World Washer: Why Whirlpool Leads in Appliances, Not Some Japanese Outfit," *Financial World,* March 20, 1990, pp. 42+.

Maruca, Regina Fazio, "The Right Way to Go Global: An Interview with Whirlpool CEO David Whitwam," *Harvard Business Review,* March/April 1994, pp. 134+.

Maurer, Mitch, "Whirlpool Cuts 3,200; Tulsa Plans Unchanged," *Tulsa World,* November 16, 1994, p. B1.

Oster, Patrick, and John Rossant, "Call It Worldpool," *Business Week,* November 28, 1994, pp. 98+.

Palmer, Jay, "Oh Boy, a Washer!," *Barron's,* September 26, 1994, pp. 17+.

Prichard, James, "Whirlpool Puts New Spin on Its Future," *Grand Rapids (Mich.) Press* (from Associated Press), September 8, 2002, p. B1.

Quintanilla, Carl, "Despite Setbacks, Whirlpool Pursues Overseas Markets," *Wall Street Journal,* December 9, 1997, p. B4.

Schiller, Zachary, et al., "Whirlpool Plots the Invasion of Europe," *Business Week,* September 5, 1988, p. 70.

Singhania, Lisa, "Whirlpool Looks to Innovation to Boost Appliance Sales," *Grand Rapids (Mich.) Press* (from Associated Press), February 6, 2000, p. F1.

Steinmetz, Greg, and Carl Quintanilla, "Tough Target: Whirlpool Expected Easy Going in Europe, and It Got a Big Shock," *Wall Street Journal,* April 10, 1998, p. A1.

Verespej, Michael A., "Whirlpool's New Kitchen Recipe," *Industry Week,* September 21, 1987, pp. 56+.

Vlasic, Bill, "Did Whirlpool Spin Too Far Too Fast?," *Business Week,* June 24, 1996, pp. 132+.

"Whirlpool: A Marketing-Minded CEO Tries to Set Sales Spinning," *Business Week,* May 16, 1983, pp. 46+.

Whirlpool Corporation, 1911–1986: Progressing Toward the 21st Century, Benton Harbor, Mich.: Whirlpool Corporation, 1986.

Woodruff, David, "Whirlpool Goes Off on a World Tour," *Business Week,* June 3, 1991, pp. 98+.

Zellner, Wendy, and Zachary Schiller, "A Tough Market Has Whirlpool in a Spin," *Business Week,* May 2, 1988, pp. 121+.

—Sandy Schusteff
—updates: Dave Mote, David E. Salamie

William Lyon Homes

4490 Von Karmen Avenue
Newport Beach, California 92660
U.S.A.
Telephone: (949) 833-3600
Fax: (949) 476-2178
Web site: http://www.lyonhomes.com

Public Company
Incorporated: 1999
Employees: 570
Sales: $613.30 million (2002)
Stock Exchanges: New York
Ticker Symbol: WLS
NAIC: 233220 Multifamily Housing Construction;
233210 Single Family Housing Construction; 233110
Land Subdivision and Land Development

William Lyon Homes designs, constructs, and markets homes in California, Arizona, and Nevada, ranking as one of the largest homebuilders, by volume, in the United States. The company generally builds three to five model homes for each product line. Sales are rarely the responsibility of independent brokers. Instead, the company maintains its own sales force, generally situating its sales offices adjacent to one of its housing developments. William Lyon Homes operates through five geographic divisions: southern California, San Diego, northern California, Arizona, and Nevada. The company derives approximately 75 percent of it business from its activities in California. The company's homes are usually sold before or during construction.

Origins

The business that became one of the largest homebuilders in the United States was founded by William Lyon, whose professional career comprised two occupations. Lyon grew up in Los Angeles, where his father was employed as a beverage wholesaler. During the 1940s, he, his brother, and his father worked together in a small construction business that provided housing for military personnel returning from World War II, but William Lyon had other dreams as a young adult. Lyon attended the

University of Southern California and dropped out in 1946 when he was 23 years old, intent on becoming a commercial airline pilot. He joined the U.S. Air Force, became a pilot, and flew combat missions during the Korean War. After serving in the war, Lyon started his own residential construction firm in 1956, but remained active in the Air Force Reserve. Lyon's service in the Reserve went far beyond the part-time commitment of a typical Reserve soldier. In 1975, he was appointed Chief of the Air Force Reserve, a title he held during both the Ford and the Carter Administrations. Lyon retired in 1979 as a major general, earning a rank he clearly coveted. In company press releases and in documents filed with the Securities and Exchange Commission, Lyon was referred to as "General Lyon," a designation that befitted the stewardship of his eponymous homebuilding company.

Lyon succeeded in home construction by concentrating his efforts in the fastest-growing construction region in the United States during the second half of the 20th century. California, and southern California in particular, recorded explosive population growth during the formative decades of Lyon's business. The state had 13.6 million residents the year Lyon started his company. By 2000, there were nearly 35 million people in California. Lyon, especially during the later stages of California's population growth, focused on developing properties in largely undeveloped regions. He built communities of homes in what would become the suburban regions that embraced metropolitan areas, the "satellite" cities that cropped up inland of the state's major cities. Lyon specialized in master-planned communities that provided affordable housing primarily to first-time home buyers, creating a mass-produced product and marketing the homes primarily through his own sales force. "A Lyon community," wrote *Forbes* reporter Ralph King, Jr., in a February 5, 1990 article, "is a latter-day Levittown marketed with a Sam Walton flair. Like William Levitt, Lyon uses assembly-line techniques, but instead of unadorned cookie-cutter houses, he offers several fully decorated models to choose from. Like Walton, he undercuts competitors' prices and dresses his customer service people in distinctive blue uniforms."

Over time, a formulaic approach to developing a Lyon community was evident. Typically, undeveloped land acquired by the company surrounded a particular unifying feature such as a parkway, or a community center, or a lake. The homes were basic and compact, but several "extra" features were included, amenities such as dormer windows or nine-foot ceilings. The company was profitable largely because it was able to keep its costs to a minimum. One of the most effective ways of keeping costs down was limiting the time each project took to complete. Lyon acquired large tracts of land and developed the property as quickly as possible, usually selling the homes before construction was complete. By adhering to a strict time schedule, the company kept the costs of possessing empty land to a minimum.

By the end of the 1980s, Lyon presided over a substantial construction empire. His interests, which generated an estimated $1.5 billion in revenue in 1989, were divided among three companies: Presley Cos., recognized as one of California's oldest homebuilders; William Lyon Homes Inc.; and Lyon Communities. Although William Lyon Co. and Presley Cos. operated as separate companies, the two entities would later share the same future. The union of the two companies was precipitated by developments that occurred during the late 1980s and early 1990s.

Difficulties Surfacing in the Early 1990s

The Lyon empire stood strong as the 1980s ended. William Lyon sold more than 6,000 apartments and single-family homes in 1989, when the average price for one of his detached, single-family homes was $190,000, or nearly 20 percent below the resale value of the average California home. In total, Lyon had constructed roughly 55,000 apartments and houses during the previous 35 years. There was every expectation that the prodigious output would continue into the 1990s. His confidence high, Lyon aggressively acquired land during the last three years of the 1980s, accumulating what he referred to as his "gold bars in the bank," in a February 5, 1990 interview with *Forbes*. As he entered the 1990s, Lyon possessed enough raw land to last for an estimated eight years, controlling an inventory of 65,000 lots, which represented more than 10,000 acres. The amount of land Lyon held was uncharacteristically high, representing twice the amount normally retained for development. His "gold bars in the bank" reference reflected his confidence, however, indicative of his faith in the continued growth of California's housing market. Unfortunately for Lyon, economic forces worked against him, leading to a decade-long struggle to regain the stability and growth of the late 1980s.

The early 1990s were difficult years for businesses nationwide. An economic recession delivered a debilitative blow to industries of all types, the homebuilding industry included. In

California, where the bulk of Lyon's interests were located, the pernicious economic conditions were particularly harsh. The state's housing market was slow to recover, hobbling Lyon's ability to withstand the downturn. In the May 7, 2002 issue of *Investor's Business Daily*, an analyst at Standard & Poor's explained the predicament: "They ran into difficulties because they had this long position in land that had been acquired in the late 1980s. It took longer for markets like California to recover. They couldn't buy (land) at the low end of the market because they didn't have any cash." The Lyon empire's strident growth slowed, its inventory of raw land weighing it down.

Repercussions from the economic slump of the early 1990s hit Lyon during the mid-1990s. Lyon gave up his controlling share of Presley in 1994, when he ceded control of the company to lenders. The transfer of control was part of a major restructuring program effected by the company. The restructuring effort included the sale of $190 million in junk bonds. Lyon's stake in the company, after lenders such as Foothill Capital Corp. were given control, was reduced to 15 percent. Lyon continued to serve as chairman of Presley. At William Lyon Homes, financial distress was evident. The company lost money in 1995, posted a negligible profit in 1996, and lost money again in 1997. Meanwhile, the restructuring effort at Presley had failed to improve the company's situation. By the summer of 1997, a $20 million payment on the company's loan agreements loomed. The company was losing money—registering an $89.9 million loss in 1997, for example—and all of its assets were pledged as collateral for its bank loans. "They've been holding on for so long," a real estate consultant remarked in the August 27, 1997 issue of *Knight Ridder/Tribune Business News*, "it's just catching up with them."

By the late 1990s, Lyon was forced to consider more comprehensive measures to keep his construction holdings afloat. Presley, perhaps only because its status as a publicly traded concern required public disclosure of its financial health, appeared to be ailing more than William Lyon Homes. Presley held roughly $250 million in high-interest debt and $160 million in bond debt. Lyon responded to the situation by proposing a buyout plan in the summer of 1998. His plan involved purchasing Presley's outstanding stock through privately held William Lyon Homes. The details of the proposed buyout plan called for William Lyon Homes to borrow $17 million to buy all of Presley's 52 million shares for $.40 per share, well below the more than $.60 per share price at the time. Once the two companies merged, the combined entity would be responsible for repaying the loan Lyon used to acquire Presley. Lyon waited for his deal to be approved, with perhaps the greatest resistance coming from Presley shareholders, some of whom had purchased the company's stock for more than $17 per share five years earlier. One shareholder, a retired artist named Nick Trone, typified the negative reaction to Lyon's proposal in the July 5, 1998 issue of *Knight Ridder/Tribune Business News*. "How do I know as an investor that as chairman of the board he did what he could do to make Presley succeed," Trone said, "since he's the one who's now trying to buy it at a cheaper price?"

Lyon's $.40-per-share offer was rejected, but he persisted in his efforts to take control of Presley and merge it with William Lyon Homes. In January 1999, according to documents filed with the Securities and Exchange Commission, the two com-

Key Dates:

1956: William Lyon founds his own residential construction firm.
1990: Lyon completes three-year spree of aggressive land acquisition.
1991: An affiliated company, Presley Cos., converts to pubic ownership.
1994: William Lyon gives up his controlling stake in Presley Cos.
1999: Presley Cos. and William Lyon Homes merge.

panies reached an agreement to merge, an agreement that called for Presley to acquire William Lyon Homes for $48 million. At the same time, Lyon promised to invest as much as $16 million in the beleaguered Presley, paying approximately $.62 per share. Lyon was expected to be chairman of the combination, which also was expected to use both the Presley and the William Lyon brand names. The merger was completed in November 1999.

Recovery in the 21st Century

The merged companies, operating under the name William Lyon Homes, rebounded in 1999 and entered the 21st century exhibiting renewed vigor. The troubles of the 1990s seemed to be behind the company, as growth returned. In 2001, William Lyon Homes generated $468 million in revenues, a 12 percent increase from the previous year's total. More impressively, the company's earnings were up during the year as well, increasing 20 percent. In 2002, the company's revenues experienced another substantial surge, jumping to $613 million. When the company's unconsolidated joint ventures were included in its sales volume, revenues reached nearly $1 billion, a total produced by delivering more than 2,500 homes. At this juncture in the company's development, it was offering homes for between $110,000 to slightly more than $1 million, with the average William Lyon Homes residence selling for $379,200.

As the company prepared to conclude its first half-century of business, it represented one of the most venerable names in California's residential construction market. In an exceptionally capricious industry, William Lyon Homes' travails during the 1990s were an expected part of competing in the residential construction business. As it moved forward, the historical cyclicality of the business promised to present itself again, but the company could take confidence in its ability to withstand the recession of the early 1990s and all the vicissitudes of its nearly 50 years in business.

Principal Subsidiaries

William Lyon Homes, Inc.; Presley Homes; California Equity Funding, Inc.; PH Institutional Ventures; Duxford Interiors; PH Ventures—San Jose; Presley CMR, Inc.; HSP Inc.; Duxford Financial, Inc.; The Presley Companies; Presley Southwest, Inc.; William Lyon Southwest, Inc.; Mountain Gate Ventures, Inc.; PH—LP Ventures; PH—Rielly Ventures; Duxford Title Reinsurance Co.; Sycamore CC, Inc.

Principal Operating Divisions

Southern California; Northern California; San Diego; Arizona; Nevada.

Principal Competitors

KB Home; Lennar Corporation; M.D.C. Holdings, Inc.

Further Reading

Barron, Kelly, "Cash-Starved Southland Builders Are Going Public," *Los Angeles Business Journal,* August 26, 1991, p. 33.
——, "Orange County, Calif., Home Builder Negotiates with Bondholders," *Knight Ridder/Tribune Business News,* August 27, 1997.
King, Ralph, Jr., " 'Rats or . . . People?,' " *Forbes,* February 5, 1990, p. 88.
LePage, Andrew, "Chairman Offers to Buy Ailing California Homebuilder," *Knight Ridder/Tribune Business News,* July 5, 1998.
Linecker, Adelia Cellini, "William Lyon Homes Newport Beach, California Strong Demand in West Helps Builder Rally from Mid-'90s Woes," *Investor's Business Daily,* May 7, 2002, p. A09.
Mouchard, Andre, "California-Based Home Builders to Merge," *Knight Ridder/Tribune Business News,* January 4, 1999.

—Jeffrey L. Covell

Winn-Dixie Stores, Inc.

5050 Edgewood Court
Jacksonville, Florida 32254-3699
U.S.A.
Telephone: (904) 783-5000
Fax: (904) 783-5294
Web site: http://www.winn-dixie.com

Public Company
Incorporated: 1928 as Winn & Lovett Grocery Company
Employees: 99,200
Sales: $12.17 billion (2003)
Stock Exchanges: New York
Ticker Symbol: WIN
NAIC: 445110 Supermarkets and Other Grocery (Except Convenience) Stores; 311412 Frozen Specialty Food Manufacturing; 311421 Fruit and Vegetable Canning; 311511 Fluid Milk Manufacturing; 311520 Ice Cream and Frozen Dessert Manufacturing; 311611 Animal (Except Poultry) Slaughtering; 311821 Cookie and Cracker Manufacturing; 311920 Coffee and Tea Manufacturing; 311941 Mayonnaise, Dressing, and Other Prepared Sauce Manufacturing; 312111 Soft Drink Manufacturing

Winn-Dixie Stores, Inc. is one of the largest supermarket chains in the southeastern United States. The company operates more than 1,070 stores in 12 southeastern states and the Bahamas in two general formats: more than 1,000 combination food and drugstores under the Winn-Dixie, Marketplace, Thriftway, and City Markets banners and about 60 grocery warehouse stores under the Save Rite and Sack & Save brands. About three dozen of the supermarkets also feature gas stations, while 44 contain separate liquor stores. The company maintains 16 facilities to produce or process such products as soft drinks, frozen pizza, sausage, eggs, milk, ice cream, crackers, and cookies. As the company has increasingly emphasized larger stores—the average one now taking up more than 44,000 square feet—Winn-Dixie outlets have added additional services, including banking, ATMs, photo processing, and restaurants. The fifth largest supermarket operator in the United States as late as the mid-1990s, Winn-Dixie Stores saw its position rapidly fall over the next several years as a massive consolidation drive in the industry bypassed the company, in large part, and left it in the number 13 position by the early 2000s.

Early History

Winn-Dixie's founder, William M. Davis, was the owner of an old-fashioned charge-and-deliver general store in Idaho before World War I. The advent of self-serve, cash-and-carry chain stores after the war drove many old-fashioned independent grocers out of business. Davis, however, saw the potential of this new kind of grocery store. He moved his family to Miami, Florida, and, borrowing $10,000, entered the self-serve grocery business. He bought his first store, the Rockmoor Grocery, in the Miami suburb of Lemon City in 1925. Davis, his wife, and their four sons ran the store; the Davis family has provided the leadership for Winn-Dixie ever since.

In the early years Davis found it difficult to expand. Three times he attempted to open a second store and three times the store failed. Chain stores had demonstrated their ability to deliver a wider variety of high-quality goods at lower prices than had ever before been possible, but many a tradition-bound consumer preferred the old way of doing business. Independent grocers had local support and political connections, but life could be made rather difficult for a chain store or supermarket operator. After consumers' initial resistance was overcome, however, it was impossible to deny that supermarkets were the wave of the future. By 1927 the Rockmoor Grocery had expanded to five stores, which were renamed Table Supply Stores that year. Having expanded to Tampa in 1931 with the $10,000 purchase of Lively Stores, the company operated 34 stores in south Florida by 1934, the year W.M. Davis died.

Davis's four sons took control of the company at their father's death and set out on a course of further expansion. In 1939 they acquired control of the 78 stores of the Winn & Lovett Grocery Company of Florida and Georgia, and in 1944 the company established its headquarters in Jacksonville, Florida, and officially adopted the Winn & Lovett name.

The war years brought a lull in the supermarket industry. Food rationing, labor shortages, and price increases forced

Company Perspectives:

Our efforts are focused on delivering total customer satisfaction and low price leadership. And this goal, we believe, is the key to gaining new customers and increasing sales and profit. We will accomplish this by being flexible and responsive to the ever-changing needs of our customers.

supermarkets to tighten their belts with the rest of the nation. Winn & Lovett, along with most of the supermarket industry, cooperated with the government by maintaining a lid on prices during and immediately following the war. During this time nonfood products filled what would otherwise have been empty shelves, and began to assume a more prominent place in supermarkets. The higher profit margins on nonfood products allowed supermarkets to maintain food prices at relatively low levels without jeopardizing overall profitability.

Merger with Dixie Home Stores in 1955 Creating Winn-Dixie

Once the economy had returned to normal, Winn & Lovett picked up where it had left off before the war. In 1945 the company expanded into Kentucky with the purchase of 31 Steiden Stores. An additional 46 Florida stores were gained in 1949 through the acquisition of Margaret Ann Stores. Winn & Lovett became the first Florida industrial corporation to gain a listing on the New York Stock Exchange in 1952. Three years later the company added several more grocery chains to its company rolls: Penney Stores in Mississippi and two South Carolina chains, Ballentine Stores and Eden Stores. Later in 1955, Winn & Lovett merged with Dixie Home Stores of Greenville, South Carolina, which operated 117 stores, and changed its name to Winn-Dixie Stores, Inc. With this merger, Winn-Dixie broke into the top ten supermarket chains and from the mid-1950s through to the mid-1960s was the most profitable company in the industry. Profits in the supermarket industry are more dependent on high volume than high profit margins, but Winn-Dixie's profit margins in this period were exceptionally high. This was due to both an increase in sales (fourfold between 1954 and 1964) and lower labor costs in the nonunion South.

Winn-Dixie continued to expand and prosper in the late 1950s and early 1960s. In 1956 alone, Winn-Dixie acquired 24 North Carolina stores from Ketner-Milner Stores, Inc.; 42 Hill Stores in the New Orleans area; and nine Kings outlets in Georgia. In 1962 the company acquired Hill Grocery Co., Inc. and its 35 stores in the Birmingham, Alabama, area. In addition to acquiring more retail outlets, Winn-Dixie also branched out into processing, manufacturing, and distribution, producing a wide variety of store brand products from these support facilities. With profits increasing each year and with 23 consecutive years of cash dividend increases, Chairman J.E. Davis (one of W.M. Davis's sons) could confidently predict in the *Wall Street Journal* in 1966 that Winn-Dixie would shatter all previous sales and profit records in fiscal 1967.

The year 1966 also brought some bad news, however. The Federal Trade Commission (FTC) had been investigating the increasing concentration in the supermarket industry and had concluded that mergers and acquisitions in the industry had unfairly limited competition, in violation of the Clayton Anti-Trust Act. Winn-Dixie, as the most profitable and one of the fastest-growing chains, was an obvious target. The investigation showed that, in fact, a third of Winn-Dixie's increase in sales over the previous ten years had been generated by stores acquired during that period. As a result, the FTC ruled that for ten years Winn-Dixie was forbidden to acquire any retail grocery stores in the United States without FTC approval. The ruling was not as much a punishment of Winn-Dixie as it was a settlement between the firm and the FTC. "The principal practical effect," Winn-Dixie President Bert L. Thomas told the *Wall Street Journal* at the time, "is to clear all Winn-Dixie's past mergers and acquisitions from future challenge." All that was required of Winn-Dixie was obedience to the ruling. Winn-Dixie used the ten-year period for "internal" expansion, adding stores by leasing new stores and improving existing retail and support facilities. Winn-Dixie did acquire 11 City Markets in the Bahamas that were not covered by the FTC order.

When the ban was lifted in 1976, Winn-Dixie acquired the 135 stores and the support facilities of Kimbell, Inc. in Texas, Oklahoma, and New Mexico. The stores in New Mexico, which were unionized, posed a problem for the traditionally nonunion Winn-Dixie. After the company refused to negotiate with the union and a pro-union boycott began, Winn-Dixie sold its New Mexico stores in 1979.

Reacting to Increased Competition in the 1980s

In 1983 J.E. Davis stepped down as chairman of Winn-Dixie, and a member of the third generation of the Davis family, Robert D. Davis, assumed control. Robert's five years at the helm were marked by a virtually flat rate of growth in gross profits, although net earnings did not suffer because of lower tax rates. Winn-Dixie faced increasing competition in the 1980s, not only from its traditional competitors—the other large chains—but also from convenience stores, which made a large dent in the market. In 1988 Robert stepped down as chairman (but remained vice-chairman) and his cousin, A. Dano Davis, was elected to succeed him.

Dano Davis's new management team implemented measures to cut operating costs and raise gross profit margins. Management costs were also pared, and 60 management positions were eliminated. Winn-Dixie began selling off its smaller, less efficient stores and also unloaded some of its less productive baking facilities. The prevailing trend was toward larger, more modern stores offering more merchandise.

Despite these very positive moves, Winn-Dixie faced some problems in the late 1980s. It was notified by the Environmental Protection Agency that it was a PRP (potentially responsible party) for the cleanup of two dumping grounds designated as "superfund sites" in Florida; the company estimated cleanup costs at about $200,000. Winn-Dixie also spearheaded a battle between grocery retailers and large producers of packaged goods over who would determine the shape of the market for retail food. Winn-Dixie announced in 1988 that it would no longer accept promotion allowances for products on a market by market basis, but only chainwide. Winn-Dixie demanded a consistent national pricing policy from major suppliers such as Campbell Soup, General Mills, Quaker, Procter & Gamble, and

Key Dates:

1925: William M. Davis enters the self-serve grocery business through the purchase of Rockmoor Grocery in Miami, Florida.

1927: The company, now operating five stores, changes its name to The Table Supply Stores.

1939: The company gains control of the Winn & Lovett Grocery Company, which operates 78 stores in Florida and Georgia.

1944: The company adopts the Winn & Lovett name and moves its headquarters to Jacksonville, Florida.

1952: The company lists its stock on the New York Stock Exchange.

1955: Dixie Home Stores of Greenville, South Carolina, is acquired; the company changes its name to Winn-Dixie Stores, Inc.

1966: The Federal Trade Commission forbids Winn-Dixie from acquiring any retail grocery stores in the United States for ten years.

1976: Kimbell, Inc. and its 135 stores in Texas, Oklahoma, and New Mexico are acquired; the New Mexico outlets are soon divested.

1984: The first Winn-Dixie Marketplace store opens.

1995: Winn-Dixie acquires the Thriftway Food Drug chain, operator of 25 outlets in the greater Cincinnati area.

2000: The company launches a major restructuring involving the closure of more than 110 stores and the elimination of 11,000 workers from the payroll.

2002: Winn-Dixie divests its operations in Texas and Oklahoma.

others. The companies initially refused to meet Winn-Dixie's demands and Winn-Dixie retaliated by dropping certain of their products from its inventory. According to *Fortune,* Winn-Dixie's crusade was a response to the declining profitability of the preceding five years. Winn-Dixie negotiated with each of the producers separately, hoping to solve the impasse and preserve its market position.

Emphasizing Low Prices and Building Larger Stores in the 1990s

In January 1990 Winn-Dixie abandoned the acquisition of 24 B&B Cash Grocery Stores in the Tampa, Florida, area that had been announced the previous October. The Federal Trade Commission was concerned about the antitrust implications of the deal, which could have provided Winn-Dixie a virtual monopoly in a couple of southern Florida counties, and launched an investigation. The deal was called off when both parties became concerned about the cost of complying with the FTC's inquiry.

By the early 1990s, Winn-Dixie had essentially won the producers over to its position, a victory that was crucial to the company's emphasis on chainwide low prices that began in 1991. The chain quickly became the "low price leader" within the markets it served. Keeping prices low helped Winn-Dixie compete in the increasingly crowded markets it served.

That accomplished, Winn-Dixie next aimed to attain a further leg up on the competition by increasing the size of its stores. During the previous decade, the company had increased average store size from 22,000 square feet in 1982 to 30,000 square feet in 1989; it had also introduced larger, 44,000-square-foot "Marketplace" stores, which were grocery stores with the addition of such services as pharmacies and photofinishing. After the first had been opened in Valdosta, Georgia, in 1984, about 55 Marketplaces had been built by the end of the 1980s.

Starting in 1991, Winn-Dixie increased its store sizes even further, renovated or closed hundreds of its older and smaller stores, and altered the layout and conception of the Marketplace stores, some of which were as large as 55,000 square feet. By 1996, average store size was up to 38,800 square feet. Although Winn-Dixie did open a number of new stores during this period and also acquired in early 1995 the Thriftway Food Drug chain, which had 25 units in the greater Cincinnati area, overall Winn-Dixie actually had fewer stores in its chain in 1996 (1,178) than in 1991 (1,207) thanks to the large number of older stores it closed. The company spent large sums of money on renovations and new store openings—$650 million in fiscal 1994 alone—and converted more and more of its stores to the new Marketplace design. By 1996 there were 504 Marketplaces in the chain (compared to 634 Winn-Dixies), and many of these larger format stores included a "Food Pavilion," which was a large single aisle featuring a bakery, produce, deli, a combination meat-seafood service area, and a sit-down eating area. The Food Pavilion was aimed to offer customers a convenient layout and more convenience food, especially targeted for the more time-stressed customer. Also in 1996, Winn-Dixie began experimenting with self-checkout lanes.

After net income hit a peak of $255.6 million in the fiscal year ending in June 1996, Winn-Dixie saw its earnings steadily erode in the face of heightening competition. In addition to its traditional rival Publix Super Markets, Inc., which was aggressively targeting many of Winn-Dixie's main markets, Winn-Dixie saw two new competitors enter its territory in the late 1980s: Food Lion, Inc., which expanded into Florida, and Wal-Mart Stores, Inc., which began a massive move into the grocery trade through its combination discount and grocery outlets that were eventually dubbed Supercenters. Given that the Arkansas-based Wal-Mart's main territory was in the South, Winn-Dixie was hit particularly hard by the discount giant's food foray. Despite Winn-Dixie's shift to the Marketplace format, same-store sales were constantly on the decline in the late 1990s. During fiscal 1999, the company's 52-year streak of increasing its dividends came to an end, and the following year the company's overall revenues fell for the first time in more than 60 years. Further bad news came in mid-1999 when the company reached an agreement to spend $33 million to settle a class-action discrimination lawsuit. The suit was similar to suits filed against other large grocery chains, charging the companies with systematically discriminating against female and African American workers in hiring and promotion.

Restructuring in the New Century

Late in 1999 Dano Davis relinquished his position as chief executive to Allen Rowland, who was named president and CEO, with Davis remaining chairman. The first Winn-Dixie leader ever to be hired from outside the company, Rowland had most recently been president and COO of Smith's Food & Drug Centers, Inc. Just a few months later, in April 2000, Winn-Dixie announced a major restructuring involving the shuttering of more than 110 underperforming stores, the slashing of the workforce by 8 percent (or 11,000 employees), the closure of paper bag and detergent manufacturing plants, and the consolidation of some division offices and warehouse facilities. The company also centralized its procurement, marketing, and merchandising, and it began a $144 million remodeling program to overhaul about 650 of the remaining 1,000-plus stores. Winn-Dixie also wanted to exit from the Texas and Oklahoma markets, where operations were only marginally profitable and market share was falling, but a deal to sell the 74 stores in those states to the Kroger Co. was nixed by the FTC, which was concerned about the potential erosion in competition in the Fort Worth, Texas, market. In connection with the restructuring, Winn-Dixie recorded charges of $396 million; as a result, Winn-Dixie suffered a net loss of $228.9 million for fiscal 2000.

At the same time that this strategic downsizing was being implemented, Winn-Dixie took the unusual step of expanding through two acquisitions. In October 2000 nine supermarkets in the Orlando, Florida, area were acquired from Gooding's Supermarkets, Inc., and in January 2001 Winn-Dixie spent $85 million to acquire 68 grocery stores from the bankrupt Jitney Jungle Stores of America, Inc. The latter outlets were located in Mississippi, Alabama, and Louisiana, and that deal also included gas stations that operated in conjunction with 32 of the stores. Later in 2001 Winn-Dixie announced that it was slashing its dividend from $1.02 per share to 20 cents in order to improve earnings and free up cash for debt reduction and reinvesting in the business. In October 2001 the company launched a new advertising campaign called "The Real Deal" that touted "real good food, from real good people, at a real good price." The next year Winn-Dixie followed an industry trend by launching a customer loyalty card.

During the early 2000s Winn-Dixie converted more than 50 of its stores to the Save Rite Grocery Warehouse format. Typically located in lower-income neighborhoods, Save Rites sold a limited selection of low-priced groceries in sparsely furnished stores. The biggest shift to this format was in Atlanta, where 38 locations began sporting the Save Rite banner in 2002. Also in 2002 the manufacturing operations were reduced still further with the sale of Deep South Products, Inc., operator of a cheese plant in Gainesville, Georgia, to Schreiber Foods, Inc. Winn-Dixie also divested its troubled operations in Texas and Oklahoma, which included 76 stores, a dairy plant, and a distribution center. This cut the workforce by another 5,300 jobs and also resulted in a $172.8 million net loss from discontinued operations, which cut net earnings for fiscal 2002 to $86.9 million.

As it looked toward the future, Winn-Dixie aimed to increasingly tailor its stores to the particular neighborhoods in which they were located. This was a growing trend among food retailers attempting to differentiate themselves from the likes of Wal-Mart. The Save Rite chain was a step in this direction, as were newer more upscale Winn-Dixie outlets—serving more affluent communities—that included special features, such as sushi bars, full-time wine stewards, and organic food sections. Early in 2003 the company said that it would accelerate its

development of new stores, with this neighborhood-focused strategy in mind. In June of that year Rowland retired from the company. Rowland had certainly succeeded in stabilizing the company's financial position, but observers were not entirely convinced that Winn-Dixie had been fully turned around. The new president and CEO was Frank Lazaran, whom Rowland had brought onboard as COO a little more than a year earlier. Lazaran had previously been president of Randalls Food Markets, Inc., a division of Safeway Inc. Net earnings of $239.2 million for fiscal 2003 represented the company's best showing since 1996. In June 2003 Winn-Dixie also announced that it would consolidate its private-label product lines from the more than 60 brands that had been in use to just three: the premium-quality Prestige line; the new Winn-Dixie brand, which would be used for moderately priced items; and the value-priced Thrifty Maid brand.

Principal Subsidiaries

Astor Products, Inc.; Crackin' Good, Inc.; Deep South Products, Inc.; Dixie Packers, Inc.; Economy Wholesale Distributors, Inc.; Save Rite Grocery Warehouse, Inc.; Superior Food Company; W-D (Bahamas) Limited; Winn-Dixie Charlotte, Inc.; Winn-Dixie Logistics, Inc.; Winn-Dixie Louisiana, Inc.; Winn-Dixie Montgomery, Inc.; Winn-Dixie Procurement, Inc.; Winn-Dixie Raleigh, Inc.; Winn-Dixie Supermarkets, Inc.

Principal Divisions

Bahamas; Charlotte; Jacksonville; Montgomery; New Orleans; Central Florida; South Florida; Raleigh.

Principal Competitors

Wal-Mart Stores, Inc.; Publix Super Markets, Inc.; Ahold USA, Inc.; Delhaize America, Inc.; Costco Wholesale Corporation; The Kroger Co.; Albertson's, Inc.

Further Reading

Albright, Mark, "FTC Rejects Winn-Dixie Store Sale," *St. Petersburg (Fla.) Times,* June 3, 2000, p. 1E.
——, "Is Winn-Dixie Next on Shopping List?," *St. Petersburg (Fla.) Times,* August 22, 1999, p. 1H.
Baljko, Jennifer L., "Winn-Dixie Cuts Prices on 3,000 Items," *Supermarket News,* October 7, 1996, p. 4.
Calnan, Christopher, "Winn-Dixie to Replace President: Rowland Steps Aside for Lazaran," *(Jacksonville) Florida Times-Union,* May 3, 2003, p. A1.
Daniels, Earl, "Winn-Dixie to Exit Two States," *(Jacksonville) Florida Times-Union,* May 7, 2002, p. F1.
Davis, J.E., *Don't Make A&P Mad,* [Montana]: J.E. Davis, 1990.
Dowdell, Stephen, "Winn-Dixie's New Blueprint," *Supermarket News,* March 1, 1993, pp. 1, 40–41, 45.
Finotti, John, "What's Eating Winn-Dixie?," *Florida Trend,* March 1999, pp. 52+.
Gordon, Mitchell, "Winn-Dixie Stores Has Another Peak Year in the Bag," *Supermarket News,* May 24, 1982, p. 44.
Klepacki, Laura, "Winn-Dixie Is Satisfied with Price-Cut Results," *Supermarket News,* May 25, 1992, pp. 17, 20.
Marcial, Gene G., "Ringing Up Gains at Winn-Dixie," *Business Week,* September 12, 1988, p. 102.
Mehlman, William, "Winn Dixie Revises Strategy for Tough Sunbelt Market," *Insiders' Chronicle,* June 26, 1989, pp. 1, 10–12.

Merrefield, David, "Winn-Dixie's Next Battle," *Supermarket News,* December 7, 1992, pp. 1, 12–13.

Northrup, Herbert R., et al., *Restrictive Labor Practices in the Super-Market Industry,* Philadelphia: University of Pennsylvania Press, 1967.

Paul, Peralte C., "Winn-Dixie Plans to Cut 11,000 Jobs," *(Jacksonville) Florida Times-Union,* April 21, 2000, p. A1.

Richards, Gregory, "Is Winn-Dixie Turned Around?," *(Jacksonville) Florida Times-Union,* May 5, 2003, p. FB12.

——, "Winn-Dixie's New CEO Plans to Build on Store's Progress," *(Jacksonville) Florida Times-Union,* May 8, 2003, p. D1.

——, "Winn-Dixie Stores Consolidate, Revamp Private Label Products," *(Jacksonville) Florida Times-Union,* June 28, 2003, p. D1.

Sachdev, Ameet, "Winn-Dixie Settles Discrimination Suit," *St. Petersburg (Fla.) Times,* July 17, 1999, p. 1E.

Saporito, Bill, "Shopping-Cart Battle in Winn-Dixieland," *Fortune,* October 3, 1983, p. 206.

Spurgeon, Devon, "Winn-Dixie to Close Stores, Cut 11,000 Jobs," *Wall Street Journal,* April 21, 2000, p. A3.

Taylor, John H., "King No More," *Forbes,* April 18, 1988, p. 37.

Tibbits, Lisa A., "Winn-Dixie to Stress Expansion, Upgrade," *Supermarket News,* October 9, 1995, pp. 1, 110.

Turcsik, Richard, "PG Profile: Winn-Dixie," *Progressive Grocer,* September 1, 2002, pp. 18–20, 22, 24.

Zimmerman, M., *The Supermarket: A Revolution in Distribution,* New York: McGraw-Hill, 1955.

Zwiebach, Elliot, "Winn-Dixie Completes Thriftway Buy," *Supermarket News,* April 3, 1995, pp. 4, 54.

——, "Winn-Dixie's New Direction," *Supermarket News,* June 20, 1988, pp. 1+.

——, "Winn-Dixie to Close 114 Stores, Cut 11,000 Jobs," *Supermarket News,* May 1, 2000, p. 1.

—Robin Carre
—update: David E. Salamie

WOLVERINE
WWW WORLD WIDE

Wolverine World Wide, Inc.

9341 Courtland Drive N.E.
Rockford, Michigan 49351-0001
U.S.A.
Telephone: (616) 866-5500
Toll Free: (800) 789-8586
Fax: (616) 866-0257
Web site: http://www.wolverineworldwide.com

Public Company
Incorporated: 1906 as Hirth-Krause Company
Employees: 4,426
Sales: $827.1 million (2002)
Stock Exchanges: New York Pacific
Ticker Symbol: WWW
NAIC: 316213 Men's Footwear (Except Athletic)
   Manufacturing; 316214 Women's Footwear (Except
   Athletic) Manufacturing; 316213 House Slipper
   Manufacturing; 316110 Leather and Hide Tanning and
   Finishing; 448210 Shoe Stores; 454111 Electronic
   Shopping; 533110 Lessors of Nonfinancial Intangible
   Assets (Except Copyrighted Works)

Wolverine World Wide, Inc. is one of the world's leading producers and marketers of nonathletic footwear, including casual, work, and outdoor shoes and boots as well as moccasins and slippers. The company sells more than 37 million pairs of footwear per year, under such brands as Wolverine (work, outdoor sport, and rugged casual categories), Bates (uniform), Hy-Test (work), Merrell (hiking, rugged outdoor, and outdoor-inspired casual), and the famous Hush Puppies (casual). Wolverine produces additional lines under brands licensed from other firms, including Caterpillar, Coleman, Harley-Davidson, Karen Neuburger, and Stanley. More than 90 percent of the company's revenues are generated from the sale of branded footwear. The company's products are sold worldwide through department stores, footwear chains, specialty and independent retailers, and international licensees and distributors. More than 20 percent of sales originate outside the United States, the vast majority coming from Europe and Canada. Other Wolverine businesses contribute about 10 percent of revenues; these include a pigskin tannery in the company's headquarters city of Rockford in west Michigan; a licensing operation through which the Wolverine and Hush Puppies brands appear on non-footwear products produced by other companies, including apparel, eyewear, watches, and plush toys; and a retailing business, which operates more than 60 factory outlet stores under the Hush Puppies and Family name as well as a couple of Track 'n Trail mall-based stores. The company also maintains several web sites selling its footwear directly to consumers. On the manufacturing side, 85 percent of the company's shoes are sourced via third-party manufacturers mainly located in the Asia-Pacific region and Central and South America; the balance are produced at company-owned facilities in Michigan, Arkansas, the Dominican Republic, and Mexico.

Family-owned from its inception in 1883 until 1965, Wolverine struggled to compete with athletic and imported shoes in the 1970s and 1980s. A combination of shrewd marketing, fresh-yet-retro design, and pure luck contributed to the company's spectacular comeback in the early 1990s. More recent developments have included acquisitions of the Hy-Test and Merrell brands in 1996 and 1997, respectively; the 1990s launching of footwear lines under licensed brands, including Caterpillar and Harley-Davidson; and the overhaul of the company's global sourcing and manufacturing operations, begun in 2000.

The Late 19th and Early 20th Centuries

Wolverine was established in 1883 by G.A. Krause and his uncle, Fred Hirth, and named the Hirth-Krause Company. The son of Prussian immigrants, Krause brought a two-century heritage of leather tanning to the enterprise. The company originally sold leather, buttonhooks, lacing, and soles at wholesale, and purchased finished shoes for retail sale.

Krause began to consolidate vertically after the turn of the century, placing his sons in independent, but related, shoe-making and leather tanning businesses. In 1903, he established a shoe manufacturing business in Rockford, Michigan. His eldest son, Otto, who had a degree in engineering from the University of Michigan, operated this arm of the family enterprise, which supplied finished footwear to the Hirth-Krause retail outlets. Five years later, G.A. and younger son Victor created the Wolverine Tanning Company, also based in Rockford, to supply leather to the shoemaking business.

Victor, whose postsecondary education had included apprenticeships in tanning, would be a driving force behind Wolverine's establishment as a premiere American shoe company. In 1909, he traveled to Milwaukee, Wisconsin, to study a chrome tanning and retanning process developed by master tanner John Pfingsten. By 1914, Victor's own experiments had resulted in a tanning process for "shell horsehide," a cheap, durable, but heretofore unworkably stiff section of hide taken from the horse's rear. The company soon stopped using cowhide in favor of their unique new material.

Promoted as "1,000 mile shoes," sales of the heavy-duty Wolverine boots helped increase corporate earnings almost 700 percent from 1916 to 1923. A centennial company history noted that "Wolverine boots and shoes became one of rural and small-town America's most popular brands."

In 1921, Hirth-Krause and the Rockford shoe factory—which had previously merged under the name Michigan Shoe Makers—were united with Wolverine to form Wolverine Shoe and Tanning Corporation. The company acquired a glovemaking business that same year and began manufacturing horsehide work gloves. Over the course of the decade, Wolverine built its first warehouse, created an employee profit-sharing plan, launched a nationwide advertising campaign, and erected its first consolidated headquarters.

Depression and World War Spark Innovation

Although Wolverine survived the Great Depression intact, the accelerating transition from horse-drawn transportation to gasoline-powered transport severely diminished the need for horses in the United States. As a result, the company was compelled to turn to less reliable international markets for its hides.

When the United States entered World War II, the federal government's War Production Board assigned Wolverine to manufacture gloves for the troops and suggested that the company try pigskin as a raw material. It seemed like a fine idea until the company discovered the inadequacy of pigskinning methods, which were not satisfactory to either the tanners or the

meat processors. Not only was it difficult to remove the skin without taking some of the flesh with it, but separating all the flesh from the skin often damaged the hide. Sometimes the only useful pieces were barely large enough to make a glove. A company history quoted one employee in the project who remarked, "It looked like these pigs didn't care to be skinned." Nevertheless, Wolverine did manage to manufacture enough gloves to keep the military happy and its books in the black throughout the war years.

But when the global conflict ended, demand for pigskin gloves fizzled and Wolverine was forced to revert to cowhide, which was in steadier supply than horsehide and in more reliable condition than pigskin. Then Chairman Victor Krause was convinced that pigskin could be a viable alternative to cowhide; it was softer than either cowhide or horsehide, widely available, woefully underused, breathable, and easy to dye and clean. He became so obsessed with "the pigskin processing dilemma" that he resigned Wolverine's chairmanship to dedicate his full attention to the question. His son, Adolph, advanced to corporate leadership.

Working as an unpaid consultant, Victor Krause assembled a team of engineers who spent two years designing a device that separated the pigskin from the flesh without damaging either product. Wolverine patented the machine, which was created to fit neatly into the pig production process. By the early 1980s, Wolverine would have one of the world's largest pigskin tanneries.

When tanned, pigskin was soft and flexible, but it was not tough enough to be used in Wolverine's traditional work boots and shoes. In a radical departure from the company's historical emphasis, Krause designed a pair of casual shoes from the pigskin and presented them to Wolverine's board of directors. The board was not particularly enthusiastic about the new product, but decided that market research would determine whether and how to proceed.

According to corporate legend, the genesis of the Hush Puppies brand name came at a southern-style fish fry where deep-fried nuggets of dough commonly known as "hush puppies" were served. When Wolverine Sales Manager Jim Muir asked his host about the origins of the strange name, he was told that farmers used the treats "to quiet their barking dogs." That conversation reminded Muir of another colloquial meaning for "barking dogs": sore feet. It occurred to him that Wolverine's new shoes worked on sore feet just like hush puppies worked on yelping dogs, so he proposed the name as a new trademark. In 1957 Wolverine President Adolph Krause, son of Victor Krause, chose the canine name and basset hound logo from a field of ten possibilities.

After a brief period of test marketing, the company launched a national advertising campaign in 1958 that was unprecedented in the shoe industry. Hush Puppies proved a timely innovation in footwear. With workers moving from farms to offices and from the countryside to the suburbs, Wolverine faced a decline in the sale of heavy-duty work shoes, but looked forward to a boom in more casual shoes. Hush Puppies became the footwear phenomenon of the late 1950s and early 1960s. Wolverine took the brand international via licensing agreements, the first of which was sold to Canada's Greb Shoes, Ltd. in 1959. Renamed

Key Dates:

1883: G.A. Krause and his uncle, Fred Hirth, found the Grand Rapids, Michigan-based Hirth-Krause Company, selling leather and shoe accessories at wholesale and purchasing finished shoes for retail sale.

1903: Krause establishes a shoe factory in nearby Rockford, placing his eldest son, Otto, in charge; Hirth-Krause and the shoe factory are later operated under the name Michigan Shoe Makers.

1908: Krause and younger son Victor create Wolverine Tanning Company, also based in Rockford, to supply leather to the shoemaking business.

1921: Michigan Shoe Makers and Wolverine Tanning are united to form Wolverine Shoe and Tanning Corporation.

1958: The Hush Puppies brand of casual shoes is launched nationally.

1965: Company goes public with a listing on the New York Stock Exchange.

1966: Company is renamed Wolverine World Wide, Inc.

1972: Leadership reign of the Krause family comes to an end.

1976: Company enters specialty retailing with the launch of the Little Red Shoe House chain.

1981: Wolverine enters the athletic shoe sector with the purchase of the Brooks brand.

Late 1980s: Company begins making hiking and outdoor boots under both the Wolverine and the licensed Coleman brand.

Early 1990s: Retailing operations are scaled back and the Brooks brand is divested, with the company intent on focusing on the Wolverine and Hush Puppies brands.

1993: More than 100 retail outlets are closed; the remaining 60 are revamped into factory outlets.

1994: Wolverine acquires the worldwide license to market footwear under the Caterpillar name.

1996: The Hy-Test line of industrial work boots is acquired.

1997: Wolverine purchases the Merrell brand of performance-outdoor footwear.

1998: Another license deal leads to the debut of the Harley-Davidson footwear line.

2000: Major restructuring of manufacturing operations involves the closure of five plants and a workforce reduction of 25 percent.

2003: Wolverine agrees to acquire Sebago Inc., maker of penny loafers and docksiders boat shoes.

Wolverine World Wide, Inc. in 1966, the parent company's sales nearly quintupled from 1958 to 1965, when it made its initial public offering on the New York Stock Exchange.

Decline in the 1970s and 1980s

Hush Puppies put Wolverine at the top of the casual shoe industry, but the branded shoes could not keep it there very long. Sales flattened in the late 1960s, as Hush Puppies' core market matured and the brand failed to win younger customers. The company attempted to diversify via acquisition during this period, acquiring Bates, Frolic, and Tru-Stitch shoes and slippers. In spite of these efforts, however, Wolverine World Wide's nearly 90 years of Krause family management came to an end after the company experienced a net loss in 1972. Wolverine appeared to recover in the later years of the decade, as sales increased from about $125 million in 1975 to about $250 million in 1980.

But the new decade brought increased competition from imported and athletic shoes that seriously undermined the already weakened business. In 1981 the Reagan administration dropped import quotas in favor of freer trade, prompting a deluge of inexpensive shoes from Asia and Latin America. Rita Koselka of *Forbes* magazine noted in a 1992 article that, ''Among U.S. industries, few have been hit harder by foreign competition than shoemaking.'' Half of the country's footwear manufacturers went bankrupt over the course of the 1980s, as the imports share of the U.S. market grew from 50 percent to 86 percent. During the same period, consumers began to turn from Hush Puppy-type shoes to athletic shoes for casual wear, further eroding Wolverine's potential market.

Unlike so many of its compatriots, Wolverine survived the 1980s, but not without its share of fits and starts. Under the

direction of Thomas Gleason from 1972 to 1992, the company struggled to meet the challenge by diversifying its footwear lineup, expanding its direct retail operation, leveraging the Hush Puppies brand via licensing, and moving some production overseas.

Wolverine World Wide had launched its own chain of ''Little Red Shoe House'' specialty stores, which emphasized children's shoes, in 1976. Acquisitions and internal growth expanded the company's retail operation to more than 100 stores by 1983. The well-known Hush Puppies logo was licensed to manufacturers of clothing, umbrellas, luggage, hats, and handbags, and could be found in 56 countries by 1987.

From its well established base in work shoes and ''career casual'' footwear, Wolverine diversified via acquisition and internal development. The company entered the athletic market with the 1981 purchase of Brooks Shoe Manufacturing Co., a struggling maker of running shoes. Wolverine acquired Town & Country and Viner Bros. shoes in 1982 and added Kaepa dual-laced, split-vamp specialty athletic shoes the following year. The company also developed its own new shoes, including the Body Shoe, which featured an ergonomic ''comfort curve,'' and Cloud 10 shoes, with special cushioning for the ball of the foot. Wolverine hoped that its expanded line of comfortable yet fashionable footwear would attract more 30- to 45-year-olds to its stores.

But in spite of these apparently well-thought-out efforts, Wolverine's bottom line continued to show signs of stress: net income slid from $15.5 million in 1981 to $2.1 million in 1984. After a slight recovery in 1985, the company suffered a $12.6 million loss on sales of $341.7 million. The shortfall sparked a restructuring and reorganization that included the closure of five U.S. factories, the sale of two small retail chains and shuttering of 15 other outlets, the spinoff of Kaepa, and divestment of a relatively new West German footwear manufacturing and 105-store retail operation. The domestic factory closings helped increase the proportion of Wolverine's shoes manufactured overseas to about 50 percent.

Analysts found plenty to blame at Wolverine. Some said that the company's new casual and career-oriented brands—Town & Country, Harbor Town of Maine, and Wimzees Casuals—were cannibalizing Hush Puppies' sales. One analyst told *Footwear News* in September 1985 that top executives "have lost their direction in recent years and can't get either manufacturing or retailing back on track." Another said the company had grown "too big to run effectively." Thomas Jaffe of *Forbes* was more direct, blaming "impulsive management, silly diversification, and finally, the flood of cheap imports that has knocked the socks off most of the U.S. shoe industry." Analyst Sheldon Grodsky told *Business Week*'s Keith Naughton, "Dullness permeated the company and they just missed the entire 1980s."

In 1987, the company hired Geoffrey B. Bloom, a marketing and product development expert with 12 years of experience at Florsheim Shoe Co., as president and chief operating officer. In the waning years of the decade, Wolverine made another attempt at revitalization. The company leveraged its basic lines of work shoes and boots, dress shoes, and casual footwear to fit the multiple fashion and function demands of younger customers. For example, the company's 100-plus years of expertise in making durable work boots gave it insight into the development of hiking and outdoor boots. Wolverine used its own venerable brand and licensed the Coleman name for this new venture. The company hired new designers to update its athletic and casual shoes, and it even contracted with a Michigan State University laboratory for new footwear innovations.

Although Wolverine World Wide's net income rose to $7.7 million on sales of $324 million by 1988, other nagging problems stole the spotlight from this modest recovery. Most infamous of these was a 1989 lawsuit charging that Wolverine and Fred Goldston, a pigskin and cowhide broker, had conspired to steal cowhide from Southwest Hide Co. Goldston had been hired by Wolverine to raise the quantity and quality of pigskin rinds to supply the company's tannery. Southwest originally accused Goldston of exchanging their high-grade cowhides with lower-quality skins, but when Goldston went bankrupt, the plaintiff added partner Wolverine to the suit. Faced with a jury verdict of more than $39.3 million, Wolverine elected to settle the suit for $8.5 million in cash and bonds in 1992. CEO Gleason continued to assert his company's innocence in spite of the settlement, telling *Forbes*'s Rita Koselka, "We were just the deep pockets around." Wolverine was also plagued with quality control and inventory problems in the late 1980s.

Dramatic Recovery in the Early 1990s

In the fall of 1990, Wolverine announced another restructuring, including plans to scale back its retail operations, shutter a manufacturing plant, and eliminate certain shoe lines. After multiple reorganizations, infrequent profitability, and sliding market share, the company elected to divest its Brooks athletic shoe division to Rokke Group, a U.S.-Norway joint venture, in 1992. The restructuring shrunk Wolverine's overall revenues from more than $320 million in 1990 to $282.9 million in 1992, but allowed it to concentrate on its Wolverine and Hush Puppies brands, which made near miraculous recoveries in the early 1990s.

Wolverine's revitalization after more than a decade of lackluster performance came about through a combination of rejuvenated designs, savvy marketing, strict cost controls, and a healthy dose of good luck. From 1990 to 1995, Geoffrey Bloom, who succeeded Thomas Gleason as chief executive officer in 1993, closed more than 100 of the company's retail outlets, designating the remaining 60 as factory outlets. He also consolidated Wolverine's 16 divisions into five streamlined operating units, thereby increasing productivity (measured in revenue per employee) by nearly one-fourth from 1992 to 1994.

Taking a cue from fashion designer John Bartlett, newly hired designer Maggie Mercado revived 1950s-era styles such as the "Wayne" (nee Duke) oxford and "Earl" slip-on, offering the waterproof suede shoes in a rainbow of new colors such as Pepto-Bismol pink and Day-Glo green. Both Bartlett and designer Anna Sui featured the shoes in their 1995 collections. Hush Puppies soon began to turn up on the famous feet of stars such as Jim Carrey, Sharon Stone, David Bowie, Tom Hanks, and Sylvester Stallone. Hush Puppies also benefited from the trend toward dressing-down at work, filling the fashion gap between tennis shoes and dress shoes. Wolverine sent videotapes with tips for casual dressing at work to 200 businesses throughout the United States. In the ultimate retro coup, the company revived the "We invented casual" tagline that had launched Hush Puppies in 1958. By 1995, tony stores such as Barneys in New York and Pleasure Swell in California struggled to keep the shoes in stock.

While its Hush Puppies conquered the world of fashion, Wolverine World Wide's work boots and hikers tackled more mundane markets. In spite of steadily declining employment in American construction and manufacturing sectors, sales of Wolverine work boots reached record levels in 1991. The high-tech, relatively lightweight footwear featured DuraShock shock absorbers and slip-resistant treads. Smart new ads told prospective customers that they could "hunt 'til hell freezes over." Coleman hiking boots gave Wolverine entree into the mass market via distribution in Wal-Mart stores. In 1994 Wolverine added another licensed brand to its stable when it acquired the worldwide license to market footwear under the Caterpillar name from Caterpillar Inc., the manufacturer of earthmoving equipment. Leveraging Caterpillar's rugged image, Wolverine promoted the new line as "walking machines, the toughest equipment on earth." Annual sales of the Caterpillar line reached nearly eight million pairs by 1997—eclipsing sales of the Wolverine brand—with sales being made in more than 100 countries. According to one Wolverine executive, the Caterpillar boots had become a trendy item with younger consumers looking for "funky" footwear.

A focus on international growth increased the geographic distribution of the company's sales to about 50 percent international by 1995. Wolverine was the only American shoemaker to achieve a comprehensive contract in Russia. It had also established a Hush Puppies store in China, and its branded shoes were offered in more than 60 countries around the world. By mid-1995, *Forbes* had declared Wolverine "a dog no more."

Sales had risen by more than 46 percent from $282.9 million in 1992 to $414 million in 1995, and net income more than tripled from $4.7 million to $24.1 million during the same period.

Expanding the Brand Portfolio in the Late 1990s

In 1996 Bloom was rewarded for his remarkable turnaround achievement by being named chairman. He also remained CEO but relinquished the presidency to Timothy O'Donovan, who was named chief operating officer as well the following year. O'Donovan had held a series of marketing, sales, and management positions since joining Wolverine in 1969, and as president of the Hush Puppies Company from 1992 to 1996, he played a key role in the turnaround led by Bloom.

Expansion was clearly still on the agenda for Bloom and O'Donovan in the later years of the 1990s. Wolverine paid $22.8 million in cash to the Florsheim Shoe Company in 1996 for the Hy-Test line of industrial work boots. That fall a line of Hush Puppies men's and women's slippers began reaching store shelves. The company's stable of outdoor footwear brands was augmented via the October 1997 acquisition of Merrell, a brand of performance footwear designed for backpacking, day hiking, and everyday use. Wolverine's aggressive drive into foreign markets continued in 1997 with the introduction of the Hush Puppies brand into Russia, China, France, and Scandinavia and the Caterpillar line into Russia, China, Brazil, and India. During 1998 the company began producing a Harley-Davidson line of motorcycle, casual, fashion, and western footwear for men, women, and children under a license agreement with the Harley-Davidson Motor Company. The next year Wolverine launched its first full line of children's shoes and boots, including the Hush Puppies, Caterpillar, Harley-Davidson, and Coleman labels.

The growth initiatives helped revenues and profits increase smartly in 1996 and 1997, but the company managed only marginal increases in 1998 because of a weak fourth quarter. The economic crisis that erupted in Russia that year battered Wolverine's nascent moves into that market. The company took the difficult decision of closing down its Russian subsidiary, taking a $14 million charge in 1999 to do so, which in turn led to a decline in profits for the year.

Restructuring in Early 2000s

In April 2000 Bloom handed over the CEO reins to O'Donovan, with Bloom continuing as chairman. A month later Wolverine announced that it had entered into a license agreement with the Stanley Works, the famous U.S. toolmaker, to develop a line of Stanley brand work boots. In a first for Wolverine, the line, which was to be value priced at under $60 per pair, was to be sold through Payless ShoeSource, Inc., operator of the biggest chain of shoe stores in the United States.

O'Donovan next faced the challenge of implementing a major restructuring of the company's global sourcing and manufacturing operations. Aiming to reduce operating costs by $10 million per year, Wolverine closed five of its manufacturing plants in New York, Missouri, Canada, Puerto Rico, and Costa Rica, shifting production to its remaining seven plants. Nearly 1,400 employees were cut from the payroll by the time the restructuring was complete in mid-2001, representing one-

quarter of the workforce. In the end, the initiative substantially shifted more of the company's production outside the United States, a shift that many other U.S. footwear makers had made in the 1990s. Prior to the restructuring, 40 percent of Wolverine's shoes and boots were made in the United States, but by 2003 this figure was down to 5 percent.

Wolverine recorded $28 million in restructuring charges during 2000, resulting in a net income figure for the year of just $10.7 million. Revenues for the year, however, increased a respectable 6 percent thanks in large part to phenomenal sales of the Merrell brand. Wolverine sold nearly 4.5 million pairs of Merrell shoes in 2000, doubling the previous year's total, and the brand garnered sales in excess of $100 million, an increase of 80 percent. Driving these stellar results was Merrell's move beyond hiking boots. In late 1998 Merrell invented a new footwear category when it began selling "aftersport" shoes—comfortable moccasins or sandals with all-weather treads. As O'Donovan told the *Grand Rapids Business Journal* in 2001, "We found that after these hardcore users of Merrell products got off the ski slopes or mountain bikes, or finished trail running, we had an opportunity to sell them another pair of footwear they could wear after all those activities. That was the concept." In 2002 Wolverine sold more than seven million pairs of Merrell footwear, which was now distributed in more than 130 countries. Revenues for the brand reached $180 million.

Wolverine World Wide recorded its third straight year of record revenues in 2002, with sales increasing 14.9 percent that year, to $827.1 million. Profits increased 7.5 percent, reaching a record $47.9 million. That year Wolverine reached a license agreement with Karen Neuburger to develop a line of slippers and casual footwear for women under the name of the lifestyle designer. The company purchased the rights to the Track 'n Trail name, which had been the name of a shoe store chain before it declared bankruptcy in 2001. Wolverine's two existing mall-based retail outlets, which had been called UpFootgear, were rebranded Track 'n Trail. Wolverine also acquired its CAT (the Caterpillar line) and Merrell distribution businesses in Europe during 2002.

Continuing to seek new avenues for growth, Wolverine reached an agreement in July 2003 to acquire Sebago, Inc., a privately held footwear maker based in Portland, Maine. This acquisition would expand Wolverine into more preppy footwear given Sebago's output of penny loafers and its flagship product, docksiders boat shoes. Concurrently, workers at the Wolverine tannery in Rockford went on strike that same month, the first such action at the plant in 23 years. The workers were mainly concerned about their jobs being subcontracted out or shifted to China as the company wanted them to agree to contract language giving Wolverine just those rights. Ironically, Wolverine was in the process of buying a company that made 75 percent of its shoes in two plants in Maine and that prominently touted many of its brands as "Made in the USA." Sebago was known for the high quality of its shoes, which were handcrafted and handstitched.

Principal Subsidiaries

Aguadilla Shoe Corporation; Brooks France, S.A.; BSI Shoes, Inc.; Dominican Wolverine Shoe Company Limited (Cayman

Islands); Hush Puppies Canada Footwear Ltd.; Hush Puppies Retail, Inc.; Hush Puppies (U.K.) Ltd.; Hy-Test, Inc.; Merrell Europe B.V. (Netherlands); Merrell (Europe) Limited (U.K.); Spartan Shoe Company Limited (Cayman Islands); Wolverine de Costa Rica, S.A.; Wolverine de Mexico S.A. de C.V.; Wolverine Design Center, Inc.; Wolverine Europe Limited (U.K.; 95%); Wolverine International GP, LLC; Wolverine International, L.P. (Cayman Islands); Wolverine International S.a.r.l. (Luxembourg); Wolverine International, S.L. (Spain); Wolverine Outdoors, Inc.; Wolverine Procurement, Inc.; Wolverine Russia, Inc.; Wolverine Slipper Group, Inc.; Wolverine Sourcing, Inc.; Wolverine World Wide Europe Limited (U.K.).

Principal Divisions

Wolverine Footwear Group; Merrell Performance Footwear Group; CAT Footwear Group; Hush Puppies Company; Wolverine Slipper Group; Global Operations Group; Wolverine Leathers Division.

Principal Competitors

The Timberland Company; Red Wing Shoe Company, Inc.; R. Griggs Limited; C&J Clark International Ltd.; L.L. Bean, Inc.; Reebok International Ltd.; The North Face, Inc.; Rocky Shoes & Boots, Inc.; LaCrosse Footwear, Inc.

Further Reading

Carr, Debra, "Hot Dogs," *Footwear News*, August 7, 1995, p. 108.

"CEO Interview: Geoffrey B. Bloom," *Wall Street Transcript*, December 15, 1997.

"A Dog No More," *Forbes*, May 8, 1995, p. 16.

Emrich, Anne Bond, "Wolverine Continues Building Global Brands," *Grand Rapids (Mich.) Business Journal*, February 5, 2001, p. 7.

——, "Wolverine World Wide Embraces Life After Realignment," *Grand Rapids (Mich.) Business Journal*, September 25, 2000, p. 7.

Ghering, Mike, "WWW Chief Gets New Title, Responsibility," *Grand Rapids (Mich.) Business Journal*, January 27, 1997, p. 1.

Harger, Jim, "Wolverine in Step: New Boot, New Method," *Grand Rapids (Mich.) Press*, October 4, 1992, p. D1.

——, "WWW Shedding Money-Losing Units," *Grand Rapids (Mich.) Press*, October 2, 1990, p. C5.

Hawn, Carleen, "What's in a Name? Whatever You Make It," *Forbes*, July 27, 1998, pp. 84 +.

Jaffe, Thomas, "Fit to Be Tied?," *Forbes*, September 9, 1985, p. 2.

Kern, Beth Sexer, "Wolverine World Wide: Americana—A Long-Term Investment Portfolio," *Footwear News*, December 4, 1995, p. 23.

Lane, Amy, "Hush Puppies' Giant Step: With Foot in Door, Shoemaker Has Global Goal," *Crain's Detroit Business*, September 22, 1997, p. I3.

Knape, Chris, "Wolverine Buys Sebago, Docksiders," *Grand Rapids (Mich.) Press*, July 25, 2003, p. A1.

Koselka, Rita, "The Dog That Survived," *Forbes*, November 9, 1992, p. 82.

Lassiter, Dawn, "Wolverine Will Put Lock on Hush Puppies Plant," *Footwear News*, August 18, 1986, p. 4.

——, "WWW Picks Hartmax Exec As New Prexy," *Footwear News*, April 6, 1987, p. 1.

——, "WWW's Balance Sheet Shapes Up As Sales Drop," *Footwear News*, April 20, 1987, p. 4.

Miller, Cyndee, "Hush Puppies: All of a Sudden They're Cool," *Marketing News*, February 12, 1996, p. 10.

Min, Janice, "Puttin' on the Dog," *People Weekly*, December 11, 1995, p. 163.

Naughton, Keith, "Don't Step on My Blue Suede Hush Puppies," *Business Week*, September 11, 1995, p. 84.

Plotkin, Amanda, "Fighting Back, WWW Shows Wall Street Its Sharpened Claws," *Footwear News*, December 20, 1999, p. 1.

Radigan, Mary, "Putting on the Dog: Hush Puppies Going Upscale, Hoping to Attract New Buyers," *Grand Rapids (Mich.) Press*, August 8, 1993, p. E1.

Rooney, Ellen, "Gleason Will Drop WWW CEO Hat by '93," *Footwear News*, May 11, 1992, p. 2.

——, "Hush Puppies Seeks Fountain of Youth," *Footwear News*, May 31, 1993, p. 15.

Rooney, Ellen, and Rich Wilner, "Norway's Rokke Dealing for the Purchase of Brooks," *Footwear News*, September 28, 1992, p. 1.

Sabo, Mary Ann, "These Boots Are Made for Profit," *Grand Rapids (Mich.) Press*, May 18, 1997, p. F1.

Schneider-Levy, Barbara, "New Bites and Barks from Hush Puppies," *Footwear News*, February 15, 1993, p. 27.

Sender, Isabelle, "WWW to Capitalize on Hush Puppies," *Footwear News*, April 22, 1996, p. 2.

Silverman, Dick, "Solid 1st Half Buoys WWW's Prospects," *Footwear News*, August 9, 1993, p. 28.

Tedeschi, Mark, "The SGB Interview: Dean Estes," *Sporting Goods Business*, November 10, 1997, pp. 52–53.

Weldon, Michele, "Brooks: Off and Running with Innovation," *Footwear News*, September 1983, p. 35.

——, "Hush Puppies Is Having a Facelift to Raise Sales," *Footwear News*, February 13, 1984, p. 14.

——, "Imports Won't Let Wolverine Rest on Its Laurels," *Footwear News*, May 2, 1983, p. 21.

Wieland, Barbara, "It's in the Shoes: Wolverine Soars on Success of Its Products," *Grand Rapids (Mich.) Press*, April 20, 2001, p. A5.

Wieland, Barbara, and Barton Deiters, "Pension, Job Security Behind Wolverine Strike," *Grand Rapids (Mich.) Press*, July 18, 2003, p. A1.

Wieland, Barbara, and Scott Leith, "Wolverine to Slash 1,357 Jobs," *Grand Rapids (Mich.) Press*, July 12, 2000, p. A1.

Wilner, Rich, "Hush Puppies Out to Learn New Tricks," *Footwear News*, August 17, 1992, p. 55.

"Wolverine Plans to Restructure," *Footwear News*, October 8, 1990, p. 1.

Wolverine Worldwide, Inc.: A Tradition of Success, Rockford, Mich.: Wolverine World Wide, Inc., 1983.

"WWW Posts Record Work Boot Sales," *Footwear News*, February 3, 1992, p. 53.

—April Dougal Gasbarre
—update: David E. Salamie

INDEX TO COMPANIES

Index to Companies

Listings in this index are arranged in alphabetical order under the company name. Company names beginning with a letter or proper name such as Eli Lilly & Co. will be found under the first letter of the company name. Definite articles (The, Le, La) are ignored for alphabetical purposes as are forms of incorporation that precede the company name (AB, NV). Company names printed in bold type have full, historical essays on the page numbers appearing in bold. Updates to entries that appeared in earlier volumes are signified by the notation (**upd.**). Company names in light type are references within an essay to that company, not full historical essays. This index is cumulative with volume numbers printed in bold type.

GenRad, Inc., **24** 179–83
GenSet, **19** 442
Genstar, **22** 14; **23** 327
Genstar Gypsum Products Co., **IV** 273
Genstar Rental Electronics, Inc., **58** 110
Genstar Stone Products Co., **III** 735; **15** 154; **40** 176
GenTek Inc., **37** 157; **41** 236
Gentex Corporation, 26 153–57; 35 148–49
Gentex Optics, **17** 50; **18** 392
GenTrac, **24** 257
Gentry Associates, Inc., **14** 378
Gentry International, **I** 497; **47** 234
Genty-Cathiard, **39** 183–84; **54** 306
Genuardi's Family Markets, Inc., 35 **190–92**
Genuin Golf & Dress of America, Inc., **32** 447
Genuine Parts Company, 9 253–55; 45 **176–79 (upd.)**
Genung's, **II** 673
Genus, **18** 382–83
Genzyme Corporation, 13 239–42; 38 **203–07 (upd.); 47** 4
Genzyme Transgenics Corp., **37** 44
Geo. H. McFadden & Bro., **54** 89
GEO SA, **58** 218
Geo Space Corporation, **18** 513
GEO Specialty Chemicals, Inc., **27** 117
geobra Brandstätter GmbH & Co. KG, **48 183–86**
Geodynamics Oil & Gas Inc., **IV** 83
Geographics, Inc., **25** 183
Geomarine Systems, **11** 202
The Geon Company, 11 158–61
Geon Industries, Inc. *See* Johnston Industries, Inc.
Geophysical Service, Inc., **III** 499–500; **IV** 365
GeoQuest Systems Inc., **17** 419
Georesources, Inc., **19** 247
Georg Fischer Foundries Group, **38** 214
George A. Hormel and Company, II **504–06;** **7** 547; **12** 123–24; **18** 244. *See also* Hormel Foods Corporation.
George A. Touche & Co., **9** 167
George Booker & Co., **13** 102
George Buckton & Sons Limited, **40** 129
The George F. Cram Company, Inc., 55 **158–60**
George Fischer, Ltd., **III** 638
George H. Dentler & Sons, **7** 429
The George Hyman Construction Company, **8** 112–13; **25** 403
George J. Ball, Inc., **27** 507
George K. Baum & Company, **25** 433
George Kent, **II** 3; **22** 10
George Newnes Company, **IV** 641; **7** 244
George R. Rich Manufacturing Company. *See* Clark Equipment Company.
George S. May International Company, **55 161–63**
George Smith Financial Corporation, **21** 257
George W. Neare & Co., **III** 224
George Weston Limited, II 631–32; 36 **245–48 (upd.); 41** 30, 33
George Wimpey plc, 12 201–03; 28 450; **51 135–38 (upd.)**
Georges Renault SA, **III** 427; **28** 40
Georgetown Group, Inc., **26** 187
Georgetown Steel Corp., **IV** 228
Georgia Carpet Outlets, **25** 320

Georgia Cotton Producers Association. *See* Gold Kist Inc.
Georgia Credit Exchange, **6** 24
Georgia Federal Bank, **I** 447; **11** 112–13; **30** 196
Georgia Gulf Corporation, IV 282; **9** **256–58**, 260
Georgia Hardwood Lumber Co., **IV** 281; **9** 259
Georgia International Life Insurance Co., **III** 218
Georgia Kraft Co., **IV** 312, 342–43; **8** 267–68; **19** 268
Georgia Natural Gas Corporation, **6** 447–48
Georgia-Pacific Corporation, IV 281–83, 288, 304, 345, 358; **9** 256–58, **259–62** **(upd.); 12** 19, 377; **15** 229; **22** 415, 489; **31** 314; **44** 66; **47 145–51 (upd.); 51** 284
Georgia Power & Light Co., **V** 621; **6** 447, 537; **23** 28; **27** 20
Georgia Power Company, **38** 446–48; **49** 145
Georgia Railway and Electric Company, **6** 446–47; **23** 28
Georgie Pie, **V** 35
GeoScience Corporation, **18** 515; **44** 422
Geosource Inc., **III** 182; **21** 14; **22** 189
Geotec Boyles Brothers, S.A., **19** 247
Geotecnia y Cimientos SA, **55** 182
Geotek Communications Inc., 21 238–40
GeoTel Communications Corp., **34** 114
Geothermal Resources International, **11** 271
GeoVideo Networks, **34** 259
Geoworks Corporation, **25** 509
Geraghty & Miller Inc., **26** 23
Gerald Stevens, Inc., 37 161–63
Gérard, **25** 84
Gerber Products Company, II 481; **III** 19; **7 196–98**, 547; **9** 90; **11** 173; **21** 53–55, **241–44 (upd); 25** 366; **34** 103; **36** 256
Gerber Scientific, Inc., 12 204–06
Gerbes Super Markets, Inc., **12** 112
Gerbo Telecommunicacoes e Servicos Ltda., **32** 40
Gerdau S.A., 59 200–03
Geren Associates. *See* CRSS Inc.
Geriatrics Inc., **13** 49
Gericom AG, 47 152–54
Gerling-Konzern Versicherungs- **Beteiligungs-Aktiengesellschaft, III** 695; **51 139–43**
Germaine Monteil Cosmetiques Corp., **I** 426; **III** 56
German American Bancorp, 41 178–80
German-American Car Company. *See* GATX.
German-American Securities, **II** 283
German Cargo Service GmbH., **I** 111
The German Society. *See* The Legal Aid Society.
Germania Refining Co., **IV** 488–89; **50** 351
Germplasm Resource Management, **III** 740
GERPI, **51** 16
Gerresheimer Glas AG, II 386; **IV** 232; **43 186–89**
Gerrity Oil & Gas Corporation, **11** 28; **24** 379–80
Gervais Danone, **II** 474
GESA. *See* General Europea S.A.

Gesbancaya, **II** 196
Geschmay Group, **51** 14
Gesparal, **III** 47; **8** 342
Gestettner, **II** 159
Gestione Pubblicitaria Editoriale, **IV** 586
GET Manufacturing Inc., **36** 300
Getronics NV, 39 176–78
Getty Images, Inc., 31 216–18
Getty Oil Co., **II** 448; **IV** 367, 423, 429, 461, 479, 488, 490, 551, 553; **6** 457; **8** 526; **11** 27; **13** 448; **17** 501; **18** 488; **27** 216; **41** 391, 394–95; **47** 436; **50** 353
Getz Corp., **IV** 137
Gevaert. *See* Agfa Gevaert Group N.V.
Geyser Peak Winery, **58** 196
Geysers Geothermal Co., **IV** 84, 523; **7** 188
GFI Informatique SA, 49 165–68
GfK Aktiengesellschaft, 49 169–72
GFS. *See* Gordon Food Service Inc.
GFS Realty Inc., **II** 633
GGT Group, **44** 198
GHH, **II** 257
GHI, **28** 155, 157
Ghirardelli Chocolate Company, 24 480; **27** 105; **30 218–20**
GI Communications, **10** 321
GI Export Corp. *See* Johnston Industries, Inc.
GIAG, **16** 122
Gianni Versace SpA, 22 238–40
Giant Bicycle Inc., **19** 384
Giant Cement Holding, Inc., 23 224–26
Giant Eagle, Inc., **12** 390–91; **13** 237
Giant Food Inc., II 633–35, 656; **13** 282, 284; **15** 532; **16** 313; **22 241–44 (upd.);** **24** 462
Giant Industries, Inc., 19 175–77
Giant Resources, **III** 729
Giant Stores, Inc., **7** 113; **25** 124
Giant TC, Inc. *See* Campo Electronics, Appliances & Computers, Inc.
Giant Tire & Rubber Company, **8** 126
Giant Video Corporation, **29** 503
Giant Wholesale, **II** 625
GIB Group, V 63–66; 22 478; **23** 231; **26** **158–62 (upd.)**
Gibbons, Green, van Amerongen Ltd., **II** 605; **9** 94; **12** 28; **19** 360
Gibbs Automatic Molding Co., **III** 569; **20** 360
Gibbs Construction, **25** 404
GIBCO Corp., **I** 321; **17** 287, 289
Gibraltar Casualty Co., **III** 340
Gibraltar Financial Corp., **III** 270–71
Gibraltar Steel Corporation, 37 164–67
Gibson, Dunn & Crutcher LLP, 36 **249–52; 37** 292
Gibson Greetings, Inc., 7 24; **12 207–10;** **16** 256; **21** 426–28; **22** 34–35; **59** 35, 37
Gibson Guitar Corp., 16 237–40
Gibson McDonald Furniture Co., **14** 236
GIC. *See* The Goodyear Tire & Rubber Company.
Giddings & Lewis, Inc., 8 545–46; **10** **328–30; 23** 299; **28** 455
Giftmaster Inc., **26** 439–40
Gil-Wel Manufacturing Company, **17** 440
Gilbane, Inc., 34 191–93
Gilbert & John Greenall Limited, **21** 246
Gilbert-Ash Ltd., **I** 588
Gilbert Lane Personnel, Inc., **9** 326
Gilde-Verlag, **IV** 590

India General Steam Navigation and
Railway Co., **III** 522
Indian Airlines Corporation. *See* Air-India.
Indian Airlines Ltd., 46 240–42
Indian Archery and Toy Corp., **19** 142–43
Indian Oil Corporation Ltd., IV 440–41,
483; **48 210–13 (upd.)**
Indian Point Farm Supply, Inc., **IV** 458–59
Indiana Bearings, Inc., **13** 78
**Indiana Bell Telephone Company,
Incorporated, 14 257–61; 18** 30
Indiana Board and Filler Company, **12** 376
Indiana Electric Corporation, **6** 555
Indiana Energy, Inc., 27 233–36
Indiana Gaming Company, **21** 40
Indiana Gas & Water Company, **6** 556
Indiana Group, **I** 378
Indiana Oil Purchasing Co., **IV** 370
Indiana Parts and Warehouse, **29** 86, 88
Indiana Power Company, **6** 555
Indiana Protein Technologies, **55** 233
Indiana Refining Co., **IV** 552
Indiana Tube Co., **23** 250
Indianapolis Air Pump Company, **8** 37
Indianapolis Brush Electric Light & Power
Company, **6** 508
Indianapolis Cablevision, **6** 508–09
Indianapolis Light and Power Company, **6**
508
**Indianapolis Motor Speedway
Corporation, 9** 16; **46 243–46**
Indianapolis Power & Light Company, **6**
508–09
Indianapolis Pump and Tube Company, **8**
37
Indianhead Truck Lines, **6** 371
IndianOil Companies. *See* Indian Oil
Corporation Ltd.
Indigo Books & Music Inc., 58 185–87
Indigo NV, 26 212–14, 540–41
Indo Mobil Ltd., **48** 212
Indola Cosmetics B.V., **8** 16
Indonesia Petroleum Co., **IV** 516
Indresco, Inc., **22** 285; **52** 215
Induba, S.A. de C.V., **39** 230
Induban, **II** 196
Indura SA Industria Y Commercio, **25** 82
Industri Kapital, **27** 269
Industria Gelati Sammontana, **II** 575
Industria Metalgrafica, **I** 231
Industria Raffinazione Oli Minerali, **IV** 419
Industrial & Commercial Bank, **56** 363
Industrial & Trade Shows of Canada, **IV**
639
Industrial Acceptance Bank, **I** 337
Industrial Air Products, **19** 380–81
Industrial Air Tool, **28** 387
Industrial Airsystems Inc., **56** 247
Industrial Bancorp, **9** 229
**Industrial Bank of Japan, Ltd., II
300–01,** 310–11, 338, 369, 433, 459; **17**
121; **58** 228
Industrial Bank of Scotland, **10** 337
Industrial Cartonera, **IV** 295; **19** 226
Industrial Chemical and Equipment, **16** 271
Industrial Circuits, **IV** 680
Industrial Computer Corp., **11** 78
Industrial Development Corp. of Zambia
Ltd., **IV** 239–41
Industrial Development Corporation, **IV**
22, 92, 534; **57** 185
Industrial Devices Inc., **48** 359
Industrial Engineering, **III** 598

Industrial Engineering Associates, Inc., **II**
112
Industrial Equity Ltd., **I** 438; **17** 357
Industrial Fuel Supply Co., **I** 569
Industrial Gas Equipment Co., **I** 297
Industrial Gases Lagos, **25** 82
Industrial Instrument Company. *See*
Foxboro Company.
Industrial Light & Magic, **12** 322; **50** 320
Industrial Mutual Insurance, **III** 264
Industrial National Bank, **9** 229
Industrial Powder Coatings, Inc., **16** 475
Industrial Publishing Company, **9** 413; **27**
361
Industrial Reorganization Corp., **III** 502,
556
Industrial Resources, **6** 144
Industrial Services Group, Inc., **56** 161
**Industrial Services of America, Inc., 46
247–49**
Industrial Shows of America, **27** 362
Industrial Tectonics Corp., **18** 276
Industrial Trade & Consumer Shows Inc.,
IV 639; **26** 272
Industrial Trust Co. of Wilmington, **25** 540
Industrial Trust Company, **9** 228
Industrial Vehicles Corp. B.V., **III** 543–44
**Industrias Bachoco, S.A. de C.V., 39
228–31**
Industrias del Atlantico SA, **47** 291
Industrias Nacobre, **21** 259
Industrias Negromex, **23** 170
**Industrias Penoles, S.A. de C.V., 22
284–86**
Industrias Resistol S.A., **23** 170–71
Industrias y Confecciones, S.A. **V** 51; **26**
129
Industrie-Aktiengesellschaft, **IV** 201
Industrie Natuzzi S.p.A., 18 256–58
Industrie Regionale du Bâtiment, **IV** 108
Les Industries Ling, **13** 443
Industriförvaltnings AB Kinnevik, **26**
331–33; **36** 335
AB Industrivärden, **II** 366; **32** 397
Induyco. *See* Industrias y Confecciones,
S.A.
Indy Lighting, **30** 266
Indy Racing League, **37** 74
Inelco Peripheriques, **10** 459
Inespo, **16** 322
Inexco Oil Co., **7** 282
Infineon Technologies AG, 50 269–73; 57
323
**Infinity Broadcasting Corporation, 11
190–92; 22** 97; **23** 510; **28** 72; **35** 232;
48 214–17 (upd.)
Infinity Enterprises, Inc., **44** 4
Infinity Partners, **36** 160
INFLEX, S.A., **8** 247
Inflight Sales Group Limited, **11** 82; **29**
511
InfoAsia, **28** 241
Infobase Services, **6** 14
Infocom, **32** 8
**Infogrames Entertainment S.A., 35
227–30; 41** 407
Infonet Services Corporation, **6** 303; **27**
304
Infoplan, **14** 36
Informa Group plc, 58 188–91
Informatics General Corporation, **III** 248;
11 468; **25** 86
Informatics Legal Systems, **III** 169; **6** 285

Information Access Company, 12
560–62; **17 252–55; 34** 438. *See also*
The Thomson Corporation.
Information and Communication Group, **14**
555
Information Associates Inc., **11** 78
Information Builders, Inc., 14 16; **22
291–93**
Information Consulting Group, **9** 345
Information, Dissemination and Retrieval
Inc., **IV** 670
Information Holdings Inc., 47 183–86
Information International. *See* Autologic
Information International, Inc.
Information Management Reporting
Services. *See* Hyperion Software
Corporation.
Information Management Science
Associates, Inc., **13** 174
Information Please LLC, **26** 216
**Information Resources, Inc., 10 358–60;
13** 4; **25** 366
Information Spectrum Inc., **57** 34
Information Unlimited Software, **6** 224
Informix Corporation, 10 361–64, 505;
30 243–46 (upd.)
Infoseek Corporation, **27** 517; **30** 490
InfoSoft International, Inc. *See* Inso
Corporation.
Infostrada S.p.A., **38** 300
Infosys Technologies Ltd., 38 240–43
Infotech Enterprises, Ltd., **33** 45
Infotechnology Inc., **25** 507–08
Infotel, Inc., **52** 342
Infrasud, **I** 466
Infun, S.A., **23** 269
ING Australia Limited, **52** 35, 39
ING, B.V., **14** 45, 47
Ing. C. Olivetti & C., S.p.A., III 122,
144–46, 549, 678; **10** 499; **16** 122; **25**
33. *See also* Olivetti S.p.A
Ingalls Quinn and Johnson, **9** 135
Ingalls Shipbuilding, Inc., I 485; **11**
264–65; **12** 28, **271–73; 36** 78–79; **41**
42
Ingear, **10** 216
Ingefico, S.A., **52** 301
**Ingenico—Compagnie Industrielle et
Financière d'Ingénierie, 46 250–52**
Ingenious Designs Inc., **47** 420
Ingersoll-Rand Company, III 473,
525–27; 10 262; **13** 27, 523; **15** 187,
223–26 (upd.); 22 542; **33** 168; **34** 46;
55 218–22 (upd.)
Ingka Holding B.V. *See* IKEA
International A/S.
Ingleby Enterprises Inc. *See* Caribiner
International, Inc.
Inglenook Vineyards, **13** 134; **34** 89
Ingles Markets, Inc., 20 305–08
Inglis Ltd., **III** 654; **12** 549
Ingram Book Group, **30** 70
Ingram Corp. Ltd., **III** 559; **IV** 249
Ingram Industries, Inc., 10 518–19; **11
193–95; 13** 90, 482; **49 217–20 (upd.);
52** 178. *See also* Ingram Micro Inc.
Ingram Micro Inc., 24 29; **52 178–81**
AB Ingredients, **II** 466
Ingredients Technology Corp., **9** 154
Ingres Corporation, **9** 36–37; **25** 87
Ingwerson and Co., **II** 356
INH. *See* Instituto Nacional de
Hidrocarboros.
Inha Works Ltd., **33** 164

Mobile TeleSystems OJSC, **48** 419; **59**
    300–03
Mobilefone, Inc., **25** 108
MobileMedia Corp., **39** 23, 24
MobileStar Network Corp., **26** 429
Mobu Company, **6** 431
Mobujidosha Bus Company, **6** 431
Mochida Pharaceutical Co. Ltd., **II** 553
Modar, **17** 279
Mode 1 Communications, Inc., **48** 305
Modell's Shoppers World, **16** 35–36
Modell's Sporting Goods. *See* Henry
    Modell & Company Inc.
Modeluxe Linge Services SA, **45** 139–40
Modem Media, **23** 479
Modern Equipment Co., **I** 412
Modern Furniture Rentals Inc., **14** 4; **27**
    163
Modern Handling Methods Ltd., **21** 499
Modern Maid Food Products, **II** 500
Modern Merchandising, Inc., **19** 396
Modern Patterns and Plastics, **III** 641
Modern Times Group AB, 36 335–38
Modernistic Industries Inc., **7** 589
Modine Manufacturing Company, 8
    372–75; 56 243–47 (upd.)
Modis Professional Services. *See* MPS
    Group, Inc.
MoDo. *See* Mo och Domsjö AB.
MoDo Paper AB, **28** 446; **52** 164
Moen Incorporated, 12 344–45
Moët-Hennessy, 10 397–98; **23** 238, 240,
    242. *See also* LVMH Moët Hennessy
    Louis Vuitton SA.
Mogen David. *See* The Wine Group, Inc.
Mogul Corp., **I** 321; **17** 287
The Mogul Metal Company. *See* Federal-
    Mogul Corporation.
Mohasco Corporation, **15** 102; **26** 100–01
Mohawk & Hudson Railroad, **9** 369
Mohawk Airlines, **I** 131; **6** 131
Mohawk Carpet Corp., **26** 101
Mohawk Industries, Inc., 19 274–76; 31
    199
Mohawk Rubber Co. Ltd., **V** 256; **7** 116;
    19 508
Mohegan Tribal Gaming Authority, 37
    254–57
Mohr-Value Stores, **8** 555
Moilliet and Sons, **II** 306
Mojave Foods Corporation, **27** 299
Mojo MDA Group Ltd., **11** 50–51; **43** 412
Moksel. *See* A. Moskel AG.
Mokta. *See* Compagnie de Mokta.
MOL. *See* Mitsui O.S.K. Lines, Ltd.
Molecular Biosystems, **III** 61
Molerway Freight Lines, Inc., **53** 250
Molex Incorporated, II 8; **11 317–19; 14**
    27; **54 236–41 (upd.)**
Molfino Hermanos SA, **59** 365
Molinera de México S.A. de C.V., **31** 236
Molinos Nacionales C.A., **7** 242–43; **25**
    241
Molins plc, IV 326; **51 249–51**
Molkerie-Zentrak Sud GmbH, **II** 575
Moll Plasticrafters, L.P., **17** 534
Molloy Manufacturing Co., **III** 569; **20**
    360
Mölnlycke AB, **IV** 338–39; **28** 443–45; **36**
    26
The Molson Companies Limited, I
    273–75, 333; **II** 210; **7** 183–84; **12** 338;
    13 150, 199; **21** 320; **23** 404; **25** 279; **26**
    303–07 (upd.); **36** 15

Molycorp, **IV** 571; **24** 521
Momentus Group Ltd., **51** 99
Mon-Dak Chemical Inc., **16** 270
Mon-Valley Transportation Company, **11**
    194
Mona Meyer McGrath & Gavin, **47** 97
MONACA. *See* Molinos Nacionales C.A.
Monaco Coach Corporation, 31 336–38
Monadnock Paper Mills, Inc., 21 381–84
Monarch Air Lines, **22** 219
Monarch Development Corporation, **38**
    451–52
Monarch Foods, **26** 503
Monarch Marking Systems, **III** 157
MonArk Boat, **III** 444; **22** 116
Mondadori. *See* Arnoldo Monadori Editore
    S.p.A.
Mondex International, **18** 543
Mondi Foods BV, **41** 12
Mondi Paper Co., **IV** 22
Moneris Solutions Corp., **46** 55
Monet Jewelry, **II** 502–03; **9** 156–57; **10**
    323–24
Money Access Service Corp., **11** 467
Money Management Associates, Inc., **53**
    136
Monfort, Inc., 13 350–52
Monheim Group, **II** 521
Monier Roof Tile, **III** 687, 735
Monis Wineries, **I** 288
Monitor Dynamics Inc., **24** 510
Monitor Group Inc., **33** 257
Monk-Austin Inc., **12** 110
Monmouth Pharmaceuticals Ltd., **16** 439
Monneret Industrie, **56** 335
Monochem, **II** 472; **22** 93
Monogram Aerospace Fasteners, Inc., **11**
    536
Monogram Models, **25** 312
Monogramme Confections, **6** 392
Monolithic Memories Inc., **6** 216; **16**
    316–17, 549
Monon Corp., **13** 550
Monon Railroad, **I** 472
Monongahela Power, **38** 40
Monoprix, **V** 57–59
Monro Muffler Brake, Inc., 24 337–40
Monroe Auto Equipment, **I** 527
Monroe Calculating Machine Co., **I** 476,
    484
Monroe Savings Bank, **11** 109
Monsanto Company, I 310, 363, **365–67**,
    402, 631, 666, 686, 688; **III** 741; **IV**
    290, 367, 379, 401; **8** 398; **9** 318,
    355–57 (upd.), 466; **12** 186; **13** 76, 225;
    16 460–62; **17** 131; **18** 112; **22** 107; **23**
    170–71; **26** 108; **29 327–31 (upd.)**; **33**
    135; **34** 179; **41** 306; **52** 312; **53** 261; **59**
    149
Monsoon plc, 39 287–89
Mont Blanc, **17** 5; **27** 487, 489
Montabert S.A., **15** 226
Montan TNT Pty Ltd., **27** 473
Montana Alimentaria S.p.A., **57** 82
Montana-Dakota Utilities Co., **7** 322–23;
    37 281–82; **42** 249–50, 252
Montana Group, **54** 229
The Montana Power Company, 6 566; **7**
    322; **11 320–22**; **37** 280, 283; **44**
    288–92 (upd.); **50** 367
Montana Refining Company, **12** 240–41
Montana Resources, Inc., **IV** 34
Montaup Electric Co., **14** 125
MontBell America, Inc., **29** 279

Montecatini, **I** 368; **IV** 421, 470, 486
Montedison S.p.A., I 368–69; **IV** 413,
    421–22, 454, 499; **14** 17; **22** 262; **24**
    341–44 (upd.); **26** 367; **36** 185–86, 188
Montefibre, **I** 369
Montefina, **IV** 499; **26** 367
Montell N.V., **24** 343
Monterey Homes Corporation. *See*
    Meritage Corporation.
Monterey Mfg. Co., **12** 439
Monterey Pasta Company, 58 240–43
Monterey's Acquisition Corp., **41** 270
Monterey's Tex-Mex Cafes, **13** 473
Monterrey, Compania de Seguros sobre la
    Vida. *See* Seguros Monterrey.
Monterrey Group, **19** 10–11, 189
Montfort of Colorado, Inc., **II** 494
Montgomery Elevator Company, **27** 269
Montgomery Ward & Co., Incorporated,
    III 762; **IV** 465; **V 145–48; 7** 353; **8**
    509; **9** 210; **10** 10, 116, 172, 305, 391,
    393, 490–91; **12** 48, 309, 315, 335, 430;
    13 165; **15** 330, 470; **17** 460; **18** 477; **20**
    263, **374–79 (upd.)**, 433; **22** 535; **25**
    144; **27** 428–30; **43** 292
Montiel Corporation, **17** 321
Montinex, **24** 270
Montreal Bank, **II** 210
Montreal Engineering Company, **6** 585
Montreal Light, Heat & Power
    Consolidated, **6** 501–02
Montreal Mining Co., **17** 357
Montres Rolex S.A., 8 477; **13 353–55**;
    19 452; **34 292–95 (upd.)**
Montrose Capital, **36** 358
Montrose Chemical Company, **9** 118, 119
Montrose Chrome, **IV** 92
Monument Property Trust Ltd., **IV** 710
Monumental Corp., **III** 179
MONYCo., **III** 306
Moody's Investment Service, **IV** 605; **16**
    506; **19** 133; **22** 189
Moog Inc., 13 356–58
Mooney Aerospace Group Ltd., 52
    252–55
Mooney Chemicals, Inc. *See* OM Group,
    Inc.
Moonlight Mushrooms, Inc. *See* Sylvan,
    Inc.
Moonstone Mountaineering, Inc., **29** 181
Moore and McCormack Co. Inc., **19** 40
Moore Corporation Limited, IV 644–46,
    679; **15** 473; **16** 450; **36** 508
Moore Gardner & Associates, **22** 88
The Moore Group Ltd., **20** 363
Moore-Handley, Inc., IV 345–46; **39**
    290–92
Moore McCormack Resources Inc., **14** 455
Moore Medical Corp., 17 331–33
Moorhouse, **II** 477
Moquin Breuil. *See* Smoby International
    SA.
Moran Group Inc., **II** 682
Moran Health Care Group Ltd., **25** 455
MoRan Oil & Gas Co., **IV** 82–83
Moran Towing Corporation, Inc., 15
    301–03
Morana, Inc., **9** 290
Moretti-Harrah Marble Co., **III** 691
Morgan & Banks Limited, **30** 460
Morgan & Cie International S.A., **II** 431
Morgan Construction Company, **8** 448
Morgan Edwards, **II** 609
Morgan Engineering Co., **8** 545

INDEX TO INDUSTRIES

Index to Industries

639

ADVERTISING & OTHER BUSINESS SERVICES (continued)

The Ogilvy Group, Inc., I
Olsten Corporation, 6; 29 (upd.)
Omnicom Group, I; 22 (upd.)
On Assignment, Inc., 20
1-800-FLOWERS, Inc., 26
Opinion Research Corporation, 46
Outdoor Systems, Inc., 25
Paris Corporation, 22
Paychex, Inc., 15
PDI, Inc., 52
Pei Cobb Freed & Partners Architects LLP, 57
Penauille Polyservices SA, 49
Phillips, de Pury & Luxembourg, 49
Pierce Leahy Corporation, 24
Pinkerton's Inc., 9
PMT Services, Inc., 24
Priceline.com Incorporated, 57
Publicis S.A., 19
Publishers Clearing House, 23
Randstad Holding n.v., 16; 43 (upd.)
RemedyTemp, Inc., 20
Rental Service Corporation, 28
Rentokil Initial Plc, 47
The Richards Group, Inc., 58
Right Management Consultants, Inc., 42
Ritchie Bros. Auctioneers Inc., 41
Robert Half International Inc., 18
Roland Berger & Partner GmbH, 37
Ronco, Inc., 15
Russell Reynolds Associates Inc., 38
Saatchi & Saatchi, I; 42 (upd.)
Securitas AB, 42
ServiceMaster Limited Partnership, 6
Shared Medical Systems Corporation, 14
Sir Speedy, Inc., 16
Skidmore, Owings & Merrill, 13
SmartForce PLC, 43
SOS Staffing Services, 25
Sotheby's Holdings, Inc., 11; 29 (upd.)
Spencer Stuart and Associates, Inc., 14
Spherion Corporation, 52
Steiner Corporation (Alsco), 53
Strayer Education, Inc., 53
Superior Uniform Group, Inc., 30
Sykes Enterprises, Inc., 45
Sylvan Learning Systems, Inc., 35
TA Triumph-Adler AG, 48
Taylor Nelson Sofres plc, 34
TBWA Advertising, Inc., 6
TBWA\Chiat\Day, 43 (upd.)
Thomas Cook Travel Inc., 33 (upd.)
Ticketmaster Group, Inc., 13; 37 (upd.)
TMP Worldwide Inc., 30
TNT Post Group N.V., 30
Towers Perrin, 32
Trader Classified Media N.V., 57
Transmedia Network Inc., 20
Treasure Chest Advertising Company, Inc., 32
TRM Copy Centers Corporation, 18
True North Communications Inc., 23
24/7 Real Media, Inc., 49
Tyler Corporation, 23
U.S. Office Products Company, 25
UniFirst Corporation, 21
United Business Media plc, 52 (upd.)
United News & Media plc, 28 (upd.)
Unitog Co., 19
Valassis Communications, Inc., 37 (upd.)
ValueClick, Inc., 49
Vebego International BV, 49
Vedior NV, 35
W.B Doner & Co., 56
The Wackenhut Corporation, 14

Waggener Edstrom, 42
Warrantech Corporation, 53
Wells Rich Greene BDDP, 6
Westaff Inc., 33
Whitman Education Group, Inc., 41
William Morris Agency, Inc., 23
WPP Group plc, 6; 48 (upd.)
Young & Rubicam, Inc., I; 22 (upd.)

AEROSPACE

A.S. Yakovlev Design Bureau, 15
Aeronca Inc., 46
The Aerospatiale Group, 7; 21 (upd.)
Alliant Techsystems Inc., 30 (upd.)
Antonov Design Bureau, 53
Aviacionny Nauchno-Tehnicheskii Komplex im. A.N. Tupoleva, 24
Avions Marcel Dassault-Breguet Aviation, I
B/E Aerospace, Inc., 30
Banner Aerospace, Inc., 14
Beech Aircraft Corporation, 8
Bell Helicopter Textron Inc., 46
The Boeing Company, I; 10 (upd.); 32 (upd.)
Bombardier Inc., 42 (upd.)
British Aerospace plc, I; 24 (upd.)
CAE USA Inc., 48
Canadair, Inc., 16
Cessna Aircraft Company, 8
Cirrus Design Corporation, 44
Cobham plc, 30
Daimler-Benz Aerospace AG, 16
DeCrane Aircraft Holdings Inc., 36
Ducommun Incorporated, 30
EADS SOCATA, 54
EGL, Inc., 59
Empresa Brasileira de Aeronáutica S.A. (Embraer), 36
European Aeronautic Defence and Space Company EADS N.V., 52 (upd.)
Fairchild Aircraft, Inc., 9
Fairchild Dornier GmbH, 48 (upd.)
First Aviation Services Inc., 49
G.I.E. Airbus Industrie, I; 12 (upd.)
General Dynamics Corporation, I; 10 (upd.); 40 (upd.)
GKN plc, 38 (upd.)
Goodrich Corporation, 46 (upd.)
Groupe Dassault Aviation SA, 26 (upd.)
Grumman Corporation, I; 11 (upd.)
Grupo Aeropuerto del Sureste, S.A. de C.V., 48
Gulfstream Aerospace Corporation, 7; 28 (upd.)
HEICO Corporation, 30
International Lease Finance Corporation, 48
N.V. Koninklijke Nederlandse Vliegtuigenfabriek Fokker, I; 28 (upd.)
Learjet Inc., 8; 27 (upd.)
Lockheed Corporation, I; 11 (upd.)
Lockheed Martin Corporation, 15 (upd.)
Loral Space & Communications Ltd., 54 (upd.)
Magellan Aerospace Corporation, 48
Martin Marietta Corporation, I
McDonnell Douglas Corporation, I; 11 (upd.)
Meggitt PLC, 34
Messerschmitt-Bölkow-Blohm GmbH., I
Moog Inc., 13
Mooney Aerospace Group Ltd., 52
The New Piper Aircraft, Inc., 44
Northrop Grumman Corporation, I; 11 (upd.); 45 (upd.)
Orbital Sciences Corporation, 22
Pemco Aviation Group Inc., 54

Pratt & Whitney, 9
Raytheon Aircraft Holdings Inc., 46
Robinson Helicopter Company, 51
Rockwell International Corporation, I; 11 (upd.)
Rolls-Royce Allison, 29 (upd.)
Rolls-Royce plc, I; 7 (upd.); 21 (upd.)
Sequa Corp., 13
Shannon Aerospace Ltd., 36
Sikorsky Aircraft Corporation, 24
Smiths Industries PLC, 25
Snecma Group, 46
Société Air France, 27 (upd.)
Spacehab, Inc., 37
Spar Aerospace Limited, 32
Sukhoi Design Bureau Aviation Scientific-Industrial Complex, 24
Sundstrand Corporation, 7; 21 (upd.)
Textron Lycoming Turbine Engine, 9
Thales S.A., 42
Thiokol Corporation, 9; 22 (upd.)
United Technologies Corporation, I; 10 (upd.)
Vought Aircraft Industries, Inc., 49
Whittaker Corporation, 48 (upd.)
Woodward Governor Company, 49 (upd.)
Zodiac S.A., 36

AIRLINES

Aer Lingus Group plc, 34
Aeroflot—Russian International Airlines, 6; 29 (upd.)
Aerolíneas Argentinas S.A., 33
Air Canada, 6; 23 (upd.); 59 (upd.)
Air China, 46
Air Jamaica Limited, 54
Air New Zealand Limited, 14; 38 (upd.)
Air Wisconsin Airlines Corporation, 55
Air-India Limited, 6; 27 (upd.)
AirTran Holdings, Inc., 22
Alaska Air Group, Inc., 6; 29 (upd.)
Alitalia-Linee Aeree Italiana, S.p.A., 6; 29 (upd.)
All Nippon Airways Company Limited, 6; 38 (upd.)
Aloha Airlines, Incorporated, 24
America West Holdings Corporation, 6; 34 (upd.)
American Airlines, I; 6 (upd.)
AMR Corporation, 28 (upd.); 52 (upd.)
Amtran, Inc., 34
Arrow Air Holdings Corporation, 55
Asiana Airlines, Inc., 46
Atlantic Coast Airlines Holdings, Inc., 55
Atlantic Southeast Airlines, Inc., 47
Atlas Air, Inc., 39
Austrian Airlines AG (Österreichische Luftverkehrs AG), 33
Aviacionny Nauchno-Tehnicheskii Komplex im. A.N. Tupoleva, 24
Avianca Aerovías Nacionales de Colombia SA, 36
Banner Aerospace, Inc., 37 (upd.)
Braathens ASA, 47
Bradley Air Services Ltd., 56
British Airways PLC, I; 14 (upd.); 43 (upd.)
British Midland plc, 38
British World Airlines Ltd., 18
Cargolux Airlines International S.A., 49
Cathay Pacific Airways Limited, 6; 34 (upd.)
Chautauqua Airlines, Inc., 38
China Airlines, 34
China Eastern Airlines Co. Ltd., 31
China Southern Airlines Company Ltd., 33
Comair Holdings Inc., 13; 34 (upd.)

AUTOMOTIVE

Hochtief AG, 33
Horton Homes, Inc., 25
Hospitality Worldwide Services, Inc., 26
Hovnanian Enterprises, Inc., 29
J.A. Jones, Inc., 16
J.F. Shea Co., Inc., 55
Jarvis plc, 39
JLG Industries, Inc., 52
John Brown PLC, I
John Laing plc, I; 51 (upd.)
John W. Danforth Company, 48
Kajima Corporation, I; 51 (upd.)
Kaufman and Broad Home Corporation, 8
KB Home, 45 (upd.)
Kitchell Corporation, 14
The Koll Company, 8
Komatsu Ltd., 16 (upd.)
Kraus-Anderson, Incorporated, 36
Kumagai Gumi Company, Ltd., I
L'Entreprise Jean Lefebvre, 23
Ledcor Industries Limited, 46
Lennar Corporation, 11
Lincoln Property Company, 8
Lindal Cedar Homes, Inc., 29
Linde A.G., I
MasTec, Inc., 55
McCarthy Building Companies, Inc., 48
Mellon-Stuart Company, I
Michael Baker Corp., 14
Morrison Knudsen Corporation, 7; 28
   (upd.)
New Holland N.V., 22
NVR L.P., 8
Ohbayashi Corporation, I
Opus Group, 34
The Parsons Corporation, 56 (upd.)
PCL Construction Group Inc., 50
The Peninsular & Oriental Steam
   Navigation Company (Bovis Division), I
Perini Corporation, 8
Peter Kiewit Sons' Inc., 8
Philipp Holzmann AG, 17
Post Properties, Inc., 26
Pulte Homes, Inc., 8; 42 (upd.)
Pyramid Companies, 54
Redrow Group plc, 31
RMC Group p.l.c., 34 (upd.)
Rooney Brothers Co., 25
The Rottlund Company, Inc., 28
The Ryland Group, Inc., 8; 37 (upd.)
Sandvik AB, 32 (upd.)
Schuff Steel Company, 26
Shorewood Packaging Corporation, 28
Simon Property Group, Inc., 27
Skanska AB, 38
Standard Pacific Corporation, 52
Sundt Corp., 24
Swinerton Inc., 43
Taylor Woodrow plc, I; 38 (upd.)
Thyssen Krupp AG, 28 (upd.)
Toll Brothers Inc., 15
Trammell Crow Company, 8
Tridel Enterprises Inc., 9
The Turner Corporation, 8; 23 (upd.)
U.S. Aggregates, Inc., 42
U.S. Home Corporation, 8
VA TECH ELIN EBG GmbH, 49
Veit Companies, 43
Walbridge Aldinger Co., 38
Walter Industries, Inc., 22 (upd.)
The Weitz Company, Inc., 42
Willbros Group, Inc., 56
William Lyon Homes, 59
Wilson Bowden Plc, 45
Wood Hall Trust PLC, I

CONTAINERS

Ball Corporation, I; 10 (upd.)
BWAY Corporation, 24
Clarcor Inc., 17
Continental Can Co., Inc., 15
Continental Group Company, I
Crown Cork & Seal Company, Inc., I; 13
   (upd.); 32 (upd.)
Gaylord Container Corporation, 8
Golden Belt Manufacturing Co., 16
Greif Bros. Corporation, 15
Grupo Industrial Durango, S.A. de C.V.,
   37
Hanjin Shipping Co., Ltd., 50
Inland Container Corporation, 8
Kerr Group Inc., 24
Keyes Fibre Company, 9
Libbey Inc., 49
Liqui-Box Corporation, 16
The Longaberger Company, 12
Longview Fibre Company, 8
The Mead Corporation, 19 (upd.)
Metal Box PLC, I
Molins plc, 51
National Can Corporation, I
Owens-Illinois, Inc., I; 26 (upd.)
Packaging Corporation of America, 51
   (upd.)
Primerica Corporation, I
Reynolds Metals Company, 19 (upd.)
Royal Packaging Industries Van Leer N.V.,
   30
Sealright Co., Inc., 17
Shurgard Storage Centers, Inc., 52
Smurfit-Stone Container Corporation, 26
   (upd.)
Sonoco Products Company, 8
Thermos Company, 16
Toyo Seikan Kaisha, Ltd., I
U.S. Can Corporation, 30
Ultra Pac, Inc., 24
Viatech Continental Can Company, Inc., 25
   (upd.)
Vitro Corporativo S.A. de C.V., 34

DRUGS/PHARMACEUTICALS

A.L. Pharma Inc., 12
Abbott Laboratories, I; 11 (upd.); 40 (upd.)
Akorn, Inc., 32
Alpharma Inc., 35 (upd.)
ALZA Corporation, 10; 36 (upd.)
American Home Products, I; 10 (upd.)
Amersham PLC, 50
Amgen, Inc., 10
Andrx Corporation, 55
Astra AB, I; 20 (upd.)
AstraZeneca PLC, 50 (upd.)
Barr Laboratories, Inc., 26
Bayer A.G., I; 13 (upd.)
Biovail Corporation, 47
Block Drug Company, Inc., 8
Bristol-Myers Squibb Company, III; 9
   (upd.); 37 (upd.)
C.H. Boehringer Sohn, 39
Caremark Rx, Inc., 10; 54 (upd.)
Carter-Wallace, Inc., 8; 38 (upd.)
Cephalon, Inc., 45
Chiron Corporation, 10
Chugai Pharmaceutical Co., Ltd., 50
Ciba-Geigy Ltd., I; 8 (upd.)
D&K Wholesale Drug, Inc., 14
Discovery Partners International, Inc., 58
Dr. Reddy's Laboratories Ltd., 59
Eli Lilly and Company, I; 11 (upd.); 47
   (upd.)
Express Scripts Inc., 44 (upd.)
F. Hoffmann-La Roche Ltd., I; 50 (upd.)

Fisons plc, 9; 23 (upd.)
Forest Laboratories, Inc., 52 (upd.)
FoxMeyer Health Corporation, 16
Fujisawa Pharmaceutical Company Ltd., I
G.D. Searle & Co., I; 12 (upd.); 34 (upd.)
GEHE AG, 27
Genentech, Inc., I; 8 (upd.)
Genetics Institute, Inc., 8
Genzyme Corporation, 13
Glaxo Holdings PLC, I; 9 (upd.)
GlaxoSmithKline plc, 46 (upd.)
Groupe Fournier SA, 44
H. Lundbeck A/S, 44
Hauser, Inc., 46
Heska Corporation, 39
Huntingdon Life Sciences Group plc, 42
ICN Pharmaceuticals, Inc., 52
IVAX Corporation, 55 (upd.)
Johnson & Johnson, III; 8 (upd.)
Jones Medical Industries, Inc., 24
The Judge Group, Inc., 51
King Pharmaceuticals, Inc., 54
Kyowa Hakko Kogyo Co., Ltd., 48 (upd.)
Leiner Health Products Inc., 34
Ligand Pharmaceuticals Incorporated, 47
Marion Merrell Dow, Inc., I; 9 (upd.)
McKesson Corporation, 12; 47 (upd.)
Medicis Pharmaceutical Corporation, 59
MedImmune, Inc., 35
Merck & Co., Inc., I; 11 (upd.)
Miles Laboratories, I
Millennium Pharmaceuticals, Inc., 47
Monsanto Company, 29 (upd.)
Moore Medical Corp., 17
Murdock Madaus Schwabe, 26
Mylan Laboratories Inc., I; 20 (upd.); 59
   (upd.)
National Patent Development Corporation,
   13
Natrol, Inc., 49
Natural Alternatives International, Inc., 49
Novartis AG, 39 (upd.)
Noven Pharmaceuticals, Inc., 55
Novo Industri A/S, I
Omnicare, Inc., 49
Perrigo Company, 59 (upd.)
Pfizer Inc., I; 9 (upd.); 38 (upd.)
Pharmacia & Upjohn Inc., I; 25 (upd.)
Quintiles Transnational Corporation, 21
R.P. Scherer, I
Roberts Pharmaceutical Corporation, 16
Roche Bioscience, 14 (upd.)
Rorer Group, I
Roussel Uclaf, I; 8 (upd.)
Sandoz Ltd., I
Sankyo Company, Ltd., I; 56 (upd.)
The Sanofi-Synthélabo Group, I; 49 (upd.)
Schering AG, I; 50 (upd.)
Schering-Plough Corporation, I; 14 (upd.);
   49 (upd.)
Sepracor Inc., 45
Serono S.A., 47
Shionogi & Co., Ltd., 17 (upd.)
Sigma-Aldrich Corporation, I; 36 (upd.)
SmithKline Beckman Corporation, I
SmithKline Beecham plc, 32 (upd.)
Squibb Corporation, I
Sterling Drug, Inc., I
Sun Pharmaceutical Industries Ltd., 57
The Sunrider Corporation, 26
Syntex Corporation, I
Takeda Chemical Industries, Ltd., I
Teva Pharmaceutical Industries Ltd., 22; 54
   (upd.)
The Upjohn Company, I; 8 (upd.)
Vitalink Pharmacy Services, Inc., 15
Warner-Lambert Co., I; 10 (upd.)

ENGINEERING & MANAGEMENT SERVICES

ENTERTAINMENT & LEISURE

ENTERTAINMENT & LEISURE
(continued)

FINANCIAL SERVICES: BANKS

FOOD PRODUCTS

HEALTH CARE SERVICES

MATERIALS

PAPER & FORESTRY

PERSONAL SERVICES

PUBLISHING & PRINTING

TEXTILES & APPAREL

UTILITIES

GEOGRAPHIC INDEX

Geographic Index

Germany

Hongkong Electric Holdings Ltd., 6; 23 (upd.)
Hongkong Land Holdings Limited, IV; 47 (upd.)
Hutchison Whampoa Limited, 18; 49 (upd.)
Kerry Properties Limited, 22
New World Development Company Limited, IV; 38 (upd.)
Playmates Toys, 23
Singer Company N.V., The, 30 (upd.)
Swire Pacific Limited, I; 16 (upd.); 57 (upd.)
Tommy Hilfiger Corporation, 20; 53 (upd.)

Hungary

Malév Plc, 24

Iceland

Icelandair, 52

India

Air-India Limited, 6; 27 (upd.)
Bajaj Auto Limited, 39
Coal India Limited, IV; 44 (upd.)
Dr. Reddy's Laboratories Ltd., 59
Indian Airlines Ltd., 46
Indian Oil Corporation Ltd., IV; 48 (upd.)
Infosys Technologies Ltd., 38
Minerals and Metals Trading Corporation of India Ltd., IV
MTR Foods Ltd., 55
Oil and Natural Gas Commission, IV
Steel Authority of India Ltd., IV
Sun Pharmaceutical Industries Ltd., 57
Tata Iron & Steel Co. Ltd., IV; 44 (upd.)
Wipro Limited, 43

Indonesia

Garuda Indonesia, 6; 58 (upd.)
PERTAMINA, IV
Pertamina, 56 (upd.)
PT Astra International Tbk, 56

Iran

National Iranian Oil Company, IV

Ireland

Aer Lingus Group plc, 34
Allied Irish Banks, plc, 16; 43 (upd.)
Baltimore Technologies Plc, 42
Bank of Ireland, 50
Dunnes Stores Ltd., 58
eircom plc, 31 (upd.)
Fyffes Plc, 38
Glanbia plc, 59
Harland and Wolff Holdings plc, 19
IAWS Group plc, 49
IONA Technologies plc, 43
Irish Life & Permanent Plc, 59
Jefferson Smurfit Group plc, IV; 19 (upd.); 49 (upd.)
Kerry Group plc, 27
Musgrave Group Plc, 57
Ryanair Holdings plc, 35
Shannon Aerospace Ltd., 36
Telecom Eireann, 7
Waterford Wedgwood plc, 34 (upd.)

Isle Of Man

Strix Ltd., 51

Israel

Amdocs Ltd., 47
Bank Hapoalim B.M., II; 54 (upd.)
Blue Square Israel Ltd., 41
ECI Telecom Ltd., 18
El Al Israel Airlines Ltd., 23
Elscint Ltd., 20
Israel Chemicals Ltd., 55
Koor Industries Ltd., II; 25 (upd.)
Scitex Corporation Ltd., 24
Teva Pharmaceutical Industries Ltd., 22; 54 (upd.)

Italy

Alfa Romeo, 13; 36 (upd.)
Alitalia-Linee Aeree Italiana, S.p.A., 6; 29 (upd.)
Aprilia SpA, 17
Arnoldo Mondadori Editore S.p.A., IV; 19 (upd.); 54 (upd.)
Assicurazioni Generali SpA, III; 15 (upd.)
Autogrill SpA, 49
Automobili Lamborghini Holding S.p.A., 13; 34 (upd.)
Banca Commerciale Italiana SpA, II
Barilla G. e R. Fratelli S.p.A., 17; 50 (upd.)
Benetton Group S.p.A., 10
Bulgari S.p.A., 20
Credito Italiano, II
Cremonini S.p.A., 57
Davide Campari-Milano S.p.A., 57
Diesel SpA, 40
Ducati Motor Holding S.p.A., 30
Ente Nazionale Idrocarburi, IV
Ente Nazionale per L'Energia Elettrica, V
Fabbrica D' Armi Pietro Beretta S.p.A., 39
Ferrari S.p.A., 13; 36 (upd.)
Ferrero SpA, 54
Fiat SpA, I; 11 (upd.); 50 (upd.)
Fila Holding S.p.A., 20; 52 (upd.)
Gianni Versace SpA, 22
Giorgio Armani S.p.A., 45
Gruppo Coin S.p.A., 41
Guccio Gucci, S.p.A., 15
illycaffè SpA, 50
Industrie Natuzzi S.p.A., 18
Ing. C. Olivetti & C., S.p.a., III
Istituto per la Ricostruzione Industriale S.p.A., I; 11
Juventus F.C. S.p.A., 53
Luxottica SpA, 17; 52 (upd.)
Marchesi Antinori SRL, 42
Marzotto S.p.A., 20
Mediaset SpA, 50
Montedison SpA, I; 24 (upd.)
Officine Alfieri Maserati S.p.A., 13
Olivetti S.p.A., 34 (upd.)
Parmalat Finanziaria SpA, 50
Piaggio & C. S.p.A., 20
Pirelli S.p.A., V; 15 (upd.)
Reno de Medici S.p.A., 41
Riunione Adriatica di Sicurtè SpA, III
Safilo SpA, 54
Sanpaolo IMI S.p.A., 50
Seat Pagine Gialle S.p.A., 47
Società Finanziaria Telefonica per Azioni, V
Società Sportiva Lazio SpA, 44
Telecom Italia S.p.A., 43
Tiscali SpA, 48

Jamaica

Air Jamaica Limited, 54

Japan

Aisin Seiki Co., Ltd., III; 48 (upd.)
Aiwa Co., Ltd., 30
Ajinomoto Co., Inc., II; 28 (upd.)
All Nippon Airways Co., Ltd., 6; 38 (upd.)
Alpine Electronics, Inc., 13
Alps Electric Co., Ltd., II; 44 (upd.)
Asahi Breweries, Ltd., I; 20 (upd.); 52 (upd.)
Asahi Glass Company, Ltd., III; 48 (upd.)
Asahi National Broadcasting Company, Ltd., 9
ASICS Corporation, 57
Bandai Co., Ltd., 55
Bank of Tokyo-Mitsubishi Ltd., II; 15 (upd.)
Bridgestone Corporation, V; 21 (upd.); 59 (upd.)
Brother Industries, Ltd., 14
C. Itoh & Company Ltd., I
Canon Inc., III; 18 (upd.)
CASIO Computer Co., Ltd., III; 16 (upd.); 40 (upd.)
Central Japan Railway Company, 43
Chubu Electric Power Company, Inc., V; 46 (upd.)
Chugai Pharmaceutical Co., Ltd., 50
Chugoku Electric Power Company Inc., V; 53 (upd.)
Citizen Watch Co., Ltd., III; 21 (upd.)
Cosmo Oil Co., Ltd., IV; 53 (upd.)
Dai Nippon Printing Co., Ltd., IV; 57 (upd.)
Dai-Ichi Kangyo Bank Ltd., The, II
Daido Steel Co., Ltd., IV
Daiei, Inc., The, V; 17 (upd.); 41 (upd.)
Daihatsu Motor Company, Ltd., 7; 21 (upd.)
Daikin Industries, Ltd., III
Daimaru, Inc., The, V; 42 (upd.)
Daio Paper Corporation, IV
Daishowa Paper Manufacturing Co., Ltd., IV; 57 (upd.)
Daiwa Bank, Ltd., The, II; 39 (upd.)
Daiwa Securities Company, Limited, II
Daiwa Securities Group Inc., 55 (upd.)
DDI Corporation, 7
DENSO Corporation, 46 (upd.)
Dentsu Inc., I; 16 (upd.); 40 (upd.)
East Japan Railway Company, V
Fanuc Ltd., III; 17 (upd.)
Fuji Bank, Ltd., The, II
Fuji Electric Co., Ltd., II; 48 (upd.)
Fuji Photo Film Co., Ltd., III; 18 (upd.)
Fujisawa Pharmaceutical Company, Ltd., I; 58 (upd.)
Fujitsu Limited, III; 16 (upd.); 42 (upd.)
Furukawa Electric Co., Ltd., The, III
General Sekiyu K.K., IV
Hakuhodo, Inc., 6; 42 (upd.)
Hankyu Corporation, V; 23 (upd.)
Hino Motors, Ltd., 7; 21 (upd.)
Hitachi, Ltd., I; 12 (upd.); 40 (upd.)
Hitachi Metals, Ltd., IV
Hitachi Zosen Corporation, III; 53 (upd.)
Hokkaido Electric Power Company Inc. (HEPCO), V; 58 (upd.)
Hokuriku Electric Power Company, V
Honda Motor Company Limited, I; 10 (upd.); 29 (upd.)
Honshu Paper Co., Ltd., IV
Hoshino Gakki Co. Ltd., 55
Idemitsu Kosan Co., Ltd., IV; 49 (upd.)
Industrial Bank of Japan, Ltd., The, II
Isetan Company Limited, V; 36 (upd.)
Ishikawajima-Harima Heavy Industries Co., Ltd., III
Isuzu Motors, Ltd., 9; 23 (upd.); 57 (upd.)
Ito-Yokado Co., Ltd., V; 42 (upd.)
ITOCHU Corporation, 32 (upd.)

NOTES ON CONTRIBUTORS

Notes on Contributors

BIANCO, David P. Writer, editor, and publishing consultant.

COHEN, M. L. Novelist and researcher living in Paris.

COVELL, Jeffrey L. Seattle-based writer.

CULLIGAN, Susan B. Minnesota-based writer.

DINGER, Ed. Writer and editor based in Bronx, New York.

HALASZ, Robert. Former editor in chief of *World Progress* and *Funk & Wagnalls New Encyclopedia Yearbook*; author, *The U.S. Marines* (Millbrook Press, 1993).

HEER-FORSBERG, Mary. Minneapolis-based researcher and writer.

INGRAM, Frederick C. Utah-based business writer who has contributed to *GSA Business, Appalachian Trailway News,* the *Encyclopedia of Business,* the *Encyclopedia of Global Industries,* the *Encyclopedia of Consumer Brands,* and other regional and trade publications.

LORENZ, Sarah Ruth. Minnesota-based writer.

PEIPPO, Kathleen. Minneapolis-based writer.

RHODES, Nelson. Editor, writer, and consultant in the Chicago area.

ROTHBURD, Carrie. Writer and editor specializing in corporate profiles, academic texts, and academic journal articles.

SALAMIE, David E. Part-owner of InfoWorks Development Group, a reference publication development and editorial services company.

TRADII, Mary. Writer based in Denver, Colorado.

WOODWARD, A. Wisconsin-based writer.